Lecture Notes in Computer Science

Vol. 49: Interactive Systems. Proceedings 1976. Edited by A. Blaser and C. Hackl. VI, 380 pages. 1976.

Vol. 50: A. C Hartmann, A Concurrent Pascal Compiler for Minicomputers VI, 119 pages. 1977.

Vol. 51: B S Garbow, Matrix Eigensystem Routines – Eispack Guide Extension VIII, 343 pages. 1977.

Vol. 52: Automata, Languages and Programming Fourth Colloquium, University of Turku, July 1977 Edited by A Salomaa and M Steinby X, 569 pages 1977.

Vol. 53: Mathematical Foundations of Computer Science. Proceedings 1977 Edited by J Gruska. XII, 608 pages. 1977

Vol. 54: Design and Implementation of Programming Languages Proceedings 1976 Edited by J H Williams and D. A. Fisher. X, 496 pages 1977

Vol 55: A Gerbier, Mes premières constructions de programmes XII, 256 pages. 1977

Vol 56: Fundamentals of Computation Theory Proceedings 1977. Edited by M. Karpiński. XII, 542 pages. 1977

Vol 57· Portability of Numerical Software. Proceedings 1976 Edited by W Cowell VIII, 539 pages. 1977

Vol 58 M J. O'Donnell, Computing in Systems Described by Equations. XIV, 111 pages. 1977

Vol. 59 E Hill, Jr, A Comparative Study of Very Large Data Bases X, 140 pages. 1978.

Vol. 60· Operating Systems, An Advanced Course. Edited by R Bayer, R M. Graham, and G. Seegmuller. X, 593 pages. 1978

Vol 61 The Vienna Development Method The Meta-Language Edited by D Bjørner and C B Jones. XVIII, 382 pages 1978

Vol. 62: Automata, Languages and Programming. Proceedings 1978 Edited by G. Ausiello and C. Böhm. VIII, 508 pages 1978.

Vol 63 Natural Language Communication with Computers Edited by Leonard Bolc. VI, 292 pages 1978.

Vol. 64· Mathematical Foundations of Computer Science Proceedings 1978. Edited by J. Winkowski. X, 551 pages 1978

Vol. 65 Information Systems Methodology, Proceedings, 1978. Edited by G. Bracchi and P. C Lockemann XII, 696 pages 1978

Vol 66. N D Jones and S. S. Muchnick, TEMPO. A Unified Treatment of Binding Time and Parameter Passing Concepts in Programming Languages. IX, 118 pages 1978.

Vol 67 Theoretical Computer Science, 4th GI Conference, Aachen, March 1979 Edited by K Weihrauch. VII, 324 pages. 1979

Vol 68. D. Harel, First-Order Dynamic Logic. X, 133 pages 1979

Vol 69: Program Construction. International Summer School Edited by F L Bauer and M Broy VII, 651 pages 1979.

Vol 70. Semantics of Concurrent Computation Proceedings 1979 Edited by G. Kahn VI, 368 pages 1979.

Vol 71 Automata, Languages and Programming. Proceedings 1979 Edited by H. A. Maurer. IX, 684 pages. 1979

Vol. 72 Symbolic and Algebraic Computation Proceedings 1979. Edited by E W Ng XV, 557 pages. 1979

Vol 73: Graph-Grammars and Their Application to Computer Science and Biology Proceedings 1978. Edited by V. Claus, H Ehrig and G. Rozenberg. VII, 477 pages 1979

Vol. 74 Mathematical Foundations of Computer Science. Proceedings 1979. Edited by J Bečvář IX, 580 pages 1979

Vol 75: Mathematical Studies of Information Processing Proceedings 1978. Edited by E. K Blum, M. Paul and S Takasu. VIII, 629 pages. 1979

Vol. 76 Codes for Boundary-Value Problems in Ordinary Differential Equations Proceedings 1978 Edited by B Childs et al VIII, 388 pages 1979

Vol 77· G. V. Bochmann, Architecture of Distributed Computer Systems. VIII, 238 pages. 1979.

Vol. 78 M Gordon, R Milner and C. Wadsworth, Edinburgh LCF VIII, 159 pages 1979

Vol. 79 Language Design and Programming Methodology Proceedings, 1979. Edited by J. Tobias IX, 255 pages. 1980

Vol 80. Pictorial Information Systems Edited by S K Chang and K. S Fu. IX, 445 pages 1980.

Vol. 81· Data Base Techniques for Pictorial Applications. Proceedings, 1979 Edited by A Blaser. XI, 599 pages 1980.

Vol 82 J G Sanderson, A Relational Theory of Computing. VI, 147 pages. 1980.

Vol 83 International Symposium Programming Proceedings, 1980 Edited by B Robinet. VII, 341 pages. 1980

Vol 84· Net Theory and Applications. Proceedings, 1979 Edited by W Brauer XIII, 537 Seiten 1980.

Vol 85· Automata, Languages and Programming Proceedings, 1980. Edited by J de Bakker and J van Leeuwen. VIII, 671 pages 1980

Vol 86 Abstract Software Specifications. Proceedings, 1979. Edited by D Bjørner XIII, 567 pages. 1980

Vol. 87: 5th Conference on Automated Deduction Proceedings, 1980 Edited by W. Bibel and R Kowalski. VII, 385 pages 1980

Vol 88. Mathematical Foundations of Computer Science 1980 Proceedings, 1980. Edited by P. Dembiński VIII, 723 pages. 1980

Vol. 89. Computer Aided Design - Modelling, Systems Engineering, CAD-Systems. Proceedings, 1980 Edited by J Encarnacao. XIV, 461 pages 1980.

Vol. 90 D. M Sandford, Using Sophisticated Models in Resolution Theorem Proving
XI, 239 pages 1980

Vol 91 D. Wood, Grammar and L Forms. An Introduction IX, 314 pages. 1980.

Vol. 92 R Milner, A Calculus of Communication Systems. VI, 171 pages. 1980.

Vol. 93. A. Nijholt, Context-Free Grammars· Covers, Normal Forms, and Parsing VII, 253 pages 1980

Vol. 94· Semantics-Directed Compiler Generation Proceedings, 1980 Edited by N. D. Jones V, 489 pages 1980

Vol. 95· Ch D. Marlin, Coroutines XII, 246 pages 1980

Vol. 96 J L. Peterson, Computer Programs for Spelling Correction VI, 213 pages 1980

Vol. 97. S. Osaki and T. Nishio, Reliability Evaluation of Some Fault-Tolerant Computer Architectures. VI, 129 pages 1980

Vol. 98· Towards a Formal Description of Ada Edited by D. Bjørner and O. N Oest XIV, 630 pages. 1980

Vol 99 I Guessarian, Algebraic Semantics XI, 158 pages 1981

Vol 100. Graphtheoretic Concepts in Computer Science Edited by H. Noltemeier X, 403 pages. 1981

Vol 101 A. Thayse, Boolean Calculus of Differences VII, 144 pages 1981

Vol. 102 J. H Davenport, On the Integration of Algebraic Functions 1–197 pages. 1981

Vol 103: H Ledgard, A. Singer, J Whiteside, Directions in Human Factors of Interactive Systems. VI, 190 pages. 1981.

Vol. 104· Theoretical Computer Science Ed by P Deussen. VII, 261 pages 1981

Vol 105 B. W Lampson, M. Paul, H J. Siegert, Distributed Systems – Architecture and Implementation XIII, 510 pages. 1981

Vol. 106: The Programming Language Ada. Reference Manual. X, 243 pages. 1981

Lecture Notes in Computer Science

Edited by G. Goos and J. Hartmanis

154

Automata, Languages and Programming

10th Colloquium
Barcelona, Spain, July 18–22, 1983

Edited by J. Díaz

Springer-Verlag
Berlin Heidelberg GmbH 1983

Editor

Josep Díaz
Facultat d'Informàtica, Universitat Politècnica de Barcelona
Jordi Girona Salgado 31, Barcelona 34, Spain

CR Subject Classifications (1982): 4.1, 4.2, 5.2, 5.3

ISBN 978-3-540-12317-0 ISBN 978-3-540-40038-7 (eBook)
DOI 10.1007/978-3-540-40038-7

Originally published by Springer-Verlag Berlin Heidelberg New York in 1983
2145/3140-543210

PREFACE

ICALP-83 is the tenth International Colloquium on Automata, Languages and Programming in a series of meetings sponsored by the European Association for Theoretical Computer Science (EATCS). It is a conference covering all aspects of Theoretical Computer Science, including topics like automata theory, formal language theory, analysis of algorithms, computational complexity, computability theory, mathematical aspects of programming languages definition, semantics of programming languages, program verification, theory of data structure and theory of data bases. The previous meetings have been held in Paris (72), Saarbrücken (74), Edinburgh (76), Turku (77), Udine (78), Graz (79), Amsterdam (80), Haifa (81) and Aarhus (82).

ICALP-83 was organized by the Facultat d'Informàtica de la Universitat Politècnica de Barcelona, and was held in Barcelona from July 18th. to July 22nd. 1983. The organizing committee consisted of X.Berenguer, R.Casas, J.Diaz, F.Orejas and M.Verges.

ICALP-83 celebrate its tenth anniversary with a record of submitted abstracts and draft papers, 178, and a record of accepted papers, 59, that together with the two invited papers made the core of the colloquium. The program committee consisted of G.Ausiello (Roma), J.L.Boasson (Paris), C.Boehm (Roma), W.Brauer (Hamburg), J.Diaz (Barcelona)(chairman), S.Even (Haifa), P.Flajolet (Le Chesnay), E.Garcia Camarero (Madrid), R.Karp (Berkeley), B.Mayoh (Aarhus), K.Melhorn (Saarbrücken), J.Meseguer (Menlo Park), U.Montanari (Pisa), J.Nesetril (Praha), M.Nivat (Paris), C.Pair (Nancy), I.Ramos (Valencia) G.Rozenberg (Leiden), D.Scott (Pittsburgh), J.Ullman (Stanford), L.Valiant (Cambridge). Each paper was sent to at least four program committee members for evaluation. Based on these evaluations a selection committee consisting of G.Ausiello, J.L.Boasson, W.Brauer, J.Diaz, S.Even, P.Flajolet, B.Mayoh, U.Montanari, M.Nivat, I.Ramos, G.Rozenberg and D.Scott selected the papers presented at the conference We wish to express our gratitude to the members of the program committee and the referees which assisted this process (see next page) for the enormous amount of work they invested in the evaluation process.

ICALP-83 was made possible by the support from a number of sources. We thank the Generalitat de Catalunya, The Spanish Ministery of Education, IBM-Spain, Sperry-Spain and Digital Corporation. We also want to thank the support given by all the members in the secretary of the Facultat d'Informàtica, specially Montserrat Bernat who controlled most of the organizational matters related to the conference.

Josep DIAZ,
ICALP-83

CONTENTS

On Semantic Foundations for Applicative Multiprogramming

Samson Abramsky
Department of Computer Science and Statistics
Queen Mary College
Mile End Road
London E1 4NS
United Kingdom

1. Background and Motivation

By _applicative multiprogramming_ we mean the attempt to describe and construct concurrent systems in a purely applicative (or "functional") style. For work on the pragmatics of applicative multiprogramming, see e.g. [Hend82]. We are concerned with the semantic basis for this approach. Specifically, in this paper we shall consider

(i) non-discrete data domains - e.g. streams [Kah74]
(ii) unbounded non-determinism - cf. fair merge [Kel, Par].

Order-theoretic fixed-point semantics encounters serious problems with both

- non-discrete data domains, even with bounded non-determinism
- unbounded non-determinism, even with discrete domains.

We shall develop an approach which appears to overcome these problems.

General description of the approach

The now classical method of Scott's theory of computation [Sco69], of modelling domains as ordered sets, means we have

- the data elements
- relations of approximation between data elements

i.e. statements of the form "a approximates b", but no way of distinguishing between _different ways_ in which a might approximate b.

In the deterministic case, and even for bounded non-determinism over discrete domains, this seems not to matter - such fine distinctions are not relevant, at the usual level of abstraction. Thus in such restricted cases, there are satisfactory fixed-point semantics using order-theoretic powerdomain constructions [Henn81, Plo80]. When we extend _either_ to non-discrete domains, _or_ to unbounded non-determinism, such distinctions become crucial.

The mathematical framework for making these distinctions is to generalise from ordered sets to categories. Much of the groundwork for this programme of generalisation has been done by D. Lehmann in his thesis [Leh76], and also by M. Smyth. The pattern of generalisation is straightforward:

From	**To**
posets	categories
ω-chains	ω-diagrams
least upper bounds	colimits
least elements	initial objects
ω-continuous functions	ω-colimit preserving functors

The fixed point theorem generalises, as does Scott's theory of solutions of recursive domain equations [Leh76].

Lehmann also defined a categorical powerdomain construction. However, he failed to justify it mathematically, and to apply it to the semantics of programming languages. We shall attempt to remedy these omissions, and in so doing to give powerful support to this approach as overcoming many of the problems arising with order-theoretic fixed point semantics in the treatment of non-determinism.

The remainder of this paper is organised as follows. Section 2 reviews the categorical background, gives Lehmann's powerdomain construction, and presents an adjoint characterisation of it, which can be claimed to give it some justification as a mathematically canonical construction. This characterisation also suggests some of the underlying reasons why the categorical construction avoids problems which arise with its order-theoretic counterpart.

Section 3 represents a first application of the approach, to (boundedly) non-deterministic recursive program schemes, over arbitrary interpretations, including non-discrete ones. Operational and fixed point semantics are defined, and their equivalence is proved. Considerable use is made of the work of Boudol on operational semantics [Bou].

Section 4 gives a second application, to semantics of unbounded non-determinism. Problems of failure of continuity of some important semantic functionals in the order-theoretic case are discussed, and it is shown how these problems do not arise in the categorical setting. The non-deterministic recursive program schemes of the previous section are extended to allow unbounded non-determinism, and the equivalence of operational and fixed point semantics is proved again for this extended language.

2. Basic Results

2.1 Categorical preliminaries

Generalising the following categories familiar from order-theoretic semantics

pos	posets and order preserving functions
pos$_\bot$	posets with least elements, strict order preserving functions
ω-pos	posets with least upper bounds of ascending ω-sequences, and functions preserving these

we have

cat	small categories and functors
cat$_\bot$	small categories with initial objects, functors preserving these
ω-cat	small categories with colimits of ω-diagrams, functors preserving these

moreover each pos-category is a full subcategory of the corresponding cat-category.

We also extend the notion of continuous Σ-algebra [ADJ] to categories, following the generalised approach to universal algebra in [LS81].

Definition Given a functor $T:C\to C$, a **T-algebra** is a C-arrow $\alpha:Ta\to a$, for some object a in C. A **T-algebra homomorphism** $f:(\alpha:Ta\to a) \to (\beta:Tb\to b)$ is a C-arrow $f:a\to b$ such that

$$\begin{array}{ccc} Ta & \xrightarrow{\alpha} & a \\ {\scriptstyle Tf}\downarrow & & \downarrow{\scriptstyle f} \\ Tb & \xrightarrow[\beta]{} & b \end{array}$$

T-algebras and homomorphisms form a category under C-composition and identities, denoted by **T-alg-C**.

A ranked alphabet $(\Sigma, \nu:\Sigma \to \mathbf{N})$ is made into a C-endofunctor, where C has finite products and small coproducts, by

$$\Sigma : X \to \coprod_{\sigma\in\Sigma} X^{\nu(\sigma)}$$

For C = **Set**, this gives classical universal algebra. For C = ω-**pos**$_\perp$, we define a variant

$$\Sigma : X \to \coprod_{\sigma\in\Sigma} (X^{\nu(\sigma)})_\perp$$

where $(\_)_\perp$ is the $\perp$-adjoining functor [LS81, SP82], in order to allow the operations to be non-strict. The same definition is used in ω-**cat**$_\perp$. (Products in ω-**cat**$_\perp$ are ordinary products of categories, coproducts are "coalesced sums".)

Fact The initial algebra in **Σ-alg-ω-cat$_\perp$** is CT_Σ, the initial continuous Σ-algebra [ADJ].

The significance of this result is that syntax is unaffected by the broadening of semantics.

Remark CT_Σ is actually only initial in the weak sense, that any two arrows from CT_Σ to an algebra A have a unique natural equivalence between them. If we restrict to strongly skeletal categories, as defined in Section 2.3, then CT_Σ is initial in the usual sense.

2.2 The Categorical Powerdomain Construction

For simplicity, we shall define P(D) for a cpo D. Even when D is a cpo, P(D) is a non-poset category. In order to make this definition, we shall need the notion of a **function between multisets**. To make this notion precise, we represent multisets by sets. Multisets are standardly represented by functions

$D \to$ **Card**

where **Card** is the class of cardinal numbers. We use the standard representation of cardinals by ordinals.

Definition Given a multiset X over D,
$S(X) = \{\langle\alpha,d\rangle \mid d\in D \ \& \ \alpha<X(d)\}$.
A function f between multisets X and Y is a function (in the ordinary sense)
$f : S(X) \to S(Y)$

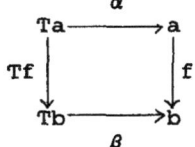

Definition of P(D):

Objects multisets over D

Arrows f:X→Y is a function from Y to X as multisets such that ∀y∈Y f(y) ⊆y.

Composition Contravariant function composition.

Identities Identity functions.

Theorem (Lehmann)
P(D) is ω-complete and initial.

(In order for P(D) to be small, we need to restrict the cardinalities of multisets. Restriction to any uncountable cardinality will preserve ω-completeness.)

Example
To see how approximations and colimits are working, consider the diagram

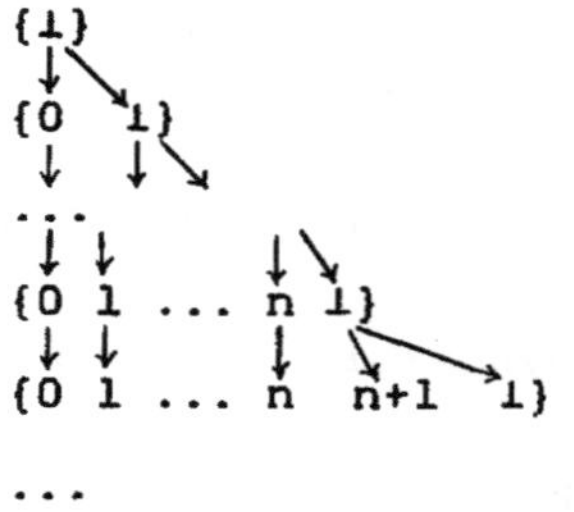

with colimit vertex $N_\perp$ and typical colimit arrows

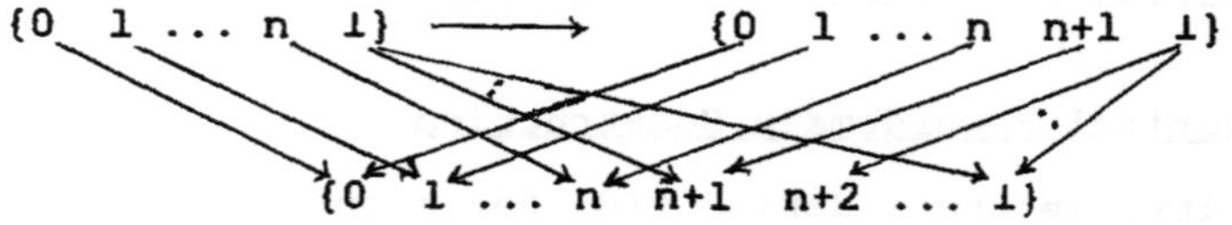

<u>Remark</u> While ω-diagrams in the categorical powerdomain correspond to computation trees, the <u>objects</u>, which will ultimately serve as program denotations, are (multi)sets, thus (almost) as abstract as could be wished. This differentiates our approach sharply from proposals to use domains of computation trees, e.g. [Bac], in which the elements carry a great deal of operational information.

<u>2.3 Characterisation of the Powerdomain construction</u>

A category is **strongly skeletal** if the only isomorphisms are the identities (poset categories are strongly skeletal).

For κ any uncountable cardinal, let P_κ be the powerdomain construction restricted to multisets of cardinality < κ. Let P^s_κ be the strongly skeletal powerdomain construction (obtained by identifying isomorphisms in P_κ, which is already skeletal).

Let C_1 be the category of small categories with distinguished products of all I-indexed families for **card**(I)<κ, such that the products satisfy generalised (I-indexed) associativity, commutativity and unit (w.r.t the terminal object) up to <u>identity</u> - products always satisfy these up to unique isomorphism - and functors preserving the distinguished products.

Let $\mathbf{C_2}$ be the category of strongly skeletal small categories with (necessarily unique) products of all I-indexed families for card(I)$<\kappa$, and functors preserving these.

$$U_i : C_i \to \mathbf{cat} \qquad i=1,2$$

are the evident forgetful functors.

Theorem

(i) $\mathbf{P}_\kappa$ is left adjoint to U_1

(ii) $\mathbf{P}^S_\kappa$ is left adjoint to U_2.

Moreover, both these constructions cut down to left adjoints on ω-$\mathbf{cat}_\perp$, so that if D is in ω-$\mathbf{cat}_\perp$ so are $\mathbf{P}_\kappa(D)$ and $\mathbf{P}^S_\kappa(D)$. In particular, multiset union is the categorical product in $\mathbf{P}_\kappa(D)$, with the empty multiset the terminal object, and singleton insertion is the unit of the adjunction.

<u>Proof Outline</u>

To show the freeness of $\mathbf{P}_\kappa(D)$, we need to show

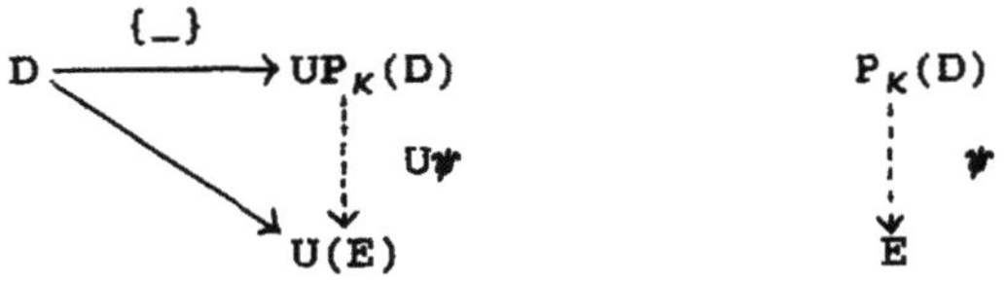

where this amounts to showing that any arrow from $\mathbf{P}(D)$ to E in $\mathbf{C}$ is uniquely determined by its action on singleton objects and arrows, i.e.

$$\begin{array}{l}\{a\}\\ \downarrow f\\ \{b\}\end{array}$$

where $f:a\to b$ is an arrow in D. For objects, the associative, commutative and unit properties clearly characterise multisets, in an "equational" fashion. For arrows, we can express each $f:X\to Y$ in $\mathbf{P}(D)$ as

$$f = \biguplus_{x\in X} f_x$$

where f_x is the "part" of f whose image is x. These parts are disjoint, since f is a (contravariant) function. There are then three cases:

(i) $\begin{array}{c}\{a\}\\ \downarrow\\ \{b\}\end{array}$ (deterministic step)

which is in the image of {_};

(ii) $\{a\}$

$\downarrow$ (discarding)

$\emptyset$

i.e. a not in the image of f, which is the unique map to the terminal object;

(iii) $\{a\}$

$\swarrow \cdots \searrow$ (non-deterministic branching)

$\{b_1 \ \ldots \ b_\mu\}$

which is just the unique map lifting

$$\begin{array}{ccc} \{a\} & \ldots & \{a\} \\ \downarrow & & \downarrow \\ \{b_1\} & \ldots & \{b_\mu\} \end{array}$$

to the categorical product of $\{b_1\},\ldots,\{b_\mu\}$. Because the arrows in C are functors preserving the product structure between categories, the unique determination of ψ by F via $\{\_\}$ follows from these observations. □

Intuitive significance of the results

The crucial property of the categorical powerdomain construction is that it involves no identification of multisets. This contrasts with the classical order-theoretic approach to powerdomains, where sets are identified both to make the approximation relation antisymmetric, and to make it complete [Plo76]. Unfortunately, this identification of sets leads to the loss of operationally significant information. The categorical powerdomain has been exposed as a purely (categorical, infinitary) "algebraic" construction, which automatically preserves ω-completeness.

3. First Application: non-discrete domains

We assume the following ranked alphabets (with ranking function ν).

- Σ - base function symbols
- Φ - user-defined function symbols
- or - a binary operation not in $\Sigma\cup\Phi$
- $\Sigma+$ - $\Sigma\cup\{or\}$.

A non-deterministic recursive program scheme (ndrps) is

$$\begin{aligned} S:\ & \varphi_1(x_1\ldots x_{\nu(\varphi_1)}) = t_1 \\ & \ldots \\ & \varphi_n(x_1\ldots x_{\nu(\varphi_n)}) = t_n \end{aligned}$$

where $t_i \in T_{\Sigma+\cup\Phi}(X_{\nu(\varphi_i)})$.

Here $X_n = \{x_1,\ldots,x_n\}$

$T_\Sigma(X)$ is the Σ-word algebra over X.

Given an interpretation A, in **Σ-alg-ω-pos$_\perp$**, we want an operational semantics

$$OP_{S,A} : T_{\Sigma+\cup\Phi}(|A|) \to P(|A|)$$

We proceed in a somewhat abstract way, following ideas of A. Poigne [Poi], with the following motivation:

1) to get away from explicit choice of a computation rule
2) to expose the canonical mathematical structures underlying the operational semantics
3) to give a priori operational meaning to infinite computations.

First we define a transition relation, $\rightarrow$, on terms, as the least satisfying

(I) $\varphi_i(t_1 \ldots t_n) \rightarrow t_i[t_1/x_1 \ldots t_n/x_n]$

(II) (i) $\underline{or}(t_1,t_2) \rightarrow t_1$ (ii) $\underline{or}(t_1,t_2) \rightarrow t_2$

(III) $t \rightarrow t' \Rightarrow t''[t] \rightarrow t''[t']$.

Let $TA = T_{\Sigma+\cup\Phi}(|A|)$. Now $(TA,\overset{*}{\rightarrow})$ is the free preorder over $(TA,\rightarrow)$. Take the ω-chains over $(TA,\overset{*}{\rightarrow})$, ordered by cofinality, i.e.

$$\langle c_n\rangle \sqsubseteq \langle c'_m\rangle \equiv \forall n \exists m\ c_n \overset{*}{\rightarrow} c'_m$$

and then factor by antisymmetry:

$$\langle c_n\rangle \approx \langle c'_m\rangle \equiv \langle c_n\rangle \sqsubseteq \langle c'_m\rangle \ \&\ \langle c'_m\rangle \sqsubseteq \langle c_n\rangle.$$

This gives us the free ω-complete poset over $(TA,\rightarrow)$, call it CS.

Then the unique homomorphism $h_A:TA\rightarrow A$ extending id_A, where A is made into a $\Sigma+\cup\Phi$-algebra by interpreting every operation not in Σ as Ω, has a unique ω-continuous extension

$$\hat{h}_A:CS\rightarrow A$$

(since $t\rightarrow t' \Rightarrow h_A(t) \sqsubseteq h_A(t')$)

given by

$$\hat{h}_A([\langle c_n\rangle]) = \bigsqcup \langle h_A(c_n)\rangle.$$

We could now define

$$Comp(t) = \{[\langle c_n\rangle]\in CS \mid c_0=t\}$$

$$OP_{S,A}(t) = \{\hat{h}_A(c) \mid c\in Comp(t)\}.$$

However, we do not want <u>all</u> the sequences in Comp(t), but only those which are not trivially underdefined because they neglect to expand some function call or choice. Poigne [Poi] proposes taking the <u>maximal</u> elements of Comp(t); however, some valid computation sequences are not maximal, e.g.

$$\varphi(x) \rightarrow \underline{or}(\varphi(x),\sigma(\varphi(x))) \rightarrow \varphi(x) \rightarrow \underline{or}(\varphi(x),\sigma(\varphi(x))) \rightarrow \ldots$$

which approximates, but is not approximated by

$$\varphi(x) \rightarrow \underline{or}(\varphi(x),\sigma(\varphi(x))) \rightarrow \sigma(\varphi(x)) \rightarrow \sigma(\underline{or}(\varphi(x),\sigma(\varphi(x)))) \rightarrow \ldots$$

Thus it turns out that in operational semantics, as in fixed-point semantics, it is necessary to consider <u>how</u> one object (computation sequence) approximates another. This can be done, using the machinery of residuals, and an important part of the work of Boudol in [Bou] is to define an appropriate notion of equivalence, and thence of approximation, between computation sequences. We can then, for a correspondingly revised definition of Comp(t), define

$$OP_{S,A}(t) = \{\hat{h}_A(c) \mid c \text{ is a maximal element of Comp}(t)\}$$

For lack of space, we omit this development, but remark that Boudol's constructions can be placed very naturally in a categorical setting.

We now illustrate the problems encountered with the order-theoretic approach to defining a fixed-point semantics, with an important example due to Boudol [Bou].

Consider the scheme

$$S: \varphi_1 = \sigma(\varphi_1)$$
$$\varphi_2(x) = \underline{or}(x, \varphi_2(\sigma(x)))$$

and terms

$$t = \varphi_2(x) \qquad u = \underline{or}(\varphi_1, t)$$

then

$$OP_{S,CT_\Sigma(X)}(t) = \{\sigma^n(x) \mid n\in\omega\} \cup \{\bot\}$$

$$OP_{S,CT_\Sigma(X)}(u) = \{\sigma^n(x) \mid n\in\omega\} \cup \{\bot\} \cup \{\sigma^\omega\}.$$

However, if we expand S in $CT_{\Sigma+}(X)$, i.e. solve it as a <u>deterministic</u> scheme, (this step is justified in the remarks on the proof of the Theorem in this section), we obtain the following infinite trees corresponding to t and u:

t: u:

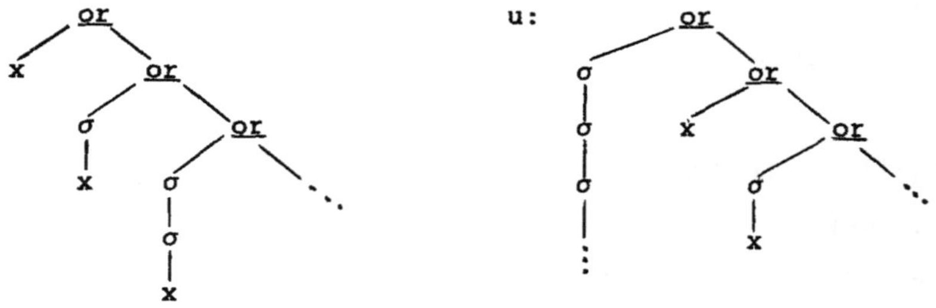

These trees are the least upper bounds of the chains of finite trees shown in Figure 1: Clearly, for all n

$$OP_{S,CT_\Sigma(X)}(t_n) = OP_{S,CT_\Sigma(X)}(u_n),$$

but

$$OP_{S,CT_\Sigma(X)}(\sqcup\langle t_n\rangle) = OP_{S,CT_\Sigma(X)}(t) \neq OP_{S,CT_\Sigma(X)}(u) = OP_{S,CT_\Sigma(X)}(\sqcup\langle u_n\rangle)$$

Thus $OP_{S,CT_\Sigma(X)}$ cannot possibly be continuous, no matter what order or topology is placed on P(|A|). This example appears to rule out any possibility of a fixed-point semantics for non-deterministic recursive program schemes which extends the classical one for deterministic schemes by means of a powerdomain construction. Broy [Bro] has given a non-standard fixed-point semantics for schemes interpreted in a domain of streams, using multiple fixed points over multiple powerdomains with different notions of approximation. However, his semantics still fails to give exact agreement with the operational semantics. We can show this by adapting the above example

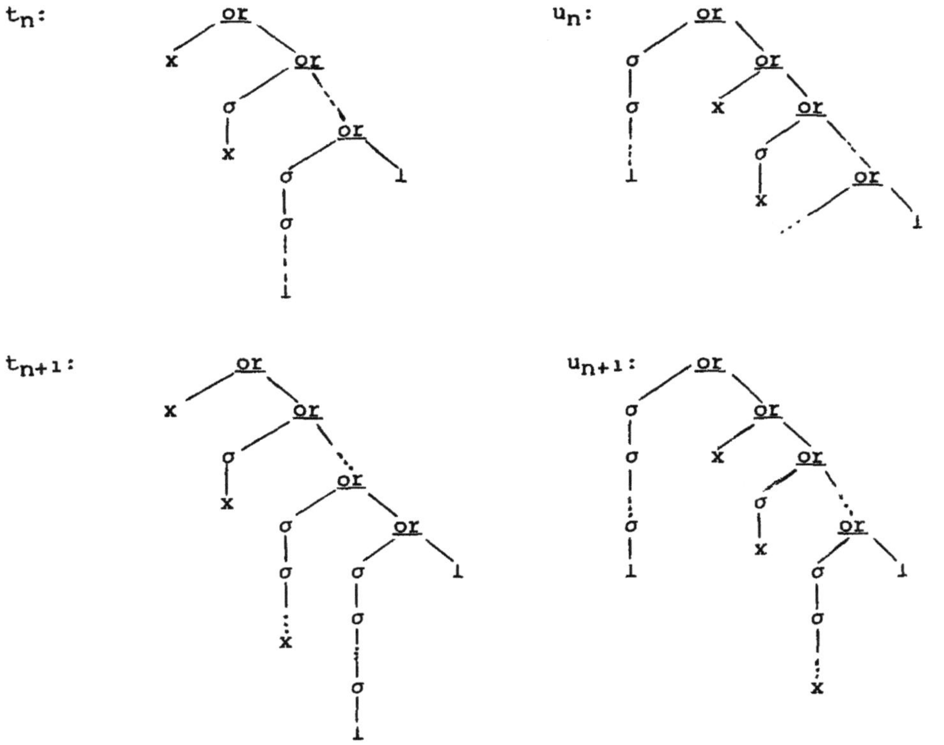

Figure 1

as follows. Fix an interpretation A with

$|A| = 1^* \cup 1^\omega$ with the prefix ordering

$\sigma^A(s) = 1s.$

Then it is clear that

$OP_{S,A}(t[\langle\rangle/x]) = 1^*$

$OP_{S,A}(u[\langle\rangle/x]) = 1^* \cup 1^\omega$

but in Broy's fixed-point semantics the sets 1^* and $1^* \cup 1^\omega$ cannot be distinguished, since only "closed" sets are allowed, and the closure of 1^* is $1^* \cup 1^\omega$.

However, in the categorical approach, we <u>can</u> differentiate between the denotations of the chains t_n, u_n if we take into account not just the sets of terms (objects), but also <u>how</u> they approximate each other (the arrows). As ω-diagrams they <u>are</u> different, and do indeed determins different colimits, as we can see:

$\langle t_n \rangle$:

$\{x \quad \sigma(x) \quad \ldots \quad \sigma^n(\bot) \quad \bot\}$

$\{x \quad \sigma(x) \quad \ldots \quad \sigma^n(x) \quad \sigma^{n+1}(\bot) \quad \bot\}$

$\langle u_n \rangle$:

$\{\sigma^n(\bot) \quad x \quad \sigma(x) \quad \ldots \quad \bot\}$

$\{\sigma^{n+1}(\bot) \quad x \quad \sigma(x) \quad \ldots \quad \sigma^n(x) \quad \bot\}$

We now give our results on semantics of non-deterministic recursive program schemes. Our fixed point semantics is factored into three parts, as illustrated below.

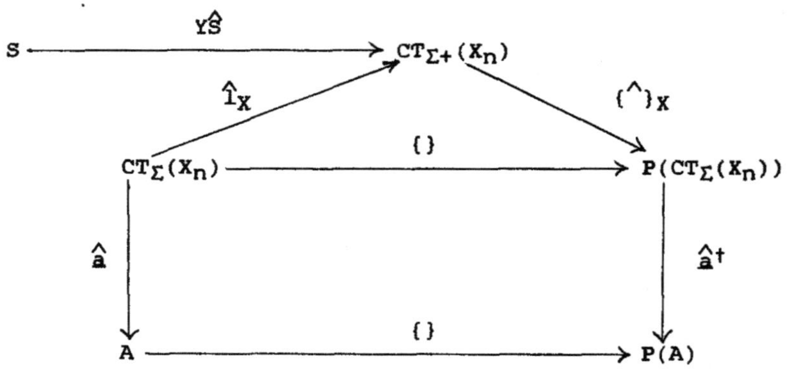

These correspond to

(i) interpreting the recursion (solving the equations in $CT_{\Sigma+}(X)$, i.e. as a deterministic program scheme with <u>or</u> left uninterpreted).

(ii) interpreting the non-determinism (via the unique continous homomorphism extending the insertion of variables $x \to \{x\}$ in $P(CT_\Sigma(X))$ - where $P(CT_\Sigma(X))$ is made into a $\Sigma+$ algebra by pointwise extending the free operations in Σ, and interpreting <u>or</u> as multiset union).

(iii) interpreting the base functions (via the pointwise extension of the unique continuous homomorphism extending the environment map $\mathbf{a}: x_i \to a_i \quad i=1,\ldots,n$).

Note that pointwise extension is the arrow part of the powerdomain construction as a free functor, while singleton insertion is the unit of the corresponding adjunction.

Theorem

$OP_{S,A} = \lambda \mathbf{a}.\ \hat{\mathbf{a}}^\dagger \circ \{\hat{}\}_X \circ Y\hat{S}$

<u>Proof Indication</u>

Boudol [Bou] established an important characterisation of $OP_{S,A}$ in terms of **choice trees**. Given a tree $t \in CT_{\Sigma+}(X)$, a choice tree on t is a tree with the same structure, but with a <u>left</u> or <u>right</u> symbol at each node where t has an <u>or</u>. Given a choice tree h on t, we can define the **application** $\hat{h}(t)$ of h to t, which maps t to the corresponding deterministic tree in $CT_\Sigma(X)$, with all choices resolved according to h. Let choice(t) be the set of all choice trees on t. We can then define a function

$\rho : CT_{\Sigma+}(X) \to P(CT_\Sigma(X))$

$\rho(t) = \{\hat{h}(t) \mid h \in choice(t)\}.$

In effect, Boudol proved that

$OP_{S,A} = \lambda \mathbf{a}.\ \hat{\mathbf{a}}^\dagger \circ \rho \circ Y\hat{S}.$

The following result is crucial:

<u>Choice Tree Lemma</u>

If ρ is redefined as a function to <u>multisets</u> over $CT_\Sigma(X)$ (i.e.

multiplicities are taken into account), then ρ is the <u>object part</u> of the functor $\{\hat{\_}\}_X$. This is a very strong agreement - at the level of multisets - with the categorical semantics, and combined with Boudol's results establishes our Theorem.

<u>Computability</u>

Nivat [Niv] has used the non-continuity of ρ to argue that a fully accurate semantics for general non-deterministic recursive program schemes cannot be effective even in an extended sense, since the set choice(t) for infinite $t \in CT_{\Sigma+}(X)$ may be uncountable, and certainly need not be recursively enumerable. His arguments derive their force from the non-continuity of ρ, since this precludes dealing with choice(t) through its finite approximants, and forces us to consider the completed infinite objects directly. However, from our perspective ρ <u>is</u> (the object part of) a continuous mapping (functor), and we can in fact easily show that our program denotations are effective in the obvious extension of the standard concepts from Scott semantics. A brief sketch must suffice.

Let D be a cpo with an effectively given basis B. In **P**(D), the finite multisets over B and the arrows between them can be recursively enumerated; moreover the operations <u>source</u>, <u>target</u>, <u>composition</u> and <u>identity</u> are recursive in the indices. An object in **P**(D) is **effectively definable** if it is the colimit vertex of a recursively enumerable diagram of finite objects and arrows; this generalises the definition in [Plo75]. Then it is clear that program denotations in our semantics (for any effectively given A, in particular for $CT_{\Sigma}(X)$), will be effectively definable - enumerate the Kleene sequence in $CT_{\Sigma+}(X)$, and take images in **P**(A).

4. Second Application - unbounded non-determinism

Recent work by Park, Apt and Plotkin [Par, AP] has shown that although order-theoretic fixed point semantics can be developed for unbounded non-determinism, serious problems arise. In particular, the property of ω-continuity of semantic functions, so central to the intuitions underlying Scott's theory of computation, fails. An important property of the categorical approach is that ω-continuity does <u>not</u> fail in these cases, so that the classical characterisation of the least fixed point as the least upper bound of ω iterates may be retained.

<u>Example 1</u>

$P_{EM}(X_\perp)$ is the Egli-Milner powerdomain over a flat domain $X_\perp$ [AP], in which all non-empty subsets, not only "finitely generable" ones, are included. The pointwise extension functional

$$\_^{\dagger} : [X \to P_{EM}(X_\perp)] \to [P_{EM}(X_\perp) \to P_{EM}(X_\perp)]$$

is **not continuous**, as the following counter-example shows.

Let $\mathbf{2} = \{false \sqsubseteq true\}$.

$\langle f_n \rangle : \mathbf{N} \to P_{EM}(\mathbf{2})$

$$f_n(m) = \begin{cases} \{true\} & m<n \\ \{false\} & m \geq n. \end{cases}$$

Then $\langle f_n \rangle$ is a chain:

$$(\bigsqcup \langle f_n \rangle)(m) = \{\mathrm{true}\} \qquad \forall m \in \mathbf{N}$$

$$(\bigsqcup \langle f_n \rangle)^{\dagger}(\mathbf{N}) = \{\mathrm{true}\}$$

$$\bigsqcup \langle f_n{}^{\dagger}(\mathbf{N}) \rangle = \bigsqcup \langle \{\mathrm{true, false}\} \rangle = \{\mathrm{true, false}\}.$$

__Example 2__

Failure of co-continuity
(E.g. pointwise extended functions need not be continuous in the Smyth powerdomain [AP], also relevant in other contexts [Bro]).

$$X_0 = \mathbf{N} \qquad X_{n+1} = X_n - \{n+1\}$$

$$\mathrm{iszero}^{\dagger}(\cap \langle X_n \rangle) = \mathrm{iszero}^{\dagger}(\{0\}) = \{\mathrm{true}\}$$

$$\cap \langle \mathrm{iszero}^{\dagger}(X_n) \rangle = \cap \langle \{\mathrm{true, false}\} \rangle = \{\mathrm{true, false}\}$$

We now look at these examples in the categorical powerdomain. See Figure 2. Note the role of __multisets__ in allowing us to distinguish between different computational occurrences of a given value.

Theorem
The semantic functionals used by Apt and Plotkin are all ω-continuous in the categorical semantics.

__First Example__

$$(\mathrm{colim}\ \langle f_n \rangle)^{\dagger}(\mathbf{N}) = \{\mathrm{true}:\infty\}$$

$$\mathrm{colim}\ \langle f_n{}^{\dagger}(\mathbf{N}) \rangle = \mathrm{colim} \quad \begin{array}{c} \{F\ F\ F\ \ldots\} \\ \downarrow\ \downarrow\ \downarrow \\ \{T\ F\ F\ \ldots\} \\ \downarrow\ \downarrow\ \downarrow \\ \{T\ T\ F\ \ldots\} \\ \downarrow\ \downarrow\ \downarrow \end{array}$$

$$= \{\mathrm{true}:\infty\}.$$

__Second Example__

$$\begin{array}{llcl}
\mathrm{iszero}^{\dagger} & \{0\ 1\ 2\ \ldots\ n\ \ n{+}1\ \ldots\} & = & \{T\ F\ F\ \ldots\ F\ F\ \ldots\} \\
& \ \downarrow\ \ \downarrow\ \qquad\ \downarrow\ \ \ \downarrow & & \ \downarrow\ \ \downarrow\ \qquad\ \downarrow\ \downarrow \\
& \{0\ \ \ 2\ \ldots\ n\ \ n{+}1\ \ldots\} & = & \{T\ \ \ F\ \ldots\ F\ F\ \ldots\} \\
& \ \downarrow\ \qquad\qquad\ \downarrow\ \ \ \downarrow & & \ \downarrow\ \qquad\qquad\ \downarrow\ \downarrow \\
& & & \\
& \ \downarrow\ \qquad\qquad\ \downarrow\ \ \ \downarrow & & \ \downarrow\ \qquad\qquad\ \downarrow\ \downarrow \\
& \{0\ \qquad\qquad n\ \ n{+}1\ \ldots\} & = & \{T\ \qquad\qquad F\ F\ \ldots\} \\
& \ \downarrow\ \qquad\qquad\qquad\ \downarrow & & \ \downarrow\ \qquad\qquad\quad\ \downarrow \\
& \{0\ \qquad\qquad\quad\ n{+}1\ \ldots\} & = & \{T\ \qquad\qquad\quad\ F\ \ldots\}
\end{array}$$

$$\mathrm{colim}\ \langle \mathrm{iszero}^{\dagger}(X_n) \rangle = \{\mathrm{true}\}$$

Figure 2

We now revise the treatment of non-deterministic recursive program schemes in the previous section to incorporate unbounded non-determinism, in the form of a choice construct which is the applicative analogue to Apt and Plotkin's "random assignment".

Definition: With Σ, Φ as in Section 3, let K be a designated non-empty set of constants (i.e. operation symbols of rank 0) in Σ. There is no restriction on the cardinality of K - this can give rise to unbounded (even uncountable) non-determinism.

Now let ? be a constant not in $\Sigma \cup \Phi$. $\Sigma? = \Sigma \cup \{?\}$.

The definition of ndrps is revised so that right-hand-sides of recursion equations are terms in $T_{\Sigma? \cup \Phi}(X)$.

The definition of the transition relation is revised by replacing clause (II) by

(II') (k) $? \rightarrow k \ \forall k \in K$.

The definition of CS is now based on this revised relation, but otherwise unchanged. A is made into a $\Sigma?\cup\Phi$-algebra by interpreting ? and each $\varphi \in \Phi$ as Ω. Then $OP_{K,S,A}$ is defined exactly as $OP_{S,A}$ in Section 3.

$P(CT_\Sigma(X))$ is made into a $\Sigma?$-algebra by interpreting each $\sigma \in \Sigma$ as the pointwise extension of the free operation, and ? as K (i.e. the designated (multi)-set of constants).

With these revisions we obtain an exact analogue of the Theorem of Section 3:

Theorem

$$OP_{K,S,A} = \lambda a.\ \hat{a}^{\dagger} \circ \{\hat{\ }\}_X \circ Y\hat{S}$$

Example

To show how this result encompasses the type of language studied by Apt and Plotkin (in an applicative setting), we consider particular choices for Σ, K and A.

$\Sigma_0 = \{k_n \mid n \in N\}$ $\Sigma_1 = \{PRED, SUCC\}$ $\Sigma_3 = \{IF\}$

$K = \{k_n \mid n \in N\}$

$|A| = N_\perp$

$IF_A = \lambda(x,y,z).x=0 \Rightarrow y,z$ $PRED_A = \lambda x.x \dot{-} 1$ $SUCC_A = \lambda x.x+1$ $k_{n_A} = n$

I.e. A is the flat domain of the natural numbers, with the obvious interpretation of the operations. This example is essentially a first-order, one-sorted PCF [Plo75], with ? our applicative analogue of "random assignment" [AP].

Acknowledgements

The ideas of Lehmann and Boudol have provided inspiration. I would particularly like to thank Tom Maibaum for his help and encouragement.

References

[ADJ] Goguen, J. Thatcher, J. Wagner, E.G. and Wright, J.B. "Initial Algebra Semantics and Continuous Algebras", JACM (1977).

[AP] Apt K. and Plotkin G. "A Cook's tour of Countable Non-determinism", 8th ICALP, Springer LNCS 115, 1981.

[Bac] Back, R. "Semantics of Unbounded Non-Determinism", ICALP '80, Springer LNCS 84, 1980.

[Bou] Boudol G. "Semantique Operationelle et Algebrique Des Programmes Recursifs Non-Deterministes" These d'Etat, Universite de Paris VII, 1980.

[Bro] Broy M. "A Fixed Point Theory for Communication and Concurrency", Munich 1982.

[Gue] Guessarian I. Algebraic Semantics, Springer LNCS 99, 1981.

[Hend82] Henderson P. "Purely Functional Operating Systems", in Functional Programming and its Applications, ed. Darlington, Henderson and Turner, Cambridge 1982.

[Henn81] Hennessy M. "Powerdomains and Nondeterministic Recursive Definitions", Springer LNCS 137, 1982.

[Kah74] Kahn G. "The Semantics of a Simple Language for Parallel Programming", IFIP Congress 74, 1974.

[Kel] Keller R.M. "Denotational Models for Parallel Programs with Indeterminate Operators", in Formal Description of Programming Concepts ed. Neuhold, North Holland 1978.

[Leh76] Lehmann D. "Categories for Fixed Point Semantics", FOCS 17, also Warwick University Theory of Computation Report, 1976.

[LS81] Lehmann D.and Smyth M.J. "Algebraic Specification of Abstract Data Types", Mathematical Systems Theory, 1981.

[Niv] Nivat M. "Nondeterministic Programs: an Algebraic Overview", IFIP Congress 80, 1980.

[Par] Park D.M.R. "On the Semantics of Fair Parallelism", Springer LNCS 86, 1980.

[Plo75] Plotkin G.D. "LCF Considered as a Programming Language", Theoretical Computer Science 1977.

[Plo76] Plotkin G.D. "A Powerdomain Construction", SIAM Journal on Computing, 1976.

[Plo80] Plotkin G.D. "Dijkstra's Predicate Transformers and Smyth's Powerdomains", Springer LNCS 86, 1980.

[Poi] Poigne A. "On Effective Computations of Non-Deterministic Schemes", Springer LNCS 137, (1982).

[Sco69] Scott D. "An Outline of a Mathematical Theory of Computation", Oxford 1969.

AN AXIOMATIZATION OF THE INTERMITTENT ASSERTION METHOD USING TEMPORAL LOGIC
(extended abstract)

Krzysztof R. APT

LITP, Université Paris 7, 2 Place Jussieu, 75251 Paris, France

Carole DELPORTE

LCR-Thomson, Domaine de Corbeville, 91401 Orsay, France

Abstract. The intermittent assertion method proposed by Burstall [B] and subsequently popularized by Manna and Waldinger [MW] is axiomatized using a fragment of temporal logic. The proposed proof system allows to reason about while-programs. The proof system is proved to be arithmetically sound and complete in the sense of Harel [H]. The results of the paper generalize a corresponding result of Pnueli [P] proved for unstructured programs.

The system decomposes into two parts. The first part allows to prove *liveness* properties using as axioms theorems of the second part allowing to prove simple *safety* properties.

The completeness proof is constructive and provides a heuristic for proving specific liveness formulas.

1. INTRODUCTION

In 1977 Pnueli [P] introduced temporal logic as a tool for reasoning about sequential and concurrent programs. This approach received subsequently a lot of attention and since then several proof systems based on temporal were proposed. These proof systems allow to prove more complicated properties of concurrent programs than partial correctness or deadlock freedom (see e.g. [MP 1], [MP 2], [OL]).

However, most of these systems allow to reason about *unstructured* programs only. The only exception is the proof system of Owicki and Lamport [OL]. We find that in order to reason about structured programs a firm theoretical basis should be first established. In our opinion this was not done in [OL] where various obvious or less obvious axioms and proof rules are missing.

To clarify these issues we carry out our analysis in the framework of while-programs. Several (but not all) of the introduced axioms and proof rules are also valid in the case of parallel programs.

As a byproduct of our investigations we obtain a sound and complete axiomatization of the intermittent assertion method introduced in 1974 by Burstall [B] and subsequently popularized by Manna and Waldinger [MW]. This method allows to prove total correctness of sequential programs.

Its basic idea is to consider a construct "if sometime p at l_0 then sometime q at l_1" where p,q represent assertions about the program and l_0,l_1 are labels attached to subprograms of the program in question. The interpretation of "sometime p at l_0" is as expected - each execution of the (whole) program reaches at some point the label l_0 at the moment when p holds. If start and halt are the labels attached to the beginning and to the end of the program, respectively, then total correctness of the program with respect to p and q can be expressed by the statement "if sometime p at start then sometime q at halt".

To prove total correctness of the program with respect to p and q it is now sufficient to find a sequence of (not necessarily different) labels $l_0,\dots,l_k$ and assertions $p_0,\dots,p_k$ such that l_0 = start, l_k = halt, $p_0 = p$, $p_k = q$ and for each $i=0,\dots,k-1$ the statement "if sometime p_i at l_i then sometime p_{i+1} at l_{i+1}" holds. In the examples discussed in [B] and [MW] proofs of the above statements were presented informally.

The proof system we present here allows to carry out the above proofs formally. This proof system makes use of a fragment of temporal logic. Of course, temporal interpretation of the intermittent assertion method is not new - it was already given in the original paper of Pnueli [P] where also soundness and completeness of this method under the temporal interpretation was proved for the case of unstructured programs.

We adopt here the formalism of Lamport [L] and Owicki and Lamport [OL] where the formulas "at S" and "after S" are introduced. These formulas express the fact that the control in the program is just before the statement S or just after the statement S, respectively.

The statement "if sometime p at l_0 then sometime q at l_1" is interpreted as $\text{at } S_0 \wedge p \rightsquigarrow \text{at } S_1 \wedge q$ where l_i is the label attached to the subprogram $S_i (i=0,1)$. The operator "$\rightsquigarrow$" is the "leads to" operator of temporal logic (see [P] and [OL]) which is interpreted as $p \rightsquigarrow q \equiv \Box(p \supset \Diamond q)$. This provides a rigorous interpretation of the "sometime - sometime" construct.

In the proof system which we provide, for a given program T, all true formulas of the form $\eta_0 S_0 \wedge p \rightsquigarrow \eta_1 S_1 \wedge q$ where $\eta_0, \eta_1 \in \{\text{at, after}\}$ can be proved. In terminology of [OL] our system allows thus to prove *liveness* properties of sequential programs. The formulas of the above type are called throughout the paper *liveness formulas*.

To understand the essence of the problems investigated here let us consider the liveness formula $\varphi \equiv$ at $S \wedge x = 0 \rightsquigarrow$ after $S \wedge x = 5$ where $S \equiv x{:=}x+2$. This formula is of course false if we interpret it as $\{x=0\}S\{x=5\}$ in the sense of Hoare's logic of [Ho]. However, if we consider S as a subprogram of the program $T \equiv x{:=}0$; T' where $T' \equiv$ while $x < 10$ do $x{:=}x+2$; $x{:=}x+1$ od then the formula φ is true. Thus the truth of the liveness formulas depends on the *context* in which they are considered. We indicate this dependence by attaching the context program T to the truth relation "$\models$" and the provability relation "$\vdash$".

In the course of the proofs (here of $\models_T \varphi$) we first prove the formulas in the minimal context in which they are true (here T') and subsequently extend the context to the desired one (here T).

The proof system consists of two parts. The first of them uses as axioms formulas expressing simple safety properties and allows to prove the liveness formulas. This subsystem is a mixture of axioms and proof rules motivated by [Ho], [P], [L], [OL] and [H].

The second part is designed to prove the safety properties which were adopted as axioms in the first part. This part is partially motivated by [L] and [OL]. Combining these two parts together we get a hierarchically built proof system appropriate for proving liveness formulas directly from first order assertions.

The main contribution of the paper is the proof of the arithmetical soundness and completeness of this system in the sense of Harel [H]. While the soundness proof is straightforward (and omitted here) the completeness proof requires a careful analysis of several interrelated cases.

This completeness proof is constructive in the sense that it provides a heuristic for proving specific liveness formulas. Such a heuristic helps to choose a desired chain of liveness formulas $\mu_i \rightsquigarrow \mu_{i+1}$ $(i=0,\dots,k-1)$ which breaks the proof of $\mu = \mu_0 \rightsquigarrow \mu_k = \mu'$ into k pieces.

2.- PRELIMINARIES

We are interested here in proving the formulas of the form $\eta_0 S_0 \wedge p \rightsquigarrow \eta_1 S_1 \wedge q$ where $\eta_0, \eta_1 \in \{at, after\}$, S_0, S_1 are while-programs and p,q are assertions. To this end we define various classes of formulas which will be used in the sequel.

Let L be a first order language with equality. We call the formulas of L *assertions* and denote them by the letters p,q,r. The letters x,y,z, denote the variables of L, the letter t denotes the terms (*expressions*) of L, the letter b denotes a quantifier-free formula (a *Boolean expression*) of L.

By W we denote the class of while-programs which is defined as usual. The programs from W use variables, expressions and Boolean expressions of the language L. They are denoted by the letters S,T.

We allow formulas of the form at S and after S for $S \in W$. They are called *control formulas* and are denoted by the letter C.

From assertions and control formulas we can built up certain formulas which will be called *mixed formulas*. They are of the form $C \wedge p$. Mixed formulas are denoted by the letter μ.

The first subsystem discussed in section 4 allows two type of formulas : $C \wedge p \supset C' \wedge q$ and $C \wedge p \rightsquigarrow C' \wedge q$. If in the first type of a formula $C \equiv C'$ we omit C'. We also omit all assertions of the form true. The formulas of the form $\mu_1 \rightsquigarrow \mu_2$ will be of main interest. We call them *liveness formulas*.

3.- SEMANTICS

To interpret the meaning of the formulas allowed in the proof system we provide an appropriate class of models for them. These models have to take into account the semantics of programs as the formulas refer directly to them. Therefore we define first the semantics of programs appropriate for our purposes. This semantics is a slight variant of the one introduced in [HP].

Let I be an interpretation of the assertion language L with a nonempty domain D. By an *assignation* we mean a function assigning to each variable x of L a value from the domain D. By a ***state*** we mean a pair which consists of a program $S \in W$ or an empty program E and an assignation. We denote states by the letter s. If s is a state then by $\bar{s}$ we denote the assignation being its component. For a set C of states we define $\bar{C}$ to be the corresponding set of assignations: $\bar{C} = \{\bar{s} : s \in C\}$.

The value of a term t in an assignation $\bar{s}$ (written as $\bar{s}(t)$) and a truth of a formula p of L in an assignation $\bar{s}$ (written as $\models_I p(\bar{s})$) are defined as usual.

We define now a transition relation "$\rightarrow$" between states. Intuitively, for $s_0 = \langle S_0, \bar{s}_0 \rangle$ and $s_1 = \langle S_1, \bar{s}_1 \rangle$ $s_0 \rightarrow s_1$ means that one step in execution of S_0 in assignation $\bar{s}_0$ leads to assignation $\bar{s}_1$ with S_1 being the remainder of S_0 to be executed. If S_0 terminates in $\bar{s}_1$ then S_1 is empty, i.e. $S_1 \equiv E$. We assume that for any program $S: (E\ ;\ S) = (S\ ;\ E) = S$.

We define the relation $s \rightarrow s_1$ by the following clauses

i) $\langle x:=t, \bar{s} \rangle \rightarrow \langle E, \bar{s}_1 \rangle$

where $\bar{s}_1(y) = \bar{s}(y)$ for $y \not\equiv x$ and $\bar{s}_1(x) = \bar{s}(t)$

ii) If $\langle S, \bar{s} \rangle \rightarrow \langle S_1, \bar{s}_1 \rangle$ then for any program T $\langle S\ ;\ T, \bar{s} \rangle \rightarrow \langle S_1\ ;\ T, \bar{s}_1 \rangle$

iii) $<$if b then S_1 else S_2 fi, $\bar{s}> \to <S_1,\bar{s}>$ if $|=_I b(\bar{s})$

iv) $<$if b then S_1 else S_2 fi, $\bar{s}> \to <S_2,\bar{s}>$ if $|\neq_I b(\bar{s})$

v) $<$while b do S od, $\bar{s}> \to <S$; while b do S od, $\bar{s}>$ if $|=_I b(\bar{s})$

vi) $<$while b do S od, $\bar{s}> \to <E,\bar{s}>$ if $|\neq_I b(\bar{s})$

vii) $<E,\bar{s}> \to <E,\bar{s}>$

Let $\to^*$ denote the transitive closure of $\to$.

Given now a program T by an *execution sequence* of T we mean a maximal sequence of states $s_0, s_1, \ldots$ such that $s_0 = <T,\bar{s}_0>$ and for $i = 0,1,\ldots$ $s_i \to s_{i+1}$ holds. Clause vii) implies that each execution sequence is infinite. Execution sequences are denoted by the letters σ, τ . If $\sigma = s_0, s_1, \ldots$ then by definition $\sigma^i = s_i, s_{i+1}, \ldots$.

For a program T we denote by Σ_T the set of all of its execution sequences closed under the truncation operation σ^i, i.e. $\sigma \in \Sigma_T$ implies that for any $i \geq 0$ $\sigma^i \in \Sigma_T$. Of course Σ_T depends on the interpretation I.

Having defined semantics of the programs we now define semantics of the control formulas.

Let S be a subprogram of T. We define

$|=_{T,I}$ at S(s) iff $\exists \sigma \in \Sigma_T$ (s is an element of σ) and $s = <S;S',\bar{s}>$ for some S' ;

$|=_{T,I}$ after S(s) iff $\exists s_1 \exists \sigma \in \Sigma_T$ (s, s_1 are element of σ)

$<S;S',\bar{s}_1> = s_1 \to^* s = <S',\bar{s}>$ for some S'

and if $S' \not\equiv E$ then for no s_2 such that $s_1 \to^* s_2 \to^* s$ $s_2 = <S',\bar{s}_2>$.

Intuitively, $|=_{T,I}$ at S(s) holds if s is a state in an execution sequence of T such that the subprogram S is just to be executed in s. And $|=_{T,I}$ after S(s) holds if s is a state in an execution sequence of T such that the execution of the subprogram S has just terminated in s. (Note that our interpretation of after S, differs from that of [OL].) Of course the above definitions are not sufficiently precise as various occurrences of S and S' in σ do not need to correspond with the same program. To avoid the confusion we should actually assign to each subprogram of T a unique label. It is clear how to perform this process and we leave it to the reader.

Note that

$|=_{T,I}$ at T(s) iff $s = <T,\bar{s}>$ and

$|=_{T,I}$ after T(s) iff $s = <E,\bar{s}>$ and $\exists \sigma \in \Sigma_T$ (s is an element of σ).

The truth of assertions does not depend on the programs and we naturally put

$\models_{T,I} p(s)$ iff $\models_I p(\bar{s})$

where p is a formula of L.

The truth of mixed formulas and formulas of the form $\mu \supset p$ and $C \supset C'$ is now defined in a natural way.

Finally we define the truth of liveness formulas. It depends on an execution sequence as it states a property of execution sequences and not states. We define

$\models_{T,I} \mu_1 \leadsto \mu_2(\sigma)$ iff $\sigma \in \Sigma_T$ and

$\forall_j\ [\models_{T,I} \mu_1(s_j) \Rightarrow \exists\ k \geq j \models_{T,I} \mu_2(s_k)]$

where $\sigma = s_0, s_1, \ldots$

To make the definition of truth uniform for all types of formulas considered here we define

$\models_{T,I} \varphi\ (\sigma)$ iff $\models_{T,I} \varphi(s_0)$ where $\sigma = s_0, s_1, \ldots$

for all formulas φ whose definition of truth depended on a state only.

We now say that a formula φ of any type *is true with respect to* T *and* I, written as $\models_{T,I} \varphi$, if for all $\sigma \in \Sigma_T$ $\models_{T,I} \varphi\ (\sigma)$ holds.

This completes the definition of semantics.

4.- A SUBSYSTEM FOR PROVING LIVENESS FORMULAS

We present here the first part of the proof system called L which is designed to prove the liveness formulas from a certain set of hypotheses. The proof system L consists of two parts. The first part specifies how the control moves through the program. It is motivated by similar proof rules and axioms given in [L] and [OL]. The while rule shows how to prove the liveness properties of a while loop. It is an obvious adaptation of the rule given in [H] appropriate for proving the termination of while loops.

The second part axiomatizes the temporal operator "   " and shows how to manipulate the liveness formulas.

The first part consists of the following axioms and rules :

ASSIGNMENT AXIOM

A1 : $\vdash_T$ at $S \wedge p[t/x]$ after $S \wedge p$

where $S \equiv x:=t$ is a subprogram of T.

Here as usual, p[t/x] stands for the result of substituting t for the free occurrences of x in p.

CONCATENATION AXIOMS and RULE

Let $S \equiv S_1;S_2$ be a subprogram of T

A2 : $\vdash_T$ at $S \supset$ at S_1

A3 : $\vdash_T$ at $S_1 \supset$ at S

A4 : $\vdash_T$ after $S_1 \supset$ at S_2

A5 : $\vdash_T$ at $S_2 \supset$ after S_1

if S_2 is not a while construct

A6 : $\vdash_T$ after $S_2 \supset$ after S

A7 : $\vdash_T$ after $S \supset$ after S_2

R1 : concatenation rule

$$\frac{\vdash_T \text{ after } S_0 \supset \neg p}{\vdash_T \text{ at } S_2 \wedge p \supset \text{after } S_1}$$

where $S_2 \equiv$ while b do S_0 od

SELECTION AXIOMS AND RULES

Let $S \equiv$ if b then S_1 else S_2 fi be a subprogram

A8 : $\vdash_T$ at $S \wedge b \wedge p \rightsquigarrow$ at $S_1 \wedge p$

A9 : $\vdash_T$ at $S \wedge \neg b \wedge p \rightsquigarrow$ at $S_2 \wedge p$

A10 : $\vdash_T$ after $S_1 \supset$ after S

A11 : $\vdash_T$ after $S_2 \supset$ after S

R2 : $$\frac{\vdash_T \text{ after } S_1 \supset \neg q}{\vdash_T \text{ after } S \wedge q \supset \text{after } S_2}$$

R3 : $$\frac{\vdash_T \text{ after } S_2 \supset \neg q}{\vdash_T \text{ after } S \wedge q \supset \text{after } S_1}$$

WHILE AXIOMS AND RULES

Let $S \equiv$ while b do S_0 od be a subprogram of T.

A12 : $\vdash_T$ at $S \wedge b \wedge p \rightsquigarrow$ at $S_0 \wedge p$

A13 : $\vdash_T$ at $S \wedge \neg b \wedge p \rightsquigarrow$ after $S \wedge p$

A14 : $\vdash_T$ after $S_0 \supset$ at S

R4 : $$\frac{\vdash_T at^+S \supset \neg q}{\vdash_T at\ S \wedge q \supset after\ S_0}$$

The formula at^+S attempts to describe the fact that the control is at the beginning of S for the first time.

The form of at^+S depends on the direct context of the <u>while</u> loop S within T. It is defined as follows

If S appears in T in the form :

$S_1;S$ then $at^+S \equiv after\ S_1$,

$T_1 \equiv$ <u>if</u> b_1 <u>then</u> $S(;S_1)$ <u>else</u> S_2 <u>fi</u> then $at^+S \equiv at\ T_1 \wedge b_1$,

$T_1 \equiv$ <u>if</u> b_1 <u>then</u> S_1 <u>else</u> $S(;S_2)$ <u>fi</u> then $at^+S \equiv at\ T_1 \wedge \neg b_1$,

$T_1 \equiv$ <u>while</u> b_1 <u>do</u> $S(;S_1)$ <u>od</u> then $at^+S \equiv at\ T_1 \wedge b_1$.

If none of the above cases arises then T is of the form $S;S_1$ and we put $at^+S \equiv at\ T$.

R5 : <u>while-rule</u>

$$\frac{\vdash_T at\ S \wedge p(n+1) \supset b,\ \vdash_T at\ S_0 \wedge p(n+1) \rightsquigarrow after\ S_0 \wedge p(n)}{\vdash_T at\ S \wedge \exists\ n\ p(n) \rightsquigarrow at\ S \wedge p(0)}$$

Here $p(n)$ is an assertion with a free variable n which does not appear in S and ranges over natural numbers.

The second part of the system L consists of the following rules :

R6 : reflexivity rule

$$\frac{\vdash_T \mu_1 \supset \mu_2}{\vdash_T \mu_1 \rightsquigarrow \mu_2}$$

R7 : transitivity rule

$$\frac{\vdash_T \mu_1 \rightsquigarrow \mu_2,\ \vdash_T \mu_2 \rightsquigarrow \mu_3}{\vdash_T \mu_1 \rightsquigarrow \mu_3}$$

R8 : confluence rule

$$\frac{\vdash_T \mu_1 \wedge b \rightsquigarrow \mu_2,\ \vdash_T \mu_1 \wedge \neg b \rightsquigarrow \mu_2}{\vdash_T \mu_1 \rightsquigarrow \mu_2}$$

We also adopt without mentioning all axioms and proof rules of classical logic concerning $\supset$ and $\wedge$ applied to formulas $\mu_1 \supset \mu_2$ and their special cases.

The system L allows to prove $\vdash_T C \wedge p \supset C'$ whenever $\models_{T,I} C \wedge p \supset C'$. Thus if we wish to prove $\vdash_{T,I} C \wedge p \supset C' \wedge q$ it suffices to prove $\vdash_T C \wedge p \supset q$.

In section 7 we present another part of the proof system which allows to prove such formulas directly from assertions. For a moment we accept these formulas as axioms.

Let A be a set of the formulas of the form $|-_T \mu \supset p$. Given a liveness formula φ we say that φ *can be proved from* A, written as $A \,|-_T \varphi$, if there exists a proof of φ in the proof system L which uses some of the elements of A as axioms.

5.- SOUNDNESS

In order to prove soundness of the proof system L we should interpret the formulas in a model. However, not all models are appropriate here. The reason for it is that the while rule R5 refers to natural numbers. To ensure a correct interpretation of this rule we should restrict ourselves to models which contain natural numbers. This leads us to *arithmetical interpretations* defined in [H]. We recall the definition :

let L^+ be the minimal extension of L containing the language L_p of Peano arithmetic and a unary relation nat(x). Call an interpretation I of L^+ *arithmetical* if its domain includes the set of natural numbers, I provides the standard interpretation for L_p, and nat(x), is interpreted as the relation "to be a natural number". Additionally, we require that there exists a formula of L^+ which, when interpreted under I, provides the ability to encode finite sequences of elements from the domain of I into one element. (The last requirement is needed only for the completeness proof.) Our proof system is suitable only for assertion languages of the form L^+, and an expression such as p(n) is actually a shorthand for nat(n) $\wedge$ p(n).

Given now a program T and an arithmetical interpretation I denote by Th(T,I) the set of all formulas of the form $|-_T \mu \supset q$ for which $|=_{T,I} \mu \supset q$.

We have the following theorem :

SOUNDNESS THEOREM

Let T be a program from W and let I be an arithmetical interpretation. For any liveness formula φ if $Th(T,I) \,|-_T \varphi$ then $|=_{T,I} \varphi$. □

Note that any liveness formula true or provable in a context of T refers to subprograms of T only.

6.- COMPLETENESS

The following theorem states completeness of the subsystem L.

COMPLETENESS THEOREM

Let T be a program from $\mathcal{W}$ and let I be an arithmetical interpretation. For any liveness formula φ if $\models_{T,I} \varphi$ then $Th(T,I) \vdash_T \varphi$.

The proof of the theorem relies on the following important proposition.

Proposition 1 : Let S be a subprogram of T. Then for any liveness formula φ if $Th(S,I) \vdash_S \varphi$ then $Th(T,I) \vdash_T \varphi$.

Proof : The proof of $\vdash_S \varphi$ becomes a proof of $\vdash_T \varphi$ if we replace everywhere in it "$\vdash_S$" by "$\vdash_T$". □

This proposition has a semantic counterpart.

Proposition 2 : Let S be a subprogram of T. Then for any liveness formula φ if $\models_{S,I} \varphi$ then $\models_{T,I} \varphi$. □

The proof of the theorem proceeds by structural induction with respect to T. Given $\varphi \equiv \mu \leadsto \mu'$ we find in each case a chain of the intermediate mixed formulas $\mu_o, \mu_1, \ldots, \mu_k$ such that $\mu = \mu_o, \mu_k = \mu'$ and for each $i=0,\ldots,k-1$ $\models_T \mu_i \leadsto \mu_{i+1}$. This chain is so chosen that for every $i=0,\ldots,k-1$ either $\models_S \mu_i \leadsto \mu_{i+1}$ for a proper subprogram S of T or $\mu_i \quad \mu_{i+1}$ can be proved directly. In the first case by the induction hypothesis $Th(S,I) \vdash_S \mu_i \leadsto \mu_{i+1}$ so $Th(T,I) \vdash_T \mu_i \leadsto \mu_{i+1}$ by proposition 1. In the latter case one either applies the axioms or proof rules directly or makes use of the induction hypothesis. Depending on the case the length of the chain varies between 2 and 5. In some cases more than one chain is needed and the confluence rule is used to obtain the desired result.

7.- A SUBSYSTEM FOR PROVING FORMULAS OF THE FORM $\vdash_T \mu \supset p$

The subsystem presented in section 4 used as axioms formulas of the form $\vdash_T \mu \supset p$. Such a choice of axioms is unsatisfactory for our purposes as these formulas refer to programs and the properties expressed by them are not always easy to verify. Note for example that $\models_{T,I}$ after $T \wedge p \supset q$ is equivalent to $\models_{T,I} \{true\}\ T\ \{p \supset q\}$ in the sense of Hoare's logic (see e.g. [A]).

To remedy this deficiency we provide now another part of the proof system called $\mathcal{S}$ appropriate for proving this type of formulas.

The system $\mathcal{S}$ allows to prove arbitrary true formulas of the form $\vdash_T C \supset p$ so also $\vdash_T C \wedge p \supset q$ since $C \wedge p \supset q \equiv C \supset (p \supset q)$.

Two types of formulas are allowed in the system $\mathcal{S}$: $\mu \supset p$ and $C \supset C'$.

The system consists of the following axioms and rules :

ASSIGNMENT RULE

S1 : let $S \equiv x:=t$ be a subprogram of T

$$\frac{\vdash_T \text{at } S \supset p\,[t/x]}{\vdash_T \text{after } S \supset p}$$

SELECTION RULES

Let $S \equiv \underline{\text{if}}\ b\ \underline{\text{then}}\ S_1\ \underline{\text{else}}\ S_2\ \underline{\text{fi}}$ be a subprogram of T

S2 : $$\frac{\vdash_T \text{at } S \supset p}{\vdash_T \text{at } S_1 \supset p \wedge b}$$ if S_1 does not begin with a while loop

S3 : $$\frac{\vdash_T \text{at } S \supset p}{\vdash_T \text{at } S_2 \supset p \wedge \neg b}$$ if S_2 does not begin with a while loop

S4 : $$\frac{\vdash_T \text{after } S_1 \supset p,\ \vdash_T \text{after } S_2 \supset r}{\vdash_T \text{after } S \supset p \vee r}$$

CONCATENATION AXIOMS

Axioms A2 - A7

WHILE RULES

Let $S \equiv \underline{\text{while}}\ b\ \underline{\text{do}}\ S_0\ \underline{\text{od}}$ be a subprogram of T

S5 : $$\frac{\vdash_T \text{at } S \supset p}{\vdash_T \text{at } S_0 \supset p \wedge b}$$ if S_0 does not begin with a while loop

S6 : $$\frac{\vdash_T \text{at } S \supset p}{\vdash_T \text{after } S \supset p \wedge \neg b}$$

S7 : $$\frac{\vdash_T \text{at}^+ S \supset p,\quad \text{at } S_0 \supset p \wedge b \vdash_T \text{after } S_0 \supset p}{\vdash_T \text{at } S \supset p}$$

The second premise of rule S7 means that there exists a proof of $\vdash_T$ after $S_0 \supset p$ in the system from the assumption $\vdash_T$ at $S_0 \supset p \wedge b$. This expresses in the system a property corresponding to $\{p \wedge b\}\ S_0\ \{p\}$ in the sense of Hoare's logic. Note that for any I : $\models_I \{p \wedge b\} S_0 \{p\}$ implies $[\models_{T,I} \text{at } S_0 \supset p \wedge b \Rightarrow\ \models_{T,I} \text{after } S_0 \supset p]$ but not necessarily conversely. $\text{at}^+ S$ is defined in section 4.

INITIALIZATION AXIOM

B1 : $\vdash_T$ at $T \supset \underline{\text{true}}$.

Let A be a set of assertions. We say that a formula $\vdash_T C \supset p$ *can be proved from* A, written as $A \vdash_T C \supset p$, if there exists a proof in the above system which uses some of the elements of A as axioms.

We denote by Th(I) the set all assertions true in I.

The following theorem states arithmetical soundness and completeness of the system $\mathcal{S}$.

THEOREM Let T be a program from $\mathcal{W}$ and let I be an arithmetical interpretation. Then for any formula $C \supset p$

$$Th(I) \vdash_T C \supset p \text{ iff } \models_{T,I} C \supset p.$$

The completeness proof, i.e. the implication "$\Leftarrow$" proceeds by induction with respect to a certain well-ordering defined on the control formulas. This ordering is defined as follows. Consider the directed graph representing the flowchart of T with nodes being the control formulas. Remove now from this graph all edges causing cycles, i.e. edges leading from after S_0 to at S for any subprogram S ≡ while b do S_0 od of T. The resulting graph defines the well-ordering in question. Due to the lack of space the details of the proof are omitted.

The converse implication, i.e. the soundness proof is straightforward. A precise proof requires techniques similar to those of section 3.7 of [A] to deal properly with rule S7.

COROLLARY Let T be a program from $\mathcal{W}$ and let I be an arithmetical interpretation. Then for any liveness formula φ

$$Th(I) \vdash_T \varphi \text{ iff } \models_{T,I} \varphi. \qquad \square$$

Here $\vdash_T$ refers to the provability in the final proof system which contains all mentioned axioms and rules.

Proofs will appear in the full version of the paper.

Acknowledgements. We are grateful to D. Lehmann for suggesting a simplified completeness proof of the system $\mathcal{L}$ and to E.-R. Olderog for critical remarks concerning the first version of the paper.

REFERENCES

[A] Apt, K.R., Ten Years of Hoare's logic, a survey, part I, TOPLAS, vol. 3,4, pp. 431-483, 1981.

[B] Burstall, R.M., Program proving as hand simulation with a little induction, in : Proceedings IFIP 74, pp. 308-312, North Holland, Amsterdam, 1974.

[H] Harel, D., First order dynamic logic, Lecture Notes in Computer Science, 68, Springer Verlag, 1979.

[HP] Hennessy, M.C.B., Plotkin G.D., Full abstraction for a simple programming language, in : Proceedings 8th Symposium MFCS, Lecture Notes in Computer Science, 74, pp. 108-120, 1979.

[Ho] Hoare, C.A.R., An axiomatic basis of computer programming, Communications ACM, vol. 12, 10, pp. 576-580, 583, 1969.

[L] Lamport, L., The "Hoare Logic" of concurrent programs, Acta Informatica, vol. 14, 1, pp. 21-37, 1980.

[MP1] Manna Z., Pnueli A., Verification of concurrent programs ; The temporal framework, in : The Correctness Problem in Computer Science, International Lecture Series in Computer Science, Academic Press, London, 1981.

[MP2] Manna Z., Pnueli A., Verification of concurrent programs ; Temporal proof principles, in : Logic of Programs, Lecture Notes in Computer Science, 131, pp. 200-252, 1982.

[MW] Manna Z., Waldinger R., Is "Sometime" sometimes better than "Always" ?, Communications ACM, vol. 21, 2, pp. 159-172, 1978.

[OL] Owicki S., Lamport L., Proving liveness properties of concurrent programs, TOPLAS, vol. 4, 3, pp. 455-495, 1982.

[P] Pnuéli, A., The temporal logic of programs, in : Proceedings 18th Symposium FOCS, pp. 46-57, IEEE, Providence, R.I., 1977.

TOPOLOGICAL CHARACTERIZATIONS OF INFINITE BEHAVIOURS OF TRANSITION SYSTEMS

André ARNOLD
Laboratoire d'Informatique
Université de Poitiers and L.I.T.P.

Abstract

Different kinds of infinite behaviours of different kind of transition systems are characterized by their topological properties.

INTRODUCTION

In [5], processes are represented by non deterministic automata with a possibly infinite number of states, called "transition systems". Then the infinite behaviour of a process is the infinite behaviour of the transition system it is represented by, ie the set of infinite words recognized by the transition system, which are defined exactly in the same way as infinite words recognized by a (finite) automaton [3].

These transition systems are assumed in [5] to be "finitely branching" (in each state there is only a finite number of possible transition). This property, obviously satisfied by finite automata, allows to apply Koenig's lemma and thus has strong consequences when studying behaviours of such transition systems. Then a natural question arises : how restrictive is this assumption ? Or, in other words, what is exactly the class L of infinite behaviours of finitely branching transition systems ?

Some useful hints are supplied by obvious answers to similar questions (proofs of these facts will nevertheless be given in this paper).
- any set of infinite words is the behaviour of a continuously branching transition system.
- the class of closed sets of infinite words (for the topology on infinite words used in [5]) is exactly the class of infinite behaviours of deterministic transition systems, where the recognition criterion is

slightly strengthened, and, for the same topology, the class G_δ was given a similar characterization by Landweber [4].
- topological characterizations of infinite words recognized in different ways are given in [6,7].

Thus we are led to try to characterize by topological properties various classes of infinite behaviours of transition systems. These classes are related to
- the "branching type" of the transition system (deterministic, finitely branching, countably branching, continuously branching)
- the criterion of recognition : an infinite word is recognized if it goes through designed states infinitely often (it is the classical definition for finite automata [3]), or if it goes always, or if it goes almost always.

In each of these classes we can define the subclass of non ambiguous behaviours : a behaviour is non ambiguous if there is at most one way to recognize each word in the behaviour.

The results in this paper are summarized in the following chart (or theorem) :

branching type / recognition	determin.	finitely branching		countably branching		continuously branching	
		n.a.		n.a.		n.a.	
always	F	F	F	B	S	T	T
almost always	F_σ	F_σ	F_σ	B	S	T	T
infinitely often	G_δ	B	S	B	S	T	T

where F is the class of closed sets, F_σ is the class of countable unions of closed sets, G_δ is the class of class of countable intersections of open sets, B is the class of Borel Sets, S is the class of Souslin sets, T is the class of all sets.

In particular, the class L we wanted to characterize is S, and its subclass L^{na} of non ambiguous behaviours is B.

Now, classical properties of the classes S and B have their immediate counterpart for L and L^{na} ; for example
- $B = L^{na}$ is the closure of F under complement and countable union ;
- $S = L$ is closed under countable union and countable intersection ;
- $L \in B = L^{na}$ if and only if L and its complement are in $S = L$.

At last let us mention some connection with the famous Büchi-Mac-Naughton Theorem [3]. The class Rat^{ω} of sets recognized by non deterministic finite automata is the boolean closure of the class $DRat^{\omega}$ of sets recognized by deterministic finite automata. Then, since $DRat^{\omega} \subset G_{\delta} \subset \mathcal{B}$, Rat^{ω} is included in $\mathcal{B}$. Therefore, each set in *Rat* can be recognized by a non ambiguous transition system. This remark led us to the conjecture that it is also recognized by a non ambiguous finite automaton, which was proved to be true in [1].

This paper is divided in four parts. The first one contains preliminary definitions about infinite words and transition systems. In the second one we establish some general results on inclusion of various classes of behaviours. In the third part we prove some equalities between these classes and we characterize some of them. And in the last one we introduce Souslin sets and Borel sets.

1. PRELIMINARIES

1.1 Infinite words

Let A be a *countable* alphabet. As usual A^* and A^{ω} are the sets of finite and infinite sequences of letters of A. If $u \in A^{\omega}$ we denote by u(i) and u[i] the ith letter of u and the sequence of the first i letters of u.

Let us define the distance d on A^{ω} by

$$d(u,v) : \begin{cases} o & \text{if } u = v \\ 2^{-\inf\{n/u(n)\neq v(n)\}} & \text{otherwise.} \end{cases}$$

It can be easily proved that d is a ultrametric distance (ie $d(x,y) \leq \max(d(x,z),d(z,y))$). With this distance, A^{ω} is a complete metric space. Moreover the open ball $B(u,2^{-k}) = \{v \in A^{\omega}/d(u,v)<2^{-k}\}$ is $\{v \in A^{\omega}/u[k] = v[k]\} = u[k]A^{\omega}$. It follows that A^{ω} has a countable number of open balls, in other words it is a separable space.

A complete metric space which is separable is called a Polish space [2], hence

Proposition 1.1 A^{ω} *is a Polish space.*

Let now, for $u \in A^{\omega}$, FG(u) be the set $\{u[n]/n \geq o\} \subset A^*$, and for $L \subset A^*$, $FG(L) = \bigcup_{u \in L} FG(u)$. For any subset L of A^{ω} (also called ω-language) we denote by Adh(L) the set $\{u \in A^\omega / FG(u) \subset FG(L)\}$.

Proposition 1.2 For any ω-language L, Adh(L) is the topological closure of L.

Proof The topological closure of L is the set of limit points of L ie the set of points u such that any open ball of center u intersects L, ie $\forall n : u[n]A^\omega \cap L \neq \emptyset$ which is equivalent to $FG(u) \subset FG(L)$. □

1.2 Transition systems

A transition system (TS for short) A over the finite alphabet A is a 4-uple $<Q,Q_o,Q_f,\rightarrow>$ where Q is a set of states, $Q_o \subset Q$ is the set of initial states, $Q_f \subset Q$ is the set of final states, and $\rightarrow \subset Q \times A \times Q$ is the transition relation and we will denote by $q \overset{a}{\rightarrow} q'$ the fact that $(q,a,q') \in \rightarrow$.

With a ST we associate its set D(A) of degrees : $\{Card(Q_o)\} \cup \{Card\{q'/q \overset{a}{\rightarrow} q'\}/q \in Q, a \in A\}$.

The TS A is said to be

deterministic	if $\forall d \in D(A)$,	$d \leq 1$
finitely branching	if $\forall d \in D(A)$,	$d \in \mathbb{N}$
countably branching	if $\forall d \in D(A)$,	$d \leq \omega_o$
continuously branching	if $\forall d \in D(A)$,	$d \leq \omega_1$

Remark If A is countably branching, we can assume that its number of states is countable.

Let u be a finite word in A^* and let n = length(u). A *computation of* u *in* A (or a u-*computation in* A) is a sequence $q_o,q_1,\ldots,q_n$ of states such that : $q_o \in Q_o$ and $\forall i \in \{1,\ldots,n\}$, $q_{i-1} \xrightarrow{u(i)} q_i$.

An infinite u-computation $q_o,q_1,\ldots,q_n,\ldots$ in A is said to be 1-*successful* (*resp* : 2-*successful* ; 3-*successful*) if

(1) $\forall i \geq 0$, $q_i \in Q_f$; (*resp* : (2) $\exists n \geq 0$, $\forall i \geq n, q_i \in Q_f$;
(3) $\forall n \geq 0$, $\exists i \geq n$, $q_i \in Q_f$).

For i = 1,2,3, an infinite word u is i-*recognized* by A if there exists a i-successful u-computation in A and the i-*behaviour* of A is the set $L_i(A)$ of infinite words i-recognized by A. If for every u in $L_i(A)$ there exists only one i-successful u-computation in A, then A is said to be *non i-ambiguous*. Obviously any deterministic TS is non i-ambiguous for i = 1,2,3.

1.3 Classes of behaviours

For each class C of TS (deterministic, finitely branching,...) and each type of recognition we define the class $L_i(C)$ of all the i-behaviours of TS in C and its subclass $L_i^{na}(C)$ of all the i-behaviours of non i-ambiguous TS in C.

Thus the various classes we are considering are summarized in the following chart :

branching type / Type of recognition	determin.	finitely branching		countably branching		continuously branching	
		n.a.		n.a.		n.a.	
1	L_{11}	L_{12}^{na}	L_{12}	L_{13}^{na}	L_{13}	L_{14}^{na}	L_{14}
2	L_{21}	L_{22}^{na}	L_{22}	L_{23}^{na}	L_{23}	L_{24}^{na}	L_{24}
3	L_{31}	L_{32}^{na}	L_{32}	L_{33}^{na}	L_{33}	L_{34}^{na}	L_{34}

which reads as follows : for example, L_{32}^{na} is the class of all 3-behaviours of finitely branching non 3-ambiguous TS ; L_{13} is the class of all 1-behaviours of countably branching TS.

2. PRELIMINARY INCLUSIONS

From the very definitions, immediately, it follows :

<u>*Proposition 2.1*</u> *For* i=1,2,3, $L_{i1} \subset L_{i2} \subset L_{i3} \subset L_{i4}$ and $L_{i1} \subset L_{i2}^{na} \subset L_{i3}^{na} \subset L_{i4}^{na}$

For i=1,2,3, j=2,3,4, $L_{ij}^{na} \subset L_{ij}$.

We can also prove easily, by restricting any TS A to its set of final states.

<u>*Proposition 2.2*</u> *For* j=1,2,3,4, $L_{1j} \subset L_{2j}$ and $L_{1j} \subset L_{3j}$;

For j=2,3,4, $L_{1j}^{na} \subset L_{2j}^{na}$ and $L_{1j}^{na} \subset L_{3j}^{na}$.

<u>*Proposition 2.3*</u> *For* j=2,3,4, $L_{2j} \subset L_{3j}$ and $L_{2j}^{na} \subset L_{3j}^{na}$

Proof Let $A = \langle Q, Q_o, Q_f, \rightarrow\rangle$ be a TS and let A' be $\langle Q', Q'_o, Q'_f, \twoheadrightarrow\rangle$ with $Q' = Q \times \{o,\infty\}$, $Q'_o = Q_o \times \{o,\infty\}$, $Q'_f = Q_f \times \{\infty\}$ and $\twoheadrightarrow$ defined by $\langle q,n\rangle \overset{a}{\twoheadrightarrow} \langle q',n'\rangle$ iff $q \overset{a}{\rightarrow} q'$ and ($n=o$ and $n'=o$) or ($n=o, n'=\infty$, $q \notin Q_f, q' \in Q_f$) or ($n=\infty, n'=\infty, q \in Q_f$, $q' \in Q_f$).

Let us firstly notice that $\mathrm{Card}(Q'_o) = \mathrm{Card}\,(Q_o)$ and $\mathrm{Card}\,\{\langle q',n'\rangle / \langle q,n\rangle \overset{a}{\twoheadrightarrow} \langle q',n'\rangle\} \leq 2 \times \mathrm{Card}\,\{q'/q \overset{a}{\rightarrow} q'\}$, hence if A is not deterministic, A' is of the same branching type as A.

It can be proved that the sequence $(\langle q_i, n_i\rangle)_i$ where $n_i = o$ if $i \leq k$ for some k and ∞ otherwise, is a 3-successful u-computation in A' iff $(q_i)_i$ is a 2-successful u-computation in A. Moreover the previous correspondence between 3-successful u-computations in A' and 2-successful u-computations in A' is obviously bijective, thus if A is not 2-ambiguous, A' is not 3-ambiguous. □

The previous results are collected together in the following chart, where arrows represent inclusion.

Proposition 2.4

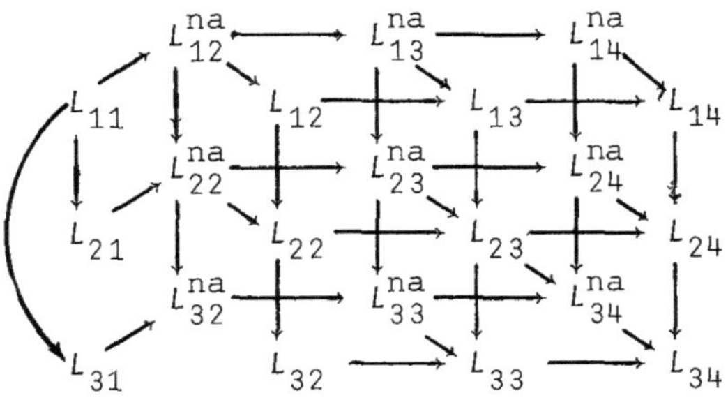

3. FURTHER RESULTS

3.1 Continuously branching transition systems

The case of continuously branching transition systems is very simple : they recognize any ω-language.

Let T be the class of all ω-languages.

Proposition 3.1 $T = L_{i4} = L^{na}_{i4}$ *for* $i = 1,2,3$

Proof Because of proposition 2.4, it suffices to prove $\mathcal{T} \subset \mathcal{L}^{na}_{14}$. Let $L \subset A^\omega$ be an ω-language. Let $\mathcal{A} = \langle Q, Q_o, Q_t, \rightarrow \rangle$ with $Q = \{\langle u,n\rangle / u \in L, n \in \mathbb{N}$, $Q_o = \{\langle u,o\rangle / u \in L\}$, $Q_f = Q$ and $\langle u,n\rangle \xrightarrow{a} \langle u,n+1\rangle$ iff $u(n+1) = a$

Then $\mathcal{A}$ is ω_1-branching and the unique u-computation in $\mathcal{A}$ is $(\langle u,n\rangle)_n$ with $u \in L$, which is 1-successful. □

3.2 Deterministic transition systems

We characterize here the behaviours of deterministic TS, and also behaviours of finitely branching TS when they have close connections with the former ones.

First let us notice that we can identify a deterministic TS $\mathcal{A} = \langle Q, Q_o, Q_f, \rightarrow \rangle$ with the set $K_\mathcal{A} \subset A^*$ defined by $u \in K_\mathcal{A}$ iff the unique u-computation $q_o, \ldots, q_n$ (if it exists at all) satisfies $q_n \in Q_f$. Then $L_i(\mathcal{A}) = L_i(A) = L_i(K_\mathcal{A})$ for $i=1,\ldots,3$ where, for $K \subset A^*$, $L_1(K) = \{u \in A^\omega / \forall n \geq 0, [u]n \in K\}$, $L_2(K) = \{u \in A^\omega /\ m \geq 0, \forall n \geq m, u[n] \in K\}$, $L_3(K) = \{u \in A^\omega / \forall m \geq 0,\ n \geq m, u[n] \in K\}$.

Conversely to every subset K of A^*, we associate the deterministic TS $\mathcal{A}_K = \langle A, \{\wedge\}, K, \rightarrow \rangle$ where $u \xrightarrow{a} v$ iff $v = ua$. Then $L_i(K) = L_i(\mathcal{A}_k)$ for $i = 1,2,3$.

Let now $\mathcal{F}$ be the class of all closed sets.

Proposition 3.2 $\mathcal{F} = \mathcal{L}_{11} = \mathcal{L}^{na}_{12} = \mathcal{L}_{12}$.

Proof From proposition 2.4 it suffices to prove $\mathcal{L}_{12} \subset \mathcal{F} \subset \mathcal{L}_{11}$.

i) $\mathcal{L}_{12} \subset \mathcal{F}$. Let $\mathcal{A}$ be a finite branching TS and $L = L_1(\mathcal{A})$. The fact that L is closed, ie $Adh(L) \subset L$, follows from Koenig's lemma.

ii) $\mathcal{F} \subset \mathcal{L}_{11}$. Let L be a closed set and let $\mathcal{A}$ be the deterministic TS associated with $K = FG(L)$. Then $L_1(\mathcal{A}) = L_1(K) = \{u \in A^\omega / \forall n, u[n] \in K\}$ $= \{u \in A^\omega / FG(u) \subset K\} = Adh(L) = L$. □

Let $\mathcal{F}_\sigma$ be the class of countable unions of closed sets, and $\mathcal{G}_\delta$ be the class of countable intersections of open sets.

Proposition 3.3 $\mathcal{L}_{21} = \mathcal{L}^{na}_{22} = \mathcal{L}'_{22} = \mathcal{F}_\sigma$; $\mathcal{L}_{31} = \mathcal{G}_\delta$

Proof

1) Let us prove firstly that $\mathcal{L}_{22} \subset \mathcal{F}_\sigma$. Let $\mathcal{A}<Q,Q_o,Q_f,\rightarrow>$ be a finitely branching TS, where Q is countable. For any $q \in Q - Q_f$ we define the two sets $X(q) \in A^*$ and $Y(q) \in A^\omega$ by

$u \in X(q)$ iff there exists a u-computation $q_o,\ldots,q_n$ with $q_n = q$;

$v \in Y(q)$ iff there exists a sequence $(q_i)_i$ such that $q_o = q, i \geq 1$

$\Rightarrow \quad q_i \in Q_f$ and $q_{i-1} \xrightarrow{v(i)} q_i$.

It is obvious that $L_2(\mathcal{A}) = \bigcup_{q \in Q-Q_f} X(q).Y(q)$. From proposition 3.2, all Y(q) are closed sets ; hence $L_2(\mathcal{A}) \in \mathcal{F}_\sigma$.

2) Lemma 2.2 of Landweber [4] just amounts to say $\mathcal{L}_{31} = \mathcal{G}_\delta$.

3) At last, since $\mathcal{G}_\delta$ is the class of complements of sets in $\mathcal{F}_\sigma$, and since $L = L_3(K)$ iff $A^\omega - L = L_2(A^*-K)$, we get $\mathcal{L}_{21} = \mathcal{F}_\sigma$. □

3.3. Remaining classes

It remains to characterize the behaviours of countably branching TS and 3-behaviours of finitely branching ones. We prove they are equal

Proposition 3.4 $\mathcal{L}_{32} = \mathcal{L}_{13} = \mathcal{L}_{23} = \mathcal{L}_{33}$; $\mathcal{L}^{na}_{32} = \mathcal{L}^{na}_{13} = \mathcal{L}^{na}_{23} = \mathcal{L}^{na}_{33}$.

Proof With proposition 2.4, it suffices to prove $\mathcal{L}_{33} \subset \mathcal{L}_{32} \subset \mathcal{L}_{13}$ and $\mathcal{L}^{na}_{33} \subset \mathcal{L}^{na}_{32} \subset \mathcal{L}^{na}_{13}$.

1) Let $\mathcal{A} = <Q,Q_o,Q_f,\rightarrow>$ be a countably branching TS. We can assume that Q is countable, ie $Q = \{q_o,q_1,\ldots,q_n,\ldots\}$. Let $\mathcal{A}' = <Q',Q'_o,Q'_f,\rightarrow>$ be the TS defined by $Q' = \{<u,\alpha>/u \in A^*, \alpha \in \{0,1\}^*$, length(n) = length($\alpha$)$\}$, $Q'_o = \{<\wedge,\wedge>\}$, $Q'_f = \{<u,0^{i_o}1\, 0^{i_1}1\ldots 0^{i_n}1> \,/\, q_{i_n} \in Q_f$, $q_{i_o} \in Q_o$ and $q_{i_o},\ldots,q_{i_n}$ is a u[n]-computation in $\mathcal{A}$ and $<u,\alpha> \xrightarrow{a} <u\,a,\beta>$ iff $\beta = \alpha 0$ or $\beta = \alpha 1$. Obviously $\mathcal{A}'$ is finitely branching. Then $L_3(\mathcal{A}) = L_3(\mathcal{A}')$ and if $\mathcal{A}$ is not 3-ambiguous, nor is $\mathcal{A}'$.

It follows that $\mathcal{L}_{33} \subset \mathcal{L}_{32}$ and $\mathcal{L}^{na}_{33} \subset \mathcal{L}^{na}_{32}$.

2) Let $\mathcal{A}$ $<Q,Q_o,Q_f,\rightarrow>$ be a finitely branching TS. Let $\mathcal{A}' = <Q',Q'_o,Q'_f,\twoheadrightarrow>$ be the countably branching TS defined by $Q' = Q \times \mathbb{N}$, $Q'_f \times \{0\} \cup (Q-Q_f) \times (\mathbb{N}-\{0\})$, $Q'_o = Q_o \times \mathbb{N}$ and $<q,n> \twoheadrightarrow <q',n'>$ iff $q \xrightarrow{a} q'$ and $n = n'+1$ or $n = 0$.

Then $L_3(A) = L_1(A')$ and if A is not 3-ambiguous, nor is A'.

It follows that $\mathcal{L}_{32} \subset \mathcal{L}_{13}$ and $\mathcal{L}_{32}^{na} \subset \mathcal{L}_{13}^{na}$. □

Then denoting by $\mathcal{S}$ the class $\mathcal{L}_{32}$ and by $\mathcal{B}$ the class $\mathcal{L}_{32}^{na}$, the previous propositions make the chart in § 1.3 to become the chart in the introduction. It remains to characterize by topological properties these two classes $\mathcal{B}$ and $\mathcal{S}$.

4. BOREL SETS AND SOUSLIN SETS

A subset of a metric space E is a *Souslin set* (*resp Lusin set*) if it is the image of a polish space P under a continuous (*resp* injective continuous) mapping. Clearly every Lusin set is a Souslin set and every polish space is a Lusin set. A subset of a metric space E is a Borel set if it is in the least class of subsets of E containing closed sets and closed under complement and countable union (and then also under countable intersection).

But

Theorem 4.1 [2] *A subset of a Lusin set is a Borel set if and only if it is a Lusin set.*

Hence, since A^ω is a polish space, and thus a Lusin set, any ω-language is a Borel set iff it is a Lusin set.

Denoting by $\mathcal{B}$ the class of ω-languages which are Borel sets (or Lusin sets) and by $\mathcal{S}$ the class of those which are Souslin sets, we can achieve our characterization by :

Proposition 4.2 $\mathcal{L}_{13} = \mathcal{S}$, $\mathcal{L}_{13}^{na} = \mathcal{B}$.

Proof

1) Let A be a countably branching TS. With every 1-successful u-computation $(q_i)_i$ in A we associate the infinite word $q_o\ u(1)q_1\ u(2)q_2 \ldots u(n)q_n \ldots$ in $(A \cup Q_f)^\omega$. The set Δ of such words is obviously a closed subset of the Polish space $(A \cup Q_f)^\omega$ thus it is also a Polish space [2]. Now the mapping $\varepsilon : \Delta \to A^\omega$ defined by $\varepsilon(q_o\ u(1)q_1\ u(2)q_2 \ldots u(n)q_n \ldots)$ $= u(1)u(2)\ldots u(n)\ldots$ is obviously continuous, and injective if A is not

1-ambiguous, so that $L_1(A) = \varepsilon(\Delta)$ is a Souslin set, and a Lusin set if A is not 1-ambiguous.

2) We know from [2] that a Souslin (*resp* Lusin) set L is the image, under a continuous (*resp* injective continuous) mapping f, of some closed subset S of C for some countable C. Then, adaptating a proof of [2], we can construct a countably branching automaton , states of which are pairs (u,U) with $u \in A^*$ such that U is a maximal open ball of radius less than $2^{-|u|}$ satisfying : $f(U) \subset u A^\omega$. $(u,U) \xrightarrow{a} (ua,V)$ iff $V \subset U$. Obviously $(u[i], U_i)_i$ is a u-computation in A iff $f(\bigcap_i U_i) = u$, hence the result. □

Let us end this paper with some properties of the classes S and B which are of interest when interpreted in term of 3-behaviours of finitely branching TS (ie $S = L_{32}$ and $B = L_{32}^{na}$).

Proposition 4.3 [2]

- *S is closed under countable union and countable intersection.*
- *If* $L \subset A^\omega$ *is a Souslin set, then* $A^\omega - L$ *is a Souslin set iff* L *is a Borel set.*

Acknowledgement

In a discussion about these matters G. Plotkin suggested that $L_{32} = L_{13}$. Not only he was right, but this equality turns out to be of greatest importance.

REFERENCES

1 A. Arnold. Rational ω-languages are non ambiguous. To appear in Theor. Comput. Sci.

2 N. Bourbaki. Topologie générale, ch. IX., Hermann, Paris (1958).

3. S. Eilenberg. Automata, languages and machines, Vol. A. Academic Press, New York (1974).

4. L.H. Landweber. Decision problems for ω-automata. Math. System Theory 3 (1969) 376-384.

5. M. Nivat, A. Arnold. Comportements de processus. In Colloque AFCET "Les mathématiques de l'Informatique", Paris (1982) 35-68.

6. M. Takahashi, H. Yamasaki. A note on ω-Regular languages. Report C-44, Tokyo Institute of Technology (1982).

7. K. Wisniewski. A notion of the acceptance of infinite sequences by finite automata. Bull. Acad. Pol. Sci. Math. 27(1979) 331-332.

LINEAR TIME AND BRANCHING TIME SEMANTICS FOR RECURSION WITH MERGE

J.W. de Bakker
Mathematical Centre, Kruislaan 413, 1098 SJ Amsterdam
Free University, Amsterdam

J.A. Bergstra
Mathematical Centre, Amsterdam

J.W. Klop
Mathematical Centre, Amsterdam

J.-J.Ch. Meyer
Free University, Amsterdam

ABSTRACT

We consider two ways of assigning semantics to a class of statements built from a set of atomic actions (the 'alphabet'), by means of sequential composition, nondeterministic choice, recursion and merge (arbitrary interleaving). The first is linear time semantics (LT), stated in terms of trace theory; the semantic domain is the collection of all closed sets of finite and infinite words. The second is branching time semantics (BT), as introduced by de Bakker and Zucker; here the semantic domain is the metric completion of the collection of finite processes. For LT we prove the continuity of the operations (merge, sequential composition) in a direct, combinatorial way.

Next, a connection between LT and BT is established by means of the operation trace which assigns to a process its set of traces. If the alphabet is finite, the trace set of a process is closed and trace is a continuous operation. Using trace, we then can carry over BT into LT.

1. INTRODUCTION

We study two ways of assigning meaning to a simple language $\mathcal{L}$ which has elementary actions (a,b,c,...), sequential composition, nondeterministic choice, *recursion* and *merge* (arbitrary interleaving) as its constituent concepts. This type of language may be seen as the core of various current approaches to parallellism (mostly to be extended with further concurrent concepts such as synchronization and communication, and often with simple iteration rather than full recursion), and it deserves in our opinion a full study of its associated semantics. There are a number of issues one encounters in developing a rigorous theory for this purpose.

Firstly, there is the issue of "linear time" versus "branching time", a terminology one finds, e.g., in investigations of the model theory of temporal logic. In fact, an important motivation for our investigation was to better understand this phenomenon. "Linear time" is easy: it is nothing but trace theory. For example, in the linear time model both the statements $(a;b) \cup (a;c)$ and $a;(b \cup c)$ obtain as associated meaning the so-called trace set {ab,ac}. "Branching time" refers to an approach where one wants to distinguish between these two statements. Here for the two statements we obtain as meaning the two trees: 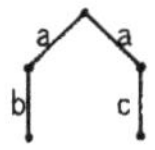 and 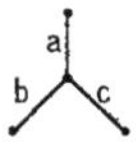

(Trees are not quite what we want, though. The statement a ∪ a should yield the object a| rather than a/\a as its meaning, and there are further differences - to be explained below - between trees and the objects in the branching time universe.)

Secondly, the appearance of merge (||) introduces various questions. For traces, "||" is to be defined as the usual shuffle in the sense of language theory; for the branching time model a new definition is required. Also, various known results about context free (or algebraic) languages, possibly with infinite words, have to be extended due to the addition of the "||" operator.

Thirdly, in accordance with the emphasis which in the study of concurrency is put onto nonterminating computations, we want to include a mathematical rigorous treatment of finite *and infinite* actions specified by the programs in our language. For example, employing the μ-notation for recursion, we want as (linear time) meaning of $\mu x[a;x]$ the sequence a^{ω} (the infinite sequence of a's), and for $\mu x[(a;x) \cup b]$ the set of sequences $(a^*b) \cup a^{\omega}$. The trace theory to be developed below is a continuation of the investigation of languages of infinite words by Nivat and his school [10 - 13]. The inclusion of the "||" operation is responsible for further technical problems which - as far as we know - are not dealt with in their work in a way resembling our approach. (Also, in cases where Nivat addresses questions of semantics, these concern languages which are completely different from our $\mathcal{L}$.)

The development of the models for linear time and branching time semantics (from now on abbreviated to LT and BT) starts with a few tools from metric topology. For LT, not much more is used than the definition of *distance* between words. E.g., $d(abc,abde) = 2^{-3}$, where 3 is the index where the sequences exhibit their first difference. Next, a notion of *closed* set (closed with respect to d) is introduced. For example, the set a^* is not closed since it does not contain its limit point a . The framework for LT semantics is then taken as the complete partially ordered set of closed sets, with "$\supseteq$" (set containment) as the "$\sqsubseteq$" ordering of the cpo. For BT we use the (mathematical) notion of *process* which is an element of a *domain* of processes obtained as solution of a domain equation by topological *completion* techniques. Domain equations have been studied extensively by Scott ([15,16]) and, in a nondeterministic setting and using category theory, by Plotkin [14] and Smyth [17]. The theory of processes has been described elsewhere ([3,4]), and is included here to facilitate comparison between the LT and BT semantics.

Section 2 is devoted to LT semantics, Section 3 to BT semantics, and Section 4 to the relationship between the two, and to some variations on the preceding definitions. The proof of Lemma 4.4 is omitted here and can be found in [2].

2. LT SEMANTICS: MATHEMATICAL BACKGROUND AND SEMANTICAL EQUATIONS

Let A be an alphabet with elements a,b,... . (Most of the results below hold when A is finite or infinite. In a few cases, we require A to be finite.) Let x,y,... be statement variables from a set *Stmv*, which we shall use in the formation of *recursive* or μ-statements. The syntax for the language L is given (in a self-explanatory BNF notation) in

2.1. DEFINITION. $S ::= a \mid S_1;S_2 \mid S_1 \cup S_2 \mid S_1 \| S_2 \mid x \mid \mu x[S]$.

2.1.1. EXAMPLES. $(a;b) \cup (a\|c)$, $\mu x[(a;\mu y[(b;y)\|x]) \cup c]$.

2.1.2. REMARKS. (1) Syntactic ambiguities should be remedied by using parentheses or conventions for the priority of the operations.

(2) (For the reader who isn't familiar with the μ-notation.) A term such as $\mu x[(a;x) \cup b]$ has the same meaning as a *call* of the procedure declared (in an ALGOL-like language) by $P \Leftarrow (a;P) \cup b$, or, alternatively, generates the same language (of finite and infinite words) as the grammar $X \rightarrow aX \mid b$.

(3) In a term $\mu x[S]$, x may occur "guarded" in S, i.e., when S has the form a;(--x--): a recursive "call" of x is guarded by at least one elementary action $a \in A$. Terms like $\mu x[x]$, $\mu x[x;b]$ or $\mu x[a\|x]$ contain unguarded occurrences of x. (In language theory, the equivalent notion is the "Greibach condition", as in Nivat [12].) Certain results below are - though mathematically correct - not necessarily semantically satisfactory for statements with unguarded variables.

We now turn to the development of the underlying semantic framework.

2.2. DEFINITION. (a) $A^\infty = A^* \cup A^\omega$, where A^* is the set of all finite words over A, and A^ω the set of all infinite words.

(b) $\leqslant$ denotes the usual prefix relation (a partial order) on A^∞. The prefix of $x \in A^\infty$ of length n will be denoted by $x[n]$.

(Examples: abc $\leqslant$ abccb; abccb[3] = abc; abc[5] = abc; abc[0] is the empty word.)

(c) Let $x,y \in A^\infty$. The distance or *metric* $d: A^\infty \rightarrow [0,1]$ is defined by

$$d(x,y) = \begin{cases} 2^{-\min\{n \mid x[n] \neq y[n]\}+1} & \text{if } \exists n\ x[n] \neq y[n] \\ 0 \text{ otherwise (i.e. if } x = y) \end{cases}$$

(d) $\mathcal{P}_c(A^\infty)$ denotes the collection of all *closed* subsets of A^∞. Here 'closed' refers to the metric d, i.e., $X \in \mathcal{P}_c(A^\infty)$ whenever each Cauchy sequence $\langle x_n \rangle_n$ has a limit in X. (By definition, the elements of a Cauchy sequence have arbitrarily small distances for sufficiently large index.) In the sequel we write C for the collection $\mathcal{P}_c(A^\infty)$.

We define the order "$\sqsubseteq$" on C by putting $X \sqsubseteq Y$ iff $X \supseteq Y$ (with "$\supseteq$" set-containment).

2.3. LEMMA. d *is a metric on* A^∞, *and* C *is a complete partially ordered set with respect to* $\sqsubseteq$, *with* A^∞ *as bottom element and with* $\bigsqcup_n X_n = \bigcap_n X_n$, *for* $\langle X_n \rangle_n$ *a* $\sqsubseteq$*-chain.*

For later use (in Section 4) we introduce one further definition with a theorem and a corollary:

2.4. DEFINITION. (Hausdorff distance)

For any metric space (M,d), $x,y \in M$ and $X,Y \subseteq M$ we define distances $\hat{d}$, $\tilde{d}$:

(a) $\hat{d}(x,Y) = \inf \{d(x,y) \mid y \in Y\}$, where $\inf \emptyset = 1$

(b) $\tilde{d}(X,Y) = \max (\sup \{\hat{d}(x,Y) \mid x \in X\}, \sup \{\hat{d}(y,X) \mid y \in Y\})$ where $\sup \emptyset = 0$.

2.5. THEOREM. (a) *$\tilde{d}$ is a metric for $\mathcal{P}_c(M)$.*

(b) *If (M,d) is complete, then so is $(\mathcal{P}_c(M),\tilde{d})$. Also, for $\langle X_n\rangle_n$ a Cauchy sequence in $\mathcal{P}_c(M)$, we then have that* $\lim_n X_n = \{x \mid x_n \to x, \text{ with } x_n \in X_n\}$.

PROOF. See e.g. [6]. A complete proof of (b) is contained in [4]. □

2.6. COROLLARY. *The Hausdorff metric on C turns it into a complete metric space.* □

The Hausdorff metric on C will be written as d_L (to be contrasted with the Hausdorff metric d_B on $\mathcal{P}$, in Section 3).

In Section 4 we will need the following connection between the metric on C and its cpo structure:

2.7. PROPOSITION. *Let $\langle X_n\rangle_n$ be both a Cauchy sequence in C and a $\sqsubseteq$-chain. Then:*

$$\bigsqcup_n X_n = \lim_n X_n.$$

PROOF. By Theorem 2.5 we must prove that $\bigcap_n X_n = \{x \mid x = \lim_n x_n, \text{ for some } x_n \in X_n\}$. Here $(\subseteq)$ is trivial. $(\supseteq)$: let $x = \lim_n x_n$ for some sequence $\langle x_n\rangle_n$ such that $x_n \in X_n$. Since $X_n \subseteq X_0$ for all n, we have $x_n \in X_0$. Since X_0 is closed, $x \in X_0$. Likewise $x = \lim_n x_{n+1}$ is an element of X_1, etc. Hence $x \in \bigcap_n X_n$. □

We shall use C *with its cpo structure* as semantic domain for the trace semantics of L. (By Corollary 2.6, C is also a complete metric space. However, contrary to the situation for BT semantics, we find the cpo structure more convenient for the LT semantics.) We need two theorems to support C as model. (Technically, these two theorems are among the main results of the paper.) First we give the natural definitions of the basic operations on A^∞ and C:

2.8. DEFINITION. (a) For $x,y \in A^\infty$, $x \cdot y$ (mostly written as xy) is the usual *concatenation* of sequences (including the convention that $xy = x$ for $x \in A^\omega$).
Further, $x \| y$ is the set of all *shuffles* of x with y (extending to the infinite case the classical definition of the shuffle of two finite words).

(b) $X \cup Y$ is the set-theoretic union of X and Y; $X \cdot Y = \{x \cdot y \mid x \in X, y \in Y\}$, and $X \| Y = \bigcup \{x \| y \mid x \in X, y \in Y\}$. We will write also XY for $X \cdot Y$.

The main theorems of this section state that the operations $\cdot$, $\cup$, $\|$ preserve closedness and are *continuous* (in the usual cpo sense) in both their arguments. (But note the proviso in Theorem 2.10.)

2.9. THEOREM. *For X,Y in C, $X \cdot Y$, $X \cup Y$ and $X \| Y$ are in C.*

PROOF. See Appendix. □

2.10. THEOREM. *Let* A *be finite. Then the operations* $\cdot$, $\cup$, $\|$ *from* $C \times C$ *to* C *are continuous in both their arguments.*

PROOF. See Appendix. □

2.10.1. REMARK. The finiteness condition on A ensures *compactness* of A^∞ (as observed in [12]). We then have that each sequence in A^∞ has a convergent subsequence. It is readily seen that this implies that, for each $\sqsubseteq$-chain $\langle X_n \rangle_n$ such that $X_n \neq \emptyset$ for all n, we have that $\bigcap_n X_n \neq \emptyset$, and this fact is needed in the proof of Theorem 2.10.

We proceed with the definition of the linear time semantics for L. We adopt the usual technique with environments to deal with (free) statement variables. Let $\Gamma = Stmv \to C$, and let γ range over Γ. Let, as before, X range over C, and let $\gamma\{X/x\}$ stand for the environment which is like γ, but for its value in x which is now X. Let $[C \to C]$ stand for the collection of all continuous functions from C to C, and let, for Φ $[C \to C]$, $\mu\Phi$ denote its least fixed point. We have

2.11. DEFINITION. The semantic mapping $[\![\ ]\!]_L : L \to (\Gamma \to C)$ is given by

$[\![a]\!]_L(\gamma) = \{a\}$, $[\![s_1;s_2]\!]_L(\gamma) = [\![s_1]\!]_L(\gamma) \cdot [\![s_2]\!]_L(\gamma)$

$[\![s_1 \cup s_2]\!]_L(\gamma) = [\![s_1]\!]_L(\gamma) \cup [\![s_2]\!]_L(\gamma)$, $[\![s_1 \| s_2]\!]_L(\gamma) = [\![s_1]\!]_L(\gamma) \| [\![s_2]\!]_L(\gamma)$

$[\![\mu x[s]]\!]_L(\gamma) = \mu\Phi_{s,\gamma}$ where $\Phi_{s,\gamma} = \lambda X.[\![s]\!]_L(\gamma\{X/x\})$.

This definition is justified by the following Lemma:

2.12. LEMMA. (i) $\lambda X_1 \ldots X_n . [\![s]\!]_L(\gamma\{X_i/x_i\}_{i=1}^n) \in [C \to [C \to \ldots \to [C \to C]\ldots]]$ (n factors C)
(ii) *The functions in (i) are monotonic.*

PROOF. (i) Routine (see, e.g., [1] Theorem 7.9), once Theorem 2.10 is available.
(ii) By a simple inductive proof. Or: note that C is also a complete lattice, and use the fact that in a complete lattice continuous functions are monotonic (see e.g. [1]).□

2.13. COROLLARY. $[\![\mu x[s]]\!]_L(\gamma) = \bigcap_n \Phi^n_{s,\gamma}(A^\infty)$ *where* $\Phi_{s,\gamma}$ *is as in Definition 2.11.*

PROOF. By Definition 2.11, Lemma 2.12(i) and the Tarski-Knaster fixed point theorem.□

2.14. EXAMPLE. $[\![\mu x[(a;x) \cup b]]\!]_L(\gamma) = \mu[\lambda X.[\![(a;x) \cup b]\!]_L(\gamma\{X/x\})] = \mu[\lambda X.((a \cdot X) \cup b)] = \bigcap_n X_n$, where $X_0 = A^\infty$, and $X_{i+1} = (a \cdot X_i) \cup b$. Hence, $\bigcap_n X_n = a^*b \cup a^\omega$.

2.15. REMARK. For statements which have unguarded μ-terms, the semantics $[\![\ ]\!]_L$ may not be the most natural one. E.g. we have - for any γ - that $[\![\mu x[x]]\!]_L(\gamma) = A^\infty$ and $[\![\mu x[x;b]]\!]_L(\gamma) = A^\omega$. We shall return to this point in Section 4, where we are in a position to compare both LT and BT semantics for such unguarded μ-terms.

3. BT SEMANTICS: MATHEMATICAL BACKGROUND AND SEMANTIC EQUATIONS

The *branching time* semantics for L is based on the theory of processes as sketched in [3] and described more fully in [4]. We briefly recall the main facts from this theory (in the terminology of [3,4] referring only to uniform processes).

For an approach to uniform processes via projective limits, see [5]; and for an approach where processes are congruence classes of trees ('behaviours'), see Milner [8,9]. (See [2] for a comparison between the present uniform processes and Milner's behaviours.)

Here, processes are objects which are best compared to labeled unordered trees without repetitions in successor sets. Considering the examples

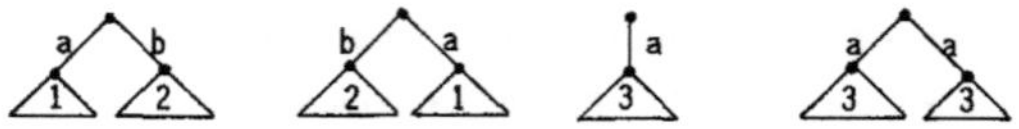

we have that the first and second, and the third and fourth represent the same process. Also, processes are closed objects: they contain all their limit points, in a sense to be made precise in a moment. E.g., the tree t_1 does not represent a process, but tree t_2 does, since it contains also the limit process "a^ω ".

t_1
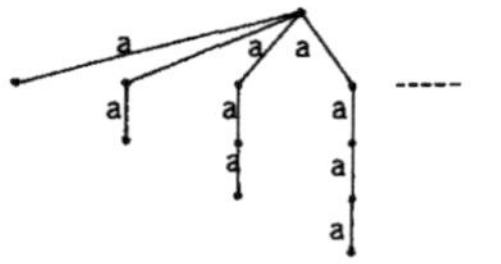

t_2
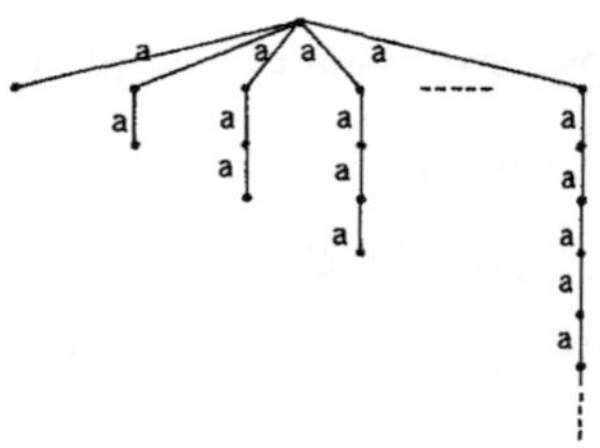

Technically, processes are obtained as follows:

0. Start from alphabet A as before; moreover, a so-called nil-process p_0 is assumed.
1. Define P_n, $n=0,1,\ldots$, by $P_0 = \{p_0\}$, $P_{n+1} = \mathcal{P}(A \times P_n)$, where $\mathcal{P}(.)$ stands for the collection of all subsets of (.). Write $P_\omega = \bigcup_n P_n$.
2. Introduce a metric on P_n (by suitably combining Definition 2.2(c) and 2.4) and take $\mathcal{P}$ as the *completion* of P_ω. Let d_B be the metric on $\mathcal{P}$.

We can then show

3.1. THEOREM. $\mathcal{P} \cong \{p_0\} \cup \mathcal{P}_c(A \times \mathcal{P})$

where $\mathcal{P}_c(.)$ refers to the collection of all closed subsets of (.) - with respect to d_B -, and $\cong$ denotes isometry.

The next definition gives the main operations upon processes. We distinguish the cases $p=p_0$, $p=X\subseteq\mathcal{P}(A\times P_n)$ for some $n\geq 0$, or $p=\lim_i p_i$, with $\langle p_i\rangle_i$ a Cauchy sequence of elements p_i in P_i.

3.2. DEFINITION. (a) $p\circ p_0 = p$, $p\circ X = \{p\circ x \mid x\in X\}$, $p\circ\langle a,q\rangle = \langle a,p\circ q\rangle$, $p\circ\lim_i q_i = \lim_i (p\circ q_i)$

(b) $p\cup p_0 = p_0\cup p = p$, and, for $p,q\neq p_0$, $p\cup q$ is the set-theoretic union of p and q

(c) $p \| p_0 = p_0 \| p = p$, $X \| Y = \{x \| Y \mid x \in X\} \cup \{X \| y \mid y \in Y\}$,

$\langle a,p\rangle \| Y = \langle a, p\|Y\rangle$, $X \| \langle a,q\rangle = \langle a, X\|q\rangle$, $(\lim_i p_i) \| (\lim_j q_j) = \lim_k (p_k \| q_k)$.

3.3. LEMMA. *The above operations are well-defined and continuous in both arguments.*

This lemma is the counterpart of the results in the Appendix for the LT framework. For the proof - which does not require more effort than the LT case - see [4].

By way of preparation for the definition of the recursive case we need a classical result. A mapping $T: \mathcal{P} \to \mathcal{P}$ is called *contracting* whenever $d_B(T(p), T(p')) \leq c \cdot d_B(p,p')$ with $0 \leq c < 1$. We will need Banach's fixed point theorem:

3.4. THEOREM. *If* T *is continuous and contracting, then for each* $q \in \mathcal{P}$, *the sequence* $q, T(q), T^2(q), \ldots$ *is a Cauchy sequence converging to the unique fixed point of* T.

As final preparatory step for the semantic definition we extend the alphabet A with a special so-called unobservable action τ and take as process domain the domain $\mathcal{P}_2$ given by $\mathcal{P}_2 \cong \{p_0\} \cup \mathrm{P}_c((A \cup \{\tau\}) \times \mathcal{P}_2)$. As before, we apply the familiar environment technique. Let $\Gamma = \mathit{Stmv} \to \mathcal{P}_2$. We define the BT-semantics for $\mathcal{L}$ in

3.5. DEFINITION. The semantic mapping $[\![\ ]\!]_B : \mathcal{L} \to (\Gamma \to \mathcal{P}_2)$ is given by

$[\![a]\!]_B(\gamma) = \{\langle a,p_0\rangle\}$

$[\![s_1;s_2]\!]_B(\gamma) = [\![s_2]\!]_B(\gamma) \circ [\![s_1]\!]_B(\gamma)$

$[\![s_1 \cup s_2]\!]_B(\gamma) = [\![s_1]\!]_B(\gamma) \cup [\![s_2]\!]_B(\gamma)$

$[\![s_1 \| s_2]\!]_B(\gamma) = [\![s_1]\!]_B(\gamma) \| [\![s_2]\!]_B(\gamma)$

$[\![x]\!]_B(\gamma) = \gamma(x)$

$[\![\mu x[S]]\!]_B(\gamma) = \lim_i p_i$, where p_0 is the nil-process and $p_{i+1} = \{\langle \tau, [\![S]\!]_B(\gamma\{p_i/x\})\rangle\}$.

3.6. EXAMPLES. (For simplicity we omit γ.)

(1) $[\![a_1;a_2]\!]_B = \{\langle a_2,p_0\rangle\} \circ \{\langle a_1,p_0\rangle\} = \{\langle a_1, \{\langle a_2,p_0\rangle\}\rangle\}$

(2) $[\![a \| (b \cup c)]\!]_B =$ (in a natural picture representation)

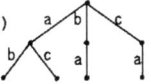

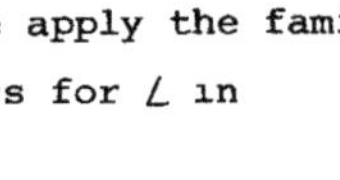

(3) $[\![\mu x[(a;x) \cup b]]\!]_B = \lim_i p_i$, where $p_{i+1} = \{\langle \tau, \{\langle a,p_i\rangle, \langle b,p_0\rangle\}\rangle\}$; =

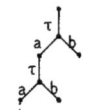

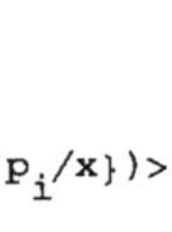

(4) $[\![\mu x[x]]\!]_B = [\![\mu x[x;b]]\!]_B = \{\langle \tau, \{\langle \tau, \{\langle \tau, \ldots\rangle\}\rangle\}\rangle\}$.

3.7. REMARK. The central clause is the definition of recursion $\mu x[S]$. We have solved this by introducing for each S an associated *contracting* mapping $T = \lambda p.\{\langle \tau, [\![S]\!]_B(\gamma\{p/x\})\rangle\}$. Contractivity is enforced by the $\langle \tau, \ldots\rangle$ construct. Operationally, the $\langle \tau, \ldots\rangle$ action corresponds to the action of procedure entrance, which does not involve any "observable" action in A. For such T, $\lim_i T^i(p_0)$ is its unique fixed point (p_0 is only chosen for definiteness; other choices would of course yield the same result.) We shall return to the motivation for adopting this strategy in the next section.

4. LT AND BT COMPARED

In this section we compare the two semantics presented in Sections 2 and 3. More specifically, we discuss the relationship between LT and BT both for statements with *guarded* μ-terms only, and for statements with any form of recursion.

The main result of the section is stated in terms of the notion of *trace set* of a process. Roughly, the trace set of process p is the set of branches (terminating or infinite) obtained by viewing p as a labelled tree. In order to establish a correspondence between LT and BT semantics, we will only consider processes whose terminating branches all terminate in p_0 and not in $\emptyset$, which according to the definition of processes is also possible. (Termination in $\emptyset$ is used in [3,4] to model failure, but in the present context this issue is not yet at stake.) That is, we adopt the natural restriction to the closure of

$$\mathcal{P}_{[\![\,]\!]} = \{[\![S]\!]_B(\gamma) \mid S \text{ not containing free statement variables, } \gamma \in \mathit{Stmv} \to \mathcal{P}\}.$$

(Note that $\mathcal{P}_{[\![\,]\!]}$ itself is not yet closed.) We will write $\mathcal{P}^+$ for this closure. Obviously, $\mathcal{P}^+$ is a complete metric subspace of $\mathcal{P}$. An alternative characterization of $\mathcal{P}^+$ is:

$$\mathcal{P}^+ = \{p \in \mathcal{P} \mid \text{all terminating paths of p end in } p_0\}.$$

For use in Theorem 4.7, we note that $\mathcal{P}^+ = \{[\![S]\!]_B(\gamma) \mid \text{all } S, \gamma \in \mathit{Stmv} \to \mathcal{P}^+\}$.

4.1. DEFINITION. Let $p \in \mathcal{P}^+$. (1) A *path* π for p is a (finite or infinite) sequence $\langle a_1,p_1\rangle, \langle a_2,p_2\rangle, \ldots$ such that $\langle a_1,p_1\rangle \in p$ and $\langle a_{i+1},p_{i+1}\rangle \in p_i$, $i = 1,2,\ldots$

(2) (i) Let $\pi = \langle a_1,p_1\rangle, \langle a_2,p_2\rangle, \ldots$ be an infinite path of $p \in \mathcal{P}^+$. Then $a_1a_2\ldots \in A^\omega$ is called a *trace* of p.

(ii) Let $\pi = \langle a_1,p_1\rangle, \ldots, \langle a_n,p_0\rangle$ be a finite path of $p \in \mathcal{P}^+$. Then $a_1a_2\ldots a_n \in A^*$ is a *trace* of p.

(3) *trace*(p) is the set of traces of p.

4.2. EXAMPLES. $\mathit{trace}(\{\langle a,\{\langle b,p_0\rangle\}\rangle,\langle a,\{\langle c,p_0\rangle\}\rangle\}) = \{ab,ac\}$,

$\mathit{trace}(\{\langle a,\{\langle a,\ldots\rangle\}\rangle\}) = \{a^\omega\}$, $\mathit{trace}([\![\mu x[(a;x) \cup b]]\!]_B(\gamma)) = (\tau a)^\omega \cup (\tau a)^*\tau b$.

Now we would like to assert that *trace* is an operation from $\mathcal{P}^+$ to $\mathcal{C}$, i.e. for $p \in \mathcal{P}^+$, *trace*(p) is a closed set. Surprisingly, this need not to be the case if A is infinite; say $A = \{a\} \cup \{b_i \mid i \geq 1\}$:

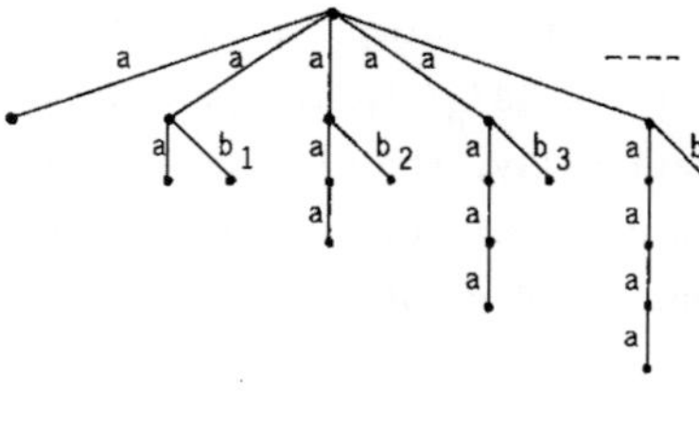

4.3. EXAMPLE. Consider $p \in \mathcal{P}^+$ as given by the tree i.e.: $p = \{\langle a,p_i\rangle \mid i \geq 0\}$ where p_0 is the nil-process and for $n > 0$: $p_n = \{\langle b_n,p_0\rangle,\langle a,q_{n-1}\rangle\}$,

$q_n = \{\langle a,\langle a,\langle a,\ldots,\langle a,p_0\rangle\}\rangle\ldots\rangle\}$ (n times a).

Then *trace*(p) = $\{a^n \mid n \geq 1\} \cup \{aa_m \mid m \geq 1\}$, which is not closed as it lacks a^ω.

However, with the additional assumption that A is finite, we have (by a nontrivial proof which is omitted here and can be found in [2]) that *trace*(p) is closed indeed. In fact we have:

4.4. LEMMA. *Let* A *be finite. Then: (i)* *trace*(p) $\in C$,
(ii) *trace is continuous (with respect to the Hausdorff metrics in* $\mathcal{P}^+$ *and C).* □

We will also need the following fact, whose proof is routine and omitted here:

4.5. PROPOSITION. *trace:* $\mathcal{P}^+ \longrightarrow C$ *is an homomorphism (with respect to the operations* $\cdot$, $\cup$, $\|$ *on* $\mathcal{P}^+$ *and C).* □

We also need the notion of *universal process* for $\mathcal{P}^+$:

4.6. DEFINITION. The universal process for $\mathcal{P}^+$, called p_u, is the (unique) solution of the equation $p = \{\langle a,p\rangle \mid a \in A\} \cup \{\langle a,p_0\rangle \mid a \in A\}$.
(Note that *trace*(p_u) = A^∞.)

In the following, it will be convenient to restrict ourselves to *closed* statements, i.e., statements without free statement variables. Now the natural question which suggests itself concerning the relationship between LT and BT is whether, for each closed S - omitting γ which is then superfluous - we have that

(¶) $\qquad$ *trace*($[\![S]\!]_B$) = $[\![S]\!]_L$.

Taken as it stands, the answer to the question is *no*. For example, taking $S \equiv \mu x[x]$ we have that

$$trace([\![\mu x[x]]\!]_B = trace(\{\langle\tau,\{\langle\tau,\ldots\rangle\}\rangle\}) = \{\tau^\omega\} \neq A^\infty = [\![\mu x[x]]\!]_L.$$

This discrepancy is not an essential phenomenon, but due to the special role of the unobservable action τ for BT semantics. Remember that τ was introduced to enforce contractivity of the mapping T as defined in Remark 3.7, which in turn was necessary to allow us to apply Banach's fixed point theorem 3.4. However, another approach may also be adopted which will lead to a positive answer to the question (¶). It is convenient to treat separately the cases where
(i) S has only guarded μ-terms, and
(ii) S may have unguarded μ-terms.

Case (i). *(Only guarded μ-terms.)* In this case the "τ-trick" for BT is in fact superfluous. Taking $T' = \lambda p.[\![S]\!]_B(\gamma\{p/x\})$, T' is now contracting for each S, and $\lim_{i\geq 1} T'(p_i)$, with p_1 arbitrary, $p_{i+1} = T'(p_i)$, converges to the unique fixed point of T' independent of the initial p_1 - which we may therefore choose as p_u to facilitate the proof of

4.7. THEOREM. *Assume statement* S *is closed and involves only guarded* μ*-terms. Let* $[\![S]\!]_L$ *be as before, and let* $[\![S]\!]_B$ *be as in Definition 3.5, except that in the clause for* $\mu x[S]$*, we replace* p_0 *by* p_u *and define*

$$p_{i+1} = [\![S]\!]_B(\gamma\{p_i/x\}).$$

Then:

$$\mathit{trace}([\![S]\!]_B) = [\![S]\!]_L.$$

PROOF. We will prove the following stronger fact, necessary for the induction on the structure of statements S' (which now need not to be closed):
for every S' containing only guarded μ-terms, and for every $\gamma \in \mathit{Stmv} \to \mathcal{P}^+$:

$$[\![S']\!]_L(\mathit{trace} \circ \gamma) = \mathit{trace}([\![S']\!]_B(\gamma)).$$

Case (i). $S' \not\equiv \mu x[S]$. Now the result follows easily by the induction hypothesis and and the homomorphism properties of *trace*.

The interesting case is

Case (ii). $S' \equiv \mu x[S]$.

Some notation: $\mathit{trace} \circ \gamma = \gamma'$. Further, we employ again the notation of Definition 2.11: $\Phi_{S,\gamma'} = \lambda X.[\![S]\!]_L(\gamma'\{X/x\})$. Finally, p_n is defined as in the statement of the theorem.

First we prove

CLAIM 1. $\mathit{trace}(p_n) = \Phi^n_{S,\gamma'}(A^\infty)$.

Proof of Claim 1. $\mathit{trace}(p_n) = \mathit{trace}([\![S]\!]_B(\gamma\{p_{n-1}/x\}))$ = (by the induction hypothesis) $[\![S]\!]_L(\gamma'\{\mathit{trace}(p_{n-1})/x\}) = (\lambda X.[\![S]\!]_L(\gamma'\{X/x\}))(\mathit{trace}(p_{n-1})) = \Phi_{S,\gamma'}(\mathit{trace}(p_{n-1}))$.
Hence $\mathit{trace}(p_n) = \Phi^n_{S,\gamma'}(\mathit{trace}(p_u)) = \Phi_{S,\gamma'}(A^\infty)$.

CLAIM 2. $\bigcap_n \Phi^n_{S,\gamma'}(A^\infty) = \lim_n \Phi^n_{S,\gamma'}(A^\infty)$.

Proof of Claim 2. By the fact that only guarded μ-terms are considered, $\{p_n\}$ is a Cauchy sequence. By the continuity of *trace* (Lemma 4.4), $\{\mathit{trace}(p_n)\}$ is therefore also a Cauchy sequence. So by Claim 1, $\{\Phi^n_{S,\gamma'}(A^\infty)\}$ is a Cauchy sequence.

Furthermore, the $\Phi^n_{S,\gamma'}$ are monotonic (Lemma 2.12(ii)). Since A^∞ is the maximal element of $\mathcal{C}$, the sequence $\{\Phi^n_{S,\gamma'}(A^\infty)\}$ is therefore decreasing (w.r.t. $\subseteq$). Now Claim 2 follows by Proposition 2.7.

Now we have: $[\![S']\!]_L(\mathit{trace}\circ\gamma) \equiv [\![\mu x[S]]\!]_L(\gamma')$ = (Coroll.2.13)

$\bigcap_n \Phi^n_{S,\gamma'}(A^\infty)$ = (Claim 2) $\lim_n \Phi^n_{S,\gamma'}(A^\infty)$ = (Claim 1)

$\lim_n \mathit{trace}(p_n)$ = (Lemma 4.4) $\mathit{trace}(\lim_n p_n)$ = (definition in the

present theorem) $\mathit{trace}[\![\mu x[S]]\!]_B(\gamma) \equiv \mathit{trace}[\![S']\!]_B(\gamma)$.

□

We continue with

Case (ii). (S involves at least one unguarded μ-term.) Now two ways of achieving (¶) are available.

Firstly, we can maintain the definition of $[\![S]\!]_L$, and use the revised definition of $[\![S]\!]_B$ as stated in Theorem 4.7. The crucial difference is that the mapping T' is now no longer contracting in general, and we cannot use Banach's fixed point theorem to show that the sequence p_u, $T'(p_u)$, $T'^2(p_u)$,... converges to a fixed point of T'. However, this fact has indeed - with some effort, and for arbitrary initial q - been established in Bergstra & Klop [5]. Thus, we can base our revised definition on their theorem, and again obtain - by the same reasoning as in the proof of Theorem 4.7 - that (¶) holds.

Secondly, we may also keep the definition of $[\![S]\!]_B$ as in Definition 3.5, and revise that of $[\![S]\!]_L$. We then replace the last clause of Definition 2.11 by

$$[\![\mu x[S]]\!]_L(\gamma) = \mu[\lambda X.[\![\tau;S]\!]_L(\gamma\{X/x\})].$$

All this amounts to the idea of replacing, both for LT and for BT, $\mu x[S]$ by $\mu x[\tau;S]$, thus ensuring that all statements have only guarded terms, so that Theorem 4.7 applies again.

APPENDIX: Well-definedness and continuity of the operations $\cdot$, $\cup$, $\|$ on C.

We will now give the proofs of Theorem 2.9 and 2.10. For both theorems the case of '$\cup$' is trivial; this leaves us with the following four propositions, which we will treat together since their proofs have a common structure.

THEOREM 2.9, 2.10. (i) $X,Y \in C \Longrightarrow X\|Y \in C$, (ii) $X,Y \in C \Longrightarrow X\cdot Y \in C$,

(iii) *Let* A *be finite. Let* $X_n, Y_m \in C$ $(n,m \geq 0)$ *be such that* $X_0 \supseteq X_1 \supseteq \cdots$ *and* $Y_0 \supseteq Y_1 \supseteq \cdots$. *Then:*

$$(\bigcap_{n\geq 0} X_n) \| (\bigcap_{m\geq 0} Y_m) = \bigcap_{k\geq 0} (X_k \| Y_k).$$

(iv) *As (iii) with* $\|$ *replaced by* $\cdot$.

PROOF. The proofs of (i),...,(iv) all start with a Cauchy sequence $\{z_i | i \geq 0\}$, where the z_i are elements of $X\|Y$, $X\cdot Y$, $\bigcap_{k\geq 0}(X_k\|Y_k)$, $\bigcap_{k\geq 0} X_k\cdot Y_k$, respectively. Since we will need to specify which parts from z_i originate from X (resp. X_k) and which from Y (resp. Y_k), we introduce two disjoint copies A_ξ and A_η of the alphabet A. Intuitively, A_ξ and A_η are colored copies of A, say 'blue' resp. 'red'. The sequence $\{z_i\}$ is then colored, i.e. lifted to a sequence $\{\zeta_i\}$ where $\zeta_i \in (A_\xi \cup A_\eta)^\infty = B^\infty$ and $h(\zeta_i) = z_i$; h is the 'decoloring homomorphism' whose precise definition is left to the reader.

The sequence $\{\zeta_i\}$ is however in general no longer a Cauchy sequence in $P_c(B^\infty)$. But it contains a subsequence $\{\zeta_{g(i)}\}$ which is a Cauchy sequence. The (colored) limit ξ of this subsequence is then used to prove the result.

More precisely:

Proof of (i). Let $\{z_i | i \geq 0\}$ be a Cauchy sequence such that $z_i \in X||Y$ $(i \geq 0)$. So $z_i \in x_i||y_i$ for some $x_i \in X$, $y_i \in Y$. Lifting to the alphabet B we find colored versions ζ_i, ξ_i, η_i such that $\xi_i \in A_\xi^\infty$, $\eta_i \in A_\eta^\infty$ and $\zeta_i \in \xi_i||\eta_i$.

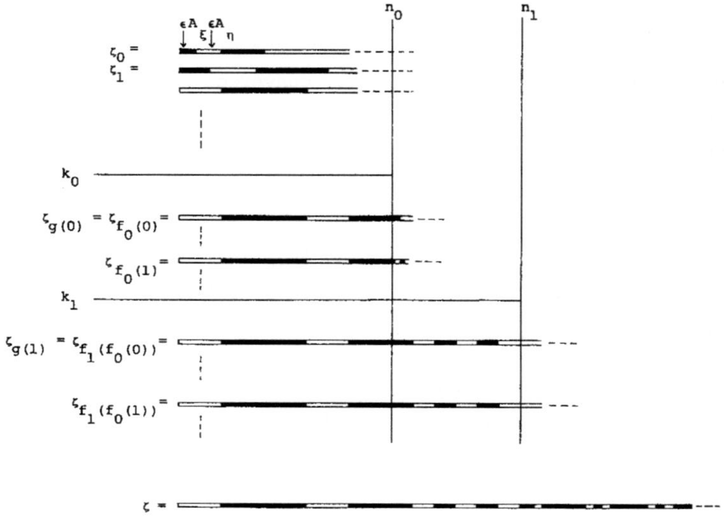

Consider $n = n_0$. Since $\{z_i\}$ is a Cauchy sequence, there is a k_0 such that the prefixes $z_i[n_0]$ are constant for $i \geq k_0$, namely equal to $z_{k_0}[n_0]$. This need not to be the case for $\zeta_i[n_0]$. However, since there are only finitely many colorings of $z_{k_0}[n_0]$, there is (by the pigeon-hole principle) a subsequence $\{\zeta_{f_0(i)}\}$ of $\{\zeta_i | i \geq k_0\}$ such that the prefixes $\zeta_{f_0(i)}[n_0]$ are constant for all i. (Here f_0 is some monotonic function from $\mathbb{N}$ to $\mathbb{N}$.)

Now consider $n_1 > n_0$. From the sequence $\{\zeta_{f_0(i)}\}$ we can in the same way extract a subsequence $\{\zeta_{f_1(f_0(i))}\}$ whose n_1-prefixes are constant. Continuing this procedure we find a sequence $\{\zeta_{g(j)}\}$ where g is a monotonic function such that $g(j) = (f_j \circ \ldots \circ f_1 \circ f_0)(0)$, which evidently is a Cauchy sequence in $\mathcal{P}_c(B^\infty)$. Call the limit ζ. Then ζ can be decomposed (by projections to A_ξ, resp. A_η) into ξ, η such that $\zeta \in \xi||\eta$. Decoloring, we have $z \in x||y$. Since z is the limit of $\{z_i\}$, we are through if $x \in X$ and $y \in Y$. This follows easily because X,Y are closed.

Proof of (ii). The proof is almost identical to that of (i): we only have to replace $X||Y$ by $X \cdot Y$, and $z_i \in x_i||y_i$ by $z_i = x_i \cdot y_i$ etc. (In the figure: the 'blue' parts precede the 'red' parts, instead of being mixed.)

Proof of (iii). ($\subseteq$) is trivial. ($\supseteq$): take $z \in \bigcap (X_i \| Y_i)$, so for all i: $z \in x_i \| y_i$ for some $x_i \in X_i$ and $y_i \in Y_i$. Again, find colored versions ζ_i, ξ_i, η_i such that $\zeta_i \in B^{\infty}$, $\xi_i \in A_{\xi}^{\infty}$, $\eta_i \in A_{\eta}^{\infty}$, $h(\zeta_i) = z$, $h(\xi_i) = x_i$, $h(\eta_i) = y_i$ and $\zeta_i \in \xi_i \| \eta_i$. Construct ζ, ξ, η such that $\zeta \in \xi \| \eta$ as in (i).

Let $h(\xi) = x$ and $h(\eta) = y$. It remains to show that $x \in \bigcap X_n$ and $y \in \bigcap Y_m$. This follows because for each prefix x' of x there is a p such that $x' \leq x_p \in X_p \subseteq X_0$. Since X_0 is closed, it follows that $x \in X_0$; likewise $x \in X_1$, and so on.

The finiteness condition on A is used to ensure that $\bigcap X_n \neq \emptyset$ and $\bigcap Y_m \neq \emptyset$. The non-emptiness of these intersections is needed in the case that $\zeta \in A_{\xi}^{\infty}$ or $\zeta \in A_{\eta}^{\infty}$ (i.e. ζ is entirely 'blue' or 'red'). In that case we need to pick an arbitrary η resp. ξ such that $h(\eta) = y \in \bigcap Y_m$ resp. $h(\xi) = x \in \bigcap X_n$, to be able to write $\zeta \in \xi \| \eta$ and $z \in x \| y$.

Proof of (iv): mutatis mutandis identical to that of (iii). □

REFERENCES

[1] DE BAKKER, J.W., Mathematical Theory of Program Correctness, Prentice-Hall International, 1980.

[2] DE BAKKER, J.W., J.A. BERGSTRA, J.W. KLOP & J.-J.CH. MEYER, Linear time and branching time semantics for recursion with merge. Report IW 211/82, Mathematical Centre, Amsterdam 1982.

[3] DE BAKKER, J.W. & J.I. ZUCKER, Denotational semantics of concurrency, Proc. 14th ACM Symp. on Theory of Computing, pp.153-158, 1982.

[4] DE BAKKER, J.W. & J.I. ZUCKER, Processes and the denotational semantics of concurrency, Report IW 209/82, Mathematisch centrum, Amsterdam 1982.

[5] BERGSTRA, J.A. & J.W. KLOP, Fixed point semantics in process algebras, Report IW 206/82, Mathematisch Centrum, Amsterdam 1982.

[6] ENGELKING, R., General Topology, Polish Scientific Publishers, 1977.

[7] FRANCEZ, N., D.J. LEHMANN & A. PNUELI, Linear history semantics for distributed languages, Proc. 21st Symp. Foundations of Computer Science, IEEE 1980, pp.143-151.

[8] MILNER, R., A Calculus for Communicating Systems, Springer LNCS 92, 1980.

[9] MILNER, R., A complete inference system for a class of regular behaviours, Preprint, Edinburgh 1982.

[10] NIVAT, M., Mots infinis engendrés par une grammaire algébrique, RAIRO Informatique Théorique Vol.11 (1977) pp.311-327.

[11] NIVAT, M., Sur les ensembles des mots infinis engendrés par une grammaire algébrique, RAIRO Informatique Théorique Vol.12 (1978) pp.259-278.

[12] NIVAT, M., Infinite words, infinite trees, infinite computations, Foundations of Computer Science III.2 (J.W. de Bakker & J. van Leeuwen,eds.) pp.3-52, Mathematical Centre Tracts 109, 1979.

[13] NIVAT, M., Synchronization of concurrent processes, Formal Language Theory (R.V. Book, ed.),pp.429-454, Academic Press, 1980.

[14] PLOTKIN, G.D., A power domain construction, SIAM J. on Comp., 5 (1976), pp.452-487.

[15] SCOTT, D.S., Data types as lattices, SIAM J. on Comp., 5 (1976), pp.522-587.

[16] SCOTT, D.S., Domains for denotational semantics, Proc. 9th ICALP (M. Nielsen & E.M. Schmidt, eds.), pp.577-613, Springer LNCS 140, 1982.

[17] SMYTH, M.B., Power domains, J. Comp. Syst. sciences, 16 (1978), pp.23-36.

PROCESSES AND A FAIR SEMANTICS FOR THE ADA RENDEZ-VOUS

J.W. de Bakker
Department of Computer Science
Mathematisch Centrum
Kruislaan 413, Amsterdam

J.I. Zucker
Department of Computer Science
SUNY at Buffalo
Amherst, N.Y. 14226, U.S.A.

ABSTRACT

Processes are mathematical objects which are elements of domains in the sense of Scott and Plotkin. Process domains are obtained as solutions of equations solved by techniques from metric topology as advocated by Nivat. We discuss how such processes can be used to assign meanings to languages with concurrency, culminating in a definition of the ADA rendez-vous. An important intermediate step is a version of Hoare's CSP for which we describe a process semantics and which is used, following Gerth, as target for the translation of the ADA fragment. Furthermore, some ideas will be presented on a mathematically tractable treatment of fairness in the general framework of processes.

1. INTRODUCTION

This paper presents a case study in the area of the semantics of concurrency. In the initial years of the theory of concurrency, most of the attention was devoted to notions such as composition and *synchronization* of parallel processes - often established through suitably restricted interleaving of the elementary actions of the components, and mostly referring to a shared variable model. More recently there has been a considerable increase in the interest for *communication* between processes - often referring to a model where the individual processes have disjoint variables which interact only through the respective communication mechanisms. Instrumental in this development have been the studies of BRINCH HANSEN [6], HOARE [10] and MILNER [15], where a variety of forms of communication was proposed and embedded in a language design or studied with the tools of operational and denotational semantics. The incorporation of the notions of tasking and rendez-vous in the language ADA ([1]) provides additional motivation for the study of communication, and it is the latter notion in particular which we have chosen as the topic of our investigation.

The main purpose of our paper is firstly to provide a rigorous definition for the ADA rendez-vous with the tools of *denotational* semantics, and secondly to introduce a mathematically tractable approach to fairness which is applicable in general in various situations where choices have to be made on a fair basis, and in particular to the ADA rendez-vous definition.

The general framework we apply in our paper was first outlined in DE BAKKER & ZUCKER [3], and later described in detail in DE BAKKER & ZUCKER [4]. In order to keep the present paper self-contained, we shall provide a summary description of the main points of the latter paper, without going into much mathematical detail. Our approach to the ADA rendez-vous and to fairness owes much to two contributions to ICALP 82.

In GERTH [8] the idea of translating the ADA fragment to a version of CSP was proposed; the same approach will be applied by us in section 6. In PLOTKIN [19], the fundamental idea of specifying a fair merge through suitable use of - essentially - an appropriate succession of random choices was proposed and embedded in a category - theoretic setting. (The suggestion of applying a version of such random choice in the framework of processes arose in a discussion with Plotkin during an IFIP WG 2.2 meeting.)

The structure of the paper is the following. After this introduction we present in section 2 an outline of the underlying semantic framework, though without most of the mathematics. In denotational semantics, language constructs are provided with mathematical objects (functions, operators, etc.) as their meanings. In the present paper, these meanings are so-called *processes* (in our paper a technical term for certain mathematical objects rather than for -syntactic- components of a program). Processes are elements of domains in the general sense as introduced by SCOTT [21,22]. Technically, domains of processes are obtained as solutions of *domain equations*. The solution of such equations in a context with nondeterminacy and concurrency was first studied in detail by PLOTKIN [18] (see [4] for more recent references). We have based our solution techniques on completion methods in metric topology (as advocated recently by Nivat and his school, see e.g. [16]). Throughout our paper, we shall introduce a variety of processes, corresponding to a variety of programming concepts we encounter on the way to our understanding of the ADA rendez-vous. In section 2, processes are still simple. We call them *uniform*, and they bear a close resemblance to trees - though there are also a few crucial differences. Section 2 further introduces various operations upon processes - which will undergo successive refinements in later sections. We moreover illustrate uniform processes by using them in the semantics of a very simple language with parallel merge as its only concurrent notion. In section 3 we use uniform processes as a vehicle to explain the key idea of our approach to fairness, viz. suitable alternation of random choices. (Ultimately, this idea may be traced back to the use of *oracles* to handle fairness. Fundamental studies of the semantics of fairness were made by PARK [17]; proof - theoretic investigations are described, e.g., in [2,11,12,20].) Section 4 describes a number of ways of providing processes with additional structure. Firstly, we enrich them with a synchronization mechanism in the sense of MILNER's ports ([15]). We then obtain structures which are close to his synchronization trees. Next, we add a functional flavor to uniform processes, and obtain objects which have PLOTKIN's resumptions ([18]) as forerunners. Finally, we add a communication feature to processes yielding a counterpart for Milner's communication trees ([15]). Whereas in section 4 we introduce each extension independently, we need their combination in section 5 to define the semantics of a language with both parallel merge, (synchronization through) communication, and a version of Milner's restriction operator. This language is an abstraction of HOARE's CSP ([10]), and we use it to provide a translation of the ADA fragment featuring its rendez-vous concept ([1], chapter 9) in section 6. Section 7, finally, extends the fairness-definition ideas of section 3 to a situation with communication.

2. UNIFORM PROCESSES AND A SIMPLE LANGUAGE WITH MERGE

A uniform process is a variation on the notion of tree. It is used, e.g., to assign meaning to a program when one is primarily interested in the structure of the sequences of elementary actions generated during its execution, rather than in the relation between input and output states of the program. Processes (and trees) constitute a more refined tool than just sets of sequences: we distinguish between the two objects

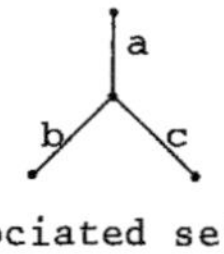

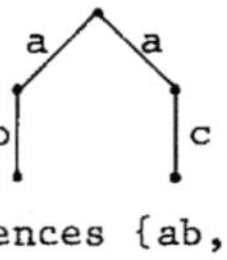

which have the same associated sets of sequences {ab,ac}. Also, uniform processes are only the first on a list of gradually more complex constructs to be studied in subsequent sections.

Let A be any (finite or infinite) alphabet. Let a,b,... be elements of A. Uniform processes p,q,... wil be described as certain constructs over the alphabet A. We introduce

1. The *nil process* p_0. Roughly, its role is that of neutral element for various operations; also, it may be seen as label of the leaves of a process in case this is viewed as a tree-like construct.
2. The set of all *finite* processes $P_\omega \overset{df.}{=} \bigcup_n P_n$, where P_n, n = 0,1,..., are given by $P_0 = \{p_0\}$, $P_{n+1} = \mathcal{P}(A\times P_n)$, where $\mathcal{P}$ (·) denotes all subsets of (·). Finite processes are for example p_0,$\{<a,p_0>,<b,p_0>\}$, or $\{<a,\{<b,p_0>,<c,p_0>\}>\}$ and $\{<a,\{<b,p_0>\}>,<a,\{<c,p_0>\}>\}$. Note that these examples are elements of P_0,P_1,P_2 and P_2. Note also that the latter two processes correspond to the pictures at the beginning of the section.
3. The set of all finite or infinite processes (over A) as solution of the domain equation

(2.1) $\quad P = \{p_0\} \cup \mathcal{P}_c(A\times P)$.

We shall not give the full explanation here, but restrict ourselves to the following: We may introduce a distance or *metric* d on the space P_ω of all finite processes, and consider the *completion* of P_ω with respect to this metric (cf. Cantor's completion of the set of rationals to that of the reals). Essentially, this amounts to adding to the space P_ω all limits of so-called Cauchy sequences (sequences $<p_n>_{n=0}^{\infty}$ with $p_n \in P_n$, such that distances between elements get arbitrarily small with increasing index). E.g., infinite objects such as $\{<a,\{<a,\{<a,...>\}>\}>\}$ or $\{<a,\{<a,...>,<b,...>\}>,<b,\{<a,...>,<b,...>\}>\}$ belong to P. Furthermore $\mathcal{P}_c(\cdot)$ now stands for the collection of all *closed* - with respect to the metric - subsets of (·), and one can show that for P the completion of P_ω, it indeed satisfies equation (2.1). In summary, each proces is either finite and element of some P_n, or infinite and limit of a Cauchy sequence $<p_n>_n$, with $p_n \in P_n$. Throughout the paper, we shall pay little attention to the infinite case, not because we want to ignore it but rather since, based on the firm foundation of (2.1) - or similar equations below -, the infinite case always follows straightforwardly from the finite case.

The reader should observe the difference between processes and trees. Firstly, in processes we have nor order. Trees  and 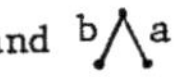 are different; as processes they are both equal to $\{<a,p_0>,<b,p_0>\}$. Secondly, processes have no multiple occurrences of elements. The trees  and 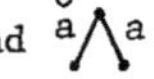 are different, but as processes they coincide (non-nil processes are sets, not multisets).

We continue with the definition of the main *operations* on processes. Throughout the paper, we shall distinguish the cases of the nil process p_0, finite processes $p,q,\ldots$ which are *sets* $X,Y \in \mathcal{P}(A\times P_n)$ for some n, and infinite processes $\lim_n p_n$, with $p_n \in P_n$. Observe that elements x,y of sets X,Y are *pairs* $<a,p'>,<b,q'>$, etc. We now define three important operations on processes.

DEFINITION 2.1.

a. *Composition* "$\circ$" is defined by

$$p\circ p_0 = p,\ p\circ X = \{p\circ x \mid x \in X\},\ p\circ <a,q> = <a,p\circ q>,\quad p\circ \lim_n q_n = \lim_n (p\circ q_n)$$

b. *Union* "$\cup$" is defined by

$p \cup p_0 = p_0 \cup p = p$, and, for $p,q \neq p_0$, $p \cup q$ is the set theoretic union of the sets p,q

c. *Merge* "$\|$" is defined by

$$p \,\|\, p_0 = p_0 \,\|\, p = p,\quad X \,\|\, Y = (X \,\|_L Y) \cup (X \,\|_R Y),$$
$$X \,\|_L Y = \{x \,\|\, Y \mid x \in X\},\ X \,\|_R Y = \{X \,\|\, y \mid y \in Y\},$$
$$<a,p> \,\|\, Y = <a,p \,\|\, Y>,\quad X \,\|\, <b,q> = <b,X \,\|\, q>,$$
$$(\lim_i p_i) \,\|\, (\lim_j q_j) = \lim_k (p_k \,\|\, q_k).$$

LEMMA 2.2. *The above operations are all well-defined and associative,* $\cup$, $\|$ *are commutative, and they all have the usual continuity properties.*

Examples

1. Let $p = \{<a,p_0>,<b,p_0>\}$, $\quad q = \{<c,\{<d,p_0>,<e,p_0>\}>\}$.
   Then $p\circ q = \{<c,\{<d,p>,<e,p>\}>\}$. In pictures we have

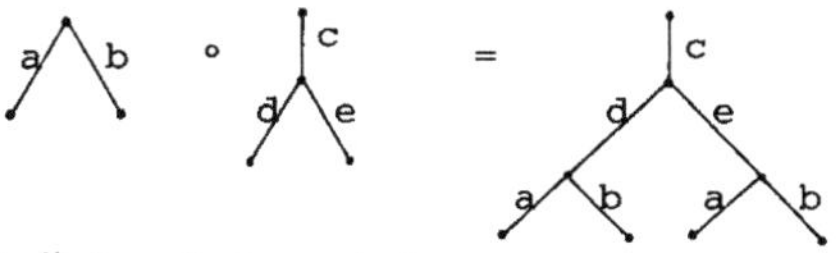

2. $\{<a,\{<b,p_0>\}>\} \,\|\, \{<c,\{<d,p_0>\}>\}$
   =

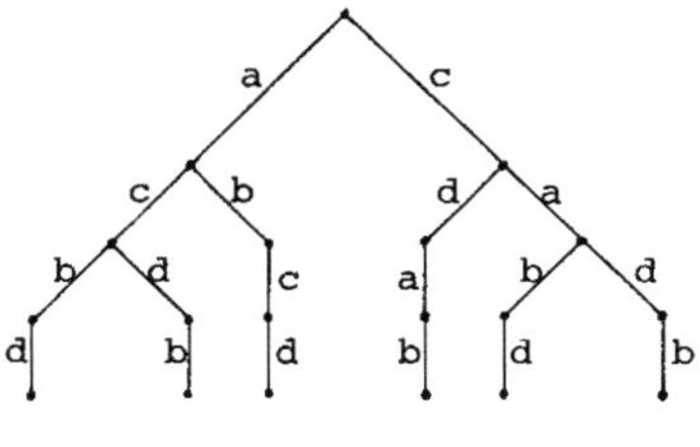

We next introduce the important notion of a so-called *contracting* mapping. A mapping $T: P \to P$ is called contracting whenever, for all p', p'', $d(T(p'),T(p'')) \le c \times d(p',p'')$, with $0 \le c < 1$. (The mapping T brings points closer to each other.) We have a classical theorem which will be very useful in the sequel:

THEOREM 2.3 (Banach). *Let* T *be contracting, and let* q *be an arbitrary element of* P. *Then the sequence* $q, T(q), T^2(q), \ldots$ *is a Cauchy sequence which converges to the unique fixed point of* T.

Remarks

1. Observe that $\lim_n T^n(q)$ is independent of q.
2. Convergence of the sequence $q, T(q), \ldots$ in cases where T is not necessarily contracting is studied in [5].

We close this section with the introduction of a simple language with parallel composition (i.e. the merge "$\|$") as its only non-sequential concept and we show how uniform processes can be used to define its semantics. More specifically, the simple language L_1 has elementary actions (for simplicity taken from the alphabet A), sequential composition, nondeterministic choice, merge, and (finite or infinite) iteration. In BNF like notation, its syntax is given in

DEFINITION 2.4. Statements $S \in L_1$ are defined by

$$S ::= a \,|\, \underline{skip} \,|\, S_1;S_2 \,|\, S_1 \cup S_2 \,|\, S_1 \parallel S_2 \,|\, S^*.$$

Remark. We ignore possible syntactic ambiguities.

Let τ be a special element added to A (Milner would call it the unobservable action), and let P_1 solve the equation

$$(2.2) \qquad P_1 = \{p_0\} \cup \mathcal{P}_c((A\cup\{\tau\})\times P_1).$$

We define the semantic mapping $M: L_1 \to P_1$ in

DEFINITION 2.5. The mapping $M: L_1 \to P_1$ is given in
$M(a) = \{\langle a,p_0\rangle\}$, $M(\underline{skip}) = \{\langle\tau,p_0\rangle\}$,
$M(S_1;S_2) = M(S_2) \circ M(S_1)$, $M(S_1 \cup S_2) = M(S_1) \cup M(S_2)$, $M(S_1 \parallel S_2) = M(S_1) \parallel M(S_2)$, and
$M(S^*) = \lim_i p_i$, where p_0 is the nil process and $p_{i+1} = (p_i \circ M(S)) \cup \{\langle\tau,p_0\rangle\}$.

Remarks.

1. We see that the syntactic operations $;$, $\cup$, $\parallel$ are mapped directly onto the semantic operations $\circ$, $\cup$, $\parallel$.
2. The definition of S^* is explained by observing the intended equivalence $S^* = (S;S^*) \cup \underline{skip}$. Semantically, we have, by theorem 2.3, for $p \overset{df.}{=} \lim_i p_i$, the fixed point property $p = (p \circ M(S)) \cup \{\langle\tau,p_0\rangle\}$.

Examples.

1. $M(a_1;a_2) = M(a_2) \circ M(a_1) = \{\langle a_2,p_0\rangle\}\circ\{\langle a_1,p_0\rangle\} = \{\langle a_1,\{\langle a_2,p_0\rangle\}\rangle\}$
2. $M(a_1;(a_2 \cup a_3)) = \{\langle a_1,\{\langle a_2,p_0\rangle,\langle a_3,p_0\rangle\}\rangle\} \ne M((a_1;a_2) \cup (a_1;a_3))$
3. $M(a^*) = \{\langle\tau,p_0\rangle,\langle a,\{\langle\tau,p_0\rangle,\langle a,\ldots\rangle\}\rangle\}$.

The reader should observe that L_1 could also be provided with a semantics in terms of sets of sequences rather than of processes. In this case $a_1;(a_2 \cup a_3)$ and $(a_1;a_2) \cup (a_1;a_3)$ - and also statements such as $(a \cup b) \parallel c$ and $(a \parallel c) \cup (b \parallel c)$ - would obtain the same meaning. In subsequent applications we shall be able to profit from the more refined process structure, which is why we already used them for providing meaning to L_1.

3. FAIRNESS FOR UNIFORM PROCESSES

We present a definition of fair merge for uniform processes which is based essentially on the well-known idea of implementing fair scheduling through systematic alternation of random choice (see [2] and, in particular, [19]). We first discuss the idea using a simple example (in which it is convenient to use sequences rather than processes). Consider the two infinite sequences of actions a^ω and b^ω, and suppose we want to write a program scheduling their fair merge $a^\omega \parallel_f b^\omega$ (which should therefore exclude sequences with almost all a's or almost all b's). Now this is achieved by the following program with random assignments - where x := ? means that x is assigned an arbitrary non-negative integer:

$x_1 := ?;\ x_2 := ?;$

$L_1 : a;\ \underline{\text{if}}\ x_1 > 0\ \underline{\text{then}}\ x_1 := x_1 - 1;\ \underline{\text{goto}}\ L_1\ \underline{\text{else}}\ x_2 := ?;\ \underline{\text{goto}}\ L_2\ \underline{\text{fi}}$

$\cup$

$L_2 : b;\ \underline{\text{if}}\ x_2 > 0\ \underline{\text{then}}\ x_2 := x_2 - 1;\ \underline{\text{goto}}\ L_2\ \underline{\text{else}}\ x_1 := ?;\ \underline{\text{goto}}\ L_1\ \underline{\text{fi}}$

Observe that this program determines $a^\omega \parallel_f b^\omega$ as an infinite sequence of *either* subsequences of $x_1^{(i)}$ a's and then $x_2^{(i)}$ b's, $i = 1,2,\ldots$, $x_1^{(i)}$ and $x_2^{(i)}$ successive results of the random choices $x_1 := ?$ and $x_2 := ?$, *or* of a similar sequence of subsequences of $x_2^{(j)}$ b's and $x_1^{(j)}$ a's, $j = 1,2,\ldots$.

In PLOTKIN [19], this idea was embedded in the setting of category theory. What we shall describe here is the same approach in the framework of process theory. At first sight, the random assignment is an extraneous element for the process notion. However, there is a natural way to link it to the process framework. We start with the observation that the *infinite* union $\bigcup_n p_n$, for processes $p_n \in P$, is, in general, not well-defined (technically, this is the case because the infinite union of a family of closed sets is not necessarily closed). What we can do, however, is to extend P in the following way. Let $\mathbb{N}$ be the set of natural numbers. Now instead of using equation (2.1) we take process domain P_f as solution of

$$P_f = \{p_0\} \cup \mathcal{P}_c((A \cup \mathbb{N}) \times P_f). \tag{3.1}$$

Within P_f we can define a new construct $\bigsqcup_n p_n$ by the definition

$$\bigsqcup_n p_n = \{\langle n, p_n \rangle \mid n \in \mathbb{N}\}.$$

(In this expression, p_0 is some arbitrary process rather than the nil process.) In a picture we have for $\bigsqcup_n p_n$:

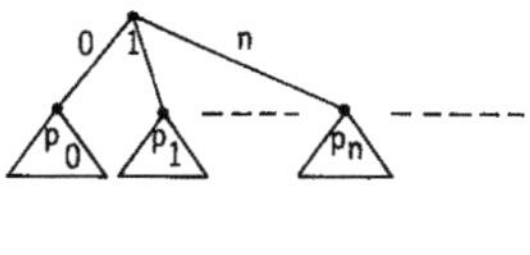

which simulates a random choice between the p_n. It can be verified that $\bigsqcup_n p_n$ is a well-defined element of P_f (since the only non-trivial Cauchy sequences must be wholly within some p_n). We are now sufficiently prepared for

DEFINITION 3.1 (fair merge). Let $p,q \in P_f$, and let, as usual, X,Y be finite processes. Let b range over $B \overset{df.}{=} A \cup \mathbb{N}$. We shall define $p\|_f q$ in terms of a number of auxiliary constructs $p\|_\alpha q$, for α any of the subscripts of $\|$ occurring in the clauses below.

a. $p\|_\alpha p_0 = p_0\|_\alpha p = p$
b. $X\|_f Y = (X\|_L Y) \cup (X\|_R Y)$
c. $X\|_L Y = \{<n, X\|_{L,n} Y> \mid n \in \mathbb{N}\}$, and similarly for $X\|_R Y$
d. $X\|_{L,n} Y = \{x\|_{L,n} Y \mid x \in X\}$, and similarly for $X\|_{R,n} Y$
e. $<b,p> \|_{L,n+1} Y = <b, p \|_{L,n} Y>$, and symmetric
f. $<b,p> \|_{L,0} Y = <b, p\|_R Y>$, and symmetric
g. $(\lim_i p_i) \|_f (\lim_j q_j) = \lim_k (p_k \|_f q_k)$

LEMMA 3.2. *The above definition of* $\|_f$ *is well-formed (e.g., if* $<p_i>_i$ *and* $<q_j>_j$ *are Cauchy sequences, then so is* $<p_k\|_f q_k>_k$, *etc.*

Remark. The reader who has understood the program in the beginning of this section will recognize that definition 3.1 is the exact counterpart of that program, with the random choice x_i := ?, i = 1,2, replaced by a choice <n,...> for some $n \in \mathbb{N}$.

We need additional study to link the notion of fair merge of two processes to that of a "fair process". The following definitions and property seem plausible here (though we have no full supporting proofs):

1. Let $p \in P_f$, and let b range over $B \overset{df.}{=} A \cup \mathbb{N}$. A *path* for p is a (finite or infinite) sequence (*): $<b_1,p_1>, <b_2,p_2>, \ldots$ such that $<b_1,p_1> \in p$, and $<b_{i+1},p_{i+1}> \in p_i$, $i = 1,2,\ldots$.
2. b is *enabled* in (*) whenever, for some i and q, $<b,q> \in p_i$.
   b *occurs* in (*) whenever, for some i, $b = b_i$.
3. A path (*) is *fair* with respect to some $B' \subseteq B$ whenever, for all $b' \in B'$, if b' is infinitely often enabled in (*), it infinitely often occurs in (*). Process p is called fair with respect to B' whenever all its paths are fair with respect to B'.
4. We conjecture that, for p,q fair with respect to A, $p\|_f q$ is fair with respect to A.

The above ideas can be modified for *regular* processes. Without going into details, let us call a process regular whenever it has only finitely many different subprocesses. We expect that results extending the above can be obtained for regular processes, where the above definitions are replaced by conditions imposed upon "moves" of pairs <b,q> rather than simply of elementary actions b.

4. PROCESSES WITH ADDITIONAL STRUCTURE

In this section, we discuss three ways in which to extend the uniform processes of section 2. We shall deal with

- processes exhibiting synchronization

- processes which are (also) functions
- processes which communicate.

We begin with synchronization. (The ideas for this stem from MILNER's CCS [15].) Let Γ be a set of *ports*, the elements of which appear in pairs $\gamma,\bar{\gamma},\ldots$ (pairs are symmetric in the sense that $\bar{\bar{\gamma}} = \gamma$). We introduce processes with synchronization as elements of the set P_s which solves

(4.1) $\quad P_s = \{p_0\} \cup \mathcal{P}_c((A\cup\{\tau\}\cup\Gamma) \times P_s)$.

Let β range over $A \cup \{\tau\} \cup \Gamma$. We define the operations of section 2, together with the new operation of restriction $p\backslash\gamma$, in

DEFINITION 4.1.

a. $p\circ p_0$, $p\circ X$, $p\circ \lim_n p_n$ are as before, and $p\circ\langle\beta,q\rangle = \langle\beta,p\circ q\rangle$.

b. $\cup$ is defined as before

c. $p\| q$ is defined as before, except for the (central) clause

$X\|Y = (X\|_L Y) \cup (X\|_R Y) \cup (X\|_s Y)$, where $\|_L$ and $\|_R$ are as in def.2.1, and

$X\|_s Y = \{\langle\tau,p'\| p''\rangle \mid \langle\gamma,p'\rangle \in X, \langle\bar{\gamma},p''\rangle \in Y$, for some pair of corresponding ports $\gamma,\bar{\gamma}\}$

d. $p\backslash\gamma$ is defined by: $p_0\backslash\gamma = p_0$, $(\lim_n p_n)\backslash\gamma = \lim_n (p_n\backslash\gamma)$, and

$X\backslash\gamma = \{\langle\beta,p'\backslash\gamma\rangle \mid \langle\beta,p'\rangle \in X,\ \beta \neq \gamma,\bar{\gamma}\}$.

Remarks.

1. The definition of $p\|q$ is the essential new element for synchronizing processes. Succesful synchronization of p,q results from pairs $\langle\gamma,p'\rangle$, $\langle\bar{\gamma},p''\rangle$ in p and q, respectively, and the outcome of composing these pairs yields an invisible τ, followed by $p'\| p''$. $X\|Y$ also includes the full merge $(X\|_L Y) \cup (X\|_R Y)$ as introduced in definition 2.1. Pairs $\langle\gamma,\ldots\rangle$ and $\langle\bar{\gamma},\ldots\rangle$ in this full merge can be removed by applying the $\backslash\gamma$ operation. (All this is extensively discussed in [15].)
2. In [4] we discuss how the "$\backslash\gamma$" operation can be defined to model deadlock. In our view, this appears in situations where applying the "$\backslash\gamma$" operation would yield an empty set as outcome; in that case, the refined restriction operator yields a "dead process" as result. We omit further discussion of this.

LEMMA 4.2. *The operations* $\circ$, $\cup$, $\|$, $\backslash$ *are well-defined, and satisfy (where relevant) the usual properties such as associativity, continuity etc.*

We continue with the treatment of *functional* processes. Let A,B be two (arbitrary) sets. We take P_{fn} as solution of

(4.2) $\quad P_{fn} = \{p_0\} \cup (A\to \mathcal{P}_c(B\times P_{fn}))$.

The various definitions of operations on P_{fn} are collected in the next definition (where we omit the standard cases when the operands are nil or infinite). We use the lambda - notation $\lambda a\cdot\ldots a\ldots$ for the function which maps a to $\ldots a\ldots$.

DEFINITION 4.3.

a. $p\circ q = \lambda a.(p\circ q(a))$, $p\circ X = \{p\circ x \mid x \in X\}$, $p\circ\langle b,q\rangle = \langle b,p\circ q\rangle$

b. $p\cup q = \lambda a.(p(a) \cup q(a))$

c. $p \| q = \lambda a.((p \| q(a)) \cup (p(a) \| q))$

$X \| q = \{x \| q \mid x \in X\}$, $p \| Y = \{p \| y \mid y \in Y\}$

$\langle b,p\rangle \| q = \langle b, p \| q\rangle$, $p \| \langle b,q\rangle = \langle b, p \| q\rangle$

Remark. Note the (essential) difference between clauses b and c, in that $p \| q$ is *not* defined as $\lambda a.\ (p(a) \| q(a))$.

<u>LEMMA 4.4</u>. *The operations of definition* 4.3 *have the usual properties.*

We conclude with the introduction of processes with *communication*. We take P_c as solution of

(4.3) $\quad P_c = \{p_0\} \cup \mathcal{P}_c((B \times P_c) \cup (B \to P_c))$.

Let π range over the set $B \to P_c$. The operations on P_c are given in

<u>DEFINITION 4.5</u>.

a. $p \circ X = \{p \circ x \mid x \in X\}$, $p \circ \langle b,q\rangle = \langle b, p \circ q\rangle$, $p \circ \pi = \lambda b.\ (p \circ \pi(b))$

b. $\cup$ is as usual

c. $X \| Y = (X \|_L Y) \cup (X \|_R Y) \cup (X \|_c Y)$, with $X \|_L Y$, $X \|_R Y$ as usual. Moreover,

$X \|_c Y = \{\pi(b) \| p' \mid \pi \in X, \langle b,p'\rangle \in Y\} \cup \{p'' \| \pi(b) \mid \langle b,p''\rangle \in X, \pi \in Y\}$.

Remark. A process p may *communicate* with process q in case p contains some $\langle b,p'\rangle$, and q some function π (or vice versa). The process $\pi(b)$ is then used to continue the operation with the merge $\pi(b) \| p'$ (or symmetric). Applications of this idea (which we first saw in [14]) appear in the next section.

5. A CSP LIKE LANGUAGE

We introduce syntax and semantics of a CSP - like language (CSP for Hoare's Communicating Sequential Processes [10]). In the next section we shall use this language as target for the translation of the ADA fragment containing the rendez-vous construct. In the CSP - like language L_2 we expand the elementary actions of L_1 to assignments and tests; in the next section we explain how tests are used in selection and while statements. L_2 has the same program-forming operations as L_1 and, in addition, communication commands c?x and c!s. Here c is a *channel*, c?x means that variable x is to receive a value from channel c, and c!s means that the current value of expression s is to be transmitted over the channel c. The actual "hand-shake" communication over the channel c takes place provided (i) c?x and c!s appear as substatements in the statements S_1 and S_2 of some parallel composition $S \equiv S_1 \| S_2$, and (ii) in the execution of S, the flow of control in S_1 has arrived at c?x, and control in S_2 has arrived at c!s. The result of the communication is then equivalent to the assignment x:=s. Besides the communication commands we also have in L_2 a restriction S\c which enables us to delete unsuccesful attempts at communication from (the process which is the meaning of) S, and a special construct $b \Rightarrow S$ which in case test b is true will initiate execution of S without allowing a possible interleaving action from some parallel S'.

DEFINITION 5.1 (syntax of L_2).

a. Let x,y,... be variables in a set *Var*, s,t,... expressions, b,... boolean expressions, and c,... channels. (We omit specifying a syntax for (boolean) expressions.)

b. Let ($S\in$) L_2 be the class of statements defined by

$$S ::= x{:=}s \mid \underline{skip} \mid b \mid S_1;S_2 \mid S_1 \cup S_2 \mid S_1 \parallel S_2 \mid S^* \mid c?x \mid c!s \mid S\backslash c \mid b \Rightarrow S.$$

Remark. We hope no confusion will arise from our using $x \in Var$ in the syntax, and $x \in X$ in the semantics.

We next turn to the semantics of L_2. Let V be a set of *values* (meanings of variables and expressions), and let α range over V. Let $\Sigma = Var \to V$ be the set of *states*, with elements $\sigma \in \Sigma$, and let $\sigma\{\alpha/x\}$ be a state which is like σ, but for its value in x which equals α. Let V,W be functions which for each s, b and σ determine values $V(s)(\sigma) \in V$, and $W(b)(\sigma)$ in {tt,ff} (the set of truth-values). We take P_2 as solution of

$$(5.1) \qquad P_2 = \{p_0\} \cup (\Sigma \to P_c((\Sigma\times P_2) \cup (\Gamma\times V\times\Sigma\times P_2) \cup (\Gamma\times(V\to(\Sigma\times P_2))))).$$

In this process domain equation we recognize elements of the three types of extensions discussed separately in section 4. Firstly, terms $\Gamma \times \ldots$ reflect synchronization ports ($\gamma \in \Gamma$ will correspond to channels c in the syntax). Secondly, the $\Sigma \to P_c(\cdot)$ term indicates that processes in P_2 are functional. Thirdly, terms $V \times (\Sigma\times P)$ combined with $V \to (\Sigma\times P)$ correspond to terms $B\times P$ together with $B \to P$ in the case of communicating processes treated previously. In fact, certain variations on equation (5.1) would also lead to a feasible semantics. However, we have chosen the present form since it provided the best model for our fairness considerations in section 7.

DEFINITION 5.2 (semantics of L_2).

a. $M(x{:=}s) = \lambda\sigma.\{<\sigma\{V(s)(\sigma)/x\},p_0>\}$, $M(\underline{skip}) = \lambda\sigma.\{<\sigma,p_0>\}$

$M(b) = \lambda\sigma.\ \underline{if}\ W(b)(\sigma)\ \underline{then}\ \{<\sigma,p_0>\}\ \underline{else}\ \emptyset\ \underline{fi}$

b. $M(S_1;S_2) = M(S_2) \circ M(S_1)$, $M(S_1 \cup S_2) = M(S_1) \cup M(S_2)$

$M(S_1 \parallel S_2) = M(S_1) \parallel M(S_2)$, with $\parallel$ to be defined in definition 5.3

$M(S^*) = \lim_i p_i$, with p_0 as always, and $p_{i+1} = (p_i \circ M(S)) \cup \lambda\sigma.\{<\sigma,p_0>\}$

c. $M(c?x) = \lambda\sigma.\{<\gamma,\lambda\alpha.<\sigma\{\alpha/x\},p_0>>\}$, $M(c!s) = \lambda\sigma.\{<\bar{\gamma},V(s)(\sigma),\sigma,p_0>\}$

d. $M(S\backslash c) = M(S)\backslash\gamma$, with $\backslash$ to be defined in definition 5.3

$M(b \Rightarrow S) = \lambda\sigma.\ \underline{if}\ W(b)(\sigma)\ \underline{then}\ M(S)(\sigma)\ \underline{else}\ \emptyset\ \underline{fi}$

Remarks.

1. We use associativity of tupling, and identify constructs such as <1,2,<3,4>>, <1,2,3,4>, etc.
2. In part c, note that $M(c?x)(\sigma) \in \Gamma \times (V\to(\Sigma\times P))$, $M(c!s)(\sigma) \in \Gamma\times V\times\Sigma\times P$.
3. The definition of $M(b\Rightarrow S)$ should be contrasted with the result of $M(b;s)$: $M(b;S) = \lambda\sigma.\ \underline{if}\ W(b)(\sigma)\ \underline{then}\ \{<\sigma,M(S)>\}\ \underline{else}\ \emptyset\ \underline{fi}$. The reader should ponder the reasons why the latter semantics indeed allows what amounts to an interleaving action at the ";" in b;S, contrary to what is the case for $b \Rightarrow S$.

Definition 5.2 assumes the definition of $\|$ and $\backslash$ in (omitting the nil and infinite cases as usual):

DEFINITION 5.3.

a. $p\| q = \lambda\sigma.((p(\sigma)\| q) \cup (p\| q(\sigma)) \cup (p(\sigma)\|_c q(\sigma)))$

$X\| q = \{x\| q \mid x \in X\}$, $\pi \| q = \lambda\alpha.(\pi(\alpha)\| q)$

$\langle\sigma,p\rangle \| q = \langle\sigma,p\| q\rangle$

$\langle\bar{\gamma},\alpha,\sigma,p\rangle \| q = \langle\bar{\gamma},\alpha,\sigma,p \| q\rangle$, $\langle\gamma,\pi\rangle \| q = \langle\gamma,\pi \| q\rangle$

(and, for the last three lines, the symmetric cases)

$X\|_c Y = \{\pi(\alpha) \| p' \mid \langle\gamma,\pi\rangle \in X, \langle\bar{\gamma},\alpha,\sigma,p'\rangle \in Y\} \cup \{p''\| \pi(\alpha) \mid \langle\bar{\gamma},\alpha,\sigma,p''\rangle \in X, \langle\gamma,\pi\rangle \in Y\}$

b. $p\backslash\gamma = \lambda\sigma.\ (p(\sigma)\backslash\gamma)$, $\pi\backslash\gamma = \lambda\alpha.(\pi(\alpha)\backslash\gamma)$, $x\backslash\gamma = \{x\}\backslash\gamma$,

$X\backslash\gamma = \{\langle\sigma,p'\backslash\gamma\rangle \mid \langle\sigma,p'\rangle \in X\} \cup \{\langle\gamma',\pi\backslash\gamma\rangle \mid \langle\gamma',\pi\rangle \in X,\ \gamma' \neq \gamma,\bar{\gamma}\} \cup$

$\{\langle\gamma',\alpha,\sigma,p'\backslash\gamma\rangle \mid \langle\gamma',\alpha,\sigma,p'\rangle \in X,\ \gamma' \neq \gamma,\bar{\gamma}\}$.

Example. We evaluate $M((c?x \| c!1)\backslash c)$. We obtain $M(c?x\| c!s) \overset{df.}{=} p =$
$\lambda\sigma.\{\langle\gamma,\lambda\alpha.\langle\sigma\{\alpha/x\},p_0\rangle\rangle\} \| \lambda\sigma.\{\langle\bar{\gamma},1,\sigma,p_0\rangle\} =$
$\lambda\sigma.\{\langle\gamma,\ldots\rangle,\langle\bar{\gamma},\ldots\rangle,\lambda\alpha.(\langle\sigma\{\alpha/x\},p_0\rangle)(1) \| p_0\} =$
$\lambda\sigma.\{\langle\gamma,\ldots\rangle,\langle\bar{\gamma},\ldots\rangle,\sigma\{1/x\},p_0 \| p_0\rangle\}$.
Hence, $M(c?x\| c!1)\backslash c) = p\backslash\gamma = \lambda\sigma.\{\langle\sigma\{1/x ,p_0\rangle\}$, which is, indeed, the same process as $M(x:=1)$.

Note that in the above definitions the role of σ in fourtuples $\langle\bar{\gamma},\alpha,\sigma,p\rangle$ is in fact superfluous. However, we have included it to facilitate the definition of *path* in section 7.

6. THE ADA RENDEZ-VOUS

We consider an ADA fragment which centers around the notion of rendez-vous between (calls and accepts of) entries occurring in ADA tasks, and we exhibit a denotational semantics for the fragment by establishing a translation to L_2. We begin with the syntax:

DEFINITION 6.1.

a. (programs formed from tasks). Programs $S \in L_A$ are defined by

$S ::= T_1 \| T_2 \| \ldots \| T_m$

b. (tasks). Tasks T are defined by

T ::= x:=s | skip | if b then T_1 else T_2 fi | while b do T od | e(s,z) | $T_1;T_2$ |
accept e(x,y) do T end
select $b_1 \rightarrow$ accept $e_1(x_1,y_1)$ do T_1' end; T_1'' $\square\ldots\square$
$b_n \rightarrow$ accept $e_n(x_n,y_n)$ do T_n' end; T_n'' end

Remarks.

1. e(s,z) is an entry call statement, with actual parameters s and z. Also, accept e(x,y) do T end is an entry accept statement. At the moment of a (successful) rendez-vous, statement T is executed with actuals s and z corresponding to the formals x,y. The "hand-shake" communication follows the CSP principle. The select statement allows a nondeterministic choice between the guarded accept branches as listed.

2. To avoid problems of naming and scope, we assume a fixed number of distinct entry names $e_1,\ldots,e_s$ occurring in the tasks $T_1,\ldots,T_m$ of program S. Thus, we ignore the notion of entry declarations; neither do we deal with the selected component notation $T_i.e$.
3. In entry calls e(s,z) we encounter - for simplicity's sake - only two actual parameters, viz. expression s and variable z. We also ignore complications arising from parameter passing, and concentrate our interest on cases where the parameter mechanism is equivalent to call-by-value for s and to call-by-value-result - the definition of which is implied by the clauses in part c of definition 6.2 - for the parameter z.

We now present a translation from the statements (and tasks) in L_A to those in L_2. (The idea of such a translation is due to GERTH [8]; the main difference between our approach and [8] is that the latter paper ultimately considers an operational rather than a denotational semantics.) For $S \in L_A$ and tasks T we define their translation $S^\circ, T^\circ \in L_2$. Compared to L_2 as introduced in section 5 we have, in fact, a few minor amendments. We use e rather than c for channels (to stick more closely to the convention for entries in L_A); moreover, we use a version of *simultaneous* restriction $S\backslash\{e_1,\ldots,e_s\}$ with the obvious meaning. Furthermore, we introduce an error statement Δ to be used to indicate failure when all guards in a select statement have the value false. The meaning of Δ is given by $M(\Delta) = \lambda\sigma.\{\langle\delta,p_0\rangle\}$, where δ is a special *dead* state (to be accompanied by natural definitions such as $M(x:=s)(\delta) = \{\langle\delta,p_0\rangle\}$, etc.). The translation from L_A to L_2 is given in

DEFINITION 6.2.

a. $(x:=s)^\circ \equiv (x:=s)$, $\underline{\text{skip}}^\circ \equiv \underline{\text{skip}}$, $(T_1;T_2)^\circ \equiv (T_1^\circ;T_2^\circ)$

b. $(\underline{\text{if}}\ b\ \underline{\text{then}}\ T_1\ \underline{\text{else}}\ T_2\ \underline{\text{fi}})^\circ \equiv (b;T_1^\circ) \cup (\neg b;T_2^\circ)$

$(\underline{\text{while}}\ b\ \underline{\text{do}}\ T\ \underline{\text{od}})^\circ \equiv (b;T^\circ)^*;\ \neg b$

c. $e(s,z)^\circ \equiv e!s;\ e!z;\ e?z$

$(\underline{\text{accept}}\ e(x,y)\ \underline{\text{do}}\ T\ \underline{\text{end}})^\circ \equiv e?x;\ e?y;\ T^\circ;\ e!y$

$$(\underline{\text{select}}\ \ldots\ \underline{\text{end}})^\circ \equiv \bigcup_{i=1}^{n} (b_i \Rightarrow e_i?\,x_i;\ e_i?\,y_i;\ (T_i')^\circ;\ e_i!\,y_i;(T_i'')^\circ) \cup (\neg b_1 \wedge\ldots\wedge \neg b_n);\ \Delta$$

d. $S^\circ \equiv (T_1^\circ \parallel \ldots \parallel T_m^\circ)\backslash\{e_1,\ldots,e_s\}$

where $e_1,\ldots,e_s$ are all names of entries appearing in the tasks $T_1,\ldots,T_m$.

The reader will be able to convince himself that, indeed, the translation results in elements of L_2. Since L_2 obtained a denotational semantics in section 5, we have now established a denotational semantics - situated in the process framework - for the ADA fragment as well. What remains to be done is to develop a *fair* semantics, and this we shall present in the next section.

Remark (due to I. Mearns). We observe that the above translation assumes the ADA revision stating that an accept statement for an entry cannot appear within another accept statement for the same entry.

7. A FAIR SEMANTICS FOR THE ADA RENDEZ-VOUS

This section brings the final result of the paper: a fair semantics for the ADA rendez-vous concept. Since the ADA reference manual does not mention the word fair, let us explain why we are interested in such a semantics. We distinguish two aspects concerning the proper execution of a number of ADA tasks. Firstly, following the argument from PNUELI & DE ROEVER [20], such execution should be what they call *just*, i.e., it should satisfy the requirement that every task which is continuously enabled from a certain point in the computation should *move* infinitely often in that computation. (For the notions "enabled" and "move" cf. our notions of "enabled" and "occur" described in section 3; refinements for the present context follow soon.) It is this justice property which is achieved by the fair merge schedule to be defined below. Basically, it is motivated by the idea that modelling simultaneous execution of a number of parallel processors by an interleaving of their constituent individual actions should imply that each process should contribute eventually each of its enabled moves to this interleaving. Secondly, the manual stipulates a scheduling which honours different calls for the same entry in their order of arrival. Now one of the benefits of our treatment is that this requirement is met automatically. The crucial property here is that interleavings of the elementary actions where the synchronization does not fit - which in an operational approach leads to extension of the queue of calls for the entry concerned - in the denotational approach disappear through the restriction operator; hence, no special measures to impose the right queuing discipline are in order.

We proceed with the definition proper of $T_1 \|_f T_2$ - which is all that remains for the fair semantics of the ADA rendez-vous. Firstly, we have to extend the process domain in a fashion similar to the construction in section 3: we add a suitable $\mathbb{N} \times (\ldots)$ term:

$$P_A = \{p_0\} \cup (\Sigma \to \mathcal{P}_c((\Sigma \times P_A) \cup (\Gamma \times V \times \Sigma \times P_A) \cup (\Gamma \times (V \to \Sigma \times P_A)) \\ \cup\ \mathbb{N} \times ((\Sigma \times P_A) \cup (\Gamma \times V \times \Sigma \times P_A) \cup (\Gamma \times (V \to \Sigma \times P_A)))))$$

Next, we give the definition of $p \|_f q$ for $p,q \in P_A$.

<u>DEFINITION 7.1</u>. As before, we define $p \|_\beta q$, for β as encountered below, and we omit treatment of the nil and infinite cases.

a. $p \|_f q = (p \|_L q) \cup (p \|_R q)$, $p \|_L q = \lambda\sigma.((p(\sigma) \|_L q) \cup (p(\sigma) \|_f q(\sigma)))$
$\quad p \|_{L,n} q = \lambda\sigma.((p(\sigma) \|_{L,n} q) \cup (p(\sigma) \|_f q(\sigma)))$

b. $X \|_L q = \{\langle n, x \|_{L,n} q\rangle \mid x \in X, n \in \mathbb{N}\}$, $X \|_{L,n} q = \{x \|_{L,n} q \mid x \in X\}$

c. $\langle\sigma,p\rangle \|_{L,n+1} q = \langle\sigma, p \|_{L,n} q\rangle$, $\langle\sigma,p\rangle \|_{L,\underline{0}} q = \langle\sigma, p \|_R q\rangle$
$\quad \langle\bar{\gamma},\alpha,\sigma,p\rangle \|_{L,n+1} q = \langle\bar{\gamma},\alpha,\sigma,p \|_{L,n} q\rangle$, $\langle\bar{\gamma},\alpha,\sigma,p\rangle_{L,0} q = \langle\bar{\gamma},\alpha,\sigma,p \|_R q\rangle$

d. $\langle\gamma,\pi\rangle \|_{L,n} q = \langle\gamma, \pi \|_{L,n} q\rangle$, $\langle m,x\rangle \|_{L,n} q = \langle m, x \|_{L,n} q\rangle$
$\quad \pi \|_{L,n} q = \lambda\alpha.(\pi(\alpha) \|_{L,n} q)$

e. $X \|_f Y = \{\pi(\alpha) \|_f q \mid \langle\gamma,\pi\rangle \in X, \langle\bar{\gamma},\alpha,\sigma,q\rangle \in Y\} \cup$
$\qquad \{q \|_f \pi(\alpha) \mid \langle\bar{\gamma},\alpha,\sigma,q\rangle \in X, \langle\gamma,\pi\rangle \in Y\}$
$\quad \langle\sigma,p\rangle \|_f q = \langle\sigma, p \|_f q\rangle$

(We omit symmetric clauses for $\|_R$ and $\|_{R,n}$.)

We see that the definition is based on the same L/R alternation of random choices, but now embedded in a more complex setting due to the increased complexity of P_A.

Next, we make some remarks on the question - again generalizing section 3 - as to whether fair merge preserves fair processes. The following definitions and properties seem plausible here:

1. Let $\sigma,\sigma' \in \Sigma$, $p,p' \in P_A$. We say that the relationship $\langle\sigma,p\rangle \to \langle\sigma',p'\rangle$ holds whenever one of the following four cases applies:
   (i) $\langle\sigma',p'\rangle \in p(\sigma)$
   (ii) $\langle\bar{\gamma},\alpha,\sigma',p'\rangle \in p(\sigma)$, for some $\bar{\gamma},\alpha$
   (iii) $\langle\gamma,\pi\rangle \in p(\sigma)$, and $\langle\sigma',p'\rangle \in \pi(\alpha)$, for some γ,π,α
   (iv) $\langle n,x\rangle \in p(\sigma)$ for some n, and $\langle\sigma',p'\rangle$ can be derived from x according to (i) to (iii) above.

   Note how clause (ii) is only meaningful due to the presence of σ' in the fourtuple on the left-hand side.
2. Let $\sigma \in \Sigma, p \in P_A$. A *path* for p and σ is a (finite or infinite) sequence
   (*) $\langle\sigma_1,p_1\rangle,\langle\sigma_2,p_2\rangle,\ldots$, such that $\langle\sigma_1,p_1\rangle = \langle\sigma,p\rangle$, and $\langle\sigma_i,p_i\rangle \to \langle\sigma_{i+1},p_{i+1}\rangle$, $i = 1,2,\ldots$
3. Let $\phi \in \Sigma \to \Sigma$. We say that ϕ is *enabled* in (*) whenever there exist i,σ and p such that $\langle\sigma_i,p_i\rangle \to \langle\sigma,p\rangle$, and $\sigma = \phi(\sigma_i)$.
4. We call a path (*) *fair* with respect to ϕ whenever, if ϕ is infinitely often enabled in (*), it infinitely often occurs in (*). We say that p is fair with respect to a collection Φ of functions ϕ whenever, for all σ and $\phi \in \Phi$, all paths for σ and p are fair with respect to ϕ.

Now we conjecture that

5. If p,q are fair with respect to Φ then so is $p \|_f q$.
6. (The meaning of) each program S of the ADA fragment (with syntax as in definition 6.1) is fair with respect to the collection of functions Φ defined as follows: (i) Φ contains the identity function $\lambda\sigma.\sigma$ and the error function $\lambda\sigma.\delta$. (ii) For $x := s$ occurring in S, Φ contains the function $\lambda\sigma.\sigma\{V(s)(\sigma)/x\}$. (iii) For each (syntactically matching) pair e?y, e!t occurring in S, Φ contains the function $\lambda\sigma.\sigma\{V(t)(\sigma)/y\}$.

By way of final remark let us add that the fairness notion appearing in ADA is only one out of a large number of variations on the theme of fairness. We have some ideas on how to apply techniques resembling those of sections 3 and 7 to, e.g., fair iteration in a framework of guarded commands ([2]) or fair communication as discussed in KUIPER & DE ROEVER ([11]). We hope to describe these techniques in a future publication.

REFERENCES

[1] ADA, *The Programming Language* ADA, Reference Manual, LNCS 106, Springer, 1981.
[2] APT, R.R. & E.R. OLDEROG, *Proof rules dealing with fairness*, Proc. Logic of Programs 1981 (D. Kozen, ed.), 1-9, LNCS 131, Springer, 1982.
[3] DE BAKKER, J.W. & J.I. ZUCKER, *Denotational semantics of concurrency*, Proc 14th ACM Symp. on Theory of Computing, pp. 153-158, 1982.
[4] DE BAKKER, J.W. & J.I. ZUCKER, *Processes and the denotational semantics of concurrency*, Report IW 209/82, Mathematisch Centrum, 1982, to appear in Information & Control.
[5] BERGSTRA, J.A. & J.W. KLOP, *Fixed point semantics in process algebras*, Report IW 206/82, Mathematisch Centrum, 1982.
[6] BRINCH HANSEN, P., *Distributed processes: a concurrent programming concept*, C. ACM 21 (1978), 934-941.
[7] DUGUNDJI, J., *Topology*, Allen & Bacon, 1966.
[8] GERTH, R., *A sound and complete Hoare-like axiomatization of the* ADA *rendez-vous*, Proc. 9th ICALP (M. Nielsen & E.M. Schmidt, eds), 252-264, LNCS 140, Springer, 1982.
[9] HENNESSY, M. & W. LI, *Translating a subset of Ada into* CCS, Proc. IFIP Working Conference on Formal Description of Programming Concepts II (D. Bjørner, ed.), North-Holland, to appear.
[10] HOARE, C.A.R., *Communicating sequential processes*, C. ACM 21 (1978), 666-677.
[11] KUIPER, R. & W.P. DE ROEVER, *Fairness assumptions for* CSP *in a temporal logic framework*, Proc. IFIP Working Conference on Formal Description Programming Concepts, II (D. Bjørner, ed.), North-Holland, to appear.
[12] LEHMANN, D.A. PNUELI & J. STAVI, *Impartiality, justice and fairness: the ethics of concurrent computation*, Proc. 8th ICALP (S. Even & O. Kariv, eds.), 264-277, LNCS 115, Springer, 1981.
[13] LI, W., *An operational semantics of tasking and exception handling in* ADA, proc. ACM ADA Tec and Tutorial Conference, to appear.
[14] MILNE, G. & R. MILNER, *Concurrent processes and their syntax*, J. ACM 26 (1979), 302-321.
[15] MILNER, R., *A Calculus for Communicating Systems*, LNCS 92, Springer, 1980.
[16] NIVAT, M., *Infinite words, infinite trees, infinite computations*, Foundations of Computer Science III.2 (J.W. de Bakker & J. van Leeuwen, eds.) 3-52, Mathematical Centre Tracts 109, 1979.
[17] PARK, D., *On the semantics of fair parallelism*, in Abstract Software Specifications (D. Bjørner, ed.) pp. 504-526, LNCS 86, Springer, 1980.
[18] PLOTKIN, G.D., *A power domain construction*, SIAM J. on Comp. 5 (1976), 452-487.
[19] PLOTKIN, G.D., *A power domain for countable nondeterminism*, Proc. 9th ICALP (M. Nielsen & E.M. Schmidt, eds.), 418-428, LNCS 140, Springer, 1982.
[20] PNUELI, A. & W.P. DE ROEVER, *Rendez-vous with* ADA, *a proof theoretical view*, Proc. ACM ADA Tec and Tutorial Conference, to appear.
[21] SCOTT, D.S., *Data types as lattices*, SIAM J. on Comp., 5 (1976), 522-587.
[22] SCOTT, D.S., *Domains for denotational semantics*, Proc. 9th ICALP (M. Nielsen & E.M. Schmidt, eds.), 577-613, LNCS 140, Springer, 1982.

CONDITIONAL DEPENDENCIES FOR HORIZONTAL DECOMPOSITIONS

P. De Bra* – J. Paredaens
Department of Mathematics
University of Antwerp, U.I.A.
Universiteitsplein 1
B-2610 Antwerp, Belgium

*This author is supported by the IWONL.

ABSTRACT

A new decomposition theory for functional dependencies in the Relational Database Model is given. It uses a method to break up a relation into two subrelations whose union is the given relation. This horizontal decomposition is based on a new constraint: the ***conditional-functional dependency***. It indicates how to decompose a relation into two restrictions of this relation. The only difference between the two subrelations is a functional dependency that holds in one subrelation but not in the other. Functional dependencies can be expressed as special conditional-functional dependencies.

The membership problem is solved for this new constraint, and also for another constraint, induced by the horizontal decomposition: the ***afunctional dependency***.

An algorithm is described that performs the decomposition. It uses a new normal form: the ***Conditional Normal Form***. The link between the horizontal- and the traditional vertical decomposition is explained.

1. INTRODUCTION

The vertical decomposition of relations into projections of these relation was introduced by Codd [Co], together with the Relational Database Model. The horizontal decomposition of relations into restrictions of these relations, using the union as composition operator, was suggested later on in [Sm]. In [De1,De2,Pa] the horizontal decomposition has been formalized and used to treat "exceptions" to functional dependencies (fd's).

In this paper we introduce a new constraint, the ***conditional-functional dependency*** (cfd) which induces the same horizontal decomposition as that of [De1,De2,Pa]. The conditional-functional dependencies contain the (ordinary) functional dependencies as a subclass. Also the concept of "goals", used in [De1,De2,Pa] to formalize "fd's with exceptions", can be expressed by means of cfd's. The horizontal decomposition, based on cfd's, induces a new constraint: the ***afunctional dependency*** (ad), which also occurs in the decompositions of [De1,De2,Pa]. We suppose the reader is aware of the basic definitions of the Relational

Database Model [Ul].

In Section 2 we define the horizontal decomposition, based on cfd's. We also propose two theoretical tools: the ***Armstrong relation*** and the ***conflict concept***. In Section 3 the membership problem is solved, for mixed cfd's and ad's. In Section 4 the inheritance of dependencies is described. In Section 5 finally, a new normal form for horizontal decompositions is proposed: the ***Conditional Normal Form***, and a decomposition algorithm is described informally. This algorithm can be used as a preprocessor for any decomposition algorithm for the traditional vertical decomposition.

2. HORIZONTAL DECOMPOSITIONS

The success of the traditional vertical decomposition, based on functional dependencies (fd's), is due to the presence of fd's in the real world. Fd's are rather strong constraints. In many "real world" situations there exist "almost functional dependencies", or "functional depedencies with exceptions". In [De1,De2,Pa] it is shown how to treat such situations by means of horizontal decompositions. The exceptions are put in a separate subrelation, inducing the fd in the remaining (and main) part of the relation. Because the fd holds in this main part, it can be used to decompose this subrelation vertically.

When decomposing a relation horizontally, it may become obvious that some additional constraints must hold in one of the subrelations. For instance, if (in a company) employees can hire parking boxes for their car(s), it is obvious that employees who have only one car will not hire more than one parking box. We now show how to express this constraint formally, and we then treat the parking-example in detail.

Definition 2.1.

Let X be a set of attributes. A set of tuples S in an instance is called ***X-complete*** iff the tuples not belonging to S all have other X-projections than those belonging to S. Formally, for all $t_1 \in S, t_2 \notin S$ holds $t_1[X] \neq t_2[X]$. ∎

In particular, the empty set of tuples is X-complete for every set X of attributes.

Definition 2.2.

The ***conditional-functional dependency*** (cfd) $X \rightarrow Y \supset\!\!- X \rightarrow Z$ means that in every X-complete set of tuples (in every instance) in which the fd $X \rightarrow Y$ holds, the fd $X \rightarrow Z$ must hold too. ∎

The constraint of the parking-example is the cfd

$$employee \rightarrow car \supset\!\!- employee \rightarrow parking\ box.$$

It means that the employees who have only one car also hire only one parking box.

The cfd's contain the fd's as a subclass. Indeed a cfd $X \rightarrow Y \supset\!\!- X \rightarrow Z$ is equivalent to the fd $X \rightarrow Z$ iff $Y \subseteq X$. In the sequel we shall usually denote fd's as fd's and not as these special cfd's.

The horizontal decomposition separates the employees having only one car from the others. Assuming that most employees have only one car, the part of the relation, that contains these employees, is almost the entire relation. Hence not much efficiency is lost by allowing some employees to have more than one car, since the fd's ***employee→car*** and ***employee→parking box*** still hold in the main part of the relation.

When separating the exceptions to an fd $X \rightarrow Y$ from the main part of the relation (instance) the X-complete sets must not be split. This "separation" is formalized by defining a new restriction operator:

Definition 2.3.

Let $\mathcal{R}(C)$ be a (relation) scheme with a set C of cfd's. Let X,Y be sets of attributes.

For every instance R of $\mathcal{R}$, the *restriction for $X \rightarrow Y$ of R, $\sigma_{X \rightarrow Y}(R)$*, is the largest X-complete subset (of tuples) of R in which $X \rightarrow Y$ holds.

The *restriction for $X \rightarrow Y$ of $\mathcal{R}$, $\sigma_{X \rightarrow Y}(\mathcal{R})$*, is a scheme $\mathcal{R}_1$, (with the same attributes as $\mathcal{R}$,) of which the instances are exactly the restrictions for $X \rightarrow Y$ of the instances of $\mathcal{R}$. ∎

Definition 2.4.

The *horizontal decomposition of a scheme $\mathcal{R}$, according to the cfd $X \rightarrow Y \supset\!\!- X \rightarrow Z$*, is the pair $\{\mathcal{R}_1, \mathcal{R}_2\}$, where $\mathcal{R}_1 = \sigma_{X \rightarrow Y}(\mathcal{R})$ and $\mathcal{R}_2 = \mathcal{R} - \mathcal{R}_1$.

In general, we say that $\{\mathcal{R}_1, \ldots, \mathcal{R}_n\}$ is a horizontal decomposition of $\mathcal{R}$ iff $\mathcal{R}_1 \ldots \mathcal{R}_n$ are subschemes of $\mathcal{R}$, and $\mathcal{R} = \mathcal{R}_1 \cup \ldots \cup \mathcal{R}_n$. ∎

Note that the horizontal decomposition of a scheme, according to $X \rightarrow Y \supset\!\!- X \rightarrow Z$ does not depend on the set Z.

We shall give an example of the new restriction operator, and of the horizontal decomposition according to a cfd, after we have examined the structure of the subscheme $\mathcal{R}_2 = \mathcal{R} - \sigma_{X \rightarrow Y}(\mathcal{R})$. In $\mathcal{R}_2$, which contains the "exceptions", the fd $X \rightarrow Y$ is violated for every X-value. This is formalized by means of a new constraint: the ***afunctional dependency***.

Definition 2.5.

The ***afunctional dependency*** (ad) $X \not\rightarrow Y$ means that in every nonempty X-complete set of tuples, in every instance, the functional dependency $X \rightarrow Y$ does not hold. [De1,De2,Pa] ∎

From now on we let a relation scheme $\mathcal{R}$ have a set $\mathcal{A}$ of ad's (that hold in $\mathcal{R}$) as well as a set C of cfd's. For the sake of completeness we define:

Definition 2.6.

Let $\mathcal{R}(C, \mathcal{A})$ be a relation scheme.

For every instance R of $\mathcal{R}$ the ***restriction for $X \not\rightarrow Y$ of R***, $\sigma_{X \not\rightarrow Y}(R)$, is $R - \sigma_{X \rightarrow Y}(R)$. Note that this also is the largest X-complete set of tuples of R in which $X \not\rightarrow Y$ holds.

The ***restriction for $X \not\rightarrow Y$ of $\mathcal{R}$***, $\sigma_{X \not\rightarrow Y}(\mathcal{R})$, is $\mathcal{R} - \sigma_{X \rightarrow Y}(\mathcal{R})$. ∎

Remark 2.7.

In $\sigma_{X \not\to Y}(\mathcal{R})$ $X \not\to Y$ holds, $\mathcal{R} = \sigma_{X \to Y}(\mathcal{R}) \cup \sigma_{X \not\to Y}(\mathcal{R})$, hence the horizontal decomposition of $\mathcal{R}$, according to the cfd $X \to Y \supset\!\!- X \to Z$ (for any Z), is the pair of schemes $\{\sigma_{X \to Y}(\mathcal{R}), \sigma_{X \not\to Y}(\mathcal{R})\}$. ∎

The calculation of the constraints that hold in the restrictions of $\mathcal{R}$ is described in section 4. The main problem with this calculation is that cfd's and ad's (which hold in $\mathcal{R}$) may not hold in some restrictions of $\mathcal{R}$.

To illustrate the new restriction operators, and the horizontal decomposition, based on cfd's, consider the following example:

Example 2.8.

Let *PARKING* be a relation scheme, with attributes E, PB and C, representing *E*mployees hiring *P*arking *B*oxes for their *C*ar(s). Most (but not all) employees have only one car and hire only one parking box. We assume that an employee who has only one car must not hire more than one parking box. This is the cfd $E \to C \supset\!\!- E \to PB$.

Hence the scheme $PARKING(\{E \to C \supset\!\!- E \to PB\}, \emptyset)$ is decomposed in $\sigma_{E \to C}(PARKING) = PARKING_1(\{E \to C\ PB\}, \emptyset)$ and $\sigma_{E \not\to C}(PARKING) = PARKING_2(\emptyset, \{E \not\to C\})$.

In $PARKING_2$ the number of parking boxes, hired by these employees is completely unknown. However, most employees will probably hire only one parking box, even if they have two or more cars. The fd $E \to PB$ does not necessarily hold in $PARKING_2$, but the number of "violations" of this fd is likely to be very small. Therefore let us add the trivial cfd $E \to PB \supset\!\!- E \to PB$ to the set C of cfd's that hold in *PARKING*. $PARKING_1$ cannot be decomposed by $E \to PB \supset\!\!- E \to PB$ since $E \to PB$ holds in $PARKING_1$. However $PARKING_2$ can be decomposed by $E \to PB \supset\!\!- E \to PB$. The subschemes, resulting from the decomposition of $PARKING_2$ are:

$\sigma_{E \to PB}(PARKING_2) = PARKING_{21}(\{E \to PB, E \to PB \supset\!\!- E \to PB\}, \{E \not\to C\})$ and
$\sigma_{E \not\to PB}(PARKING_2) = PARKING_{22}(E \to PB \supset\!\!- E \to PB, \{E \not\to PB, E \not\to C\})$.

By decomposing a scheme according to a trivial cfd (to handle exceptions to a functional dependency) one can simulate the decomposition theory of [De1,De2,Pa], which represents the fd's with exceptions as so called "goals".

Note that the two fd's $E \to C$ and $E \to PB$ are equivalent to the fd $E \to C\ PB$, but that the ad's $E \not\to C$ and $E \not\to PB$ must not be replaced by the ad $E \not\to C\ PB$, since this ad is weaker than the two given ad's.

Consider the following instance of *PARKING* :
$PARKING(\{E \to C \supset\!\!- E \to PB, E \to PB \supset\!\!- E \to PB\}, \emptyset) =$

E	PB	C
Jones	1	FIAT 500
Smith	2	RABBIT
Harvey	3	ESCORT
Harvey	3	GRANADA
Johnson	4	SILVERGHOST
Johnson	5	MERCEDES 600

After the decomposition we have the instances :

$PARKING_1(\{E \rightarrow CPB, E \rightarrow PB \supset\!\!- E \rightarrow PB\}, \emptyset) = \sigma_{E \rightarrow C}(PARKING) =$

E	PB	C
Jones	1	FIAT 500
Smith	2	RABBIT

$PARKING_{21}(\{E \rightarrow PB, E \rightarrow PB \supset\!\!- E \rightarrow PB\}, \{E \not\twoheadrightarrow C\}) = \sigma_{E \rightarrow PB}(\sigma_{E \not\twoheadrightarrow C}(PARKING)) =$

E	PB	C
Harvey	3	ESCORT
Harvey	3	GRANADA

$PARKING_{22}(\{E \rightarrow PB \supset\!\!- E \rightarrow PB\}, \{E \not\twoheadrightarrow C, E \not\twoheadrightarrow PB\}) = \sigma_{E \not\twoheadrightarrow PB}(\sigma_{E \not\twoheadrightarrow C}(PARKING)) =$

E	PB	C
Johnson	4	SILVERGHOST
Johnson	5	MERCEDES 600

∎

The presence of ad's in a database scheme may cause some problems. Not every combination of cfd's and ad's can hold in a nonempty instance. E.g. an fd $X \rightarrow Y$ (which is a cfd too) and its "corresponding" ad $X \not\twoheadrightarrow Y$ cannot both hold in a nonempty instance. The "bad" combinations of cfd's and ad's, which must be avoided when designing a database, are defined below.

Definition 2.9.

A set $\mathcal{C} \cup \mathcal{A}$ of cfd's ($\mathcal{C}$) and ad's ($\mathcal{A}$) is said to be ***in conflict*** iff the empty set of tuples is the only instance in which all dependencies of $\mathcal{C} \cup \mathcal{A}$ hold. ∎

In section 3 it is shown how the detection of conflict can be reduced to the membership problem for fd's, (which is well known). The following property of ***Armstrong relations for fd's*** (described in [Ar,Fa], and proved in [De1]) is used to prove that reduction, and also some other theorems.

Theorem 2.10.

Let $Arm(\mathcal{F})$ denote the ***Armstrong relation*** for a set $\mathcal{F}$ of fd's. In $Arm(\mathcal{F})$ every fd, that is a consequence of $\mathcal{F}$, holds, and for every other fd $X \rightarrow Y$, the "corresponding" ad $X \not\twoheadrightarrow Y$ holds. ∎

3. THE MEMBERSHIP PROBLEM FOR CFD'S AND AD'S

For fd's, a number of membership algorithms have been developed [Be,Ber]. In the sequel we shall reduce the membership problem for cfd's and ad's to the membership problem for fd's only.

We use the symbol $\models$ to denote the (logical) implication of a dependency by a set of dependencies (cfd's, or cfd's and ad's). The symbol $\vdash$ is used to denote that a cfd can be derived from a set of cfd's, using the following inference rules:

$(C1)$: if $Z \subseteq XY$ or $XY \rightarrow Z$ then $X \rightarrow Y \supset\!\!- X \rightarrow Z$.
$(C2)$: if $X \rightarrow Y \supset\!\!- X \rightarrow Z$ and $X \rightarrow Y \supset\!\!- X \rightarrow T$ then $X \rightarrow Y \supset\!\!- X \rightarrow ZT$.
$(C3)$: if $X \rightarrow Y \supset\!\!- X \rightarrow Z$ and $Z \rightarrow T$ then $X \rightarrow Y \supset\!\!- X \rightarrow T$.
$(C4)$: if $X \rightarrow Y \supset\!\!- X \rightarrow Z$ and $X \rightarrow Z \supset\!\!- X \rightarrow T$ then $X \rightarrow Y \supset\!\!- X \rightarrow T$.
$(C5)$: if $X \rightarrow Y \supset\!\!- X \rightarrow Z$ and $W \rightarrow Y \supset\!\!- W \rightarrow X$ and $X \rightarrow W$ then $W \rightarrow Y \supset\!\!- W \rightarrow Z$.

∎

As fd's are special cfd's the use of fd's in these rules is allowed. The reader is invited to deduce the "classical" inference rules for fd's, (i.e. reflexivity, augmentation and transitivity [Ul]) from $C1 \ldots C5$.

Theorem 3.1.
The rules $C1 \ldots C5$ are sound.

Proof
For $C1 \ldots C4$ this is very easy, and left to the reader. We only prove $C5$:
Let S be an arbitrary W-complete set of tuples. Since $X \rightarrow W$ holds, S is also X-complete [Del]. If $W \rightarrow Y$ holds in S then so does $X \rightarrow Y$ by transitivity on $X \rightarrow W$ and $W \rightarrow Y$. $X \rightarrow Y$ in S induces $X \rightarrow Z$ in S and $W \rightarrow Y$ in S induces $W \rightarrow X$ in S. By transitivity on $W \rightarrow X$ and $X \rightarrow Z$, $W \rightarrow Z$ holds in S.

∎

In the sequel we prove that $C1 \ldots C5$ are complete for cfd's, i.e. $C1 \ldots C5$ generate all the consequences of a given set C of cfd's. This however does not provide an efficient way to verify whether some cfd is a consequence of C.

The link between the inference (or "generation") problem and the membership problem is indicated by the following definition.

Definition 3.2.
$FSAT_C(X,Y)$ is the smallest possible set of fd's, such that:
1) $X \rightarrow Y \in FSAT_C(X,Y)$.
2) If $T \rightarrow U \in FSAT_C(X,Y)$ and $T \rightarrow U \supset\!\!- T \rightarrow V \in C$ then $T \rightarrow V \in FSAT_C(X,Y)$.
3) If $FSAT_C(X,Y) \models T \rightarrow V$ then $T \rightarrow V \in FSAT_C(X,Y)$.

∎

$FSAT_C(X,Y)$ can be constructed starting from $\{X \rightarrow Y\}$ by repeatedly trying to satisfy 2) and 3) of the definition. Hence it is obvious that $FSAT_C(X,Y)$ contains fd's that are a consequence of $C \cup \{X \rightarrow Y\}$ only.

Furthermore one can easily see that in $Arm(FSAT_C(X,Y))$ $C \cup \{X \rightarrow Y\}$ holds, hence (by theorem 2.10) this set is precisely the set of all fd's that are consequences of $C \cup \{X \rightarrow Y\}$.

Note that for all X, Y the sets $FSAT_C(X,Y)$ and $FSAT_{C \cup \{X \rightarrow Y\}}(\emptyset,\emptyset)$ are equal. If $Y \subseteq X$ then $FSAT_C(X,Y)$ is the set of all fd's that are consequences of C. We usually denote this set by $FSAT_C(\emptyset,\emptyset)$.

Lemma 3.3.
If $T \rightarrow V \in FSAT_C(X,Y)$ then $C \vdash T \rightarrow V$ or $C \vdash T \rightarrow X$.

Proof
For $T \rightarrow V = X \rightarrow Y$ this property is trivial. We prove that the property remains valid during the construction of $FSAT_C(X,Y)$ by repeatedly trying to satisfy 2) and 3) of definition 3.2.

Let $C = \{X_i \rightarrow Y_i \supset\!\!- X_i \rightarrow Z_i : i = 1 \dots n\}$.

Let step 2) be the reason that $T \rightarrow V \in FSAT_C(X,Y)$. Then for some i $T = X_i$ and $V = Z_i$ and by induction $C \vdash X_i \rightarrow Y_i$ or $C \vdash X_i \rightarrow X$. If $C \vdash X_i \rightarrow Y_i$ (the other case being trivial) we have $C \vdash X_i \rightarrow X_i \supset\!\!- X_i \rightarrow Y_i$ (equivalent to $C \vdash X_i \rightarrow Y_i$), $C \vdash X_i \rightarrow Y_i \supset\!\!- X_i \rightarrow Z_i$ (since $X_i \rightarrow Y_i \supset\!\!- X_i \rightarrow Z_i \in C$) and hence by $C4$ $C \vdash X_i \rightarrow X_i \supset\!\!- X_i \rightarrow Z_i$, i.e. $C \vdash X_i \rightarrow Z_i$.

Let step 3) be the reason that $T \rightarrow V \in FSAT_C(X,Y)$. Then there are three possibilities:

a. If $V \subseteq T$, then, by $C1$ $C \vdash T \rightarrow T \supset\!\!- T \rightarrow V$, i.e. $C \vdash T \rightarrow V$.

b. If $T = T_1 T_2$ and $V = V_1 V_2$ with $T_1 \rightarrow V_1 \in FSAT_C(X,Y)$ and $V_2 \subseteq T_2$ we have that $C \vdash T_1 \rightarrow V_1$ or $C \vdash T_1 \rightarrow X$.
   If $C \vdash T_1 \rightarrow V_1$ then $C \vdash T \rightarrow V$ by augmentation. (This can be demonstrated explicitly, using $C1 \dots C5$.
   If $C \vdash T_1 \rightarrow X$ then $C \vdash T \rightarrow X$, also by augmentation.

c. If $T \rightarrow U$ and $U \rightarrow V \in FSAT_C(X,Y)$ we have ($C \vdash T \rightarrow U$ or $C \vdash T \rightarrow X$) and ($C \vdash U \rightarrow V$ or $C \vdash U \rightarrow X$).
   Using the transitivity rule for fd's (that is expressed by $C4$ for cfd's) we obtain $C \vdash T \rightarrow V$ or $C \vdash T \rightarrow X$.

The proof is completed by remarking that reflexivity, augmentation and transitivity are complete for fd's [Ul]. ∎

Lemma 3.4.
If $T \rightarrow V \in FSAT_C(X,Y)$ then $C \cup \{X \rightarrow Y \supset\!\!- X \rightarrow T\} \vdash X \rightarrow Y \supset\!\!- X \rightarrow V$.

Proof
For $T \rightarrow V = X \rightarrow Y$ this property is trivial (by $C1$). As in lemma 3.3 we prove that the property remains valid during the construction of $FSAT_C(X,Y)$ by repeatedly trying to satisfy 2) and 3) of definition 3.2.

Let $C = \{X_i \rightarrow Y_i \supset\!\!- X_i \rightarrow Z_i : i = 1 \dots n\}$.

Let step 2) be the reason that $T \rightarrow V \in FSAT_C(X,Y)$. Then for some i $T = X_i$ and $V = Y_i$ and by induction $C \cup \{X \rightarrow Y \supset\!\!- X \rightarrow X_i\} \vdash X \rightarrow Y \supset\!\!- X \rightarrow Y_i$.

By lemma 3.3 we have that $C \vdash X_i \rightarrow Z_i$ or $C \vdash X_i \rightarrow X$.

If $C \vdash X_i \to Z_i$ then $X \to Y \supset\!\!-X \to X_i$ and $X_i \to Z_i$ induce $X \to Y \supset\!\!-X \to Z_i$ by $C3$.
If $C \vdash X_i \to X$ then we have:
$X \to Y \supset\!\!-X \to Y$ holds by $C1$, $X \to Y \supset\!\!-X \to X_i$ induces $X \to Y \supset\!\!-X \to Y_i$ by induction, and hence $X \to Y \supset\!\!-X \to YY_i$ holds by $C2$.

$X \to YY_i \supset\!\!-X \to Y$ (holding by $C1$) and $X \to Y \supset\!\!-X \to X_i$ induce $X \to YY_i \supset\!\!-X \to X_i$ by $C4$, and $X_i \to YY_i \supset\!\!-X_i \to Y_i$ (holding by $C1$) and $X_i \to Y_i \supset\!\!-X_i \to Z_i$ induce $X_i \to YY_i \supset\!\!-X_i \to Z_i$ by $C4$.

$X_i \to YY_i \supset\!\!-X_i \to Z_i$ and $X \to YY_i \supset\!\!-X \to X_i$ and $X_i \to X$ induce $X \to YY_i \supset\!\!-X \to Z_i$ by $C5$, and finally $X \to Y \supset\!\!-X \to YY_i$ and $X \to YY_i \supset\!\!-X \to Z_i$ induce $X \to Y \supset\!\!-X \to Z_i$ by $C4$.

Let step 3) be the reason that $T \to V \in FSAT_C(X,Y)$. Then there are three possibilities:
a. If $V \subseteq T$, then $X \to Y \supset\!\!-X \to T$ and $T \to V$ (reflexivity) induce $X \to Y \supset\!\!-X \to V$ by $C3$.
b. Suppose $T = T_1 T_2$ and $V = V_1 V_2$ with $T_1 \to V_1 \in FSAT_C(X,Y)$ and $V_2 \subseteq T_2$.
$X \to Y \supset\!\!-X \to T$ and $T \to T_1$ (reflexivity) induce $X \to Y \supset\!\!-X \to T_1$ by $C3$,
and $C \cup \{X \to Y \supset\!\!-X \to T_1\} \vdash X \to Y \supset\!\!-X \to V_1$ by induction.

$X \to Y \supset\!\!-X \to T$ and $T \to T_2$ (reflexivity) induce $X \to Y \supset\!\!-X \to T_2$ by $C3$,
and $X \to Y \supset\!\!-X \to T_2$ and $T_2 \to V_2$ (reflexivity) induce $X \to Y \supset\!\!-X \to V_2$ by $C3$.

Finally $X \to Y \supset\!\!-X \to V_1$ and $X \to Y \supset\!\!-X \to V_2$ induce $X \to Y \supset\!\!-X \to V$ by $C2$.
c. If $T \to U$ and $U \to V \in FSAT_C(X,Y)$ we have that
$C \cup \{X \to Y \supset\!\!-X \to T\} \vdash X \to Y \supset\!\!-X \to U$
and $C \cup \{X \to Y \supset\!\!-X \to U\} \vdash X \to Y \supset\!\!-X \to V$ by induction,
hence $C \cup \{X \to Y \supset\!\!-X \to T\} \vdash X \to Y \supset\!\!-X \to V$ by concatenating both derivations. ∎

Using these two lemmas the link between the membership problem for cfd's and the set $FSAT_C(X,Y)$ can be easily established:

Theorem 3.5.
$C \models X \to Y \supset\!\!-X \to Z$ iff $X \to Z \in FSAT_C(X,Y)$.

Proof
Let $C = \{X_i \to Y_i \supset\!\!-X_i \to Z_i : i = 1\ldots n\}$.

If $X \to Z \in FSAT_C(X,Y)$ then $C \vdash X \to Y \supset\!\!-X \to Z$ by lemma 3.4 (since $X \to Y \supset\!\!-X \to X$ is trivial). Hence $C \models X \to Y \supset\!\!-X \to Z$ because $C1 \ldots C5$ are sound.

Conversely, if $X \to Z \notin FSAT_C(X,Y)$ then consider $Arm\bigl(FSAT_C(X,Y)\bigr)$.
In $Arm\bigl(FSAT_C(X,Y)\bigr)$ $X \to Z$ does not hold, $X \to Y$ holds and C holds too because for every i holds that:
- if $X_i \to Y_i \in FSAT_C(X,Y)$ then $X_i \to Z_i \in FSAT_C(X,Y)$, and hence both fd's hold in $Arm\bigl(FSAT_C(X,Y)\bigr)$, and
- if $X_i \to Y_i \notin FSAT_C(X,Y)$ then $X_i \not\to Y_i$ holds, hence $X_i \to Y_i \supset\!\!-X_i \to Z_i$ holds trivially.
Since $X \to Y \supset\!\!-X \to Z$ does not hold in $Arm\bigl(FSAT_C(X,Y)\bigr)$ $C \not\models X \to Y \supset\!\!-X \to Z$. ∎

From the proof of the above theorem immediately follows:

Corollary 3.6.

$C1 \ldots C5$ are complete for cfd's. ∎

Theorem 3.5 shows that the membership problem for cfd's is very closely related to that of fd's. In fact one can imagine a cfd as an ad-hoc implication between two fd's. The construction of $FSAT_C(X,Y)$ indeed consists of generating the "closure" of a set of fd's, using the normal inference rules (in step 3) and some "additional" rules (the cfd's in step 2). It is not obvious that cfd's should behave this way, since the cfd $X \rightarrow Y \supset\!\!- X \rightarrow Z$ is a stronger constraint than the expression that "if the fd $X \rightarrow Y$ holds (in the entire relation) then also $X \rightarrow Z$ holds".

Because of the completeness of rules $C1 \ldots C5$ we shall abandon the symbol $\vdash$ in the sequel, and only use the symbol $\models$.

From theorem 3.5 one can deduce a membership algorithm which simply calculates $FSAT_C(X,Y)$ and verifies whether $X \rightarrow Z$ is an element of this set of fd's. A "clever" implementation of this algorithm need not take more than $O(n^3 r^2)$ time, where n is the number of cfd's of C and r is the number of attributes.

In the sequel we consider the presence of ad's as well as cfd's. First we show how conflict can be detected algoritmically.

Lemma 3.7.

$C \cup \mathcal{A}$ is in conflict iff for some $T \not\twoheadrightarrow U \in \mathcal{A}$ holds $C \models T \rightarrow U$.

Proof

The if-part is trivial.

For the only-if part consider the instance $Arm(FSAT_C(\emptyset,\emptyset))$. In $Arm(FSAT_C(\emptyset,\emptyset))$ C holds, hence if $C \cup \mathcal{A}$ is in conflict, then some ad $T \not\twoheadrightarrow U \in \mathcal{A}$ does not hold in $Arm(FSAT_C(\emptyset,\emptyset))$. By theorem 2.9 this means that $T \rightarrow U$ holds. Hence $T \rightarrow U \in FSAT_C(\emptyset,\emptyset)$. By theorem 3.5 this means that $C \models T \rightarrow U$. ∎

The time-complexity of a conflict detection algorithm, based on lemma 3.7 is m times the time-complexity for the membership problem for cfd's, where m is the number of ad's of $\mathcal{A}$; i.e. $O(n^3 r^2 m)$.

The membership problem for ad's (considering the presence of cfd's) is easy to describe, but its proof is somewhat complicated.

Theorem 3.8.

Let $C \cup \mathcal{A}$ be not in conflict, $X \not\twoheadrightarrow Y$ an ad. Then $C \cup \mathcal{A} \models X \not\twoheadrightarrow Y$ iff $C \cup \mathcal{A} \cup \{X \rightarrow Y\}$ is in conflict.

Proof

The only-if-part is trivial.

For the if-part, suppose that $C \cup \mathcal{A} \cup \{X \rightarrow Y\}$ is in conflict. Then, by lemma 3.7

$C \cup \{X \rightarrow Y\} \models \{T \rightarrow U\}$ for some $T \not\twoheadrightarrow U \in \mathcal{A}$. We prove that $C \cup \{T \not\twoheadrightarrow U\} \models X \not\twoheadrightarrow Y$.

Suppose $C \cup \{X \rightarrow Y\} \models T \rightarrow U$ and $C \cup \{T \not\twoheadrightarrow U\} \not\models X \not\twoheadrightarrow Y$.

Without loss of generality we may assume that C is minimal for the property $C \cup \{X \rightarrow Y\} \models T \rightarrow U$, i.e. all cfd's of C are used during the construction of $FSAT_{C \cup \{X \rightarrow Y\}}(T,T)$. "Being used" means that the cfd $X_i \rightarrow Y_i \supset\!\!- X_i \rightarrow Z_i$ satisfies the condition of step 2) of definition 3.2. Hence both $X_i \rightarrow Y_i$ and $X_i \rightarrow Z_i$ are in $FSAT_{C \cup \{X \rightarrow Y\}}(T,T)$ for all $X_i \rightarrow Y_i \supset\!\!- X_i \rightarrow Z_i \in C$.

After definition 3.2 it is proved that $FSAT_{C \cup \{X \rightarrow Y\}}(T,T) = FSAT_C(X,Y)$. Hence from the argument above and from lemma 3.3 follows that for all $X_i \rightarrow Y_i \supset\!\!- X_i \supset\!\!- Z_i \in C$ holds that $C \models X_i \rightarrow Y_i$ or $C \models X_i \rightarrow X$ and $C \models X_i \rightarrow Z_i$ or $C \models X_i \rightarrow X$.

Since $C \cup \{T \not\twoheadrightarrow U\} \not\models X \not\twoheadrightarrow Y$ there exists an instance R in which $C \cup \{T \not\twoheadrightarrow U\}$ holds, but in which $X \not\twoheadrightarrow Y$ does not hold. Consider $R' = \sigma_{X \rightarrow Y}(R.)$

If for $X_i \rightarrow Y_i \supset\!\!- X_i \rightarrow Z_i \in C$ $X_i \rightarrow Y_i$ (and hence also $X_i \rightarrow Z_i$) holds in R then $X_i \rightarrow Y_i$ and $X_i \rightarrow Z_i$ also hold in R' since fd's cannot be violated by taking a restriction of R.

If for $X_i \rightarrow Y_i \supset\!\!- X_i \rightarrow Z_i \in C$ $X_i \rightarrow Y_i$ does not hold in R then $X_i \rightarrow X$ holds in R. Consider an X_i-complete set S of tuples of R, with only one X_i-value. Such a set is called "X_i-unique" and X_i-complete. By taking $\sigma_{X \rightarrow Y}(R)$, S becomes a part of $\sigma_{X \rightarrow Y}(R)$ or is disjoint with it, because of $X_i \rightarrow X$. Hence $X_i \rightarrow Y_i \supset\!\!- X_i \rightarrow Z_i$ cannot be violated in R' (i.e. in an X_i-complete subset of R') without being violated in R too. (This is shown more clearly by the "inheritance rules" in section 4.) Hence C holds in R'.

Since C and $X \rightarrow Y$ hold in R', $T \rightarrow U$ must hold too because $C \cup \{X \rightarrow Y\} \models T \rightarrow U$. However, since $C \not\models T \rightarrow U$ and $C \cup \{X \rightarrow Y\} \models T \rightarrow U$ we have that $C \models T \rightarrow X$ by lemma 3.3. Hence the above argument for the X_i also holds for T, i.e. R' is a T-complete subset of R. Hence $T \not\twoheadrightarrow U$ does not hold in R if it does not hold in R', a contradiction.

∎

Using lemma 3.7 a membership algorithm for ad's (considering the presence of cfd's) can be easily deduced from theorem 3.8. The time needed to perform a membership test for ad's is the same as for the conflict detection: $O(n^3 r^2 m)$ where $n = \# C$, $m = \# \mathcal{A}$ and $r = \# \Omega$.

The membership problem for cfd's is affected by the presence of ad's.

Theorem 3.9.

Let $C \cup \mathcal{A}$ be not in conflict. Then $C \cup \mathcal{A} \models X \rightarrow Y \supset\!\!- X \rightarrow Z$ iff $C \models X \rightarrow Y \supset\!\!- X \rightarrow Z$ or $C \cup \mathcal{A} \models X \not\twoheadrightarrow Y$.

Proof

The if-part is trivial.

For the only-if-part, assume that $C \not\models X \rightarrow Y \supset\!\!- X \rightarrow Z$ and $C \cup \mathcal{A} \not\models X \not\twoheadrightarrow Y$. By theorem 3.8 $C \cup \mathcal{A} \cup \{X \rightarrow Y\}$ is not in conflict. Consider $Arm(FSAT_C(X,Y))$. In $Arm(FSAT_C(X,Y))$ $C \cup \{X \rightarrow Y\}$ holds by definition (of Armstrong relations and of $FSAT_C(X,Y)$). If some ad $T \not\twoheadrightarrow U$ of $\mathcal{A}$ does not hold then $C \cup \{X \rightarrow Y\} \models T \rightarrow U$, a contradiction with $C \cup \mathcal{A} \cup \{X \rightarrow Y\}$ not being in conflict. In $Arm(FSAT_C(X,Y))$ $X \rightarrow Z$ does not hold by theorem 3.5. Hence

$Arm(FSAT_{\mathcal{C}}(X,Y))$ is an instance in which $\mathcal{C} \cup \mathcal{A}$ holds and in which $X \rightarrow Y \supset\!\!- X \rightarrow Z$ does not hold.

Hence $\mathcal{C} \cup \mathcal{A} \not\models X \rightarrow Y \supset\!\!- X \rightarrow Z$.

∎

Because of this theorem a membership algorithm for cfd's takes as much time as a membership algorithm for ad's: $O(n^3 r^2 m)$ with $n = \# \mathcal{C}$, $m = \# \mathcal{A}$ and $r = \# \Omega$, where Ω is the set of attributes.

4. THE INHERITANCE OF DEPENDENCIES

The membership problem has been studied to decide whether a decomposition according to a cfd is trivial or not (i.e. whether for the cfd $X \rightarrow Y \supset\!\!- X \rightarrow Z$ the fd $X \rightarrow Y$ or the ad $X \not\rightarrow\!\!\!\!\rightarrow Y$ holds). When performing several decomposition steps (i.e. decomposing the subschemes further on) it is necessary to know which dependencies hold in the subschemes that are the result of a decomposition step. This is called the ***inheritance problem***. The inherited dependencies determine whether further decomposition step is necessary.

Notation 4.1.

In the sequel we treat the horizontal decomposition of a scheme $\mathcal{R}$, with cfd's $\mathcal{C}$ and ad's $\mathcal{A}$, according to $X \rightarrow Y \supset\!\!- X \rightarrow Z$, into the schemes $\mathcal{R}_1 = \sigma_{X \rightarrow Y}(\mathcal{R})$, with cfd's $\mathcal{C}_1$ and ad's $\mathcal{A}_1$, and $\mathcal{R}_2 = \sigma_{X \not\rightarrow\!\!\!\!\rightarrow Y}(\mathcal{R})$, with cfd's $\mathcal{C}_2$ and ad's $\mathcal{A}_2$. We assume that $\mathcal{C} \cup \mathcal{A}$ is not in conflict, $\mathcal{C} \cup \mathcal{A} \not\models X \rightarrow Y$ and $\mathcal{C} \cup \mathcal{A} \not\models X \not\rightarrow\!\!\!\!\rightarrow Y$. We do not consider "complete" sets of dependencies. The sets of dependencies, holding in $\mathcal{R}$ or in one of its subschemes are only "generating" for the set of all dependencies, holding in the scheme.

∎

Since fd's cannot be violated by taking a restriction of a relation we have:

Remark 4.2.

All the fd's that hold in $\mathcal{R}$ also hold in both $\mathcal{R}_1$ and $\mathcal{R}_2$.

∎

The fd's of $\mathcal{R}$ are not the only fd's that hold in the subschemes. In $\mathcal{R}_1$ for instance the fd $X \rightarrow YZ$ holds (which does not hold in $\mathcal{R}$ if the decomposition is not trivial, i.e. if $\mathcal{C} \cup \mathcal{A} \not\models X \rightarrow Y$ and $\mathcal{C} \cup \mathcal{A} \not\models X \not\rightarrow\!\!\!\!\rightarrow Y$).

When considering cfd's and ad's there always is the danger of introducing conflict, when modifying the sets of cfd's and ad's. However, the non-trivial horizontal decomposition of a (nonempty) relation cannot generate sets of dependencies that are in conflict, since the subschemes are nonempty too. Indeed, if neither $X \rightarrow Y$ nor $X \not\rightarrow\!\!\!\!\rightarrow Y$ holds in $\mathcal{R}$, then in most instances R of $\mathcal{R}$ the subinstances $\sigma_{X \rightarrow Y}(R)$ an $\sigma_{X \not\rightarrow\!\!\!\!\rightarrow Y}(R)$ will be nonempty. Therefore we do not have to consider the danger of generating conflict by decomposing a scheme in the sequel.

For cfd's ad's the inheritance problem is more complicated than for fd's. We first show some inclusions.

Lemma 4.3.

Using the notations of 4.1 we have:

$\mathcal{C}_1 \subseteq \{T \rightarrow U \supset\!\!- T \rightarrow V : \mathcal{C} \cup \mathcal{A} \cup \{X \rightarrow Y\} \models T \rightarrow U \supset\!\!- T \rightarrow V\}$.

$\mathcal{C}_2 \subseteq \{T \rightarrow U \supset\!\!- T \rightarrow V : \mathcal{C} \cup \mathcal{A} \cup \{X \not\twoheadrightarrow Y\} \models T \rightarrow U \supset\!\!- T \rightarrow V\}$.

$\mathcal{A}_1 \subseteq \{T \not\twoheadrightarrow U : \mathcal{C} \cup \mathcal{A} \cup \{X \rightarrow Y\} \models T \not\twoheadrightarrow U\}$.

$\mathcal{A}_2 \subseteq \{T \not\twoheadrightarrow U : \mathcal{C} \cup \mathcal{A} \cup \{X \not\twoheadrightarrow Y\} \models T \not\twoheadrightarrow U\}$.

Proof

Let $T \rightarrow U \supset\!\!- T \rightarrow V$ be such that $\mathcal{C} \cup \mathcal{A} \cup \{X \rightarrow Y\} \not\models T \rightarrow U \supset\!\!- T \rightarrow V$. We show that $T \rightarrow U \supset\!\!- T \rightarrow V \not\in \mathcal{C}_1$, by constructing an instance R for which $T \rightarrow U \supset\!\!- T \rightarrow V$ does not hold in $R_1 = \sigma_{X \rightarrow Y}(R)$.

$\mathcal{C} \cup \mathcal{A} \cup \{X \rightarrow Y\} \not\models T \not\twoheadrightarrow U$ by theorem 3.9. Hence by theorem3.8 $\mathcal{C} \cup \mathcal{A} \cup \{X \rightarrow Y\} \cup \{T \rightarrow U\}$ is not in conflict and holds in $Arm(FSAT_{\mathcal{C} \cup \{X \rightarrow Y\}}(T, U))$. Since $\mathcal{C} \cup \mathcal{A} \cup \{X \rightarrow Y\} \not\models T \rightarrow U \supset\!\!- T \rightarrow V$, $T \not\twoheadrightarrow V$ holds in $Arm(FSAT_{\mathcal{C} \cup \{X \rightarrow Y\}}(T, U))$.

We also have that in $Arm(FSAT_{\mathcal{C}}(\emptyset, \emptyset))$ $\mathcal{C} \cup \mathcal{A}$ holds.

Suppose (without loss of generality) that the domain(s) of $Arm(FSAT_{\mathcal{C} \cup \{X \rightarrow Y\}}(T, U))$ and $Arm(FSAT_{\mathcal{C}}(\emptyset, \emptyset))$ are disjoint. Then in $R = Arm(FSAT_{\mathcal{C} \cup \{X \rightarrow Y\}}(T, U)) \cup Arm(FSAT_{\mathcal{C}}(\emptyset, \emptyset))$ $\mathcal{C} \cup \mathcal{A}$ holds. When this instance is decomposed according to $X \rightarrow Y \supset\!\!- X \rightarrow Z$ then $R_1 = \sigma_{X \rightarrow Y}(R) = Arm(FSAT_{\mathcal{C} \cup \{X \rightarrow Y\}}(T, U))$, in which $T \rightarrow U \supset\!\!- T \rightarrow V$ does not hold.

The three other inclusions can be proved in a similar way. Their proof is left to the reader.

∎

In the proof of the inheritance of cfd's and ad's a special instance is needed, of which the construction is partially described below.

Lemma 4.4.

Consider a set $\mathcal{C} \cup \mathcal{A}$, not being in conflict. Let S be an instance in which $\mathcal{C} \cup \mathcal{A}$ holds.

If $\mathcal{C} \cup \mathcal{A} \cup \{P \not\twoheadrightarrow Q\}$ is not in conflict, then there is an instance T, containing S as a subset, in which the ad $P \not\twoheadrightarrow Q$ holds (and also every cfd $P \rightarrow Q \supset\!\!- P \rightarrow O$).

Proof

A T-complete set of tuples, all having the same T-projection, in which the ad $T \not\twoheadrightarrow U$ does not hold (hence in which $T \rightarrow U$ holds) is called a ***violation of*** $T \not\twoheadrightarrow U$. A T-complete set of tuples, all having the same T-projection, in which $T \rightarrow U$ and $T \not\twoheadrightarrow V$ hold is called a ***violation of*** $T \rightarrow U \supset\!\!- T \rightarrow V$.

Let $P \not\twoheadrightarrow Q$ not hold in S. Construct $Arm(FSAT_{\mathcal{C}}(\emptyset, \emptyset))$, and suppose that the domains of $Arm(FSAT_{\mathcal{C}}(\emptyset, \emptyset))$ and S are disjoint. Suppose also that in $Arm(FSAT_{\mathcal{C}}(\emptyset, \emptyset))$ the domains of the attributes all are disjoint.

Let $\overline{P} = \{A : \mathcal{C} \models P \rightarrow A\}$. Let t be a tuple in an arbitrary violation of $P \not\twoheadrightarrow Q$ (in S). Let r be an arbitrary tuple of $Arm(FSAT_{\mathcal{C}}(\emptyset, \emptyset))$. The domain of $Arm(FSAT_{\mathcal{C}}(\emptyset, \emptyset))$ is changed such that $r[\overline{P}] := t[\overline{P}]$. Let the adapted Armstrong relation be called S'.

Let $T = S \cup S'$. In T $\mathcal{C}$ holds, since $\mathcal{C}$ holds in S and S', and since if $V \not\subseteq \overline{P}$ then

$V \rightarrow W$, for which $C \models V \rightarrow W$, still holds because no tuple of S' has the same V-projection as any tuple of S, and if $V \subseteq \overline{P}$ then $V \rightarrow W$, for which $C \models V \rightarrow W$, still holds because also $W \subseteq \overline{P}$ and if the V-projection of a tuple of S and of a tuple of S' are equal then this projection is $t[V]$, and hence for the tuple of S and the tuple of S' then W-projection is $t[W]$ by the construction of S'. If for $V \rightarrow W \supset\!\!- V \rightarrow W' \in C$ $V \rightarrow W$ does not hold, then in S' $V \not\rightarrow\!\!\!\!\not\rightarrow W$ holds, hence in T $V \rightarrow W \supset\!\!- V \rightarrow W'$ still holds.

In T $\mathcal{A}$ holds since $\mathcal{A}$ holds in S and S' and since ad's cannot be violated by taking a union.

In S' $P \not\rightarrow\!\!\!\!\not\rightarrow Q \in \mathcal{A}$ holds, hence S' does not contain any violation of $P \not\rightarrow\!\!\!\!\not\rightarrow Q$. In T the violation of $P \not\rightarrow\!\!\!\!\not\rightarrow Q$ (in S) that contains t is no longer a violation of $P \not\rightarrow\!\!\!\!\not\rightarrow Q$. Hence in T the number of violations of $P \not\rightarrow\!\!\!\!\not\rightarrow Q$ is (strictly) less than in S.

By repeating the above construction until there are no violations of $P \not\rightarrow\!\!\!\!\not\rightarrow Q$ anymore (in the final T), one establishes an instance T in which $P \not\rightarrow\!\!\!\!\not\rightarrow Q$ holds, and which still contains S as a subset.

It is obvious that when $P \not\rightarrow\!\!\!\!\not\rightarrow Q$ holds, then also $P \rightarrow Q \supset\!\!- P \rightarrow O$, by the definition of cfd's.

∎

Some dependencies are inherited by both $\mathcal{R}_1$ and $\mathcal{R}_2$. They are described by the following "inheritance rules":

$(H1)$: if $T \not\rightarrow\!\!\!\!\not\rightarrow U$ and $T \rightarrow X$ then $T \not\rightarrow\!\!\!\!\not\rightarrow U$ is inherited by both $\mathcal{R}_1$ and $\mathcal{R}_2$.
$(H2)$: if $T \rightarrow U \supset\!\!- T \rightarrow V$ and $T \rightarrow U$ or $T \rightarrow X$ then $T \rightarrow U \supset\!\!- T \rightarrow V$ is inherited by both $\mathcal{R}_1$ and $\mathcal{R}_2$.

∎

These rules have been used in the proof of theorem 3.8 already. We leave the (formal) proof of their soundness to the reader.

In the sequel we denote the set of the ad's of $\mathcal{A}$, that are inherited by rule $H1$, by $\hat{\mathcal{A}}$. The set of the cfd's of C, that are inherited by rule $H2$ or that are trivial, is denoted by $\hat{C}$. The trivial cfd's are included because they represent the "goals" of [De1,De2,Pa]. They are of no importance for the inheritance problem, and are neglected in the following lemmas and theorem.

Lemma 4.5.

Let $C \cup \mathcal{A}$ be not in conflict. Let S be an instance in which $\hat{C} \cup \hat{\mathcal{A}}$ holds. Then there exists an instance T, containing S as a subset, and in which $C \cup \mathcal{A}$ holds.

Proof

T can be obtained by repeating the construction of the proof of lemma 4.4 for every ad of $\mathcal{A} - \hat{\mathcal{A}}$ and every cfd of $C - \hat{C}$. The final instance T satisfies $C \cup \mathcal{A}$.

∎

Theorem 4.6.

A cfd or ad must hold in $\mathcal{R}_1$ (resp. $\mathcal{R}_2$) iff it is a consequence of $\hat{C} \cup \hat{\mathcal{A}} \cup \{X \rightarrow Y\}$ (resp. $\hat{C} \cup \hat{\mathcal{A}} \cup \{X \not\rightarrow\!\!\!\!\not\rightarrow Y\}$).

Proof

From lemma 4.3, rules $H1$ And $H2$ and the definition of the horizontal decomposition according to $X \to Y \supset\!\!- X \to Z$ it follows that $(\hat{C} \cup \hat{A} \cup \{X \to Y\})^* \subseteq (C_1 \cup A_1)^* \subseteq (C \cup A \cup \{X \to Y\})^*$ and $(\hat{C} \cup \hat{A} \cup \{X \not\to Y\})^* \subseteq (C_2 \cup A_2)^* \subseteq (C \cup A \cup \{X \not\to Y\})^*$, where * means the "closure" operator, i.e. taking all the consequences of a set of dependencies.

Consider an ad $T \not\to U \in (C \cup A \cup \{X \to Y\})^* - (\hat{C} \cup \hat{A} \cup \{X \to Y\})^*$. We prove that $T \not\to U \notin (C_1 \cup A_1)^*$.

Since $T \not\to U \notin (\hat{C} \cup \hat{A} \cup \{X \to Y\})^*$, $\hat{C} \cup \hat{A} \cup \{X \to Y\} \cup \{T \to U\}$ is not in conflict, by theorem 3.8. Hence there exists an instance S in which $\hat{C} \cup \hat{A} \cup \{X \to Y\} \cup \{T \to U\}$ holds. By the construction of lemma 4.5 an instance R can be build which contains S and in which $C \cup A$ holds. In this construction (explained in the proof of lemma 4.4) a number of modified copies of $Arm(FSAT_C(\emptyset, \emptyset))$ are added to S. Since $X \not\to Y$ holds in $Arm(FSAT_C(\emptyset, \emptyset))$, and since $C \not\models T \to X$ (hence certainly $X \not\subset \overline{T}$), $R_1 = \sigma_{X \to Y}(R) = S$. Hence in R_1 $T \not\to U$ does not hold, which means that $T \not\to U \notin (C_1 \cup A_1)^*$.

Consider a cfd $T \to U \supset\!\!- T \to V \in (C \cup A \cup \{X \to Y\})^* - (\hat{C} \cup \hat{A} \cup \{X \to Y\})^*$. We prove that $T \to U \supset\!\!- T \to V \notin (C_1 \cup A_1)^*$.

Since $T \to U \supset\!\!- T \to V \notin (\hat{C} \cup \hat{A} \cup \{X \to Y\})^*$, $\hat{C} \cup \hat{A} \cup \{X \to Y\} \cup \{T \to U\}$ cannot be in conflict. (Otherwise $\hat{C} \cup \hat{A} \cup \{X \to Y\} \models T \not\to U$ which contradicts with $\hat{C} \cup \hat{A} \cup \{X \to Y\} \not\models T \to U \supset\!\!- T \to V$ (by theorem 3.9).) $\hat{C} \cup \hat{A} \cup \{X \to Y\} \cup \{T \to U\} \cup \{T \not\to V\}$ cannot be in conflict either, since $T \to V \notin FSAT_{\hat{C} \cup \{X \to Y\}}(T, U)$, (hence $\hat{C} \cup \hat{A} \cup \{X \to Y\} \cup \{T \to U\} \cup \{T \not\to V\}$ holds in $Arm(FSAT_{\hat{C} \cup \{X \to Y\}}(T, U))$).

There exists a set S of tuples, in which $\hat{C} \cup \hat{A} \cup \{X \to Y\} \cup \{T \to U\} \cup \{T \not\to V\}$ holds. By lemma 4.5 one con construct an instance R, containing S, in which $C \cup A$ holds. $R_1 = \sigma_{X \to Y}(R) = S$, hence $T \to U \supset\!\!- T \to V$ does not hold in R_1. This means that $T \to U \supset\!\!- T \to V \notin (C_1 \cup A_1)^*$.

Consider an ad $T \not\to U \in (C \cup A \cup \{X \not\to Y\})^* - (\hat{C} \cup \hat{A} \cup \{X \not\to Y\})^*$. We prove that $T \not\to U \notin (C_2 \cup A_2)^*$.

Since $T \not\to U \notin (\hat{C} \cup \hat{A} \cup \{X \not\to Y\})^*$, $\hat{C} \cup \hat{A} \cup \{X \not\to Y\} \cup \{T \to U\}$ is not in conflict, by theorem 3.8. Hence there exists an instance S in which $\hat{C} \cup \hat{A} \cup \{X \not\to Y\} \cup \{T \to U\}$ holds. By a construction, very similar to that of lemma 4.5 an instance R can be build which contains S and in which $C \cup A$ is satisfied. To obtain that $\sigma_{X \not\to Y}(R) = S$ one must use modified copies of $Arm(FSAT_{\hat{C}}(X, Y))$ instead of $Arm(FSAT_{\hat{C}}(\emptyset, \emptyset))$. In $R_2 = \sigma_{X \not\to Y}(R)$ $T \to U$ holds, hence $T \not\to U \notin (C_2 \cup A_2)^*$.

The above argument relies on the fact that $T \not\to U$ holds in $Arm(FSAT_{\hat{C}}(X, Y))$, i.e. that $\hat{C} \cup \{X \to Y\} \not\models T \to U$. Suppose $\hat{C} \cup \{X \to Y\} \models T \to U$ (hence $T \to U \in FSAT_{\hat{C}}(X, Y)$). We also have that $C \cup A \cup \{X \not\to Y\} \models T \not\to U$. $T \to U \in FSAT_{\hat{C}}(X, Y)$ means that $\hat{C} \models T \to X$, by lemma 3.3. If $C \cup A \models T \not\to U$ then $T \not\to U$ is inherited by rule $H1$. Since $T \not\to U \notin \hat{A}$, this is not the case, hence $C \cup A \not\models T \not\to U$. By the proof of theorem 3.8 $C \cup A \cup \{X \not\to Y\} \models T \not\to U$ and $C \cup A \not\models T \not\to U$ imply $C \cup \{X \not\to Y\} \models T \not\to U$, and hence also $C \cup \{T \to U\} \models X \to Y$ (by the proof of theorem 3.8 again). To deduce $X \to Y$ from $C \cup \{T \to U\}$, only cfd's $P \to Q \supset\!\!- P \to O \in C$ for which $C \models P \to Q$ or $C \models P \to T$ can be used. Since $\hat{C} \models T \to X$

these cfd's all are in $\hat{\mathcal{C}}$ ($P \to T$ and $T \to X$ induce $P \to X$). Hence $\hat{\mathcal{C}} \cup \{T \to U\} \models X \to Y$, or, by the proof of theorem 3.8, $\hat{\mathcal{C}} \cup \{X \not\twoheadrightarrow Y\} \models T \not\twoheadrightarrow U$, which contradicts with $\hat{\mathcal{C}} \cup \hat{\mathcal{A}} \cup \{X \not\twoheadrightarrow Y\} \not\models T \not\twoheadrightarrow U$.

The proof for $T \to U \supset\!\!- T \to V \in (\mathcal{C} \cup \mathcal{A} \cup \{X \not\twoheadrightarrow Y\})^* - (\hat{\mathcal{C}} \cup \hat{\mathcal{A}} \cup \{X \not\twoheadrightarrow Y\})^*$ is similar, and left to the reader.

∎

Note that $\mathcal{C}_1, \mathcal{C}_2, \mathcal{A}_1$ and $\mathcal{A}_2$ need not contain all cfd's and ad's of $\mathcal{C}$ and $\mathcal{A}$ that are inherited. However, the cfd's and ad's of $\mathcal{C} \cup \mathcal{A}$ that are inherited and not in the $\mathcal{C}_i$ or $\mathcal{A}_i$ are generated by the $\mathcal{C}_i$ and $\mathcal{A}_i$. To illustrate this, consider the following example:

Let $\mathcal{R}$ have a set $\mathcal{C} = \{A \to C, A \to D \supset\!\!- A \to C\}$ of (fd's and) cfd's, and a set $\mathcal{A} = \{A \not\twoheadrightarrow B, C \not\twoheadrightarrow B\}$. When $\mathcal{R}$ is decomposed according to $A \to D \supset\!\!- A \to C$ $\;C \not\twoheadrightarrow B \notin \hat{\mathcal{A}}$, but this ad is inherited anyway, since it is a consequence of $A \to C$ and $A \not\twoheadrightarrow B$; $A \to C \in \mathcal{C}_1$ (and $\mathcal{C}_2$) and $A \not\twoheadrightarrow B \in \mathcal{A}_1$ (and $\mathcal{A}_2$) [De2].

If $n = \#\mathcal{C}$, $m = \#\mathcal{A}$ and $r = \#\Omega$, one can deduce from theorem 4.6 that the time-complexity of an algorithm that performs a horizontal decomposition step is n times the complexity of a cfd-membership test (for calculating $\hat{\mathcal{C}}$) plus m times the complexity of an ad-membership test (for calculating $\hat{\mathcal{A}}$), i.e. $O(n^4 r^2 + n^3 m^2 r^2)$.

5. THE CONDITIONAL NORMAL FORM

When decomposing a relation scheme both horizontally (according to goals) and vertically (according to fd's) one should decide which kind of decomposition is to be performed first. Our approach, to perform the horizontal decomposition steps first, is based on remark 4.2, which states that the horizontal decomposition, according to a goal, preserves fd's.

We first define a normal form for horizontal decompositions.

Definition 5.1.

A scheme $\mathcal{R}$ is said to be in *Conditional Normal Form (CNF)* iff for all cfd's $X \to Y \supset\!\!- X \to Z$ of $\mathcal{C}$ holds $\mathcal{C} \cup \mathcal{A} \models X \to Y$ or $\mathcal{C} \cup \mathcal{A} \models X \not\twoheadrightarrow Y$.

A decomposition $\{\mathcal{R}_1, \ldots, \mathcal{R}_n\}$ is in *CNF* iff all the $\mathcal{R}_i$, $i = 1 \ldots n$, are in CNF.

∎

From this definition one can easily construct a decomposition algorithm, which decomposes a relation scheme according to a cfd, and then decomposes the subschemes further on, until all subschemes are in CNF. In the "final" subschemes, for every cfd $X \to Y \supset\!\!- X \to Z$ either $X \to Y$ (and $X \to Z$) or $X \not\twoheadrightarrow Y$ holds. Hence there are no "real" cfd's anymore in the subschemes. Therefore one can decompose the subschemes vertically (hereby neglecting the ad's), using the fd's that hold in these subschemes.

6. CONCLUSIONS

A new way to decompose a relation in the Relational Database Model has been proposed, formalized and illustrated. This horizontal decomposition is based on a new constraint: the ***conditional-functional dependency***. It is compatible with the traditional vertical decomposition, based on functional dependencies, since it preserves fd's.

The new decomposition theory includes the horizontal decompositions, used for handling exceptions to fd's, described in [De1,De2,Pa].

A normal form for this new horizontal decomposition has been proposed: the ***Conditional Normal Form.*** A nontrivial example has been used to illustrate how to decompose a relation scheme. Such an algorithm can be used as a preprocessor for a decomposition algorithm for the traditional vertical decomposition.

References

[Ar] Armstrong W., Dependency structures of database relationships, *Proc. IFIP 74*, North Holland, pp. 580–583, 1974.

[Be] Beeri C., Bernstein P.A., Computational Problems related to the Design of Normal Form Relation Schemes, *ACM TODS*, vol. **4.1**, pp. 30–59, 1979.

[Ber] Bernstein P.A., Normalization and Functional Dependencies in the Relational Database Model, *CSRG-60*, 1975.

[Co] Codd E., Further normalizations of the database relational model, In *Data Base Systems* (R. Rustin, ed.) Prentice Hall, N.J., pp. 33–64, 1972.

[De1] De Bra P., Paredaens J., The membership and the inheritance of functional and afunctional dependencies, Dept. of Math., Univ. of Antwerp, Belgium, report 81-39, 1981.

[De2] De Bra P., Paredaens J., Horizontal Decompositions for Handling Exceptions to Functional Dependencies, *CERT-82* workshop "Logical Bases for Data Bases", France, 1982.

[Fa] Fagin R., Armstrong Databases, *IBM RJ 3440*, 1982

[Pa] Paredaens J., De Bra P., On Horizontal Decompositions, *XP2-Congress*, State Univ. of Pennsylvania, 1981.

[Sm] Smith J., Smith D., Data base abstractions: Aggregation and generalization, *ACM TODS*, vol. **2.2**, pp. 105–133, 1977.

[Ul] Ullman J., Principles of Database Systems, Pitman, 1980.

ON THE RELATIONSHIP OF CCS AND CSP

Stephen D. Brookes
Department of Computer Science
Carnegie-Mellon University
Pittsburgh
Pennsylvania 15213

Abstract.

This paper compares two models of concurrency, Milner's Calculus of Communicating Systems (CCS) and the *failures* model of Communicating Sequential Processes (CSP) developed by Hoare, Brookes and Roscoe. By adapting Milner's synchronisation trees to serve as notation for both CCS and CSP, we are able to define a representation mapping for CSP processes. We define an equivalence relation on synchronisation trees which corresponds precisely to the notion of *failure equivalence*. Milner's calculus is founded on a different notion, *observation equivalence*. We show how these two equivalences are related. Just as Milner's equivalence can be characterised as the smallest relation satisfying a set of axioms, we find a suitable set of axioms for the failures equivalence relation. This again makes explicit the differences between the two systems, as well as revealing that the semantic models underlying CCS and CSP are comparable.

1.0. Introduction.

This paper considers the similarities and differences between two abstract models of concurrent behaviour, Milner's synchronisation trees for CCS [1], and the failures model of CSP (Hoare, Brookes, Roscoe [2]). We begin by listing the principal characteristics of the two systems. Milner's original formulation of his calculus introduced synchronisation trees, with arcs labelled by action names drawn from an alphabet Σ or by a special symbol τ standing for an invisible action; paths through a tree then correspond to a sequence of visible actions, possibly with some invisible actions on the way. Each node of a tree defines a possible sequence of visible actions up to some moment, and the subtree rooted there represents a possible future behaviour. Milner defines a notion of behaviour for synchronisation trees and constructs an equivalence relation on trees known as *observation equivalence*. Terms in the language CCS can then be taken to denote equivalence classes of trees under observation equivalence.

In the failures model of Hoare, Brookes and Roscoe the behaviour of a process is defined in terms of the sequences of visible actions the process may perform, and the sets of actions the process may (as the result of making a nondeterministic decision) refuse to perform. A failure is simply a pair consisting of a finite sequence of visible actions possible for the process and a set of actions which the process may be able to refuse on the next step after this sequence. The behaviour of a process is then determined by its failure set. There is a natural partial order on behaviours which captures precisely the notion of nondeterminism and turns the set of all process behaviours into a complete semi-lattice. Terms in the language CSP can then be taken to denote failure sets.

We will give an alternative formulation of processes equivalent to the failures definition. The new version is designed in order to facilitate comparison with CCS. Specifically, we define a mapping from CSP to synchronisation trees, and an equivalence relation (called failure equivalence) on trees which reflects the failure semantics of processes. Two processes have the same failure sets if and only if the trees representing them are identified by the failure equivalence relation. We also define operations on synchronisation trees which mirror the process operations of CSP. This leads to a discussion of which CSP operations are definable in terms of Milner's CCS operations. We also show that the failure equivalence relation is the relation characterised by a set of axioms, and compare these axioms with the defining axioms of observation equivalence.

1.1. Milner's synchronisation trees.

This section contains a summary of the definitions and results of Milner. More details can be found in [1]. We begin with a set Σ of *actions*, also known as *events*. This set is called the *alphabet*. There is also a special symbol τ, which does not belong to Σ : τ represents an *invisible* action. The set $\Sigma \cup \{\tau\}$ will be called the *extended alphabet*, and we use meta-variables a, b to range over the alphabet, and λ, μ to range over the extended alphabet. The meta-variables s, t, u range over finite sequences of events, and w ranges over finite sequences of extended events.

A *synchronisation tree* S is an rooted, unordered, finitely branching tree all of whose arcs are labelled with either τ or an event. We use the notation

$$\sum_{i=1}^{n} \mu_i T_i$$

for the tree whose initial arcs are labelled $\mu_1, \ldots, \mu_n$, and which has subtrees $T_1, \ldots, T_n$ at the ends of these arcs. The trivial tree with no arcs is denoted *NIL*, and the result of joining two trees S and T at their roots is denoted $S+T$. The meta-variables S, T, U range over trees. The *branches* of a tree are defined in the usual way. Note that NIL has no non-trivial branches, and the non-trivial branches of $S+T$ are either branches of S or of T. The following axioms reflect our assumption that a tree is uniquely determined by its set of branches.

PROPOSITION 1.1.1. *Addition is commutative, idempotent and associative; NIL is an additive identity element.*

$$\begin{array}{ll} (A1) & S+T=T+S \\ (A2) & (S+T)+U=S+(T+U) \\ (A3) & S+S=S \\ (A4) & S+NIL=S \end{array}$$

If S has a branch of the form wT, we write $S \xrightarrow{w} T$, and say that S has a w-branch (to T.) As far as an observer of a tree is concerned, the τ actions are invisible; we use the notation $w\,/\,\tau$ for the sequence of visible actions obtained by deleting all occurrences of τ from w, and write

$$S \stackrel{t}{\Longrightarrow} T$$

when S has a branch to T on which the sequence of visible actions is t; we say that S has a *t-derivation* (to T). A t-derivation represents a possible behaviour in which the sequence of visible actions t occurs and where the behaviour thereafter may be any consistent with T. The behaviour of a process will be modelled by a synchronisation tree, and two processes will be distinguishable only if their possible derivations differ. In making this more precise, Milner defines a sequence of equivalence relations $\{\approx_n \mid n \geq 0\}$ on trees, with the idea being that the nth relation represents equivalence up to depth n.

DEFINITION 1.1.2. The equivalence relations $\approx_n$ $(n \geq 0)$ are defined by:

$$\begin{array}{lll} \text{(i)} & S \approx_0 T & \text{for all } S, T. \\ \text{(ii)} & S \approx_{n+1} T & \text{iff, for all } s \in \Sigma^*, \\ & & \text{(a)}\quad S \stackrel{s}{\Longrightarrow} S' \Rightarrow \exists T'.T \stackrel{s}{\Longrightarrow} T' \;\&\; S' \approx_n T' \\ & & \text{(b)}\quad T \stackrel{s}{\Longrightarrow} T' \Rightarrow \exists S'.S \stackrel{s}{\Longrightarrow} S' \;\&\; S' \approx_n T'. \end{array}$$

It is clear that each of these relations is indeed an equivalence, and that they form a decreasing chain of finer and finer relations: $\approx_{n+1} \subset \approx_n$, for all n. Milner regards two trees as observationally equivalent if and only if they cannot be distinguished by any finite experiment; this is the case when no $\approx_n$ relation can distinguish between them. This motivates the following definition.

DEFINITION 1.1.3. Two trees S and T are observationally equivalent, written $S \approx T$, iff $\forall n, S \approx_n T$.

Milner notes the following laws of observation equivalence [1]. They are easily verified; one uses induction on n to prove that the appropriate pairs of trees are n-equivalent for all n.

PROPOSITION 1.1.4. *The following laws hold for observation equivalence:*

$$\begin{array}{ll} (1) & S + \tau S \approx \tau S \\ (2) & \tau S \approx S \\ (3) & \mu S + \mu(\tau S + T) \approx \mu(\tau S + T) \end{array}$$

Milner also defines an inference rule, known as ***guarded inference.***

PROPOSITION 1.1.5. *The following inference rule, (R), is valid:*

$$(R) \qquad \frac{S \approx T}{\mu S + U \approx \mu T + U}.$$

As Milner shows, there is a sense in which these laws and inference rule *characterize* observation equivalence, at least on *finite* trees. One can use these laws to prove every true equivalence on finite trees, provided one allows use of laws (1) and (3), (A1)–(A4), in any additive context. Law (2), however, is not valid in all contexts, so its use must be restricted. The reason for this is that there are trees which are observation equivalent but which do not remain so when placed in some additive contexts. Although the law $S \approx \tau S$ is valid, it is not always the case that $S + T \approx \tau S + T$.

PROPOSITION 1.1.6. *The following set of axioms, together with rule (R) and laws (A1)–(A4), is complete for observation equivalence of finite trees.*

$$\begin{array}{ll} (M1) & S + \tau S + T \approx \tau S + T \\ (M2) & \tau S \approx S \\ (M3) & \mu S + \mu(\tau S + T) + U \approx \mu(\tau S + T) + U \end{array}$$

Proof. These are (essentially) Milner's τ-laws, and the completeness result is stated in [1]. ∎

Milner uses synchronisation trees and the observation equivalence relation in constructing a mathematical model of concurrent processes. He introduces a simple language, called CCS, whose terms can be taken to denote (equivalence classes of) synchronisation trees. For our purposes, the terms in this language can be thought of as being generated by the following grammar:

$$S ::= NIL \mid aS \mid S_1 + S_2 \mid S_1 \mid S_2 \mid S\backslash a \mid S[a \setminus b].$$

We have already dealt with the first three forms. Milner calls $S \mid T$ the *composition* of S and T, and for trees $S = \sum_{i=1}^{n} \lambda_i S_i$, $T = \sum_{i=1}^{m} \mu_i T_i$, with $\lambda_i, \mu_j \in \Sigma \cup \{\tau\}$, the composition is defined by

$$S \mid T = \sum_{i=1}^{n} \lambda_i (S_i \mid T) + \sum_{j=1}^{m} \mu_j (S \mid T_j) + \sum_{\lambda_i = \overline{\mu_j}} \tau(S_i \mid T_j).$$

Here the events a and $\overline{a}$ are *matching* or *complementary* actions. It will simplify our presentation without losing any generality to assume that the only actions which have complements are visible actions, and that $a = \overline{\overline{a}}$ for all visible actions a. The final two types of CCS process are interpreted thus, using the same notation as above for S :

$$S\backslash b = \sum_{\lambda_i \neq b} \lambda_i (S_i \backslash b),$$

$$S[a \setminus b] = \sum_{i=1}^{n} \lambda_i [a \setminus b] S_i [a \setminus b],$$

where for an event μ, $\mu[a \setminus b]$ is a if $\mu = b$ and μ otherwise. These operations are called *restriction* ($\backslash b$) and *relabelling* ($[a \setminus b]$) by Milner. Restricting prunes away branches involving the particular event b, while relabelling replaces all occurrences of one label by another. Note that these operations are defined recursively, and these definitions can be thought of as *expansion theorems* which allow a term involving composition, relabelling or restriction to be manipulated into a summation form. Milner shows that addition of these expansion laws to the logical system of Proposition 1.1.6 produces a complete system for the full language of (finite) CCS terms.

1.2. The failures model of CSP.

In the failures model of process behaviour, a process is characterised as a *failure set*. Each possible failure of a process represents a finite piece of behaviour in which the process has engaged in a sequence of visible actions up to some moment and has since then refused to participate in some set of actions, *i.e.* the process has *refused* a set of actions. This refusal comes about as the result of an autonomous decision by the process, and models the possibility of nondeterministic behaviour. Failures are intended to capture precisely the situations in which a process can *deadlock*.

Again we begin with a set Σ of *events*, and events stand for process actions which are visible to the process's environment. In the CSP model we are thinking of events as standing for synchronised *communications* or *interactions* between a process and its environment. Instead of using τ as a special symbol for an unobservable action, and allowing occurrences of τ to represent nondeterministic behaviour, the presence of nondeterminism manifests itself as follows. After each finite sequence of visible actions, a process has a set of *refusal sets* which represents the possible consequences, for the next step, of the various nondeterministic decisions available to the process. We imagine that a nondeterministic decision has the effect of *removing* a set of events from the set of actions in which the process might have participated on the next step. In other words, each nondeterministic decision restricts the process's future behaviour. Thus it is appropriate to represent this effect as a *refusal set*.

A failure is a *pair* consisting of a sequence s of events and a set X of events. We will refer to s as the *trace* and X as the *refusal set*. Intuitively, if a particular failure (s, X) is possible for a process then the process may, once it has performed the sequence s, refuse to participate in any event in X on the next step. Thus we say that the process may do s and then refuse X. If (s, X) is a possible failure of a process and the process is run in an environment in which the sequence of events s is allowed and then the environment only allows events in X as the next step, there is a possibility of deadlock: the process can refuse all of the events which the environment is willing to perform next.

A process P will be characterised as a set of failures, or (equivalently) as a relation between traces and refusal sets. The domain dom(P) of this relation will define the trace set of the process. The following definition says that the traces of a process form a non-empty set (P1), which is also prefix-closed (P2). If P can refuse a set Y at some stage then it can also refuse any subset X of Y (P3). An *impossible* event can always be included in a refusal set (P4). These conditions are intuitively appealing, given our model of behaviour.

DEFINITION 1.2.1. A process is a set of failures P satisfying:

$$
\begin{array}{ll}
\text{(P1)} & (\langle\rangle, \emptyset) \in P \\
\text{(P2)} & (st, \emptyset) \in P \Rightarrow (s, \emptyset) \in P \\
\text{(P3)} & X \subseteq Y \;\&\; (s, Y) \in P \Rightarrow (s, X) \in P \\
\text{(P4)} & (s, X) \in P \;\&\; s\langle b\rangle \notin \mathrm{dom}(P) \Rightarrow (s, X \cup \{b\}) \in P
\end{array}
$$

DEFINITION 1.2.2. For any set P of failures,

$$
\begin{array}{ll}
\text{(i)} & \mathrm{traces}(P) = \{\, s \mid (s, \emptyset) \in P \,\} \\
\text{(ii)} & \mathrm{refusals}(P) = \{\, X \mid (\langle\rangle, X) \in P \,\} \\
\text{(iii)} & \mathrm{initials}(P) = \{\, a \mid \langle a\rangle \in \mathrm{traces}(P) \,\}
\end{array}
$$

If P and Q are two processes such that $P \supseteq Q$, then every possible failure of Q is also possible for P. Intuitively this means that it is possible for P to behave like Q, but it may also be the case that P can behave in a manner impossible for Q, either by refusing or performing more than Q could at the same stage. In such circumstances we say that P is more nondeterministic than Q, and write $P \sqsubseteq Q$. It is easy to see that processes are partially ordered by this relation. In fact the set of processes becomes a *complete semi-lattice* under this ordering.

PROPOSITION 1.2.3. *Processes, ordered by* $\sqsubseteq$, *form a complete semi-lattice; that is,* $\sqsubseteq$ *is a partial order, there is a least element (known as CHAOS), every non-empty set of processes has a greatest lower bound, and every directed set of processes has least upper bound.*

Proof. The union of any non-empty set of processes is again a process, and the intersection of any directed set of processes is a process. The bottom element is CHAOS $= \Sigma^* \times \mathcal{P}(\Sigma)$. Details can be found in [2]. ∎

In [2] we introduced a denotational semantics for a simplified version of Hoare's CSP language, in which CSP processes were identified with failure sets. We defined a set of operations on failure sets which correspond to the syntactic constructs of the language, and showed that all of these operations are continuous with respect to the nondeterminism ordering. This fact justified our use in [2] of recursively defined processes, since least fixed points of continuous functions on complete semi-lattices exist.

The syntax of the language is simple. The syntactic category of *processes* P is defined thus:

$$P ::= \text{STOP} \mid (a \to P) \mid P \sqcap P \mid P \Box P \mid P \| P \mid P ||| P \mid P / b$$

STOP is intended to be a process which is unable to perform any action; this corresponds to *deadlock*. We refer to the other syntactic constructs as *prefixing, unkind choice, kind choice, strict parallel composition, interleaving* and *hiding*. The result of prefixing an event a to a process P is a process which must initially perform a and then behaves like P. The difference between the two forms of *choice* operation manifests itself only on the initial step: $P \Box Q$ is not allowed to refuse an event unless both constituent processes refuse it; $P \sqcap Q$ can refuse an event if either of the constituents chooses to do so. In both forms of choice, once an event has occurred, only one of the constituent processes is still active. The reader familiar with Hoare's original language might recognise that a kind choice corresponds to a guarded command in which all the guards are communications, so that the process's environment must be consulted before determining which guard to pass; likewise, an unkind choice represents the case where all guards are purely boolean, so that a guard can be passed without consulting the environment. The process $P \| Q$ is a form of parallel composition in which each event occurs only if both constituents perform it together; this obviously represents a very tightly coupled form of parallelism. In contrast, the interleaving of two processes allows them to execute events independently of each other, so that the traces of $P ||| Q$ will be obtained by interleaving traces from P and Q. The hiding operator renders an event invisible to the environment, and allows its action to take place nondeterministically. For further details the reader is referred to [2].

The semantic function F maps a process P to its failure set $F(P)$, and is defined by a structural induction in the usual way. Thus for the "terminal" cases (*i.e.* STOP) we define the failures explicitly while in general the failures of P are built up from the failures of its immediate syntactic components.

DEFINITION 1.2.4. The failures semantic function F is defined by structural induction as follows:

$$
\begin{aligned}
F[\![\text{STOP}]\!] &= \{ (\langle\rangle, X) \mid X \subseteq \Sigma \} \\
F[\![a \to P]\!] &= \{ (\langle\rangle, X) \mid a \not\in X \} \cup \{ (\langle a\rangle s, X) \mid (s, X) \in F[\![P]\!] \} \\
F[\![P_1 \sqcap P_2]\!] &= F[\![P_1]\!] \cup F[\![P_2]\!] \\
F[\![P_1 \Box P_2]\!] &= \{ (\langle\rangle, X) \mid (\langle\rangle, X) \in F[\![P_1]\!] \cap F[\![P_2]\!] \} \cup \{ (s, X) \mid s \neq \langle\rangle \;\&\; (s, X) \in F[\![P_1]\!] \cup F[\![P_2]\!] \} \\
F[\![P_1 \| P_2]\!] &= \{ (s, X \cup Y) \mid (s, X) \in F[\![P_1]\!] \;\&\; (s, Y) \in F[\![P_2]\!] \} \\
F[\![P_1 ||| P_2]\!] &= \{ (u, X) \mid \exists s, t. (s, X) \in F[\![P_1]\!] \;\&\; (t, X) \in F[\![P_2]\!] \;\&\; u \in \text{merge}(s, t) \} \\
F[\![P / b]\!] &= \{ (s / b, X) \mid (s, X \cup \{ b \}) \in F[\![P]\!] \}
\end{aligned}
$$

Notice that the intuition behind each syntactic operation is captured in this semantic definition. Thus, for instance, X is a refusal of $(a \to P)$ iff X does not contain a : this process cannot refuse a. And the difference between the two forms of choice operation is exemplified by the fact that the process

$$(a \rightarrow \mathrm{STOP}) \square (b \rightarrow \mathrm{STOP})$$

must initially perform either a or b, and cannot commit itself to one of these events over the other; although $\{a\}$ is a refusal of $(b \rightarrow \mathrm{STOP})$, the other component process $(a \rightarrow \mathrm{STOP})$ cannot refuse a. On the other hand, the process

$$(a \rightarrow \mathrm{STOP}) \sqcap (b \rightarrow \mathrm{STOP})$$

can choose arbitrarily whether or not to allow a or b, and $\{a\}$ and $\{b\}$ are refusals of this process; the fact that one or other of the events must occur initially is reflected in the process's inability to refuse $\{a, b\}$.

We have given here the definition of hiding appropriate for finite processes: when the language is extended to allow infinite processes there are several alternative definitions of hiding, all of which agree on finite processes; it would not be appropriate to give details here, since we are only dealing with finite terms. More details can be found in [2].

In the next section we will link the failure set semantics with the synchronisation tree model, by defining an equivalence relation on synchronisation trees which naturally represents failure sets. This will enable us to define a semantic mapping from CSP to (equivalence classes of) trees which matches precisely the failure set semantics. In doing so, we will define tree operations analogous to the syntactic CSP operations.

1.3. The failure equivalence relation on synchronisation trees.

We begin by defining some basic attributes of synchronisation trees. The ***traces*** of a tree are simply the sequences of visible actions that appear on the branches of the tree, and (similarly) the initials are the visible events appearing first on the branches. A tree can ***refuse*** a set X of events if there is a τ-branch from the root to a subtree whose initials are disjoint from X. Equivalently, S can refuse X if it has an invisible transition to a tree which has no x-actions, for all $x \in X$. Finally, the pair (s, X) is a ***failure*** of T if T has an s-derivation to a subtree whose initials are disjoint from X.

DEFINITION 1.3.1. For any synchronisation tree S,

(i) $\mathrm{traces}(S) = \{ s \mid \exists T.\, S \stackrel{s}{\Longrightarrow} T \}$

(ii) $\mathrm{initials}(S) = \{ a \mid \langle a \rangle \in \mathrm{traces}(S) \}$

(iii) $\mathrm{refusals}(S) = \{ X \mid \exists T.\, S \stackrel{\langle\rangle}{\Longrightarrow} T \;\&\; X \cap \mathrm{initials}(T) = \emptyset \}$

(iv) $\mathrm{failures}(S) = \{ (s, X) \mid \exists T.\, S \stackrel{s}{\Longrightarrow} T \;\&\; X \cap \mathrm{initials}(T) = \emptyset \}$

The ***failure equivalence relation*** on trees identifies two trees if and only if they have identical failure sets. The formal definition is:

DEFINITION 1.3.2. Failure equivalence $\equiv$ is the relation $S \equiv T \Leftrightarrow \mathrm{failures}(S) = \mathrm{failures}(T)$.

It is clear that this is an equivalence relation. From the definition, a comparison with the definitions of Milner's first and second relations shows that:

(1) $S \approx_1 T \quad \Leftrightarrow \quad$ for all $s \in \Sigma^*$, $\quad (\exists S'.\, S \stackrel{s}{\Longrightarrow} S' \Leftrightarrow \exists T'.\, T \stackrel{s}{\Longrightarrow} T')$

(2) $S \equiv T \quad \Leftrightarrow \quad$ for all $s \in \Sigma^*$ and $X \subseteq \Sigma$,
$\exists S'.\, S \stackrel{s}{\Longrightarrow} S' \;\&\; X \cap \mathrm{initials}(S') = \emptyset$
$\Leftrightarrow \exists T'.\, T \stackrel{s}{\Longrightarrow} T' \;\&\; X \cap \mathrm{initials}(T') = \emptyset$

(3) $S \approx_2 T \quad \Leftrightarrow \quad$ for all $s \in \Sigma^*$, and $U \subseteq \Sigma^*$,
$\exists S'.\, S \stackrel{s}{\Longrightarrow} S' \;\&\; \mathrm{traces}(S') = U$
$\Leftrightarrow \exists T'.\, T \stackrel{s}{\Longrightarrow} T' \;\&\; \mathrm{traces}(T') = U$

Thus it follows that failure equivalence implies trace equivalence ($\approx_1$) and is implied by $\approx_2$. Hence, failure equivalence is a weaker relation than observation equivalence, because it makes more identifications and cannot distinguish between some pairs of trees which observation equivalence separates. Moreover, the failure relation is distinct from $\approx_1$ and $\approx_2$, as shown by the example:

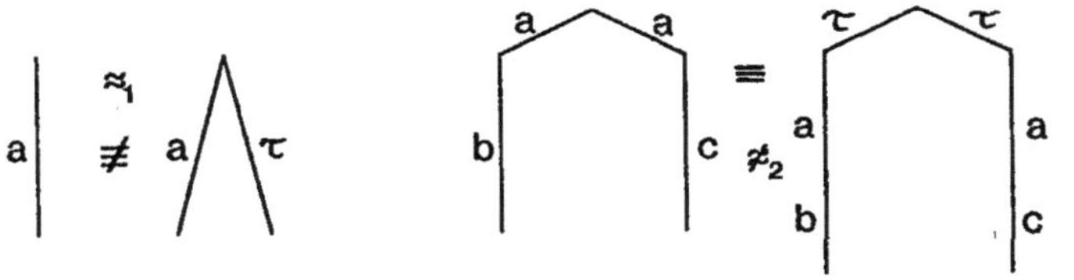

PROPOSITION 1.3.3. *Failure equivalence lies between Milner's first and second equivalences, and is implied by observation equivalence:*

$$\approx_1 \supset \; \equiv \; \supset \; \approx_2 \; \supset \; \approx .$$

It is clear that we can define a pre-order $\sqsubseteq$ on trees which corresponds precisely to the nondeterminism ordering on processes, as follows.

DEFINITION 1.3.4. The pre-order $\sqsubseteq$ on trees is defined by $S \sqsubseteq T \quad \Leftrightarrow \quad \text{failures}(T) \subseteq \text{failures}(S)$.

COROLLARY 1.3.5. *For any pair of trees S and T,* $\quad S \equiv T \Leftrightarrow S \sqsubseteq T \;\&\; T \sqsubseteq S.$

Failure equivalence, like observation equivalence, can be axiomatized. We begin with a set of true equivalence laws and a valid rule of inference.

PROPOSITION 1.3.6. *The following laws hold for failure equivalence:*

$$\begin{array}{ll} (B1) & S + \tau T + U \equiv \tau(S+T) + \tau T + U \\ (B2) & \tau S \equiv S \\ (B3) & \mu S + \mu T + U \equiv \mu(\tau S + \tau T) + U \qquad (\mu \in \Sigma \cup \{\tau\}) \\ (B4) & \tau(\mu S + T) + \tau(\mu S' + T') \equiv \tau(\mu S + \mu S' + T) + \tau(\mu S + \mu S' + T') \end{array}$$

Proof. Verify for each law that the failures of the left-hand and right-hand side are identical. The details are omitted, as the proof is straightforward. ∎

PROPOSITION 1.3.7. *The following inference rule (R) is valid:*

$$(R) \qquad \frac{S \equiv T}{\mu S + U \equiv \mu T + U} \qquad (\mu \in \Sigma \cup \{\tau\})$$

Note that we use the same name for this rule as for the corresponding rule in Milner's system.

As with the corresponding result for Milner's equivalence, these axioms and inference rule are complete for establishing equivalence of finite trees, provided we again allow use of the laws of Proposition 1.1.1 in any context. The proof that this system is complete is based on a simple algorithm for converting a tree to a "normal form," in which the arcs at each node have a special property known as *uniformity:* either the labels on the arcs are distinct and visible (*i.e.* not τ), or all the arcs are labelled with τ. It is clear that one can use (B1) and (B3) at a non-uniform node to produce uniformity; in each case any non-uniformity is pushed deeper into the tree, so that this method will definitely terminate on finite depth trees. One then shows that this process can be continued until the tree is in a *pre-normal form,* in which successive τ arcs have been collapsed down to single arcs (using (B3) again), and where the tree is "convex." Convexity can best be explained by observing that in a uniform tree each node without τ arcs corresponds to a sequence of visible events (the visible path from the root) and, conversely, each visible sequence s of actions corresponds to a set of such s-nodes (because the same sequence of actions may occur on different paths). Say that the set X of actions appears at an s-node of T if one of the s-nodes has arcs labelled by the events in X. The convexity condition is that, for each s, whenever X and Z appear at (different) s-nodes and $X \subseteq Y \subseteq Z$, then Y also appears at some s-node; and that whenever X and Y appear at some s-node so does $X \cup Y$. Axioms (B1) and (B3) are used to fill out a tree in this way. Finally one proves that any tree in pre-normal form can be converted, using (B4), into a normal form in which, for each sequence s all s-nodes have identical trees attached and these trees are also in normal form. Then it is easy to show that failure equivalence on trees in normal form is essentially the identity relation. Thus, each tree can be proven equivalent to a *unique* tree in full normal form; this establishes completeness of the system. The full proof is included in the appendix.

PROPOSITION 1.3.8. *The axiom system consisting of laws (A1)-(A4), (B1)-(B4), and rule (R) is complete for failure equivalence on finite trees.*

The following property of $\sqsubseteq$ enables us to obtain a complete proof system for the failures preorder on finite trees, by modifying the above axiom system.

PROPOSITION 1.3.9. *For all trees S and T, $S \sqsubseteq T$ iff $\tau S + \tau T \equiv S$.*

We regard each of the above axioms for $\equiv$ as a pair of axioms involving $\sqsubseteq$, in the obvious way. We replace rule (R) by the rule given below:

$$(R') \qquad \frac{S \sqsubseteq T}{\mu S + U \sqsubseteq \mu T + U}.$$

And we add enough axioms and rules to give us that $\sqsubseteq$ is a pre-order satisfying Proposition 1.3.9:

$$\begin{array}{ll} (O1) & S \sqsubseteq T \sqsubseteq S \Leftrightarrow S \equiv T \\ (O2) & S \sqsubseteq T \sqsubseteq U \Rightarrow S \sqsubseteq U \\ (O3) & S \sqsubseteq T \Leftrightarrow \tau S + \tau T \equiv S \end{array}$$

The proof of completeness for the earlier system can easily be modified to establish the truth of the following proposition.

PROPOSITION 1.3.10. *The proof system generated by axioms* $(A1)$–$(A4)$, $(B1)$–$(B4)$, $(O1)$–$(O3)$ *and rule* (R'), *is complete for the failure pre-order on finite trees.*

1.4. Mapping CSP to synchronisation trees.

Now we can define a mapping from CSP syntax to synchronisation trees. If P is a CSP process then $\mathcal{T}[\![P]\!]$ will be a synchronisation tree having the same failure set as P. This will mean that two CSP processes have the same meaning in the failure set semantics if and only if their images under $\mathcal{T}$ are equivalent. The mapping $\mathcal{T}$ is defined by structural induction on the syntax, as usual.

DEFINITION 1.4.1. The map $\mathcal{T}$ from CSP to synchronisation trees is given by the following clauses:

$$\begin{aligned} \mathcal{T}[\![\mathrm{STOP}]\!] &= NIL \\ \mathcal{T}[\![a \rightarrow P]\!] &= a\mathcal{T}[\![P]\!] \\ \mathcal{T}[\![P_1 \sqcap P_2]\!] &= \tau\mathcal{T}[\![P_1]\!] + \tau\mathcal{T}[\![P_2]\!] \\ \mathcal{T}[\![P_1 \Box P_2]\!] &= \mathcal{T}[\![P_1]\!] \Box \mathcal{T}[\![P_2]\!] \\ \mathcal{T}[\![P_1 \| P_2]\!] &= \mathcal{T}[\![P_1]\!] \| \mathcal{T}[\![P_2]\!] \\ \mathcal{T}[\![P_1 ||| P_2]\!] &= \mathcal{T}[\![P_1]\!] ||| \mathcal{T}[\![P_2]\!] \\ \mathcal{T}[\![P \,/\, b]\!] &= \mathcal{T}[\![P]\!][\tau \backslash b] \end{aligned}$$

where the tree operations $\Box$, $\|$, $|||$ are defined so that for the trees

$$S = \sum_{i=1}^{n} a_i S_i + \sum_{i=1}^{N} \tau S_i', \qquad T = \sum_{j=1}^{m} b_j T_j + \sum_{j=1}^{M} \tau T_j',$$

we have

$$S \Box T = \sum_{i=1}^{n} a_i S_i + \sum_{j=1}^{m} b_j T_j + \sum_{i=1}^{N} \tau(S_i' \Box T) + \sum_{j=1}^{M} \tau(S \Box T_j')$$

$$S \| T = \sum_{a_i = b_j} a_i(S_i \| T_j) + \sum_{i=1}^{N} \tau(S_i' \| T) + \sum_{j=1}^{M} \tau(S \| T_j')$$

$$S ||| T = \sum_{i=1}^{n} a_i(S_i ||| T) + \sum_{j=1}^{m} b_j(S ||| T_j) + \sum_{i=1}^{N} \tau(S_i' ||| T) + \sum_{j=1}^{M} \tau(S ||| T_j')$$

and the tree $S[\tau \setminus b]$ denotes the result of replacing every label b by τ in S. This is an instance of Milner's relabelling operation.

As examples, we can see that the trees representing the processes

$$(a \to \text{STOP}) \Box (b \to \text{STOP}) \quad \text{and} \quad (a \to \text{STOP}) \sqcap (b \to \text{STOP})$$

are $aNIL + bNIL$ and $\tau aNIL + \tau bNIL$.

To show that these tree operations do correspond to the original CSP operations, first we establish some results on the way transitions of a composite tree are built up from the transitions of the component trees.

Firstly, it is obvious that $aS \stackrel{a}{\Longrightarrow} S$ and that $\tau S + \tau T$ has an invisible transition to S and to T. The behaviour of the tree operation $\Box$ is expressed by:

$$S \stackrel{\langle\rangle}{\Longrightarrow} S',\ T \stackrel{\langle\rangle}{\Longrightarrow} T' \ \Rightarrow\ (S \Box T) \stackrel{\langle\rangle}{\Longrightarrow} (S' \Box T'),$$
$$S \stackrel{s}{\Longrightarrow} S',\ s \neq \langle\rangle \ \Rightarrow\ (S \Box T) \stackrel{s}{\Longrightarrow} S',$$
$$T \stackrel{t}{\Longrightarrow} T',\ t \neq \langle\rangle \ \Rightarrow\ (S \Box T) \stackrel{t}{\Longrightarrow} T'.$$

For parallel composition we have: $S \stackrel{s}{\Longrightarrow} S',\ T \stackrel{s}{\Longrightarrow} T' \ \Rightarrow\ (S \| T) \stackrel{s}{\Longrightarrow} (S' \| T')$. For interleaving: if $S \stackrel{s}{\Longrightarrow} S'$, $T \stackrel{t}{\Longrightarrow} T'$, and u merges s & t then $(S ||| T) \stackrel{u}{\Longrightarrow} (S' ||| T')$. Finally, let s / b denote the result of deleting all occurrences of b from the sequence s. Then

$$S \stackrel{s}{\Longrightarrow} S' \ \Rightarrow\ S[\tau \setminus b] \stackrel{s/b}{\Longrightarrow} S'[\tau \setminus b].$$

These facts can be used to prove the following result.

PROPOSITION 1.4.3. *The mapping $\mathcal{T}$ respects failure sets: $failures(\mathcal{T}[\![P]\!]) = F[\![P]\!]$.*

Proof. By structural induction on P. The base case is trivial, since $\mathcal{T}[\![\text{STOP}]\!] = NIL$ and NIL has no non-trivial derivations. We give details for one of the inductive steps. The other cases are similar.

Case 1. When $P = Q \| R$, let S and T be the trees representing Q and R respectively. The inductive hypothesis is that

$$\text{failures}(S) = F[\![Q]\!], \qquad \text{failures}(T) = F[\![R]\!].$$

We must prove that $\text{failures}(S \| T) = F[\![Q \| R]\!]$. But (s, X) is a failure of $S \| T$ if and only if there is a U such that

$$(S \| T) \stackrel{s}{\Longrightarrow} U \ \&\ X \cap \text{initials}(U) = \emptyset.$$

From the definition of parallel composition on trees there must be some trees S' and T' such that

$$U = (S' \| T') \ \& \ S \stackrel{s}{\Longrightarrow} S' \ \& \ T \stackrel{s}{\Longrightarrow} T'.$$

But initials$(S' \| T')$ = initials$(S') \cap$ initials(T'). Let $Y = X -$ initials(S'), and $Z = X -$ initials(T'). Then $X = Y \cup Z$ and by definition, $(s, Y) \in$ failures(S) & $(s, Z) \in$ failures(T). By inductive hypothesis, this gives

$$(s, Y) \in F[\![P]\!] \ \& \ (s, Z) \in F[\![Q]\!],$$

and hence $(s, Y \cup Z) = (s, X) \in F[\![P \| Q]\!]$. ∎

COROLLARY 1.4.4. *Two processes have the same failure sets if and only if their images under $\mathcal{T}$ are equivalent:*

$$F[\![P]\!] = F[\![Q]\!] \quad \Leftrightarrow \quad \mathcal{T}[\![P]\!] \equiv \mathcal{T}[\![Q]\!].$$

This result shows that the failure equivalence relation partitions the set of synchronisation trees into a set of equivalence classes which correspond precisely to the meanings of CSP processes under the failure set semantic function. Moreover, the preorder $\sqsubseteq$ on trees corresponds exactly to the nondeterminism order on processes. It is also clear that failure equivalence on trees respects the tree operations which represent CSP operations. Thus, unlike Milner's system, here we have an equivalence relation which is a *congruence* with respect to the operations of our language. Of course, it is still not the case that the equivalence relation is well behaved with respect to +. Again, $S \equiv \tau S$ always holds, but it is not in general true that $S + T \equiv \tau S + T$. But this does not matter to us, since + is not a CSP operation.

2. Conclusions.

We have described two alternative languages for concurrency, CCS and CSP, using a common basis for a semantic model: Milner's synchronisation trees. We gave a semantics to CSP by mapping terms in this language to synchronisation trees and factoring out by an equivalence relation. Milner's semantics for CCS was also constructed in a similar fashion, although his equivalence relation was chosen in accordance with different criteria. We established a simple relationship between these two equivalence relations, and defined a complete axiom system for proving equivalence of finite CSP terms. Since the CCS equivalence is finer than the failure equivalence of CSP, and therefore makes fewer identifications on trees, all of the axioms of CCS are true also of failure equivalence. The converse is not true, of course, and the axioms of failure equivalence reflect very clearly the reasons.

Interesting topics for future work include extending these ideas to cope with infinite processes and infinite synchronisation trees; such an extension would be necessary if a form of recursion were added to the syntax of the language of processes. It then becomes necessary to treat problems associated with *divergence,* and there are several alternative models here to consider: for example, see [3,4,6] for CCS and [7,8] for CSP. To illustrate some of the problems introduced by divergence, consider the following. If we identify divergence with the ability to perform arbitrarily long sequences of hidden actions, without ever interacting with the environment, then one can model divergence as the presence in a synchronisation tree of an infinite path of τ arcs. Under the standard observational equivalence and failure equivalence presented here, the divergent tree τ^{ω} would be identified with *NIL*. Intuitively, such an inability to distinguish between divergence and deadlock is unappealing. One would therefore have to change the definitions of equivalence of trees to allow for such distinctions to be made. It is not yet clear which methods of modelling divergence are likely to be most successful.

An interesting area for research is to investigate the possibility of axiomatising other semantic models for concurrency, in much the same way as was done here for the failures model of CSP. A concise, complete proof system summarises the essential properties of a semantic model in a way that might clarify the differences and similarities between various models. Darondeau [9] gives an axiomatization of an equivalence on processes; these axioms can be simply derived from (B1)-(B4), showing that the same underlying model is being used, even though the constructions differ. In [6] the authors give complete proof systems for a variety of preorders (and hence for the associated equivalences) on CCS, which are shown in [7] to be related closely to the failures model. [7] also shows the connections between failure sets and the model proposed by Kennaway for communicating processes. It should be possible to axiomatize Kennaway's model, since it is so closely related to failure sets. Similar possibilities should also exist for the *possible futures* model of processes, described in [10]; this model is essentially based on the equivalence $\approx_2$ as given above.

3. Appendix.

In this section we prove the results stated earlier about normal forms, and justify our claim that the CSP axiom system based on (B1)-(B4) and (R) is complete for finite trees. First it will be useful to give some derived laws and rules.

PROPOSITION A.1. *The following laws are derivable in our proof system:*

$$\text{(G1)} \qquad S + \sum_{i=1}^{n} \tau T_i + U \equiv \sum_{i=1}^{n} \tau(S + T_i) + \sum_{i=1}^{n} \tau T_i + U$$

$$\text{(G3)} \qquad \sum_{i=1}^{n} \mu S_i + U \equiv \mu \sum_{i=1}^{n} \tau S_i + U$$

$$\text{(G4)} \qquad \sum_{i=1}^{n} \tau(\mu S_i + T_i) \equiv \sum_{i=1}^{n} \tau(\mu S + T_i),$$

where $S = \sum_{i=1}^{n} \tau S_i$.

Proof. In each case an induction on n will establish the result; the base case, $n = 1$, is an instance of an axiom. Details are left to the reader. ∎

PROPOSITION A.2. *The following inference rule is a derived rule in our system:*

$$\frac{\sum_{i=1}^{n} \tau S_i \equiv \sum_{j=1}^{m} \tau T_j}{\sum_{i=1}^{n} \tau S_i + U \equiv \sum_{j=1}^{m} \tau T_j + U.}$$

Proof. Let us introduce abbreviations $S = \sum_{i=1}^{n} \tau S_i$, $T = \sum_{j=1}^{m} \tau T_j$. Assume that $S \equiv T$ is provable. Then by (G3) with $\mu = \tau$, we can prove

$$\text{(1)} \quad \tau S + U \equiv S + U,$$
$$\text{(2)} \quad \tau T + U \equiv T + U.$$

But from $S \equiv T$ applying rule (R) gives us

$$\text{(3)} \qquad \tau S + U \equiv \tau T + U.$$

The result follows from (1) and (2). ∎

PROPOSITION A.3. *The following convexity laws are derivable:*

$$\text{(C1)} \qquad \tau S + \tau T \equiv \tau S + \tau T + \tau(S + T)$$
$$\text{(C2)} \quad \tau S + \tau(S + T + U) \equiv \tau S + \tau(S + T) + \tau(S + T + U).$$

DEFINITION A.4. A tree T is *uniform* iff at each node in T if any (outgoing) arc is labelled τ then all are.

Thus, a tree T is uniform iff it has one of the two forms:

$$T = \sum_{i=1}^{n} \tau T_i, \quad \text{or} \quad T = \sum_{i=1}^{n} a_i T_i,$$

where each a_i is in Σ, and each T_i is also uniform.

PROPOSITION A.5. *Any finite tree T is provably equivalent to a uniform tree.*

Proof. Let T be the tree $T = \sum_{i=1}^{n} a_i S_i + \sum_{j=1}^{m} \tau T_j$, where the a_i are all in Σ. The proof is by induction on the depth of T. When T has depth zero it is trivial, because $T = NIL$ and this tree is already uniform. For the inductive step, assume that every tree of smaller depth than T is equivalent to a uniform tree. In particular, this means that there are uniform trees S_i', T_j' such that the relations $S_i \equiv S_i'$, $T_j \equiv T_j'$, are provable. Using rule (R) this gives us

$$T \equiv \sum_{i=1}^{n} a_i S_i' + \sum_{j=1}^{m} \tau T_j'.$$

If any T_j' has τ branches at its root, we can use (G3) to contract successive τ labels; hence, we may assume without loss of generality that each T_j' has visible labels at its root. Writing S for the first term above, we have

$$T = S + \sum_{j=1}^{m} \tau T_j' \equiv \sum_{j=1}^{m} \tau(S + T_j') + \sum_{j=1}^{m} \tau T_j' \qquad \text{by (G1)}.$$

But S and each T_j' are uniform, and they all have visible labels at the root; this means that each $(S + T_j')$ is also uniform, so the result follows. ∎

DEFINITION A.6. A set $\mathcal{B}$ of subsets of Σ is *convex* iff $\mathcal{B}$ is non-empty and for all $X, Z \in \mathcal{B}$,

$$X \cup Z \in \mathcal{B}$$
$$X \subseteq Y \subseteq Z \Rightarrow Y \in \mathcal{B}.$$

For example, the set $\{\{a\}, \{b\}\}$ is not convex, because it does not contain $\{a, b\}$. And the set $\{\emptyset, \{a, b\}\}$ is not convex because it does not contain $\{a\}$ and $\{b\}$.

DEFINITION A.7. A tree T is in *normal form* iff T has the structure $T = \sum_{B \in \mathcal{B}} \tau T_B$, with $\mathcal{B}$ convex, and each T_B having the form $T_B = \sum_{b \in B} b T_b$, where each T_b is also in normal form.

Notice that in a normal form, for each sequence of visible actions there is (at most) one derivative. For example, the tree

$$T = \tau a NIL + \tau(a \tau b NIL + b NIL)$$

is not in normal form, because there are two distinct a-derivatives. It can, however, be transformed by the axioms to the normal form

$$\tau a S + \tau(a S + b NIL),$$

where $S = \tau NIL + \tau b NIL$.

PROPOSITION A.8. *Any uniform tree is provably equivalent to a normal form.*

Proof. Any multiple occurrences of a visible label at a node can be combined into a single occurrence by the law (G3):

$$\sum_{i=1}^{n} a S_i + T \equiv a\left(\sum_{i=1}^{n} \tau S_i\right) + T.$$

Note that this transformation preserves uniformity. Sequences of τ arcs can always be pruned down to a set of single τ arcs by the same law (using τ for a.) We can use the convexity laws (C1) and (C2), to introduce convexity at each node of the tree; finally, one uses (G4) to produce a unique s-derivative for each trace s of the tree. ∎

The completeness theorem rests upon the fact that equivalence on normal forms is provable. Indeed, it turns out that two normal forms are failure equivalent iff they are identical trees, up to order of summation. The proof will rely on a lemma.

PROPOSITION A.9. *For trees S and T in normal form, say*

$$S = \sum_{B \in \mathcal{B}} \tau \sum_{b \in B} bS_b, \qquad T = \sum_{C \in \mathcal{C}} \tau \sum_{c \in C} cT_c,$$

$S \sqsubseteq T$ holds iff $\mathcal{C} \subseteq \mathcal{B}$, and for all $c \in C \in \mathcal{C}$, $S_c \sqsubseteq T_c$.

Proof. Using the above notation, suppose $S \sqsubseteq T$. Then failures$(S) \supseteq$ failures(T). This immediately gives

$$\text{initials}(S) = \bigcup \mathcal{B} \supseteq \bigcup \mathcal{C} = \text{initials}(T).$$

If $\mathcal{C} \not\subseteq \mathcal{B}$, let C be a set in $\mathcal{C}$ but not in $\mathcal{B}$. Let $X = \Sigma - C$, so that $(\langle\rangle, X)$ is a failure of T. By hypothesis, this is also a failure of S, so there must be a $B \in \mathcal{B}$ such that $B \cap X = \emptyset$; equivalently, $B \subseteq C$. But then we have

$$B \subseteq C \subseteq \bigcup \mathcal{C} \subseteq \bigcup \mathcal{B},$$

and we know that B and $\bigcup \mathcal{B}$ belong to the convex set $\mathcal{B}$. Hence, $C \in \mathcal{B}$, which contradicts our assumption. It follows that $\mathcal{C}$ is a subset of $\mathcal{B}$.

Since S and T are in normal form, they have unique derivatives for each initial event. We have shown that initials$(S) \supseteq$ initials(T). It follows easily from the assumption that $S \sqsubseteq T$ that for all $a \in$ initials(T), $S_a \sqsubseteq T_a$. To complete the proof the above argument can be reversed to obtain the converse implication. ∎

COROLLARY A.10. *Two normal forms S and T as above are equivalent iff $\mathcal{B} = \mathcal{C}$ and for every $a \in \mathcal{B}$ the trees S_a and T_a are equivalent.*

PROPOSITION A.11. *(Completeness) Two finite trees S and T are failure equivalent iff $S \equiv T$ is provable in the above proof system.*

Proof. By Propositions A.5 and A.8 S and T are provably equivalent to normal forms, say S^* and T^*. Because the proof system is *sound*, we can assume that S^* and T^* are failure equivalent. We will prove by induction on the depth of the trees that equivalence of normal forms is provable. The basis is trivial, because the only normal form of depth 0 is *NIL*. Let the two normal forms be

$$S^* = \sum_{B \in \mathcal{B}} \tau \sum_{b \in B} bS_b^*, \qquad T^* = \sum_{C \in \mathcal{C}} \tau \sum_{c \in C} cT_c^*.$$

By Corollary A.10 we have $\mathcal{B} = \mathcal{C}$ and $S_a^* \equiv T_a^*$, for all a. Since S_a^* and T_a^* are also in normal form, and have smaller depth than S and T, we may assume by the inductive hypothesis that $S_a^* \equiv T_a^*$ is provable, for all a. An application of rule (R) then proves $S \equiv T$. ∎

4. Acknowledgements.

The author has benefitted from discussions with C.A.R.Hoare, Robin Milner, Bill Roscoe, Bill Rounds and Glynn Winskel. This work was supported in part by a grant from the Science Research Council of Great Britain, and by Carnegie-Mellon University Computer Science Department.

5. References.

[1] Milner, R., A Calculus for Communicating Systems, Springer LNCS Vol. 92 (1980).

[2] Hoare, C.A.R., Brookes, S.D., and Roscoe, A.W., A Theory of Communicating Sequential Processes, Technical Report PRG-16, Oxford University Computing Laboratory, Programming Research Group (1981).

[3] Hennessy, M.C.B. and Plotkin, G.D., A Term Model for CCS, Proceedings of 9th MFCS Conference, Springer LNCS Vol. 88 (1980).

[4] Hennessy, M.C.B. and Milner, R., On observing nondeterminism and concurrency, in: Springer LNCS Vol. 85 (1979).

[5] Hoare, C.A.R., Communicating Sequential Processes, CACM 21, Vol. 8 (1978).

[6] Hennessy, M., and de Nicola, R., Testing equivalences for processes, Technical Report, University of Edinburgh (July 1982).

[7] Brookes, S.D., A Model for Communicating Sequential Processes, Ph.D thesis, University of Oxford (submitted 1983).

[8] Roscoe, A.W., A Mathematical Theory of Communicating Sequential Processes, Ph.D thesis, University of Oxford (1982).

[9] Darondeau, Ph., An enlarged definition and complete axiomatization of observational congruence of finite processes, Proceedings of International Symposium on Programming, Springer LNCS 137 (1982).

[10] Rounds, W.C., and Brookes, S.D., Possible futures, acceptances, refusals, and communicating processes, Proceedings of 22nd IEEE Symposium on Foundations of Computer Science (October 1981).

BEHAVIOURAL EQUIVALENCE RELATIONS INDUCED BY PROGRAMMING LOGICS

Stephen D. Brookes
Carnegie-Mellon University
Pittsburgh, Pa.

William C. Rounds
University of Michigan
Ann Arbor, Mi.

1.0. Abstract.

In this paper we compare the descriptive power of three programming logics by studying the elementary equivalence relations which the logics induce on nondeterministic state-transition systems. In addition, we compare these relations with other natural state-equivalence relations for nondeterministic systems. We find that the notions of ***bisimilarity*** (Park [P], Ogden [O]) and ***observation equivalence*** (Milner [M]) are very strong equivalences compared with those induced by the logics. These three comprise ***regular trace logic*** (RTL), ***propositional dynamic logic*** (PDL), and ***Hennessy-Milner logic*** (HML). Regular trace logic is a new logic which can be used to give behavioural specifications for concurrent systems (*e.g.* Wolper [W], but with significant differences). It is a way of formalising those properties of programs which have been given informally in terms of path expressions [CH]. The model theory and axiomatics of this logic are interesting in their own right. Propositional dynamic logic is well-known; our treatment differs from the standard one only in that we regard the modalities as specifying intended behaviour instead of being programs. Hennessy-Milner logic is a simplified modal logic which those authors used as a characterisation of their notion of observation equivalence, which we call weak observation equivalence in this paper. We also include a brief treatment in this context of two other natural equivalences for nondeterministic systems: ***failure*** equivalence [HBR] and ***trace*** equivalence [H], both of which are weaker than the relations induced by the logics but can be characterised using appropriate logical subsets.

1.1. Introduction.

In this paper we generalise the notion of state-equivalence, familiar from the theory of sequential machines, to the case of nondeterministic transition systems, and use it to investigate some issues in the semantics of parallel processes. We are motivated by several recent studies of parallelism and concurrency. In particular we are interested in modelling systems which can be controlled through interactions with a surrounding environment, but which are also capable of making internal or hidden moves, in a way which cannot be influenced by an outside agent. This sort of behaviour naturally demands a nondeterministic model, especially when no probabilities can reasonably be attached to the internal actions.

Hennessy and Milner [HM] seem to have been the first to consider this modelling problem explicitly. They give a general definition of ***observational equivalence*** and prove a basic characterization of the property in terms of a simple modal logic. Milner subsequently considered several variations of the definition in his CCS [M]. These studies rely on the idea of a ***transition system*** with explicitly named actions and hidden actions. A similar model was used by Keller [K] in his early work on formalizing the notion of concurrent computations. The present work differs from Keller's in that the result of a single transition may be nondeterministic, and in having implicit or hidden transitions as well.

Our work can be seen as a direct extension of the Hennessy-Milner results. We introduce several alternatives to the definition of observational equivalence. The first was suggested to us by W. Ogden, and we subsequently learned from R. Milner that the same definition was independently given by David Park, who called it *bisimulation.* This mathematically appealing relation is the strongest of our equivalence relations. Next we consider a class of equivalences based on *distinguishability by logical formulae.* These formulae are drawn from three logics: the first is the original Hennessy-Milner logic (HM); the second, is a version of Pratt-Fischer-Ladner's *propositional dynamic logic* (PDL); and the third, called *regular trace logic,* is a new logic intended to express the nondeterministic capabilities of transition systems in a way not possible with PDL. We do not treat temporal logic in this respect since our semantics deals only with finite sequences of states and actions. Indeed, because our logics talk only about what properties of a system can be observed during the occurrence of a finite sequence of transitions, this treatment cannot cope with eventualities and fairness conditions as can temporal logics [Pn] and process logics [HKP]. We hope that our techniques can be extended to these systems. Milner and Hoare, however, have emphasised that the concept of *finite observability* is all that one could ever reasonably use in practice to detect behavioural differences between concurrent systems.

We compare the strength of these various equivalence relations, including the one already proposed by Hennessy and Milner. Under the hypothesis that all transitions have a finite number of possible outcomes, the definitions all coincide; a theorem amounting to this was proved by Hennessy and Milner. In the absence of this hypothesis, however, significant differences emerge. Perhaps the most interesting of these is the one which states that observational equivalence is a strictly stronger relation than the relation of indistinguishability by formulae of regular trace logic. The proof of this fact uses a rather delicate argument involving the pumping lemma for regular sets.

1.2. Fundamental definitions.

Our fundamental model of computation is the *labelled transition system.* This very general model was first used by Keller to study concurrent systems, although its origins can be traced back to Petri nets and to the nondeterministic automata of Rabin and Scott [RS]. Formally, a labelled transition system is a tuple

$$(Q, \Sigma, q_0, \rightarrow)$$

where Q is a set of *states* (at most countable), Σ is a finite *alphabet,* $q_0 \in Q$ is the *initial state* and $\rightarrow$ is a transition relation, *i.e.* a ternary relation on $Q \times (\Sigma \cup \{\tau\}) \times Q$. The special symbol τ (not in Q) is used to denote a *hidden action.* We will write Δ for the set $\Sigma \cup \{\tau\}$. The variable μ will range over Δ. If $(q, \mu, q') \in \rightarrow$, we write $q \xrightarrow{\mu} q'$.

As usual, Σ^* (resp. Δ^*) denotes the set of finite strings over Σ (resp. Δ); the empty sequence is ϵ, and we use s, t, u to range over Σ^*, and v, w over Δ^*. The operation $\backslash\tau$ of deleting all occurrences of τ in a sequence converts $w \in \Delta^*$ into $w\backslash\tau \in \Sigma^*$. The transition relation extends in the usual way to a relation on $Q \times \Delta^* \times Q$. For $s \in \Sigma^*$ we define the relation $\stackrel{s}{\Longrightarrow}$ on $Q \times Q$ by:

$$q \stackrel{s}{\Longrightarrow} q' \quad \Leftrightarrow \quad \exists w \in \Delta^*.\, q \xrightarrow{w} q' \;\&\; w\backslash\tau = s.$$

Notice that the symbol τ does not appear in any of the strings s used in the previous definition. This is because we are only interested in the aspects of behaviour which can be inferred from "experimenting" with externally visible events. We need to retain the possibility of uncontrolled behaviour in the underlying system, however; this behaviour might be caused, for example, by an unfair scheduler or some other unfriendly agent.

A transition system can be "unrolled" into a tree in the usual way. The initial state labels the root, states label the nodes, and elements of $\Sigma \cup \{\tau\}$ label the arcs. The resulting tree is called a *synchronisation tree* (ST). Often, where the set of states is implicit, we will identify this tree with the transition system. When we do this, the transition relation on trees is as given by Milner [M]. A transition system (or ST) has *finite branching* iff for each $q \in Q$ and each $s \in \Sigma^*$ the set $\{q' \mid q \stackrel{s}{\Longrightarrow} q'\}$ is finite. This property obviously holds if Q is finite, but note that it is not implied by the condition that the set $\{q' \mid q \xrightarrow{\mu} q'\}$ is finite for all $\mu \in \Sigma \cup \{\tau\}$. This latter condition is known as *image-finiteness* of the transition system.

We write aS for the synchronisation tree with a unique initial branch labelled $a \in \Delta$ and subtree S attached. If $\{ S_i \mid i \in I \}$ is a family of STs we denote by

$$\sum_{i \in I} S_i$$

the tree obtained by identifying the root nodes of all the S_i. The trivial tree, with a single node and no arcs, is *NIL*.

Finally, we will use α to denote a regular subset of Σ^*. We will not generally distinguish between a regular expression and the language it denotes.

1.3. Equivalences.

(i) Bisimulation.

Let $S = (Q, \Sigma, q_0, \rightarrow)$ be a transition system. A relation $\gamma \subseteq Q \times Q$ is *invariant* if whenever $p\gamma q$, $a \in \Delta$ and $p \xrightarrow{a} p'$, then there is a q' such that $q \xrightarrow{a} q'$ and $p'\gamma q'$. A *bisimulation* is a relation γ such that both γ and its inverse relation γ^{-1} are invariant. Two states p and q are *bisimilar* if there is a bisimulation γ such that $p\gamma q$. We write pBq in this case. This definition can be used to extend bisimulation to a relation on synchronisation trees, with initial states, in the obvious way. Note that if γ is invariant, then whenever $p\gamma q$ and $s \in \Sigma^*$ any transition sequence $p \stackrel{s}{\Longrightarrow} p'$ corresponds to a sequence $q \stackrel{s}{\Longrightarrow} q'$ for which $p'\gamma q'$. This can be shown by induction on the length of the transition sequence. The following properties of bisimulation are elementary.

PROPOSITION 1.3.1. *The relation of bisimulation is an equivalence relation.*

Proof. The composition of two bisimulations is again a bisimulation. ∎

PROPOSITION 1.3.2. *The relation B is itself a bisimulation, and any bisimulation on Q is a subset of B.*

Example 1. Consider the two STs $a(b+c)$ and $a(b+c)+a(b+c)$. If the root nodes of these two trees are states in some transition system, then there is an obvious bisimulation. However, there is no bisimulation between $ab+ac$ and $a(b+c)$.

(ii) Observational equivalence.

DEFINITION 1.3.3. Let p and q be states of some transition system. We define a sequence $\approx_n$ of equivalence relations as follows:

$$\begin{aligned} &p \approx_0 q \quad \text{always} \\ &p \approx_{n+1} q \Leftrightarrow \forall s \in \Sigma^*. \\ &\qquad (i) \quad p \stackrel{s}{\Longrightarrow} p' \Rightarrow \exists q'.q \stackrel{s}{\Longrightarrow} q' \;\&\; p' \approx_n q' \\ &\qquad (ii) \quad q \stackrel{s}{\Longrightarrow} q' \Rightarrow \exists p'.p \stackrel{s}{\Longrightarrow} p' \;\&\; p' \approx_n q'. \end{aligned}$$

We define $pOq \quad \Leftrightarrow \quad \forall n.p \approx_n q$.

Example 1. We present a sequence (S_k, T_k) of pairs of trees in which the nth pair is n-equivalent but not $(n+1)$-equivalent, for all n.

$$\begin{aligned} S_0 &= a\mathit{NIL} & T_0 &= \mathit{NIL} \\ S_{n+1} &= aS_n + aT_n & T_{n+1} &= aS_n \end{aligned}$$

It is easy to check that these pairs have the desired properties.

DEFINITION 1.3.4. (Weak observational equivalence) Let p and q be states in Q as above. Say that p is weakly equivalent to q iff $p \approx_n^W q$ for all n, where $\approx_n^W$ is defined inductively by

$$
\begin{aligned}
p \approx_0^W q & \quad \text{always} \\
p \approx_{n+1}^W q & \Leftrightarrow \forall a \in \Sigma \cup \{\epsilon\}. \\
& (i) \quad p \stackrel{a}{\Longrightarrow} p' \Rightarrow \exists q'.q \stackrel{a}{\Longrightarrow} q' \ \& \ p' \approx_n q' \\
& (ii) \quad q \stackrel{a}{\Longrightarrow} q' \Rightarrow \exists p'.p \stackrel{a}{\Longrightarrow} p' \ \& \ p' \approx_n q'.
\end{aligned}
$$

Weak observational equivalence is obtained by restricting attention at each stage in the construction to sequences of visible actions of length at most one. The relation W of weak observational equivalence is in general weaker than observation equivalence, although, as Milner states, the two relations coincide on image-finite trees. We are not making the assumption that all transition systems are image-finite.

(iv) Failure equivalence.

In the failure set semantics of nondeterministic communicating processes [HBR], the behaviour of a process is described in terms of so-called *failures:* each failure is a pair (s, X) in which s records a possible sequence of visible transitions and X is a set of transitions which the process *may*, as the result of a nondeterministic decision, be incapable of performing on the next step. This leads naturally to a failure equivalence relation on synchronisation trees (see also [B1]).

DEFINITION 1.3.5. The failure set of a synchronisation tree S is

$$\text{failures}(S) = \{(s, X) \mid \exists S'.S \stackrel{s}{\Longrightarrow} S' \ \& \ \forall x \in X \ S' \stackrel{x}{\not\Longrightarrow}\}.$$

We use the abbreviation $S \stackrel{x}{\not\Longrightarrow}$ for $\neg\exists S'(S \stackrel{x}{\Longrightarrow} S')$. The failure equivalence relation is defined as follows:

DEFINITION 1.3.6. Trees S and T are failure equivalent iff failures(S) = failures(T). An extensive discussion of the properties enjoyed by this equivalence relation, and its use in giving a semantics to concurrent processes, can be found in [HBR] and [RB]; fuller accounts are provided in [B2] and [R].

(v) Trace equivalence.

An early model for process semantics was based on the notion of *traces* [H]. A trace is a finite sequence of visible transitions, and two synchronisation trees are trace-equivalent iff they have the same set of possible traces:

DEFINITION 1.3.7. Two trees S and T are trace-equivalent iff

$$\forall s \in \Sigma^*.(\exists S'.S \stackrel{s}{\Longrightarrow} S') \Leftrightarrow (\exists T'.T \stackrel{s}{\Longrightarrow} T').$$

This is a very simple equivalence relation, and coincides with Milner's $\approx_1$ above.

(vi) Logical equivalences.

We present three logics which can be interpreted in state transition systems, and which describe aspects of the behaviour of such systems. The behaviour equivalences induced by these logics are exactly the elementary equivalences for the corresponding models.

These logics are all specializations of *regular trace logic* (Rounds and Gurevich), with which we begin our definitions.

Syntax. The formulas ϕ, ψ, of regular trace logic (RTL) are built up from *constants* T and F, by means of boolean combinations using $\&, \vee$ and $\neg$, and by modal combinations $\forall\alpha\langle\phi\rangle$ and $\forall\alpha[\phi]$. Here α is a regular expression over Σ.

Semantics. We interpret RTL formulas in state transition systems. A *structure* for RTL consists of a transition system $S = (Q, \Sigma, q_0, \rightarrow)$ and a state $q \in Q$. The system S will usually be understood. We define the *satisfaction* relation as follows, by structural induction on the formulas:

$$
\begin{array}{rcl}
q \models T & & \text{always} \\
q \models F & & \text{never} \\
q \models \phi \,\&\, \psi & \Leftrightarrow & q \models \phi \text{ and } q \models \psi \\
q \models \phi \vee \psi & \Leftrightarrow & q \models \phi \text{ or } q \models \psi \\
q \models \neg\phi & \Leftrightarrow & \text{not } q \models \phi \\
q \models \forall\alpha\langle\phi\rangle & \Leftrightarrow & \forall s \in \alpha . \exists q' \, q \stackrel{s}{\Longrightarrow} q' \;\&\; q' \models \phi \\
q \models \forall\alpha[\phi] & \Leftrightarrow & \forall s \in \alpha . \forall q' \, q \stackrel{s}{\Longrightarrow} q' \Rightarrow q' \models \phi
\end{array}
$$

Remarks:

1. α is a regular expression for the syntax, and denotes a regular subset of Σ^* for the semantics.

2. Propositional variables have been omitted. We are interested in purely behavioural properties, and not in the conditions holding of a state.

3. We may define two further modalities:

$$
\begin{array}{rcl}
\exists\alpha\langle\phi\rangle & \equiv & \neg(\forall\alpha[\neg\phi]) \\
\exists\alpha[\phi] & \equiv & \neg(\forall\alpha\langle\neg\phi\rangle)
\end{array}
$$

Clearly,

$$
\begin{array}{rcl}
q \models \exists\alpha\langle\phi\rangle & \Leftrightarrow & \exists s \in \alpha . \exists q' \, q \stackrel{s}{\Longrightarrow} q' \;\&\; q' \models \phi, \\
q \models \exists\alpha[\phi] & \Leftrightarrow & \exists s \in \alpha . \forall q' \, q \stackrel{s}{\Longrightarrow} q' \;\Rightarrow\; q' \models \phi.
\end{array}
$$

DEFINITION 1.3.8. PDL (propositional dynamic logic) is obtained from RTL by omitting the modality $\forall\alpha\langle\cdot\rangle$.

DEFINITION 1.3.9. HML (Hennessy-Milner logic) is obtained from RTL by restricting the sets α used in modalities to be singletons.

Notice that if $\alpha = \{ s \}$ is a singleton set then the existential and universal quantifiers have the same effect. We abbreviate $\forall\{ s \}[\phi]$ and $\exists\{ s \}[\phi]$ to $s[\phi]$ and similarly for the other modality.

We will be interested in the possibility of distinguishing between states of a transition system by the sets of formulas which they satisfy. If L is a subset of the class of RTL formulas, we define L-equivalent states to be states which satisfy precisely the same formulas from L. In the sequel we will use the name L to denote these equivalence relations, where L can be HML, PDL or RTL.

2. Classifying equivalence relations.

In this section we compare the various equivalence relations introduced so far. We consider the following relations on transition systems:

B	bisimulation
O	observational equivalence
W	weak observational equivalence
RTL	
PDL	equivalence w.r.t. formulas of a logic
HML	
F	failure equivalence
T	trace equivalence

We obtain the following diagram, in which the strongest equivalences are at the top:

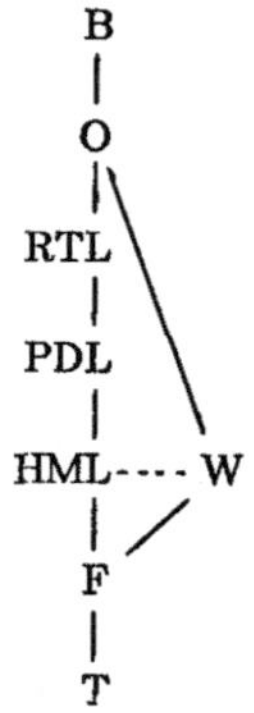

We will show that the equality $HML = W$ holds when Σ is finite. Hennessy and Milner's results established that $B = O = HML = W$ in case all relations are of finite image.

THEOREM 2.1. $B \subseteq O \subseteq RTL \subseteq PDL \subseteq HML \subseteq F \subseteq T$.

Proof. We only prove in detail the inclusions $B \subseteq O \subseteq RTL$. First we indicate briefly the reasons for the final two inclusions in our diagram. The other cases are also straightforward.

($HML \subseteq F \subseteq T$) Trace equivalence is clearly the elementary equivalence induced by the set of formulas of the form $s\langle T\rangle$ of HML, and failure equivalence is characterised similarly by the set of formulas of the form $s\langle\psi\rangle$, where ψ has the form $a_1[F] \,\&\, \ldots a_n[F]$ for some set $\{a_1, \ldots, a_n\} \subseteq \Sigma$. (We adopt the convention that an empty conjunction denotes T.) Thus it follows easily that $HML \subseteq F \subseteq T$.

($B \subseteq O$) To prove that bisimilarity implies observation equivalence, let γ be a bisimulation. We show that $p\gamma q \Rightarrow p \approx_n q$, for all n. We proceed by induction on n. The case $n = 0$ is trivial, since $\approx_0$ is the universal relation. Suppose the result holds for $n = k$. Let $p\gamma q$. If $p \stackrel{s}{\Longrightarrow} p'$, then by bisimilarity of p and q there is a state q' such that $q \stackrel{s}{\Longrightarrow} q'$ and $p'\gamma q'$. By the inductive hypothesis, this implies $p' \approx_k q'$, which is the conclusion we need for $k+1$-equivalence of p and q. The converse (for q) goes through similarly. Thus we have proved by induction that $p\gamma q \Rightarrow \forall n.p \approx_n q$. Thus, $p\gamma q \;\Rightarrow\; pOq$.

($O \subseteq RTL$) For the inclusion $O \subseteq RTL$, we argue by induction on the length of formulas, showing that

$$\forall k.(p \approx_k q \;\Rightarrow\; \forall\phi(\text{length}(\phi) \leq k \Rightarrow (p \models \phi \Leftrightarrow q \models \phi)))$$

Again the base case is trivial. Assume the result for length k. Let ϕ have length $k+1$, and assume that $p \approx_{k+1} q$. There are several cases, depending on the structure of ϕ.

Case 1: ϕ is $\neg\psi$, with $\text{length}(\psi) \leq k$. In this case we use the fact that $p \approx_{k+1} q \Rightarrow p \approx_k q$, easily established by induction. Then we have by inductive hypothesis that $p \models \psi \Leftrightarrow q \models \psi$, giving also $p \models \neg\psi \Leftrightarrow q \models \neg\psi$, as required.

Case 2: ϕ is $\forall\alpha\langle\psi\rangle$, with $\text{length}(\psi) \leq k$. Suppose $p \models \phi$ and let $s \in \alpha$. Then there is a state p' such that $p \stackrel{s}{\Longrightarrow} p'$ and $p' \models \psi$. Since we are assuming that $p \approx_{k+1} q$, there is also a q' such that $q \stackrel{s}{\Longrightarrow} q'$ and $p' \approx_k q'$. By the inductive hypothesis, we must have $q' \models \psi$. Since we chose s arbitrarily in α this argument shows that $q \models \forall\alpha\langle\psi\rangle$, as required. The converse $(q \models \phi \Rightarrow p \models \phi)$ is similar.

Case 3: ϕ is $\forall\alpha[\psi]$, with $\text{length}(\psi) \leq k$. Suppose $p \models \phi$. We want $q \models \phi$. Let $s \in \alpha$ and suppose $q \stackrel{s}{\Longrightarrow} q'$, for some q'. Then we know there is a state p' such that $p \stackrel{s}{\Longrightarrow} p'$ and $q' \approx_k p'$, because p and q are assumed to be $k+1$-equivalent. Since $p \models \phi$, we know that $p' \models \psi$. By the inductive hypothesis, $q' \models \psi$. This gives $q \models \forall\alpha[\psi]$,b as required. The converse is again similar. ∎

The rest of this section is devoted to establishing that the inclusions of Theorem 2.1 are proper.

THEOREM 2.2. *Observation equivalence properly includes bisimulation, $O \supset B$.*

Proof. We find U and V which are observation equivalent but not bisimilar. To begin, let us define some auxiliary trees. Let (S_n, T_n) be a sequence of pairs in which the nth pair is $\approx_{n-1}$ equivalent but not $\approx_n$ equivalent, for each n. An example of such a sequence was given in the previous section. If S is an ST and $s \in \Sigma^*$, we write sS for the tree obtained by prefixing a path s to the root of S. Let $c \in \Sigma$. Define for each $i \geq 0$,

$$U_i = \sum_{j=1}^{\infty} c^j T_j + \sum_{j=1}^{i-1} c^j S_j$$

and let

$$U_\omega = \sum_{j=1}^{\infty} c^j T_j + \sum_{j=1}^{\infty} c^j S_j.$$

Let $U = \sum_{i=1}^{\infty} aU_i$ and $V = U + aU_\omega$. Now we show that

$$(\dagger) \qquad \forall i.(U_i \not\approx_{i+1} U_\omega \ \&\ U_{i+1} \approx_i U_\omega)$$

This is easy to establish. For each i, $U_\omega \stackrel{c^i}{\Longrightarrow} S_i$, but the subtree S_i is missing from U_i. In fact, if $U_i \stackrel{c^i}{\Longrightarrow} T$ and $T \approx_i S_i$ then the only possibility would be that $T = T_i$, which cannot happen by construction. On the other hand, for $j \geq i$, we know that $S_j \approx_i T_j$. Thus, $(c^j S_j + c^j T_j) \approx_i c^j T_j$ for each such j. It follows that

$$U_\omega \approx_i (\sum_{j=1}^{\infty} c^j T_j + \sum_{j=1}^{i} c^j S_j) = U_{i+1}.$$

This shows that $(\dagger)$ holds. To see why $(\dagger)$ implies the desired conclusion, suppose for a contradiction that U and V are bisimilar. Let γ be a bisimulation such that $U \gamma V$. Since $V \stackrel{a}{\Longrightarrow} U_\omega$, by construction of U there must be an i such that $U \stackrel{a}{\Longrightarrow} U_i$ and $U_i \gamma U_\omega$. But this implies $U_i B U_\omega$, which contradicts Theorem 1, since we have $U_i \not\approx_i U_\omega$, by $(\dagger)$. Thus U and V are not bisimilar. On the other hand, $U \approx_i V$ for each i. Indeed, let i be fixed and let $V \stackrel{s}{\Longrightarrow} V'$ for some $s \in \Sigma^*$. We show that U has a similar transition sequence to some U' with $U' \approx_{i-1} V'$. The only interesting case is when the transition of V enters the subtree U_ω, clearly. In this case, s must have the form at, and $U_\omega \stackrel{t}{\Longrightarrow} V'$. By $(\dagger)$, $U_{i+1} \approx_i U_\omega$. Therefore $U \stackrel{a}{\Longrightarrow} U_{i+1} \stackrel{t}{\Longrightarrow} U'$ for some subtree U' of U_{i+1} with $U' \approx_{i-1} V'$. This is the conclusion needed for $\approx_i$-equivalence of U and V. So U and V are observation equivalent but not bisimilar, as required. ∎

Next we investigate the logical equivalences.

THEOREM 2.3. *RTL properly contains O: $RTL \supset O$.*

Proof. The proof of this theorem is quite intricate, and is deferred until we have established some definitions and lemmas.

For any set $L \subseteq \Sigma^*$, we let S^L be the synchronisation tree determined by L: having one branch for each $s \in L$;

$$S^L = \sum_{s \in L} sNIL.$$

When L is a singleton $\{ s \}$ it determines the tree $sNIL$ with a single branch; we will identify this tree with the string s where there is no possibility of confusion.

LEMMA 2.4. *Let $\phi \in RTL$. Then the set $L(\phi) = \{ s \in \Sigma^* \mid sNIL \models \phi \}$ is regular.*

Proof. Induction on the structure of RTL formulas. The base case, when ϕ is either T or F, is trivial: $L(T) = \Sigma^*$, $L(F) = \emptyset$. The boolean combinations go through because regular sets are closed under complement, intersection and union:

$$L(\neg\phi) = \Sigma^* - L(\phi),$$
$$L(\phi \,\&\, \psi) = L(\phi) \cap L(\psi),$$
$$L(\phi \vee \psi) = L(\phi) \cup L(\psi).$$

If α denotes an infinite regular set, then $L(\forall\alpha[\phi]) = L(\forall\alpha\langle\phi\rangle) = \emptyset$, because each tree under consideration here is finite. Otherwise, let α denote the finite set $\{ s_1, \ldots, s_k \}$. Then $L(\forall\alpha\langle\phi\rangle) = \bigcap_{i=1}^{k} s_i L(\phi)$. The same holds for the other modality, because the trees here have only a single branch. That concludes the proof of Lemma 1. ∎

LEMMA 2.5. *Suppose α denotes a regular set not containing the empty sequence. Let ϕ be of the form $\forall\alpha[\psi]$ or $\exists\alpha[\psi]$. Then for all L, if $S(L) \models \phi$ then $S(L') \models \phi$, for all $L' \subseteq L$.*

Proof. Routine application of the definitions. ∎

Now consider the language

$$K = \{ a^{n^2} b^{n+j} \mid n \geq 1, 0 \leq j \leq n \}.$$

Let $W = S^K$, and for each pair n, j let W_j^n be the tree obtained from W by removing the branch $a^{n^2} b^{n+j}$. Notice that K is not a regular language. We will use the properties of this set in constructing two trees which cannot be distinguished by any RTL formula, but which are not observation equivalent. First we establish an important property of the synchronisation tree W determined by K.

LEMMA 2.6. *Let ϕ be an RTL formula. If $W \models \phi$ then for all but finitely many pairs n, j the tree W_j^n also satisfies ϕ.*

Proof. First put ϕ into *monotonic form,* by moving all the negations through to the inside. Then ϕ has one of the forms:

$$T,\ F,\ (\psi \vee \theta),\ (\psi \,\&\, \theta),$$
$$\exists\alpha\langle\psi\rangle,\ \exists\alpha[\psi],\ \forall\alpha\langle\psi\rangle,\ \forall\alpha[\psi],$$

where ψ and θ are also in monotonic form. We proceed by induction on the structure of monotonic formulas. The base case and the boolean combinations are straightforward. The first three modalities are simple, with the help of Lemma 2.5. The final case is when ϕ is $\forall\alpha\langle\psi\rangle$. Notice that the structure of W allows us to assume without loss of generality that α does not contain the empty string, as W has no nontrivial empty transitions. We therefore assume $\epsilon \not\in \alpha$. Moreover, we claim that without loss of generality we can assume that $\alpha \subseteq a^+$. To show this, first notice that because $W \models \forall\alpha\langle\psi\rangle$, every string in α is a prefix of some string in K; thus $\alpha \subseteq a^* b^*$. Suppose that $\alpha \cap a^* b^+$ is infinite. For each n, the number of strings of the form $a^{n^2} b^j$ which are prefixes of members of K is finite, because j can be at most $2n$. Therefore, the set

$$\{ t \in a^* b \mid \exists u (tu \in \alpha \cap a^* b^+) \}$$

is an infinite regular subset of $\{ a^{n^2} b \mid n \geq 0 \}$, which is impossible. Therefore $\alpha \cap a^* b^+$ is finite, say $\{ t_1, \ldots t_m \}$. We may therefore write

$$\forall\alpha\langle\psi\rangle \equiv \forall\beta\langle\psi\rangle \,\&\, t_1\langle\psi\rangle \,\&\, \ldots t_m\langle\psi\rangle,$$

where $\beta \subseteq \alpha^+$. The claim follows using the inductive reasoning for the & connective.

Now suppose the conclusion of Lemma 2.6 to be false for $\forall\alpha\langle\psi\rangle$, where $\alpha \subseteq a^+$. Then $W \models \forall\alpha\langle\psi\rangle$, but for infinitely many pairs n, j $W_j^n \models \neg\forall\alpha\langle\psi\rangle$. Let $s = a^{n^2} b^{n+j}$ be a trace corresponding to such a pair. For each such s there must therefore be a prefix $t \leq s$ such that $t \in \alpha$ and $W_j^n \models t[\neg\psi]$. This t must be a prefix of s because $W \models t\langle\psi\rangle$ and W_j^n differs from W only in the s-branch. We may therefore write $s = tu$, where $t \in a^*$ and $u \models \psi$. Furthermore, for any $w \neq s$ in K if $w = tv$ for some v then $v \models \neg\psi$.

Recall that $L(\psi)$ is a regular language. Let k be the number of states of a FSA accepting this language. Choose an $s \in K$ as above but such that it has the form $a^{n^2}b^{n+j}$ with $n > 2k$. Decomposing s into tu as above, the number i of b's in u must satisfy

$$n \leq i \leq 2n,$$

because $0 \leq j \leq n$. Since $u \in L(\psi)$, the FSA accepting u must repeat a state while reading across the b's. Further, this happens in at most p steps, where $p \leq k$. We then have

$$u = a^r b^i,$$

for some r, and hence $a^r b^{i-p} \in L(\psi)$. If $i-p \geq n$ we have a contradiction, because then $ta^r b^{i-p} \in K$, and $a^r b^{i-p} \models \neg\psi$, which is impossible. But if $i-p < n$ we have

$$i + p < n + 2p \leq n + 2k \leq 2n,$$

because $2k \leq n$. Therefore $a^r b^{i+p} \in L(\psi)$ and $ta^r b^{i+p} \in K$. Therefore $a^r b^{i+p} \models \neg\psi$, again a contradiction. That completes the proof of Lemma 2.6. ∎

Now we are ready to prove Theorem 2.2. Define the two trees

$$U = \sum_{n,j} aW_j^n,$$
$$V = U + aW.$$

It is clear that $U \not\approx_2 V$, because $V \overset{a}{\Longrightarrow} W$, and for each n, j pair we have $W_j^n \not\approx_1 W$. So U and V are not observation equivalent. We claim that U and V satisfy precisely the same RTL formulas:

$$\forall \phi \in RTL.\, (U \models \phi \;\Leftrightarrow\; V \models \phi).$$

The proof is again by induction on the structure of ϕ. The base case and the boolean connectives are trivial. We consider the cases $\phi = \exists\alpha\langle\psi\rangle$ and $\phi = \exists\alpha[\psi]$ in detail. The other modalities can be deduced using the argument for negation.

Case 1. Let $\phi = \exists\alpha\langle\psi\rangle$. Clearly if $U \models \phi$ then so does V. Conversely, if $V \models \phi$ then choose $t \in \alpha$ and V' such that $V \overset{t}{\Longrightarrow} V'$ and $V' \models \psi$. If $t = \epsilon$ then we must have $V = V'$, and $V \models \psi$; then by inductive hypothesis, $U \models \psi$, from which we get $U \models \phi$. The only other possibility is that $t = au$ for some u. If $V \overset{a}{\Longrightarrow} W_j^n \overset{u}{\Longrightarrow} V'$ there is no problem, because U has a similar subtree. Suppose that $V \overset{a}{\Longrightarrow} W \overset{u}{\Longrightarrow} V'$. Then $W \models u\langle\psi\rangle$, so by Lemma 2.6 there is a W_j^n also satisfying this formula. Hence, $U \models au\langle\psi\rangle$ and $U \models \phi$.

Case 2. Let $\phi = \forall\alpha\langle\psi\rangle$. Consider the possibilities for $s \in \alpha$. In each case we must show that U has an s-branch leading to a subtree where ψ holds. If $s = \epsilon$ we can use the inductive hypothesis. If s is traceable into some W_j^n there is no problem, because U has a corresponding transition. If s is traceable into W, then $s = at$ for some t which must be a prefix of a string w in K. If $t = \epsilon$ then $s = a$ and $W \models \psi$; by Lemma 2.6 there is a pair n, j with $W_j^n \models \psi$. Otherwise, t is a prefix of some string in K, and for all but one pair n, j the tree W_j^n has a branch t. In each case we have shown that U has a corresponding s-branch. That completes the proof. ∎

THEOREM 2.7. ***RTL is properly contained in PDL.***

Proof. We give only an example to show that the inclusion cannot be reversed. The proof that PDL cannot distinguish the two trees follows the lines of Theorem 2.2 but is much easier. Define

$$S_n = \sum_{i=1}^{n} b^i NIL,$$
$$S_\omega = \sum_{i=1}^{\infty} b^i NIL.$$

Let U and V be the trees

$$U = \sum_{n=1}^{\infty} aS_n,$$
$$V = U + aS_\omega.$$

Then the RTL formula $a\langle\forall b^+\langle T\rangle\rangle$ is satisfied by V but not U, since only V has an a-branch to a place where arbitrarily many B-transitions can be made. (Here we have used the notation b^+ for $b^*-\{\epsilon\}$.) However, all PDL formulas agree on U and V. The relevant lemma is: for any PDL formula ϕ, if $S_\omega \models \phi$ then for all but finitely many n $S_n \models \phi$. ∎

THEOREM 2.8. *PDL properly is contained in HML.*

Proof. Again we exhibit an example. Let $U = \sum_{i\geq 1} a^i bNIL$, and $V = U + a^\omega NIL$. Then the PDL formula $a[\exists a^*\langle b\langle T\rangle\rangle]$ is satisfied by U but not V, because V has an a-branch to a place where no future b-transitions are possible. However, all HML formulas agree on U and V, because if ψ is an HML formula and $a^\omega \models \psi$, then $a^n \models \psi$ also holds for all but finitely many n. ∎

Theorem 2.8 will also follow from the fact that U and V are weakly observation equivalent, once we have established that $W = HML$. Hennessy and Milner proved this result in the case when the underlying system has the *finite-image property:* for each $a \in \Delta$ and each $q \in Q$ the set

$$\{\, q' \mid q \xrightarrow{a} q' \,\}$$

is finite. They also showed the identity $HML = B$ under the finite-image hypothesis. We now show that the result $W = HML$ still holds when the finite-image hypothesis is not assumed, provided we assume that Σ is finite. Since we are allowing infinitely branching systems, finiteness of Σ does not, of course, imply the finite-image property. Our proof makes use of normal-form arguments for HML which are of independent interest. Indeed, these normal form results can be used to show that a natural pseudometric structure on synchronisation trees induces a compact metric topology on the set of W-equivalence classes (see [GR]).

THEOREM 2.9. *If Σ is finite, then $HML \subseteq W$.*

Proof. Let $\equiv$ denote the relation of logical equivalence between HML formulas:

$$\phi \equiv \psi \;\Leftrightarrow\; \forall p\,(p \models \phi \;\Leftrightarrow\; p \models \psi).$$

Define the ***depth*** of an HML formula as follows:

$$\begin{aligned} \text{depth}(T) &= \text{depth}(F) = 0 \\ \text{depth}(\neg\phi) &= \text{depth}(\phi) \\ \text{depth}(\phi \vee \psi) &= \text{depth}(\phi \,\&\, \psi) = \max(\text{depth}(\phi), \text{depth}(\psi)) \\ \text{depth}(a\langle\phi\rangle) &= 1 + \text{depth}(\phi). \end{aligned}$$

The depth of a formula is the maximum number of nested modalities. We let $H_k = \{\,\theta \mid \text{depth}(\theta) \leq k\,\}$, for each $k \geq 0$. Then for each k there is an integer E_k such that $\equiv$ partitions H_k into at most E_k equivalence classes. To show this, we give an algorithm for converting an arbitrary $\phi \in H_k$ into a disjunctive normal form ϕ^* such that distinct normal forms are logically inequivalent and the number of distinct normal forms is less than or equal to E_k. We use induction on depth. Every HML formula is either ***basic,*** which we define to mean of the form T or F or $a\langle\psi\rangle$ for some ψ, or else a boolean combination of such basic formulas. It is easy to see that a depth 0 fomula is logically equivalent to either T or F, so that H_0 is partitioned into two distinct equivalence classes. We may, therefore, put $E_0 = 2$. For the inductive step, let $\phi \in H_{k+1}-H_k$, and suppose that H_k is partitioned into E_k equivalence classes. Let the modal subformulas of ϕ be $a_i\langle\theta_i\rangle$; each a_i can be assumed to belong to the set $\Sigma \cup \{\epsilon\}$, and each θ_i has lower depth than ϕ. Put each θ_i into normal form. There are at most E_k possible normal forms for each θ_i, and we may replace logically equivalent formulas. We can then treat ϕ as a propositional combination of at most $m = E_k \times (|\Sigma| + 1)$ variables, and as such put it into disjunctive normal form. In order to guarantee that H_{k+1} has no more than E_{k+1} equivalence classes, we may take $E_{k+1} = 2^{2^m}$. Now we prove by induction on k that

$$(1)\quad \forall k.\forall p,q\,(p \not\approx_k^W q \Rightarrow \exists\phi(\text{depth}(\phi) \leq k \;\&\; p \models \phi \;\&\; q \models \neg\phi)).$$

The base case is trivial, as we may choose $\phi = T$. Assume the result for k, and suppose $p \not\approx_{k+1}^W q$. Then for some $a \in \Sigma \cup \{\epsilon\}$ there is a p' for which $p \stackrel{a}{\Longrightarrow} p'$ and p' is not $\approx_k^W$ to any q' such that $q \stackrel{a}{\Longrightarrow} q'$. Let the set of possible a-derivatives of q be $\{ q_i \mid i \in I \}$. Notice that we are not assuming this set to be finite. By hypothesis there are distinguishing formulas θ_i, each of depth at most k, such that for each $i \in I$ we have

$$p' \models \neg\theta_i \;\&\; q_i \models \theta_i.$$

For each $i \in I$ let θ_i^* be a normal form logically equivalent to θ_i. Note that $\text{depth}(\theta_i) = \text{depth}(\theta_i^*) \leq k$. Only finitely many of these normal forms can be logically inequivalent, say $\theta_1^*, \ldots, \theta_m^*$. Let $\phi = a\langle\theta_1^* \;\&\; \ldots \;\&\; \theta_m^*\rangle$. Then $p \models \neg\phi$ and $q \models \phi$. That completes the proof. ▮

COROLLARY 2.10. *If Σ is finite, $HML = W$.*

Proof. The inclusion $W \subseteq HML$ follows by a straightforward induction, using the converse to the inductive hypothesis of Theorem 2.8. This does not depend on the finiteness hypothesis. ▮

3. Conclusions.

We have investigated the descriptive power of three programming logics by examining the elementary equivalence relations induced on nondeterministic state transition systems by the logics. These equivalence relations have also been examined in the context of some other natural behavioural equivalence relations from the literature. An exact characterisation of a behavioural equivalence as the elementary equivalence induced by a particular logic provides an indication of the essential semantic properties of the equivalence; equally, delineating the relationships between the various existing equivalences serves to illuminate their differences.

We have shown that in general the three logical equivalences are not as discriminating as other natural behavioural equivalences such as Milner's observation equivalence, but are themselves finer than failure equivalence and trace equivalence. These latter two relations are, in fact, characterizable as the elementary equivalences generated from restricted sets of logical formulas.

We finish with a remark on complexity. If we interpret the logics in nondeterministic finite state automata, the finite-branching condition holds, and all of the logical equivalence relations coincide with observation equivalence and the bisimulation relation; moreover, it can be shown that these equivalences are decidable in polynomial time. In contrast, failure equivalence of finite automata turns out to be a PSPACE-complete problem.

4. Acknowledgements.

The research of the first author was supported in part by the Defense Advanced Research Projects Agency, ARPA Order No. 3597, under contract F33615-81-K-1539. The second author was supported by NSF Grant No. MCS-8102286.

We would like to thank Joyce Friedman for suggesting the proof of Theorem 2.9. Our original proof was much more complicated.

5. References.

[B1] Brookes, S.D., On the relationship of CCS and CSP, this volume.

[B2] Brookes, S.D., A Model for Communicating Sequential Processes, Ph.D. thesis, University of Oxford (submitted 1983).

[CH] Campbell, R., and Habermann, N., The Specification of Process Synchronization by Path Expressions, Springer LNCS Vol. 16.

[GR] Golson, W.G., and Rounds, W.C., Connections between Two Theories of Concurrency: Metric Spaces and Synchronisation Trees, Technical Report, Computing Research Laboratory, University of Michigan (January 1983)

[H] Hoare, C.A.R., A model for Communicating Sequential Processes, Technical Report PRG-22, University of Oxford, Programming Research Group (1981).

[HBR] Hoare, C.A.R., Brookes, S.D., and Roscoe, A.W., A Theory of Communicating Sequential Processes, Technical Report PRG-16, Oxford University, Programming Research Group (1981).

[HKP] Harel, D., Kozen, D., and Parikh, R., Process Logic: Expressiveness, Decidability and Completeness Proceedings of IEEE Symposium on Foundations of Computer Science (1980).

[HM] Hennessy, M., and Milner, R., On Observing Nondeterminism and Concurrency, Proc. 7th ICALP, Springer LNCS Vol. 85 (1980).

[K] Keller, R., Formal Verification of Parallel Programs, CACM 19, Vol. 7 (July 1976).

[M] Milner, R., A Calculus of Communicating Systems, Springer LNCS Vol. 92.

[O] Ogden, W.F., Private communication.

[P] Park, D.M.R., Concurrency and Automata on Infinite Sequences, Computer Science Department, University of Warwick.

[Pn] Pnueli, A., The Temporal Logic of Programs, Proceedings of IEEE Symposium on Foundations of Computer Science (1977).

[RS] Rabin, M.O., and Scott, D.S., Finite Automata and their Decision Problems, IBM J. Res. 3:2 (1959).

[R] Roscoe, A.W., A Mathematical Theory of Communicating Processes, Ph.D. thesis, Oxford University (1982).

[RB] Rounds, W.C., and Brookes, S.D., Possible Futures, Acceptances, Refusals, and Communicating Processes, Proc. 22nd IEEE Symposium on Foundations of Computer Science (October 1981).

[W] Wolper, P., Temporal Logic can be more expressive, Proc. 22nd IEEE Symposium on Foundations of Computer Science.

Lower Bounds for Constant Depth Circuits for Prefix Problems

Ashok K. Chandra (†)
Steven Fortune (†)
Richard Lipton (††)

Abstract

A prefix-or circuit has n inputs and n outputs; the ith output is the OR of the first i inputs. A prefix-carry circuit has $2n$ inputs, interpreted as two n-bit numbers, and n outputs; the ith output is the carry in the ith position of the sum of the two numbers. We show a nonlinear lower bound for constant-depth, unbounded-fanin implementations of prefix-or. However, with negation, linear size circuits are possible. For prefix-carry, we show nonlinear lower bounds for arbitrary circuits. In both cases the lower bounds exhibit a size/depth tradeoff: the circuit size must be at least $\Omega(nf_d^{-1}(n))$ for depth a constant times d. Here the functions f_d form an increasing hierarchy coextensive with the primitive recursive functions. The lower bounds match the known upper bounds for these problems, to within a constant factor for depth.

1 Introduction

Most models of parallel computation can be characterized as being bounded fanin. In a bounded fanin parallel computation, at each step each process computes a new value, where the value computed depends on previously computed values of only a bounded number of other processes. By contrast, in unbounded fanin parallelism the value computed by a process at a particular step can depend on the values previously computed by arbitrarily many other processes.

At least two models of unbounded fanin parallelism have been proposed: combinational circuits, where the AND and OR gates are allowed to have arbitrary fanin, and parallel random access machines with multiple concurrent writes to global memory [G, Vis, SV]. These two models have been shown to be equivalent, in the following sense[CSV]. An algorithm on the parallel random access machines can be transformed to a circuit, and conversely, with number of processors corresponding to size of circuit and running time corresponding to depth of circuit. Furthermore, both measures can be preserved simultaneously.

With bounded fanin parallelism, it is usually possible to show that at least logarithmic time is necessary to examine all inputs, though the proof may be nontrivial[CD,R]. With unbounded fanin parallelism it is often possible to devise sublogarithmic and even constant time algorithms for various computational problems.

(†) Mathematical Sciences Department, IBM T.J. Watson Research Center, Yorktown Heights, NY 10598

(††)Department of EECS, Princeton University, Princeton, NJ 08544. Research supported by DARPA contract N00014082-K-0549.

However, the speedup may not be without cost: an algorithm requiring a linear number of processors in logarithmic depth may become nonlinear when executed in constant depth.

The most striking example of an increase in size is the lower bound due to Furst, Sipser, and Saxe [FSS] They show that any constant depth implementation of the parity function must require more than polynomial size. Of course, parity can be implemented using linear circuitry in logarithmic depth.

We continue the examination of lower bounds for constant depth, unbounded fanin circuits. We are motivated by constructions for various prefix problems that are almost linear in size. For example, the prefix-or problem is "given n inputs, produce n outputs, where the ith output is the OR of the first i inputs." It is possible to construct monotone circuits for prefix-or that are of depth $2d$ and size $O(nf_d^{-1}(n))$ [CFL], where f_d is the dth function in a natural hierarchy that is coextensive with the primitive recursive functions. Monotone circuits of similiar size exist for prefix-carry, the function that indicates the carries in the sum of two n-bit numbers. Clearly it is possible to construct a circuit for the sum of two n-bit numbers from a circuit for computing carries, adding only constant depth and $O(n)$ new gates. Of course, addition is itself not monotone and cannot be implemented using monotone circuits.

We show that bounded depth monotone circuits for these prefix problems must be nonlinear in size. In fact, any monotone implementation of prefix-or of depth $d+1$ must be of size at least $O(nf_d^{-1}(n))$. Hence the lower and upper bounds are tight to within a constant factor for the depth. A similiar bound applies for monotone implementations of prefix carry and other prefix functions.

What happens with negation? For the problem of prefix-or, we show how to construct linear size circuits of constant depth. For prefix carry, however, linear size circuits are not possible. We show that any circuit for prefix-carry must contain a graph called a weak superconcentrator. Dolev, Dwork, Pippenger, and Wigderson[DDPW] have recently shown that weak superconcentrators of constant depth must be nonlinear in size, in fact must have size at least $\Omega(nf_d^{-1}(n))$ for depth $2d$. Hence the lower and upper bounds for prefix-carry match to within a constant factor for the depth, even for circuits with negation.

2. Preliminaries

A *boolean circuit* is a directed acyclic graph whose nodes of indegree 0 are *inputs* and whose other nodes are *gates*. Input nodes are labelled with variables $\{x_1,x_2,\ldots\}$. Gate nodes are labelled with boolean functions; the usual set is $\wedge$, $\vee$, and $\neg$. Nodes labelled with $\neg$ have indegree one; nodes labelled with $\wedge$ and $\vee$ may have arbitrary indegree; the indegree of other nodes depends upon the function with which they are labelled. Certain nodes are selected as output nodes; with each output node is associated a boolean function in the obvious way. The *size* of a circuit is the number of edges in it. The *depth* of a circuit is the length of a longest path from an input node to an output node.

A *problem* is an infinite family of multi-input boolean functions, at most one function for each number of inputs. A problem P is *reducible* to problem Q if P has a constant-depth, linear size circuit constructed using gates labelled with $\wedge$, $\vee$, $\neg$, functions from Q, and the constants 0 and 1. Problem P is *monotone reducible* to

Q if not gates are unnecessary. Problems P and Q are *equivalent* if P is reducible to Q and Q is reducible to P; similiarly, problems P and Q are *monotone equivalent* if the reducibilities are monotone.

We remark that this reducibility should properly be called "constant depth linear size arbitrary nesting" reducibility. Other reducibilities include constant depth truth table reducibility [CSV], where the circuit size may be polynomial but gates from Q may not be nested, and projection reducibility [SV], where no additional circuitry is allowed, but inputs may be identified or fixed at 0 or 1.

The *threshold-k function* is the function of n inputs that has value one exactly if at least k inputs have value 1. The *prefix-threshold-k function* has n inputs and n outputs; the ith output is the threshold-k function of the first i inputs. The *prefix-or function* is prefix-threshold-1.

The *addition function* has $2n$ inputs $x_1,\dots,x_n,y_1,\dots,y_n$, and $n+1$ outputs; these are the $n+1$ bit sum of $x_1x_2\dots x_n$ and $y_1y_2\dots y_n$. The *carry function* has the same inputs as addition and has value 1 if the sum of $x_1x_2\dots x_n$ and $y_1y_2\dots y_n$ is at least 2^n, that is, there is a carry out. The *prefix carry function* also has $2n$ inputs $x_1,\dots,x_n,y_1,\dots,y_n$ and has n outputs; the ith output is the carry function of $x_1,\dots,x_i,y_1,\dots,y_i$.

Proposition 2.1

1. Prefix-or is monotone equivalent to prefix-threshold-k, for any k.
2. Addition is equivalent to prefix carry.
3. Prefix-or is monotone reducible to prefix carry.

Proof:

Parts 2 and 3 are trivial. For part 1, first note that a prefix-or circuit can be obtained from a prefix-threshold-k circuit by fixing the first k-1 inputs to one; hence prefix-or is reducible to prefix-threshold-k. For the converse, we construct prefix-threshold-2 circuits from circuits for prefix-or; the case for arbitrary k is similiar. Compute $p_1,\dots,p_n$ as the prefix-or of $x_1,\dots,x_n$. Now compute $z_i = x_i \wedge p_{i-1}$, for $i = 2,\dots,n$ and $q_2,\dots,q_n$ as the prefix-or of $z_2,\dots,z_n$. Now $q_2,\dots,q_n$ are the prefix-threshold-2 of $x_1,\dots,x_n$.

□

How big are constant depth circuits for prefix-or and prefix-carry? We define a family of functions f_i, $i = 1,2,\dots,$ as follows.

$$f_1(n) = 2^n$$
$$f_{i+1} = f_i^{(n)}(2)$$

where $g^{(n)}$ is the n-fold iterate of g. It is clear that each f_i is monotone increasing and that $f_{i+1}(n) \geq f_i(n) \geq 2^n$. Each of these functions is primitive recursive and the function $f_\omega(n) = f_n(n)$ grows as Ackermann's function, that is, it majorizes the primitive recursive functions. The inverse of a monotone increasing function g, g^{-1}, is defined by $g^{-1}(n) =$ the least x so that $g(x) \geq n$.

Theorem 2.2 [CFL] There are circuits of size $O(nf_d^{-1}(n))$ and depth $2d$ that compute prefix-or. There are circuits of size $O(nf_d^{-1}(n)$ and depth $6d + 6$ that compute prefix carry.

3. Lower bounds

This section contains the lower bounds for prefix circuits. First we consider monotone circuits; we demonstrate a lower bound for prefix-or and prefix-carry by showing a lower bound on the size of prefix graphs. Then we consider circuits with negation. It turns out to be possible to implement prefix-or in constant depth and linear size. Prefix-carry, however, is still nonlinear. The lower bound proof for prefix-carry depends on recently discovered lower bounds for constant-depth weak superconcetrators[DDPW]; these are graphs with slightly weaker connectivity properties than superconcentrators[GG, Val].

A *prefix graph of size n* is a directed acyclic graph with n vertices of indegree 0, called inputs, and n vertices of outdegree 0, called outputs. Both the inputs and the outputs are numbered from 1 to n. For each i and j, $1 \leq i,j \leq n$, there is a directed path from input i to output j exactly if $i \leq j$. The *depth* of a prefix graph is the length of a longest path from an input vertex to an output vertex. The *size* of a prefix graph is the number of edges in it. It is possible to construct prefix graphs of depth $2d$ and size $O(nf_d^{-1}(n))$ [CFL].

Note that a circuit for prefix-or is exactly a prefix graph with vertices labelled with OR gates. This correspondence will be exploited for the lower bound proof.

Lemma 3.1 A prefix graph of size n and depth d requires at least $O(nf_{d-1}^{-1}(n))$ edges.

Proof: We begin by making some observations about the structure of prefix graphs.

First, we can assume that the prefix graph is a level graph. The *level* of a vertex is the length of a longest path to it from an input. In a *level graph*, every edge is directed from a vertex at level i to a vertex at level $i+1$. If in a prefix graph some edge is directed from a vertex v at level i to a vertex at level $j>i+1$, then we can create a new vertex w at level $i+1$, direct an edge from v to w, and replace edges directed from v to vertices at levels greater than $i+1$ by edges directed from w. Performing this modification as much as possible makes the prefix graph into a level graph and only multiplies its size by d, a constant. By a similiar argument we can assume every output is at level d.

Second, at each level l and for each i between 1 and n there must be a unique vertex reachable from input i but not input $i+1$; we call this vertex *vertex i at level l*. To see this, notice that a simple inductive argument shows that at each level there must be at least one vertex reachable from input i but not input $i+1$. Then if in fact there are two such vertices, they can be merged.

Third, notice that all edges are directed from "left to right," that is, if there is an edge between vertex i at level l and vertex j at level $l+1$, then $j \geq i$. Also, there is always an edge between vertex i at level l and vertex i at level $l+1$.

Finally, notice that each block of a prefix graph is itself a prefix graph. A block is the subgraph whose vertices are the vertices i at at all levels, where the index i ranges over a consecutive sequence $k, k+1, \ldots, l$, for some k and l between 1 and n, and whose edges are the connecting edges.

The proof now proceeds by induction on d. The case $d=1$ corresponds to a size of $O(n^2)$ and is trivial.

Case 1 *d=2*.

This step is simpler than the general inductive step and is handled differently. We show that the number of edges in a prefix graph of depth 2 and size *n*, *e(n)*, satisfies the recurrence $e(n) \geq 2e(n/2) + n/2$. The lower bound $\Omega(n \log n)$ follows.

Partition the graph into two blocks, the first with the vertices $1,2,\ldots,n/2$; the second with vertices $n/2 + 1,\ldots,n$. Each such block is a prefix graph of size *n/2* and must have *e(n/2)* edges; all these edges are within block boundaries. We show that there must be at least *n/2* edges that cross block boundaries; the recurrence and lower bound follow.

Consider the output vertices in the second block. The first case is that every such output vertex is incident to some vertex at level 1 in the first block. Then *n/2* edges cross block boundaries. The second case is that some output vertex *y* is incident to only vertices at level 1 in the second block. Then every input in the first block must be incident to one of the vertices in the second block that is incident to *y*. Thus *n/2* edges cross block boundaries.

Case 2 The inductive step, *d>2*.

We show that the number of edges in a prefix graph of size *n* and depth *d*, *e(n)*, satisfies the recurrence $e(n) \geq (n/f_{d-2}^{-1}(n))e(f_{d-2}^{-1}(n)) \; + \; O(n)$. From this it follows that $e(n)$ is $\Omega(nf_{d-1}^{-1}(n))$.

The graph is partitioned into $n/f_{d-2}^{-1}(n)$ blocks each of size $f_{d-2}^{-1}(n)$. Each block solves a prefix problem of size $f_{d-2}^{-1}(n)$ and hence must have $f_{d-2}^{-1}(n))$ edges within block boundaries. To obtain the recurrence we show that there must be $O(n)$ edges that cross block boundaries.

An output vertex is *local* if all its immediate predecessors are vertices in the same block; otherwise it is *nonlocal*. A block is *local* if some output vertex within it is local.

Case 2a There are $1/2 \; n/f_{d-2}^{-1}(n)$ nonlocal blocks.

Each vertex in a nonlocal block has an incident edge that crosses block boundaries; all these edges are distinct. Hence there must be at least $(1/2 \; n/f_{d-2}^{-1}(n)) \; (f_{d-2}^{-1}(n)) \; = \; n/2$ such edges.

Case 2b There are $1/2 \; n/f_{d-2}^{-1}(n)$ local blocks.

Clearly there are at least $1/2 \; n/f_{d-2}^{-1}(n)$ local output vertices. Consider the graph obtained as follows. First, delete every nonlocal ouptut vertex, the corresponding input vertices, and adjacent edges. Second, for each block of vertices, for each level collapse all vertices in the block at that level into a single vertex.

What are the properites of the collapsed graph? First, it is a prefix graph of size *m*, where $m \geq 1/2 \; n/f_{d-2}^{-1}(n)$. Second, each output vertex is connected to only a single vertex at level *d-1*; hence by deleting the output vertices and considering the vertices at level *d-1* the output vertices, a prefix graph of depth *d-1* and size *m* results.

By the inductive hypothesis the collapsed graph has at least $O(mf_{d-2}^{-1}(m)) = O(n)$ edges. Now every edge in the collapsed graph is the image of at least one edge in the original graph. Of these, how many cross block boundaries? There are $O(n)$ edges in the collapsed graph between a vertex i at level l and a vertex j at level $l+1$, for $j>i$, since there are only $O(n/f_{d-2}^{-1}(n))$ edges between a vertex i at level l and a vertex i at level $l+1$. All of the preimages of these $O(n)$ edges must cross block boundaries.

□

A *monotone boolean circuit* is a boolean circuit where nodes are labelled with monotone boolean functions. Note that since there can be many more than two inputs to a gate, there are many more boolean functions that can label a gate than simply AND and OR.

Theorem 3.2 A monotone circuit of depth d for the prefix-or problem must have size $\Omega(nf_{d-1}^{-1}(n))$.

Proof We show that every gate in a monotone circuit for prefix-or that is not an OR gate can be replaced by an OR gate without changing the function computed by the circuit. The Theorem then follows from Theorem 3.1.

Suppose C is a monotone circuit for prefix-or containing gates besides OR gates. Choose G not an OR gate so that there are only OR gates on any path from G to an output. Let y_i be the smallest numbered output that depends upon G, $y_i = x_1 \vee \ldots \vee x_i$. The input assignment $x_1 = x_2 = \ldots = x_i = 0$, $x_{i+1} = \ldots = x_n = 1$ does not satisfy G, else it would satisfy y_i. Let Z be the set of inputs to G that are not satisfied by this assignment. Two facts follow by monotonicity. First, any input assignment that actually satisfies G must satisfy some element of Z. Second, any assignment that has all of $x_1,\ldots,x_i$ zero cannot satisfy any element of Z.

We claim that the circuit C' obtained by replacing G with an OR gate G' with inputs Z still computes prefix-or. To see this, fix an input assignment. Suppose it satisfies G in C. Since the inputs assignment must satisfy some element of Z, it must also satisfy G'. Hence any output satisfied in C is also satisfied in C', by monotonicity. Conversely, suppose some output y_j in C' is satisfied. If y_j does not depend on G', or if G and G' have identical values, then y_j is satisfied in C as well. Now it cannot be that G is satisfied and G' is not, since by construction of G', any assignment that satisfies G satisfies some element of Z and hence G'. The final possibility is that y_j depends on G', G' is satisfied, and G is not. But by choice of i, $j \geq i$, and by choice of Z, some one of $x_1,\ldots,x_i$ must be nonzero. Since C computes prefix-or, y_j must be satisfied in C.

□

Since prefix-carry is reducible to prefix-or, Theorem 3.2 implies a nonlinear lower bound on monotone implementations of prefix-carry as well. However, Theorem 3.6 below is stronger, since it indicates a better bound and applies to circuits with negation.

Theorem 3.4 There are linear size circuits of constant depth for prefix-or.

Proof Number the inputs x_{ij}, $1 \leq i,j \leq m = \sqrt{n}$, using the lexicographic ordering. The case where the number of inputs is not a square requires simple modifications. Compute

$$y_i = \bigvee_j x_{ij} \qquad i = 1,\ldots,\sqrt{n}$$

$$p_i = \bigvee_{k \leq i} y_k \qquad i = 1,\ldots,\sqrt{n}$$

$$f_i = y_i \wedge \neg p_{i-1} \qquad i = 1,\ldots,\sqrt{n}.$$

Informally, the y's are ors of blocks of size $\sqrt{n}$; the p's are prefixes of the blocks, and the single f that is a one indicates the first block that contains a one. The p's are accurate for every block except the block containing the first one. The remaining computation patches that block.

$$z_j = \bigvee_i (x_{ij} \wedge f_i) \qquad j = 1,\ldots,\sqrt{n}$$

$$g_j = \bigvee_{k \leq j} z_j$$

$$out_{ij} = \neg f_i \wedge p_i \ \vee \ f_i \wedge g_j \qquad i = 1,\ldots,\sqrt{n},\ j = 1,\ldots,\sqrt{n}.$$

The size of the circuit is clearly $O(n)$ and its depth constant.

□

Let G be a directed acyclic graph with n inputs (vertices of indegree 0) numbered from 1 to n and n outputs (vertices of outdegree 0) numbered from 1 to n. An *ordered matching of size k* is a set of pairs of input and output vertices $\{(i_1,j_1), (i_2,j_2), \ldots, (i_k,j_k)\}$ so that $i_1 < j_1 < i_2 < j_2 < \ldots < i_k < j_k$. Graph G is a *weak n-superconcentrator* if for every ordered matching of size k, there are k node-disjoint paths from the inputs in the matching to the outputs in the matching. The *size* of G is the number of edges in it. An n-superconcentrator (or circuit) is *synchronous* if all paths between inputs and outputs are the same length.

Thereom 3.5 [DDPW] A weak n-superconcentrator of depth $2d$ has size at least $\Omega(nf_d^{-1}(n))$. Any synchronous weak superconcentrator has size at least $\Omega(nf_\omega^{-1}(n))$.

Theorem 3.6 A prefix-carry circuit of depth $2d$ has size at least $\Omega(nf_d^{-1}(n))$. Any synchronous prefix-carry circuit has size at least $\Omega(nf_\omega^{-1}(n))$.

Proof: Suppose C is a prefix-carry circuit. Then C has $2n$ inputs $x_1,\ldots,x_n,y_1,\ldots,y_n$ and n outputs $c_1,\ldots,c_n$, indicating the carries. We will show that the graph obtained by merging x_i with y_i for each i is a weak n-superconcentrator. The theorem then follows from Theorem 3.5.

Choose an ordered matching M, say of size m. Let I be $\{i{:}\exists j(i,j)\in M\}$ and J be $\{j{:}\exists i(i,j)\in M\}$. Construct circuit C'' by merging inputs x_i and y_i into a new vertex, say z_i, for each $i\in I$. We identify the set I with the vertices z_i, for $i\in I$, and J with the outputs c_j, for $j\in J$. We will show that there are m vertex disjoint paths from I to J in C''; it then follows that there are m vertex disjoint paths from I to J in C'. Since the ordered matching M is arbitrary, C' is a weak n-superconcentrator.

Consider all assignments A to C'' obtained by fixing $x_i = 0$ and $y_i = 1$ for i not in I and varying the assignments to I. Clearly there are 2^m such assignments. Notice that for any such assignment and $(i,j)\in M$, if $z_i = 0$ then $c_j = 0$ and if $z_i = 1$ then $c_j = 1$. Thus there are 2^m different combinations of the outputs J.

We claim that the minimum size of a cutset between I and J is m. It then follows by Menger's theorem [Har] that there are m node-disjoint paths between I and J. To establish the claim, consider the subgraph of C'' consisting of those gates that take on both the value 0 and the value 1 as assignments vary over A. This subgraph is connected and contains both I and J. Furthermore, the minimum size of a cutset in this subgraph is m. For if there is a cutset of size $k<m$, then the number of different combinations of values to the gates in the cutset is at most 2^k. But then the number of different combinations of values for the outputs J is at most 2^k, a contradiction since $2^k < 2^m$.

□

Discussion

This paper was originally motivated by the almost-linear, constant-depth constructions for prefix-or and prefix-carry [CFL]. It is interesting that those constructions have turned out to be essentially optimal, though by different arguments for the two problems. Apparently, the similiarity of the size/depth tradeoffs for monotone implementations of prefix-or and arbitrary implementations of prefix-carry is coincidental, since neither seems to be reducible to the other.

Bibliography

[CD] S. Cook and C. Dwork, "Bounds on the Time for Parallel RAM's to Compute Simple Functions," *Proceedings of the 14th ACM Symposium on Theory of Computing*, 1982, 231-233.

[CFL] A.K. Chandra, S.J. Fortune, R. Lipton, "Unbounded Fanin Circuits and Associative Functions," *Proceedings of the 15th ACM Symposium on Theory of Computing*, 1983.

[CSV] A.K. Chandra, L.J. Stockmeyer, U. Vishkin, "A Complexity Theory for Unbounded Fan-in Parallelism," *Proceedings 23rd Annual Symposium on the Foundations of Computer Science*,1982, pp. 1-13.

[DDPW] D. Dolev, C. Dwork, N. Pippenger, A. Wigderson, "Superconcentrators, Generalizers and Generalized Connectors with Limited Depth," *Proceedings of the 15th ACM Symposium on Theory of Computing*, 1983.

[FSS] M. Furst, J. Saxe, M. Sipser, "Parity, Circuits, and the Polynomial-time Hierarchy," *Proceedings of the 22nd Annual Symposium on the Foundations of Computer Science*, 1981, pp. 260-270.

[GG] O. Gabber and Z. Galil, "Explicit Constructions of Linear Size Concentrators," *Proceedings of the 20th Annual Symposium on the Foundations of Computer Science*, 1979, pp. 364-370.

[G] L.M. Goldschlager, "A Unified Approach to Models of Synchronous Parallel Machines," *Proceedings of the Tenth ACM Symposium on Theory of Computing*, 1978, pp. 89-94.

[Har] F. Harary, *Graph Theory*, Addison-Wesley Publishing Co., Reading, Mass, 1971.

[MP] R. McNaughton, S. Papert, *Counter-Free Automata*, Research Monograph No. 65, The MIT Press, Cambridge, Mass., 1971.

[R] R. Reischuk, "A Lower Time Bound for Parallel Random Access Machines without Simultaneous Writes," Report RJ3431, IBM Research Lab, San Jose, Ca, 1982.

[SV] Y. Shiloach and U. Vishkin, "Finding the Maximum, Merging, and Sorting in a Parallel Computation Model," *J. of Algorithms* 2 (1981), pp. 88-102.

[Val] L.G. Valiant, "On Non-linear Lower Bounds in Computational Complexity," *Proceedings of the Seventh Annual ACM Symposium on Theory of Computing*, 1975, pp. 45-53.

[Vis] U. Vishkin "Implementation of Simultaneous Memory Access in Models that Forbid it," Tech Report No 210, Dept of Computer Science, Technion, Haifa, Israel, 1981.

TEST SETS FOR MORPHISMS WITH BOUNDED DELAY

Christian CHOFFRUT
Université Paris VII U.E.R. de Mathématiques
2, Place Jussieu 75251 Paris Cedex 05, France

Juhani KARHUMAKI
Department of Mathematics
University of Turku
20500 Turku 50, Finland

Abstract Let p be a fixed nonnegative integer. We prove the Ehrenfeucht conjecture for morphisms having deciphering delay bounded by p. In other words, we show that for each language L over a finite alphabet there exists a finite subset F of L such that for arbitrary morphisms h and g having deciphering delay bounded by p, the equation h(x) = g(x) holds for all x in L if and only if it holds for all x in F.

Résumé Soit p un entier positif ou nul. Nous prouvons la conjecture de Ehrenfeucht pour les morphismes ayant un délai de déchiffrage borné par p. En d'autres termes, nous montrons que pour tout langage L sur un alphabet fini, il existe un sous-ensemble fini F de L tel que pour tout couple h,g de morphismes ayant un délai de déchiffrage borné par p, l'équation h(x) = g(x) est satisfaite pour tout x dans L, ssi elle l'est pour tout x dans F.

Resumen Sea p un entero positivo o nulo. Se demuestra aquí la conjetura de Ehrenfeucht para los morfismos con plazo de descodificación acotado por p. En otras palabras, establecemos que para cada lenguage L sobre un alfabeto finito, existe un subconjunto finito F de L, tal que para todo par h,g de morfismos con plazo de descodificación acotado por p, la ecuación h(x) = g(x) es válida para todo x en L, ssi es válida para todo x en F.

I. INTRODUCTION

In recent years it has been a vivid interest among formal language theoreticians to study problems involving morphisms of free monoids (cf. e.g. [C] and [S]). Examples of such problems are morphic representation results of language families, the DOL equivalence problem, the Post Correspondence Problem (cf.[EKR2]) and the following problem which is our topic here and which is usually referred to as the :

Ehrenfeucht Conjecture Each language L over a finite alphabet Σ has a finite subset F such that, for any pair h,g of morphisms from Σ^* into some other free monoid, the equation $h(x) = g(x)$ holds for all x in L if and only if it holds for all x in F.

In [CS 2] such a finite subset F is called a test set for L. With this terminology the conjecture states : each language over a finite alphabet has a test set.

The purely algebraic importance of the Ehrenfeucht Conjecture was emphasized when it was noticed in [CK 2] that the conjecture is equivalent to the following statement : each system of equations over a finitely generated free monoid and containing only a finite number of variables possesses an equivalent finite subsystem. Here the equivalence means, of course, that the systems have exactly the same solutions, and a subsystem refers to a subset of equations.

As another connection of the Ehrenfeucht Conjecture with other problems we mention the following. In [CK 2] it was also proved that the validity of the Ehrenfeucht Conjecture implies the decidability of the so-called HDOL sequence equivalence problem, as well as the decidability of the so-called DTOL sequence equivalence problem (cf. [C] or [RS]). Moreover, for these reductions it is enough that the Ehrenfeucht Conjecture holds (even noneffectively !) for DOL and DTOL languages, respectively.

In spite of the importance of the Ehrenfeucht Conjecture it is known to hold only in some special cases. In [CS 2] it was proved for all languages over a two-letter alphabet. Later a shorter proof was given in [EKR 1]. Over general alphabets the conjecture has been proved only for rather restrictive classes of languages, such as for context-free languages in [ACK] and for positive DOL languages in [CK 1]. A sufficient condition for a language to possess a test set is given in [CK 1].

Common to all the above results is that the family of languages for which the Ehrenfeucht Conjecture has been established is heavily restricted. Our approach of the problem is in the opposite direction. We restrict the class of morphims and prove that the conjecture holds for such a class.

More precisely, for each nonnegative integer p, let H_p denote the class of all morphisms whose deciphering delay is bounded by p. We prove that the Ehrenfeucht Conjecture holds for H_p, to wit :

Theorem Let p be a nonnegative integer. For each language L over a finite alphabet there exists a finite subset F of L such that, for all pairs h,g of morphisms in H_p, the equation h(x) = g(x) holds for all x in L if and only if it holds for all x in F.

Of course, the above F can not be found effectively in general. However, we show that under relatively mild conditions (shared e.g. by indexed languages, cf. [HU]) the above F can be effectively constructed. This implies some (known) decidability results concerning the so-called morphism equivalence problem on languages (cf. [CS 1]).

II. PRELIMINARIES

We use the standard formal language theory terminology, cf. e.g. [H] or [La]. Mainly to fix our notations we recall the following.

1.- Basic definitions

Given an arbitrary set Σ, we denote by $|\Sigma|$ is cardinality, Σ^* the free monoid it generates. The identity of Σ^*, or the empty word, is denoted by 1. For pure notational reasons it will be convenient to consider Σ^* as embedded in the free group $\Sigma^{(*)}$ generated by Σ. In other words, Σ^* is as submonoid of $\Sigma^{(*)}$

Given any word $w \in \Sigma^*$ we denote by $|w|$ its length. In particular $|1| = 0$ and $|a| = 1$ for all $a \in \Sigma$. We write $u \leq v$ whenever $u \in \Sigma^*$ is a prefix of $v \in \Sigma^*$, i.e., whenever $uw = v$ holds for some $w \in \Sigma^*$. We denote by $u \wedge v$ the longest common prefix of u and v.

A set $R \subseteq \Sigma^*$ is rational (or regular) and we write $R \in \text{Rat}\, \Sigma^*$ if R can be obtained from singletons of Σ^* by applying finitely many times the rational operations of union, product and star.

Given a morphism h of Σ^* into some free monoid and a nonnegative integer p, we say that h has a (from left to right) deciphering delay bounded by p (cf. e.g. [Ni]) if the following holds for all $u,v \in \Sigma^*$ and $a,b \in \Sigma$:

(1) $h(au) \leq h(bv)$ and $|u| \geq p$ implies $a = b$.

We will shortly say that h is a p-bounded morphism, or a morphism with bounded delay when no reference to p is necessary, and we will denote by H_p the set of all p-bounded morphisms. Observe that h is a 0-bounded morphism iff the restriction of h to Σ is injective, and if the set $h(\Sigma)$ is a prefix.

2.- Equality sets

From now on, Σ is a fixed finite alphabet.

Given two arbitrary morphisms h, g of Σ^* into some free monoid, we denote by $E(h,g)$ their equality language (cf. [RS]) i.e. the set of all words on which they agree :

$$E(h,g) = \{w \in \Sigma^* \mid h(w) = g(w)\}$$

Assume h and g map Σ^* into some free monoid Δ^*. We recall how we can obtain the minimal deterministic automaton redognizing the equality set $E(h,g)$. Observe that for arbitrary morphisms, this automaton is not necessarily finite.

Let 0 be an element not belonging to the free group $\Delta^{(*)}$. To every word $w \in \Sigma^*$ we assign its overflow $\varphi(w) \in \Delta^{(*)} \cup \{0\}$ defined as follows :

$$\varphi(w) = \begin{cases} g(w)^{-1}h(w) & \text{if there exists } u \in \Sigma^* \text{ such that } h(wu) = g(wu) \\ 0 & \text{otherwise} \end{cases}$$

Observe that when $\varphi(w) \neq 0$, its value does not depend upon the word u, and that either itself or its inverse in the free group, belongs to Δ^* according to whether $g(w) \leq h(w)$ or $h(w) \leq g(w)$ (cf. fig.)

We set $\Delta_0 = \{\varphi(w) \mid w \in \Sigma^*\}$ and we define an action λ of Σ into Δ_0 by setting for all $x \in \Delta_0$ and $a \in \Sigma$:

$$\lambda(x,a) = \begin{cases} 0 & \text{if } x = 0 \text{ or else if } g(a)^{-1}\, x\, h(a) \notin \Delta_0 \\ g(a)^{-1}\, x\, h(a) & \text{otherwise} \end{cases}$$

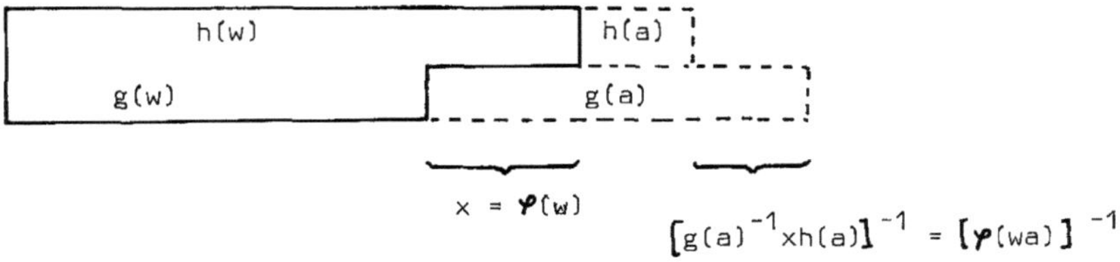

Taking Δ_0 as the set of states, 1 as initial and final states, and λ as the transition finition, completely determines the minimal automaton recognizing $E(h,g)$.

We introduce now the crucial notion of critical overflow which is defined as a state $x \in \Delta_0$ for which there exist two different transitions $a, b \in \Sigma$, taking x into some non-0 states :

$$\lambda(x,a) \in \Delta_0 \setminus \{0\} \quad \text{and} \quad \lambda(x,b) \in \Delta_0 \setminus \{0\} \quad \text{with } a \neq b.$$

In other words, there must exist three words $w, w_1, w_2 \in \Sigma^*$ such that :

(2) $h(w) = g(w)\, x$

(3) $\begin{cases} h(waw_1) = g(waw_1) \\ \text{and} \quad h(wbw_2) = g(wbw_2) \end{cases}$

Setting

$y = h(aw_1) \wedge h(bw_2)$

$z = g(aw_1) \wedge g(bw_2)$

we obtain

$h(waw_1) \wedge h(wbw_2) = h(w)y = g(w)xy$

and $g(waw_1) \wedge g(wbw_2) = g(w)z$

i.e., because of (3) a necessary condition for x to be a critical overflow is that

(4) $x (= zy^{-1}) = [g(aw_1) \wedge g(bw_2)]\,[h(aw_1) \wedge h(bw_2)]^{-1}$ holds for some $w_1, w_2 \in \Sigma^*$.

III. PROOF OF THE THEOREM

The theorem is proven via two Lemmas which we proceed to state.

The first Lemma says that when Σ and p are fixed, all equality sets of p-bounded morphisms are morphic images of some unique "universal" rational set.

<u>Lemma 1</u> <u>Let p be a nonnegative integer. Then there exists a rational set R over a finite alphabet V such that for any pair h,g of p-bounded morphisms there exists a morphism $\tau : V^* \to \Sigma^*$ satisfying</u> :

$$E(h,g) = \tau(R)$$

<u>Proof</u>

Observe first that it is sufficient to prove that there exists a finite collection $R_1, \ldots, R_n$ of rational sets over (pairwise disjoint) alphabets $V_1, \ldots, V_n$ such that for every equality set $E(h,g)$ there exists $1 \le i \le n$ and a morphism $\sigma : V_i^* \to \Sigma^*$ such that $\sigma(R_i) = E(h,g)$.

Indeed, assume this is the case. Since all equality sets contain the empty word, without loss of generality we may assume that $R_1, \ldots, R_n$ contain the empty word as well. We set $V = \bigcup_{1 \le i \le n} V_i$ and $R = \bigcup_{1 \le i \le n} R_i$ and we consider the morphism $\tau : V^* \to \Sigma^*$ defined by :

$$\tau(a) = \begin{cases} \sigma(a) & \text{if } a \in V_i \\ 1 & \text{otherwise} . \end{cases}$$

Then we obtain $\tau(R) = \sigma(R_i) \cup \{1\} = \sigma(R_i)$ as claimed.

Consider thus the equality set $E(h,g)$ of two p-bounded morphisms $h,g : \Sigma^* \to \Delta^*$. Now denote by Δ_1 the union of the empty word and of all critical overflows. Let M be the set of all triples $(z,q,z') \in \Delta_1 \times \Sigma \times \Delta_1$ satisfying the following :

There exists a word $u \in \Sigma^*$ such that :

i) $\lambda(z,au) = z'$

ii) for every factorization $u = u_1u_z$, $\lambda(z,au_1) \in \Delta_1$ implies $u_1 = u$.

Observe that because of the definition of the critical overflow and of the fact that ii) guarantees that we take the shortest word taking z into some critical overflow or the empty word, u is uniquely determined.

Thus we may assign to every $(z,a,z') \in M$ the word $\sigma(z,a,z') = au$.

We set :

$$I = M \cap (\{1\} \times \Sigma \times \Delta_1)$$
$$F = M \cap (\Delta_1 \times \Sigma \times \{1\})$$
$$L = \{(z,a,z')(t,b,t') \mid z' \neq t\} \subseteq M^2$$

Consider the set :

$$R = IM^* \cap M^*F \setminus M^*LM^*$$

Then the equality $\sigma(R) = E(h,g)$ is a direct consequence of the fact that every word $w \in E(h,g)$ has a unique factorization $w = w_1 \ldots w_n$ where all $w_1 \ldots w_i$ $(1 \leq i \leq n)$ are exactly these prefixes of w for which $\varphi(w_1 \ldots w_i)$ is a critical overflow or the empty word.

Now observe that because h and g are p-bounded morphisms, then (1) applies and all possible values of x in (4) are obtained when w_1 and w_2 run over all words of length at most $p+1$: $|\Delta_1| \leq 1 + |\Sigma|^{2(p+2)}$. Thus not only the number of different critical overflows for a fixed pair h,g is finite (and therefore R is rational) but it is bounded by a function depending only on p, which proves that there are only finitely many different R's, as claimed. □

Before stating the second Lemma we need more terminology. We consider a fixed finite set V and denote by $\mathcal{F}$ the family of all morphisms $\tau : W^* \to \Sigma^*$ where W is a subset of V. Let τ_o denote the only element in $\mathcal{F}$ for which $W = \emptyset$.

Define a partial ordering on $\mathcal{F}$ by setting for all $\tau : W^* \to \Sigma^*$ and $\sigma : U^* \to \Sigma^*$:

$\tau \leq \sigma$ iff $W \subseteq U$ and $\tau(w) = \sigma(w)$ for all $w \in W^*$.

For convenience, given any subset $R \subseteq V^*$ we write $\tau(R)$ instead of the more correct $\tau(R \cap W^*)$.

<u>Lemma 2</u> <u>Let</u> $R \subseteq V^*$ <u>be an arbitrary set. Then for each language</u> $L \subseteq \Sigma^*$ <u>there exists a finite subset</u> $F \subseteq L$ <u>such that for each</u> $\tau : V^* \to \Sigma^*$ <u>one has</u> :

$$L \subseteq \tau(R) \quad \text{\underline{iff}} \quad F \subseteq \tau(R).$$

<u>Proof</u> We define by induction a sequence :

$$F_o \subseteq F_1 \subseteq \ldots \subseteq F_i \subseteq \ldots$$

of finite subsets of L and a sequence

$$\theta_o, \ldots \theta_1, \ldots, \theta_i, \ldots$$

of finite subsets of $\mathcal{F}$ as follows :

$$F_o = \emptyset$$

$$\theta_o = \{\tau_o\}$$

and for $i > 0$:

F_i contains all elements of F_{i-1} and contains for each element $\tau \in \theta_{i-1}$ such that $L - \tau(R) \neq \emptyset$, an arbitrary element x in $L - \tau(R)$.

$$\theta_i = \mathrm{Min}\{\tau \mid F_i \subseteq \tau(R)\}$$

where Min refers to the partial ordering defined on $\mathcal{F}$.

Clearly, if $i > 0$ and $\tau \in \theta_i$ then there exists $\tau' \in \theta_{i-1}$ such that $\tau' \leq \tau$. We claim that :

(5) $\tau' = \tau$ iff $L \subseteq \tau'(R)$

Indeed, assume that $L \subseteq \tau'(R)$. Because of $F_i \subseteq L$ we have $F_i \subseteq \tau'(R)$. By the minimality of τ we get : $\tau' = \tau$. Conversely, assume by contradiction that we have $\tau' = \tau$ and $L - \tau'(R) \neq \emptyset$. Then there exists $x \in F_i - F_{i-1}$ such that $x \in L - \tau'(R)$ and $x \in \tau(R)$, contradicting $\tau' = \tau$.

Consider now $\tau : W^* \to \Sigma^*$ an element of θ_i and assume $L - \tau(V^*) \neq \emptyset$. Then we claim :

(6) $|W| \geq i$

Indeed, by definition there exists a sequence

$$\tau_o \leq \tau_1 \leq \ldots \leq \tau_i$$

such that $\tau_j \in \theta_j$ for all $0 \leq j \leq i$. Because of (5) we may not have any equality, which implies (6).

Setting $|V| = n$, we claim that F_{n+1} is the required subset F. Indeed, if $\sigma : V^* \to \Sigma^*$ satisfies $F_{n+1} \subseteq \sigma(R)$ then there exists τ' and τ such that : $\tau' \in \theta_n$, $\tau \in \theta_{n+1}$ and $\tau' \leq \tau \leq \sigma$.

By (5) and (6) we obtain $\tau' = \tau$, i.e., $L \subseteq \tau'(R)$ and thus $L \subseteq \sigma(R)$. This proves the Lemma. □

Now, our Theorem is a direct consequence of Lemmas 1 and 2.

IV. CONCLUDING REMARKS

In Lemma 1 we showed that each equality language of two p-bounded morphisms, for some fixed nonnegative integer p is obtained as a morphic image of a fixed rational language L_p. Moreover, this language can be effectively constructed for each $p \geq 0$. It follows immediately from the results in [EKR 1] that in the case when Σ is binary, the language L_p can be chosen to be $(\alpha + \beta\gamma^*\delta)^*$ independently of p where α, β, γ are arbitrary words.

Despite the fact that L_p can be effectively constructed, we know practically nothing about the problem of which of the morphic images of L_p are actually equality languages of morphisms in H_p. It is even not known whether there exist in the binary case, bounded morphisms, or equivalently, injective morphisms such that their equality language would be infinitely generated, or more sharply whether $(\alpha + \beta\gamma^*\delta)^*$ above could be replaced by $(\alpha + \beta)^*$ (cf. [CK 3] and [EKR 1]).

Not only the problem of deciding whether a given morphic image of L_p is an equality language of morphisms in H_p, but also the "converse" problem of determining the equality language of two morphisms in H_p is extremely difficult. Indeed, for a given pair h, g of morphisms in H_p, the equality language $E(h,g)$ can not be constructed effectively in general (cf. [ERR]).

As regards the effectiveness of our Theorem we have :

Corollary 1 Let p be a nonnegative integer and $\mathcal{L}$ a family of languages satisfying

(i) each L in $\mathcal{L}$ is recursively enumerable,

(ii) for each L in $\mathcal{L}$ and R in $Rat(\Sigma^*)$, $L \cap R$ is in $\mathcal{L}$,

(iii) it is decidable whether a given L in $\mathcal{L}$ is empty.

Then for each L in $\mathcal{L}$ there effectively exists a finite subset F of L such that, for all pairs h, g of morphisms in H_p, the equation $h(x) = g(x)$ holds for all x in L if and only if it holds for all x in F.

Proof The result follows from the proofs of Lemmas 1 and 2. Indeed, what is essential is that the sequence $F_o \subseteq F_1 \subseteq \ldots$ in the proof of Lemma 2 can be constructed effectively, and this certainly follows from (ii) and (iii).

As consequences of our Corollary 1 we give new proofs for some decidability results of [CS 1]. We recall that the morphism equivalence problem for a family $\mathcal{L}$ of languages is to decide whether two given morphisms h and g agree (word by word) on a given language L in L, i.e., whether $L \subseteq E(h,g)$. Based on the fact that the minimal delay of a morphism with bounded delay can be effectively found we obtain :

Corollary 2 Let L be a family of languages satisfying conditions (i), (ii) and (iii) of Corollary 1. The morphism equivalence problem restricted to morphisms with bounded delay is decidable in L.

Observe that in Corollary 2 the class $\bigcup_{p \geq o} H_p$ is used instead of the class H_p for some $p \geq o$.

An example of quite a large family of languages satisfying conditions (i), (ii) and (iii) is the family of indexed languages (cf. [HU]). Hence Corollary 2 yields :

Corollary 3 It is decidable whether two morphisms with bounded delay agree on a given indexed language.

Corollary 3 is a slight, but not essential, generalization of a result in [CS 1]. This is because each elementary morphism has effectively findable bounded delay, although the delay depends upon the morphism (cf. [S]).

REFERENCES

[ACK] Albert, J., Culik, K.II, Karhamäki, J., Test sets for context-free languages and algebraic systems of equations, Information and Control (to appear).

[C] Culik, K. II, Homomorphisms : Decidability, Equality and Test Sets, in : R. Book, ed., Formal Language Theory, Perspectives and Open Problems (Academic Press, New York 1980).

[CK 1] Culik, K. II, Karhamäki, J., On test sets for DOL Languages, RAIRO, Theoretical Informatics (to appear).

[CK 2] Culik, K. II, Karhumäki, J., Systems of equations and Ehrenfeucht Conjecture, Discrete Mathematics 43 (1983) 139-153.

[CK 3] Culik, K. II, Karhumäki, J., On the equality sets for homomorphisms on free monoids with two generators, RAIRO, Theoretical Informatics 14 (1980) 340-369.

[CS 1] Culik, K. II, Salomaa, A., On the decidability of homomorphism equivalence on Languages, JCSS 17 (1978) 163-175.

[CS 2] Culik, K. II, Salomaa, A., Test sets and checking words for homomorphism equivalence, JCSS 19 (1980) 379-395.

[EKR 1] Ehrenfeucht, A., Karhumäki, J., Rozenberg, G., On binary equality languages and a solution to the test set conjecture in the binary case, J. of Algebra (to appear).

[EKR 2] Ehrenfeucht, A., Karhumäki, J., Rozenberg, G., The (generalized) Post Correspondence Problem with lists consisting of two words is decidable, Theoretical Computer Science 21 (1982), 119-144.

[ERR] Ehrenfeucht, A., Rozenberg, G., Ruohonen, K., Maximal solutions of language equations involving morphisms, manuscript (1983).

[H] Harrison, M., Introduction to formal language theory, (Addison-Wesley, Mass. Reading 1978).

[HU] Hopcroft, J., Ullman, J., Introduction to Automata Theory, Languages and Computation, (Addison-Wesley, Mass. Reading, 1979).

[La] Lallement, G., Semigroups and Combinatorial Applications (Wiley Interscience, New York, 1979).

[Ni] Nivat, M., Elements de la théorie générale des Codes, in : E.R. Caianello, ed., Automata Theory (Academic Press, New York, 1966).

[RS] Rozenberg, G., Salomaa, A., The Mathematical Theory of L Systems, (Academic Press, New York, 1980).

[S] Salomaa, A., Jewels of Formal Language Theory, (Computer Science Press, 1981).

Symmetric and economical solutions to the mutual exclusion problem in a distributed system

(Extended Abstract)

by

Shimon Cohen[1], Daniel Lehmann[1] and Amir Pnueli[2]

Abstract:

The mutual exclusion problem in a distributed system, in which each process has a memory of its own, into which it has exclusive write privileges but from which others may read, is reconsidered. Symmetric solutions are looked for. It is shown that, though no such solution may be deterministic, there are probabilistic solutions. Different solutions are provided for two processes, and then a solution is proposed for any number of processes. The solutions offered are amenable to a formal proof of their correctness with a small effort. The solutions are correct even against a very well informed scheduler, unlike Rabin's probabilistic solution to the mutual exclusion problem in a centralized system. Some of the solutions are correct even against an evil scheduler that knows in advance the results of the future random draws, in sharp contrast with the algorithms of [LR]. The solutions are economical: mutual exclusion between two processes may be achieved with variables capable of holding four different values (to be compared with Peterson and Fischer's three), mutual exclusion between n processes may be achieved with variables capable of holding ten different values (to be compared with Peterson and Fischer's fourteen). All solutions have been attained by careful reasoning and not by an exhaustive computer search, they exhibit general principles of design that may be useful in solving other similar problems.

1. The mutual exclusion problem in a distributed environment

The mutual exclusion problem is a now classical problem in concurrent programming, first proposed by E. W. Dijkstra (see [D1], [D2] and [K] for early work and [LA], [RP], [PF] and [R2] for recent work on this problem). For the notions of critical section, remainder, trying and exit sections the reader is referred to the papers quoted above.

Relative to the mutual exclusion problem, we define a lockout as a computation in which one of the processes wishes to enter its critical section, but will never do so. A deadlock is a computation in which, at some point, some process wishes to enter its critical section and no process ever enters its critical section beyond that point. A computation is said to exhibit

[1]Institute of Mathematics and Computer Science, Hebrew University, Jerusalem 9104 (Israel)

[2]Department of Applied Mathematics, Weizmann Institute, Rehovoth (Israel)

overtaking bounded by k, if every process that wishes, at any time, to enter its critical section, gets access to its critical section before any other process gets to enter its critical section $k+1$ times.

We are interested in solving the mutual exclusion problem in a distributed environment as introduced in [LA]. We assume the existence of n processors, each containing its own memory unit. In each of those memory units, there is a special area that may be read (but not written) by any processor. Except for this special area, a processor has exclusive access to its own memory. Deterministic solutions to the mutual exclusion problem in a distributed environment have been proposed by [LA], [RP] and [PF]. The quality of a proposed solution is assessed by reference to different criteria, among them the size of the special area of memory used by the processors for communicating, the speed with which an interested processor will be allowed to enter its critical section and the immunity of the system to the possible failure of a processor. We concentrate on the first two criteria. The best solution proposed so far is that of [PF], where a solution is proposed for two processors that requires a special memory area capable of holding three different values (this number is also shown to be a lower bound), and a solution for n processors requiring an area capable of holding fourteen values. The solution also guarantees bounded waiting time.

2. Symmetric solutions

The solutions mentioned above are not symmetric, i.e. either the different processors follow different routines or the initial values of the memories of the different processors are not the same. Nevertheless one expects a solution not to favour one of the processors among its competitors. This requirement of symmetry has been first formulated by Dijkstra and an up-to-date study may be found in [BU].

A very simple symmetry argument can show that many problems do not have a deterministic symmetric solution, see for example [LR] and [LY]. The centralized version of the mutual exclusion problem has a symmetric deterministic solution The distributed version does not.

There is wide agreement as to the necessity of behavioural symmetry, but not quite, yet, general agreement about the use of totally symmetric solutions. Symmetry is aesthetically pleasing (and that **is** important), but even more important is the fact that symmetric solutions automatically ensure behavioural symmetry (thus short-cutting a possibly delicate proof) and that their proofs of correctness tend to be eased by the symmetry. Symmetric solutions should also be prefered for economy reasons. A non-symmetric solution to the mutual exclusion problem for n processes, such as that of [PF], though it requires a shared (for reading only) variable of only constant (independent of n) size, requires each process to somehow remember some kind of identity number of size $\log(n)$. A symmetric solution, such as ours, does not. Also, it is always easier to manufacture a system consisting of identical parts, than a system consisting of a large number of different parts that have to be assembled in a specific fixed layout. The rest of the paper is devoted to studying probabilistic symmetric solutions.

3. Probabilistic solutions

The main notions concerning probabilistic solutions, such as schedule, may be found in [LR]. The basic idea of all our solutions is to let all processes compete for the shared resource by drawing a random value and let the process that obtained the "highest" random value enter its critical section. The loosers of a competition will then compete between themselves. If there is a tie the processes go through another competition. The two main problems that arise in implementing this idea are: to make sure that processes compare up-to-date results of random draws and not out-of-date values and to define precisely the group of processes competing, so as not to wait for results of draws of processes that are not interested in competing.

4. A first solution for two processes

At first, we shall present a solution for the mutual exclusion problem between two processes, that guarantees that no process has ever more than one turn to wait. The solution is not economical, since the private variable of each process must be able to hold nine different values. Its interest lies in its simplicity and the simplicity of its proof of correctness. This solution ensures mutual exclusion with certainty, absence of deadlock with probability one and bounded overtaking with certainty. This is much stronger than finite expected overtaking. The solution below guarantees absence of deadlock, with probability one, even against an evil clairvoyant scheduler that knows in advance the results of future random draws; it is the first example of such a "robust" solution (the algorithms of [LR], for example, do not enjoy this property).

Each process uses a private variable *my* on which it has exclusive write privileges and refers to the private variable of the competing process by *hers*. The basic commands are assignments and wait statements. The wait statement has to be understood as busy waiting: looking from time to time until *hers* is found in a favourable state, and then, branch depending on the value found. The general version of the **wait** statement is:

wait until *condition* **and then goto** *label*
  or *condition* **and then goto** *label*
  or ...
endwait

An absent **goto** part means go to the textually next statement.

Nothing is assumed concerning the rate at which checking is performed, except that it is performed an infinite number of times or until successful. The variables *my* and *hers* may take seven different values, in addition to the set of random values from which processes draw. Since this set of random values must contain at least two different values, the most economical (in space) version of our first algorithm uses three-bits variables. We name those seven values: ***uninterested***, ***interested***, ***going-in***, ***ready-to-draw***, ***won***, ***lost***, ***tie***. The initial value of the variables *my* and *hers* is ***uninterested***. The set of values from which values are randomly drawn is totally ordered, and denoted *Random*.

Algorithm 1

Exit section :
  30· my := uninterested

Trying section:
  1: **wait until**
        hers **in** {uninterested, interested, going-in}
      endwait;
  2: my := interested;
  3: **wait until**
      hers = uninterested **and then goto** 4
      or hers **in** {interested,ready-to-draw} **and then goto** 6
      endwait;
  4: my := going-in;
  5: **if** hers = uninterested **then goto** Critical Section
                                   else goto 6
      fi;
  6: my := ready-to-draw;
  7: **wait until** hers **in** {ready-to-draw} $\cup$ Random **endwait**;
  8: my := a random element of Random;
  9: **wait until**
        hers = won $\vee$ my < hers **and then goto** 10

```
         or hers = lost v my > hers and then goto 12
         or hers = tie v my = hers and then goto 14
         endwait;
10:  my := lost;
11:  wait until
           hers = uninterested and then goto Critical Section
         endwait;
12:  my := won;
13:  wait until
          hers = lost and then goto Critical Section
         endwait;
14:  my := tie;
15:  wait until
          hers in {tie, ready-to-draw} and then goto 6
         endwait;
```

Note that the condition *my > hers* holds only if both values are in the set *Random*. Otherwise the condition is well defined and evaluates to false.

The proof of correctness proceeds the following way. First some invariant properties may be easily proved, in particular mutual exclusion. A first observation is that if one process is in its critical section with the value *lost*, then the competitor must be in its remainder section or at statement 1 (in both cases with value *uninterested*). There are only three entries to the critical section: statements 5, 11 and 13. If our process has entered its critical section from statement 5 or from statement 11, at entry time *my* was *going-in* or *lost* (respectively) and *hers* was *uninterested*, therefore the competitor was either at statement 1 or at statement 2; in any case it will not pass statement 3. If our process has entered its critical section from statement 13, at entry time *my* was *won* and *hers* was *lost*. Therefore the competitor was either at statement 11 or in the critical section. If it was at statement 11, it could not pass it. It could not be in the critical section with *hers* equal to *lost* due to our observation above. We proved that a violation of mutual exclusion may occur only as a consequence of a previous violation and therefore mutual exclusion is guaranteed.

The more interesting part of the proof concerns liveness properties. First let us show that no process will wait indefinitely in one of the **wait** statements. Suppose we wait indefinitely at statement 1 (with *my* equal *uninterested*). Then we can show, with the help of some invariants, that our competitor will, sometime, attain its remainder section. From then on, since we do not move, it will always stay in statements 1, 2, 3, 4, 5, critical section, 30 and remainder. At all times then its variable *hers* will stay in the set {*uninterested*, *interested*, *going-in*}, and we shall test *hers*, find its value favourable and proceeed to statement 2. Contradiction.

Suppose now that we wait indefinitely at statement 3 (with *my* equal to *interested*). Invariant properties show that our competitor may only be at one of the statements: 1, 2, 3, 4, 5, 6, 7, critical section, 30 and remainder. It will then either stay indefinitely in its remainder section (with *hers* equal to *uninterested*) or move to statement 7 and get stuck there indefinitely with *hers* equal to *ready-to-draw*. In any case, after a certain time the variable *hers* will stay indefinitely with a value that allows us to go on. Contradiction.

The reasoning concerning statements 7, 9, 11, 13 and 15 are very similar to the previous one.

It follows that a process that is interested in getting access to its critical section will eventually enter its critical section, unless it loops indefinitely in the only loop of the program: 6, 7, 8, 9, 14, 15. Invariant analysis shows that whenever a process is at statement 14, its competitor is at one of statements 9, 14, or 15. Our process will therefore move to 15, and to 6, but will not attain statement 6 before its competitor has attained at least 15, and at most 7. We see that our process may loop indefinitely only when its competitor also loops indefinitely and both processes keep in step: they draw the same number of times and compare (in statement 9) always freshly drawn values. Such looping may happen only as long as the two processes draw the same random value at each turn: this clearly has probability zero.

The maximum waiting time may be easily analyzed: as soon as our process executes statement 2, its competitor may enter its critical section, before our process does, at most once.

5. An economical algorithm

The previous algorithm used relatively large variables. Can we do better ? A straightforward generalization of an argument of [PF] can show that no solution (even probabilistic and not symmetric) can be worked out, that uses variables capable of holding only two different values. We do not know whether there are symmetric solutions using variables capable of holding only three different values ([PF] offers such a solution that is not symmetric). We propose a symmetric solution using four-values variables.

The basic idea is to use liberal policies regarding the synchronisation of the competition process: we shall allow competing processes to draw at very different rates and compare their random values to values drawn long ago by the competitor. Obviously, random values will be drawn from a set of two values only: *{high, low}*.

The algorithm we propose guarantees mutual exclusion with certainty (not with high probability) , absence of deadlock with probability one and bounded overtaking with certainty. This obviously implies absence of lockout with probability one. Absence of deadlock, with probability one, is guaranteed against an evil scheduler that knows everything about the past. In comparison with the previous algorithm, the current one does not enjoy the robust feature of being deadlock free even against a clairvoyant scheduler. The possible values for the variables *my* and *hers*, in addition to the two random values already mentioned, are *{uninterested, interested}*. The first one is the initial value for both variables.

Algorithm 2

```
Exit section:
 30: if my = interested
          then goto 33
          else wait until hers in {uninterested, high, low}
                    and then goto 31
               endwait
      fi;
 31: my := interested;
 32: wait until hers in {uninterested, high} endwait;
 33: my := uninterested;

Trying section:
  1: wait until
          hers in {uninterested, interested}
     endwait;
  2: my := interested;
  3: wait until
             hers = uninterested and then goto Critical Section
             or hers = interested and then goto 4
             or hers = high and then goto 8
     endwait;
  4: my := a random element of {high, low};
```

```
 5: if my = high
      then
       wait until hers in {low, uninterested}
            and then goto Critical Section
         or hers = high and then goto 4
       endwait
      else
        if hers in {uninterested, interested} then goto 6
             elsif hers = low then goto 4
           else goto 9
        fi
    fi;
 6: my := high;
 7: wait until
      hers in {uninterested, low} and then goto Critical Section
     endwait;
 8: my := low;
 9: wait until hers in {uninterested, interested} endwait;
10: my := high;
11: goto Critical Section;
```

A complete proof will be given in the full paper. We present only a sketch here. No special problems occur in the proof of mutual exclusion.

One may then prove that our process has to wait indefinitely in a **wait** statement only with probability zero. As an example, let us prove that one cannot be stuck for ever in statement 9. Suppose we get stuck in statement 9, with value *low* for ever. Invariant reasoning shows that, while we are at one of statements 8 or 9, our competitor cannot be at one of statements: 8 or 9. If our competitor is at one of statements: 11, 10, 7 or 6, it will eventually enter its critical section and then either move to statement 33 and the remainder section or move to statements 31, 32 and get stuck indefinitely in statement 32 with value *interested*. In this last case, we should move and we have a contradiction. In the first case, our competitor may either stay indefinitely in its remainder section with value *uninterested*, but in this case we should move (a contradiction) or it will get to statement 1 and be stuck there for ever with value *uninterested* (a contradiction). If our competitor is at one of statements 2 or 3, it will move to statement 3 and get stuck there with value *interested* and we will move (a contradiction). If our competitor is at one of statements 4 or 5, it will move to statement 5. If it draws *high* it will enter its critical section and we are in a case already treated. If it draws *low* it will move back to statement 4 and be given another chance of drawing *high*. With probability one, our competitor will eventually draw *high* and move to its critical section.

The most delicate part of the proof is that our process cannot be looping indefinitely in the only loop of the program: 4, 5. If it did its value would be, after a certain time, always *high* or *low*. The first step is to show that if our process is at one of statements 4 or 5, with value *high* or *low* and its competitor is not at one of statements 4 or 5, then our process will eventually, with probability one, leave those statements and, by previous results, enter eventually its critical section.

Suppose, indeed, that our process is staying indefinitely in statements 4 and 5, with value *high* or *low*, and that our competitor is not at one of statements 4 or 5. By previous reasoning, our competitor will either
1) attain statement 9 and stay there until we move, or
2) attain its remainder section and stay there for ever, or
3) attain statement 1 and stay there until we move.
In case 1, we shall find *hers* equal to *low*, and go on drawing until we eventually draw *high*,

and then enter our critical section. In case 2 or 3, we shall find ***hers*** equal to ***uninterested*** and move either to our critical section or to statement 6 and then 7. At this point, our competitor would still be unable (or unwilling) to move and therefore we would move to our critical section.

The crux of the proof is that, if both competitors are at one of statements 4 or 5, one of them will, with probability one, eventually leave those statements (by previous results, the other one will eventually leave too). Suppose, indeed, that both competitors are at one of statements 4 or 5, and none of them will ever leave those statements. Clearly, both processes will draw an infinite number of times. Now we wish to show that, whenever a process (call it A) draws a random value, there is a fixed, positive probability that one of the competitors (A or B) will leave the loop before A draws a second time.
Case 1: B is at statement 5. Here, if A draws the value (***high*** or *low*) that is different from that of B (and this event has probability 1/2), whoever will be next to perform its own statement 5 will leave the loop.
Case 2: B is at statement 4. Here, if A draws the value that is different from that of B (and this event has probability 1/2), then either A will be next to act, execute statement 5 and leave the loop, or B will be next to act, and, by the analysis of Case 1, somebody will leave the loop immediately with probability at least 1/2. It follows that, in any situation, the probability that somebody will leave the loop, before any further draw of A, is at least 1/4. Since A draws an infinite number of times, somebody leaves the loop, with probability one.

By a slight refinement of the proof above, one may see that as soon as process A has performed statement 2, its competitor will not enter its critical section more than once before process A does.

6. Mutual exclusion for n competitors

We present now an algorithm that solves the mutual exclusion problem for *n* processes in a distributed environment. Each process has a private variable ***my***, that it can write into and reading privileges on the private variables of other processes. The private variables may take, in addition to at least two values used for random draws, the following values: ***{uninterested, waiting, competing, goingin, lost, again, tie, breaktie}***. The initial value is ***uninterested***. We use a slight generalization of the **wait** statement used previously: **wait until all in** *Set* waits until all private variables of other processes are in *Set*. Its execution implies a repetition of simple waits. Thus the values of the variables belonging to other processes may be tested at different times, and we may decide on a positive answer while, in fact, the values never were in *Set* all at the same time. The reserved word **some** refers to any one of the private variables of the other processes; its use implies some hidden loop. The reserved word **none** is similarly understood.

Algorithm 3

```
Exit section:
 30: my := uninterested;

Trying section:
  1: my := waiting;
  2: wait until
         all in {uninterested, waiting}
         or some in {goingin}
       endwait;
  3: my := competing;
  4: if some in {lost, again, tie, breaktie} ∪ Random
         then goto 1;
  5: my := a random element of Random;
```

```
6:  wait until
        all in {uninterested, waiting, tie, lost} ∪ Random
    endwait;
7:  if some > my then goto 17;
8:  wait until
        all in {uninterested, waiting, tie, lost, my}
    endwait;
9:  my := tie;
10: wait until
        all in {uninterested, waiting, tie, breaktie, lost}
    endwait;
11: if some in {tie, breaktie} then goto 15;
12: if some in {lost} then goto Critical Section;
13: my := goingin;
14: wait until
        all in {uninterested} ∪ Random
        and then goto Critical Section
    endwait;
15: my := breaktie;
16: wait until
        all in {uninterested, waiting, lost, breaktie} ∪ Random
        and then goto 5
    endwait;
17: my := lost;
18: wait until
        all in {uninterested, waiting, lost, again}
    endwait;
19: my := again;
20: wait until
        all in {uninterested, waiting, again} ∪ Random
        and then goto 5
    endwait;
```

A full proof of correctness will appear in the full paper, we present here only a sketch. A process may enter its critical section only from statement 12 or 14, after putting its variable to the value *tie* in statement 9, and checking that no one else has value *tie* in statement 11. This proves mutual exclusion.

The next step is to prove a number of invariant properties, showing that, essentially processes proceed in an almost synchronized way, in the competition part, starting at statement 5.

Then one shows that the set of processes that take part in the competition is (those at statements 5..20) is closed once the competition begins and that each one has a positive chance of entering its critical section. It follows that, with probability one, somebody enters its critical section, leaving a smaller set of competitors. The last one of a competition to enter its critical section, goes through statements 13 and 14 and makes sure that all waiting processes enter the next turn of the competition. It is left to show that if nobody is in the competition, and somebody is waiting then somebody will enter the competition.

7. Conclusion

We provide attractive alternatives to classical solutions. We suggest to interested researchers to have a look into formal proof techniques for probabilistic simple programs.

8. Acknowledgements

We are grateful to Sergiu Hart and Micha Sharir for discussions on the subject of probabilistic algorithms.

References

[BR] de Bruijn, G. Additional comments on a problem in concurrent programming control, Comm. ACM Vol.10, No.3 (1967) pp. 137-138.

[BU] Burns, J. E. Symmetry in systems of asynchronous processes, Proc. 22nd Annual ACM Symposium on Foundations of Computer Science, Nashville, Tennessee (1981), pp. 169-174.

[D1] Dijkstra, E. W. Solution of a problem in concurrent programming control, Comm. ACM Vol.8, No.9 (1965), p. 569.

[D2] Dijkstra, E. W. Co-operating sequential processes, in Programming Languages (Genuys, F. ed.) Academic Press, New York, pp. 43-112 (1968).

[EG] Eisenberg, A. and McGuire, M. R. Further comments on Dijkstra's concurrent programming control problem, Comm. ACM Vol.15, No.11 (1972), p. 999.

[K] Knuth, D. E. Additional comments on a problem in concurrent programming control, Comm. ACM Vol.9, No.5 (1966), pp.321-322.

[HSP] Hart, S., Sharir, M. and Pnueli, A. Termination of probabilistic concurrent programs, Conf. Record 9th Annual ACM Symposium on Principles of Programming Languages, Albuquerque, New Mexico (1982), pp.1-6.

[LA] Lamport, L. A new solution of Dijkstra's concurrent programming problem, Comm. ACM Vol.17, No 8 (1974), pp. 453-455

[LR] Lehmann, D. and Rabin, M. O. On the advantages of free choice. a symmetric and fully distributed solution to the dining philosophers problem (extended abstract), Conf. Record of 8th Annual ACM Symposium on Principles of Programming Languages, Williamsburg, Va. (Jan. 1981), pp 133-138.

[LY] Lynch, Nancy A. Fast allocation of nearby resources in a distributed system, Proc. of the 12th Annual ACM Symposium on the Theory of Computing, Los Angeles, April 1980, pp. 70-81.

[PF] Peterson, Gary L. and Fischer, Michael J. Economical solutions to the critical section problem in a distributed system, Proc. 9th Annual ACM Symposium on Theory of Computing, Boulder, Colorado (1977), pp.91-97.

[R1] Rabin, M.O. Theoretical impediments to artificial intelligence, Information Processing 74 (Jack L. Rosenfeld ed.) pp.615-619.

[R2] Rabin, M.O. N-process mutual exclusion with bounded waiting time by 4 logN-valued shared variable, Journal of Computer and System Sciences, Vol. 25 (1982), pp.66-75.

[R3] Rabin, M.O. The choice coordination problem, Memo. UCB/ERL M80/38, Electronics Research Lab. Univ. of California at Berkeley, Aug. 1981.

[RP] Rivest, R. L. and Pratt, V. R. The mutual exclusion problem for unreliable processes: preliminary report, Proc. 17th Annual Symposium on Foundations of Computer Science, Houston, Texas (1976), pp.1-8.

AMBIGUITY AND DECISION PROBLEMS CONCERNING NUMBER SYSTEMS*

Karel Culik II
Department of Computer Science
University of Waterloo
Waterloo, Ontario, Canada N2L 3G1

Arto Salomaa
Mathematics Department
University of Turku
Finland

ABSTRACT

The representation of integers in arbitrary number systems is considered. The main emphasis is on problems concerning ambiguity, completeness and equivalence. We develop a rather general automata-theoretic method for solving such, in essence, purely number-theoretic problems. The method seems to be applicable in a variety of different situations.

1. INTRODUCTION

Recent work in the theory of codes (see, for instance, [4]) as well as in cryptography, has led to problems dealing with the representation of positive integers in arbitrary number systems. Here "arbitrary" means that the digits may be larger than the base and that some integers may have several representations or none at all. Typical questions arising are: Do the sets of numbers represented by two given number systems coincide? Is the representation of numbers according to a given number system ambiguous or unambiguous?

Very little is known about the solution of such problems in spite of their fundamental number-theoretic nature and also in spite of the fact that the representation of integers is fundamental also in the theory of computing. Moreover, such problems seem to be closely connected with the theory of arithmetical codes, in particular with the work of P. Elias (see [2] and also [3]). Unfortunately there fails to be a general framework or theory for dealing with such problems although there are some scattered results such as the one by Honkala, [1].

---

* This work was supported by Natural Sciences and Engineering Research Council of Canada, Grant Nos. A7403 and A1617. The work was done while the second author was visiting the University of Waterloo during the academic year 1981-82.

The purpose of the present paper is to lay the foundations for such a theory by discussing the basic notions in a systematic way and introducing a technique for solving decision problems. It is interesting to note that this technique is based on results in automata theory, and we do not know any other way of solving the purely number-theoretic problems we are dealing with! Of course, the constructions can be "translated" into a language which does not use automata theory but they may then become very complicated.

2. DEFINITIONS AND EXAMPLES

We begin by defining the fundamental notions of this paper.

A number system is a $(v+1)$-tuple

$$N = (n, m_1, \ldots, m_v)$$

of positive integers such that $v \geq 1$, $n \geq 2$ and $1 \leq m_1 < m_2 < \ldots < m_v$. The number n is referred to as the base and the numbers m_i as digits.

A nonempty word

$$m_{i_k} m_{i_{k-1}} \ldots m_{i_1} m_{i_0} , \quad 1 \leq i_j \leq v ,$$

over the alphabet $\{m_1, \ldots, m_v\}$ is said to represent the integer

$$[m_{i_k} \ldots m_{i_0}] = m_{i_0} + m_{i_1} \cdot n + m_{i_2} \cdot n^2 + \ldots + m_{i_k} \cdot n^k .$$

The set of all represented integers is denoted by $S(N)$. A set of positive integers is said to be representable by a number system, shortly RNS, if it equals the set $S(N)$, for some number system N.

Two number systems N_1 and N_2 are called equivalent if $S(N_1) = S(N_2)$. A number system N is called complete if $S(N)$ equals the set of all positive integers. It is called almost complete if there are only finitely many positive integers not belonging to $S(N)$.

A number system N is termed ambiguous if there are two distinct words w_1 and w_2 over the alphabet $\{m_1, \ldots, m_v\}$ representing the same integer: $[w_1] = [w_2]$. Otherwise, N is termed unambiguous.

An RNS set is termed unambiguous if it equals $S(N)$, for some unambiguous number system N. Otherwise, it is termed inherently ambiguous. (Thus, an RNS set S being inherently ambiguous means that whenever $S = S(N)$ then N is ambiguous.)

Example 2.1: For each $n \geq 2$, the number system

$$N = (n,1,2,\dots,n)$$

is complete and unambiguous. Consequently, for different values of n we get equivalent systems. Representation according to N is customarily referred to as the n-adic representation of integers.

Example 2.2: Consider the number system $N = (2,2,3,4)$. We claim that S(N) consists of all positive integers that are not of the form $2^k - 3$, for some $k = 2,3,4,\dots$. Thus, 1, 5, 13, 29, 61 are the first few numbers missed.

In fact, no number of the form $2^k - 3$ can be in S(N) because if $x = 2^k - 3$ is the smallest such number in S(N), we consider the representation $[a_1 \dots a_m] = x$. Here obviously $m \geq 2$ and $a_m = 3$ (because otherwise the represented number is even). But now $[a_1 \dots a_{m-1}] = 2^{k-1} - 3$, contradicting the choice of x.

On the other hand, for any $k \geq 1$, an arbitrary integer x satisfying $2^{k+1} - 2 \leq x \leq 2^{k+2} - 4$ is represented by some word of length k over the digit alphabet. This can be easily established by induction on k. Observe that

$$[2^k] = 2^{k+1} - 2 \quad \text{and} \quad [4^k] = 2^{k+2} - 4 \,.$$

Hence, our claim concerning S(N) follows. Note also that N is ambiguous, 8 being the smallest number with two representations. We'll see in Section 6 that S(N) is, in fact, inherently ambiguous. In the "dyadic" number system $N_2 = (2,1,2)$, S(N) is represented by all words over $\{1,2\}$ that are not of the form $2^i 1$, for some $i \geq 0$. Thus, a regular expression can be given for the set of words representing S(N) in dyadic notation.

Example 2.3: The number system $N = (2,1,4)$ is unambiguous. This is easy to verify directly.

We claim that S(N) equals the set of numbers incongruent to 2 modulo 3. We show first that all numbers in S(N) are of this type. This is clearly true of numbers represented by words of length 1 over the digit alphabet. On the other hand, whenever x is congruent to 0 (resp. 1) modulo 3, then both $2x + 1$ and $2x + 4$ are congruent to 1 (resp. 0) modulo 3. Hence, induction on the length of the representing words shows that every number in S(N) is incongruent to 2 modulo 3.

Conversely, to show that all such numbers are in S(N), we assume the contrary. Let x be the smallest number incongruent to 2 (mod 3) which is not in S(N). Hence, $x = 3k$ or $x = 3k + 1$, for some k. Assume first that $x = 3k$. Then if k is odd (resp. even), the last digit in the representation of x must be 1 (resp. 4) and the number $(3k-1)/2 = 3(k-1)/2 + 1$

(resp. $(3k-4)/2$) is congruent to 1 modulo 3 and not in $S(N)$ (because, otherwise, x would be in $S(N)$). This contradicts the choice of x. Assume, secondly, that $x = 3k + 1$. A similar contradiction now arises by considering the number $(x - 1)/2$ or $(x - 4)/2$, depending whether k is even or odd.

Observe, finally, that in unary notation the set $S(N)$ of Example 2.2 is non-regular, whereas the set $S(N)$ of Example 2.3 is regular.

Example 2.4: This example is a more general one. Consider, for $k \geq 3$, the number system $N(k) = (2,2,k)$. When is $N(k)$ unambiguous? Clearly, $N(k)$ is unambiguous if k is odd. Thus, assume that $k = 2m$. It is easy to see that if m is even, then $N(k)$ is unambiguous. The first odd values of m yielding an unambiguous $N(k)$ are: 11, 19, 23, 27, 35, 37, 39, 43, 45, 47, 51, 53, 55, 59, 67, 69, 71, 75, 77, 79, 83, 87, 89, 91, 93, 95, 99. The reader is referred to [4] for more information as regards this example.

3. PRELIMINARY LEMMAS

This section contains lemmas dealing with ambiguity and the construction of some classes of RNS sets. Note that all our constructions are effective, although this is not explicitly stated.

Lemma 3.1. A number system $N = (n, m_1, \ldots, m_v)$ is ambiguous if $v > n$. N is unambiguous if the digits m_j lie in different residue classes modulo n.

Lemma 3.2. No finite set is RNS, whereas every cofinite set is RNS.

Lemma 3.3. Let $n \geq 2$ be arbitrary. Then every (nonempty) union of some residue classes modulo n is RNS. Consequently, both odd and even numbers form an RNS set.

Lemma 3.3 shows that the set $S(N)$ of Example 2.3 is represented also by the number system (3, 1, 3, 4, 6, 7). In some sense, this number system is more "natural" for the set consisting of all integers incongruent to 2 modulo 3. However, it is ambiguous, whereas the set of Example 2.3 is unambiguous!

4. TRANSLATION LEMMA AND COROLLARIES

We shall now introduce the method which will be basic for our decidability results. It consists of representing the sets S(N) as regular languages. The following result is referred to as the "translation lemma".

Lemma 4.1: For every number system $N=(n,m_1,\ldots,m_v)$, one can construct a regular expression p(N) over the alphabet $\{1,\ldots,n\}$ such that the set of words in the language denoted by p(N), when these words are viewed as n-adic numbers, equals the set S(N).

Proof: We construct a generalized sequential machine M translating words over the alphabet $\{m_1,\ldots,m_v\}$ into equivalent (i.e., representing the same number "over" the base n) words over the alphabet $\{1,\ldots,n\}$. The construction is based on the fact that the "carry" will always be bounded in such computations. The input and output format of M will be explained below.

The state set of M consists of the states $q_0,q_1,\ldots,q_{2t}$, where $t=\max(n,m_v)$, and of a special final state q. The input alphabet is $\{m_1,\ldots,m_v,\#\}$, and the output alphabet $\{1,\ldots,n\}$. q_0 is the initial state and q the only final state. The behavior of M is specified as follows. Intuitively, being in the state q_i means that there is a carry i in the computation so far.

Thus, when reading the letter j in the state q_i, M produces the output letter j' and goes to the state $q_{i'}$, where i' and j' are unique integers satisfying

$$i+j=j'+i'n\ ,\ 1\leqslant j'\leqslant n\ .$$

It is easy to verify inductively that, in this procedure, i' never becomes greater than 2t, so M has the required state $q_{i'}$. Finally, when reading the letter # in the state q_i, M produces the output i in reverse n-adic notation (i.e., the rightmost digit represents the highest power) and goes to the state q. Thus, proper translations are obtained only for words from $\{m_1,\ldots,m_v\}^*\#$. Moreover, M translates such words, viewed as numbers represented according to N in reverse notation and provided with the boundary marker #, into words over $\{1,\ldots,n\}$, representing the same number in reverse n-adic notation. Consequently, the mirror image of the language $M(\{m_1,\ldots,m_v\}^+\#)$ represents the set S(N) in n-adic notation, and clearly a regular expression p(N) can be constructed as required. □

As an example, consider the number system $N = (2,a,b)$ where $a = 13$ and $b = 22$. The computation of M for the input aba# is given below:

STATE:	q_0	q_6	q_{13}	q_{12}
INPUT:	a	b	a	#
OUTPUT:	1	2	2	212
NEW STATE:	q_6	q_{13}	q_{12}	

Clearly, the dyadic word 212221 represents the same number (109) as the word aba (which happens to be its own mirror image) according to N. Of course, the reason for the reverse n-adic notation and mirror images in the proof of Lemma 4.1 is merely the fact that we have followed the customary operational mode of gsm's: inputs are read from left to right. On the other hand, in number system notation, the digits representing the highest numbers are customarily on the left.

Observe also that the sequential machine M in the proof of Lemma 4.1 is deterministic. It is also almost a Mealy machine: the only time it may produce more than one output letter (or none at all) is the end of the computation when it scans #.

The following two results are now immediate corollaries of Lemma 4.1.

Theorem 4.2: It is decidable whether or not a given number system is almost complete.

Deciding the completeness of a giving number system is trivial: a number system is complete if and only if every number less than or equal to the base is among the digits.

Theorem 4.3: The equivalence problem is decidable for number systems with the same base.

5. EQUIVALENCE AND CHARACTERIZATION

We shall establish in this section the decidability of the equivalence of two number systems in the general case. We shall also consider some problems dealing with the characterization of RNS sets. We begin with a lemma useful in many considerations involving number systems. The lemma resembles some fixed-point results in language theory.

Lemma 5.1: Let $n \geq 2$ and $1 \leq m_1 < \ldots < m_v$ $(v \geq 1)$ be given integers. Consider the number system $N = (n, m_1, \ldots, m_v)$. Then the set $X = S(N)$

satisfies the equation

$$X = \{nx + m_j \mid x \in X,\ 1 \leq j \leq v\} \cup \{m_1, \ldots, m_v\}$$

and, moreover, S(N) is the only set of positive integers satisfying this equation.

<u>Proof:</u> Clearly S(N) is a solution: the first term on the right side represents the operation of adding one digit to the right. To show that the solution is unique, we let X be an arbitrary solution. Then clearly m_j is in X, for $1 \leq j \leq v$. Thus, all one-digit numbers (we are considering the representation according to N) are in X. We make the following inductive hypothesis: all k-digit numbers are in X. But now the first term of the union shows that all (k+1)-digit numbers are in X. Consequently, S(N) is included in X.

To establish the reverse inclusion $X \subseteq S(N)$, we assume the contrary, and let x be the smallest number in $X - S(N)$. Since x is in X, it must belong to one of the terms of the union. Because x is not in S(N), it cannot be in $\{m_1, \ldots, m_v\}$. Consequently, there are numbers $x_1 \in X$ and j such that $x = nx_1 + m_j$. Here x_1 cannot belong to S(N) because, otherwise, x is in S(N), a contradiction. Consequently, x_1 is in $X - S(N)$. Because clearly $x_1 < x$, this contradicts the choice of x. This implies that $X = S(N)$. □

We introduce the following notation in order to avoid confusion and cumbersome terminology. Consider a word w over the alphabet $\{1, \ldots, n\}$. We denote by $\nu(w)$ the integer denoted by w in n-adic notation. Thus, if $n = 2$ then $\nu(212221) = 109$.

<u>Lemma 5.2:</u> Let A be a regular language over the alphabet $\{1, \ldots, n\}$, $n \geq 2$, and let a and b be positive integers. Then the language

$$L(A,a,b) = \{w \in \{1, \ldots, n\}^+ \mid \nu(w) = a \cdot \nu(x) + b, \text{ for some } x \text{ in } A\}$$

is also regular.

<u>Theorem 5.3:</u> The equation $S(N) = \{\nu(w) \mid w \in A\}$ is decidable for a given regular language A over the alphabet $\{1, \ldots, m\}$, $m \geq 2$, and for a given number system $N = (n, m_1, \ldots, m_v)$.

<u>Proof:</u> By Lemma 5.1, $S(N) = \{\nu(w) \mid w \in A\}$ holds if and only if

$$A = \bigcup_{1 \leq i \leq v} L(A,n,m_i) \cup \{\nu^{-1}(m_1),\ldots,\nu^{-1}(m_v)\} .$$

(Clearly, if A and B are regular languages over the alphabet $\{1,\ldots,m\}$, then $A = B$ holds if and only if $\{\nu(w) \mid w \in A\} = \{\nu(w) \mid w \in B\}$ holds. This follows by the unambiguity of the m-adic representation.) Finally, use Lemma 5.2. □

Theorem 5.4: It is decidable whether or not two given number systems are equivalent.

Lemma 4.1 associates a regular expression to each RNS set. Conversely, not every regular expression gives rise (in this sense) to an RNS set (see, for instance, Lemma 3.2). The following characterization problem is open: characterize the regular expressions giving rise to RNS sets. Indeed, we do not even know the solution for the following decision problem: decide of a regular expression whether or not it gives rise to an RNS set.

We mention, finally, that the decidability of the following problem is open: given a number system N and an integer $m \geq 2$, is there a number system N_1 with base m such that $S(N) = S(N_1)$? A solution for the case where N_1 is assumed to be unambiguous is given in the next section.

6. AMBIGUITY AND INHERENT AMBIGUITY

Our first theorem gives another proof for the decidability of the ambiguity of a given number system.

Theorem 6.1: Let $N = (n,m_1,\ldots,m_v)$ be a number system and A the corresponding regular language according to Lemma 4.1. Let $L(A,a,b)$ be the regular language considered in Lemma 5.2. Then N is unambiguous if and only if, for all distinct i and j,

$$L(A,n,m_i) \cap L(A,n,m_j) = \phi .$$

Proof: The intersection being nonempty means that there two words, one ending with m_i and the other with m_j, over the digit alphabet representing the same number according to N. Hence, the intersection being empty is a necessary and sufficient condition for the unambiguity. □

An analogous argument can be used also to solve a problem related to the one mentioned at the end of Section 5.

<u>Theorem 6.2:</u> It is decidable of a given number system N and an integer $m \geq 2$ whether or not there exists an unambiguous number system N_1 with base m satisfying $S(N) = S(N_1)$.

The decidability of the inherent ambiguity of a given RNS set is open. By Theorem 6.2, it suffices to find an effective bound for the base.

One can also introduce for number systems in a natural fashion (as for context-free grammars, see [5]), the notions of the degree of ambiguity and the degree of inherent ambiguity. The resulting existence and decision problems are all open.

In the remainder of this section, we consider some special cases of ambiguity and inherent ambiguity.

<u>Theorem 6.3:</u> The set of even numbers is unambiguous. The set of odd numbers is inherently ambiguous.

<u>Proof:</u> Consider the number system $N = (2,2,4)$. Clearly, for any $m \geq 1$, there is a one-to-one correspondence between dyadic representations of m and representations of 2m according to N. (The former are obtained from the latter through division by 2.) Since the dyadic representation is unambiguous and complete, the first sentence follows. (In fact, one can prove in the same way that, for every $k \geq 1$, the set

$$\{ik \mid i \geq 1\}$$

is unambiguous.)

The second sentence is easily established by an exhaustive argument leading to a contradiction in each case. □

We now return to Example 2.2 and show that the set S(N) is inherently ambiguous. Consider any number system N_1 with base n, representing S(N). Since the number 1 is not of the proper form, it cannot appear as a digit. Consequently, all numbers of the proper form among the numbers $1,\dots,2n+1$ must appear as digits. (Observe that $2n+2$ is the smallest number we can get using the first power of n.) We now choose i in such a way that $2 \leq i \leq 3$ and $n+i$ is of the proper form. (This is possible because no two consecutive numbers are of the improper form.) Since 2 and 3 are among the digits, the equation

$$2n + (n+i) = 3n + i$$

shows that N_1 is ambiguous. Hence, S(N) is inherently ambiguous.

The last result in this section shows that in some cases ambiguity depends essentially on the base.

Theorem 6.4: There is an RNS set S possessing representations with different bases m and n such that it has an unambiguous representation with the base m, whereas every representation of S with base n is ambiguous.

Proof. The set $S = S(N)$ in Example 2.3 satisfies the required conditions.

7. CONCLUSION

We have studied in a systematic way representability, ambiguity and decision problems dealing with number systems. Some important questions still remain open, as pointed out above. Another open problem area is to develop some useful "normal forms" for number systems. Also open is to what extent our results carry over to number systems having arbitrary integers as digits. A rather surprising fact is that our main results are based entirely on automata theory. This can be viewed as another indication of the diverse applicability of automata theory! It remains to be seen whether these results can be obtained also by purely number-theoretic arguments.

REFERENCES

[1] Honkala, J. (1982) Unique representation in number systems and L codes. Discrete Applied Mathematics, 4, 229-232.

[2] Jelinek, F. (1968) Probabilistic Information Theory. McGraw-Hill, New York.

[3] Jürgensen, H. and Kunze, M. (1980) Redundanzfreie Codes als Kryptocodes. Technical Report TI 8/80, Darmstadt Technical University.

[4] Maurer, H.A., Salomaa, A. and Wood, D. (1982) L codes and number systems. Theoretical Computer Science, 22, 331-346.

[5] Salomaa, A. (1973) Formal Languages. Academic Press, New York.

ON THE OBSERVATIONAL SEMANTICS OF FAIR PARALLELISM

Ph. Darondeau and L. Kott
IRISA
Campus de Beaulieu
F-35042 RENNES CEDEX

1. INTRODUCTION

The work reported below stems from several remarks upon Milner's calculus of communicating systems (CCS) [Mi80].

- Among conditions to be fulfilled by observationally equivalent systems S and S', it is required that for any sequence ρ of observable actions, and possible state σ of S after experiment ρ, there exists some equivalent state σ' of S' possibly reached after identical experiment. Systems may happen to be discriminated that way although no experiment makes any difference between them.
- The observational equivalence is not a congruence, which bears evidence of the weaknesses of principles assumed for observing systems.
- The unrestricted power of the programming language entails incompleteness of the calculus, so that it is impossible to decide wether its parallel composition is fair or unfair.
- Parallelism is reduced to sequential nondeterminism, which involves debts in the fairness issue.

In the case of finite behaviours, the first remark already led us to enhance an enlarged equivalence and an associated proof system [Da82]. In the vein of Hoare's theory of CSP [Ho81], our proposal excludes the sum operator (+) to the benefit of n-ary guarding operators $(\mu_1,\ldots,\mu_n)$ and makes the assumption of a sequential observer which presents ambiguous action demands such as $(\mu_1,\ldots,\mu_n)$. By the way, the observer is able to simulate any non-deterministic program context, whence the identity between the equivalence and the adjoined congruence : both relations are defined as the equality between the alternated demand and response languages which represent the observations of programs. In that framework, the observational semantics of programs can no more be expressed by the conditional rewriting systems suggested by Plotkin [Pl81], as it was the case in [He80, Mi80, HeP80].

The present work aims to extend our previous approach to infinite behaviours and to achieve fairness of the parallel composition, which requirement has been evaded as yet in all studies inspiring from CCS. The intended kind of fairness is one of possible derivatives of the original property described by Park, several interpretations of which make sense when applied to communicating systems [KuR82]. Our acknowledged intention is to validate the following statement

PARALLELISM = FAIRNESS ≠ SEQUENTIAL NON DETERMINISM

For example, we take it as granted that the machine H+T which repeats indefinitely the non deterministic choice between two actions "head" and "tail", equally looked for by an observer, has some extra behaviours which do not pertain to the parallel composition H|T of two machines H and T, each of which iterates the corresponding action "head" or "tail". A subtle distinction is then established between asynchronous parallelism and non-determinism, much more refined than the usual difference which lays in the occasional simultaneity of events [Wi80, Da80, CMF82] : although asynchronous systems with finite behaviours have always purely sequential equivalents, some infinite asynchronous systems have the prerogative not to support any sequential equivalent. Nor will be considered here the strong simultaneity of events, taken as a basic phenomenon in synchronized calculi such as [Mi82, AuB82]. The fact is that, although the history of interactions approach might still be used, strong simultaneity of events would require a much more refined expression of the condition of fairness, since a process could be waiting for several resources used one at a time by other concurrent processes.

By showing that for synchronization programs with bounded parallelism, languages of observations may be composed according to the structure of programs and still remain in the well known class of rational languages, this paper establishes the existence of a decision procedure for the observational congruence of fairly communicating processes. This result makes it reasonable to search for a corresponding formal proof system ; the main difficulty lies in the axiomatization of infinitary rational expressions.

The remaining sections are organized as follows. Section 2 states our principles of observation. Section 3 describes the programming language and builds its operational semantics. Section 4 derives the observational semantics of programs from their operational semantics and contains the main results of the paper.

2. PRINCIPLES OF OBSERVATION

Programs in our scope are pure synchronization programs. A particular system comes from joining a program with an initial agent. An agent is said composite when it is programmed as the parallel composition of other agents, else it is atomic. M, the vocabulary of actions $\{\mu_1,\ldots,\mu_i,\ldots\}$, is the disjoint union of two subsets Δ and $\overline{\Delta}$, related to each other by a pair of bijections $\overline{}$: $\lambda \in \Delta \Rightarrow \overline{\lambda} \in \overline{\Delta} \Rightarrow \overline{\overline{\lambda}} = \lambda \in \Delta$. Given an agent p composed of atomic agents q_i, $i=1,\ldots,n$, an operation of p is either an action μ of one of q_i's, which responds to some demand from the outer, or an interaction $(\mu,\overline{\mu})$ between a pair of agents (q_i,q_j). Actions of atomic agents are directed according to the communication capabilities $(\mu_1,\ldots,\mu_n)$ allowed by their programs. When using such a capability μ_i, an atomic agent disappears from the embedding agents to the benefit of a new agent, possibly atomic or composite. The presentation of capabilities $(\mu_1,\ldots,\mu_n)$ by one of the agents amounts for the other agents to a complementary action demand $(\overline{\mu}_1,\ldots,\overline{\mu}_n)$ issued from the global environment of the system. Bounded parallelism and bounded sequential non determinism are assumed.

Experimenting over a system amounts to involve it in an environment made of one or several agents, the observers, which it may consequently interact with. The system of observers obeys the same communication laws as the observed system does obey, but the behaviour of an observer is not constrained by a program. Observers submit to the observed system freely chosen action demands $(\mu_1,\ldots,\mu_n)$, possibly answered by the observed agents which display sufficient capabilities to perform one of the actions μ_i. Since an action demand $(\mu_1,\ldots,\mu_n)$ of an observer amounts, for the other observers, to the presentation of complementary capabilities $(\overline{\mu}_1,\ldots,\overline{\mu}_n)$ by the observed system, observers cannot avoid to interact by mutual answering. That property of observers is quite essential : under the assumption of a fair execution of the closed system made of both kinds of agents, infinite sequences of interactions between observers provide default information upon the observed system. We call an experience any fair processing of such a closed system : an atomic agent who infinitely often has the possibility to interact with other agents in the course of an experience will necessarily do so. We shall assume a constant number of observers and exclude the case of observers which could compete on non disjoint action demands. Let the observers date and record their individual acts, then the history of the system of observers may be gathered into a finite or infinite word over the alphabet of demands and responses, on condition that pairs of identically dated responses $\lambda,\overline{\lambda}$ are confused into simple elements $\tilde{\lambda}$ which represent interactions between observers. For a program p with sort $\Lambda \subseteq M$, let $Exp_\Lambda(p)$ be the set of the words which are constructed so. $Exp_\Lambda(p)$ will be called a language of experiments.

Let w in $Exp_\Lambda(p)$ - e.g. $w = (\alpha,\beta)(\gamma,\delta)\alpha(\alpha)(\overline{\gamma},\beta)\hat{\gamma}$ - ; let Fail(w) be the set union of unsuccessful demands which occur in w - e.g. (α) - intersected with $(\Lambda \cup \overline{\Lambda})$; let Div(w) be the subset of the action names which infinitely often occur in the demands of w intersected with $(\Lambda \cup \overline{\Lambda})$; let Resp(w) be the sequence of responses μ_i in Λ which occur in w, postfixed with a special symbol χ and excluding $\hat{\chi}$ symbols - e.g. $\alpha\chi$ -. For such a sequence ρ, let Act(ρ) - resp. Ult(ρ) - be the subset of the action names which occur - resp. occur infinitely often - in ρ. Using the notations $d = Div(w)$, $\delta = Fail(w)$ and $\rho = Resp(w)$, we define the application Ψ : $\Psi(w) = (d,\delta,\rho)$ then the following properties are verified by $\Psi(w)$ for any word of experiments w :

1. $d \subseteq \Lambda \cup \overline{\Lambda}$, $\delta \subseteq \Lambda \cup \overline{\Lambda}$, $\rho \in \Lambda^\omega \cup \Lambda^* \chi$
2. $Ult(\rho) \subseteq d$
3. $d \cap (\delta \cup \overline{\delta}) = \emptyset$

Define Obs(Λ) as the set of triples (d,δ,ρ) which satisfy conditions 1 to 3, then Obs(Λ) may be ordered by the relation $(d,\delta,\rho) \leqslant (d',\delta',\rho')$ if and only if ($\rho = \rho'$ and $\delta \subseteq \delta'$ and $d \subseteq d' \cup \delta'$) or ($\rho = \rho''\chi$ and $\rho'' < \rho'$ and $d \cup \delta = \emptyset$) where $<$ is the prefix order over words. We call a language of observations any downwards and non empty subset of Obs(Λ). A huge amount of combinatorial developments shows that the fonction Ψ is actually a bijection between languages of experiments and languages of observations. Let $Obs_\Lambda(p)$ denote $\Psi(Exp_\Lambda(p))$; for any program p with sort Λ, $Obs_\Lambda(p)$ will be considered from now on as the observational semantics associated with program p.

3. THE PROGRAMMING LANGUAGE AND ITS OPERATIONAL SEMANTICS

3.1. THE SYNTAX OF PROGRAMS

Given the set $M = \Delta \cup \overline{\Delta}$ of action names and a set X of variables, the syntactic categories of terms and programs in the language are the least families constructed from the following rules, where we let MS(t) and FV(t) respectively denote the minimal sort and set of free variables of term t (μ_i, x_i, t_i stand for an action name, a variable, a term) :

- NIL is a term, $MS(NIL)=\emptyset$, $FV(NIL)=\emptyset$
- x is a term , $MS(x)=\emptyset$, $FV(x)=\{x\}$
- $(\mu_1,\ldots,\mu_n)(t_1,\ldots,t_n)$ is a term, let t that term, $MS(t) = \{\mu_1,\ldots,\mu_n\} \cup (\bigcup_i MS(t_i))$, $FV(t) = \bigcup_i FV(t_i)$
- $Y(x_1 \leftarrow t_1,\ldots,x_n \leftarrow t_n)$ is a term if $\bigcup_i FV(t_i) \subseteq \{x_1,\ldots,x_n\}$, Let t that term then $MS(t) = \bigcup_i MS(t_i)$ and $FV(t) = \emptyset$
- $(t_1 | t_2)$ is a term if $FV(t_1) = FV(t_2) = \emptyset$, let t that term then

$MS(t) = MS(t_1) \cup MS(t_2)$ and $FV(t) = \emptyset$

- if $FV(t) = \emptyset$ then $t[/\mu_1 \ldots \mu_n]$ is a term, let t',
  $MS(t') = MS(t) \setminus (\{\mu_1 \ldots \mu_n\} \cup \{\overline{\mu}_1 \ldots \overline{\mu}_n\})$ and $FV(t') = \emptyset$
- if $FV(t) = \emptyset$ and $MS(t) \subseteq \Lambda$ then t is a program with MS(t) as its minimal sort, and t_Λ is a program with minimal sort Λ.

Two kinds of construction operations are provided in the syntax :

- operations which define the *elementary* behaviours of programs (constant NIL, n-ary guarded selection $(\mu_1, \ldots, \mu_n)$, recursion (Y)) ;
- *flow-operations* which allow the composition of programs (parallel composition $|$, and restrictions $[/\mu_1 \ldots \mu_n]$.

3.2. HISTORIES

We call histories of a program the records of operation of the observed system in every possible experience upon a system initialized with that program. Given an history h_p of some program p of sort Λ, and an action name μ in $\Lambda \cup \overline{\Lambda}$, we say that μ is : *blocked* in h_p if some observed agent has remained endlessly inactive while displaying capability μ, *transient* in h_p if no observed agent shows capability μ beyond some step of the execution, *persistent* in h_p if neither blocked nor transient, *satiated* in h_p if corresponding responses μ have been issued infinitely often. From the assumption of fairness, we take it for granted that satiated labels are persistent and therefore not blocked. It follows that an history h_p of a program p with sort Λ may be represented by a triple (d, δ, ρ) : d, resp. δ, is the set of the action labels which are persistent, resp. transient, in h_p, so that $(\Lambda \cup \overline{\Lambda}) \setminus (d \cup \delta)$ contains exactly the labels of actions which are blocked in h_p. $H(\Lambda)$ will denote the set of such histories (d, δ, ρ) which verify conditions 1 and 2 of section 2 together with condition (3') : $d \cap \delta = \emptyset$. Define $H_\Lambda(p)$ as the set of histories of a program p with sort Λ ; from now on, $H_\Lambda(p)$ will be regarded as the operational semantics of p.

3.3. THE OPERATIONAL SEMANTICS

<u>definition 1</u>. For $W \subseteq M$ and $\mu \in W$, we let $\xrightarrow{W,\mu}$ be the least binary relation over programs such that

- $(\mu_1, \ldots, \mu_n)(t_1, \ldots, t_n) \xrightarrow{(\mu_1, \ldots, \mu_n), \mu_i} t_i$, $1 \leq i \leq n$
- $Y(x_1 \leftarrow t_1, \ldots, x_n \leftarrow t_n) \xrightarrow{W,\mu} t$ if

$t_1[Y(x_j \leftarrow t_j, \ldots, x_n \leftarrow t_n, x_1 \leftarrow t_1, \ldots)/x_j] \xrightarrow{W,\mu} t$
where the replacement of free variables applies for every j, $1 \leq j \leq n$.

<u>definition 2</u>. For elementary programs of sort Λ, $H_\Lambda(p)$ is the least set of histories determined by the following rules.

- if $p \xrightarrow{W,\mu} q$ for no W,μ and q, then $(\emptyset, \Lambda \cup \overline{\Lambda}, \chi) \in H_\Lambda(p)$
- if $p \xrightarrow{W,\mu} q$, then $(d,\delta,\mu\rho) \in H_\Lambda(\rho)$ for any (d,δ,ρ) in $H_\Lambda(q)$, and
  $(\emptyset, (\Lambda \cup \overline{\Lambda})\setminus W, \chi) \in H_\Lambda(p)$
- if $p \xrightarrow{W_1,\mu_1} p_1 \xrightarrow{W_2,\mu_2} p_2 \ldots \xrightarrow{W_i,\mu_i} p_i \ldots$, $i \in \mathbb{N}$, then
  $(\lim_i(\bigcup_{j \geq i} W_j), \lim_i(\bigcap_{j \geq i} (\Lambda \cup \overline{\Lambda})\setminus W_j), \mu_1 \mu_2 \ldots \mu_i \ldots) \in H_\Lambda(p)$

<u>definition 3</u>. Given histories h_p and h_q in $H(\Lambda)$, h_p and h_q are compatible ($h_p \# h_q$) iff for any action μ blocked in h_p (resp. h_q), neither μ is satiated in h_q (resp. h_p) nor $\overline{\mu}$ is blocked or persistent in h_q (resp. h_p).
Clearly, given programs p and q, incompatible histories h_p and h_q cannot record the individual behaviors of p and q in a common experience upon their parallel compound $p|q$.

<u>definition 4</u>. Let f and g be two words of M*, their parallel composition $f|g$ is inductively defined as follows, $\mu,\nu \in M$: either $f|g = \mu(f'|g)+\nu(f|g')$ with $f = \mu f'$, $g = \nu g'$ and $\mu \neq \overline{\nu}$ or $f|g = \mu(f'|g)+\nu(f|g')+(f'|g')$ with $f = \mu f'$, $g = \nu g'$ and $\mu = \overline{\nu}$.

<u>definition 5</u>. Let f and g be two words of M^∞, their parallel composition $f|g$ is the greatest subset of M^∞ such that $f|g = \sum_{n,m>0} (f\langle n\rangle | g\langle m\rangle)(f{>}n | g{>}m)$
where $f\langle n\rangle$ is the longest left factor of f of length less than or equal to n, and $f = (f\langle n\rangle)(f{>}n)$.

<u>definition 6</u>. Given compatible histories $h_p = (d_p, \delta_p, \rho_p)$ and $h_q = (d_q, \delta_q, \rho_q)$ in $H(\Lambda)$ $(h_p|h_q)$ is the set of histories (d,δ,ρ) which verify conditions i to iii :
i) $\delta = \delta_p \cap \delta_q$ ii) $d \cup \delta = (d_p \cup \delta_p) \cap (d_q \cup \delta_q)$
iii) $\rho\setminus\chi \in ((\rho_p\setminus\chi)|(\rho_q\setminus\chi))$

Let h_p and h_q record behaviours of p and q in a common experience on their compound $p|q$, then the set of blocked (resp. transient) actions in the history of $p|q$ is the union (intersection) of their respective sets of blocked (transient) actions.

<u>definition 7</u>. $H_\Lambda(p|q) = \bigcup \{(h_p|h_q) | h_p \in H_\Lambda(p), h_q \in H_\Lambda(q), h_p \# h_q\}$.

<u>definition 8</u>. Let the restriction $R \equiv /\mu_1 \ldots \mu_n$ and let sets of lablels $\Lambda, \Lambda', \Lambda''$ be such that $\Lambda' = \{\mu_1 \ldots \mu_n\}$, $\Lambda'' = \Lambda \cup \Lambda' \cup \overline{\Lambda}'$, then
$H_\Lambda(q[R]) = ((H_{\Lambda''}(q)) \downarrow (\Lambda' \cup \overline{\Lambda}')) \uparrow ((\Lambda \cup \overline{\Lambda}) \cap (\Lambda' \cup \overline{\Lambda}'))$

where $(d,\delta,\rho) \uparrow \Omega = (d,\delta \cup \Omega,\rho)$ and $(d,\delta,\rho) \downarrow \Omega$ is equal to $(d\backslash\Omega,\delta\backslash\Omega,\rho)$ if $\rho \in (M\backslash\Omega)^{\omega} \cup (M\backslash\Omega)^{*}\chi$ or else is empty.

proposition 9. For any program p and for any triple (d,δ,ρ) in $H_{\Lambda}(p)$, $\overline{d} \subseteq d \cup \delta$. (In clear, the complement of a persistent label cannot be blocked).

4. THE OBSERVATIONAL SEMANTICS OF PROGRAMS

Let the order relation $\leqslant$ of section 2 be extended from $Obs(\Lambda)$ to $H(\Lambda)$; we state that for any possible history $h_p = (d_p,\delta_p,\rho_p)$ of a program p with sort Λ, the observations which are produced by experiences in which p behaves according to h_p are exactly the elements of the set $\{(d,\delta,\rho) \in Obs(\Lambda) \mid (d,\delta,\rho) \leqslant (d_p,\delta_p,\rho_p)\}$.

As an example, let Λ be $\{\alpha,\beta\}$ and h_p be $(\emptyset,\alpha,\beta\chi)$; let us consider some pair of complementary labels $\gamma,\overline{\gamma}$ which do not belong to Λ, then a possible experience upon p is described by the infinite word w equal to $(\beta)\beta(\alpha,\gamma)(\overline{\gamma})\tilde{\gamma}(\alpha,\gamma)(\overline{\gamma})\tilde{\gamma}\ \ldots$, which produces the observation $\Psi(w)$ equal to $(\alpha,\emptyset,\beta\chi) < (\emptyset,\alpha,\beta\chi)$. At the opposite, let now h_p be $(\overline{\alpha}\beta\overline{\beta},\alpha,\beta^{\omega})$, then $(\overline{\alpha}\beta\overline{\beta},\alpha,\beta^{\omega})$ is not an observation of p : no word such as $(\alpha)(\overline{\alpha},\beta,\overline{\beta})\beta(\overline{\alpha},\beta,\overline{\beta})\beta\ \ldots$ describes a possible experience since one of the observers would be endlessly deprived of a possible interaction with the other observers.

At the present time, the observational meanings of programs are indirectly defined by the law $Obs_{\Lambda}(p) = \{o \in Obs(\Lambda) \mid (\exists h \in H_{\Lambda}(p))(o \leqslant h)\}$ that has just been assumed. The remaining of the paper intends to show that these meanings are in fact a pre-semantics and to derive a direct calculus of that semantics. Preliminary definitions are needed.

4.1. PARTIAL OBSERVATIONS AND RATIONAL LANGUAGES

definition 1. pre-$Obs(\Lambda)$, the set of pre-observations, is constituted by the triples (d,δ,ρ) whose elements verify :

1'. $d \subseteq \Lambda \cup \overline{\Lambda}$, $\delta \subseteq \Lambda \cup \overline{\Lambda}$, $\rho \in \Lambda^{\omega} \cup \Lambda^{*}\chi \cup \Lambda^{*}$

2'. $Ult(\rho) \subseteq d$ if ρ is complete, i.e. $\rho \in \Lambda^{*}\chi \cup \Lambda^{\omega}$, or else $Act(\rho) \subseteq d$

3'. $d \cap \delta = \emptyset$

3". $Ult(\rho) \cap \overline{\delta} = \emptyset$ if ρ is complete, or else $Act(\rho) \cap \overline{\delta} = \emptyset$

<u>definition 2.</u> We call a language of pre-observations any non-empty subset of pre-Obs(Λ) downwards closed for the generalized order $\leqslant$ of section 2. We adopt the convention that a language of pre-observations (resp. observations) may be given the notation $\lfloor L \rfloor$ (resp. $\lfloor L \rfloor_o$) where L is any subset of the language which includes its maximal elements and $\lfloor\ \rfloor$ (resp. $\lfloor\ \rfloor_o$) is the downwards closure operation in pre-Obs(Λ) (resp. Obs(Λ)).

<u>definition 3.</u> For any pair of pre-observations $o_1 = (d_1,\delta_1,\rho_1)$ and $o_2 = (d_2,\delta_2,\rho_2)$, the association $o_1.o_2$ of o_1 and o_2 is the pre-observation o given by :
$o = o_1$ if o is complete, i.e. $\rho_1 \in \Lambda^*\chi \cup \Lambda^\omega$, or else
$o = (d_2,\delta_2,\rho_1\rho_2)$ if o_1,o_2 are respectively incomplete and complete, or else
$o = (d_1 \cup d_2 \cup (\delta_1\setminus\delta_2) \cup (\delta_2\setminus\delta_1),\ \delta_1 \cap \delta_2,\ \rho_1\rho_2)$

<u>definition 4.</u> P-obs(Λ), the set of partial observations, is the monoid with carrier pre-Obs(Λ) $\cup$ {$\mathbb{1}$}, neutral element $\mathbb{1}$, concatenation . extending the association . in pre-Obs(Λ), and order $\leqslant$ defined as the minimal extension of the order $\leqslant$ on pre-Obs(Λ). By way of enlargement, we call a language of partial observations any non empty and downwards closed subset $\lfloor L \rfloor$ of P-obs(Λ) such that $\lfloor L \rfloor = \{\mathbb{1}\}$ or $\mathbb{1} \notin \lfloor L \rfloor$.

<u>definition 5.</u> I : $(\text{pre-Obs}(\Lambda))^\infty \to$ P-obs(Λ) is the function s.t.
- for finite words $o_1o_2\ldots o_k$, $I(o_1o_2\ldots o_k) = o_1.o_2.\ \ldots\ .o_k$ if $k\geqslant 1$
  or else $I(\mathbb{1}) = \mathbb{1}$, the neutral element of P-obs(Λ),
- for infinite words $o_1o_2\ldots o_i\ldots$, let $o_i = (d_i,\delta_i,\rho_i)$, then
  $I(o_1o_2\ldots o_i\ldots) = I(o_1o_2\ldots o_k)$ if ρ_k is complete for some k,
  or else $I(o_1o_2\ldots o_i\ldots)$ is the triple (d,δ,ρ) defined by :

$$d = \operatorname{Lim}_j\Big(\bigcup_{i\geqslant j} d_i\Big) \cup \operatorname{Lim}_j\Big(\bigcup_{i\geqslant j} \delta_i\Big)\setminus \operatorname{Lim}_j\Big(\bigcap_{i\geqslant j} \delta_i\Big)$$

$$\delta = \operatorname{Lim}_j\Big(\bigcap_{i\geqslant j} \delta_i\Big)$$

$$\rho = \rho_1\rho_2\ldots\rho_i\ldots\chi$$

<u>proposition 6.</u> I is a monoid homomorphism.

<u>definition 7.</u> According to [Ei74], we note Rat(Z^∞) the least family of subsets of Z^∞ which contains the finite subsets of Z^* and is closed under concatenation, set union, star and ω-star operations. (The following characterization is proved in [Ei74]).

<u>proposition 8.</u> Let L be a language over Z, L is a rational set of Z^∞ iff there exist finitary rational sets of Z^*, say B, B_i, C_i, $1\leqslant i\leqslant n$, such that $L = B + \sum_i B_i.C_i^{\ \omega}$.

definition 9. For $\mathcal{L} \subseteq \Lambda^{\omega} \cup \Lambda^{*}\chi \cup \Lambda^{*}$, we define $\hat{\mathcal{L}} = \mathcal{L} \cap (\Lambda^{\omega} \cup \Lambda^{*}\chi)$ and $\dot{\mathcal{L}} = \mathcal{L} \cap \Lambda^{*}$. A response-language $\mathcal{L}$ is bi-rational if both its complete and incomplete parts $\hat{\mathcal{L}}$ and $\dot{\mathcal{L}}$ are rational sets in $Rat((\Lambda \cup \{\chi\})^{\infty})$. $\mathcal{L}$ is rational if $\hat{\mathcal{L}}$ is rational and $\dot{\mathcal{L}}$ is empty.

Notational equivalence will be assumed in the sequel between $(d,\delta,\mathcal{L})$ and $\{(d,\delta,p) \mid p \in \mathcal{L}\}$ for any response-language $\mathcal{L}$.

definition 10. A language of partial observations (resp. observations) is rational if it can be expressed as $\lfloor L \rfloor$ (resp. $\lfloor L \rfloor_o$), $L = \sum_i (d_i, \delta_i, \mathcal{L}_i)$, $1 \leq i \leq n$, where the $\mathcal{L}_i$'s are bi-rational (resp. rational) response-languages.

proposition 11. Let $X \in Rat(\text{pre-Obs}(\Lambda)^{\infty})$, then $I(X)$ is a rational language of partial observations. Moreover, there exists an effective procedure which, given the rational expression of X, computes $I(X)$ in the form $\sum_i ((d_i, \delta_i, \hat{\mathcal{L}}_i) + (d_i, \delta_i, \dot{\mathcal{L}}_i))$, where $\mathcal{L}_i$'s are bi-rational response-languages.

proposition 12. If $\lfloor L \rfloor$ is a rational language of partial observations, then $\lfloor L \rfloor \cap Obs(\Lambda)$ is a rational language of observations, let $\lfloor \varphi(L) \rfloor_o$. Moreover, there exists an effective procedure which, given the expression of L as in proposition 11, computes $\varphi(L)$ in the form $\sum_i (d_i, \delta_i, \mathcal{L}_i)$ where $\mathcal{L}_i$'s are rational response-languages.

proposition 13. Let S be a system of linear equations over Z^{∞}, such as $X_i = A_{i1}X_1 + \dots + A_{in}X_n + C_i$; $1 \leq i \leq n$; $A_{ij}, C_i \in Rat(Z^{\infty})$. Let $Y(S)$ denote the greatest solution of S, then $Y(S)$ is a vector of rational languages, and there exists an effective procedure for computing that extremal solution.

definition 14. Let L and L' be two languages on M^{∞}, their parallel composition $L|L'$ is the set $\Sigma((f|g)$, f in L and g in L').

proposition 15. If L and L' are rational, their parallel composition $L|L'$ is rational; moreover, there exists an effective procedure for computing the parallel composition of rational languages.

4.2. THE SEMANTIC LAWS

definition 16. For any elementary program p of sort Λ, we let the associated language of partial observations $P\text{-obs}_{\Lambda}(p)$ be equal to $\lfloor I(\mathcal{M}(p)) \rfloor$ where $\mathcal{M}$ is inductively defined as follows, using X_i's as variables ranging over subsets of $(\text{pre-Obs}(\Lambda))^{\infty}$:

$\mathcal{M}$ (NIL) = $(\emptyset, \Lambda\cup\overline{\Lambda}, \chi)$

$\mathcal{M}(x_i) = (\emptyset, \Lambda\cup\overline{\Lambda}, \mathbf{1}).X_i$

$\mathcal{M}((\mu_1,\ldots,\mu_n)(t_1,\ldots,t_n)) = (\emptyset, (\Lambda\cup\overline{\Lambda})\setminus\{\mu_1,\ldots,\mu_n\},\chi) +$

$$\sum_{i=1}^{n} (\{\overline{\mu}_i\} \cup \{\mu_1,\ldots,\mu_n\}, (\Lambda\cup\overline{\Lambda})\setminus\{\overline{\mu}_i\}\setminus\{\mu_1,\ldots,\mu_n\},\mu_i).\mathcal{N}(t_i)$$

where either $\mathcal{N}(t_i)$ is taken as a constant given by $Obs_\Lambda(t_i) = \lfloor\mathcal{N}(t_i)\rfloor_o$ if t_i is the result of a flow-operation, or else $\mathcal{N}(t_i) \equiv \mathcal{M}(t_i)$.

$\mathcal{M}(Y(x_1{\leftarrow}t_1,\ldots,x_n{\leftarrow}t_n)) = Y_1(X_1 = \mathcal{M}(t_1),\ldots,X_n = \mathcal{M}(t_n))$

where Y_1 denotes the first component of the greatest solution of the corresponding system of linear equations over $(\text{pre-Obs}(\Lambda))^\infty$.

<u>proposition 17.</u> Let p be an elementary program of sort Λ, then the following relations hold : $Obs_\Lambda(p) = P\text{-}obs_\Lambda(p) \cap Obs(\Lambda) = \lfloor\varphi(I(\mathcal{M}(p))\rfloor_o$. Let $q_1 \ldots q_n$ be the outermost subprograms of p which are direct results of flow operations ; if $Obs_\Lambda(q_i)$ is rational for any i, then $\mathcal{M}(p)$, $P\text{-}obs_\Lambda(p)$ and $Obs_\Lambda(p)$ are rational, and there exists an effective procedure for computing $\varphi(I(\mathcal{M}(p))$ in the rational form $\sum_j(d_j,\delta_j,\mathcal{L}_j)$, given the syntax of p and the rational expressions of the sets $Obs_\Lambda(q_i)$.

Next result shows a little more suprising property, since it states that the set of observations of a system of parallel processes can be synthesized from the sets of observations of the parallel components : fairness conditions can still be taken into full account despite the loss of information on operational properties which comes from considering observations instead of histories (for instance, given the history $(\alpha,\overline{\alpha},\chi)$, none of the corresponding observations $(\alpha\overline{\alpha},\emptyset,\chi)$ and $(\emptyset,\overline{\alpha},\chi)$ tells us that the system can indefinitely escape action α without offering $\overline{\alpha}$).

<u>proposition 18.</u> Let observations $o_p = (d_p,\delta_p,\rho_p)$ and $o_q = (d_q,\delta_q,\rho_q)$ in Obs(Λ) ; o_p and o_q are compatible $(o_p{*}o_q)$ iff the following property holds for any $\lambda \in \Lambda$: $(\{\lambda,\overline{\lambda}\} \subseteq \delta_p$ or $\{\lambda,\overline{\lambda}\} \subseteq \delta_q$ or $\lambda \in \delta_p \cap \delta_q$ or $\overline{\lambda} \in \delta_p \cap \delta_q$ or $\{\lambda,\overline{\lambda}\} \subseteq d_p \cap d_q)$.

<u>definition 19.</u> Given rational response languages $\mathcal{L}$ and $\mathcal{L}'$, we let $\mathcal{L}||\mathcal{L}'$ stand for $((\mathcal{L}\setminus\chi)|(\mathcal{L}'\setminus\chi))\chi$, where operations $|$ and $\setminus$ are respectively the parallel composition and right division in $Rat((\Lambda \cup \{\chi\})^\infty)$.

<u>proposition 20.</u> If $Obs_\Lambda(p)$ and $Obs_\Lambda(q)$ are rational languages of observations, let $Obs_\Lambda(p) = \lfloor L_p\rfloor_o$, $L_p = \sum_i(d'_i,\delta'_i,\mathcal{L}'_i)$ and $Obs_\Lambda(q) = \lfloor L_q\rfloor_o$, $L_q = \sum_j(d''_j,\delta''_j,\mathcal{L}''_j)$ where the $\mathcal{L}'_i$'s and $\mathcal{L}''_j$'s are rational, then $Obs_\Lambda(p|q)$ is the rational language of observations $\lfloor L_p||L_q\rfloor_o$ defined by $L_p||L_q$ =

$\sum_{ij}((d'_i \cap d''_j) \cup (d'_i \cap \delta''_j) \cup (\delta'_i \cap d''_j),\ \delta'_i \cap \delta''_j,\ \mathcal{L}'_i \,||\, \mathcal{L}''_j)$, i and j such that $(d'_i, \delta'_i, \chi) * (d''_j, \delta''_j, \chi)$.

As a consequence, there exists an effective procedure for computing $Obs_\Lambda(p|q)$ in the form $\lfloor \sum_k (d_k, \delta_k, \mathcal{L}_k) \rfloor_o$, given $Obs_\Lambda(p)$ and $Obs_\Lambda(q)$ in similar forms.

<u>proposition 21</u>. Let programs p and q such that $p \equiv q[R]$ where $R \equiv /\mu_1 \ldots \mu_n$. Let sets of labels Λ, Λ', Λ'' be such that $\Lambda' = \{\mu_1 \ldots \mu_n\}$ and $\Lambda'' = \Lambda \cup \Lambda' \cup \overline{\Lambda}'$. If $Obs_{\Lambda''}(q)$ is a rational language of observations, put $Obs_{\Lambda''}(q) = \lfloor L_q \rfloor_o$, $L_q = \sum_i (d_i, \delta_i, \mathcal{L}_i)$ where the $\mathcal{L}_i$'s are rational, then $Obs_\Lambda(p)$ is the rational language of observations $\lfloor (L_q \downarrow (\Lambda' \cup \overline{\Lambda}')) \uparrow ((\Lambda \cup \overline{\Lambda}) \cap (\Lambda' \cup \overline{\Lambda}')) \rfloor_o$, where $\uparrow$ is the same as in section 3, and $(d_i, \delta_i, \mathcal{L}_i) \downarrow \Omega$ equals $(d_i \setminus \Omega, \delta_i \setminus \Omega, \mathcal{L}_i \setminus \Omega)$ with $\mathcal{L}_i \setminus \Omega$ defined as $\mathcal{L}_i \cap ((M \setminus \Omega)^\omega \cup (M \setminus \Omega)^* \chi)$.
As a consequence, there exists an effective procedure for computing $Obs_\Lambda(p)$ in the form $\lfloor \sum_k (d'_k, \delta'_k, \mathcal{L}'_k) \rfloor_o$, given $Obs_{\Lambda''}(q)$ in similar form.

The induction on the structure of programs may now be used to prove the following facts.

<u>proposition 22</u>. For any program p_Λ, $Obs_\Lambda(p)$ is rational, and there exists an effective procedure which computes Obs_Λ.

<u>proposition 23</u>. Let programs q and q' with identical minimal sorts $MS(q) = MS(q')$. If $Obs_\Lambda(q) = Obs_\Lambda(q')$ for any sort Λ such that $MS(q) \subseteq \Lambda$, then $Obs_\Lambda(p[q]) = Obs_\Lambda(p[q'])$ for any program context p[ ] and for any set Λ s.t. $MS(p[q]) \subseteq \Lambda$.

For our simple language with bounded parallelism, we have precisely proved that languages of observations may be composed according to derived semantic laws, and that they moreover remain in the well known class of rational languages. The outcome is two-sided. First, we obtain an observational congruence of programs under the assumption of fairness : programs p and q are observationally congruent iff they are observationally equivalent, that is $Obs_\Lambda(p) = Obs_\Lambda(q)$. Second, due to the effectiveness of the semantic calculus, and since there exists a decision procedure for the equality of infinitary rational expressions, we can affirm the following

<u>proposition 24</u>. There exists a decision procedure for the observational congruence of programs.

This result motivates further work towards the axiomatization of the observational congruence of programs under the assumption of fairness,which task is perhaps unfeasible for more general programming languages without resorting to arithmetics or to ordinals.

5. SHORT EXAMPLES

Let $p \equiv Y(x \leftarrow (\alpha,\bar{\alpha})(x,x))$, $q \equiv Y(y \leftarrow (\alpha)(y))$, $r \equiv Y(z \leftarrow (\bar{\alpha})(z))$, then the following equalities hold for sort Λ equal to $\{\alpha,\bar{\alpha}\}$.

$$H_\Lambda(p) = (\emptyset,\emptyset,(\alpha+\bar{\alpha})*\chi) + (\alpha\bar{\alpha},\emptyset,(\alpha+\bar{\alpha})^\omega)$$
$$H_\Lambda(q) = (\emptyset,\bar{\alpha},\alpha*\chi) + (\alpha,\bar{\alpha},\alpha^\omega)$$
$$H_\Lambda(r) = (\emptyset,\alpha,\bar{\alpha}*\chi) + (\bar{\alpha},\alpha,\bar{\alpha}^\omega)$$
$$H_\Lambda(q|r) = (\alpha\bar{\alpha},\emptyset,(\alpha^\omega \,||\, \bar{\alpha}^\omega)) = (\alpha\bar{\alpha},\emptyset,(\alpha+\bar{\alpha})*\chi) + (\alpha\bar{\alpha},\emptyset,(\alpha+\bar{\alpha})^\omega)$$
$$Obs_\Lambda(p) = \lfloor(\emptyset,\emptyset,(\alpha+\bar{\alpha})*\chi) + (\alpha\bar{\alpha},\emptyset,(\alpha+\bar{\alpha})^\omega)\rfloor_o$$
$$Obs_\Lambda(q) = \lfloor(\emptyset,\bar{\alpha},\alpha*\chi) + (\alpha\bar{\alpha},\emptyset,\alpha^\omega)\rfloor_o$$
$$Obs_\Lambda(r) = \lfloor(\emptyset,\alpha,\bar{\alpha}*\chi) + (\alpha\bar{\alpha},\emptyset,\bar{\alpha}^\omega)\rfloor_o$$
$$Obs_\Lambda(q|r) = \lfloor(\alpha\bar{\alpha},\emptyset,(\alpha^\omega \,||\, \bar{\alpha}^\omega)\rfloor_o = \lfloor(\alpha\bar{\alpha},\emptyset,(\alpha+\bar{\alpha})*\chi) + (\alpha\bar{\alpha},\emptyset,(\alpha+\bar{\alpha})^\omega\rfloor_o$$

p and $(q|r)$ are therefore not equivalent.

Let now $p = Y(x \leftarrow (\alpha,\beta)(x,x)$, $q = Y(y \leftarrow (\alpha)(y))$, $r = Y(z \leftarrow (\beta)(z))$, with $\alpha \neq \bar{\beta}$. Taking $\Lambda = \{\alpha,\beta\}$, one gets $Obs_\Lambda(p) = \lfloor U\rfloor_o$ and $Obs_\Lambda(q|r) = \lfloor V\rfloor_o$ with U and V as follows :

$$V = (\emptyset,\bar{\alpha}\ \bar{\beta},(\alpha+\beta)*\chi) + (\alpha\bar{\alpha}\beta\bar{\beta},\emptyset,(\alpha^+\beta^+ + \beta^+\alpha^+)^\omega) + (\beta\bar{\beta},\bar{\alpha},(\alpha+\beta)*\beta^\omega) + (\alpha\bar{\alpha},\bar{\beta},(\alpha+\beta)*\alpha^\omega)$$

$$U = (\emptyset,\bar{\alpha}\ \bar{\beta},(\alpha+\beta)*\chi) + (\alpha\bar{\alpha}\beta\bar{\beta},\emptyset,(\alpha+\beta)^\omega) + (\beta\bar{\beta},\bar{\alpha},(\alpha+\beta)*\beta^\omega) + (\alpha\bar{\alpha},\bar{\beta},(\alpha+\beta)*\alpha^\omega)$$

As a consequence, $(\alpha\bar{\alpha}\beta\bar{\beta},\emptyset,\alpha^\omega) \in \lfloor U\rfloor_o \quad \lfloor V\rfloor_o$, which shows that parallelism cannot be reduced to sequential non-determinism.

REFERENCES

[AuB82] Austry,D. and Boudol,G. Algèbre de processus et synchronisation. (private communication).

[CFM82] Castellani,I., Franceschi,P. and Montanari,U. Labelled event structures : a model for observable concurrency. IFIP TC-2 Working Conference, Garmisch-Partenkirchen, 1982.

[Da80] Darondeau,Ph. Processus non séquentiels et leurs observations en univers non centralisé. in LNCS 83, 1980.

[Da82] Darondeau, Ph. An enlarged definition and complete axiomatization of observational congruence of finite processes. in LNCS 137, 1982.

[Ei74] Eilenberg,S. Automata, Languages and Machines, Vol. 1. Academic Press ed.

[He80] Hennessy,M. and Milner,R. On observing non determinism and concurrency. in LNCS 85, 1980.

[He80] Hennessy,P. and Plotkin,G. A term model for CCS. in LNCS 88, 1980.

[Ho81] Hoare,C.A.R., Brookes,S.D., and Roscoe,A.D. A theory of communicating sequential processes. Technical Monograph PRG-16, Computing Laboratory, University of Oxford, 1981.

[KuR82] Kuiper,R. and de Roever,W.P. Fairness assumptions for CSP in a temporal logic framework. IFIP TC-2 Working Conference, Garmisch-Partenkirchen, 1982.

[Mi80] Milner,R. A calculus of communicating systems. LNCS 92, 1980.

[Mi82] Milner,R. Calculi for synchrony and asynchrony. CSR-104-82, Computer Science Department, Edinburgh, 1982.

[Pa80] Park, D. On the semantics of fair parallelism. in LNCS 86, 1980.

[Pl81] Plotkin,G. A structural approach to operational semantics. Daimi FN-19, Computer Science Department, Aarhus University, 1981.

[Wi80] Winskel,G. Events in computation. PhD Thesis, CST-10-80, Edinburgh, 1980.

AN $O(N^4)$ ALGORITHM TO CONSTRUCT ALL VORONOI DIAGRAMS FOR K NEAREST NEIGHBOR SEARCHING

by

Frank Dehne

Lehrstuhl für Informatik I

Bayerische Julius-Maximilians-Universität Würzburg

Am Hubland

8700 Würzburg

W.-Germany

ABSTRACT

This paper presents an algorithm, that constructs all Voronoi diagrams for k nearest neighbor searching in the Euclidean plane simultaneously. Its space and time complexity of $O(N^4)$ is shown to be optimal.

1. INTRODUCTION

In /ShHo75/ Shamos and Hoey introduce the idea of generalized Voronoi diagrams to get an optimal solution of the k nearest neighbor problem and give an $O(N \log N)$ algorithm to construct the order one diagram.
Lee /Le81/ extends this to an algorithm, that computes an order k diagram in $O(k^2 N \log N)$.

To answer k nearest neighbor queries with arbitrary k we now want to construct all Voronoi diagrams.
This paper presents a simple solution of this problem.
The given algorithm has time and space complexity $O(N^4)$ and is shown to be optimal. Its implementation is not very difficult and the constant factors for the complexity are expected to be quite good.

2. K NEAREST NEIGHBOR SEARCHING AND GENERALIZED VORONOI DIAGRAMS

Let $S:=\{s_1,\ldots,s_N\}$ be a set of $N\geq 3$ points in the Euclidean plane $\mathbb{E}^2$ (with distance measure d).
We shall assume that no more than three of these points lie on a circle and that they are not all collinear.
To answer a query for the k nearest neighbors of a point $q\in\mathbb{E}^2$, we have to find a subset $A\subset S$ with $|A|=k$ and $(\forall x\in A, y\in S-A): d(q,x)\leq d(q,y)$.
With $B(x,y):=\{z\in\mathbb{E}^2 / d(x,z)=d(y,z)\}$ and $h(x,y):=\{z\in\mathbb{E}^2 / d(x,z)\leq d(y,z)\}$ we call $v(A):=\bigcap_{\substack{x\in A\\ y\in S-A}} h(x,y)$

the Voronoi polygon of $A\subset S$ and
$V_k(S):=\{v(A) / A\subset S \text{ and } |A|=k\}-\{\phi\}$ the (generalized) Voronoi diagram of order k.

It is easy to see that $V_k(S)$ can be described by a straight line graph, that divides the Euclidean plane into a finite number of convex polygons* (the Voronoi polygons) and that $A \subset S$ is a set of k nearest neighbors of all query points $q \in v(A) \in V_k(S)$.
With these postulates we can solve the k nearest neighbor problem in the following way:

A. Construct all $V_k(S)$ for $1 \leq k \leq N-1$ (preprocessing)

B. For every query $(q \in \mathbb{E}^2, k \in \{1, \ldots, N-1\})$ find a $v(A) \in V_k(S)$ with $q \in v(A)$.

For part B Kirkpatrick (/Ki81/) has already found an optimal algorithm that answers a query in $O(k+\log N)$ steps.
The next two sections of this paper will describe an optimal solution of part A.

3. PROPERTIES OF GENERALIZED VORONOI DIAGRAMS

Every Voronoi edge (edge of a Voronoi diagram) is part of a bisector $B(x,y)$ with $x,y \in S$.
So let $\overline{B}_k(x,y)$ be the part of $B(x,y)$ that is Voronoi edge of $V_k(S)$.
With every Voronoi polygon being convex and only up to three points of S lying on a circle, every Voronoi point (point of a Voronoi diagram) has degree three and is the center of exactly three points of S.

---

*In the following this paper only will operate with this diagram also called $V_k(S)$.

Now we can prove the following theorem.

Theorem 1:
Let $x \in \mathbb{E}^2$ be the center of $a,b,c \in S$ and $H := \{z \in S / d(x,z) < d(x,a)\}$ with $|H| =: k \leq N-3$, then x is Voronoi point of $V_{k+1}(S)$ and $V_{k+2}(S)$.
The Voronoi edges and polygons that are incident upon x are given by the following diagram.

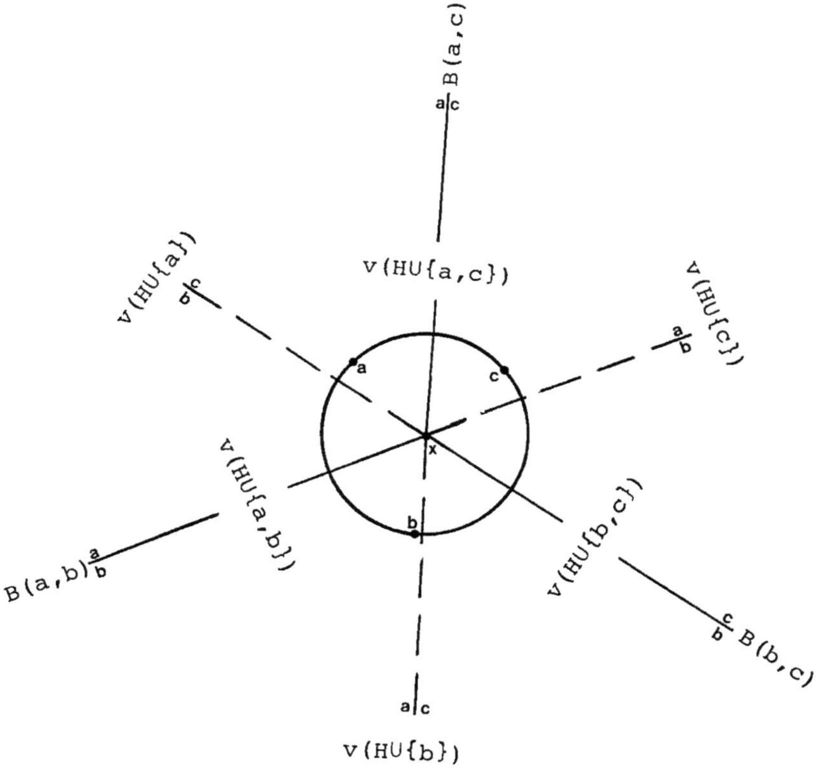

----: Voronoi edge of $V_{k+2}(S)$

——: Voronoi edge of $V_{k+1}(S)$

Proof:
$H\cup\{a\}$, $H\cup\{b\}$ and $H\cup\{c\}$ are sets of k+1 nearest neighbors of x. So $x \in v(H\cup\{a\}) \cap v(H\cup\{b\}) \cap v(H\cup\{c\})$ is a Voronoi point of $V_{k+1}(S)$. Because $H\cup\{a,b\}$, $H\cup\{b,c\}$ and $H\cup\{a,c\}$ are sets of k+2 nearest neighbors of x, it is also a Voronoi point of $V_{k+2}(S)$. With this the construction of the above diagram is trivial. □

The next theorem will demonstrate, that every Voronoi point can be constructed as described in theorem 1.

<u>Theorem 2:</u>

Let a Voronoi point $x \in v(A) \cap v(B) \cap v(C)$ with $v(A), v(B), v(C) \in V_i(S)$ be the center of $a,b,c \in S$ and $H := \{z \in S / d(x,z) < d(x,a)\}$ with $|H| =: k \leq N-3$, then

$(\{A,B,C\} = \{H \cup \{a\}, H \cup \{b\}, H \cup \{c\}\}$ and $i = k+1)$

or

$(\{A,B,C\} = \{H \cup \{a,b\}, H \cup \{b,c\}, H \cup \{a,c\}\}$ and $i = k+2)$.

<u>Proof:</u>

Let without loss of generality $v(A) \cap v(B) = \overline{B}_i(a,b)$, $v(B) \cap v(C) = \overline{B}_i(b,c)$ and $v(A) \cap v(C) = \overline{B}_i(a,c)$, then theorem 2 follows from the next three statements.

(1) Because $v(A) = \bigcap_{\substack{x \in A \\ y \in S-A}} h(x,y)$ and $\overline{B}_i(a,b)$ borders $v(A)$, there exists a $x \in A$ and $y \in S-A$ with $\{x,y\} = \{a,b\}$, getting $A \cap \{a,b,c\} \neq \phi$ and $\{a,b,c\} \not\subset A$. In the same way we get $B \cap \{a,b,c\} \neq \phi$, $\{a,b,c\} \not\subset B$, $C \cap \{a,b,c\} \neq \phi$ and $\{a,b,c\} \not\subset C$.

(2) $H \subset A$, $H \subset B$, $H \subset C$.
Proof of $H \subset A$ with $a \in A$ and $b \notin A$ (see (1)):
If there would be a $z \in H$ with $z \notin A$, this would be a contradiction to $x \in v(A)$ because of $d(x,z) < d(x,a)$.

(3) $A,B,C \subset H \cup \{a,b,c\}$.
Proof of $A \subset H \cup \{a,b,c\}$ with $a \in A$ and $b \notin A$ (see (1)):
If there would be a $z \in A$ with $z \notin H \cup \{a,b,c\}$, we would have $d(x,z) > d(x,a) = d(x,b)$ with $z \in A$ and $b \notin A$; a contradiction to $x \in v(A)$.

□

With theorem 2 we know theorem 1 describing all Voronoi points, edges and polygons of all $V_k(S)$ $(1 \leq k \leq N-1)$. This is the main idea for the algorithm in section 4.

For the analysis of this algorithm the next theorem gives us the number of Voronoi points, edges and polygons we have to compute.

Theorem 3:

Let I_k be the number of Voronoi points, E_k the number of edges and N_k the number of polygons of $V_k(S)$ $(1 \leq k \leq N-1)$, then we get

(i) $(\forall 1 \leq k \leq N-1): \theta(I_k) = \theta(E_k) = \theta(N_k)$ *

(ii) $(\forall 1 \leq k \leq N-1): N_k \in O(k(N-k)) \subset O(kN)$

(iii) $\sum_{k=1}^{N-1} N_k \in \theta(N^3)$

(iv) $\sum_{k=1}^{N-1} kN_k \in \theta(N^4)$.

Proof:

(i),(ii),(iii): see /ShHo75/ and /Le81/.

(iv):

From (ii) and $k \leq N$ we get $N_k \in O(N^2)$. So let us take an $a \in \mathbb{N}$ with $N_k \leq aN^2$ (for large N), then we get

$$\sum_{k=1}^{N-1} kN_k \leq \sum_{k=1}^{N-1} kaN^2 = \frac{a}{2}(N-1)N^3 \in O(N^4).$$

To prove $\sum_{k=1}^{N-1} kN_k \in \Omega(N^4)$ we define $I := \{1 \leq k \leq N-1 / N_k \in \Omega(N^2)\}$ and $J := \{1 \leq k \leq N-1 / N_k \notin \Omega(N^2)\}$ and show $|I| \in \Omega(N)$.

Assuming $|I| \notin \Omega(N)$ we would get $\sum_{k \in I} N_k \notin \Omega(N^3)$ from $N_k \in O(N^2)$.

---

*Having two functions $f,g: \mathbb{N} \rightarrow \mathbb{R}$ we say

$f \in O(g) :\Longleftrightarrow (\exists m \in \mathbb{N}, c \in \mathbb{N})(\forall n \geq m): f(n) \leq c \cdot g(n)$,

$f \in \Omega(g) :\Longleftrightarrow (\exists m \in \mathbb{N}, c \in \mathbb{N})(\forall n \geq m): f(n) \geq c \cdot g(n)$ and

$f \in \theta(g) :\Longleftrightarrow (f \in O(g) \wedge f \in \Omega(g))$.

By definition of J we get $\sum_{k\in J} N_k \notin \Omega(N^3)$ and further more

$$\sum_{k=1}^{N-1} N_k = \sum_{k\in I} N_k + \sum_{k\in J} N_k \notin \Omega(N^3);$$ a contradiction to (iii).

Let b and c be two numbers with $|I| \geqq bN$ and $N_k \geqq cN^2$ for $k\in I$ and large N, then we get

$$\sum_{k=1}^{N-1} kN_k \geq \sum_{k\in I} kN_k \geq cN^2 \sum_{k\in I} k \geq cN^2 \sum_{k=1}^{|I|} k \geq cN^2 \sum_{k=1}^{bN} k$$

$$= \frac{cb}{2} N^3 (bN+1) \in \Omega(N^4).$$

|_|

4. THE ALGORITHM

This section will give a description of the algorithm to construct all $V_k(S)$.
It needs $\theta(N^4)$ time and $\theta(N^4)$ storage. Theorem 3 No.(iv) showed that all Voronoi diagrams have a space complexity of at least $\theta(N^4)$ and therefore we need at least $\theta(N^4)$ steps to construct them. So the algorithm has optimal time and space complexity.
The data structure for the $V_k(S)$ is the same Kirkpatrick defines for the input data of his region location algorithm (see /Ki81/). Every $V_k(S)$ is stored by a list of its Voronoi points, each of wich contains the information about the incident Voronoi edges and polygons.

The basic idea is, to take all triples of points $a,b,c \in S$ and compute all Voronoi points in the way theorem 1 describes. Theorem 2 makes sure, that we get all of them. In a second step we have to link the points of each $V_k(S)$ together.
Before coming to a detailed description of the algorithm, we need some more definitions.

Definition:

For every $(s_a, s_b, s_c) \in S^3$ let

(i) $M(a,b,c)$ be the center of s_a, s_b, s_c (if exists)

(ii) $H(a,b,c) := \{y \in S - \{s_a, s_b, s_c\} / d(M(a,b,c), y) < d(M(a,b,c), s_a)\}$

(iii) $\nabla := \{(u,v,w) \in \{1,\ldots,N\}^3 / u > v > w\}$.

With this we can construct all $V_k(S)$ as follows:

(1) Construct an array L of all $M(a,b,c)$ with $(a,b,c) \in \nabla$ in wich every $M(a,b,c)$ can be found in $O(1)$ steps (store $M(a,b,c)$ with $(a,b,c) \in \nabla$ at the adress $\binom{a-1}{3} + \binom{b-1}{2} + c)$.

(2) Traverse L.
For every $M(a,b,c)$ calculate $H(a,b,c)$ and the incident rays and polygons as described by theorem 1 and add them to the lists of $V_{|H(a,b,c)|+1}(S)$ and $V_{|H(a,b,c)|+2}(S)$. Note the two adresses in L.

(3) Traverse L again.
Every $M(a,b,c)$ is a Voronoi point in two lists $V_i(S)$ and $V_{i+1}(S)$ with at most 6 incident rays.
With each ray r do the following steps:
Let r be in $V_j(S)$ and be part of $B(s_a, s_b)$.
Take all $M(a,b,x)$ with $s_x \in S - \{s_a, s_b, s_c\}$ and check, whether $M(a,b,x)$ is a Voronoi Point of $V_j(S)$ and lies on r. If there are more such points, take the $M(a,b,x_0)$ with minimum distance from $M(a,b,c)$. Reduce r to an edge $(M(a,b,c), M(a,b,x_0))$ and the corresponding ray of $M(a,b,x_0)$ to an edge $(M(a,b,x_0), M(a,b,c))$.

With theorem 3 the analysis of the algorithm is easy. The space complexity is

$$\theta\left(\sum_{k=1}^{N-1} (I_k + kE_k)\right) = \theta\left(\sum_{k=1}^{N-1} kN_k\right) = \theta(N^4).$$

L contains $\theta(N^3)$ points. So part (1) of the algorithm needs time $\theta(N^3)$. In part (2) for each of these points we need $\theta(N)$ steps and so the whole part takes $\theta(N^4)$ steps. In the same way you see evidently part (3) needing time $\theta(N^4)$ too. So the time complexity of the whole algorithm is $\theta(N^4)$.
This short description of the algorithm yields already so many details, that it is easy to be implemented.
We don´t need very much overhead (compared with the algorithms in /Le81/ and /ShHo75/) and the multiplicative constants for the complexity are expected to be quite good.

5. AN EXAMPLE

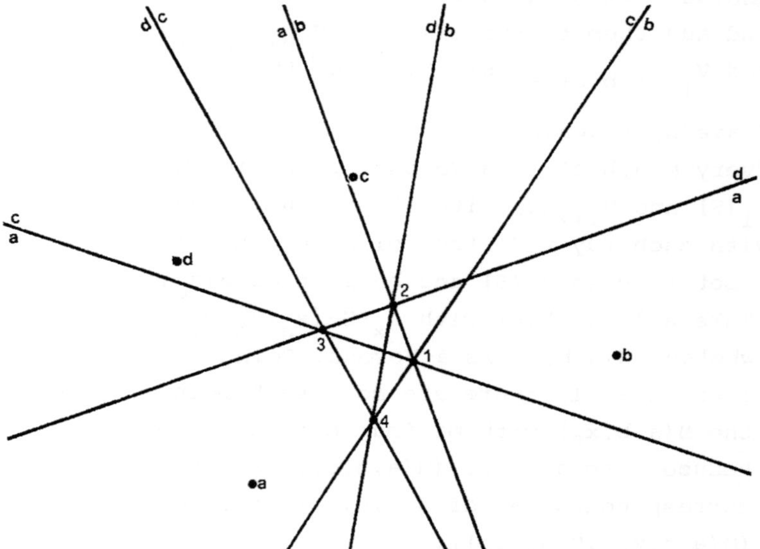

This picture shows a set $S:=\{a,b,c,d\}\subset\mathbb{E}^2$ and all possible bisectors.

With these points the array L looks as follows:

Voronoi point No.	center of	H	$\|H\|+1$	$\|H\|+2$
1	{a,b,c}	ϕ	1	2
2	{a,b,d}	{c}	2	3
3	{a,c,d}	ϕ	1	2
4	{b,c,d}	{a}	2	3

Now we can construct all Voronoi points and diagrams at once.

$\underline{V_1(S):}$

Voronoi points

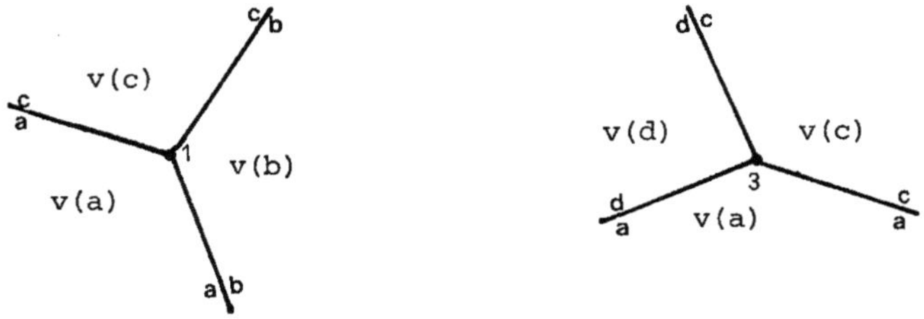

diagram

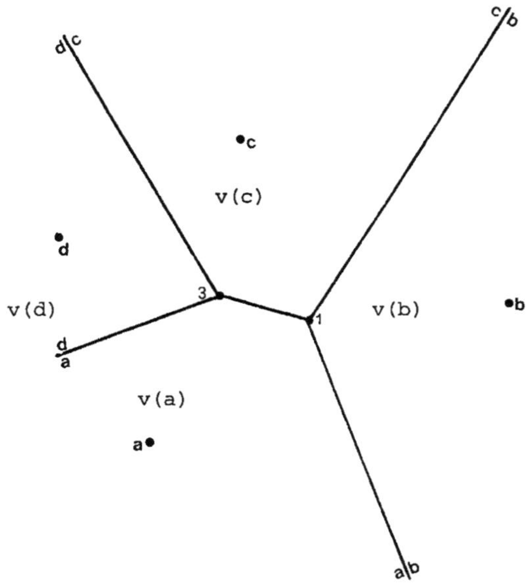

$\underline{V_2(S):}$

Voronoi points

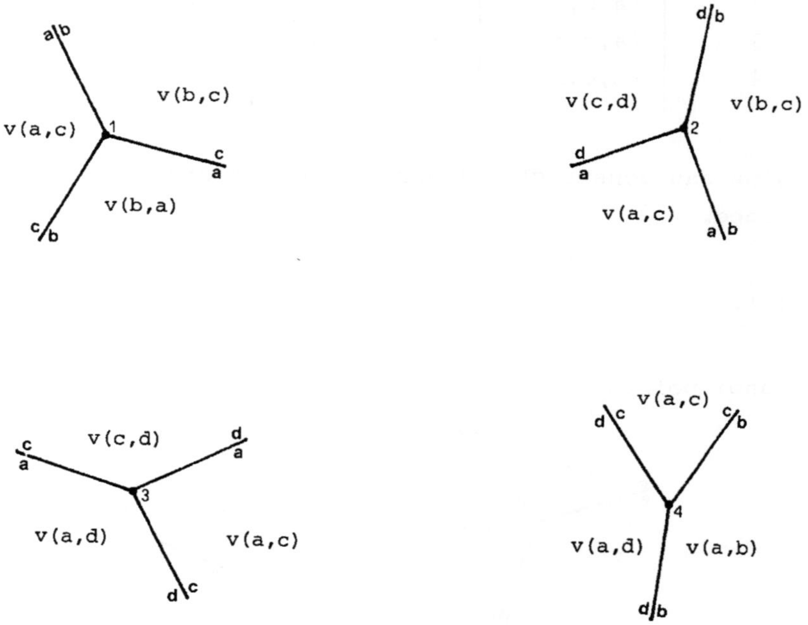

diagram

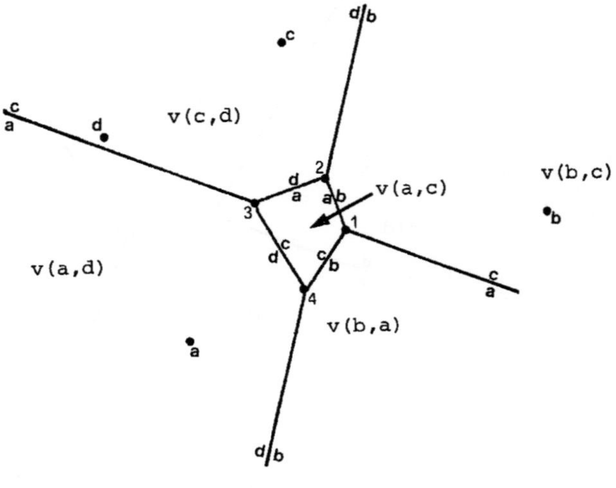

$\underline{V_3(S)}$

Voronoi points

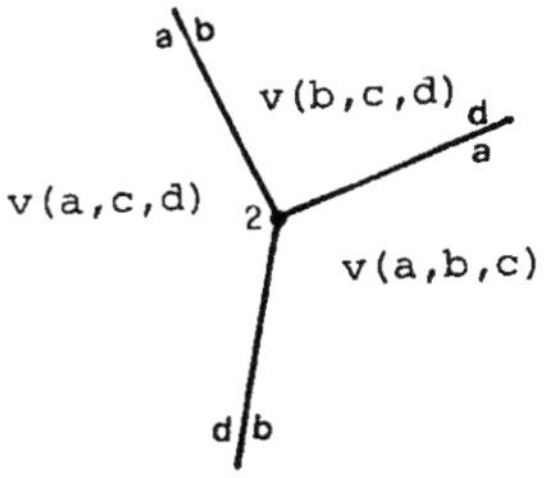

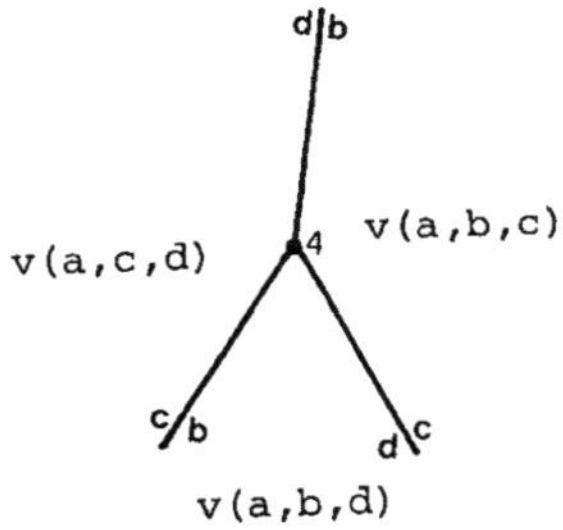

diagram

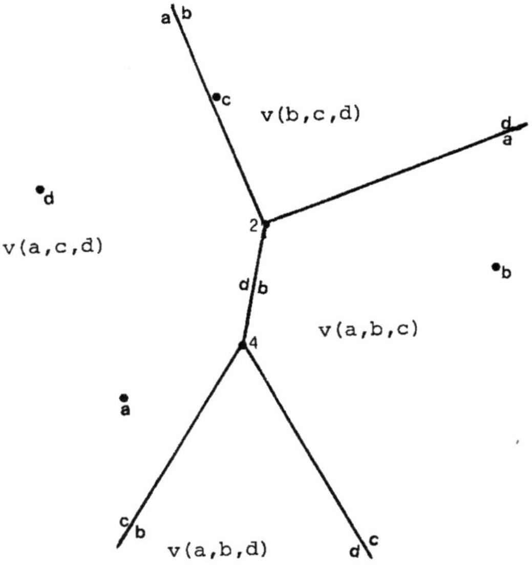

6. ACKNOWLEDGMENT

The author wishes to thank Prof. Dr. H. Noltemeier for his encouragement and helpfull discussions.

7. REFERENCES

/Ki81/ Kirkpatrick: OPTIMAL SEARCH IN PLANAR SUBDIVISIONS, Department of Computer Science, Univ. of British Columbia, Vancouver, B.C., Canada, Report 81-13, 1981

/Le81/ Lee: AN APPROACH TO FINDING THE K-NEAREST NEIGHBOR IN THE EUCLIDEAN PLANE, Department of Electrical Engineering and Computer Science, Northwestern Univ., Evanston, Il. 60201, USA, Report 1981

/Ma80/ Maurer: THE POST-OFFICE PROBLEM AND RELATED QUESTIONS, in Noltemeier (ed.): GRAPHTHEORETIC CONCEPTS IN COMPUTER SCIENCE, Proceedings of the International Workshop WG80, Bad Honnef, June 1980, Lecture Notes in Computer Science 100, Springer 198'

/Sh75a/ Shamos: COMPUTATIONAL GEOMETRY, Yale University, New Haven, Connecticut,USA, Ph.D.Thesis, 1975

/Sh75b/ Shamos: GEOMETRIC COMPLEXITY, Proceedings of the 7th Annual ACM Symposium on Theory of Computing, 1975, pp.224-233

/ShHo75/ Shamos,Hoey: CLOSEST-POINT PROBLEMS, Proceedings of the 16th IEEE Symposium on Foundations of Computer Science, 1975, pp.151-162

ALGEBRAIC LANGUAGES AND POLYOMINOES ENUMERATION

M. P. DELEST
Université Bordeaux II
33076 BORDEAUX Cedex, France

G. VIENNOT
Université Bordeaux I
33405 Talence, France

Abstract
The purpose of this paper is to show the use of algebraic languages theory in solving an open problem in combinatorics : give a formula for the number of convex polyominoes.

1- Introduction

Let Ω_n be a class of combinatorial objects enumerated by the integer a_n and suppose that the corresponding generating function $f(t) = \sum_{n\geq 0} a_n t^n$ is algebraic. An old idea dear to M.P. Schützenberger is to explain this algebricity by giving a bijection between Ω_n and the words L_n of length n of a certain algebraic (context free) language L defined by a non-ambiguous grammar.

Usually, an explicit formula is known for a_n or f(t) by means of classical calculus technics (recurrence relation, Lagrange inversion formula, etc...). With the non-ambiguous grammar, one can associate classically a proper algebraic system of equations (see for example Salomaa, Soittola [13]) in non-commutative power series. The unique solution contains the generating function $\underline{\underline{L}} = \sum_{w \in L} w$, of the language $L \subseteq X^*$ (free monoid generated by the alphabet X). By sending all variables $x \in X$ on t, one obtains an (ordinary) algebraic system of equations and $\underline{\underline{L}}$ becomes $f(t) = \sum_{n\geq 0} a_n t^n$. The coding with words gives more light inside the combinatorial comprehension of Ω_n.

A trivial example is with Ω_n for the set of binary trees with n vertices. Here $a_n = \frac{1}{n+1}\binom{2n}{n}$, the well known Catalan numbers, with generating function $d(t) = \frac{1-(1-4t)^{1/2}}{2t}$ satisfying the equation $d = 1 + t\,d^2$. The coding with words of the restricted Dyck language $D'^{*}_1 = D$ on two letters $x, \bar{x}$ is very classical. The non-commutative corresponding equation is $\underline{\underline{D}} = 1 + x\,\underline{\underline{D}}\,\bar{x}\,\underline{\underline{D}}$. Other examples can be found in Goldman [7] .

Deep examples are found in the work of Cori and Vauquelin [4] [5] following the numerous Tutte formulae for enumeration of planar maps (see for example [14]).

In this paper the method is reversed. Let P_n be the set of convex polyominoes (definition below) with perimeter 2n. Knuth raised the problem [9] to give some informations about the number of such polyominoes. We give an exact formula for this number p_{2n}. This formula is deduced from a coding between convex polyominoes and words of an algebraic language.

The method is in 3 steps :

(i) bijection between convex polyominoes and words. In fact three different types of polyominoes have to be considered.

(ii) solving the three corresponding algebraic systems and obtaining the generating functions f(t). These systems have about 20 to 40 equations each. We are thus forced to employ more carefully algebraic languages theory and use auxilliary languages, operators, substitutions and also multiheaded finite (or pushdown) automata The final solution has been possible with the use of the symbolic manipulation system MACSYMA from MIT.

(iii) expanding the generating function f(t) in order to obtain the formula for p_{2n}.

To the knowledge of the authors, this is the first time an open combinatoric problem is solved by using algebraic languages. These results were given in a talk at the combinatoric meeting in Oberwolfach (May 1982), and since, apparently, no "classical" analytic proof has been given.

2- CONVEX POLYOMINOES

A polyominoe is a connected, with no "cut point", union of elementary squares (or cells) of the plane $\mathbb{Z} \times \mathbb{Z}$. The polyominoe π is said to be convex if the intersection with π of any vertical or horizontal line is a connected segment (possibly empty).

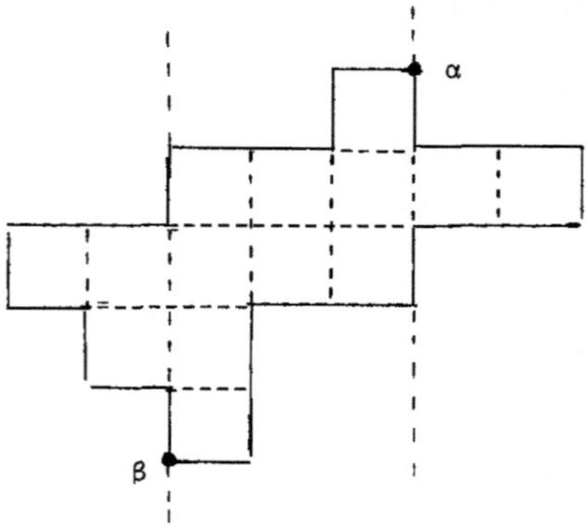

Fig. 1 - A convex polyominoe

Polyominoes are defined up to a translation. Polyominoes enumeration problems are well known in combinatorics (see for example Golomb [8]) but very few exact results are known, except for special cases or asymptotic formulae (mainly obtained by physicists, in connection with self-avoiding path problems). Some asymptotic formulae are known for the number of convex polyominoes (counted according to the area) see Bender [2] and Klarner, Rivest [9] .

Our formula has the surprising simple following form :

Theorem 1. The number p_{2n} of convex polyominoes with perimeter $2n$ is :

$$p_4 = 1,\ p_6 = 2, \text{ and for perimeter } \geq 8.$$

$$p_{2n+8} = (2n + 11)\, 4^n - 4(2n+1) \binom{2n}{n}.$$

Any coding obtained by following the border of the convex polyominoe would immediately give non-algebraic languages : as shown from Ogden's iteration lemma [11] or Boasson's overlaping iterative pairs lemma [3] , and geometric considerations.

As in [9] , we cut a polyominoe into three parts, along the vertical lines containing the point α (rightmost of the topmost points) and the point β (leftmost of the lowest points). Three cases have to be considered, according to the fact the absciss of α is strictly bigger (type I), equal (type II) or strictly less (type III) than the absciss of β.
Each part of this trisection can be encoded by words of algebraic language. The main problem is to "glue" them together into a single word, keeping the convex and algebraic properties.

3- PARALLELOGRAM AND STACK POLYOMINOES

The middle part in the trisection of type I polyominoes is called a parallelogram polyominoe, or pair of two disjoint paths, except at the endpoints, with elementary North and East steps (see figure 2). It is well known that such pairs are enumerated by Catalan numbers C_n, see Polya [12] . Coding with Dyck words is classical [6] .
The two extreme parts of the trisection are (up to a rotation) called stack polyominoes .They are enumerated by the Fibonacci numbers F_{2n} and thus encoded by a rational language.
With these codings it would be very difficult to keep the convex and algebraic properties through the "gluing" process and the corresponding algebraic system would be intractable for computations.
We introduce a new coding between parallelogram polyominoes and Dyck words of D (see below). This coding is related to (finite) binary trees and new considerations about the classical concepts of prefix order, symmetric order and height of a vertex.

4- THE LANGUAGES CODING CONVEX POLYOMINOES

By a "gluing" process, we obtain a bijection between type I polyominoes with perimeter $2n + 2$ and the so-called pigmented Dyck words of length $2n$, defined by the following conditions :

(i) $w \in \{a, x, \bar{x}\}^*$ and the word $\alpha(w)$ obtained by deleting the letters a is a Dyck word of D,

(ii) w has a factorization in the form
$w = x\,u\,h\,v\,\bar{x}$, $u \in \{a,x\}^*\, x$ or $u = e$ (empty word)
$h \in \{x,\bar{x}\}^*$, $v \in \bar{x}\,\{a,\bar{x}\}^*$ or $v = e$,

(iii) the numbers $|u|_a$ (resp. $|v|_a$) of occurrences of the letter a in the word u (resp. v) is even.

We describe briefly this bijection on the following example.

Let w be the pigmented Dyck word :

$$w = xaxaaaxxxxxxxxxxxxaaaax.$$

We first construct the parallelogram polyominoe coded by the Dyck word $\alpha(w)$. This polyominoe is displayed on figure 2.

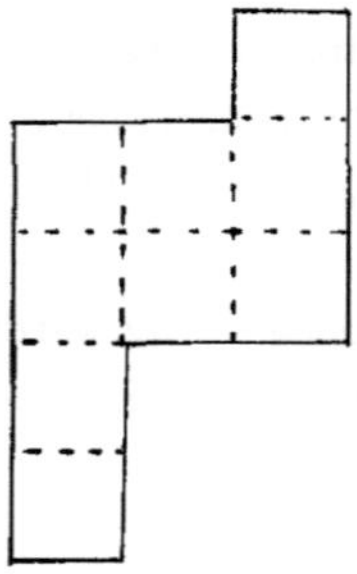

Fig. 2 - A parallelogram polyominoe

The number of vertical strips is the number of factors $x\bar{x}$ in the word $\alpha(w)$. Thus each of these strips corresponds to a factorization $\alpha(w) = ux\bar{x}v$. The number of elementary squares of the strip is $\delta(ux) = |ux|_x - |ux|_{\bar{x}}$.

Between the $i^{\underline{th}}$ and $(i+1)^{\underline{th}}$ factors $x\bar{x}$, there exists a factor $\bar{x}x$. Denote the corresponding factorization by $\alpha(w) = f\bar{x}xg$. The $i^{\underline{th}}$ and $(i+1)^{\underline{th}}$ strips are then "glued" together along $\delta(f)$ squares. A unique parallelogram polyominoe is thus obtained (see figure 2).

In a second step, we extract the longest left factor $\lambda(w)$ of the word w, not containing the letter $\bar{x}$. Here $\lambda(w) = xaxaaaxx$.

Denote by $2p = |\lambda(w)|_a$. If $p \neq o$, we define a unique factorization $\lambda(w)=xuavx$ with $|u|_a = p-1$, and the word $\lambda'(w) = xuaxv$.

Reading this word $\lambda'(w)$ from left to right, we construct a path in $\mathbb{Z} \times \mathbb{Z}$, as shown on figure 3.

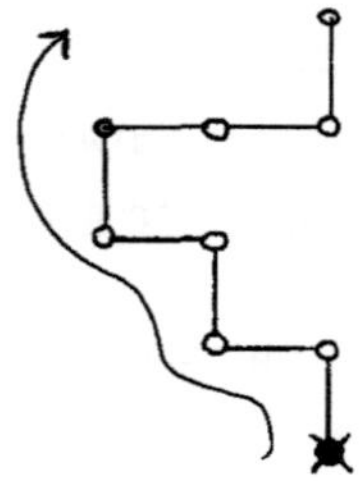

Fig. 3. The path coded by $\lambda'(w)=xaxaxaax$.

Each occurrence of the letter x corresponds to a North elementary step. Each occurren ce of one of the first (resp. last) p occurrences of the letter a corresponds to a West (resp. East) elementary step.
Remark that the first step of the path is a North step, and that the endpoints are on the same vertical line, the distance between them is equal to the number of elementary squares of the first vertical strip of the parallelogram polyominoe coded by α (w). We can "glue" the path on the left side of this par
Dually we define and "glue" a path on the right side of the par
We thus obtained a type I convex polyominoe, which is displayed on figure 1.
By "gluing" together two stack polyominoes, similar considerations lead to encode type II polyominoes with words w of the language defined by the three following conditions :

(i) $w \in \{a,x,y,z\}^*$ and has a factorization
$w = u\,z\,v$, with $u, v \in \{a,y\}^* . \{a,xx\}^*$,

(ii) $|u|_y = |u|_y \neq 0$,

(iii) $|u|_a$ and $|v|_a$ are even.

The middle part of type III polyominoes is obtained from a parallelogram polyominoe by a symmetry with respect to a vertical axis. The "gluing" process is more complicated and the coding is a mixture of type I and type II polyominoes.
It is easy to describe a pushdown automaton accepting pigmented Dyck words. This language is algebraic, and similarly for type III. The type II language is obviously a linear language.

5- SOLVING THE ALGEBRAIC SYSTEMS

It is a long but routine task to write down the corresponding proper algebraic systems, in non-commutative power series with coefficients in $\mathbb{N}$, for the three algebraic languages defined in § 4. Note that type III language needs about 40 equations. By brute force, and a high use of the symbolic manipulation system MACSYMA from MIT, it would be possible to solve these systems (in commutative variables). This resolution is made possible because, in a certain sense, these languages are "rationally closed" to the Dyck language : the system can be reduced to a succession of linear systems with coefficients of the form R(d(t)), where R(u) is a rational power serie and d(t) is the generating function of Dyck words.
Nevertheless, following a suggestion of R. Cori, it is better to introduce auxilliary algebraic languages (with small solvable algebraic systems) and some operators on these languages, reducing the MACSYMA computation.
We give an idea of the method for type I polyominoes.

Let Φ be the morphism $\Phi : \{x,\bar{x},y,\bar{y}\}^* \longrightarrow \{x,\bar{x}\}^*$ defined by the relations $\Phi(x) = \Phi(y) = x$, $\Phi(\bar{x}) = \Phi(\bar{y}) = \bar{x}$. Let $S \subseteq \{x,\bar{x},y,\bar{y}\}^*$ be the set of words w defined by the two following conditions :

(i) $\Phi(w)$ is a Dyck word of $\{x,\bar{x}\}^*$,

(ii) w has one of following form : $w = y^k\bar{y}^k$ for $k \neq 0$, or $w = f\bar{x}gxh$ with $f \in \{y\}^*$, $g \in \{x,\bar{x}\}^*$, $h \in \{\bar{y}\}^*$.

The language S is obviously algebraic. The (non-commutative) generating function $\underline{\underline{S}}$ is solution of the algebraic system

$$\begin{cases} \underline{\underline{S}} = y\bar{y} + y\,\underline{\underline{S}}\,\bar{y} + y\,\underline{\underline{L}}\,\bar{x}\,\underline{\underline{D}}\,x\,\underline{\underline{R}}\,\bar{y}\,, \\ \underline{\underline{L}} = 1 + y\,\underline{\underline{L}}\,\bar{x}\,\underline{\underline{D}}\,, \\ \underline{\underline{R}} = 1 + \underline{\underline{D}}\,x\,\underline{\underline{R}}\,\bar{y}\,, \\ \underline{\underline{D}} = 1 + x\,\underline{\underline{D}}\,\bar{x}\,\underline{\underline{D}}\,. \end{cases}$$

Denote by $s(x,\bar{x},y,\bar{y})$ (resp. $d(x,\bar{x})$) the commutative image of the power serie $\underline{\underline{S}}$ (resp. $\underline{\underline{D}}$). From the system, we get

$$s(x,\bar{x},y,\bar{y}) = \frac{y\,\bar{y}}{1 - y\,\bar{y}} \left(1 + \frac{x\,\bar{x}\,d\,(x,\bar{x})}{(1 - \bar{y}\,x\,d(x,\bar{x}))\,(1 - y\bar{x}\,d(x,\bar{x}))} \right)$$

Now we introduce the operator T defined on the words w of S. This operator substitutes the first y (resp. last $\bar{y}$) of w by x (resp. $\bar{x}$), and every other letter y (resp. $\bar{y}$) by the language $\{a\}^*x$ (resp. $\bar{x}\,\{b\}^*$). The image by T of the language S is the pigmented Dyck, coding type I polyominoes. This operator "goes through" the commutative image of the generating function, and we obtain the generating function $Ts\,(x,\bar{x},a,b)$ of the words $w \in \{x,\bar{x},a,b\}^*$ satisfying the two following conditions :

(i) $\alpha(w)$, the word obtained by deleting the letters a and b, is a Dyck word of D,

(ii) w has a factorization in the form
$w = x\,u\,h\,v\,\bar{x}$, $u \in \{a,x\}^*x$ or $u = e$,
$h \in \{x,\bar{x}\}^*$, $v \in \bar{x}\{b,\bar{x}\}^*$ or $v = e$,

$$Ts\,(x,\bar{x},a,b) = (1-a)\,(1-b)\quad s(x,\bar{x},\frac{x}{1-a},\frac{\bar{x}}{1-b}).$$

Then, taking the even parts for the variables a and b, we get the generating function

$$ETs\,(x,\bar{x},a,b) = \frac{1}{4}\,(Ts\,(x,\bar{x},a,b) + Ts(x,\bar{x},-a,b) + Ts(x,\bar{x},a,-b) + Ts(x,\bar{x},-a,-b))\,.$$

Substituting each variables by t, we get the generating function for type I convex polyominoes :

$$p_I(t) = \frac{t^4 (1-8t^2 + 21t^4 - 19t^6 + 4t^8)}{(1-2t)^2 (1+2t)^2 (1-2t^2)} - 2t^8 (1-4t^2)^{-3/2}.$$

The generating function for type II polyominoes is rational. It is possible to define a finite automaton, using two heads, which recognize the words w coding these polyominoes. At the beginning, these heads are positioned in the word w. At each step, the automaton reads a letter with one of the heads, moves the head, the next state determines which will be the next head to be used. At the end, each letter have been read once and only once by one of the heads .

For type II polyominoes, the problem is thus reduced to compute the generating function of a rational language. It is also possible to apply similar methods introduced for type I polyominoes. The generating function for type II convex polyominoes is the following

$$p_{II}(t) = \frac{t^{10} (1-3t^2 + 2t^4 + t^6)}{(1-2t)(1+2t)(1-2t^2)(1+t-t^2)^2 (1-t-t^2)^2}.$$

For type III polyominoes, the computations are similar, but more complicated. Using MACSYMA, we get an explicit expression for the corresponding generating function $p_{III}(t)$:

$$p_{III}(t) = \frac{t^8(2-20t^2+75t^4-127t^6+95t^8-27t^{10}+4t^{12})}{(1-2t)^2 (1+2t)^2 (1-2t^2)(1+t-t^2)^2 (1-t-t^2)^2} - 2t^8 (1-4t^2)^{-3/2}.$$

By adding the three generating functions $p_I(t)$, $p_{II}(t)$, and $p_{III}(t)$ (and thus restoring the original symmetry of the polyominoe problem), we get the generating function for convex polyominoes :

$$p(t) = \frac{t^4 (1-t^2+11t^4-4t^6)}{(1-4t^2)^2} - 4t^8 (1-4t^2)^{-3/2}.$$

Expanding p(t) gives the exact formula of theorem 1.

6- CONCLUSION

We have solved an open enumerative problem in combinatorics by using algebraic languages, while tentatives using "classical" analytic technics have not yet succeeded.

Apart from purely combinatorial considerations, we believe that the interest in such method, is in the confrontation between two different points of view : combinatorists are looking for enumeration formulae while algebraic language theorists are motivated by computer science considerations. In particular the combinatorist is looking the languages up to a commutation of the letters and manipulate languages (not necessarily algebraic) but which are in bijection with an algebraic or even rational language. Multiheads pushdown autom a are of special use in producing these bijections. Note that these ideas are different from the theoretical concepts of commutative languages introduced by Latteux [2], [10].

Also note that the final expressions for the generating functions can be expressed as rational expressions in term of the Dyck language generating function (in commutative variables). A theorical investigation about such languages, "rationally close" to the Dyck language, would be of interest.

ACKNOWLEDGEMENT :

We thank R. Cori for useful suggestions and H. Cohen for MACSYMA help.

REFERENCES

[1] E. BENDER : Convex n-ominoes Discrete Maths, 8 (1974) 31-40.

[2] BLATTNER, M. LATTEUX : Parikh-bounded languages, in Proc. 8th ICALP, Lecture Note in Computer Science n°115, Springer (1981) 316-323.

[3] L. BOASSON : Langages algébriques, paires itérantes et transductions rationnelles, Theor. Comp. Sci. 2 (1976) 209-223.

[4] R. CORI : "Un code pour les graphes planaires et ses applications", Astérisque, Société Mathématique de France 27 (1975).

[5] R. CORI, B. VAUQUELIN : Planar maps are well labeled trees, Can. Jour. Math., 33(1981) 1023-1042.

[6] I. GESSEL : A noncommutative generalization and q-analog of the Lagrange inversion formula, Trans. Amer. Math. Soc., 257 (1980) 455-482.

[7] J. GOLDMAN : Formal languages and enumeration, Jour. of Comb. Th., (A) 24 (1978) 318-338.

[8] S. GOLOMB : "Polyominoes", Scribner"s, New-York, (1965).

[9] D. KLARNER, R. RIVEST : Asymptotic bounds for the number of convex n-ominoes, Discrete Maths, 8 (1974) 31-40.

[10] M. LATTEUX : Cones rationnels commutatifs, J.C.S.S., 18 (1979) 307-333.

[11] W. OGDEN : A helpful result for proving inherent ambiguity, Math. Syst. The., 2 (1968) 191-194.

[12] G. POLYA : On the number of certain lattice polygons, J. of Comb. Th. 6 (1969) 102-105.

[13] A. SALOMAA, M. SOITTOLA : "Automa-Theoretic aspects of formal power series", Springer Verlag, (1978).

4] W. T. TUTTE : A census of planar maps, Can. Jour. Math., 15 (1963) 249-271.

ON THE NUMBER OF EQUAL-SIZED SEMISPACES OF A SET OF POINTS IN THE PLANE

(extended abstract)

by

Herbert Edelsbrunner and Emmerich Welzl
Institutes for Information Processing, Technical University of Graz, Schießstattgasse 4a, A-8010 Graz, Austria.

1. Introduction.

We present some results on a geometric problem which deals with sets of points in the plane. The motivation for the problem stems from a host of applications in the design of algorithms.

Let S denote a set of n points in the plane. A halfplane h defines the semispace $S(h) = S \cap h$. We call S(h) a k-set of S if it contains exactly k points. Let now $f_k(S)$ denote the number of k-sets of S, for $1 \leq k \leq n-1$, and let $f_k(n)$ be the maximum of $f_k(S)$, for all sets S of n points. We are interested in asymptotic bounds for $f_k(n)$, in particular we will show that $f_k(n)$ is in $\Omega(n\log k)$ and also in $O(nk^{1/2})$. Before we present the proofs for the two bounds some problems of computational geometry are sketched to which $f_k(n)$ applies.

1.1. Halfplanar Range Estimation.

Let S denote a set of n points in the plane. A typical halfplanar estimation query requires the decision whether or not more than $\lfloor n/2 \rfloor$ points lie in a specified halfplane. The halfplanar range estimation problem asks for an accommodation of S such that such a query can be answered efficiently.

Edelsbrunner and Welzl [EW] showed:

> There exists a data structure for S which requires $O(f_{\lfloor n/2 \rfloor}(n))$ space and $O(f_{\lfloor n/2 \rfloor}(n)\log^2 n)$ time for construction such that $O(\log n)$ time suffices to answer a halfplanar estimation query.

1.2. Center Point.

Let S denote a set of n points in the plane. Then a point c(S) which is in general not in S is called a centerpoint of S if each line through c(S) has at least $\lfloor n/3 \rfloor$ of the point in S in both closed halfplanes defined. The methods in [EW] imply:

There exists an algorithm which constructs the region of centerpoints of S in $O(f_{\lfloor n/3 \rfloor}(n)\log^2 n)$ time and $O(f_{\lfloor n/3 \rfloor}(n))$ space.

A centerpoint can also be used for halfplanar range estimation.

1.3. Moving Points.

Let M denote a set of n moving points on a horizontal line. Each point p of M moves with constant speed s(p) in either direction. If p moves towards the right then s(p) is positive, if it moves towards the left then s(p) is negative. Some problems arising from this concept are discussed in Ottmann and Wood [OW].

We say that a point p is at position k at some point t in time if p is the only k-th point from the right at time t. The geometric transform which maps each point p of M with location p_1 at time 0 and speed p_2 into a point $p = (p_1, p_2)$ in the plan implies:

The length of the sequence of points in M at position k, for the time interval from minus to plus infinity, is bounded above by $f_{k-1}(n)+f_k(n)+1$ and this bound is asymptotically tight.

1.4. High-Order Voronoi Diagrams.

Let S denote a set of n points in the plane. The Voronoi diagram of order k, for $1 \leq k \leq n-1$, is a subdivision of the plane such that each subset T of k points in S is associated with the region r(T) such that x in r(T) implies $d(x,p) \leq d(x,q)$ with p in T and q in S-T. Those diagrams are investigated in Shamos and Hoey [SH] and Lee [L]. It is readily seen that the region r(T) is properly unbounded, that is, r(T) does not fit in between two parallel lines, if and only if T is a k-set of S.
This implies:

The order-k Voronoi diagram of S contains $f_k(S)$ properly unbounded regions.

2. Asymptotic Bounds for $f_k(n)$.

First, $f_k(n)$ is shown to be in $\Omega(n\log k)$ by exhibiting a point-set which realizes that many k-sets. Then $f_k(n)$ is proved to be in $O(nk^{1/2})$ which is proved using combinatorial concepts related to sets of points in the plane.

2.1. A Lower Bound.

We proceed as follows: First we show that the lower bound is correct for the special case when $n = 2.3^m$, m a positive integer, and $k = n/2$. Then the general result is obtained by generalizing the result to arbitrary k and n.

Theorem 2.1: Let $n = 2.3^m$, m a positive integer. Then there exists a exists a set S of n points in the plane such that $f_{n/2}(S) = n(\log_3(n/2)+1)$.

Sketch of proof: Let r, s, and t be three rays emanating from the origin such that any two enclose an angle of $2\pi/3$, see Figure 2-1. The points in S are chosen such that near each ray there are one third of the points. Let S^r, S^s, and S^t denote the subsets of points near r, s, and t, that is $S = S^r \cup S^s \cup S^t$.

For each permutation (A,B,C) of (r,s,t), we choose the points in S^A such that

(i) they are in general position, that is, no three lie on a common line, and

(ii) each line through two points of A separates the points in B from those in C.

A straightforward counting argument yields now $f_{n/2}(S) = n+f_{n/6}(S^r)+f_{n/6}(S^s)+f_{n/6}(S^t)$. Thus S realizes many n/2-sets if S^r, S^s and S^t realize many n/6-sets. Indeed, examinations of particular affine transformations of point-sets show that it is possible to choose S^r, S^s, and S^t recursively like S itself without violating conditions (i) and (ii). To be able to formulate this idea in terms of a recursive equation let S(n) denote a set of n points chosen in the scheme of S. Then $f_{n/2}(S) =$

$f_{n/2}(S(n)) = n+3f_{n/6}(S(n/3)) = 2.3^m(m+1) = n(\log_3(n/2)+1)$. This completes the sketch of proof.

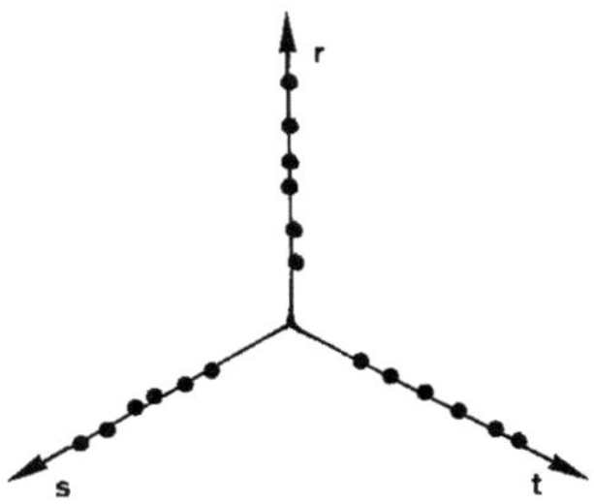

Figure 2-1. S for $n = 2.3^2$ points.

Theorem 2.1 can easily be generalized to arbitrary k and n with $1 \le k \le n-1$. We state this result but omit the proof.

Theorem 2.2: $f_k(n) = f_{n-k}(n) = \Omega(n\log k)$, for $1 \le k \le \lfloor n/2 \rfloor$.

2.2. An Upper Bound.

In order to develop an upper bound for $f_k(n)$, we transform the geometric problem into a combinatorial one. To this end it is essential that we can restrict ourselves to point-sets in general position, that is, no three points lie on a common line and no two connecting lines are parallel. Let S be a set of n points in general position and let us label the points with the numbers 1,...n.

Let now L be a directed line not orthogonal to a line through two points of S. The orthogonal projection of S into L determines a unique permutation of 1,...n. As L rotates counterclockwise about some fixed point it defines an infinite sequence of permutations in an obvious way. With Goodman and Pollack [GP] we term this sequence the circular sequence of S and say that S induces its circular sequence.

Evidently an n-sequence has period n(n-1) and (1) two successive permutations differ only by having the order of two adjacent numbers switched, and (2) each one of the n(n-1)/2 unordered switches occurs exactly once in any halfperiod, that is, a subsequence of n(n-1)/2+1 permutations. A sequence of permutations of 1,...n satisfying (1) and (2) is called an allowable circular sequence of 1,...n or simply an n-sequence. The main result in [GP] tells us that there are n-sequences which are not induced by point-sets, nevertheless, there is a close relationship between those two concepts. This relationship will be exploited for establishing an upper bound for $f_k(n)$.

To this end let C be an n-sequence and let A be a subset of {1,...n} containing k numbers. A is called an allowable k-set of C if there is a permutation in C such that the k numbers of A occur ot the leftmost k positions. We denote by $g_k(C)$ the number of allowable k-sets realized by C, and let $g_k(n)$ denote the maximum of $g_k(C)$ for all n-sequences C. Evidently, $f_k(n) \leq g_k(n)$, thus, an upper bound for $g_k(n)$ is also an upper bound for $f_k(n)$.

Observation 2.3: Let C be an n-sequence. Then $g_k(C)$ equals the number of switches at positions k and k+1 among a period of C.

Let C^k_{max} denote an n-sequence such that $g_k(C^k_{max}) = g_k(n)$. We choose a halfperiod H of C^k_{max} such that H realizes at least $g_k(n)/2$ allowable k-sets. Note that each unordered switch occurs exactly once in H thus H ends with the reverse permutation it begins with. Without loss of generality let $P_0 = 1,\dots n$ be the first permutation of H and let X, Y, and Z such that P_0 = XYZ, that is, X = 1,...i-1, Y = i,...j, and Z = j+1,...n, for some $1 \leq i \leq j \leq n$. Let y = j-i+1 denote the length of Y.

Lemma 2.4: At most $\frac{y}{2}(y-1)+\min\{n-y,2k\}$ of the switches in H at position k and k+1 involve a number of Y.

Sketch of proof: Clearly, at most $\frac{y}{2}(y-1)$ switches involve two numbers of Y. Thus, let us consider the number of switches at positions k and k+1 involving exactly one number of Y. It can be shown that for H there exists another halfperiod H' of an n-sequence such that

(1) P_0 = XYZ is the first permutation of H',

(2) the number of switches at positions k and k+1 involving a number of Y equals the corresponding number in H, and

(3) no switch involving two numbers of either of X and Z is performed before the last switch involving a number of Y is completed.

In H' each number in X or Z can only once be the partner of a number in Y when it switches at positions k and k+1. In addition, at most k numbers of X and k of Z can actually realize such a switch. This completes the argument.

From Lemma 2.4, the upper bound follows almost immediately.

Theorem 2.5: $f_k(n) = f_{n-k}(n) = O(nk^{1/2})$, for $1 \leq k \leq \lfloor n/2 \rfloor$.

The assertion follows from the relation $f_k(n) \leq g_k(n)$ and from Lemma 2.4 by partitioning P_0 into about $n/k^{1/2}$ subsequences of about $k^{1/2}$ numbers each. Taking each subsequence for Y once yields the assertion.

References.

[EW] Edelsbrunner,H. and Welzl,E. Halfplanar Range Estimation. F98, Inst. for Inf. Proc., Techn. Univ. of Graz, Austria (1982).

[GP] Goodman,J.E. and Pollack,R. On the Combinatorial Classification of Nondegenerate Configurations in the Plane. J. of Comb. Theory, Ser.A, 29 (1980), 220-235.

[L] Lee,D.T. On k-Nearest Neighbor Voronoi Diagrams in the Plane. IEEE Tr. on Comp. C-31 (1982), 487-487.

[OW] Ottmann,Th. and Wood,D. Dynamical Sets of Points. Manuscript (1982).

[SH] Shamos,M.I. and Hoey,D. Closest-Point Problems. Proc. 16th Ann. IEEE Symp. on Found. of Comp. Sci. (1975). 151-162

ALGEBRAIC SPECIFICATIONS WITH GENERATING CONSTRAINTS

H. Ehrig
Technische Universität
Berlin (Germany)

E.G. Wagner, J.W. Thatcher
IBM T.J.W. Research Center
Yorktown Heights (U.S.A.)

ABSTRACT

In this paper we take a new look at one of the basic principles of abstract data types. Due to this principle the domain of an abstract data type must be generated by the operations. In the initial algebraic approach as well as in the loose case with initial restrictions or data constraints this principle is satisfied because of initiality resp. free construction. Actually initiality makes sure that the data under consideration are not only generated but even freely generated by the operations. In this paper we do not consider free generation but only generation leading to the new concept of algebraic specifications with generating constraints.

This new look was also motivated by the notion of hierarchy constraints, introduced by the CIP-group in Munich, but there are two main differences between hierarchy and generating constraints: First of all we remove the consistency condition "TRUE≠FALSE" for bool. This part of hierarchy constraints can be expressed (if necessary) in the axiom part of the specifications. Secondly we give a mechanism how to construct generating constraints and how to translate or reflect them from one part of a specification to other parts. More precisely we define syntax and semantics of a language building up generating constraints together with the stepwise construction of an algebraic specification. The main result of this paper shows how an arbitrary generating constraint built up in this way can be transformed to a very simple constraint in canonical form which is equivalent to the given one. Equivalence of two generating constraints on the same algebraic specification means that they have the same semantics, i.e. they define the same class of algebras.

Finally we discuss how concepts and results of this paper could be used for the design of algebraic specification languages where not only the specifications but also the constraints are built up in a stepwise way.

1. INTRODUCTION

It is one of the basic principles of abstract data types that the domain of an abstract data type should be generated by the operations (see /LZ 75/). This generating principle together with the principle of representation independence was the main motivation for the initial algebraic approach to the specification of abstract data types given in /ADJ 76-78/. This was a first mathematical precise formulation of algebraic specifications as introduced by Zilles in /Zil 74/ and Guttag in /Gut 75/. The generalization of this idea to the parameterized case in /ADJ 78/ was that parameterized data types are freely generated by their formal parameter parts. Since the formal parameter part itself is not assumed to be generated by parameter operations the generating principle is already relaxed in this case.

fications with most general requirements for the formal parameter part including algebraic constraints as mentioned above as well as logical requirements. The key for this generality in /Ehr 81/ was that requirements are only considered to be sets where each element is assumed to define a subclass of algebras. The idea to consider subcategories of algebras (which are closed under isomorphism) was picked up in /WEB 82/ to start a rigorous algebraic treatment of constraints which are generated by free constructions and algebraic functors. These constraints are generalizing initial restrictions (/HKR 80/) as well as data constraints (/BG 80/). Especially it is shown that each set of data constraints built up by some very general constructors can be transformed into a single data constraint equivalent to the given set of constraints.

In this paper we extend the algebraic treatment of constraints by considering generating constraints instead of free generating constraints as in /WEB 82/. Let us reconsider the specification string-pick(data) defined above. But now we assume that the constraint is a generating constraint instead of a data or free generating constraint. Formally this generating constraint is given by

$$\text{data} \xrightarrow[\text{GEN}]{f1} \text{string(data)} \xrightarrow[\text{TRA}]{f2} \text{string-pick(data)}$$

where f1 and f2 are inclusions of specifications, GEN means that the string(data)-part is GENerated by the data-part, and TRA means that the constraint on string(data) is TRAnslated to string-pick(data). The semantics of this generating constraint is the class of all string-pick(data)-algebras B, such that the string(data)-part S of B with sort $S_{string}=B_{string}$ is generated by the data-part A of B with sort $A_{data}=B_{data}=S_{data}=A$. This includes the case $B_{string}=A^*$ of free generation but allows also that B_{string} is the set of all strings over A without repetition of elements, or that B_{string} is the set of all finite subsets of A. The main point is that S with $S_{string}=B_{string}$ is generated by A in the following sense: Each string(data)-subalgebra S' of S, where the data-part A' of S' is equal to the data-part A of S, is already equal to S, i.e. S'=S. In general the data-part A of S is defined by $A=U_{f1}(S)$ where U_{f1} is the forgetful functor from string(data)-algebras S to data-algebras A associated with f1:data$\longrightarrow$string(data) considered as a presentation morphism. In this case we say that S is U_{f1}-generated, i.e. generated by $A=U_{f1}(S)$. The treatment of generating constraints is motivated by the original generating principle for abstract data types which allows but does not force free generation. A similar idea was already developed by the CIP-group in /BDPPW 79/ and most recently in /SW 82/ where parameterized data types with hierarchy constraints are studied. In /SW 82/ it is argued that hierarchy constraints are more suitable than data constraints. We would not like to make any judgment before a rigorous treatment of both cases is carried out and is applied to a number of partical examples.

Consider for example the simple parameterized specification

string(data) = data +
    sorts: string
    opns: EMPTY: $\longrightarrow$ string
        LADD: data string $\longrightarrow$ string

with formal parameter part data consisting of the sort "data" only. The corresponding parameterized data type STRING(DATA) defined by string(data) is a function, or more precisely a functor, assigning to each data-algebra A, i.e. a set A, the string(data)-algebra B with $B_{data}=A$, $B_{string}=A^*$ (free monoid), $EMPTY_B$=empty word, and $LADD_B$=left concatenation. Obviously A* is freely generated by the parameter part A but A itself is not even generated by operations.

Even more relaxed is the generating principle in the case of "loose semantics" with initial restrictions in /HKR 80/ or data constraints in /BG 80/. In both cases the semantics is the class of all those data types B where only designated subtypes of B are assumed to be initially or freely generated. If in our example above the designated subtype of string(data) is data the semantics is the class of all string(data)-algebras B as defined above where A is the data-part of B, i.e. $A=B_{data}$. In other words the semantics in this case is the image of the function STRING(DATA) defined above.
The situation is different if we consider the specification

string-pick(data) = string(data) +
    opns: PICK:string $\longrightarrow$ data

again with a data constraint which makes sure that the string(data)-part is freely generated by the data-part. In this case the semantics consists of the class of all algebras B as defined above, where, however, each B has an arbitrary additional operation $PICK_B:A^* \longrightarrow A$ (which implies also that A must not be empty).
If, on the other hand, we would consider string-pick(data) as a parameterized specification with parameter part data the operation $PICK_B:B_{string} \longrightarrow B_{data}$ would also be freely generated, i.e. $PICK_B$ would generate new elements $PICK_B(W)$ in B_{data} for each W in B_{string}. This means, provided that we are interested to obtain an additional operation $PICK_B:A^* \longrightarrow A$, we have to consider string-pick(data) as a specification with data constraint and loose semantics.

The concept of initial restriction resp. data constraints turned out to be very useful also in the context of parameterized data types as studied in /ADJ 78+81/ in order to restrict the data types which are allowed in the formal parameter part. Especially this concept can be used to make sure that a bool-part in the formal parameter is really two-valued and not just any bool-algebra. In /Ehr 81/ we have allowed requirements of this kind. We were able to show that all the results concerning parameter passing (see /ADJ 81/) can be extended to parameterized speci-

Our notion of generating constraints is different from hierarchy constraints in the sense of /SW 82/ with respect to two main points:

1. The consistency condition "TRUE≠ FALSE" included in hierarchy constraints seems unnatural because it claims that bool is a designated specification among all others. The same effect, however, could be achieved assuming "0≠1" in the specification nat of natural numbers or any other specification. The main point is that we should be able to formulate distinctness of terms in some way. This can be done using initiality but can also be done using inequalities in the axioms.
2. There are syntactical rules to construct new generating constraints from given ones in a stepwise way. More precisely we give syntactic rules to define a language of constraints in much the same way as compound specifications are defined using the syntactical rules of a specification language. The syntactical rules include generation, translation, reflection and union of constraints while the semantics of each constraint defines a subclass of all algebras with given signature and axioms.

The main intention of this language is a precise syntax and semantics as given in Section 2 such that it can be used as a reference language in connection with some other algebraic specification language. In Section 3 we prove the main result of this paper showing that each constraint can be transformed into an equivalent constraint of a very simple canonical form. This canonical form result seems to be of great theoretical and practical significance: It allows to calculate the semantics of complex constraints by calculation of the corresponding equivalent canonical constraints. The basic concept for the semantics is that of an "U_f-generated algebra", as introduced above, where f:PRES$\longrightarrow$ PRES' is a presentation morphism and U_f:PRES'$^b\longrightarrow$ PRES^b the corresponding forgetful functor between the categories PRES'^{b} of PRES'- and PRES^b of PRES-algebras. A presentation in this paper consists of sorts, operations and equations or other axioms while a specification is a presentation together with a set of constraints. In Section 4 we give a construction and characterization of U_f-generated algebras including a "GENERATION LEMMA" which is the key for the proof of the canoncial form result in Section 3. Finally in Section 5 we discuss how generating constraints or free generating constraints can be used for the design of algebraic specification languages like CLEAR (/BG 80/) and LOOK (/ZLT 82/), and some other languages which are in preparation. In this paper we only give selected proofs. For full technical detail and comparison of generating and free generating constraints we refer to our technical report /EWT 82/. The part concerning free generating constraints in /EWT 82/ will be revised and combined with the final version of /WEB 82/. Finally let us mention that there is also a useful normal form result in /Cip 82/ which seems to be closely related to our technical lemma 3.3.7 for the case of free generation.

2. SYNTAX AND SEMANTICS OF GENERATING CONSTRAINTS

In the following we define a language for the construction of constraints for specifications which is based on the following operators: generation (GEN), translation (TRA), reflection (REF) and union (+). More precisely constraints are defined to be the (equivalence classes of) terms in some higher level presentation of constraints, called GENCONSTRAINT, where each finite presentation PRES corresponds to one sort in GENCONSTRAINT and for each presentation morphism f there are operations GEN_f, TRA_f and REF_f in GENCONSTRAINT. In addition we have an operation $\emptyset$ (initialization) of arity zero and a binary union operator + for each sort in GENCONSTRAINT together with axioms for commutativity and associativity of + and $\emptyset$ being neutral with respect to +. Since the syntax of our constraints language for specifications is itself a presentation the class of all constraints becomes an algebra in a natural way, namely the initial algebra defined by the presentation GENCONSTRAINT. This makes it easy to define the semantics of the constraints language. Due to the idea of initial algebra semantics of languages (/ADJ 77/) it sufficies to define a semantical algebra with the same presentation GENCONSTRAINT such that the semantics of the language is the uniquely defined homomorphism from the initial algebra to the semantical algebra. As shown in /ETLZ 82/ this initial algebra approach to languages is equivalent to a strong compositional denotational semantics which will be given in this paper. For each sort PRES in GENCONSTRAINT the corresponding semantical domain is the class of all full subcategories of the category $PRES^b$ of all PRES-algebras. More precisely we only take all full replete (i.e. closed under isomorphisms) subcategories of $PRES^b$ which corresponds exactly to the semantical framework in our paper /WEB 82/. The semantics of the operators GEN_f, TRA_f and REF_f will be defined as given in the introduction.

The main result in the next section shows that for each constraint in the constraints language there is an equivalent constraint (i.e. with same semantics) in canonical form.

Now we are able to give the syntax of our constraints language. We also give a graphical notation (shown for a number of examples). In 2.4 the semantics of the language is given.

2.1 DEFINITION (SYNTAX OF THE CONSTRAINTS LANGUAGE GENCONSTRAINT)

The syntax of the constraints language is the following (infinite) presentation

GENCONSTRAINT =

sorts: PRES — one sort for each finite presentation PRES

opns: GEN_f:PRES' $\longrightarrow$ PRES
TRA_f:PRES' $\longrightarrow$ PRES
REF_f:PRES $\longrightarrow$ PRES'
— one operation GEN_f, TRA_f and REF_f for each presentation morphism f:PRES' $\longrightarrow$ PRES respectively

$\emptyset: \longrightarrow$ PRES
+:PRES PRES$\longrightarrow$ PRES } one operation $\emptyset$ and + for each finite presentation PRES respecitvely

eqns: $\emptyset + C = C$

$C1+C2 = C2+C1$

$C1+(C2+C3)=(C1+C2)+C3$

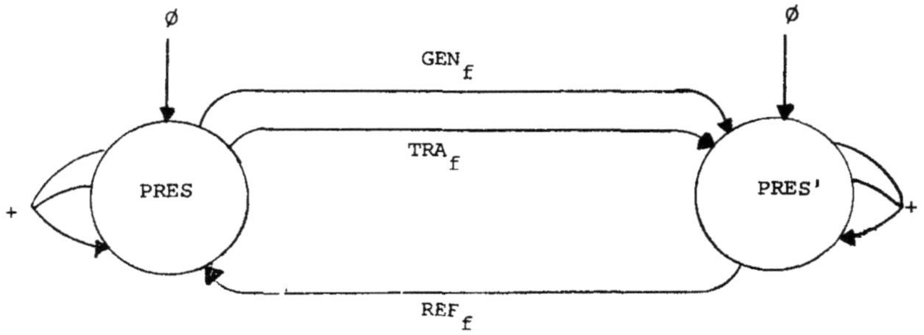

A constraint for a presentation PRES is a term of sort PRES in GENCONSTRAINT. A constraint is called linear if it is built up by GEN_f, TRA_f, REF_f and $\emptyset$ only, constraints including the union operator + are called compound.

The operations of GENCONSTRAINT will be called operators in the sequel in order to distinguish them from the operations in the presentations PRES. The operators $\emptyset$ resp. + are in fact abbreviations for the operators $\emptyset: \longrightarrow$ PRES and +:PRES PRES$\longrightarrow$PRES and might be indexed by the corresponding presentation PRES if there are problems of confusion, e.g. $\emptyset_{PRES}$ resp. $+_{PRES}$.

A specification SPEC=$\langle S,\Sigma,E,C\rangle$ is a presentation PRES=$\langle S,\Sigma,E\rangle$ together with a constraint C for PRES.

2.2 EXAMPLES AND NOTATION

There is a straight forward graphical notation of linear constraints in terms of sequences which is used in the following examples (see 2.5 for the semantics):

1) $\emptyset \xrightarrow[GEN]{f}$ nat means $GEN_f(\emptyset)$ or more precisely $GEN_f(\emptyset_{\emptyset})$ where the index $\emptyset$ corresponds to the empty source specification of f

2) $\emptyset \xrightarrow[GEN]{f}$ bool means $GEN_f(\emptyset)$ of sort bool

3) $\emptyset \xrightarrow[GEN]{f1}$ bool $\xrightarrow[TRA]{f2}$ data $\xrightarrow[GEN]{f3}$ string(data) $\xrightarrow[TRA]{f4}$ string-pick(data)

means $TRA_{f4}(GEN_{f3}(TRA_{f2}(GEN_{f1}(\emptyset))))$ also written as

$TRA_{f4} \circ GEN_{f3} \circ TRA_{f2} \circ GEN_{f1}(\emptyset)$

where string-pick(data) is string(data) together with an operation PICK:string$\longrightarrow$data which is intended to pick an arbitrary element of each non-empty string.

4) $\emptyset \xrightarrow[\text{GEN}]{f1} \underline{\underline{\text{bool}}} \xrightarrow[\text{REF}]{f2} \langle\{s\},\emptyset,\emptyset\rangle$ means $\text{REF}_{f2}(\text{GEN}_{f1}(\emptyset))$ also written as
$\text{REF}_{f2} \circ \text{GEN}_{f1}(\emptyset)$

Since compound constraints are built up by sets of linear constraints they can be represented by the following tree-like structure

5) $\emptyset \xrightarrow[\text{GEN}]{f1} \underline{\underline{\text{bool}}} \xrightarrow[\text{TRA}]{f2\,3} \underline{\underline{\text{string}(\text{data})}} \xrightarrow[\text{TRA}]{f4} \underline{\underline{\text{string-pick}(\text{data})}}$

$\underline{\underline{\text{data}}} \xrightarrow[\text{GEN}]{f3} \nearrow$

means $\text{TRA}_{f4}(\text{TRA}_{f2\,3}(\text{GEN}_{f1}(\emptyset))+\text{GEN}_{f3}(\emptyset))$ also written
as $\text{TRA}_{f4}(\text{TRA}_{f2\,3} \circ \text{GEN}_{f1}(\emptyset)+\text{GEN}_{f3}(\emptyset))$

Before we are going to define the semantics of our constraint language we have to make some general assumptions concerning the algebraic foundations. We are not going to fix a specific kind of axioms and specification morphisms in this paper but only some general properties which are needed in the constructions and proofs.

2.3 GENERAL ALGEBRAIC ASSUMPTIONS

A presentation $\text{PRES}=\langle S,\Sigma,E\rangle$ consists of a set S of sorts, a set Σ of operation symbols, short operations, and a set E of equations or axioms . A presentation morphism $f:\text{PRES}' \longrightarrow \text{PRES}$, where $\text{PRES}=\langle S,\Sigma,E\rangle$ and $\text{PRES}'=\langle S',\Sigma',E'\rangle$ are presentations, is a signature morphism $f=(f_s:S' \longrightarrow S, f:\Sigma' \longrightarrow \Sigma)$ which "preserves" equations resp. axioms. In the simplest case we take equations in the sense of /ADJ 76-78/ and assume that the translated equations $f(E')$ are included in E (see /ADJ 81/). But we could also consider more general axioms, like conditional axioms or universal Horn (see /ADJ 78/), and more general morphisms, e.g. E implies $f(E')$, if only the following weak assumptions are valid.

1. (Existence of Model Category)
For each presentation PRES there is a well-defined category PRES^b of PRES-algebras and PRES-homomorphisms.

2. (Existence of Forgetful Functor)
For each presentation morphism $f:\text{PRES}' \longrightarrow \text{PRES}$ there is a <u>forgetful functor</u> $U_f:\text{PRES}^b \longrightarrow \text{PRES}'^b$ defined by $U_f(A)=A'$ with $A'_{s'}=A_{f(s')}$ and $\sigma'_{A'}=f(\sigma')_A$ for all $A \in \text{PRES}^b$, similarly for morphisms. Moreover we assume that U_f <u>creates isomorphisms</u> (see 2.4.2), i.e. for all $A \in \text{PRES}^b$, $B' \in \text{PRES}'^b$ with $B' \cong U_f(A)$, there is $B \in \text{PRES}^b$ with $U_f(B)=B'$ and $B \cong A$.

3. (Existence of Syntactical and Semantical Categories)
All presentations PRES and presentation morphisms $f:\text{PRES} \longrightarrow \text{PRES}'$ are defining a syntactical category SYNTPRES with finite coproducts, constructed by disjoint union and pushouts. The corresponding categories PRES^b and forgetful functors $U_f:\text{PRES}^b \longrightarrow \text{PRES}'^b$ are defining a semantical category SEMPRES with finite products,

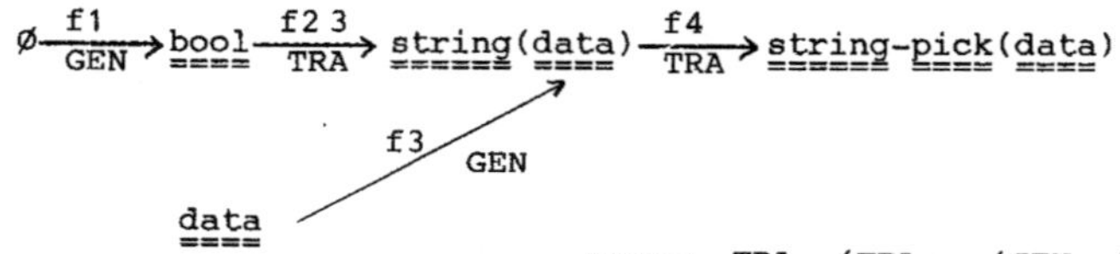

constructed by cartesian products, and pullbacks.
Moreover the contravariant functor FPRES:SYNTPRES$\longrightarrow$SEMPRES defined by FPRES(PRES)=$PRES^b$ and FPRES(f)=U_f transforms finite coproducts and pushouts in SYNTPRES into finite products and pullbacks respectively.

For the verification of these properties in the equational case we refer to /BW 82/. Note that in the short version of /BW 82/ only the unsigned case is considered, i.e. without designated set of operations, but the signed case as needed to show assumption 3 above will be given in the full version.

The main notation in this section depends only on the existence of the forgetful functor $U_f:PRES^b \longrightarrow PRES'^b$:
A PRES-algebra A is called generated w.r.t.U_f, short U_f-generated, if for all PRES-algebras B with $U_f(A)=U_f(B)$ we have

$$B \subseteq A \Longrightarrow B = A$$

For the construction of U_f-generated algebras we refer to Section 4.

2.4 DEFINITION (SEMANTICS OF THE CONSTRAINTS LANGUAGE GENCONSTRAINT)

Let us consider the following semantical domains:
For each presentation PRES we take the class of all full replete (i.e. closed under isomorphisms) subcategories of the category $PRES^b$ (see 2.3.1).
The semantical equations for the operators of GENCONSTRAINT are the following where f:PRES'$\longrightarrow$PRES is a presentation morphism and C' resp. C,C1,C2 constraints on PRES' resp. PRES

$$[\![GEN_f(C')]\!] = \{A \in PRES^b / A \text{ is } U_f\text{-generated} \wedge U_f(A) \in [\![C']\!]\}$$

$$[\![TRA_f(C')]\!] = \{A \in PRES^b / U_f(A) \in [\![C']\!]\}$$

$$[\![REF_f(C)]\!] = \{U_f(A) \in PRES'^b / A \in [\![C]\!]\}$$

$$[\![\emptyset]\!] = PRES^b \qquad \text{for } \emptyset: \longrightarrow PRES$$

$$[\![C1+C2]\!] = [\![C1]\!] \cap [\![C2]\!] \qquad \text{for } +: PRES\ PRES \longrightarrow PRES$$

Remarks:

1. The denotational semantics given above is strong compositional in the sense of /ETLZ 82/ and hence equivalent to an initial algebra semantics for the language GENCONSTRAINT.
2. If $[\![C']\!]$ resp. $[\![C]\!]$, $[\![C1]\!]$, $[\![C2]\!]$ are closed under isomorphisms then also the right hand sides of the equations above. This is easy to check in the first two and the last two equations. For the middle equation we need the property that U_f creates isomorphisms (see 2.3.2). Hence all constraints are defining full replete subcategories of the corresponding category $PRES^b$ which are the elements of the semantical domains defined above.

2.5 EXAMPLES

In the following we give the semantics of the constraints defined in 2.2 where T_{PRES} denotes the initial PRES-algebra:

1) $[\![GEN_f(\emptyset)]\!] = \{A \in \underline{nat}^b / A$ generated by O and SUCC$\}$
$= \{A \in \underline{nat}^b / \exists$ surj. $\underline{nat}$-hom $f: T_{\underline{nat}} \longrightarrow A\}$ (see Section 4)

2) $[\![GEN_f(\emptyset)]\!] = \{A \in \underline{bool}^b / A$ generated by TRUE and FALSE $\}$
$= \{A / A \cong T_{\underline{bool}} \vee card(A)=1\}$ if $\underline{bool}$ has equations only
$\{A / A \cong T_{\underline{bool}}\}$ if TRUE$\neq$FALSE is axiom in $\underline{bool}$ which will be assumed in the following

3) $[\![TRA_{f4} \circ GEN_{f3} \circ TRA_{f2} \circ GEN_{f1}(\emptyset)]\!] =$
$= \{A \in \underline{string\text{-}pick}(\underline{data})^b / A_{\underline{string}(\underline{data})}$ is generated by $A_{\underline{data}}, A_{\underline{bool}} \cong T_{\underline{bool}}\}$

4) $[\![REF_{f2} \circ GEN_{f1}(\emptyset)]\!] =$ class of all sets with two distinct elements.

Note, that this example shows that constraints including REF are strictly more powerful than those without REF. Actually it can be shown that all constraints on PRESO$=\langle\{s\},\emptyset,\emptyset\rangle$ using only the operators GEN_f, TRA_f, $\emptyset$ and + can only define the class of all sets, e.g. by $\emptyset \xrightarrow[TRA]{} PRESO$, or the class consisting of the empty set only, e.g. by $\emptyset \xrightarrow[GEN]{} PRESO$ (see Thm. 3.6).

5) $[\![TRA_{f4}(TRA_{f23} \circ GEN_{f1}(\emptyset) + GEN_{f3}(\emptyset))]\!] =$
$= \{A \in \underline{string\text{-}pick}(\underline{data}) / A_{\underline{string}(\underline{data})}$ is generated by $A_{\underline{data}}, A_{\underline{bool}} \cong T_{\underline{bool}}\}$

Note, that this value coincides with that given under 3 above. This is a consequence of Lemma 3.3 which shows that the corresponding constraints are equivalent.

3. CANONICAL FORM RESULTS

In this section we give two canoncial form results for generating constraints and the technical lemmas to prove these results. Before we are able to state the main result we have to define equivalence and canonical constraints.

3.1 DEFINITION (EQUIVALENCE AND CANONICAL CONSTRAINTS)

1. Two constraints C1 and C2 for PRES are called equivalent, written C1$\sim$C2, if they have the same semantics, i.e. $[\![C1]\!] = [\![C2]\!]$.
2. A constraint C for PRES is called canonical if C is a linear constraint of the form $C=REF_{f3} \circ TRA_{f2} \circ GEN_{f1}(\emptyset)$, i.e.

$$PRES1 \xrightarrow[GEN]{f1} PRES2 \xrightarrow[TRA]{f2} PRES3 \xleftarrow[REF]{f3} PRES$$

for some presentations PRESi and presentation morphisms fi (i=1,2,3).

Now we are able to state the main result of this section:

3.2 THEOREM (CONSTRUCTION OF EQUIVALENT CANONICAL CONSTRAINTS)

There is an effective algorithm to construct for each constraint in GENCONSTRAINT an equivalent canonical one.

For the proof of this theorem we need a number of technical lemmas which will be given first. For first reading we advice to skip 3.3 and go immediately to the proof of Theorem 3.2 in 3.4.

3.3 TECHNICAL LEMMAS

The following elementary results concerning equivalence of constraints on PRES are true for all presentations PRESi, PRESi' all presentation morphisms fi for i=1,2,3,4 and all constraints C1, C1' on PRES1 resp. PRES1':

The notation of constraints follows mainly that given in 2.2. However, we allow in addition to begin with an arbitrary constraint C1 on PRES1 (resp. C1' on PRES1') s.t. the given sequence defines a constraint on PRES.

1. $\underset{C1}{\mathrm{PRES1}} \xrightarrow[\mathrm{TRA}]{f1} \mathrm{PRES2} \xrightarrow[\mathrm{TRA}]{f2} \mathrm{PRES} \sim \underset{C1}{\mathrm{PRES1}} \xrightarrow[\mathrm{TRA}]{f2 \circ f1} \mathrm{PRES}$

2. $\underset{C1}{\mathrm{PRES1}} \xleftarrow[\mathrm{REF}]{f1} \mathrm{PRES2} \xleftarrow[\mathrm{REF}]{f2} \mathrm{PRES} \sim \underset{C1}{\mathrm{PRES1}} \xleftarrow[\mathrm{REF}]{f1 \circ f2} \mathrm{PRES}$

3. $\underset{C1}{\mathrm{PRES1}} \xrightarrow[\mathrm{GEN}]{f1} \mathrm{PRES2} \xrightarrow[\mathrm{GEN}]{f2} \mathrm{PRES} \not\sim \underset{C1}{\mathrm{PRES1}} \xrightarrow[\mathrm{GEN}]{f2 \circ f1} \mathrm{PRES}$ (in general)

4. $\underset{C1}{\mathrm{PRES1}} \xrightarrow[\mathrm{GEN}]{f1} \mathrm{PRES2} \xrightarrow[\mathrm{TRA}]{f2} \mathrm{PRES3} \xleftarrow[\mathrm{REF}]{f3} \mathrm{PRES} \quad \sim$

   $\underset{C1'}{\mathrm{PRES1'}} \xrightarrow[\mathrm{GEN}]{f1'} \mathrm{PRES2'} \xrightarrow[\mathrm{TRA}]{f2'} \mathrm{PRES3'} \xleftarrow[\mathrm{REF}]{f3'} \mathrm{PRES}$ (see next line)

$$\underset{C1 \oplus C1'}{\mathrm{PRES1+PRES1'}} \xrightarrow[\mathrm{GEN}]{f1+f1'} \mathrm{PRES2+PRES'} \xrightarrow[\mathrm{TRA}]{f2+f2'} \mathrm{PRES3+PRES3'} \xleftarrow[\mathrm{REF}]{f3+f3'} \mathrm{PRES+PRES} \xrightarrow[\mathrm{TRA}]{f4} \mathrm{PRES}$$

where + is the coproduct (disjoint union) in SYNTPRES, f4 the morphism induced by identities, $C1 \oplus C1' = TRA_{inj}(C1) + TRA_{inj'}(C1')$ for the coproduct injections $inj: \mathrm{PRES1} \to \mathrm{PRES1+PRES1'}$ and $inj': \mathrm{PRES1'} \to \mathrm{PRES1+PRES1'}$.

5. $\underset{C1}{\mathrm{PRES1}} \xrightarrow[\mathrm{GEN}]{f1} \mathrm{PRES2} \xrightarrow[\mathrm{TRA}]{f2} \mathrm{PRES3} \xrightarrow[\mathrm{GEN}]{f3} \mathrm{PRES4} \xrightarrow[\mathrm{TRA}]{f4} \mathrm{PRES} \quad \sim$

   $\underset{C1 \oplus \emptyset}{\mathrm{PRES1+PRES3}} \xrightarrow[\mathrm{GEN}]{f1+f3} \mathrm{PRES2+PRES4} \xrightarrow[\mathrm{TRA}]{f5} \mathrm{PRES}$

where + is again the coproduct and f5 the unique morphism induced by $f4 \circ f3 \circ f2: \mathrm{PRES2} \to \mathrm{PRES}$ and f4 and $C1 \oplus \emptyset$ is defined in the same way as above.

6. $\underset{C1}{\mathrm{PRES1}} \xleftarrow[\mathrm{REF}]{f1} \mathrm{PRES2} \xrightarrow[\mathrm{TRA}]{f2} \mathrm{PRES} \sim \underset{C1}{\mathrm{PRES1}} \xrightarrow[\mathrm{TRA}]{f3} \mathrm{PRES3} \xleftarrow[\mathrm{REF}]{f4} \mathrm{PRES}$

where (f3,f4) is pushout of (f1,f2) in SYNTPRES .

7. $\underset{C1}{\mathrm{PRES1}} \xleftarrow[\mathrm{REF}]{f1} \mathrm{PRES2} \xrightarrow[\mathrm{GEN}]{f2} \mathrm{PRES} \sim \underset{C1}{\mathrm{PRES1}} \xrightarrow[\mathrm{GEN}]{f3} \mathrm{PRES3} \xleftarrow[\mathrm{REF}]{f4} \mathrm{PRES}$

where (f3,f4) is pushout of (f1,f2) in SYNTPRES.

Proofs:

We only give the proofs for parts 1 and 7 in this paper. For the remaining parts we refer to /EWT 82/.

1. $[\![TRA_{f2} \circ TRA_{f1}(C1)]\!] = \{A \in PRES^b / U_{f2}(A) \in [\![TRA_{f1}(C1)]\!]\}$
$= \{A \in PRES^b / U_{f1} \circ U_{f2}(A) \in [\![C1]\!]\}$
$= \{A \in PRES^b / U_{f2 \circ f1}(A) \in [\![C1]\!]\}$
$= [\![TRA_{f2\ f1}(C1)]\!]$

If $C1=\emptyset$ then both sides are equal to $PRES^b$ which means that using $\emptyset$ and TRA-constructors only is trivial because they do not restrict the class of algebras. But they are meaningful in connection with other constructors.

7. $[\![GEN_{f2} \circ REF_{f1}(C1)]\!] = \{A \in PRES^b / A\ U_{f2}\text{-generated} \wedge U_{f2}(A) \in [\![REF_{f1}(C1)]\!]\}$
$= \{A \in PRES^b / A\ U_{f2}\text{-generated} \wedge \exists A1 \in [\![C1]\!]\ U_{f1}(A1) = U_{f2}(A)\}$
$= \{A \in PRES^b /\ A3 \in PRES3^b\ A3\ U_{f3}\text{-generated} \wedge U_{f3}(A3) \in [\![C1]\!] \wedge U_{f4}(A3) = A\}$ (see 4.3)
$= \{A \in PRES^b / \exists A3 \in [\![GEN_{f3}(C1)]\!] \wedge A = U_{f4}(A3)\}$
$= [\![REF_{f4} \circ GEN_{f3}(C1)]\!]$

3.4 SKETCH OF PROOF OF THEOREM 3.2

According to the recursive definition of terms in GENCONSTRAINT it sufficies to give explicit constructions for an equivalent canonical constraint in each of the following cases:

1. $\emptyset$ — for each PRES
2. $C1+C2$ — for canonical constraints C1,C2 on PRES
3. $GEN_f(C)$ — for each $f:PRES \longrightarrow PRES'$ and canonical C on PRES
4. $TRA_f(C)$ — dto.
5. $REF_f(C)$ — for each $f:PRES' \longrightarrow PRES$ and canonical C on PRES

This can be done using lemmas 3.3.1, 3.3.4, 3.3.6 in case 2, 2.8.7, 3.3.5 in case 3, 3.3.1, 3.3.6 in case 4 and 3.3.2 in case 5 respectively. For the complete proof see /EWT 82/.

3.5 COROLLARY

If we consider all constraints built up by the operators $\emptyset$,+,GEN_f and TRA_f only, i.e. not using REF_f, then each constraint on PRES is equivalent to one in the following canonical form:

$$\underset{\emptyset}{PRES1} \xrightarrow[GEN]{f1} PRES2 \xrightarrow[TRA]{f2} PRES$$

Proof: All steps in the proof of Theorem 3.2 involving TRA can be considered to be identities and hence omitted. Especially we do not need Lemma 3.3.6 and 3.3.2.

4.3 GENERATION LEMMA

Given the following pushout of presentation morphisms

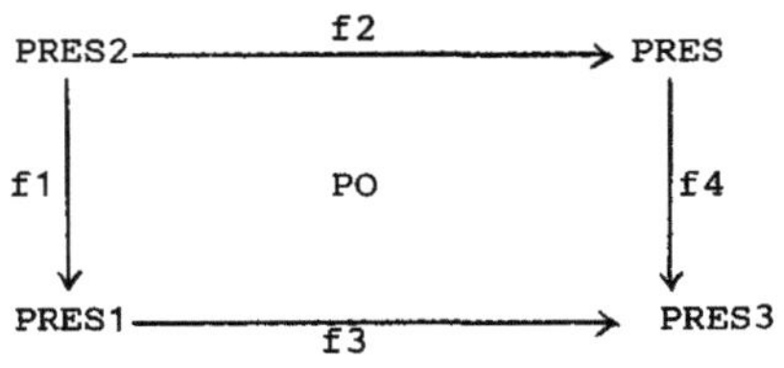

then we have:

For all $A \in PRES^b$ and $A1 \in PRES1^b$ with $U_{f2}(A)=U_{f1}(A1)$ we have

$$A \text{ is } U_{f2}\text{-generated} \iff A3 \text{ is } U_{f3}\text{-generated}$$

where $A3 \in PRES3^b$ is the unique PB-object with $U_{f3}(A3)=A1$ and $U_{f4}(A3)=A$ (see 2.3.3)

5. CONCLUSION

In this paper we have started a systematic discussion of constraints which have been used in connection with algebraic specifications in the last few years. On one hand constraints are necessary in the framework of algebraic specifications with initial algebra semantics in order to study a sufficiently large class of parameterized specifications (see /Ehr 81/). A number of basic examples, however, can be studied in the basic algebraic case without constraints (see /ADJ 81/) which is considered in the algebraic specification language ACT ONE in /EFH 83/. But in our next language ACT TWO we will also allow constraints.

Experience has shown that we need constraints for the formal parameter part once we have bool in the formal part and an if-then-else operation in the body part of the specification. In most of these cases simple constraints, i.e. $TRA_{f1} \circ GEN_{f2}(\emptyset)$, or simple free generating constraints, seem to be sufficient for the specification of the formal parameter parts. Looking also at parameter passing we obtain in a natural way general linear and compound constraints (see /EWT 82/) including the REF-operator. The situation after parameter passing is characterized by the corresponding equivalent canonical constraints resp. free generating, short F-constraints.

On the other hand constraints are necessary in the framework of algebraic specifications with loose semantics as used in the algebraic specification languages by Hupbach, Kaphengst and Reichel (/HKR 80/), Burstall and Goguen (CLEAR in /BG 80/) and Zilles, Lucas and Thatcher (LOOK in /ZLT 82/). Up to now in all these languages only sets of simple F-constraints are used. Since sets of simple constraints are shown to be equivalent to just one simple F-constraint it would be theoretically sufficient to consider just one simple F-constraint for each presentation. Building up specifications with F-constraints, however, general

3.6 THEOREM

Constraints not using REF_f are strictly less powerful then all constraints in GENCONSTRAINT.

Proof: We are going to calculate the semantics of all constraints not using REF_f on the presentation PRESO= $\langle\{s\},\emptyset,\emptyset\rangle$. Using Corollary 3.5 we only have to consider canonical constraints of the form

$$\langle S1,\Sigma 1,E1\rangle \xrightarrow[\text{GEN}]{f1} \langle S2,\Sigma 2,E2\rangle \xrightarrow[\text{TRA}]{f2} \langle\{s\},\emptyset,\emptyset\rangle$$
$$\emptyset$$

Since ΣO and EO are empty in PRESO also $\Sigma 2$,E2 and hence $\Sigma 1$,E1 must be empty because f2 resp. f1 are presentation morphisms. The semantics of this canonical constraint can be calculated directly (see /EWT 82/) leading to

$$[\![TRA_{f2} \circ GEN_{f1}(\emptyset)]\!] = \begin{cases} PRESO^b & \text{if } S2=S1=\emptyset \text{ or } S2\neq\emptyset \wedge S1\neq\emptyset \\ \{\emptyset\} & \text{if } S2\neq\emptyset \text{ and } S1=\emptyset \end{cases}$$

On the other hand the constraint $REF_{f2} \bullet GEN_{f1}(\emptyset)$ given in 2.2.4 has as semantics the class of all sets with two distinct elements (see 2.5.4). Due to the calculation above this class cannot be generated without REF.

4. CONSTRUCTION AND CHARACTERIZATION OF U_f-GENERATED ALGEBRAS

In this section we give a characterization of U_f-generated objects in terms of the free construction F_f. This allows also to show that all the U_f-generated objects are defining a coreflexive subcategory. Moreover, we present the basic lemma for Section 3, the GENERATION LEMMA. We assume to have the general assumptions stated in 2.3. In addition we assume for 4.1 and 4.2 to have for each forgetful functor $U_f:PRES^b \longrightarrow PRES'^b$ a left adjoint functor $F_f:PRES'^b \longrightarrow PRES^b$, called free construction. The proofs of the results are given in /EWT 82/.

4.1 THEOREM (CHARACTERIZATION OF U_f-GENERATION)

Given a presentation morphism f:PRES'$\longrightarrow$ PRES an object $A \in PRES^b$ is U_f-generated iff the counit morphism $\varepsilon_A:F_f \circ U_f(A) \longrightarrow A$ of the adjunction $F_f \dashv U_f$ is surjectiv.

4.2 THEOREM (CONSTRUCTION OF U_f-GENERATED ALGEBRAS)

For each algebra $A \in PRES^b$ there is a unique U_f-generated subalgebra G(A) of A. G(A) can be constructed as the image of the counit morphism $\varepsilon_A:F_f \bullet U_f(A) \longrightarrow$ of the adjunction $F_f \dashv U_f$. Moreover all U_f-generated algebras in $PRES^b$ are defining a coreflexive subcategory of $PRES^b$.

Remark: There is also a construction of G(A) without using the free construction F_f:G(A) is the intersection of all $B \in PRES^b$ satisfying $U_f(B)=U_f(A)$.

linear and compound F-constraints arise naturally. The results of /EWT 82/ can be used to reduce compound F-constraints to equivalent canonical forms which are much easier to calculate.
The same arguments are true for generating constraints as discussed in this paper. We are not going to argue about the question whether constraints or F-constraints are more adequate in practice. Moreover it would be possible to use both of them in combined form. That means we would have to define a constraints language built up by the operators $\emptyset$, +, GEN_f, $FGEN_f$, TRA_f, $FREF_f$ and REF_f. That could be done in a subsequent paper. At the moment, however, we are not sure whether this would be the right direction to follow. We would rather suggest to have more experience with generating constraints in practice first.

There are, however, some suggestions for the design of algebraic specification languages which we can give independent of the question whether to take constraints or F-constraints. In any case there should be a feature in the language to build up compound constraints on the syntactical level and to reduce compound constraints to equivalent canonical ones on the syntactical or at least the first semantical level. Our language GENCONSTRAINT in this paper may be used as a reference language for this purpose. It is not intended for convenient practical use.

In LOOK (see /ZLT 82/) it is suggested to consider only sets of simple injective F-constraints, i.e. $TRA_{f2} \circ FGEN_{f1}(\emptyset)$ where f1 and f2 are inclusions. On one hand this simplifies the notation of constraints. On the other hand the generative power is properly restricted: Actually a set of simple injective F-constraints is equivalent to a single simple F-constraint but this will not be injective in general (see lemma 3.3.4). Moreover there are simple noninjective F-constraints having no equivalent set of simple injective F-constraints (see /EWT 82/).

REFERENCES

/ADJ 76-78/ Goguen, J.A., Thatcher, J.W., Wagner, E.G.: An initial algebra approach to the specification, correctness, and implementation of abstract data types, IBM Research Report RC-6487, Oct. 76, Current Trends in Progr. Method., IV: Data Structuring (R.T.Yeh, Ed.) Prentice Hall, New Jersey (1978), 80-149

/ADJ 77/ --, Wright, J.B.: Initial algebra semantics and continous algebras, J.ACM 24, 68-95 (1977)

/ADJ 78/ Thatcher, J.W., Wagner, E.G., Wright, J.B.: More on advice on structuring compilers and proving them correct, TCS 15 (1981), 223-249

/ADJ 81/ Ehrig, H., Kreowski, H.-J., Thatcher, J.W., Wagner, E.G., Wright, J.B.: Parameter Passing in Algebraic Specification Languages, Proc. Aarhus Workshop on Prog. Spec., 1981, LNCS 134 (1982), 322-369

/BDPPW 79/ Broy, M., Dorsch, N., Partsch, H., Pepper, P., Wirsing, M.: Existential quantifiers in abstract data types; Proc. 6th ICALP, LNCS 71, 73-87 (1979)

/BG 80/ Burstall, R., Goguen, J.: The semantics of CLEAR, a Specification Language, Proc. Advanced Course on Abstr. Software Spec., LNCS 86 (1980), 294-332

/BW 82/ Bloom, S.L., Wagner, E.G.: Many sorted theories and their algebras, with examples from Comp. Sci. (working paper), IBM Research Center, 1982

/Ehr 82/ Ehrich, H.-D.: On the theory of specification,implementation and parameterization of abstract data types, J. ACM 29, No.1 (1982), 206-227

/Ehr 81/ Ehrig, H.: Parameterized Specifications with Requirements, Proc. CAAP'81, LNCS 112 (1981), 1-24

/EFH 83/ Ehrig, H., Fey, W., Hansen, H.: ACT ONE: An Algebraic Specification Language with Two Levels of Semantics, Techn. Report TU Berlin, No. 83-03, 1983

/EKP 80/ Ehrig, H., Kreowski, H.-J., Padawitz, P.: Algebraic Implementation of Abstract Data Types: Concept, Syntax, Semantics and Correctness, Proc. 7th ICALP, LNCS 85 (1980),142-156; long version to appear in TCS

/EK 82/ Ehrig, H., Kreowski, H.-J.: Parameter Passing Commutes with Implementation of Parameterized Data Types, Proc. 9th ICALP, LNCS 140 (1982), 197-211

/ETLZ 82/ Ehrig, H., Thatcher, J., Lucas, P., Zilles, S.: Denotational and initial algebra semantics of the algebraic specification language LOOK (draft paper), IBM Research Center (1982)

/EWT 82/ Ehrig, H., Wagner, E.G., Thatcher, J.W.: Algebraic Constraints for Specifications and Canonical Form Results, Techn.Report TU Berlin, No. 82-09, 1982

/Gut 75/ Guttag, J.V.: The specification and application to programming of abstract data types, Univ. Toronto, Techn.Report CSRG-59, (1975)

/HKR 80/ Hupbach, U.L., Kaphengst, M., Reichel, H.: Initial algebraic specifications of data types, parameterized data types and algorithms, VEB Robotron ZFT, Techn. Report, Dresden, 1980

/Lip 82/ Lipeck, U.: Ein algebraischer Kalkül für einen strukturierten Entwurf von Datenabstraktionen, PhD Thesis, Univ. Dortmund, 1982

/LZ 75/ Liskov, B.H., Zilles, S.N.: Specification Techniques for Data Abstraction, IEEE Trans.on Soft.Eng.,Vol.SE-1,No.1 (1975),7-19

/SW 82/ Sanella, D.,Wirsing, M.: Implementation of parameterized specifications, Proc. 9th ICALP, LNCS 140 (1982), 473-488

/WEB 82/ Wagner, E.G., Ehrig, H., Bloom, S.: Parameterized data types, parameter passing and canonical constraints (working paper) IBM Research Center (1982)

/Zil 74/ Zilles, S.N.: Algebraic specifications of data types, Project MAC Prog. Rep. 11, MIT (1974), 52-58

/ZLT 82/ Zilles, S.N., Lucas, P., Thatcher, J.W.: A look at algebraic specifications, IBM Research Report RJ 3568, 1982

WYTHOFF GAMES, CONTINUED FRACTIONS, CEDAR TREES AND FIBONACCI SEARCHES

Aviezri S. Fraenkel
Department of Applied Mathematics
The Weizmann Institute of Science
Rehovot, 76100 Israel

ABSTRACT.

Recursive, algebraic and arithmetic strategies for winning generalized Wythoff games in misère play are given. The notion of cedar trees, a subset of binary trees, is introduced and used for consolidating these and the normal play strategies. A connection to generalized Fibonacci searches is indicated.

1. INTRODUCTION

Let a be a positive integer. Given two piles of tokens, two players move alternately in a generalized Wythoff game. The moves are of two types: a player may remove any positive number of tokens from a single pile, or he may take from both piles, say k (>0) from one and ℓ (>0) from the other, provided that $|k-\ell| < a$. Note that passing is not allowed: each player at his turn has to remove at least one token. In normal play, the player first unable to move is the loser, his opponent the winner. In misère play, the outcome is reversed: the player first unable to move is the winner, his opponent the loser.

In this paper we show how to beat our adversary recursively, algebraically and arithmetically in misère play, analogously to the three strategies given in [3] for normal play. In addition we introduce the notion of cedar trees and use it to consolidate the strategies of normal play and of misère play. This permits us to beat our adversary in both normal and misère play from the top of a single cedar tree. A connection between cedar trees and generalized Fibonacci searches is also indicated.

The classical Wythoff game (see e.g. Wythoff [9] or Yaglom and Yaglom [10]) is the normal play version for the parameter choice $a = 1$, that is a player taking from both piles has to take the same number from both. Denote by S_1 and S_2 the previous-player-winning positions of normal and misère play respectively. Our results imply, in particular, the interesting fact that S_1 is identical to S_2 except for the first two positions when $a = 1$ (for which case the game is tame in the sense of Berlekamp, Conway and Guy [1]), whereas $S_1 \cap S_2 = \emptyset$ for every $a > 1$.

The recursive and algebraic characterizations of the previous-player-winning positions are presented in Sections 2 and 3 respectively. Some prerequisite results on continued fractions and systems of numeration are briefly presented in Section 4. These results are used for giving the arithmetic characterization of the previous-player-winning positions in Section 5. In Section 6 the notion of cedar trees is introduced, and in the final section 7 it is used for consolidating normal and misère play strategies.

Notation. Unless otherwise specified, we assume misère play. Game positions are denoted by (x,y) with $x \le y$, where x denotes the number of tokens in one pile and y the number of tokens in the other pile. Positions from which the Previous player can win whatever move his opponent will make are called P-positions, and those from which the Next player can win whatever his opponent will make are called N-positions. Thus $(0,1)$ is a P-position for every a, because the Next player has to move to $(0,0)$ and so Previous wins; $(1,b)$, $b > 1$ is an N-position for every a: the Next player moves to $(0,1)$ and wins. For $a = 2$, the position $(2,5)$ is a P-position: if Next moves to $(0,2),(0,3),(0,4),(0,5),(1,2),(1,3),(1,4)$ or $(1,5)$, then Previous, using a move of the first type, moves to $(0,1)$ and wins. If Next moves to $(2,2),(2,3)$ or $(2,4)$, then Previous, using a move of the second type, can again move to $(0,1)$.

The set of all P-positions is denoted by P, and the set of all N-positions by N.

2. RECURSIVE CHARACTERIZATION OF THE P-POSITIONS

A list of the first few P-positions (E_n,H_n) for the cases $a = 1$ and $a = 3$ is displayed in Tables 1 and 2. The tables have an interesting structure. First note that (at least for $n \le 11$), $H_n - E_n = n$ in Table 1, $3n + 1$ in Table 2. It is a bit harder to notice that $E_n = \text{mex}\{E_i,H_i : 0 \le i < n\}$ for both, where, for any set S, if $\bar{S}$ denotes the complement of S with respect to the nonnegative integers, then $\text{mex}\, S = \min \bar{S}$ = least nonnegative integer not in S. (mex stands for minimum excluded value.) Thus $\text{mex}\, \emptyset = 0$. If we define (E_n,H_n) in the indicated manner for all n, then $(E_{12},H_{12}) = (19,31)$ for $a = 1$ and $(16,53)$ for $a = 3$.

Table 1. The first few P-positions of the misère Wythoff game for $a = 1$.

n	E_n	H_n
0	2	2
1	0	1
2	3	5
3	4	7
4	6	10
5	8	13
6	9	15
7	11	18
8	12	20
9	14	23
10	16	26
11	17	28

Table 2. The first few P-positions for the misère Wythoff game for $a = 3$.

n	E_n	H_n
0	0	1
1	2	6
2	3	10
3	4	14
4	5	18
5	7	23
6	8	27
7	9	31
8	11	36
9	12	40
10	13	44
11	15	49

We now prove that the pairs (E_n, H_n) constitute the set P of P-positions for every $n \geq 0$.

THEOREM 1. The P-positions for misère Wythoff games are:

(i) For $a = 1$: $(E_0, H_0) = (2,2)$,

$$E_n = \text{mex}\{E_i, H_i : 0 \leq i < n\}, \quad H_n = E_n + n \quad (n \geq 1).$$

(ii) For $a > 1$: $E_n = \text{mex}\{E_i, H_i : 0 \leq i < n\}$, $H_n = E_n + an + 1$ $(n \geq 0)$.

PROOF. From the definition of E_n and H_n as given in the theorem it follows that if $E = \bigcup_{n=0}^{\infty} E_n$ and $H = \bigcup_{n=0}^{\infty} H_n$, then for every $a > 1$ E and H are complementary sets of numbers, that is, $E \cup H = Z^0$ (the set of nonnegative integers), and $E \cap H = \emptyset$. The last equality is true since if $E_n = H_m$, then $n > m$ implies that E_n is the mex of a set containing $H_m = E_n$, a contradiction; and $n \leq m$ is impossible since $H_m = E_m + am + 1 \geq E_n + an + 1 > E_n$. For $a = 1$, E and H are covering sets, that is, $E \cup H = Z^0$. (In fact, $E \cap H = \{2\}$ is easily proved as above.) Thus E and H are covering for every $a \geq 1$.

In order to prove the theorem it evidently suffices to show two things: I. A player moving from some (E_n, H_n) lands in a position not of the form (E_i, H_i). II. Given any position $(x,y) \neq (E_i, H_i)$ (except for $(x,y) = (0,0)$), there is a move to some (E_n, H_n). (It is useful to note that these two conditions are also necessary: the definition of P and N implies that all positions reachable in one move from a P-position are N-positions; whereas at least one P-position is reachable in one move from an N-position.)

I. A move of the first type from (E_n, H_n) clearly produces a position not of the form (E_i, H_i). Suppose that a move of the second type from (E_n, H_n) produces a position (E_i, H_i). Then $i \neq n$. A move of the second type satisfies

$$|(H_n - H_i) - (E_n - E_i)| = |(H_n - E_n) - (H_i - E_i)| = |(n-i)a| < a,$$

which implies $i = n$, a contradiction.

II. Let (x,y) with $x \leq y$ be a position not of the form (E_i, H_i) $(i \geq 0)$. If $(x,y) = (0,0)$, then Next wins without doing anything. So we may assume $(x,y) \neq (0,0)$. Since E and H are covering, every nonnegative integer appears in one of $\{E_n\}$ or $\{H_n\}$. Therefore either $x = H_n$ or $x = E_n$ for some $n \geq 0$.

Case (i). $x = H_n$. Then move $y \to E_n$. (This move always exists since $y \geq x = H_n \geq E_n$, and at least one inequality is strict.)

Case (ii). $x = E_n$. If $y > H_n$, then move $y \to H_n$. If $y = E_n$, then move to (E_0, H_0). We may thus assume that $E_n < y < H_n$. In particular, $n > 1$ for $a = 1$. Let $d = y - x - \varepsilon$, $m = \lfloor d/a \rfloor$, where

$$\varepsilon = \varepsilon(a) = \begin{cases} 0 & \text{if } a = 1 \\ 1 & \text{if } a > 1. \end{cases}$$

Then move $(x,y) \to (E_m,H_m)$. This is a legal move, since:

(a) $m \geq 0$.

(b) $d = y - E_n - \varepsilon < H_n - E_n - \varepsilon = an$, hence

$$m = \lfloor d/a \rfloor \leq d/a < n.$$

(c) $y = E_n + d + \varepsilon > E_m + d + \varepsilon \geq E_m + am + \varepsilon = H_m$.

(d) $|(y-H_m) - (x-E_m)| = |(y-x) - (H_m-E_m)| = |d-am| < a$.

Note that whereas the statement of Theorem 1 characterizes the P-positions, its proof indicates explicitly how to win, starting from an N-position. The characterization and move-specification constitute together a strategy for the game. Thus Theorem 1 and its proof provide a strategy for misère Wythoff games in which each P-position can be computed from the previous ones.

For computing a strategy, consider a position (x,y) with $0 \leq x \leq y$ $((x,y) \neq (0,0))$. We may assume, here and in the sequel, that $y \leq x + ax+1$, since for $y > x + ax+1$ we have $(x,y) \in N$; and (x,y) and $(x,x+ax+1)$ have then the same winning strategy. At most $O(x)$ computation steps are needed for computing the table of P-positions. Once the table is given, only $O(\log x)$ steps are required to locate x in it by binary search. Since also the next move can be computed in $O(\log x)$ steps, the total number of steps for computing the strategy is only $O(\log x)$, which is linear in the input size $O(\log x)$. However, a given table permits to compute the strategy for piles of bounded size only, and the table itself has exponential size. In the next section we give a closed form for the n-th P-position, which enables us to beat our adversary using an explicit rather than only an implicit recursive strategy, which is always polynomial (in time and space).

3. AN ALGEBRAIC CHARACTERIZATION OF THE P-POSITIONS

Let

$$\alpha = \alpha(a) = \frac{2-a+\sqrt{a^2+4}}{2}, \quad \beta = \beta(a) = \alpha + a .$$

α is the positive root of the quadratic equation $\xi^{-1} + (\xi+a)^{-1} = 1$. Thus α and β are irrational for every positive integer a, and satisfy $\alpha^{-1} + \beta^{-1} = 1$. Let $\gamma = \gamma(a) = \alpha^{-1}$, $\delta = \delta(a) = \gamma + 1$. Then

$$\frac{\gamma}{\alpha} + \frac{\delta}{\beta} = \gamma(\frac{1}{\alpha} + \frac{1}{\beta}) + \frac{1}{\beta} = \frac{1}{\alpha} + \frac{1}{\beta} = 1 .$$

It thus follows immediately from [2, Theorem II] that the sets

$$E' = \{E'_n: n = 0,1,2,\ldots\}, \quad H' = \{H'_n: n = 0,1,2,\ldots\}$$

are complementary, where $E'_n = \lfloor n\alpha+\gamma \rfloor$, $H'_n = \lfloor n\beta+\delta \rfloor$.

Let $a > 1$. Note that $E'_0 = 0 = E_0$, $H'_0 = 1 = H_0$, and $H'_n = E'_n + an + 1$. Moreover, $\text{mex}\{E'_i, H'_i: 0 \le i < n\} = E'_n$ $(n \ge 0)$, since $\{E'_n\}$ and $\{H'_n\}$ are increasing sequences and E' and H' are complementary: if the mex were not E'_n, then E'_n would never be obtained! This shows that $E'_n = E_n$, $H'_n = H_n$ $(n \ge 0)$. We have proved the second part of:

THEOREM 2. The P-positions of misère Wythoff games are:

(i) For $a = 1$: $(E_0,H_0) = (2,2)$ $(E_1,H_1) = (0,1)$,

$$(E_n,H_n) = (\lfloor n\alpha \rfloor, \lfloor n\beta \rfloor) \quad (n \ge 2),$$

where $\alpha = \alpha(1)$, $\beta = \beta(1)$.

(ii) For $a > 1$: $(E_n,H_n) = (\lfloor n\alpha+\gamma \rfloor, \lfloor n\beta+\delta \rfloor) \quad (n \ge 0)$,

where $\alpha = \alpha(a)$, $\beta = \beta(a)$, $\gamma = \gamma(a)$, $\delta = \delta(a)$.

The first part is proved in essentially the same way. ∎

A strategy based on this observation can be realized as follows for every $a > 1$. It is easy to see that $n\alpha+\gamma$ is irrational for every n. Since $\alpha > 1$,

$$x = \lfloor n\alpha+\gamma \rfloor \iff x < n\alpha+\gamma < x+1$$

$$\iff \frac{x-\gamma}{\alpha} < n < \frac{x-\gamma+1}{\alpha} \iff \left\lfloor \frac{x-\gamma+1}{\alpha} \right\rfloor = \left\lfloor \frac{x-\gamma}{\alpha} \right\rfloor + 1,$$

where (x,y) with $x \le y$ is a game position. Therefore either $x = \lfloor n\alpha+\gamma \rfloor = E_n$ where $n = \lfloor (x-\gamma+1)/\alpha \rfloor$, or else, by complementarity, $x = \lfloor n\beta+\delta \rfloor = H_n$ where $n = \lfloor (x-\delta+1)/\beta \rfloor$. We have thus reduced the situation to that considered in cases (ii) and (i) in the proof of Theorem 1, and hence the move selection made there can be followed. The strategy is similar for $a = 1$, hence the details are omitted. For implementing this strategy, α,β,γ and δ have to be computed and stored to a precision of $O(\log x)$ digits, such that $(x-\gamma+1)\alpha^{-1}$ and $(x-\delta+1)\beta^{-1}$ have still at least one significant digit to the right of the (decimal, say) point.

In order to give yet another, unexpected, way for beating our opponent, we resort to the theory of continued fractions.

4. CONTINUED FRACTIONS AND SYSTEMS OF NUMERATION

Let α be an irrational number satisfying $1 < \alpha < 2$. Denote its simple continued fraction expansion by

$$\alpha = 1 + \cfrac{1}{a_1 + \cfrac{1}{a_2 + \cfrac{1}{a_3 + \ddots}}} = [1,a_1,a_2,a_3,\ldots],$$

where the a_i are positive integers. Its <u>convergents</u> $p_n/q_n = [1,a_1,\ldots,a_n]$ satisfy the recursion

$$p_{-1} = 1,\ p_0 = 1,\ p_n = a_n p_{n-1} + p_{n-2} \qquad (n \geq 1)$$

$$q_{-1} = 0,\ q_0 = 1,\ q_n = a_n q_{n-1} + q_{n-2} \qquad (n \geq 1)\ .$$

For the basic facts of the theory of continued fractions see for example Hardy and Wright [4], Olds [7] or Perron [8].

In the next theorem we present two systems of numeration, one based on the numerators p_i and one on the denominators q_i of the convergents of α. The two systems are called <u>p-system</u> and <u>q-system</u> in the sequel.

<u>THEOREM 3</u>. Every positive integer can be written uniquely in the form

$$N = \sum_{i=0}^{m} s_i p_i\ , \quad 0 \leq s_i \leq a_{i+1}\ , \quad s_{i+1} = a_{i+2} \Rightarrow s_i = 0 \quad (i \geq 0)\ ,$$

and also in the form

$$N = \sum_{i=0}^{n} t_i q_i\ , \quad 0 \leq t_0 < a_1,\quad 0 \leq t_i \leq a_{i+1},\quad t_i = a_{i+1} \Rightarrow t_{i-1} = 0 \quad (i \geq 1).$$

Table 3 displays the representation of the first few nonnegative integers in the p and q-systems for the case $a_i = 3$ $(i \geq 1)$.

For the proof of Theorem 3 and Lemma 1 below (which is needed later), see [3].

<u>Table 3</u>. The representation of the first few nonnegative integers in the p and q-systems for the case $a_i = 3$ $(i \geq 1)$.

	p_2	p_1	p_0	q_2	q_1	q_0
n	13	4	1	10	3	1
0	0	0	0	0	0	0
1			1			1
2			2			2
3			3		1	0
4		1	0		1	1
5		1	1		1	2
6		1	2		2	0
7		1	3		2	1
8		2	0		2	2
9		2	1		3	0
10		2	2	1	0	0
11		2	3	1	0	1
12		3	0	1	0	2
13	1	0	0	1	1	0
14	1	0	1	1	1	1
15	1	0	2	1	1	2
16	1	0	3	1	2	0
17	1	1	0	1	2	1
18	1	1	1	1	2	2
19	1	1	2	1	3	0
20	1	1	3	2	0	0

LEMMA 1. Let

$$G_{i+1} = a_{i+1}p_i + a_{i-1}p_{i-2} + \dots + a_{k+1}p_k ,$$

where $k = 0$ if i is even, $k = 1$ if i is odd. Then $G_{i+1} = p_{i+1} - 1$. (Informally, G_{i+1} is the equivalent in the p-system of 99⋯9 in the decimal system.)

We close this short section with three definitions which will be useful in the next sections.

(i) Representations and their interpretations. Relative to a simple continued fraction $\alpha = [1,a_1,a_2,\dots]$, define a representation R to be an (m+1)-tuple

$$R = (d_m,d_{m-1},\dots,d_1,d_0),$$

where

$$0 \leqslant d_i \leqslant a_{i+1} \quad \text{and} \quad d_{i+1} = a_{i+2} \Rightarrow d_i = 0 \quad (i \geqslant 0).$$

If it is known that $d_{i-1} = d_{i-2} = \dots = d_0 = 0$, we also write $R = (d_m,\dots,d_i)$ instead of $(d_m,\dots,d_i,0,\dots,0)$. The p-interpretation I_p of a representation $R = (d_m,\dots,d_0)$ is the number $I_p = \sum_{i=0}^{m} d_i p_i$. The q-interpretation of R is the number $I_q = \sum_{i=0}^{m} d_i q_i$, provided that $d_0 < a_1$; otherwise R has no q-interpretation. Given any positive integer k, we say that its p-representation $R_p(k)$ (or q-representation $R_q(k)$) is $(d_m,\dots,d_0)$ if

$$k = \sum_{i=0}^{m} d_i p_i \quad \left(\text{or } k = \sum_{i=0}^{m} d_i q_i,\ d_0 < a_1\right).$$

We shall later be interested in p-interpretations of q-representations! Thus for $\alpha = [1,\dot{3}]$ where $\dot{x}$ denotes the infinite concatenation of x with itself, the decimal number 15 has q-representation 112 (see Table 3), whose p-interpretation is 19. Thus $I_p(R_q(15)) = I_p(112) = 19$.

(ii) Left and right shifts of representations. If $R = (d_m,\dots,d_0)$ is any representation (which might be $R_p(k)$ or $R_q(k)$ for some positive integer k), then the representation $R' = (d_m,\dots,d_0,0)$ is called a left shift of R. In other words, R' is obtained from R by shifting each digit d_i of R left by one place and inserting a zero at the right. If $R = (d_m,\dots,d_1,d_0)$ is any representation, then the representation $R'' = (d_m,\dots,d_1)$ is called a right shift of R.

(iii) Lexicographic ordering of representations. Given two representations $R_1 = (d_m,\dots,d_0)$ and $R_2 = (c_m,\dots,c_0)$, we say that R_1 is larger than R_2 or R_2 is smaller than R_1 ($R_1 > R_2$ or $R_2 < R_1$) if there is some $j \in [0,m]$ such that $d_j > c_j$ and $d_i = c_i$ $(i > j)$.

Note that $R_1 > R_2$ if and only if $I_p(R_1) > I_p(R_2)$.

5. AN ARITHMETIC CHARACTERIZATION OF THE P-POSITIONS

We use the numeration systems introduced in the previous section to give a quite different characterization of the P-positions. Comparing Tables 2 and 3 we notice three interesting patterns. To make them more conspicuous, we unite Tables 2 and 3 in the form of Table 4. Below we prove that these patterns do indeed hold for every $\alpha = [1,\dot{a}]$, $a > 1$, in the form of the following three properties.

Whenever we say that a representation R ends in a certain string, we mean that this string constitutes the right-hand end of R.

Table 4. The representation of the first few P-positions (E_n, H_n) and n in the p and q-systems for $\alpha = [1,\dot{3}]$ ($a = 3$, misère play).

			$R_p(E_n)$			$R_p(H_n)$				$R_q(n)$		
			p_2	p_1	p_0	p_3	p_2	p_1	p_0	q_2	q_1	q_0
n	E_n	H_n	13	4	1	43	13	4	1	10	3	1
0	0	1	0	0	0				1	0	0	0
1	2	6			2			1	2			1
2	3	10			3			2	2			2
3	4	14		1	0		1	0	1		1	0
4	5	18		1	1		1	1	1		1	1
5	7	23		1	3		1	2	2		1	2
6	8	27		2	0		2	0	1		2	0
7	9	31		2	1		2	1	1		2	1
8	11	36		2	3		2	2	2		2	2
9	12	40		3	0		3	0	1		3	0
10	13	44	1	0	0	1	0	0	1	1	0	0
11	15	49	1	0	2	1	0	1	2	1	0	1
12	16	53	1	0	3	1	0	2	2	1	0	2
13	17	57	1	1	0	1	1	0	1	1	1	0
14	19	62	1	1	2	1	1	1	2	1	1	1
15	20	66	1	1	3	1	1	2	2	1	1	2
16	21	70	1	2	0	1	2	0	1	1	2	0
17	22	74	1	2	1	1	2	1	1	1	2	1
18	24	79	1	2	3	1	2	2	2	1	2	2
19	25	83	1	3	0	1	3	0	1	1	3	0
20	26	87	2	0	0	2	0	0	1	2	0	0
21	28	92	2	0	2	2	0	1	2	2	0	1
22	29	96	2	0	3	2	0	2	2	2	0	2
23	30	100	2	1	0	2	1	0	1	2	1	0
24	32	105	2	1	2	2	1	1	2	2	1	1
25	33	109	2	1	3	2	1	2	2	2	1	2
26	34	113	2	2	0	2	2	0	1	2	2	0
27	35	117	2	2	1	2	2	1	1	2	2	1
28	37	122	2	2	3	2	2	2	2	2	2	2
29	38	126	2	3	0	2	3	0	1	2	3	0
30	39	130	3	0	0	3	0	0	1	3	0	0
31	41	135	3	0	2	3	0	1	2	3	0	1
32	42	139	3	0	3	3	0	2	2	3	0	2

PROPERTY 1. The set $\{E_n : n \geq 0\}$ is identical to the set of numbers with p-representations ending in one of: (i) $3,4,\ldots,a$; (ii) $01\cdots1$even, $01\cdots12$even; (iii) $c1\cdots1$odd, $c1\cdots12$odd, where c denotes any digit in the range $1 < c < a$, and even (odd) at the end of a string means that the number of consecutive trailing 1's is even (odd), followed by the digit 2 where indicated. The set $\{H_n : n \geq 0\}$ is identical to

the set of numbers with p-representations ending in one of: (iv) $01\cdots 1$odd, $01\cdots 12$odd; (v) $c1\cdots 1$even≥ 2, $c1\cdots 12$even.

PROPERTY 2. Denote the least significant digit of $R_p(E_n)$ by t. Then $R_p(H_n)$ is the left shift $R'_p(E_n)$ of $R_p(E_n)$ with the last digit (zero) replaced by 1 (if $t=0$ or 1) or by 2 and t replaced by $t-1$ (if $1<t\leq a$) $(n\geq 0)$.

PROPERTY 3. Let n be any nonnegative integer. If $R_q(n)$ ends in $01\cdots 1$even or in $c1\cdots 1$odd $(1<c<a)$, then $E_n = I_p(R_q(n))$. If $R_q(n)$ ends in $01\cdots 1$odd or in $c1\cdots 1$even, then $E_n = I_p(R_q(n))+1$ $(n\geq 0)$.

For proving these properties we need two further auxiliary results. Let $\alpha=[b, a_1,a_2,\ldots]$ with convergents $\{p_i/q_i\}$, where b is any integer. Let $D_i = \alpha q_i - p_i$ $(i\geq -1)$. From the theory of continued fractions it is known that

$$-1=D_{-1}<D_1<D_3<\ldots<0<\ldots<D_4<D_2<D_0=\alpha-b,\quad |D_{i-1}|>|D_i| \qquad (i\geq 0).$$

LEMMA 2. $D_j + \sum_{i=1}^{m} a_{j+2i}D_{j+2i-1} = D_{j+2m}$ $(j\geq -1)$.

See [3] for a proof.

LEMMA 3. Let b be any integer, a any positive integer and $\alpha=[b,\dot{a}]$. Then

$$\sum_{i=0}^{m} D_i = a^{-1}(D_m+D_{m+1}+b+1-\alpha) \quad (m\geq 0).$$

PROOF. True for $m=0$. If it is true for m, then

$$\sum_{i=0}^{m+1} D_i = a^{-1}(D_m+D_{m+1}+b+1-\alpha)+D_{m+1} = a^{-1}(aD_{m+1}+D_m+D_{m+1}+b+1-\alpha)$$

$$= a^{-1}(D_{m+1}+D_{m+2}+b+1-\alpha), \quad \text{since } aD_{m+1}+D_m=D_{m+2}. \quad \blacksquare$$

For proving Property 3 it evidently suffices to show that the following four relations hold for every $j\geq 0$:

$$\text{(i)}\quad n=\sum_{i=0}^{2j-1} q_i + \sum_{i=2j+1}^{k} d_iq_i \Rightarrow \lfloor n\alpha+\alpha^{-1}\rfloor = \sum_{i=0}^{2j-1} p_i + \sum_{i=2j+1}^{k} d_ip_i \qquad (k\geq 0)$$

$$\text{(ii)}\quad n=\sum_{i=0}^{2j} q_i + \sum_{i=2j+1}^{k} d_iq_i,\ d_{2j+1}>1 \Rightarrow \lfloor n\alpha+\alpha^{-1}\rfloor = \sum_{i=0}^{2j} p_i + \sum_{i=2j+1}^{k} d_ip_i \quad (k\geq 1),$$

$$\text{(iii)}\quad n=\sum_{i=0}^{2j} q_i + \sum_{i=2j+2}^{k} d_iq_i \Rightarrow \lfloor n\alpha+\alpha^{-1}\rfloor = 1+\sum_{i=0}^{2j} p_i + \sum_{i=2j+2}^{k} d_ip_i \qquad (k\geq 0),$$

$$\text{(iv)}\quad n=\sum_{i=0}^{2j-1} q_i + \sum_{i=2j}^{k} d_iq_i,\ d_{2j}>1 \Rightarrow \lfloor n\alpha+\alpha^{-1}\rfloor = 1+\sum_{i=0}^{2j-1} p_i + \sum_{i=2j}^{k} d_ip_i \quad (k\geq 0).$$

Relation (i) is evidently equivalent to

$$0\leq n\alpha+\alpha^{-1}-\sum_{i=0}^{2j-1} p_i - \sum_{i=2j+1}^{k} d_ip_i < 1$$

for n as given in (i). This is equivalent to:

$$\text{(v)}\quad 0 \leq \sum_{i=0}^{2j-1} D_i + \sum_{i=2j+1}^{k} d_i D_i + \alpha^{-1} < 1 \qquad (k \geq 0).$$

Similarly, (ii), (iii) and (iv) are equivalent, respectively, to:

$$\text{(vi)}\quad 0 \leq \sum_{i=0}^{2j} D_i + \sum_{i=2j+1}^{k} d_i D_i + \alpha^{-1} < 1 \qquad (d_{2j+1}>1,\ k\geq 1),$$

$$\text{(vii)}\quad 1 \leq \sum_{i=0}^{2j} D_i + \sum_{i=2j+2}^{k} d_i D_i + \alpha^{-1} < 2 \qquad (k\geq 0),$$

$$\text{(viii)}\quad 1 \leq \sum_{i=0}^{2j-1} D_i + \sum_{i=2j}^{k} d_i D_i + \alpha^{-1} < 2 \qquad (d_{2j}>1,\ k\geq 0).$$

We proceed to prove (v). By Lemma 2,

$$\sum_{i=2j+1}^{k} d_i D_i \leq \sum_{i=1}^{k} aD_{(2j+1)+(2i-1)} = D_{2j+2k+1} - D_{2j+1} < -D_{2j+1},$$

$$\sum_{i=2j+1}^{k} d_i D_i \geq \sum_{i=1}^{k} aD_{2j+2i-1} = D_{2j+2k} - D_{2j} > -D_{2j}.$$

Hence by Lemma 3 (with $b=1$ here and below),

$$\sum_{i=0}^{2j-1} D_i + \sum_{i=2j+1}^{k} d_i D_i < a^{-1}(D_{2j-1} + D_{2j} + 2 - \alpha) - D_{2j+1}$$

$$= a^{-1}(2 - \alpha - (a-1)D_{2j-1} - (a^2-1)D_{2j}).$$

Now

$$D_{2j+1} = aD_{2j} + D_{2j-1} = (a+1)D_{2j} + D_{2j-1} - D_{2j}.$$

Since $D_{2j} > -D_{2j+1}$, we thus get

$$-D_{2j-1} < D_{2j+1} + D_{2j} - D_{2j-1} = (a+1)D_{2j}.$$

Thus $-(a-1)D_{2j-1} \leq (a^2-1)D_{2j}$, hence

$$\sum_{i=0}^{2j-1} D_i + \sum_{i=2j+1}^{k} d_i D_i < a^{-1}(2-\alpha).$$

Let α_2 be the negative root of $\xi^2 + (a-2)\xi - a = 0$ (α is the positive root). Then $\alpha\alpha_2 = -a$, $\alpha+\alpha_2 = 2-a$. Therefore

$$a^{-1}(2-\alpha) = a^{-1}(a+\alpha_2) = a^{-1}(a-a\alpha^{-1}) = 1-\alpha^{-1},$$

proving the right-hand side of (v). For proving the left-hand side, write

$$\sum_{i=1}^{2j-1} D_i + \sum_{i=2j+1}^{k} d_i D_i \geq a^{-1}(D_{2j-1} + D_{2j} + 2 - \alpha) - D_{2j}$$

$$= a^{-1}(D_{2j-1} - (a-1)D_{2j} + 2 - \alpha) \geq a^{-1}(D_{-1} - (a-1)D_0 + 2 - \alpha)$$

$$= 1-\alpha = a+\alpha_2 - 1 = a(1-\alpha^{-1}) - 1 \geq -\alpha^{-1}. \quad \blacksquare$$

For proving (vi) we use $d_{2j+1} > 1$ and Lemma 2 to get

$$\sum_{i=2j+1}^{k} d_i D_i < 2D_{2j+1} + \sum_{i=1}^{k} aD_{(2j+1)+(2i-1)} = D_{2j+1} + D_{2j+2k+1} < D_{2j+1},$$

and, as above, $\sum_{i=2j+1}^{k} d_i D_i > -D_{2j}$. Hence by Lemma 3,

$$\sum_{i=1}^{2j} D_i + \sum_{i=2j+1}^{k} d_i D_i < a^{-1}(D_{2j}+D_{2j+1}+2-\alpha)+D_{2j+1}$$

$$= a^{-1}(D_{2j+1}+D_{2j+2}+2-\alpha) = \sum_{i=0}^{2j+1} D_i \leq 1 - \alpha^{-1},$$

where the last inequality follows as in the proof of (v). On the other hand,

$$\sum_{i=0}^{2j} D_i + \sum_{i=2j+1}^{k} d_i D_i > a^{-1}(D_{2j}+D_{2j+1}+2-\alpha) - D_{2j}$$

$$= a^{-1}(2-\alpha-(a-1)D_{2j}+D_{2j+1}) \geq a^{-1}(2-\alpha-(a-1)D_0+D_1) = 0 > -\alpha^{-1}. \blacksquare$$

For proving (vii) we again start with Lemma 2:

$$\sum_{i=2j+2}^{k} d_i D_i \leq \sum_{i=1}^{k} aD_{(2j+1)+(2i-1)} = D_{2j+2k+1} - D_{2j+1} < -D_{2j+1},$$

$$\sum_{i=2j+2}^{k} d_i D_i \geq \sum_{i=1}^{k} aD_{(2j+2)+(2i-1)} = D_{2j+2k+2} - D_{2j+2} > -D_{2j+2}.$$

Thus

$$\sum_{i=0}^{2j} D_i + \sum_{i=2j+2}^{k} d_i D_i < a^{-1}(D_{2j}+D_{2j+1}+2-\alpha) - D_{2j+1}$$

$$= a^{-1}(2-\alpha+D_{2j}-(a-1)D_{2j+1}) \leq a^{-1}(2-\alpha+D_0-(a-1)D_1)$$

$$= \alpha+a-a\alpha = 1-(\alpha-1)(a-1).$$

Since $\alpha > 1$, we have $-(\alpha-1)(a-1) \leq 0 < 1 - \alpha^{-1}$. Thus

$$1 - (\alpha-1)(a-1) < 2-\alpha^{-1},$$

proving the right-hand side of (vii). In the other direction,

$$\sum_{i=0}^{2j} D_i + \sum_{i=2j+2}^{k} d_i D_i > a^{-1}(D_{2j}+D_{2j+1}+2-\alpha)-D_{2j+2}$$

$$= a^{-1}(2-\alpha-(a-1)D_{2j}-(a^2-1)D_{2j+1}).$$

We proceed in a way similar to the proof of (v):

$$D_{2j+2} = (a+1)D_{2j+1} + D_{2j} - D_{2j+1},$$

hence

$$-D_{2j} > D_{2j+2} + D_{2j+1} - D_{2j} = (a+1)D_{2j+1},$$

so

$$-(a-1)D_{2j} - (a^2-1)D_{2j+1} \geq 0 .$$

Hence $\sum_{i=0}^{2j} D_i + \sum_{i=2j+2}^{k} d_i D_i > a^{-1}(2-\alpha) = 1-\alpha^{-1}$. ■

Finally we prove (viii) by writing

$$\sum_{i=2j}^{k} d_i D_i \leq \sum_{i=1}^{k} aD_{(2j-1)+(2i-1)} = D_{2j+2k-1} - D_{2j-1} < -D_{2j-1}.$$

Since $d_{2j} > 1$,

$$\sum_{i=2j}^{k} d_i D_i > 2D_{2j} + \sum_{i=1}^{k} aD_{2j+2i-1} = D_{2j} + D_{2j+2k} > D_{2j}.$$

Thus

$$\sum_{i=0}^{2j-1} D_i + \sum_{i=2j}^{k} d_i D_i < a^{-1}(D_{2j-1}+D_{2j}+2-\alpha) - D_{2j-1}$$

$$= a^{-1}(2-\alpha-(a-1)D_{2j-1}+D_{2j}) \leq a^{-1}(2-\alpha-(a-1)D_{-1}+D_0)$$

$$= 1 < 2-\alpha^{-1},$$

since $\alpha > 1$. In the other direction,

$$\sum_{i=0}^{2j-1} D_i + \sum_{i=2j}^{k} d_i D_i > a^{-1}(D_{2j-1}+D_{2j}+2-\alpha) + D_{2j}$$

$$= a^{-1}(D_{2j}+D_{2j+1}+2-\alpha) = \sum_{i=0}^{2j} D_i > 1-\alpha^{-1},$$

as in (vii). ■

The first part of Property 3 implies that if $R_q(n)$ ends in $01\cdots1$even or in $c1\cdots1$odd, then also $R_p(E_n) = R_q(n)$ ends in the same strings. The second part of Property 3 implies that if $R_q(n)$ ends in $01\cdots1$odd then $R_p(E_n)$ ends in $01\cdots12$even; and if $R_q(n)$ ends in $c1\cdots1$even, then $R_p(E_n)$ ends in $3,4,\ldots,a$ or in $c1\cdots12$ odd. Since the sets $\{E_n : n \geq 0\}$ and $\{H_n : n \geq 0\}$ are complementary, the latter set of numbers has representations which are the complement of the representations of the former set. This proves Property 1. ■

For proving Property 2, note that the transformation of f defined in its statement is a bijection since it has an inverse f^{-1}: Shift $f(R_p(E_n))$ right; if $d_0 = 2$, then put $d_1 \leftarrow d_1 + 1$ ($d_1 d_0$ is the right trailing end of $f(R_p(E_n))$). This evidently produces E_n. Moreover, by Property 1, the sets $\{R_p(E_n) : n \geq 0\}$ and $\{f(R_p(E_n)) : n \geq 0\}$ are complementary.

We now proceed by induction. The assertion is true for $n = 0$. If it is true for all $n < m$, then $f(R_p(E_m)) \neq R_p(H_n)$, $n < m$. In fact $I_p(f(R_p(E_m)))$ is the smallest number of $\{H_n\}$ not yet obtained for $n < m$. If $H_m \neq I_p(f(R_p(E_m)))$, then $I_p(f(R_p(E_m)))$ can never be obtained for $n > m$, contradicting the complementarity of $\{R_p(E_n)\}$ and $\{f(R_p(E_n)\}$. ■

Now suppose we are given a position (x,y) with $0 \leqslant x \leqslant y$ $(a > 1)$. We may assume $(x,y) \neq (0,0)$. To obtain a strategy based on Properties 1,2 and 3, compute $R_p(x)$. If it ends in one of the strings (iv) or (v) of Property 1, then $x = H_k$ for some $k \geqslant 0$, and a winning move is $(x,y) \to (I_p(f^{-1}(R_p(x))),x) \in P$. If $R_p(x)$ ends in one of the strings (i), (ii) or (iii) of Property 1, then $x = E_k$ for some $k \geqslant 0$. If $y > I_p(f(R_p(x)))$, then the move $(x,y) \to (x,I_p(f(R_p(x)))) \in P$ is a winning move. If $y = I_p(f(R_p(x)))$, then $(x,y) \in P$, so we cannot win when starting from the given position (x,y). If $x = y$, then the move $(x,y) \to (0,1) \in P$ is winning. Finally, if $x < y < I_p(f(R_p(x)))$, then let $m = \lfloor (y-x-1)/a \rfloor$. If $R_q(m)$ ends in $01\cdots1$even or $c1\cdots1$odd $(1 < c < a)$, then $E_m = I_p(R_q(m))$ by Property 3. Otherwise $E_m = I_p(R_q(m))+1$. In either case a winning move is $(x,y) \to (E_m,E_m+am+1) \in P$. The strategy for $a = 1$ is similar and is therefore omitted.

The complexity analysis of this algorithm is very similar to that performed at the end of [3], and is based on the fact that $p_n \sim Kg^{n+1}$, where $K = \alpha/\sqrt{a^2+4}$, $g = (a+\sqrt{a^2+4})/2$. Since $n \sim \log_g(x/K)$ and g increases with a, this strategy implementation, which requires $n = O(\log x)$ steps, is more efficient than even the algebraic one of Section 3 when a is large.

In order to consolidate the above strategies of misère Wythoff games as well as those of normal Wythoff games, we now proceed to introduce the notion of a cedar tree.

6. CEDAR TREES

Relative to a simple continued fraction $\alpha = [1,a_1,a_2,\ldots]$ we define the following subclass of binary tree. The subclass consists of continued fraction representation trees (cedar trees). A cedar tree $C_{m,d} = C_{m,d}(\alpha)$ of order m is defined as follows: (i) For $m < 0$ or $d = d_m$ outside the range $(1,2,\ldots,a_{m+1})$, $C_{m,d}$ is empty. (ii) For $1 \leqslant d = d_m \leqslant a_{m+1}$ and $m \geqslant 0$, the root of $C_{m,d}$ is any representation of the form $(d_n,\ldots,d_m)$. Note that the order m of the tree is the index m of the least significant nonzero digit d_m of the representation of the tree's root. The root of the left subtree is the representation $(d_n,\ldots,d_{m+1},d_m-1,1)$ of order $m-1$ $(m \geqslant 1)$. If $d = d_m < a_{m+1}$, then the root of the right subtree is the representation $(d_n,\ldots,d_m+1)$ of order m. If $d_m = a_{m+1}$, then the root of the right subtree is the representation $(d_n,\ldots,d_m,0,1)$ of order $m-2$ $(m \geqslant 2)$. This inductive definition is illustrated schematically in Figure 1 for the case $m = 2$ and $a_3 = 4$. If the root of $C_{m,d}$ is the re-

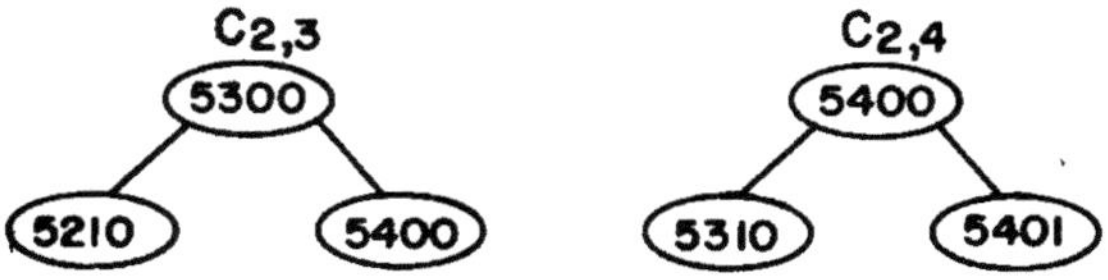

Figure 1. The inductive construction of a cedar tree for $m = 2$, $a_3 = 4$.

presentation (d_m), we denote the tree by $C^0_{m,d}$. Figure 2 illustrates the unique cedar tree $C^0_{2,1}([1,\dot{3}])$ in which the numbers above and below the nodes should be ignored for the moment.

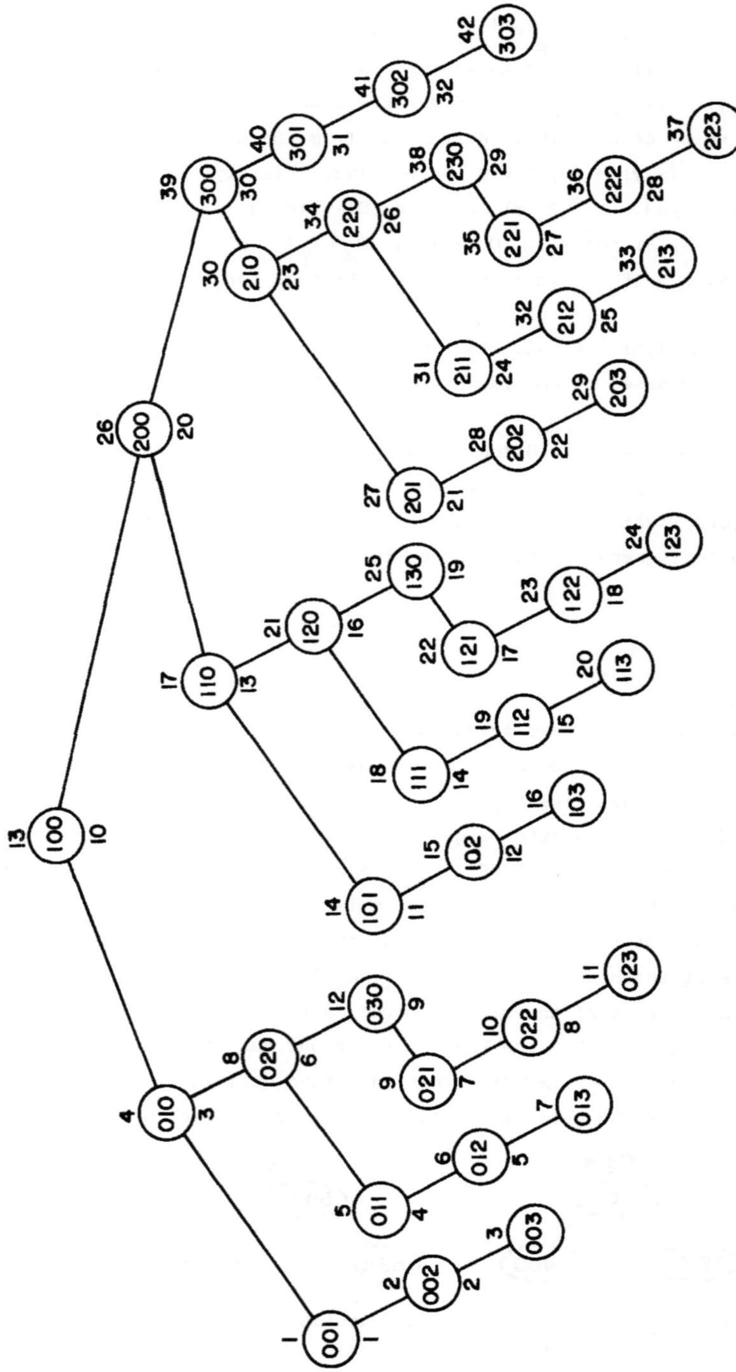

Figure 2: Illustration of the cedar tree $C^0_{2,1}([1,\dot{3}])$.

We now derive two subfamilies of trees from the family of cedar trees. A <u>p-tree</u> $T_{m,d}$ derived from a cedar tree $C_{m,d}$ is the p-interpretation of $C_{m,d}$, that is, every node of $C_{m,d}$ is replaced by its p-interpretation to make up $T_{m,d}$. Similarly, a <u>q-tree</u> $\tau_{m,d}$ derived from $C_{m,d}$ is the q-interpretation of $C_{m,d}$, but with one proviso: since $t_0 < a_1$ (see Theorem 3 above) and the nodes of $C_{m,d}$ ending in a_1 are precisely the leaves of $C_{m,d}$, the form of a $\tau_{m,d}$-tree is that of $T_{m,d}$, but without the leaves of the latter. Thus a $T_{m,d}$-tree turns into a $\tau_{m,d}$-tree in the fall, after having shed all its leaves, and the process is reversed in the spring! The notation $C^0_{m,d}$ carries over to $T^0_{m,d}$ and $\tau^0_{m,d}$ in an obvious manner.

For example, the numbers above the nodes in Figure 2 are the p-interpretations of the nodes. Replacing the nodes of $C^0_{2,1}([1,\dot{3}])$ by these p-interpretations gives $T^0_{2,1}([1,\dot{3}])$. The numbers under the nodes of $C^0_{2,1}([1,\dot{3}])$ are the q-interpretations. So pruning the leaves of $C^0_{2,1}([1,\dot{3}])$ and replacing its remaining nodes by their q-interpretations gives $\tau^0_{2,1}([1,\dot{3}])$.

We need the following definitions. The <u>rightmost</u> (<u>leftmost</u>) <u>descendant</u> v of a node u is the descendant at the end of a chain of right (left) descendants of u which has no further right (left) son. (Note that v is not necessarily a leaf.) A <u>label</u> of an edge (u,v) of a cedar tree is a bit 0 or 1 attached to the edge according to whether v is a left or right son of u. If w is any vertex of a cedar tree and $(e_1,\ldots,e_m)$ is the path of edges between the root and w, then $m+1$ is the <u>length</u> of the path and $(c_1,\ldots,c_m) \in \{0,1\}^m$ is the <u>trace</u> $tr(w)$ of w, where c_i is the label of edge e_i $(1 \le i \le m)$. The order of the sequence is such that c_1 is the label of the edge e_1 from the root to its son, and c_m is the label of the edge e_m leading into w. Note that the trace of the root of a cedar tree is the empty sequence. If $tr(u) = (0,c_2,\ldots c_k)$, then $tr(v) = tr'(u) = (c_2,\ldots,c_k)$ is a <u>left shift</u> of $tr(u)$. Also $tr(u) = tr''(v) = (0,c_2,\ldots c_k)$ is a <u>right shift</u> of $tr(v)$.

The basic properties of cedar trees and some other properties needed for the applications are enunciated in the "cedar tree ten commandments" theorem below.

The reader may find it useful to verify the properties on the cedar tree of Figure 2 while reading the theorem.

To simplify the notation we write $tr(R_p\lfloor x\rfloor)$ instead of $tr(R_p(\lfloor x\rfloor))$.

<u>THEOREM 4</u>. Let $\alpha = [1,a_1,a_2,\ldots]$ be an irrational number and $C_{m,d} = C_{m,d}(\alpha)$ a cedar tree $(d = d_m,\ m \ge 0)$. For assertions (ix) and (x) we assume: $a_i = a$ $(i \ge 1)$ where a is any positive integer (since the proof rests on Lemma 3), $\gamma = \alpha^{-1}$, $\beta = \alpha + a$, and we restrict attention to a cedar tree $C^0_{m,1}(\alpha)$.

(i) Let u be any node in $C_{m,d}$ or in the $T_{m,d}$ or $\tau_{m,d}$-tree derived from $C_{m,d}$. Then every node in the left subtree of u is smaller than u and every node in the right subtree of u is larger than u.

(ii) The trees $C_{m,d}$ and $T_{m,d}$ have $p_{m+1} - (d-1)p_m - 1$ nodes each and $\tau_{m,d}$ has $q_{m+1} - (d-1)q_m - 1$ nodes.

(iii) Every number from among $\{1,2,\ldots,p_{m+1}-1\}$ appears exactly once in $T^0_{m,1}$

and every number from among $\{1,2,\dots,q_{m+1}-1\}$ appears exactly once in $\tau^0_{m,1}$.

(iv) Pruning the leaves of $C_{m,d}$ and replacing the nodes by their q-interpretations gives $\tau_{m,d}$. Moreover, the number of leaves of $C_{m,1}$ (or $T_{m,1}$) is $p_{m+1}-q_{m+1}$; this number is q_m if $a_i = a$ ($i \geq 1$, a any positive integer).

(v) Let $R_1 = (d_n,\dots,d_{k+1},d_k)$ be a node of $C_{m,d}$ with $d_k \neq 0$, $k > 0$. Then the leftmost descendant of the right subtree of R_1, if any, is $R_2 = (d_n,\dots,d_{k+1},d_k,0,\dots,0,1)$ ($k-1$ intervening 0's), and $I_p(R_2) = I_p(R_1)+1$. The rightmost descendant of the left subtree of R_1 is $R_3 = (d_n,\dots,d_{k+1},d_k-1,a_k,0,\dots,0,a_1)$ (k odd) or $(d_n,\dots,d_{k+1},d_{k-1},a_k,0,\dots,a_2,0)$ (k even). In either case, $I_p(R_3)=I_p(R_1)-1$

(vi) The longest path from the root of $C_{m,1}$ to a leaf has length $L_m = \sum_{i=1}^{m+1} a_i$; the shortest path has length $\ell_m = a_1+m$ (if $a_i > 1$ for $i \geq 1$) or $\lfloor (m+3)/2 \rfloor$ (if $a_i = 1$ for $i \geq 1$).

(vii) If $tr(u) = (0,c_2,\dots,c_k)$ for u in $C^0_{m,1}$, then there exists a node v in $C^0_{m,1}$ with $tr(v) = tr'(u) = (c_2,\dots,c_k)$, and v is a left shift of u. Conversely, if v is a node in $C^0_{m,1}$ ending with 0 and $tr(v) = (c_2,\dots,c_k)$, then the right shift u of v is in $C^0_{m,1}$ and $tr(u) = (0,c_2,\dots,c_k)$.

(viii) If $R_q(n)$ ends in an even number of zeros in $C^0_{m,1}$, then $tr(R_p\lfloor n\alpha\rfloor) = tr(R_q(n))$. Otherwise $tr(R_p\lfloor n\alpha\rfloor)$ is $tr(R_q(n))$ followed by 0 and as many 1's as possible until a rightmost descendant is reached.

(ix) Let u be a node in $C^0_{m,1}$ ending in a digit t with $tr(u) = (0,c_2,\dots,c_k)$. If $t < a$, then there exists a node v in $C^0_{m,1}$ with $tr(v) = (c_2,\dots,c_k,1,0,\dots,0)$ (maximal number of trailing o's until a leftmost descendant is reached) and $v = u'$, except that the last digit 0 of v is replaced by 1. Suppose $a > 1$. If $t > 0$, then there exists a node v in $C^0_{m,1}$ with $tr(v) = (c_2,\dots,c_k,0,1)$ and $v = u'$, except that the last two digits $(t,0)$ of v are replaced by $(t-1,2)$. Conversely, if v and $tr(v)$ have the specified forms, then $(0,c_2,\dots,c_k)$ is the trace of a node in $C^0_{m,1}$ which is the right shift v'' of v with the last digit t of v'' replaced by $t+1$, if the last digit of v is 2.

(x) If $R_q(n)$ ends in $01\cdots1$even or in $c1\cdots1$odd ($1 < c < a$), then $tr(R_p\lfloor n\alpha+\gamma\rfloor) = tr(R_q(n))$. Otherwise $tr(R_p\lfloor n\alpha+\gamma\rfloor)$ is $tr(R_q(n))$ followed by 1 ($n > 0$).

<u>PROOF</u>. (i) We prove the result for $T_{m,d}$. The proof for $\tau_{m,d}$ and $C_{m,d}$ is the same. If u in $T_{m,d}$ has the form $K_{m+1}+dp_m$ for some $1 \leq d \leq a_{m+1}$ where $R_p(K_{m+1})$ has the form $(d_n,\dots,d_{m+1})$, then it follows from the definition of cedar trees that every node in the right subtree of u contains the summand $K_{m+1}+dp_m$, in addition to other summands. The left subtree T' of u has root $v = K_{m+1}+(d-1)p_m+p_{m+1}$. Assuming the result inductively for T', the largest node of T' is a rightmost descendant of v, whose value is $K_{m+1}+(d-1)p_m+a_m p_{m-1}+a_{m-2}p_{m-3}+\dots = K_{m+1}+dp_m-1 < u$ by Lemma 1. ■

(ii) Again we prove the assertion for $T_{m,d}$ only. Since obviously $T_{m,d}$ and $T^0_{m,d}$ have the same number of nodes, it suffices to restrict attention to $T^0_{m,d}$. We proceed by induction on m for any d. A tree $T^0_{0,d}$ has obviously $a_1-d+1=p_1-(d-1)p_0-1$

vertices. Given $T^0_{m,d}$ $(m \geq 1)$. Each of the nodes $dp_m, (d+1)p_m, \ldots, a_{m+1}p_m$ in the branch emanating from the root on the right has a left subtree of the form $T_{m-1,1}$ (see Figure 3). The number of nodes in the branch and in the $(a_{m+1} - d + 1)$ left subtrees is $(a_{m+1} - d + 1)p_m$ by the induction hypothesis. In addition, the node $a_{m+1}p_m$ has a right subtree of the form $T_{m-2,1}$, which has $p_{m-1} - 1$ nodes. Hence the total number of nodes of $T_{m,d}$ is $(a_{m+1} - d + 1)p_m + p_{m-1} - 1 = p_{m+1} - (d-1)p_m - 1$. ■

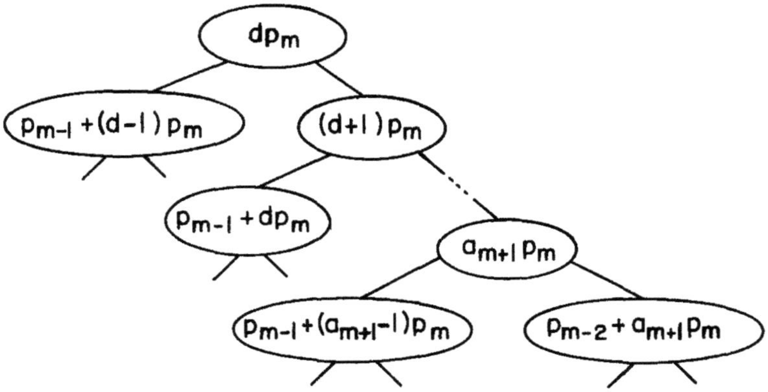

Figure 3. The first few branches of $T^0_{m,d}$.

(iii) Once again we prove the result for $T^0_{m,1}$ only. From (i) it follows that the smallest element in $T^0_{m,1}$ is the leftmost descendant which is evidently 1. The largest element is the rightmost descendant, and it is $a_{m+1}p_m + a_{m-1}p_{m-2} + \ldots = p_{m+1} - 1$ by Lemma 1. It also follows from (i) that all values in $T_{m,d}$ are distinct. Since the number of nodes is $p_{m+1} - 1$ by (ii) and all are in the range $[1, p_{m+1} - 1]$, every integer in this range must appear precisely once in $T^0_{m,1}$. (Induction on m without using (i) and Lemma 1 could have been used as an alternative proof.) ■

(iv) The first part was already proved. By (ii), the number of leaves of $T_{m,1}$ is $(p_{m+1} - 1) - (q_{m+1} - 1) = p_{m+1} - q_{m+1}$. For $\alpha = [1, \dot{a}]$ we have $p_i = q_i + q_{i-1}$ $(i \geq 0)$. This is indeed the case for $i = 0$ and 1 by inspection. Assume true for $i < n$ $(n \geq 2)$ Then $p_n = ap_{n-1} + p_{n-2} = a(q_{n-1} + q_{n-2}) + (q_{n-2} + q_{n-3}) = q_n + q_{n-1}$. ■

(v) The results follow directly from the definition of cedar trees and from Lemma 1. ■

(vi) It suffices to compute the longest and shortest path from the root of $T^0_{m,1}$ — rather than $C_{m,1}$ — to a leaf. By inspection, $L_0 = \ell_0 = a_1$, $L_1 = a_2 + a_1$, $\ell_1 = \ell_0 + 1$. Since $L_{m-1} \geq L_{m-2}$ we have (see Figure 3 in which we now put $d = 1$),

$$L_m = \max(1 + L_{m-1}, a_{m+1} + L_{m-1}) = a_{m+1} + L_{m-1},$$

and the result $L_m = \sum_{i=1}^{m+1} a_i$ follows by induction on m. Since also $\ell_{m-1} \geq \ell_{m-2}$ we have,

$$\ell_m = \min(1 + \ell_{m-1}, a_{m+1} + \ell_{m-2}) .$$

If $a_i > 1$ $(i \geq 1)$, then, assuming the result inductively, we get $\ell_m = \min(a_1 + m, a_{m+1} + a_1 + m - 2) = a_1 + m + \min(0, a_{m+1} - 2) = a_1 + m$. If $a_i = 1$ $(i \geq 1)$, then $\ell_m = 1 + \ell_{m-2} = 1 + \lfloor (m+1)/2 \rfloor = \lfloor (m+3)/2 \rfloor$ by the induction hypothesis. ■

(vii) For traces of length 1, $tr(u) = (c_1) = (0)$. The desired vertex v in this case is the root with the empty trace. Moreover, $u = (0,1,0,\ldots,0)$ $(m-1$ trailing zeros) and $v = (1,0,0,\ldots,0)$ (m trailing zeros), and so v is a left shift of u. Given u with $tr(u) = (0,c_2,\ldots,c_k)$ $(k \geq 2)$. By the induction hypothesis on the trace length, for the father u_1 of u with $tr(u_1) = (0,c_2,\ldots,c_{k-1})$, there exists a node v_1 with $tr(v_1) = (c_2,\ldots,c_{k-1})$, and v_1 is a left shift of u_1. Thus if $u_1 = (d_n,\ldots,d_\ell,0,\ldots,0)$, $d_\ell \neq 0$ (ℓ trailing zeros), then $v_1 = (d_n,\ldots,d_\ell,0,\ldots,0)$ (ℓ+1 trailing zeros). If u is a left son of u_1, then $\ell > 0$ and so a fortiori v_1 has a left son v. The trace of u is then $(0,c_2,\ldots,c_k)$ $(c_k = 0)$ and that of v is $(c_2,\ldots,c_k)$. Moreover, $u = (d_n,\ldots,d_\ell - 1,1,0,\ldots,0)$ (ℓ-1 trailing zeros) and v has the same form but with ℓ trailing zeros, and so v is a left shift of u. A similar argument holds if u and v are right sons of u_1 and v_1 respectively.

Now let v be a node ending in zero and let u be the right shift of v. Since $I_p(u) < I_p(v)$, (iii) implies that $I_p(u)$ appears in $T^0_{m,1}$, the p-tree derived from $C^0_{m,1}$. Hence u appears in $C^0_{m,1}$. Since $I_p(v) < p_{m+1}$, we have $I_p(u) < p_m$. Hence if $tr(v) = (c_2,\ldots,c_k)$ and $tr(u) = (b_1,b_2,\ldots,b_k)$, then $b_1 = 0$. By the first part of (vii), we know that the left shift v of u has trace $(b_2,\ldots,b_k) \equiv (c_2,\ldots,c_k)$. Hence u has trace $(0,c_2,\ldots,c_k)$. ■

(viii) The result follows from [3, Theorem 4]. The first part of that theorem implies that if $R_q(n)$ ends in an even number of zeros, then $R_p\lfloor n\alpha \rfloor = R_q(n)$ is represented by a single node of $C^0_{m,1}$. The second part of the theorem and (v) imply that if $R_q(n)$ ends in an odd number of zeros, then $R_p\lfloor n\alpha \rfloor$ is a rightmost descendant of the left subtree of $R_q(n)$, which implies the result. ■

(ix) From (vii) we know that the left shift $w = u'$ is in $C^0_{m,1}$ and $tr(w) = (c_2,\ldots,c_k)$. If $t < a$, then w has a right son x, hence a leftmost descendant v of x (which may be x itself). Clearly $tr(v) = (c_2,\ldots,c_k,1,0,\ldots,0)$; and $I_p(v) = I_p(w) + 1$ by (v). This implies that replacing the last digit of w by 1 gives v, completing the proof of the first part. For proving the second part, note that since w ends in 0, w has a left son y. If $t > 0$, then y ends in $t-1,1$. Since $a > 1$, y has a right son z which ends in $t-1,2$, and $tr(z) = (c_2,\ldots,c_k,0,1)$. The converse of the first two parts is clear. ■

(x) The result follows directly from Property 3. ■

7. SOME USES OF CEDAR TREES

A. Search decision trees

A tree $T^0_{m,1}([\dot{1}])$ is the decision tree of a so-called Fibonacci search. See e.g. Knuth [6, Sect. 6.2.1]. More generally, a tree $T^0_{m,1}([1,\dot{a}])$ ($a \geq 1$ any integer) can be considered as the decision tree of a generalized Fibonacci search algorithm which, given a table of n numbers in increasing order, starts by comparing the argument searched for with the (n/g)-th number (where $g = (p_{m+1} - 1)/p_m$), and iterates this procedure on the smaller blocks. See [6, Sect. 6.2.1, Ex. 20]. A generalized search in this sense is in fact defined by $T^0_{m,1}(\alpha)$ and by $\tau^0_{m,1}(\alpha)$ for every real number α. A use of such searches is indicated below.

B. Wythoff games

In order to show how cedar trees can be used to consolidate Wythoff game strategies, it is useful to take stock of the main results obtained so far.

Normal Play

Three characterizations of the P-positions (A_n, B_n)

I. $A_n = \text{mex}\{A_i, B_i : 0 \leq i < n\}$, $B_n = A_n + an$ $(n \geq 0)$.

II. $A_n = \lfloor n\alpha \rfloor$, $B_n = \lfloor n\beta \rfloor$, $\alpha = (2-a+\sqrt{a^2+4})/2$, $\beta = \alpha + a$ $(n \geq 0)$.

III. (a) $\{A_n\}$ $(\{B_n\})$ is the set of all numbers whose representation relative to $\alpha = [1,\dot{a}]$ ends in an: (1) even ((2) odd) number of zeros.

(b) $R_p(B_n) = R'_p(A_n)$.

(c) If $R_q(n)$ ends in: (1) an even number of zeros, then $A_n = I_p(R_q(n))$; if it ends in: (2) an odd number of zeros, then $A_n = I_p(R_q(n)) - 1$ $(n \geq 0)$.

Misère Play

Three characterizations of the P-positions (E_n, H_n)

IV. (i) For $a = 1$: $(E_0, H_0) = (2,2)$,

$$E_n = \text{mex}\{E_i, H_i : 0 \leq i < n\}, \quad H_n = E_n + n \quad (n \geq 1).$$

(ii) For $a > 1$: $E_n = \text{mex}\{E_i, H_i : 0 \leq i < n\}$, $H_n = E_n + an + 1$ $(n \geq 0)$.

V. (i) For $a = 1$: $(E_0, H_0) = (2,2)$, $(E_1, H_1) = (0,1)$,

$$E_n = \left\lfloor n\frac{1+\sqrt{5}}{2} \right\rfloor, \quad H_n = \left\lfloor n\frac{3+\sqrt{5}}{2} \right\rfloor \quad (n \geq 2).$$

(ii) For $a > 1$: $E_n = \lfloor n\alpha + \gamma \rfloor$, $H_n = \lfloor n\beta + \delta \rfloor$ $(n \geq 0)$, where $\alpha = \dfrac{2-a+\sqrt{a^2+4}}{2}$, $\beta = \alpha + a$, $\gamma = \alpha^{-1}$, $\delta = \gamma + 1$.

VI. (i) For $a = 1$: E_n, H_n are the same as A_n, B_n in III above $(n \geq 2)$, except that $(E_0, H_0) = (2,2)$, $(E_1, H_1) = (0,1)$.

(ii) For $a > 1$: (a) E_n is the set of all numbers with p-representation ending in one of: (1) $3,4,\ldots,a$, $01\cdots1$even, $01\cdots12$even, $c1\cdots1$odd or $c1\cdots12$odd $(1 < c < a)$, and H_n is the set of all numbers with p-representation ending in one of: (2) $01\cdots1$odd, $01\cdots12$odd, $c1\cdots1$even≥ 2 or $c1\cdots12$even $(n \geq 0)$. (b) $R_p(H_n)$ is $R'_p(E_n)$ with the last digit (zero) replaced by 1 (if the last digit t of $R_p(E_n)$ is 0 or 1) or by 2 and t replaced by $t-1$ (if $1 < t \leq a$) $(n \geq 0)$. (c) If $R_q(n)$ ends in: (1) $01\cdots1$even or in $c1\cdots1$odd, then $E_n = I_p(R_q(n))$. If $R_q(n)$ ends in: (2) $01\cdots1$odd or in $c1\cdots1$even, then $E_n = I_p(R_q(n)) + 1$ $(n \geq 0)$.

Note. Consider the following alternative definition of Wythoff games. The rules are as defined in Section 1, with the additional requirement that no player is ever permitted to move to a position of the form (x,x) $(x \geq 0)$. The player first unable to move is the loser, his opponent the winner. Then obviously the last position of the game is $(0,1)$. Moreover, it is easy to see that this class S_2 of normal Wythoff games is equivalent to the class S_1 of misère Wythoff games according to the definition of Section 1 for every $a > 1$. But for $a = 1$ we get a different game, whose P-positions are consistent with those for $a > 1$ rather than different from them. For the alternative definition, the above summary for misère play can thus be simplified by omitting IV(i), V(i) and VI(i), and omitting $a > 1$ in IV(ii), V(ii) and VI(ii). (Note that the inequalitites (V) - (VIII) in Section 5 hold also for $a = 1$; the proofs did not use $a > 1$).

Table 5. The representation of the first few P-positions (E_n, H_n) and n in the p and q-systems for $\alpha = [\dot{1}]$ in the alternatively defined Wythoff game ($a = 1$, normal play).

			$R_p(E_n)$						$R_p(H_n)$							$R_q(n)$					
			p_5	p_4	p_3	p_2	p_1	p_0	p_6	p_5	p_4	p_3	p_2	p_1	p_0	q_5	q_4	q_3	q_2	q_1	q_0
n	E_n	H_n	13	8	5	3	2	1	21	13	8	5	3	2	1	8	5	3	2	1	1
0	0	1	0	0	0	0	0	0	0	0	0	0	0	0	1	0	0	0	0	0	0
1	2	4					1	0					1	0	1					1	0
2	3	6				1	0	0				1	0	0	1				1	0	0
3	5	9			1	0	0	0			1	0	0	0	1			1	0	0	0
4	7	12			1	0	1	0			1	0	1	0	1			1	0	1	0
5	8	14		1	0	0	0	0		1	0	0	0	0	1		1	0	0	0	0
6	10	17		1	0	0	1	0		1	0	0	1	0	1		1	0	0	1	0
7	11	19		1	0	1	0	0		1	0	1	0	0	1		1	0	1	0	0
8	13	22	1	0	0	0	0	0	1	0	0	0	0	0	1	1	0	0	0	0	0
9	15	25	1	0	0	0	1	0	1	0	0	0	1	0	1	1	0	0	0	1	0
10	16	27	1	0	0	1	0	0	1	0	0	1	0	0	1	1	0	0	1	0	0
11	18	30	1	0	1	0	0	0	1	0	1	0	0	0	1	1	0	1	0	0	0

As an illustration for the alternative definition we present the first few P-positions for $a = 1$ of the alternatively defined game in Table 5. But in the remaining part of this section we shall resort back to our original definition of misère Wythoff games given in Section 1.

We shall now apply cedar trees to consolidate Wythoff game strategies. A connection between cedar trees and the first, second and third characterizations of the

P-positions is given by the following algorithm:

While traversing a $C^0_{m,1}([1,\mathring{a}])$ cedar tree $(a \geq 1)$ in <u>inorder</u> (see e.g. Horowitz and Sahni [5, Sect. 6.1.1]), put $I_p(n)$ of every node u visited into a list A', B', E' or H' according to whether u ends in one of the strings of the form (III,a,1), (III,a,2), (VI,ii,a,1) or (VI,ii,a,2). Then A',B',E' and H' are the beginning segment of an $A_n = \lfloor n\alpha \rfloor$-sequence, a $B_n = \lfloor n\beta \rfloor$-sequence, an $E_n = \lfloor n\alpha+\gamma \rfloor$-sequence and an $H_n = \lfloor n\beta+\delta \rfloor$-sequence. There are some "boundary conditions": The A_n, B_n sequences have to be preceded by $A_0 = 0$, $B_0 = 0$; the E_n sequence by $E_0 = 0$. For $a = 1$, the E_n and H_n sequences should be replaced by the A_n and B_n sequences $(n \geq 2)$ and preceded by $(E_0, E_1) = (2,0)$ and $(H_0, H_1) = (2,1)$. In practice, this procedure is simulated without actually constructing $C^0_{m,1}([1,\mathring{a}])$: Start with a vector $(0,\ldots,0)$ $(m+1$ 0's) and, by "adding 1", cycle through all representation vectors up to $(a0a0\cdots b)$, where $b = a$ (m even), $b = 0$ (m odd).

The correctness of this algorithm is a direct consequence of the strategies summarized above and the fact that an inorder traversal of a cedar tree with property (i) of Theorem 4 sorts the entries in increasing lexicographic order.

A more intimate connection between cedar trees and the third characterizations of the P-positions will now be presented. We assume $a > 1$ for misère play, since for $a = 1$ the strategy is the same as for normal play except that the first two P-positions are different.

Given a position (x,y) in a normal or misère Wythoff game. We may assume $0 < x < y$, since for $x = 0$ and for $x = y$, the situation is quite clear. Let m be the smallest positive integer satisfying $p_m > x$, and let $u = R_p(x)$. We can compute u and $tr(u)$ simultaneously by "searching for u" in an (imaginary) p-tree with root p_m, proceeding in binary search tree fashion: "Turn left" ("right") whenever x is smaller (larger) than the current node z. This simply means that if $z = \sum_{i=k}^{m} d_i p_i$ $(d_k \neq 0)$, then "turning left" amounts to replacing d_k by $d_k - 1$ and adding p_{k-1} $(k \geq 1)$; and "turning right" means replacing d_k by $d_k + 1$ (if $d_k < a_{k+1}$) or adding p_{k-2} (if $d_k = a_{k+1}$, $k \geq 2$).

The following algorithm is based on representations. Other variants, based on traces or a mixture of traces and representations can easily be formulated. An algorithm based on traces instead of representations has the advantage that binary sequences rather than representations are being handled and compared.

Statements in parentheses and in brackets refer to normal and misère play respectively. Comments appear in curly brackets.

1 {Compute u}. Using the above search method, compute $u = R_p(x)$.

2 $\{x = (B_n)[H_n]\}$. If u ends in a string of the form (III,a,2) [VI,ii,a,2], make the move $(x,y) \rightarrow (I_p(w), x) \in P$, where $w = u''$ [with the rightmost digit t of u'' replaced by $t+1$ if the rightmost digit of u is 2]. End.

3 $\{x = (A_n)[E_n]\}$. Denote by (s,t) the two rightmost digits of u. If u ends in a string of the form (III,a,1) [VI,ii,a,1], let $v = u$ if $(t < a)$ [$t = 0$ or 1] ($v = u$ except that $(s+1,0) \leftarrow (s,t)$ if $t = a$) [$v = u$ except that $t-1 \leftarrow t$ if $t > 1$]. Compute

$I_q(v) = n$. Then $(B_n)[H_n] = x + an[+1]$. If $y = (B_n)[H_n]$, then $(x,y) \in P$. End.

4 $\{y > (B_n)[H_n]\}$. If $y > (B_n)[H_n]$, make the move $(x,y) \to (x,(B_n)[H_n]) \in P$. End.

5 $\{(A_n < y < B_n)[E_n < y < H_n]\}$. Compute $d = \lfloor (y - x[-1])/a \rfloor$. Using the above search method, compute $w = R_q(d)$. If w ends in a string of the form (III,c,1) [VI,c,1], make the move $(x,y) \to (I_p(w), I_p(w) + ad[+1]) \in P$. End. If w ends in a string of the form (III,c,2) [VI,c,2], make the move $((x,y) \to (I_p(w) - 1, I_p(w) + ad - 1) \in P)$ $[(x,y) \to (I_p(w) + 1, I_p(w) + ad + 2) \in P]$. End.

Verification. We shall verify the algorithm for misère play only, since the argument for normal play is very similar.

In step 2 we have $x = H_n$ for some $n \geq 0$ by Property 1. The node w constructed in step 2 is $R_p(E_n)$ by the inverse of Property 2. In step 3 we have $x = E_n$ by Property 1. The inverse of Property 3 implies that $I_q(v) = n$; and $H_n = x + an + 1$ by Theorem 1. The correctness of step 4 is obvious. The correctness of step 5 follows from Property 3 and case II(ii) in the proof of Theorem 1. It remains only to show that there is a node w in $C^0_{m,1}$ satisfying $w = R_q(d)$. This follows from

$$
\begin{aligned}
d &= \left\lfloor \frac{y-x-1}{a} \right\rfloor \leq \frac{y-x-1}{a} < \frac{H_n - E_n - 1}{a} && \{\text{since } E_n = x < y < H_n\} \\
&= n \leq E_n && \{\text{since } \alpha > 1 \Rightarrow E_n = \lfloor n\alpha \rfloor \geq n\} \\
&= x < p_m = q_m + q_{m-1} && \{\text{by the last part of Theorem 4(iv)}\} \\
&\leq aq_m + q_{m-1} = q_{m+1}\,.
\end{aligned}
$$

Hence $d \leq q_{m+1} - 1$, so d appears in $\tau^0_{m,1}$ by Theorem 4(iii), hence $R_q(d)$ appears in $C^0_{m,1}$. ■

The complexity of the algorithm is the same as that of the algorithm based on the arithmetic characterization, and the space requirement is also limited to $O(\log x)$.

Note. The paper [3] originally contained the analysis of normal Wythoff games and the basic theory of cedar trees and their use for consolidating normal play. Since the two referees of [3] recommended to publish the cedar tree part separately, the present paper resulted, to which we have added, however, the misère analysis, which, as shown above, is also consolidated by means of cedar trees.

REFERENCES

1. E.R. Berlekamp, J.H. Conway and R.K. Guy, Winning Ways, Academic Press, London, 1982.
2. A.S. Fraenkel, The bracket function and complementary sets of integers, Can. J. Math. 21 (1969), 6-27.
3. A.S. Fraenkel, How to beat your Wythoff games' opponent on three fronts, Amer. Math. Monthly 89 (1982), 353-361.
4. G.H. Hardy and E.M. Wright, An Introduction to the Theory of Numbers, Oxford University Press, 4-th Edition, 1960.

5. E. Horowitz and S. Sahni, Fundamentals of Computer Algorithms, Computer Science Press, Potomac, MD, 1978.

6. D.E. Knuth, The Art of Computer Programming, Vol. 3; Sorting and Searching, Addison-Wesley, Reading, MA, Second Printing, 1975.

7. C.D. Olds, Continued Fractions, Random House, New York, 1963.

8. O. Perron, Die Lehre von den Kettenbrüchen, Band I, Teubner, Stuttgart, 1954.

9. W. Wythoff, A modification of the game of Nim, Nieuw Arch. Wisk. 7 (1907), 199-202.

10. A.M. Yaglom and I.M. Yaglom, Challenging Mathematical Problems with Elementary Solutions, translated by J. McCawley, Jr., revised and edited by B. Gordon, Vol. II, Holden-Day, San Francisco, 1967.

INITIAL INDEX : A NEW COMPLEXITY FUNCTION FOR LANGUAGES

J. GABARRO

L.I.T.P. et Université Pierre et Marie Curie - U.E.R. 50, Tour 55-65
4, Place Jussieu, 75230 PARIS Cedex 05 - France

Abstract A new complexity measure for languages is defined, called the initial index. This measure is of combinatorial nature ; it is a function defined by counting the minimal number of states of automata recognizing approximations of a language.
The family of polynomial initial languages is defined, and it is proved that it is an intersection-closed A.F.L. The relations between this family and on-line multicounter Turing-machines, Petri-net languages and context-free languages are investigated. The family of exponential initial index languages is defined. The relations of this family with generators of usual families under usual operations are studied. At the end of the paper we relate the initial index with other complexity measures such as growth functions, rational index and straight-line programs.

1. Introduction

The theory of families of formal languages, in the sense of S. Ginsburg and S. Greibach [11] , is a classical framework for the study of languages. The main idea in this way is the study of families of languages closed under some fixed set of operations. For example a rational cone (full trio in [11] is a family of languages closed under rational transduction, and a full-AFL is a rational cone closed under union, product and star.
In that framework one of the most important problems is the principality problem, which can be stated as follows : A family of languages $\mathcal{L}$ is principal under some set of operations O, or O-principal, if there exists a language L in $\mathcal{L}$ such that its closure under O is the family $\mathcal{L}$. We note then $\mathcal{L} = O(L)$.
Another method to study formal languages is by complexity measures. For a given complexity measure, we can associate to every language its complexity with respect to this measure. The most important case arises when this measure is an integer valued function ; we call then this function a "complexity-function".
Given a complexity-function, we can sort the languages with respect to the asymptotic behaviour of their function. Many complexity-functions have been defined : growth function [18] rational index [3] , height of derivations trees [6] , T-measure [20] , concise description of finite languages [5] , costof straight-line languages [12] , circuit size [22] . In that framework it is possible to reformulate Milnor's problem [18,23] in the following way : "for every family of languages has the complexity function of a given language a polynomial upper bound or an exponential lower bound ?. " So, for every function measure, it is possible to define two new families of languages, the family of polynomial languages and the family of exponential languages. The main problem is then to compare these families with the families of languages given in the classical framework. In [3,10,20] there are some results in that way.
In this paper we define a new complexity function, the initial index. This function is of combinatorial nature : it is a function defined by counting the minimal number of states of an automaton recognizing approximations of a language. For a given language L we note its initial index μ_L .
In order to place the families defined with the initial index in the framework given by S. Ginsburg and S. Greibach we study their behaviour through the operations on languages.
We prove that the initial index behaves properly through the rational cone and A.F.L. operations. In particular, if L is the image of L' by rational transduction, then μ_L and $\mu_{L'}$ are polynomially related. Thus, we can define rational cones and AFL's in terms of this complexity. In that sense, the initial index seems to be very useful in formal language theory.
One interesting result is that the family of polynomial initial index languages is

an intersection closed AFL containing on-line multicounter languages. This family also contains the sets of computation sequences of Petri-nets languages [21], and the Szilard languages [7] of context-free grammars.
Then, we focus our attention on the initial index of context-free languages. We obtain that the family of polynomial context-free languages is a non principal substitution-closed full-A.F.L. containing the iterated counter languages [1].
Then, we study exponential languages. We prove that every faithful generator of the families of respectively linear, single reset, context-free and Post languages is exponential. The paper end with the study of the relation between initial index and other complexity functions such as growth function, rational index and straight-line programs.
We prove that every polynomial growth-function language is also polynomial initial index language. We have also that every polynomial initial index language is straight line polynomial. It seems that there is no relation between initial index and rational index.

2. Initial index ; definitions and exemples

We shall measure each language by an integer valued function. In order to define that function, we need first to give "approximations" of a language. These approximations are defined by :

Definition 1. [5]. Let L be a language ; we call n-initial segment of L the set

$$nL = \{ w \in L \mid |w| \leq n \}$$

Remark that nL is a finite language, so we can find a finite automaton $\mathcal{A}$ accepting nL. We denote by $\|\mathcal{A}\|$ the number of states of $\mathcal{A}$. We can define a complexity-function by :

Definition 2. Let L be a language ; we call initial index μ_L the mapping given by :

$$\mu_L(n) = \min\{ \|\mathcal{A}\| \mid nL = L(\mathcal{A}) \}$$

Remark that, in this last definition, the automata are non deterministic. So μ_L is the smallest number of states of a non deterministic automaton accepting nL
In the sequel we call smallest automaton any automaton $\mathcal{A}$ for nL with a number of states equal to $\mu_L(n)$. We use Θ, Ω, O [17] to deal with the magnitude of $\mu_L(n)$. The next lemma proves the existence of an exponential gap between deterministic and non deterministic automat for nL. So, if we want to have economical functions we have to take non deterministic-automata.

Lemma 1. Consider the language $L \subset \{0,1\}^* \# \{0,1\}^*$ defined by :

$$L = \{ f \# g / |f| = |g| \text{ et } f \neq \tilde{g} \}$$

where $\tilde{g}$ is the reverse of g.

(i) There exists a smallest non deterministic automaton with $O(n^3)$ states.

(ii) The minimal deterministic automaton for nL has $\Omega(2^{\frac{n}{2}})$ states.

In the following lemma we look at the behaviour of initial index. We have that initial index is "roughly increasing" :

Lemma 2. Let L be an infinite language over $\{x_1,x_2,\dots,x_p\}^*$ then :

1. μ_L is at most exponential : $\mu_L(n) = O(p^n)$.

2. There exists $n_1 < \dots\ n_i < \dots$ such that $\mu_L(n_i) \geq n_i$ for all $i > 1$.

3. For all $n \geq 1$, we have $\mu_L(n) \leq 2\mu_L(n+1)$.

We give now the initial index of $D_2'^*$, the Dyck language over two pairs of letters $a,\bar{a},b,\bar{b}$. For a word w, let $\theta(w)$ be the reduced word of w. Denote by $LF(D_2'^*)$ the set of left factors of words in $D_2'^*$. When $w \in LF(D_2'^*)$ the $\theta(w) \in \{a,b\}^{|\theta(w)|}$

Example 1. We shall prove that $\mu_{D_2'^*}(n) = \Theta(2^{\frac{n}{2}})$. They are two steps.

(i) First step. Consider the automaton

$$\mathcal{A}_n = (\{a,\bar{a},b,\bar{b}\},\ Q,\ q_-\ ,\ Q_+,\ .)$$

$$Q = \{(w,\ 2p + |w|\ )\ |\ w \in n\ \{a,b\}^*,\ \ 0 \leq p \leq n - |w|\}$$

$$q_- = (\varepsilon,0),\ Q_+ = \{(\varepsilon,2p)\ |\ 0 \leq p \leq n\}$$

The transition function is :

$$(w,\ y).\ u = (w\ u,\ y + 1)\quad,\ 2n > |w| + y\ ,\quad u \in \{a,\ b\}$$

$$(wu,y).\ \bar{u} = (w,\ y+1)\quad,\quad u \in \{a,b\}$$

Then $(\varepsilon,0).f = (\theta(f),\ |f|)$ for $f \in LF(D_2'^*)$ and $|f| + |\theta(f)| \leq n$, the transition function is undefined otherwise. From this we have $L(\mathcal{A}_n) = 2n\ D_2'^*$.
We will count $\|Q\|$. We call $Q_x = \{(w,y) \in Q\ |\ |w| = x\}$, $0 \leq x \leq n$, oviously $\|Q_x\| = (n+1-x)2^x$, whence

$$\|Q\| = \sum_{x=0}^{n} \|Q_x\| = \sum_{x=0}^{n} (n+1-x)\ 2^x = \Theta(2^n)$$

(ii) Second step. We will prove that every smallest automaton for $2n\ D_2'^*$ has at least $\sum_{x=0}^{n} (n+1-x)2^x$ states.

Let $\mathcal{B}_n = (\{a,\ \bar{a},\ b,\ \bar{b}\},\ Q,\ Q_-,\ Q_+\ ,\ .)$ be a smallest automaton for $2\ n\ D_2'^*$.
All the words leading to the same state q have the same reduced word. Formally, let q_1, q_2 in Q_- , w, w' in $\{a,\ \bar{a}\ ,\ b,\ \bar{b}\}^*$,if $q_1 . w = q_2.w' = q$ then $\theta(w) = \theta(w') = u_1\ u_2 \dots u_r$. Also $w\ \bar{u}_r \dots \bar{u}_2\ \bar{u}_1$ or $w'\ \bar{u}_r \dots \bar{u}_2\ \bar{u}_1$ are not in $D_2'^*$.
We cannot merge two states with different reduced word.
We give now a lower bound to the number of states having the same reduced word. Consider for $0 \leq x \leq n$ the words $u_1u_2 \dots u_x (a\bar{a})^{p-x}$, $u_i \in \{a,\ b\}$, $0 \leq p \leq x$, then $\theta(u_1u_2 \dots u_x\ (a\ \bar{a})^{p-x}) = u_1u_2 \dots u_x$. We can complete these words to obtain a word in $2n\ D_2'^*$ in the way

$$u_1\ u_2 \dots u_x\ (a\ \bar{a})^{p-x}\ \ \bar{u}_x \dots\ \bar{u}_2 \dots \bar{u}_1$$

We conclude that $\|Q_- . \{u_1\ u_2 \dots u_x (a\ \bar{a})^{p-x}\ |\ 0 \leq p \leq x\}\| = (n+1-x)$.

They are at least $(n+1-x)$ states with the reduced word $u_1 u_2 \dots u_x$.

$$\| Q_{-} \cdot \{u_1 u_2 \dots u_x (a\bar{a})^{p-x} \mid 1 \leq x \leq n \,,\ 0 \leq p \leq x\} \| = \sum_{x=0}^{n} (n+1-x)\, 2^x$$

Then $\|Q\| \geq \sum_{x=0}^{n} (n+1-x) 2^x$. We conclude that the automaton $\mathcal{A}_n$ given in (i) is smallest.

Exemple 2. Let E be the language generated by the grammar $S \to a\, SbSc + d$. This language is the class of the d in the congruence adbdc = d. Consider the infinite minimal automaton for E and split every state to take in account the lenght of word arriving to it. By inspection we come to $\mu_E(n) = \Theta(2^{\frac{n}{4}})$.

3. Initial index and A.F.L. Operations

Considering the asymptotic behavior of the initial index we can define two new families of languages.

Definition 3. Let $\underline{Pol}_{\mu}$ the family of languages of initial index at most polynomial :

$$\underline{Pol}_{\mu} = \{L \,/\, \exists\, k \text{ such that } \mu_L(n) = O(n^k)\}$$

Let $\overline{Exp}_{\mu}$ be the family of languages of initial index at least exponential :

$$\overline{Exp} = \{L / \exists \alpha \in R_+ \text{ such that } \mu_L(n) = \Omega(2^{\alpha n})\}$$

Example 3. The following are polynomial languages :

$S_1 = \{a^n b^n \mid n \geq 1\}$, $D_1'^{*}$ and D_1^{*} , $\{a^n b^n c^n \mid n \geq 1\}$.

Among the exponential languages we have :

PAL = $\{w\tilde{w} \,/\, w \in \{a,b\}^*$ and $\tilde{w}$ reverse of $w\}$, COPY = $\{ww \mid w \in \{a,b\}^*\}$,
$D_n'^{*}$, D_n^{*} , $TWIN_n = \{f \sqcup\!\sqcup \bar{f} \mid f \in \{a_1,\dots,a_n\}^*$ and $\bar{f}$ is a copy of $f\}$, $n > 1$,
$FIFO_n = \{w \in TWIN_n \mid w = u_1 v_1 u_2 v_2 \dots u_n v_n \,,\ u_i \in \{a_1, a_2, \dots, a_n\}^*$,
$v_i \in \{\bar{a}_1, \bar{a}_2, \dots, \bar{a}_n\}^*$ and for every $i = 1,\dots, n$ we have
$|u_1 \dots u_i| \geq |v_1 \dots v_i|\}$.

In order to place the families of languages defined by the initial index in the framework of families of languages we need to study their behaviour through rational transductions and A.F.L. operations.

Recall from Nivat [19] that a rational transduction $\tau : X^* \to Y^*$ can be writen $\tau(f) = \psi(\varphi^{-1}(f) \cap R)$ where R is a rational language over some finite alphabet Z and φ, ψ are morphisms of $Z^* \to X^*$ and of $Z^* \to Y^*$ respectively. When the number of consecutive letters erased in R by ψ is bounded then τ is called faithful [2]. We call rational cone, or full trio [11], a family closed under rational transduction, and faithful cone, or trio, a family closed under faithful transductions. A full A.F.L. [11] is a rational cone closed under rational operations and an A.F.L. is a faithful cone closed under union, product and the plus operation.

The following lemma explains that the initial index behaves properly through usual operations such as union, product, star, intersection, inverse morphism and ε-free substitution. In particular if L' is the image of L by one of these operations, then μ_L and $\mu_{L'}$ are polynomialy related.

Lemma 3. Let L_1, L_2, L a languages. Then for all $n \geq 1$ the following inequalities hold :

$$\mu_{L_1 \cup L_2}(n) \leq \mu_{L_1}(n) + \mu_{L_2}(n) - 2 \ , \ \mu_{L_1 . L_2}(n) \leq (n + 1).(\mu_{L_1}(n) + \mu_{L_2}(n))$$

$$\mu_{L^*}(n) \leq (n + 1).\mu_L(n) \quad , \ \mu_{L_1 \cap L_2}(n) \leq \mu_{L_1}(n).\mu_{L_2}(n)$$

If R is a rational language, then there exists a k such that

$$\mu_{L \cap R}(n) \leq k.\mu_{L_1}(n)$$

Let φ be a morphism, and $k = \max\{|\varphi(x)| \mid x \text{ a letter}\}$, then

$$\mu_{\varphi^{-1}(L)}(n) \leq (n+1).\mu_L(kn)$$

Let σ be an ε-free subsitution then

$$\mu_{\sigma(L)}(n) \leq (n+1).\mu_L(n).\max\{\mu_{\sigma(x)}(n) \mid x \text{ a letter}\}$$

We are going now to study the behaviour of initial index through morphism. This operation is more difficult to handle. There are two cases where it is possible to give a precise result.

The first case arises when we have a context-free language. In that case the pumping lemma allows us to explicit the behaviour of initial segments through the morphism. The second case arises when we bound directly the erasing power of the morphism. That is the case when the morphism is k-limited of pol-limited over a language. Recall that φ is k-limited over L if φ erases at most k consecutive letters in a word of L, and φ is pol-limited over L if there exists k and p such that $k|\varphi(f)|^p \geq |f|$ for every f in L.

The next lemma shows the behaviour of initial index throught morphisms.

Lemma 4. Let φ be a morphism and L be a language.

1) If L is context-free, then there exists k such that

$$\mu_{\varphi(L)}(n) \leq (n+1) \ .\mu_L(k\,n)$$

2) If φ is k-limited, then

$$\mu_{\varphi(L)}(n) \leq (n+1).\ \mu_L(k(n+1) + n)$$

If φ is pol-limited, there exist k and p such that :

$$\mu_{\varphi(L)}(n) \leq (n+1)\mu_L(k\,n^p)$$

Putting together lemmas 3,4 obtain that initial index behaves properly through rational transductions in two large cases.

Theorem 1. 1) Let L be context-free language and τ a rational transduction.
There exist k_1, k_2 such that :

$$\mu_{\tau(L)}(n) \leq k_1 . (n+1) \mu_L (k_2\, n)$$

2) Let L be a language and τ a faithful transduction.
There exists k_1 , k_2 such that :

$$\mu_{\tau(L)}(n) \quad k_1 . (n+1) \mu_L (k_2 (n+1) + n)$$

This theorem is important because it allows us to relate the family of polynomial languages to the classical theory of abstract families of languages. In that sense, the initial index is an interesting tool in formal language theory.

Theorem 2. The family of polynomial languages in an intersection closed AFL.

4. Initial index and classical families of languages

In this part, we will consider the relation between polynomial and exponential languages and the classical families of languages.

4.1. Polynomial languages. We begin to focus our attention on polynomial context free languages. Recall that iterated counter languages, noted Fcl in [1], are defined as the least substitution closed full-A.F.L. containing $D_1'^{*}$. We have the theorem :

Theorem 3 : The polynomial context free languages family is a non-principal substitution closed full-A.F.L. containing the iterated counter languages.

Proof. It is easy to see, from lemma 3 and theorem 1 that the family ot polynomial context-free languages is a substitution closed full-A.F.L.

Considering the infinite chain of languages

$$P_k = \{ a_1^{n_1} a_2^{n2} \ldots a_k^{n_k} \# a_k^{n_k} \ldots a_2^{n2} \; a_1^{n_1} \mid n_i \geq 1, \; i = 1, \ldots, k \}$$

satisfying $\mu_{P_k}(n) = \Theta(n^k)$ we can see that the full A.F.L. of polynomial languages is non principal.

As $D_1'^{*}$ is a polynomial language, the family Fcl is contained in Polμ.

The strict inclusion of iterated counter language in polynomial language is an open question. We conjecture.

Conjecture 1 : The inclusion of iterated counter languages in polynomial context-free languages is strict.

In the sequel we will study polynomial multicounter languages [9,13,14] Among the multicounter languages the computations sequences sets [21] , that noted CSS, have one important place. Recall CSS is the set of firing sequences leading some ε-free labeled Petri net from an initial marking to a set of final markings.

As examples of CSS we have $D_1'^{*}$ and $\{ a^n\, eb^n\, e\, c^n\, e \mid n \geq 1 \}$.

Alternative way to define CSS is to consider the least intersection closed rational cone containing $D_1'^{*}$, we come to theorem :

Theorem 4. [14, 15, 16] . CSS = $(\mathcal{H}, \hat{\mathcal{H}}^{-1}, \wedge \underline{Rat}, \wedge)\, D_1'^{*} = \mathcal{H}(\wedge \underline{Rocl})$, where $\underline{Rocl} = (\mathcal{H}, \hat{\mathcal{H}}^{-1}, \wedge \underline{Rat})\, D_1'^{*} = (\hat{\mathcal{H}}, \hat{\mathcal{H}}^{-1}, \wedge \underline{Rat})\, D_1'^{*}$

Recall from lemma 3 that polynomial languages are closed under intersection an non-erasing morphism. As a corollary we have :

Corollary 1. The computations sequence sets are polynomial languages.
One interesting case of computations sequence sets are the Szilard languages [7]. For a given context-free grammar, its Szilard language is the set of skelettons of valid derivations. This language may be not context-free as in the next grammar G, of axiome S

$$t_1 : S \to a S b T d U \; ; \; t_2 : T \to c \; ; \; t_3 : U \to f \; ; \; t_4 : S \to g$$

Using the Crespi-Reghizzi construction [7] we come to

$$SZ(G) = \{ w \in \{t_1, t_2, t_3\}^* t_4 \{t_2, t_3\}^* \mid |w|_{t_1} = |w|_{t_2} = |w|_{t_3} \; ;$$
$$w' \text{ proper left factor of } w \text{ has } |w'|_{t_2} \leq |w'|_{t_1} \; ; \; |w'|_{t_3} \leq |w'|_{t_1} \}$$

Consider morphisms φ and ψ defined by $t_1 \to x$; $t_2 \to \bar{x}$; $t_4 \to \varepsilon$; $t_3 \to \varepsilon$ and by $t_1 \to x$; $t_2 \to \varepsilon$; $t_3 \to \bar{x}$; $t_4 \to \varepsilon$ respectively. Then

$$SZ(G) = \psi^{-1}(D_1'^{*}) \cap \varphi^{-1}(D_1'^{*}) \cap \{t_1, t_2, t_3\}^* t_4 \{t_2, t_3\}^*$$

Recall [7,16] that every Szilard language, when a grammar is context-free, is in $\wedge \underline{Rocl}$. Then :

Corollary 2 : For every context-free grammar, its Szilard language has polynomial initial index.
We now consider the on-line quasi-real-time multicounter languages [9] . One alternative way to define the languages of this family is to consider the least intersection closed A.F.L. containing $D_1'^{*}$, we come to theorem :

Theorem 5 [14] : The on-line quasi-real-time multicounters languages are

$$\mathcal{H}(\wedge \underline{Ocl}) = \mathcal{H}(\wedge \underline{Fcl}) = (\mathcal{H}, \hat{\mathcal{H}}^{-1}, \wedge \underline{Rat}, \cup, \cdot, *, \wedge)\, D_1'^{*}$$

The on-line polynomial-time multicounters languages are $\mathcal{H}^{pol}(\wedge \underline{Ocl})$
Then we have.

Corollary 3 The on line quasi-real-time and polynomial time multicounters languages have polynomial initial index.

4.2. Exponential languages After the polynomial initial index we are going to study the exponential initial index. This languages are closely related to generators of most usual families of languages [4]. Recall that a family $\mathcal{L}$ has a faithful generator G iff :

$$\mathcal{L} = \{ L \mid \text{there is a faithful transduction } \tau \text{ such that } L = \tau(G) \}.$$

In this case $\mathcal{L}$ is the trio or the faithful cone generated by G , we note $\mathcal{L} = \mathcal{T}^f(G)$.

The relation between generators and exponential languages is given in the next theorem :

Theorem 6. Every faithful generator of the following families :

$\mathcal{T}^f(PAL)$ = Lin ; $\mathcal{T}^f$ (COPY) = Single Reset ; $\mathcal{T}^f(D_2'^*)$ = Context-free ; $\mathcal{T}^f(FIFO_2)$ = Post-languages has an exponential initial index.

Proof :Obvious from example 3 and theorem 1

5. Comparaison with other complexity measures

We shall compare the initial index with other complexity measures. The first is the growth function introduced by Milnor [18,23] . It is defined by :

Definition 4 : For a language L its growth-function g_L is given by

$$g_L(n) : n \longrightarrow \text{Card } n\, L$$

The relation between initial index and growth function is explicited by :

Theorem 7

1) When a language has a polynomial growth function its initial index is polynomial.
2) When a language has a exponential initial index its growth function is exponential.

Proof. Obvious considering the automata given by the list of words of n L

As a corollary, the generators of the families defined above have exponential growth functions.

The second measure we mention is the rational index, introduced by Boasson, Courcelle, Nivat [3] defined by

Definition 5 : For a language $L \subset X^*$ its rational index is given by :

$\rho_L(n) = \max \{ \min \{ |w| \mid w \in L \cap K \} \mid L \cap K \neq \emptyset$ and $K \in Rat_n(X) \}$ where $Rat_n(X)$ is the family of all languages recognized by a non deterministic automata with at most n states.

For arbitrary languages there is no relation between rational and initial indexes : There exist languages with a "small" rational index, but with a "big" initial index and conversely for exemple :

Lemma 3 : Consider the language $L = \{a^x b^{f(x)} \mid x \in N_+\}$. Then $\rho_L(n) \geqslant n + f(n)$ and $\mu_L(n) \leqslant n$

Consider the language $S_2 = \{w \in \{0,1\}^* \mid w = \tilde{w}\}$. Then

$$\mu_L(n) = \Theta(n^2) \quad \text{and} \quad \mu_L(n) = \Theta(2^{\frac{n}{2}})$$

We can also give one interesting example due to Deleage [8].
There exists an infinite chain of languages with polynomial rational index which collapse into only one degree in initial index.

$$L_p = \{a_1^x \; a_2^x \ldots a_p^x \mid x \in N_+\}, \; p \geqslant 2$$

$$\rho_{L_p}(n) = \Theta(n^p) \quad \text{and} \; \mu_{L_p}(n) = \Theta(n^2)$$

We call Pol ρ the family of languages with rational index at most polynomial. Then Gre $\subsetneq$ Pol ρ, [10], Fcl $\subseteq$ Pol μ and Fcl $\subsetneq$ Gre [1]. We conjecture for the case of algebraic languages that :

Conjecture 2 : Every algebraic language with polynomial initial index has polynomial rational index.
The third measure we want to mention has been introduced by Goodrich, Ladner and Fischer [12]. It is based on the cost of straight-line programs computing finite languages.
Let P_{sl} be a straight-line program computing $L \subset X^n$ using only

$$\{\cup, \cdot, \{\varepsilon\}\} \cup \{\{x\} \mid x \in X\},$$

call $C_{UC}(P_{sl})$ the number of unions and concatenation in this program.
For every $L \subset X^*$ we define their cost-function as :

$$C_{UC}(L_n) = \min\{C_{UC}(P_{sl}) \mid P_{sl} \text{ compute } L_n = L \cap X^n\}$$

In some aspects μ_L and C_{UC} are very differents, as we see considering PAL and COPY.

$$\mu_{PAL}(n) = \mu_{COPY}(n) = \Theta(2^{\frac{n}{2}})$$

$$C_{UC}(PAL_n) = \Theta(n^2) \; ; \; C_{UC}(COPY_n) \geqslant \frac{2^{n+1}}{n} - 1$$

Recal that every algebraic language has C_{UC} - measurebounded by n^2 [12]. This is false for the initial index.
Calling Pol_{UC} the polynomial languages C_{UC} - measure we have.

Theorem 8 : $Pol_\mu \subsetneq Pol_{UC}$

Proof. When $L \in Pol_\mu$, there is a finite automaton with a polynomial number of states. Consider their Chomsky normal form :

$[q_i, q_j] \rightarrow [q_i, q_k]\ [q_k, q_j]$ and $[q_i, q_j] \rightarrow x$ if $q_j \in q_i \cdot x$.

We can easily transforms that grammar in a straight-line program using variables $[q_i, q_j]$ (1), $1 \leq 1 \leq n$, where $[q_i, q_j]$ (1) computes the strings of length 1 derivable from $[q_i, q_j]$.

References

[1] Berstel, J. [1979] . "Transductions and Context free languages", Teubner Studienbücher, Stuttgart.

[2] Boasson, L. [1971] . "Cones rationnels et familles agreables de langages - application aux langages a compteur". Thèse de 3ème cycle. Paris VII.

[3] Boasson, L ; B. Courcelle ; M. Nivat [1981] . "The rational index a complexity measure for languages". SIAM Journal on computing 10, 2, 284-296.

[4] Book, R. [1982] . "Intersection of CFL's and related structures" in Actes de l'école de printemps de théorie de langages. Editeur Blab. M. publication of LITP n° 82-14.

[5] Bucher. W ; K. Culik ; H. Maurer ; D. Wotschke. "Concise description of finite languages". Theor. Comput. Sci. 14, 3, 211-347 (1981).

[6] Culik II. K ; H.A. Maurer. "On the derivation trees". Internal report.

[7] Crespi-Reghizzi, S. ; D. Mandrioli [1977] "Petri nets and Szilard languages", Inf. and Control, 33, 177-192.

[8] Deleage, J.L. [1982] . "Memoire de D.E.A.", Paris VII, unpublihed manuscript.

[9] Fischer, P.C. ; A.R. Meyer ; A.L. Rosenberg [1968], Math. Syst. Theor.2.3,265.

[10] Gabarro, J. [1982] . "Une application des notions de centre et index rationnel à certains langages algébriques". RAIRO Inf. Theor. 16,4, 317-329.

[11] Ginsburg, S. ; Greibach, S. [1969] . "Abstract families of languages" in Abstract families of languages . Mem. of the Amer. Math. Soc. 87, 1-32.

[12] Goodrich, G.B. ; Ladner, R.E. ; Fischer, M. J. [1977] . "Straight-Line programs to compute finite languages", A conference on Theorethical Computer Science, Aug. 1977, Waterloo, Canada.

[13] Greibach, S.A. [1976] . Remarks on the complexity of non deterministic counter languages", Theor. Comput. Sci. 1, 269-288.

[14] Greibach, S.A. [1978] . Remarks on blind and partially blind one-way multicounter machines", Theor. Comput. Sci. 7, 311-324.

[15] Hack, M. [1975] . "Petri nets languages", Computation Structures Group Memo 124, Project MAC, MIT Cambridge, Mass.

[16] Jantzen, M. [1973] . "One hierarchy of Petri net languages", RAIRO Inf. Theor. 13, 1, 19-30.

[17] Knuth, D.E. [1976]. "Big omicron and big omega and big theta". Sigact News Apr-June 18-24.

[18] Milnor, J. [1968]. "A note on curvature and fundamental group", J. Differential Geometry 2, 1-7.

[19] Nivat, M. [1968]. "Transductions des langages de Chomsky". Ann. de l'Inst. Fourier 18, 339-456.

[20] Paredaens, J. ; R. Vyncke [1977] . "A class of measure on formal languages". Acta Informatica, I, 73-86.

[21] Peterson, J.L. [1976]. "Computations sequence sets", J. Comput. and Syst. Sci. 13, 1, 1-24.

[22] Savage, J.E. 1972 . "Computational work and time on Finite Machines". J.A.C.M. 19,4, 660-674.

[23] Trofimov, V.I. [1980]. "The growth function of finitely generated semigroup", Semigroup Forum 21, 351-360.

Modular Compiler Descriptions Based on Abstract Semantic Data Types[1]
(Extended Abstract)

Harald Ganzinger

Institut für Informatik, Technische Universität München
Postfach 202420, D-8000 München 2, Fed. Rep. of Germany

Abstract

In this paper we introduce a method for modularizing descriptions of compilers. Modules correspond to basic language concepts such as binding of identifiers, control constructs, type concept. This allows compiler descriptions to be more easily adapted to different but related languages. The formal treatment of the method is by extending known models of abstract data type theory.

1. Introduction

The aim of this paper is to introduce a method for obtaining modular compiler descriptions that: (i) exhibit a semantic processing based on fundamental concepts of languages and compiling; (ii) are easily modifiable and adaptable to different but related languages; (iii) are combinations of language-independent modules; (iv) are subject to automatic compiler generation.

The work reported here is based on ideas from (modular) algebraic specifications of abstract data types [Zil75], [ADJ78a], [BG80], [Lip82], abstract semantic algebras [Mos80], [Mos82], and compiler descriptions based on attribute grammars [Knu68]. Many papers have utilized ideas of abstract data type theory to improve the structure of semantics definitions and/or compiler descriptions. In [ADJ79], following [CP67] and [Mor73], the fundamental algebraic structure of denotational semantics definitions and syntax-oriented compiler descriptions has been recognised. Following [Wan79], in [BW80], [Gau82], and [GP81] the use of abstract data types has been suggested. In particular the latter paper is concerned with structuring compiler definitions hierarchically, using the specification language OBJ [Gog78]. In addition, many authors of denotational descriptions have tried to impose structure on their descriptions. In particular [RS82] and [Wan82] proposed general language independent combinators, abbreviating pieces of λ-notation.

We agree with [Mos82] in that none of the mentioned approaches has succeeded in reaching the goals that have been stated above. A detailed justification of this claim can be found in [Mos82]. We give the intuitive reason for the principal problem that arises in semantics and compiler descriptions.

The theory of abstract data types in the classical sense [Zil75], [ADJ78a] views a software module as a package of functions which the user of the module may call. The data elements themselves are only implicitly given by the set of all terms in the functions. Compiler modules decorate nodes of parse trees with semantic information. E.g., a module that handles the declarations associates declaration information with applied occurrences of identifiers. So, it has to handle data of sorts Stat, Id, DeclInfo and to provide a function find : Stat Id $\longrightarrow$ DeclInfo, where Stat represents all

[1] The work reported in this paper has been partially supported by the Sonderforschungsbereich 49 - Programmiertechnik - at the Technical University of Munich.

statement nodes in a parse tree. find(s,x) is supposed to find that declaration for x that is visible at s. Specifying the properties of the elements of Stat requires to model this set of nodes together with their syntactic relationships in the program. E.g., it has to be specified that find(s,x) = d, if s is a statement in a scope p containing a declaration c that binds the identifier x to d. Thus, it is not sufficient to know the internal structure of a statement s; the context of s in the program is relevant, too.

Authors of algebraic specifications of languages and compilers, [BW80], [Gau82], [GP81], [Wan79], usually consider the syntax of a language as a system of operators, e.g.

if Exp then Stat else Stat $\longrightarrow$ Stat

Var := Exp $\longrightarrow$ Stat

...

In any model, Stat is, then, the set of all objects that can be represented as terms in if_then_else_, _:=_, etc. The context in which a syntactic construct occurs in a program is not available. As a consequence, this technique is not adequate to model an algebra of nodes in parse trees. Rather, something that establishes the following equation would be needed:

$$Stat = \{ (t,v) \mid t \text{ parse tree, } v \text{ node in } t \text{ labelled by } Stat \}$$

Mosses [Mos80], [Mos82], circumvents this difficulty by indexing semantic operators, such as find in the above example, by the semantic abstractions of the context in which it is applied. This goes beyond the classical technical and, as we believe, methodological framework of abstract data type specifications. Mosses' specifications are two-levelled: One level provides the specification of the index algebras and a second level contains the specification of the properties of the semantic operators. The mathematical basis for specifications of this kind is in this author's view not fully developed yet. Moreover, Mosses does not yet provide a formal basis for combining his "semantic algebras". (Such a framework exists for specifications in the classical sense [BG80], [ADJ78b], [ADJ80], [Lip82].) In [Mos82], it is not at all clear, how language specifications can be obtained as combinations of the specified language concepts. Nevertheless, Mosses' approach has motivated a great deal of this work. To get around the problems that exist with Mosses' approach, we will suggest a different modification of the classical concepts. The formal model behind are signatures and signature morphisms in the sense of the next section.

Lack of space does not permit to include realistic examples nor to provide a detailed presentation of the aspects of the formal model. The interested reader is referred to [Gan83]. We also assume the reader to be familiar with the basic definitions of a category and a functor.

2. Signature Morphisms

(2.1) Definition:

Signatures $\Sigma=(S,\Omega,R)$ consist of a set of sorts S, an $S^* \times S$-indexed family of sets $\Omega_{s_1 \dots s_n s_0}$ of operators, and an S^*-indexed family of sets $R_{s_1 \dots s_n}$ of relation symbols. □

Operators f with parameter sorts $s_1,\ldots,s_n$ and result sort s_0 are denoted by $f{:}s_1\ldots s_n s_0$ or $f{:}s_1\ldots s_n \text{->} s_0$. Similarly, relation symbols r with argument sorts $s_1,\ldots,s_n$ are written as $r{:}s_1\ldots s_n$. Let X be an S-indexed family of sets (of variables). Furthermore, let $T_\Omega(X)$ be the free Ω-algebra over X and let $T_\Omega(X)_s$ denote the set of terms with result sort s. Then, for $u,v \in S^*$, $u = s_1\ldots s_n$, $v = s'_1\ldots s'_m$, we set

$$T_\Omega(u{:}v) = \{\lambda\ x.1,\ldots,x.n\ .\ (t_1,\ldots,t_m) \mid t_i \in T_\Omega(Y)_{s'_i}\},$$

where $Y = \{\ x.i : s_i \mid i = 1,\ldots,n\ \}$.[2)]

$T_\Omega(u{:}v)$ is the set of (tupels of) terms with parameter sequence of sort u and with a result sequence of sort v.

The set $F_\Sigma(X)$ of formulas over X is defined as

(1) $x{:}s,\ y{:}s \in X \Rightarrow x{:}s = y{:}s \in F_\Sigma(X)$,

(2) $f{:}s_1\ldots s_n s_0 \in \Omega$, $x_i{:}s_i \in X \Rightarrow x_0{:}s_0 = f(x_1{:}s_1,\ldots,x_n{:}s_n) \in F_\Sigma(X)$

(3) $r{:}s_1\ldots s_n \in R$, $x_i{:}s_i \in X \Rightarrow r(x_1{:}s_1,\ldots,x_n{:}s_n) \in F_\Sigma(X)$

(4) $q1,q2 \in F_\Sigma(X) \Rightarrow q1 \wedge q2 \in F_\Sigma(X)$.

Formulas become relation expressions by making some of their variables to be bound variables. Given $u = s_1\ldots s_n \in S^*$, $E_\Sigma(u)$ is the set of relation expressions

$$E_\Sigma(u) = \{\ \lambda\ x_1{:}s_1,\ldots,x_n{:}s_n.\ q \mid q \in F_\Sigma(X), \text{ for any X that contains the } x_i{:}s_i\ \}.$$

The prefix λ makes the x_i to be the bound variables of q. The remaining variables in q are the free variables of q. Thus q denotes a (derived) relation of sort u. For $Q = \lambda\, x_1,\ldots,x_n.\ q$, $Q(y_1,\ldots,y_n)$, y_i pairwise distinct, denotes the result of replacing in q any occurrence of the i-th bound variable x_i by y_i. In what follows we will consider two relation expressions Q1, Q2 to be equal, if Q1 can be obtained from Q2 by consistently renaming all its variables.

(2.2) Definition:
Given two signatures Σ and Σ', a signature morphism $\sigma : \Sigma \longrightarrow \Sigma'$ consists of three components:

- a sort map $\sigma_S : S \longrightarrow S'^+$ sending any sort s to a nonempty tupel $\sigma_S(s)$ of sorts,[3)]
- a $S^* \times S$-indexed family of operator maps $\sigma_{\Omega_{us}}$ sending any operator $f \in \Omega_{us}$ with parameter sorts u and result sort s to a term $\sigma_{\Omega_{us}}(f) \in T_{\Omega'}(\sigma_S(u){:}\sigma_S(s))$,
- a S^*-indexed family of relation symbol maps σ_{R_u} sending any relation symbol $r \in R_u$ to a relation expression $\sigma_{R_u}(r) \in E_{\Sigma'}(\sigma_S(u))$.

□

Example 1:
Let $\Sigma_{\text{SymbolTable}}$ be given as

sorts StStates, Id, DeclInfo

ops

```
init : ⟶ StStates
openScope : StStates ⟶ StStates
closeScope : StStates ⟶ StStates
enter : StStates Id DeclInfo ⟶ StStates
```

2) Generally, if $(Y_i)_{i \in I}$ is a family of sets, Y will also denote the disjoint union $\{\ y{:}i \mid i \in I,\ y \in Y_i\ \}$ of the Y_i. We will also omit the index i, if no confusion arises.

3) We do not allow sorts to be mapped to the empty sequence of sorts as this would later require to introduce operators with possibly empty result sequences. In principle, however, this restriction could be removed.

lookup : StStates Id ⟶ DeclInfo
rel <no relation symbols> .
Then the following defines a signature morphism $\sigma_{BR} : \Sigma_{BindingRules} \longrightarrow \Sigma_{SymbolTable}$:
sorts
Bindings ↦ (inSt : StStates, outSt : StStates)
Id ↦ Id
DeclInfo ↦ Declinfo
ops
find(Bindings, Id) : DeclInfo ↦ λ B.inSt, B.outSt, I . lookup(B.outSt,I)
rel
program is _ : (Bindings) ↦ λ B.inSt, B.outSt . (B.inSt = init)
_ is scope with body _ : (Bindings, Bindings) ↦
λ B0.inSt, B0.outSt, B1.inSt, B1.outSt .
(B1.inSt = openScope(B0.inSt) ∧ B0.outSt = closeScope(B1.outSt))
_ is _ followed by _ : (Bindings, Bindings, Bindings) ↦
λ B0.inSt, B0.outSt, B1.inSt, B1.outSt, B2.inSt, B2.outSt .
(B1.inSt = B0.inSt ∧ B2.inSt = B1.outSt ∧ B0.outSt = B2.outSt)
_ binds _ to _ : (Bindings, Id, DeclInfo) ↦
λ B.inSt, B.outSt, I, D . (B.outSt = enter(B.inSt,I,D))
_ contains no bindings : (Bindings) ↦ λ B.inSt, B.outSt . (B.outSt = B.inSt)

In the example we have used the notation $X \mapsto \sigma(X)$, for sorts, operators, and relation symbols X. The left sides of ↦ constitute the signature $\Sigma_{BindingRules}$. For relations we employ a mixfix-notation where the "_" serve as placeholders for the parameters of the relations. Instead of numbers we have introduced identifiers (inSt, outSt) to denote the projections to the components in the sort map part. E.g., σ(Bindings) = StStates StStates, where the projections 1 and 2 are named inSt and outSt, respectively. (For the intuitive meaning of this signature morphism cf. next section.)

To be able to compose signature morphisms, we extend σ to expressions $Q \in E_{\Sigma}(u)$ by

$$\sigma(x_0 = f(x_1,\ldots,x_n)) \equiv$$
$$x_0.1 = g_1(x_1.1,\ldots,x_1.k_1,\ldots \ldots,x_n.1,\ldots,x_n.k_n)$$
$$\wedge \ldots \wedge$$
$$x_0.k_0 = g_k(x_1.1,\ldots,x_1.k_1,\ldots \ldots,x_n.1,\ldots,x_n.k_n)$$
$$\text{if } \sigma(f) = \lambda\, x_1,\ldots,x_n \,.\, (g_1,\ldots,g_k),\ x_j{\equiv}x_j{:}s_j, \text{ and } |\sigma(s_j)|{=}k_j,$$
$$\sigma(x_0 = x_1) \equiv x_0.1 = x_1.1 \wedge \ldots \wedge x_0.k_1 = x_1.k_1$$
$$\sigma(r(x_1,\ldots,x_n)) \equiv \sigma(r)(x_1.1,\ldots,x_1.k_1,\ldots \ldots,x_n.1,\ldots,x_n.k_n)\ ,$$
$$\sigma(q1 \wedge q2) \equiv \sigma(q1) \wedge \sigma(q2),$$
$$\sigma(\lambda\, x_1,\ldots,x_n.\ q) \equiv \lambda\, x_1.1,\ldots,x_1.k_1,\ldots \ldots,x_n.1,\ldots,x_n.k_n \,.\, \sigma(q)\ .$$

In the above it is assumed that, if given σ and a variable x of sort s, then x.i is a new variable of sort s_i, if $\sigma(s) = s'_1 \ldots s'_n$ and $1 \le i \le n$.

Example 2:
σ_{BR} sends
(S is scope with body B) ∧ (B is B1 followed by B2) ∧ (B1 binds x to D) ∧
(D' = find(B2, x))
to
(B.inSt = openScope(S.inSt) ∧ S.outSt = closeScope(B.outSt)) ∧
(B1.inSt = B.inSt ∧ B2.inSt = B1.outSt ∧ B.outSt = B2.outSt) ∧
(B1.outSt = enter(B1.inSt,x,D)) ∧ (D' = lookup(B2.outSt,x))

(2.3) Theorem:
Signatures together with signature morphisms form a category denoted SIG. □

The proof is obvious. The composition $\sigma = \sigma'\sigma''$ is defined by composing the sort, operator, and relation symbol maps, respectively.[4]

Semantically, signatures represent classes of algebraic structures. Signature morphisms define maps between such classes, thereby representing formally the process of implementing a module in terms of the constituents of pregiven modules.

By Σ-struct we denote the class of Σ-structures together with Σ-homomorphisms between them. A Σ-structure A consists of (carrier) sets s_A, for any $s \in S$, of functions $f_A : s1_A \times \dots \times sn_A \longrightarrow s0_A$, for any operator symbol $f : s_1 \dots s_n s_0$, and of relations $r_A \subseteq s1_A \times \dots \times sn_A$, for any relation symbol $r : s_1 \dots s_n$. A Σ-homomorphism $h : A \longrightarrow B$ between Σ-structures A and B is a S-sorted family of maps $h_s : s_A \longrightarrow s_B$ for which

$$h_{s0}(f_A(x_1,\dots,x_n)) = f_B(h_{s1}(x_1),\dots,h_{sn}(x_n))$$
$$r_A(x_1,\dots,x_n) \Rightarrow r_B(h_{s1}(x_1),\dots,h_{sn}(x_n)),$$

for operators f and relation symbols r as above.

Semantically, relation expressions denote relations. Given a Σ-structure A and $Q \in E_\Sigma(u)$, $Q_A \subseteq u_A$ is defined as follows. If $Q \equiv \lambda\, x_1{:}s_1,\dots,x_n{:}s_n.\ q$, then Q_A is the set of all $(a_1,\dots,a_n)$ such that there exist values $(x{:}s)_A \in s_A$ for the variables $x{:}s$ in q such that $(x_i{:}s_i)_A = a_i$ and q becomes a valid assertion in A. For $u = s1\dots sn \in S^*$, we assume $u_A = s1_A \times \dots \times sn_A$.

(2.4) Theorem:
Let $\sigma : \Sigma \longrightarrow \Sigma'$ be a signature morphism. Then there exists a functor σ-struct : Σ'-struct $\longrightarrow$ Σ-struct such that the map that sends any signature Σ to Σ-struct and any signature morphism σ to σ-struct is a (contravariant) functor struct : SIG $\longrightarrow$ CAT, where CAT is the category of all categories. □

Proof.
Let $A' \in \Sigma'$-alg. We define σ-struct(A') = A as follows. $s_A = \sigma(s)_{A'}$, i.e. the product of the A'-carriers of the sorts in $\sigma(s)$. For $f \in \Omega$, $f_A = g1_{A'} \times \dots \times gn_{A'}$, if $\sigma(f) = (g_1,\dots,g_n)$. For $r \in R$, $r_A = \sigma(r)_{A'}$. □

An observation, which was in fact a major goal of this research, is that attribute grammars as introduced in [Knu68] are a particular subclass of signature morphisms.

(2.5) Theorem:
Any attribute grammar is a signature morphism. □

The following example illustrates this fact by reformulating Σ_{BR}, cf. example 1, in attribute grammar notation. Here, "is" in relation symbols has been replaced by "$\longrightarrow$" and terminal symbols are assumed to have one standard attribute symbol conveying lexical information.

---

4) The composition of morphisms is written from right to left, i.e. $\sigma'\sigma''(x) = \sigma'(\sigma''(x))$.

Example 3:

grammar symbol	term./nonterm.	attribute	type	class
program	nonterm.	-	-	-
Bindings	nonterm.	inSt	StStates	inherited
		outSt	StStates	synthesized
Id	terminal	symbol	Id	lexical
DeclInfo	terminal	symbol	DeclInfo	lexical

Rules (indexes [i] disambiguate multiple occurrences of grammar symbols) :

```
program ⟶ Bindings
    Bindings.inSt = init
Bindings[0] ⟶ scope with body Bindings[1]
    Bindings[1].inSt = openScope(Bindings[0].inSt)
    Bindings[0].outSt = closeScope(Bindings[1].outSt)
Bindings[0] ⟶ Bindings[1] followed by Bindings[2]
    Bindings[1].inSt = Bindings[0].inSt
    Bindings[2].inSt = Bindings[1].outSt
    Bindings[0].outSt = Bindings[2].outSt
Bindings ⟶ binds Id to DeclInfo
    Bindings.outSt = enter(Bindings.inSt,Id.symbol,DeclInfo.symbol)
Bindings ⟶ contains no bindings
    Bindings.outSt = Bindings.inSt
```

The following table lists corresponding notions of attribute grammars and signature morphisms.

(2.6) Table: (attribute grammars as signature morphisms)

attribute grammar	signature morphism $\sigma : \Sigma \longrightarrow \Sigma'$
grammar symbols X having	
- at least 1 attribute	sorts X in S
- no attributes	parts of names of relations in R
syntactic rule r = X ⟶ Y ... Z	relation r : (X',Y',...,Z') ∊ R, where the X',...,Z' are those among the X,...,Z that have at least one attribute
association of attributes with grammar symbols	sort map part σ_S; attribute names are the names of projections
types of attributes and signature of semantic actions	codomain signature (S',Ω')
conjunction of semantic rules associated with production p	$\sigma_R(p)$

□

Note that the converse of the theorem is not true, i.e. our notion of compiler modules is more general that what is captured by attribute grammars. Note also that in contrast to existing approaches to algebraic definitions of languages and compilers, syntactic constructs are viewed as relations rather than operators. This allows to associate context information with them. This will be the key to the kind of modularization we have in mind.

3. The Representation of Basic Compiler Modules

In this section we briefly indicate, taking σ_{BR} as an example, how signature morphisms in our sense will be viewed as defining the representation of compiler modules over already given modules. The formal treatment of this process will be summarized in the next section.

The morphism σ_{BR} represents a compiler module that handles the binding rules in block-structured languages. These languages are assumed to define a concept of scopes that specify the regions in which declarations are visible. Scopes may contain inner scopes where identifiers can be redeclared. A scope must not contain more than one declaration of an identifier. At any application of an identifier, a declaration of this identifier has to preceed that application and it has to be found in an enclosing scope. The declaration contained in the innermost such scope is, then, the one to which the identifier is bound to. The relevant constructs of any such language with respect to binding are, thus, programs, scopes, sequences (representing the order of constructs), and declarations. These correspond to the relations program is _, _ is scope with body _, _ is _ followed by _, and _ binds _ to _, respectively. The relation _ contains no declarations represents all constructs of a program that are irrelevant with respect to the binding process. The operator find is the "output"-operation of the module, rendering information about the visible declaration of a given identifier at a given point in the program. The fact that these relations project from concrete language constructs to module-specific abstract constructs guarantees for considerably increased language-independency. Vice-versa, concrete language constructs can be represented as expressions in these relations. E.g. for-loops in ALGOL68 that are at the same time scopes and implicit declarations of the loop variable can be viewed as some conjunction of the is-scope and binds-to relations. We will return to this aspect in section 4.

In order to implement this compiler module, the existence of a module SymbolTable, encapsulating operations on symbol tables, has been assumed. In this module, StStates is the domain of all states of the symbol table. Id is the domain of identifiers. DeclInfo is the domain of objects to which an identifier can be bound to. init initializes the symbol table. openScope marks the begin of a new scope. closeScope marks the end of a scope. enter enters a new declaration into the symbol table. lookup searches the symbol table for the declaration of the Id. SymbolTable does not provide relations, i.e. it is a module in the "classical" sense so that we could have given a formal specification of this module in the style of [GHM78] or [GP81].

The morphism σ_{BR} now specifies the implementation of the binding relations as relations over symbol table states. In particular, the binding contexts of program constructs (i.e. the objects of sort Binding) are represented as pairs of symbol table states. inSt is the state before and outSt is the state after analysing the construct. Therefore, the scope construct (relation is-scope) is implemented by opening and closing a new region in the symbol table into which the local declarations will be entered from left to right. Constructs containing no scopes and declarations do not change the symbol table. The operator find(b,x) finds the declaration of the identifier x in a set b of bindings by applying lookup. The functor σ_{BR}-struct is the formal model of this implementation process.

In this paper, (compiler) modules are assumed to be parameterized. Sorts, operators, and relation symbols are allowed as parameters of a module. In the above case, we can assume that identifiers Id and declaration information DeclInfo are the parameters of both the module SymbolTable and the module BindingRules. The representation of a module must be the identity on the parameter part.

In order to provide for some more illustration, we give the representation $\sigma_A : \Sigma_{Alloc} \longrightarrow \Sigma_{Integer}$ of a simple memory allocation module in terms of the predefined standard type of integers.

Example 4:
sorts
Data ↦ (address : Integer, end : Integer)
Integer ↦ Integer
ops
address : Data ⟶ Integer ↦ λ D.address, D.end . (D.address)
rel
program data is _ : (Data) ↦ λ D.address, D.end . (D.address = 0)
_ is _ overlapped _ : (Data, Data, Data) ↦
 λ D0.address, D0.end, D1.address, D1.end, D2.address, D2.end .
 (D1.address = D0.address ∧ D2.address = D1.end ∧ D0.end = D2.end)
_ is _ disjoint _ : (Data, Data, Data) ↦
 λ D0.address, D0.end, D1.address, D1.end, D2.address, D2.end .
 (D1.address = D0.address ∧ D2.address = D0.address ∧ D0.end = max(D1.end,D2.end))
_ is of size _ : (Data, Integer) ↦ λ D.address, D.end, I . (D.end = D.address + I)

In this example we refer to languages where some of the data which the programmer manipulates can be allocated statically. (Variables in PASCAL-procedures would be an example.) It is assumed that storage will be occupied by elementary as well as structured data. Data of the first kind have some statically known size (relation is-of-size). Structured data consist of components whose lifetimes can either be overlapping, i.e. require disjoint memory (relation overlapped) or disjoint, i.e. may be allocated to overlapping memory (relation disjoint). Again, these four given relations define a module-specific abstraction of the concrete constructs of a specific language.

For the implementation of this module, a simple storage allocation technique has been adopted. The program data elements (i.e. objects of sort Data) are represented by their address address and the address of the next free unit end in memory. Data overlapping in lifetime are allocated to consecutive memory cells. Data with disjoint lifetimes are allocated to the same memory unit. The operator address renders the address of a data structure.

4. Combining Modules to Make Compilers

According to [BG80] and [Lip82], signature morphisms are the only syntactic mechanism needed for structuring data types. Semantically there are two aspects of signature morphisms σ: the forgetful functor σ-struct and σ-persistent type generators $T : \Sigma\text{-struct} \longrightarrow \Sigma'\text{-struct}$. Combining data types means, therefore, applying a type generator or a forgetful functor. Our application to compilers has required to define a version of signatures and signature morphisms that, in contrast to the standard approach, also includes relation symbols. Moreover, our signature morphisms map sorts to sequences of sorts. So it needs to be demonstrated that these morphisms satisfy some basic requirements, allowing to adopt the structuring principles of abstract data type theory. In the following we will briefly state that these requirements are, in fact, satisfied. In the formal presentation we follow Lipeck [Lip82]. The proofs of the theorems given below are straightforward extensions to signature morphisms in our sense of Lipeck's proofs. The reader is assumed to be familiar with the basic notions and techniques of parameterized data types.

A (class of) data type(s) is a pair $D = (\Sigma, C)$, consisting of a signature Σ and a full sub-category $C \subseteq \Sigma\text{-struct}$ of Σ-structures that is closed under isomorphism.[5] A parameterized data type is a triple $P = (D, D1, T)$, where D and $D1$ are classes of data types such that

- $\Sigma 1 = \Sigma + (S1, \Omega 1, R1)$ and $i\text{-struct}(C1) \subseteq C$, if i is the inclusion morphism $\Sigma \subseteq \Sigma 1$,
- $T : C \longrightarrow C1$ is a functor.

Σ is the parameter signature, C the class of parameter structures. $\Sigma 1$ is the body signature and $C1$ the class of structures that is the range of the type constructor T. P is called persistent, if $i\text{-struct}\ T = id_C$.

Given parameterized types P and P' and given a signature morphism $\alpha : \Sigma \longrightarrow \Sigma 1'$, P' is called an (admissible) actual parameter for P with respect to α, if $\alpha\text{-struct}(C1') \subseteq C$. Passing an actual parameter to a given parameterized type has a syntactic (resulting signature) and a semantic aspect (resulting type constructor). The result signature is modelled by pushouts. In contrast to signature morphisms in the classical sense, our category SIG of signature morphisms does not have all pushouts. However, if one of the morphisms is an inclusion, pushouts do exist:

(4.1) Theorem:
Given $\sigma i : \Sigma \longrightarrow \Sigma i$, $i=1,2$, such that $\Sigma \subseteq \Sigma 1$ and $\sigma 1$ is the inclusion morphism, then there exists a signature Σ_{po} and simple morphisms $\sigma' 1 : \Sigma 2 \longrightarrow \Sigma_{po}$ and $\sigma' 2 : \Sigma 1 \longrightarrow \Sigma_{po}$ such that

$$\begin{array}{ccc} \Sigma & \xrightarrow{\sigma 1} & \Sigma 1 \\ {\scriptstyle \sigma 2}\downarrow & & \downarrow{\scriptstyle \sigma' 2} \\ \Sigma 2 & \xrightarrow{\sigma' 1} & \Sigma_{po} \end{array}$$

is a pushout diagram. □

(4.2) Theorem:
Let be given a pushout diagram as above. Furthermore, let K be an arbitrary category. Then, to any pair of functors $Ti : K \longrightarrow \Sigma i\text{-struct}$ for which

$$\sigma 1\text{-struct}\ T1 = \sigma 2\text{-struct}\ T2$$

there exists exactly one functor $T1 \cup T2 : K \longrightarrow \Sigma_{po}\text{-struct}$ for which

$$\sigma' 1\ (T1 \cup T2) = T2 \text{ and } \sigma' 2\ (T1 \cup T2) = T1.$$

□

Parameter passing is now defined as follows. If P' is an admissible parameter for P wrt. α (both persistent parameterized types), then consider the pushout diagram where $\sigma 1$ is the inclusion $\Sigma \subseteq \Sigma 1$ and where $\sigma 2 = \alpha$. Then, the result of applying P' to P according to α is given as

$$\mathbf{apply}(P, P', \alpha) = (D2, D', T2),$$

where $D2 = (\Sigma_{po}, T2(C'))$, $T2 = (id_{C1'} \cup (T\ \alpha\text{-struct}))\ T'$.

The second basic operation on parameterized data types is called abstraction (or reduction). Abstraction models the implementation of a data type of signature $\Sigma 2$ over a data type of signature $\Sigma 1$.
Given P, $\Sigma \subseteq \Sigma 2$, and arbitrary $\sigma : \Sigma 2 \longrightarrow \Sigma 1$ such that $\sigma|_{\Sigma} = id_{\Sigma}$, then

[5] This general semantic assumption makes the treatment independent of specification languages.

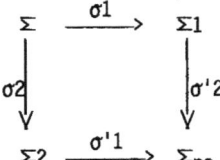

abstract(P,σ) = (D2,D,T2),
where D2 = (Σ2,σ-struct(C1)), T2 = σ-struct T.

Combinations of data types are terms in **apply** and **abstract** over basic data types and signature morphism. These terms can mechanically be reduced to terms in which **abstract** occurs exactly once, namely at the root of the term. This is the assertion of the following normal form theorem that was proved in [Lip82] and which can be adapted to our case.

(4.3) Theorem:
If **apply**(**abstract**(P_1,σ_1),**abstract**(P_2,σ_2),α) is defined, then there exists a signature morphism σ such that this term is equal to

abstract(**apply**(P_1,P_2, σ_2 α),σ) .

□

We give some illustration by referring to the above examples. For these modules it holds

BindingRules = **abstract**(SymbolTable,σ_{BR})
Alloc = **abstract**(Standard,σ_A)

To provide a simple example for a possible combination of these two modules, consider a compiler module that handles record type definitions in languages such as PASCAL or ADA. Such a module has to provide, e.g., an operation yielding the offset of a record field when given its name. Obviously, the problem is a combination of binding rules in the presence of block structure (inner records may contain redeclarations of field names) and of allocating storage for structured data. The combination is such that the declaration information about a field name is its offset in the record. Thus we want to apply BindingRules to Alloc by passing address information (of type integer) to DeclInfo. Then, the question is where to map the parameter Id to. As we want Id to be a parameter of the resulting module, we first add Id to the so far empty parameter[6]) of the module Alloc. For this purpose we assume that Ident is a module that is simply the identity on its only parameter Id. Then,

Alloc+Id = **apply**(Alloc,Ident,∅)

is the old module Alloc with Id added to its parameter. Then,

Bindings+Alloc = **apply**(BindingRules,Alloc+Id,{Id↦Id, DeclInfo↦Integer})

is the wanted combination of the given modules to implement the new module RecordTypes. The corresponding morphism σ_{RT} : $\Sigma_{RecordTypes} \longrightarrow \Sigma_{Bindings+Alloc}$ is given in the following example.

Example 5:
sorts
Field ↦ (names : Bindings, data : Data)
Type ↦ (names : Bindings, data : Data)
Id ↦ Id
Integer ↦ Integer
ops
offset : Field Id ⟶ Integer ↦ λ f.names, f.data, I . (find(f.names,I))
rel
record is _ : (FieldStructure) ↦
λ f.names, f.data . ((program is f.names) ∧ (program data is f.data))

6) With the kind of formal framework given above one would have to consider globally given standard types such as Integer as parameters of a module. This is, however, irrelevant here.

_ has variants _ , _ : (FieldStructure, FieldStructure, FieldStructure) $\mapsto$
  λ f0.names, f0.data, f1.names, f1.data, f2.names, f2.data .
    ((f0.names is f1.names followed by f2.names) $\wedge$ (f0.data is f1.data disjoint f2.data))
_ has components _ ; _ : (FieldStructure, FieldStructure, FieldStructure) $\mapsto$
  λ f0.names, f0.data, f1.names, f1.data, f2.names, f2.data .
    ((f0.names is f1.names followed by f2.names) $\wedge$ (f0.data is f1.data overlapped f2.data))
_ is field _ : _ : (FieldStructure, Id, Type) $\mapsto$
  λ f.names, f.data, I, t.names, t.data .
    ((f.names is N followed by t.names) $\wedge$ (N binds I to A)
    $\wedge$ (A = address(f.data)) $\wedge$ (f.data = t.data))
_ has size _ : (Type, Integer) $\mapsto$
  λ t.names, t.data, s . ((t.names contains no bindings) $\wedge$ (T.data is of size s))
_ is record _ : (Type, FieldStructure) $\mapsto$
  λ t.names, t.data, f.names, f.data .
    ((t.names is scope with body f.names) $\wedge$ (t.data = f.data))

Abstract records in the sense of RecordTypes consist of a field structure. This may either consist of two variants (relation variants), two consecutive components (relation components), or be elementary. In the latter case, an identifier names the field (relation is-field). The type of an elementary field is either elementary (relation has-size) or again a record. The implementation of the module as given by σ_{RT} establishes the relations between the name and the data structures as defined by a record. Declarations of field names establish the interaction between the two relation structures: the address of the field becomes the object the field name is bound to. Id is the parameter of RecordTypes.

According to the above normal form theorem it holds

RecordTypes = **abstract**(**abstract**(Predefined,σ),σ_{RT})
  = **abstract**(Predefined,$\sigma\ \sigma_{RT}$), for some σ,

where Predefined is an **apply**-term that combines the elementary data types Standard, Ident, and SymbolTable and passes Integer to DeclInfo. The following example shows part of the composition of the two representation maps $\sigma'_{RT} = \sigma\ \sigma_{RT}$ as it is implicit in the proof of the normal form theorem.

Example 6:
FieldStructure, Type $\mapsto$
  (names.inSt : StStates, names.outSt : StStates, data.address : Integer, data.end : Integer)
...
_ has components _ ; _ : (FieldStructure, FieldStructure, FieldStructure) $\mapsto$
  λ f0.names.inSt, f0.names.outSt, f0.data.address, f0.data.end,
    f1.names.inSt, f1.names.outSt, f1.data.address, f1.data.end,
      f2.names.inSt, f2.names.outSt, f2.data.address, f2.data.end .
    ((f1.names.inSt = f0.names.inSt) $\wedge$ (f2.names.inSt = f1.names.outSt)
    $\wedge$ (f0.names.outSt = f2.names.outSt) $\wedge$ (f1.data.address = f0.data.address)
    $\wedge$ (f2.data.address = f1.data.end) $\wedge$ (f0.data.end = f2.data.end))
...
_ has size _ : (Type, Integer) $\mapsto$
  λ t.names.inSt, t.names.outSt, t.data.address, t.data.end, I .
    ((t.names.outSt = t.names.inSt) $\wedge$ (t.data.end = t.data.address + I))

In this example, σ'_{RT} is again an attribute grammar although σ_{RT} is not, i.e. the definition of RecordTypes could be subject to automatic compiler generation. In applications of the concept in a compiler generating system based on attribute grammars it should be allowed that some intermediate levels of the compiler definition can be described by arbitrary signature morphisms such as σ_{RT}, as it may still be possible to automatically transform the definition into an attribute grammar by applying the algebraic laws for **apply** and **abstract**.

The reader should realize that descriptions such as σ'_{RT} do not exhibit the fact that record types are a combination of at least two elementary language facets. It should be obvious that the possibility of deriving such descriptions out of modules that correspond to these facets increases flexibility and modifiability considerably.

5. Conclusions

The main contribution of this paper is the introduction of a concept for modular definition of software for language implementation. The basic idea was to employ relations to characterize program constructs with respect to both internal structure and context.[7] The relation symbols can be viewed as defining an abstract syntax that is specifically tailored to the module being defined. Thereby, modules become independent of the concrete (syntax of the) language. Modules in our sense encapsulate implementation decisions that correspond to fundamental semantic concepts and compiling techniques. This increases flexibility of language implementation considerably.

The main technical achievements are due to the formal system which we employ for specifying the implementation of relations. Rather than adopting a general logical framework such as the one provided by PROLOG, we introduced an extended version of the concept of a signature morphism which is the basic formal tool of known approaches to structuring specifications of abstract data types. As we have demonstrated, this allows to apply basic results of abstract data type theory concerning the structuring and parameterizing of data types: Basic compiler modules can be defined according to the specific language concepts a compiler has to deal with. Then, the modules can be combined (using **apply** and **abstract**) such that they, finally, make the complete compiler for the concrete language. Secondly, and this is important from a practical point of view, we have indicated that attribute grammars are a particular subclass of such signature morphisms. This way we are able to apply the structuring techniques to compiler descriptions as they are input to today's compiler generating systems. (In such applications one has to find ways to guarantee that a compiler description which has been combined out of library modules can in fact be viewed as an attribute grammar. A step towards a practical solution to this problem can be found in [Gan83].) We have, thus, also given a new algebraic view of attribute grammars, different from that of [CM77]. Whereas in the latter paper attributes are functionalized into attribute dependencies to obtain denotational semantics definitions in the sense of [ADJ79], we view the dependencies between attribute values as relations. Solving these relations is what a compiler does, namely compiling semantic information characterizing program constructs in their contexts.

References

[ADJ78a] Goguen, J.A., Thatcher, J.W., and Wagner, E.G.: An initial algebra approach to the specification, correctness, and implementation of abstract types. Current trends in Programming Methodology, IV: Data Structuring (R.T. Yeh, ed.), Prentice Hall, 1978, pp. 80-149.

[ADJ78b] Thatcher, J.W., Wagner, E.G., and Wright, J.B.: Data type specification:

[7] Note that this corresponds to the syntactic meaning of grammar rules as defining a relation of derivation between sentential forms.

parameterization and the power of specification techniques. Proc. SIGACT 10th Annual Symp. on Theory of Comp., May 1978, pp. 119-132.

[ADJ79] Thatcher, J.W., Wagner, E.G., and Wright, J.B.: More on advice on structuring compilers and proving them correct. Proc. ICALP 1979, LNCS 71, 1979.

[ADJ80] Ehrig, H., Kreowski, H.-J., Thatcher, J.W., Wagner, E.G., and Wright, J.B.: Parameter passing in algebraic specification languages. Proc. ICALP 1980, LNCS 85, 1980.

[BG80] Burstall, R.M., and Goguen, J.A.: The semantics of CLEAR, a specification language. Version of Feb. 80. Proc. 1979 Copenhagen Winter School in Abstract Software Specifications.

[BW80] Broy, M., and Wirsing, M.: Algebraic definition of a functional programming language and its semantic models. Techn. Univ. München, Rep. TUM-I8008, 1980.

[CM77] Chirica, L.M., Martin, D.F.: An algebraic formulation of Knuthian semantics. Proc. 17th IEEE Symp. on FOCS, 1977, pp.127-136.

[CP67] McCarthy, J., Painter, J.: Correctness of a compiler for arthmetic expressions. Math. Aspects of Comp. Sci., Proc. Symp. in Appl. Math., 19 (1967), pp.33-41.

[Gan83] Ganzinger, H.: Increasing modularity and language-independency in automatically generated compilers. Report TUM-I83.., TU München, 1983, in print.

[Gau82] Gaudel, M.-C.: Correctness proof of programming language translation. In D. Bjørner (ed.): Proc. IFIP TC2 Work. Conf. on Formal Description of Programming Concepts II, Garmisch-Partenkirchen 1982, to be published by North-Holland Publ. Co.

[GHM78] Guttag, J., Horowitz, W., and Musser, D.: Abstract data types and software validation. Com. ACM, 21, 12 (1978), 1043-1064.

[Gog78] Goguen, J.A.: Some design principles and theory for OBJ-O. Proc. Int. Conf. on Math. Studies of Inf. Proc., Kyoto, 1978.

[GP81] Goguen, J.A., Parsay-Ghomi, K.: Algebraic denotational semantics using parameterized abstract modules. LNCS 107, Springer 1981, 292-309.

[Knu68] Knuth, D.E.: Semantics of context-free languages. Math. Systems Theory 2, (1968), 127-145.

[Lip82] Lipeck, U.: An algebraic calculus for structured design of data abstractions (in German). PhD-Thesis, Univ. Dortmund, 1982.

[Mor73] Morris, F.L.: Advice on structuring compilers and proving them correct. Proc. POPL, Boston 1973, pp. 144-152.

[Mos80] Mosses, P.: A constructive approach to compiler correctness. LNCS 94, Springer 1980.

[Mos82] Mosses, P.: Abstract semantic algebras! In D. Bjørner (ed.): Proc. IFIP TC2 Work. Conf. on Formal Description of Programming Concepts II, Garmisch-Partenkirchen 1982, to be published by North-Holland Publ. Co.

[RS82] Raoult, J.-C., Sethi, R.: On metalanguages for a compiler generator. Proc. ICALP 1982, Aarhus.

[Wan79] Wand, M.: First-order identities as a defining language. Techn. Rep. 29, Comp. Sci. Dept., Indiana Univ., Bloomington, Indiana, 1979.

[Wan82] Wand, M.: Semantics-directed machine architecture. Proc. POPL 1982.

[Zil75] Zilles, S.N.: An introduction to data algebras. Working draft paper. IBM Research, San Jose, 1975.

POLYNOMIAL-TIME FACTORIZATION OF MULTIVARIATE POLYNOMIALS OVER FINITE FIELDS

J. von zur Gathen and E. Kaltofen

Department of Computer Science
University of Toronto
Toronto, Ontario M5S 1A4, Canada

Abstract.

We present a probabilistic algorithm that finds the irreducible factors of a bivariate polynomial with coefficients from a finite field in time polynomial in the input size, i.e. in the degree of the polynomial and *log* (cardinality of field). The algorithm generalizes to multivariate polynomials and has polynomial running time for densely encoded inputs. Also a deterministic version of the algorithm is discussed whose running time is polynomial in the degree of the input polynomial and the size of the field.

1. Introduction and Summary of Results

Polynomials with coefficients from a finite field and their factorization properties have been considered for a long time. In 1846, Schönemann proved that univariate polynomials over $\mathbf{Z}_p$ have the unique factorization property (Schönemann [1846], p.276). Since there is only a finite number of factor candidates, the factorization problem is immediately shown to be computable. However, an efficient algorithm to compute these factors was not presented until the late 1960's. Berlekamp [67] then devised an algorithm which factors univariate polynomials over a finite field F with q elements in $O(qn^3)$ field operations, where n is the degree of the polynomial (see Knuth [81], Sec.4.6.2). This running time is polynomial both in n and q. Soon after, Berlekamp [70] made the running time polynomial in the input size, i.e. using $\log q$ rather than q, at the expense of introducing a probabilistic rather than deterministic method. It seems natural to ask whether this can also be accomplished for multivariate, say bivariate polynomials, over F. In particular, given a bivariate polynomial of total degree n with coefficients in F, can one find (probabilistically) its factors in sequential running time polynomial in n and $\log q$?

Older algorithms proposed for this problem (e.g. Musser [71], 2.7.2, and Davenport-Trager [81]) had an exponential worst case running time. The same was true of the Berlekamp-Zassenhaus approach to factoring integer polynomials, until Lenstra-Lenstra-Lovász [82] (for the univariate case) and Kaltofen [82, 83] (for the multivariate case) provided a polynomial-time solution. In this paper, we give a polynomial-time factorization algorithm for bivariate polynomials over a finite field, based on the methods from Kaltofen [82]. Chistov-Grigoryev [82] and Lenstra [83] have also presented polynomial-time algorithms for this problem. Both these papers are based on the short vector algorithm for lattices from Lenstra-Lenstra-Lovász [82], and are quite different from ours.

Our algorithm has two variants: a probabilistic one (Las Vegas) with running time $(n \log q)^{O(1)}$, and a deterministic one with running time $(nq)^{O(1)}$, where n is the degree of the input polynomials and q the cardinality of the coefficient field (section 4.2). In our deterministic version, q could be replaced by $\log q$ if one could factor univariate polynomials over finite fields in deterministic time polynomial in $\log q$. Observe that $n \log q$ is the input size in a natural "dense" encoding of polynomials. Our description concentrates on the probabilistic variant, which may be the more important one for practical purposes.

We also give a parallel variant (section 4.1) for our algorithm which runs in parallel time $O(\log^2 n \, \log q)$, based on the results for univariate factorization in von zur Gathen [83]. It is not known whether the other proposed factorization algorithms yield a fast parallel version.

It is straightforward to generalize our algorithm for factoring multivariate polynomials (section 4.3). Again the running time is polynomial in the input size, provided the inputs are encoded as dense polynomials. Chistov-Grigoryev [82] and Lenstra [83] also present multivariate factoring algorithms of polynomial running time. Using an effective Hilbert Irreducibility Theorem and the results presented here, von zur Gathen [83a] presents a polynomial-time factoring procedure for sparsely encoded multivariate polynomials.

2. Factoring a Nice Polynomial

The algorithm for factoring an arbitrary polynomial $f \in F[x,y]$ proceeds in two stages. We first preprocess f into a "nice format", and then factor the nice polynomial. We start by describing the crucial second stage.

We assume that an algorithm for factoring univariate polynomials over F is given. This algorithm will be allowed to be probabilistic (Las Vegas), so that it either returns the correct answer or "failure", the latter with small probability.

Definition 2.1. Let F be a field, and $f \in F[x,y]$. We call f nice if the following conditions hold:

(N_1) $f(x,0) \in F[x]$ is squarefree.

(N_2) f is monic with respect to x.

Algorithm QUICK FACTORING.

Input: A nice polynomial $f \in F[x,y]$.

Output: An irreducible factor $g \in F[x,y]$ of f.

1. Compute an irreducible monic factor $h \in F[x]$ of $f(x,0)$. If $h = f(x,0)$, then return f. If the probabilistic univariate procedure returns failure, then return "failure". (This should happen with probability at most 2^{-n-1}.)

2. Set $d_x = deg_x f$, $d_y = deg_y f$, and $d = 2d_x d_y$. Set $E = F[t]/(h(t))$, and $a_0 = (t \bmod h(t)) \in E$. We use the Newton iteration in steps 3 and 4 to compute $b \in E[y]$ such that
$$f(b,y) \equiv 0 \bmod y^{d+1}$$
in $E[y]$.

3. Set $t = \dfrac{1}{f_x(a_0,0)} \in E$, where $f_x = \dfrac{\partial f}{\partial x} \in F[x,y]$. (Note that $f_x(a_0,0) \neq 0$, since otherwise a_0 would be a double zero for $f(x,0)$, contradicting its squarefreeness.)

4. For $k = 1,\ldots,d$ compute
$$a_k = a_{k-1} - tf(a_{k-1},y) \in E[y].$$
("$\bmod y^{k+1}$", i.e. truncating the powers y^l of y with $l>k$. Then $f(a_k) \equiv 0 \bmod y^{k+1}$.) Set $b = a_d$.

5. Find the minimal i, $deg h \leq i \leq d_x$, for which there exist $u_0,\ldots,u_{i-1} \in F[y]$ such that
$$deg_y u_j \leq d_y \quad \text{for } 0 \leq j < i,$$
$$b^i + \sum_{0 \leq j < i} u_j b^j \equiv 0 \bmod y^{d+1}.$$
Compute the corresponding $u_0,\ldots,u_{i-1}$.

6. Return
$$g = x^i + \sum_{0 \leq j < i} u_j x^j \in F[x,y].$$

For the timing analysis, we assume that the factorization procedure used in step 1 to factor a univariate polynomial of degree e takes at most $\tau(e)$ operations in F. We will later allow a probabilistic procedure (Las Vegas), which either correctly returns an irreducible factor, or "failure".

Theorem 2.2. Let $f \in F[x,y]$ be nice, and assume that step 1 of algorithm QUICK FACTORING does not return "failure". Then the following hold:

(i) The output is an irreducible factor of f.

(ii) Let n be the total degree of f, and d_x the degree of f with respect to x. The algorithm can be performed in $O(n^3 d_x^4) + \tau(d_x)$ or $O(n^7) + \tau(n)$ operations in F.

Proof. The correctness claim (i) follows just as in Kaltofen [82], section 4. The output g will be the irreducible factor of f such that h divides $g(x,0)$.

In applying (ii), we will need the first estimate, which clearly implies the second one. First observe that step 3 can be performed in $O(d_x)$ operations in E. Each a_k in step 4 takes $O(d_x)$ operations in $E[y]$ (computing $mod\ y^{k+1}$). By Lemma 2.3, step 4 then takes $O(d^2 d_x log^4 d)$ operations in E.

In step 5, we first compute $b^2, b^3, \ldots, b^{d_x}$ in $O(d_x)$ operations in $E[y]$ (again $mod\ y^{d+1}$) or $O(d_x d\ log^4 d)$ operations in E. Then we have to solve a system of at most $(d+1)d_x$ linear equations in at most $d_x(d_y+1)$ unknowns over F. (Note that one equation in E corresponds to less than d_x equations in F.) Gaussian elimination solves the system in $O((d_x(d_y+1))^2\ (d+1)d_x)$ or $O(d^3 d_x)$ operations in F. Noting that $[E:F] < d_x$, $d \le nd_x \le n^2$, and using Lemma 2.3, we get a total of $O(d^3 d_x + d^2 d_x^2 log^4 d\ log^4 d_x)$ or $O(n^3 d_x^4)$ operations in F. □

The following lemma gives an upper bound on the time to perform arithmetic in finite field extensions. Lempel-Seroussi-Winograd [83] give a quasi-linear bound on the number of nonscalar operations needed for multiplication.

Lemma 2.3. Let F be an arbitrary field, and $h \in F[x]$ of degree d. Then an arithmetic operation (+, -, *, division by an invertible element) in $F[x]/(h)$ can be performed in $O(d\ log^4 d)$ operations in F. If the cardinality $\#F$ of F is at least $2d$, then it can be performed in $O(d\ log^2 d)$ operations.

Proof. Let $q = \#F$. We consider the elements of $F[x]/(h)$ as being represented by polynomials in $F[x]$ of degree less than d (i.e. by its sequence of d coefficients). The last claim is well-known (see Aho-Hopcroft-Ullman [74], 8.3). If $q < 2d$, we can (deterministically) compute an irreducible polynomial $w \in F[t]$ of degree $\lceil log_q 2d \rceil$ (see Theorem 3.1). Setting $K = F[t]/(w)$, an operation in $F[x]/(h) \subseteq K[x]/(h)$ can be simulated in $O(dlog^2 d)$ operations in K, and an operation in K costs $O(log^2 d)$ operations in F, giving a total of

$O(d\log^4 d)$ operations in F for each operation in $F[x]/(h)$. □

Remark 2.4. Some simplifications of the algorithm may be of practical interest. Step 4 only has to be executed for $k = 1,...,\bar{d}$, where

$$\bar{d} = \left\lceil \frac{d_y(2d_x-1)}{\deg h} \right\rceil .$$

(See Kaltofen [82], Theorem 4.1.) The algorithm can also be performed without the assumption that f is monic with respect to x. If $c \in F[y]$ is the leading coefficient, then step 4 has to be executed for $k = 1,...,\delta$, where

$$\delta = \left\lceil \frac{d_y(2d_x-1) + \deg c\,(d_x+1)}{\deg h} \right\rceil .$$

In step 5, we then have to consider

$$\deg_y u_j \le d_y \deg c \quad \text{for } 0 \le j < i ,$$

$$c b^i + \sum_{0 \le j < i} u_j b^j \equiv 0 \bmod y^{\delta+1} ,$$

and in step 6, we have to compute

$$v = \gcd(c, u_0,...,u_{i-1}) \in F[y]$$

and return

$$g = \frac{c}{v} x^i + \sum_{0 \le j < i} \frac{u_j}{v} x^j .$$

3. The Preprocessing Stage

In this section we describe the algorithm for factoring an arbitrary bivariate polynomial over a finite field. It converts the input polynomial into a nice polynomial, calls QUICK FACTORING, and then determines a factor of the input polynomial.

We first need an algorithm for the *gcd* of two bivariate polynomials. We use a modular approach for this; see Brown [71].

Algorithm BIVARIATE GCD.

Input: Two polynomials $f, g \in F[x,y]$, where f is monic with respect to x, and F is an arbitrary field.

Output: The monic (with respect to x) *gcd* $h \in F[x,y]$ of f and g.

1. Set $d_x = max(deg_x f, deg_x g)$, $d_y = max(deg_y f, deg_y g)$, and $d = 2d_x d_y$. If $d = 0$, use a procedure for univariate gcd's. If $q = \#F < 3d$, then do the following. Choose an irreducible monic polynomial $w \in F[t]$ of degree $\lceil log_q 3d \rceil$, and replace F by the extension field $F[t]/(w)$.

2. Choose any pairwise distinct $a_1, \ldots, a_{2d} \in F$ such that $g(x, a_i)$ has the same degree in x as g. (We need at most $2d + d_y < 3d$ elements in F to locate such evaluation points.)

3. For all i, $1 \le i \le 2d$, compute the monic
$$h_i = gcd(f(x,a_i), g(x,a_i)) = \sum_{0 \le j} h_{ij} x^j \in F[x].$$

4. Set $m = min\{deg h_i : 1 \le i \le 2d\}$, and choose some $M \subseteq \{1, \ldots, 2d\}$ with $\#M = d_y + 1$ and $deg\ h_i = m$ for all $i \in M$.

5. For $0 \le j \le m$, interpolate the h_{ij}'s: compute $b_j \in F[y]$ of degree at most d_y with $b_j(a_i) = h_{ij}$ for all $i \in M$. (In particular, $b_m = 1$.)

6. Return $h = \sum_{0 \le j \le m} b_j x^j$.

Theorem 3.1. Let $f, g \in F[x,y]$, where f is monic with respect to x, and let d be as in step 1 above. Then algorithm BIVARIATE GCD has the following properties:

(i) It correctly computes a gcd of f and g,

(ii) It can be performed in $O(d^2 log^4 d)$ operations in F. If $\#F \ge 3d$, then it takes $O(d^2 log^2 d)$ operations.

Proof. Let $h_0 = gcd(f, g) \in F[x,y]$ be monic with respect to x, and $f = uh_0$, $g = vh_0$ with $u, v \in F[x,y]$. Then the resultant
$$r = res_x(u,v) \in F[y]$$
is a polynomial of degree less than d, and for any $a \in F$ with $r(a) \ne 0$ and $deg\ g(x,a) = deg_x g$ we have
$$gcd(f(x,a), g(x,a)) = h_0(x,a).$$
Thus for at least d among $h_1, \ldots, h_{2d}$ we have
$$h_i = h_0(x, a_i),$$
and $deg\ h_i \ge deg_x h_0$ for all i. Therefore some M as in step 4 can be found, and steps 5 and 6 correctly compute $h = h_0$.

If $q < 3d$, then we can find w as in step 1 deterministically by testing each monic polynomial $w \in F[t]$ of degree $l = \lceil log_q 3d \rceil$ for irreducibility. There are at most $q^l \leq 3dq < 9d^2$ such polynomials, and each irreducibility test takes $O(log^2 d\ log^2 logd\ logloglogd\ logq)$ or $O(log^4 d)$ operations in F (Rabin [80]). Any operation in $F[t]/(w)$ can be simulated by $O(log^2 d)$ operations in F. This factor $log^2 d$ has to be multiplied to the estimates for steps 3 to 6 only if $q < 3d$.

In step 3, the number of operations is $O(d)$ for each $f(x, a_i)$ and $g(x, a_i)$, and $O(d_x log^2 d_x)$ for each h_i (Aho-Hopcroft-Ullman [74], 8.9), for a total of $O(d(d + d_x log^2 d_x))$ operations. Obviously $m \leq d_x$, and the interpolations in step 5 take $O(d_x(d_y log^2 d_y))$ operations (Aho-Hopcroft-Ullman [74], 8.7). The total is $O(d^2 log^2 d\ log^2 d)$ operations, and $O(d^2 log^2 d)$ if $q \geq 3d$. □

We now describe the algorithm for computing a factor of a bivariate polynomial over a finite field.

Algorithm BIVARIATE FACTORING

Input: A polynomial $f \in F[x,y]$, where F is a finite field with q elements, and $p = charF$, the characteristic of F.

Output: Either a non-constant factor $g \in F[x,y]$ of f, or "failure".

1. (Check primitivity) Set $d_x = deg_x f$, and write $f = \sum_{0 \leq i \leq d_x} f_i x^i$ with $f_i \in F[y]$. Compute the content

$$c = cont_x(f) = gcd(f_0, \ldots, f_{d_x}) \in F[y].$$

If c is non-constant, then return c.

2. (Check squarefreeness) Compute $f_x = \frac{\partial f}{\partial x}$ and $f_y = \frac{\partial f}{\partial y}$. If $f_x = f_y = 0$, then write $f = \sum_{0 \leq i,j} f_{ij} x^{ip} y^{jp}$, set $g = \sum_{0 \leq i,j} f_{ij}^{q/p} x^i y^j$ and return g. (We have $g^p = f$.) If $f_x = 0$ and $f_y \neq 0$, then interchange the role of x and y and goto step 1. Now we have $f_x \neq 0$. Compute $g = gcd(f, f_x)$. If $g \neq 1$, then return g.

3. (Monic version of f) Let $f_0 \in F[y]$ be the leading coefficient of f with respect to x. Set

$$v = f_0^{d_x - 1} f\left(\frac{x}{f_0}, y\right) \in F[x,y].$$

(v is monic of degree d_x with respect to x.)

4. (Extend F) Set $d_y = deg_y v$, $m = max\{d_x, d_y\}$, and $d = 2d_x d_y$. If $q = \#F > d$, then set $F^* = F$. Otherwise choose a prime number l with $m < l \leq 2m$, and an irreducible monic polynomial $w \in F[t]$ of degree l. Set $F^* = F[t]/(w)$.

5. (Good evaluation point) Set

$$r = disc_x(v) = res_x(v, \frac{\partial v}{\partial x}) \in F[y].$$

(r is a nonzero polynomial of degree $\leq (2d_y - 1)d_x < d$.) Choose $c \in F^*$ such that $r(c) \neq 0$, and set

$$f^* = v(x, y-c) \in F^*[x,y].$$

(f^* is nice.)

6. Call procedure QUICK FACTORING with input $f^* \in F^*[x,y]$, to return $g^* \in F^*[x,y]$.

7. Set

$$e = deg_x g^*,\ g_1 = f_0^{-e+1}\, g^*(xf_0, y+c) \in F^*[x,y],$$

$$g_0 = cont_x(g_1) \in F^*[y],\ g = g_1/g_0 \in F[x,y],$$

and return g.

For a concrete estimate of the running time, we have to implement step 1 of the procedure QUICK FACTORING. The probabilistic version of Berlekamp's univariate algorithm due to Cantor-Zassenhaus [82] (see also Knuth [81], 4.6.2) factors a polynomial of degree e in

$$O(e^3 + e^2 \log e \log q)$$

operations in F, where $q = \#F$. Other algorithms for this problem are due to Berlekamp [70], Rabin [80], Ben-Or [81]. This algorithm can be written as a Las Vegas procedure, so that it either returns an irreducible factor or "failure" - the latter with probability at most ½. The algorithm requires $O(e \log e)$ random choices from F, and we assume that they can be performed in $O(e \log e \log q)$ random bit choices. The cost of the Las Vegas univariate factoring procedure in step 1 of QUICK FACTORING is dominated by the cost of other steps. So we can apply that procedure several times, say $n+1$ times, to obtain failure probability at most 2^{-n-1}, where n is the total degree of f.

Theorem 3.2. Let F be a finite field with q elements, and $f \in F[x,y]$ of total degree n. Algorithm BIVARIATE FACTORING with input f has the following properties.

(i) If f is irreducible, it either returns f or "failure".

(ii) If f is reducible, it either returns a proper factor of f or "failure".

(iii) Failure occurs with probability at most 2^{-n}.

(iv) The algorithm can be performed with

$$O(n^7 \log^4 n \log^2 q (n^5 + \log n \log q))$$

bit operations, and $O(n^5 \log q)$ random bit choices.

Proof. It is well-known how the factorization of f and v in $F[x,y]$ are related; see Knuth [81], exercise 4.6.2-18, using the coefficient domain $F[y]$.

By a result of von zur Gathen [83a], section 5, the factorizations of v in $F[x,y]$ and $F^*[x,y]$ are the same. The relation between factors of v and f^* in $F^*[x,y]$ is obvious. Also, f^* is nice.

Note that an l as in step 4 exists by Bertrand's Postulate (see Hardy-Wright [79]). In order to see that some c as in step 5 can be found, it is sufficient to show that $\#F^* = q^l \geq d$:

$$q^l \geq 2^{m+1} \geq 2m^2 \geq d.$$

(The second inequality holds for all $m \geq 1$ with $m \neq 3$. But for $m = 3$ we have $l \geq 5$ and $q^l \geq d$.) We have now proven (i) and (ii) in the case where no failure occurs.

Failure can either occur in step 6 - with probability at most 2^{-n-1} by the remark before theorem 3.2 - or in the computation of w in step 4. This step is executed by taking $8ln$ random monic polynomials in $F[t]$ of degree l, and testing them for irreducibility. If all of them are reducible, "failure" is returned. This happens with probability at most

$$(1 - \frac{1}{2l})^{8ln} \leq e^{-2n} \leq 2^{-n-1}$$

since a random polynomial is reducible with probability at most $1 - \frac{1}{2l}$ (Rabin [80], Lemma 2). Therefore the total failure probability is at most 2^{-n}.

For the timing estimate, first note that $d_x \leq n$, $d_y \leq n^2$, $d = 2d_x d_y \leq 2n^3$, $l \leq 2m \leq 2n^2$, and the total degree n^* of f^* is not more than n^2. Step 1 takes $O(n^3)$ operations, and step 3 $O(n^4)$ operations. In step 2, the gcd can be computed in $O(d^2 \log^4 d)$ operations in F by Theorem 3.1, and the p-th root in $O(d \log \frac{q}{p})$ operations in F, since $deg_y f \leq d_y$ with d_y from step 4. The prime number l can be found deterministically in $O(m^{3/2} \log^2 m)$ bit operations, and w in $O(8ln\, m^2 \log^2 m \log\log m \log q)$ or $O(n^7 \log^3 n \log q)$ operations in F

(Rabin [80]). Steps 5 and 7 both take $O(d_x d^2)$ operations. The cost of the algorithm is dominated by the running time for step 6, which is

$$O((n^*)^3 d_x^4 + n(d_x^3 + d_x^2 \log d_x \log(q^l))$$

or $O(n^{10} + n^5 \log n \log q)$ operations in F^*. Each operation in F^* can be simulated by $O(l \log^4 l)$ operations in F by Lemma 2.3, and $O(l \log^4 l \log^2 q)$ bit operations. Thus the total cost is

$$O(n^7 \log^4 n \log^2 q (n^5 + \log n \log q))$$

bit operations.

The number of random bit choices is $O(8ln\ l \log q)$ or $O(n^5 \log q)$ in step 4, and $O(nd_x \log d_x \log q)$ or $O(n^2 \log n \log q)$ in step 5. □

We note that if $q > d$, then the algorithm uses $F^* = F$ and runs in $O(n^3 \log^2 q (n^7 + \log n \log q))$ bit operations.

Once we have found one nontrivial factor using BIVARIATE FACTORING, we can of course apply the algorithm to this partial factorization. Repeating this yields a probabilistic algorithm which returns either the complete factorization of the input polynomial, or "failure". The total number of bit operations is

$$O(n^8 \log^4 n \log^2 q (n^5 + \log n \log q)),$$

and the number of random bit choices is $O(n^6 \log q)$. The failure probability can be made as small as $n2^{-2n} \le 2^{-n}$ by repeating the algorithm twice at each stage. So we have

Corollary 3.3. Let F be a finite field with q elements. Polynomials in $F[x,y]$ of total degree n can probabilistically (Las Vegas) be factored completely in time polynomial in n and $\log q$.

4. Some Variants

4.1. A parallel version. The basic subroutines for algorithm BIVARIATE FACTORING are a univariate factoring procedure over finite fields, computing univariate gcd's, and solving systems of linear equations over a finite field (which also solves the interpolation step in BIVARIATE GCD). In von zur Gathen [83], all these tasks have been shown to be probabilistically solvable in parallel with $O(\log^2 n)$ operations in F (respectively $O(\log^2 n \log^2 k \log p)$ for factoring). Here n is the total degree of the input polynomial, $p = \mathrm{char} F$, and $q = p^k = \#F$. For a complete factorization, one would lift all irreducible factors of $f(x,0)$ from step 1 of QUICK FACTORING in parallel, using a quadratic Newton procedure (see e.g. von zur Gathen [81]), and then discard duplicate ones. As our model of parallel computation we can take algebraic circuits, with one arithmetic operation or test in F as the basic operation of a gate. Also a prime number l as in step 4 of BIVARIATE FACTORING can be found in parallel with $O(\log^2 n)$ bit operations.

The resulting Las Vegas algorithm returns either the complete factorization of the input polynomial, or "failure"; the latter with probability no more than 2^{-n}. The number of processors required is polynomial in n and $\log q$. Thus we have

Theorem 4.1. Let F be a finite field with $q = p^k$ elements, where $p = \mathrm{char}F$. Polynomials in $F[x,y]$ of total degree n can probabilistically be factored completely in parallel time $O(\log^2 n \log^2(kn) \log p + \log n \log q)$.

The second summand comes from the computation of p-th roots in step 2 of BIVARIATE FACTORING, and the first summand from step 1 of QUICK FACTORING, where a univariate polynomial of degree at most n over a field with not more than p^{kn^2} elements has to be factored. In step 4 of QUICK FACTORING, each step of the quadratic Newton iteration has to compute $t \in E[y]$ such that $t f_k(a_k,y) \equiv 1 \bmod y^{2k}$. This congruence can be considered as a system of linear equations over the ground field, and solved in parallel time $O(\log^2 n)$.

4.2. A deterministic version. Algorithm BIVARIATE FACTORING can be viewed as a reduction from bivariate factoring to univariate factoring over finite fields. All steps of this reduction are deterministic, except the choice of $w \in F[t]$ in step 4. We need w in order to construct F^* with $\#F^* \geq d$, so that step 5 can be executed. But it is sufficient to have $w^+ \in F[t]$ with $l = \deg w^+ \geq \log_q d$, and use $F^+ = F[t]/(w^+)$. Such an w^+ can be found deterministically in time polynomial in d. The problem is that we are not guaranteed that an irreducible factor of f is irreducible in $F^+[x,y]$. Our choice for the degree of w was motivated by the fact that then irreducible factors remain irreducible in $F^*[x,y]$ (von zur Gathen [83a]), and we can avoid the costly norm computation below.

However, the case of w^+ as above can be salvaged by introducing the norm

$$N(g) = N_{F^+(x,y)/F(x,y)}(g) = (-1)^u \mathrm{res}_t(w,\bar{g})$$

for $g \in F^+[x,y]$, where we choose $\bar{g} \in F[x,y,t]$ of degree $i<l$ in t such that $g \equiv \bar{g} \bmod w$ (see van der Waerden [53], p.89). It is well-known that if $g \in F^+[x,y]$ is an irreducible factor of f, then $N(g) \in F[x,y]$ is a power of an irreducible factor of f (Weyl [40], I.5). This irreducible factor is easily found as the $\gcd$ of f and $N(g)$. Thus we have

Theorem 4.2. Let F be a finite field with q elements.

(i) Factoring bivariate polynomials over F of total degree n is deterministically reducible to factoring univariate polynomials of degree at most n (over a small finite extension field of F). The number of operations for the reduction is polynomial in n and $\log q$.

(ii) Bivariate polynomials over F of degree n can be factored deterministically with a number of operations that is polynomial in n and q.

Proof. The above discussion has proven (i); we have to factor a univariate polynomial over a finite extension field F^+ of F. For (ii), we use any of the deterministic variants of Berlekamp's algorithm. □

4.3. A multivariate version. The algorithm can easily be modified for factoring multivariate polynomials over a finite field with q elements. One variable is selected as the main variable, and constants are substituted for the remaining variables. The resulting univariate polynomial is then factored and this factorization lifted. See Kaltofen [83] for details.

The running time of the resulting probabilistic algorithm is polynomial in the input size, and polynomial in the input size and q for the deterministic version. The input size for a polynomial $f \in F[x_1,\ldots,x_k]$ of degree d is $O(d^k \log q)$ in a "dense encoding".

Another measure of size - of greater practical relevance - is the length of a "sparse encoding" of a multivariate polynomial, which is proportional to the number of nonzero terms in the polynomial. Multivariate polynomials can be factored in polynomial time also under this measure, taking input and output size into account (von zur Gathen [83a]).

4.4. Remark. Our techniques do not allow to reduce the exponent 7 in the estimate for QUICK FACTORING in Theorem 2.2(ii). However, it would be easy to improve the running time of algorithm BIVARIATE FACTORING. In remark 2.4 we have indicated how to avoid the necessity of monic inputs. This would result in an $O(n^7 \log^4 n \log^2 q)$ probabilistic algorithm for factoring a bivariate polynomial of degree n over a finite field with q elements.

We close with two open questions.

1. Given a polynomial $f \in \mathbb{Z}_p[x,y]$, can one decide the irreducibility of f deterministically in time polynomial in $\deg f$ and $\log p$?

2. Let F be a finite field with q elements. We have (deterministically) reduced the factorization of a bivariate polynomial $f \in F[x,y]$ of total degree n to factoring univariate polynomials of degree at most n over a (small) finite extension of F. The reduction is polynomial in n and $\log q$. Does a similar reduction exist to factoring univariate polynomials over F itself?

References

A.V. Aho, J.E. Hopcroft and J.D. Ullman, The design and analysis of computer algorithms. Addison-Wesley, Reading MA, 1974.

M. Ben-Or, Probabilistic algorithms in finite fields. Proc. 22nd Symp. Foundations Comp. Sci. IEEE, 1981, 394-398.

E.R. Berlekamp, Factoring polynomials over finite fields. Bell System Tech. J. **46** (1967), 1853-1859.

E.R. Berlekamp, Factoring polynomials over large finite fields. Math. Comp. **24** (1970), 713-735.

W.S. Brown, On Euclid's algorithm and the computation of polynomial Greatest Common Divisors. J. ACM **18** (1971), 478-504.

D.G. Cantor and H. Zassenhaus, On algorithms for factoring polynomials over finite fields. Math. Comp. **36** (1981), 587-592.

A.L. Chistov and D.Yu. Grigoryev, Polynomial-time factoring of the multivariable polynomials over a global field. LOMI preprint E-5-82, Leningrad, 1982.

J.H. Davenport and B.M. Trager, Factorization over finitely generated fields. Proc. 1981 ACM Symp. Symbolic and Algebraic Computation, ed. by P. Wang, 1981, 200-205.

J. von zur Gathen, Hensel and Newton methods in valuation rings. Tech. Report 155(1981), Dept. of Computer Science, University of Toronto. To appear in Math. Comp.

J. von zur Gathen, Parallel algorithms for algebraic problems. Proc. 15th ACM Symp. Theory of Computing, Boston, 1983.

J. von zur Gathen [83a], Factoring sparse multivariate polynomials. Manuscript, 1983.

G.H. Hardy and E.M. Wright, An introduction to the theory of numbers. Clarendon Press, Oxford, 1962.

E. Kaltofen, A Polynomial Time Reduction from Bivariate to Univariate Integral Polynomial Factorization. Proc. 23rd Symp. Foundations of Comp. Sci., IEEE, 1982, 57-64.

E. Kaltofen, Polynomial-time Reduction from Multivariate to Bivariate and Univariate Integer Polynomial Factorization. Manuscript, 1983, submitted to SIAM J. Comput.

D.E. Knuth, The Art of Computer Programming, Vol.2, 2nd Ed. Addison-Wesley, Reading MA, 1981.

A. Lempel, G. Seroussi and S. Winograd, On the complexity of multiplication in finite fields. Theor. Comp. Science **22** (1983), 285-296.

A.K. Lenstra, Factoring multivariate polynomials over finite fields. Proc. 15th ACM Symp. Theory of Computing, Boston, 1983.

A.K. Lenstra, H.W. Lenstra, and L. Lovász, Factoring polynomials with rational coefficients. Math. Ann. **261** (1982), 515-534.

D.R. Musser, Algorithms for Polynomial Factorization. Ph.D. thesis and TR 134, Univ. of Wisconsin, 1971.

M.O. Rabin, Probabilistic algorithms in finite fields. SIAM J. Comp. **9** (1980), 273-280.

T. Schönemann, Grundzüge einer allgemeinen Theorie der höheren Congruenzen, deren Modul eine reelle Primzahl ist. J. f. d. reine u. angew. Math. **31** (1846), 269-325.

B.L. van der Waerden, Modern Algebra, vol. 1. Ungar, New York, 1953.

H. Weyl, Algebraic theory of numbers. Princeton University Press, 1940.

PROCESSES OF PLACE/TRANSITION-NETS

U. Goltz and W. Reisig
Lehrstuhl für Informatik II
RWTH Aachen
Büchel 29 - 31, 5100 Aachen

Abstract

The idea of representing nonsequential processes as partially ordered sets (occurrence nets), is applied to place/transitions-nets (Petri-nets), generalizing the well known notion of process for condition/event-systems. For occurrence nets some theorems relating K-density, cut-finiteness and discreteness are proved. With these theorems we get the result that a place/transition-net is bounded if and only if its processes are K-dense.

1. Introduction

C.A. Petri suggested the representation of non-sequential processes as occurrence nets (causal nets) [P1]. The elements of such nets are event occurrences and condition holdings. Two elements a, b are ordered ($a<b$), if a is a prerequisite for b. Consequently, a and b are unordered, if they are causally independent (concurrent). Similar partially ordered structures are widely used for the description of processes, for instance in [Wi, Ma].

Many properties of occurrence nets (cut-finiteness, density, continuity, coherence, etc.) have been studied and related to each other [P2,Be,BM, FT]. It has been asked which of them are adequate for a characterization of "reasonable" processes. One of the most significant properties in this respect is K-density. It has been introduced by Petri in [P1] in order to "ensure that for every new, real observation a place can be found in an ordering scheme according to its relation to precisely made observations". Best [Be] motivates K-density by the intuitive idea that every sequential subprocess of a process should always be in a well defined state.

In this paper we will not only consider occurrence nets as abstract models of some kind of real processes. Rather we also want to talk about processes which run on special kinds of systems, represented as place/transitions-nets (usually called Petri nets). The relationship between processes and systems corresponds to the connection between finite automata and character strings in the sequential case. There have been some approaches [St,Gr,Wi,RV] which define processes of place/transition-nets by adopting concepts of formal language theory. In contrast, we define processes as mappings from occurrence nets into the underlying place/transition-net. This is a proper generalization of the well known notion of processes of condition/event-systems [P1,GS] and allows for precise reasoning about concurrency and causality.

In order to study this notion of processes of place/transition-nets in detail, we examine properties of the underlying occurrence nets. It turns out that there is a close relationship between the boundedness of a Petri net (i.e. the existence of an upper bound for the number of tokens for all markings) and the K-density of its processes. To establish this relationship, we prove a theorem relating K-density and cut-finiteness of occurrence nets, using the results about K-density of [Be]. Then we characterize the boundedness of a Petri net by the cut-finiteness of its processes. We then get the result that a Petri net is bounded if and only if each of its processes is based on a K-dense occurrence net.

2. Occurrence Nets

a) Basic Notions

The basic notions introduced in this part are well known, e.g. from [GS] and [BM].

2.1 Definition

(i) $N=(S,T,F)$ is called a <u>net</u> iff
  - (a) S and T are disjoint sets (S-elements and T-elements, resp.),
  - (b) $F\subseteq(S\times T)\cup(T\times S)$, F is called the <u>flow relation</u> ,
  - (c) $T\subseteq \mathrm{dom}(F)\cup\mathrm{cod}(F)$.

(ii) For $x\in S\cup T$ $^{\bullet}x:=\{y\mid yFx\}$ is called the <u>pre-set</u> of x ,
  $x^{\bullet}:=\{y\mid xFy\}$ is called the <u>postset</u> of x .
  For $X\subseteq S\cup T$, let $^{\bullet}X:=\bigcup_{x\in X}{^{\bullet}x}$, $X^{\bullet}:=\bigcup_{x\in X}x^{\bullet}$.

(iii) Let $^{\circ}N:=\{x\in S\cup T\mid {^{\bullet}x}=\emptyset\}$ and $N^{\circ}:=\{x\in S\cup T\mid x^{\bullet}=\emptyset\}$.

(iv) $x\in S\cup T$ is called <u>isolated</u> iff $^{\bullet}x\cup x^{\bullet}=\emptyset$.

Notice that property 2.1(i)(c) excludes isolated transitions, but in contrast to [GS], we do not exclude isolated places. This has no influence on the validity of the theorems of Section 2.

Graphically we represent places and transitions as circles and boxes, respectively. The flow relation is indicated by arcs between the corresponding circles and boxes. Given a net $N=(S,T;F)$ we often write S_N,T_N,F_N instead of S,T,F . We denote $S\cup T$ by N if no confusion is possible.

2.2 Definition

(i) A net K is an occurrence net iff

(a) $\forall x,y \in K \quad xF_K^+y \Rightarrow \neg(yF_K^+x)$,

(b) $\forall s \in S_K \quad |{}^\bullet s| \leq 1 \wedge |s^\bullet| \leq 1$.

(ii) Let K be an occurrence net.

(a) $<_K := F_K^+$ is the order relation of K .
The index K is omitted if it is obvious from the context.

(b) Let $\underline{li} \subseteq K \times K$ and $\underline{co} \subseteq K \times K$ be given by

$$x\,\underline{li}\,y \quad :\Leftrightarrow \quad x<y \;\vee\; y<x \;\vee\; x=y \;,$$
$$x\,\underline{co}\,y \quad :\Leftrightarrow \quad \neg(x\,\underline{li}\,y) \;\vee\; x=y \;.$$

$\underline{li}$ and $\underline{co}$ denote the orderedness and unorderedness of elements, respectively. Maximal sets of pairwise ordered or unordered elements, resp., are called lines and cuts :

(iii) $M \subseteq K$ is called a line iff $\forall x,y \in M \quad x\,\underline{li}\,y \;\wedge$
$\forall z \in K \setminus M \quad \exists x \in M \neg(x\,\underline{li}\,z)$.

$M \subseteq K$ is called a cut iff $\forall x,y \in M \quad x\,\underline{co}\,y \;\wedge$
$\forall z \in K \setminus M \quad \exists x \in M \neg(x\,\underline{co}\,z)$.

(iv) A cut $M \subseteq K$ is called a slice iff $M \subseteq S_K$.

The following lemma follows from the axiom of choice :

2.3 Lemma Let K be an occurrence net.

(i) Let $L_\circ \subseteq K$ such that $\forall x,y \in L_\circ : x\,\underline{li}\,y$.
Then there is a line L of K with $L_\circ \subseteq L$.

(ii) Let $C_\circ \subseteq K$ such that $\forall x,y \in C_\circ : x\,\underline{co}\,y$.
Then there is a cut C of K with $C_\circ \subseteq C$.

The following is obvious :

2.4 Lemma Let K be a finite occurrence net. Then ${}^\circ K$ and K° are cuts.

b) K-dense Occurrence Nets

K-dense occurrence nets (and, more general, K-dense partially ordered sets) have been studied in several papers, e.g. [Be,BM,FT,Ni,P1,Pl]. We relate K-density to other properties, i.e. to cut finiteness, degree finiteness and discreteness. Hereby we apply a theorem of Best which is stated in [Be]. Two key notions of this paper, K-density and cut-finiteness, are given as follows :

2.5 Definition Let K be an occurrence net.

(i) K is K-dense iff for every line L and every cut C of K :
$L \cap C \neq \emptyset$.

(ii) K is cut-finite iff each cut of K is finite.

As $x \,\underline{li}\, y \wedge x \,\underline{co}\, y \Rightarrow x=y$, we get for lines L and cuts C of K-dense occurrence nets immediately : $|L \cap C| = 1$.
A first characterization of K-density requires the notion of causal components of occurrence nets.

<u>2.6 Definition</u> Let K be an occurrence net. A net K' is a <u>causal component</u> of K iff

(i) $T_{K'} \subseteq T_K \wedge S_{K'} \subseteq S_K$,
(ii) $\forall x,y \in K' \quad s <_{K'} y \Leftrightarrow x <_K y$.

The main theorem proved in [Be] shows that K-density can be characterized by means of the nets N_1 and N_2 shown in Fig. 1.

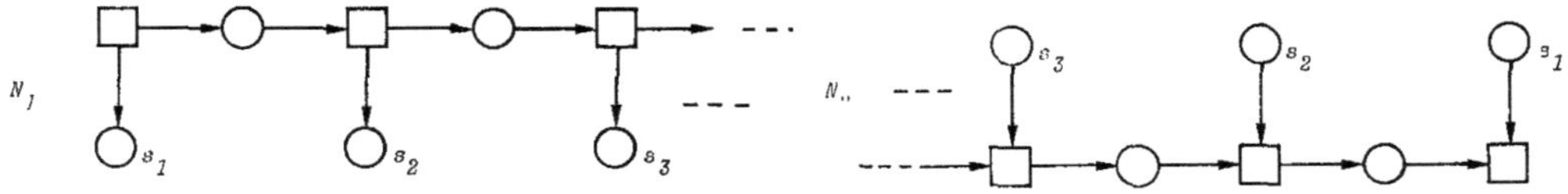

Fig. 1 Non-K-dense occurrence nets

<u>2.7 Theorem</u> Let K be an occurrence net and let N_1 and N_2 be as shown in Fig. 1. K is K-dense iff there is no causal component of K shaped like N_1 or N_2 .
Using this theorem, we immediately see that cut-finiteness implies K-density. Furthermore we can show that an occurrence net is K-dense if all its slices are finite.

<u>2.8 Corollary</u> If all slices of an occurrence net K are finite then K is K-dense.
It is easy to find an example which shows that the converse of Corollary 2.8 is not true.
We now introduce two more properties of occurrence nets, discreteness and degree-finiteness [BM,FT]. Processes of place/transition-nets, as introduced in Section 3, are based on degree-finite occurrence nets, which are not necessarily discrete.

<u>2.9 Definition</u> Let K be an occurrence net, let $x,y \in K$ and let L be a line of K .

(i) $[x,y] := \{z \in K \mid x \leq z \leq y\}$.
(ii) $[x,y;L] := [x,y] \cap L$.
(iii) K is <u>discrete</u> iff, for all $x,y \in K$ and each line L, $[x,y;L]$ is finite.

(iv) K is <u>degree-finite</u> iff $\forall t \in T_K$ $^{\bullet}t$ and $t^{\bullet}$ are finite.

As a direct consequence of a theorem stated in [BM], we find that K-density implies discreteness.

<u>2.10 Theorem</u> Each K-dense occurrence net is discrete.

Now all preliminaries are given in order to relate K-density, degree-finiteness and cut-finiteness.

<u>2.11 Theorem</u> Let K be a degree-finite, K-dense occurrence net and let $°K$ be a finite cut. Then all cuts of K are finite.

<u>Proof</u> Assume an infinite cut C of K and let $C' := C \setminus °K$. We construct inductively elements z_i of K and infinite subsets $D_i \subseteq C'$ as follows : As $°K$ is a cut, $\forall x \in C'$ $\exists y \in °K$ $y<x$. Since $°K$ is finite and C' is infinite there exists some $z_o \in °K$ such that the set $D_o := \{x \in C' \mid z_o < x\}$ is infinite.
Now assume z_i be given such that the set $D_i := \{x \in C' \mid z_i < x\}$ is infinite. Since K is degree-finite, $z_i^{\bullet}$ is finite, and hence there exists an element $z_{i+1} \in z_i^{\bullet}$ such that $D_{i+1} := \{x \in C' \mid z_{i+1} < x\}$ is infinite.
In this way we obtain an infinite totally ordered set $Z = \{z_1, z_2, \ldots\}$ and according to Lemma 2.3(i) there is a line L such that $Z \subseteq L$. As K is K-dense, there is an element $z \in L \cap C$. Assume, there is $i_o \in \mathbb{N}$ such that $z < z_{i_o}$. There is $x \in C$ such that $z_{i_o} < x$, so $z < z_{i_o} < x$. This is impossible, since C is a cut. So $z_i < z$ for all $i \in \mathbb{N}$, and $[y_o, z; L]$ is infinite. Hence K is not discrete and therefore not K-dense (Theorem 2.10). ■

This theorem can also be derived from some results on partial orders of [P1].

<u>2.12 Corollary</u> Let K be a degree-finite occurrence net such that $°K$ is a finite cut. K is K-dense iff all slices of K are finite.

<u>c) Foundedness and Discrete Initial Subnets</u>

We turn now back to the property of discreteness defined in 2.9 . We shall show that a degree-finite occurrence net starting with a cut is discrete if and only if all its elements have "a finite history".

<u>2.13 Definition</u> Let K be an occurrence net, let $x \in K$ and let $A \subseteq K$.

(i) $\downarrow x := \{y \in K \mid y \leq x\}$, $\downarrow A := \bigcup_{x \in A} \downarrow x$.

(ii) x is called <u>founded</u> iff $\downarrow x$ is finite.

<u>2.14 Theorem</u> Let K be a degree-finite occurrence net such that $°K$ is a finite cut. K is discrete iff all $x \in K$ are founded.

Proof

"⇒" Assume an element $y\in K$ which is not founded. Since $\downarrow y$ is infinite and K is degree-finite we find an infinite set $L_0\subseteq\downarrow y$ such that $\forall x,y\in L_0\ x\,\underline{li}\,y$ (analogously to the proof of König' s Lemma, see [Kn]). Using Lemma 2.3(i), there exists a line L with $L_0\subseteq L$. Since $°K$ is a finite cut, the set $L_x:=\{z\in L_0 \mid x\leq z\}$ is infinite for some $x\in °K$. Then $x\leq z\leq y$ for all $z\in L_x\subseteq L$ and therefore $[x,y;L]$ is infinite. Hence K is not discrete.

"⇐" Assume that K is not discrete. Then there exists $x,y\in K$ and a line L such that $[x,y;L]$ is infinite. Since $\downarrow y\subseteq[x,y;L]$, y is not founded. ■

Now we consider initial subnets of occurrence nets.

2.15 Definition Let K be an occurrence net and let $A\subseteq K$.

(i) $K_A:=°K\cup\downarrow A\cap(A\cap T_K)$.

(ii) A is called left closed iff $K_A=A$.

(iii) If A is left closed then $A=(S_K\cap A,T_K\cap A;F_K\cap(A\times A))$ is called initial subnet of K .

Clearly, an initial subnet of an occurrence net K is a causal component of K . The following lemma is an immediate consequence of the definitions.

2.16 Lemma Let K be a degree-finite occurrence net and let $A\subseteq K$.

K discrete, $°K$ finite cut, A finite $\Rightarrow K_A$ finite .

If an occurrence net contains an infinite slice, we can find an infinite slice contained in a discrete initial subnet. In order to show this, we need the following lemma, which again is an immediate consequence of the definitions.

2.17 Lemma Let K be a degree-finite occurrence net, let $x,y\in K$.

(i) x founded and $y<x \Rightarrow y$ founded.

(ii) x not founded $\Rightarrow$ there exists $y<x$, y not founded.

(iii) x not founded, $y\in {}^\bullet x$ founded $\Rightarrow x\in T_K$.

2.18 Theorem Let K be a degree-finite occurrence net with an infinite slice, $°K$ a finite cut. Then K has a discrete initial subnet with an infinite slice.

Proof Assume an arbitrary element x of K which is not founded. Then we construct two elements x' and x'' for this element x as follows : Since $°K$ is a cut, there exists an element $y\in °K$ with $y<x$ and a line L such that $x,y\in L$ and $[y,x,L]$ is finite. Since $x\in[y,x,L]$,

the set $\{z\in[y,x,L] \mid z$ is not founded$\}$ has a minimal element x' (obviously $x'\leq x$) . Using Lemma 2.17(iii), $x'\in T_K$ and there exists a unique S-element $x''\in {}^{\bullet}x'\cap L$ which is founded, while x' is not founded (cf Fig. 2).

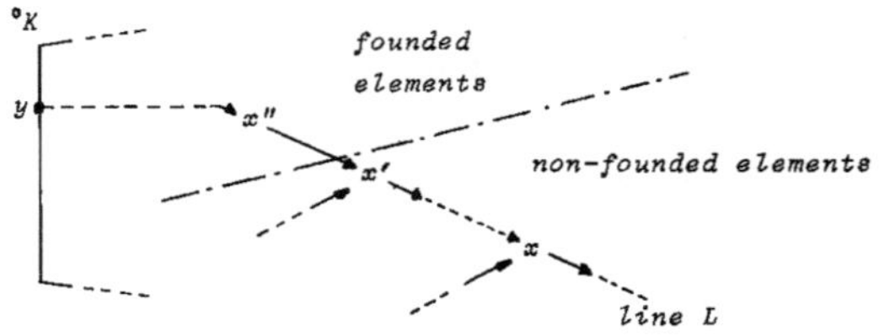

Fig. 2 *The construction of x' and x'' for a non-founded element x.*

Now we prove the result as follows :
If K is discrete, the proposition is trivially true, since K is an initial subnet of itself.
Assume K is not discrete. We construct inductively not founded elements $x_o, x_1, \ldots$ as follows : According to 2.14 there exists a non-founded element x_o . Let now a non-founded element x_n be given. By the construction above we find a non-founded T-element $x'_n<x_n$ and a founded S-element $x''_n\in {}^{\bullet}x'_n$. Using Lemma 2.17(ii) there exists a non-founded element $x_{n+1}<x'_n$.
Next we show $\forall i,j\in \mathbb{N} : i\neq j \Rightarrow x''_i\neq x''_j$: Assume $x''_i=x''_j$. Since x''_i and x''_j are S-elements and therefore unbranched, we have $\{x'_i\}=x''^{\bullet}_i = x''^{\bullet}_j = \{x'_j\}$, hence $x'_i=x'_j$. But if (w.l.o.g.) $j<i$, we get from the above construction immediately $x'_i<x_i<x'_j$.
It is easy to show that $\forall i,j\in\mathbb{N}\ x''_i \ \underline{co}\ x''_j$: Assume (w.l.o.g.) $x''_i<x''_j$. Because $x''^{\bullet}_i=\{x'_i\}$, we obtain $x''_i<x'_i<x''_j$. This contradicts Lemma 2.17(i), since x''_j is founded, but x'_i is not.
Thus, $S=\{x''_o,x''_1,\ldots\}$ is an infinite set of founded, pairwise concurrent S-elements of K . By definition of K_S and using Lemma 2.17(i), all elements of K_S are founded. Hence, K_S yields a discrete initial subnet of K (Theorem 2.14) and $S\subseteq K_S$ is contained in some infinite slice of K_S . ■

3. Processes of Place/Transition Nets

In part a) of this section we introduce the well known model of place/transition nets, often called Petri nets. Furthermore, as the central concern of this part, we define processes for such nets as mappings from occurrence nets to place/transition nets and we discuss the intuition of this notion. In part b) we consider processes which are based on occurrence nets with special properties, as defined in Section 2. We show that a place/transition net is bounded if and only if all its processes are based on K-dense occurrence nets.

a) Place/Transition Nets and their Processes

Place/transition nets, also called marked nets or Petri nets, are the most widespread model of Net Theory. Such nets consist of S-elements (called places) which hold tokens, and of T-elements (called transitions) which can be fired. Upon firing a transition, the token count of all places in its preset is decreased, and the token count of all places in its postset is increased. Continuing firing of transitions is usually represented as a firing sequence [Pe]. We suggest an alternative representation as a process in order to represent precisely concurrency and causality of transition firings.

According to [GS] we define :

3.1 Definition A 5-tuple $N=(S,T;F,W,M)$ is a marked place/transition net (a marked net, for short) iff

(i) $(S,T;F)$ is a net, $S\cup T$ finite (the elements of S and T are called places and transitions, respectively),

(ii) $W:F\to\mathbb{N}$ assigns a positive weight to each arc,

(iii) $M:S\to\mathbb{N}$ is the initial marking of N.

We omit place capacities. (If wanted, they can be simulated by complementary places, cf [GS].) According to the shorthands of 2.1 we denote the components of N by S_N, T_N, F_N, W_N, M_N, respectively. In graphical representations of marked nets, arcs are inscribed by their weights and markings M are represented by $M(s)$ dots (called tokens) in each place s.

The dynamic behaviour of marked nets is given by the usual firing rule :

3.2 Definition Let N be a marked net.

(i) A mapping $M:S_N\to\mathbb{N}\cup\{\omega\}$ is a marking.

(ii) Let M be a marking.
A transition $t\in T_N$ is M-activated $:\Leftrightarrow \forall s\in {}^{\bullet}t \;\; M(s)\geq W(s,t)$.

(iii) Each M-activated transition t yields a follower marking M' by $\forall s\in S \;\; M'(s)=M(s)-W_N(s,t)+W_N(t,s)$ (whereby we assume $W_N(x,y)=0$ for all $(x,y)\notin F_N$).
In this case, t fires from M to M' and we write $M[t>M'$.

(iv) The set $[M_N>$ of reachable markings of N is the smallest set of markings such that (a) $M_N\in[M_N>$ and (b) $M\in[M_N>, M[t>M' \Rightarrow M'\in[M_N>$.

As mentioned above, a common way to trace consecutive transition firings is the construction of firing sequences $M_o[t_1>M_1 \dots M_{n-1}[t_n>M_n$, whereby t_i fires from M_{i-1} to M_i .
As an example consider Fig. 3 .

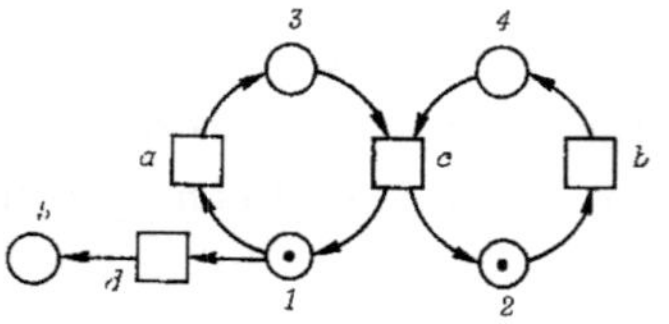

$$\begin{pmatrix}1\\1\\0\\0\\0\end{pmatrix} a \begin{pmatrix}0\\1\\1\\0\\0\end{pmatrix} b \begin{pmatrix}0\\0\\1\\1\\0\end{pmatrix} c \begin{pmatrix}1\\1\\0\\0\\0\end{pmatrix} d \begin{pmatrix}0\\1\\0\\0\\1\end{pmatrix} b \begin{pmatrix}0\\0\\0\\1\\1\end{pmatrix}$$

Fig. 3   *A Petri Net N and a firing sequence, whereby markings M are represented by* $\begin{pmatrix}M(1)\\ \vdots \\ M(5)\end{pmatrix}$.

In the net N of Fig. 3, *a* and *b* may fire concurrently, but *c* is delayed until both *a* and *b* have fired. The concurrency between *a* and *b* , and the causal dependency of *a* and *c* , and of *b* and *c*, cannot be derived from the firing sequence shown in Fig. 3. The net K of Fig. 4 suggests an alternative representation : The S- and T-elements of K are inscribed by places and transitions of N , respectively, indicating the places which change their token count and the transitions which fire. Obviously, K is a (labelled) occurrence net. Its initial slice represents the initial marking of N : One token on place *1* , one token on place *2* and no token on all other places. In this way, all slices of K represent markings of N .

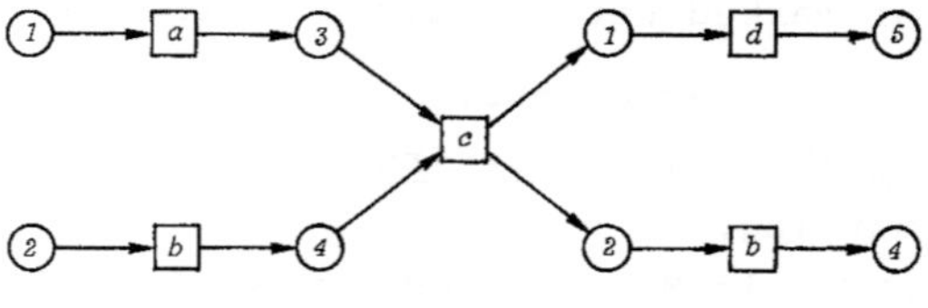

Fig. 4   *A process of the net N shown in Fig. 3*

K represents a process of N . To be more precisely, a process maps the elements of an occurrence net to the elements of a marked net. It is obvious that occurrence nets are adequate to represent such processes. If a place s is branched, e.g. the place *1* in the net N , one of

the transitions in $s^{\bullet}$ is fired in each actual situation. In the above example, first *a* and then *d* is choosen. Hence, S-elements of process representations are not branched. Furthermore, process representations are acyclic, because each instance of firing a transition is represented separately.
In the above example, the net N is a contact free condition/event-system. For such systems, the notion of process is, for instance, defined in [GS].
We shall define processes of place/transition-nets as a proper generalization of this notion of process. As an example, Fig. 5 shows a marked net and a process of this net.

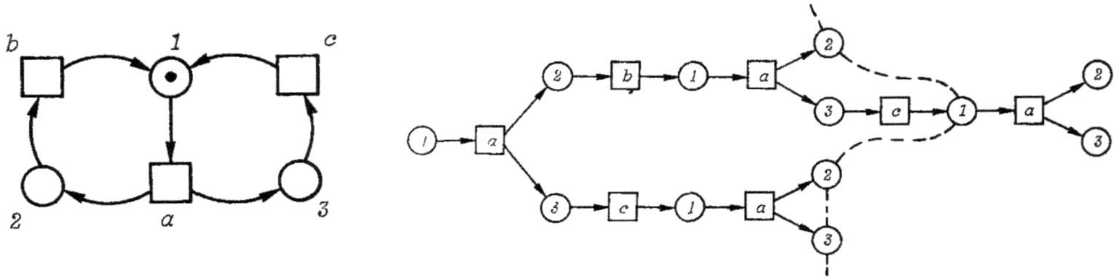

Fig. 5 *A marked net which is no condition/event-system and a process of this net. The dotted line reflects the marking M(1) = M(3) = 1, M(2) = 2.*

The key properties of processes are : (1) The initial places represent the initial marking and (2) the mapping respects the environments of transitions.

3.3 Definition Let N be a marked net and let K be an occurrence net. A mapping $p:K \to N$ is a process (of N) iff

(i) $p(S_K) \subseteq S_N \wedge p(T_K) \subseteq T_N$,

(ii) $°K$ is a cut and $\forall s \in S_N \quad M_N(s) = |p^{-1}(s) \cap °K|$,

(iii) $\forall t \in T_K : \forall s \in {}^{\bullet}p(t) \quad W_N(s,p(t)) = |p^{-1}(s) \cap {}^{\bullet}t|$,

$\qquad \forall s \in p(t)^{\bullet} \quad W_N(p(t),s) = |p^{-1}(s) \cap t^{\bullet}|$.

As in the examples shown above, we represent processes graphically by labelling each element x of the occurrence net K with its image p(x) .
In a process $p:K \to N$, each T-element t of K , together with its inscription, denotes a firing of the transition $p(t) \in T_N$. On the other hand, each S-element s of K , with its inscription, denotes a token in the place $p(s) \in S_N$. Furthermore, we shall show now that each slice of a finite process (K finite) corresponds to a reachable marking of N .

<u>3.4 Definition</u> Let $p:K\to N$ be a process, let S be a finite slice of K . We define the marking $M(p,S):S_N\to\mathbb{N}$ of N by $M(p,S)(s)=|p^{-1}(s)\cap S|$ for each $s\in S_N$.

As an example, consider Fig. 5. We obtain the marking corresponding to a slice by counting, how often each place is represented in this slice.

<u>3.5 Corollary</u> Let K be finite, let $p:K\to N$ be a process and let S be a slice of K . Then $M(p,S)\in M_N$.

To conclude part a) of this section, we shall discuss now some consequences of the notion of process as defined in 3.3.

As marked nets are finite, requirement 3.3(iii) implies immediately that the occurrence net underlying a process is always degree-finite.

The representation of dynamic behaviour as processes shows immediately, which transition firings are concurrent and which ones are ordered : by application of the relations <u>li</u> and <u>co</u> given in 2.2. In order to compare concurrent and ordered transition firings, consider the net N_1 of Fig. 6 with the following interpretation : Each token in place *1* represents a file to be printed ; each token in place *2* represents a file after being printed and each firing of transition *a* represents the action of printing a file. In the situation given in Fig. 6, two files are to be printed. There is no order specified for printing them, and assuming two printers being available, both files may be printed concurrently. This is represented by the process given in Fig. 6. Now let us assume that only one printer is available. In the net of Fig. 7 this printer is represented as a token in place *3* and the two firings of *a* are sequentialized (the process shown in Fig. 7 has a sequential subprocess (3) → [a] → (3) → [a] → (3)).

Clearly, the two marked nets of Fig. 6 and Fig. 7 represent two different real systems with different behaviours (concurrent or sequential firings of *a* , respectively). In contrast to firing sequences, processes reflect this difference. As a further example , skipping both arrows between place *3* and transition *a* in the net of Fig. 7 has much impact on the behaviour, but no impact on the firing sequences.

the net N_1 *a process of* N_1

<u>*Fig. 6*</u> *A transition firing concurrently to itself.*

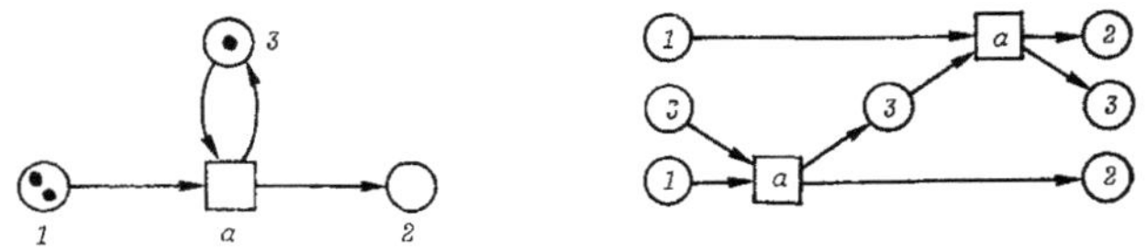

the net N_2 *a process of* N_2

Fig. 7 Sequentialization by means of loops

As motivated by these examples, we allow a transition to fire concurrently to itself (this is excluded in [GS] and in the approach of [St]).

b) Boundedness of Place/Transition Nets and K-density of Processes

A marked net is called bounded if and only if there exists a natural number $n \in \mathbb{N}$ such that each place contains under each reachable marking not more than n tokens. This is equivalent to the requirement that the set of reachable markings is finite.

3.6 Definition A marked net N is called bounded iff

$\exists n \in \mathbb{N} \; \forall M \in [M_N\rangle \; \forall s \in S_N \; M(s) \leq n$.

In general, processes $p:K \to N$ may be infinite ($S_K \cup T_K$ may be infinite). Furthermore there may be infinite slices of K. These slices do not correspond to reachable markings, since all those markings are finite.
We will show now that a marked net N is bounded if and only if all slices of all processes of N are finite. As a consequence we get, using the results of Section 2, that a marked net is bounded if and only if all its processes are based on K-dense occurrence nets.

3.7 Lemma and Definition Let $p:K \to N$ be a process, let K' be an initial subnet of K . Then $p' := p|K'$ is a process of N . p' is called initial subprocess of p .

3.8 Theorem Let $p:K \to N$ be a process of a marked net N such that K has an infinite slice. Then N is not bounded.

Proof using 2.16, 2.18, 3.5 and 3.7.■

3.9 Theorem If all slices of all processes of a marked net N are finite then N is bounded .

Proof Because of space restrictions we only give the idea : Assume N is not bounded. Then it is possible to construct an infinite process with initial subprocesses containing arbitrary many concurrent S-elements. These are contained in some infinite slice of p .■

From Theorem 3.8 and Theorem 3.9 we get :

3.10 Corollary A marked net N is bounded iff all slices of all processes of N are finite.

We shall show now that the boundedness of a net can also be characterized by the K-density of its processes. Using Corollary 3.10 and Corollary 2.8, we immediately have :

3.11 Corollary Let N be a marked net. If there is a non-K-dense process on N , then N is not bounded.

We can prove the converse of this corollary, under one restriction : We do not allow the preset of transitions to be empty. A transition with an empty preset is always enabled and produces "something out of nothing" (cf Fig. 8).

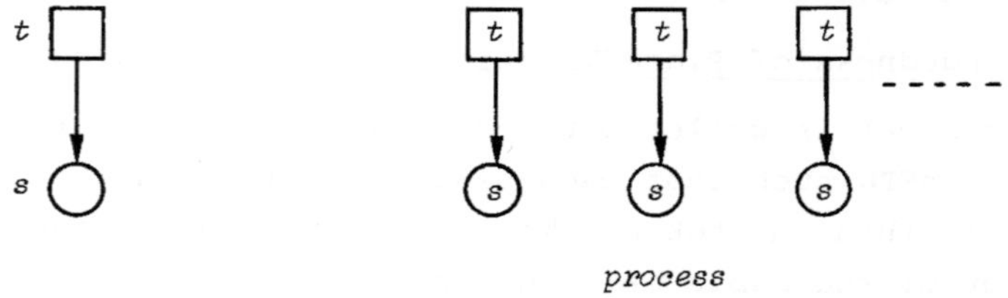

Fig. 8 All processes of the net are K-dense, but it is not bounded.

3.12 Theorem Let N be a marked net and $^\circ N \subseteq S_N$.
If all processes of N are K-dense, then N is bounded.

Proof using 2.12 and 3.10. ■

Acknowledgements

The first ideas for this paper appeared in a discussion with P.S. Thiagarajan. Eike Best contributed to this paper by many discussions and helpful suggestions. In particular, we owe to him an idea to shorten the proof of Theorem 2.11.

References

[Be] E.Best : A Theorem on the Characteristics on Non-Sequential Processes. Fund. Informaticae, Vol. 3, No 1, pp.77-94 (1980).

[BM] E. Best, A. Merceron : Discreteness, K-Density and D-Continuity of Occurrence Nets. 6th GI-Conference on theoretical computer science (January 1983), to appear.

[FT] C. Fernandez, P.S. Thiagarajan : Some Properties of D-continuous Causal Nets. ICALP 1982, Lecture Notes in Computer Science 140 (July 1982).

[GS] H.J. Genrich, E. Stankiewicz-Wiechno : A Dictionary of Some Basic Notions of Net Theory. Advanced Course on General Net Theory of Processes and Systems Hamburg, Lecture Notes in Computer Science 84, Springer Verlag 1980.

[Gr] J. Grabowski : On Partial Languages. Preprint No. 40/79, Sekt. Mathematik, Humboldt-Univ. (October 1979).

[Kn] D.E. Knuth : The Art of Computer Programming, Vol. 1 : Fundamental Algorithms. Addison-Wesley Publishing Company, second edition 1973.

[Ma] A. Mazurkiewicz : Concurrent Program Schemes and their Interpretation. Report DAIMI PB-78, Computer Science Department, Aarhus University, Aarhus, Denmark (1977).

[Ni] M. Nielsen, G. Plotkin, G. Winskel : Petri Nets, Event Structures and Domains. Theoretical Computer Science, Vol. 13, pp. 85-108 (1981).

[Pe] J.L. Peterson : Petri Net Theory and the Modeling of Systems, Prentice-Hall, Inc. 1981.

[P1] C.A. Petri : Non-Sequential Processes. GMD-ISF Report 77-05 (1977).

[P2] C.A. Petri : Concurrency. Lecture Notes in Computer Science Vol. 84, pp. 251-260 (1980).

[Pl] H. Plünnecke : Schnitte in Halbordnungen. GMD-ISF Report 81-09 (April 1981).

[Re] W. Reisig : Processes of Marked, Arc-Weighted Nets. In : Petri Nets and Related System Models, Newsletter No. 5 (June 1980).

[RV] G. Rozenberg, R. Verreadt : Subset Languages of Petri Nets. Third European Workshop on Applications and Theory of Petri Nets. Varenna, Sept. 27-30, 1982, to appear.

[St] P. Starke : Processes in Petri Nets. In : Elektronische Informationsverarbeitung und Kybernetik, Vol. 17, No. 8-9 (1981).

[Wi] J. Winkowski : An Algebraic Description of System Behaviours. Theoretical Computer Science, Vol. 21, Number 3, December 1982 pp. 315-340

A Hardware Semantics Based on Temporal Intervals

Joseph Halpern[1] Zohar Manna[2,3] and Ben Moszkowski[2]

[1]IBM Research Center, 5600 Cottle Road, San Jose, CA 95193, USA
[2]Department of Computer Science, Stanford University, Stanford, CA 94305, USA
[3]Applied Mathematics Department, Weizmann Institute of Science, Rehovot, Israel

Abstract

We present an interval-based temporal logic that permits the rigorous specification of a variety of hardware components and facilitates proving properties such as correctness of implementation. Conceptual levels of circuit operation ranging from detailed quantitative timing and signal propagation up to functional behavior are integrated in a unified way.

After giving some motivation for reasoning about hardware, we present the propositional and first-order syntax and semantics of the temporal logic. In addition we illustrate techniques for describing signal transitions as well as for formally specifying and comparing a number of delay models. Throughout the discussion, the formalism provides a means for examining such concepts as device equivalence and internal states.

§1 Introduction

Computer systems continue to grow in complexity and the distinctions between hardware and software keep on blurring. Out of this has come an increasing awareness of the need for behavioral models suited for specifying and reasoning about both digital devices and programs. Contemporary hardware description languages (for example [1,22,29]) are not sufficient because of various conceptual limitations:

- Most such tools are intended much more for simulation than for mathematically sound reasoning about digital systems.
- Difficulties arise in developing circuit specifications that out of necessity must refer to different levels of behavioral abstraction.
- Existing formal tools for such languages are in general too restrictive to deal with the inherent parallelism of circuits.

The formalism presented in this paper overcomes these problems and unifies in a single notation digital circuit behavior that is generally described by means of the following techniques:

- Register transfer operations
- Flowgraphs and transition tables
- Tables of functions
- Timing diagrams
- Schematics and block diagrams

Using the logic, we can describe and reason about qualitative and quantitative properties of signal stability, delay and other fundamental aspects of circuit operation.

We develop an extension of linear-time temporal logic [18,25] based on intervals. The behavior of programs and hardware devices can often be decomposed into successively smaller periods (intervals) of activity. These intervals provide a convenient framework for introducing quantitative timing details. State transitions can be characterized by properties relating the initial and final values of variables over intervals of time. In fact, we feel that interval-based temporal logic provides a sufficient basis for directly describing a wide range of devices and programs. For our purposes, the distinctions made in dynamic logic [10,24] and process logic [6] between programs and propositions seem unnecessary.

The temporal logic's applicability is not limited to the goals of computer-assisted verification and synthesis of circuits. This type of notation, with appropriate "syntactic sugar," can provide a fundamental and rigorous basis for communicating, reasoning or teaching about the behavior of digital devices, computer programs and other discrete systems. Moszkowski [20,21] has applied it to describing and comparing devices ranging from delay elements up to a clocked multiplier and the Am2901 ALU bit slice developed by Advanced Micro Devices, Inc. Temporal logic also provides a basic framework for exploring the computational complexity of reasoning about time. Simulation-based languages can perhaps use such a formalism as a vehicle for describing the intended semantics of delays and other features. Manna and Moszkowski [17] show how temporal logic can itself serve as a programming language.

This work was supported in part by the National Science Foundation under a Graduate Fellowship, Grants MCS79-09495 and MCS81-11586, by DARPA under Contract N00039-82-C-0250, and by the United States Air Force Office of Scientific Research under Grant AFOSR-81-0014.

§2 Propositional Temporal Logic with Intervals

We first present the propositional part of the temporal logic; this provides a basis for the first-order part.

Syntax

The propositional temporal logic consists of propositional logic with the addition of modal constructs to reason about intervals of time.

Formulas are built inductively out of the following:

- Propositional variables: $P, Q, \ldots$
- Logical connectives: $\neg w$ and $w_1 \wedge w_2$, where w, w_1 and w_2 are formulas.
- Next: $\bigcirc w$ (read "*next w*"), where w is a formula.
- Semicolon: $w_1; w_2$ (read "w_1 *semicolon* w_2" or "w_1 *followed by* w_2"), where w_1 and w_2 are formulas.

Models

Our logic can be viewed as linear-time temporal logic with the addition of the "chop" operator of process logic [6,11]. The truth of variables depends not on states but on intervals. A model is a pair $(\Sigma, \mathcal{M})$ consisting of a set of states $\Sigma = s, t, \ldots$ together with an interpretation $\mathcal{M}$ mapping each propositional variable P and nonempty interval $s_0 \ldots s_n \in \Sigma^+$ to a some truth value $\mathcal{M}_{s_0 \ldots s_n}[\![P]\!]$. In what follows, we assume Σ is fixed.

The length of an interval $s_0 \ldots s_n$ is n. An interval consisting a single state has length 0. It is possible to permit infinite intervals although for simplicity we will omit them here. An interval can also be thought of as the sequence of states of a computation. In the language of Chandra et al. [6], our logic is "non-local" with intervals corresponding to "paths."

Interpretation of Formulas

We now extend the meaning function $\mathcal{M}$ to arbitrary formulas:

- $\mathcal{M}_{s_0 \ldots s_n}[\![\neg w]\!] = \textit{true}$ *iff* $\mathcal{M}_{s_0 \ldots s_n}[\![w]\!] = \textit{false}$
  The formula $\neg w$ is true in an interval iff w is false.
- $\mathcal{M}_{s_0 \ldots s_n}[\![w_1 \wedge w_2]\!] = \textit{true}$ *iff* $\mathcal{M}_{s_0 \ldots s_n}[\![w_1]\!] = \textit{true}$ and $\mathcal{M}_{s_0 \ldots s_n}[\![w_2]\!] = \textit{true}$
  The conjunction $w_1 \wedge w_2$ is true in $s_0 \ldots s_n$ iff w_1 and w_2 are both true.
- $\mathcal{M}_{s_0 \ldots s_n}[\![\bigcirc w]\!] = \textit{true}$ *iff* $n \geq 1$ and $\mathcal{M}_{s_1 \ldots s_n}[\![w]\!] = \textit{true}$
  The formula $\bigcirc w$ is true in an interval $s_0 \ldots s_n$ iff w is true in the subinterval $s_1 \ldots s_n$. If the original interval has length 0, then $\bigcirc w$ is false.
- $\mathcal{M}_{s_0 \ldots s_n}[\![w_1; w_2]\!] = \textit{true}$ *iff* $\mathcal{M}_{s_0 \ldots s_i}[\![w_1]\!] = \textit{true}$ and $\mathcal{M}_{s_i \ldots s_n}[\![w_2]\!] = \textit{true}$, for some i, $0 \leq i \leq n$.
  Given an interval $s_0 \ldots s_n$, the formula $w_1; w_2$ is true if there is at least one way to divide the interval into two adjacent subintervals $s_0 \ldots s_i$ and $s_i \ldots s_n$ such that the formula w_1 is true in the first one, $s_0 \ldots s_i$, and the formula w_2 is true in the second, $s_i \ldots s_n$.

A formula w is *satisfied* by a pair $(\mathcal{M}, s_0 \ldots s_n)$ iff

$$\mathcal{M}_{s_0 \ldots s_n}[\![w]\!] = \textit{true}$$

This is denoted as follows:

$$(\mathcal{M}, s_0 \ldots s_n) \models w.$$

If all pairs of $\mathcal{M}$ and $s_0 \ldots s_n$ satisfy w then w is *valid*, written $\models w$.

§3 Expressing Temporal Concepts in the Propositional Logic

We illustrate the temporal logic's descriptive power by giving a variety of useful temporal concepts. The connectives $\neg$ and $\wedge$ clearly suffice to express other basic logical operators such as $\vee$ and $\equiv$.

Examining Subintervals

For a formula w and an interval $s_0 \ldots s_n$, the construct $\Diamond w$ is true if w is true in at least one subinterval $s_i \ldots s_j$ contained within $s_0 \ldots s_n$ and possibly the entire interval $s_0 \ldots s_n$ itself. Note that the "a" in $\Diamond_a$ simply stands for "any" and is not a variable.

$$\mathcal{M}_{s_0 \ldots s_n}[\![\Diamond_a\, w]\!] = \textit{true} \quad \textit{iff} \quad \mathcal{M}_{s_i \ldots s_j}[\![w]\!] = \textit{true}, \text{ for some } 0 \le i \le j \le n$$

Similarly, the formula $\Box_a\, p$ is true if the formula p itself is true in all subintervals of $s_0 \ldots s_n$:

$$\mathcal{M}_{s_0 \ldots s_n}[\![\Box_a\, w]\!] = \textit{true} \quad \textit{iff} \quad \mathcal{M}_{s_i \ldots s_j}[\![w]\!] = \textit{true}, \text{ for all } 0 \le i \le j \le n$$

These constructs can be expressed as follows:

$$\Diamond_a\, w \quad \equiv \quad (\textit{true}; w; \textit{true})$$

$$\Box_a\, w \quad \equiv \quad \neg \Diamond_a \neg w$$

Because *semicolon* is associative, the definition of $\Diamond_a$ is unambiguous. Together, $\Diamond_a$ and $\Box_a$ fulfill all the axioms of the modal system *S4* [12], with $\Diamond_a$ interpreted as *possibly* and $\Box_a$ as *necessarily*.

Initial and Terminal Subintervals

For a given interval $s_0 \ldots s_n$ the operators $\Diamond_i$ and $\Box_i$ are similar to $\Diamond_a$ and $\Box_a$ but only look at *initial* subintervals of the form $s_0 \ldots s_i$ for $i \le n$. We can express $\Diamond_i\, w$ and $\Box_i\, w$ as shown below:

$$\Diamond_i\, w \quad \equiv \quad (w; \textit{true})$$

$$\Box_i\, w \quad \equiv \quad \neg \Diamond_i \neg w$$

For example, the formula $\Box_i(P \wedge Q)$ is true on an interval if P and Q are both true in all initial subintervals. The connectives $\Diamond_t$ and $\Box_t$ refer to *terminal* subintervals of the form $s_i \ldots s_n$ and are expressed as follows:

$$\Diamond_t\, w \quad \equiv \quad (\textit{true}; w)$$

$$\Box_t\, w \quad \equiv \quad \neg \Diamond_t \neg w$$

Both pairs of operators satisfy the axioms of *S4*. The operators $\Diamond_t$ and $\Box_t$ correspond directly to $\Diamond$ and $\Box$ in linear-time temporal logic [18].

The *Yields* Operator

It is often desirable to say that within an interval $s_0 \ldots s_n$ whenever some formula w_1 is true in any initial subinterval $s_0 \ldots s_i$, then another formula w_2 is true in the corresponding terminal interval $s_i \ldots s_n$ for any i, $0 \le i \le n$. We say that w_1 *yields* w_2 and denote this by the formula $w_1 \leadsto w_2$:

$$\mathcal{M}_{s_0 \ldots s_n}[\![w_1 \leadsto w_2]\!] = \textit{true} \quad \textit{iff} \quad \mathcal{M}_{s_0 \ldots s_i}[\![w_1]\!] = \textit{true} \text{ implies } \mathcal{M}_{s_i \ldots s_n}[\![w_2]\!] = \textit{true} \text{ for all } 0 \le i \le n$$

The yields operator can be viewed as ensuring that no counterexample of the form $w_1; \neg w_2$ exists in the interval:

$$(w_1 \leadsto w_2) \equiv \neg(w_1; \neg w_2)$$

This is similar to interpreting the implication $w_1 \supset w_2$ as the formula $\neg(w_1 \wedge \neg w_2)$.

Temporal Length

The construct *empty* checks whether an interval has length 0:

$$\mathcal{M}_{s_0 \ldots s_n}[\![\textit{empty}]\!] \equiv \textit{true} \quad \textit{iff} \quad n = 0$$

Similarly, the construct *skip* checks whether the interval's length is exactly 1:

$$\mathcal{M}_{s_0 \ldots s_n}[\![\textit{skip}]\!] \equiv \textit{true} \quad \textit{iff} \quad n = 1$$

These operators are expressible as shown below:

$$\textit{empty} \equiv \neg \bigcirc \textit{true}$$

$$\textit{skip} \equiv \bigcirc \textit{empty}$$

Combinations of the operators *skip* and *semicolon* can be used to test for intervals of some fixed length. For example, the formula

$$\textit{skip}; \textit{skip}; \textit{skip}$$

is true exactly for intervals of length 3. Alternatively, the connective *next* suffices:

$$\bigcirc \bigcirc \bigcirc\, \textit{empty}$$

Initial and Final States

The construct *beg* w tests if a formula w is true in an interval's starting state:

$$\mathcal{M}_{s_0 \ldots s_n}[\![beg\ w]\!] \equiv \mathcal{M}_{s_0}[\![w]\!]$$

The connective *beg* can be expressed as follows:

$$beg\ w \equiv \Diamond(empty \wedge w)$$

This checks that w holds for an initial subinterval of length 0, *i.e.*, at the interval's first state. By analogy, the final state can be examined by the operator *fin* w:

$$fin\ w \equiv \Diamond(empty \wedge w)$$

This checks that w holds for a terminal subinterval of length 0, *i.e.*, at the interval's final state.

§4 Some Complexity Results

We prove that satisfiability for arbitrary propositional formulas is undecidable but demonstrate the decidability of a useful subset.

Theorem: Satisfiability for propositional temporal logic with *semicolon* is undecidable.
Chandra et al. [6] show that satisfiability for process logic with an operator called *chop* is undecidable. Our *semicolon* construct acts like *chop* and therefore our theorem strengthens their result since we do not require programs in order to obtain undecidability.

If we restrict all propositional variables to be *local* (that is, each propositional variable P is true of an interval $s_0 \ldots s_n$ iff P is true of the first state s_0), then we get a decidable logic:

Theorem: Local temporal logic with *semicolon* has a decision procedure that is elementary in the depth of the operators $\neg$ and *semicolon*.
This is the best we can do since Kozen (private communication) has shown that the validity problem for local temporal logic with *semicolon* is nonelementary. The proofs of these theorems will appear in the full paper.

§5 First-Order Temporal Logic with Intervals

We now give the syntax and semantics of the first-order temporal logic. Expressions and formulas are built inductively as follows:

Syntax of Expressions

- Individual variables: $U, V, \ldots$
- Functions: $f(e_1, \ldots, e_k)$, where $k \geq 0$ and $e_1, \ldots, e_k$ are expressions. In practice, we use functions such as $+$ and $\vee$ (bit-or). Constants like 0 and 1 are treated as zero-place functions.

Syntax of Formulas

- Predicates: $p(e_1, \ldots, e_k)$, where $k \geq 0$ and $e_1, \ldots, e_k$ are expressions. Predicates include $\leq$ and other basic relations.
- Equality: $e_1 = e_2$, where e_1 and e_2 are expressions.
- Logical connectives: $\neg w$ and $w_1 \wedge w_2$, where w, w_1 and w_2 are formulas.
- Universal quantification: $\forall V. w$, where V is a variable and w is a formula.
- Next: $\bigcirc w$, where w is a formula.
- Semicolon: $w_1; w_2$, where w_1 and w_2 are formulas.

Models

A model consists of a set of states $\Sigma = s, t, \ldots$ and domain D together with an interpretation $\mathcal{M}$ mapping each variable V and interval $s_0 \ldots s_n$ to some value $\mathcal{M}_{s_0 \ldots s_n}[\![V]\!]$ in D. Furthermore, each function and predicate symbol is given some meaning. Each k-place function symbol f has an interpretation $\mathcal{M}[\![f]\!]$ which is a function mapping k elements in D to a single value:

$$\mathcal{M}[\![f]\!] \in (D^k \rightarrow D)$$

Interpretations of predicate symbols are similar but map to truth values:

$$\mathcal{M}[\![p]\!] \in (D^k \rightarrow \{true, false\})$$

The semantics given here keeps the interpretations of function and predicate symbols independent of intervals and thus time-invariant. The semantics can however be extended to take into account the dynamic behavior of parameters.

Interpretation of Expressions and Formulas

We now extend the interpretation $\mathcal{M}$ to arbitrary expressions and formulas:

- $\mathcal{M}_{s_0\ldots s_n}[\![f(e_1,\ldots,e_k)]\!] = \mathcal{M}[\![f]\!](\mathcal{M}_{s_0\ldots s_n}[\![e_1]\!],\ldots,\mathcal{M}_{s_0\ldots s_n}[\![e_k]\!])$,
  The interpretation of the function symbol f is applied to the interpretations of $e_1,\ldots,e_k$.
- $\mathcal{M}_{s_0\ldots s_n}[\![p(e_1,\ldots,e_k)]\!] = \mathcal{M}[\![p]\!](\mathcal{M}_{s_0\ldots s_n}[\![e_1]\!],\ldots,\mathcal{M}_{s_0\ldots s_n}[\![e_k]\!])$
- $\mathcal{M}_{s_0\ldots s_n}[\![e_1 = e_2]\!] = \textit{true} \quad \textit{iff} \quad \mathcal{M}_{s_0\ldots s_n}[\![e_1]\!] = \mathcal{M}_{s_0\ldots s_n}[\![e_2]\!]$
- $\mathcal{M}_{s_0\ldots s_n}[\![\neg w]\!] = \textit{true} \quad \textit{iff} \quad \mathcal{M}_{s_0\ldots s_n}[\![w]\!] = \textit{false}$
- $\mathcal{M}_{s_0\ldots s_n}[\![w_1 \wedge w_2]\!] = \textit{true} \quad \textit{iff} \quad \mathcal{M}_{s_0\ldots s_n}[\![w_1]\!] = \mathcal{M}_{s_0\ldots s_n}[\![w_2]\!] = \textit{true}$
- $\mathcal{M}_{s_0\ldots s_n}[\![\forall V.\, w]\!] = \textit{true} \quad \textit{iff} \quad \mathcal{M}'_{s_0\ldots s_n}[\![w]\!] = \textit{true}$,
  for every interpretation $\mathcal{M}'$ that agrees with $\mathcal{M}$ on the assignments to all variables, function and predicate symbols except possibly the variable V.
- $\mathcal{M}_{s_0\ldots s_n}[\![\bigcirc w]\!] = \textit{true} \quad \textit{iff} \quad n \geq 1$ and $\mathcal{M}_{s_1\ldots s_n}[\![w]\!] = \textit{true}$
- $\mathcal{M}_{s_0\ldots s_n}[\![w_1; w_2]\!] = \textit{true} \quad \textit{iff} \quad \mathcal{M}_{s_0\ldots s_i}[\![w_1]\!] = \textit{true}$ and $\mathcal{M}_{s_i\ldots s_n}[\![w_2]\!] = \textit{true}$, for some i, $0 \leq i \leq n$.

Satisfiability and validity of formulas are as in the propositional case.

All the other temporal operators mentioned earlier are expressible as before. In addition, existential quantification can be introduced as the dual of universal quantification:

$$\exists V.w \quad \equiv \quad \neg\forall V.\neg w$$

Values in the Data Domain

It is sufficient for our purposes that the data domain D contain natural numbers and nested finite tuples. Both 0 and 1 serve as numbers and bits, with 0 standing for low voltage and 1 standing for high voltage. The data domain does not contain any intermediate voltages or "undefined" values.* The following are sample values:

$$0, \quad 3, \quad \langle 0\rangle, \quad \langle 1,2\rangle, \quad \langle\rangle, \quad \langle 6,3,\langle\rangle,9\rangle$$

We adapt the convention that an n-element tuple has subscripts ranging from 0 on the left to $n-1$ on the right.

It is assumed that $\mathcal{M}$ contains standard interpretations of function and predicate symbols such as $+$, $\leq$ and $\vee$ (bit-or). We also include conditional expressions and conventional operators for constructing, subscripting and determining the length of tuples.

Naming Conventions of Variables

Within an interpretation $\mathcal{M}$, a variable's values can differ from interval to interval. For convenience, we will use naming conventions to distinguish certain types of dynamic behavior.

- General variables: $\mathcal{A}, \mathcal{N}, \mathcal{X}, \ldots$
  These can vary in value from interval to interval and are also known as ***non-local, path*** or ***interval*** variables.
- Signal variables: $A, N, X, \ldots$
  The value of such a variable in an interval $s_0 \ldots s_n$ depends solely on the initial state s_0:

  $$\mathcal{M}_{s_0\ldots s_n}[\![A]\!] = \mathcal{M}_{s_0}[\![A]\!]$$

  Thus, signals can change from state to state and are a special case of general variables. Signals can also be referred to as ***local*** or ***state*** variables.
- Static variables: $a, n, x, \ldots$
  A static variable a has a single interpretation $\mathcal{M}[\![a]\!]$, independent of any particular interval:

  $$\mathcal{M}_{s_0\ldots s_n}[\![a]\!] = \mathcal{M}_{t_0\ldots t_m}[\![a]\!]$$

  All static variables are signals and are often called ***global*** or ***frame*** variables.

In general, variables such as $\mathcal{A}$, B and c range over all elements of the data domain D. On the other hand, $\mathcal{J}$, K and n range over natural numbers. The variables $\mathcal{X}$, Y and z always equal one of the bit values 0 and 1. If desired, the naming style suggested here can also be used in the propositional logic.

*The approach taken earlier in Moszkowski [20] included undefined values. However, their omission results in no loss of generality and simplifies the underlying logic.

§6 Some First-Order Temporal Concepts

Within the framework of first-order temporal logic, we can explore a variety of qualitative and quantitative timing issues. The constructs given below are useful for describing and reasoning about circuits.

Temporal Assignment

The formula $A \to B$ is true for an interval if the signal A's initial value equals B's final value:

$$A \to B \quad \equiv_{\text{def}} \quad \forall c.\, \big[beg(A = c) \supset fin(B = c)\big]$$

We call this *temporal assignment*. Unlike in conventional programming languages, it is perfectly acceptable to have an arbitrary expression on the receiving end of the arrow.

Properties:

$$\models \quad (A \to B) \supset \big[f(A) \to f(B)\big]$$

If A is assigned to B, then any time-invariant function application $f(A)$ is passed to $f(B)$.

$$\models \quad [(\neg Z \to Z); (\neg Z \to Z)] \supset (Z \to Z)$$

If a bit signal is twice complemented, it ends up with its original value.

Temporal Equality

Two signals A and B are *temporally equal* in an interval if they have the same values in all states. This is written $A \approx B$ and differs from the constructs for initial and terminal equality, which only examine signals' values at the extremes of the interval:

$$A \approx B \quad \equiv_{\text{def}} \quad \boxdot(A = B)$$

Properties:

$$\models \quad [A \approx B] \supset [f(A) \approx f(B)]$$

If A temporally equals B, then $f(A)$ temporally equals $f(B)$.

$$\models \quad [\langle A, B\rangle \approx \langle A', B'\rangle] \equiv (A \approx A' \wedge B \approx B')$$

The pair $\langle A, B\rangle$ temporally equals $\langle A', B'\rangle$ exactly if the signal A temporally equals A' and B temporally equals B'.

Temporal Stability

A signal A is *stable* if it has a fixed value. The notation used is $stb\, A$ and can be expressed as shown below:

$$stb\, A \quad \equiv_{\text{def}} \quad \exists b.\, (A \approx b)$$

It follows from this that every static variable is stable.

The Temporal Function *len*

Quantitative timing properties are handled by a 0-place function *len* whose value for any interval $s_0 \ldots s_n$ equals the length n:

$$\mathcal{M}_{s_0 \ldots s_n}[\![len]\!] = n$$

Examples

Concept	*Formula*
The signal A is stable and the interval has at least $m+n$ units	$stb\, A \wedge len \geq m+n$
In some subinterval of length $\geq m$, X is stable	$\diamondsuit([len \geq m] \wedge stb\, X)$

Blocking

It is useful to specify that as long as a signal A remains stable, so does another signal B. We say that A *blocks* B and write this as $A \; blk \; B$. The predicate *blk* can be expressed using the temporal formula

$$A \; blk \; B \quad \equiv_{\text{def}} \quad \boxdot(stb\, A \supset stb\, B)$$

The predicate $A \; blk \; B$ can be extended to allow for quantitative timing. When describing the behavior of digital circuits, it is often useful to express that in any initial interval where A remains stable up to within the last m units of time, B is stable throughout:

$$A \; blk^m \; B \quad \equiv_{\text{def}} \quad \boxdot[(stb\, A;\, len \leq m) \supset stb\, B]$$

This modification has utility in situations where B is known to be slow in responding to changes in A.

Initial and Terminal Stability

The predicate $istb^m A$ is true for an interval $s_0 \ldots s_n$ if the signal A is stable in the initial states $s_0 \ldots s_m$. The next definition has this meaning:

$$istb^m A \quad \equiv_{\text{def}} \quad \diamondplus(stb\, A \wedge len = m)$$

Note that the formula is false on an interval of length less than m. By analogy, $tstb^m A$ is true if A ends up stable for at least m units of time.

Rising and Falling Signals

A rising bit signal can be described by the predicate $\uparrow X$:

$$\uparrow X \quad \equiv_{\text{def}} \quad [(X \approx 0);\, skip;\, (X \approx 1)]$$

This says that X is 0 for a while and then jumps to 1. The gap of quantum length represented by the test *skip* is necessary here since a signal cannot be 0 and 1 at the same instant. Falling signals are analogously described by the construct $\downarrow X$:

$$\downarrow X \quad \equiv_{\text{def}} \quad [(X \approx 1);\, skip;\, (X \approx 0)]$$

These operators can be extended to include quantitative information specifying minimum periods of stability before and after the transitions. For example, timing details can be added to the operator $\uparrow$:

$$\uparrow^{m,n} X \quad \equiv_{\text{def}} \quad [(X \approx 0 \wedge len \geq m);\, skip;\, (X \approx 1 \wedge len \geq n)]$$

This can also be expressed as shown below:

$$\models \quad \uparrow^{m,n} X \equiv (\uparrow X \wedge istb^m X \wedge tstb^n X)$$

Thus, the extended form of $\uparrow$ can be reduced to the original one with separate details concerning initial and terminal stability.

A negative pulse with quantitative information can be described as shown below:

$$\downarrow\uparrow^{l,m,n} X \quad \equiv_{\text{def}}$$
$$[(X \approx 1 \wedge len \geq l);\, skip;\, (X \approx 0 \wedge len \geq m);\, skip;\, (X \approx 1 \wedge len \geq n)]$$

These constructs can be further modified to provide for noninstantaneous rise and fall times.

Smoothness

A bit signal X is smooth if it is either stable or has a single transition. The following illustrates one way to express smoothness:

$$sm\, X \quad \equiv_{\text{def}} \quad (stb\, X \vee \uparrow X \vee \downarrow X)$$

Since digital devices generally require clock inputs to be smooth, it is sometimes important to ensure that a signal has this property.

§7 Delays and Combinational Elements

Delay is a fundamental phenomenon in dynamic systems and an examination of it touches upon basic issues ranging from feedback and parallelism to implementation and internal device states. Such concepts also come into play in descriptions of more complicated devices. In addition, a key design decision in building any hardware simulator centers around the treatment of delay (see, for example, Breuer and Friedman [5]). For these and other reasons, it is worth taking a detailed look at various models of signal propagation.

Unit Delay

One of the simplest and most important types of delay elements can modeled as having the following structure:

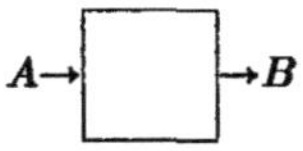

Here A is the input bit signal and B is the associated output. The following statement uses intervals to characterize the desired behavior:

In every subinterval of length exactly one unit, the initial value of the input A equals the final value of the output B.

The next predicate *del* formalizes this:

$$A \; del \; B \quad \equiv_{\text{def}} \quad \boxdot[(len = 1) \supset (A \rightarrow B)]$$

Property:

$$\models \quad (A \; del \; A) \;\equiv\; stb \; A$$

A signal is fed back to itself iff it is stable.

Transport Delay

It is natural to extend the predicate *del* to cover delays over m-unit intervals:

$$A \; del^m \; B \quad \equiv_{\text{def}} \quad \boxdot(len = m \;\supset\; [A \rightarrow B])$$

Breuer and Friedman [5] refer to this as ***transport delay.***

Properties:

$$\models \quad A \; del^0 \; B \;\equiv\; A \approx B$$

Zero delay is equivalent to temporal equality.

$$\models \quad (A \; del^m \; B \;\wedge\; B \; del^n \; C) \;\supset\; A \; del^{m+n} \; C$$

Delay is cumulative.

$$\models \quad \langle A1, A2 \rangle \; del^m \; \langle B1, B2 \rangle \;\equiv\; (A1 \; del^m \; B1 \;\wedge\; A2 \; del^m \; B2)$$

Delay between pairs is equivalent to component-wise delay. This generalizes to tuples of arbitrary length.

Functional Delay

Often, one signal receives a delayed function of another. The following examples illustrate this and are based on the predicate *del* although other delay models can be used.

Examples

Concept	*Formula*
X keeps on being complemented	$(\neg X) \; del \; X$
B either accepts A or itself, depending on X	$[\text{if } (X = 1) \text{ then } A \text{ else } B] \; del \; B$

Properties:

$$\models \quad A \; del^m \; B \;\supset\; f(A) \; del^m \; f(B)$$

If A has a delay to B then it follows that $f(A)$ is delayed to $f(B)$.

$$\models \quad [f(A) \; del^m \; B \;\wedge\; g(B) \; del^n \; C] \;\supset\; g(f(A)) \; del^{m+n} \; C$$

Composition applies.

$$\models \quad [(\neg X) \; del^m \; Y \;\wedge\; (\neg Y) \; del^n \; Z] \;\supset\; X \; del^{m+n} \; Z$$

Two inverters cancel.

$$(I + 1) \; del \; I \;\supset\; [(I + len) \rightarrow I]$$

If the variable I keeps incrementing by 1, its final value is greater than its initial value by the length of the interval.

Delay Based on Shift Register

A shift register R storing $m+1$ values can be specified as follows:

$$R[0]\ \mathit{del}\ R[1] \ \wedge\ \cdots\ \wedge\ R[m-1]\ \mathit{del}\ R[m]$$

Over each unit of time, the contents of R shift right by one element. That is, the value of $R[0]$ is passed to $R[1]$ and so forth. This description is more formally expressed by means of quantification:

$$\forall i \in [0, m-1].\,(R[i]\ \mathit{del}\ R[i+1])$$

The next formula has the same meaning but is more concise:

$$R[0 \text{ to } m-1]\ \mathit{del}\ R[1 \text{ to } m]$$

The following property shows how to achieve an m-unit delay by means of such a shift register:

$$\models \quad R[0 \text{ to } m-1]\ \mathit{del}\ R[1 \text{ to } m] \ \supset\ R[0]\ \mathit{del}^m\ R[m] \qquad (*)$$

This suggests an implementation of $A\ \mathit{del}^m\ B$ of the form $A\ \mathit{shdel}^m_R\ B$:

$$A\ \mathit{shdel}^m_R\ B \quad \equiv_{\text{def}} \quad (A \approx R[0]\ \wedge\ R[m] \approx B\ \wedge\ R[0 \text{ to } m-1]\ \mathit{del}\ R[1 \text{ to } m])$$

Here, the value of A is fed into $R[0]$ and B receives the value $R[m]$. The correctness of this implementation is given by the following property:

$$\models \quad A\ \mathit{shdel}^m_R\ B \ \supset\ A\ \mathit{del}^m\ B$$

We can localize R in the formula $A\ \mathit{shdel}^m_R\ B$ by defining a variant $A\ \mathit{shdel}^m\ B$ which existentially quantifies over R:

$$A\ \mathit{shdel}^m\ B \quad \equiv_{\text{def}} \quad \exists R.\,(A\ \mathit{shdel}^m_R\ B)$$

The register is assumed to exist without being externally visible to an observer. The quantifier's effect on scoping is similar to that of a *begin*-block in a conventional block-structured programming language. We call $A\ \mathit{shdel}^m\ B$ an *external* specification of the implementation. In fact, this is logically equivalent to the basic delay predicate $A\ \mathit{del}^m\ B$ as the next property demonstrates:

$$\models \quad A\ \mathit{shdel}^m\ B \ \equiv\ A\ \mathit{del}^m\ B$$

The proof that *shdel* implies *del* follows from the implementation theorem (*) given above. The converse requires demonstrating that some R exists. Perhaps the easiest way to do this is by direct construction. At each instant of time, the values of the $m+1$ elements of R can be those of the next $m+1$ values of B in appropriate order:

$$R[i] \approx \bigcirc^{m-i} B, \quad \text{for } 0 \le i \le m$$

The output value $R[m]$ always equals the expression $\bigcirc^0 B$, which is defined to be B's current value. Similarly, $R[0]$ always equals $\bigcirc^m B$, that is, the value B will have m units later. This technique works even if the interval has length less than m.

Variable Transport Delay

A batch of delay elements may have varying characteristics although each individual device is rather fixed in its timing behavior. The predicate $A\ \mathit{vardel}^{m,n}\ B$ specifies that A's value is propagated to B by transport delay with some uncertain factor between m and n:

$$A\ \mathit{vardel}^{m,n}\ B \quad \equiv_{\text{def}} \quad \exists i \in [m,n].\,(A\ \mathit{del}^i\ B)$$

Delay with Sampling

Digital circuits often require that inputs remain stable and be sampled for some minimum amount of time in order to ensure proper device operation. The delay model $A\ \mathit{sadel}\ B$ has this characteristic:

$$A\ \mathit{sadel}^m\ B \quad \equiv_{\text{def}} \quad \boxdot[(\mathit{stb}\,A\ \wedge\ \mathit{len} \ge m)\ \supset\ \mathit{fin}(A = B)]$$

Here the input A must be stable at least m units of time for the output B to equal A. Behavior during changes in A is left unspecified. The properties below illustrate two other ways of expressing *sadel*. We present them to demonstrate other possible styles:

$$\models \quad A\ \mathit{sadel}^m\ B \ \equiv\ \boxdot(\mathit{tstb}^m\,A\ \supset\ \mathit{fin}(A = B))$$

$$\models \quad A\ \mathit{sadel}^m\ B \ \equiv\ [\mathit{tstb}^m\,A \leadsto \mathit{beg}(A = B)]$$

Properties:

$\models \; A\ del^m\ B \supset A\ sadel^m\ B$

Basic delay implements sampling delay.

$\models \; A\ sadel^m\ B \equiv \big(tstb^m A \leadsto [beg(A = B) \land A\ blk\ B]\big)$

Once the device stabilizes, the input A blocks the output B.

The predicate *sadel* can be extended to associate some factor with the blocking of B by A:

$$A\ sadel^{m,n}\ B \quad \equiv_{\text{def}} \quad \big(tstb^m A \leadsto [beg(A = B) \land A\ blk^n\ B]\big)$$

In a sense, m is the maximum delay and n is the minimum delay.

An Equivalent Delay Model with an Internal State

A related delay model $A\ stdel_X^{m,n}\ B$ is based on a bit flag X that is set to 1 after the input A has been held stable m units. Whenever X is 1, the input A equals the output B and blocks X, which in turn blocks B by the factor n:

$$\begin{aligned} &A\ stdel_X^{m,n}\ B \quad \equiv_{\text{def}} \\ &\quad \boxdot([stb\ A \land len \geq m] \supset fin(X = 1)) \\ &\quad\quad \land \boxdot(beg(X = 1) \supset [beg(A = B) \land A\ blk\ X \land X\ blk^n\ B]) \end{aligned}$$

In the manner described earlier, we internalize X by existentially quantifying over it:

$$A\ stdel^{m,n}\ B \equiv \exists X.\,(A\ stdel_X^{m,n}\ B)$$

This external form is in fact logically equivalent to $A\ sadel^{m,n}\ B$:

$\models \; A\ stdel^{m,n}\ B \equiv A\ sadel^{m,n}\ B$

The following construction for X can be used:

$$X \approx \text{if } [beg(A = B) \land A\ blk^n\ B] \text{ then } 1 \text{ else } 0$$

There are a variety of specifications that use different internal signals such as X and yet are externally equivalent.

Delay with Separate Propagation Times for 0 and 1

Sometimes it is important to distinguish between the propagation times for 0 and 1. The following variant of *sadel* does this by having separate timing values for the two cases:

$$\begin{aligned} &A\ sadel01^{m,n}\ B \quad \equiv_{\text{def}} \\ &\quad \boxdot([A \approx 0 \land len \geq m] \supset fin(A = B)) \\ &\quad \land \boxdot([A \approx 1 \land len \geq n] \supset fin(A = B)) \end{aligned}$$

Smooth Delay Elements

It is possible to specify that between times when the delay element is stable, if the input changes smoothly, then so does the output. We call such a device a *smooth* delay element. This type of delay has utility in systems which must propagate clock signals without distortion. Here is a predicate based on the earlier specification *stdel*:

$$\begin{aligned} &A\ smdel_X^{m,n}\ B \quad \equiv_{\text{def}} \\ &\quad A\ stdel_X^{m,n}\ B \\ &\quad\quad \land \boxdot\big([beg(X = 1) \land fin(X = 1) \land sm\ A] \supset sm\ B\big) \end{aligned}$$

The external form quantifies over X:

$$A\ smdel^{m,n}\ B \quad \equiv_{\text{def}} \quad \exists X.\,(A\ smdel_X^{m,n}\ B)$$

Delay with Tolerance to Noise

Sometimes it is important to consider the affects of transient noise during signal changes. A signal A is *almost smooth* with factor l if A is continuously stable all but at most l contiguous units of time:

$$stb\,A; (len \le l); stb\,A$$

The delay model *toldel* is similar to *smdel* but has an additional timing coefficient l for showing how almost smooth input changes result in smooth output transitions:

$$\begin{aligned} &A\ toldel_X^{m,n,l}\ B \quad \equiv_{\text{def}} \\ &\quad A\ stdel_X^{m,n}\ B \\ &\quad \wedge\ \boxdot[(beg(X=1)\ \wedge\ fin(X=1)\ \wedge\ [stb\,A; (len \le l); stb\,A]) \supset\ sm\,B] \end{aligned}$$

From this we can obtain the external form

$$A\ toldel^{m,n,l}\ B$$

The predicate *smdel* is a special case of *toldel* with a noise tolerance of 1 time unit:

$$\models\quad A\ smdel^{m,n}\ B \equiv A\ toldel^{m,n,1}\ B$$

Gates with Input and Output Delays

One might specify an and-gate with both input and output delays as follows:

$$(X, X')\ saand^{m,n}\ Y \quad \equiv_{\text{def}} \quad \exists Z, Z'.\ [X\ sadel^m\ Z\ \wedge\ X'\ sadel^m\ Z'\ \wedge\ (Z\ \wedge\ Z')\ sadel^n\ Y]$$

Here a delay exists from the input X to an internal signal Z and another delay occurs from X' to Z'. The bit-and of Z and Z' is propagated to Y. The input delays are given by m and the output one by n. If we choose to ignore input delays, the model reduces to a single occurrence of *sadel*:

$$\models\quad (X, X')\ saand^{0,n} \equiv (X\ \wedge\ X')\ sadel^n\ Y$$

If the internal propagation is modeled by transport delay, things are even simpler. Here is an and-gate specified in this manner:

$$(X, X')\ tand^{m,n}\ Y \quad \equiv_{\text{def}} \quad \exists Z, Z'.\ [X\ del^m\ Z\ \wedge\ X'\ del^m\ Z'\ \wedge\ (Z\ \wedge\ Z')\ del^n\ Y]$$

The predicate *tand* simplifies even if internal input delay is not ignored:

$$\models\quad (X, X')\ tand^{m,n}\ Y \equiv (X\ \wedge\ X')\ del^{m+n}\ Y$$

§8 Simple Latch

A latch is a simple memory element for storing and maintaining a single bit of data. The two inputs S and R determine what value is stored with S standing for *Set* and R standing for *Reset*. When the latch is stable, the outputs Q and $\overline{Q}$ are complements. Note that the bar in "$\overline{Q}$" is part of the name and not an operator. Such elements are among the simplest storage devices that can be built out of TTL gates and provide a basis for building counters and other sequential components. Here is one way to specify such a latch:

$$\begin{aligned} &(S, R)\ latch^{m,n}\ (Q, \overline{Q}) \quad \equiv_{\text{def}} \\ &\quad \boxdot[(S \approx 0\ \wedge\ R \approx 1\ \wedge\ len \ge m) \leadsto ([Q = 0\ \wedge\ \overline{Q} = 1]\ \wedge\ S\ blk^n\ (Q, \overline{Q}))] \\ &\wedge\ \boxdot[(S \approx 1\ \wedge\ R \approx 0\ \wedge\ len \ge m) \leadsto ([Q = 1\ \wedge\ \overline{Q} = 0]\ \wedge\ R\ blk^n\ (Q, \overline{Q}))] \end{aligned}$$

For example, the specification states that after S is 1 and R is 0 for at least m units of time, Q equals 1, $\overline{Q}$ equals 0 and R blocks both with factor n. That is, the outputs are stable as long as R remains "inactive" at 0, independent of S's behavior. A logically equivalent specification based on an internal state is given in the full paper.

A latch can be constructed out of two nor-gates that feed back to one another:

$$\models\quad [\neg(R\ \vee\ \overline{Q})\ sadel^{m,n}\ Q\ \wedge\ \neg(S\ \vee\ Q)\ sadel^{m,n}\ \overline{Q}\ \wedge\ n \ge 1] \supset [(S, R)\ latch^{2m,n}\ (Q, \overline{Q})]$$

The gates' blocking factor n must be nonzero in order to achieve a feedback loop that maintains a stored value.

§9 Some Variants of Temporal Logic

There are a variety of operators and concepts that can be added to the temporal logic. We discuss a few here.

Iteration

The logic can be generalized to include iteration. In the proposition case, this involves adding the Kleene closure of *semicolon*. This does not affect our basic complexity results. Loop operators such as *while* can be expressed by means of such a construct.

Ignoring Intervals

The concepts presented here can generally be expressed in linear-time temporal logic [18] with $\bigcirc$, $\Box$, $\Diamond$ and $\mathcal{U}$. The satisfiability of propositional formulas for such a logic is PSPACE-complete [28]. However, the conciseness and clarity provided by *semicolon* and other interval-dependent constructs are often lost.

Infinite Intervals

In the semantics already given, all intervals are restricted to being finite. It can however be advantageous to consider infinite intervals arising out of nonterminating computations. The inclusion of such intervals does not alter the complexity of satisfiability.

Projection

Sometimes it is desirable to examine to behavior of a device at certain points in time and ignore all intermediate states. This can be done using the notion of *temporal projection*. The formula $w_1 \,\Pi\, w_2$ in an interval forms a subinterval consisting of those states where w_1 is true and then determines the value of w_2 in this subinterval:

$$\mathcal{M}_{s_0\ldots s_n}[\![w_1 \,\Pi\, w_2]\!] = \mathcal{M}_{t_0\ldots t_m}[\![w_2]\!],$$

where $t_0 \ldots t_m$ is the sequence of the states in $s_0 \ldots s_n$ that satisfy w_1:

$$\mathcal{M}_{t_i}[\![w_1]\!] = \textit{true}, \quad \text{for } 0 \le i \le m$$

Note that $t_0 \ldots t_m$ need not be a contiguous subsequence of $s_0 \ldots s_n$. If no states can be found, the projection is *false*. In the semantics given here, the formula w_1 examines states, not intervals. For example, the formula

$$(X = 1) \,\Pi\, \textit{stb}\, A$$

is true is A has a constant value throughout the states where X equals 1. Variables like X act as metrics for measuring time and facilitate different levels of atomicity. If two parts of a system are running as different rates, metrics can be constructed to project away the asynchrony. Other definitions of projection are also possible.

Additional Modifications

Further possible extensions include quantification over propositional variables as well as interval-oriented temporal logics based on branching or probabilistic models of time.

§10 Related Work

We now mention some related research on the semantics of hardware. Gordon's work [8] on register-transfer systems uses a denotational semantics with partial values to provide a concise means for reasoning about clocking, feedback, instruction-set implementation and bus communication. Talantsev [30] as well as Betancourt and McCluskey [3] examine qualitative signal transition concepts corresponding to $\uparrow X$ and $\downarrow X$. Wagner [31] also uses such constructs as $\uparrow X$ in a semi-automated proof development system for reasoning about signal transitions and register transfer behavior. Malachi and Owicki [16] utilize a temporal logic to model self-timed digital systems by giving a set of axioms. Bochmann [4] uses a linear-time temporal logic to describe and verify properties of an arbiter, a device for regulating access to shared resources.

Leinwand and Lamdan [14] present a type of Boolean algebra for modeling signal transitions. Applications include systems with feedback and critical timing constraints. Patterson [23] explores the verification of firmware from the standpoint of sequential programming. Meinen [19] discusses a semantics of register transfer behavior. McWilliams [15] develops computational techniques for determining timing constraints in hardware. Eveking [7] uses predicate calculus with explicit time variables to explore verification in the hardware specification language Conlan.

A number of people have used temporal logics to describe computer communication protocols [9,13,26]. Bernstein and Harter [2] augment linear-time temporal logic with a construct for expressing that one event is followed by another within some specified time range. This facilitates the treatment of various quantitative timing issues. Recently Schwartz et al. [27] have introduced a temporal logic for reasoning about intervals. They distinguish intervals from propositions.

For our purposes, much of this work either has difficulties in treating quantitative timing, lacks rigor, is unintuitive or does not easily generalize. In particular, we believe that in many papers on applications of temporal logic, various basic aspects of discrete-time systems have be neglected in favor of more "glamorous" protocols and distributed algorithms. Furthermore, the computational models used generally interleave the executions of different processes. In the treatment of digital circuits, this approach seems inappropriate.

It has been argued by some that temporal logic is simply a subset of dynamic logic. However, once interval-dependent constructs are added, this is no longer the case. Operators such as *semicolon* and *yields* are not directly expressible in dynamic logic. Furthermore, the descriptive styles used in dynamic logic and temporal logic differ rather greatly. Dynamic logic and process logic stress the interaction between programs and propositions. Temporal logic is expressive enough to conveniently and directly specify a variety of useful programs. Our current view is that the addition of program variables would be redundant.

§11 Conclusion

Standard temporal logics and other such notations are not designed to concisely handle the kinds of quantitative timing properties and signal transitions that occur in the examples considered. Temporal intervals provide a unifying means for presenting the various features. Even without intervals, many of the dynamic concepts discussed here have utility in specifications and properties about discrete-time systems.

Moszkowski [21] uses the logic for describing and comparing a variety of digital devices. Manna and Moszkowski [17] show how to program directly in temporal logic. Future work will explore microprocessors, buses and protocols, DMA, firmware and instruction sets, as well as the combined semantics of hardware and software. We also plan to examine compilers and other systems that transmit and manipulate commands and programs.

References

1. M. R. Barbacci. "Instruction Set Processor Specifications (ISPS): The notation and its applications." *IEEE Trans. Comp. C-30*, 1 (Jan. 1981), 24–40.
2. A. Bernstein and P. Harter. "Proving real-time properties of programs with temporal logic." Proc. 8-th Symp. on Operating Systems Principles, Pacific Grove, California, Dec., 1981, pp. 1–11.
3. R. Betancourt and E. J. McCluskey. Analysis of sequential circuits using clocked flip-flops. Tech. Rept. 82, Digital Systems Laboratory, Stanford Univ., Aug., 1975.
4. G. V. Bochmann. "Hardware specification with temporal logic: An example." *IEEE Trans. Comp. C-31*, 3 (March 1982), 223–231.
5. M. A. Breuer and A. D. Friedman. *Diagnosis and Reliable Design of Digital Systems.* Computer Science Press, Inc., Woodland Hills, California, 1976.
6. A. Chandra, J. Halpern, A. Meyer, and R. Parikh. Equations between regular terms and an application to process logic. Proc. 13-th ACM Symp. on Theory of Computing, Milwaukee, Wisconsin, May, 1981, pp. 384–390.
7. H. Eveking. The application of Conlan assertions to the correct description of hardware. Proc. 5-th Int'l Conf. on Computer Hardware Description Languages, Kaiserslautern, West Germany, Sept., 1981, pp. 37–50.
8. M. Gordon. Register transfer systems and their behavior. Proc. 5-th Int'l Conf. on Computer Hardware Description Languages, Kaiserslautern, West Germany, Sept., 1981, pp. 23–36.
9. B. T. Hailpern and S. Owicki. Verifying network protocols using temporal logic. Tech. Rept. 192, Computer Systems Laboratory, Stanford Univ., June, 1980.
10. D. Harel. *First-Order Dynamic Logic.* Springer-Verlag, Berlin, 1979. No. 68 of *Lecture Notes in Comp. Sci.*
11. D. Harel, D. Kozen, and R. Parikh. Process logic: Expressiveness, decidability, completeness. 21-th Symp. on Foundations of Comp. Sci., Syracuse, New York, Oct., 1980, pp. 129–142.

12. G. E. Hughes and M. J. Cresswell. *An Introduction to Modal Logic*. Methuen and Co., Ltd., London, 1968.
13. L. Lamport. Specifying concurrent program modules. Opus 60, Comp. Sci. Lab., SRI International, June, 1981.
14. S. Leinwand and T. Lamdan. Algebraic analysis of nondeterministic behavior. Proc. 17-th Design Automation Conf., Minneapolis, June, 1980, pp. 483–493.
15. T. M. McWilliams. Verification of timing constraints on large digital systems. Proc. 17-th Design Automation Conf., Minneapolis, June, 1980, pp. 139–147.
16. Y. Malachi and S. S. Owicki. Temporal specifications of self-timed systems. In H.T. Kung, B. Sproul, and G. Steele, editors, *VLSI Systems and Computations*, pp. 203–212, Computer Science Press, Inc., Rockville, Maryland, 1981.
17. Z. Manna and B. Moszkowski. Temporal logic as a programming language, forthcoming.
18. Z. Manna and A. Pnueli. Verification of concurrent programs: the temporal framework. In R. S. Boyer and J. S. Moore, editors, *The Correctness Problem in Computer Science*, pp. 215–273, Academic Press, New York, 1981.
19. P. Meinen. Formal semantic description of register transfer language elements and mechanized simulator construction. Proc. 4-th Int'l Symp. on Computer Hardware Description Languages, Palo Alto, California, Oct., 1979, pp. 69–74.
20. B. Moszkowski. A temporal logic for multi-level reasoning about hardware. Proc. 6-th Int'l Symp. on Computer Hardware Description Languages, Pittsburgh, Pennsylvania, May, 1983.
21. B. Moszkowski. *Reasoning about Digital Circuits*. Ph.D. Thesis, Dept. of Comp. Sci., Stanford Univ., forthcoming.
22. A. C. Parker and J. J. Wallace. "SLIDE: An I/O hardware description language." *IEEE Trans. Comp. C-30*, 6 (June 1981), 423–439.
23. D. A. Patterson. "Strum: Structured microprogram development system for correct firmware." *IEEE Trans. Comp. C-25*, 10 (Oct. 1976), 974–985.
24. V. R. Pratt. Semantical considerations on Floyd-Hoare logic. 17-th IEEE Symp. on Foundations of Comp. Sci., Houston, Texas, Oct., 1976, pp. 109–121.
25. N. Rescher and A. Urquart. *Temporal Logic*. Springer-Verlag, New York, 1971.
26. R. L. Schwartz and P. M. Melliar-Smith. Temporal logic specification of distributed systems. Proc. 2-nd Int'l Conf. on Distributed Computing Systems, Paris, France, April, 1981, pp. 446–454.
27. R. L. Schwartz, P. M. Melliar-Smith, and F. H. Vogt. An interval logic for higher-level temporal reasoning: language definition and examples. Tech. Rept. CSL-138, Comp. Sci. Lab., SRI International, Feb., 1983.
28. A. P. Sistla and E. M. Clarke. The complexity of propositional linear temporal logics. Proc. 14-th ACM Symp. on Theory of Comp., San Francisco, California, May, 1982, pp. 159–168.
29. S. Y. H. Su, C. Huang, and P. Y. K. Fu. A new multi-level hardware design language (LALSD II) and translator. Proc. 5-th Int'l Conf. on Computer Hardware Description Languages, Kaiserslautern, West Germany, Sept., 1981, pp. 155–169.
30. A. D. Talantsev, "On the analysis and synthesis of certain electrical circuits by means of special logical operators." *Automation and Remote Control* 20, 1959, pp. 874–883.
31. T. Wagner. *Hardware Verification*. Ph.D. Thesis, Dept. of Comp. Sci., Stanford Univ., 1977.

LOWER BOUNDS FOR SOLVING UNDIRECTED GRAPH PROBLEMS ON VLSI

Susanne E. Hambrusch
Department of Computer Sciences
Purdue University
West Lafayette, IN 47907

Janos Simon*
Department of Computer Science
The Pennsylvania State University
University Park, PA 16802

Abstract

We study VLSI solutions to the connected component problem on networks that have area too small to store all the edges of the graph for the entire computation. We give lower bounds on the time needed to solve this problem on such networks. The lower bounds use a new proof technique combining adversary strategy, information flow, and Kolmogorov complexity arguments. The lower bounds obtained for the connected components problem hold for a number of other undirected graph problems.

1. Introduction

The potential use of VLSI technology for direct hardware implementation of algorithms has motivated much recent research in parallel computation and in the design of special purpose chips tailored to a particular problem ([AA], [BK], [GKT], [LS], [T]). In this paper we study to the *connected component problem* (ccp), which is a paradigm for many other graph problems. We consider solutions on chips of small area; i.e., area too small to store all the edges of the graph explicitly within the chip for the entire computation. The assumption is interesting for both upper and lower bounds: for algorithms because small area may mean that actual implementation of the design could be attempted; and for lower bounds, because our solution yielded a new proof technique.

Many lower bounds on the quantity AT^2 for VLSI chips have been obtained, using information flow arguments ([BK], [T], [V]). These arguments are, in a sense, 'static': information is localized in some parts of the chip, and must eventually reach certain other areas of the chip by 'flowing' across an imaginary cut on the chip. More dynamic information theoretic arguments are desirable - both to prove stronger lower bounds on VLSI, and eventually to yield techniques that could be applied to other problems in complexity theory (for example, extending the results of [PSS] to the non-real-time case). We take the first step in this direction by introducing a new lower bound technique for VLSI that gives strong lower bounds in a dynamic setting. Such a situation arises on chips that cannot store all the information about the graph for the entire computation.

Applying the information transfer technique to undirected graph problems yields $AT^2=\Omega(n^2(\log n)^2)$ [J]. This lower bound is tight within factors of $\log n$ for chips of $\Omega(n^2)$ area: [H1] presents an algorithm for the ccp that achieves $AT^2 = O(n^2(\log n)^6)$ on a network of $O(n^2(\log n)^2)$ area. (A similar result can also be found in [NMB].) For chips of small area the lower bound of $AT^2=\Omega(n^2(\log n)^2)$ is far from optimal. For example, on networks of $O(n)$ area, the time required to read n^2 inputs is $\Omega(n)$, which gives $AT^2 = \Omega(n^3)$.

Our lower bound technique combines adversary, Kolmogorov complexity, and information flow arguments. We obtain lower bounds for verification problems (i.e., given a solution to the problem and a graph, verify that the solution is the correct solution for the given graph). In general it seems to be harder to prove lower bounds for verification problems than for problems where the solution must be computed and multiple outputs are produced. We show that the lower bounds for the verification problem also hold for the original problem.

* Research supported in part by NSF grant MCS81-04876 and USARO Contract Number DAAG29-82-K-0110.

We examine several forms of input for a graph: adjacency matrix, adjacency lists, and an unordered sequence of edges. We show that the form of input is crucial for the performance of the algorithm. For networks of small area the input mode is also of importance: in this paper we only consider the *when oblivious* mode; i.e., the environment, rather than the network, determines the moments in time at which the input is given to the network. Networks of area large enough to store all the inputs before and during the actual computation are not sensitive to the when obliviousness of the model. This does not hold for all problems solved on networks of small area: while the performance of the algorithms presented in [KL] does not depend on when obliviousness, efficient algorithms for undirected graph problems seem to be harder to find in the when oblivious model ([H1], [LV]). Furthermore, for undirected graph problems we will prove stronger lower bounds for the when oblivious model. Other parallel algorithms for the ccp and for other graph problems can be found in [AK], [GKT], and [NMB].

We prove that for every when oblivious chip of $o(n^2)$ area there exists a graph in the class of adversary graphs for which we can obtain a lower bound on the time needed to process this graph. We show that a certain amount of time must elapse between successive input sequences, because there will always be a segment on the chip that has an information deficiency about the input supplied to it. The next wave of input must then wait until enough information flows into the deficient segment. For networks of $O(n)$ area having constant width and input in the form of adjacency lists or edges, we prove that for some n vertex graph, the time elapsing between two consecutive input sequences is at least $\Omega(n)$. Since there may be n input sequences, we have $T=\Omega(n^2)$, and $AT^2=\Omega(n^5)$, which can be achieved by an algorithm presented [H1]. The results obtained for chips of $O(n)$ area extend to chips of $O(nm)$ area, $m=o(n)$, and to problems that allow the produced solution to be 'close' (in a probabilistic sense) to the correct solution.

The paper is organized as follows. In section 2 we describe the model of computation and the different forms of input for graphs. Section 3 contains the lower bound results. We first prove the lower bounds for the verification problem of the ccp and show that a lower bound on the time needed to solve the verification problem of the ccp on a network of $O(n)$ area is $\Omega(n^2/k)$, when the network can be circumscribed by a rectangle of size $k \times n/k$, $1 \le k \le n^{1/2}$. We generalize this technique to obtain lower bounds on the time for networks of $O(nm)$ area. We then show that the connected component problem is at least as hard as its verification problem. Thus a lower bound on the verification problem is also a lower bound for the ccp.

2. Model of Computation and Forms of Input

In a number of recent papers, ([BK],[CM],[LS],[S],[T]), parallel models suitable for VLSI implementation have been developed and refined. Our model follows the one of [LS] and is discussed below.

(1) Each *processing element* (PE) of the chip contains r registers, r constant, and is able to execute a simple set of instructions. Each register consists of $\log n$ bits, where n is the number of vertices in the graph. Each PE is connected to a constant number of other PE's, and the PE's operate synchronously.
(2) The chip communicates with its environment through the input/output ports (I/O ports). Since we are interested in the information flow requirements of the problem, and not in the information flow requirements based on the I/O restrictions of the chip, we assume each PE of the chip can read input and produce output.
(3) Each input is read once, and each output is generated once.
(4) The chips are *when and where oblivious*. A chip is when and where oblivious when the time and locations at which the inputs arrive (and the outputs are generated) are independent of the input data. On a when oblivious chip the time elapsing between the reading of two successive input waves is fixed by the environment of the chip and is the same for all successive input waves.

The complexity measures are *time* and *area*. Two definitions of time have been used in the VLSI literature. One defines time as the number of *steps* required to generate all the outputs, where one step is either an operation on two bits of a PE, or the transmission of a bit from one PE to an adjacent PE. Many algorithms for VLSI networks perform operations on entire registers rather than on bits of the registers, and this motivated a second definition, which is the one used in this paper. In this definition time is the total number of *cycles* needed to generate all the outputs, where one cycle is either an operation on two registers of a PE, or the transmission of the content of a register of a PE to an adjacent PE. See [AK], [GKT], [LV].

The area is the space necessary to lay out the PE's with their interconnections on a small, constant number of parallel layers. When time is measured in terms of steps a bit is considered to have unit size, and thus each PE occupies $\log n$ area. When time is measured in terms of cycles we consider a register to have unit size, and thus each PE occupies a constant number of units of area.

In this paper we will measure time in terms of cycles. Thus, in order to compare our results with results obtained in the other model, the area needs to be multiplied by a factor of $\log n$. The time needs to be multiplied by a factor of $(\log n)^{1/2}$ or $\log n$, depending on whether or not in the model PE's have $(\log n)^{1/2}$ or constant bandwidth. The issue of whether time is proportional to the wire length (synchronous versus diffusion model) is avoided. In the time bounds unit time is charged for the communication between two PE's, and the lower bounds hold in either model.

Three common representations for a graph are: adjacency matrix, adjacency lists and unordered edge list. When the graph is given to the chip in form of an ***adjacency matrix*** it reads the n rows of the matrix. Let $PE_1, \ldots, PE_m$ be the m processing elements receiving inputs, V be the vertex set, $V=\{1,2,\ldots,n\}$, and E be the set of edges. If $(i,j)\in E$, $i<j$. When the graph is given in the form of ***adjacency lists*** the edges are read in lexicographic order; i.e., if PE_i reads (u_i,v_i) and PE_{i+1} reads (u_{i+1},v_{i+1}), then $u_i<u_{i+1}$, or, $u_i=u_{i+1}$ and $v_i<v_{i+1}$. Thus PE_i reads the $((j-1)m+i)-th$ edge of the list of edges in lexicographic order in the j-th input sequence, $1\le i<m$, $1\le j\le e/m$, where e is the number of edges in the graph. When the graph is given in the form of an ***unordered edge list*** (hereafter called input in the form of edges) the edges (i,j) are read into the chip in arbitrary order. See Fig. 2.1. In this paper we primarily discuss input in the form of adjacency lists and edges. We refer to [H1] for results when the input is in the form of an adjacency matrix.

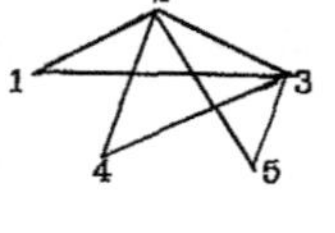

Input sequences	adjacency matrix	adjacency lists	edges
1.	1 1 1 0 0	(1,2) (1,3) (2,3) (2,4) (2,5)	(3,5) (1,2) (2,4) (3,4) (2,5)
2.	1 1 1 1 1	(3,4) (3,5)	(1,3) (2,3)
3.	1 1 1 1 1		
4.	0 1 1 1 0		
5.	0 1 1 0 1		

Fig. 2.1
The input sequences for the 3 forms of input ($m=5$)

A chip receiving the input in the form of adjacency lists or edges reads only e inputs, as compared with n^2 inputs for the adjacency matrix. Every graph represented in the form of a matrix or lists has a unique description, while different input sequences can describe the same graph when represented in the form of edges. Graphs given in the form of an adjacency matrix allow the PE's of the chip to know before the computation what inputs they will read (i.e. PE_i reads the i-th column). This is no longer possible when the graph is given in the form of lists or edges, since the inputs PE_i receives depend on the graph in the first case and are arbitrary in the second case.

3. Lower Bound Results

We prove lower bounds on the time needed to solve undirected graph problems on when oblivious chips of small - $o(n^2)$ - area, when the graph is given in the form of adjacency lists or edges. In this paper we only deal with the connected component problem (i.e., two vertices are in the same connected component if and only if there is a path between them), but the results extend to many other problems (e.g., biconnectivity, bridgeconnectivity, minimum-cost spanning tree). The proof technique combines adversary, Kolmogorov complexity, and information flow arguments, and the lower bounds obtained hold also for verification problems.

3.1. The Verification Problem

In the *verification problem* of the ccp we are given as input an encoding of a solution to the ccp and a description of a graph G. We have to determine whether or not the connected components of graph G are those specified in the solution and produce a 0/1 answer. The minimal length of an encoding describing the solutions to the ccp is $n\log n$, and $n\log n$ bits are sufficient; (see [H1]). Verification is easy when input is given in the form of an adjacency matrix. In [H1] it is shown how to verify in time $O(n)$ on a network of $O(n)$ area. This time is optimal for a network of $O(n)$ area. We will define a class of graphs, and show that the verification problem of the ccp is harder when input is given in the form of adjacency lists or edges.

An *adversary graph* G^* consists of $n/6+1$ connected components, where $n/6$ components consist of a single edge, and one component is a connected subgraph on the remaining $2n/3$ vertices, which we term the *filler graph*. See Fig. 3.1.

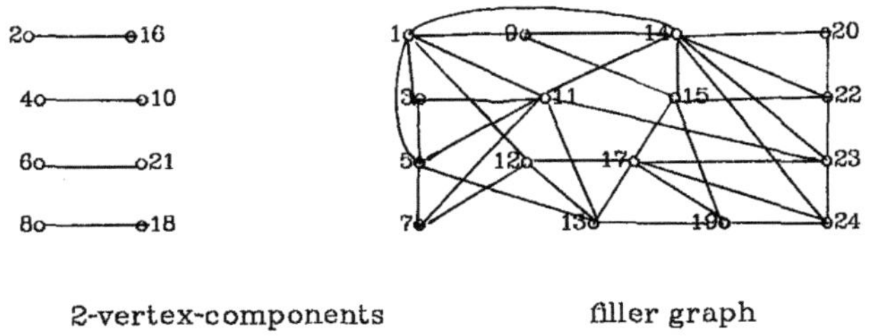

Fig. 3.1
An adversary graph with 24 vertices

Let the vertex set $V^*=\{1,2,\ldots,n\}$. Each one of the $n/6$ edges representing a 2-vertex-component is adjacent to an even numbered vertex less than or equal to $n/3$ and a vertex greater than $n/3$. The first $n/3$ odd numbered vertices and the vertices not used in the 2-vertex-components are the vertices of the filler graph. Formally, the set of edges E^* of G^* is defined as $E^*=\{(2i,x_i) \mid 1 \le i \le n/6, x_i \in \{n/3+1,...,n\}, x_i \ne x_j \text{ for } i \ne j\} \cup E'$, where E' is $E' \subseteq \{(2i+1,y_i) \mid 0 \le i < n/6, y_i \in V_x\} \cup V_x \times V_x$, and V_x is the set of vertices greater than $n/3$, not used in the 2-vertex-components. The edges of E' are ***filler edges***; they will be used to 'fill up' input sequences (i.e., make them sufficiently long for the lower bound argument). The edges representing 2-vertex-components are the ones of interest for the adversary.

Kolmogorov complexity, also known under the term descriptional complexity, measures the minimal number of bits needed for descriptions. We refer to [PSS] for formal definitions. We use Kolmogorov complexity to measure the length of the minimal encoding describing the connected components of the adversary graphs. The next two lemmas formalize the intuitively obvious fact that at least $\alpha n \log n$ bits must be used to encode an adversary graph, for some $\alpha > 0$.

Lemma 3.1 There are $2^{\alpha n \log n}$ different adversary graphs G^*, for some constant α, and thus at least $\alpha n \log n$ bits are needed to encode all different adversary graphs.

Proof: There are $(2n/3)(2n/3-1) \cdots (2n/3-n/3+1)$ different ways to choose the $n/3$ 2-vertex-components, which is $2^{\alpha n \log n}$ for some constant α. Thus encoding all adversary graphs with different 2-vertex-components (without counting the bits needed to encode the filler graph) requires $\alpha n \log n$ bits, and the lemma follows. ▪

It does not immediately follow that the chip will need $\alpha n \log n$ bits of its registers for the encoding, since the chip may use the fixed network configuration in the encoding of the solution (e.g. use the indices of the PE's or the interconnection pattern or the fact that a given register is not used in the encoding). While an encoding of the solution of length $\alpha n \log n$ is input, the chip is allowed to modify (and, possibly compress) the solution before the graph is being input. But it still must be able to distinguish between the $2^{\alpha n \log n}$ different solutions, each one describing an adversary graph with different connected components.

In lemma 3.2 we show that for chips of $O(n)$ area there cannot be sufficiently clever encodings of the input solution on the chip: $\alpha' n \log n$ bits of the registers are needed to distinguish between all different solutions, for some constant α'.

Lemma 3.2 Let N be a chip of $O(n)$ area that reads a minimal length encoding. Let the length of the encoding be $\alpha n \log n$. Then in order to be able to distinguish between all $2^{\alpha n \log n}$ different encodings, $\alpha' n \log n$ bits of the registers of the PE's of the chip are needed, for some constant α'.

Proof: For simplicity assume the chip has n PE's and each PE has one register ($r=1$). If the network has cn PE's, for some constant c, or $r>1$, the results will hold with different constants.

Assume the chip needs s bits to store the (possibly modified) encoding on the chip. Let the *configuration* C of the chip be the encoding formed by those s bits. Each different input must have a different configuration, and thus there have to be at least $2^{\alpha n \log n}$ different configurations. To prove the lemma we show that s, the number of bits needed, has to be at least $\alpha' n \log n$, for some constant α'.

Let $A(s,n)$ be the number of ways s bits can be distributed into n registers of size $\log n$. Then the number of different final configurations is $2^s A(s,n)$. In [H1] it is shown that $A(s,n) = O(2^{O(n \log\log n)})$, and thus the number of different final configurations is $2^s 2^{O(n \log\log n)}$. Since we need $2^{\alpha n \log n}$ final configurations, $s = \alpha' n \log n$, for some constant α'. This proves lemma 3.2. ▪

3.2. Networks of O(n) Area

We will now give the lower bound for networks of $O(n)$ area that solve the verification problem of the ccp.. In the lower bound proofs we make a constant number of cuts through the chip and then choose a particular section S of the chip. After having stored (and possibly modified) the solution read as input, we start reading the edges of the adversary graph in the form of adjacency lists or edges. The adversary graph will be such that all the edges representing 2-vertex-components are fed into section S in a constant number of input sequences. Since section S can hold at most half of the information needed by the 2-vertex-components during the verification process, an information exchange between the PE's in section S and the PE's outside section S has to occur. In order to be able to continue reading the edges of the filler graph (after having read all 2-vertex-components) and to correctly verify the connected components, a certain time has to elapse between the reading of two consecutive input sequences. This will give the lower bound on the time.

We first present the bound for input given in the form of edges. Note that in the lower bound arguments we measure the exchange of information in bits, but in the final results we express the time in terms of cycles (as described in section 2).

Theorem 3.3 Let N be a network of $O(n)$ area that can be circumscribed by a rectangle of size $k \times n/k$, $1 \le k \le n^{1/2}$. Then solving the verification problem of the ccp on N with edges as input requires time $\Omega(n^2/k)$, or, expressed in terms of the edges of the graph, time $\Omega(e/k)$.

Proof: W.l.o.g. assume the network has n PE's. (If the network has cn PE's, for some constant c, the proof below will hold, provided we multiply the appropriate constants by c.) Consider the adversary graphs G^* whose minimal length encoding of the input solution describing the $n/6$ 2-vertex-components requires $\alpha n \log n$ bits on the chip, $0<\alpha<1$. According to lemma 3.2 such graphs exist. Assume the input solution has been read and stored in the chip using $\alpha n \log n$ bits.

Let r be the constant denoting the number of registers in each PE. Make $\max(2r/\alpha - 1, 12r - 1)$ cuts through the network such that each cut is of length $O(k)$ and each section between two cuts contains $\min(\alpha/2r.n, 1/12r.n)$ PE's. See Fig. 3.2. It is always possible to make such a cut: PE's lying on the cut are counted either to the section to the left or to the right of the cut depending on the number of PE's in the section left of the cut. Each section between two cuts can hold a total of $\min(\alpha/2.n\log n, 1/12.n\log n)$ bits. Let S be an arbitrary section.

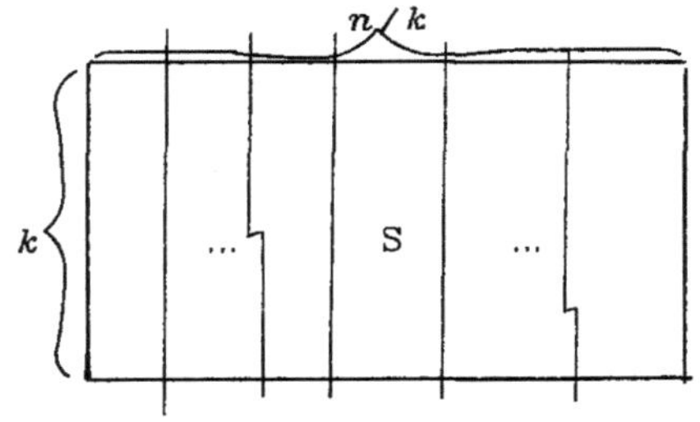

Fig. 3.2
The cuts through the chip

Consider first the case when $2r/\alpha > 12r$. Then $\alpha < 1/6$, and section S has $\alpha/2r.n$ PE's and can hold a total of $\alpha/2.n\log n$ bits. In the extreme case all the $\alpha/2.n\log n$ bits available in section S contain bits of the encoding describing the input solution, which contains the connected components of the edges representing 2-vertex-components. Thus at least $\alpha/2.n\log n$ bits of the encoding describing the input solution are stored outside section S.

In a constant number of input sequences all the edges representing 2-vertex-components are read into section S, while the PE's outside section S will read edges of the filler graph. Since there are $n/6$ 2-vertex-components and section S contains $\alpha/2r.n$ PE's, $r/3\alpha$ input sequences are needed to read all the 2-vertex-components into section S.

We first give the intuition behind the proof. During the entire verification process an encoding of the input solution has to be compared with an encoding of the connected components of the graph read as input. We expect that while for some of the edges representing 2-vertex-components and read into section S verification might be easy (i.e., their verification can be done without knowing anything about the part of the input solution stored outside section S), other edges will need to know something about the part of the encoding stored outside section S. We are able to verify at most half of the 2-vertex-components without knowing anything about the encoding stored outside section S. The communication needed between section S and the rest of the chip will cause the delay. More formally, we argue as follows.

There exist adversary graphs G^* such that their 2-vertex-components generate in section S at least $\alpha/2.n\log n$ bits that have to be compared with the $\alpha/2.n\log n$ bits stored outside section S, which are part of the encoding of the input solution. Assume by contradiction that fewer than $\alpha/2.n\log n$ bits are generated from section S. Then there exist two adversary graphs G_1^* and G_2^* with different 2-vertex-components where the sequence of bits that flows out of section S or into section S is the the same. Thus the chip cannot distinguish between G_1^* and G_2^* and will produce the wrong answer for one of the graphs.

The verification process of the 2-vertex-components does not have to be finished by the time the $(r/3\alpha+1)$st input sequence is read. This input sequence (and all subsequent input sequences) consists of edges of the filler graph only. But at the time the $(r/3\alpha+1)$st input sequence is read, section S has to contain $\alpha/2r.n\log n$ 'free' bits; i.e., bits that can be used to store the edges of this input sequence.

Recall that k is the width of the circumscribing rectangle. Let t be the uniform delay between two successive input sequences. In each cycle $\beta k\log n$ bits can leave or enter section S, for some constant β. Altogether, the first $r/3\alpha$ input sequences generate $\alpha/2.n\log n$ bits initially stored in section S. Those bits either have to leave section S, or wait for the corresponding bits from outside section S before they can be reused. Thus, at the time the $(r/3\alpha+1)$st input sequence is read at most $\beta.r/3\alpha.k.t.\log n$ of the $\alpha/2.n\log n$ bits generated in section S can be reused. Section S contains only $\alpha/2n\log n$ bits, and in order to have $\alpha/2r.n\log n$ 'free' bits we need:

$$\frac{\alpha}{2}n\log n \; - \beta\,\frac{r}{3\alpha}k\;t\;\log n \; + \; \frac{\alpha}{2r}n\log n \;\le\; \frac{\alpha}{2}n\log n$$

The only variable in the inequality that is not fixed is t (α, β and r are constants, and k is fixed by the network). When distributing the amount of time it takes to 'free' $\alpha/2r.n\log n$ bits evenly among the $r/3\alpha$ time intervals (each one of length t) elapsing between the reading of two input sequences, we obtain a lower bound on t. We need $\alpha/2r.n \le \beta.r/3\alpha.k.t$ in order to be able to read the $(r/3\alpha+1)$st input sequence, which gives $t=\Omega(n/k)$. Thus $T=\Omega(n^2/k)$, or $\Omega(e/k)$. This concludes the proof in the case when $2r/\alpha>12r$.

Consider now the case when $12r \ge 2r/\alpha$. Then $\alpha \ge 1/6$ and section S contains $1/12r.n$ PE's and can hold a total of $1/12.n\log n$ bits. In this case we need to read $2r$ input sequences to feed all the 2-vertex-components into section S. Since $1/12.n\log n < \alpha/2.n\log n$, more than half of the bits of the encoding of the input solution describing the connected components of the 2-vertex-components are stored outside section S. By an argument similar to the one used in the first case we obtain $T=\Omega(n^2/k)$, or $\Omega(e/k)$. ▪

Our argument used the fact that the algorithm was where oblivious in a crucial way. One could dislike the idea of using where obliviousness in such an inimical fashion: one can easily agree with the idea of the chip's environment having control of where the input will be read, but one does not expect the environment to act as an adversary. The lower bound, however, does not depend on a possibly bad definition. Consider a more realistic model: the input given in the form of adjacency lists, with the edges arriving into the input ports in lexicographic order. Now, clearly, the environment is not an adversary, yet the same bounds hold, as we show below.

Theorem 3.4 Let N be a network of $O(n)$ area that can be circumscribed by a rectangle of size $k \times n/k$, $1 \le k \le n^{1/2}$. Then solving the verification problem of the ccp on N with input given in the form of adjacency lists requires time $\Omega(n^2/k)$, or, expressed in terms of edges $\Omega(e/k)$.

Proof: We will show how to find a section S and an adversary graph G^* so that all the edges representing 2-vertex-components are fed into section S in a constant number of input sequences. Again, as in the proof of theorem 3.3, the filler edges will be used to fill up input sequences and are read by the PE's outside section S. One has to be more careful with the selection of the filler edges and the order in which all the edges are input, since the lexicographic ordering of all the edges has to be preserved.

Make the cuts through the network as in theorem 3.3. Let S be the section containing $PE_{n/2}$. Let $i_1, i_2, \ldots, i_{\delta n}$ be the indices of the PE's in section S, $\delta = \min(\alpha/2r, 1/12r)$. Thus section S contains $PE_{i_1}, \ldots, PE_{n/2}, \ldots, PE_{i_{\delta n}}$. In the first input sequence PE_{i_1} reads the edge $(2, x_1)$, PE_{i_2} the edge $(4, x_2)$, ... ,$PE_{i_{\delta n}}$ reads the edge $(2\delta n, x_{\delta n})$. The edges $(2i, x_i)$ are the first δn edges of the adjacency list representing 2-vertex-components. See Fig. 3.3, where section S contains PE_1, PE_5, PE_7, $PE_{n/2-1}$, $PE_{n/2}$, ..., and the input for the first $n/2$ PE's in the first input sequence is given. ($PE_i \leftarrow (x, y)$ stands for PE_i reads the edge (x, y)).

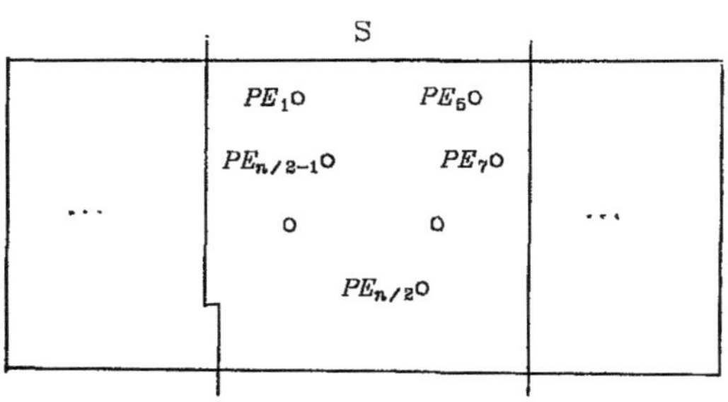

$PE_1 \leftarrow (2, x_1)$
$PE_2 \leftarrow (3, y_1)$, $PE_3 \leftarrow (3, y_2)$, $PE_4 \leftarrow (3, y_3)$ $\quad y_1 < y_2 < y_3$
$PE_5 \leftarrow (4, x_2)$
$PE_6 \leftarrow (5, y_4)$
$PE_7 \leftarrow (6, x_3)$
$PE_8 \leftarrow (7, y_5)$, $PE_9 \leftarrow (7, y_6)$, $\cdots$, $PE_{n/2-2} \leftarrow (7, y_{n/2-5})$
$y_5 < y_6 < \cdots < y_{n/2-5}$
$PE_{n/2-1} \leftarrow (8, x_4)$
$PE_{n/2} \leftarrow (10, x_5)$

$x_i, y_j \in \{n/3+1, \ldots, n\}$
$x_i \ne y_j$, for all i, j
$x_i \ne x_k$ for $i \ne k$

Fig. 3.3
Section S for input in the form of adjacency lists

Let i_p and i_{p+1} be two consecutive indices of PE's in section S; i.e., all PE_k with $i_p < k < i_{p+1}$ are outside section S, $1 \le p \le \delta n - 1$. If $i_p < i_{p+1} - 1$, $1 \le p \le \delta n - 1$, $PE_{i_p+1}, \ldots, PE_{i_{p+1}-1}$, which are the PE's outside section S, have to read edges of the filler graph. They will read $i_{p+1} - i_p - 1$ edges adjacent to vertex $2p+1$ (PE_{i_p} reads the edge $(2p, x_p)$, $PE_{i_{p+1}}$ the edge $(2(p+1), x_{p+1})$).

Since $i_{p+1}-i_p-1 \le n/2$ and vertex $2p+1$ can choose from at least $n/2$ vertices with greater index that are not used in the 2-vertex-components, this can always be done.

If $i_p = i_{p+1}-1$, vertex $2p+1$ is adjacent to no other vertex. In this case the filler graph is not one connected component, which does not affect the proof. Furthermore $PE_1,\dots,PE_{i_1-1}$ read the edges adjacent to vertex 1, and $PE_{i_{\delta n}+1},\dots,PE_n$ read the edges adjacent to vertex $2\delta n+1$.

The succeeding input sequences are formed in the same way: each time the next δn edges of the adjacency list representing 2-vertex-components are read into section S, while the PE's outside section S read the edges of the filler graph as described above.

After all the 2-vertex-components have been read into section S, the $\Omega(n^2)$ edges (i,x_i) of the filler graph, $i>n/3$, $i<x_i$, remain to be read. The same argument as used in the proof of theorem 3.3 yields $T=\Omega(n^2/k)$ for chips of $O(n)$ area with input given in the form of adjacency lists. ▪

3.3. Networks of O(nm) Area

The result of the previous theorems can be generalized to networks of $O(nm)$ area that have $O(np)$ PE's. The area determines the amount of information that can flow in and out section S in one time pulse, the number of PE's determines the number of input sequences required to read n^2 inputs.

Theorem 3.5 Let N be a network of $O(nm)$ area containing $O(np)$ PE's, that can be circumscribed by a rectangle of size $k \times nm/k$, $1 \le k \le (nm)^{1/2}$, $m=o(n)$, $p=o(n)$, $m \ge p$. Then solving the verification problem of the ccp on N with input given in the form of edges requires time $\Omega(n^2/pk)$. When input is given in the form of adjacency lists the time required is $\Omega(n^2/(p^2k)+n/p)$.

Proof: For chips containing $O(np)$ PE's, $p>o(1)$, it is no longer true that an encoding of the solution on the chip requires $\alpha n\log n$ bits of the registers of the PE's. (The use of the indices of the PE's in the encoding or the use of the fact that some bits are not used in the encoding allows the chip to encode with fewer bits.)

When the graph G^* is given in the form of edges consider a section of the chip containing $\alpha/2r.n$ PE's. Such a section S contains $\alpha/2.n\log n$ bits and by lemma 3.2 at most half of the information about the encoding of the solution can be stored in S. The 'other half' of the encoding is stored outside section S. Even when the 'other half' is encoded by the PE's outside section S using $o(\alpha/2.n\log n)$ bits, at least $\alpha/2.n\log n$ bits are required to send this information into section S. Section S is obtained by making $max(2pr/\alpha-1, 12pr-1)$ cuts through the network so that each section between two cuts contains $min(\alpha/2r.n, 1/12r.n)$ PE's. Input all the edges representing 2-vertex-components into section S in a constant number of input sequences. Choose G^* as in the proof of theorem 3.3 and obtain $T=\Omega(n^2/np.n/k) = \Omega(n^2/pk)$, $1 \le k \le (nm)^{1/2}$, when the input is given in the form of edges.

Consider now the case when the graph G^* is given in the form of adjacency lists. Again, as in the proof of theorem 3.4, it must be possible to feed the PE's outside a section S with filler edges while preserving the lexicographic ordering of the input edges. Let PE_{i_k} and $PE_{i_{k+1}}$ be two succeeding PE's in section S, $i_k<i_{k+1}$ and for no i_p, $i_k<i_p<i_{k+1}$, PE_{i_p} is in section S. In theorem 3.4 we never needed to fill in more than $n/2$ edges adjacent to one vertex between PE_{i_k} and $PE_{i_{k+1}}$. Assume $PE_{np/2}$ to be in section S, then we must now be able to fill in $np/2$ edges between PE_{i_k} and $PE_{i_{k+1}}$. Since it is not possible to have $np/2$ edges adjacent to one vertex, we define the modified adversary graph G_m^*.

G_m^* consists of $n/6p$ 2-vertex-components and a filler graph on $n-2n/6p = n(1-1/3p)$ vertices. $E_m^* = \{(i(p+1),x_i) \mid 1 \le i \le n/6p,\ n(p+1)/6p<x_i \le n\} \cup E'$. Let V_x be the set of vertices greater than $n(p+1)/6p$ not used in the 2-vertex components. Then

$E' \subseteq \{((i-1)p+i+j, x_{ij}) \mid 1 \le i \le n/6p,\ 0 \le j \le p-1,\ x_{ij} \in V_x\} \cup V_x \times V_x$. Between two succeeding 2-vertex-components $(i(p+1), x_i)$ and $((i+1)(p+1), x_{i+1})$ in the adjacency list we can have the edges adjacent to $(i+1)(p+1)-i(p+1)-1 = p$ vertices. This allows us to fill up the input sequences correctly (each one of the p vertices can be adjacent to at least $n/2$ vertices with higher index not used in the 2-vertex-components). It can be shown that $\alpha/p.n\log n$ bits are needed for the encoding of the 2-vertex-components of G_m^*.

Make cuts through the network, so that each section between two cuts contains $\alpha/2pr.n$ PE's Choose as section S the section containing $PE_{np/2}$. By applying the ideas of theorem 3.3 and theorem 3.4 we obtain $t=\Omega(n/kp)$. Since n/p time pulses are needed to read all the input sequences T = $\Omega(n^2/np.n/kp + n/p) = \Omega(n^2/p^2k+n/p)$, which proves theorem 3.5. ▪

Note that for $p>O(1)$ the lower bound achieved for input in the form of adjacency lists is weaker than the one for edges. But we don't know of an algorithm that achieves a better time when the input is in the form of adjacency lists than when input is in the form of edges.

The reader may want to compare our results with those reported in [J], where a different technique, based on 'mutual information transmission' arguments (as in [JK] and [Y]) was used to obtain lower bounds for the ccp on a different VLSI model. The important difference between the models used in [J] and ours is that the model in [J] assumes that the information about the previous input sequence is completely processed at the time a new input sequence is read. Under this assumption the lower bounds hold also for input in the form of an adjacency matrix, which we were not able to prove in our model. In our model, a new technique will be necessary for a lower bound proof, since the idea of using the verification problem to obtain lower bounds for the ccp cannot be used for input in the form of an adjacency matrix, as verification is easier than computation for this form of input.

The lower bounds proven in theorem 3.4 and 3.5 hold even if the verification is allowed to be approximate: given as input an encoding of the solution and a graph G the answer to the verification problem is 1 if and only if G contains at most δn vertices that are in different connected components than the ones specified in the solution (i.e., a 1 is produced if the connected components of G are 'close' to the ones of the given solution). For the proofs of the approximate verification we refer to [H1].

3.4. Verifying is no harder than Computing

In a sequential model of computation, verification of problems with unique solutions is never harder than computing, since one can always verify by computing the actual solution and comparing it with the given input solution. In a parallel setting, this argument does not hold: both the input solution and the computed solution will be scattered among different processing elements. Nevertheless, we show that the lower bounds obtained for the verification problem of the ccp hold also for the ccp; i.e., computing the connected components is at least as hard as verifying them. For all networks solving the ccp we assume that the solution describing the connected components can be stored entirely within the network; i.e., length of the solution $\le A.\log n$, where A is the area of the network. This seems to be a reasonable assumption. There are graphs where the connected components cannot be determined until all the input has been read, and a description of the connected components formed so far has to be stored in the network in order to solve the ccp correctly. For example, networks of $O(n)$ area that output the connected components in form of an $n \times n$ adjacency matrix have to keep a description of the connected components of length $O(n\log n)$ bits in the network before generating the matrix.

Assume network N computes the connected components. We show how to construct a new network N_v that verifys the connected components and whose time and area requirements differ from network N only by a constant factor. Network N_v uses N as a subnetwork.

Theorem 3.6 Let N be a network of area A, $A=\Omega(n)$, that solves the ccp in time T. Then there exists a network N_v of area $\Theta(A)$ solving the verification problem of the ccp in time $\Theta(T)$.

Proof: Network N has area A and produces the solution to the ccp in form of an encoding E in time T. Since $A=\Omega(n)$ we can assume that one PE produces at most $\log n$ bits of the solution.

Let $\mathcal{N}(A, T, E_v)$ be the class of networks solving the verification problem of the ccp in time $O(T)$ on a network of area $O(A)$ when the input solution is given in the form of the encoding E_v. We show that this class is not empty and outline how to construct a network $N_v \in \mathcal{N}$ that uses network N as a subnetwork.

Network N_v contains the same number of PE's and the same interconnections as network N, and each PE contains an additional register. Let the encoding of the ~solution read by the network N_v be of the same form as the encoding of the solution generated by the network N; i.e., $E_v=E$. Input the bits of E into those PE's of the network N that will contain the corresponding output bits of the solution of the ccp generated by the algorithm for the ccp. After storing the input solution in the additional register run the algorithm for the ccp. When all the output bits have been generated by the algorithm compare in each PE the generated encoding with the encoding given as input and set a flag in the PE in case of inequality.

Assume w.l.o.g. that PE_1 produces the 0/1 answer to the verification problem. Then PE_1 produces a 0 if one (or more) flags have been set to 0. Let each PE that contains a set flag send the value of its flag to PE_1. If two or more flags meet at a PE on the path to PE_1, the 'and' of all the incoming flags is produced and send to PE_1. (Since each PE is connected only to a constant number of other PE's, this step takes constant time.) It can easily be shown that in any network N_v, where each PE is needed at some point during the computation, the number of steps required to generate the connected components is larger than the longest shortest distance between any two PE's. Thus the area (and the time) to determine the answer to the verification problem does not increase the time (and area) needed to solve the ccp by more than a constant factor, and the theorem follows. ▪

Acknowledgements

We would like to thank Helmut Alt, Thomas Lengauer and Joseph Ja'Ja' for reading the early version of this paper and for making helpful suggestions.

References

[AA] H. Abelson, P. Andreae, 'Information Transfer and Area-Time Tradeoffs for VLSI Multiplication', CACM, Vol. 23, pp 20-23, Jan. 1980.

[AK] M.J. Atallah, S.R. Kosaraju, 'Graph Problems on a Mesh-Connected Processor Array', Proc. of the 14-th Ann. Symp. on Th. of Comp., pp 345-353, 1982.

[BK] R.P. Brent, H.T. Kung, 'The Area-Time Complexity of Binary Multiplication', JACM, Vol.28, pp 521-534, July 1981.

[CM] B. Chazelle, L. Monier, 'A Model of Computation for VLSI with Related Complexity Results', 13-th Ann. Symp. on Th. of Comp., pp 318-325, 1981.

[FJ] G.N. Frederickson, D.B. Johnson, 'Generalized Selection and Ranking: Sorted Matrices', Tech. Report of The Pennsylvania State University, CS-81-12, 1981.

[GKT] L.J. Guibas, H.T. Kung, C.D. Thompson, 'Direct VLSI Implementations for Combinatorial Algorithms', Proc. of Conf. VLSI Tech. Design and Fabrication, Caltech 1979.

[H1] S.E. Hambrusch, 'The Complexity of Graph Problems on VLSI', Ph.D. thesis, The Pennsylvania State University, 1982.

[H2] S.E. Hambrusch, 'VLSI Algorithms for the Connected Components Problem', SIAM J. on Computing, Vol. 12, No. 2, May 1983.

[J] J. Ja'Ja', 'The VLSI Complexity of Graph Problems', Tech. Report of The Pennsylvania State University, CS-81-25, October 1981.

[JK] J. Ja'Ja', V.K. Kumar, 'Information Transfer in Distributed Computing with Applications to VLSI', Tech. Report of The Pennsylvania State University, CS-81-14, 1981.

[KT] H.T. Kung, C.E. Leiserson, 'Systolic Arrays for VLSI', appeared in Introduction to VLSI Systems', C. Mead, L. Conway, Addison-Wesley, pp 260-292, 1980.

[LS] R.J. Lipton, R.S. Sedgewick, 'Lower Bounds for VLSI', 13-th Ann. Symp. on Th. of Comp., pp 300-307, 1981.

[LV] R.J. Lipton, J. Valdes, 'Census Function: An Approach to VLSI Upper Bounds', Proc. of the 22-nd Ann. Symp. on Found. of Comp. Sc., pp 13-22, 1981.

[MC] C. Mead, L. Conway, Introduction to VLSI Systems, Addison-Wesley, 1980.

[NMB] D. Nath, S.N. Maheshwari, P.C.P. Bhatt, 'Efficient VLSI Networks for Parallel Processing based on Orthogonal Trees', Techn. Report of the Indian Inst. of Techn., Delhi, April 1981.

[P] W. Paul, 'On Heads versus Tapes', 22-nd Ann. Symp. on Found. of Comp. Sc., pp 68-73, 1981.

[PSS] W. Paul, J. Seiferas, J. Simon, 'An Information Theoretic Approach to Time Bounds on On-line Computation', 12-th Ann. Symp. on Th. of Comp., pp 357-367, 1980.

[PV] F.P. Preparata, J.E. Vuillemin, 'The Cube Connected Cycles: a Versatile Network for Parallel Computation', Proc. of 20-th annual IEEE FOCS Conf., pp 140-147, 1979.

[S] L. Snyder, 'Overview of the CHiP Computer', in John P. Gray, VLSI 1981, pp 237-246, Academic Press, 1981.

[T] C.D. Thompson, 'Area-Time Complexity for VLSI', 11-th Ann. Symp. on Th. of Comp., pp 81-88, 1979.

[V] J.E. Vuillemin, 'A Combinatorial Limit to the Computing Power of VLSI Circuits', 21-st Ann. Symp. on Found. of Comp. Sc., pp 294-300, 1980.

[Y] A. Yao, 'Some Complexity Questions related to Distributed Computing', Proc. 11-th Ann. Symp. on Th. of Comp., pp 209-213, 1979.

Concurrent Probabilistic Program, or: How to Schedule if You Must

Sergiu Hart and Micha Sharir(*)
School of Mathematical Sciences
Tel-Aviv University

ABSTRACT: Given a finite set of concurrent processes executing asynchronously, such that each process may use randomization in its course of execution, we consider the problem of computing the worst-case probability for the program which consists of these processes to terminate (i.e. to converge to a specified set of common goal states), under a fair interleaving scheduling of the processes. Several methods for computing this probability are presented, and characterizations of the special case in which this probability is 1 are derived. Specializations of these characterizations to the case of deterministic and nondeterministic programs are also discussed.

INTRODUCTION.

This paper continues the study, begun in [HSP], of termination of concurrent probabilistic programs. The model that we assume is that of a finite set K of concurrent processes, each of which is allowed to use randomization, i.e., draw randomly according to fixed probability distributions. These processes execute asynchronously, and we consider each process $k \in K$ as a discrete Markov chain (with stationary transition probability matrix P^k) on the set I of common execution states. The overall execution behavior of these processes is described in terms of the interleaving pattern in which they are scheduled by some imaginary scheduler σ. Each process k scheduled at a state i can reach more than one subsequent state, so that to specify σ we need to consider all these transitions simultaneously. We may therefore represent σ as a tree (referred to as the execution-tree or the transition-tree induced by σ) each of whose nodes is labeled by a pair (i,k), where $i \in I$ is the state reached at that node, and where $k \in K$ is the process to be scheduled there next. A node (i_1,k_1) will be a son of (i,k) in the tree if there exists a positive transition probability of reaching i_1 from i under a single execution step of process k, and if process k_1 will be next scheduled at i_1, provided that this transition has indeed taken place.

(*) Work by the second author on this paper has been supported in part by the Bat-Sheva Fund at Tel-Aviv University, and by ONR Grant N00014-75-C-0571 at the Courant Institute.

Given such a σ, it induces a probability measure μ_σ on the space of all infinite sequences of states, such that the μ_σ-measure of each cylinder consisting of all sequences having a prescribed initial segment π_n is the product of all transition probabilities along the path in the transition tree of σ going in order through the states of π_n (or 0 if no such path exists). We consider here general schedules σ of this sort, with the sole restriction that they be fair, meaning that no process stops being scheduled; i.e.,that the μ_σ-measure of the set of all tree paths on which each process $k \in K$ is scheduled infinitely often is 1. (Strictly speaking, this is called impartiality in [LPS]; however, since we assume that processes are continuously enabled, there is no real distinction between these two notions.)

This model is discussed and justified more fully in [HSP]. We note that it coincides with the models assumed by Rabin in [Ra_2], by Lehmann and Rabin in [LR], and is similar to that used by Dubins and Savage [DS] in their study of optimal gambling strategies (although they do not require fairness). It does differ though, from various other models used in the literature (cf. [Ra1], [RS1], [RS2]). The crucial distinction between these models lies in the degree to which the imaginary scheduler can "base its scheduling decisions" on the outcome of random draws made by the processes, or, more generally on their internal states. These and other scheduling models used in the literature are more restrictive and usually correspond to situations in which the execution time of a single step of a process is independent of its current state and of the outcome of the random draws it has made. Our model is more general, and allows for such dependence, thereby being a more realistic model for general concurrent or distributed probabilistic execution. Moreover, properties established for concurrent probabilistic programs under our model will continue to hold under the more restrictive models mentioned above, but not necessarily vice-versa (for example, Rabin's synchronization algorithm described in [Ra1] is shown in [HSP] to fail in our model.)

In the preceding paper [HSP], we have analyzed termination of concurrent probabilistic programs having a finite state space. We have obtained there necessary and sufficient conditions for such a program to reach (with probability 1) a given set X of goal states from some initial state, under any fair schedule. These conditions can be checked mechanically, and are independent of the particular values of nonzero transition probabilities of the processes involved.

In this paper we generalize and extend these results to programs with infinite state spaces. As in the case of a single Markov chain, the analysis of program termination is much more complicated in the general case, and becomes dependent upon the actual values of the nonzero transition probabilities involved. The basic problem that we treat in this paper is the computation of the function ω on the set of states I, where, for each $i \in I$, $\varphi(i)$ is the minimum probability of program termination starting at state i, under any fair schedule. We establish various properties and characterizations of φ, and derive from them several techniques for the calculation of this function. This theorey enables us to gain a better understanding of the structure of the (worst-case) convergence of the program towards termination. For example, one can interpret this convergence process as a game between the program and the scheduler, in which each move of the program requires the scheduler to schedule one of the processes, and the scheduler responds by scheduling this process eventually, but only after shceduling some other processes prior to it, in a way which would lower as much a possible the program's probability to terminate. We show that the optimal payoff for the program in this game is the function φ, provided that the game is long enough, where the length of such a game is measured by some (infinite) ordinal.

The various characterizations of φ are next used to obtain necessary and sufficient conditions for the special case $\varphi \equiv 1$ (i.e. for worst-case almost-sure termination from any initial state) to hold. Some of these conditions generalize similar conditions given in the preceding paper [HSP] for programs with finite state spaces. These characterizations of program termination are also specialized to the case in which the processes are deterministic or nondeterministic. Some of the derived characterizations are shown to reduce to the conditions given by Lehmann, Pnueli and Stavi [LPS] for the termination of nondeterministic programs, while others appear to be new. The results of this paper are exemplified on several running sample programs. The techiques developed in this paper can be immediately interpreted as (sound and complete) proof methods for almost sure program termination (although we do not state them explicitly as such), and can be used to prove various properties of concurrent probabilistic algorithms, e.g., freedom from deadlock or from lockout of synchronization protocols.

PRELIMINARY RESULTS

We go on to describe the main results of this paper in more detail. For each $i \in I$ let $\Sigma(i)$ (resp. $\Sigma F(i)$) denote the set of all (infinite) schedules (resp. fair schedules) starting at i, and let $H^*(i)$ denote the set of all infinite execution paths starting at i. Without loss of generality, we assume that the goal set X is a set of absorbing states (i.e., once $j \in X$ is reached, the program stays at j forever). The function φ that we wish to compute is defined as

$$\varphi(i) = \inf_{\sigma\in\Sigma F(i)} E_\sigma(\chi_X) = \inf_{\sigma\in\Sigma F(i)} \mu_\sigma \text{ (X is eventually reached)}$$

where χ_X, the characteristic functions of X, is extended to $H^*(i)$, so that $\chi_X(\pi)$ is 1 if X is ever reached along π, and is 0 otherwise, and where $E_\sigma(\chi_X)$ is the expectation of this extended function under μ_σ. Note that $\varphi(i) = 1$ iff the program terminates a.s. from i under any fair schedule.

Proposition 1: (a) $0 \leq \varphi \leq 1$ and $\varphi|_X \equiv 1$

(b) $\varphi(i) = \min_{k \in K}(P^k\varphi)(i)$, for each $i \in I$.

Sketch of Proof: (a) is trivial. To prove (b), use the fact that each $\sigma \in \Sigma F(i)$ is equivalent to scheduling some $k \in K$ at i, and continuing after each successor state j of i under k with some $\sigma_j \in \Sigma F(j)$. The inequality $\leq$ in (b) is then obvious; to prove the converse inequality, take a sequence σ_n of schedules in $\Sigma F(i)$ such that μ_{σ_n} (X reached) $\rightarrow \varphi(i)$, and take $k \in K$ to be a process which is scheduled at the starting state i by infinitely many σ_n's.

Extending standard terminology in Markov chain theory, we call functions satisfying (b) min-harmonic functions; these functions are special case of the more general subharmonic functions, i.e., functions ψ satisfying $\psi(i) \leq (P^k\psi)(i)$, for each $k \in K$, $i \in I$.

Unlike the case of a single process (see e.g., [SPH1]) (i.e., sequential program) φ is not the smallest function satisfying (a) and (b) above, because of our restriction to fair schedules only. Indeed, consider the following simple example: Let $I = \{0,1\}$, $X = \{0\}$, and $K = \{1,2\}$, with the nonzero transition probabilities $p^1_{1,0} = p^2_{1,1} = 1$. Obviously, any fair execution of this program brings it into X with certainty, so that $\varphi \equiv 1$, yet the function $\psi(0) = 1$, $\psi(1) = 0$ is a smaller nonnegative min-harmonic function which is 1 on X.

Theorem 2 (Zero-One Law): $\inf_{i \in I} \varphi(i)$ is either 0 or 1. Moreover, for each $i \in I$, $\sigma \in \Sigma F(i)$ and $n \geq 0$ define f_n on $H^*(i)$ by putting $f_n(\pi) = \varphi(i_n)$, where i_n is the n-th state along π. Then f_n converges μ_σ- a.s. to the characteristic function χ_X of X.

Proof: Let $i \in I$ and $\sigma \in \Sigma F(i)$ be given. We will use the following terminology: For each $n \geq 0$, τ_n denotes the first n steps of σ. For each $\pi \in H^*(i)$ and each $n \geq 0$ we denote by σ_{π_n} the restriction of σ to the subtree rooted at i_n. The sub-harmonicity of φ implies that the sequence $\{f_n\}$ is a submartingale*) on $H^*(i)$. Since $0 \leq f_n \leq 1$ for each $n \geq 0$, it follows from the (sub)martingale convergence theorem that $\{f_n\}$ converges μ_σ- a.s. to a limit f_∞. Then

*) i.e., for all $n \geq 0$, $E_\sigma(f_{n+1}|\pi_n) \geq f_n$, where π_n is any history of length n with $\mu_\sigma(\pi_n) > 0$.

for each $n \geq 0$,

$$E_\sigma(\chi_X) = E_{\tau_n}(E_{\sigma_{\pi_n}}(\chi_X)) \geq E_{\tau_n}(\varphi) = E_\sigma(f_n)$$

(since each σ_{π_n} is fair). Letting $n \to \infty$, we obtain

$$E_\sigma(\chi_X) \geq E_\sigma(f_\infty) \geq 1.\ \mu_\sigma\{\pi : f_\infty(\pi) = 1\}.$$

But for each $\pi \in H^*(i)$, if X is ever reached along π then $f_n(\pi) = \varphi(i_n) = 1$ for all sufficiently large n, so that $f_\infty(\pi) = 1$. Thus

$$\mu_\sigma\{\pi : f_\infty(\pi) = 1\} \geq \mu_\sigma\{\pi : X \text{ reached along } \pi\} = E_\sigma(\chi_X).$$

Therefore we must have equalities throughout; that is

$$E_\sigma(\chi_X) = E_\sigma(f_\infty) = \mu_\sigma\{\pi : f_\infty(\pi) = 1\} .$$

This, however, implies that almost everywhere f_∞ **is** either 0 or 1, and that $f_\infty(\pi) = 1$ if and only if X is ever reached along π. The zero-one law is now immediate, because if φ is not identically 1, take $i \in I$, $\sigma \in \Sigma F(i)$ such that $E_\sigma(\chi_X) = c < 1$. Then $\varphi(i_n) \to 0$ on a set of paths whose μ_σ-measure is $1 - c > 0$, thus there exist states with arbitrarily small φ, or $\inf_{i \in I} \varphi(i) = 0$. Q.E.D.

φ- ITERATES

Next we establish some useful characterizations of φ, which will also facilitate methods for its computation. For each $i \in I$ let $T(i)$ denote the class of all subschedules starting at i; these are initial portions of schedules in $\Sigma(i)$ which contain only a finite segment of almost every execution path. Special subclasses of $T(i)$ are $T(i,k)$, $k \in K$, which consist of those subschedules which end immediately after scheduling k. Define operators Q^k, $k \in K$, and Q on the space of bounded real functions on I by

$$(Q^k\alpha)(i) = \inf_{\tau \in T(i,k)} E_\tau(\alpha), \quad i \in I,$$

where $E_\tau(\alpha)$ is the expectation of α over its values at the end states of τ, and

$$(Q\alpha)(i) = \max_{k \in K} (Q^k\alpha)(i)$$

The operators Q^k and Q are all monotone, positively homogeneous, and map the functions 0 and 1 to themselves. Moreover, it is easily seen that

Lemma 3: $Q^k\alpha$ is the largest subharmonic function which does not exceed $P^k\alpha$.

Intuitively, $(Q^k\alpha)(i)$ is the minimum expected value of α after an a.s. finite portion of program execution which ends just after scheduling k. We will use these operators to construct a transfinite sequence of functions in I, called the φ-iterates, whose limit will be shown to be φ. These functions are denoted γ_a^k, $k \in K$, and γ_a, where a is an ordinal, and are defined as follows:

$$\gamma_0^k = \gamma_0 = \chi_X;$$

$$\gamma_{a+1}^k = Q^k\gamma_a, \quad k \in K, \ a \text{ an ordinal};$$

$$\gamma_a^k = \sup_{b<a} \gamma_b^k, \quad k \in K, \ \text{for limit ordinals } a;$$

$$\gamma_a = \max_{k\in K} \gamma_a^k, \quad \text{for each ordinal } a.$$

The sequences $\{\gamma_a^k\}_{a\geq 0}$, $k \in K$, and $\{\gamma_a\}_{a\geq 0}$ are all non-decreasing and bounded between 0 and 1 (note that we also have $\gamma_{a+1} = Q\gamma_a$ for any a, and $\gamma_a = \sup_{b<a} \gamma_b$ for limit ordinals a). Thus γ_a converges to a limit γ which is attained at some ordinal c, called the convergence ordinal of the program, i.e., $\gamma = \gamma_c$.

Theorem 4: $\gamma = \varphi$.

The proof of this theorem is quite involved, and uses methods from martingale theory. An intuitive interpretation of this theorem is as follows: $\gamma_a(i)$ is equal to the minmax value of a two-person zero-sum game $\Gamma_a(i)$ between "the program", whose goal is to reach X, and "the scheduler", whose goal is to prevent the program from reaching X. $\Gamma_a(i)$ is played according to the following transfinite inductive rules:

(a) $\Gamma_0(i)$ is an "empty" game. The program receives a payoff of 1 unit from the scheduler if $i \in X$, and 0 otherwise.

(b) If a is not a limit ordinal, say $a = b+1$, the program chooses some $k \in K$ and requires the scheduler to schedule k. The scheduler must do so eventually a.s., but can schedule other processes in between so as to prevent the program from reaching X as much as possible. In other words, the scheduler responds by choosing some subschedule τ in $T(i,k)$ and runs the program according to τ. When τ ends at some state j, the game continues as $\Gamma_b(j)$ (we refer to this stage of the game as imposing one fairness constraint on the scheduler.)

(c) If a is a limit ordinal, the program chooses some ordinal $b < a$, and the game continues as $\Gamma_b(i)$.

It is easily seen that each play of any of the games $\Gamma_a(i)$ consists of finitely many steps, always ending at playing Γ_o at some state; it also follows by definition that the value (expected payoff) of the game $\Gamma_a(i)$ is $\gamma_a(i)$. Theorem 4 therefore implies that if the program imposes "sufficiently many" fairness constraints on the scheduler, it can achieve a payoff equal to φ, i.e., realize the (worst-case) effect of infinite (adversary) fair schedules. To see that this result is not at all obvious, we will exhibit later a simple 2-process deterministic program in which $\varphi = \gamma_{\omega+1} > \gamma_\omega$.

Proof of Theorem 4: We first sketch the proof of the "easier" ineqality $\gamma \leq \varphi$. This proof consists of showing the following claims:

I. Each of the φ-iterates γ_a^k and γ_a is subharmonic (use transfinite induction and Lemma 3).

II. $Q^k\varphi \leq \varphi$ for each $k \in K$ (follows from the definitions of Q^k and φ).

III. $\varphi = Q\varphi = Q^k\varphi$ for each $k \in K$ (use II, Lemma 3, and subharmonicity of φ).

IV. $\gamma \leq \varphi$ (prove that $\gamma_a \leq \varphi$ for all a, using transfinite induction, I and III).

To prove the converse inequality $\varphi \leq \gamma$ we note that, since $\gamma = \max_{k\in K} Q^k\gamma$, we have

$$(*)\qquad \gamma(i) \geq \inf_{\tau\in T(i,k)} E_\tau(\gamma), \qquad i \in I,\ k \in K.$$

Let $i \in I$ be given. Choose $\varepsilon > 0$ and a sequence $\varepsilon_n \downarrow 0$ such that $\sum_n \varepsilon_n = \varepsilon$. Let $\{k_n\}_{n\geq 1}$ be a fixed sequence of processes in which each $k \in K$ appears infinitely many times. We will use (*) to construct a fair schedule σ starting at i by building it layer-by-layer from subschedules, as follows: Suppose that the first n layers of σ have already been constructed, the union of which being some subschedule τ_n starting at i (initially, τ_o is "empty"). The $(n+1)$-th layer of σ is defined by appending to τ_n at each of its end-nodes j a subschedule $\rho_j \in T(j, k_{n+1})$ such that $\gamma(j) \geq E_{\rho_j}(\gamma) - \varepsilon_n$ (such a subschedule exists by (*)). Repeating this process inductively, we obtain the required (infinite) schedule σ, which is fair by our choice of the sequence $\{k_n\}_{n\geq 1}$.

Let $\{N_n\}_{n\geq 0}$ be the increasing sequence of stopping times defined by our construction; namely, the n-th layer (i.e., τ_n) ends at N_n (in particular $N_o \equiv 0$). For each $n \geq 0$ define the function

$$g_n(\pi) = \gamma(\pi_{N_n}), \qquad \pi \in H^*(i);$$

in particular, $g_o \equiv \gamma(i)$. By the choice of the subschedules ρ_j we have

(**) $\quad g_n \geq E_\sigma(g_{n+1} \mid \pi_{N_n}) - \varepsilon_{n+1}, \qquad n \geq 0.$

Hence, the sequence of functions $\{g'_n\}_{n\geq 0}$ given by

$$g'_n \equiv g_n - \sum_{m=1}^{n} \varepsilon_m, \qquad n \geq 0$$

forms a supermartingale, which is bounded between 1 and $-\varepsilon$. Hence it converges almost surely to a limit g'_∞, so that $\{g_n\}$ also converges almost surely to the function

$$g_\infty \equiv g'_\infty + \sum_{m=1}^{\infty} \varepsilon_m = g'_\infty + \varepsilon.$$

Note that $\gamma|_X \equiv 1$; thus, if X is reached along π, then $g_\infty(\pi) = 1$, because for all sufficiently large n we will have $g_n(\pi) = 1$. Hence, by (**),

$$\gamma(i) = g'_0 \geq E_\sigma(g'_\infty) = E_\sigma(g_\infty) - \varepsilon \geq \mu_\sigma(g_\infty = 1) - \varepsilon$$

$$\geq \mu_\sigma(X \text{ is reached}) - \varepsilon = E_\sigma(\chi_X) - \varepsilon \geq \varphi(i) - \varepsilon.$$

Since ε was arbitrary, the proof is complete. Q.E.D.

Example: Let $K = \{1,2\}$, and let $I = I_1 \cup I_2$, where $I_1 = N \times \{1\}$, $I_2 = N \times \{2\}$, and $X = \{(0,1)\}$. The nonzero transition probabilities are

$$p^1_{(n,1),(n-1,1)} = p^2_{(n,1),(n,1)} = 1 \qquad n > 0;$$

$$p^1_{(n,2),(n+1,2)} = p^2_{(n,2),(n,1)} = 1, \qquad n \geq 0.$$

These transitions are displayed in the following diagram:

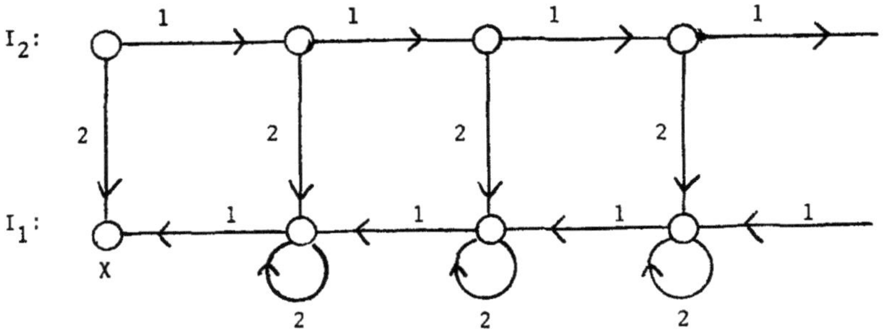

Let us first comupte the φ-iterates on I_1. We claim that for each integer n

$$\gamma_n(i,1) = \begin{cases} 0 & i \geq n \\ 1 & i < n \end{cases}, \quad i \in N$$

This is easily checked by induction on n: For $n = 0, \gamma_0 = \chi_X$ as required. Suppose that γ_n has this form. Then $(Q^2\gamma_n)(i,1) = \gamma_n(i,1)$ and $(Q^1\gamma_n)(i,1) = \gamma_n(i-1,1)$, where in both cases the subschedule that yields the required infimum is the corresponding trivial one-step subschedule. It follows that γ_{n+1} has the asserted form on I_1. By definition of γ_ω we thus have

$$\gamma_\omega(i,1) = 1, \qquad i \in N.$$

Next consider I_2: We claim that $\gamma_n(i,2) = 0$ for each $i,n \in N$. This is again proven by induction on n: Suppose it is true for some $n \in N$. Then, scheduling process 1 immediately at $(i,2)$ yields $(Q^1\gamma_n)(i,2) = \gamma_n(i+1,2) = 0$. On the other hand, to obtain $(Q^2\gamma_n)(i,2)$, schedule process 1 sufficiently many times so as to reach a state $(j,2)$ with $j \geq n$, and then schedule process 2, obtaining $\gamma_n(j,1)=0$. Hence $(Q^2\gamma_n)(i,2) = 0$, so that $\gamma_{n+1}(i,2) = 0$. Thus

$$\gamma_\omega(i,2) = 0, \qquad i \in N.$$

But $\gamma_{\omega+1} = Q\gamma_\omega > \gamma_\omega$. Indeed, for each $(i,2) \in I_2$ we have

$$\gamma_{\omega+1}(i,2) = (Q\gamma_\omega)(i,2) = (Q^2\gamma_\omega)(i,2) = \gamma_\omega(j,1) = 1 \qquad (\text{where} \quad j \geq i).$$

Thus $\varphi = \gamma_{\omega+1} \equiv 1$, and convergence of the φ-iterates is attained at the ordinal $\omega+1$.

CHARACTERIZATIONS OF φ

So far, in order to compute φ, we need to compute the transfinite sequence of the φ-iterates, which may be a difficult task in practice. We can provide better (though less "constructive") methods of computing φ, by the following theorem (the first part of which is an immediate corollary to Theorem 4):

Theorem 5: (a) φ is the smallest fixpoint, which is $\geq \chi_X$, of the operator Q.
(b) φ is the smallest simultaneous fixpoint, which is $\geq \chi_X$, of all the operators Q^k, $k \in K$.

Now the condition $\varphi = Q^k\varphi$ can be restated as follows: Since φ is subharmonic (so that $\varphi \leq P^k\varphi$) and since, by Lemma 3, $Q^k\varphi$ is the largest subharmonic function $\leq P^k\varphi$, we obtain the following

Corollary 6: φ is the smallest subharmonic (or min-harmonic) function which is $\geq \chi_X$, and which satisfies the following property:

(A) For each $k \in K$, the only subharmonic function lying between φ and $P^k\varphi$ is φ itself.

We demonstrate the use of Corollary 6 in the following

Example: Let $K = 1,2$. The following program arises in an analysis of freedom from lockout in the following simple synchronization protocol (cf., [HSP], example 1): In this example, the two processes use a "test-and-set" shared variable c, having 3 possible values: 0 - designating a neutral state, and j - a state in which process j will enter its critical section, $j = 1,2$. The code for process j is

```
T : --trying region--
    if  c = j  then  go to X
    else  if  c=0  then  c: = Random (1,2)  fi; go to  T
    fi
X:  -- critical region --
    c: = 0; go to  T
```

Let X denote the state in which process 1 has entered its critical section. Then only four additional states need be considered, each of which is denoted as (c,ℓ_1,ℓ_2) where c is the value of the shared variable, and where $\ell_j = T$ or X denote the location in process j, $j = 1,2$. The states are

$$i_1 = (1,T,T); \quad i_2 = (0,T,T); \quad i_3 = (2,T,X); \quad i_4 = (2,T,T)$$

The nonzero transition probabilities are

$$P^1_{i_1,X} = P^2_{i_1,i_1} = P^1_{i_3,i_3} = P^2_{i_3,i_2} = P^1_{i_4,i_4} = P^2_{i_4,i_3} = 1$$

$$P^1_{i_2,i_1} = P^1_{i_2,i_4} = P^2_{i_2,i_1} = P^2_{i_2,i_4} = \frac{1}{2}$$

To compute φ, we first write down the form of the general subharmonic function which is 1 on X. Such a function $\alpha = (\alpha_1,\alpha_2,\alpha_3,\alpha_4)$ (where α_t is a shorthand for $\alpha(i_t)$, $1 \leq t \leq 4$) must satisfy

$$\alpha_1 \leq 1; \quad \alpha_2 \leq \tfrac{1}{2}\alpha_1 + \tfrac{1}{2}\alpha_4 \; ; \quad \alpha_3 \leq \alpha_2 \; ; \quad \alpha_4 \leq \alpha_3.$$

Next, we spell out condition (A) for such an α: First consider $k=1$. It is easily checked that the function

$$P^1\alpha = (1, \tfrac{1}{2}\alpha_1 + \tfrac{1}{2}\alpha_4, \alpha_3, \alpha_4)$$

is also subharmonic. Hence we must have $\alpha = P^1\alpha$, i.e.

$$\alpha_1 = 1; \qquad \alpha_2 = \frac{1}{2}\alpha_1 + \frac{1}{2}\alpha_4 = \frac{1}{2} + \frac{1}{2}\alpha_4$$

Similarly, for $k = 2$ we have

$$P^2\alpha = (\alpha_1, \frac{1}{2}\alpha_1 + \frac{1}{2}\alpha_4, \alpha_2, \alpha_3),$$

which is also seen to be subharmonic. Hence $\alpha = P^2\alpha$, i.e.

$$\alpha_2 = \alpha_3; \quad \alpha_3 = \alpha_4.$$

Thus we have $\alpha_1 = \alpha_2 = \alpha_3 = \alpha_4 = 1$. That is, the only -- and thus, the smallest-- subharmonic function $\geq \chi_X$ satifying (A) is $\varphi \equiv 1$.

Example ("The Two Combs"): Let $K = \{1,2\}$, $I = X \cup Z$, (Z = integers), and let the nonzero transition probabilities be

$$\begin{aligned} P^1_{n,n+1} &= p_n, & P^1_{n,X} &= p'_n = 1 - p_n \\ P^2_{n,n-1} &= q_n, & P^2_{n,X} &= q'_n = 1 - q_n \end{aligned} \qquad n \in Z$$

To avoid degeneracy, we assume that $0 < p_n q_{n+1} < 1$ for each $n \in Z$. A fairly involved analysis, based on Corollary 6, yields the following computation of φ: Put

$$\hat{P}_n = \prod_{m=n}^{\infty} p_m; \quad \hat{Q}_n = \prod_{m=-\infty}^{n} q_m; \qquad n \in Z$$

and consider the following thwo conditions:

(C^+) $\quad \prod_{n>0} p_n > 0$ and $\limsup_{n\to\infty} q_n = 1$,

(C^-) $\quad \prod_{n<0} q_n > 0$ and $\limsup_{n\to-\infty} p_n = 1$.

Then we have the following

Proposition 7: (a) If neither (C^+) nor (C^-) hold, then $\varphi \equiv 1$.

(b) If (C^+) holds but (C^-) does not hold, then $\varphi_n = 1 - \hat{P}_n$, $\quad n \in Z$.

(c) If (C^-) holds but (C^+) does not hol1, then $\varphi_n = 1 - \hat{Q}_n$, $\quad n \in Z$

(d) If both (C^+) and (C^-) hold, then $\varphi_n = 1 - \max\{\hat{P}_n, \hat{Q}_n\}$, $\quad n \in Z$.

ALMOST-SURE PROGRAM TERMINATION

As already noted, in many cases the only question of interest is whether $\varphi \equiv 1$, i.e., whether the program terminates almost surely from any initial state under any fair schedule. By specializing Theorem 4 and Corollary 6 to this case, we obtain immediately two characterizations for almost-sure program termination, one of which states that the φ-iterates (or relaxed and more general forms of this sequence) converge to 1, while the other states that for every subharmonic function α which lies between χ_X and 1, and which is not identically 1, there exist $k \in K$ and another subharmonic function between α and $P^k\alpha$.

There is, however, a third characterization generalizing that given in [HSP] for programs with finite state space. To state it, we first define a K-ergodic chain to be a non-increasing sequence $\{E_n\}_{n\geq 1}$ of non-empty subsets of $I - X$ such that

$$\lim_{n\to\infty} \sup_{i\in E_n,\ m\geq 1} (Q\chi_{E_m^c})(i) = 0$$

Intuitively, from each $i \in E_n$ the scheduler can satisfy any single fairness constraint, and then reach states in E_m (for any $m \geq 1$) with probability which tends to 1 uniformly as $n\to\infty$. It is easy to see that with such a structure available in $I - X$, an adversary fair scheduler can prevent the program from reaching X with some positive probability (i.e., $\varphi \not\equiv 1$). The converse is also true (the proof can be found in the full version of the paper):

Theorem 8: $\varphi \equiv 1$ if and only if $I - X$ does not contain any K-ergodic chain.

TERMINATION OF DETERMINISTIC/NONDETERMINISTIC PROGRAMS.

Next we specialize the preceding results to the case of deterministic programs. Since nondeterministic programs can be simulated by deterministic programs consisting of additional processes, our results apply to nondeterminsitic programs as well.

As it turns out, the specialized form of Theorem 4 for deterministic/nondeterministic programs with $\varphi \equiv 1$ reduces precisely to the known characterization for termination of "just" concurrent programs, as given by Lehmann, Pnueli and Stavi [LPS].

Indeed, in the deterministic case, each of the φ-iterates γ_a^k, $k \in K$, (resp. γ_a) is a characteristic function of the form $\chi_{G_a^k}$ (resp. χ_{G_a}). Note also that a characteristic function χ_A is subharmonic if and only if for each $k \in K$ and each $i \in A$ the (unique) k-transition from i is to a state in A, i.e., there are no transitions from states in A to states outside A. Hence, it follows from the definition of φ- iterates, and from Theorem 4 that termination of a deterministic program is equivalent to the existence of transfinite (increasing) sequences $\{G_a^k\}_{a\geq 0}$, $k \in K$, and $\{G_a\}_{a\geq 0}$ of subsets of I such that (1) $G_0 = G_0^k = X$, $k \in K$; (2) There are no transitions from states in G_a^k to states outside G_a^k, for each ordinal a and each $k \in K$; (3) $G_a = \bigcup_{k\in K} G_a^k$, for each ordianl a; (4) For each $k \in K$ and each ordinal a, all k-transitions from states in G_{a+1}^k are to states in G_a; (5) $G_a^k = \bigcup_{b<a} G_b^k$, for each limit ordinal a and each $k \in K$; and (6) There exists an ordinal c such that $G_c = I$. However, these conditions can easily be shown to be equivalent to the conditions of [LPS].

However, the specialization of Corollary 6 to this case yields a new characterization for the termination of deterministic (and nondeterministic) programs. To obtain this characterization, use again the fact that a characteristic function χ_A is subharmonic iff there are no transitions from A to A^c. With this in mind, we define a cut of I to be a partition (I_0, I_1) of I into two disjoint sets I_0, I_1 such that $X \subseteq I_1$ and such that there are no transitions from states in I_1 to states in I_0 (so that χ_{I_1} is subharmonic). For each cut (I_0, I_1) and each $k \in K$, define I_0^k to be the set of all $i \in I_0$ for which there exist k-transitions from i to states in I_0. Corollary 6 then yields the following:

Theorem 9: A deterministic/nondeterministic program terminates from every initial state if and only if for each non-trivial cut (I_0, I_1) (i.e., such that $I_0 \neq \emptyset$) there exists $k \in K$ and another cut (J_0, J_1) such that $I_0^k \subseteq J_0 \subsetneq I_0$.

Proof: Since this result may be of independent interest, we give a direct nonprobabilistic proof of it.

Assume first that the program is deterministic, but that the condition of the theorem does not hold, i.e., that there exists a nontrivial cut (I_0, I_1) such that for each $k \in K$ and each set $I_0^k \subseteq J \subsetneq I_0$, the pair (J, J^c) is not a cut, that is, there exist transitions from J^c to J (these transitions can only be from states in $I_0 - J$). Let $i \in I_0$, and let $F(i)$ denote the set of all states in I_0 (including i) reachable from i by some finite sequence of process activations. We claim that for each $k \in K$, $F(i)$ interesects I_0^k. For otherwise, put $J = I_0 - F(i)$, so that $I_0^k \subset J \underset{\neq}{\subset} I_0$. By our assumption there exist transitions from $I_0 - J = F(i)$ into J, which contradicts the definition of $F(i)$. This implies that I_0 is ergodic, i.e., that there exists a fair schedule σ which can keep the program in I_0 forever. To prove this it suffices to show that for each $i \in I_0$ and each $k \in K$ there exists a finite scheduling sequence starting at i and ending by scheduling k and reaching a state in I_0. Since $F(i) \cap I_0^k \neq \emptyset$, take a finite sequence of process activations which takes the program form i into some state in $F(i) \cap I_0^k$, and then schedule k, thereby reaching a state in I_0.

Next suppose that the condition of the theorem does hold. We will construct a "ranking" function ρ from I to the ordinals and an "assistance" function $h : I \to K$ which will satisfy the conditions of [LPS] for program termination. These functions will be constructed in the following transfinite inductive manner. Put initially $\rho|_X = 0$, and define $h|_X$ in an arbitrary manner. Suppose inductively that ρ and h have already been defined on some subset M of I such that (L,M) is a cut (where $L = M^c$). By the above condition, there exists $k \in K$ and another cut (J,J^c) such that $L^k \subseteq J \subsetneq L$. Put $H = L - J \neq \emptyset$, and define $\rho|_H = 1 + \sup \rho|_M$, and $h|_H = k$. Note that since (J,J^c) is a cut, there are no transitions from H into J, and since H is disjoint from L^k, each k-transition from H is into M. Repeating this construction transfinitely, we obtain everywhere-defined functions ρ and h whose properties imply by [LPS] that the program terminates. The same proof will also work for nondeterministic programs. Q.E.D.

Example : Let us apply Theorem 9 to the deterministic program given in the first example. As is easily checked, a cut (I_0, I_1) of I must be one of the following three types:

(a) $I_0 = [0,n] \times \{2\}$, for some $n \in N$:

(b) $I_0 = N \times \{2\}$;

(c) $I_0 = N \times \{2\} \cup [n,\infty] \times \{1\}$ for some $n \geq 1$.

In cases (a) and (b), $I_0^2 = \emptyset$, so that $(I_0^2, (I_0^2)^c) = (\emptyset, I)$ is a cut satisfying the condition of Theorem 9. In case (c), $I_0^1 = N \times \{2\} \cup [n+1,\infty] \times \{1\}$, so that $(I_0^1, (I_0^1)^c)$ is the required cut. Thus program termination is ensured by Theorem 9.

REFERENCES

[DS] L.E. Dubins and L.J. Savage, "Inequalities for Stochastic Processes; How to Gamble if You Must", Dover, N.Y. 1976.

[HSP] S. Hart, M.Sharir and A. Pnueli, "Termination of Concurrent Probabilistic Programs", Proc. 9th POPL Conference, 1982, pp. 1-7. (also to appear in TOPLAS 1983).

[LPS] D. Lehmann, A. Pnueli and J. Stavi, "Impartiality, Justice, Fairness: The Ethics of Concurrent Termination", Proc. 8th ICALP Conference, 1981, pp. 264-277.

[LR] D. Lehmann and M.O. Rabin, "On the Advantages of Free Choice: A Symmetric and Fully Distributed Solution to the Dining Philosophers' Problem", Proc. 8th POPL Conference, 1981, pp. 133-138.

[Ra1] M.O. Rabin, "N Process Synchronization by a 4 $\log_2 N$ - valued Shared Variable", JCSS 25 (1982) pp. 66-75.

[Ra2] M.O. Rabin, "The Choice Coordination Problem" Acta Informatica 17 (1982) pp.121-134.

[RS1] J.Reif and P. Spirakis, "Distributed Algorithms for Synchronizing Interprocess Communication Within Real Time", Proc. 13th STOC Conference, 1981, pp. 133-145.

[RS2] J.Reif and P. Spirakis, "Unbounded Speed Variability in Distributed Communication Systems", Proc. 9th POPL Conference, 1982, pp. 46-56.

[SPH] M.Sharir, A. Pnueli and S. Hart, "The Verification of Probabilistic Programs", to appear in SIAM J. Computing.

Computation Times of NP Sets of Different Densities

J. Hartmanis and Y. Yesha
Department of Computer Science
Cornell University
Ithaca, New York 14853

Abstract

In this paper we study the computational complexity of sets of different densities in *NP*. We show that the deterministic computation time for sets in *NP* can depend on their density if and only if there is a collapse or partial collapse of the corresponding higher nondeterministic and deterministic time bonded complexity classes. We show also that for *NP* sets of different densities there exist complete sets of the corresponding density under polynomial time Turing reductions. Finally, we show that these results can be interpreted as results about the complexity of theorem proving and proof presentation in axiomatized mathematical systems. This interpretation relates fundamental questions about the complexity of our intellectual tools to basic structural problems about *P*, *NP*, *CoNP*, and *PSPACE*, discussed in this paper.

This research was supported in part by National Science Foundation Grant MCS78-00418. Furthermore, the work of the second author was supported in part by a Dr. Chaim Weizmann Post-Doctoral Fellowship for Scientific Research.

Introduction

The general motivation for this work is the need and desire to understand what makes the solution of *NP* problems hard, provided $P \neq NP$. The fundamental question is whether the deterministic computation time required to solve *NP* problems could depend on the density of the set of problems under consideration. In other words, is the problem of finding satisfying assignments for Boolean formulas in conjunctive normal form, *SAT*, computationally hard because there are exponentially many formulas up to size n and that no one single method can solve them all easily? Or is the satisfiability problem still hard if we consider only "thinned out" sets of formulas whose density is much lower than exponential?

It has been shown recently that the structural properties of lower density sets in *NP* are directly determined by the relations between the corresponding higher deterministic and nondeterministic time bounded complexity classes. We cite one such result next [Ha, HIS].

A set S is said to be *sparse* if S contains only polynomially many elements up to size n, i.e. $|S \cap (\epsilon + \Sigma)^n| \leq n^k + k$. Let

$$NEXPTIME = \bigcup_{c \geq 1} NTIME[2^{cn}] \text{ and } EXPTIME = \bigcup_{c \geq 1} TIME[2^{cn}].$$

Theorem A: There exist sparse sets in $NP-P$ if and only if $NEXPTIME \neq EXPTIME$.

For related results about tally sets see [Bo].

In this paper we continue this study and show that the deterministic computation speed of sets in *NP* can depend on their density if and only if the corresponding higher deterministic and nondeterministic complexity classes have collapsed or partially collapsed.

We first show that there are sets of prescribed densities in *NP* and *PSPACE* which are complete under polynomial time Turing reductions for all other sets of the same density in *NP* and *PSPACE*, respectively. We cite one such result.

Theorem B: There exists a sparse set S_0 in *NP* such that all other sparse sets in *NP* are in P^{S_0}.

This completeness result contrasts the well known results by Mahaney [Ma] and Karp-Lipton [KL]. The first result asserts that if there exists a sparse, many-one complete set for *NP* then $P=NP$. The Karp-Lipton result shows that if there exists a sparse set S such that $NP \subseteq P^S$, then the polynomial time hierarchy collapses to Σ_2^P. Our results show that as long as we restrict ourselves to sparse sets in *NP* then there exist sparse complete sets. At the same time, it is interesting to note that the same results do not seem to hold for *CoNP*, or at least they do not hold for relativized *CoNP* computations whereas the above results hold also for relativized computations [HIS]. We also show that there are relativized computations for which there do not exist sparse sets in *NP* which are complete for all other sparse sets in *NP* under many-one polynomial time reductions.

From Theorem B we immediately obtain a proof of the previously known Theorem A as well as new results about the relation between partial collapse of higher deterministic and nondeterministic computations and the recognition speed of sparse sets.

Theorem C: All sparse sets in NP are in

$$\bigcup_{c \geq 1} TIME[n^{c \log n}]$$

if and only if

$$NEXPTIME \subseteq \bigcup_{c \geq 1} TIME[2^{cn^2}].$$

Related results are derived for sets of other densities and computation times as well as for $PSPACE$ versus NP and $PSPACE$ versus P.

From all these results we see that the deterministic time complexity of sets in NP can depend on their density if and only if the corresponding higher deterministic and nondeterministic time classes have suffered a collapse or partial collapse. Since it is our sincere conviction that the density of sets in NP and $PSPACE$ cannot affect their computation time, we are lead to the *generalized complexity hypothesis*. This conjecture asserts for NP (i.e. the *generalized NP hypothesis*) that SAT requires roughly deterministic exponential time and that the deterministic recognition time of sets in NP does not depend on their density. This clearly implies, because of our results, that the higher deterministic and nondeterministic time classes have not even partially collapsed. For example, we conjecture that there exist sets in $NEXPTIME$ which require roughly double exponential deterministic recognition time. The *generalized PSPACE hypothesis* versus P as well as NP is formulated similarly.

Intuitively, the generalized NP hypothesis asserts that the computational difficulty of finding assignments for Boolean formulas in SAT does not stem from the existence of the aggregate of such formulas, but that the difficulty is inherent even in very sparse subsets of SAT.

We give an interpretation of these results in terms of the computational complexity of doing mathematics. We assume that we are using Peano Arithmetic, F. Let

L_1 = {THEOREM: "Statement of result". PROOF: b^k □ | There is a proof of length k or less of the stated theorem in F}.

It is easily seen that L_1 is an NP complete set.

Similarly the set

L_2 = {THEOREM: "Statement of result". PRESENTATION OF PROOF: b^k □ | There is a proof of the stated theorem in F which can be presented on tape of length k}

is $PSPACE$ complete. By presentation of proof we mean a formal writing down of the proof so that a simple proof checker can guarantee that the theorem has a proof, but we can erase any part of the proof not needed later. Thus, when the presentation is completed, the verifier knows that a proof exists, but there may not be a complete proof written down.

Clearly, $PSPACE \neq NP$ if and only if $L_2 \notin NP$ and this happens if and only if in Peano Arithmetic there are infinitely many theorems for which the difference in the length of the shortest proof and the space needed to present a proof is not polynomially bounded.

Similarly, the same relationship will hold for sparse subsets of L_2 which are in $PSPACE$, even if we are allowed to design specialized proof systems for these restricted subsets, if and only if $EXPSPACE \neq NEXPTIME$.

Corollary D: There exist sparse sets in $PSPACE-NP$ if and only if $EXPSPACE \neq NEXPTIME$ (and the quantitative difference between proof length and length of proof presentation depends on the quantitative difference between $EXPSPACE$ and $NEXPTIME$.)

Furthermore, we observe that the existence of sparse subsets of tautologies in $CoNP-NP$ implies that for these sparse subsets we cannot design special proof rules to prove in polynomial length that they are tautologies. This is so because if a sparse subset of $TAUT$ is not in NP then we know that there cannot exist a proof system which proves these formulas to be tautologies with polynomially long proofs.

We prove the following result:

Theorem E: There exists a sparse set S in P such that

$$S \cap TAUT \in CoNP-NP$$

if and only if

$$CoNEXPTIME \neq NEXPTIME.$$

Thus if and only if $CoNEXPTIME \neq NEXPTIME$ can we find a syntactically restricted sparse subset (a sparse set S in P) of Boolean formulas for which we cannot find a good proof system that would yield polynomially long proofs for formulas in $S \cap TAUT$. Furthermore, the actual length of the possible (not polynomially bounded) proofs for $S \cap TAUT$ is given by the disparity between $CoNEXPTIME$ and $NEXPTIME$.

Using a similar method we show that $EXPSPACE \neq EXPTIME$ if and only if there exists a language in $PSPACE$ which is not in P, but has polynomial size circuits (i.e., is in the class P/Poly as defined in [KL]). Formally:

Theorem F:

$$EXPSPACE \neq EXPTIME \Leftrightarrow PSPACE \cap P/Poly \neq P$$

As a corollary we get a "uniform upward separation" result for random polynomial time R and P (R is called ZPP in [G]):

Corollary G:

$$R \neq P \Rightarrow EXPSPACE \neq EXPTIME.$$

Thus we show that a separation of two low uniform complexity classes implies a separation higher up. This result is quite unique: usually separation above implies separation below, but whether in general separation below implies separation above is open. For instance:

$$NEXPTIME \neq EXPTIME \Rightarrow NP \neq P$$

But it is not known whether the assumption $NP \neq P$ can force $NEXPTIME \neq EXPTIME$ (see also [BWX], Theorem 5) or even the weaker separation $EXPSPACE \neq EXPTIME$.

From the above comments we see that the classic problems about $P=?NP=?PTAPE$, $NP=?CoNP$, etc., are really questions about the complexity of our intellectual tools, namely mathematics. Correspondingly, our work tries to address the fundamental question of what makes these problems hard and whether restricting them to subsets of lower density can make them simpler to compute. Our results show that the lower density problems can become computationally easier than the unrestricted problem if and only if there is a partial collapse of the differences between the corresponding higher complexity classes.

Sparse Complete Sets and the Structure of NP

In this section we show that the computational complexity of sets of different densities in NP and $PSPACE$ are completely determined by the relations between the corresponding higher complexity classes.

The main tool in this study will be the existence of sparse sets in NP which are complete for all other sparse sets in NP.

Theorem 1: There exists a tally set S_0 in NP, $S_0 \subseteq 1^*$, such that all sparse sets in NP are polynomial time Turing reducible to S_0, i.e.

$$\{S \mid S \text{ sparse and in } NP\} \subseteq P^{S_0}.$$

Proof: Let A be a complete set of $NEXPTIME$ under many-one linear time reductions and let

$$S_0 = TALLY(A) = \{1^n \mid n \in 1A\}.$$

Let S be a sparse set in NP, say

$$|S \cap (\epsilon+\Sigma)^n| \leq n^{k_0} + k_0.$$

Then the set

$$B = \{(n,r) \mid |S \cap (\epsilon+\Sigma)| \geq r\} \text{ is in } NEXPTIME,$$

since for n and r represented in binary one has enough nondeterministic time to guess r strings in S, $r \leq n^{k_0} + k_0$, and verify that they are in S. Hence, B is many-one linear time reducible to A, and the corresponding set

$$B' = \{(1^n, 1^r) \mid |S \cap (\epsilon+\Sigma)^n| \geq r\}$$

is polynomial time many-one reducible to S_0. Hence, $B' \in P^{S_0}$. Since P^{S_0} is closed under complement we see that

$$B'' = \{(1^n, 1^{r_n}) \mid |S \cap (\epsilon+\Sigma)^n| = r_n\} \text{ is in } P^{S_0}.$$

Thus in P^{S_0} we can compute the exact number of elements in S up to size n, namely r_n.

Furthermore, the set

$$C = \{(n,i,j,k,d) \mid (\exists x_1 < x_2 < \ldots < x_i = x < y_1 < y_2 < \ldots < y_j)$$

$$[\,|y_j| \leq n \text{ and } x_r,\ y_t \in S \text{ for } 1 \leq r \leq i \text{ and } 1 \leq t \leq j$$

$$\text{and } |x| = n \text{ and the } k^{th} \text{ digit of } x \text{ is } d]\}$$

is in $NEXPTIME$ since in nondeterministic time 2^{cn} one can guess the appropriate strings, verify that they satisfy the required conditions and are in S. But then the corresponding set C' obtained by replacing (n,i,j,k,d) by $(1^n, 1^i, 1^j, 1^k, d)$ is in P^{S_0}, by the same argument used to show that $B' \in P^{S_0}$. Since B'' is in P^{S_0}, for any x such that $|x|=n$ we can compute r_n and then, using C', check for $1 \le i \le r_n$, $1 \le j \le r_n$ such that $i+j=r_n$, whether $x=x_i$ for x_i in S. Therefore we conclude that

$$S \in P^{S_0},$$

as was to be shown. □

Later in this paper we will investigate the possibility that there exists an $S_0 \subseteq 1^*$ which is many-one complete for all sparse sets in NP, and show that there exist relativized computations for which this is not true (though Theorem 1 holds for relativized computations).

From the first theorem we immediately obtain a known result about the collapse of higher deterministic and nondeterministic time bounded complexity classes [Ha, HIS], as well as a set of new results about partial collapse of these classes.

Corollary 2: $EXPTIME=NEXPTIME$ if and only if there are no sparse sets in $NP-P$.

Proof: If $EXPTIME=NEXPTIME$ then a complete set A of $NEXPTIME$ is in $EXPTIME$ and therefore $TALLY(A)=S_0$ is in P. But then all sparse sets in NP are in P.

Conversely, if a sparse set S is in $NP-P$ then S_0 is not in P hence $A \notin EXPTIME$ and therefore $EXPTIME \neq NEXPTIME$. □

We say that a set S is P*-printable* if and only if for input 1^n in polynomial time we can print all the elements of S up to size n. Clearly, every P-printable set is sparse.

Similarly, we define a set S to be NP*-printable* if and only if there exists a nondeterministic polynomial time machine such that for input 1^n there exists a computation which prints exactly all the elements of S of length at most n, and every computation either prints exactly those elements or halts with indication of failure to print.

It is easily seen that the proofs of the previous results yield the following.

Corollary 3: $EXPTIME=NEXPTIME$ if and only if every sparse set in NP is P-printable.

Next we show that the upward separation method yields necessary and sufficient conditions also for NP-printability.

Theorem 4: $NEXPTIME=CoNEXPTIME$ if and only if every sparse set in NP is NP-printable.

Proof: Assume $NEXPTIME=CoNEXPTIME$, let S be a sparse set in NP and define

$$L = \{(n,i) \mid |S \cap (\epsilon+\Sigma)^n| \ge i\},$$

where n and i are represented in binary. Clearly, for any (n,i) in nondeterministic exponential time a machine can guess i different strings up to size n and verify that they are in S. Therefore, L is in $NEXPTIME$ and since $NEXPTIME=CoNEXPTIME$ we can use a nondeterministic exponential time machine to check if (n,i) is in $\overline{L}$. Clearly $i_n=|S \cap (\epsilon+\Sigma)^n|$ is given by $(n,i_n) \in L$ and $(n,i_n+1) \in \overline{L}$. Thus we see that

$$L' = \{(n,i_n) \mid |S \cap (\epsilon+\Sigma)^n| = i_n\} \in NEXPTIME$$

and therefore

$$L'' = \{(1^n, i_n) \mid |S \cap (\epsilon + \Sigma)^n| = i_n\} \in NP.$$

But then a nondeterministic polynomial time machine for input 1^n can print

$$x_1 < x_2 < \ldots < x_j < \ldots < x_{i_n}, \text{ for } 1 \leq j \leq i_n, \ |x_j| \leq n, \ x_j \in S,$$

by first guessing i_n and verifying that it is a correct guess and then guessing i_n distinct strings of S of length at most n and printing them if the guess is verified (if not the machine fails to print). Thus S is NP-printable.

Assume that every sparse set in NP is NP-printable and let A be a set in $NEXPTIME$. Then $TALLY(A) = \{1^n \mid n \in 1A\}$ is a sparse set in NP and therefore NP-printable, but then $\overline{TALLY(A)}$ is also in NP and we see that $\bar{A}$ is in $NEXPTIME$. But then $CoNEXPTIME \subseteq NEXPTIME$ and therefore

$$CoNEXPTIME = NEXPTIME. \ \square$$

From Theorem 4 we can obtain a further characterization of the $NEXPTIME = CoNEXPTIME$ collapse.

Corollary 5: $NEXPTIME = CoNEXPTIME$ if and only if for all sparse sets S in NP $\bar{S}$ is in NP.

Proof: Since $NEXPTIME = CoNEXPTIME$ implies that S in NP is NP-printable by Theorem 4 we immediately see that $\bar{S}$ is in NP.

Conversely, if for every sparse set T in NP $\bar{T}$ is also in NP then we see that for any sparse set S in NP the set

$$L'' = \{(1^n, i_n) \mid |S \cap (\epsilon + \Sigma)^n| = i_n\} \text{ is in } NP$$

and therefore S is NP-printable. Therefore

$$NEXPTIME = CoNEXPTIME$$

by Theorem 4. $\square$

The above completeness results for sparse sets in NP can be easily extended to $PSPACE$ versus NP and $PSPACE$ versus P. Furthermore, with an additional uniformity assumption these results generalize to denser sets in NP and without the uniformity assumption to denser sets in $PSPACE$. For a discussion of uniformity conditions on NP sets see [HIS].

Next we show that a partial collapse of the higher deterministic and nondeterministic complexity classes directly determines the computation time of the lower density sets in NP and $PSPACE$. We first prove, as an example, a special case of our general result.

Theorem 6: $NEXPTIME \subseteq \bigcup_{c \geq 1} TIME[2^{cn^k}]$ if and only if all sparse sets in NP are in

$$\bigcup_{c \geq 1} TIME[n^{c(\log n)^{k-1}}].$$

Proof: If $NEXPTIME \subseteq \bigcup_{c \geq 1} TIME[2^{cn^k}]$ then for a complete set A of $NEXPTIME$

$$TALLY(A) = S_0 \text{ is in } TIME[2^{d(\log n)^k}] = TIME[n^{d(\log n)^{k-1}}].$$

But then by Theorem 1 every sparse set S in NP is in P^{S_0} and

$$S \in P^{S_0} \subseteq \bigcup_{c \geq 1} TIME[n^{c(\log n)^{k-1}}].$$

Conversely, if every sparse set of NP is in

$$\bigcup_{c \geq 1} TIME[n^{c(\log n)^{k-1}}]$$

then so is S_0 and we see that

$$A \in TIME[2^{rn^k}],$$

for some r. But then

$$NEXPTIME \subseteq \bigcup_{c \geq 1} TIME[2^{cn^k}]. \square$$

Related results can easily be derived for $PSPACE$ versus NP and $PSPACE$ versus P.

We now state without proof the generalization to any well behaved computation times.

Theorem 7: Let $f(n) \geq n$ be nondecreasing and fully-time-constructible. Then:

(1) $NEXPTIME \subseteq \bigcup_{d \geq 1} TIME[2^{d(f(dn+d))}]$ if and only if every sparse set in NP is in $\bigcup_{d \geq 1} TIME[2^{d(f(d\log n+d))}]$.

(2) $CoNEXPTIME \subseteq \bigcup_{d \geq 1} NTIME[2^{d(f(dn+d))}]$ if and only if the complement of every sparse set in NP is in $\bigcup_{d \geq 1} NTIME[2^{d(f(d\log n+d))}]$. $\square$

Results about sets of higher than polynomial density are correspondingly related to higher complexity classes below exponential time.

We say that a set S has density $\sigma(n)$ if

$$| S \cap (\epsilon + \Sigma)^n | \leq \sigma(n).$$

Theorem 8: There are no $\sigma(n) = n^{\log n}$ dense sets in

$$PSPACE - NP$$

if and only if

$$\bigcup_{c \geq 1} SPACE[2^{c\sqrt{n}}] = \bigcup_{c \geq 1} NTIME[2^{c\sqrt{n}}].$$

We can derive similar results for NP if we assume that our lower density sets are uniformly distributed. (For a more detailed discussion of uniform distributions see [HIS]).

Theorem 9: There are no $\sigma(n) = n^{\log n}$ uniformly dense sets in $NP - P$ if and only if

$$\bigcup_{c \geq 1} TIME[2^{c\sqrt{n}}] = \bigcup_{c \geq 1} NTIME[2^{c\sqrt{n}}],$$

and in this case

$$SAT \in \bigcup_{c \geq 1} TIME[2^{c\sqrt{n}}].$$

Finally, we list an illustrative result about partial collapse of subexponential complexity classes.

Theorem 10: $\bigcup_{c \geq 1} SPACE[2^{c\sqrt{n}}] \subseteq \bigcup_{c \geq 1} TIME[2^{cn^k}]$ if and only if all $\sigma(n) = n^{\log n}$ dense sets of $PSPACE$ are in

$$\bigcup_{c \geq 1} TIME[n^{c(\log n)^{k-1}}].$$

On Many-One Complete Sparse Sets

The existence of a tally set S_0 in NP such that all other sparse sets in NP are in P^{S_0} raises the question whether there exists a tally set which is many-one polynomial time complete for all sparse sets in NP.

Our results show that there exist relativized computations for which no tally set S_0 can be complete for all sparse sets in NP under many-one reductions. At the same time, it is easily seen that Theorem 1 holds for relativized computations and therefore for any oracle A there exists a sparse set complete for all other sparse sets in NP^A under Turing reducibility.

Let $\leq_T^P$ and $\leq_M^P$ denote, respectively, polynomial time Turing and many-one reductions. Let Σ_i^E denote the Σ-levels of the exponential hierarchy, i.e.

$$\Sigma_0^E = EXPTIME, \quad \Sigma_1^E = NEXPTIME,$$

$$\Sigma_2^E = NEXPTIME^{\Sigma_1^P} = NEXPTIME^{SAT}, \text{ etc.}$$

We first prove a technical result which shows that for some oracle A there do not exist tally sets which are $\leq_M^P$-complete for all sparse sets in NP^A.

Lemma 11: Let $S_0 \subseteq 1^*$ and assume that for all sparse S in NP we have $S \leq_M^P S_0$. Then $NEXPTIME = \Sigma_2^E$ implies that

$$NEXPTIME = EXPTIME.$$

Proof (outline): We first observe that it is sufficient to show that every set S of the form

$$S = T \cap SAT,$$

where T is a sparse set in P, must be in P, since then by [HIS] $NEXPTIME = EXPTIME$. The assumption

$$\Sigma_2^E = \Sigma_1^E = NEXPTIME$$

implies that for any sparse set $S = T \cap SAT$, T sparse and in P, the set

$$\{(F_i, x_i) \mid F_i \in S \text{ and } x_i \text{ is the minimal solution of } F_i\}$$

is also in NP. For F_i in S let F_i^k denote F_i with its first k variables, $0 \leq k \leq |x_i|$, filled in with the values of its minimal solution x_i (we choose our syntax so that $|F_i^k| = |F_i|$). Then

$$S' = \{F_i^k \mid F_i \in S \text{ and } 0 \leq k \leq |x_i|\}$$

is seen to be a sparse set in NP.

Note that S does not necessarily have the self reducibility property but that S' has a weak form of this property, sufficient for the following proof.

If $S' \leq_M^P S_0 \subseteq 1^*$ then for any F in T in polynomial time we can find the minimal satisfying assignment of F if $F_i = F$ or determine that F is not in S. This is done by searching the tree of functions generated by F by partial assignments of variables (as in P. Berman's proof [Be, Ma]). We can discard any subtree which is assigned a string not in 1^* by the reduction. For subtrees with the same labels in 1^* we always pick the leftmost subtree to find x_i if $F_i = F$. Since there are only polynomially many labels in 1^* the reduction can assign, we see that the search is completed in polynomial time, either yielding the minimal solution or showing that F is not in S. □

Corollary 12: There exists an oracle A such that no tally set can be $\leq_M^P$-complete for all sparse sets in NP^A.

Proof: Since there exists an oracle A [S] such that

$$EXPSPACE^A = \ldots = \Sigma_2^{E(A)} = \Sigma_1^{E(A)} \neq \Sigma_0^{E(A)},$$

a relativized version of the previous lemma implies that there cannot exist a tally set $\leq_M^P$-complete for all sparse sets of NP^A. □

Furthermore, from Theorem 12 in [HIS] it follows that there exists an oracle A such that no tally set can be even $\leq_T^P$-complete for all sparse sets in $CoNP^A$.

The Computational Complexity of Mathematics

It is well known that the sets of provable theorems of sufficiently rich, axiomatized mathematical systems form complete sets for the recursively enumerable sets under recursive reductions. Thus, intuitively, we can say that the provable theorems in Peano Arithmetic form a set which is computationally as hard as any recursively enumerable set. Unfortunately, this interpretation dos not yield any real insight about the computational complexity of doing mathematics.

We believe that the proper formulation for the study of the computational complexity of mathematics and therefore the study of the computational complexity of our intellectual tools in general, is by investigating the difficulty of proving theorems by bounding the length of the desired proof. If we do this then, as will be shown below, the questions about the computational complexity of the process of doing mathematics -- finding proofs and presenting proofs -- become questions about P, NP, and $PSPACE$.

Assume that we have an axiomatized formal system F, which could be Peano Arithmetic, and that we have given a "natural" definition for the length of proofs and related concepts.

Then it is easily seen that the set

L_1 = {THEOREM: "Statement of result". PROOF: b^k □ | There is a proof of length k or less of the stated theorem in F}

is NP complete.

Similarly the set

L_2 = {THEOREM: "Statement of result". PRESENTATION OF PROOF: b^k □ | There is a proof of the stated theorem in F which can be presented on tape of length k}

is $PSPACE$ complete. By ***presentation of proof*** we mean a formal writing down of the proof so that a simple (polynomial time) proof checker can guarantee that the theorem has a proof, but we can erase any part of the proof not needed later. Thus, when the presentation is completed, the verifier knows that a proof exists, but there may not be a complete proof written down.

Clearly, $PSPACE \neq NP$ if and only if L_2 is not in NP and this happens if and only if in Peano Arithmetic there are infinitely many theorems for which the difference in the length of the shortest proof and the space needed to present a proof is not polynomially bounded.

The fundamental question is whether finding proofs of theorems in mathematics is hard because of the existence of the aggregate of all provable theorems so that no one method can prove them all easily or is it because "individual" theorems are hard to prove. Since we cannot give precise mathematical meaning to "computational complexity" of finding proofs for individual theorems, we replace this question by questions about sparse or supersparse subsets of the sets L_1 and L_2. Clearly this brings us right back to the main topic of this paper and shows that questions about sparse subsets of $NP-P$, $PSPACE-NP$ and $PSPACE-P$ are actually fundamental questions about the nature of mathematics. For example, we easily obtain the following result.

Corollary 13: There exists a sparse set S in P such that $L_2 \cap S \notin NP$ if and only if

$$EXPSPACE \neq NEXPTIME.$$

In the study of proof techniques special attention has been given to proving a Boolean formula a tautology. Let

$$TAUT = \{F \mid F \text{ Boolean formula in } DNF \text{ such that } (\forall x)[F(x)=1]\}.$$

Clearly, $TAUT$ is a complete set for $CoNP$ and the question whether some decision problem in $CoNP$ is not in NP when restricted to some sparse domain S in P can be shown to be equivalent to the question whether for some sparse set S in P we cannot design special proof rules with which in polynomial length will prove for any tautology in S that it is indeed a tautology. The following result gives necessary and sufficient conditions for this to be impossible.

Theorem 14: The following conditions are equivalent.

(1) $CoNEXPTIME \neq NEXPTIME$

(2) For some set L in $CoNP$ and some sparse set S in P, $L \cap S \in CoNP-NP$.

(3) For some P-printable set S, $TAUT \cap S \in CoNP-NP$.

Proof: It can easily be seen that if $S \in P$ and $L \cap S \in CoNP-NP$ then $\bar{L} \cap S$ is a sparse set in $NP-CoNP$. Thus, by Corollary 5, (2) implies (1). Clearly (3) implies (2). We now outline a proof that (1) implies (3): If (1) holds then there exists a tally set T in $CoNP-NP$. There exists a 1-1 length increasing polynomial time reduction g from T to $TAUT$ [BH]. Then $g(1^*)$ is the desired S in (3). □

The above theorem can be generalized to any well behaved computation times (rather than $NEXPTIME$ and NP) in a fashion similar to Theorem 7. We omit the details.

A Uniform Upward Separation

There are known separation results about uniform complexity classes of the form: "If two high uniform complexity classes are unequal then two corresponding lower uniform complexity classes are unequal", (a *downward* separation). For instance, if $NEXPTIME \neq EXPTIME$ then $NP \neq P$. We use our techniques to prove a quite unique *upward* separation of uniform complexity classes. Let R be random polynomial time. We prove

Theorem 15: $R \neq P$ implies $EXPSPACE \neq EXPTIME$.

Before we prove this theorem, we need a lemma.

Let $P/Poly$ be the class $\bigcup_{S \text{ sparse}} P^S$ [KL]. By a result due to Meyer (see [KL]), $P/Poly$ is equal to the class of languages having polynomial size circuits.

Lemma 16: $EXPSPACE \neq EXPTIME$ if and only if $PSPACE \cap P/Poly \neq P$.

Proof: If $EXPSPACE \neq EXPTIME$ then there exists a tally set $T \in PSPACE - P$. Clearly $T \in P/Poly$. Conversely, let $L \in PSPACE - P$ be in $P/Poly$. Then it can be shown that the family of minimal circuits $\{C_n\}$ for L can be computed in space polynomial in n. $\{C_n\}$ can be encoded by a sparse set S which is in $PSPACE$ such that $L \in P^S$, hence $S \notin P$. By [HIS], $EXPSPACE \neq EXPTIME$ follows. □

Theorem 15 now follows since $R \subset PSPACE$, and also by [A] $R \subset P/Poly$.

References

[A] L. Adleman, "Two Theorems on Random Polynomial Time", IEEE-FOCS Symp. (1978), 75-83.

[Be] P. Berman, "Relationship Between Density and Deterministic Complexity of *NP*-Complete Languages", 5th ICALP, Lecture Notes in Computer Science 62, Springer-Verlag, Berlin (1978), 63-71.

[BH] L. Berman and J. Hartmanis, "On Isomorphism and Density of *NP* and Other Complete Sets", SIAM J. on Computing (1977), 305-322.

[Bo] R.V. Book, "Tally Languages and Complexity Classes", Information and Control 26 (1974), 186-193.

[BWX] R. Book, C. Wilson, and M. Xu, "Relativizing Time and Space", IEEE-FOCS Symp. (1981), 254-259.

[G] J. Gill, "Computational Complexity of Probabilistic Turing Machines", SIAM J. on Computing 6 (1977), 675-695.

[Ha] J. Hartmanis, "On Sparse Sets in NP-P", Department of Computer Science, Cornell University, TR82-508, August 1982.

[HIS] J. Hartmanis, N. Immerman, and V. Sewelson, "Sparse Sets in NP-P: EXPTIME vs NEXPTIME", ACM Symposium on Theory of Computing, 1983.

[KL] R.M. Karp and R.J. Lipton, "Some Connections Between Nonuniform and Uniform Complexity Classes", Proceedings 12th Annual ACM Symposium on Theory of Computing (April 1980), 302-309.

[Ma] S. Mahaney, "Sparse Complete Sets for *NP*: Solution of a Conjecture of Berman and Hartmanis", Proceedings 21st IEEE Foundations of Computer Science Symposium (1980), 42-49.

[S] V. Sewelson, private communication.

Rewrite Methods for Clausal and Non-Clausal Theorem Proving

Jieh Hsiang
Department of Computer Science
State University of New York at Stony Brook
Stony Brook, NY 11794
U.S.A.

Nachum Dershowitz
Department of Computer Science
University of Illinois at Urbana-Champaign
Urbana, IL 61801
U.S.A.

1. Abstract

Effective theorem provers are essential for automatic verification and generation of programs. The conventional resolution strategies, albeit complete, are inefficient. On the other hand, special purpose methods, such as term rewriting systems for solving word problems, are relatively efficient but applicable to only limited classes of problems.

In this paper, a simple canonical set of rewrite rules for Boolean algebra is presented. Based on this set of rules, the notion of term rewriting systems is generalized to provide complete proof strategies for first order predicate calculus. The methods are conceptually simple and can frequently utilize lemmas in proofs. Moreover, when the variables of the predicates involve some domain that has a canonical system, that system can be incorporated as rewrite rules, with the algebraic simplifications being done simultaneously with the merging of clauses. This feature is particularly useful in program verification, data type specification, and programming language design, where axioms can be expressed as equations (rewrite rules). Preliminary results from our implementation indicate that the methods are space-efficient with respect to the number of rules generated (as compared to the number of resolvents in resolution provers).

2. Introduction

Given an equational theory E, a *term rewriting system for E* is a finite set of rewrite rules $R=\{l_i \rightarrow r_i\}_{i=1}^n$ such that $\{l_i = r_i\}_{i=1}^n$ and E are equivalent (i.e., $s=t$ is true in $\{l_i = r_i\}_{i=1}^n$ if and only if $s=t$ in E). A term t is *reduced* using rule $l \rightarrow r$ if a subterm s of t, which is an instance of the left hand side l, is replaced by the corresponding instance of the right hand side r. A term s is *reachable* from t if t can be reduced to s after a finite number of reductions. A term is *irreducible* if no rule can be applied to it. We use t^* to denote an irreducible form of t. We call a term rewriting system *terminating* if there is no infinite sequence of reductions from any term, and *confluent* if for any distinct terms t, r, and s, if r and s are both reachable from t, then there is another term u which is reachable from both r and s. A rewriting system satisfying these two properties is called a *canonical term rewriting system.* It is easy to see that if R is a canonical term rewriting system, then every term has a unique irreducible form with respect to R. Thus, to check if equation $s =_E t$ is valid, all that needs be done is to reduce both s and t to their irreducible forms and see if they are identical.

A canonical system for an equational theory, if it exists, will not only have the same theoretical power as E, but can also eliminate the unmanageable search space often encountered in equational theorem proving. The reasons for such improvement are twofold: (1) the equations are used in one direction, so terms are "simplified" when rewrite rules are applied; (2) rules may be used in arbitrary order and no backtracking is needed (since all sequences of reductions lead to the same irreducible form).

Knuth & Bendix ([KnBe70]) gave a necessary and sufficient condition for a terminating term rewriting system to be confluent (and therefore canonical). They also presented a completion procedure for extending a non-canonical system to a canonical one without changing the original theory (although the method does not always terminate successfully). Their idea has been generalized by Lankford & Ballantyne ([LaBa77]) and Peterson & Stickel ([PeSt81]) to handle the case where some operators are commutative or associative and commutative.

3. A Canonical System for Boolean Algebra

Although very effective for solving word problems, the term rewriting method has been largely ignored by the theorem proving community on account of its relatively small problem domain. Therefore it would be desirable to extend this idea to handle the full first order theory. In order to achieve this goal, we need a canonical system for the logical connectives, Boolean algebra, and a complete strategy for the first order predicate calculus.

Attempts to find a canonical system for Boolean algebra have been reported in [Hul80] and [PeSt81], where conventional axioms for Boolean algebra were converted into rewrite rules and the AC-Completion Algorithm was used. Some stronger axioms, such as the Absorption Law, have also been used ([Hul80]). The Completion Algorithm, nevertheless, failed to terminate in all experiments (i.e. generated infinitely many rules) due to the well-known fact that the prime implicant representation of Boolean terms is not unique.

The problem of non-unique representation can be finessed, however, by choosing the right kind of operators. In our approach, we use "EXCLUSIVE-OR" in place of the usual operator "OR", and construct a canonical system for Boolean algebra with the help of this operator. (A system that simplifies Boolean expressions using EXCLUSIVE-OR was also discussed in [WaCo80].) The notion of EXCLUSIVE-OR was discussed by Stone ([St36]), who defined a *Boolean ring* (B,+,*,0) to be a ring which is idempotent with respect to *, i.e. $x*x=x$ for all x in B. He proved the following:

Theorem (Stone):

(1) *Every Boolean ring is commutative (i.e.* $x*y=y*x$*).*

(2) *Every Boolean ring is nilpotent with respect to* + *(i.e.* $x+x=0$*).*

(3) *Let* $(B,+,*,0,1)$ *be a Boolean ring with unit 1. Introduce the following operators :*

$$x\vee y=x+y+x*y$$
$$x\wedge y=x*y$$
$$\neg x=x+1$$

then $(B,\wedge,\vee,\neg,0,1)$ *is a Boolean algebra. Conversely, given a Boolean algebra* $(B,\wedge,\vee,\neg,0,1)$*, define*

$$a+b=(a\wedge\neg b)\vee(\neg a\wedge b)$$
$$a*b=a\wedge b$$

then the corresponding $(B,+,*,0,1)$ *is a Boolean ring.*

The operator '+' used by Stone later became XOR in switching theory. We use + for XOR, $\vee$ for OR, $*$ for AND, $\neg$ for NOT, 1 for TRUE, and 0 for FALSE throughout this paper. We say a term s is a *normal expression* of a Boolean term t if s is 1, 0 or $s=s_1+\ldots+s_n$ where all s_i's are distinct, non-zero products of distinct positive literals. For example, a normal expression of $\neg x\vee y$ is $x*y+x+1$. It is not hard to prove that the normal expression of a Boolean term is unique up to permutation of arguments ([Hs82]).

A six-rule canonical system for Boolean rings can be obtained by executing the AC-Completion Algorithm (i.e. the Knuth-Bendix Completion Algorithm with a commutative-associative unification algorithm for finding critical pairs [PeSt81]) over the axioms of ring theory, the idempotence of $*$, and the nilpotence of +. By adding four more rules for transforming the usual Boolean connectives into Boolean ring forms, we have the following canonical term rewriting system for Boolean algebra:

$$\mathrm{BA}\left\{\begin{array}{lll} x\vee y & \to x*y+x+y & R1\\ x\supset y & \to x*y+x+1 & R2\\ x\equiv y & \to x+y+1 & R3\\ \neg x & \to x+1 & R4\\ x+0 & \to x & R5\\ x+x & \to 0 & R6\\ x*1 & \to x & R7\\ x*x & \to x & R8\\ x*0 & \to 0 & R9\\ x*(y+z) & \to x*y+x*z & R10 \end{array}\right.$$

This system, like any canonical term rewriting system, yields very simple proofs for the word problems of the underlying theory (in this case, the propositional calculus). As an example, the absorption law (i.e. $p\vee(p\wedge q)=p$) can be easily proved by observing that

$$p\vee(p\wedge q)\to p*(p*q)+p+p*q\to p*q+p+p*q\to 0+p\to p.$$

The dual system, based on $\vee$ and $\equiv$ rather than $\wedge$ and +, is also canonical and can be used in a similar fashion. This reduction process actually gives us an effective method for determining the validity problem of the propositional calculus. To be more precise, a Boolean term is valid if and only if its irreducible expression is 1; unsatisfiable if and only if its irreducible expression is 0; and satisfiable but not valid if and only if its irreducible expression is neither 1 nor 0. By the NP-completeness of the satisfiability problem ([Co71]), any systematic procedure for reducing Boolean terms to a canonical form requires exponential time in the worst case if $P \neq NP$.

4. A Complete Clausal Strategy for First Order Predicate Calculus

The "brute-force" reduction method described above is not the most convenient way of handling the validity problem for several reasons:

(1) For complicated statements with a lot of implications and disjunctions, the sentences may be expanded into long expressions by the procedure (using R1-R4 and R10) before most of the "simplification" reductions (using the rest of the rules) begin.

(2) The method cannot be easily generalized to effectively handle first order predicate calculus.

These problems can be circumvented by using a refutational proof technique. The scenario can be roughly described as follows: To prove that a first order sentence ϕ is valid, we first skolemize its negation, convert it into clause form $C_1 \wedge \cdots \wedge C_n$, add a rule $C_i + 1 \rightarrow 0$ for each clause C_i, then run the AC-Completion Algorithm over this set of rules until $1 \rightarrow 0$ is generated. The canonical system BA is used throughout to keep Boolean terms always in their normal form.

One potential problem with this approach is that both of the Boolean operators (+ and *) are AC and the unification algorithm used for finding critical pairs must deal with two AC operators at the same time. However, no AC-unification algorithm is presently known to be finite and complete (see [St81]). Fortunately, this problem does not arise in our method since we *do not* need to generate all critical pairs. In fact, by using the canonical system BA as inference rules, a new unification algorithm (BN-unification), which is considerably simpler than the AC-unification for one operator, can be achieved. Detail about this unification algorithm is in the appendices. The reader can treat the BN-unifications in the following definitions as AC-unifications and the results still hold.

Definition: *A Boolean term is an* **N-term** *if it is a conjunction of literals. A rule* $l \rightarrow 0$ *is an* **N-rule** *if* l *is an N-term.*

Definition: *Let* $l_1[t] \rightarrow 0$ *and* $l_2 \rightarrow 0$ *be two rules converted from clauses* C_1 *and* C_2*. If*

(1) $l_2 \rightarrow 0$ *is an N-rule,*

(2) *there is a (most general) BN-unifier* σ *such that* $(ut)\sigma = (vl_2)\sigma$ *(where* u *and* v *are two extra variables in the BN-unification not in* l_1 *and* l_2*),*

then

$$<(ul_1[0])\sigma, 0>$$

is an **N-critical pair** *of* $l_1 \rightarrow 0$ *and* $l_2 \rightarrow 0$*, with* $(ul_1[t])\sigma$ *as its superposition.*

In the above definition, $l_1[t]$ indicates that t is a nonvariable subterm of l_1. Note that since unifications are done only between N-terms, no unification involves the operator $+$.

The theorem proving strategy is the following:

N-Strategy: *To prove that a sentence Φ is valid:*
Convert the (skolemized) negation of Φ into a set of clauses S;
transform S into a set of rewrite rules R using BA;
repeat
Find a nontrivial N-critical pair $<t,0>$ between rules in R;
($<t,0>$ is nontrivial if t is irreducible w.r.t. BA and R, and $t \neq 0$)
Convert $<t,0>$ into the rule $t \rightarrow 0$;
$R := R \cup \{t \rightarrow 0\}$;
Use $t \rightarrow 0$ to simplify and delete rules in R;
until *(no N-critical pair can be found) or ($1 \rightarrow 0$ is generated);*
if $1 \rightarrow 0$ *is generated* **then return** *"proved"*
else return *"consistent".*

The N-strategy is essentially the same as the Knuth-Bendix Completion Algorithm except that (1) it looks only for N-critical pairs, and (2) it stops when a contradiction is generated. The canonical system BA is used throughout the process to reduce every term (such as the terms in the generated critical pairs) to its irreducible form. Like the Knuth-Bendix Completion Algorithm, the N-strategy can also produce different outcomes. It may:

(1) generate $1 \rightarrow 0$: In this case, the input clauses are inconsistent.

(2) generate finitely many rules and terminate: The clauses are consistent.

(3) generate infinitely many rules, i.e. never stop: The clauses are consistent.

Note that the case of abort (i.e. generation of a critical pair with incomparable terms) never happens in the N-strategy since one of the terms in any N-critical pair is always 0.

The completeness of the N-strategy is stated by the following theorem:

Theorem 4.1: *Given a set of clauses S in first order predicate calculus, S is inconsistent if and only if $1 \rightarrow 0$ can be produced using the N-strategy.*

We show how the strategy works by giving a proof for a verification condition of Hoare's FIND program:

$$\{ \forall x,y(x \leq y \vee y < x) \wedge j < i \wedge m \leq p \leq q \leq n$$
$$\wedge\ \forall x,y(m \leq x < i \wedge j < y \leq n \supset A[x] \leq A[y])$$
$$\wedge\ \forall x,y(m \leq x \leq y \leq j \supset A[x] \leq A[y])$$
$$\wedge\ \forall x,y(i \leq x \leq y \leq n \supset A[x] \leq A[y]) \} \supset A[p] \leq A[q].$$

The first mechanical proof of this problem was reported in [SlNo73] where resolution and some special inference rules for partial ordering were used. The proof was completed after 62 resolvents were generated. In [GrNaOrPl82], experiments using locking resolution and a certain version of natural deduction (a simplified problem reduction format) were reported.

Locking generated 173 resolvents and stopped without obtaining a proof, the natural deduction strategy found a proof after producing 223 subgoals. Using the N-strategy, the negation of the sentence is converted into 9 rules:

$A[p] \leq A[q] \rightarrow 0$ c1

$q \leq n \rightarrow 1$ c2

$p \leq q \rightarrow 1$ c3

$m \leq p \rightarrow 1$ c4

$j < i \rightarrow 1$ c5

$(A[x] \leq A[y])(i \leq x)(x \leq y)(y \leq n) + (i \leq x)(x \leq y)(y \leq n) \rightarrow 0$ c6

$(A[x] \leq A[y])(m \leq x)(x \leq y)(y \leq j) + (m \leq x)(x \leq y)(y \leq j) \rightarrow 0$ c7

$(A[x] \leq A[y])(m \leq x)(y \leq n)(j < y)(x < i) + (m \leq x)(y \leq n)(j < y)(x < i) \rightarrow 0$ c8

$(x \leq y)(y < x) + (x \leq y) + (y < x) \rightarrow 1$ c9

For convenience, we have omitted all the $*$'s between predicates. We have also moved all the 1's to the right hand sides. The latter change will not increase the number of critical pairs since such rules are not N-rules. On the contrary, it will improve the efficiency, since occurrences of the corresponding left hand sides can now be replaced by 1, and each $l_1 * l_2 * \ldots * l_n \rightarrow 1$ can be split into n new rules $l_1 \rightarrow 1, \ldots, l_n \rightarrow 1$.

By unifying p and q in c1 with x and y in c6, we have a critical pair $<(i \leq p)(p \leq q)(q \leq n), 0>$. However, this critical pair is not irreducible since subterms $p \leq q$ and $q \leq n$ can be reduced to 1 by c3 and c2. Thus we produce a rule:

$i \leq p \rightarrow 0.$ c10

By the same token, c1 and c7 yield a new rule

$q \leq j \rightarrow 0,$ c11

while c1 and c8 create

$(j < q)(p < i) \rightarrow 0.$ c12

Now c10, c11, and c12 are the N-rules we can use. The only nontrivial critical pair between c10 and the rest of the set is with c9. By unifying i and p with x and y, we get

$p < i \rightarrow 1.$ c13

Rule c13 simplifies c12 into

$j < q \rightarrow 0.$ c12'

And c11, similar to c10, also produces a new rule with c9:

$j < q \rightarrow 1.$ c14

A contradiction is reached immediately by c12' and c14. Note that the proof is obtained after producing only 6 rules (or 5 rules to be precise, since c12' is simplified from c12), and that this proof is exhaustive!

4.1. Comparisons with Resolution

The N-strategy is in itself similar to the all-negative resolution method (i.e. one of the parents of a resolvent must contain only negative literals). When the constant 1 is placed on the right hand side (as it was in the previous example), the method also contains some features of unit-resolution. Thus, our system works well in some cases, such as Horn clauses, where the all-negative strategy does not. In general, however, the efficiency of the N-strategy, as a purely syntactic method, should not be drastically different from that of other resolution strategies. Nevertheless, the example we showed seems to reveal a dramatic gain in efficiency using the N-strategy over resolution or natural deduction: achieving a proof after generating 6 rules as opposed to generating 173 resolvents without a proof (locking resolution) and generating 223 subgoals (natural deduction). The reason for such a surprising improvement is certainly worth investigating.

The basic difference between N-strategy and other resolution strategies lies in the adoption of the rewriting (reduction) method. To be more precise, the rewriting method *requires* everything to be reduced as much as possible. For example, when the critical pair $<(i \leq p)(p \leq q)(q \leq n),0>$ was generated, it was not converted immediately into a rule, since the first term can still be reduced using rules c2 and c3. When the critical pair was finally reduced to $<i \leq p,0>$ and made into a rule, all the possible intermediate "resolvents" (in this case, $(i \leq p)(p \leq q)(q \leq n) \rightarrow 0$, $(i \leq p)(p \leq q) \rightarrow 0$, and $(i \leq p)(q \leq n) \rightarrow 0$) were excluded. In a resolution strategy, however, all those resolvents are kept, and even if subsumption is included as part of the strategy, the resolvents will not be deleted until some subsuming clause is generated. In a breadth-first implementation (which seems to be the most commonly used technique), such a subsuming clause usually will not be generated early. Subsequently, the more useful resolvents (such as c10 in our example) are not generated until much later.

5. A Non-Clausal Strategy

Since the canonical system for Boolean algebra always gives us an irreducible form for any Boolean term, it seems superfluous to insist on converting sentences into clause form. In fact, by lifting the restriction of generating only N-critical pairs, non-clausal strategies can be obtained:

A non-clausal strategy: *To prove a sentence Φ is valid:*

(1) *Skolemize $\neg\Phi$; assume that the result is $M_1 \wedge M_2 \wedge \cdots \wedge M_n$ (the M_i's are not necessarily clauses).*

(2) *Add rewrite rules $M_1 \rightarrow 1$, $M_2 \rightarrow 1, \ldots, M_n \rightarrow 1$.*

(3) *Run the AC Knuth-Bendix Completion algorithm on the set of rules, using BA as additional simplification rules, until no more critical pairs can be found or $1 \rightarrow 0$ is generated.*

(4) *If $1 \rightarrow 0$ is found, then return "proved"; otherwise return "consistent".*

The AC-unification algorithm needed for finding critical pairs is, as in the N-strategy, weaker than the full AC-unification, since no variable will appear as an argument of an AC-operator. Nevertheless, both AC-operators ($*$ and $+$) are still involved in the unification, and the completeness of such a restricted algorithm remains unknown at this moment. The method can be proven complete for first order predicate calculus (as a direct consequence of the Theorem in [HuHu80]) once the completeness problem of the unification is resolved affirmatively.

We demonstrate the use of the strategy by the following example. Let Φ be:

$$\forall x[A(x)\equiv B(x)]\supset[\forall xA(x)\equiv\forall xB(x)].$$

The Skolemized negation of Φ is:

$$[A(z)\equiv B(z)]\wedge[A(x)\vee B(y)]\wedge[\neg B(a)\vee\neg A(b)]\wedge[B(a)\supset B(y)]\wedge[A(b)\supset A(x)],$$

where a and b are new Skolem constants. Since the first $\equiv$ remains intact, we can make use of the rule R4: $x\equiv y\rightarrow x+y+1$ in BA. The formulas, when converted into rules, are as follows:

$$A(z)+B(z)\rightarrow 0 \qquad \text{r1}$$
$$A(x)B(y)+A(x)+B(y)\rightarrow 1 \qquad \text{r2}$$
$$B(a)A(b)\rightarrow 0 \qquad \text{r3}$$
$$B(a)B(y)+B(a)\rightarrow 0 \qquad \text{r4}$$
$$A(b)A(x)+A(b)\rightarrow 0 \qquad \text{r5}$$

From r1 and r2, we have a superposition $A(z)B(z)+A(z)+B(z)$ by unifying both x and y with z, and a critical pair $<A(z)B(z),1>$. Since $M_1\cdots M_n=1$ can be split into equations $M_1=1,\ldots,M_n=1$, instead of converting the critical pair into one rule, we have:

$$A(z)\rightarrow 1 \qquad \text{r6}$$
$$B(z)\rightarrow 1. \qquad \text{r7}$$

Rules r6 and r7 mean that every instance of $A(z)$ and $B(z)$ in the set of rules can be replaced by 1. Therefore, all of the original five rules are deleted, and r3 becomes:

$$1\rightarrow 0,$$

the contradiction.

6. Complete Strategies for First Order Built-in Theories

In this section we generalize the previous results to a larger class of problems, namely, the first order calculus whose predicates involve some special domains. We further assume that there exist canonical term rewriting systems for such domains. Such problems are common in practice, such as theorems in group theory (or other algebraic structures), properties of data types, etc. The conventional method for dealing with such problems is to treat the axioms of the domain as extra clauses and equations, and use resolution and/or paramodulation. This method is very inefficient in general. Another possible solution is the following: since the rewriting method is very effective in manipulating terms, why not use resolution on the clauses and the rewriting method (with the canonical system for the theory) on the arguments? Feasible as it sounds, this approach is not complete ([La75]). Research along these lines has been conducted by Plotkin [Pl73], who merged the domain axioms into the unification algorithm (the same idea was adopted later by [PeSt81] and [LaBa77] for extending the Knuth-Bendix method), and Slagle [Sl74], Lankford [La75], and Lankford-

Ballantyne [LaBa79] who introduced the concept of "narrowing" to find useful instances of the arguments in the clauses.

The problem can be easily solved, with the help of BA, by using only the term rewriting method. Henceforth, S stands for a set of rewrite rules converted from a set of clauses, and R stands for a (canonical) rewriting system for the domain theory T.

Definition: *$l \rightarrow r$ is an* **RN-rule** *if it is an N-rule in S or it is a rule in R.*

Definition: *Given a rule $t_1[s] \rightarrow 0$ in S and an RN-rule $l \rightarrow r$, if either*

(i) $l \rightarrow r$ is an N-rule and there is an N-critical pair $<t_2,0>$ between the two rules,

or (ii) $l \rightarrow r$ is in R and there is a most general unifier σ such that $s\sigma = l\sigma$ (let $t_2 = (t_1[r])\sigma$),

then $<t_2,0>$ is an **RN-critical pair.**

In the above definition, the subterm s in $t_1[s]$ is a nonvariable subterm of an argument of one of the predicates in t_1. In case (ii), the most general unifier between an argument of a clause and a rule in R is obtained by applying whatever unification algorithm is appropriate for the theory T. The only difference between the making of an N-critical pair and an RN-critical pair is that in the latter, superposition is also allowed between a rule about the formulas and one about the domain axioms. The N-strategy can also be generalized to the RN-strategy by requiring the generation of RN-critical pairs:

RN-Strategy:
Given sets S and R as described above,
repeat
  Find a nontrivial RN-critical pair $<t,0>$ between rules in $R \cup S$;
  Convert $<t,0>$ into the rule $t \rightarrow 0$;
  $S := S \cup \{t \rightarrow 0\}$;
  Use $t \rightarrow 0$ to simplify and delete rules in S;
until *(no RN-critical pair can be found) or ($1 \rightarrow 0$ is generated);*
if *$1 \rightarrow 0$ is generated* **then return** *"proved"*
  else return *"consistent".*

The possible outcomes of the algorithm are similar to those for the N-strategy, and the method is also complete for its target problems:

Theorem 6.1: *Given a set of clauses S and a canonical system R, $S \cup R$ is E-unsatisfiable if and only if $1 \rightarrow 0$ can be produced from $S \cup R$ using the RN-strategy.*

To demonstrate how RN-strategy works, we proof the following problem in group theory. To save space, we list only the first three rules of the ten-rule canonical system for group theory ([KnBe70]) that is used in the proof.

$$xe \to x \qquad \text{r1}$$
$$(xy)z \to x(yz) \qquad \text{r2}$$
$$xx^{-1} \to e \qquad \text{r3}$$

...

$$P(a) \to 0 \qquad (i.e.\ \neg P(a)) \qquad \text{c1}$$
$$P(xb^{-1}) + 1 \to 0 \qquad (i.e.\ P(xb^{-1})) \qquad \text{c2}$$

The RN-strategy found a proof after generating five rules. Among them, the following three derives the proof directly:

$$P(x(yb^{-1})) + 1 \to 0 \qquad \text{(r2 and c2)} \qquad \text{c3}$$
$$P(x) + 1 \to 0 \qquad \text{(c3 and r3)} \qquad \text{c4}$$
$$1 \to 0 \qquad \text{(c4 and c1)} \qquad \text{c5}$$

The other two generated rules are $P(b^{-1}) + 1 \to 0$ and $P(e) + 1 \to 0$.

The theorem (and method) can also be generalized to the case where R is an AC-canonical system (such as the theory of abelian groups).

6.1. Extensions and Discussions

The RN-strategy will improve the efficiency (as compared with resolution and paramodulation type provers) in at least the following ways:

(1) The clauses for describing the axioms of the domain are eliminated; thus, the number of clauses and resolvents is reduced.

(2) Replacements of terms in the literals using the equational axioms are done strictly in one direction, and no elaborate arrangement of choice of proper subterms is needed since every term has a unique irreducible form; thus, the search space is reduced considerably.

(3) Once a canonical system for the domain theory is found, it can be reused each time a theorem is to be proved, and no more work on the domain need be done. The savings are most significant when several theorems are to be proved at the same time. In resolution (paramodulation) theorem proving, however, resolvents among the axioms as well as those between the axioms and the similar clauses in the theorems will usually be generated every time.

(4) The useful lemmas for T that are generated by the Completion Algorithm are fully utilized.

Experiments comparing the performance of RN and N strategies have been conducted ([HsJo82]). As an example, for the problem:

If S is a nonempty subset of a group and $x,y \epsilon S \supset xy^{-1} \epsilon S$, then $x \epsilon S \supset x^{-1} \epsilon S$,

the N-strategy generated 18 rules while the RN-strategy only generated 6. (For comparison, the locking resolution generated 76 resolvents and the simplified reduction format, SPRF, generated 52 subgoals [GrNaOrPl82].) This seems to show that the method is more efficient when used with a canonical system for the domain theory.

The RN-strategy can also be modified into a non-clausal strategy in the same fashion as in the previous section. As before, the completeness of the strategy also depends on the finiteness and completeness of the employed unification algorithm.

The RN-strategy does not apply when a canonical system for the domain theory does not exist. This requirement can be relaxed somewhat ([Hs82]) by generating RN-critical pairs and critical pairs between rules in R (a noncanonical system for the domain theory) simultaneously. Such a strategy is called the RN^+-strategy, and it is a complete strategy as long as no incomparable critical pair between rules in R can be produced. A method suggested by Lankford ([La75]) for (partially) handling incomparable critical pairs can be incorporated into RN^+-strategy and increases its power to some extent. These extensions, however, are still weaker than resolution+ paramodulation since they cannot always handle equations in non-unit clauses. An obvious remedy is to employ the modification method of Brand ([Br75]) for non-unit equations. Unfortunately, this trivial solution will undoubtedly increase the search space considerably and thus destroy the major advantage we gained by using the rewrite method. Finding an effective way to deal with equations in non-unit clauses is something worth looking into.

Acknowledgement

The authors would like to thank David Plaisted for many stimulating conversations during the development of this work, Dallas Lankford for his lively correspondence and encouragement, Francois Fages for his comments, and Alan Josephson for implementing TeRSe, a theorem prover that contains some of the strategies discussed here.

7. References

[Br75] Brand, D., Proving theorems with the modification method. *SIAM J. of Computing,* Vol 4, 1975.

[Co71] Cook, S.A., The complexity of theorem-proving procedures. *3rd. ACM Symp. on Theory of Computing,* pp151-158, 1971.

[GrNaOrPl82] Greenbaum, S., Nagasaka, A., O'Rorke, P., Plaisted, D., Comparison of natural deduction and locking resolution implementations. *6th Conf. on Automated Deduction,* Lecture Notes in CS, No. 138, 1982.

[Hs82] Hsiang, J., Topics in automated theorem proving and program generation. Ph.D. Thesis, U. of Illinois at Urbana-Champaign, 1982.

[HsJo82] Hsiang, J. & Josephson, N.A., A term rewriting theorem prover. Unpublished manuscript, 1982.

[Hul80] Hullot, J.-M., A catalogue of canonical term rewriting systems. Report CSL-113, SRI International, 1980.

[HuHu80] Huet, G. & Hullot, J.-M., Proofs by induction in equational theories with constructors. *21st FOCS,* 1980.

[KnBe70] Knuth, D.E. & Bendix, P.B., Simple word problems in universal algebra. *Computational Problems in Abstract Algebra,* J.Leech Ed. Pergamon Press, Oxford, 1970.

[KoHa69] Kowalski, R. & Hayes, P., Semantic trees in automatic theorem proving. *Machine Intelligence 4* Meltzer & Michie eds. pp87-101, 1969.

[La75] Lankford, D.S., Canonical inference. Report ATP-32, Univ. of Texas at Austin, 1975.

[LaBa77] Lankford, D.S. & Ballantyne, A.M., Decision procedure for simple equational theories with commutative-associative axioms. Report ATP-39, Univ. of Texas at Austin, 1977.

[LaBa79] Lankford, D.S. & Ballantyne, A.M., The refutation completeness of blocked permutative narrowing and resolution. *4th Conf. on Automated Deduction,* 1979.

[PeSt81] Peterson, G.E. & Stickel, M.E., Complete sets of reductions for some equational theories. *J.ACM* Vol 28, pp233-264, 1981.

[Pl73] Plotkin, G., Building in equational theories. *Machine Intelligence* 7 Meltzer & Michie Eds., pp73-90

[Ro65] Robinson, J.A., A machine oriented logic based on resolution principle. *J.ACM* Vol 12, pp23-41, 1965.

[Sl74] Slagle, J., Automated theorem proving with simplifiers, commutativity, associativity. *J.ACM* Vol 21, pp622-642, 1974.

[SlNo73] Slagle, J. & Norton, Experiments with an automatic theorem prover having partial ordering inference rules. *C.ACM* Vol 16, pp682-688, 1973.

[St81] Stickel, M.E., A unification algorithm for associative-commutative functions. *J.ACM* Vol 28, pp233-264, 1981.

[St36] Stone, M., The theory of representations for Boolean algebra. *Trans. AMS* Vol 40, pp37-111, 1936.

[WaCo80] Watts, D.E. & Cohen, J.K., Computer implemented set theory. *American Mathematical Monthly,* Vol 87, No. 7, pp557-560.

8. Appendix

8.1. BN-Unification

The unification problem for Boolean terms is considerably simpler than AC-unification since (1) a Boolean term is a sum of products of predicates and different predicates symbols cannot unify with each other, and (2) identical predicates never appear twice in a term (from the idempotence of $*$). However, in order to achieve completeness for the N-strategy, a variable needs to be attached to each term (similar treatment is also needed for obtaining canonical systems for AC-theories, see [PeSt81]). Since the N-strategy only requires unifications between N-terms, we may reformulate the unification problem into the following:

Given two (irreducible) Boolean N-terms s' and t', find the complete set of most general unifiers between $s = us'$ and $t = vt'$, where u and v are new variables.

We call this process *BN-unification.*

We now give a straightforward BN-unification algorithm. The algorithm has as inputs s' and t', which are two seperated (i.e. they do not share common literals) N-terms. The output of the algorithm is Σ, the complete set of most general unifiers. For simplicity of notation, we always assume that the variables in the predicates are properly renamed before substitution.

Proc *UNIFY(s',t'):*
    $\Sigma := \phi$;
    $s := us'$;   /*u and v are the extra variables */
    $t := vt'$;
    call *UNIFY1(s,t,ϕ);*
    return Σ.

Proc *UNIFY1(s,t,unifier):*
    separate s and t, assume that the resulting terms are:
        $s=us_1...s_n$ *and* $t=vt_1...t_m$;
    $\Sigma := \Sigma +$ *unifier* $\cup \{u \leftarrow wt_1...t_m, v \leftarrow ws_1...s_n\}$;
    for $i=1$ **to** n **do**
        for $j=1$ **to** m **do**
            if $\exists\sigma$ s.t. $s_i\sigma=t_j\sigma$ /* σ is a unifier between literals */
                then *UNIFY1(*$s\sigma, t\sigma$*, unifier*$\cup\sigma$*)*.

The unifier "σ" in the algorithm is a most general unifier between the target literals, and is *not* a unifier between the N-terms. One way to reduce the number of loops is to sort the literals in the terms beforehand. Then literals with the same predicate symbols will be grouped together and most of the useless unification attempts between different predicates will be eliminated.

As an example, terms $<s', t'> = <P(x,y)P(y,z)P(z,x), P(a,b)>$ have the following four most general unifiers: $\{u \leftarrow wP(a,b), v \leftarrow wP(x,y)P(y,z)P(z,x)\}$, $\{x \leftarrow a, y \leftarrow b, u \leftarrow w, v \leftarrow wP(b,z)P(z,a)\}$, $\{y \leftarrow a, z \leftarrow b, u \leftarrow w, v \leftarrow wP(x,a)P(b,x)\}$, and $\{z \leftarrow a, x \leftarrow b, u \leftarrow w, v \leftarrow wP(b,y)P(y,a)\}$. Note that in this example there are actually two types of variables and two kinds of unifications. The variables u, v, and w are Boolean variables; x, y, and z are variables in the arguments of the predicates, and the unification between the predicates is the conventional unification.

The extra variable w, which is added to achieve the most general unifiers, will always be replaced by 1 when used in the theorem proving strategies.

8.2. Proofs of Theorems

In order to present the proofs effectively, we use equations $l=0$ instead of rules $l \rightarrow 0$. We also need a modified notion of the semantic tree ([Ro65], [KoHa69]) for the proof.

Definition: *The* **E-atom set** *of a set of clauses S is the set* $\{P(a_1,...,a_n)=0, P(a_1,...,a_n)=1 : a_i$ *is in the Herbrand universe of S and P is a positive literal in S*$\}$.
The elements in the E-atom sets are called the **E-atoms.**

For example, the E-atom set of $\{P(a), \neg Q(fx)\}$ is
$$\{P(a)=0, P(a)=1, Q(a)=0, Q(a)=1, P(fa)=0, P(fa)=1, ...\}.$$
An *E-semantic tree* over a set of clauses S is a conventional semantic tree except that the two arcs of a node are labelled with complementary E-atoms from the E-atom set of S (i.e. $L=0$ and $L=1$ instead of L and $\neg L$). A node N of an E-semantic tree is a *failure node* if there is a ground instance $G=0$ of $C^*=0$ (where C is a clause in S, and C^* is the irreducible form

of C with respect to BA), whose normal expression becomes 1=0 when each literal L in G is replaced by 0 (resp. 1) if $L=0$ (resp. $L=1$) labels an arc on the path from the root to N. An E-semantic tree is *closed* if every leaf is a failure node. Other definitions concerning the semantic tree follow in a similar way. The Herbrand Theorem is also true for the new definitions:

Theorem (Herbrand): *A set of clauses S is unsatisfiable if and only if every complete E-semantic tree of S has a finite closed subtree.*

8.3. Completeness of N-strategy

We now prove the completeness of the N-strategy (Theorem 4.1). The 'if' part is easy since every reduction step is sound. We prove the 'only if' part by induction on the size of the closed E-semantic tree. For the simplicity of notation, we prove only the propositional case. The proof can be generalized to first order predicate calculus without difficulty.

Induction basis: If the E-semantic tree has only one node, then the node must be 1=0 and we are done.

Induction step: We order the closed E-semantic tree in such a way that the right arc is always positive, i.e. $L=0 \diagup\diagdown L=1$. Since each leaf (failure node) of the closed E-semantic tree is an instance of the canonical form of a clause in S, the rightmost leaf must be an equation with an N-term as the left hand side (which corresponds to an all-negative clause in S). Let $LL_1 ... L_n=0$ be the leaf of the rightmost path with $L=1$ as the last arc (see Figure 1). If every leaf in its neighboring subtree does not contain the literal L, the last fork labelled with L can be eliminated and the E-semantic tree will be "shrunk" to become Figure 2 (with D' the same as D). Then by the induction hypothesis, we are done. So the problem lies in the case where some of the leaves in D do contain L. Let $L*s_1+L*s_2+ ... +L*s_m+t=0$ be such a leaf where s_i's are N-terms and t does not contain L. By the BN-unification, $L*s_1$ and $LL_1 ... L_n$ have a most general unifier which unifies the

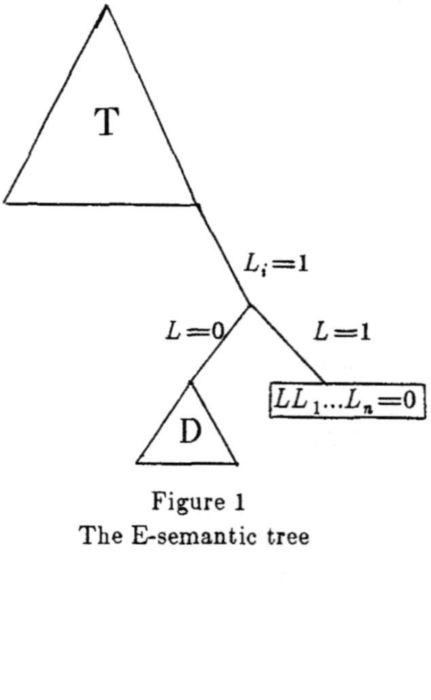

Figure 1
The E-semantic tree

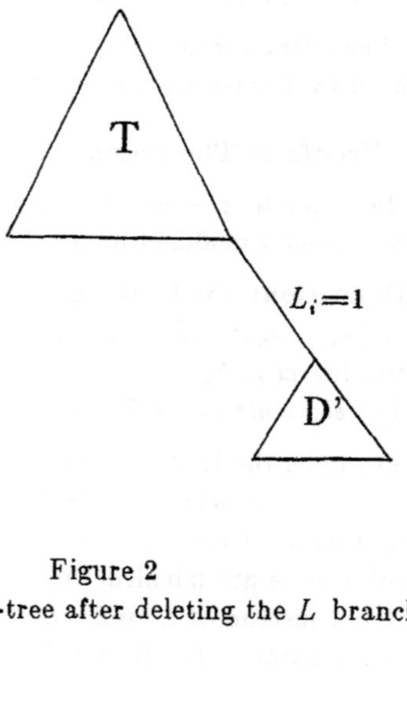

Figure 2
The E-tree after deleting the L branch

extra variable v of $L*s_1$ with part of $L_1...L_n$ (or with all of $L_1...L_n$ if none of the L_i's occur in s_1). Without loss of generality, we assume that only the literals L_{i+1} through L_n appear in s_1, and v is unified with $L_1...L_i$. We then have a superposition $LL_1...L_i*s_1+...+LL_1...L_i*s_m+L_1...L_i*t$, and a new equation (from the corresponding critical pair) $LL_1...L_i*s_2+...+LL_1...L_i*s_m+L_1...L_i*t=0$. Note that (1) this step is a legitimate rule-generating step in the N-strategy, and (2) the first subterm $L*s_1$ has been eliminated. It is not hard to show that it takes at most n superpositions to eliminate the literal L completely from this leaf and that the new failure node thus becomes $L_{i_1}...L_{i_j}*t=0$ for some j and $i_1,..., i_j$. After applying the above process to every equation in D with literal L, the subtree D becomes a new tree D' without the occurrence of L in any of its leaves. The fork labelled with L can then be eliminated and the E-semantic tree is also shrunk accordingly (as shown in Figure 2). By the induction hypothesis, we are done.

8.4. Completeness of RN-strategy

Now we prove Theorem 6.1. The 'if' part is true since all the reduction steps are sound. For the 'only if' part, we proceed by induction on the size of the E-semantic tree. As in the proof of the completeness of the N-strategy, we use equations instead of rules. First, let us look at the case of ground formulas. Let $B=\{t[a_1,...,a_m]=0\}$ be an inconsistent set of ground instances of rules in S, where a_1 to a_m are all the arguments in the literals of t. We may convert B into $B'=\{t[a_1^*,...,a_m^*]=0\}$ where a_i^* is the irreducible form of a_i. (The reductions can be done by finding RN-critical pairs between rules in R and rules in B. Note that a_i^* is unique since R is canonical.) By Theorem 4.1 we know that 1=0 can be derived from B' using BA. Let Figure 3 be an E-semantic tree corresponding to such a proof. We assume, as in the proof of Theorem 4.1, that the right branch of a node is always positive. Let $L_1L_2...L_nP(a_1^*,...,a_m^*)=0$ be the leaf of the rightmost path in the E-semantic tree. Take all the leaves of its neighboring subtree D that contain $P(a_1^*,...,a_m^*)$ and perform

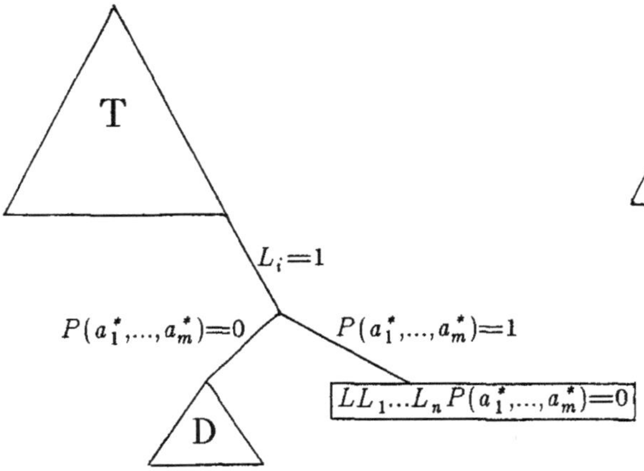

Figure 3
The E-semantic tree

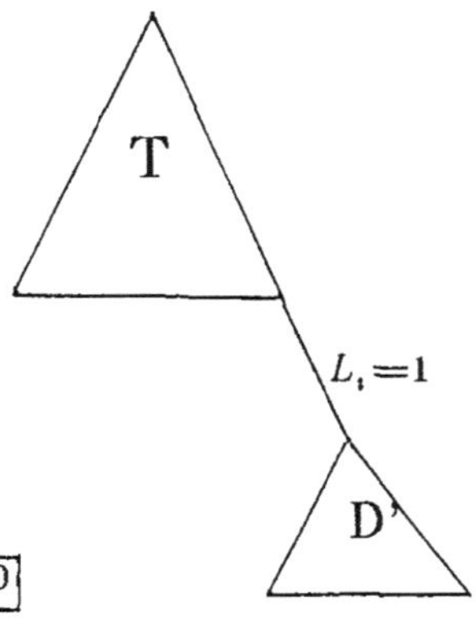

Figure 4
The E-tree after deleting the $P(a_1^*,...,a_m^*)$ branch

superpositions between each of these leaves and $L_1 L_2 ... L_n P(a_1^*,...,a_m^*)=0$ as in the proof of Theorem 4.1. Then the literal $P(a_1^*,...,a_m^*)$ will be eliminated from the tree D, and the branch labelled $P(a_1^*,...,a_m^*)$ can be eliminated (see Figure 4) accordingly. Then by the induction hypothesis, we are done.

The following problem, however, may appear when lifting the above argument to the corresponding nonground formulas of B': There might be some $P(b_1^*,...,b_m^*)t_1 + t_2=0$ where $b_i^*=a_i^*$, but $b_i \neq a_i$. To be more precise, if $P(s_1,..,s_m)$ is the nonground literal corresponding to $P(b_1,...,b_m)$ and $P(t_1,...,t_m)$ is the one corresponding to $P(a_1,...,a_m)$, then $P(b_1^*,...,b_m^*)=P(a_1^*,...,a_m^*)$ does not guarantee that s_i and t_i are unifiable. This is exactly the difficulty for which Slagle and Lankford devised additional techniques (such as narrowing).

We claim that by superimposing rules in R on $P(t_1,...,t_m)$ (i.e., finding RN-critical pairs between rules in R and S), some $P(t'_1,...,t'_m)$ which has $P(a_1^*,...,a_m^*)$ as an instance will eventually be generated. If this is true, let $P(t'_1,...,t'_m)$ and $P(s'_1,...,s'_m)$, corresponding to $P(a_1^*,...,a_m^*)$ and $P(b_1^*,...b_m^*)$ respectively, be such generated literals. They can certainly unify with each other and produce the corresponding critical pair we desire. Thus, it remains only to prove the claim.

For simplicity, we use $P(t_1,...,t_m) \rightarrow 0$ as a rule.

Lemma 6.2: *Given a canonical system R and an extra rule $P(t_1,...,t_m) \rightarrow 0$ with $P(a_1,...,a_m) \rightarrow 0$ as a ground instance, by performing the RN-strategy on $R \cup \{P(t_1,...,t_m) \rightarrow 0\}$, we will generate a rule $P(t'_1,...,t'_m) \rightarrow 0$ which has $P(a_1^*,...,a_m^*)$ as a ground instance.*

Proof: We proceed by induction on the total number (n) of steps needed to reduce all a_i to a_i^*. If n=0, nothing need be proved.

If $a_i \neq a_i^*$, there must be a subterm c of a_i which is a ground instance of the left hand side of some rule $l \rightarrow r$ in R. We denote this a_i by $a_i[c]$ and the corresponding nonground term by $t_i[l']$ (where l' is an instance of l). $P(t_1,...,t_i[l'],...,t_m) \rightarrow 0$ and $l \rightarrow r$ will produce a critical pair $\langle P(t_1,...,t_i[r'],...,t_m),0 \rangle$ and, thus, a new rule $P(t_1,...,t_i[r'],...,t_m) \rightarrow 0$. Since the corresponding ground instance of $t_i[r']$ is at least one reduction step closer to a_i^* than a_i, by the induction hypothesis, we are done.

We thus have completed lifting the argument to the nonground case and finished the proof of Theorem 6.1.

COMPLEXITY OF INFINITE TREES

K. Indermark
Lehrstuhl für Informatik II, RWTH Aachen
Büchel 29 - 31, 5100 Aachen
W.-Germany

Abstract

Rational schemes interpreted over derived algebras permit a simple algebraic analysis of higher type recursion. Their equivalence is characterized by infinite trees. Measuring their complexity by the size of finite subtrees we obtain a direct proof of the recursion hierarchy.

Introduction

Recursion is certainly a fundamental control construct of programming languages. The problem whether its auxiliary use on higher functional domains adds computational power to a language has been investigated by W. Damm in great detail. He solved this problem successfully using the typed λ-calculus with fixed-point operators and constructing hierarchies of formal languages [Dam 82].

A simplified algebraic framework for proving the recursion hierarchy was suggested in [Ind 80] by means of rational schemes with rank-free interpretations. It is the purpose of this paper to demonstrate that this suggestion in fact allows an appropriate treatment of higher type recursion.

Denotational semantics supports the view that the function computed by a program is a certain combination of given base functions. Under the influence of D. Scott's work the advantage of continuous base functions was observed : their use avoids predicates and partial functions. As a consequence, complete algebras were recognized as a basis for an algebraic theory of programming [Niv 72, 75].

In a complete algebra there is a natural class of operations definable as the closure of projections and base operations under composition and resolution. The fundamental character of resolution (regular equations with parameters) already became evident in [Bek 69], [Wag 71 a,b] and [Wan 72].

Of course, resolution is simpler than recursion - their difference corresponds to that of regular and context-free languages. However, the simple control mechanism of regular equations turns out to be powerful enough in order to model not only recursion but also higher type recursion.

Technically, this is achieved by taking derived algebras (algebras of operations) as interpretations. This technique has first been used by Maibaum in formal language theory [Mai 74].
Since the derived algebra is heterogeneous according to the arities of operations, we allow an operation to have an arbitrary number of arguments. The resulting theory of complete algebras without rank is not very different from the ranked case, but it avoids many-sortedness.
Secondly, we modify the derivation insofar as base operations of the underlying algebra are not represented by nullary constants but by left-composition. This gives some additional simplifications.
The main advantage of this approach is that the semantics of a rational scheme interpreted by a derived algebra splits into several parts which can be analyzed seperately. Since there exist initial algebras for complete algebras representable by infinite trees [Gog 77], the equivalence class of a n-rational scheme can be characterized by an infinite tree which originates from a regular infinite tree by successive elimination of composition and projection symbols. Using an appropriate complexity measure we shall see that the resulting infinite trees become more and more complex. This easily demonstrates the recursion hierarchy.

1. Ω-algebras without rank

We consider algebras whose operations have an arbitrary number of arguments, including the empty list ε . This modification is of technical advantage for dealing with higher type objects because we thus circumvent many-sortedness.

Let A be a set.
Then $\underline{\text{Ops}}(A) := \{f \mid f : A^* \longrightarrow A\}$ is the set of *operations on A.*
Let Ω be a set of *operation symbols* (without arities).
Then $\varphi : \Omega \longrightarrow \underline{\text{Ops}}(A)$ determines an *Ω-algebra* :

$$\mathcal{A} := \langle A;\varphi\rangle \in \underline{\text{Alg}}_{\Omega}$$

For any set X there exists

$$F_{\Omega}(X) \in \underline{\text{Alg}}_{\Omega} \text{ freely generated by } X \quad .$$

Hence, any assignment $\alpha : X \longrightarrow A$ with $\mathcal{A} = \langle A;\varphi\rangle \in \underline{\text{Alg}}_{\Omega}$ extends uniquely to a homomorphism

$$\bar{\alpha} : F_{\Omega}(X) \longrightarrow \mathcal{A} \quad .$$

If $X = \emptyset$, we simply write F_{Ω} instead of $F_{\Omega}(\emptyset)$, and we denote the unique homomorphism by $h_{\mathcal{A}}$.
The same situation arises when starting from a partially ordered or complete partially ordered set $\mathcal{A}$ -complete with respect to directed sub-

sets - and restricting Ops(A) to monotone or continuous operations on A . The corresponding objects are denoted by

$$\underline{\mathrm{Alg}}^{p}_{\Omega} \;,\quad F^{p}_{\Omega}(X) \;,\quad h^{p}_{A}$$

$$\text{and}\quad \underline{\mathrm{Alg}}^{c}_{\Omega} \;,\quad F^{c}_{\Omega}(X) \;,\quad h^{c}_{A} \;.$$

Although we do not need any representation of a freely generated algebra, we may of course view its elements as trees. In particular, we may assume set inclusion for the carrier sets :

$$F_{\Omega}(X) \subseteq F^{p}_{\Omega}(X) \subseteq F^{c}_{\Omega}(X)$$

Examples With $\Omega = \{F_1, F_2, \ldots\}$ we have

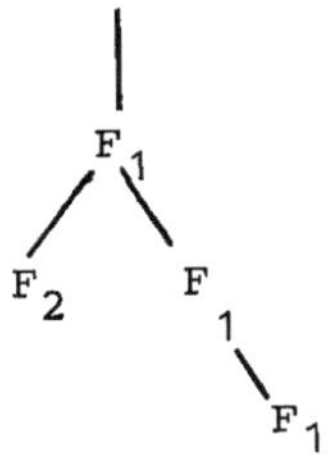

$\in F_{\Omega}$,

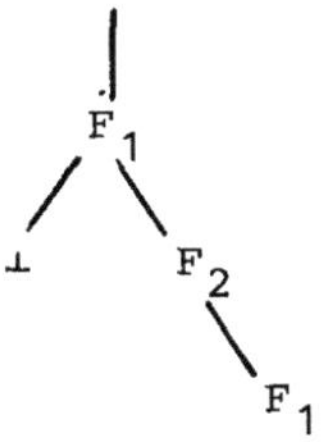

$\in F^{p}_{\Omega}$

and

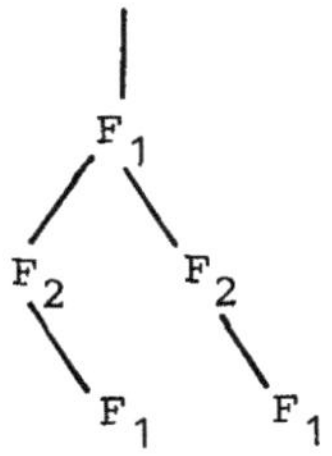

:=

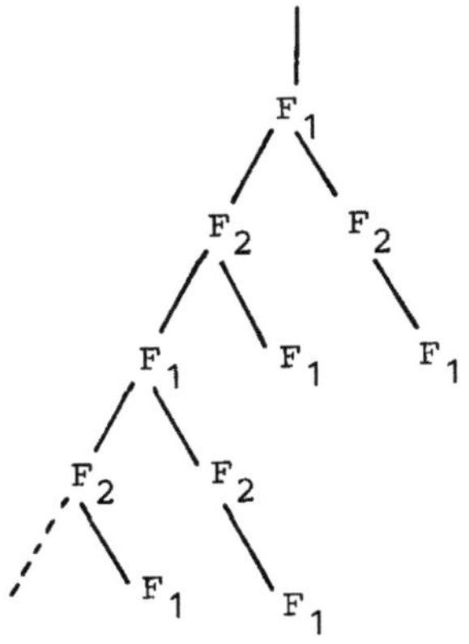

$\in F^{c}_{\Omega}$

Note that the operation symbols have no arity and can therefore occur at arbitrary nodes.

Derived operations

If we choose a standard alphabet

$$X = \{x_1, x_2, \ldots\} \quad ,$$

each infinite tree $t \in F^{c}_{\Omega}(X)$ determines for $A \in \underline{\mathrm{Alg}}^{c}_{\Omega}$ an operation.

For its definition we associate with

$$a = a_1 .. a_r \in A^*$$

the assignment

$$[a,\bot] : X \longrightarrow A$$

$$x_i \longmapsto \underline{proj}_i(a) := \begin{cases} a_i & \underline{if} \quad i \leq \underline{length}(a) \\ \bot & \underline{else} \end{cases}$$

and get the *derivation operator*

$$\underline{derop}_A : F^c_\Omega(X) \longrightarrow \underline{Ops}(A)$$

$$t \longmapsto (a \longmapsto \overline{[a,\bot]}(t)) \quad .$$

Substitution

If $A = F^c_\Omega(X)$, $\underline{derop}_A$ describes *substitution of infinite trees* :

$$\underline{derop}_{F^c_\Omega(X)} =: \underline{sbst}^\bot : F^c_\Omega(X) \longrightarrow \underline{Ops}(F^c_\Omega(X))$$

The index $\bot$ indicates that in $\underline{sbst}^\bot(t_o)(t_1..t_r)$ the variables $x_{r+1}, x_{r+2}, \ldots$ are replaced by $\bot$.

Iteration

In order to define *iteration of infinite trees* we shall also consider another kind of substitution which only substitutes given arguments and leaves the remaining arguments unchanged :

for $\quad t_1,\ldots,t_r \in F^c_\Omega(X)$ we define the assignment

$$[t_1..t_r, x_{r+1}] : X \longrightarrow F^c_\Omega(X)$$

$$x_i \longmapsto \underline{if} \quad i \leq r \ \underline{then} \ t_i \ \underline{else} \ x_i$$

and get

$$\underline{sbst} : F^c_\Omega(X) \longrightarrow \underline{Ops}(F^c_\Omega(X))$$

$$t \longmapsto (t_1..t_r \longmapsto \overline{[t_1..t_r, x_{r+1}]}(t)) \quad .$$

This is used to introduce the *iteration of infinite trees at* i , where $i \geq 1$:

$$\underline{iter}_i : F^c_\Omega(X)^* \longrightarrow F^c_\Omega(X) \quad \text{is defined by}$$

$$\underline{iter}_i(t_1..t_r) :=$$

$$\underline{proj}_i(\underline{fix}(u_1..u_r \longmapsto \underline{sbst}(t_1)(u_1..u_r)..\ \underline{sbst}(t_r)(u_1..u_r)))$$

Here, $\underline{fix}$ gives the least fixed-point of a continuous transformation of $F^c_\Omega(X)^r$.

2. Rational Ω-schemes

For an arbitrary complete algebra $A \in \underline{Alg}^c_\Omega$ there exists a natural class of operations, called *rational operations*, which can be obtained uniformly from the class of projections by means of left-composition with base operations of A, composition and resolution. The essential construction is that of resolution : it corresponds to the least solution of a system of regular equations with parameters.
For defining rational operations we choose rational schemes in their general inductive form. This is of technical advantage as we can introduce at the same time the derivation mechanism.

Abstract syntax

We enlarge the set Ω of operation symbols first to the set

$D(\Omega) := \{F' \mid F \in \Omega\} \cup \{\mathbb{P}_i \mid i > 0\} \cup \{\mathbb{C}\}$ of *derived symbols*

and next to the set

$R(\Omega) := D(\Omega) \cup \{\mathbb{R}_i \mid i > 0\}$ of *rational symbols* over Ω.

The *algebra of rational Ω-schemes* is then defined as

$$\mathrm{Rat}_\Omega := F_{R(\Omega)} \quad .$$

Initial algebra semantics

Let $A = \langle A;\varphi\rangle \in \underline{Alg}^c_\Omega$ be an *interpretation* of Ω . For the semantics of rational Ω-schemes it suffices to construct an $R(\Omega)$-algebra because of initiality of Rat_Ω in $\underline{Alg}_{R(\Omega)}$. Again we proceed in two steps : first we define the *derived algebra* of A

$$D(A) := \langle \underline{Ops}(A);\bar\varphi\rangle \in \underline{Alg}^c_{D(\Omega)}$$

where

$$\bar\varphi(F')(f_1..f_r)(a) := \varphi(F)(f_1(a)..f_r(a)) \qquad \textit{left-composition}$$

$$\bar\varphi(\mathbb{P}_i)(f_1..f_r)(a) := \underline{proj}_i(a) \qquad \textit{projection}$$

$$\bar\varphi(\mathbb{C})(f_o..f_r)(a) := f_o(f_1(a)..f_r(a)) \qquad \textit{composition}$$

$$\bar\varphi(\mathbb{C})(\varepsilon)(a) := \bot_A$$

with $r,i \in \mathbb{N}$.
Next, we augment $D(A)$ to the *rational algebra* of A

$$R(A) := \langle \underline{Ops}(A);\bar\varphi\rangle \in \underline{Alg}^c_{R(\Omega)}$$

where in addition

$$\bar\varphi(\mathbb{R}_i)(f_1..f_r)(a) := \underline{proj}_i(\underline{fix}(f)) \text{ with } f : A^r \longrightarrow A^r$$
$$b \longmapsto f_1(ba)..f_r(ba)$$

Now, the semantics of rational Ω-schemes with interpretation $A \in \underline{Alg}^c_\Omega$ is given by the initial $R(\Omega)$-homomorphism

$$[\![\ ]\!]_A := h_{R(\Omega)} : Rat_\Omega \longrightarrow R(A)$$

Equivalence, infinite trees

As it may happen that different schemes define the same rational operation in each interpretation we have a natural equivalence relation on $\underline{Rat}_\Omega$ (the carrier set of Rat_Ω) :

$$S \sim T :\Leftrightarrow (\forall\ A \in \underline{Alg}^c_\Omega)\ [\![S]\!]_A = [\![T]\!]_A$$

We shall characterize this equivalence by infinite Ω-trees. For this purpose we extend the algebra of infinite Ω-trees

$$F^c_\Omega(X) = < F^c_\Omega(X);\varphi > \in \underline{Alg}^c_\Omega$$

to an $R(\Omega)$-algebra such that the derivation operator turns out to be an $R(\Omega)$-homomorphism. For technical reasons, we proceed again in two steps.

$$F^c_\Omega(X)^D = < F^c_\Omega(X);\hat{\varphi} > \in \underline{Alg}^c_{D(\Omega)}$$

is defined by

$$\begin{aligned}
\hat{\varphi}(F') &:= \varphi(F)\\
\hat{\varphi}(\mathbb{P}_i)(t_1..t_r) &:= x_i\\
\hat{\varphi}(\mathbb{C})(t_o..t_r) &:= \underline{sbst}^\perp(t_o)(t_1..t_r)\\
\hat{\varphi}(\mathbb{C})(\varepsilon) &:= \perp
\end{aligned}$$

and extended to

$$F^c_\Omega(X)^R = < F^c_\Omega(X);\hat{\varphi} > \in \underline{Alg}^c_{R(\Omega)}$$

by
$$\hat{\varphi}(\mathbb{R}_i)(t_1..t_r) := \overline{[\perp^r,x_1]}(\underline{iter}_i(t_1..t_r))$$

where the assignment $[\perp^r,x_1] : X \longrightarrow F^c_\Omega(X)$ is a shift of variables : $x_i \longmapsto \underline{if}\ i > r\ \underline{then}\ x_{i-r}\ \underline{else}\ \perp$.

It was shown in [Ind 80] that the derivation operator now is an $R(\Omega)$-homomorphism

$$\underline{derop}_A : F^c_\Omega(X)^R \longrightarrow R(A)$$

Moreover, since Rat_Ω is initial in $\underline{Alg}_{R(\Omega)}$ there is a unique $R(\Omega)$-homomorphism
$$\underline{tree}_\Omega : Rat_\Omega \longrightarrow F^c_\Omega(X)^R$$

and we conclude the coincidence

$$[\![\ ]\!]_A = \underline{derop}_A \circ \underline{tree}_\Omega\ .$$

Now, the characterization of equivalence by infinite trees is easily obtained : $S \sim T \Leftrightarrow \underline{tree}_\Omega(S) = \underline{tree}_\Omega(T)$

3. Derived interpretations

We are now well prepared for modelling higher type recursion : we leave the control structure represented by rational schemes unchanged, but take repeatedly derived algebras as interpretations.

Abstract syntax of (n+1)-rational schemes

By induction on $n \in \mathbb{N}$ we construct the set

$D^n(\Omega)$ of *derived symbols of degree n* :

$$D^0(\Omega) := \Omega$$
$$D^{n+1}(\Omega) := D(D^n(\Omega))$$

The *algebra of (n+1)-rational Ω-schemes* is then simply defined as

$$Rat_\Omega^{(n+1)} := Rat_{D^n(\Omega)} = F_{R(D^n(\Omega))}$$

Semantics

Let $A = \langle A;\varphi\rangle \in \underline{Alg}_\Omega^c$ be an interpretation of Ω .

By induction we get *the derived algebra of degree n*

$$D^n(A) \in \underline{Alg}^c_{D^n(\Omega)} :$$
$$D^0(A) := A$$
$$D^{n+1}(A) := D(D^n(A))$$

From initiality we conclude the unique $R(D^n(\Omega))$-homomorphism

$$h_{R(D^n(A))} : Rat_\Omega^{(n+1)} \longrightarrow R(D^n(A))$$

which gives us the semantics of an (n+1)-rational Ω-scheme S by

$$[\![S]\!]_{D^n(A)} := h_{R(D^n(A))}(S) : \underline{Ops}^n(A)^* \longrightarrow \underline{Ops}^n(A)$$

where $\underline{Ops}^0(A) := A$ and $\underline{Ops}^{n+1}(A) := \underline{Ops}(\underline{Ops}^n(A))$.

O-semantics

Our interest in using fixed-points on higher functional domains originated from the question whether the possibility of high level recursion increases the relative computational power of a language - in other words : can we define more elements of a complete algebra by auxiliary fixed-point constructions on higher functional levels.

In order to prove a positive answer it suffices to consider repeated applications of higher level functions to empty argument lists ε thus

producing a low level object.
Therefore we modify the semantics.

For $S \in \underline{Rat}_\Omega^{(n+1)}$ we define *O-semantics* of S with interpretation A by

$$[\![S]\!]_A^O := [\![S]\!]_{D^n(A)} \overbrace{(\varepsilon)(\varepsilon)\dots(\varepsilon)}^{n+1} \in A$$

Now, it becomes possible to compare schemes of different functional levels.
Let $S \in \underline{Rat}_\Omega^{(n+1)}$ and $T \in \underline{Rat}_\Omega^{(m+1)}$.
Their *O-equivalence* is defined by

$$S \approx T :\Leftrightarrow (\forall\, A \in \underline{Alg}_\Omega^c) [\![S]\!]_A^\circ = [\![T]\!]_A^\circ \; .$$

Again, this equivalence can be characterized by infinite Ω-trees.
If $S \in \underline{Rat}_\Omega^{(n+1)}$, we compute its Ω-tree by taking its rational $D^n(\Omega)$-tree followed by successive elimination of derived symbols.
The initial $D(\Omega)$-homomorphism

$$\underline{yield}_\Omega : F_{D(\Omega)}^c \longrightarrow F_\Omega^c(X)^D$$

describes this elimination. Since O-semantics is given by repeated application to empty argument lists, variables in infinite trees do not have any influence and will be replaced by $\bot$. Therefore, we define the Ω-homomorphisms

$$\underline{\bot\text{-yield}}_\Omega : F_{D(\Omega)}^c \longrightarrow F_\Omega^c \quad \text{by} \quad \overline{[\varepsilon,\bot]} \circ \underline{yield}_\Omega$$

and

$$\underline{\bot\text{-tree}}_\Omega : F_{R(\Omega)} \longrightarrow F_\Omega^c \quad \text{by} \quad \overline{[\varepsilon,\bot]} \circ \underline{tree}_\Omega$$

Taking into account that $[\![\;]\!]_{D^n(A)} = \underline{derop}_{D^n(A)} \circ \underline{tree}_{D^n(\Omega)}$ we get the indicated splitting of O-semantics.

(1) Lemma For $S \in \underline{Rat}_\Omega^{(n+1)}$ we have

$$[\![S]\!]_A^O = h_A^c \underbrace{(\underline{\bot\text{-yield}}_\Omega(\dots\underline{\bot\text{-yield}}_{D^{n-1}(\Omega)}(\underline{\bot\text{-tree}}_{D^n(\Omega)}(S))\dots))}_{=:\ \underline{O\text{-tree}}_\Omega(S)}$$

This implies as an immediate consequence the desired characterization of O-equivalence.

(2) Theorem Let $S \in \underline{Rat}_\Omega^{(n+1)}$ and $T \in \underline{Rat}_\Omega^{(m+1)}$.

Then :

$$S \approx T \Leftrightarrow \underline{O\text{-tree}}_\Omega(S) = \underline{O\text{-tree}}_\Omega(T)$$

In this way, higher type recursion leads to classes of infinite trees.
Let

$$\underline{Rattree}_\Omega^{(n+1)} := \underline{O\text{-tree}}_\Omega(\underline{Rat}_\Omega^{(n+1)})$$

be the set of *(n+1)-rational Ω-trees*. In the sequel, we shall investigate their complexity and prove the hierarchy theorem :

(3) Theorem $(\forall n \in \mathbb{N})$ $\underline{\text{Rattree}}_{\Omega}^{(n+1)} \subsetneqq \underline{\text{Rattree}}_{\Omega}^{(n+2)}$

4. Representation of (n+1)-rational trees

We have seen that an (n+1)-rational Ω-tree is constructable from an 1-rational $D^n(\Omega)$-tree by successive elimination of derived symbols using $\underline{\perp\text{-yield}}$. In order to prove the hierarchy we shall investigate the impact of derived symbols on the structure of these trees. Therefore, we first choose an appropriate representation of derived symbols. In particular, we have to distinguish between different derivation levels. This will be indicated by a *level index* p and a *derivation index* q in

$$G^{p.q} \in D^n(\Omega) \qquad \text{where } p.q \text{ is short for } (p,q) :$$

$$\begin{aligned} D^0(\Omega) &:= \{F^{1.0} \mid F \in \Omega\} \\ D(D^n(\Omega)) &:= \{G^{p.q+1} \mid G^{p.q} \in D^n(\Omega)\} \\ &\cup \{\mathbb{P}_i^{n+2.0} \mid i > 0\} \qquad (\mathbb{P} := \mathbb{P}_1) \\ &\cup \{\mathbb{C}^{n+2.0}\} \end{aligned}$$

It follows that p+q = n+1 which is the "semantic level" since $\bar{\varphi}(G^{p.q}) \in \underline{\text{Ops}}^{n+1}(A)$.

Now we can explicitly describe the construction of an (n+1)-rational Ω-tree from an 1-rational $D^n(\Omega)$-tree, $n \geq 1$.

$$\underline{\perp\text{-yield}}_{D^{n-1}(\Omega)} : F^c_{D^n(\Omega)} \longrightarrow F^c_{D^{n-1}(\Omega)} \quad \text{splits into}$$

$$\overline{[\varepsilon,\perp]} \circ \underline{\text{yield}}_{D^{n-1}(\Omega)}$$

$$\text{with} \quad \underline{\text{yield}}_{D^{n-1}(\Omega)} : F^c_{D^n(\Omega)} \longrightarrow F^c_{D^{n-1}(\Omega)}(X)^D$$

Since this mapping, $\downarrow$ for short , is a $D^n(\Omega)$-homomorphism, we have

$$\begin{aligned} \downarrow(G^{p.q+1}(t_1..t_r)) &= G^{p.q}(\downarrow(t_1)..\downarrow(t_r)) \\ \downarrow(\mathbb{P}_i^{n+2.0}(t_1..t_r)) &= x_i \\ \downarrow(\mathbb{C}^{n+2.0}(t_0..t_r)) &= \underline{\text{sbst}}^{\perp}(\downarrow(t_0))(\downarrow(t_1)..\downarrow(t_r)) \\ \downarrow(\mathbb{C}^{n+2.0}(\varepsilon)) &= \perp \end{aligned}$$

Moreover, as $\downarrow$ is continuous we may carry out the computation on finite subtrees (approximations).

At this point we realize the advantage of representing a base operation on level n by its left-composition on level n+1 : the tree structure remains unchanged. As an immediate consequence we get the inclusion part of the hierarchy theorem (3) :

$$(\forall n \in \mathbb{N}) \quad \underline{\text{Rattree}}_{\Omega}^{(n+1)} \subseteq \underline{\text{Rattree}}_{\Omega}^{(n+2)}$$

For the proof we only have to replace in the defining 1-rational $D^n(\Omega)$-tree a symbol $G^{p.q}$ by $G^{p.q+1}$. The resulting 1-rational $D^{n+1}(\Omega)$-tree yields the same Ω-tree.

Next, we shall present for $n \geqslant 1$ "hierarchy candidates"

$$t_{n+1} \in \underline{\text{Rattree}}_{\Omega}^{(n+1)}$$

such that $t_{n+1} \notin \underline{\text{Rattree}}_{\Omega}^{(n)}$.

They are constructed from $t^{n+1} \in \underline{\text{Rattree}}_{D^n(\Omega)}^{(1)}$ as explained below.

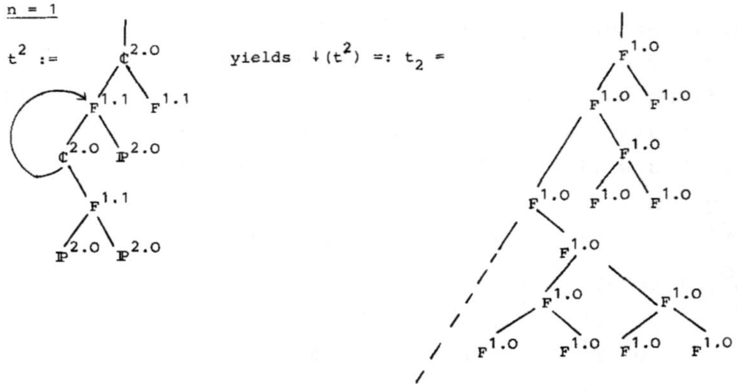

Note that during ↓-computation $\mathbb{P}^{2.0}$ is replaced by x_1 which disappears within the substitution produced by elimination of $₵^{2.0}$.
This first example already demonstrates the influence of derived symbols : iterated composition yields finite subtrees of growing size.

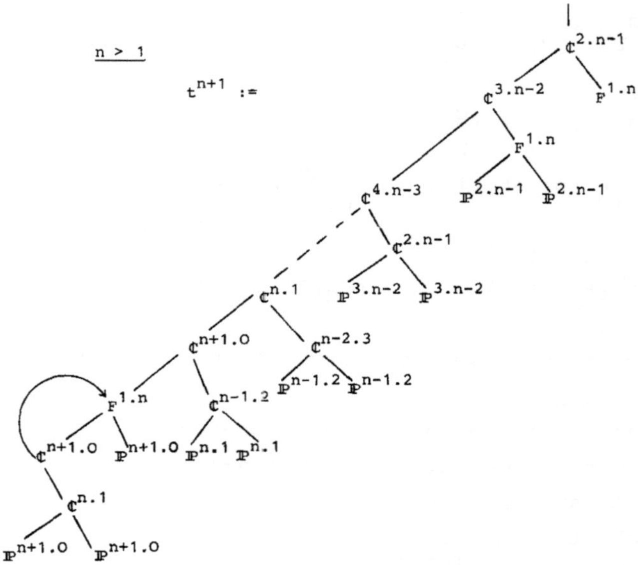

On computing t_{n+1} we carry out substitution of substitutions of ... so that the resulting tree becomes more and more complex. The growth of finite subtree size increases with level n.

As an example we compute t_3 :

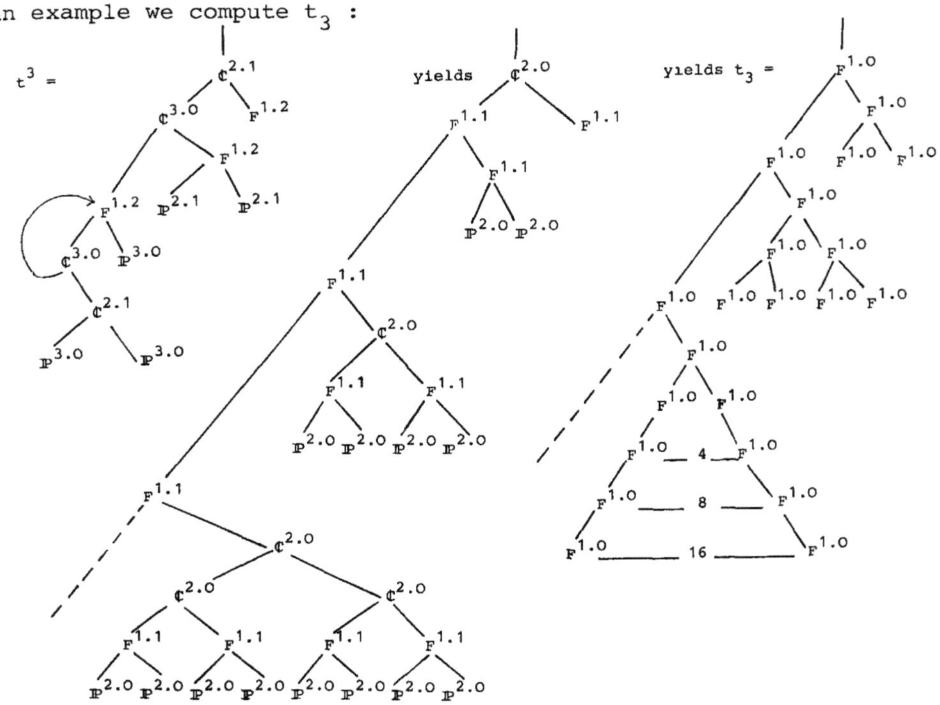

For arbitrary $n > 1$ we can prove by induction that

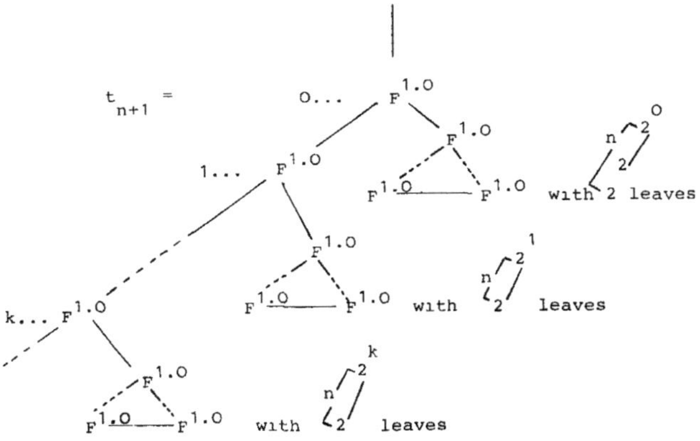

5. Complexity of (n+1)-rational Ω-trees

Obviously, it holds for our example trees that $t_{n+1} \in \underline{\text{Rattree}}_{\Omega}^{(n+1)}$. For a hierarchy proof it remains to verify that $t_{n+1} \notin \underline{\text{Rattree}}_{\Omega}^{(n)}$. Therefore, we introduce a complexity measure on infinite trees following our previous observations : we choose the breadth of finite subtrees with respect to the depth of their roots.

Let $\mathbb{N}^{\top}$ be the cpo of natural numbers with top element such that

$$0 < 1 < 2 < \dots < \top$$

and $M := \{f \mid f : \mathbb{N} \longrightarrow \mathbb{N}^{\top}\}$ be the cpo of *measures* with pointwise ordering.

The *measure algebra*

$$M = \langle M; \sim \rangle \in \underline{Alg}^{c}_{\Omega}$$

is then defined by

$$\tilde{F}(\varepsilon) := \underline{\text{if}}\ k = 0\ \underline{\text{then}}\ 1\ \underline{\text{else}}\ 0$$

$$\tilde{F}(f_1 .. f_r) := \underline{\text{if}}\ k = 0\ \underline{\text{then}}\ \text{if}\ \prod_{i=1}^{r} f_i(0) \neq 0\ \underline{\text{then}}\ \sum_{i=1}^{r} f_i(0)\ \underline{\text{else}}\ 0\ \ \underline{\text{else}}\ \max_{i=1}^{r}(f_i(k-1))$$

Clearly, F does not depend on F. Moreover, one can easily check that $\tilde{F}$ is continuous. Hence, there is a unique Ω-homomorphism

$$\Gamma : F^{c}_{\Omega}(X) \longrightarrow M$$

which extends $x_i \longmapsto \underline{\text{if}}\ k = 0\ \underline{\text{then}}\ 1\ \underline{\text{else}}\ 0$.

$\Gamma(t)$ is called *finite subtree complexity* of t.

We see that $\Gamma(t)(k) \neq 0$ iff t contains a node of depth k being the root of a finite subtree $t' \in F_{\Omega}(X)$. Of these subtrees $\Gamma(t)(k)$ takes the maximal breadth.

Computing the complexity of our example trees t_{n+1} shows :

(4) <u>Lemma</u> $\Gamma(t_{n+1})(0) = 0$

$\Gamma(t_{n+1})(k+1) = \underbrace{2^{2^{\cdot^{\cdot^{2}}}}}_{n}$ for all $n \geq 1$

Now, we determine upper bounds for the complexity of $t \in \underline{Rattree}^{(n)}_{\Omega}$.

First, we can prove that each regular tree has bounded complexity :

(5) <u>Lemma</u> For each $t \in \underline{Rattree}^{(1)}_{\Omega}$ there exists $c \in \mathbb{N}$ such that

$$\Gamma(t)(k) \leq c \quad \text{for all } k \in \mathbb{N}.$$

This relies on the fact that a regular tree has only a finite number of different subtrees.

(6) <u>Corollary</u> $\underline{Rattree}^{(1)}_{\Omega} \subsetneq \underline{Rattree}^{(2)}_{\Omega}$

Next, we analyse the increase of complexity produced by <u>$\perp$-yield</u>. So, let $t \in F^{c}_{D(\Omega)}$ be an arbitrary infinite $D(\Omega)$-tree such that $\Gamma(t) \leq f$. A look at the computation of our example trees shows what happens on elimination of derived symbols : composition symbols produce substitution of subtrees causing exponential growth of the breadth of a finite subtree. However, if f is constant, as in the case of regular trees, $2^{f(n)}$ remains constant ! But, since composition symbols can also occur on infinite branches they can produce more and more substitutions of finite subtrees :

(7) Theorem Let $t \in F^{c}_{D(\Omega)}$ such that $\Gamma(t) \leqslant f$.
Then there are c_1 , $c_2 \in \mathbb{N}$ such that $\Gamma(\underline{\bot\text{-yield}}(t))(k) \leqslant \prod_{i=1}^{c_1 \cdot k} 2^{c_2 \cdot f(i)}$

The proof proceeds by algebraic induction on the structure of finite approximations of t in $F^{p}_{D(\Omega)}$ and exploits continuity of yield.
From (5) and (7) it follows :
(8) Corollary For $n \geqslant 1$ and $t \in \underline{\text{Rattree}}_{\Omega}^{(n+1)}$ there are $c_1, c_2 \in \mathbb{N}$ such that

$$\Gamma(t)(k) \leqslant \left.2^{\cdot^{\cdot^{\cdot^{2^{c_1 \cdot k + c_2}}}}}\right\} n$$

Therefore : $t_{n+1} \notin \underline{\text{Rattree}}_{\Omega}^{(n)}$.

Conclusion

The algebraic analysis of recursion on higher functional domains shows that its computational power grows with increasing functional level. Moreover, the approach by combinators (derived symbols) clearly demonstrates the reason for this phenomenon : it is composition of higher functionals which in connection with recursion causes growing complexity.

Acknowledgement

It should be clear that this paper would not have been written without the long-standing efforts W. Damm spent on solving the recursion hierarchy problem. In numerous discussions with him I learnt a lot about the nature of higher type recursion. I gratefully acknowledge his help.

References

[Bek 69] Bekić, H : Definable operations in general algebras, and the theory of automata and flowcharts ,Research Report,IBM Lb., Vienna, 1969

[Dam 82] Damm, W. : The IO- and OI-hierarchies Theoret. Comput. Sci. 20 (1982) 2, 95 - 208

[Gog 77] Goguen, J.A. et. al. : Initial algebra semantics and continuous algebras Journal ACM 24 (1977) 1, 68 - 95

[Ind 80] Indermark, K. : On rational definitions in complete algebras without rank Theoret. Comput. Sci. 21(1982), 281 - 313

[Mai 74] Maibaum, T.S.E. : A generalized approach to formal languages Journal Comp. Syst. Sci. 8 (1974), 409 - 439

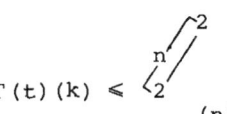

[Niv 72] Nivat, M. : Langages algébriques sur le magma libre et sémantique des schémas de programme
in : Automata, Languages, and Programming (M. Nivat, ed.)
North-Holland P.C. (1972) , 293 - 308

[Niv 75] Nivat, M. : On the interpretation of recursion polyadic program schemes - Symposia Matematica 15, Rome 1975, 255 - 281

[Wag 71a] Wagner, E.G. : An algebraic theory of recursive definitions and recursive languages - Proc. 3rd ACM Symp.
Theory of Computing (1971) ,12 - 23

[Wag 71b] Wagner, E.G. : Languages for defining sets in arbitrary algebras - Proc. IEEE Conf. SWAT 12 (1971), 192 -201

[Wan 72] Wand, M. : A concrete approach to abstract recursive definitions - in : Automata, Languages, and Programming (M. Nivat, ed.) North-Holland P.C. (1972), 331 - 344

INCREMENTAL CONSTRUCTION OF UNIFICATION ALGORITHMS IN EQUATIONAL THEORIES

Jean-Pierre Jouannaud, Claude Kirchner, Helene Kirchner

Centre de Recherche en Informatique de Nancy et GRECO Programmation
Campus scientifique. BP 239. 54506 Vandoeuvre-les-Nancy Cedex
France

1 INTRODUCTION

In this paper, we address the unification problem in equational theories. This is known to be an important, however rather hard problem. Applications may be found in various situations such as the use of paramodulation in automatic theorem proving and the computation of complete sets of criticals pairs in the Knuth and Bendix completion procedure [P&S,81].

Many important equational theories have been studied in the past, and specific unification algorithms are known for some of them, including commutativity, associativity [PLO,72], idempotence [R&S,78], associativity and commutativity [STI,81], associativity, commutativity and idempotence [L&S,77] and abelian group theory [LAN,79]. All of these algorithms are complete. Some of them are not proved to be finitely terminating.

On the other hand, Fay [FAY,79] described a complete unification algorithm for some equational theories that possess a confluent and noetherian term rewriting system as defined by Knuth and Bendix [K&B,70]. This method relies on using the narrowing process defined by Lankford [LAN,75]. More recently, Hullot [HUL,80] described an improved version of Fay's algorithm, which both allows avoiding useless computations and gives sufficient conditions for termination.

Problems arise in practice, that forbid the use of this elegant technique:

- various equational theories contain axioms that cannot be oriented without loosing the finite termination property (commutativity axiom for example).
- the completion of many equational theories generates an infinite set of rules (for example the signed trees theory [KKJ,81; K&K,82]).
- even applied to convergent sets of rules, Hullot's algorithm does not always terminate: group theory for example with the rule: -(x.y) -> -y.-x .

Against such a situation, the set A of axioms can be split into a set E of equations and a sét R of rules. This technique was still investigated by Hullot [HUL,80] when R is confluent modulo E as defined in [HUE,80], with the strong restriction of using left linear term rewriting systems, and in [JKK,82] when R is E-confluent as defined by Peterson and Stickel [P&S,81], and E-commuting, which requires in practice linear equations.

Our goal here is to generalize these results to the case where R is E-confluent and E-coherent, as defined in [JOU,83], without any linearity hypothesis.

In section 2, we recall basic notions about terms and term rewriting systems, together with Hullot's results. Peterson-Stickels's R,E-relation and the related E-confluence results are given in section 3. We describe in section 4 the link between R,E-reduction and R,E-narrowing. A complete unification algorithm is then given for the theory RuE, assuming a complete terminating unification algorithm for the theory E. Following Hullot, we define in section 5 an improved algorithm and give sufficient conditions for its termination. We discuss briefly some examples and point out in conclusion the interest of our results in order to build new unification algorithms in an incremental way. We show also how they can be applied to obtain extensions of the Knuth and Bendix completion algorithm.

2. PRELIMINARIES

Definitions 1: Given a set X of variables and a graded set F of function symbols T(F,X) denotes the free algebra (or free magma) over X. Elements of T(F,X) are called terms. Terms may be viewed as labelled trees in the following way : a term t is a partial application of N^* into FuX such that its domain Dom(t) satisfies:

(1) e ∈ Dom(t) where e is the empty word.

(2) m ∈ Dom(t_i) => im ∈ Dom(f(... t_i ...)) for all i in [1,n=arity(f)].

Dom(t) is called set of occurrences of t, O(t) denotes the subset of non variable occurrences of Dom(t), V(t) denotes the set of variables of t, t/m the subterm of t at occurrence m, and t[m<-t'] the term obtained by replacing t/m by t' in t.

A term t is said to be linear iff ∀ x ∈ V(t), ∃! m ∈ Dom(t), t(m)=x.

Definitions 2: Substitutions s are defined as endomorphisms of T(F,X) with a finite domain D(s). A substitution s is denoted by $\{(x_1\backslash t_1),\ldots,(x_n\backslash t_n)\}$.

We define the set I(s) of variables introduced by s as the union of the sets V(s(x)) for all x in D(s).

We denote by $s_{|W}$ the restriction of the substitution s to the subset W of X.

We denote by ≤ the subsumption preorder on T(F,X) defined by:
t≤t' iff t'= s(t) for a substitution s called match from t to t'.

Composition of substitutions s and r is denoted by s.r .

Given a subset V of X, we define $s\leq s'[V]$ iff $s(x)\leq s'(x)$ for any variable x in V. It is also denoted : $s'=s''.s$ [V] for some substitution s". V=X is omitted.

Definitions 3: We call axiom or equation any pair (t,t') of terms and write it $t=t'$. The A-equality $=_A$ is the smallest congruence closed under instanciation and generated by a finite set A of axioms. $|-|_A$ denotes one step of A-equality.

We are interested in solving equations in equational theories, that is in finding substitutions s such that $s(t) =_A s(t')$. To define a basis of the set of solutions, we extend the preorder on substitutions to equational theories.

Definition 4: We define $t \leq_A t'$ iff $t'=_A s(t)$ for some substitution s called A-match from t to t'. Given a subset V of X, we define $s \leq_A s'$ [V] iff

$s(x) \leq_A s'(x)$ for all x in V,

That will be also denoted : $s' =_A s''.s$ [V] for some substitution s".

Definitions 5: Given an equational theory $=_A$, two terms t and t' are said to be A-unifiable iff there exists a substitution s such that $s(t) =_A s(t')$. S is a complete set of A-unifiers of t and t' away from W such that $V=V(t)\cup V(t')\subseteq W$ iff:

(1) for all s in S, $D(s)\subseteq V$ and $I(s)\cap W = \emptyset$ (no conflicts between variables)

(2) for all s in S, $s(t) =_A s(t')$

(3) for all unifiers s', there exists s in S such that $s \leq_A s'[V]$.

In addition S is said to be minimal if it satisfies the further condition:

(4) for all s and s' in S, $s \leq_A s'$ implies $s=s'$.

We denote by SU(t,t',A) the set of all A-unifiers of t and t', by CSU(t,t',A) a complete set of A-unifiers of t and t' and by CMSU(t,t',A) a complete and minimal set of A-unifiers of t and t'. A may be omitted when known or empty. An A-unification algorithm is complete if it generates a complete set of A-unifiers. This set is not required to be finite here. In what follows, we write "finite" algorithm for a terminating and finite sets generating algorithm.

Many theoretical problems arise in equational theories (word problem,...) that can be approached by the use of rewrite rules, that is one-way-equations. Working with rules requires good properties, as shown by Knuth and Bendix.

Definitions 6: A term rewriting system R is a set of pairs $\{g_k\text{->}d_k \mid 1\leq k\leq n\}$ such that $V(d_k)\subseteq V(g_k)$. We say that a term t R-reduces at occurrence m to a term t' using the rule $g_k \text{->} d_k$ and write $t \xrightarrow[{[m,k]}]{R} t'$ iff there exists a match s from g_k to t/m and $t' = t[m \leftarrow s(d_k)]$. We may omit R or [m,k].

We denote by $\overset{*}{\text{--->}}{}^R$ the derivation relation, that is the reflexive transitive closure of --->^R and by $=_R$ the generated equational theory.

An irreducible term for --->^R is said in R-normal form. t! is a normal form of t, that is a term t' in R-normal form s.t. $t \overset{*}{\text{--->}}{}^R t'$.

Definition 7: A term rewriting system R is said to be:

(1) noetherian iff --->^R is terminating

(2) confluent iff for all t, t_1, t_2 such that
$t \xrightarrow{*} t_1$ and $t \xrightarrow{*} t_2$, there exists a term t such that
$t_1 \xrightarrow{*} t'$ and $t_2 \xrightarrow{*} t'$.

Confluent and noetherian term rewriting systems (called convergent) provide a decision procedure for equational theories because $t =_R t'$ iff t and t' have the same R-normal form. In this framework, a complete unification algorithm for the theory $=_R$ is based on the narrowing process.

Definition 8: We say that t is "R-narrowable" at occurrence m belonging to O(t) and we write $t \text{-\^{}->}^R_{[m,k,s]} t'$ iff s is a most general unifier of t/m and g_k away from $V(t) \cup V(g_k)$ and $t' = s(t[m \leftarrow d_k])$.

The relation -^-> is called narrowing and its reflexive, transitive closure denoted by $\text{-\^{}->}^*$ is called narrowing derivation.

Notice that $t \text{-\^{}->}^R_{[m,k,s]} t'$ implies $s(t) \text{--->}^R_{[m,k]} t'$.

Theorem 1[HUL,80]: Given a confluent and noetherian term rewriting system R, if the equational term t=t' , where = is a binary function symbol, satisfies:

$$t=t' \text{-\^{}->}^R_{[m_0,k_0,s_0]} t_1 \text{-\^{}->}^R \dots \text{-\^{}->}^R_{[m_{n-1},k_{n-1},s_{n-1}]} t_n = t_n'$$

with r as most general unifier of t_n and t_n', then $r.s_{n-1}...s_0$ is a R-unifier of t and t', and a complete set of R-unifiers can be obtained in this way.

A complete R-unification algorithm may thus be designed from this result.

3. R/E-REDUCTION, R,E-REDUCTION AND E-CONFLUENCE

We assume now that the set A of axioms is split into a set E of equations and a set R of rules. Such a mixed set will be called an equational term rewriting system (ETRS). To work with, a confluence property is also needed.

Definition 9 : Let $\text{--->}^{R/E}$ be the relation $=_E . \text{--->}^R$; R is said to be

(1) E-noetherian iff $\text{--->}^{R/E}$ is terminating

(2) E-confluent iff for all terms t, t_1, t_2 such that
$t \xrightarrow{*}{}^{R/E} t_1$ and $t \xrightarrow{*}{}^{R/E} t_2$, there exist t_1' and t_2' such that
$t_1 \xrightarrow{*}{}^{R/E} t_1'$, $t_2 \xrightarrow{*}{}^{R/E} t_2'$ and $t_1' =_E t_2'$.

As E-congruence classes may be infinite, R/E-reducibility is not decidable. In order to get over this problem, Peterson and Stickel introduced the R,E-reducibility, together with a property, namely the E-compatibility, which links the two relations. In what follows, we use a weaker property called E-coherence, which allows us to obtain the desired link and confluence results [JOU,83].

Definition 10 : We say that the term t is R,E-reducible at occurrence m with the rule $g_k \to d_k$ and we write $t \text{--->}^{R,E}_{[m,k]} t'$ iff there exists a E-match s from g_k to t/m such that $t' = t[m \leftarrow s(d_k)]$.

Notice that the R,E-reducibility is decidable if the E-matching is decidable. From now on, we assume the existence of a finite and complete E-unification algorithm, which is a sufficient condition for that decidability.

Definition 11 : A term t is in R,E-normal form iff t is R,E-irreducible. From now on, t! denotes the R,E-normal form of t.

A substitution s is R,E-normalized iff s(x) is R,E-irreducible, $\forall x \in D(s)$.

Definition 12 : $\xrightarrow{R,E}$ (or simply R,E) is said to be E-coherent iff :
$\forall t_1,t_2,t_3$ s.t. $t_1 =_E t_2$ and $t_1 \xrightarrow{R,E} t_3 \xrightarrow{*}{}^{R/E} t_4$,
$\exists t_5, t_6, t_7$ s.t. $t_4 \xrightarrow{*}{}^{R/E} t_5$, $t_2 \xrightarrow{R,E} t_6 \xrightarrow{*}{}^{R/E} t_7$ and $t_5 =_E t_7$.

Notice that E-compatibility [P&S,81] is a particular case of E-coherence with $t_3=t_4$ and $t_6=t_7$. In the same way, E-commutation [JKK,82] is a particular case of E-compatibility with $t_3=t_5$.

Proposition 1 [JOU,83] : Assume R is E-confluent and E-noetherian. Then R,E- and R/E-normal forms of any term t are E-equal iff R,E is E-coherent.

Thus E-coherence enables us to compute R/E-normal forms using the R,E-reduction and R/E-reducibility coincides with R,E-reducibility.

We expect that the E-termination of R can be proved in practice by refinements of the recursive path ordering of Dershowitz, Kamin, Levy [DER,79], [K&L,82], or of the recursive decomposition ordering of Jouannaud, Lescanne, Reinig [JLR,82]. On the other hand, suffisant conditions decidable on E-critical pairs defined below, can be obtained for the two properties of E-coherence and E-confluence.

Definition 13: A term t E-overlaps a term t′ at occurrence $m \in O(t)$, with a complete set S of E-overlappings iff S is a complete set of E-unifiers of t and t′/m.

Given two rules g->d and g′->d′ such that $V(g) \cap V(g') = \emptyset$ and g E-overlaps g′ at occurrence m with a complete set S of E-overlappings, then the set $\{<P,Q> \mid P=s(d'), Q=s(g'[m<-d]), \forall s \in S\}$ is called a complete set of E-critical pairs of the rule g->d on the rule g′->d′ at occurrence m.

Let CSECP(R) and CSECP(R/E) be the complete sets of non trivial E-critical pairs (that is satisfying $P \neq Q$) for respectively:

- all g->d and g′->d′ belonging both to R,
- all g->d in R together with all g′->d′ s.t. g′=d′ or d′=g′ belongs to E.

Theorem 2 [JOU,83] : Let be an ETRS such that:

(1) R is E-noetherian

(2) $=_E$ is decidable and $\forall (g=d) \in E$, $V(g)=V(d)$

(3) A complete and finite unification algorithm exists for the theory E.

Then R is E-confluent and R,E is E-coherent if :

- any E-critical pair <P,Q> of CSECP(R) satisfies $P! =_E Q!$

- any E-critical pair <P=s(d´),Q> of CSECP(R/E) satisfies $P \longrightarrow^{R,E} P'$ at some occurrence of Dom(d´) and $P'! =_E Q!$.

From this theorem, a Knuth and Bendix-like completion algorithm can be derived for equational term rewriting systems, which is more general than Peterson and Stickel one´s [P&S,81].

We end this section with examples of ETRS satisfying the previous properties.

Example 1 : 1/ E={x+y=y+x} and R={x+0 --> x} or R={x+0 --> 0} or R={x+x --> x}.

2/ E={-(x+y)=(-y)+(-x)}, R={(x+0 --> x) and (-0 --> 0)}. There is a E-critical pair between the equation and the first rule and we must add the new rule 0+(-x) --> -x (using a Knuth and Bendix-like completion algorithm).

3/ The binary signed trees theory [KKJ,81]:

E={-(x+y)=(-y)+(-x) and --x = x }, R={ (y+x)+(-x) --> y and (-x)+(x+y) --> y }.

4/ The signed trees theory with the binary symbol + and for example two additional unary symbols h and h^{-1}(see [K&K,82]):

E={ -(x+y)=(-y)+(-x), -h(x)=h(-x) and --x=x }

R={h^{-1}(h(x)) --> x, h(h^{-1}(x)) --> x, (y+x)+(-x) --> y, (-x)+(x+y) --> y }.

4. R,E-NARROWING AND RuE-UNIFICATION

Within the framework of equational term rewriting systems, the unification problem appears as a fundamental one since a complete and finite E-unification algorithm is required for proving E-confluence and E-coherence. Such algorithms are known for a number of classical theories [S&S,82]. Our goal here is to generalize the narrowing process to equational theories for which a E-confluent, E-coherent and E-noetherian ETRS is known, providing us for an automatic and universal way to obtain unification algorithms.

4.1. DEFINITIONS

The R,E-narrowing is simply defined by using E-unifiers instead of unifiers:

We denote (g_k -> d_k) the k-th rule of R and suppose that two different rules have distinct variables. By an appropriate renaming, it is always possible to get V(g_k) and V(t) disjoint for any term t.

Definitions 14 : A term t is R,E-narrowable into t´ at occurrence m, with the rule k and the substitution s, if and only if

* s belongs to a complete set of E-unifiers of t/m and g_k away from W containing V(t)UV(g_k) with V(t) and V(g_k) disjoint

* t´ = s(t[m<-d_k]).

We then write $t \ \text{-\^{}->}^{R,E}_{[m,k,s]} \ t'$ or sometimes simply $t \ \text{-\^{}->}^{R,E}_{[s]} \ t'$.

s is called a R,E-narrowing substitution.

A finite sequence of R,E-narrowings from a term t to a term t' is called a R,E-narrowing derivation and is denoted by: $t \overset{\wedge *}{\longrightarrow}{}^{R,E}_{[r]} t'$
where r is the composition (in the reverse order) of the successive R,E-narrowing substitutions, defined by:
r = Identity if $t = t'$ and $r = r'.r''$ if $t \overset{\wedge *}{\longrightarrow}{}^{R,E}_{[r'']} t'' \overset{\wedge}{\longrightarrow}{}^{R,E}_{[r']} t'$.

Example 2 : E = { $-(x+y)=(-y)+(-x)$, $--x=x$ }
and R = {rule 1: $(x+y)+(-y) \longrightarrow x$, rule 2: $(-y)+(y+x) \longrightarrow x$ }
$x+0 = 0+x \overset{\wedge}{\longrightarrow}{}^{R,E}_{[1,1,(x\backslash x'+(-0))]} x' = 0+(x'+(-0))$. (The symbol = is here considered as a binary function symbol).

Remark : Notice that $t \overset{\wedge}{\longrightarrow}{}^{R,E}_{[m,k,s]} t$ implies $s(t) \longrightarrow^{R,E}_{[m,k]} t'$.

It is our goal now to prove that a complete RuE-unification algorithm can be obtained from the computations of the R,E-narrowing derivation tree generated by the two terms t and t' to unify. More precisely, if $t=t' \overset{\wedge *}{\longrightarrow}{}^{R,E}_{[s]} t_n=t'_n$ (I) s.t. t_n and t'_n are E-unifiable and $r \in CSU(t_n,t'_n,E)$, we first prove that r.s is an RuE-unifier of t and t', which thus states the correctness of the R,E-narrowing process. Then we show that, for any RuE-unifier s' of t and t', it is possible to find a R,E-narrowing derivation (I) s.t. : $r.s \leq_{RuE} s'[V(t)UV(t')]$, which states the completeness of the R,E-narrowing process.

4.2. THE CORRECTNESS PROOF

The proof is based on the following intuition: if a term t is R,E-narrowable, then an appropriate instanciation of this term is R,E-reducible.

Lemma 1 [JKK,83]: Let $t_0 \overset{\wedge}{\longrightarrow}{}^{R,E}_{[m,k,s]} t_1$. Then for any substitution r,
$r.s(t_0) \longrightarrow^{R,E}_{[m,k]} r(t_1)$.

This lemma is now extended to derivations:

Proposition 2: If $t_0 \overset{\wedge *}{\longrightarrow}{}^{R,E}_{[s]} t_n$, then $r.s(t_0) \overset{*}{\longrightarrow}{}^{R,E} r(t_n)$ for any substitution r.
Proof: by induction on n, using lemma 1. []

This result is depicted on the following diagram:

$$\begin{array}{ccccccc}
t_0 & \overset{\wedge}{\longrightarrow}{}^{R,E}_{[m_0,k_0,s_0]} & t_1 & \overset{\wedge}{\longrightarrow} & \cdots & \overset{\wedge}{\longrightarrow}{}^{R,E}_{[m_{n-1},k_{n-1},s_{n-1}]} & t_n \\
\downarrow r_0 = r.s_{n-1}\ldots s_0 & & \downarrow r_1 = r.s_{n-1}\ldots s_1 & & & & \downarrow r_n = r \\
r.s(t_0) & \longrightarrow^{R,E}_{[m_0,k_0]} & t'_1 & \longrightarrow & \cdots & \longrightarrow^{R,E}_{[m_{n-1},k_{n-1}]} & t'_n
\end{array}$$

Notice that r_i is R,E-normalized if r_0 is R,E-normalized.

We now may state the correctness theorem:

Theorem 3 : Let t and t' be two terms and a R,E-narrowing derivation $(t=t') \overset{\wedge *}{\longrightarrow}{}^{R,E}_{[s]} (t_n=t'_n)$ such that t_n and t'_n are E-unifiable by $r \in CSU(t_n,t'_n,E)$. Then r.s is a RuE-unifier of t and t'.

Proof: Applying proposition 2 : $r.s(t=t') \overset{*}{\longrightarrow}^{R,E} r(t_n=t'_n)$

thus $r.s(t) =_{RuE} r(t_n) =_E r(t'_n) =_{RuE} r.s(t')$. []

4.3. THE COMPLETENESS PROOF

The completeness result is based on the converse construction. Let us first prove its starting step.

Lemma 2 [JKK,83]: Let t_0 be a term and r_0 a R,E-normalized substitution such that

$$r_0(t_0) \longrightarrow^{R,E}_{[m,k]} t''_0 .$$

Then there exist a substitution s and a R,E-normalized substitution r_1 such that

- $t_0 \; \text{-\^{}->}^{R,E}_{[m,k,s]} t_1$ with $r_1(t_1) =_E t''_0$
- $D(r_1) = V(t_1)$
- $r_0 =_E r_1.s \quad [V(t_0)]$

This lemma is now extended to derivations:

Proposition 3 : Let be RuE an ETRS such that R is E-confluent and E-noetherian and R,E is E-coherent. Then, for any R,E-derivation from $t'_0 = r_0(t_0)$ to any of its R,E-normal forms, say $t'_0!$, where $D(r_0) \subseteq V(t_0)$ and r_0 is a R,E-normalized substitution, there exists a R,E-narrowing derivation $t_0 \; \overset{*}{\text{-\^{}->}}^{R,E}_{[s]} t_n$ and a R,E-normalized substitution r_n such that $r_n(t_n) =_E t'_0!$ and $r_0 =_E r_n.s \; [V(t_0)]$.

Proof: by noetherian induction on the relation $\longrightarrow^{R,E}.=_E$.

Let us sketch the proof on the following diagram, where encircled numbers stand for successive steps of the proof:

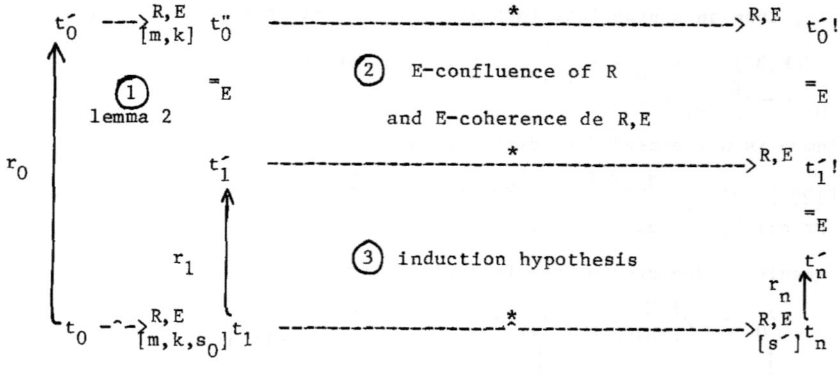

[]

We are now ready to prove the completeness theorem:

Theorem 4 : Let t and t' be two terms RuE-unifiable by s' and $V_0 = V(t) \cup V(t')$. Then there exists a R,E-narrowing derivation starting from (t=t'):

$$(t=t') \; \text{-\^{}->}^{R,E}_{[s_0]} (t_1=t'_1) \; \text{-\^{}->} \; \ldots \; \text{-\^{}->}^{R,E}_{[s_{n-1}]} (t_n=t'_n)$$

such that t_n and t'_n are E-unifiable.

Besides, if $V_n = V(t_n) \cup V(t'_n)$ and $s'_i = s_{i-1} \ldots s_0 \; \forall i, \; i=1,\ldots,n$,

- there exists $r \in CSU(t_n,t'_n,E)$ away from $V_0 \cup V_n$ such that $r.s'_n \leq_{RuE} s' \; [V_0]$.

- it is possible to only consider the R,E-narrowing derivations such that, for any i between 1 and n, s'_i is R,E-normalized.

Proof: Notice first that, if $s'(t) =_{RuE} s'(t')$, we can obtain, by R,E-normalizing s', a R,E-normalized substitution s" s.t. $s"(t) =_{RuE} s"(t')$. Let s"(t)! and s"(t')! be the respective R,E-normal forms of s"(t) and s"(t'). Thus $s"(t)! =_E s"(t')!$. Considering now the R,E-derivation

$t'_0 = (s"(t)=s"(t')) \longrightarrow^{R,E} t'_1 \longrightarrow \ldots \longrightarrow^{R,E} t'_p = (s"(t)!=s"(t')!)$

and applying proposition 3, we obtain a R,E-narrowing derivation

$$(t=t') \overset{*}{-\!\!\hat{}\!\!\rightarrow}{}^{R,E}_{[s'_n]} (t_n=t'_n)$$

and a R,E-normalized substitution r_n such that:

$$r_n(t_n=t'_n) =_E (s"(t)!=s"(t')!) \text{ and } r_n.s'_n =_E s" \quad [V_0].$$

From the first E-equality, it follows that:

$$r_n(t_n) =_E s"(t)! =_E s"(t')! =_E r_n(t'_n).$$

So there exists $r \in CSU(t_n,t'_n,E)$ away from $V_0 UV_n$ such that

$$r \leq_E r_n \quad [V_n], \text{ and } r' \text{ such that } r'.r =_E r_n \ [V_n].$$

As $s" =_E r_n.s'_n$ $[V_0]$ and $I(s'_n) \subseteq V_n$, $s" =_E r'.r.s'_n$ $[V_0]$.

Finally $r.s'_n \leq_E s" =_{RuE} s'$ $[V_0]$.

On the other hand, since $r_n.s'_n =_E s"$ $[V_0]$, and s" is R,E-normalized, it is possible to consider R,E-normalized substitutions s'_i only. []

4.4. A COMPLETE ALGORITHM OF RuE-UNIFICATION

The previous results allow us to state the main theorem:

Theorem 5 : Let R be a E-confluent and E-noetherian term rewriting system such that R,E is E-coherent and let t and t' be two terms. Assume that there exists a finite and complete E-unification algorithm. Let S be the set of all the substitutions s satisfying: there exists a R,E-narrowing derivation :

$$(t=t') -\hat{}\!\!\rightarrow^{R,E}_{[s_0]} (t_1=t'_1) -\hat{}\!\!\rightarrow \ldots -\hat{}\!\!\rightarrow^{R,E}_{[s_{n-1}]} (t_n=t'_n)$$

such that t_n and t'_n are E-unifiable,

$s'_i = s_{i-1} \ldots s_0$ is R,E-normalized for any i=1,...,n

$s = r.s'_n$ with $r \in CSU(t_n,t'_n,E)$ away from $V(t)UV(t')$.

Then S is a complete set of RuE-unifiers of t and t'.

Proof: from theorems 3 and 4. []

We thus obtain a non-deterministic algorithm which consists in building the R,E-narrowing derivations tree starting from (t=t'). Obviously termination problems arise and our aim is now to find a suffisant condition of termination.

5. BASIC R,E-NARROWING

Following [HUL,80], we now want to improve the previous algorithm by cutting useless branches out of the R,E-narrowing derivations tree. We thus have to take care of keeping completeness. As this property is based on the computation of

R,E-normal forms, we must guarantee that we use a strategy which is complete for these computations. It leads to innermost-outermost computations which are characterized by the use of R,E-normalized substitutions only. Maybe, there are other interesting strategies, and the previously developped tools are general enough to be applied to any one.

Definition 15 : Let t_0 be any term, r any R,E-normalized substitution and U_0 a prefix-closed set of occurrences included in $Dom(t_0)$.
A R,E-derivation starting from $r(t_0)$:

$$r(t_0) \dashrightarrow^{R,E}_{[m_0,k_0]} t'_1 \dashrightarrow^{R,E} \ldots \dashrightarrow^{R,E}_{[m_{n-1},k_{n-1}]} t'_n$$

or a R,E-narrowing derivation starting from t_0:

$$t_0 \ \text{-^->}^{R,E}_{[m_0,k_0,s_0]} t_1 \ \text{-^->}^{R,E} \ldots \ \text{-^->}^{R,E}_{[m_{n-1},k_{n-1},s_{n-1}]} t_n$$

is based on U_0 if and only if for any i, i=1,...,n-1, m_i belongs to U_i where:

$$U_{i+1} = U_i \setminus \{p \in Dom(t_i) \mid p \geq m_i\} \cup \{m_i p \mid p \in O(d_{k_i})\}$$

The R,E-(narrowing) derivation is said basic if $U_0 = O(t_0)$.

Example 3 : Let be R={rule 1:(h(h(x))-->h(x) and rule 2:h(a)-->a} and E=∅.
Then the following narrowing derivation

$$h(y)+y \ \text{-^->}_{[1,1,(y\backslash h(x))]} h(x)+h(x) \ \text{-^->}_{[1,2,(x\backslash a)]} a+h(a)$$

is basic since $U_0=\{e,1\}=U_1$, but the other one

$$h(y)+y \ \text{-^->}_{[1,1,(y\backslash h(x))]} h(x)+h(x) \ \text{-^->}_{[2,2,(x\backslash a)]} h(a)+a$$ is not.

Lemma 3 [JKK,83]: Let t and t´ be two terms s. t. t´=r(t) and r a R,E-normalized substitution. Any innermost-outermost R,E-derivation starting from t´ is basic.

Lemma 4 [JKK,83]: For any term t´=r(t) with r R,E-normalized, there exists a basic R,E-derivation from t´ to any R,E-normal form of t´.

We define a new relation $=_E$ <U>, more precise than the E-equality, which intends to keep trace of the performed E-equality steps. Intuitively, $t =_E t'$ <U> if and only if no axioms of E have been applied at occurrences of U.

Definition 16 : Let t and t´ be two terms and U a prefix-closed set of occurrences included in V(t)∪V(t´). We say that t is E-equal to t´ out of U and write $t =_E t'$ <U> if and only if there exists a proof

$$t=t_0 \ |\overset{E}{-}|_{[m_0]} \ t_1 \ |\overset{E}{-}|_{[m_1]} \ \ldots \ |\overset{E}{-}|_{[m_{n-1}]} \ t_n=t'$$ such that ∀i, i=1,...,n-1, $m_i \notin U$.

Example 4 : Let E = { x+y=y+x }, t = (x+y)+(x+y) and t´= (x+y)+(y+x).
$t =_E t'$<U> when U = {e,1}, but $t \neq_E t'$ <U´> when U´ = {e,2}.

Let us point out some properties of this relation, freely used in what follows:
* $=_E$<U> is a transitive relation.
* If U ⊆ U´, then $=_E$ <U´> is included in $=_E$ <U>.

In particular, $=_E$ <U> is included in $=_E$.
* If s and s´ are two substitutions such that $s =_E s'$ [V(t)], then

$s(t) =_E s'(t)$ $\langle O(t)\rangle$.

* If $t =_E t'$ $\langle U\rangle$, then $\forall m \in U$, $t/m =_E t'/m$ but the converse does not hold.

We now give the precise link between basic R,E-reduction and basic R,E-narrowing, obtained by looking more closely the results of proposition 3. But we need before the following lemmas which link together more precisely based R,E-reduction and based R,E-narrowing, stating a more accurate version of proposition 3.

Lemma 5 [JKK,83] : If $t_0 \xrightarrow{R,E}_{[m,k]} t_1$ with $m \in U_0 \subseteq O(t_0)$ and $t_0' =_E t_0$ $\langle U_0\rangle$, then $t_0' \xrightarrow{R,E}_{[m,k]} t_1'$ and $t_1' =_E t_1$ $\langle U_1\rangle$.

This result is easily extended to R,E-derivations:

Lemma 6 : Let $t_0 \xrightarrow{n}{}^{R,E} t_n$ be a R,E-derivation based on $U_0 \subseteq O(t_0)$ and and $t_0' =_E t_0$ $\langle U_0\rangle$. Then there exists a R,E-derivation $t_0' \xrightarrow{n}{}^{R,E} t_n'$ also based on U_0, such that $\forall i$, $i=1,\ldots n$, $t_i =_E t_i'$ $\langle U_i\rangle$.

Proof: Easy induction on the length n of the R,E-derivation. []

We are ready to state a result similar to proposition 3, but using based R,E-derivations.

Proposition 4 : Let t_0 be a term and r_0 a R,E-normalized substitution. For any R,E-derivation based on $U_0 \subseteq O(t_0)$: $t_0' = r_0(t_0) \xrightarrow{*}{}^{R,E} t_0'!$ there exists a R,E-narrowing derivation based on U_0: $t_0 \xrightarrow{*}{}^{R,E}_{[s]} t_n$ and a R,E-normalized substitution r_n such that $r_n(t_n) =_E t_0'!$ and $r_0 =_E r_n.s$ $[V(t_0)]$.

We are thus able to deduce a completeness theorem for basic R,E-narrowing, since Theorem 4 remains valid by replacing R,E-narrowing by basic R,E-narrowing.

Theorem 6 : Theorem 5 remains valid when restricted to basic R,E-narrowing derivations.

Thus basic R,E-narrowing improves our previous algorithm. Moreover, as in [HUL,80], it allows us to give a sufficient condition for the termination of the process.

Theorem 9 : Let R be a E-confluent and E-noetherian rewriting system such that R,E is E-coherent. Let us assume that there exists a finite complete E-unification algorithm. If any basic R,E-narrowing derivation starting from a right-hand side of rules terminates, then the R,E-narrowing process terminates.

Proof: same as in [HUL,80]. []

The last result allows us to obtain complete and finite unification algorithms for the theories of example 1, assuming a complete and finite algorithm is known for their E theories. For cases 2, 3 and 4, E-unification can be solved [K&K,82] by an extension of the Martelli and Montanari method [M&M,82]. Case 4 is interesting: a complete set of E-unifiers of two terms can be infinite but recursively enumerable. Thus by using finite descriptions of such infinite sets of E-unifiers, and a schematization of the R,E-narrowing derivations tree, we succeed in applying this method (see [K&K,82]).

We conclude this section with an algorithm which computes a complete set S of RuE-unifiers of two terms t and t´ with the basic strategy. We assume that E-UNIF(t,t´) returns ∅ if t and t´ are not unifiable in the theory E, else a finite and complete set of E-unifiers of t and t´. Notations are as above.

```
SOLVE((t=t´), U, s, S)
        IF r=E-UNIF(t,t´) THEN S:=SU{r.s}  END IF
        FOR ANY m ∈ U DO
            FOR ANY rule (g -> d) ∈ R DO
                IF (ECU := E-UNIF(g,(t=t´)/m)) ≠ ∅
                THEN FOR ANY s´∈ ECU DO
                          SOLVE(s´((t=t´)[m<-d]),U\{p∈U|p≥m}U{mp|p∈O(d)},s´.s, S)
                     END FOR
                END IF
            END FOR
        END FOR
        RETURN S
END SOLVE
```

The required result is obtained by: SOLVE((t=t´),O((t=t´)),Identity, ∅)

As pointed out by N.Dershowitz [DER,82], the narrowing process can be implemented with the help of the Knuth and Bendix completion algorithm. In the case of R,E-narrowing, we need a generalized completion algorithm [JOU,83].

6.CONCLUSION

We have shown here a powerfull method to obtain complete algorithms for A-unification. It is incremental in the following sense: starting with a finite complete E-unification algorithm (possibly E=∅), we can add new axioms, assuming they provide a set of rewrite rules R with the required good properties of theorem 6 and get a complete unification algorithm for the theory RuE by using the R,E-narrowing process. If this algorithm terminates, it is possible to start again with E=RuE.

Notice on the other hand that the method will allow us to implement various extensions of the Knuth and Bendix completion procedure: for proving consistency of hierarchical abstract data types for instance, one can start from a set E of equations such that a finite and complete E-unification algorithm is known (may be E=∅) and a set R of rules defining new operations; one can complete the set of rules in order to obtain E-confluence and E-coherence (and the consistency is proved if success is obtained); then one can start again to prove the consistency of the next enrichment, because a complete procedure for unification in the theory EuR is now available.

Acknowledgments : We thank Jean Luc Remy for his relevant remarks.

7 REFERENCES

[DER,79] DERSHOWITZ N.: "Orderings for term-rewriting systems"
Proc 20th Symposium on Foundations of Computer Science, pp 123-131 (1979).
also Theorical Computer Science 17-3 (1982).

[DER,82] DERSHOWITZ N.: "Computing with rewrite systems"
Preliminary draft (1982)

[FAY,79] FAY M.: "First order unification in equational theory"
Proc. 4th Workshop on Automata Deduction Texas (1979).

[HUE,80] HUET G.: "Confluent reductions: abstract properties and applications to term rewriting systems"
J. Assoc. Comp. Mach. 27-4, pp 797-821 (1980).

[HUL,80] HULLOT J. M.: "Canonical forms and unification"
Proc. 5th Workshop on Automated Deduction Les Arcs (1980).

[JKK,82] JOUANNAUD J.P. KIRCHNER C. KIRCHNER H.: "Incremental unification in equational theories". Proc. of the Allerton conference (1982).

[JKK,83] JOUANNAUD J.P. KIRCHNER C. KIRCHNER H.: "Incremental construction of unification algorithms in equationnal theories". Internal report 83-R-008. Centre de Recherche en Informatique de Nancy (1983).

[JLR,82] JOUANNAUD J.P., LESCANNE P., REINIG F.: "Recursive decomposition ordering" in "Formal description of programming concepts 2".
Ed. BJORNER D., North Holland (1982).

[JOU,83] JOUANNAUD J.P. : "Confluent and Coherent sets of reductions with equations. Application to proofs in data types". Proc. of the 8th Colloquium on Trees in algebra and programming. To appear in LNCS (1983).

[K&B,70] KNUTH D. BENDIX P.: "Simple word problems in universal algebras" in "Computational problems in abstract algebra"
Leech J. ed. Pergamon Press, pp 263-297 (1970).

[K&K,82] KIRCHNER C., KIRCHNER H.: "Contribution à la résolution d'équations dans les algèbres libres et les variétés équationnelles d'algèbres".
Thèse de doctorat de spécialité, C.R.I.N., Nancy (1982).

[KKJ,81] KIRCHNER C., KIRCHNER H., JOUANNAUD J.P.: "Algebraic manipulations as a unification and matching strategy for linear equations in signed binary trees". Proc. IJCAI 81 Vancouver (1981).

[K&L,82] KAMIN, LEVY J.J.: "Attempts for generalizing the recursive path ordering". To be published.

[LAN,75] LANKFORD D.S.: "Canonical inference". Report ATP-32, dpt. Math. and comp. sciences, Univ. of Texas at Austin (1975).

[LAN,79] LANKFORD D.S.: "A unification algorithm for abelian group theory"
Report MTP-1. Math. dep., Louisiana Tech. U. (1979).

[L&S,77] LIVESEY M. and SIEKMANN J.: "Unification of sets"
Report 3/76, Institut fur Informatik 1, Univ. Karlsruhe, (1977).

[M&M,82] MARTELLI A. and MONTANARI U.: "An efficient unification algorithm".
T.O.P.L.A.S., Vol. 4, No. 2, pp 258-282. (1982).

[PLO,72] PLOTKIN G.: "Building in equational theories"
Machine Intelligence 7, pp 73-90 (1972).

[P&S,81] PETERSON G.E. and STICKEL M.E.: "Complete sets of reductions for equational theories with complete unification algorithms"
J.ACM 28, no.2, pp 233-264 (1981).

[R&S,78] RAULEFS P. and SIEKMANN J.:"Unification of idempotent functions"
Report, Institut fur Informatik 1, Univ. Karlsruhe, (1978).

[S&S,82] SIEKMANN J. and SZABO P.:"Universal unification"
Report, Institut fur Informatik 1, Univ. Karlsruhe, (1982).

[STI,81] STICKEL M.E.: "A unification algorithm for associative-commutative functions". J.ACM 28, no.3, pp 423-434 (1981).

TREE AUTOMATA AND ATTRIBUTE GRAMMARS*

by

Tsutomu Kamimura
Department of Computer Science
University of Kansas
Lawrence, Kansas 66045
U.S.A.

1. INTRODUCTION

Attribute grammars, introduced by Knuth [9], provide an attractive method of formalizing the semantics of context-free languages, and introduce a general framework of the syntax-directed translation scheme of programming languages. Using attribute grammars, we can define transformations from derivation trees of context-free grammars to values of the specified attributes as the meanings of the trees, and various attribute evaluation procedures [1,8] actually perform these transformations.

A number of attempts have been made to study the transformational mechanism of attribute grammars from several different points of view. Lewis et. al [10] initiated a formal study of attribute grammars and introduced the attributed pushdown machine to characterize transformations defined by certain class of attribute grammars (called L-attribute grammars). More recently, Engelfriet and Filé [6] considered the attribute grammar as a device to define a transformation from derivation trees of a context-free grammar to trees which describe the expressions to compute the specified attribute of the derivation trees. Furthermore, to study various properties of the transformations in very formal way, Engelfriet [4] proposed the device called macro tree transducer to model the transformational mechanism of attribute grammars. Finally, Courcelle and Franchi-Zannettaci [2] advocate the viewpoint of program schemes and introduced the recursive program scheme with a tree parameter to study the mechanism of attribute grammars.

In this paper, we consider attribute values as strings over a fixed alphabet, and define attribute grammars as tree-to-string transducers. Then we propose tree-walking pushdown tree-to-string transducers with certain synchronized pushdown facility as a model of attribute transducers and study properties of this model.

Our model differs from any of those mentioned above in that it includes all the rules to compute attributes as a part of formalism and yet it is a conventional type of sequential device with iterative control. To demonstrate the utility of this model, we show that noncircular attribute grammars are equally powerful as arbitrary attribute grammars, and provide the method to show that certain type of transformations are not possible by attribute grammars.

---

*This work was supported in part by the National Science Foundation Grant NSF-MCS82-02945.

2. PRELIMINARIES

We assume that the reader is familiar with the basic concepts and results in tree automata and languages. Details can be found in [3,11].

An alphabet Σ is ranked if $\Sigma=\bigcup_{n\geq 0}\Sigma_n$ where each Σ_n is a finite set of symbols and only finitely many n has nonempty Σ_n. The maximal rank of Σ is the largest number n such that Σ_n is nonempty. We do not need to assume that Σ_n and Σ_m are disjoint for distinct n and m, but for the sake of convenience, we require that $\Sigma_0\cap\Sigma_n=\emptyset$ for every $n>0$. A tree t over Σ is an ordered tree such that each node having n sons is labeled by a symbol of Σ_n. We exclude trees of single node in our consideration for technical reasons and let T_Σ denote the set of all the non-single node trees over Σ. Given Σ, a tree language L is an arbitrary subset of T_Σ. The yield of a tree t, denoted as yield(t), is a string over Σ_0 obtained by concatenating labels of all the leaves of t from left to right, and yield(L) = $\{$yield(t)$|t\in L\}$ for a language L.

A nondeterministic parallel (top-down) tree automaton A is a construct (Q,Σ,R) where Q is a finite set of states, Σ a ranked alphabet and R is a finite set of rules of the form : $\sigma\rightarrow\sigma(q_1\ldots q_n)$ or $[p]\sigma\rightarrow\sigma(q_1\ldots q_n)$ for $\sigma\in\Sigma_n$ and $p,q_1,\ldots,q_n\in Q$, $n>0$ and $[p]\sigma\rightarrow\sigma$ for $\sigma\in\Sigma_0$ and $p\in Q$. A is deterministic if the left-hand side of each rule is distinct. A begins its computation at the root of a tree $t\in T_\Sigma$ by applying a rule $\sigma\rightarrow\sigma(q_1\ldots q_n)$ where σ is the label of the root of rank n. It creates n copies $q_1,\ldots,q_n$ of its finite control and processes i-th subtree of the root in state q_i, $1\leq i\leq n$. Processing a subtree in state p is done in a similar manner by applying a rule $[p]\sigma\rightarrow\sigma(q_1\ldots q_n)$ if the root of the subtree is labeled by σ of rank n. A can process a leaf labeled by σ in state p if it has a rule $[p]\sigma\rightarrow\sigma$. A accepts t iff there is a sequence of application of rules to successfully process all the subtrees of t. The tree language recognized by A, denoted by L(A), is the set of all the trees accepted by A. A language L is recognizable if there is a nondeterministic parallel automaton to recognize L. RECOG denotes the class of all recognizable tree languages. RECOG is closed under union, intersection and complement; where the complement of $L\subseteq T_\Sigma$, denoted by $\bar{L}$, is defined as $T_\Sigma - L$. It is well-known that yield(L) is context-free for $L\in$RECOG.

In addition to examining finite state properties of trees, if we consistently change the labels of trees to symbols of another ranked alphabet, we obtain a simple transformation device called finite state relabeling. A finite state relabeling T is a construct (Q,Σ,Δ,R), where Q is a set of states, Σ and Δ are input and output ranked alphabets respectively and R is a set of rules. Each rule is defined similarly to that of parallel tree automaton except that an alphabet symbol of the right-hand side is taken from Δ (while the left-hand side is unchanged). T is deterministic if each rule has distinct left-hand side. The transformation defined by T is $\{(t,t')\in T_\Sigma\times T_\Delta | t'$ is an output (not necessarily unique) of t by T$\}$ and $T(L)=\{t'\in T_\Delta | (t,t')\in T$ for some $t\in L\}$ for a tree language $L\subseteq T_\Sigma$. T(L) is recognizable for every recognizable language L. A (deterministic) relabeling is a total (deterministic) single-state relabeling, and REL (DREL) denotes the class of all the (deterministic) relabelings. Finally we introduce special deterministic finite state relabeling s_Σ for each ranked alphabet Σ. It changes a label $\sigma\in\Sigma$ of a node of an input tree to (σ,i) (i.e., attaches subscript i to σ), where $0\le i\le m$ and m is the maximal rank of Σ, if that node is the i-th son (from left to right) of its father; in particular, i=0 if the node is the root of the tree. SUB denotes the class of all s_Σ.

3. TREE-WALKING AUTOMATA

In this section, we discuss the sequential type of tree automaton, called a finite state tree-walking automaton. The finite state tree-walking automaton is a tree version of the finite state (two-way) automaton on strings: it has a finite control and an input pointer which points at a (present) node of input tree; the present state of finite control and the label of the present node determine the next state and the node to visit next which is either the father or one of sons of the present node.

3.1 Definition. A finite state tree-walking automaton (fsta in short) A is a construct (Q,Σ,δ,q_0,F), where Q is the finite set of states, Σ is the input ranked alphabet, $q_0\in Q$ is the initial state, $F\subseteq Q$ is the set of final states and δ is a mapping from $Q\times\Sigma$ to finite subsets of $Q\times D$ where $D=\{0,1,\ldots,M\}$ where M is the maximal rank of Σ. A is deterministic if $\delta(q,\sigma)$ has at most one element for every $q\in Q$ and $\sigma\in\Sigma$. ☒

A configuration of A on a tree $t\in T_\Sigma$ is a triple (q,n,t) where $q\in Q$ and n is a node of t. Define $(q,n,t)\vdash_A(p,n',t)$ iff $(p,i)\in\delta(q,\sigma)$ where σ is the label of n; and n' is the father of n if i=0; or n' is the i-th son of n if i>0. The node n' is called the i-th surrounding of n. $\vdash_A^*$ is the reflexive-transitive closure of $\vdash_A$.

A sequence of configurations $P=C_0,C_1,C_2,\ldots$, where $C_0=(q_0,n_0,t)$ with n_0 being the root of a tree t is called a computation path of A on t if $C_i\vdash_A C_{i+1}$ for every $i\ge0$, except for the last configuration in P if it exists. A computation path is accepting if it has some C_i which has a final state as its first component; otherwise it is nonaccepting. A computation path is maximal if either it is infinite or there is no C' for its last configuration C such that $C\vdash_A C'$. Obviously, every computation path can be extended to a maximal computation path. Given a fsta A, define $L_N(A)=\{t\in T_\Sigma|$ there is an accepting computation path of A on t$\}$ and $L_U(A)=\{t\in T_\Sigma|$every maximal computation path of A on t is accepting$\}$. Then $2N=\{L|L=L_N(A)$ by some fsta A$\}$ and $2U=\{L|L=L_U(A)$ by some fsta A$\}$. If A is deterministic, $L_N(A)=L_U(A)$ and $2D=\{L|L=L_N(A)=L_U(A)$ by a deterministic fsta A$\}$.

3.2 Example. Let $\Sigma=\Sigma_0\cup\Sigma_2$ and $\Sigma_0=\{a,b\}$, $\Sigma_2=\{C\}$. Thus, T_Σ is the set of all complete binary trees in which every interior node is labeled by 'C' and every leaf is labeled by 'a' or 'b'. Consider the following fsta $A=(\{q_0,q_F\},\Sigma,\delta,q_0,\{q_F\})$ where $\delta(q_0,C)=\{(q_0,1),(q_0,2)\}$, $\delta(q_0,a)=\{(q_F,0)\}$ and all other transitions are undefined. Then $L_N(A)=\{t\in T_\Sigma|$t has a leaf labeled by 'a'$\}$ and $L_U(A)=\{t\in T_\Sigma|$every leaf of t is labeled by 'a'$\}$. ☒

3.3 Theorem. The following inclusion diagram (Fig. 1) holds. Lines denote proper inclusion and 2N and 2U are incomparable.

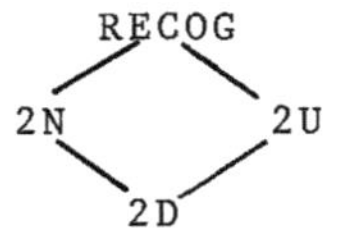

Figure 1.

Proofs. (a) It was proved in [7] that $L_N(A)$ of Example 3.2 is in 2N-2D and $L_U(A)$ is in RECOG-2N.

(b) $L_N(A)$ of Example 3.2, denoted as K, is not in 2U. The outline of this proof is as follows. Assume that $K=L_U(A)$ by some fsta $A=(Q,\Sigma,\delta,q_0,F)$ and k is the cardinality of Q. Consider a complete balanced binary tree $t\in T_\Sigma$ of height $> \log_2(2k+2)$ in which all the leaves are labeled by 'b'. Since $t\notin L_U(A)$, there is a maximal computation path $P=C_0,C_1,\ldots$ where none of C_i has a final state at the first component. Also A must visit all the leaves of t during P, since otherwise the same sequence as P (with obvious modification on the third component of each C_i's) is a nonaccepting maximal computation path for t' obtained from t by changing the labels of unvisited leaves to 'a'. Now let $n_1,n_2,\ldots$ be the sequence of leaves A visits in P in this order. As t has more than 2k+2 leaves, A must visit two leaves in the same state during P. Let n_i and n_j be the first such nodes in this sequence. Hence there are $0<\ell_i<\ell_j$ and $q\in Q$ such that $C_{\ell_i}=(q,n_i,t)$, $C_{\ell_j}=(q,n_j,t)$ and $C_{\ell_i}\overset{*}{\underset{A}{\vdash}}C_{\ell_j}$. Furthermore, A visits at most k+1 leaves during the sequence $C_0,\ldots,C_{\ell_i},\ldots,C_{\ell_j}$. Now we can construct the sequence of configurations such that $C_{\ell_j}\overset{*}{\underset{A}{\vdash}}C_{\ell_j}$ by applying exactly the same transition at each step as in $C_{\ell_i}\overset{*}{\underset{A}{\vdash}}C_{\ell_j}$, but by starting at n_j instead of n_i. This is possible because t is balanced, all the internal nodes are labeled by 'C', and all the leaves are labeled by 'b'. Hence, we obtain a maximal computation path by infinitely repeating this sequence after $C_0,\ldots,C_{\ell_j}$. Clearly, this computation path is not accepting; however A visits at most 2k+2 leaves since it visits the same leaves, the number of which is at most k+1, in the repeated portion of $C_{\ell_j}\overset{*}{\vdash}C_{\ell_j}$. This is a contradiction.

(c) To show $2U\subseteq$RECOG, we prove that $L\in 2U$ implies $\bar{L}\in$RECOG. Let $L=L_U(A)$ by a fsta A. Without loss of generality, we may assume that a computation path of A is accepting iff it is finite. Hence a tree t is in $\bar{L}$ iff A can visit some node of t more than once in the same state. Define the finite state relabeling T which nondeterministically selects one node, say n, of t and a state q of A and attaches q to n. Then we can define the fsta A' which operates on an output tree of T and checks whether A can visit n in state q more than once. If so, A' accepts the tree. Let h be the deterministic relabeling to erase the information attached by T. Then $\bar{L}$ is equal to $h(T(T_\Sigma)\cap L_N(A'))$ and hence recognizable. ☒

4. TREE-WALKING PUSHDOWN TRANSDUCERS

In this section we introduce a new tree-walking pushdown transducer with some synchronization mechanism. It uses the pushdown stack with two tracks; the first is a standard track for storing symbols out of a given stack alphabet. The additional track will contain pointers to nodes of the input tree. We will not distinguish between pointers and nodes themselves. The machine can push a pair (δ,n) on the stack while moving up or down the tree where δ is a stack symbol and n is the currently scanned node of the tree. When the stack is popped, the tree walk "backtracks", i.e., resumes at the node which currently appears at the top of the pushdown.

4.1 Definition. A (deterministic) tree-walking (synchronized) pushdown tree-to-string transducer (tw-pd) is a construct $M=(Q,\Sigma,\Delta,\Gamma,\delta,Z_0,q_0,F)$ where Q is a finite set of states, Σ is a ranked alphabet of tree labels, Δ is the output alphabet, Γ is the pushdown alphabet with Z_0 being the initial pushdown symbol, $q_0\in Q$ the initial state and $F\subseteq Q$ the set of final states. δ is the transition function from $Q\times\Sigma\times\Gamma$ to $Q\times\Delta^*\times D$ where D (the instruction set) is $\{pop\}\cup\{(i,\gamma_1\gamma_2)\mid \gamma_1,\gamma_2\in\Gamma$, and $0\le i\le m\}$ where m is the maximal rank of Σ. M is a single state (1tw-pd) if $|Q|=1$. If every pair in D has nonzero first component, M becomes the checking tree pushdown transducer (ct-pd) of [5]. ⊠

A configuration of M on an input tree t is a tuple $(q,t,u,w,(n_1,\ldots,n_k))$ where $q\in Q$, $u\in\Gamma^k$, $w\in\Delta^*$, $n_i\in V_t$ (the set of nodes of t), $i=1,2,\ldots,k$ for some $k\ge 0$. For two configurations C_1 and C_2 we let $C_1\vdash_M C_2$ if either of the following conditions is satisfied.

(i) $C_1=(q,t,u\gamma,w,(n_1,\ldots,n_k))$, $u\in\Gamma^*$, $\gamma\in\Gamma$; $\delta(q,\sigma,\gamma)=(p,v,(i,\gamma_1\gamma_2))$ where σ labels n_k, and $C_2=(p,t,u\gamma_1\gamma_2,wv,(n_0,\ldots,n_k,n_{k+1}))$ where n_{k+1} is the i-th surrounding of n_k.

(ii) $C_1=(q,t,u\gamma,w,(n_1,\ldots,n_k))$, $u\in\Gamma^*$, $\gamma\in\Gamma$; $\delta(q,\sigma,\gamma)=(p,v,pop)$ where σ labels n_k and $C_2=(p,t,u,wv,(n_1,n_2,\ldots,n_{k-1}))$.

$\vdash_M^*$ denotes the reflexive transitive closure of $\vdash_M$. The tree-to-string transformation realized by tw-pd M is:

$$T(M)=\{(t,w)\mid(q_0,t,Z_0,\varepsilon,(n_0))\vdash_M^*(p,t,\varepsilon,w,(\ ))\text{ and }p\in F\}$$

where n_0 is the root of t. The string-to-string transformation $T_S(M)$ is $\{(yield(t),w)\mid(t,w)\in T(M)\}$. We identify M with T(M) when no confusion arises. TW-PD (1TW-PD) denotes the set of all tw-pd's (1tw-pd's) as well as the set of all the tree-to-string transformations they realize. Also, $TW\text{-}PD_S$ ($1TW\text{-}PD_S$) denotes the set of all the string-to-string transformations they realize. The domain of M is $Dom(M)=\{t\in T_\Sigma\mid(t,w)\in T(M)$ for some $w\in\Delta^*\}$, and $Dom(TW\text{-}PD)=\{L\mid L=Dom(M)$ for $M\in TW\text{-}PD\}$ (similarly for Dom(1TW-PD)). Given a tree language L, the transformation of L by M is $M(L)=\{w\in\Delta^*\mid(t,w)\in T(M)$ for some $t\in L\}$.

4.2 Theorem. Dom(1TW-PD)=2U.

Proof. Let $M=(\{q\},\Sigma,\Delta,\Gamma,\delta,Z_0,\{q\},\{q\})$ be a 1tw-pd. The following fsta A=

$(\Gamma\cup\{q_F\},\Sigma,\delta',Z_0,\{q_F\})$ establishes $L_U(A)=Dom(M)$. A holds the top of the stack of M in its finite control and uses "universal branching" to verify that every stack symbol M pushes will eventually be popped. Thus, for $\sigma\in\Sigma$ and $Z\in\Gamma$,

(1) if $\delta(q,\sigma,Z)=(q,w_1,(i_1,Z_1Z_1'))$, $\delta(q,\sigma,Z_1)=(q,w_2,(i_2,Z_2Z_2'))$, ..., $\delta(q,\sigma,Z_{n-1})=(q,w_n,(i_n,Z_nZ_n'))$, $\delta(q,\sigma,Z_n)=(q,w_{n+1},pop)$ for $n>0$, $Z_i,Z_i'\in\Gamma$ for $1\le i\le n$ and $w_i\in\Delta^*$ for $1\le i\le n+1$ then $\delta'(Z,\sigma)=\{(Z_1',i_1),\ldots,(Z_n',i_n)\}$.

(2) If $\delta(q,\sigma,Z)=(q,w,pop)$ for some $w\in\Delta^*$, then $\delta'(Z,\sigma)=\{(q_F,0)\}$.

Conversely, given a fsta $A=(Q,\Sigma,\delta,q_0,F)$, define 1tw-pd M as $(\{q_a\},\Sigma,\emptyset,Q\times\{0,1,\ldots,k\},\bar{\delta},(q_0,0),q_a,\{q_a\})$, where q_a is the unique state of M ($q_a\notin Q$) and k is the maximal number of elements of set $\delta(q,\sigma)$ for every $q\in Q$ and $\sigma\in\Sigma$. M utilizes backtracking to check whether every computation path of A can be extended to an accepting computation path. Thus, $\bar{\delta}$ is defined as follows: $\bar{\delta}(q_a,\sigma,(p,0))=(q_a,\varepsilon,pop)$ for every $p\in F$ and $\sigma\in\Sigma$; if $\delta(p,\sigma)=\{(p_1,i_1),\ldots,(p_n,i_n)\}$ for $\sigma\in\Sigma$ and $p\in Q-F$, then $\bar{\delta}(q_a,\sigma,(p,j))=(q_a,\varepsilon,(i_{j+1},(p,j+1)(p_{j+1},0)))$ for $0\le j<n$ and $\bar{\delta}(q_a,\sigma,(p,n))=(q_a,\varepsilon,pop)$. ⊠

For two transformations M_1 and M_2, $M_1\circ M_2$ is the transformation obtained by applying first M_1 and then M_2. The operation $\circ$ is extended to sets of transformations in a standard manner.

4.3 Theorem. $TW\text{-}PD \subseteq REL\circ 1TW\text{-}PD$.

Proof. Let $M=(Q,\Sigma,\Delta,\Gamma,\delta,Z_0,q_0,F)$ be a tw-pd. Define the following relabeling T on T_Σ. T selects and attaches a function f: $Q\times\Gamma\times\{0,1,\ldots,k\}\to Q$ at each node of rank k in nondeterministic way. A node labeled by σ with function f gives the information of computation of M in that when M pushes Z as a top of the stack at σ and visits its j-th surrounding in state q, then it must come back to σ in state $f(q,Z,j)$ by executing a pop operation at node j. Then, construct a 1tw-pd M' which simulates M by using the information given at each node by T to establish $M=T\circ M'$. The details are omitted. ⊠

4.4 Corollary.

(a) Dom(TW-PD)=RECOG.

(b) $1TW\text{-}PD \subseteq TW\text{-}PD$

(c) $1TW\text{-}PD_S = TW\text{-}PD_S$ ⊠

5. ATTRIBUTE GRAMMARS

In our formulation of attribute grammar, initial nonterminals are allowed to have inherited attributes and separate rules are given to compute them. Also, we use context-free grammars with possibly more than one initial nonterminal; they are called generalized context-free grammars.

5.1 Definition. An attribute grammar (AG) is a construct $H=(G,N,\Delta,A,R,a_0)$ defined as follows.

(i) $G=(\Sigma_N,\Sigma_T,P,\Sigma_I)$ is the underlying generalized context-free grammar with nonterminals Σ_N, terminals Σ_T, productions P and initial nonterminals $\Sigma_I \subseteq \Sigma_N$. Σ denotes $\Sigma_N \cup \Sigma_T$.

(ii) N is a finite set of attribute names.

(iii) Δ is an alphabet of attribute values.

(iv) A is a pair of mappings (S,I) which associate with each nonterminal $X \in \Sigma_N$ disjoint subsets S(X) and I(X) of N; A(X) denotes $S(X) \cup I(X)$; elements of S(X) and I(X) are synthesized and inherited attributes of X, respectively. A pair a(X) with $a \in A(X)$ is an attribute of X.

(v) R is a mapping which associates with each production r: $X_0 \to u_0 X_1 u_1 \ldots u_{k-1} X_k u_k$ of G, where $X_i \in \Sigma_N$ and $u_i \in \Sigma_T{}^*$, $0 \le i \le k$, a set of attribute evaluation rules R(r). A pair $\langle a,i\rangle$ with $a \in A(X_i)$ for $0 \le i \le k$ is called an attribute occurrence of r; R(r) is a collection of attribute evaluation rules $\langle a,i\rangle = \alpha$ where α is a string over $\Delta \cup \bigcup_{i=0}^{k} (A(X_i) \times \{i\})$ for $\langle a,i\rangle \in S(X_0) \times \{0\} \cup \bigcup_{i=1}^{k} (I(X_i) \times \{i\})$ and for each such $\langle a,i\rangle$, R(r) has exactly one rule having $\langle a,i\rangle$ as its left-hand side.

(vi) R also associates with each $\sigma \in \Sigma_I$, a set of attribute evaluation rules $R(\sigma)$ of the form $\langle a,0\rangle = \alpha$ where α is a string over $\Delta \cup (A(\sigma) \times \{0\})$ for each $a \in I(\sigma)$. $R(\sigma)$ has exactly one rule for each $a \in I(\sigma)$.

(vii) Finally, $a_0 \in N$ is the distinguished attribute, called the output attribute of H, whose value is defined as an output of tree-to-string transformation. We require that $a_0 \in S(\sigma)$ for every $\sigma \in \Sigma_I$. ⊠

Let $H=(G,N,\Delta,A,R,a_0)$ be an AG. D_G denotes the set of derivation trees of G. For each $t \in D_G$, V_t is the set of nodes of t, and a translational instance of t is a string over $\Delta \cup (N \times V_t)$; TI(t) denotes the set of all translational instances of t. For α, $\beta \in TI(t)$ we define the relation $\alpha \underset{t}{\Rightarrow} \beta$ (we omit H throughout for simplicity) as follows. Suppose $\alpha = \alpha_1 (a,n) \alpha_2$ where n is labeled by nonterminal X and let r be a production $X_0 \to u_0 X_1 \ldots u_{k-1} X_k u_k$, $X_i \in \Sigma_N$, $u_i \in \Sigma_T{}^*$.

(a) If $a \in S(X)$, let $n=n_0$, $X=X_0$ and r be a production used at n_0. Suppose R(r) has a rule $\langle a,0\rangle = \gamma$; then $\beta = \alpha_1 \gamma' \alpha_2$ where γ' is obtained from γ by replacing each $\langle a',j\rangle$ by the pair (a',n_j), $0 \le j \le k$ and n_j is the j-th son of n_0 if $j>0$.

(b) If $a \in I(X)$ and n is not the root of t, let r be a production applied at n_0 and $n=n_j$, i.e. j-th son of n_0, $0<j\le k$. If R(r) contains a rule $\langle a,j\rangle = \gamma$, then $\beta = \alpha_1 \gamma' \alpha_2$ where γ' is defined as in (a).

(c) If $a \in I(X)$ and n is the root of t, $\beta = \alpha_1 \gamma' \alpha_2$ if R(X) has $\langle a,0\rangle = \gamma$ and γ' is as in (a).

The reflexive-transitive closure of $\underset{t}{\Rightarrow}$ is denoted by $\underset{t}{\overset{*}{\Rightarrow}}$. The (tree-to-string) transformation defined by H is

$$T(H)=\{(t,w)\,|\,(a_0,n)\underset{t}{\overset{*}{\Rightarrow}} w\in\Delta^* \text{ for } t\in D_G \text{ with root } n\}$$

As before, we also use AG to denote the class of all the transformations $\{T(H)\,|\,H\in AG\}$. The string-to-string transformation by H is $T_S(H)=\{(\text{yield}(t),w)\,|\,(t,w)\in T(H)\}$ and AG_S denotes $\{T_S(H)\,|\,H\in AG\}$. The domain of H is $Dom(H)=\{t\in D_G\,|\,(t,w)\in T(H)$ for some $w\in\Delta^*\}$ and $Dom(AG)=\{Dom(H)\,|\,H\in AG\}$. H is noncircular iff $Dom(H)=D_G$.

Remark. A noncircular AG produces an output for every $t\in D_G$. Hence, no attributes on which the output attribute depends can have a circular definition. However, it may have circularly defined attributes so long as they are never used to produce an output. In this sense, our definition of noncircularity differs from the standard notion.

5.2 Theorem. $1TW\text{-}PD \subseteq AG$.

Proof. Let $M=(\{q\},\Sigma,\Delta,\Gamma,\delta,Z_0,q,\{q\})$ is 1tw-pd. Define AG H as follows. The underlying grammar G of H is $(\Sigma_N,\Sigma_0,P,\Sigma_I)$ where $\Sigma_N=\Sigma_I=\bigcup_{n>0}\Sigma_n$ and $P=\{\sigma\rightarrow\tau_1\ldots\tau_n\,|\,\sigma\in\Sigma_n$ for $n>0$ and $\tau_i\in\Sigma$, $1\le i\le n\}$. For each $Z\in\Gamma$, we define a synthesized attribute $O[Z]$ so that: for a node n labeled by σ of a tree $t\in D_G$ and $w\in\Delta^*$, $(O[Z],n)\underset{t}{\overset{*}{\Rightarrow}} w$ if and only if, starting its translation at n with Z at the top of the stack, M produces w as an output before it pops the cell containing Z. In addition, we need an inherited attribute $U[Z]$ for $Z\in\Gamma$ to handle an output produced during which M visits the father of node n by pushing Z. The output attribute is $O[Z_0]$. For each production r: $X_0\rightarrow u_0X_1u_1\ldots u_{m-1}X_mu_m$ of G, where $X_i\in\Sigma_N$ and $u_i\in\Sigma_T^*$, $0\le i\le m$, H has the following attribute evaluation rules.

(i) $\langle U[Z],j\rangle=\langle O[Z],0\rangle$ for $Z\in\Gamma$, $1\le j\le m$.

(ii) Suppose $\delta(q,Z,X_0)=(q,w_0,(i_1,Z_1'Z_1))$, $\delta(q,Z_1',X_0)=(q,w_1,(i_2,Z_2'Z_2))$, ..., $\delta(q,Z_{k-1}',X_0)=(q,w_{k-1},(i_k,Z_k'Z_k))$, $\delta(q,Z_k',X_0)=(q,w_k,\text{pop})$ for $Z,Z_j,Z_j'\in\Gamma$, $w_j\in\Delta^*$ and $i_j\in D$ for $1\le j\le k$, $k\ge0$ (if $k=0$, $Z=Z_0'$). Define α_j for each $1\le j\le k$ as follows.

(a) If $i_j=0$ then $\alpha_j=w_{j-1}\cdot\langle U[Z_j],j\rangle$

(b) If $i_j>0$ and i_j-th symbol of the right-hand side of r is a nonterminal X_{i_j}, then $\alpha_j=w_{j-1}\cdot\langle O[Z_j],i_j\rangle$

(c) Otherwise, let σ_t be the $i_j(>0)$-th (terminal) symbol of the right-hand side of r. Since we do not use attributes for terminals, we must "summarize" the translation of M for σ_t. This requires the following definition. Suppose $\delta(q,Z_{i_j},\sigma_t)=(q,w_0',(0,Y_1'Y_1))$, $\delta(q,Y_1',\sigma_t)=(q,w_1',(0,Y_2'Y_2))$, ..., $\delta(q,Y_{\ell-1}',\sigma_t)=(q,w_{\ell-1}',(0,Y_\ell'Y_\ell))$, $\delta(q,Y_\ell',\sigma_t)=(q,w_\ell',\text{pop})$ for $Y_h,Y_h'\in\Gamma$, $w_0',w_h'\in\Delta^*$ for $1\le h\le\ell$ for some $\ell\ge0$ (if $\ell=0$, $Y_0'=Z_{i_j}$). Then, define

$$\alpha_j=w_{j-1}w_0'\langle O[Y_1],0\rangle\, w_1'\langle O[Y_2],0\rangle\ldots w_{\ell-1}'\langle O[Y_\ell],0\rangle\, w_\ell'\,.$$

Using these α_j's, the evaluation rule for $O[Z](X_0)$ is defined as $\langle O[Z],0\rangle = \alpha_1\alpha_2\ldots\alpha_k \cdot w_k$. In case that no such Z_j and Z_j' or no Y_h and Y_h' exist, define the rule simply as $\langle O[Z],0\rangle = \langle O[Z],0\rangle$. Also, define $\langle U[Z],0\rangle = \langle U[Z],0\rangle$ for $Z\in\Sigma_N$ as a rule of the root. ⊠

Hence, attribute grammars are at least as powerful as ltw-pd's in their transformational power. In the next proposition, we give an attribute grammar which has $L_N(A)$ of Example 3.2 as its domain. Hence,

<u>5.3 Proposition</u>. The inclusion of Theorem 5.2 is proper.

<u>Proof</u>. We construct the follwoing AG H such that $\mathrm{Dom}(H) = L_N(A)$ of Example 3.2. The underlying grammar of H has terminals 'a' and 'b' and a nonterminal 'C' with synthesized attribute s and inherited attributes i. 'C' is the initial nonterminal and s is the output attribute. Productions and attribute rules are defined as follows.

Productions		Attribute rules
(i) $C \to CC$	:	$\langle s,0\rangle = \langle s,1\rangle$, $\langle i,1\rangle = \langle s,2\rangle$ and $\langle i,2\rangle = \langle i,0\rangle$
(ii) $C \to bb$	:	$\langle s,0\rangle = \langle i,0\rangle$
(iii) $C \to ab$, $C \to ba$ and $C \to aa$	:	$\langle s,0\rangle = \varepsilon$
(iv) For a root C	:	$\langle i,0\rangle = \langle i,0\rangle$

To compute s of the root of a tree, we need to visit nodes in preorder until a leaf labeled by 'a' is seen. If every leaf has a label 'b', we return to the root and fall into a loop; therefore the translation is undefined. ⊠

Despite Proposition 5.3, the difference of the transformational powers between AG and 1TW-PD is not significant. In fact, relabeling a tree by s_Σ can close this gap.

<u>5.4 Theorem</u>. $AG = SUB \circ 1TW\text{-}PD$.

<u>Proof</u>. The inclusion $AG \subseteq SUB \circ 1TW\text{-}PD$ is proved by a straightforward simulation. Given $H\in AG$ and s_Σ where Σ is the set of terminals and nonterminals of H, we can construct a 1tw-pd M such that $T(H) = s_\Sigma \circ T(M)$. M first checks whether a tree is obtained from a derivation tree of H by s_Σ, and if so, it then produces the value of a_0 of the root by using appropriate rules of H. To do so, M must find a production applied at each node and an attribute evaluation rule for a specific attribute. For this purpose, M uses a number attached at each node by s_Σ. The details are omitted.

The other inclusion is shown as follows. Let M be a 1tw-pd with input alphabet $\Sigma\times\{0,\ldots,m\}$ where m is the maximal rank of Σ. By Theorem 5.2, there is $H\in AG$ with underlying grammar $G = (\Sigma_N\times\{0,\ldots,m\}, \Sigma_0\times\{0,\ldots,m\}, P, \Sigma_N\times\{0,\ldots,m\})$, where $\Sigma_N = \bigcup_{n>0}\Sigma_n$. Define $H'\in AG$ so that $T(H') = s_\Sigma \circ T(H)$ as follows. The underlying grammar G' of H is $(\Sigma_N, \Sigma_0, P', \Sigma_N)$; G' has a production r': $\sigma \to \tau_1\ldots\tau_n$ iff G has a production r: $(\sigma,k) \to (\tau_1,1)\cdots(\tau_n,n)$ for some k. σ has synthesized (inherited) attribute (a,k) if

(σ,k) has synthesized (inherited) attribute a in H. r' has attribute evaluation rule $\langle (a,k),0\rangle = \alpha'$ for σ if a is synthesized and r has $\langle a,0\rangle = \alpha$; α' is obtained from α by replacing each $\langle a',0\rangle$ by $\langle (a',k),0\rangle$ and each $\langle a',\ell_i\rangle$ by $\langle (a',i),\ell_i\rangle$ for $i>0$ with τ_i being the ℓ_i-th nonterminal in the right-hand side of r. Rules for inherited attributes are more involved as r' may be defined by more than one such r of H. We introduce synthesized attribute (b,i,k) and inherited attribute $(b,i,-1)$ of σ for each inherited attribute (b,i) of τ_i. Each (b,i,k) is to hold a value of (b,i) of τ_i computed by using the attribute rule of r. Then we use $(b,i,-1)$ to choose a correct value of (b,i) of τ_i by finding k. Hence, r' has $\langle (b,i,k),0\rangle = \alpha'$ if r has $\langle b,\ell_i\rangle = \alpha$, where ℓ_i and α' are defined as above. Also, it has $\langle (b,i),\ell_i\rangle = \langle (b,i,-1),0\rangle$. Furthermore, each production of G' having σ as the j-th symbol and the ℓ-th nonterminal of its right-hand side must have $\langle (b,i,-1),\ell\rangle = \langle (b,i,j),\ell\rangle$ for each b and i. Finally, for each $\sigma\in\Sigma_N$, the rules for a root have $\langle (b,i,-1),0\rangle = \langle (b,i,0),0\rangle$ for every b and i. For all other attributes x and $h\in\{0,\ldots,m\}$ define $\langle x,h\rangle = \langle x,h\rangle$. ☒

<u>5.5 Corollary</u>. (a) $\mathrm{Dom}(AG) \subseteq \mathrm{RECOG}$.

(b) $1TW\text{-}PD_S = TW\text{-}PD_S = AG_S$.

(c) For $H \in AG$, yield (Dom(H)) is context-free.

(d) Given $H\in AG$, there is a noncircular $H'\in AG$ such that $T_S(H')=T_S(H)$. ☒

Finally, we generalize Corollary 5.5(c) in that even if we restrict a translation of the output attribute to be an element of some regular set over the output alphabet, the yield of the set of trees satisfying this restriction is still context-free.

<u>5.6 Corollary</u>. Given $H\in AG$ with output alphabet Δ and a regular set $K\subseteq\Delta^*$, $H_s^{-1}(K) = \{x \mid (x,w)\in T_S(H) \text{ for some } w\in K\}$ is context-free.

<u>Proof</u>. By Corollary 5.5(b), there is $M\in 1TW\text{-}PD$ such that $T_S(M) = T_S(H)$. Let A be a deterministic finite state automaton to recognize K. Define $M'\in TW\text{-}PD$ as follows. M' operates in exactly the same way as M. In addition, each time M produces an output, M' computes the state of A in which A is after reading all the output strings produced until that moment. Then, M' terminates in a final state iff M terminates and the present state of A that M' is computing is a final state. By Corollary 4.4(a), Dom(M') is recognizable; therefore yield(Dom(M'))$=H_s^{-1}(K)$ is context-free. ☒

This corollary enables us to show that certain type of transformations are not possible by attribute grammars.

<u>5.7 Example</u>. Consider the following string-to-string transformation $T=\{(a^n,b^k) \mid k = \lfloor\sqrt{n}\rfloor \text{ for } n\geq 0\}$. Suppose there is $H\in AG$ such that $T = T_S(H)$. Let $K=\{b^{2\cdot i} \mid i\geq 0\} \subseteq b^*$. By Corollary 5.6, $\{a^n \mid \lfloor\sqrt{n}\rfloor = 2\cdot i \text{ for } i\geq 0\}$ is context-free. However, $S = \{n \mid \lfloor\sqrt{n}\rfloor = 2\cdot i \text{ for } i\geq 0\}$ is not semilinear; contradiction. ☒

<u>Acknowledgment</u>. The author would like to thank Giora Slutzki for stimulating discussions.

REFERENCES

[1] Bochman, G. V. (1976), Semantic evaluation from left to right. CACM 19, No. 2, 55-62.

[2] Courcelle, B. and Franchi-Zannettacci, P. (1982), Attribute grammars and recursive program schemes I. Theoretical Computer Science 17, 163-191.

[3] Engelfriet, J. (1975), Tree automata and tree grammars. Lecture Notes DAIMI FN-10, University of Aarhus, Denmark.

[4] Engelfriet, J. (1979), Some open questions and recent results on tree transducers and tree languages. In Proc. of the Symposium on Formal Language Theory, Santa Barbara, 241-286.

[5] Engelfriet, J. et. al., (1980), Tree transducers, L systems and two-way machines. JCSS 20, 150-202.

[6] Engelfriet, J. and Filé, G. (1981), Passes, sweeps and visits. Proc. of 8th ICALP, 193-207.

[7] Kamimura, T. and Slutzki, G. (1981), Parallel and two-way automata on directed ordered acyclic graphs. Information and Control 49, 10-51.

[8] Kennedy, K. and Warren, S. K. (1976), Automatic generation of efficient evaluators for attribute grammars. Proc. of 3rd POPL, 32-49.

[9] Knuth, D. E. (1968), Semantics of context-free languages. Mathematical Systems Theory 2, 127-145.

[10] Lewis, P. M., Rosenkrantz, D. J. and Stearns, R. E. (1974), Attribute translations. JCSS 9, 4, 279-307.

[11] Thatcher, J. W. (1973), Tree automata: informal survey in Currents in the Theory of Computing, (A. V. Aho, Ed.). Prentice-Hall, Engelwood Cliffs, NJ, 143-172.

Effectively Given Spaces

by

T. Kamimura & A. Tang*
Department of Computer Science
University of Kansas
Lawrence, Kansas 66045
U.S.A.

1. Introduction

The theory of domains has been presented in various formalisms by D. Scott. It ranges from continuous lattices in [6], neighborhood systems in [8], to information systems in [9]. By a domain in our context, we mean a bounded-complete cpo with a basis. The presence of a basis in a domain facilitates the reasonings about computations and paves the way for a theory of effectively given domains studied in [10] and [5]. The purpose of this paper is to show how to use the ideas in effectively given domains to formalize a theory of effectively given T_0 spaces.

Why opt for a theory of effectively given spaces and what is its significance to computer science? Recent trends in programming tend to emphasize abstraction at both the data and the control levels. In data abstraction for instance, it has been commonly accepted that the notion of a type should not depend on any particular implementation. Consequently, various encapsulation mechanisms are added to recent languages to support the notion of abstract data types. A good understanding of the abstract properties of a program would shed insight in the verification as well as the design phases. In the setting of computation in a mathematical domain, the notion of a computable domain is normally given with an operational flavor. For example, in an effectively given domain, computable objects are given by directed lubs of recursively enumerable sequences of basis elements. The question is: can such an operational notion be abstracted by a set of properties of the object which are independent of how the object is computed? To answer such a question, a certain enumerable set of properties must be carefully isolated that must be fine enough to separate distinct objects in the domain. To this end, Scott introduced a T_0 topology on domains and explained properties by Scott open sets. In [5], it was shown that computable objects in a continuous lattice can be characterized using Scott topology, showing that effectively given continuous lattices are certain effectively given T_0 spaces. The purpose of this paper is to formalize the notion of an effectively given T_0 space. In doing so, we introduce continuous spaces, a class of T_0 spaces (properly) including all the domains. Unlike domains, continuous spaces may not have a (countable) basis in the specialization ordering. We show that every continuous space can be suitably embedded

*in memory of Monica Tang [1949-1983]

as a dense subspace of some domain, the construction of which is reminiscent of Scott's construction of the interval domain from the reals [7]. A continuous space is effectively given just in case the corresponding domain is effectively given. To answer the question stated earlier, we show that in an effectively given space, there are two equivalent formulations of the notion of a computable object, an operational one and a topological one. The operational notion tells us how a computable object is obtained, whereas the topological notion defines a computable object using its properties. Consequently, the operational notion may be viewed as an implementation of the topological notion.

2. Preliminaries on Domains

Given a poset $D = (D, \sqsubseteq)$, $x \ll y$ (x is way-below y) if for every directed set H in D, $y \sqsubseteq \bigsqcup H$ implies $x \sqsubseteq h$ for some $h \in H$. $x \in D$ is compact if $x \ll x$. A basis of D is a countable subset $E = \{e_i \mid i \in \omega\}$ of D such that for every $x \in D$, the set $\{e \in E \mid e \ll x\}$ is directed and $x = \bigsqcup \{e \in E \mid e \ll x\}$. D is directed-complete if lub of every directed set exists. It is bounded-complete if glb for every non-empty set exists. By a domain, we mean a bounded-complete and directed-complete poset which has a basis.

Given a poset D, $U \subseteq D$ is Scott-open if

(i) $\uparrow x = \{y \in D \mid x \sqsubseteq y\} \subseteq U$ for every $x \in U$; and

(ii) for every directed set H, $\bigsqcup H \in U$ implies $h \in U$ for some $h \in H$.

In a domain D, the set of all $\Uparrow e_i$'s where $\Uparrow e_i = \{x \mid e_i \ll x\}$ forms a base of Scott topology. The following characterization of domains using Scott topology is useful in the sequel.

Proposition 1

A bounded-complete and directed-complete poset D is a domain iff there exists $\{e_i \mid i \in \omega\} \subseteq D$ and a countable collection of Scott open sets $\{U_i \mid i \in \omega\}$ such that:

[D1] Structural Axiom: $U_i \subseteq \uparrow e_i$ for every $i \in \omega$

[D2] Continuity Axiom: for every $x \in D$, the set $\{e_i \mid x \in U_i\}$ is directed and $x = \bigsqcup \{e_i \mid x \in U_i\}$.

Proof:

(⇒) Suppose $E = \{e_i \mid i \in \omega\}$ is a basis of a domain D. Let U_i be $\Uparrow e_i$ for every $i \in \omega$.

(⇐) From [D1], it can be shown that for every $x \in U_i$, $e_i \ll x$. Thus by [D2], $x = \bigsqcup \{e_i \mid e_i \ll x\}$. Directedness of the set $\{e_i \mid e_i \ll x\}$ also follows from [D2].

□

We say that $\langle D, \{e_i\}_{i \in \omega}, \{U_i\}_{i \in \omega} \rangle$ is a continuous presentation of the domain D if e_i's and U_i's satisfy [D1] and [D2]. We shall generalize such a notion to a topological space in the next section.

Domains can be characterized using R-structures. An <u>R-structure</u> $\langle\omega,<\rangle$ is specified by a transitive relation $<$ on ω such that for every $i\in\omega$, the set $[i] = \{j \mid j<i\}$ is $<$-directed. For example, if $\langle D, \{e_i\}_{i\in\omega}, \{U_i\}_{i\in\omega}\rangle$ is a continuous presentation of a domain D, an R-structure can be obtained as follows: $i<j$ iff $e_j \in U_i$. A subset ℓ of ω is <u>left-closed</u> if for every $i\in\ell$, $[i]\subseteq\ell$. The <u>Dedekind cut completion</u> $\overline{\langle\omega,<\rangle}$ of an R-structure $\langle\omega,<\rangle$ consists of all the left-closed directed subsets of ω; the ordering is given by subset inclusion. Smyth showed in [10] that directed-complete posets with a least element are given by Dedekind cut completions of R-structures up to isomorphism.

Given a domain D, $x\in D$ is <u>total</u> if $x \not\sqsubseteq y$ for every other y in D. Let T(D) denote the space of all the total objects in D endowed with the subspace topology. For example, if R is Scott's interval lattice [7] without the top, then T(R) is homeomorphic to the reals. A topological space X is a <u>total space</u> if X is homeomorphic to T(D) for some domain D. Every total space is metrizable. A characterization of total spaces is given in [2].

3. Continuous Spaces

All topological spaces here are T_0 and second countable. The <u>specialization ordering</u>, denoted by $\sqsubseteq_s$, is given by: $x \sqsubseteq_s y$ iff for every open set U, $x\in U$ implies $y\in U$. If $D = (D,\sqsubseteq)$ is a domain endowed with Scott topology, then $\sqsubseteq_s$ is the same as $\sqsubseteq$. However in many other topological spaces X, the poset $(X,\sqsubseteq_s)$ lacks a (countable) basis. In certain cases, fictitious partial objects can be added to X to complete it into a domain. The most notable example here is the reals R. Scott [7] used closed intervals as partial objects and complete R into the interval domain R. The lack of a basis in the specialization ordering of the reals R, Baire space ω^ω and Cantor space 2^ω presents a stumbling block in an operational formulation of the notion of computable objects in such spaces. However, each of those spaces has certain properties by which the notion of computable objects can be formulated. Our notion of effectively given spaces should include not only all the domains but also such spaces.

When $\langle D, \{e_i\}_{i\in\omega}, \{U_i\}_{i\in\omega}\rangle$ is the continuous presentation of a domain, then e_i's and U_i's are partial objects and properties respectively, and the predicate $e_i\in U_j$ means that e_i has property U_j. In generalizing the notion of a continuous presentation from a domain to a topological space which may lack a basis in the specialization ordering, we are faced with the following difficulties: (i) partial objects may no longer be given by points; (ii) properties may not be Scott open sets; and (iii) a binary relation other than $\in$ may be needed to express that a partial object has certain property. In the sequel, we introduce the notion of a continuous presentation for a topological space X as a 4-tuple $\langle X, \{\alpha_i\}_{i\in\omega}, \{U_i\}_{i\in\omega}, \triangleleft\rangle$. The α_i's are certain G_δ subsets of X used as partial objects to complete X into a domain later on (in the case of a domain, each e_i may be identified with the G_δ set $\uparrow e_i$). The U_i's are non-empty basic open sets used to describe properties. Finally, $\triangleleft$ is a binary relation between U_i's and non-empty intersections of α_j's such that $U_i \triangleleft \bigcap_{j\in J}\alpha_j$ means that the partial object $\bigcap_{j\in J}\alpha_j$ has property U_i. Obviously, some axioms are needed to say that the partial objects α_i's are plentiful enough to approximate every object in X and that the properties U_i's have the finiteness property with respect to the relation $\triangleleft$. Formally, a <u>continuous presentation</u> is a 4-tuple $\langle X, \{\alpha_i\}_{i\in\omega}, \{U_i\}_{i\in\omega}, \triangleleft\rangle$ satisfying the following axioms:

[C1] <u>Structural Axiom</u>: $U_i \subseteq \alpha_i$ for every $i\in\omega$

[C2] <u>Continuity Axiom</u>: for every indexed set $J\subseteq\omega$ such that $\bigcap_{j\in J}\alpha_j \neq \emptyset$, the collection $\{\alpha_i \mid U_i \triangleleft \bigcap_{j\in J}\alpha_j\}$ is filtered and $\bigcap_{j\in J}\alpha_j = \bigcap\{\alpha_i \mid U_i \triangleleft \bigcap_{j\in J}\alpha_j\}$.

[C3] <u>Axioms on $\triangleleft$</u>:

(i) for every $x\in X$, $x\in U_i$ iff $U_i \triangleleft \uparrow x = \bigcap\{\alpha_j \mid x\in U_j\}$;

(ii) $U_i \triangleleft \bigcap_{j\in J}\alpha_j$ implies $U_i \supseteq \bigcap_{j\in J}\alpha_j$;

(iii) $U_i \supseteq U_j \triangleleft \bigcap_{h\in H}\alpha_h \supseteq \bigcap_{k\in K}\alpha_k$ implies $U_i \triangleleft \bigcap_{k\in K}\alpha_k$; and

(iv) (finiteness property)

$U_i \triangleleft \bigcap_{j\in J}\alpha_j$ implies $U_i \triangleleft \bigcap_{j\in J'}\alpha_j$ for some finite subset J' of J

[C4] <u>Directed-completeness Axiom</u>: $\bigcap_{i\in I}\alpha_i \neq \emptyset$ whenever $\{\alpha_i \mid i\in I\}$ is filtered.

X is a <u>continuous space</u> if it has a continuous presentation. Note that if $\triangleleft$ is interpreted as $\supseteq$, then all the properties in [C3] but the finiteness property are satisfied.

Every domain is a continuous space. For if D has a basis $E = \{e_i \mid i\in\omega\}$, let α_i and U_i be $\uparrow e_i$ and $\Uparrow e_i$ respectively, and the relation $\triangleleft$ be given by: $U_i \triangleleft \bigcap_{j\in J}\alpha_j$ iff $e_i \ll \bigsqcup_{j\in J}e_j$ where $\bigcap_{j\in J}\alpha_j$ is non-empty (note that by the bounded-completeness property, $\bigsqcup_{j\in J}e_j$ exists in D). Besides all the domains, continuous spaces also include the following Hausdorff spaces.

<u>Examples of Continuous Spaces</u>

(1) <u>Reals R</u>: U_i's and α_i's are given by open intervals (x,y) and closed intervals $[x,y]$ respectively with rational endpoints x,y such that $x \leq y$. The relation $\triangleleft$ is $\supseteq$.

(2) <u>Stone spaces</u>: A Stone space is a compact Hausdorff space with a countable base of clopen sets. For example, Cantor space 2^ω is a Stone space. Since we

assume that all our spaces are separable, there can be at most countably many clopen sets in a Stone space. Let $\{U_i | i\in\omega\}$ be an enumeration of all the clopen sets. Define α_i to be U_i and $\lhd$ to be $\supseteq$. The finiteness property follows from the fact that U_i's are closed and hence compact. [C4] follows from the compactness of the whole space.

(3) Baire space ω^ω: Basic open sets U_i's are given by finite intersections of $U_{m,n} = \{f\in\omega^\omega | f(m) = n\}$. Note that each U_i is clopen. Let us consider only those non-empty U_i's. Define $\alpha_i = U_i$ and $\lhd$ to be $\supseteq$. To verify the finiteness property, suppose $U_i \supseteq \bigcap_{j\in J} U_j \ (\neq \emptyset)$ and J is infinite. This means that for some finite sequences $\{s_i\}_{1\le i\le n}$ and $\{t_i\}_{1\le i\le n}$, and some infinite sequences $\{p_i\}_{i\in\omega}$ and $\{q_i\}_{i\in\omega}$,

$$\{f\in\omega^\omega | f(s_i) = t_i \text{ for all } 1\le i\le n\} \supseteq \{f\in\omega^\omega | f(p_i) = q_i \text{ for all } i\in\omega\}$$

Since the right hand side of the above inclusion is non-empty, it must be that for each $1\le i\le n$, there exists some $\ell\in\omega$ such that $s_i = p_\ell$ and $t_i = q_\ell$, showing that $U_i \supseteq \bigcap_{j\in J'} U_j$ for some finite subset J' of J. For the directed-completeness axiom [C4], suppose $\{U_i | i\in I\}$ is filtered and

$$\bigcap_{i\in I} U_i = \{f\in\omega^\omega | f(p_i) = q_i \text{ for all } i\in\omega\}.$$

If $\bigcap_{i\in I} U_i$ is empty, then there must exist some p_i, q_i, p_j and q_j such that $p_i = p_j$ and $q_i \neq q_j$. Letting $r = \max(i,j)$, we can find $k\in\omega$ such that

$$U_k \subseteq \{f\in\omega^\omega | f(p_n) = q_n \text{ for all } 1\le n\le r\}$$

showing that U_k is empty, contradiction.

Proposition 2

(i) In a continuous presentation $\langle X, \{\alpha_i\}_{i\in\omega}, \{U_i\}_{i\in\omega}, \lhd\rangle$,

$$\alpha_j = \bigcap\{U_i | U_i \lhd \alpha_j\}$$

for every $j\in\omega$, showing that α_j is a G_δ set.

(ii) When X is Hausdorff, α_j is closed.

Proof:

(i) By [C2], $\alpha_j = \bigcap\{\alpha_i | U_i \lhd \alpha_j\}$, hence $\alpha_j \supseteq \bigcap\{U_i | U_i \lhd \alpha_j\}$ by [C1]. On the other hand, $U_i \lhd \alpha_j$ implies $\alpha_j \subseteq U_i$, hence $\alpha_j \subseteq \bigcap\{U_i | U_i \lhd \alpha_j\}$.

(ii) We need to show that α_j^c, the complement of α_j, is open. Given $x\in\alpha_j^c$, it suffices to find some U_i such that $x\in U_i \subseteq \alpha_j^c$. Suppose this is not the case. Then for every U_i containing x, $U_i \cap \alpha_j \neq \emptyset$ and hence $\alpha_i \cap \alpha_j \neq \emptyset$ (because $U_i \subseteq \alpha_i$). By [C2], the sequence $\{\alpha_i \cap \alpha_j | x\in\alpha_i\}$ is filtered and hence $\bigcap\{\alpha_i \cap \alpha_j | x\in\alpha_i\}$ is non-empty by [C4]. Since X is Hausdorff, $\uparrow x = \{x\} = \bigcap\{\alpha_i | x\in U_i\} \supseteq \bigcap\{\alpha_i \cap \alpha_j | x\in U_i\}$, hence concluding $x\in\alpha_j$, contradiction. □

From a continuous presentation, we can readily construct a domain $\bar{X}$ using the α_i's as basis elements. The elements of $\bar{X}$ consist of all the non-empty $\bigcap_{j\in J}\alpha_j$ where J ranges over all subsets of ω. The partial ordering $\sqsubseteq$ in $\bar{X}$ is given by $\supseteq$.

Proposition 3

(i) For every continuous presentation $<X, \{\alpha_i\}_{i\in\omega}, \{U_i\}_{i\in\omega}, \lhd>$, $\bar{X}$ is a domain.

(ii) Define $<$ on ω by:

$$i<j \quad \text{iff} \quad U_i \lhd \alpha_j$$

Then $<\omega,<>$ is an R-structure and $\bar{X}$ is isomorphic to the Dedekind cut completion of $<\omega,<>$.

(iii) The map: $X \to \bar{X}$ defined by:

$$i(x) = \uparrow x \quad (= \cap\{\alpha_i | x\in U_i\})$$

embeds X as a dense subspace of $\bar{X}$.

Proof:

(i) $\bar{X}$ is clearly directed-complete and bounded-complete. Now define $\bar{e}_i = \alpha_i$ and $\bar{U}_i = \{x\in\bar{X} | U_i \lhd x\}$. The finiteness property shows that $\bar{U}_i$ is Scott-open in $\bar{X}$. If $x\in\bar{U}_i$, then $\alpha_i \supseteq U_i \lhd x$, which implies $\alpha_i \sqsubseteq x$ in $\bar{D}$ and hence $\bar{U}_i \subseteq \uparrow\bar{e}_i$. Finally for every $x\in\bar{X}$, [C2] says that the set $\{\alpha_i | U_i \lhd x\} = \{\bar{e}_i | x\in\bar{U}_i\}$ is directed and $x = \cap\{\alpha_i | U_i \lhd x\} = \bigsqcup\{\bar{e}_i | x\in\bar{U}_i\}$. Therefore, $\bar{X}$ is a domain by Proposition 1.

(ii) To show that $<\omega,<>$ is an R-structure, we need to verify that $[i] = \{j | j<i\} = \{j | U_j \lhd \alpha_i\}$ is $<$-directed. Assume $U_{j_1} \lhd \alpha_i$ and $U_{j_2} \lhd \alpha_i$. By [C2], the set $\{\alpha_k | U_k \lhd \alpha_i\}$ is filtered and $\alpha_i = \cap\{\alpha_k | U_k \lhd \alpha_i\}$. By applying the finiteness property twice, we obtain α_{k_1} & α_{k_2} such that $U_{k_1} \lhd \alpha_i$, $U_{k_2} \lhd \alpha_i$, $U_{j_1} \lhd \alpha_{k_1}$ and $U_{j_2} \lhd \alpha_{k_2}$. Since $\{\alpha_k | U_k \lhd \alpha_i\}$ is filtered, there exists some k such that $U_k \lhd \alpha_i$, $\alpha_k \subseteq \alpha_{k_1}$ and $\alpha_k \subseteq \alpha_{k_2}$, thereby showing $k<i$, $j_1<k$ and $j_2<k$. To see that $\bar{X}$ is isomorphic to the Dedekind cut completion of $<\omega,<>$, define the pair of isomorphic maps ϕ: $\bar{X} \to \overline{<\omega,<>}$ and ψ: $\overline{<\omega,<>} \to \bar{X}$ as follows:

$$\phi(\bigcap_{j\in J}\alpha_j) = \{i | U_i \lhd \bigcap_{j\in J}\alpha_j\}$$

and

$$\psi(x) = \cap\{\alpha_j | j\in x\}$$

The finiteness property shows that $\phi(\bigcap_{j\in J}\alpha_j)$ is a $<$-directed left closed subset of ω.

(iii) Note: $i(U_k) = i(X) \cap \bar{U}_k$. Since U_k is non-empty for every $k\in\omega$, $i(X)$ is a dense subspace of $\bar{X}$.

$\sqcap$

A continuous space X is <u>algebraic</u> if for some continuous presentation, $\bar{X}$ has a basis of compact elements. The following proposition characterizes the algebraic spaces.

Proposition 4

A continuous space X is algebraic iff X has a base $B = \{U_i \mid i \in \omega\}$ of non-empty open sets satisfying:

[A1] $\bigcap_{j \in J} U_j \subseteq U_i$ implies $\bigcap_{j \in J'} U_j \subseteq U_i$ for some finite subset J' of J; and

[A2] Every filtered subset of B has a non-empty intersection.

Proof:

(⇐) Without loss of generality, we may assume that B is closed under consistent finite intersections, i.e. $U_i \cap U_j \neq \emptyset$ implies $U_i \cap U_j \in B$. It is easy to see that $\langle X, \{U_i\}_{i\in\omega}, \{U_i\}_{i\in\omega}, \supseteq \rangle$ is a continuous presentation. [A1] says that each U_i is compact in $\bar{X}$, hence X is algebraic.

(⇒) Suppose for some continuous presentation $\langle X, \{\alpha_i\}_{i\in\omega}, \{U_i\}_{i\in\omega}, \lhd \rangle$, $\bar{X}$ has a basis of compact elements. Since $\{\alpha_i \mid i\in\omega\}$ is a basis of X, it must contain all the compact elements.

Claim: α_i is compact iff $\alpha_i = \alpha_j$ where $U_j \lhd \alpha_j$

Proof:

(⇒) Suppose α_i is compact. Since $\alpha_i = \bigcap\{\alpha_j \mid U_j \lhd \alpha_i\}$ and the set $\{\alpha_j \mid U_j \lhd \alpha_i\}$ is filtered, there exists some j such that $\alpha_i = \alpha_j$ and $U_j \lhd \alpha_j$.

(⇐) Suppose $U_j \lhd \alpha_j$ and $\bigcap_{k\in K} \alpha_k \subseteq \alpha_j$, hence $U_j \lhd \bigcap_{k\in K} \alpha_k$. By the finiteness property, $U_j \lhd \bigcap_{k\in K'} \alpha_k$ for some finite subset K' of K, hence $\bigcap_{k\in K'} \alpha_k \subseteq \alpha_j$. □

Define $B = \{U_i \mid U_i \lhd \alpha_i\}$. Note that $U_i \in B$ implies $U_i = \alpha_i$. Since B consists of all the compact elements in X by the above claim, the open sets in B must form a base of the topology of X. Also in B, $U_i \lhd \bigcap_{j\in J} U_j$ is equivalent to $\bigcap_{j\in J} U_j \subseteq U_i$. Thus [A1] and [A2] follow from the finiteness property and the directedness completeness axiom. □

Suppose X is an algebraic space. Proposition 4 says that α_i can be chosen to be the same as U_i. When X is Hausdorff, Proposition 1 shows that α_i is closed. Thus, every algebraic Hausdorff space has a clopen base satisfying [A1] and [A2]. Stone spaces are compact Hausdorff spaces with a clopen base which trivially satisfy [A1] and [A2]. Hence Stone spaces are precisely all the compact algebraic spaces.

Suppose the continuous space X is Hausdorff. Then for every $x \in X$, $\uparrow x$ is equal to the singleton set $\{x\}$ which is a total object in the domain $\bar{X}$. By Proposition 3(iii), X is homeomorphic to the subspace of total objects in $\bar{X}$, showing that X is total. Proposition 5 below gives us a criteria to determine when a total space is continuous. And Proposition 6 shows that in the presence of compactness, total is equivalent to continuous.

Proposition 5

A total space X is continuous iff $X \simeq T(D)$ for some domain D which has a continuous presentation $\langle D, \{e_i\}_{i\in\omega}, \{U_i\}_{i\in\omega}\rangle$ satisfying the following: for every $i,j\in\omega$,

$$\text{(i)} \quad \uparrow e_i \cap T(D) = \uparrow e_j \cap T(D) \quad \text{iff } e_i = e_j$$

$$\text{(ii)} \quad U_i \cap T(D) = U_j \cap T(D) \quad \text{iff } U_i = U_j$$

Proof:

($\Rightarrow$) Suppose $\langle X, \{\alpha_i\}_{i\in\omega}, \{V_i\}_{i\in\omega}, \triangleleft\rangle$ is a continuous presentation. Let $e_i = \alpha_i$ and $U_i = \bar{V}_i$. Then:

$$\text{(i)} \ \forall x\in T(D),\ e_i \sqsubseteq x \text{ iff } e_j \sqsubseteq x \ \leftrightarrow\ \forall x\in T(D),\ x\in\alpha_i \text{ iff } x\in\alpha_j$$
$$\leftrightarrow\ \alpha_i = \alpha_j$$
$$\leftrightarrow\ e_i = e_j$$

$$\text{(ii)} \ \forall x\in T(D),\ x\in U_i \text{ iff } x\in U_j \ \leftrightarrow\ \forall x\in T(D),\ V_i \triangleleft \{x\} \text{ iff } V_j \triangleleft \{x\}$$
$$\leftrightarrow\ \forall x\in X,\ x\in V_i \text{ iff } x\in V_j$$
$$\leftrightarrow\ V_i = V_j$$
$$\rightarrow\ U_i = U_j$$

($\Leftarrow$) Given such a D, define α_i's, V_i's and $\triangleleft$ as follows:

$$\alpha_i = \uparrow e_i \cap T(D)$$

$$V_i = U_i \cap T(D)$$

and $$V_i \triangleleft \bigcap_{j\in J}\alpha_j \quad \text{iff} \quad \bigsqcup_{j\in J} e_j \in U_i$$

where $\bigcap_{j\in J}\alpha_j \neq \emptyset$ (hence $\bigsqcup_{j\in J} e_j$ exists by the bounded-completeness property of D). Note that because of (i) & (ii), $\triangleleft$ is well-defined. Showing that $\langle T(D), \{\alpha_i\}_{i\in\omega}, \{V_i\}_{i\in\omega}, \triangleleft\rangle$ forms a continuous presentation is straightforward.

□

Proposition 6

Every compact total space is continuous.

Proof:

Since every total space is metrizable [2], it suffices to show that every compact metric space X is continuous. Let $A \subseteq X$ be some countable dense subset of X and d the metric. Define U_i's to be finite intersections of open balls $B_{a,\delta} = \{x \mid d(x,a)<\delta\}$ with $a \in A$ and $\delta \in Q$ (the rationals), α_i's to be finite intersections of the corresponding closed balls $C_{a,\delta} = \{x \mid d(x,a) \leq \delta\}$ and $\triangleleft$ to be $\supseteq$. Axioms [C1] and [C2] are straightforward to show. To verify the finiteness property of $\triangleleft$ in [C3], assume that $\bigcap_{i\in\omega} C_i \subseteq B$ and $\bigcap_{i\leq n} C_i \not\subseteq B$ for every $n \in \omega$, where B is a finite intersection of open balls and each C_i is a finite intersection of closed balls. Then there is a sequence of elements $\{x_i\}_{i\in\omega}$ in X such that $x_i \in [\bigcap_{1\leq j\leq i} C_j \setminus B]$ for every $i \in \omega$. Since every infinite sequence in a compact metric space has a converging subsequence, let x be a limit of one of the converging subsequences of $\{x_i\}_{i\in\omega}$. Then $x \in \bigcap_{i\in\omega} C_i$ but $x \notin B$, contradicting $\bigcap_{i\in\omega} C_i \subseteq B$. Finally [A4] follows from the compactness of X. □

For the rest of the paper, we show how to formulate the notion of an effectively given space. The key here is that every continuous space can be suitably embedded as a dense subspace of some domain which is defined from a continuous presentation. The 5-tuple $\langle X, \{\alpha_i\}_{i\in\omega}, \{U_i\}_{i\in\omega}, \triangleleft, \text{Comp}\rangle$ is an <u>effectively given presentation</u> if $\langle X, \{\alpha_i\}_{i\in\omega}, \{U_i\}_{i\in\omega}, \triangleleft\rangle$ is a continuous presentation and Comp is a total recursive predicate on finite set of integers satisfying:

[C5] <u>Axioms on Comp</u>:

(i) for arbitrary finite sets S of integers,
$\bigcap_{i\in S} U_i \neq \emptyset \Rightarrow \text{Comp}(S) \Rightarrow \bigcap_{i\in S} \alpha_i \neq \emptyset$; and

(ii) the predicate "$\text{Comp}(S) \Rightarrow U_i \triangleleft \bigcap_{j\in S} \alpha_j$" is recursively enumberable in i and S.

X is an <u>effectively given space</u> if it has an effectively given presentation. The use of the Comp predicate is due to Smyth [10]. When we form a directed sequence of basis elements during computation, we need to know either $\bigcap_{i\in S} U_i \neq \emptyset$ or $\bigcap_{i\in S} \alpha_i \neq \emptyset$ for certain finite subsets S's. Obviously $\bigcap_{i\in S} U_i \neq \emptyset$ implies $\bigcap_{i\in S} \alpha_i \neq \emptyset$ because of the Structural axiom. Requiring either $\bigcap_{i\in S} U_i \neq \emptyset$ or $\bigcap_{i\in S} \alpha_i \neq \emptyset$ to be a recursive predicate on S seems rather strong. [C5](i) says that some recursive separation of the above two predicates is sufficient. As $\triangleleft$ is only defined for those intersections of α_j's which are non-empty, we need Comp(S) in [C5](ii) to make sure that $\bigcap_{j\in S} \alpha_j$ is non-empty. Since all the U_j's are assumed to be non-empty (hence Comp({j}) is true for every singleton set {j}), [C5](ii) says that the predicate $U_i \triangleleft \alpha_j$ is recursively enumerable in i and j.

If $\langle X, \{\alpha_i\}_{i\in\omega}, \{U_i\}_{i\in\omega}, \triangleleft, \text{Comp}\rangle$ is effectively given, then the R-structure $\langle\omega,<\rangle$ defined by: $i<j$ iff $U_i \triangleleft \alpha_j$ is obviously effective in the sense of Smyth [10], and hence the completion $\overline{\langle\omega,<\rangle}$ or $\bar{X}$ is an effectively given domain.

Every domain effectively given in the sense of Smyth [10] has an effectively given presentation. For suppose the domain D is given by the Dedekind cut completion of some effective R-structure $<\omega, <, \mathrm{Comp}>$. Define α_i's, U_i's and $\triangleleft$ as follows:

$$\alpha_i = \{\ell \in \overline{<\omega,<>} \mid [i] \subseteq \ell\}$$

$$U_i = \{\ell \in \overline{<\omega,<>} \mid i \in \ell\}$$

$$U_i \triangleleft \bigcap_{j \in J} \alpha_j \quad \text{iff} \quad i \in \bigsqcup_{\overline{<\omega,<>}} \{[j] \mid j \in J\}$$

where $\bigcap_{j\in J}\alpha_j$ is non-empty. Note that existence of $\bigsqcup_{\overline{<\omega,<>}}\{[j]\mid j\in J\}$ follows from non-emptiness of $\bigcap_{j\in J}\alpha_j$. It is routine to verify that $<\overline{\omega,<}, \{\alpha_i\}_{i\in\omega}, \{U_i\}_{i\in\omega}, \triangleleft, \mathrm{Comp}>$ is an effectively given presentation.

The concluding proposition summarizes the use of continuous spaces as topological models for computations. It says that in an effectively given space, the notion of a computable object, normally given with an operational flavor (see [OP] below), can be abstracted by a set of properties of the object which are independent of how the object is computed.

Proposition 7

If $<X, \{\alpha_i\}_{i\in\omega}, \{U_i\}_{i\in\omega}, \triangleleft, \mathrm{Comp}>$ is an effectively given presentation, then the following two notions of a computable object in X are equivalent:

[OP] $\uparrow x = \bigcap_{j\in\omega}\alpha_{p(j)}$ where $\{\alpha_{p(j)}\}_{j\in\omega}$ is filtered and $p\colon \omega \to \omega$ is a recursive function

[TOP] $\{i \mid x\in U_i\}$ (i.e. the set of all the properties of x) is recursively enumerable.

Proof:

[OP] $\Rightarrow$ [TOP] : Note

$x\in U_i$ iff $U_i \triangleleft \uparrow x$ by [C3]

iff $U_i \triangleleft \bigcap_{j\in\omega}\alpha_{p(j)}$

iff for some $j\in\omega$, $U_i \triangleleft \alpha_{p(j)}$

where the right hand side is obviously recursively enumerable in i because of [C5](ii).
[TOP] $\Rightarrow$ [OP] : If $\{i\mid x\in U_i\}$ is recursively enumerable, then by [C3], $\uparrow x = \bigcap\{\alpha_i \mid x\in U_i\}$ which is a recursively enumerable filtered intersection of α_i's.

□

The use of our topological methods in computing seems to have some limitations. Consider Kleene's (level 2) countable functionals C_2[3], or the set of all continuous functionals from ω^ω to ω. $F\in C_2$ is called a countable functional because for every

$\alpha\epsilon\omega^{\omega}$, $F(\alpha)$ depends on only finite amount of information on α. Because of the finite behavior of F on function arguments, F can be coded by some total function $\beta : \omega \to \omega$, called an associate of F, as follows: for every $\alpha\epsilon\omega^{\omega}$, there exists some $n\epsilon\omega$ such that

$$1 + F(\alpha) = \beta(\overline{\alpha(n)})$$

$$\text{and } \forall \text{ finite sequences } s, s', \ \beta(\bar{s}) > 0 \text{ and } s \subseteq s' \Rightarrow \beta(\overline{s'}) = \beta(\bar{s})$$

where $\overline{\alpha(n)}$ is the sequence number of the finite sequence $<\alpha(0),\ldots,\alpha(n)>$. The functional F is computable if it has a recursive associate. An interesting topology on the countable functionals was given by Kreisel in [4] as follows: given $n\epsilon\omega$ and some basic open set

$$\mathcal{N}_{\{(p_i,q_i) \mid 1\le i\le k\}} = \{\alpha\epsilon\omega^{\omega} \mid \alpha(p_i) = q_i \ \forall \ 1\le i\le k\} \text{ in } \omega^{\omega},$$

the sub-basic open set $\mathcal{O}$ is defined by

$$\mathcal{O} = \{F \mid F(\mathcal{N}_{\{(p_i,q_i) \mid 1\le i\le k\}}) = \{n\} \ \}$$

Now consider the following functional F: for $\alpha\epsilon\omega^{\omega}$,

$$F(\alpha) = \begin{cases} 1 & \text{if } \alpha(0) \text{ and } \alpha(1) \text{ are codes for some context-free sets L and L' and } \alpha(2) \text{ is the code of some word w such that either } w\epsilon L \cap L' \text{ or } w \epsilon (L \cup L')^{c} \\ 0 & \text{if otherwise} \end{cases}$$

Since membership question on context-free sets is decidable, the above functional F obviously has a computable associate, hence F is computable. Now if we can effectively list all the sub-basic open sets containing F, then the predicate

$$F(\mathcal{N}_{\{(0,m),(1,n)\}}) = \{1\}$$

would be recursively enumerable in m and n, meaning that we can enumerate all pairs of equivalent context-free sets, contradiction. This example shows that Kreisel's sub-basic open sets cannot correctly describe Kleene's computable functionals. It is not clear that Kleene's computable functionals can be correctly described by some other sub-base of Kreisel's topology or even of any other topology on C_2. A different approach to study C_2 using filter spaces is suggested by Hyland in [1].

References

[1] Hyland, M. [1979], "Filter spaces and continuous functionals," Annals of Mathematical Logic 16, 101-143.

[2] Kamimura, T. & Tang, A. [1983], "Total objects of domains," Technical report, University of Kansas.

[3] Kleene, S. C. [1959], "Countable functionals," Constructivity in Mathematics, North-Holland, 81-100.

[4] Kreisel, G. [1959], "Interpretation of analysis by means of contructive functionals of finite types," same as [3], 81-100.

[5] Sciore, E. & Tang, A. [1978], "Computability theory in admissible domains," Sigact, San Diego, 95-104.

[6] Scott, D. [1972], "Continuous lattices," Springer Lecture Notes in Mathematics, Vol. 274, 97-136.

[7] Scott, D. [1972], "Lattice theory, data types and semantics," Formal Semantics of Programming Languages, edited by R. Rustin, Prentice Hall, 65-106.

[8] Scott, D. [1981], "Lecture on a mathematical theory of computation," Oxford University Computing Laboratory, Technical monograph PRG-19.

[9] Scott, D. [1982], "Domains for denotational semantics," ICALP, Aarhus, Denmark.

[10] Smyth, M. [1977], "Effectively given domains," Theoretical Computer Science, Vol. 5, 257-274.

A NOTE ON INTERSECTIONS OF FREE SUBMONOIDS OF A FREE MONOID

Juhani Karhumäki
Department of Mathematics
University of Turku
Turku, Finland

ABSTRACT

According to a theorem of Tilson [7] any intersection of free submonoids of a free monoid is free. Here we consider intersections of the form $\{x,y\}^* \cap \{u,v\}^*$, where x,y,u and v are words in a finitely generated free monoid Σ^*, and show that if both the monoids $\{x,y\}^*$ and $\{u,v\}^*$ are of the rank two, then the intersection is a free monoid generated either by (at most) two words or by a regular language of the form $\beta_0 + \beta(\gamma(1+\delta+\ldots+\delta^t))^*\varepsilon$ for some words β_0, β, γ, δ and ε, and some integer $t \geq 0$. An example is given showing that the latter possibility may occur for each $t \geq 0$ with nonempty values of the words. If $\{x,y\}$ and $\{u,v\}$ are prefixes then necessarily $t = 0$ and $\beta_0 = 1$.

1. INTRODUCTION

The theory of free monoids, or codes, is of basic importance in formal language theory, cf. [6]. A typical example is a result of Tilson [7] which states that any intersection of free submonoids of a free monoid is free. In [2] an automata-theoretic proof for Tilson's theorem was given and, moreover, a method for constructing the basis for the intersection was provided.

According to the above the freeness of submonoids (of a free monoid) is preserved under the operation of intersection. The same holds also for the property of being regular (recognizable). However, in formal language theory the operation of intersection is, in general, unpleasant in the sense that it often leads from simple objects to more complicated ones. This is the situation here, too. The intersection of two finitely generated free submonoids need not be finitely generated. Of course, such an intersection is regular.

Here we study the above intersection problem in a very simple setup. More precisely, we are interested in intersections of the form

$\{x,y\}^* \cap \{u,v\}^*$, where x,y,u and v are elements (or words) in a finitely generated free monoid Σ^*. If at least one of the monoids $\{x,y\}^*$ and $\{u,v\}^*$ is of the rank 1, i.e. periodic, then the problem of determining the intersection turns out to be purely arithmetic and is handled in Theorem 1. In the other case we show that the intersection is freely generated either by at most two words or by a regular language of the form $\beta_0 + \beta(\gamma(1+\delta+\ldots+\delta^t))^*\varepsilon$ for some words β_0, β, γ, δ and ε, and some integer $t \geq 0$. Simple examples show that both the possibilities may occur with nonempty values of the parameters.

Our proof utilizes ideas from [3], where a related result characterizing so-called binary equality languages was established. Here only the case where $\{x,y\}$ and $\{u,v\}$ are prefixes is handled in details. The proof of the general case can be found in [5]. We hope that our result, as such a simple characterization, has applications not only in formal language theory but also in some other areas of discrete mathematics.

2. PRELIMINARIES

The necessary knowledge of theories of free monoids and formal languages can be found e.g. in [4] or [6]. However, to fix our notation we want to specify the following.

Let Σ be a finite alphabet. The free monoid generated by Σ is denoted by Σ^*. Elements of Σ^* are called words, in particular, the empty word 1 denotes the identity of Σ^*. We set $\Sigma^+ = \Sigma^* - \{1\}$. For technical reasons we shall also talk about infinite words (from left to right), i.e., infinite sequences of elements of Σ.

For the length of a word x we use the notation $|x|$. For two words x and y the notation yx^{-1} (resp. $x^{-1}y$) denotes the right (resp. left) quotient of y by x and the notation $x \text{pref} y$ that x is a prefix (not necessarily proper) of y. The prefix (resp. suffix) of length k of a word x is denoted by $\text{pref}_k(x)$ (resp. $\text{suf}_k(x)$). If $|x| < k$, we set $\text{pref}_k(x) = x$. By the relation $x \text{Pref} y$ we mean that either $x \text{pref} y$ or $y \text{pref} x$ holds. For a language L, $\text{pref}(L)$ (resp. $\text{suf}(L)$) denotes the set of all prefixes (resp. suffixes) of words in L and for two languages L_1 and L_2 their quotients are defined, via quotients of words, in a natural way.

In this paper we consider free submonoids of Σ^* generated by at most two words, i.e., subsets of Σ^* of the form $\{x,y\}^*$. Let $X = \{x,y\}$ for some words x and y in Σ^*. We call X <u>periodic</u> if $X \subseteq p^*$ for some word p in Σ^* and <u>marked</u> if both x and y are nonempty and, moreover, $pref_1(x) \neq pref_1(y)$. Consequently, $X = \{x,y\}$ is periodic iff X^* is of the rank 1 and nonperiodic iff X^* is of the rank 2.

The following characterization of periodic sets is well-known.

<u>Lemma 1.</u> A set $X = \{x,y\} \subsetneq \Sigma^*$ is periodic if and only if $xy = yx$. □

Lemma 1 can be generalized to the following simple result which is not only very fundamental (although hidenly) for our later considerations, but is also interesting on its own.

<u>Lemma 2.</u> Let $X = \{x,y\} \subsetneq \Sigma^*$ be nonperiodic. There exists a unique word α, with $|\alpha| \leq |xy| - 1$, such that for all words u and v, with $u \in xX^*$, $|u| > |\alpha|$, $v \in yX^*$, $|v| > |\alpha|$, we have $\alpha \in pref(u) \cap pref(v)$ and $pref_{|\alpha|+1}(u) \neq pref_{|\alpha|+1}(v)$.

<u>Proof.</u> It is not difficult to see that the lemma holds with α equal to the maximal common prefix of the words xy and yx. □

Let $X = \{x,y\}$ and $U = \{u,v\}$ be two subsets of Σ^*. We denote by $I(X,U)$ the intersection of X^* and U^*, i.e.,

$$I(X,U) = \{x,y\}^* \cap \{u,v\}^* .$$

Elements in $I(X,U)$ are called <u>(X,U)-solutions</u>, or briefly <u>solutions</u> if there is no danger of confusion. Further, for a word α in Σ^*, we define a so-called <u>α-shifted intersection of X^* and U^*</u>, in symbols $I_\alpha(X,U)$, by setting

$$I_\alpha(X,U) = (\alpha X^* \cap U^*\alpha)\alpha^{-1}$$

and we call elements in this set <u>(α,X,U)-solutions</u>, or briefly <u>solutions</u>.

Let s be an (α,X,U)-solution, i.e., there exist words $s_1, \ldots, s_n$ in U and words $r_1, \ldots, r_m$ in X such that $s = s_1 \ldots s_n$ and $s_1 \ldots s_n\alpha = \alpha r_1 \ldots r_m$. We call the solution s <u>atomic</u> if the equation $s_1 \ldots s_i\alpha = \alpha r_1 \ldots r_j$ is not satisfied by any pair (i,j) with $1 \leq i < n$ and $1 \leq j < m$.

Next we solve our problem in the case when at least one of the sets X and U is periodic.

<u>Theorem 1.</u> Let $X = \{x,y\}$ and $U = \{u,v\}$ be subsets of Σ^* such that at least one of them is periodic. Then there exist a word p, a finite subset F of p^* and integers t and N such that

$$I(X,U) = F + p^{tN} (p^N)^* .$$

Consequently, $I(X,U)$ is finitely generated.

Proof. Assume first that both X and U are periodic, say $X=\{p^n,p^m\}$ and $U=\{q^k,q^l\}$ for some words p and q and some integers n, m, k and l. We may assume that p and q are primitive, i.e., they are not proper powers of any word. Then, if $p\neq q$, $I(X,U)$ equals $\{\lambda\}$ and is thus of the required form with $F=\phi$ and $N=0$.

So we assume that $p=q$. Now the problem of determining $I(X,U)$ is purely number-theoretic, and it is not difficult to see that the required representation holds with $N = \text{l.c.m.}(\text{g.c.d.}(n,m),\text{g.c.d.}(k,l))$, where l.c.m. and g.c.d. are abbreviations for "least common multiple" and "greatest common divisor".

Secondly, assume that X is periodic, say $X=\{p^n,p^m\}$ for some word p and integers n and m, and U is not. Since U is nonperiodic, it follows from the Defect Theorem, cf. [1], that $U^*\cap p^*=(p^s)^*$ for some integer $s\geq 0$. Consequently, the problem has been reduced to the first case of this proof. □

The fact that $I(X,U)$ may be generated by more than two elements is seen e.g. from the example $X=\{a^4,a^5\}$ and $U=\{a^3\}$. Indeed, $I(X,U)=\{a^9,a^{12},a^{15}\}^*$.

3. MAIN RESULT

As our main result we state:

Theorem 2. Let $X=\{x,y\}$ and $U=\{u,v\}$ be nonperiodic subsets of Σ^*. Then $I(X,U)$ is of one of the following forms:

(*) $I(X,U) = \{\beta,\gamma\}^*$ for some (possibly empty) words β and γ in Σ^*,

(**) $I(X,U) = (\beta_0+\beta(\gamma(1+\delta+\ldots+\delta^t))^*\varepsilon)^*$ for some (possibly empty) words β_0, β, γ, δ and ε in Σ^*, and some integer $t\geq 0$.

The detailed (and lengthy) proof of Theorem 2 can be found in [5]. Here we prove only a special case when X and U are so-called prefixes. Moreover, we show how the general problem of characterizing $I(X,U)$ can be reduced to the problem of characterizing $I_\alpha(X_m,U_m)$, where α is a word and X_m and U_m are marked subsets of Σ^*.

Following [3] we define a mapping $cyc_1:\Sigma^*\to\Sigma^*$ by

$$\mathrm{cyc}_1(1) = 1 ,$$

$$\mathrm{cyc}_1(cz) = zc \quad \text{for} \quad c \in \Sigma \quad \text{and} \quad z \in \Sigma^* .$$

Let $\mathrm{cyc}_k = (\mathrm{cyc}_1)^k$. It follows that for any word z in Σ^* we have

(1) $$\mathrm{cyc}_k(z) = (\mathrm{pref}_{k_1}(z))^{-1} z \, \mathrm{pref}_{k_1}(z)$$

where $0 \leq k_1 < |z|$ and $k_1 \equiv k \bmod(|z|)$.

Since $X = \{x,y\}$ is nonperiodic Lemma 1 guarantees that $xy \neq yx$. Let α_X be the maximal common prefix of xy and yx. Thus $|\alpha_X| < |xy|$. We define

(2) $$X_m = \{\mathrm{cyc}_{|\alpha_X|}(x) , \mathrm{cyc}_{|\alpha_X|}(y)\} ,$$

and derive from (1) and the choice of α_X:

<u>Lemma 3.</u> X_m is marked. Moreover, the mapping $\mathrm{cyc}_{|\alpha_X|} : X^* \to X_m^*$ is a morphism, i.e., $\mathrm{cyc}_{|\alpha_X|}(ww') = \mathrm{cyc}_{|\alpha_X|}(w)\,\mathrm{cyc}_{|\alpha_X|}(w')$ for all w and w' in X^*. □

Now, let α_X and α_U be the words associated to X and U as above. We assume, by symmetry, that $|\alpha_X| \geq |\alpha_U|$, and prove the following auxiliary lemma.

<u>Lemma 4.</u> If α_U is not a prefix of α_X, then $I(X,U) = \{\lambda\}$.

<u>Proof.</u> We first observe, by Lemma 2, that for each w in X^* (resp. in U^*) $\alpha_X \mathrm{Pref}\, w$ (resp. $\alpha_U \mathrm{Pref}\, w$) holds true. Now, if $I(X,U)$ contains a nonempty word w_1, then it contains also the word $w_1^{|\alpha_X|}$ and thus both α_X and α_U are prefixes of a word, a contradiction. □

By Lemma 4, we may assume from now on that $\alpha_U \mathrm{pref} \alpha_X$. We set

(3) $$\alpha_{X,U} = \alpha_U^{-1} \alpha_X$$

and remind that

(4) $$|\alpha_{X,U}| < |xy| .$$

With the above notation we culminate our auxiliary considerations to:

<u>Lemma 5.</u> Let $X = \{x,y\}$ and $U = \{u,v\}$ be nonperiodic subsets of Σ^* such that $\alpha_{X,U}$ is defined. Then we have

$$\mathrm{cyc}_{|\alpha_U|}(I(X,U)) = I_{\alpha_{X,U}}(X_m,U_m) .$$

<u>Proof.</u> As in Lemma 3, $\mathrm{cyc}_{|\alpha_U|}$ is a morphism from X^* onto X_m^* and also from U^* onto U_m^*. Consequently, it is a morphism from

$I(X,U)$ onto $I(X_m,U_m)$, too. Therefore, we have

$$\begin{aligned} cyc_{|\alpha_U|}(I(X,U)) &= I(cyc_{|\alpha_U|}(X),\ cyc_{|\alpha_U|}(U)) \\ &= I((cyc_{|\alpha_X|-|\alpha_U|})^{-1}(X_m),U_m) \\ &= I_{\alpha_{X,U}}(X_m,U_m) \ . \qquad \square \end{aligned}$$

In Lemma 5 we have finished our reduction. Indeed, it follows that it suffices to show that sets of the form $I_\alpha(X_m,U_m)$, where α is a word and X_m and U_m are marked, satisfy the requirements (*) and (**) in Theorem 2. Moreover, it follows that $I_\alpha(X_m,U_m)$ is a free monoid freely generated by the atomic $(\alpha,\ X_m,U_m)$-solutions.

Now we go into a special case where X and U are so-called prefixes. We recall that a subset of Σ^* is a <u>prefix</u> if none of its words is a prefix of another. For prefixes Theorem 2 can be strengthened to the form:

<u>Theorem 3.</u> Let $X=\{x,y\}$ and $U=\{u,v\}$ be prefixes of Σ^*. Then $I(X,U)$ is of one of the following forms:

(i) $I(X,U)=\{\beta,\gamma\}^*$ for some (possibly empty) words β and γ in Σ^*,
(ii) $I(X,U)=(\beta\gamma^*\delta)^*$ for some (possibly empty) words β,γ and δ in Σ^*.

<u>Proof.</u> If $\alpha_{X,U}$ in (3) is not defined then we are done by Lemma 4. So assume that $\alpha_{X,U}$ is defined and let us denote it briefly by α. We shall show that $I_\alpha(X_m,U_m)$, where X_m and U_m are as in (2), contains at most two atomic solutions or is of the form $(\beta\gamma^*\delta)^*$ for some words β, γ and δ. From this the theorem follows. For simplicity we denote from now on $X_m=\{x,y\}$ and $U_m=\{u,v\}$. Let $pref_1(x)=pref_1(u)$.

If $\alpha=1$, then $I_\alpha(X_m,U_m)$ is of the form (i). Indeed, since X_m and U_m are marked $I(X_m,U_m)$ may contain at most as many atomic solutions as is the cardinality of U_m, and hence at most two.

So we assume that $\alpha \neq 1$. We define the following three (finite or infinite) processes P_α, P_x and P_y:

P_α: (i) $\alpha_0 = (\alpha,1)$

(ii) for $i \geq 0$, if $\alpha_i = (\mu,\nu)$ with $\mu \neq \nu$, then

$$\alpha_{i+1} = \begin{cases} (\mu\tau,\nu) & \text{if } \mu\, pref\, \nu \text{ and } \mu\tau\, Pref\, \nu \text{ for some } \tau \text{ in } X_m, \\ (\mu,\nu\tau) & \text{if } \nu\, pref\, \mu \text{ and } \mu\, Pref\, \nu\tau \text{ for some } \tau \text{ in } U_m. \end{cases}$$

P_x and P_y are defined exactly like P_α but using the initial conditions $\alpha_0=(x,y)$ and $\alpha_0=(u,v)$, respectively, Since X_m and U_m are marked the above processes are deterministic. They may be finite or infinite. We call a process <u>matching</u> if $\mu = \nu$ for some $\alpha_i = (\mu,\nu)$.

We have four subcases.

I P_α is not matching. In this case there clearly exists at most one atomic solution. Indeed, all solutions are among the prefixes of the unique maximal second component of pairs defined by P_α.

II P_α is matching but neither P_x nor P_y is matching. Now there may be at most two atomic solutions.

III P_α is matching and exactly one of the processes P_x and P_y, say P_x, is matching. Let w and w_1 be words in X_m^* and w' and w_1' in U_m^* such that $\alpha w = w'$ and $xw_1 = uw_1'$. We choose all these words minimal and illustrate our assumptions in Figure 1.

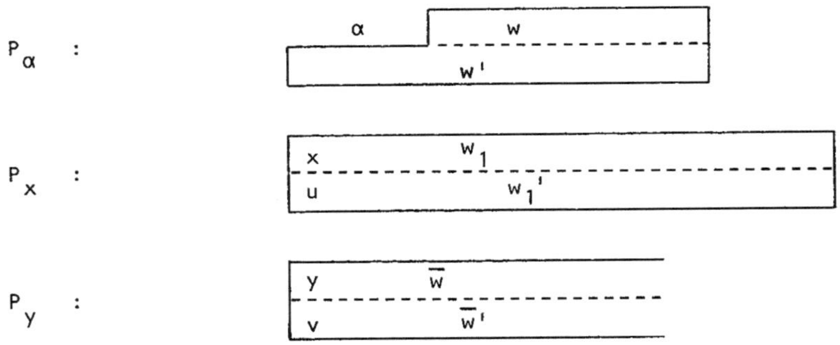

Fig. 1.

In Figure 1 (finite or infinite) words $y\bar{w}$ and $v\bar{w}'$ are determined by the process P_y.

Now we make use the fact that X and U are prefixes. This implies that (4) can be strengthened to

$$|\alpha_{X,U}| < \min\{|x| , |y|\}$$

and, consequently, we have

(4') $$|\alpha| < \min_{\substack{z \in X \\ \bar{z} \in U}}\{|z\bar{z}|\} .$$

Obviously all the elements of $I_\alpha(X_m,U_m)$ are in

$$\mathrm{pref}(w'(uw_1')^* v\bar{w}') \cap U_m{}^* .$$

Further from (4') we conclude that none of the words in

(5) $$w'(uw_1')^*(\mathrm{pref}(\alpha(\mathrm{suf}_1(\alpha)^{-1})\cap\Sigma^+)^{-1}$$

is a solution. Since all the processes are deterministic there exist at most one atomic solution both in $\mathrm{pref}(w'(uw_1')^*)$ and in $\mathrm{pref}(w'v\bar{w}')$. This means that if $I_\alpha(X_m,U_m)$ contains more than two atomic solutions it is of the form $(w'(uw_1')^*p)^*$ for some p in $\mathrm{pref}(v\bar{w}')$, which completes the proof of case III.

IV All the processes P_α, P_x and P_y are matching. Now the words w, w', w_1 and w_1' are defined as in case III. Further let w_2 in X_m^* and w_2' in U_m^* be minimal words such that $yw_2 = vw_2'$. We illustrate our assumptions in Figure 2.

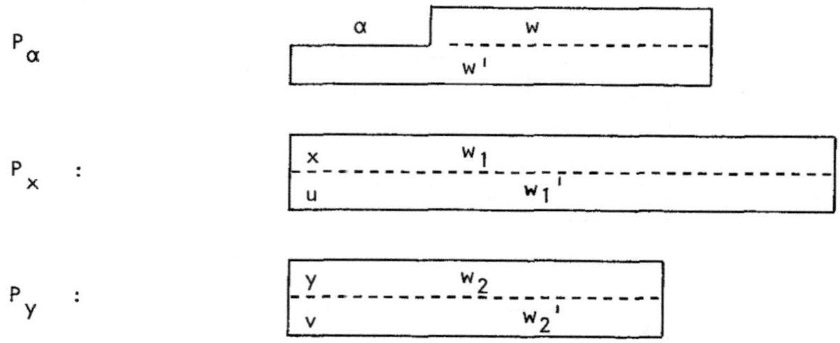

Fig. 2

Obviously all the solutions are now in

$$\mathrm{pref}(w'\{uw_1', vw_2'\}^*)\cap U_m^*$$

and, moreover, as in case III, it follows from (4') that none of the words in

(5') $$w'\{uw_1', vw_2'\}^*(\mathrm{pref}(\alpha(\mathrm{suf}_1(\alpha))^{-1})\cap\Sigma^+)^{-1}$$

is a solution. So we conclude, analogously to case III, that $I_\alpha(X_m,U_m)$ is of the form required in Theorem 2. □

The proof of the case when X and U are only nonperiodic is much longer, but not in principle very much different from that of Theorem 3. The main difficulty is that the inequality (4), contrary to the inequality (4'), does not guarantee that the sets (5) and (5') do not contain solutions - hence we need long considerations in the proof of Theorem 2, cf. [5]. Examples in Section 4 show that (5') may really contain atomic solutions, in general.

4. CONCLUDING REMARKS

We stated in the previous section a characterization result for the intersection of two free monoids freely generated by two elements. Actually, in [5] we proved even more than stated in Theorem 2, namely we proved:

Theorem 4. Let $X = \{x,y\}$ and $U = \{u,v\}$ be nonperiodic subsets of Σ^*. Then $X^* \cap U^*$ is freely generated by at most two words or by a regular language of one of the following forms:

(*) $\beta\gamma + \beta(\gamma\beta)^t(\delta(1 + \gamma\beta + \ldots + (\gamma\beta)^t)^*\delta\gamma$ for some words β,γ and δ satisfying δ and $\gamma\beta$ are nonempty and $pref_1(\delta) \neq pref_1(\gamma\beta)$, and for some integer $t \geq 0$,

(**) $\beta\gamma + \beta(\gamma\beta)^t(\delta(1 + \gamma\beta + \ldots + (\gamma\beta)^{q-1})^*\delta(\beta(\gamma\beta)^{t-q})^{-1}$ for some words β,γ and δ satisfying δ and $\gamma\beta$ are nonempty and $pref_1(\delta) \neq pref_1(\gamma\beta)$, and for some integers t and q satisfying $1 \leq q \leq t$. □

Based on the inequality (4) we can derive an estimate for t in the above theorem. Indeed,

$$t < \max\{\frac{|\underline{x}|}{|y|}, \frac{|\underline{y}|}{|x|}, \frac{|\underline{u}|}{|v|}, \frac{|\underline{v}|}{|u|}\} + 1 .$$

By the restrictions put on the words β,γ and δ, Theorem 4 yields immediately:

Corollary 1. Let $X = \{x,y\}$ and $U = \{u,v\}$ be nonperiodic subsets of Σ^*. If $X^* \cap U^*$ is finitely generated, then it is generated by at most two words. □

The fact that $X^* \cap U^*$ may be infinitely generated follows e.g. from the identity $\{ab,a\}^* \cap \{ba,a\}^* = (a(ba)^*)^*$. Furthermore, our next example shows that the possibility (*) in Theorem 4 may occur for each $t \geq 0$ with nonempty values of $\gamma\beta$ and δ (a similar example for the possibility (**) is easy to find).

Example 1. Let $X = \{a^ib,a\}$ and $U = \{ba^i,a\}$. Then it is straightforward to see that

$$X^* \cap U^* = (a + a^i(ba^i(1 + a + \ldots + a^{i-1}))^*ba^i)^*$$

and, moreover, the set $a + a^i(ba^i(1 + a + \ldots + a^{i-1}))^*ba^i$ is the basis of $X^* \cap U^*$.

Our next example (pointed out to the author by A. Restivo) shows that also Theorem 3 is optimal in the sense that both (i) and (ii) may really occur with nonempty values of parameters.

Example 2. Let $X = \{aab, aba\}$ and $U = \{a, baaba\}$. Then

$$X^* \cap U^* = (a(abaaba)^*baaba)^* .$$

We finish this paper by providing a method to decide whether $X^* \cap U^*$ for two binary nonperiodic subsets X and U of Σ^* is finitely generated or not. Of course, all what we say here is based on the proof of Theorem 2.

Let X and U be two given nonperiodic binary subsets of Σ^*. We first define the word α and the marked subsets X_m and U_m as in Section 3. Let $X_m = \{x, y\}$ and $U_m = \{u, v\}$ and, moreover, let $pref_1(x) = pref_1(u)$ and hence also $pref_1(y) = pref_1(v)$. We recall that a pair (z, z') in $X_m \times U_m$ is matching if there exist minimal words w and w' in X_m^* and U_m^*, respectively, such that (i) $zw = z'w'$ and define that it is successful if (i) is satisfied and, moreover, (ii) there exist words s and s' in $pref((zw)^*) \cap X_m^*$ and $pref((z'w')^*) \cap U_m^*$ satisfying $(s')^{-1}s = \alpha$. With this notation we have the result:

Corollary 2. $X^* \cap U^*$ is infinitely generated if and only if both the pairs (x, u) and (y, v) are matching and exactly one of them is successful. □

Corollary 2 gives a simple algorithm to decide whether for two given binary nonperiodic subsets of Σ^* their intersection is finitely generated or not.

ACKNOWLEDGEMENT. The author is grateful to T. Harju and C. Choffrut for useful comments. In particular, discussions with Choffrut revealed a gap in the original proof of the main result and also helped to sharpen the result. The completion of this paper was carried out when the author visited at the University of Pierre and Marie Curie, Paris VI, under the support of Academy of Finland and Centre National de la Recherche Scientifique (C.N.R.S.).

REFERENCES

[1] Berstel, J., Perrin, D., Perrot, J.F. and Restivo A., Sur le théorème du défaut, J. Algebra 60 (1979) 169-180.

[2] Blattner, M. and Head, T., Automata that recognize intersections of free submonoids, Information and Control 35 (1977) 173-176.

[3] Ehrenfeucht, A., Karhumäki, J. and Rozenberg, G., On binary equal-

ity sets and a solution to the test set conjecture in the binary case, J. Algebra (to appear).

[4] Harrison, M., Introduction to Formal Language Theory, Addison Wesley, Reading, Mass. (1979).

[5] Karhumäki, J., A note on intersections of free submonoids of a free monoid, Research Report 82-64, LITP, University of Paris VII

[6] Lothaire, M., Combinatorics on Words, Addison Wesley, Reading, Mass. (1983).

[7] Tilson, B., The intersection of free submonoids of a free monoid is free, Semigroup Forum 4 (1972) 345-350.

A FAST SORTING ALGORITHM FOR VLSI

Hans-Werner Lang
Manfred Schimmler
Hartmut Schmeck
Heiko Schröder

Institut für Informatik und Praktische Mathematik
Christian-Albrechts-Universität Kiel
D-2300 Kiel

Abstract: An algorithm for sorting n elements in $O(\sqrt{n})$ steps is presented. Its simple structure and the fact that it needs local communication only make it suitable for an implementation by means of VLSI technology.

1. Introduction

VLSI technology allows a large number of devices (so called special processing units, SPUs) to fit on a single chip. This situation creates a need for algorithms exploiting the potentially high degree of parallelism in networks of such SPUs.

In this paper we present an algorithm for sorting n elements on a $\sqrt{n} \times \sqrt{n}$ mesh-connected processor array that requires $O(\sqrt{n})$ comparison steps and $O(\sqrt{n})$ unit-distance routing steps (n is assumed to be a power of 4). Its simple structure and the fact that it needs local communication only make it suitable for an implementation by means of VLSI technology.

$\Omega(\sqrt{n})$ is a lower bound for sorting n elements on a mesh-connected processor array (see section 2). There are two more algorithms of time complexity $O(\sqrt{n})$ [KTh], but they are much more complex in their structure than our algorithm. Simpler algorithms like the odd-even-transposition-sort [Knuth] or the bitonic-merge-sort [Ba] require time O(n).

In section 2 some requirements concerning the design of parallel algorithms suitable for VLSI are discussed. Our new sorting algorithm and the proof of its validity are presented in section 3. In section 4 a systolic version of the algorithm is given.

2. Model of computation

Due to VLSI technology there are some properties a "good" VLSI algorithm should have [FK] :

- it can be implemented by means of only a few types of simple SPUs
- the data and control flow is simple and regular so that SPUs can be connected by a network with local and regular interconnections only
- the algorithm uses extensive pipelining and parallel processing

VLSI hardware is as usual modeled by communication graphs. The first such graph we consider for our algorithm is a grid of $\sqrt{n}$ x $\sqrt{n}$ identical SPUs, each of which is connected to its direct neighbours (Figure 1). During the sorting process every SPU contains one element of those to be sorted in some register. Observe that there are situations where two elements initially loaded at the opposite corner processors have to be transposed during the sorting. It is easy to argue that even for this simple transposition at least $2 \cdot \sqrt{n} - 2$ local exchange steps are needed. This implies that no algorithm on such a mesh-connected processor array can sort n elements in less than $O(\sqrt{n})$.

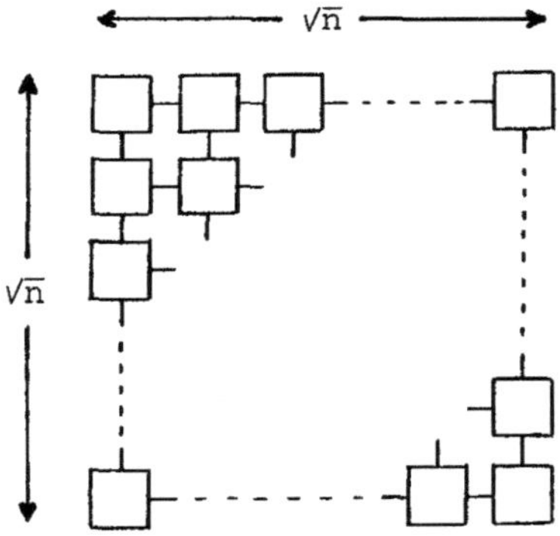

Fig. 1

For the analysis of VLSI algorithms the time requirements (T) and the area on the chip (A) have to be taken into account. There are different opinions on how to weight the time for long distant communication on a chip [Th], [CM]. The analysis of algorithms on our processor grid is independent of these differences because all interconnections have equal length. Usual complexity measures for VLSI algorithms are AT, AT^2 or ATP, where P is the period of the algorithm.

3. The sorting algorithm

A simple sorting method used as part of our algorithm is the odd-even-transposition sort:

Let $x_1, \ldots, x_n$ be a sequence of n elements to be sorted. In the odd (rsp. even) step of the algorithm all elements x_i of the sequence having an odd (rsp. even) subscript are compared with their successors x_{i+1} and exchanged if $x_i > x_{i+1}$ $(i \in \{1, \ldots, n-1\})$. The odd and even steps are executed in alternating order. After at most n steps the sequence is sorted. A simple proof of this can be found in [vL].

Example 1:

Sorting the sequence 6 5 2 3 4 1 by the odd-even-transposition-sort. A "-" indicates a comparison-exchange. After six steps the sequence is sorted.

odd	6-5 2-3 4-1
even	5 6-2 3-1 4
odd	5-2 6-1 3-4
even	2 5-1 6-3 4
odd	2-1 5-3 6-4
even	1 2-3 5-4 6
	1 2 3 4 5 6

We now give an algorithm for merging four arrays of size k/2 x k/2, where k is a power of 2 (Figure 3), and the elements of each array are in snake-like ordering (Figure 2).

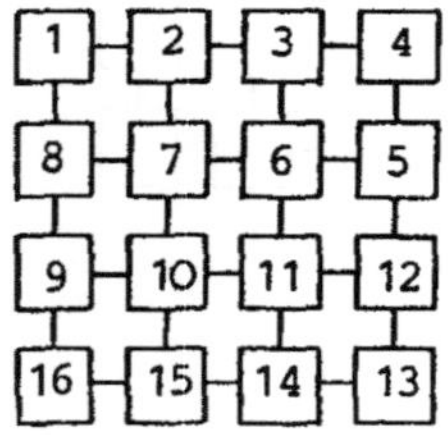

Fig. 2

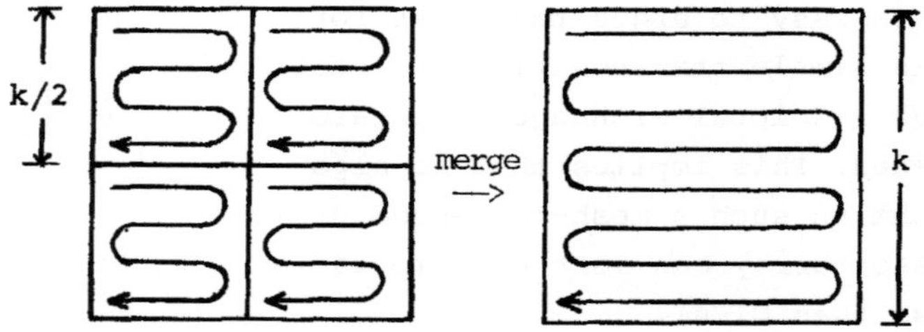

Fig. 3

For the time complexity analysis we assume t_c to be the time required by one comparison-exchange step of two adjacent processors. Furthermore we assume $t_e \le t_c$ to be the time required by a simple exchange step. We will show that our merge algorithm requires less time than $4.5 \cdot k \cdot t_c$.

The algorithm uses the "shuffle" operation transforming a sequence $x_1, \ldots, x_{2n}$ into its perfect shuffle $x_1, x_{n+1}, x_2, x_{n+2}, \ldots, x_n, x_{2n}$ [St]. This operation can be realized by n-1 parallel local exchange steps (see example 3).

Algorithm MERGE

A Shuffle in each row of the k x k array (i.e. interchange the columns according to the perfect shuffle).

B Sort all double columns, i.e. all k x 2 subarrays in snake-like ordering by application of 2•k steps of odd-even-transposition-sort in each double column (Figure 4 a).

Fig. 4a

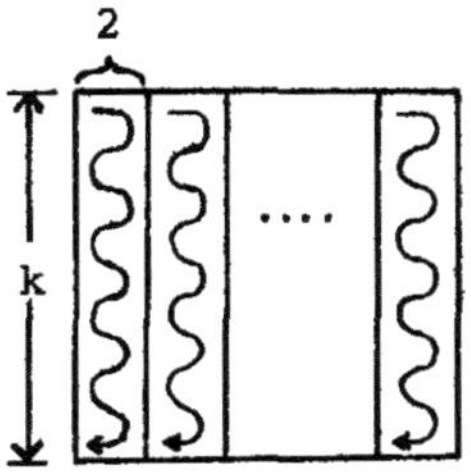

C Sort the whole k x k array in snake-like ordering by application of 2•k steps of odd-even-transposition-sort (Figure 4 b).

Fig. 4b

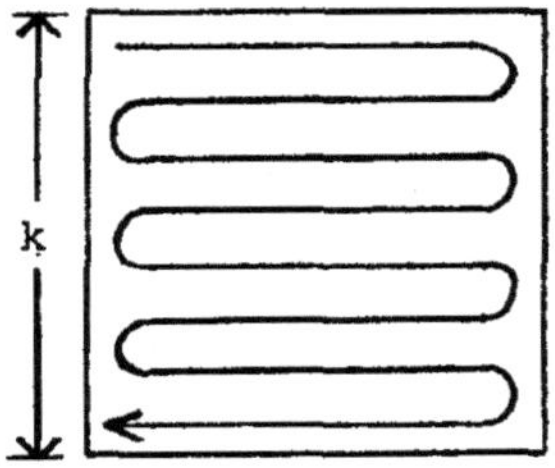

Step A requires $(k/2-1)\cdot t_e$. For step B we need 2k comparison-exchange steps, i.e. the time $2\cdot k\cdot t_c$. Step C requires $2\cdot k\cdot t_c$, too. Thus the time $T_M(k)$ needed to merge four k/2 x k/2 arrays is

$$T_M(k) = 4\cdot k\cdot t_c + (k/2-1)\cdot t_e \leq 4.5\cdot k\cdot t_c$$

Example 2:

Consider the 4 x 4 array in Figure 5a consisting of four 2 x 2 arrays sorted in snake-like ordering. Step A is an interchange of the second and the third column (Figure 5b). Eight steps of odd-even-transposition-sort on each 4 x 2 subarray in step B lead to the situation shown in Figure 5c. Now the two double columns are sorted in snake-like ordering. Application of step C yields the completely sorted array (Figure 5d - 5h). Note that the array is already sorted after four steps of odd-even-transposition-sort (Figure 5g), but the worst case takes 2k steps.

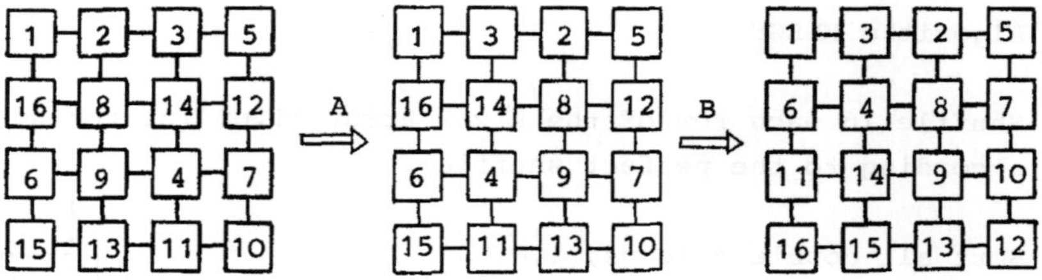

Fig. 5a 5b 5c

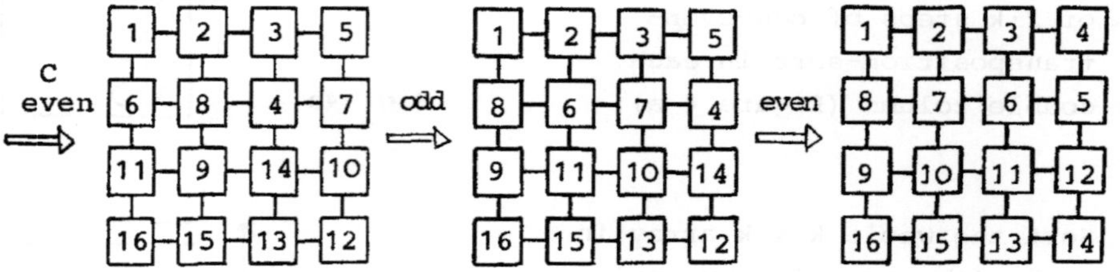

5d 5e 5f

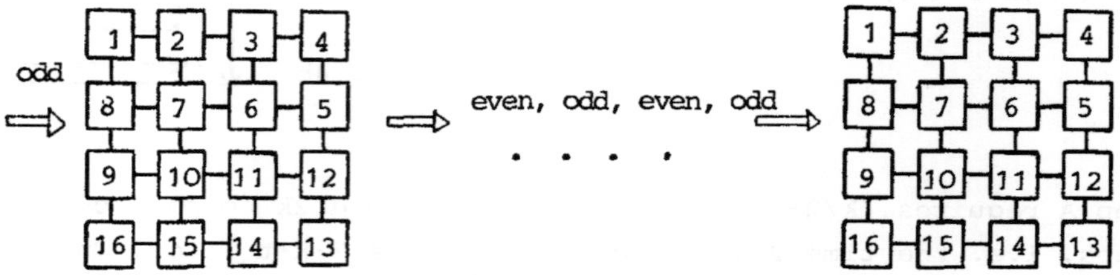

5g 5h

The correctness of this algorithm may be demonstrated by use of the 0-1-principle [Knuth]:

If a network sorts all sequences of 0's and 1's, then it will sort any arbitrary sequence of elements chosen from an ordered set.

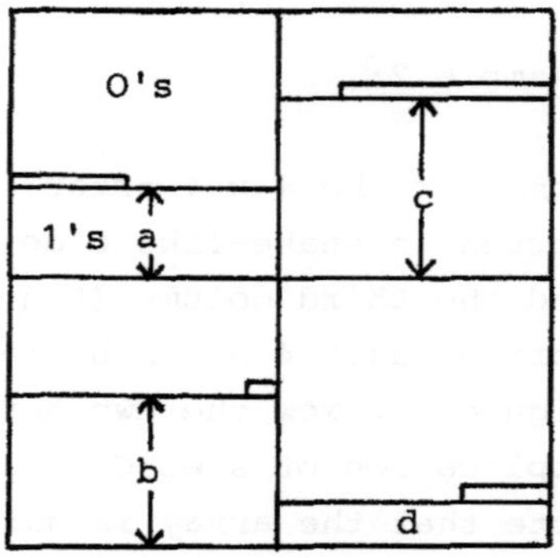

Fig. 6a

Thus we may assume that the inputs are 0's and 1's in four subarrays, each of them sorted in snake-like ordering (Figure 6a). The subarrays consist of a (rsp. b, c, d) complete 1-rows and possibly one further row beginning with some 1's. According to the snake direction these 1's can begin at the left or at the right side of the subarrays. After shuffling in step A we have in every double column at least a+b+c+d 1's and because of the incomplete 1-rows possibly one, two, three or four more 1's (Figure 6b).

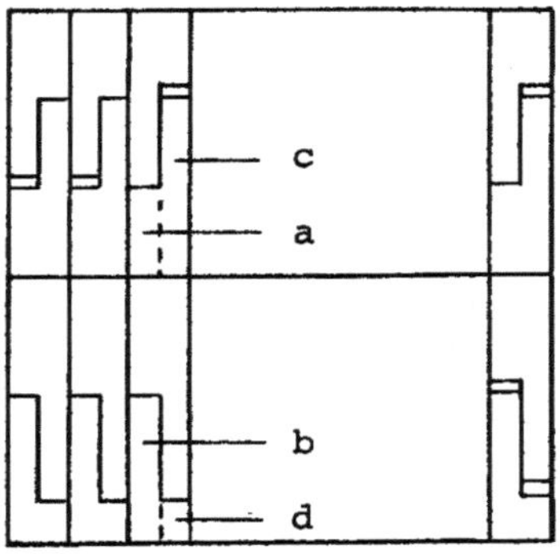

Fig. 6b

Thus, if a+b+c+d is even, the last (a+b+c+d)/2 rows of the whole array consist of 1's after sorting the double columns in step B. There are at most two more rows, in which the 1's of the incomplete 1-rows can appear (Figure 6c). These two rows consist of 2k elements. Obviously, they are sorted by 2k steps of odd-even-transposition-sort in step C of the algorithm.

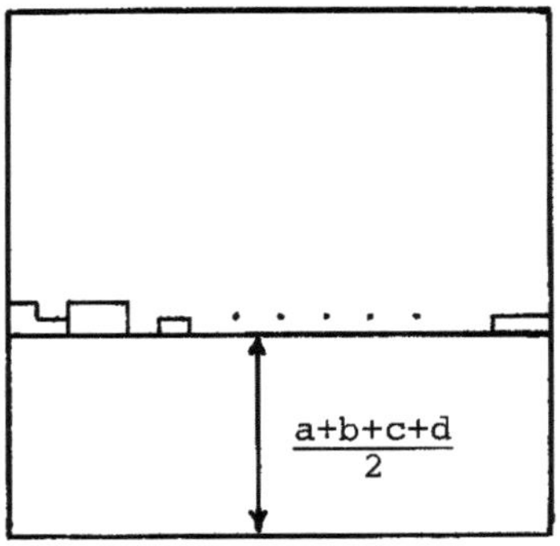

Fig. 6c

In the other case, if a+b+c+d is odd, sorting of the 1's of the complete 1-rows produces a "step" in every double column (Figure 6d). It is easy to check that in this case the incomplete 1-rows produce either at least one more 1 in every double column, or at most three more 1's in every double column. Thus after step B we have at most two unsorted rows in the whole array. Hence also in this case step C completes the sorting.

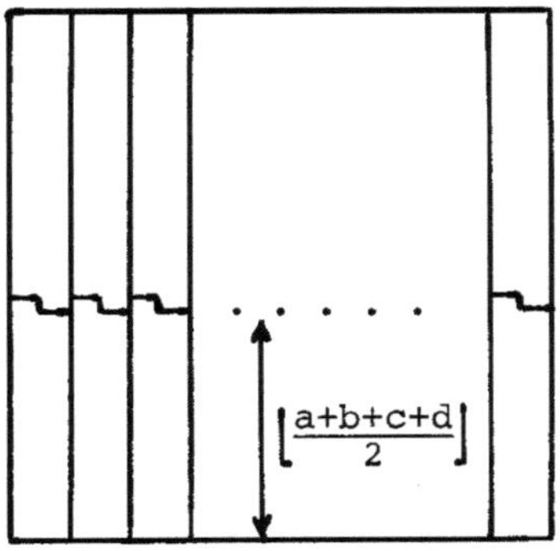

Fig. 6d

Obviously, we can sort a completely unsorted array of $n = 2^{2j}$ elements by iteratively applying the merge algorithm:

Algorithm SORT

S1 Sort all 2 x 2 arrays (in snake-like ordering) by application of four steps of odd-even-transposition-sort (Figure 7).

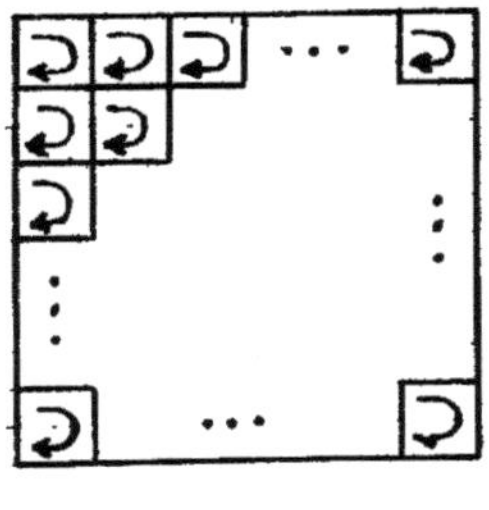
Fig. 7

S2 For m := 2,3,...,j do
sort all $2^m \times 2^m$ arrays by application of algorithm MERGE to the sorted $2^{m-1} \times 2^{m-1}$ subarrays (Figure 8).

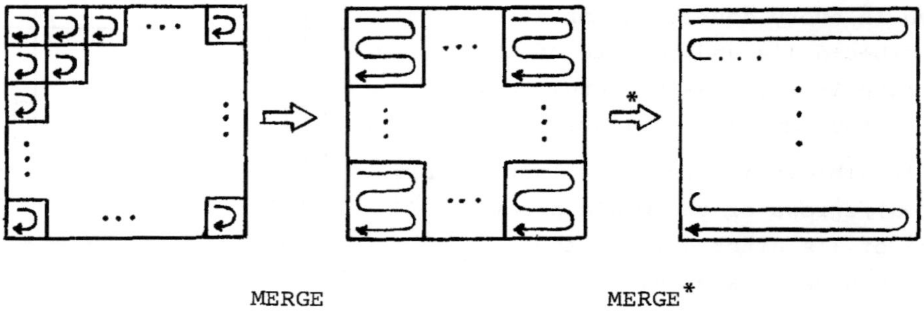

Fig. 8

Let $T_S(k)$ be the time required for sorting a k x k array. Then, according to step S1 we have

$$T_S(2) = 4t_c$$

and for k > 2

$$T_S(k) \leq T_S(k/2) + 4.5 \cdot k \cdot t_c \quad .$$

This implies

$$T_S(\sqrt{n}) \leq (9\sqrt{n} - 14) \cdot t_c \quad .$$

4. Systolic implementation of the algorithm

An implementation of our algorithm by a $\sqrt{n} \times \sqrt{n}$ grid of SPUs will not be suitable for VLSI, because each SPU has to process a complicated sequence of operations.

In this section we present a systolic version of the algorithm - data is pumped through an array of cells, each executing only one operation and then passing its data to the next cell, executing the next operation and so on. Since the operation a single cell has to execute is always the same, cells can in most cases be implemented by very simple logic (see section 5).

Example 3: Systolic computation of the perfect shuffle of eight elements

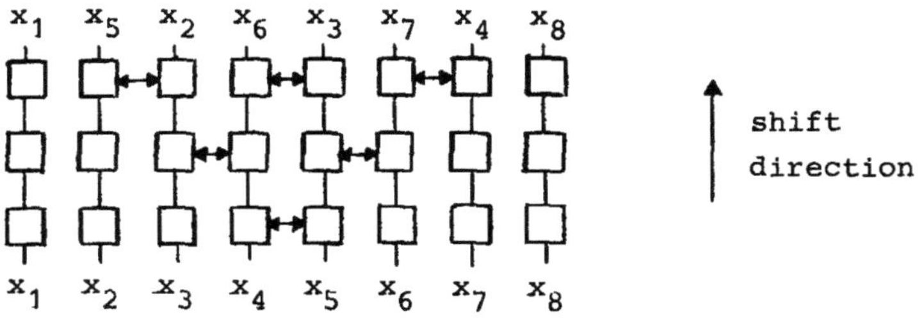

Fig. 9

Rows of 8 elements are shifted through an array of 3 x 8 cells shown in Figure 9. All cells connected by a double-headed arrow exchange their elements at each step. After three steps the shuffled input sequence appears on top of the array.

Let t_s be the time required by one step. Then, in general, this algorithm for the computation of the perfect shuffle of n elements has time complexity $T(n) = (n/2 - 1) \cdot t_s$ and period $P(n) = t_s$. If the area of one cell is a, then the array occupies area $n \cdot (n/2 - 1) \cdot a$.

Example 4: A double column of length 4 is to be sorted in snake-like ordering by the odd-even-transposition-sort. Figure 10a shows the corresponding configuration of cells, where a box denotes a cell, and an arrow between two cells indicates a comparison-exchange. At each step data is shifted through the array of cells from the bottom to the top by two rows. As an example, sorting the double column

8 7
5 6
4 3
1 2

is shown in Figure 10b.

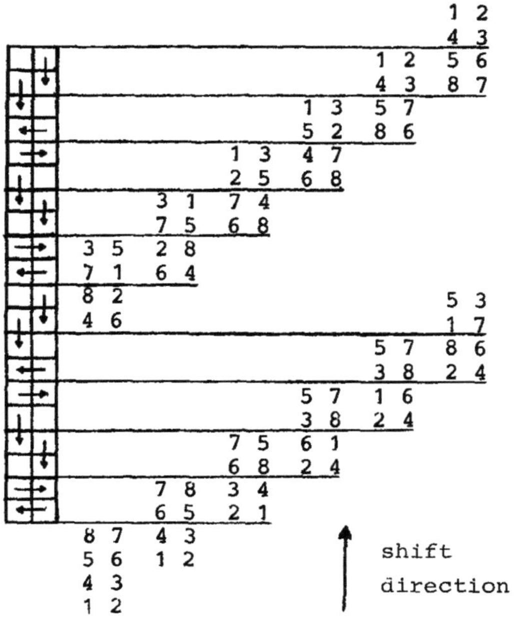

Fig. 10 (a) (b)

One difficulty arises at this point, when two double columns are consecutively shifted through the array. As the two double columns are to be sorted seperately, a comparison-exchange between the last element of the first double column and the first element of the second must be avoided (see Figure 11).

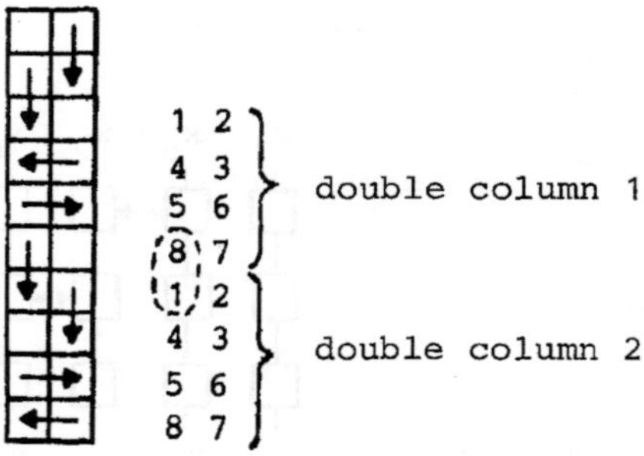

Fig. 11

Therefore, we have to mark the first element of a double column with a special bit, called stop bit. If the stop bit is set to 1, it indicates that the respective element must not be exchanged in vertical direction. If an exchange in horizontal direction occurs, the stop bit is not exchanged.

The area required by an array of cells for sorting double columns of length n/2 is $A(n) = 5 \cdot n \cdot a$. The time complexity is $T(n) = 5/4 \cdot n \cdot t_s$, while the period is $P(n) = n/4 \cdot t_s$.

Figure 12 shows the complete array of cells for sorting 64 elements. The parts that are denoted by A_i and B_i correspond to steps A and B of the merge algorithm. The configuration of the cells is the same as in examples 3 and 4. The parts of the array denoted by C_i correspond to step C of the merge algorithm. The first iteration step of the sorting algorithm, sorting squares of 4 elements, is executed in part X. Subscripts i = 2, 3 mark the following iteration steps. As shown in example 4, stop bits have to be introduced in order to avoid exchanges of elements belonging to different rectangles. In part S cells marked with s set all stop bits to 1. As the structures to be sorted double in size after each iteration step, cells r in parts R reset every second stop bit that is set to 1.

The time required by the i-th iteration step ($i \geq 2$) is

$$T_i = 5 \cdot 2^i \cdot t_s \ .$$

With steps S, X and R taken into account, the whole algorithm has time complexity

$$T(n) = (10\,\sqrt{n} + \log\sqrt{n} - 15) \cdot t_s \ .$$

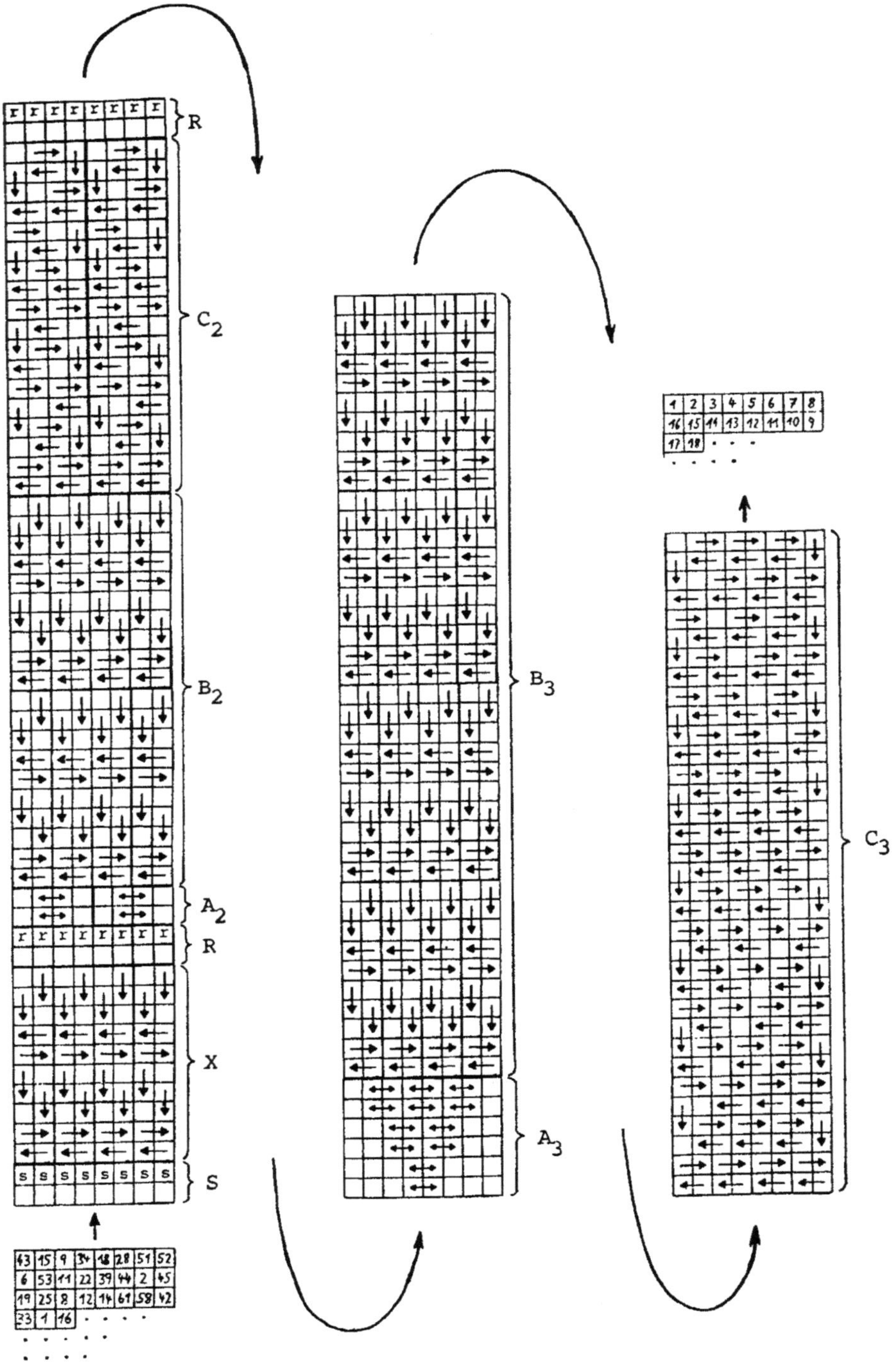
R
C2
B2
A2
R
X
S
B3
A3
C3
43 15 9 34 18 28 51 52
6 53 11 22 39 44 2 45
19 25 8 12 14 61 58 42
33 1 16
1 2 3 4 5 6 7 8
16 15 14 13 12 11 10 9
17 18

Fig. 12

The area requirements are proportional to the above value of T(n), multiplied by $\sqrt{n}\cdot a$. The period is $P(n) = \sqrt{n}/2\cdot t_s$.

This leads to complexity measures

$$AT = O(n^{3/2}\cdot a\cdot t_s)\ , \quad AT^2 = O(n^2\cdot a\cdot t_s{}^2) \quad \text{and} \quad ATP = O(n^2\cdot a\cdot t_s{}^2)\ .$$

5. Concluding remarks

Systolic computation allows a very simple cell structure. In particular, this is true in the case of bit-serial computation at the single steps. For example, two cells performing an exchange of their data - as required in a perfect shuffle network - can simply be realized by two shift registers with a cross-over of wires at their outputs (Figure 13). In a similar way, a comparison-exchange can be performed by very simple logic, switching a cross-over as soon as $x_1 > x_2$ is detected (Figure 14).

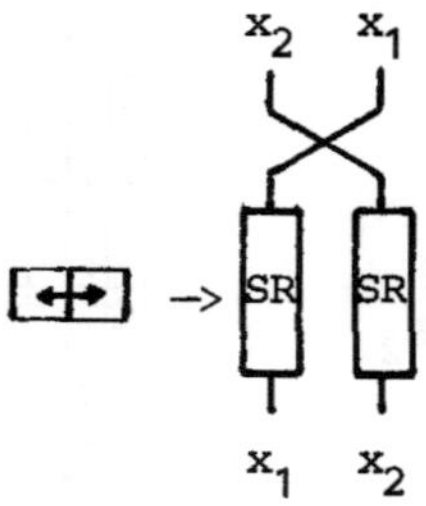

Fig. 13

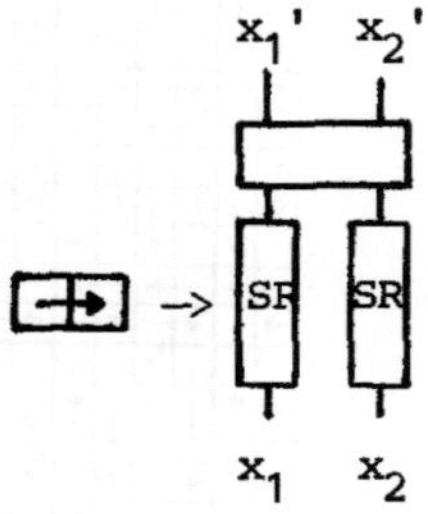

Fig. 14

Clearly the time performance of the algorithm is affected by a factor of m, the length of the input elements, if bit-serial computation is applied.

In a cost-per-bit analysis, the bit-serial version of our algorithm has complexities

$$T(n) \leq 21\cdot P(n) = O(\sqrt{n}\cdot m)$$

$$A(n) = O(n\cdot m)$$

for m-bit elements, leading to

$$ATP = O(n^2m^3)\ .$$

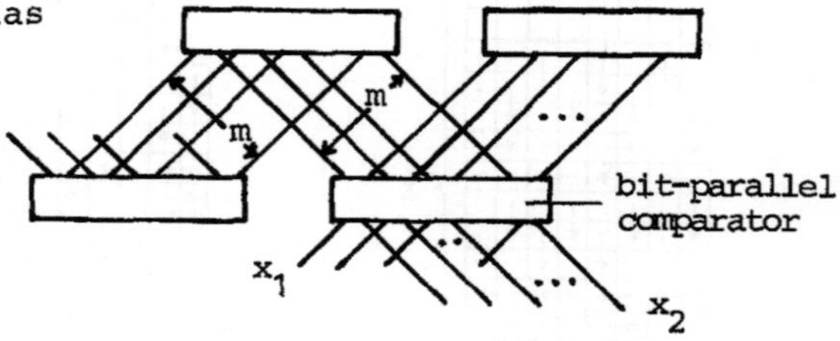

Fig. 15

In the bit-parallel version of the algorithm the interconnections between the cells in parts C_i of the algorithm require area proportional to m^2 (see Figure 15). Thus we obtain complexities

$$T(n) \leq 21\cdot P(n) = O(\sqrt{n}),\qquad A(n) = O(n\cdot m^2)\ .$$

This leads to

$$ATP = O(n^2m^2) .$$

If we assume linear instead of constant signal propagation time, in the bit-parallel version we get

$$T(n) \leq 21 \cdot P(n) = O(\sqrt{n} \cdot m) \quad \text{and} \quad ATP = O(n^2m^4) ,$$

since interconnections have length $O(m)$.

References

[Ba] Batcher, K.E.:
Sorting networks and their application.
Proc. AFIPS 1968 SJCC, Vol. 32, AFIPS Press, Montvale, N.J., 307-314 (1968)

[CM] Chazelle, B., Monier, L.:
A model of computation for VLSI with related complexity results.
Proc. 13th STOC, 318-325 (1981)

[FK] Foster, M.J., Kung, H.T.:
The design of special-purpose VLSI chips.
IEEE Computer, 26-40 (1980)

[Knuth] Knuth, D.E.:
The Art of Computer Programming
Vol. 3: Sorting and Searching.
Addison Wesley (1973)

[KTh] Kung, H.T., Thompson, C.D.:
Sorting on a mesh-connected parallel computer.
Comm. ACM 20, 263-271 (1977)

[MC] Mead, C., Conway, L.:
Introduction to VLSI Systems.
Addison Wesley (1980)

[St] Stone, H.S.:
Parallel processing with the perfect shuffle.
IEEE Trans. Comput. C-20, 153-161 (1971)

[Th] Thompson, C.D.:
A complexity theory for VLSI.
Ph.D. Thesis, Department of Computer Science, Carnegie-Mellon University, Pittsburgh (1980)

[vL] van Leeuwen, J.:
Distributed computing.
Technical report RUU-CS-82-8, Department of Computer Science, University of Utrecht (1982)

ON THE COMPOSITION OF MORPHISMS AND INVERSE MORPHISMS

M. LATTEUX and J. LEGUY
UNIVERSITE DE LILLE I,
U.E.R. I.E.E.A., Informatique,
59655 VILLENEUVE D'ASCQ CEDEX

ABSTRACT : In order to study composition of morphisms and inverse morphisms, we introduce starry transductions t which are, by definition, those verifying : $\varepsilon \in t(\varepsilon)$ and for all words u, v, $t(u)\ t(v) \subseteq t(uv)$. We show that each starry transduction can be factored with two morphisms and two inverse morphisms. Then, we study some particular starry transductions. So, we prove that each rational substitution can be factored into a single morphism and two inverse morphisms and that each decreasing starry transduction can be factored into a single inverse morphism and two morphisms. That permits us to give an answer to a question posed in [5], by showing that for every rational language R, there exist morphisms h_1, h_2, h_3, g_1, g_2, g_3 such that $R = h_3^{-1} \circ h_2 \circ h_1^{-1}(a) = g_3 \circ g_2^{-1} \circ g_1(a^*b)$.

INTRODUCTION

Morphisms and inverse morphisms are very useful operations in order to obtain representation theorems for most of the classical families of languages. For context-free languages, typical examples are given by the Chomsky-Schützenberger theorem [4] and by the Greibach's theorem [8] about the hardest context-free language. The first theorem asserts that every context-free language can be represented by $f(D_n'^*)$, where $D_n'^*$ is the Dyck language over n types of parentheses and f is an intersection with a rational language followed by a morphism. The second theorem gives a particular context-free language H such that every context-free language can be obtained from H, by using a single inverse morphism. This last result holds also for two other families in the Chomsky hierarchy, namely the family of context-sensitive languages [6] and r.e., the family of recursively enumerable languages [1, 6]. But, ćlearly, this result does not hold for the fourth family in the Chomsky hierarchy, that is Rat the family of rational languages [6]. However, it is shown in [5] that every rational language can be obtained from the single language $a^* b$ by using two morphisms and two inverse morphisms. More precisely, for every rational language R, there exist four morphisms h_1, h_2, h_3, h_4 such that $R = h_4 \circ h_3^{-1} \circ h_2 \circ h_1^{-1}(a^* b)$. Recently, in [9] and [15], this result was "explained" : for every rational transduction t, there exist four morphisms h_1, h_2, h_3, h_4 such that $t = h_4 \circ h_3^{-1} \circ h_2 \circ h_1^{-1} \circ m$, where m is a marking which adds # at the end of each word. Clearly, this marking cannot be avoided and it is impossible to simulate arbitrary rational transductions by using only morphisms and inverse morphisms. In fact, for each (inverse) morphism f the following holds : $\varepsilon \in f(\varepsilon)$, where ε is the empty word and for all words u, v, $f(u)\, f(v) \subseteq f(uv)$, these two properties being preserved under composition.

In the first section, we establish that rational transductions that hold under the two above properties, called starry transductions, admit a decomposition using only two morphisms and two inverse morphisms. Then we show that this result cannot be improved : there exists a starry transduction which cannot be factored by using a single morphisms (resp. a single inverse morphism) and two inverse morphisms (resp. two morphisms). At the end of this section, we characterize rational languages which dominate all the rational languages by starry transductions : R is such a language if and only if there exists a non empty word u such that $R \cap u^* = \{u\}$.

In the second section, we study some particular starry transductions, such as rational substitutions and decreasing starry transductions. We prove that for every rational substitution (resp. decreasing starry transduction) t, there exist three morphisms h_1, h_2, h_3 such that $t = h_3^{-1} \circ h_2 \circ h_1^{-1}$ (resp. $t = h_3 \circ h_2^{-1} \circ h_1$). As an immediate consequence, we obtain that for every rational language R, $R = h_3^{-1} \circ h_2 \circ h_1^{-1}(b)$ (resp. $R = h_3 \circ h_2^{-1} \circ h_1(a^* b)$), which gives an answer to a question in [5].

PRELIMINARIES

We assume known basic notions on formal languages [1], [14]. If w is a word, $|w|$ denotes the length of w and ε is the empty word. The families of rational and finite languages are designated respectively by Rat and Fin.

A morphism $h : X^* \to Y^*$ is *alphabetic* (resp, *strictly alphabetic*, *non-erasing*) if $h(X) \subseteq Y \cup \{\varepsilon\}$ (resp. $h(X) \subseteq Y$, $h(X) \subseteq Y^+$).

A transduction $t : X^* \to Y^*$ is *rational* if there exist an alphabet Z, a rational language R and two (alphabetic) morphisms $h : Z^* \to X^*$ and $g : Z^* \to Y^*$ such that $\forall w \in X^*$, $t(w) = g(h^{-1}(w) \cap R)$ [13]. We can write $t = g \circ \cap R \circ h^{-1}$ where $\cap R$ is defined on Z^* by $\forall w \in Z^*$, $\cap R(w) = \{w\} \cap R$, and $t^{-1} = h \circ \cap R \circ g^{-1}$.

A rational transduction is called :

- *faithful* is $\forall v \in Y^*$, $t^{-1}(v)$ is finite
- *of finite image* if t^{-1} is faithful
- *increasing* if $\forall u \in X^*$, $\forall v \in t(u)$, $|v| \geq |u|$
- *decreasing* if t^{-1} is increasing.

The set of all rational transductions is denoted by T and we define on 2^T the operation of composition by : $\forall T_1, T_2 \subseteq T$, $T_1 \circ T_2 = \{t_1 \circ t_2 \;/\; t_1 \in T_1,\ t_2 \in T_2\}$. It is clear that this operation is associative and monotone, that is, $T_1' \subseteq T_1$ and $T_2' \subseteq T_2$ imply $T_1' \circ T_2' \subseteq T_1 \circ T_2$.

For $T_1 \subseteq T$, the set $\{t^{-1} \;/\; t \in T_1\}$ is denoted by T_1^{-1}. Then, it is easy to verify that $(T_1^{-1})^{-1} = T_1$ and $(T_1 \circ T_2)^{-1} = T_2^{-1} \circ T_1^{-1}$.

For $L \subseteq \mathrm{Rat}$, $\wedge L$ denotes the subset of T defined by $\wedge L = \{\cap L \;/\; L \in L\}$ and H (resp. H_α, $H_{s\alpha}$, H_ε), $\subseteq T$, denotes the set of all morphisms (resp. alphabetic morphisms, strictly alphabetic morphisms and non-erasing morphisms).

With these notations, we can write, $T = H \circ \wedge \mathrm{Rat} \circ H^{-1} = H_\alpha \circ \wedge \mathrm{Rat} \circ H_\alpha^{-1} = T \circ T$

For $T_1 \subseteq T$ and L a family of languages, the family of languages $\{t(L) \;/\; t \in T_1,\ L \in L\}$ is denoted by $T_1(L)$. Note, for instance, that $(H^{-1} \circ H)(L)$ is not the closure of L under morphisms and inverse morphisms.

Finally, if L is a family of languages, L^* denotes $\{L^* \;/\; L \in L\}$, thus, Rat^* is the family of regular star languages.

I - STARRY TRANSDUCTIONS

In this first section, we define a new restricted rational transduction and we characterize these transductions by using only two morphisms and two inverse morphisms. As a consequence of this characterization we obtain a new proof of results established in [5], [9] and [15].

Definition : *A* *starry transduction* t *is a rational transduction which verifies* :

i) $\varepsilon \in t(\varepsilon)$,

ii) For all words u, v, $t(u)\, t(v) \subseteq t(uv)$.

Examples of starry transductions are given by the following operations : morphism, inverse morphism and rational substitution.

Notation : $T_* = \{t \in T \;/\; t \text{ is a starry transduction}\}$.

Clearly, properties i) and ii) are preserved under composition for rational transductions. Thus, the class of starry transductions is closed under composition. Now, we give a first characterization of starry transductions which explains our terminology :

Proposition 1 : $T_* = H_\alpha \circ \wedge\, \mathrm{Rat}^* \circ H_\alpha^{-1} = H \circ \wedge\, \mathrm{Rat}^* \circ H^{-1} = T_* \circ T_*$.
In other words, a transduction $t : X^* \to Y^*$ *is a starry transduction if and only if there exist a rational language* $R \subseteq Z^*$ *and two (alphabetic) morphisms* $h : Z^* \to X^*$, $g : Z^* \to Y^*$ *such that for every* $u \in X^*$, $t(u) = g(h^{-1}(u) \in R^*)$.

Proof : Clearly, H, H^{-1} and $\wedge\, \mathrm{Rat}^*$ are included in T_* which is closed under composition. Thus we obtain $H_\alpha \circ \wedge\, \mathrm{Rat}^* \circ H_\alpha^{-1} \subseteq H \circ \wedge\, \mathrm{Rat}^* \circ H^{-1} \subseteq T_*$ and it remains to establish that $T_* \subseteq H_\alpha \circ \wedge\, \mathrm{Rat}^* \circ H_\alpha^{-1}$. Let t be a starry transduction from X^* into Y^*. Since t is a rational transduction, by the Nivat's characterization [13], there exists a rational language $R \subseteq Z^*$ and two alphabetic morphisms h and g such that $t = g \circ \cap R \circ h^{-1}$. Set $t' = g \circ \cap R^* \circ h^{-1}$. Clearly, $t' \in H_\alpha \circ \wedge\, \mathrm{Rat}^* \circ H_\alpha^{-1}$ and for every $u \in X^*$, $t(u) \subseteq t'(u)$. Now take $v \in t'(u)$. Then there exists $n \in \mathbb{N}$ such that $v \in g(h^{-1}(u) \cap R^n)$. If $n = 0$, $u = v = \varepsilon$ and, by property i), we obtain $v \in t(u)$. If $n \geq 1$, there exist factorizations for u and v, $u = u_1 \ldots u_n$, $v = v_1 \ldots v_n$ such that $\forall i \in [1, n]$, $v_i \in t(u_i)$. Then, property ii) implies, by induction,

$v = v_1 \ldots v_n \in t(u_1) \ldots t(u_n) \subseteq t(u_1 \ldots u_n)$. Therefore, $t = t' \in H_\alpha \circ \wedge \mathrm{Rat}^* \circ H_\alpha^{-1}$. □

In order to establish our second characterization of starry transduction, we need two lemmas.

Lemma 2 : $H \circ H^{-1} = H \circ \wedge \mathrm{Fin}^* \circ H^{-1} = H_\alpha \circ \wedge \mathrm{Fin}^* \circ H_\alpha^{-1}$.

Proof : Let $F = \{f_1, \ldots, f_n\} \subseteq X^*$ be a finite set. Define the alphabet $Z = \{z_1, \ldots, z_n\}$ and the morphism $h : Z^* \to X^*$ by $h(z_i) = f_i$, $\forall i \in [1, n]$. Then, for every $u \in X^*$ $h^{-1}(u) \neq \emptyset$ if and only if $u \in h(Z^*) = F^*$. Thus, $h \circ h^{-1}(u) = \emptyset$ if $u \notin F^*$ and $h \circ h^{-1}(u) = u$ if $u \in F^*$. Hence, $u \cap F^* = h \circ h^{-1}(u)$ and $\wedge \mathrm{Fin}^* \subseteq H \circ H^{-1}$ which implies $H \circ H^{-1} = H \circ \wedge \mathrm{Fin}^* \circ H^{-1}$.

Now, it remains to prove that $H \circ H^{-1} \subseteq H_\alpha \circ \wedge \mathrm{Fin}^* \circ H_\alpha^{-1}$. For that, take two morphisms $h : Z^* \to X^*$ and $g : Z^* \to Y^*$. Set $\overline{Y} = \{\overline{y} / y \in Y\}$ with $X \cap \overline{Y} = \emptyset$, $\Delta = X \cup \overline{Y}$ and $F = \{h(z)\, \overline{g(z)} / z \in Z\}$. Define the morphisms $h_1 : \Delta^* \to X^*$ and $h_2 : \Delta^* \to Y^*$ by $h_1(u) = x$ if $u = x \in X$, $h_1(u) = \varepsilon$ if $u \in \overline{Y}$, $h_2(u) = \varepsilon$ if $u \in X$, $h_2(u) = y$ if $u = \overline{y} \in \overline{Y}$. It is easy to verify that, for every $u \in X^*$, $g \circ h^{-1}(u) = h_2(h_1^{-1}(u) \cap F^*)$, which implies $g \circ h^{-1} \in H_\alpha \circ \wedge \mathrm{Fin}^* \circ H_\alpha^{-1}$. □

Now, by using similar reasoning to that in [5], [9] and [15], we obtain :

Lemma 3 : *Let* R *be a language included in* X^*. *Then* R^* *is rational if and only if there exist two finite languages* F_1, F_2 *and a (strictly alphabetic) morphism* g *such that* $R^* = g(F_1^* \cap F_2^*)$.

Proof : The "if" part is obvious. For the "only if" part, let us consider $A = (X, Q, q_0, \{q_0\}, \delta)$ a finite non deterministic automaton which recognizes R^* where Q is the set of states, δ is the next state function and q_0 is the initial state and the single final state. Take $\overline{X} = \{\overline{x} / x \in X\}$ and $Z = Q \times (X \cup \overline{X}) \times Q$ and define the morphism $g : Z^* \to X^*$ by $\forall q, q' \in Q$, $\forall x \in X$, $g(q, x, q') = g(q, \overline{x}, q') = x$. It remains to define the two finite sets F_1 and F_2.

$$F_1 = \{(q_0, \overline{x}, q') / x \in X,\ q' \in \delta(q_0, x)\} \cup \{(q, x, q_0) / x \in X,\ q_0 \in \delta(q, x)\}$$
$$\cup \{(q, x, q')(q', \overline{y}, q'') / q \in Q,\ x, y \in X,\ q' \in \delta(q, x),\ q'' \in \delta(q', y)\}$$

$F_2 = \{(q, \bar{x}, q')(q', y, q'')/q \in Q, x, y \in X, q' \in \delta(q, x), q'' \in \delta(q', y)\}$
$\cup \{(q, \bar{x}, q_0)/x \in X, q_0 \in \delta(q, x)\}$.

It is straighforward to prove that $F_1^* \cap F_2^* = A^*$ with
$A = \{(q_0, u_1', q_1)\ (q_1, u_2', q_2)\ \dots\ (q_{n-1}, u_n', q_n)\ /\ q_n = q_0,$
$\forall i \in [1, n], u_i' = \bar{u}_i$ if i is odd, $= u_i$ if i is even and $q_i \in \delta(q_{i-1}, u_i)\}$.
Clearly, $R^* = g(A^*) = g(F_1^* \cap F_2^*)$. □

Proposition 4 : $T_* = (H \circ H^{-1})^2$, *that is* t *is a starry transduction if and onlyifthere exist four morphisms* h_1, h_2, h_3, h_4 *such that* $t = h_4 \circ h_3^{-1} \circ h_2 \circ h_1^{-1}$.

Proof : Since morphisms and inverse morphism are particular starry transductions and T_* is closed under composition, $(H \circ H^{-1})^2 \subseteq T_*$. In order to prove the reverse inclusion, it suffices, in view of proposition 1, to show that $\wedge\ \text{Rat}^* \subseteq (H \circ H^{-1})^2$. For that consider a rational language $R^* \subseteq X^*$. From lemma 3, $R^* = g(F_1^* \cap F_2^*)$ with F_1, F_2 finite languages. Since, for every $u \in X^*$, $u \cap g(F_1^* \cap F_2^*) = g(g^{-1}(u) \cap F_1^* \cap F_2^*)$, we obtain $\cap R^* = g \circ \cap F_2^* \circ \cap F_1^* \circ g^{-1} \in H \circ \wedge\ \text{Fin}^* \circ \wedge\ \text{Fin}^* \circ H^{-1}$. Since, by lemma 2, $\wedge\ \text{Fin}^* \subseteq H \circ H^{-1}$, we can conclude that $\cap R^* \in (H \circ H^{-1})^2$. □

Since a rational substitution is clearly a starry transduction, we get :

Corollary 5 : *A family of languages closed under morphism and inverse morphism is closed under rational substitution.*

Now, consider a rational transduction $t : X^* \to Y^*$. Then, $t = g \circ \cap R \circ h^{-1}$, where h and g are alphabetic morphisms and $R \subseteq Z^*$ a rational language. Let # be a new letter and m the marking which assigns to each word u the word u#. Then, clearly, we obtain $t = g' \circ \cap (R\#)^* \circ h'^{-1} \circ m$, where h' and g' are defined by : $\forall z \in Z$, $h'(z) = h(z)$ and $g'(z) = g(z)$, $h'(\#) = \#$ and $g'(\#) = \varepsilon$. Thus, we find again the result of Karhumäki and Linna [9] and Turakainen [15] :

Corollary 6 [9] [15] : *A transduction* t *is a rational transduction if and only if there exist four morphisms* h_1, h_2, h_3, h_4 *such that* $t = h_4 \circ h_3^{-1} \circ h_2 \circ h_1^{-1} \circ m$, *where* m *denotes the marking.*

As an immediate consequence of the above result, we can deduce :

Corollary 7 : *Let* $L \subseteq X^*$ *be a language and* $\#$ *a letter not in* X. *Then* $\mathcal{T}(L) = \mathcal{T}_*(L\#)$.

Thus, for every rational language R, $Rat = \mathcal{T}_*(R\#)$. For instance, $Rat = \mathcal{T}_*(a^*b)$ [5], but also $Rat = \mathcal{T}_*(b)$. On the other hand, if $L \in \mathcal{T}_*(\varepsilon)$, $L = L^*$, hence $\mathcal{T}_*(\varepsilon) = Rat^* \subsetneq Rat$. However, it is easy to characterize the rational languages R such that $\mathcal{T}_*(R) = Rat$.

Proposition 8 : *Let* $R \subseteq X^*$ *be a rational language. Then* $\mathcal{T}_*(R) = Rat$ *if and only if there exists a non empty word* u *such that* $R \cap u^* = u$.

Proof : Clearly, $\mathcal{T}_*(R) = Rat$ if and only if $\{b\} \in \mathcal{T}_*(R)$. Assume, first, that $R \cap u^* = u$ with $u \neq \varepsilon$. Consider the morphism h defined by $h(b) = u$. Since $u \neq \varepsilon$, $h^{-1}(u) = b$ and $\{b\} = h^{-1}(R) \in \mathcal{T}_*(R)$.

Reciprocally, if $\{b\} \in \mathcal{T}_*(R)$, from proposition 1, there exist two morphisms h, g and a rational language A such that $\{b\} = g(h^{-1}(R) \cap A^*)$. Thus $b = g(v)$, with $v \in A^*$ and $u = h(v) \in R$. Clearly, $u \neq \varepsilon$, otherwise $v^* \subseteq h^{-1}(R) \cap A^*$ and $b^* \subseteq g(h^{-1}(R) \cap A^*)$. Moreover, since $v^* \subseteq A^*$, $\{b\} = g(h^{-1}(R) \cap v^*)$, which implies $h^{-1}(R) \cap v^* = v$ and $R \cap u^* = h(h^{-1}(R) \cap v^*) = h(v) = u$. □

Now, we conclude this section by showing that proposition 4 is optimal in the sense that starry transductions do not admit a factorization using a single morphism or a single inverse morphism.

Proposition 9 : $\mathcal{H} \circ \mathcal{H}^{-1} \circ \mathcal{H}$ *and* $\mathcal{H}^{-1} \circ \mathcal{H} \circ \mathcal{H}^{-1}$ *are incomparable. Thus,* $\mathcal{H} \circ \mathcal{H}^{-1} \circ \mathcal{H}$ *(resp.* $\mathcal{H}^{-1} \circ \mathcal{H} \circ \mathcal{H}^{-1}$*)* $\subsetneq (\mathcal{H}^{-1} \circ \mathcal{H})^2$.

Proof : First, we will prove that $\mathcal{T}_1 = \mathcal{H} \circ \mathcal{H}^{-1} \circ \mathcal{H}$ and $\mathcal{T}_2 = \mathcal{H}^{-1} \circ \mathcal{H} \circ \mathcal{H}^{-1}$ are strictly included in $\mathcal{T}_*$. Let $R^* \subseteq X^*$ be a language in $Rat^* \setminus Fin^*$. Let us consider the rational transduction $t : X^* \to X^*$ given by its graph $\hat{t} = \{(u, v) \,/\, u, v \in R^*\}$. Clearly, $t = t^{-1} \in \mathcal{T}_*$. Assume that $t \in \mathcal{H} \circ \mathcal{H}^{-1} \circ \mathcal{H}$. Then $R^* = t(\{\varepsilon\}) \in \mathcal{H} \circ \mathcal{H}^{-1}(\{\varepsilon\}) = Fin^*$, a contradiction. On the other hand, if $t \in \mathcal{H}^{-1} \circ \mathcal{H} \circ \mathcal{H}^{-1}$, then $t^{-1} \in (\mathcal{H}^{-1} \circ \mathcal{H} \circ \mathcal{H}^{-1})^{-1} = \mathcal{H} \circ \mathcal{H}^{-1} \circ \mathcal{H}$, a contradiction, since $t^{-1} = t$.

Now, assume that $\mathcal{T}_1 \subseteq \mathcal{T}_2$. Then, $\mathcal{T}_1 \circ \mathcal{H}^{-1} = \mathcal{T}_* \subseteq \mathcal{T}_2 \circ \mathcal{H}^{-1} = \mathcal{T}_2$, a contradiction. If $\mathcal{T}_2 \subseteq \mathcal{T}_1$, we get also a contradiction, since we would have $\mathcal{H} \circ \mathcal{T}_2 = \mathcal{T}_* \subseteq \mathcal{H} \circ \mathcal{T}_1 = \mathcal{T}_1$. Clearly, we can deduce that $\mathcal{T}_1$ and $\mathcal{T}_2$ are strictly included in $(\mathcal{H}^{-1} \circ \mathcal{H})^2$. □

Let us denote by Cod, the set of one-to-one strictly alphabetic morphisms. In the following diagram $L \to L'$ means that $L' \subsetneq L$ and L --- L' means that L and L' are incomparable (for the set-theoretic inclusion). By using the above proposition, it is easy to prove that the following diagram holds. Thus, concerning the composition of morphisms and inverse morphisms, there remains a single open question : Is $(H^{-1} \circ H)^2 = T_*$?

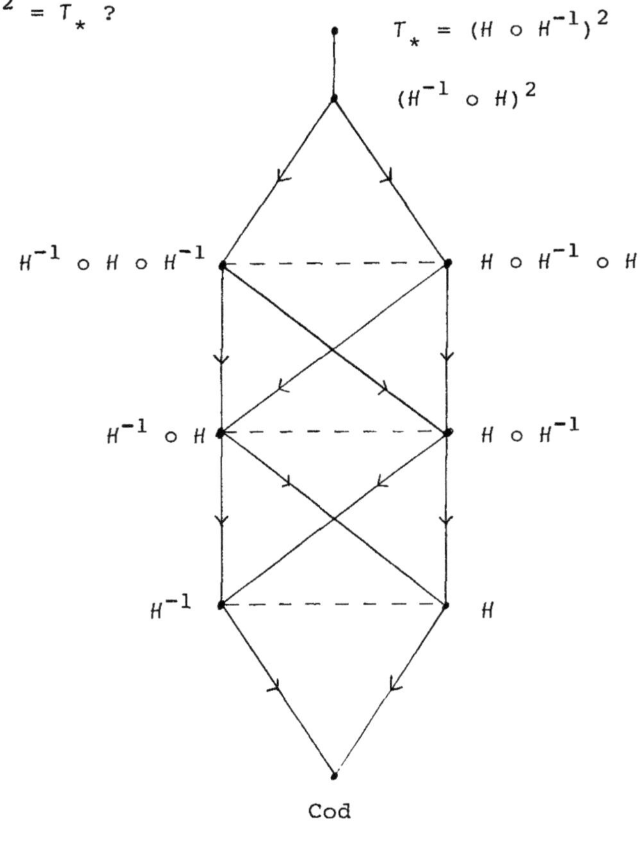

II - RESTRICTED STARRY TRANSDUCTIONS

At the end of the preceding section, we have proved that there exist starry transductions which do not admit a factorization with only one (inverse) morphism. In this section we give some restrictions on starry transductions in order that such a factorization does exist. From that, we deduce an answer to a question in [5] and some refinements for results of section 1.

Definition : *A morphism* $h : X^* \to Y^*$ *is* *uniform* *if there exists* $u \in (Y \setminus X)^*$ *such that* $\forall x \in X$, $h(x) = xu$. *The set of uniform morphisms will be designated by* H_u *and the set of non-erasing morphisms by* H_ε.

The following lemma, like lemma 3, gives a characterization of Rat^* using Fin^*. It proves the equality between Rat^* and $H^{-1}(Fin^*)$. More precisely, we obtain :

Lemma 10 : *Let* R *be a language included in* X^*. *Then* R^* *is rational if and only if there exist a finite language* F *and a (uniform) morphism* h *such that* $R^* = h^{-1}(F^*)$.

Proof : The "if" part is obvious. For the "only if" part, let us consider $A = (X, Q, q_0, T, \delta)$ a finite deterministic automaton which recognizes R^* with $Q = \{q_0, q_1, \dots, q_n\}$. Let us define the morphism h on X by : $\forall x \in X$, $h(x) = x\, a^n$, where a is a new letter. Set
$F = \{a^i x a^{n-j} \,/\, x \in X,\ q_j = \delta(q_i, x)\} \cup \{a^i x a^n \,/\, x \in X,\ \delta(q_i, x) \in T\}$.

Then, it is easy to show, by recurrence on the length of u, that $\forall i \in [0, n]$, $\forall u \in X^*$, $\delta(q_i, u) \in T \iff a^i\, h(u) \in F^*$. Hence, $u \in R^*$ if and only if $h(u) \in F^*$ and $R^* = h^{-1}(F^*)$. □

Lemma 11 : $\wedge\, Rat^* \subseteq H_{s\alpha} \circ H_\varepsilon^{-1} \circ H_u$ (*resp.* $\subseteq H_u^{-1} \circ H_\varepsilon \circ H_{s\alpha}^{-1}$).

Proof : Let $R^* \subseteq X^*$ be a rational language and a be a new letter. Then, $R^* = h^{-1}(F^*)$ with h and F defined as in the proof of lemma 9. Let us consider the morphism g defined on $X \cup \{a\}$ by : $g(a) = \varepsilon$ and $\forall x \in X$, $g(x) = x$. Set $F = \{f_1, \dots, f_t\}$ and define the morphism Θ on the alphabet $Z = \{z_1, \dots, z_t\}$ by : $\forall i \in [1, t]$, $\Theta(z_i) = f_i$. By definition of the f_i's, $g \circ \Theta$ is a strictly alphabetic morphism and it is easy to verify that $\cap R^* = g \circ \Theta \circ \Theta^{-1} \circ h \in H_{s\alpha} \circ H_\varepsilon^{-1} \circ H_u$.

At last, if $t \in \wedge\, Rat^*$, $t = t^{-1} \in (H_{s\alpha} \circ H_\varepsilon^{-1} \circ H_u)^{-1} = H_u^{-1} \circ H_\varepsilon \circ H_{s\alpha}^{-1}$.

Lemma 12 : *Let* $t : X^* \to Y^*$ *be an increasing (resp. decreasing) starry transduction. Then,* $t \in H_u^{-1} \circ H_\varepsilon \circ H_\alpha^{-1}$ (*resp.* $H_\alpha \circ H_\varepsilon^{-1} \circ H_u$).

Proof : Since t is an increasing rational transduction, there exists a rational language $R \subseteq Z^*$, an alphabetic morphism h_1, and a strictly alphabetic morphism h_2 such that $t = h_2 \circ \cap R \circ h_1^{-1}$ [12]. But, t is also a starry transduction, hence, $t = h_2 \circ \cap R^* \circ h_1^{-1}$. From lemma 11, $t \in H_{s\alpha} \circ H_u^{-1} \circ H_\varepsilon \circ H_{s\alpha}^{-1} \circ H_\alpha^{-1}$. On the other hand, it is easy to verify that $H_{s\alpha} \circ H_u^{-1}$ is included in $H_u^{-1} \circ H_{s\alpha}$ and we obtain $t \in H_u^{-1} \circ H_\varepsilon \circ H_\alpha^{-1}$.

Now, if t is a decreasing starry transduction, t^{-1} is an increasing starry transduction and $t^{-1} \in H_u^{-1} \circ H_\varepsilon \circ H_\alpha^{-1}$, which implies $t \in H_\alpha \circ H_\varepsilon^{-1} \circ H_u$. □

By using the preceding lemma, we can improve proposition 4 and, also, prove that rational substitutions do admit a factorization using a single morphism.

Proposition 13 : $T_* = H_\alpha \circ H_u^{-1} \circ H_\varepsilon \circ H_\alpha^{-1} = H_\alpha \circ H_\varepsilon^{-1} \circ H_u \circ H_\alpha^{-1}$.

Proof : Let t be in T_*. Then, there exist an increasing starry transduction t' and an alphabetic morphism h such that $t = h \circ t'$. From lemma 12, we get $t \in H_\alpha \circ H_u^{-1} \circ H_\varepsilon \circ H_\alpha^{-1}$ and $T_* = H_\alpha \circ H_u^{-1} \circ H_\varepsilon \circ H_\alpha^{-1}$ which implies $T_* = T_*^{-1} = (H_\alpha \circ H_u^{-1} \circ H_\varepsilon \circ H_\alpha^{-1})^{-1} = H_\alpha \circ H_\varepsilon^{-1} \circ H_u \circ H_\alpha^{-1}$. □

Proposition 14 : *Every rational substitution belongs to* $H_u^{-1} \circ H \circ H_\alpha^{-1}$.

Proof : Let s be a rational substitution defined on X. Set $\bar{X} = \{\bar{x} \mid x \in X\}$ and define the morphisms h and g on $X \cup \bar{X}$ by : $\forall x \in X$, $h(x) = g(x) = h(\bar{x}) = x$ and $g(\bar{x}) = \varepsilon$ if $\varepsilon \in s(x)$, $g(\bar{x}) = x$ if $\varepsilon \notin s(x)$. Then, $s = s' \circ g \circ h^{-1}$, where s' is a non erasing rational substitution defined on X by : $\forall x \in X$, $s'(x) = s(x) \setminus \{\varepsilon\}$. Hence s' is an increasing starry transduction and, from lemma 12, $s \in H_u^{-1} \circ H_\varepsilon \circ H_\alpha^{-1} \circ H_\alpha \circ H_\alpha^{-1}$. But, $H_\alpha^{-1} \circ H_\alpha \subseteq H_\alpha \circ H_\alpha^{-1}$ and we obtain $s \in H_u^{-1} \circ H_\varepsilon \circ H_\alpha \circ H_\alpha^{-1} \circ H_\alpha^{-1} = H_u^{-1} \circ H \circ H_\alpha^{-1}$. □

In [11], it was shown that every rational transduction of finite image t such taht $t(\varepsilon) \subseteq \{\varepsilon\}$ admits a decomposition in terms of non-erasing morphism and decreasing rational transduction. If t is a starry transduction of finite image, then, clearly, $t(\varepsilon) = \{\varepsilon\}$ and it is easy to verify that the construction in the proof of lemma 8 of [11] gives a decreasing starry transduction. So, we have :

Lemma 15 : *For every starry transduction* t, *the three following properties an equivalent* :

i) t *is a starry transduction of finite image,*

ii) $t = t_1 \circ h$, *where* t_1 *is a decreasing starry transduction and* h *a non-erasing morphism,*

iii) $t = h \circ t_1$, *where* t_1 *is a decreasing starry transduction and* h *a non-erasing morphism.*

Now, let us consider t a starry transduction of finite image. In view of lemma 12 and lemma 15, $t \in H_\alpha \circ H_\varepsilon^{-1} \circ H_\varepsilon$. At last, if t' is a faithful starry transduction, t'^{-1} is a starry transduction of finite image and $t'^{-1} \in H_\alpha \circ H_\varepsilon^{-1} \circ H_\varepsilon$, which implies $t' \in H_\varepsilon^{-1} \circ H_\varepsilon \circ H_\alpha^{-1}$. So, we can conclude :

Proposition 16 : *Every faithful starry transduction (resp. starry transduction of finite image) belongs to* $H_\varepsilon^{-1} \circ H_\varepsilon \circ H_\alpha^{-1}$ *(resp.* $H_\alpha \circ H_\varepsilon^{-1} \circ H_\varepsilon$*).*

The sequel of this section will be devoted to the consequence of these results on some classical languages families such as Rat, Alg, the family of algebraic or context-free languages and r.e., the family of recursively enumerable languages.

First, for every rational language R, R = s(b) where s is a rational substitution. Moreover, if $\varepsilon \notin R$, s is an increasing starry transduction. Let $Rat_\varepsilon = \{R \in Rat \ / \ \varepsilon \notin R\}$. Then proposition 14 and lemma 12 imply :

Proposition 17 : $Rat = H_u^{-1} \circ H \circ H_\alpha^{-1}(b)$ *and* $Rat_\varepsilon = H_u^{-1} \circ H_\varepsilon \circ H_\alpha^{-1}(b)$.

Note that the above proposition gives an answer to a question of [5]. On the other hand, it is easy to prove that $H \circ H^{-1} \circ H(b) \neq Rat$. However, for every rational language R, there exists a decreasing rational transduction t such as $t(a^*) = R$. From corollary 6, $t = t' \circ m$ where m is the marking and t a starry transduction which is clearly decrasing. Then, an immediate consequence of lemma 12 is :

Proposition 18 : $Rat = H_\alpha \circ H_\varepsilon^{-1} \circ H_u(a^*b)$.

Now, let us consider $L \subseteq X^*$ a generator of Alg. It is well known [2], [7], that for every algebraic language L', there exists a faithful rational transduction (resp. rational transduction of finite image) t such that L' = t(L) and from proposition 16, we obtain :

Proposition 19 : *Let* L *be an algebraic generator and* # *a new letter. Then,* Alg = $H_\varepsilon^{-1} \circ H_\varepsilon \circ H_\alpha^{-1}(L\#) = H_\alpha \circ H_\varepsilon^{-1} \circ H_\varepsilon(L\#)$.

By using the Greibach substitution lemma in its generalized version [10], one can prove the following results :

Lemma 20 : *Let* L *be a language such that* $T(L)$ *is closed under substitution. Then, for every* L' $\in T(L)$, *There exists a rational transduction of finite image such that* L' = t(L).

Since Alg and r.e. are rational cones closed under substitution, from this lemma and proposition 16 we can deduce :

Proposition 21 : *Let* L *be a language such that* $T(L)$ = Alg *(resp.* $T(L)$ = r.e.*) and* # *a new letter. Then,* $H_\alpha \circ H_\varepsilon^{-1} \circ H_\varepsilon(L\#)$ = Alg *(resp.* r.e.).

REFERENCES

[1] J. BERSTEL, "*Transductions and context-free languages*", Teubner Verlag, Stuttgart, 1979.

[2] L. BOASSON and M. NIVAT, "*Sur diverses familles de langages fermées par transduction rationnelle*", Acta Informatica 2 (1973), pp. 180-188.

[3] R.V. BOOK, "*Comparing complexity classes*", J. Comput. System Sc. 9 (1974), pp. 213-229.

[4] N. CHOMSKY and M.P. SCHÜTZENBERGER, "*The algebraic theory of context-free language*", in Computer programming and formal systems (P. Braffort and D. Hirschberg Eds.), Amsterdam, North-Holland 1963, pp. 118- 161.

[5] K. CULIK II, F.E. FICH and A. SALOMAA, "*A homomorphic characterization of regular languages*", Discrete Appl. Math. 4 (1982), pp.149-152.

[6] K. CULIK II, and H. MAURER, "*On simple representation of language families*", RAIRO Theor. Informatics 13 (1979), pp. 241-250.

[7] S. GINSBURG, J. GOLDSTINE and S. GREIBACH, *"Some uniformly erasable families of languages"*, Theoretical Computer Science 2 (1976), pp. 29-44.

[8] S. GREIBACH, *"The hardest CF language"*, SIAM J. Comput. 2 (1973), pp. 304-310

[9] J. KARHUMÄKI and M. LINNA, *"A note on morphic characterization of languages"*, Discrete Appl. Math. 5 (1983), pp. 243-246.

[10] M. LATTEUX, *"A propos du lemme de substitution"*, Theoretical Computer Science 14 (1981), pp. 119-123.

[11] M. LATTEUX and J. LEGUY, *"On the usefulness of bifaithful rational cones"*, Publication I.T. 40-82, Lille, 1982.

[12] J. LEGUY, *"Transductions rationnelles décroissantes"*, RAIRO Theor. Informatics 5 (1981), pp. 141-148.

[13] M. NIVAT, *"Transductions des langages de Chomsky"*, Ann. Inst. Fourier 18 (1968), pp. 339-455.

[14] A. SALOMAA, *"Formal languages"*, Academic Press, New-York, 1973.

[15] P. TURAKAINEN, *"A homomorphic characterization of principal semi AFLs without using intersection with regular sets"*, 1982, Technical report, University of Oulu.

ON THE GROUP COMPLEXITY OF A FINITE LANGUAGE

Evelyne Le Rest
Laboratoire d'informatique
Université de Rouen
76130 Mont-Saint-Aignan
FRANCE

Stuart W. Margolis
Department of Computer Science
University of Vermont
Burlington, Vermont, U.S.A.
05405

I. Introduction

Let A be a finite alphabet and let X be a finite subset of A^*. The study of languages of the form X^* is one of the classic topics in formal language theory. This is especially true in the case that X is a code, that is when X^* is freely generated by X. This, of course, follows from the seminal work of Schützenberger [17] and his students. See [5, Chapter 8] and [13] for a recent survey. See also the recent book by Salomaa [16] where the theory of codes is applied to the study of regularity of equality sets.

Recently, a number of papers have initiated a classification of finite languages X based on a study of certain combinatorial and algebraic properties of the "obvious" nondeterministic automaton $A(X^*)$ which recognizes X^* has one "petal" for each element of X and is called the flower automaton of X (automate petaloidique, en français). See [6-8,18]. $A(X^*)$ reflects properties related to the periodicity of words in X. This allows one to use the deep results of Cesari-Vincent and Duval [2,3,9] to study X.

It is well known that an important tool for studying X^* is the syntactic monoid $M(X^*)$. We define $M(X^*)$ here to be the transition monoid of the minimal (deterministic) automaton of X^*. It is a trivial consequence of Kleene's Theorem that $M(X^*)$ is finite. It is a result of [6] that $B(X^*)$ the transition monoid of $A(X^*)$ is very close to $M(X^*)$ and is much easier to study. We use this fact in this paper.

Our main results apply the decomposition theorem of Krohn and Rhodes to classify X. Recall that this important theorem asserts that every sequential machine M decomposes into a cascade combination of permutation and permutation-free machines. The least number of permutation machines in any decomposition of M is called the <u>group complexity</u> of M. Recall also that cascade decompositions of M correspond exactly to wreath product decompositons of T(M), the transition monoid of M. See [4] or [5] for an exposition of these results.

We define Xc, the group complexity of X, to be the group complexity of $M(X^*)$. Our main result states that $Xc \leq card(X)$. This is surprising in that Xc can be bounded by the number of elements in X and does not depend on the size of the alphabet A or the length of words in X. We also show that for each $n \geq 0$ there is a language X_n such that card $(X_n)=2n$ and $(X_n)c=n-1$. We suspect that asympotically this is the best result possible. We show that if X is a biprefix code, then $Xc \leq 1$. Finally we show that if card $(X) \leq 2$, then $Xc \leq 1$.

The interest in studying Xc is a result of [12] which asserts that given any finite monoid M one can effectively construct a finite language X such that M and X have the same group complexity. Thus the decision problem for complexity, one of the major open problems for regular languages [1], is reduced to computing Xc for finite X. It is hoped that the special nature of these languages will shed some light on the decidability problem.

II Préliminaries

1. Complexity Theory

We outline the main results from the complexity theory of finite sequential machines and finite semigroups needed here. For more details see [20]. All notation follows [4] or [5].

A finite semigroup S has complexity $\leq$ n (written $S_c \leq n$) if

$$S < A_0 o G_1 o A_1 \ldots o G_n o A_n \qquad (1)$$

where each A_i is a finite aperiodic (group-free) semigroup, each G_i is a finite group, o denotes wreath product and < denotes division.

It follows from the Krohn-Rhodes Theorem that $Sc \leq n$ for some n. The least value of n for which (1) is true is called the complexity of S. It is known that the semigroup of all maps on an n element set has complexity n-1, so that there are semigroups of arbitrary complexity. The following Theorems give some upper bounds to complexity.

<u>Theorem 2.1</u> Let S be a finite semigroup and let I be an ideal of S. Then $Sc \leq (S/I)c + Ic$. <u>Proof</u> See [20].

<u>Theorem 2.2</u> Let S be a finite semigroup and let St denote the maximum number of R equivalent idempotents in S. Then $Sc \leq St$. <u>Proof</u> See [10].

Let S be a finite semigroup. An idempotent $e \in S$ is called <u>essential</u> if the maximal subgroup G_e of S_δ containing e is not the trivial group. The depth of S, S_δ, is the length of the longest chain of idempotents in the usual idempotent ordering (i.e. $e \leq f$ iff $ef=fe=e$).

Theorem 2.3 $Sc \lesssim S\delta$.
Proof See [19].■

Let $D_1 \ldots, D_n$ be maximal (in the usual ordering) D-classes containing-essential idempotents. Let $e_i \in D_i$ be an idempotent, $1 \leq i \leq n$ and let $E=\{e_i \mid 1 \leq i \leq n\}$. The semigroup R=ESE is called a reduction of S. The following is due to Rhodes and Tilson.

Theorem 2.4 (Reduction Theorem) There is an aperiodic semigroup A such that $S < R^1 o A$.
Proof See 19 .■

Corollary Sc = Rc.

2.Monoids of Binary Relations.

Let M be a monoid of relations on a finite set Q. If $R \in M$ we let, $\mathrm{Im}R=QR=\{q' \in Q \mid \exists q \in Q \text{ and } (q,q') \in R\}$ $\mathrm{Dom}R=QR^{-1}=\{q \in Q / \ q' \in Q \text{ and } (q,q') \in R\}$.

We define the rank of R to be rank $(R)=\min\{|T| \mid \exists U,V \in M$ with $R=UV$ and $\mathrm{Im}U=\mathrm{Dom}V=T\}$.

It is easy to show that if R, $R' \in M$, then rank $(RR') \leq \min\{\mathrm{rank}\ (R), \mathrm{rank}(R')\}$.

Let E be an idempotent in M. Let $Q_E=\{q \in Q \mid (q,q) \in E\}$. It is easy to see that $R_E=\{(q,q') \mid (q,q') \in E \text{ and } (q',q) \in E\}$ is an equivalence relation on Q_E. The following Lemma is proved in [6].

Proposition 2.5 Let E be an idempotent in M. Then

1) rand $(E)=\mathrm{card}(Q_E/R_E)$.

2) The maximal subgroup G_E in M containing E has a faithful representation by permutations on Q_E/R_E.

Let n=Card(Q). Then every R in M can be represented by an nxn Boolean Matrix. We let rowrank (R) (columnrank (R)) be the maximal number of rows (columns) of R which are Boolean independent. It is known that if E is an idempotent of M, then rank(E)=rowrank(E)=columnrank(E). These results depend on the following Lemma.

Lemma 2.6 Let E be an idempotent of M. If $(q,p) \in E$ then there is a $q' \in Q_E$ such that $(q,q') \in E$ and $(q',p) \in E$. ■

We will say that M is <u>unambiguous</u> if for all R_1, R_2 in M, if $(q,p) \in R_1R_2$, then if (q,p)there exists a unique $q' \in Q$ such that $(q,q') \in R_1$ and $(q',p) \in R_2$. In this case, if E is an idempotent of M, then the element guaranteed by Lemma 2.6 is unique. Furthermore, R_E is the identity relation on Q_E. Thus rank (E)=card (Q_E).

Notice that if M is unambiguous, then M can be considered to be a monoid of nxn matrices over any semiring with $0 \neq 1$. We will use this identification in the following.

<u>Theorem 2.7</u> Let M be an unambiguous monoid of relations on a finite set Q. If E_1 and E_2 are idempotents of M, then $E_1 <_J E_2$ implies that rank $(E_1) <$ rank (E_2).

<u>Proof</u> By the above remark we can consider M to be a submonoid of $M_n(F)$ the monoid of nxn matrices over a field F, where n=card(Q). It is easy to see that the rank of E_i, i=1,2 can be taken to be in the usual sense of linear algebra.

Let $E_1 = XE_2Y$ for some $X,Y \in M$. It is easy to verify that $F = E_2YE_1XE_2$ is an idempotent J-equivalent to E_1 in M such that $F \leq_H E_2$. Thus if rank (E_1)=rank(E_2), then rank(F)=rank(E_2). This implies by using well known facts about Green's relations [5] that FJE_2 in $M_n(F)$. Since Q is finite it follows that $F=E_2$. Therefore E_1JE_2 in M, a contradiction, and it follows that rank$(E_1)<$rank(E_2).

We remark that the assumption of unambiguity is necessary in Theorem 2.7. For example, if $E_1 = \begin{bmatrix} 01 \\ 01 \end{bmatrix}$ and $E_2 = \begin{bmatrix} 10 \\ 01 \end{bmatrix}$, then $M=\{E_1,E_2\}$ is a monoid of relations with $E_1 <_J E_2$ and rank(E_1)=rank(E_2)=2.

It is clear that if M is a monoid of relations, then any two D-equivalent elements of M have the same rank. Thus we can define the rank of a D-class D_0 of M by rank(D)=rank(R) for some $R \in D$.

<u>Corollary 2.8</u> Let M be unambigous monoid of relations. If D_1 and D_2 are regular D classes of M such that $D_1 <_J D_2$ in M, then rank$(D_1) <$ rank(D_2).

Let $Q=\{1,\ldots,n\}$ and let B_n be the monoid of all relations on Q. Let $B_{n,k} = \{R \in B_n \mid \text{rank}(R) \leq k\}$ and let $E_K = \{(i,i) \mid 1 \leq i \leq k\}$. The following is easy to prove.

<u>Lemma 2.9</u> $B_{n,k} = B_nE_kB_n$

<u>Lemma 2.10</u> $B_nc = n-1$.

Proof See [20], example 6.2.

Corollary $B_{n,k}c=k-1$.

Proof The reduction $E_kB_nE_k$ of $B_{n,k}$ is clearly isomorphic to B_k. The result follows from Lemma 2.10 and the Corollary to Therorem 2.4.■

III The flower Monoid of a Finitely Generated Submonoid.

Let X be a finite subset of the free monoid A^* where A is a finite alphabet. Let

$$P=\{v \mid vA^+\cap X\neq\emptyset\}$$
$$Q=\{v \mid A^+v\cap X\neq\emptyset\}$$
$$F=\{v \mid A^+vA^+\cap X\neq\emptyset\}$$

We will assign a monoid of relations on $S=\{(p,q)\ Pxq \mid p\neq 1,q\neq 1,pq_s\ X\}\cup\{(1,1)\}$ to X by defining a relation $w\Psi$ as follows :

$$(p,q)w\Psi(p',q') \text{ iff } w=qdp' \text{ with } d\in X^* \text{ or } pwq=pq=p'q'\in X.$$

It is shown in [6] that $\Psi : A^* \to B_S$ is a morphism. The image $B(X^*)=A^*\Psi$ is called the flower monoid (in French : monoide pétaloidique) of X. It can be shown that X is a code if and only if $B(X^*)$ is unambigous.

The term flower monoid comes from the fact that $B(X^*)$ is the transition monoid of the "obvious" nondeterministic automaton recognizing X^*. (i.e. the flower automaton !)

Example

Let X={ab,ba,aa}. The flower automaton of X^* is

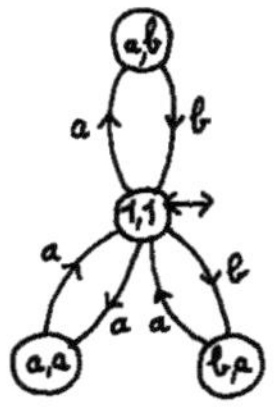

Since the flower automaton recognizes X^*, it folloows that there is a surjective morphism $f:B(X^*)\to M(X^*)$ where $M(X^*)$ is the syntactic monoid of X^*. Recall that a morphism $\emptyset:M\to N$ is aperiodic if it is 1-1 on subgroups of M.

Lemma 3.1 The morphism $f:B(X^*)\to M(X^*)$ is aperiodic. Furthermore, f induces a bijection between the regular D-classes of $B(X^*)$ and $M(X^*)$.

Proof See [6]■

Corollary 1) Every maximal subgroup of $B(X^*)$ is isomorphic to a maximal subgroup of $M(X^*)$.
2) $B(X^*)c=M(X^*)c$.

Proof 1) is obvious and 2) follows from the Fundamental Lemma of Complexity [20]■

Thus, from the point of view of this paper it suffices to study $B(X^*)$. We will now interpret the work of Schützenberger [18] in terms of $B(X^*)$. We call an idempotent e $B(X^*)$ strongly cyclic if e^{-1} is contained in a cyclic submonoid of A^*.

Lemma 3.2 The maximal subgroup G_e containing a strongly cyclic idempotent is cyclic. Moreover, $G_e\Psi^{-1}$ is contained in a cyclic submonoid of A^*.

Proof First recall that a word $h\in A^+$ is primitive if $h=w^i$ implies $i=1$ and that every $w\in A^+$ is the power of a unique primitive word. [9]. It follows that $e\Psi^{-1}$ is contained in h^* for a unique primitive word h.
Let $w\in G_e\Psi$-1. Then $w^n\in e\Psi^{-1}$ for some $n>0$ and it follows that w h^*. Therefore, $G_e\leq h^*\Psi$ and the result follows.■

We say that G_e is a strongly cyclic group with root h. We now will show that if e is an idempotent in a D class of $B(X^*)$ of rank greater than card(X), then e is strongly cyclic. We do this by relating the rank of e to the periodicity of words in $e\Psi^{-1}$.

Recall that if $w\in A^+$, then the period of w, p(w), is the length of the shortest word h such that $w=h^ih_1$, with $i\in N$ and h_1 a left factor of h. For example, the word w=aabaaba has p(w)=3. The following result of Fine and Wilf is fundamental.

Theorem 3.3 Let $x,y\in A^*$, $n=|x|$, $m=|y|$, $d=gcd(n,m)$. If two powers x^p and y^q of x and y have a common left factor of length at least equal to n+m-d, then x and y are powers of the same word.

Proof See [9]

Lemma 3.4 Let T be subsemigroup of A^+. If there is an n such that $p(w)\leq n$ for all $w\in T$, then $T\leq(h)^+$ for some primitive word h.

Proof Let $w\in T$. Write $w=h^i$ where h is primitive. We can assume, by considering a power of w if necessary, that $i\geq 2$ and $|w|\geq 2n$. Furthermore $|h|\leq n$.

Now let u be any member of T. Then $wuw\in T$, so that $p(wuw)\leq n$. Thus $wuw=g^j g_1$ where g is primitive, $g_1 f$ is a left factor of g and $|g|\leq n$. Therefore the primitive words h and g have powers h^i and g^j which have a common left factor w with $|w|\geq 2n\geq|h|+|g|$. It follows from Theorem 3.3 that h=g.

Now $wuw=h^i uh^i=h^j g_1$ where $g_1 x=h$ for some $x\in A^*$. Therefore $k=j-i>0$ and $uh^i x=h^{k+1}$. If $u\notin(h)^+$, it follows from the fact that $i\geq 2$ that h is a proper factor of h^2. This easily contradicts the primitivity of h and thus $u\in(h)^+$ as desired. ■

Corollary Let $e\in B(X^*)$ be an idempotent. If $p(w)\leq n$ for all $w\in e\Psi^{-1}$ and some $n\in\mathbb{N}$, then e is strongly cyclic.

Recall that two elements x,y of a semigroup S are conjugate if there are elements $u,v\in S$ such that x=uv and y=vu. It is well known that two idempotents in S are D-related if and only if they are conjugate. It follows that if G is a strongly cyclic group of $B(X^*)$ with root h, then every group in the D-class of G is strongly cyclic with root a conjugate of h. We call such a D-class strongly cyclic. We call a D-class D of a semigroup Brandt if every R-class and every L-class of D has exactly one idempotent.

Lemma 3.5 Every strongly cyclic D-class in $B(X^*)$ is Brandt.

Proof Let D be a strongly cyclic D-class of $B(X^*)$ and let e,f be R-equivalent idempotents in D. Then $e=h^i$, $f=g^j$ for conjugate primitive words h,g and $i,j\in\mathbb{N}$. Since ef=f it follows that $h^i g^j\in(g)^+$. Therefore h=g and it follows that e=f. A dual result works if e is L-equivalent to f.

The following definitions will help us compute the rank of an idempotent e in $B(X^*)$ by counting certain factorizations of a word $w\in e\Psi^{-1}$.

An X-interpretation of a word $w\in A^*$ is a triple $(q,d,p)\in Q\times X^*\times P$ such that w=qdp. Two X-interpretations (q,d,p) and (q',d',p') of w are crossed if there also exist X-interpretations (q,d_1,p') and (q',d_2,p) of w.

Otherwise, (q,d,p) and (q',d',p') are said to be parallel. An X-interpretation (q,d,p) is a conjugate if $pq\in X\cup\{1\}$. The following was first proved in [6].

Proposition 3.6 Let $w\in A^+$ be such that $e=w\Psi$ is an idempotent in $B(X^*)$. Then rank (e) is equal to the cardinality of the largest set of pairwise parallel conjugate X-interpretations of w.

Proof Clearly $(p,q)\in Q_e$ iff there is a conjugate X-interpretation of w of the form (q,d,p). Furthermore, if (p,q), $(p',q')\in Q_e$, then $(p,q)R_e(p',q')$ iff the associated conjugate X-interpretations are crossed. The result follows from Proposition 2.5.■

Two X-interpretations (q,d,p) and (q',d',p') of w are adjacent if there exist $d_1,d_2,d'_1,d'_2\in X^*$ such that $d=d_1d_2$, $d'=d'_1d'_2$, $qd_1=q'd'_1$:

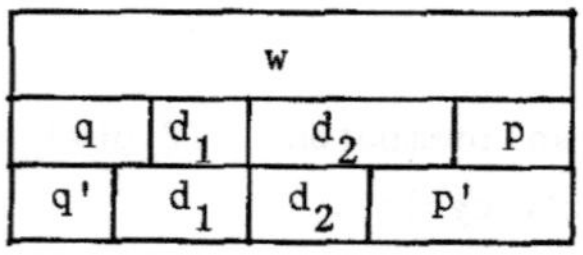

Otherwise (q,d,p) and (q',d',p') are said to be disjoint. Clearly, if (q,d,p) and (q',d',p') are adjacent, then they are crossed, but the converse is not true. 6

The following deep result is due to Duval [3], and Cesari-Vincent [2]. See also [ ]. Let k=Card(X).

Theorem 3.7 Let $w\in A^+$ have more than k pairwise disjoint interpretations. Then there is $x\in X$ such that $p(w)\leq p(x)$.

Corollary Let $e\in B(X^*)$ have rank (e)>k. Then e is strongly cyclic.

Proof Let $w\in e\Psi^{-1}$. By Proposition 3.6 w has at least K+1 parallel X-interpretation and thus at least K+1 disjoint X-interpretations. By Theorem 3.7 $p(w)\leq\max\{p(x)\mid x\in X\}$. The result follows from the corollary to Lemma 3.4.■

Define the complexity Xc of X to be the complexity of $M(X^*)$. We can now put everything together to prove :

Theorem 3.8 $Xc\leq Card(X)$.

Proof It suffices to show $B(X^*)\leq k$. Let I be the ideal $I=\{s\in B(X^*) \mid rank(s)\leq k\}$.

By theorem 2.1,

$$B(X^*)\leq(B(X^*/I)c+Ic.$$

However, by the corollary to Lemma 2.10 we have $Ic\leq k-1$. By Lemma 3.5 and Theorem 2.2 we have $(B(X^*)_{/I})_{c\leq 1}$ and the result follows.■

In the case of a code we can say even more. Let $X\delta$, the depth of X, be $M(X^*)\delta$.

Theorem 3.9 If X is a code, then $X\delta\leq card(X)$.

Proof It suffices to proves that $B(X^*)\delta\leq card(X)$.
Let I be as in Theorem 3.8. Since $B(X^*)$ is unambiguous, and idempotents of rank 1 are inessential it follows from Theorem 2.7 that $I\delta\leq k-1$. It suffices then to show that if $e,f\in B(X^*)-1$ are distinct idempotents, then they are inequivalent in the idempotent ordering.

Since e and f are strongly cyclic, there exist unique primitive words h,g and $i,j\geq 0$ such that $e=h^i$, $f=g^j$.
If $e\leq f$, then $h^i g^j \in \{h\}^+$ and it follows that h=g and thus e=f.■

By decomposing the ideal I we can refine the above result. Define the *spectrum of X*, $\Omega(X)=\{i/\exists e=e^2\in B(X)$ an essential idempotent with $rank(e)=i\}$.

Theorem 3.10 $Xc\leq 1+card(\Omega(X))$. If X is a code, then $X\delta\leq card(\Omega(X))+1)$.
Proof Let $n=card(\Omega(X))$, and let $\Omega(X)= i_j/1\leq j\leq n$ with $i_j<i_{j+1}$ for $j=1,\ldots,n-1\}$.
Let $I_j=\{s\in B(X^*)/rank(s)\leq i_j\}$. It suffices to prove that $(I_{j+1}/I_j)c\leq 1, 1\leq j\leq n-1$.

Since every essential idempotent in I_j-I_{j-1} has rank i_j we need only show that for all $m\geq 1$ and $r\leq m$, $(B_{m,r}/B_{m,r-1})c\leq 1$;

But $B_{m,r}=B_m E_r B_m$ so by Theorem 2.4 we need only consider

$$(E_r B_m E_r)/(E_r B_{m,r-1} E_r) \approx B_r/B_{r,r-1}$$

However, it is shown in [20], example 6.2 that $B_r/B_{r,r-1}$ is U_2-free and thus has complexity ≤ 1..■

Similarly, if X is a code $B(X^*)$ is unambiguous so that $(I_{j}/I_{j-1})\delta=1$ and the result follows.■

IV. A lower Bound and the Case of a Biprefix Code.

Define a function $f:\mathbb{N}\to\mathbb{N}$ by $kf=\max\{Xc \mid |X|=k\}$.

The result of the last section show that f is a well defined function and that $kf\leq k$ for all k. Here we show that $kf \geq \frac{k-1}{2}$. Our idea uses a technique of Pin [14, 15]which is refined in [12].

Theorem 4.1 Let S be a semigroup generated by m functions on an n element set. Then one can effectively find a prefix code C(S) such that :

1) $|C(S)|=mn$
2) $C(S)c=Sc$.

Proof See[12].

Let $n=\{0,\dots n-1\}$. It can be shown using standard techniques of complexity theory that the semigroup generated by the n cycle $a=(0,\dots,n-1)$ and the function $b:n\to n$ such that $0b=1b=0$ and $ib=i$ if $i\geq 1$ has complexity n-1.- Therefore,

Corollary $kf \geq \frac{k-1}{2}$.

Theorem 4.1 also shows that there are finite prefix codes of arbitrary complexity

On the other hand,

Theorem 4.2 Let X be a finite biprefix. Then $Xc \leq 1$.

Proof In [11] it is proved that U_2, the semigroup consisting of an identity and two right zeroes does not divide $S=\mathrm{Synt}(X^+)$.

It follows from [20] that $Sc \leq 1$. Therefore $Xc=S^1c \leq 1$.

Finally we remark that by an in-depth analysis of the classification in [6] of X such that card(X)=2, that it follows that if $\mathrm{card}(X)\leq 2$, then $Xc\leq 1$.

BIBLIOGRAPHIE

1 J.Brzozowski, Open Problems about regular languages, in normal Languages Perspectives and Open Problems, R. Book editor, Academic press, New York, 1980.

2 Y. Cesari, M.Vincent, Une caracterisation des mots périodiques, C.R.Acad. Sci. Paris, 286, A, 1175-1177.

3 J.P. Duval, Périodes et répétitions des mots du monoide libre, 1979 Theoret. Comp. Sci., 9,17-26.

4 S. Eilenberg, Automata Languages and Machines, Vol.b, 1976, Academic Press, New York.

5 G. Lallement, Semigroups and Combinatorial applications, 1979, Wiley Interscience.

6 E. LeRest et M. LeRest, Thèse, 1979, Université de Rouen.

7 E. LeRest, et M. LeRest, Une représentation fidèle des groupes d'un monoide de relations sur un ensemble fini, Semigroup Foum 21, 167-172,1980.

8 E. LeRest et M. LeRest, Sur le calcul du monoïde syntaxique d'un sous monoïde finiment engendré, Semigroup Forum 21, 173-185,1980.

9 M. Lothaire, Combinatorics on Words, Encyclopedia of Mathematics and its Applications, Vol.17, Addison Wesley, Reading Mass., 1983.

10 S.W. Margolis, K-transformation semigroups and a Conjecture of Tilson, J.Pure and Appl. Alg., 17 (1980) 313-322.

11 S.W. Margolis, On the syntactic transformation semigroup of a language generated by a finite biprefix code, Theor. Comp. Sci. 21(1982) 225-230.

12 S.W. Margolis, J.E. Pin, On Varieties of rational languages and variable length codes II, to appear.

13 D.Perrin, Theorie des codes, to appear.

14 J.E. Pin, On varieties of rational languages and variable length codes I,J. Pure and Appl. Alg.(23) 1982, 169-196.

15 J.E. Pin, Sur le monoïde syntactique de L lorsque L est un langage fini. Theor. Comp. Sci..

16 A. Salomaa, Jewels of Formal Language Theory, Computer Science Press, Rockville Maryland, 1981.

17 M.P. Schutzenberger, Une théorie algébrique du codage, C.R.Acad.Sci.Paris (242)1956, 862-864.

18 M.P. Schützenberger, A property of finitely generated submonoids, Algebraic Theory of Semigroups, G. Pollack Ed. North Holland (1979) 545-576.

19 B. Tilson, Depth decomposition theorem. Chap. XI in S. Eilenberg, Automata Languages and Machines, Vol. B.Academic Press, New York, 1976.

20 B. Tilson, Complexity of semigroups and morphisms, Chap. XII in S. Eilenberg,
Automata Languages and Machines, Academic press, New York, 1976.

Reasoning with Time and Chance
(Extended abstract)

by

Daniel Lehmann and Saharon Shelah

Institute of Mathematics and Computer Science,
Hebrew University, Jerusalem 9104 (Israel)

Abstract:

The temporal propositional logic of linear time is generalized to an uncertain world, in which random events may occur. The formulas do not mention probabilities explicitly, i.e. the only probability appearing explicitly in formulas is probability one. This logic is claimed to be useful for stating and proving properties of probabilistic programs. It is convenient for proving those properties that do not depend on the specific distribution of probabilities used in the program's random draws. The formulas describe properties of execution sequences. The models are stochastic systems, with state transition probabilities. Three different axiomatic systems are proposed and shown complete for general models, finite models and models with bounded transition probabilities respectively. All three systems are decidable, by the results of Rabin [Ra1].

1. Introduction

Probabilistic algorithms have recently been advocated for solving problems in different areas, and especially for enforcing efficient cooperation between asynchronous parts of a large system. Some of those algorithms exhibit efficiency, elegance and robustness but proofs of correctness were often delicate. This had not been considered surprising since such proofs must combine the difficulties of both parallel programming and probability theory.

Since the framework of temporal logic has proved itself useful to analyze parallel programs, we extend it to deal with chance on top of time and present a decidable logic in which a great many interesting properties of probabilistic parallel programs can be expressed. We hope that this work will lead to automatic or semi-automatic proof systems that will help the designer of simple probabilistic algorithms for distributed systems.

Our logic is a strict extension of the temporal logic of linear time advocated and described in [Pn]: all formulas of the temporal logic of linear time are formulas of our system, they describe the same sets of execution sequences in both systems and such a formula is valid in our system if and only if it is valid in the logic of linear time. Therefore a user of our system may use all he knows about classical temporal logic without any change; all he has to do is to express the aspects of his program that depend on chance. It is a fundamental and striking feature of our system that it deals with probabilistic programs in the framework of linear time. In this respect our work differs from recent efforts to use branching time (see for example [La], [BMP], [CE], [EH]). We think that, for probabilistic processes, *sometimes* should be *not never* ([La]). A finer analysis of the relation between linear and branching time logics may be found in section 14.

This work also differs from previous attempts to tackle probabilistic programs by quantitative methods, for example [Ko], [Re], [HSP], [FH] and [MT]. Our basic claim is that there is a large family of useful probabilistic algorithms that may be analyzed by purely qualitative methods. Clearly, some sophisticated probabilistic algorithms require a quantitative analysis. A similar effort to develop qualitative and not quantitative techniques, for a different class of problems, has been pursued by [HR].

2. Probabilistic algorithms

The analysis of asynchronous systems of programs (parallel programs) is known to be more difficult than that of sequential programs by one order of magnitude. The analysis of probabilistic asynchronous systems has, so far, been considered as another order of magnitude harder (see, in particular [LR]). We think that this first evaluation could have been too pessimistic, and that the problems encountered arose more from the novelty of the tool than from some intrinsic complexity. Together with the effort towards clarifying the concepts that can be found, for example, in [HSP], the framework proposed here should prove that, for at least a class of probabilistic asynchronous systems, probabilistic systems are not much harder than deterministic asynchronous systems.

The authors of [LR] and [CLP] quickly realized two things:
1) the properties they wanted to prove about their algorithms did not explicitly involve numeric probabilities, except probability one, and
2) the algorithms studied satisfied those properties independently of the exact numeric distribution used to implement the random draws.

A case in point is [LR] where the basic claim is that the system is, with probability one, free of deadlock, and this is true whatever the positive probabilities α and β, with which the two sides are chosen, may be. The algorithms of [CLP], [Ra3] and [Ra4] exhibit similar properties.

Noticeable exceptions are the algorithms for testing primality of [SS], [Ra2] and [Le] for which the interesting properties to be shown are of the type: if n is composite then a witness to that fact will be found with a probability greater than $f(n)$. Some finer properties of the solution described in [Ra3] also demand explicit mention of numeric probabilities.

If one divides the probabilistic algorithms in two broad classes:
(1) algorithms that are guaranteed to give correct results with probability one, and
(2) algorithms that may make mistakes with a probability smaller than any ε fixed in advance

one may say that the method proposed here is suited to prove the correctness of algorithms of the first class and not of the second.

Since so many interesting properties could be expressed without explicit mention of probabilities, and did not depend on the exact probability distribution used, we set to ourselves to provide a logical system for the analysis of those properties. In our system numerical probabilities cannot be expressed at all. Chance appears as a modality qualifying those assertions that are certainly true, i.e. true whatever the results of the random draws could be. The modality expressing that an assertion is possibly true, i.e. that it holds with a strictly positive probability, is the dual of the previous one.

Our system is therefore very rudimentary and simple and well in line with the feelings of those who have dealt with the algorithms mentioned above, that only very basic facts about probability theory are required to prove the needed properties. Essentially one does not need anything more than: "if I throw a coin an infinite number of times then it *will* fall an infinite number of times on heads". The completeness result below gives a precise meaning to this claim.

3. The models

We begin by describing the models we shall be dealing with. We suppose that a set **Pvar** of propositional variables is given. If one wants to study the truth of propositions that say something about the passing of time, it is natural to consider, as models, linear sequences of "instantaneous states of affairs" (in short states), where a state is (or is labelled by) a subset of **Pvar**. This is the class of models proposed in [Pn]. Since we want to study the truth of propositions that describe the passing of time in an uncertain universe, i.e. a universe in which the moves from one state to the next one are probabilistic in nature, we shall consider models that are essentially Markov chains.

In the case of deterministic parallel programs, each possible execution of the program defines a model. A program, therefore, defines a set of models. This set may be characterized by a formula. To prove that a given program enjoys a property, one shows that each one of the models corresponding to a possible execution satisfies the formula expressing the desired property. Similarly, in the case of probabilistic parallel programs, a program defines a set of models. This set is definable by a formula and to prove that a given program enjoys a property, one shows that all models of the set satisfy the formula corresponding to the property of interest.

We shall now define three classes of models and, later on, the notion of validity of a formula in those models. In a word, our models are Markov systems, i.e. states and transition probabilities (see [KSK], for example, for a reference on Markov chains). Similar models for different, richer, languages have been proposed in [FH], [Ko], [MT] and [Re].

A word on notation first. If A is a set, $A^{\mathbb{N}}$ is the set of all infinite sequences over A. If $\sigma \in A^{\mathbb{N}}$ and $n \in \mathbb{N}$, we denote $\sigma(n)$ by σ_n and we shall use σ^n to denote the sequence defined by : $\sigma^n_m = \sigma_{m+n}$ for all $m \in \mathbb{N}$.

Definition 1: A g-model (where g stands for *general*) is a quadruple $\langle \mathcal{S}, u, l, p \rangle$, where the following holds.
1) $\mathcal{S}$ is an arbitrary (non-empty) denumerable set. Elements of $\mathcal{S}$ are called states and denoted by: s, t, $\cdots$.
2) $u \in \mathcal{S}$ is called the initial state
3) $l : \mathcal{S} \to 2^{\mathbf{Pvar}}$ is a labelling function, associating to every state the set of propositional variables that hold in that state ($2^{\mathbf{Pvar}}$ denotes the set of all subsets of **Pvar**)
4) $p : \mathcal{S} \times \mathcal{S} \to [0,1]$ associates with every possible transition a probability, in such a way that for every $s \in \mathcal{S}$, we have $\sum_{t \in \mathcal{S}} p(s,t) = 1$. The sum is finite or infinite. We use here real probabilities but could as well, without affecting theorems or proofs, have used rational probabilities.

Definition 2: A g-model $\mathcal{U}$ is said to be a b-model (bounded), if there is a $\alpha \in \mathbb{R}$, $\alpha > 0$ such that for every $s, t \in \mathcal{S}$, if $p(s,t) > 0$ then $p(s,t) > \alpha$.

Definition 3: A g-model $\mathcal{U}$ is said to be an f-model (finite), if its state set $\mathcal{S}$ is finite.

An f-model is clearly a b-model. As in the theory of Markov chains (see [KSK] or any text on the subject for a formal definition), in a model $\mathcal{U}$, the transition function p yields, for any state s, a probability distribution on the set P_s of all sequences σ of $\mathcal{S}^{\mathbb{N}}$ that begin at s, i.e. such that $\sigma_0 = s$. We shall denote this probability distribution by $\tilde{p}_s$. It suffices to know that the set Q of all sequences σ of $\mathcal{S}^{\mathbb{N}}$, satisfying $\sigma_0 = s_0$, $\sigma_1 = s_1$, $\cdots$, $\sigma_n = s_n$, $(0 \le n)$, is measurable and such that :

$$\tilde{p}_{s_0}(Q) = p(s_0,s_1) \times p(s_1,s_2) \times \cdots \times p(s_{n-1},s_n).$$

4. The language

Our formulas are built-out of propositional variables, classical connectives, temporal connectives and modal connectives.

We define formally the set of all formulas Γ. We shall denote propositional variables by p, q, $\cdots$. Formulas will be denoted by a, b, $\cdots$. They are defined by the following rules.

1) A propositional variable $p \in$ **Pvar** is a formula. A propositional variable denotes a basic proposition, that does not mention time.
2) If a and b are formulas, then:
   a) $\neg a$ is a formula. The symbol $\neg$ denotes logical negation and is read **not**.
   b) $a \vee b$ is a formula. The symbol $\vee$ denotes logical disjunction and is read **or**.
   c) $\bigcirc a$ is a formula. The symbol $\bigcirc$ is read **next** and denotes the next instant of time.
   d) $\Box a$ is a formula The symbol $\Box$ is read **always** and denotes all the instants of times from the present (included) and on.
   e) $a\,\mathcal{U}\mathbf{ntil}\,b$ is a formula. The symbol $\mathcal{U}\mathbf{ntil}$ is read **until**. It was introduced in [GPSS]. The formula $a\,\mathcal{U}\mathbf{ntil}\,b$ denotes the fact that, there is a instant of time in the future when b is true and until the first such instant of time, say t, a stays continuously true at all intermediate instants of time (t not necessarily included).
   f) ∇a is a formula. The symbol ∇ is read **certainly** and denotes a probability of one. It has been chosen for its typographical proximity to the universal quantifier symbol $\forall$.

One may look at our language as a generalization of the one proposed by [EH], if one identifies our modal connective **certainly** (∇) and their **for all** ($\forall$). Our language is an extension of theirs since we allow the application of any connective to any formula, where they make a distinction between state and path formulas and enforce certain restrictions in the way one may build formulas related to that distinction. Their semantics is different from ours, though. More on the relation between the system presented here and that of [EH] is to be found in section 14.

We shall use the classical abbreviations: $a \wedge b$ for $\neg(\neg a \vee \neg b)$, **true** for $p \vee \neg p$, **false** for $\neg$**true**, $a \rightarrow b$ for $\neg a \vee b$ and $a \leftrightarrow b$ for $(a \rightarrow b) \wedge (b \rightarrow a)$. We shall also use two other abbreviations: $\Diamond a$ is read **sometime a** and stands for $\neg\Box\neg a$, Δa is read **possibly a** and stands for $\neg\nabla\neg a$. The usual rules of precedence are assumed. We assume also that $\rightarrow$ associates to the right.

5. The semantics

We shall now attach a truth-value ***true*** or ***false*** , to every formula and every sequence of states of a model. All formulas are path formulas, in the terminology of [EH].

Definition 4: Let $\mathcal{U}$ be a g-model $\langle \mathcal{S}, u, l, p \rangle$, $\sigma \in \mathcal{S}^{\mathbf{N}}$ a sequence of states and $a \in \Gamma$ a formula:

$p \models^{\sigma}_{\mathcal{U}} = \textit{true} \iff p \in l(\sigma_0)$

Notice that the truth value of a propositional variable, relative to a sequence σ, depends only on the first state of the sequence: σ_0.

$\neg a \models^{\sigma}_{\mathcal{U}} = \textit{true} \iff a \models^{\sigma}_{\mathcal{U}} = \textit{false}$

$a \vee b \models^{\sigma}_{\mathcal{U}} = \textit{true} \iff a \models^{\sigma}_{\mathcal{U}} = \textit{true}$ or $b \models^{\sigma}_{\mathcal{U}} = \textit{true}$

$\bigcirc a \,|^{\sigma}_{\mathcal{U}} = \textbf{\textit{true}} \iff a \,|^{\sigma^1}_{\mathcal{U}} = \textbf{\textit{true}}$

$\Box a \,|^{\sigma}_{\mathcal{U}} = \textbf{\textit{true}} \iff \forall\, n \in \mathbb{N} \quad a \,|^{\sigma^n}_{\mathcal{U}} = \textbf{\textit{true}}$

$a\, \mathcal{U}\mathbf{ntil}\, b \,|^{\sigma}_{\mathcal{U}} = \textbf{\textit{true}} \iff$

$\exists\, n \in \mathbb{N}$ such that $b \,|^{\sigma^n}_{\mathcal{U}} = \textbf{\textit{true}}$ and $\forall k < n$, $a \,|^{\sigma^k}_{\mathcal{U}} = \textbf{\textit{true}}$

$\nabla a \,|^{\sigma}_{\mathcal{U}} = \textbf{\textit{true}} \iff \tilde{p}_{\sigma_0}(\{\tau \mid \tau \in P_{\sigma_0},\ a \,|^{\tau}_{\mathcal{U}} = \textbf{\textit{true}}\}) = 1$

One may readily check that the set of paths considered above is indeed measurable. Notice now that the truth of a formula of the type ∇a at a sequence σ in a model $\mathcal{U}$ depends only on the state σ_0 and the model $\mathcal{U}$, i.e. ∇a is really a state formula.

With the assumptions above, we shall denote $\tilde{p}_s(\{\tau \mid \tau \in P_s,\ a \,|^{\tau}_{\mathcal{U}} = \textbf{\textit{true}}\})$ by $\tilde{p}_s(a)$.

6. Satisfaction and Validity

We shall now propose a notion of satisfiability that, in essence, says that a model satisfies a formula a if a holds for **almost** all paths beginning at the initial state. Our choice of definition expresses our view that there is no practical difference between satisfaction and satisfaction with probability one. This definition expresses our belief that a formula that holds with probability one does, really, holds. Anybody who does not share this belief will find an alternative approach in section 12.

Definition 5: Let $\mathcal{U}$ be a g-model and $a \in \Gamma$ a formula. We say that $\mathcal{U}$ satisfies a and write $\mathcal{U} \models a$, if $\tilde{p}_u(\{\tau \mid \tau \in P_u,\ a \,|^{\tau}_{\mathcal{U}} = \textbf{\textit{true}}\}) = 1$.

One immediately sees that: $\mathcal{U} \models a \iff \mathcal{U} \models \nabla a$. One should also notice that it may happen that $\mathcal{U} \not\models a$ and $\mathcal{U} \not\models \neg a$.

In the next definition, and from now on, γ may be any one of {g, b, f}.

Definition 6: If $a \in \Gamma$, we say that a is γ-valid if every γ-model $\mathcal{U}$ satisfies a. We shall denote γ-validity by $\models_{\gamma}$.

7. The logical system

Three different logical systems: TCg, TCb and TCf will be proposed now, each one of them corresponding to one of the notions of γ-validity defined above. The logical systems we propose contain schemata for axioms and rules of inference. An axiom schema denotes all formulas obtained from it by consistent substitution of arbitrary formulas for the formula variables (a, b, c) appearing in it, and consistent substitution of arbitrary propositional variables for the variables (p, q, ...) that stand up for propositional variables. We do not allow the replacement of a propositional variable by an arbitrary formula. The symbol $\vdash_{\gamma}$ denotes provability in the system corresponding to γ. Most of the axioms and all of the inference rules are common to all three systems. When something is claimed to hold in any one of our three systems we use $\vdash$. In other words $\vdash$ may be replaced *consistently* by any one of our three deducibility symbols.

Our systems are best viewed as composed of a number of levels.

The first level concerns classical propositional calculus.

A0) A suitable axiomatization of the propositiónal calculus

R0) (Modus Ponens) If $\vdash a$ and $\vdash a \to b$ then $\vdash b$.

The second level concerns the temporal logic of linear time, as found in [GPSS]. The axiomatization presented here is not the most economical.

A1) $\bigcirc[a \to b] \to \bigcirc a \to \bigcirc b$

A2) $\neg\bigcirc a \leftrightarrow \bigcirc\neg a$

A3) $\Box[a \to b] \to \Box a \to \Box b$

A4) $a\ \mathcal{U}\mathbf{ntil}\ b \to \Diamond b$

A5) $\Box a \leftrightarrow a \wedge \bigcirc\Box a$

A6) $a\ \mathcal{U}\mathbf{ntil}\ b \leftrightarrow b \vee a \wedge \bigcirc[a\ \mathcal{U}\mathbf{ntil}\ b]$

A7) $\Box[a \to \bigcirc a] \to a \to \Box a$

R1) ($\Box$generalization) If $\vdash a$ then $\vdash \Box a$.

The third level concerns general truths about certainty.

A8) $\nabla[a \to b] \to \nabla a \to \nabla b$

A9) $\Delta\nabla a \leftrightarrow \nabla a$

A10) $\nabla a \to a$

R2) (∇ generalization) If $\vdash a$ then $\vdash \nabla a$.

This third level amounts to the modal system S5, that is well known and well suited for the notion of certainty if we accept that there is no difference between satisfaction and satisfaction with probability one.

The fourth level expresses the fact that propositional variables denote *state* propositions, i.e. propositions that do not mention future instants of time. For this reason, if the propositional variable p is true for some path σ it is true for all paths τ of P_{σ_0}.

A11) $p \to \nabla p$

In A11 p stands for a propositional variable and cannot be replaced by an arbitrary formula. Because of A11, our system does not enjoy the substitution property.

The last and most interesting level describes the interrelation between time and chance. The following axiom expresses a general property, and is part of all three systems we propose.

A12) $\nabla\bigcirc a \to \bigcirc\nabla a$

Axiom A12 expresses the fact that the passing of time can only reduce the span of the possible, as can be seen on its contrapositive.

$$\bigcirc\Delta a \to \Delta\bigcirc a \qquad (1)$$

The schema we shall consider next is suitable for *b*-models, i.e. models in which the probabilities of the basic transitions that are not zero are bounded from below, by some positive number. Since the final formulation of the axiom for this case is slightly intricate, let us introduce first some special case of the axiom. In a system with bounded probabilities, any transition that is possible an infinite number of times will eventually be taken (with probability one). We may express the above remark by the following schema.

$$\Box\Diamond\,\Delta\bigcirc\nabla a \rightarrow \Diamond\, a \qquad (2)$$

Notice that we need the ∇ in the hypothesis to ensure that the formula a has, an infinite number of times, a probability at least α (α is the number that bounds from below the probabilities of the basic transitions) to be true at the next instant of time. Notice also that the schema above implies both:

$$\Box\Diamond\,\Delta\bigcirc\nabla a \rightarrow \Box\Diamond\,\nabla a \qquad (3)$$

(Hint: $\Box$-generalize (2), use A3 and T1 below, next section) and

$$\Box\Diamond\,\Delta\bigcirc a \rightarrow \Box\Diamond\,\Delta a \qquad (4)$$

(Hint: replace a by Δa in (2), use the contrapositive of A9 in the hypothesis to get rid of ∇ and the contrapositive of A10 to get rid of the inner Δ)

Schema (2) is not strong enough, since it does not allow to speak about a specific subset of instants of time at which $\Delta\bigcirc\nabla a$ holds. Formula (5) remedies this defect.

$$\Box\Diamond\,(\nabla a \wedge \Delta\bigcirc\nabla b\,) \rightarrow \Diamond\,(a \wedge \bigcirc b\,) \qquad (5)$$

The reader is now ready for the final form of the axiom. It really should be considered as a sequence of schemata. It is a k-steps unfolding of the previous schema and expresses the fact that successive random draws are independent.

A13) $\Box\Diamond\left[\nabla a_0 \wedge \Delta\bigcirc(\nabla a_1 \wedge \Delta\bigcirc(\nabla a_2 \wedge \Delta\bigcirc(\cdots \wedge \Delta\bigcirc\nabla a_k)))\right] \rightarrow$

$\Diamond\,(a_0 \wedge \bigcirc a_1 \wedge \bigcirc\bigcirc a_2 \wedge \cdots \wedge \bigcirc^{(k)} a_k\,)$

The following (6), is equivalent to A13, and more concise.

$$\Box\Diamond\,\Delta\left[\bigwedge_{i=0}^{k} \bigcirc^{(i)}\nabla a_i\right] \rightarrow \Diamond\left[\bigwedge_{i=0}^{k} \bigcirc^{(i)}\nabla a_i\right] \qquad (6)$$

To see the equivalence, notice first that one may as well precede each a_i of the conclusion of A13 by ∇, and then use

$$\left[\nabla a_0 \wedge \Delta\bigcirc(\nabla a_1 \wedge \Delta\bigcirc(\cdots\ \Delta\bigcirc\nabla a_k\,))\right] \leftrightarrow \Delta\left[\bigwedge_{i=0}^{k} \bigcirc^{(i)}\nabla a_i\right]$$

One may not do with Axiom A13 restricted to a finite subset of indexes k. It is indeed possible, for any k, to build a model (unbounded) that satisfies A13 for k but does not satisfies it for $k+1$. The construction is too lengthy to be included here. It is however possible that one (other) single schema may imply the whole sequence A13.

The algorithm presented in Section 5 of [Ra4] is a good example of a system with bounded transition probabilities but an infinite state set. It will be shown in section 9 that most real life systems should be treated as having an infinite state set, even when they seem to be "finite".

Our last axiom is suitable only for finite systems, is stronger than A13 and expresses the fact that, in a finite system, if something has, an infinite number of times, a positive chance of happening, it certainly happens sometime.

A14) $\Box\Diamond\Delta a \rightarrow \Diamond a$

It is useful to record also the contrapositive of A14.

$$\Box a \rightarrow \Diamond\Box\nabla a \quad (7)$$

We define three different systems, from the weakest to the strongest:
1) TCg: A0-A12 and R0-R2
2) TCb: A0-A13 and R0-R2
3) TCf: A0-A12, A14 and R0-R2.

8. An example

We shall use the system above to express and prove an interesting property on a toy program. For reasons of space economy, we satisfy ourselves with a very simple example. Nevertheless we expect that our example is telling enough to suggest how our system can be used to prove properties about parallel probabilistic programs. But, for sure, much additional work is needed before the feasibility of using our system can be assessed.

Suppose we consider a system of two processes P_1 and P_2. The system has three states s_i, for i=1,..,3. The initial state is s_1. If process P_1 is activated while the system is in s_1, it leaves it in s_1. If it is activated while the system is in s_2, with probability $\frac{1}{2}$ it leaves it in the same state and with the same probability it moves it to s_3. If process P_2 is activated in state s_1, with probability $\frac{1}{2}$ it leaves it in s_1 and with the same probability it moves the system to s_2. If it is activated in s_2, then with probability $\frac{1}{10}$, it moves the system to s_3 and with probability $\frac{9}{10}$ it moves it to s_1. The diagrams of Fig. 1 are an equivalent description of the system.

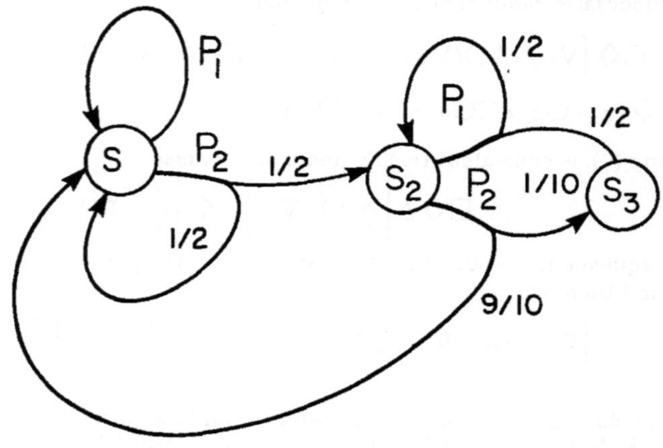

Figure 1

We claim that, with probability one, the system will, sometime, enter state s_3, under the hypothesis of fairness (all three notions of impartiality, justice and fairness of [LPS] are equivalent here).

The basic assertions we shall use are $at\ s_i$. The claim we want to make about the system may be formalized in the following proposition.

$$(C) \quad at\ s_1 \to \Diamond\ at\ s_3$$

Notice that the proposition does not mention probabilities explicitly, though we expect (C) to be correct only with probability one.

The following propositions will describe our system. Our first formula (E) has only a technical role. It expresses the fact that the system cannot be at the same time in two different states.

$$(E) \quad \Box\left[\bigwedge_{\substack{i,j=1,3 \\ i\neq j}} at\ s_i \to \neg at\ s_j\right]$$

Our next formula (M1) will describe the possible moves from state s_1. It says that, when at state s_1, one of two things must occur: either P_1 operates and then the next state is s_1, or P_2 operates and then the next state is either s_1 or s_2, but both states have a strictly positive probability of occurring.

$$(M1) \quad \Box\left[at\ s_1 \to \bigcirc at\ s_1 \vee \bigcirc\left[at\ s_1 \vee at\ s_2\right] \wedge \Delta\bigcirc at\ s_1 \wedge \Delta\bigcirc at\ s_2\right]$$

Similarly (M2) describes the possible moves from s_2.

$$(M2) \quad \Box\left[at\ s_2 \to \bigcirc\left[at\ s_2 \vee at\ s_3\right] \wedge \Delta\bigcirc at\ s_2 \wedge \Delta\bigcirc at\ s_3\right.$$

$$\left. \vee \bigcirc\left[at\ s_1 \vee at\ s_3\right] \wedge \Delta\bigcirc at\ s_1 \wedge \Delta\bigcirc at\ s_3\right]$$

Two more propositions are needed, that express the assumption of impartiality: each one of the processes operates an infinite number of times.

$$(B1) \quad \Box\Diamond\left[at\ s_1 \wedge \bigcirc at\ s_1 \ \vee\ at\ s_2 \wedge \Delta\bigcirc at\ s_2 \wedge \Delta\bigcirc at\ s_3 \ \vee\ at\ s_3\right]$$

$$(B2) \quad \Box\Diamond\left[at\ s_1 \wedge \Delta\bigcirc at\ s_1 \wedge \Delta\bigcirc at\ s_2 \ \vee\ at\ s_2 \wedge \Delta\bigcirc at\ s_1 \wedge \Delta\bigcirc at\ s_3 \ \vee\ at\ s_3\right]$$

In general, a formula expressing that the execution sequence is a possible execution in which process i is activated an infinite number of times may always be build by writing that, in the execution sequence, there is an infinite number of states in which all possible results of activating process i are indeed possible tomorrow. The careful reader noticed that we do not care to insist that process i has been activated an infinite number of times, but only that the execution sequence is identical with one in which it has been executed an infinite number of times (the execution sequence must not reveal, in general, which process has been activated at every step, though the name of the process activated last could be made part of the state).

Our claim about the system is that the proposition

$$E \wedge M1 \wedge M2 \wedge B1 \wedge B2 \to C \tag{9}$$

is valid in any b-model. Our proof proceeds the following way. First, classical temporal logic shows that proposition (10) is g-valid.

$$M1 \wedge M2 \to at\ s_1 \to \Diamond\Box at\ s_1 \vee \Box\Diamond\ at\ s_2 \vee \Diamond\ at\ s_3 \tag{10}$$

Indeed, if the system is in state s_1 and never attains s_3, it must stay forever in s_i, for $i=1,2$, since it cannot move to any other state unless it passes through s_3. Then it either ends up continuously in s_1, after some time, or is an infinite number of times in s_2.

Then, again classical temporal logic would show proposition (11) is g-valid.

$$E \wedge B2 \wedge \Diamond \Box at\ s_1 \rightarrow \Box \Diamond \Delta \bigcirc at\ s_2 \tag{11}$$

Now, we should notice that (12) is b-valid.

$$\Box \Diamond \Delta \bigcirc at\ s_2 \rightarrow \Box \Diamond \bigcirc at\ s_2 \tag{12}$$

To prove (12), use A11 to prove $at\ s_2 \rightarrow \nabla at\ s_2$, and then A13 to prove that $\Box \Diamond \Delta \bigcirc \nabla at\ s_2 \rightarrow \Diamond\ at\ s_2$. Now, putting all together, we see that (13) is b-valid.

$$E \wedge M1 \wedge M2 \wedge B2 \wedge at\ s_1 \rightarrow \Box \Diamond\ at\ s_2 \vee \Diamond\ at\ s_3 \tag{13}$$

But clearly (14) is g-valid.

$$M2 \wedge \Box \Diamond\ at\ s_2 \rightarrow \Box \Diamond \Delta \bigcirc at\ s_3 \tag{14}$$

Notice that the conclusion does not depend on the assumption of impartiality. Now, by a reasoning similar to the one that lead us to (12), we see that (15) is b-valid.

$$\Box \Diamond \Delta \bigcirc at\ s_3 \rightarrow \Diamond \bigcirc at\ s_3 \tag{15}$$

We conclude that (9) is b-valid.

Is it enough to convince us that the system enjoys the desired property? The answer is yes, since any possible (fair) execution of our program must result in a b-model that satisfies E, M1, M2, B1 and B2. It would have been slightly simpler to show that (9) is f-valid. Would that be enough to convince us that the system enjoys the desired property? The answer is no. In spite of the fact that the system can be in only a finite number of states, it is possible that some of its possible executions cannot be described as a finite model, since the schedule may be inherently "infinite", e.g. remember an amount of the past history of the system that cannot be bounded a priori and base its decision as to which process to schedule on that history. To be fully satisfied we must show that formula (9) is b-valid.

9. Soundness and Completeness

Theorem 1: For any $\gamma \in \{g,b,f\}$ and for any $a \in \Gamma$, $\vdash_{\gamma} a \iff \models_{\gamma} a$.

The proof of theorem 1 will appear in the full paper. It proceeds by the method known as *selective filtration*. It also provides a write-up and an extension of the completeness proof of [GPSS]. It is smooth and uniform enough to allow similar proofs for similar logics. We consider selective filtration to be more elegant and clearer than the tableau method that essentially amounts to brute force.

10. Alternative systems for unbelievers

Anybody who does not believe that formulas that hold with probability one *really* hold should, instead of Definition 5, use the following definition of satisfiability.

Definition 21: Let $\mathcal{U}$ be a g-model and $a \in \Gamma$ a formula. We say that $\mathcal{U}$ satisfies a and write $\mathcal{U} \models a$, iff for any $\tau \in P_u$, $a|_{\mathcal{U}}^{\tau} = \textit{true}$.

The definition of validity stays unchanged. The logical system should be changed in the following way. Essentially, instead of basing our system on S5, we should base it on *deontic* S5 (see [Ch]). More specifically, one notices that the rules R0-R2 are still sound and that, except A10, A12, A13 and A14, all axioms are still valid. Therefore we keep the rules R0-R2 and the axioms A0-A9 and A11. For the other axioms, we just prefix them by $\nabla\Box$. Instead of A10 use the following A10'.

A10') $\nabla\Box\left[\nabla a \rightarrow a\right]$

Instead of A12, use the following A12'.

A12') $\nabla\Box\left[\nabla O\alpha \rightarrow O\nabla\alpha\right]$

Instead of A13 and A14, use the following A13' and A14'.

A13') $\nabla\Box\left[A13\right]$

A14') $\nabla\Box\left[A14\right]$

We think that the resulting systems NTCγ are sound and complete for the stricter notion of validity of Definition 21. The proof should be very similar to the one presented above, the only basic difference being that the relation $\equiv$ behaves slightly differently and that theories T that do not satisfy $T \equiv T$ must be treated as a special case. The relation $\equiv$ is transitive (by T10) but not reflexive or symmetric. It, nevertheless, satisfies the property: if $T \equiv T'$, then $\nabla\alpha \in T$ iff $\nabla\alpha \in T'$.

11. Linear time versus branching time

One may remark that our language is also suitable for interpretation in non-probabilistic models. Indeed it may be interpreted on tree models similar to those used in branching time temporal logic, the symbol ∇ being taken to mean ***for all paths***. With this interpretation our language contains branching time logic as it is defined in [BMP] and [EH]. If one takes the natural definition of satifiability that says that a model satisfies a formula if the formula holds for all the branches that begin at the initial state, one immediately notices that our system TCg is sound also for those models. It is not complete, though. Notice, for example, that the formula $p \wedge \nabla\Box\Delta O p \rightarrow \Delta\Box p$ is valid for our new non-probabilistic interpretation, but is not valid in our probabilistic interpretation. To find the additional axioms needed to obtain a complete axiomatization of this non-probabilistic interpretation is an open problem.

Another non-probabilistic interpretation of our connective ∇ has been suggested by M. Magidor. Interpret ∇ as : for a "co-meagre" family of paths, where the term "co-meagre" refers to a set whose complement is of the first category in Baire's classification, assuming the natural topology for paths in models of arbitrary size. Perhaps surprisingly, our system TCf is sound and complete for this interpretation, showing that arbitrary categorical models behave exactly as finite probabilistic models. The proof of this result is outside the scope of this paper.

12. Conclusion and open problems

The main practical conclusion of this work is that there is a large class of probabilistic programs for which a qualitative analysis is sufficient, and that this analysis may be completed without any need to use sophisticated probability theory.

The three systems we presented are decidable by reduction to SωS and the results of Rabin [Ra1]. The reduction is standard and extremely inefficient as a practical decision method and therefore we shall not describe the reduction in detail.

The question of the complexity of decision procedures for our systems is interesting and open. It follows from the results of [SC] that satisfiability is Pspace-hard. Our conjecture is that the three systems above are in Pspace.

References

[BMP] Ben-Ari, M., Manna, Z. and Pnueli, A. The temporal logic of branching time, Conf. Record 8th Annual ACM Symposium on Principles of Programming Languages, Williamsburg, Va. (Jan. 1981), pp. 164-176.

[CE] Clarke, E.M. and Emerson, E.A. Design and synthesis of synchronization skeletons using branching time temporal logic, Proc. Workshop on Logics of Programs, Kozen ed., Springer-Verlag (1982) (to appear).

[Ch] Chellas, B. F. Modal logic, an introduction, Cambridge University Press, Cambridge (1980).

[CLP] Cohen, S., Lehmann D. and Pnueli, A. Symmetric and economical solutions to the mutual exclusion problem in a distributed system (in preparation).

[EH] Emerson, E. A. and Halpern, J. Y. Decision procedures and expressiveness in the temporal logic of branching time, Conf. Record 14th Annual ACM Symposium on Theory of Computing, San Francisco, CA (May 1982), pp. 169-179.

[FH] Feldman, Y. A. and Harel, D. A probabilistic dynamic logic, Conf. Record 14th Annual ACM Symposium on Theory of Computing, San Francisco, CA (May 1982), pp. 181-195. (also Tech. Report CS82-07, Dept. of Applied Mathematics, the Weizmann Institute of Science).

[GPSS] Gabbay, D., Pnueli, A., Shelah, S. and Stavi, J. On the temporal analysis of fairness, Conf. Record of 7th Annual ACM Symposium on Principles of Programming Languages, Las Vegas, Nevada (Jan. 1980), pp. 163-173.

[HC] Hughes, G. E. and Cresswell, M J., An introduction to modal logic, Methuen, London (1972).

[HR] Halpern, J. Y. and Rabin, M. O., A logic to reason about likelihood, Proc. 15th Annual ACM Symposium on Theory of Computing (April 1983).

[HSP] Hart, S., Sharir, M. and Pnueli, A. Termination of probabilistic concurrent programs, Conf. Record 9th Annual ACM Symposium on Principles of Programming Languages, Albuquerque, New Mexico (1982), pp.1-6.

[Ko] Kozen, D. Semantics of probabilistic programs, J. of Computer and System Sciences Vol. 22 (1981), pp. 328-350.

[KSK] Kemeny, J.G., Snell, J.L. and Knapp, A.W., Denumerable Markov chains, Van Nostrand, Princeton, NJ (1966).

[La] Lamport, L. "Sometimes" is sometimes "not never", Conf. Record of 7th Annual ACM Symposium on Principles of Programming Languages, Las Vegas, Nevada (Jan. 1980), pp. 174-183.

[Le] Lehmann, D. On primality tests, SIAM Journal on Computing Vol. 11 (1982), pp. 374-375.

[LPS] Lehmann, D., Pnueli, A. and Stavi, J. Impartiality, Justice and Fairness: the ethics of concurrent termination, Proceedings of 8th International Colloquium on Automata, Languages and Programming, July 1981, Acco, Israel, pp. 264-277.

[LR] Lehmann, D. and Rabin, M. O. On the advantages of free choice: a symmetric and fully distributed solution to the dining philosophers problem (extended abstract), Conf. Record of 8th Annual ACM Symposium on Principles of Programming Languages, Williamsburg, Va. (Jan. 1981), pp. 133-138.

[MT] Makowski, J.A. and Tiomkin, M. A probabilistic propositional dynamic logic (Extended Abstract), manuscript 1982.

[Pn] Pnueli, A. The temporal semantics of concurrent programs, Theoretical Computer Science Vol. 13 (1981), pp. 45-60.

[Ra1] Rabin, M. O. Decidability of second order theories and automata on infinite trees, Trans. AMS Vol. 141 (1969), pp. 1-35.

[Ra2] Rabin, M.O. Probabilistic algorithms, in Algorithms and Complexity, New Directions and Recent Results, J.F. Traub, ed., Academic Press, New York, 1976.

[Ra3] Rabin, M.O. N-process mutual exclusion with bounded waiting by 4.log N-valued shared variable, Journal of Computer and System Sciences Vol.25 (1982) pp. 66-75.

[Ra4] Rabin, M.O. The choice coordination problem, Acta Informatica Vol. 17 (1982), pp. 121-134.

[Re] Reif, J. H. Logics for probabilistic programming, Proc 12th ACM Symposium on Theory of

Computing,

Los Angeles, CA (April 1980), pp. 8-13.
[SC] Sisla, A. P. and Clarke, E. M. The complexity of propositional linear temporal logics, Proc. 14th Annual ACM Symposium on Theory of Computing, San Francisco, CA (May 1982), pp. 159-168.
[SS] Solovay, R. and Strassen V., A fast Monte-Carlo test for primality, SIAM Journal on Computing Vol. 6 (1977), pp. 84-85; erratum Vol. 7 (1978), pp. 118.

Factoring multivariate integral polynomials

A.K. Lenstra
Mathematisch Centrum
Kruislaan 413
1098 SJ Amsterdam
The Netherlands

Abstract.

We present an algorithm to factor polynomials in several variables with integral coefficients that is polynomial-time in the degrees of the polynomial to be factored. Our algorithm generalizes the algorithm presented in [7] to factor integral polynomials in one variable.

1. Introduction.

The problem of factoring polynomials with integral coefficients remained open for a long time, i.e. no polynomial-time factoring algorithm was known. The best known algorithms took exponential-time in the worst case; these algorithms had to consider a possibly exponential number of combinations of p-adic factors before the true factors could be found or irreducibility could be decided. In [1] it was proven that the problem of factorization in $\mathbb{Z}[X]$ belongs to $NP \cap co\text{-}NP$, which made its membership of P quite likely [2]. That this was indeed the case, was proven in [7] where a polynomial-time algorithm for factoring in $\mathbb{Z}[X]$ was given. This algorithm is based on the following three observations:

(1.1) The multiples of degree $< m$ of a p-adic factor together form a lattice in $\mathbb{Z}^m$;

(1.2) If this p-adic factor is computed up to a high enough precision, then the factor we are looking for is the shortest vector in this lattice;

(1.3) An approximation of the shortest vector in such a lattice can be found in polynomial-time by means of the so-called *basis reduction algorithm*.

In this paper we show that (1.1) and (1.2) can be generalized to polynomials in $\mathbb{Z}[X_1, X_2, \ldots, X_t]$ in an elementary way, for any $t \geq 2$. Combined with the same basis reduction algorithm as in (1.3), this leads to a polynomial-time algorithm for factoring in $\mathbb{Z}[X_1, X_2, \ldots, X_t]$. In [8, 9, 10] we show that the above three points can be applied to various other kinds of polynomial factoring problems as well (like multivariate polynomials over finite fields or over algebraic number fields). Another approach to multivariate integral polynomial factorization is given in [5]. There the multivariate case is first reduced in polynomial-time to the bivariate case, next bivariate is reduced to univariate.

For practical purposes we do not recommend any of these polynomial-time algorithms; their running time will be dominated by the rather slow basis reduction algorithm. For polynomials in $\mathbb{Z}[X_1, X_2, \ldots, X_t]$ the algorithm from [12] for instance is very useful, although it is exponential-time in the worst case.

We restrict ourselves in this paper to integral polynomials in two variables; the multivariate case follows immediately from this. In Section 2 we present an important result from [7: Section 1] concerning the basis reduction algorithm mentioned in (1.3). The generalizations of (1.1) and (1.2) to polynomials in $\mathbb{Z}[X,Y]$ are described in Section 3, and in Section 4 we give an outline of the factoring algorithm, and we analyze its running time.

2. The basis reduction algorithm.

The basis reduction algorithm from [7: Section 1] makes it possible to determine in polynomial-time a reasonable approximation of the shortest vector in a lattice. We will not give a description of the algorithm here. It will suffice to summarize those results from [7: Section 1] that we will need here.

Let $b_1, b_2, \ldots, b_n \in \mathbb{Z}^n$ be linearly independent. For our purposes we may assume that the $n \times n$ matrix having $b_1, b_2, \ldots, b_n$ as columns is upper-triangular. The i-dimensional lattice $L_i \subset \mathbb{Z}^i$ with basis $b_1, b_2, \ldots, b_i$ is defined as $L_i = \Sigma_{j=1}^{i} \mathbb{Z} b_j = \{\Sigma_{j=1}^{i} r_j b_j\colon\ r_j \in \mathbb{Z}\}$. We put $L = L_n$.

(2.1) Proposition. (cf. [7: (1.11), (1.26), (1.37)]) Let $B \in \mathbb{Z}_{\geq 2}$ be such that $|b_j|^2 \leq B$ for $1 \leq j \leq n$, where $|\,|$ denotes the ordinary Euclidean length. The basis reduction algorithm as described in [7: (1.15)] determines a vector $\tilde{b} \in L$ such that $\tilde{b}$ belongs to a basis for L, and such that $|\tilde{b}|^2 \leq 2^{n-1}|x|^2$ for every $x \in L$, $x \neq 0$; the algorithm takes $O(n^4 \log B)$ elementary operations on integers having binary length $O(n \log B)$. Furthermore, during the first $O(i^4 \log B)$ operations (on integers having binary length $O(i \log B)$), vectors $\tilde{b}_i \in L_i$, belonging to a basis for L_i, are determined such that $|\tilde{b}_i|^2 \leq 2^{i-1}|x_i|^2$ for every $x_i \in L_i$, $x_i \neq 0$, for $1 \leq i \leq n$. □

So, we can find a reasonable approximation of the shortest vector in L in polynomial-time. But also we find, during this computation, approximations of the shortest vectors of the lattices L_i without any time loss.

3. Factors and lattices.

We describe how to generalize (1.1) and (1.2) to polynomials in $\mathbb{Z}[X,Y]$. Let $f \in \mathbb{Z}[X,Y]$ be the polynomial to be factored; we may assume that f has no multiple factors, i.e. f is *square-free*. Furthermore we assume that f is *primitive* with respect to X, i.e. the greatest common divisor of the coefficients in $\mathbb{Z}[Y]$ of f equals one. We denote by $\delta_X f$ and $\delta_Y f$ the degrees of f in X and Y respectively, and by $\ell c(f)$ the *leading coefficient* of f with respect to X. We put $n_X = \delta_X f$ and $n_Y = \delta_Y f$.

Suppose that we are given a prime number p, an integer s and a positive integer k. By (s_1) we denote the ideal generated by p and $(Y-s)$, and by (s_k) we denote the ideal generated by p^k and $(Y-s)^{n_Y+1}$. In Section 4 we will see how to find a polynomial $h \in \mathbb{Z}[X,Y]$ such that:

(3.1) $\ell c(h) = 1$,

(3.2) $(h \bmod (s_k))$ divides $(f \bmod (s_k))$ in $\mathbb{Z}[X,Y]/(s_k)$,

(3.3) $(h \bmod (s_1)) \in (\mathbb{Z}/p\mathbb{Z})[X]$ is irreducible in $(\mathbb{Z}/p\mathbb{Z})[X]$,

(3.4) $(h \bmod (s_1))^2$ does not divide $(f \bmod (s_1))$ in $(\mathbb{Z}/p\mathbb{Z})[X]$.

We put $\ell = \delta_X h$; so $0 < \ell \leq n_X$.

Let $h_0 \in \mathbb{Z}[X,Y]$ be the irreducible factor of f for which $(h \bmod (s_1))$ divides $(h_0 \bmod (s_1))$ in $(\mathbb{Z}/p\mathbb{Z})[X]$ (or equivalently $(h \bmod (s_k))$ divides $(h_0 \bmod (s_k))$ in $\mathbb{Z}[X,Y]/(s_k)$, cf. [7: (2.5)]); notice that h_0 is unique up to sign.

(3.5) Let m_X and m_Y be two integers with $\ell \leq m_X < n_X$ and $0 \leq m_Y \leq \delta_Y \ell c(f)$. We define L as the collection of polynomials $g \in \mathbb{Z}[X,Y]$ such that

(i) $\delta_X g \leq m_X$,

(ii) $\delta_Y g \leq n_Y$,

(iii) $\delta_Y \ell c(g) \leq m_Y$,

(iv) $(h \bmod (s_k))$ divides $(g \bmod (s_k))$ in $\mathbb{Z}[X,Y]/(s_k)$.

Putting $M = m_X(n_Y+1)+m_Y+1$ it is not difficult to see that L is an M-dimensional lattice contained in $\mathbb{Z}^M$, where we identify polynomials in L and M-dimensional vectors in the usual way (i.e. $\Sigma_{i=0}^{m_X-1} \Sigma_{j=0}^{n_Y} a_{ij} X^i Y^j + \Sigma_{j=0}^{m_Y} a_{m_X j} X^{m_X} Y^j$ is identified with $(a_{00}, a_{01}, \ldots, a_{0n_Y}, a_{10}, \ldots, a_{m_X-1\, n_Y}, a_{m_X 0}, \ldots, a_{m_X m_Y})$). Because of (3.1) a basis for L is given by

$$\{p^k Y^j X^i:\ 0 \le j \le n_Y,\ 0 \le i < \ell\} \cup$$
$$\{(hY^j \bmod (s_k))X^{i-\ell}:\ (0 \le j \le n_Y \text{ and } \ell \le i < m_X) \text{ or } (0 \le j \le m_Y \text{ and } i = m_X)\}.$$

This generalizes (1.1) (cf. [7: (2.6)]). We now come to (1.2). The *height* g_{max} of a polynomial g is defined as the maximal absolute value of any of its integral coefficients. We prove that, if k and s are suitably chosen, then a vector of small height in L must lead to a factorization of f.

(3.6) Proposition. Suppose that $g \in L$ satisfies

$$(3.7)\qquad |s|^{n_Y+1} > (e^{n_X+n_Y} f_{max}\sqrt{(n_X+1)(n_Y+1)})^{m_X}(g_{max}\sqrt{(m_X+1)(n_Y+1)})^{n_X}$$

and

$$(3.8)\qquad p^k > (e^{n_X+n_Y} f_{max}\sqrt{(n_X+1)(n_Y+1)})^{m_X}(g_{max}\sqrt{(m_X+1)(n_Y+1)})^{n_X}(1+(1+|s|)^{n_Y+1})^{n_Y(n_X+m_X-1)}.$$

Then h_0 divides g in $\mathbb{Z}[X,Y]$, and in particular $\gcd(f,g) \ne 1$.

Proof. Suppose that $\gcd(f,g) = 1$. This implies that the resultant $R \in \mathbb{Z}[Y]$ of f and g is unequal to zero. Using the result from [4] one proves that

$$(3.9)\qquad |R| < (f_{max}\sqrt{(n_X+1)(n_Y+1)})^{m_X}(g_{max}\sqrt{(m_X+1)(n_Y+1)})^{n_X},$$

where $|R|$ denotes the ordinary Euclidean length of the vector identified with R. Since $(h \bmod (s_k))$ divides both $(f \bmod (s_k))$ and $(g \bmod (s_k))$, the polynomials f and g have a non-trivial common divisor in $\mathbb{Z}[X,Y]/(s_k)$, so that R must be zero modulo the ideal generated by p^k and $(Y-s)^{n_Y+1}$. The polynomial $(Y-s)^{n_Y+1}$ cannot divide R, because this would imply, according to [11: Theorem 1], that $|s|^{n_Y+1} \le |R|$, which is, combined with (3.9), a contradiction with (3.7). Therefore $(R \bmod (Y-s)^{n_Y+1})$ has to be zero modulo p^k. Using induction on n_Y+1 it is easy to prove that

$$(R \bmod (Y-s)^{n_Y+1})_{max} \le R_{max}(1+(1+|s|)^{n_Y+1})^{n_Y(n_X+m_X-1)},$$

so that, with $R_{max} \le |R|$ and (3.8), it follows that $(R \bmod (Y-s)^{n_Y+1})$ cannot be zero modulo p^k. We conclude that $\gcd(f,g) \neq 1$.

Suppose that h_0 does not divide g. So h_0 does not divide $r = \gcd(f,g)$, so $(h \bmod (s_k))$ divides $((f/r) \bmod (s_k))$. Because f/r divides f, we find from [3] that $(f/r)_{max} \leq e^{n_X+n_Y} f_{max}$. This implies that the above reasoning applies to f/r and the same polynomial g in L, so that $\gcd(f/r,g) \neq 1$. This is a contradiction with $r = \gcd(f,g)$, because f is square-free. □

(3.10) Proposition. Suppose that s and k are chosen in such a way that (3.7) and (3.8) are satisfied with g_{max} replaced by $2^{(M-1)/2}\sqrt{M}\, e^{n_X+n_Y} f_{max}$. Let $\tilde{b}$ be as in (2.1) the result of an application of the basis reduction algorithm to the M-dimensional lattice L as defined in (3.5). Then $h_0 \in L$ if and only if (3.7) and (3.8) are satisfied with g replaced by $\tilde{b}$.

Proof. To prove the "if"-part, assume that (3.7) and (3.8) hold with g_{max} replaced by $\tilde{b}_{max}$. According to (3.6) this implies that h_0 divides $\tilde{b}$, so that $h_0 \in L$.

To prove the "only if"-part, assume that $h_0 \in L$. Because h_0 divides f, we find from [3] that $(h_0)_{max} \leq e^{n_X+n_Y} f_{max}$. So there exists a non-zero vector in L with Euclidean length bounded by $\sqrt{M}\, e^{n_X+n_Y} f_{max}$. Application of (2.1) yields that $\tilde{b}_{max} \leq |b| \leq 2^{(M-1)/2}\sqrt{M}\; e^{n_X+n_Y} f_{max}$. Combined with the above choices of s and k, this implies that (3.7) and (3.8) hold with g replaced by $\tilde{b}$. □

4. Description of the algorithm.

In this section we present the polynomial-time algorithm to factor f. First we give an algorithm to determine the factor h_0, given p, s and h. After that, we will see how p and s have to be chosen.

(4.1) Let p, s and h be as in Section 3, such that (3.1), (3.3), (3.4) and (3.2) with k replaced by 1 are satisfied. Assume that s satisfies the condition in (3.10) with m_X and m_Y replaced by n_X-1 and $\delta_Y \ell c(f)$ respectively:

$$(4.2) \qquad |s|^{n_Y+1} > (e^{n_X+n_Y} f_{max}\sqrt{(n_X+1)(n_Y+1)})^{n_X-1}\,(2^{(M-1)/2}\sqrt{M}\, e^{n_X+n_Y} f_{max}\sqrt{n_X(n_Y+1)})^{n_X}$$

where $M = (n_X-1)(n_Y+1)+\delta_Y \ell c(f)+1$. We describe an algorithm that determines h_0, the irreducible factor of f such that $(h \bmod (s_1))$ divides $(h_0 \bmod (s_1))$ in $(\mathbb{Z}/p\mathbb{Z})[X]$.

We may assume that $\ell = \delta_X h < n_X$. Take k minimal such that the condition from (3.10) is satisfied with m_X and m_Y replaced by n_X-1 and $\delta_Y \ell c(f)$ respectively:

$$(4.3) \qquad p^k > \left(e^{n_X+n_Y} f_{max} \sqrt{(n_X+1)(n_Y+1)}\right)^{n_X-1} \left(2^{(M-1)/2}\sqrt{M}\, e^{n_X+n_Y} f_{max} \sqrt{n_X(n_Y+1)}\right)^{n_X} \cdot (1+(1+|s|)^{n_Y+1})^{2n_Y(n_X-1)}.$$

Next modify h in such a way that (3.2) also holds for this value of k; because of (3.4) this can be done by means of Hensel's lemma [13].

Apply Proposition (2.1) to the M-dimensional lattice L as defined in (3.5) for each of the values of $M = \ell(n_Y+1)+1, \ell(n_Y+1)+2, \ldots, \ell(n_Y+1)+\delta_Y \ell c(f)+1, (\ell+1)(n_Y+1)+1, \ldots, (n_X-1)(n_Y+1)+\delta_Y \ell c(f)+1$ in succession (so, for $m_X = \ell, \ell+1, \ldots, n_X-1$ in succession and for every value of m_X the values $m_Y = 0, 1, \ldots, \delta_Y \ell c(f)$ in succession). But stop as soon as a vector $\tilde{b}$ is found satisfying (3.7) and (3.8) with g replaced by $\tilde{b}$.

If such a vector $\tilde{b}$ is found for a certain value of M $(m_X = m_{X0}$ and $m_Y = m_{Y0})$, then we know from (3.10) that $h_0 \in L$. Since we try the values of M in succession this implies that $\delta_X h_0 = m_{X0}$ and $\delta_Y \ell c(h_0) = m_{Y0}$. By (3.6) h_0 divides $\tilde{b}$, so that $\delta_X \tilde{b} = m_{X0}$ and $\delta_Y \ell c(\tilde{b}) = m_{Y0}$. So $\tilde{b} = ch_0$ for some $c \in \mathbb{Z}$, but $h_0 \in L$ and $\tilde{b}$ belongs to a basis for L, so $\tilde{b} = \pm h_0$.

If no such vector $\tilde{b}$ was found, then (3.10) implies that $\delta_X h_0 > n_X-1$, so that $h_0 = f$, because f is primitive.

This finishes the description of Algorithm (4.1).

(4.4) Proposition. Denote by $m_{X0} = \delta_X h_0$ the degree in X of the irreducible factor h_0 of f that is found by Algorithm (4.1). Then the number of arithmetic operations needed by Algorithm (4.1) is $O(m_{X0}(n_X^5 n_Y^5 + n_X^4 n_Y^4 \log(f_{max}) + n_X^4 n_Y^6 \log(|s|) + n_X^3 n_Y^4 \log p))$ and the integers on which these operations have to be performed each have binary length $O(n_X^3 n_Y^2 + n_X^2 n_Y \log(f_{max}) + n_X^2 n_Y^3 \log(|s|) + n_X n_Y \log p)$.

Proof. Let M_1 be the largest value of M for which (2.1) is applied; so $M_1 = O(m_{X0} n_Y)$ It follows from (2.1) that the number of operations needed for the applications of the basis reduction algorithm for $\ell(n_Y+1)+1 \le M \le M_1$ is equal to the number of operations needed for $M = M_1$ only. Assuming that the coefficients of the initial basis for L are reduced modulo p^k, we find, using (4.3), that the following holds for the bound

B on the length of these vectors:

$$\log B = O(n_X^2 n_Y + n_X \log(f_{max}) + n_X n_Y^2 \log(|s|) + \log p).$$

With $M_1 = O(m_{X0} n_Y)$ and (2.1) this gives the estimates in (4.4).

The verification that the same estimates are valid for the application of Hensel's lemma is straightforward [13]. □

We now describe how s and p have to be chosen. First, s must be chosen such that $(f \bmod (Y-s)) = f(X,s)$ remains square-free, and such that (4.2) holds. The resultant R of f and its derivative f' with respect to X is a non-zero polynomial in $\mathbb{Z}[Y]$ of degree $\le n_Y(2n_X-1)$. Therefore we can find in $O(n_X n_Y)$ trials the minimal integer s such that s is not a zero of R, and such that (4.2) holds. It is easily verified that $\log(|s|) = O(n_X^2 + n_X \log(f_{max}))$.

Next we choose p as the smallest prime number not dividing the resultant of $f(X,s)$ and $f'(X,s)$. Since $\log(f(X,s)_{max}) = O(n_X^2 n_Y + n_X n_Y \log(f_{max}))$, it follows as in the proof of [7: (3.6)] that $p = O(n_X^3 n_Y + n_X^2 n_Y \log(f_{max}))$.

The complete factorization of $(f \bmod (s_1))$ can be determined by means of Berlekamp's algorithm [6: section 4.6.2]; notice that (3.4) holds for every factor $(h \bmod (s_1))$ of $(f \bmod (s_1))$, because of the choice of p, and that this factorization can be found in polynomial-time, because of the bound on p. The algorithm to factor f completely now follows by repeated application of Algorithm (4.1). The above bounds on $\log(|s|)$ and p, combined with (4.4) and the fact that a factor g of f satisfies $\log(g_{max}) = O(n_X + n_Y + \log(f_{max}))$ (cf. [3]), yields the following theorem.

(4.5) Theorem. The number of arithmetic operations needed to factor f completely is $O(n_X^7 n_Y^6 + n_X^6 n_Y^6 \log(f_{max}))$, and the integers on which these operations have to be performed each have binary length $O(n_X^4 n_Y^3 + n_X^3 n_Y^3 \log(f_{max}))$. □

5. Conclusion.

We have shown that basically the same ideas that were used for the polynomial-time algorithm for factoring in $\mathbb{Z}[X]$ lead to a polynomial-time factoring algorithm in $\mathbb{Z}[X,Y]$ (Theorem (4.5)). Our method can be generalized to polynomials in $\mathbb{Z}[X_1, X_2,$

$\ldots, X_t]$. The evaluation $(Y=s)$ is then replaced by $(X_2=s_2, X_3=s_3, \ldots, X_t=s_t)$, where the integers s_i have to satisfy conditions similar to (4.2). It will not be surprising that in this case the estimates become rather complicated.

A somewhat simpler algorithm results if we use the algorithm from [7]; the details of this algorithm, which is similar to the one described in this paper, can be found in [10].

References.

1. D.G. Cantor, Irreducible polynomials with integral coefficients have succinct certificates, J. of Algorithms 2 (1981), 385-392.

2. M.R. Garey, D.S. Johnson, Computers and intractability, Freeman, San Francisco 1979.

3. A.O. Gel'fond, Transcendental and algebraic numbers, Dover Publ., New York 1960.

4. A.J. Goldstein, R.L. Graham, A Hadamard-type bound on the coefficients of a determinant of polynomials, SIAM Rev. 16 (1974), 394-395.

5. E. Kaltofen, On the complexity of factoring polynomials with integer coefficients, Ph.D. thesis, Rensselaer Polytechnic Institute, August 1982.

6. D.E. Knuth, The art of computer programming, vol. 2, Seminumerical algorithms, Addison Wesley, Reading, second edition 1981.

7. A.K. Lenstra, H.W. Lenstra, Jr., L. Lovász, Factoring polynomials with rational coefficients, Math. Ann. 261 (1982), 515-534.

8. A.K. Lenstra, Factoring polynomials over algebraic number fields, Report IW 213/82, Mathematisch Centrum, Amsterdam 1982 (also Proceedings Eurocal 83).

9. A.K. Lenstra, Factoring multivariate polynomials over finite fields, Report IW 221/83, Mathematisch Centrum, Amsterdam 1983 (also Proceedings 15th STOC).

10. A.K. Lenstra, to appear.

11. M. Mignotte, An inequality about factors of polynomials, Math. Comp. 28 (1974), 1153-1157

12. P.S. Wang, An improved multivariate polynomial factoring algorithm, Math. Comp. 32 (1978), 1215-1231.

13. D.Y.Y. Yun, The Hensel lemma in algebraic manipulation, MIT, Cambridge 1974; reprint: Garland publ. Co., New York 1980.

ON THE STUDY DATA STRUCTURES :
BINARY TOURNAMENTS WITH REPEATED KEYS.

P. LESCANNE
CRIN
Campus Scientifique
BP 239
54506 - VANDOEUVRE LES NANCY (France)

J.M. STEYAERT
Ecole Polytechnique
Laboratoires de Mathématiques Appliquées
91128 - Palaiseau Cedex (France)

ABSTRACT :

In this paper we develop a systematic way of analyzing tree like data structures and recursive algorithms on them ; the method is shown on binary tournaments with repeated keys extending previous applications to term trees. Tournaments are studied both as a combinatorial and as a computational object ; the main line of our approach consists in showing strong correspondences between recursive definition of combinatorial parameters and of procedures on one hand and equations over generating power series on the other hand ; we can then conclude by deriving closed formulae or asymtotic estimates for the average values of various quantities and running times of procedures.

1. INTRODUCTION

Since D.E. Knuth [K 68] [K 73], a great amount of work has been devoted to the study of various data structures and of the behaviour of the basic algorithms related to them in the goal of improving efficiency. Whereas the worst case behaviour of an algorithm is most of the time easily shown on extremal configurations, the analysis of the average performence requires combinatorial or probabilistic methods which can become really intricate in many situations ; as illustrated in [K 73] the computer scientist has

(i) to find the good combinatorial representation of the data structure,

(ii) to extract from the algorithm the parameters related to its behaviour and express them on the data structure

(iii) finally by use of recurrences, generating functions, real or complex analysis... to derive the desired explicit formulae or asymptotics which allow to conclude on the average behaviour.

This general attitude may look quite tricky in several cases unless the user has a good knowledge of the various methods that have been developped in the field of combinatorics.

In the same manner that combinatorialists (e.g. Rota, Stanley, Schutzenberger, etc...) have developped general methods (umbral calculus, combinatorial algebra, etc...), it may seem desirable to propose general frameworks to handle the problems which are specific of the analysis of algorithms. Such an approach has been sketched by Burge [B 76] and Flajolet [F 79] ; a more general framework has been proposed in [FS 81] to analyse a variety of algorithms over terms or expressions represented by trees.
In this paper we propose a unified framework for analyzing binary tournaments with repeated keys, which generalize tournaments associated to permutations [FR 79]. This data structure is introduced in [L 82b] to represent monadic function terms in the context of recursive decomposition ordering ; moreover it provides a means for handling priority queues when equal priorities are allowed thus generalizing results of [FVV 78]. More generally binary tournaments with repeated keys can be viewed as unbalanced heaps satisfiing additional properties. In this respect they happen to be a convenient tree representation for studiing various conbinatorial parameters of permutations over a multi-set [L 82a].
We shall focus our attention on the problems that arise when one wants to analyze algorithms running over this data structure.
Section 2 is devoted to basic definitions. In section 3 we consider the problem of building efficiently the tournament associated to a sequence of keys ; two algorithms are studied which proceed by inserting new keys on the right (resp. left) branch of the tournaments : the analysis developed here shows that they are almost equivalent. An interesting by product of this treatment is to show how several parameters of tournaments can be systematically analyzed.
In section 4 we study the problem of comparing two tournaments which is directly related to the recursive decomposition ordering of [L 82b] : two algorithms are proposed which recursively match tournaments either left to right or right to left : we show that on the average the running times are linear in the input size for the first one, but constant for the second one.
All these results are based on a general framework, which allows analysis of recursive top down algorithms on many other data structures similar to binary tournaments.

2. BINARY TOURNAMENTS WITH REPEATED KEYS : BASIC DEFINITIONS

Let $[m] = \{1,2,\dots,m\}$ be a set of keys naturally ordered by $1 < 2 < \dots < m$. A tournament over $[m]$ is a binary tree whose nodes are labelled by keys in $[m]$ in such a may that, whenever a node is labelled by i, then the left subtree at this node is a tournament (possibly enmpty) whose keys are taken in the set $[i]$ and the right subtree at this node is a tournament (possibly empty) whose keys are taken in the set $[i-1]$; (see figure 1 for an example).

Let us denote by T_m the set of tournaments over alphabet $[m]$; we then have :

- $T_0 = \{\Lambda\}$, the empty tree

- $T_1 = T_0 + ① (T_1, T_0)$
- $T_m = T_0 + ① (T_1, T_0) + ② (T_2, T_1) + \ldots + ⓜ (T_m, T_{m-1})$

Where ① (t,t') denotes the tree whose root is labelled with i and has t as left subtree and t' as right subtree (this notation is trivially extended to sets).
The sets T_m are therefore defined by the recurrence :

$$T_0 = \Lambda$$
$$T_{i+1} = T_i + ⓘ{+}① (T_{i+1}, T_i), \quad i \geq 0 \qquad (1)$$

It is well known that tournaments with distinct keys are in one-to-one correspondence with permutations, whenever the keys form an initial segment of N^+. A similar construction can be realized when we consider possibly repeated keys.

Let $a = a_1 a_2 \ldots a_n$ be a sequence over $[m]$. From a we construct a tournament $T(a)$ in the following way :

(i) if $a = \Lambda$ then $T(\Lambda)$ is the empty tree.

(ii) otherwise let i, $1 \leq i \leq n$, be the rank of the rightmost largest key in a
($\forall j \; a_i \geq a_j$ and $\forall j > i \; a_i > a_j$) ; then :

$$T(a) = a_i (T(a \ldots a_{i-1}), T(a_{i+1} \ldots a_n))$$

or in a more pictorial manner

$$T(a) = \quad \begin{array}{c} a_i \\ \diagup \quad \diagdown \\ T(a_1 \ldots a_{i-1}) \quad (T(a_{i+1} \ldots a_n) \end{array}$$

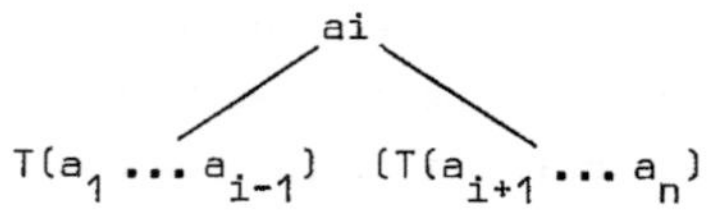

Figure 1 shows an example of tournament associated to a given sequence.
It is clear that we thus establish a one-to-one correspondence between sequences and tournaments, since given a tournament one gets the associated sequence by traversing the tree in symmetric order.

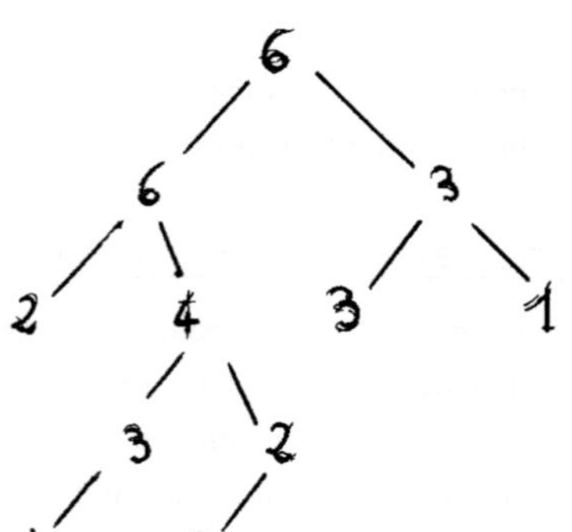

Figure 1 : The binary tournament associated to sequence
a = 26134226331

Since sequences over $[m]$ can be viewed as multiset permutations, tournaments constitute a geometric representation of permutations which allows an easy analysis of several combinatorial parameters ; for instance lengths of left (right) branches are in bijection with numbers of weak (strong) cycles or lengths of sequences of weak (strong) maxima etc ... [FoSc] [L 82] ; the number of leaves can be related to relative minima etc ... In [B 77] Bruge considered binary search trees associated to sequences with repeated keys ; it is wellknown that in the case of distinct keys, BST and tournaments are in strong correspondence via the tree skeletons (labels are omitted) ; this no longer holds in the case of repeated keys although many parameters still have the same distributions.

To conclude with general remarks, we show how generating power series can be used to solve enumerating problems ; this method will be of constant use in the following sections and will be applied to analysis of algorithms as well.
As an easy example we derive the generating power series of tournaments in T_m starting from equation (1).

Given a sequence $a = a_1 \dots a_n \in [m]^*$,
we define its type $\nu(a) = \langle n_1, n_2, \dots n_m \rangle$ as the m-tuple such that n_i is the number of keys i in a ; when T is a tournament $\nu(T)$ is the type of the sequence a associated to T.
The enumerating power series of T_m is defined by :

$$t_m(x_1,\dots,x_m) = \sum_{A \in T_m} \underset{\sim}{x}^{\nu(A)} \qquad (2)$$

Where

$$\underset{\sim}{x}^{\underset{\sim}{n}} = x_1^{n_1}\, x_2^{n_2} = x_m^{n_m} \quad †$$

Using a standard morphism (see [BR 80] [F 79], [FS 81] e.g.) it is obvious to transform equations (1) into a family of equations on power series $t_i(\underset{\sim}{x})$, obtaining :

$$t_o(\underset{\sim}{x}) = 1$$
$$t_{i+1}(\underset{\sim}{x}) = t_i(\underset{\sim}{x}) + x_{i+1}\, t_{i+1}(\underset{\sim}{x})\, t_i(\underset{\sim}{x}) \qquad (3)$$

This set of equations solves easily, yielding :

$$t_m(x_1,\dots,x_m) = \frac{1}{1-(x_1+\dots+x_m)} \qquad (4)$$

Which is precisely the generating power series of sequences over alphabet $[m]$.
Although various statistics have been considered on multiset permutations [S 77], this one looks quite natural, and enables nice developments in the analyses of sections 3 and 4.

---

† Throughout the paper we shall make an extensive use of this "vectorial" notation:
$\underset{\sim}{x} = \langle x_1,\dots,x_m \rangle$,
$\underset{\sim}{x}^{\underset{\sim}{n}} = x_1^{n_1}\, x_2^{n_2} \dots x_m^{n_m}$ etc ... The length m of the vectors will be implicit.

3. BUILDING TOURNAMENTS EFFICIENTLY.

Given a sequence $a = a_1 \dots a_n \in [m]^*$ the recursive algorithm suggested in section 2 provides us with a means of constructing the associated tournament T(a) ; however it is not very efficient since its worst case behaviour is $O(n^2)$, whereas on the average it costs O (nlogn). Following [Fr 80] it is certainly better to build T(a) on-line by inserting keys successively on the branches of the tournament.

Two strategies are offered depending on the branch (left or right) chosen for insertion : they happen to be both linear, but a detailed analysis shows they are equivalent.

Figure 2 gives the two procedures.

```
procedure rbin (x,var : rightmost) :
{key x is to be inserted in the tournament whose rightbranch extremity is pointed by
rightmost}
y := rightmost ; z := nil ;
while  x > y.label  do  z := y  ; y := y.father  od
new (rightmost) ;          rightmost.label  := x ;
if x = y.label  then       rightmost.father := y.father
                           rightmost.left   := y
                else       rightmost.father := y
                           rightmost.left   := z    fi
end  rbi.

procedure lbins (x,var : leftmost) :
{ keys x is to be inserted in the tournament whose left branch extremity is pointed by
leftmost }
y := leftmost ; z := nil ;
while x > y.label  do  z := y  ;  y := y.father  od  new (leftmost) ;
leftmost.label := x  ; leftmost.father := y ; leftmost.right := z
end lbi.
```

Figure 2   Procedures for left and right bottom up insertion in a Pascalike language.

The main result of the section states as follows :

Theorem 1 : The average numbers of comparisons performed by left bottom-up insertion algorithm (lbi) and right bottom-up insertion algorithm (rbi) for building a tournament of size n in T_m are respectively, as $n \to \infty$:

$$\overline{lbi_m}\,[n] = n\,(2 - \frac{1}{m}) - H_{m-1} + O(1)$$

$$\overline{lbi_m}\,[n] = n\,(2 - \frac{H_m}{m}) - H_m + H_m^{[2]} + O(1)$$

where $H_m = 1 + \frac{1}{2} + \dots + \frac{1}{m}$ is the m - th harmonic number

$$H_n^{[2]} = 1 + \frac{1}{4} + \dots + \frac{1}{m^2}$$

The two procedures are therefore linear in the input size on the average, and right insertion proves to be slightly better than left insertion.

In order to express the above quantities we need a few more notions :

Definition : Let T be a tournament :

- the lenght of its right (left) branch, denoted rb (T) (lb(T)) is the number of nodes on this branch
- the number of non separated pairs, nsp(T), is the total number of pairs (u,v) of nodes such that v is the left son of u and their labels are identical.

For instance, on figure 1, we have :

- the right branch 1-3-6 has length 3
- The left branch 2-6-6 has length 3
- the non separated pairs are $\frac{6}{6}$ / $\frac{3}{3}$ and $\frac{2}{2}$, so that nsp(T) = 3.

We can then state ; generalizing previous results of [FVV] to the case of repeated keys.

Proposition 1 :

The number of comparisons necessary to build a tournament T by ***left*** *insertion is*

$$lbi\ (T) = 2|T| - lb(T)$$

The number of comparisons necessary to build a tournament T by ***right*** *insertion is*

$$rbi\ (T) = 2|T| - rb(T) - nsp(T)$$

Proof :

Let us consider the case of right insertion, and let us charge comparisons to keys in the following way ; let x be the new key to be inserted : each key $< x$ on the right branch is charged by 1 (and since it will be removed from this branch will not be charged any more), and x itself is charged by 1 for the last comparison. Therefore each key is ultimately charged by 2 except those that stay on the right branch or are left sons in non-separated pairs.

A similar argument works for left insertion. □

We are now left with the question of evaluating mean values for lb(T), rb(T) and nsp(T) the average being taken over tournaments of size n in T_m.

Let L_m, R_m and P_m be the multisets of tournaments T in T_m, affected respectively with coefficients lb(T), rb(T), nsp(T), which we write formally as :

$$\begin{cases} L_m = \sum_{T \in T_m} lb(T).T \\ R_m = \sum_{T \in T_m} rb(T).T \\ P_m = \sum_{T \in T_m} nsp(T).T \end{cases} \qquad (5)$$

The multisets satisfy, the following equations :

$$\begin{cases} L_o = 0 \\ L_{i+1} = L_i + \textcircled{i+1}\ (L_{i+1} + T_{i+1}, T_i) \quad i \geq 0 \end{cases} \qquad (6)$$

$$\begin{cases} R_o = 0 \\ R_{i+1} = R_i + \textcircled{i+1}\ (T_{i+1}, R_i + T_i) \quad i \geq 0 \end{cases} \qquad (7)$$

and

$$\begin{cases} P_0 = 0 & (8) \\ P_{i+1} = P_i + \textcircled{i+1}\,(T_{i+1}, P_i) + \textcircled{i+1}\,(P_{i+1}, T_i) & \\ \qquad\quad + \textcircled{i+1}\,(T_{i+1} - T_i, T_i) \qquad i \geq 0 & \end{cases}$$

These equations express the fact that lb(T), rb(T), nsp(T) can be recursively defined on tournaments using left and right subtrees and local properties at the root. For instance equation (8) expresses that

nsp(T) = nsp(T.right) + nsp(T.left) + δ , where $\delta = 1$ if the root of T.left is labelled by i+1.

We apply arguments similar to section 2 to obtain the generating powers series $L_m(\underset{\sim}{x})$, $R_m(\underset{\sim}{x})$, $P_m(\underset{\sim}{x})$, such that e.g.,

$$L_m(\underset{\sim}{x}) = \sum_{A \in T_m} \mathrm{lb}(A) \ \underset{\sim}{x}^{\nu(A)}$$

Systems of equations (6) (7) and (8) are then transformed into systems of linear equations defining L_m, R_m and P_m by induction. These systems can be solved by iteration giving :

Proposition 2 :

The generating power series for length of left branch, length of right branch and number of non-separated pairs are given by :

$$L_m(\underset{\sim}{x}) = \frac{1}{1-X_m} \sum_{1<i<m} \frac{x_i}{1-X_i}$$

$$R_m(\underset{\sim}{x}) = \frac{1}{1-X_m} \sum_{1\leq i\leq m} \frac{x_i}{1-X_{i-1}}$$

$$P_m(\underset{\sim}{x}) = \frac{1}{(1-X_m)^2} \sum_{1\leq i\leq m} \frac{x_i^2}{1-X_{i-1}} \qquad \textit{where } X_i = X_1 + X_2 + \ldots + X_i.$$

Since we are interested in taking the average over all tournaments of a given size, irrespective of their type, we just have to identify all variables to a simple one -say z- in the above espression. We thus obtain (with obvious notations).

$$L_m(z) = \frac{1}{1-mz} \sum_{1\leq i\leq m} \frac{z}{1-iz} \qquad (9)$$

$$R_m(z) = \frac{1}{1-mz} \sum_{1\leq i\leq m} \frac{z}{1-(i-1)z} \qquad (10)$$

$$P_m(z) = \frac{1}{(1-mz)^2} \sum_{1\leq i\leq m} \frac{z^2}{1-(i-1)z} \qquad (11)$$

We then have :

Proposition 3 :

The average values of length of left branch, length of right branch, number of non separated pairs of tournaments of size n in T_m are respectively :

$$\overline{lb_m}[n] = \frac{n}{m} + H_{m-1} - \frac{1}{m^n} \sum_{1\leq i<m} \frac{i^n}{m-i}$$

$$\overline{rb_n}[n] = H_m - \frac{1}{m^n} \sum_{1\leq i<m} \frac{i^n}{m-i}$$

$$\overline{nsp_m}[n] = \frac{n}{m} H_m - H_m^{[2]} + \frac{1}{m^n} \sum_{1\leq i<m} \frac{i^n}{(m-i)^2}$$

Proposition 3 is obtained from equations (9) (10) and (11) by extracting the coefficients of the Taylor expansions of the series and the fact that the number of possible tournaments is :

$$[z^n] \quad t_m(z) = m^n.$$

We now let n tend to infinity ; the expressions $\frac{1}{m^n} \Sigma \frac{i^n}{m-i}$ and $\frac{1}{m^n} \Sigma \frac{i^n}{(m-i)^2}$ vanishe. With Proposition 1 that completes the proof of Theorem 1.

Our method can be used to derive many other combinatorial results on multiset permutations, some of which can be found in [K 68] [K 73]. It is possible to give closed formulae for variance and to evaluate parameters according to the type of the permutation.

4. TOURNAMENT COMPARISON

Comparing tournaments associated to monadic terms arises naturally in recursive decomposition ordering problems [L 82b]. It is easy to design a recursive linear time algorithm -see Figure 3- but since there are a priori two ways of traversing trees -left to right (lr) and right to left (rl)- we have to compare these two possible procedures. It happens that, although the running times are both linear in the input size in the worst case, one of them (rl) becomes constant on the average, whereas the other one (lr) keeps linear. This section is devoted to the detailed analysis of both procedures, and extends the general approach of [SF 81] on this particular showcase.

The basic idea is to associate to any procedure - say $A(X_1,\ldots,X_p)$ where $X_i \in \mathcal{E}_i$ - a cost powerseries $\tau a(\underset{\sim}{x})$ which sums the costs $\tau A(\underset{\sim}{X})$ of running procedure A over possible inputs $\underset{\sim}{X}$ (we suppose that each $\mathcal{E}_i$ is provided with a notion of size ν such that there are finitely many elements of any given size) :

$$\tau a(\underset{\sim}{x}) = \sum_{\underset{\sim}{X} \in \underset{\sim}{\mathcal{E}}} \tau A(\underset{\sim}{X}) \quad \underset{\sim}{x}^{\nu(\underset{\sim}{X})}.$$

similarly when $B(\underset{\sim}{X})$ is a boolean function or a predicate we consider its caracteristic powerseries

$$\chi b(\underset{\sim}{x}) = \sum_{\substack{\underset{\sim}{X} \in \underset{\sim}{\mathcal{E}} \\ \text{and } B(\underset{\sim}{X})}} \underset{\sim}{x}^{\nu(\underset{\sim}{X})}$$

```
Boolean function  lrc (X,Y:T_m)
case
root (X) ≠ root (Y)          : assign (false)
root (X) = root (Y) = Λ      : assign (true)
root (X) = root (Y) = 1      : assign (lrc (X.left,Y.Left))
otherwise : if lrc (X.left,Y.left)
            then assign (lrc(X.right,Y.right))
            else assign (false) fi
end lrc.
```

<u>Boolean function</u> rlc(X,Y:T_m) :
<u>case</u>
root (X) ≠ root (Y) : assign (false)
root (X) = root (Y) = Λ : assign (true)
root (X) = root (Y) = 1 : assign (rlc(X.left,Y.left))
otherwise : <u>if</u> rlc(X.right,Y.right)
<u>then</u> assign (lrc(X.left,Y.left))
<u>else</u> assign (false) <u>fi</u>
<u>end rlc</u>.

<u>Figure 3</u> : Procedures for tournament comparison.

Following this scheme we study cost power series associated to each algorithm that is, with obvious notations :

$$\tau lrc_m(\underset{\sim}{x},\underset{\sim}{y}) = \sum_{X,Y \in T_m} \tau LRC_m(X,Y)\ \underset{\sim}{x}^{\nu(X)}\ \underset{\sim}{y}^{\nu(Y)} \qquad (12)$$

and

$$\tau rlc_m(\underset{\sim}{x},\underset{\sim}{y}) = \sum_{X,Y \in T_m} \tau RLC_m(X,Y)\ \underset{\sim}{x}^{\nu(X)}\ \underset{\sim}{y}^{\nu(Y)} \qquad (13)$$

where τLRC_m (X,Y) (resp. τRLC_m (X,Y)) is the running time of procedure lrc (resp. lrc) over inputs X and Y taken in T_m.

We shall translate the procedures into a set of equations defining the cost powerseries ; it will then be possible to obtain estimations of their coefficients and thus of the average behaviour of the procedures.

We first recall a few basic features from [FS 81] :

(i) when Q(A) is a boolean procedure, $Xq(\underset{\sim}{x})$ denotes its characteristic power series :

$$\chi q(\underset{\sim}{x}) = \sum_{\substack{A \in T \\ \text{and } Q(A)}} \underset{\sim}{x}^{\nu(A)}$$

(ii) the cost power series of a conditional instruction

A(X) = <u>if</u> Q(X) <u>then</u> B(X) <u>else</u> C(X)

is related to conditional costs $\tau b(|Q)$ and $\tau c(|\bar{Q})$ by :

$$\tau a(\underset{\sim}{x}) = \tau q(\underset{\sim}{x}) + \tau b(\underset{\sim}{x}|Q) + \tau c(\underset{\sim}{x}|\bar{Q})$$

(iii) for simplicity we assume that elementary local tests have unit cost and that assign operator has cost zero.

The new feature concerning tournaments deals with descent in the structure. Let T_m be the set of inputs ; since $T_m = T_{m-1} + ⓜ (T_m, T_{m-1})$ we can state when X is a tournament. (X.left denotes its left subtree and X.right its right subtree) :

<u>Rule</u> : When A(X:T_m) := B(X.left) then

$$\tau a_m(\underset{\sim}{x}) = \sum_{1\le i\le m} x_i\ \tau b_i(\underset{\sim}{x})\ t_{i-1}(\underset{\sim}{x}) \ ;$$

when A(X:T_m) := B(X.right) then

$$\tau am(\underset{\sim}{x}) = \sum_{1\le i\le m} x_i\ t_i(\underset{\sim}{x})\ \tau b_{i-1}(\underset{\sim}{x}) \ ;$$

where $\tau a_i(\underset{\sim}{x})$ denotes the cost power series of procedure A restricted to inputs in T_i.

The proof of this rule can be established directly by considering multisets and applying the standard morphism, or by establishing recurrences on coefficients and then coming back to power series.

Combining these facts we can now derive from procedures of Figure 3 the equations for cost power series :

$$\tau lrc_0\,(\underset{\sim}{x},\underset{\sim}{y}) = 1$$

$$\begin{aligned}\tau lrc_i\,(\underset{\sim}{x},\underset{\sim}{y}) &= t_i\,(\underset{\sim}{x})\;\; t_i\,(\underset{\sim}{y}) \\ &+ \sum_{1\le j\le i} x_j\, y_j\; \tau lrc_j\,(\underset{\sim}{x},\underset{\sim}{y})\; t_{j-1}(\underset{\sim}{x})\; t_{j-1}(\underset{\sim}{y}) \\ &+ \sum_{2\le j\le i} x_j\, y_j\; \chi lrc_j\,(\underset{\sim}{x},\underset{\sim}{y})\; \tau lrc_{j-1}\,(\underset{\sim}{x},\underset{\sim}{y}) \qquad \text{for } i \ge 1\end{aligned} \qquad (14)$$

and

$$\tau rlc_0\,(\underset{\sim}{x},\underset{\sim}{y}) = 1$$

$$\begin{aligned}\tau rlc_i\,(\underset{\sim}{x},\underset{\sim}{y}) &= t_i(\underset{\sim}{x})\;\; t_i(\underset{\sim}{y}) + x_1 y_1\;\; \tau rlc_1\,(\underset{\sim}{x},\underset{\sim}{y}) \\ &+ \sum_{2\le j\le i} x_j y_j\;\; t_j(\underset{\sim}{x})\;\; \tau rlc_{j-1}\,(\underset{\sim}{x},\underset{\sim}{y}) \\ &+ \sum_{2\le j\le i} x_j y_j\; \tau rlc\,(\underset{\sim}{x},\underset{\sim}{y})\;\; \chi rlc_{i-1}\,(\underset{\sim}{x},\underset{\sim}{y}) \qquad \text{for } i > 1\end{aligned} \qquad (15)$$

One checks easily that

$$\chi\, rlc_i(\underset{\sim}{x},\underset{\sim}{y}) = \chi lrc_i(\underset{\sim}{x},\underset{\sim}{y}) = t_i(\underset{\sim}{xy})$$

where $\underset{\sim}{xy} = \langle x_1y_1, x_2y_2, \ldots, x_iy_i, \ldots\rangle$

We solve now linear equations (14) and (15), and identify all variables to z (thus obtaining cost power series relative to the total size of input (X,Y)).

<u>Proposition 4</u> : The cost power series $\tau lrc_m(z)$ and $\tau rlc_m(z)$ of comparison procedures (relative to the total size of the input) satisfy recurrences :

$$\tau lrc_0(z) = 1$$

$$\tau lrc_m(z) = \frac{(1-(m-1)z)^2}{(1-mz)(1-(m-2)z)}\;\left(\frac{1}{(1-mz)^2} + z^2 \sum_{1\le i\le m} \alpha_i(z)\;\; \tau lrc_i(z)\right)$$

and

$$\tau rlc_0(z) = 1$$

$$\tau rlc_m(z) = \frac{1-(m-1)z^2}{1-mz^2}\;\left(\frac{1}{(1-mz)^2} + z^2 \sum_{1\le i\le m} \beta_i(z)\;\; \tau rlc_i(z)\right)$$

where $\alpha_i(z) = \dfrac{1}{1-(i-1)z^2} + \dfrac{1}{(1-(i+1)z)^2}$

and $\beta_i(z) = \dfrac{1}{(1-(i-1)z)^2} + \dfrac{1}{(1-(i+1)z^2}$

Power series $\tau rlc_m(z)$ and $\tau lrc_m(z)$ are therefore rational fractions in z ; however it seems intractable to obtain closed formulae for the coefficients of their Taylor expansions, so that we now look for estimates of their asymptotic behaviour ; this is done by studying the dominant singularities (that is the pole closest to the origin with highest order) of τrlc_m and τlrc_m considered now as analytic functions.

From the expressions of Proposition 3 we obtain by induction that this singularity is located in both cases at $z = \frac{1}{m}$ and that we have local expansions :

$$\tau lrc_m(z) = \frac{1}{(1-mz)^3} \left[\frac{1}{2m} \quad (1 + \frac{1}{m^2} \quad \tau lrc_{m-1} \; (\frac{1}{m})\right] \quad (1 + (1 - mz) \; h_m \; (z)) \qquad (16)$$

and

$$\tau rlc_m(z) = \frac{1}{(1-mz)^2} \left[(1 - \frac{1}{m^2 - m}) \quad (1 + \frac{1}{m^2} \; \tau rlc_{m-1} \quad (\frac{1}{m}))\right] (1 + (1-mz) \; k_m \; (z)) \qquad (17)$$

Where h_m and k_m regular.

It is well known from complex function theory that the leadling terms in the asymptotic expansions of coefficients come from these local expansions.

We can therefore state.

Theorem 2 : The average running time of lr comparaison is linear in the size of the inputs taken in T_m :

$$\tau lrc_m \; [n] = \frac{n}{4m} \; \alpha_m + O \; (1) \quad \text{as } n \to \infty$$

The average running time of rl comparison is constant in the size of the inputs taken in T_m, m 1

$$\tau rlc_m \; [n] = \beta_n + O \; (\frac{1}{n}) \qquad \text{as } n \to \infty$$

Where $\beta_m = (1 - \frac{1}{m^2 - m}) \quad (1 + \frac{1}{m^2} \quad \tau rlc_{m-1} \; (\frac{1}{m}))$

$\alpha_m = 1 + \frac{1}{m^2} \quad \tau lrc_{m-1} \quad (\frac{1}{m})$

For large m, β_m is numerically close to $\beta_\infty = 1.33$

α_m is numerically close to $\alpha_\infty = 2.84$

Proof :

From equations (16) and (17) we derive asymptotic equivalents for the coefficients

$$[z^n] \; \tau lrc_m(z) = (\frac{\alpha_m}{2m} \quad [z^n] \; \frac{1}{(1-mz)^3} \;) \quad (1 + O \; (\frac{1}{n}))$$

and

$$[z^n] \; \tau rlc_m(z) = (\beta_m \; [z^n] \; \frac{1}{(1-mz)^2} \;) \quad (1 + O \; (\frac{1}{n}))$$

Since the number of possible inputs of size n in $T_m \times T_m$ is precisely $[z^n] \; \frac{1}{(1-mz)^2}$, we conclude with the asymptotic behaviour.

A detailed study of α_m proves the last assertion. □

Some light can be shed on this result by remarking that left branches have average lenght $\frac{n}{m} + H_{m-1}$ whereas right branches have average lenght H_m.

This method applies to many situations where search procedures are to be analyzed and especially when no obvious combinatorial parameter represents the cost of the algorithm.

Acknowledgments : We are indebted to P. Flajolet for many discussions and suggestions.

REFERENCES

[B 76] W.H. BURGE : "An analysis of binary search trees formed from sequence of nondistinct keys" J. ACM 23 (1976), 451-454.

[BR 80] J. BERSTEL, C. REUTENAUER :"Recognizable formal power series on trees", rapport LITP n° 80-26

[F 79] Ph. FLAJOLET "Analyse d'algorithmes de manipulations d'arbres et de fichiers" Thèse Université de Paris-Orsay Septembre 1979, Also published in Cahiers du Bureau Universitaire de Recherche Opérationnelle BURO, 34-35, (1981).

[FS 81] Ph. FLAJOLET, J.M. STEYAERT :"A complexity calculus for classes of recursive search programs over tree structures", in Proc. of ACM 22nd FOCS Symp., Nashville TN (1981).

[Fo C 69] D. FOATA, P. CARTIER : "Problèmes combinatoires de commutations et réarrangements", Lecture Notes in Mathematics, 85 (1969), Springer Verlag, Berlin.

[FoSc 70] D. FOATA, M.P. SCHUTZENBERGER : "Théorie géométrique des polynômes eulériens" Lecture Notes in Mathematics, 138 (1970), Springer Verlag, Berlin.

[Fr 79] J. FRANÇON : "Combinatoire des structures de données", Thèse, Université Louis Pasteur, Strasbourg 1979.

[FVV 78] J. FRANÇON, G. VIENNOT, J. VUILLEMIN :"Description and analysis of an efficient priority queue algorithms", in Proc of 19th ACM Symp on FOCS (1978) pp. 1-7.

[K 68] D.E. KNUTH : "The art of computer programming, vol 1 : Fundamental algorithms", addison Wesley, Reading, Mass (1968).

[K 73] D.E. KNUTH : "The art of computer programming, vol. 3 : Sorting and Searching", Addison Wesley, Reading Mass (1973).

[L 82a] P. LESCANNE : "Analysis of data structures with non distinct keys" Rapport CRIN 82-R-039 Centre de Recherche en Informatique de Nancy (1982).

[L 82b] P. LESCANNE : "Some properties of the recursive decomposition ordering" RAIRO Informatique théorique vol. 16, n° 4 (1982).

[S 77] R. SEDGEWICK : "Quicksort with equal keys" SIAM J. Comput 6, (1977), 240-267.

MINIMIZING WIDTH IN LINEAR LAYOUTS

F. S. Makedon[*,1]
Dept. of Computer Science
Illinois Institute of Tech.
Chicago, Illinois
U. S. A.

I. H. Sudborough[*,1]
Electrical Eng. and Computer Sci.
Northwestern University
Evanston, Illinois 60201
U. S. A.

Abstract: A (linear) layout of an undirected graph G is a one-to-one function mapping the vertices of G to integers. The cutwidth of G under a linear layout L, denoted by cw(G,L), is the maximum, taken over all possible i, of the number of edges connecting vertices assigned to integers less than i to vertices assigned to integers at least as large as i. The cutwidth of a graph G, denoted by cw(G), is the minimum of cw(G,L), taken over all possible linear layouts L. The problem of determining the cutwidth of a graph, called the Min Cut Linear Arrangement problem, has applications in VLSI, for example in the minimization of interconnection channels in Weinberger arrays [16].

We describe a relationship between the cutwidth of a graph G and its "search number" [10], denoted by s(G). We show that, for all graphs G, $s(G) \le cw(G) \le \lfloor deg(G)/2 \rfloor \cdot s(G)$, where deg(G) denotes the maximum degree of any vertex in G. In particular, this means that, for any graph G with maximum vertex degree 3, s(G) = cw(G).

The earlier dynamic programming algorithm of Gurari and Sudborough [5] is improved to show that, for any $k \ge 2$, the problem of deciding if a given graph has cutwidth at most k can be done in $O(n^{k-1})$ steps. We also characterize the classes of graphs with cutwidth 2 and cutwidth 3. The latter characterization strongly suggests a linear time algorithm to determine whether a given graph has cutwidth at most three.

I. Introduction

In 1967 Arnold Weinberger of the IBM Corporation [16] described a method for large scale integration of MOS complex logic circuits by a horizontal row layout of circuit elements and interconnections made along parallel horizontal channels. This approach has been referred to by the phrases "Gate Matrix" [8] and "Uncommitted Logic Array" [15]. An objective of this approach is to minimize the number of horizontal channels (and hence the total amount of chip area needed

---

* a portion of this work was completed while at the National Technical University of Athens, in Athens, Greece

1 supported in part by NSF Grant number MCS 81-09280

for wiring) by an optimal arrangement of circuit elements. This problem has been the subject of several papers in the literature [1 ,2 , 8 , 11,17]; most of which describe heuristic algorithms for gate placement.

It is known that the Min Cut Linear Arrangement problem, which is the problem of deciding, given a graph G and an integer k, whether $cw(G) \leq k$, is NP-complete [4 ,14]. In fact, it is known to remain NP-complete even when restricted to graphs with maximum vertex degree 3 [9]. Lengauer [7] described an algorithm that, for any tree T, produces a layout L such that $cw(T,L) \leq 2 \cdot cw(T)$. Lengauer's approximation algorithm works in $O(n \cdot \log n)$ time. Lengauer also described a linear time algorithm for obtaining the optimal layout of a complete m-ary tree, for each $m \geq 2$. Chung, Makedon, Sudborough, and Turner [2] give an algorithm which obtains an optimal layout for an arbitrary tree. It works in time $O(n \cdot \log^{d-2} n)$, where d is the maximum vertex degree of the tree. Thus, a polynomial time algorithm is known for the Min Cut problem on any class of trees with a fixed integer degree restriction. Chung et. al. also showed that cutwidth and search number are the same for all degree three trees.

In Figure 1.1 below we describe a graph with cutwidth 3 and an optimal layout. In Figures 1.2 -1.3 we describe a circuit of NOR gates and two distinct placements of gates in corresponding Weinberger arrays.

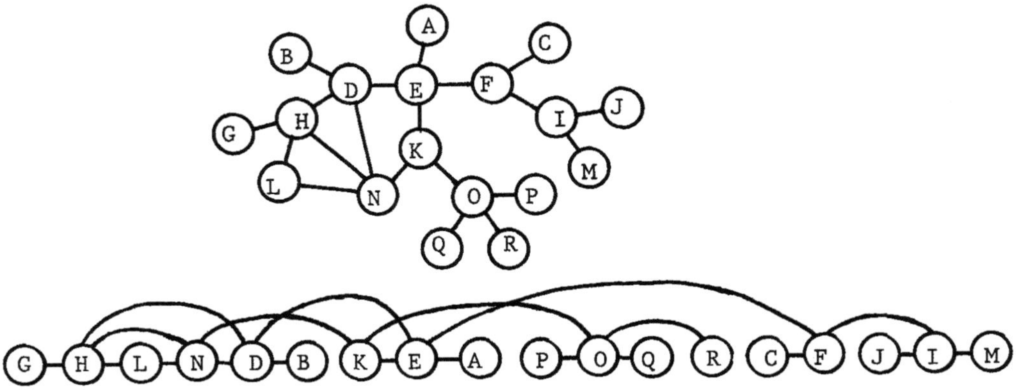

Figure 1.1. A graph with cutwidth 3 and an optimal layout.

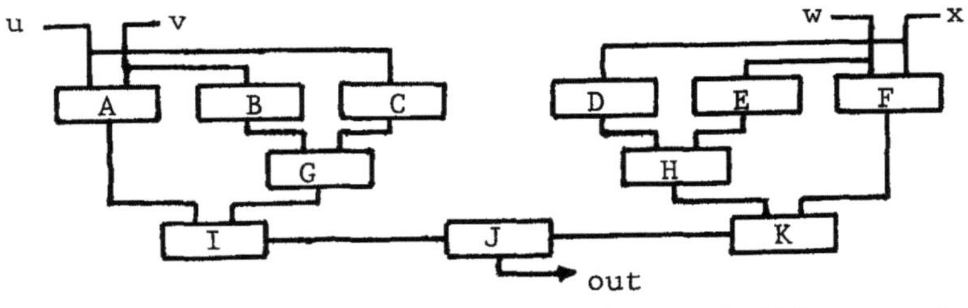

Figure 1.2. A circuit of NOR gates with out=1 iff u=v and w=x.

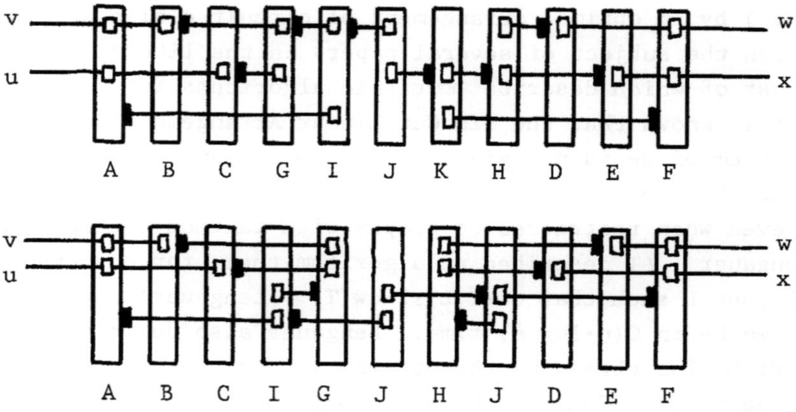

Figure 1.3. Two distinct arrangements for a Weinberger array of the NOR gates shown in Figure 1.2.

II. Relating Cutwidth to Search Number

As indicated in the introduction, search number and cutwidth are known to be identical for all binary trees [2]. In Figure 2.1 we show that search number can be smaller than cutwidth in trees with maximum vertex degree 4.

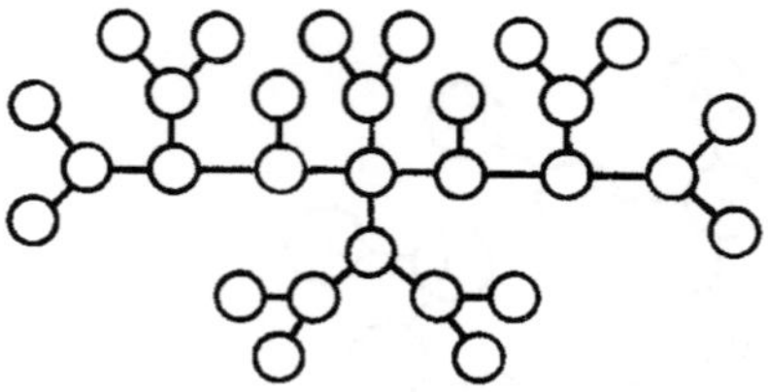

Figure 2.1. A tree with search number 3 and cutwidth 4.

The "search number" of a graph is the smallest number of searchers needed to clear all of the edges of the graph. An edge is clear when a fugitive, who has complete knowledge of his pursuers and unlimited speed to travel through the edges of the graph, cannot be on that edge due to previous movements of the searchers. Searchers are placed in an arbitrary manner on vertices of the graph and, whenever desired, moved through an edge of the graph to a neighboring vertex. Searchers may also be deleted at any time. "Recontamination" is said to occur when an edge has been clear and, because of movements of the searchers, the fugitive may again enter this edge. It is known that the problem of determining, for a given graph G and integer k, whether the search number is at most k is NP-complete [10,12]. That the problem falls in the class NP is due to A. LaPaugh, who has shown that allowing recontamination does not reduce the number of searchers needed [6]. Thus, we may assume, without loss of generality, that any sequence of search game steps does not allow recontamination. Let s(G) denote the search number of a graph G.

Theorem 2.1. For any graph G, $s(G) \leq cw(G)$.

Proof: An algorithm SEARCH is presented for searching a graph G in which the number of searchers is bounded by G's cutwidth. Let G be an arbitrary graph and L an arbitrary layout of G. Let $cw(G,L)=k$. An edge $e=\{x,y\}$ is dangling at the i-th cut (under the layout L) if $L(x) \leq i$ and $L(y)>i$. The algorithm SEARCH has as its "loop invariant" the property that during the i-th loop a searcher is located on a vertex at the lower order end of each edge that is dangling at the i-th cut. The basic searching strategy is to move searchers through all edges that are dangling at the i-th cut and are incident to the (i+1)-st vertex. The number of searchers is then adjusted to maintain the loop invariant.

```
procedure SEARCH(G)
begin  for j = 1 step 1 until |G| do
       begin  let y be the j-th vertex under the layout L;
       for each vertex x such that L(x)<L(y) and {x,y} is an
           edge in G do
           move a searcher from x to y through the edge {x,y};
       let m be the number of edges incident to y that are
           dangling at the i-th cut;
       while there are fewer than m searchers on y do
           add a searcher to y;
       while there are more than m searchers on y do
           delete a searcher from y;
       end
end
```

The correctness of the algorithm follows from the observation that the loop invariant is maintained throughout and the fact that all edges are cleared by the movement of the searchers. Furthermore, the algorithm never uses more than k searchers, since there are never more than k edges dangling from the i-th cut, for i=1,2,... □

So, the search number of a graph is never larger than its cutwidth. In fact, as we shall see, the search number of a graph is identical with its cutwidth in the special case that the graph has maximum vertex degree 3. To show such a result one must go from a sequence of steps in the search game to a linear layout of the graph. The most natural approach would be to lay out the vertices of a graph in the order that they are visited by the searchers. However, this natural approach does not work; one can easily construct examples of graphs, even graphs with maximum vertex degree three, such that the cutwidth is much larger than the number of searchers used. The correct approach is to lay out the vertices of the graph in the order that they reach the condition that at least half of their incident edges are clear. This is shown in the following theorem.

Theorem 2.2. For any graph G, $cw(G) \leq \lfloor deg(G)/2 \rfloor \cdot s(G)$, where deg(G) denotes the maximum degree of any vertex in G.

Proof: Let S be a sequence of search game steps that completely clears all the edges of an undirected graph G and uses at most k searchers. We assume, without loss of generality [6], that there is no "recontamination" in the sequence S.

Define the function f_S mapping vertices of G into natural numbers by: $f_S(x)=i$ if and only if i is the smallest integer such that after step i of the sequence S at least half of the edges incident to x have been cleared. The function f_S is not in general a layout, since the i-th step of S might clear an edge between vertices x and y and might, therefore, cause $f_S(x)$ to be equal to $f_S(y)$. So, we simply pick a layout L_S such that, if $L_S(x) < L_S(y)$, then either $f_S(x)=f_S(y)$ or $f_S(x) < f_S(y)$. We show that, for any such layout L_S, $cw(G,L_S) \leq \lfloor deg(G)/2 \rfloor \cdot k$.

We show first that, for all i, each edge that is dangling at the i-th cut (of G under the layout L_S) must be incident to a vertex that contains a searcher at step t_i, where t_i denotes that step in S when the i-th vertex first has at least half of its incident edges clear. The edges dangling at the i-th cut can be partitioned into two subsets: (a) those that are clear by step t_i, and (b) those that are contaminated at step t_i. If $e=\{x,y\}$ is a clear edge that is dangling at the i-th cut, then one can see that there must be a searcher on the vertex to the right of the i-th vertex that this edge is incident to. There must be a searcher on this vertex at step t_i, since there is at least one contaminated edge incident to this vertex, too, and the searcher must separate the contaminated edge from the clear one. (Note that there must be a contaminated edge incident to this vertex to the right of the i-th vertex or it would be assigned to a position to the left of the i-th vertex by the layout L_S. Actually, there is an exception to this. The (i+1)-st vertex might be one that is assigned to the same integer as the i-th vertex under the function f_S and, therefore, need not be incident to any more contaminated edges. However, in this case, the (i+1)-st vertex must have degree one, or it would have half of its incidents edges cleared earlier, since now all its incident edges are clear. Furthermore, if the i-th vertex and the (i+1)-st vertex are mapped to the same integer by f_S, as we have in this case, then the edge connecting them must contain a searcher during step t_i. We may take this searcher to be the one associated with the newly cleared edge, which connects the i-th vertex and the (i+1)-st vertex, and is dangling at the i-th cut.)

On the other hand, if $e=\{x,y\}$ is a contaminated edge that is dangling at the i-th cut, then there must be a searcher on the vertex to the left of the i-th cut that this vertex is incident to. There must be a searcher on this vertex at step t_i, since this vertex is incident to cleared edges and a searcher must separate these cleared edges from the contaminated one to avoid recontamination.

So, each edge that is dangling at the i-th cut is incident to a vertex that contains a searcher at step t_i. How many of these edges can be incident to the same vertex? Well, at most $\lfloor deg(G)/2 \rfloor$ contaminated edges can be incident to the same vertex to the left of the i-th cut and at most $\lfloor deg(G)/2 \rfloor$ clear edges can be incident to the same vertex to the right of the i-th cut. Otherwise, there would be a contradiction to the fact that the vertices are laid out in the order according to which at least half of their incident edges are clear. Since there only k searchers used in the sequence S, there cannot be more than $\lfloor deg(G)/2 \rfloor \cdot k$ edges that are dangling at the i-th cut. Since this is true for all i, it follows that $cw(G,L_S) \leq \lfloor deg(G)/2 \rfloor \cdot k$. And, since this is true for all search sequences S, it follows that $cw(G) \leq \lfloor deg(G)/2 \rfloor \cdot s(G)$.

□

Corollary 2.1. For any graph G with maximum vertex degree 3, $s(G) = cw(G)$.

The corollary follows immediately from Theorems 2.1 and 2.2.

II. An Improved Dynamic Programming Algorithm for Cutwidth

In [5] Gurari and Sudborough described a dynamic programming algorithm, which for an arbitrary graph G, and for the fixed integer value k, decides whether $cw(G) \leq k$ or not. Their algorithm requires $O(n^k)$ steps, where n is the number of vertices in the graph G. We improve the running time of this dynamic programming algorithm and obtain an algorithm that requires $O(n^{k-1})$ steps, for all $k \geq 2$. Thus, we obtain a linear time algorithm to determine if a graph has cutwidth 2. This is reminiscent of the linear time bandwidth 2 algorithm of Garey, Graham, Johnson, and Knuth [3]. The improvement in the running time of the earlier algorithm would also seem to be of some practical importance, due to the fact that it can be used to speed up the task of finding an optimal layout in Weinberger arrays.

The basic idea initially is to augment the dynamic programming algorithm with a procedure that reduces the given graph. That is, if x is a degree two vertex that is incident to the edges $\{x,y\}$ and $\{x,z\}$, then we replace the vertex x and its two incident edges by a direct edge connecting y and z. It is easily seen that such an operation does not change the cutwidth of the graph. However, to understand this, it should be noted that reducing a graph, i.e. performing all possible such eliminations of degree 2 vertices, may create multiple edges and self loops. Multiple edges between a given pair of vertices does not cause any ambiguity in the definition of cutwidth; each of the edges contributes to the size of any cut it is in. However, the meaning of cutwidth in a graph with a self loop may not be obvious. We adopt the convention that the cutwidth of a graph with a self loop on a vertex x is identical to the cutwidth of the graph formed by adding a degree 2 vertex to the self loop.

So, the algorithm we describe will assume that the graph has no degree 2 vertices, i.e. that the input graph has been completely reduced.

A partial layout of a graph G is a one-to-one function L mapping some of the vertices of G into the natural numbers. The cutwidth of a partial layout L of G, denoted by cw(G,L), is the maximum over all possible integers i of the number of edges which connect vertices x and y such that $L(x)<i$ and either $L(y)>i$ or y is not in the domain of the mapping L. An edge $e=\{x,y\}$ is dangling (from the partial layout L) if L(x) is defined and L(y) is undefined. A vertex x is active (in the partial layout L), if x is incident to a dangling edge. The set of dangling edges and active vertices for a partial layout L are denoted by dangling(L) and active(L), respectively.

Two partial layouts L_1 and L_2 are cutwidth equivalent if (a) (active(L_1), dangling(L_1)) = (active(L_2),dangling(L_2)) and (b) cw(G,L_1)=cw(G,L_2). It is known [5] that cutwidth equivalent partial layouts must be defined on the same set of vertices and, in addition, one can be extended to a cutwidth k layout of the entire graph if and only if both of them can be so extended. The algorithm we describe works with equivalence classes of the above relation.

Clearly, no partial layout L can be extended to a complete cutwidth k layout of a graph G if dangling(L) contains more than k edges. In fact, we show that it is not necessary to consider partial layouts with more than k-1 active vertices. Obviously, a partial layout with k active vertices can only be produced by adding another vertex to a partial layout with k-1 active vertices. So, let L be any partial layout with k-1 active vertices and at most k dangling edges. There are only two cases: (1) L has k dangling edges and (2) L has k-1 dangling edges.

Case (1): L has k dangling edges.

In this case, the next vertex must be incident to one of the dangling edges, since there can be no isolated vertices (we assume, without loss of generality, that G is connected) and the number of dangling edges after assigning the next vertex cannot be greater than k. If the next vertex has degree one, then the new partial layout has k-1 dangling edges and then either there are fewer than k-1 active vertices or case 2 of this argument applies. If the next vertex has three or more incident edges (it cannot have two, since the graph is reduced), then at least two of these edges are dangling from L (for otherwise the new partial layout would have more than k dangling edges) and, consequently, the number of active vertices cannot increase. That is, at least one vertex that was active in L is no longer active. Thus, in this case, we do not produce a layout with more than k-1 active vertices.

Case (2): L has k-1 dangling edges.

In this case, each active vertex is incident to exactly one of the dangling edges. If the next vertex is incident to one of these dangling edges, then the number of active vertices cannot increase in passing on to the next partial layout. So, we assume that the next vertex x is incident to a new edge. Assigning the vertex x does create a partial layout L' with k active vertices. However, this partial layout need not be explicitly considered in the algorithm. That is, consider the next vertex, say y, assigned after x. If y has one incident edge, then the positions of x and y can be reversed without increasing the cutwidth. That is, y must be incident to one of the dangling edges of L' (for otherwise there would be more than k dangling edges in the new partial layout) and this edge cannot be incident to x, since both x and y have degree one and the graph must be connected. So, y is connected to one of the vertices to the left of x and, consequently, x and y can be switched without increasing the cutwidth. So, the partial layout L' need not be considered. Thus, assume that y has degree at least 3.

If y has degree 3, then y must be incident to at least 2 of the dangling edges. If the dangling edges incident to y do not include the edge incident to x, then again the position of x and y can be switched without increasing the cutwidth. So, the resulting partial layout L' need not be considered. So, assume that the edge incident to x is also incident to y. Then, the number of active vertices in the new partial layout L", when the vertex y is assigned, is at most k-1. That is, at least 2 of the formerly active vertices become inactive. So, one can simply proceed directly from the partial layout L to the new partial layout L". L" has at most k-1 active vertices. Moreover, there is not much choice for the vertices x and y that are assigned in going from L to L". That is, y must be incident to one of the dangling edges of L and x must be connected to y.

Our algorithm is designed to exploit these observations. A pair p=(A,D), consisting of a set of vertices A and a set of edges D, is a <u>cutwidth-k-plausible</u> pair, if A contains at most k-1 vertices and D contains at most k edges. Such a pair p=(A,D) represents an equivalence class of partial layouts, <u>i.e</u>. the set of all partial layouts L such that (active(L),dangling(L))=(A,D). Our algorithm uses two data structures: (1) a queue Q whose elements are cutwidth-k-plausible pairs, and (2) a boolean array T with one element for each cutwidth-k-plausible pair. The item T(p) is <u>true</u>, where p is the pair (A,D), if and only if p=(A,D) represents an equivalence class that has already been considered; otherwise, T(p) is <u>false</u>. At the start, T(p) is <u>false</u> for all possible pairs p. Our algorithm also uses the procedures Unassigned and Successor, described in [5] . Unassigned(A,D) returns the set of unassigned vertices for partial layouts in the equivalence class denoted by the pair (A,D). Successor(p,z), for a given pair p=(A,D) and vertex z, gives the pair p'=(A',D') for the new equivalence class of all partial layouts obtained from the class of layouts denoted by the pair p when the vertex z is assigned next. The procedure Successor takes constant time; the procedure Unassigned takes at most O(n) steps, where n is the number of vertices in the graph.

The algorithm starts by considering the partial layout with no active vertices and no dangling edges. That is, it considers the equivalence class which contains this partial layout. The equivalence class is the one denoted by the pair (∅,∅), where ∅ is the empty set.

The algorithm is described on the next page.

```
procedure CUTWIDTH_k(G)
/ A dynamic programming algorithm to test whether a graph G has cutwidth k.  It is
assumed that the input graph G is completely reduced. /
begin
add the pair p=(∅,∅) to Q;
while Q is not empty do
    begin  delete a pair p=(A,D) from Q;
    if A is a set of k-1 vertices then
            begin
            for all unassigned vertices z incident to an edge in D do
                 begin
                 p' ← Successor(p,z);   / let p'=(A',D') /
                 if D'=∅ then stop and return answer "G has cutwidth k";
                 if p' is cutwidth-k-plausible and T(p) is false then
                      begin  T(p') ← true; add p' to Q end
                 for all unassigned vertices w adjacent to z do
                      begin
                      p'' ← Successor(p,w);
                      p' ← Successor(p'',z);   / let p'=(A',D') /
                      if D'=∅ then stop and return answer "G has cutwidth k";
                      if p' is cutwidth-k-plausible and T(p') is false then
                           begin T(p') ← true;  add p' to Q end
                      end
                 end
            end
    if A is a set of fewer than k-1 vertices then
            begin
            V ← Unassigned(A,D);
            for all vertices s in the set V do
                 begin
                 p' ← Successor(p,s);   / let p'=(A',D') /
                 if D'=∅ then stop and return answer "G has cutwidth k";
                 if p' is cutwidth-k-plausible and T(p') is false then
                      begin  T(p') ← true;  add p' to Q  end
                 end
            end
    end
stop and return answer "G has cutwidth larger than k"
end
```

The analysis of the running time of this algorithm is straightforward. The only pairs ever placed in the queue Q are cutwidth-k-plausible pairs. Since any cutwidth-k-plausible pair consists of at most k-1 active vertices and the edges that are incident to them which are dangling, there are at most $O(n^{k-1})$ pairs placed in Q. These pairs can be separated into those having exactly k-1 active vertices and those having fewer than k-1 active vertices. There are $O(n^{k-1})$ of the first type and $O(n^{k-2})$ of the second type. It can be seen that the procedure uses O(1), i.e. constant, time processing each pair of the first type and O(n) steps, in the worst case, processing pairs of the second type. Thus the total time needed is $O(n^{k-1}).O(1) + O(n^{k-2}).O(n)$. That is, $O(n^{k-1})$ time is sufficient for determining if a graph with n vertices has cutwidth k.

IV. Characterizing Graphs with Cutwidth 2 and Cutwidth 3

We describe characterizations of graphs with cutwidth 2 and cutwidth 3. The latter characterization strongly suggests that there is a linear time algorithm to recognize graphs with cutwidth 3.

We consider first some operations on graphs and their effect on cutwidth. The first operation is "node splitting". Let x be an arbitrary vertex in a graph and let E_{x1} and E_{x2} be an arbitrary partition of all of the edges incident to x. Construct the graph which has the same set of vertices as the original, except that node x is replaced by two vertices x1 and x2, and has the same set of edges as the original graph, except that the edges in E_{x1} are made incident to x1 and the edges in E_{x2} are made incident to x2. It is straightforward to verify that, if G' is obtained from G by node splitting, then $cw(G') \leq cw(G)$. That is, let L be a layout of G. Define a layout L' of G' such that, for all vertices u,v in G, if $L(u) < L(v)$, then $L'(u) < L'(v)$ and, if x is the vertex in G that is split into the two vertices x1 and x2, then x1 and x2 occupy successive positions in the layout L' and in the same relative position to the other vertices as x did in the layout L. Furthermore, let k be the maximum number of edges in the two cuts just before x and just after x in the layout L. Then, the two vertices x1 and x2 are arranged, relative to each other, so that no more than k edges cross the gap between them. It is always possible to do this. All other cuts in the linear layout L' are of the same size as the corresponding cuts in L. Thus, $cw(G') \leq cw(G)$.

Note also that the operation of coalescing vertices cannot decrease cutwidth. However, in order to understand this assertion, it must be made clear that when two vertices joined by an edge are coalesced, then the edge becomes a self loop on the coalesced vertex. The operation of coalescing vertices is the inverse of the node splitting operation.

Next consider the operation of "edge subdivision". Let e be an edge in a graph connecting vertices x and y. Construct the new graph by inserting a degree 2 vertex into the edge e. It is straightforward to see that the cutwidth of a graph does not change by this operation. It is the inverse of the operation of reduction that we described before.

Theorem 4.1. Let G be a finite undirected graph. Then the following statements are equivalent:

(1) G has cutwidth at most 2,

(2) G does not contain a homeomorphic image of any of the graphs shown in Figure 4.1 or of any of the graphs that can be obtained from any of these graphs by the operations of coalescing vertices and reduction, and

(3) The reduced graph G' of G has vertex degree at most 4 and consists of a sequence of vertices $a_1, a_2, \dots, a_r$ (some $r \geq 1$) such that, for all i ($1 \leq i < r$), a_i is joined to a_{i+1} by either one or two edges, together with attachments of the following type to the vertices of this sequence: (a) single edges and (b) a self loop added to one of the vertices a_1, a_2, a_{r-1}, a_r, provided that, if a self loop is attached to a_2 (a_{r-1}), then a_1 (a_r) has degree one.

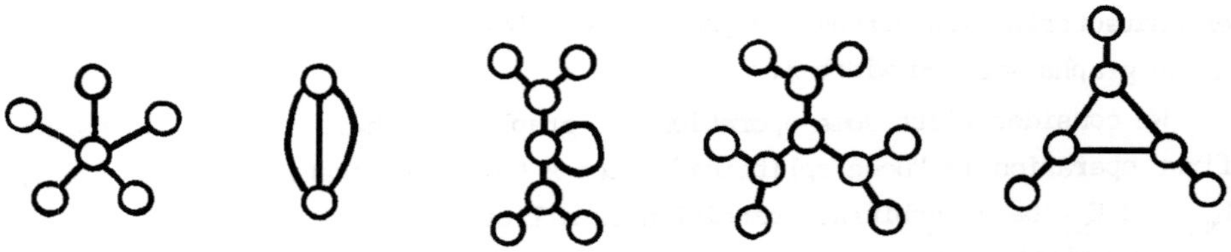

Figure 4.1. Forbidden subgraphs for cutwidth 2.

The proof of Theorem 4.1 will be given in the subsequent full paper. Let G be a reduced graph with cutwidth 2. By the above theorem there is a chain of vertices $a_1, a_2, \dots, a_r$ such that, for all i ($1 \leq i < r$), a_i is connected to a_{i+1} by one or two edges and G consists of this chain together with single edge attachments and self loops (in the manner specified) such that no vertex has degree greater than 4. An "endpoint" of such a graph G is a vertex such that, for some chain of vertices, as specified above, it is (1) either the first or last vertex in the sequence, when there is no self loop at that end of the sequence, or (2) a new degree 2 vertex inserted into one of the permitted self loops of G. It can be seen that an endpoint of such a graph G is a vertex that can be the first or last vertex in some cutwidth 2 layout.

A graph is outerplanar if it has a planar embedding in which a single face includes all of its vertices. The edges of that face (ordinarily taken to be the external face) are called sides and all of the remaining edges are called chords. A graph G is biconnected if the removal of any single vertex from G (and all of its incident edges) leaves a connected graph. A biconnected outerplanar graph satisfies the collinear chord property if it is possible to add some chords to form an outerplanar graph in which all of the chords form a simple chain. In other words, a biconnected outerplanar graph satisfies the collinear chord property if in an outerplanar representation of G one can draw a line, never entering the external region or picking up the pencil, and pass through all the chords without one part of the line touching or crossing another part of the line. Examples of outerplanar biconnected graphs which satisfy and do not satisfy the collinear chord property are given in Figure 4.2.

Figure 4.2. Biconnected graphs which (a) do and (b) do not satisfy the collinear chord property.

Lemma 4.1. Let G be a finite biconnected graph. The following statements are equivalent: (a) $cw(G) \leq 2$, and (b) the reduction of G is outerplanar and satisfies the collinear chord property.

The proof of Lemma 4.1 will be given in the subsequent complete paper. Let G be a graph. A biconnected component of G is "simple" if it consists of a single edge; otherwise, the biconnected component is "nonsimple". A vertex is "simple" if it does not belong to any nonsimple biconnected component; it is "semisimple" if it belongs to a simple and a nonsimple component.

Theorem 4.2. Let G be a finite undirected graph. Then, $cw(G) \leq 3$ if and only if G can be obtained by the operations of node splitting, edge subdivision, reduction, and edge deletion from a chain $C = C_1, C_2, \ldots, C_m$ ($m \geq 1$) of biconnected graphs, which has various cutwidth 2 graphs attached to its vertices, and which satisfies the following properties:

1. for all i ($1 \leq i < m$), C_i and C_{i+1} share an articulation point a_i,
2. for all i ($1 \leq i \leq m$), C_i satisfies the conditions of Lemma 4.1; in fact, all of the chords in C_i are part of a line drawn from a_{i-1} to a_i,
3. for all i ($1 \leq i < m$), if a_i is simple, then a single cutwidth 2 graph can be attached to a_i and, if a_i is semisimple, then a single cutwidth 2 graph can be attached by an endpoint to a_i, and
4. no attachments except those explicitly allowed in (3) are permitted.

The proof of Theorem 4.2 will be given in the subsequent complete paper. In Figure 4.3 we give a graph with cutwidth 3 and a graph with cutwidth greater than 3.

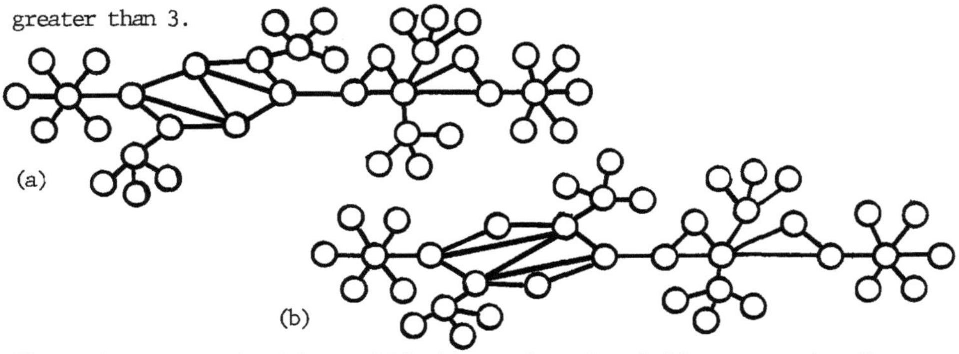

Figure 4.3. A graph with cutwidth (a) equal to 3 and (b) greater than 3.

References:

1. M. A. Breuer, "Min Cut Placement", J. Design Automation and Fault Tolerant Computing 1,4 (1977), pp. 343-362.
2. M.-J. Chung, F. S. Makedon, I. H. Sudborough, J. Turner, "Polynomial Time Algorithms for the Min Cut Linear Arrangement Problem on Degree Restricted Trees", Proc. 23rd Annual IEEE Foundations of Computer Science Symp. (1982).
3. M. R. Garey, R. L. Graham, D. S. Johnson, and D. E. Knuth, "Complexity Results for Bandwidth Minimization", SIAM J. Applied Math. 34 (1978), pp. 477-495.
4. F. Gavril, "Some NP-complete Problems on Graphs", Proc. 11th Annual Conf. on Info. Science and Systems, The Johns Hopkins University, Baltimore, Md., U.S.A., (1977), pp. 91-95.
5. E. M. Gurari and I. H. Sudborough, "Improved Dynamic Programming Algorithms for Bandwidth Minimization and the Min Cut Linear Arrangement Problem", manuscript.
6. A. S. LaPaugh, "Recontamination Does Not Help", manuscript, Princeton University, Computer Science Dept., Princeton, N.J., U.S.A., 1982.
7. T. Lengauer, "Upper and Lower Bounds on the Complexity of the Min Cut Linear Arrangement Problem on Trees", Tech. Report TM-80-1272-9, Bell Laboratories, Murray Hill, New Jersey, U.S.A. (1980).
8. A. D. Lopez and H.-F. S. Law, "A Dense Gate Matrix Layout Method for MOS VLSI", IEEE Trans. on Electronic Devices, ED-27,8 (1980), pp. 1671-1675.
9. F. S. Makedon, C. H. Papadimitriou, and I. H. Sudborough, "Topological Bandwidth", manuscript (1983).
10. N. Megiddo, S. L. Hakimi, M. R. Garey, D. S. Johnson, and C. H. Papadimitriou, "The Complexity of Searching a Graph", Proc. IEEE Foundations of Computer Science Symp. (1981), pp. 376-385.
11. T. Ohtsuki, H. Mori, E. S. Kuh, T. Kashiwabara, and T. Fujisawa, "One-Dimensional Logic Gate Assignments and Interval Graphs", IEEE Trans. on Circuits and Systems, CAS-26,9 (1979), pp. 675-684.
12. T. D. Parsons, "Pursuit Evasion in a Graph", Theory and Applications of Graphs, Y. Alavi and D. R. Lick, eds., Springer Verlag, Berlin (1976), pp. 426-441.
13. J. B. Saxe, "Dynamic Programming Algorithms for Recognizing Small Bandwidth Graphs", SIAM J. Algebra and Discrete Math. (1980).
14. L. Stockmeyer, personal communication to M. R. Garey and D. S. Johnson, (1974), cited in Computers and Intractability: A Guide to the Theory of NP-completeness, Freeman Publ. (1979).
15. S. Trimberg, "Automating Chip Layout", IEEE Spectrum (1982), pp. 38-45.
16. A. Weinberger, "Large Scale Integration of MOS Complex Logic: A Layout Method", IEEE J. Solid State Circuits, SC-2 (1967), pp. 182-190.
17. H. Yoshizawa, H. Kawanishi, and K. Kani, "A Heuristic Procedure for Ordering MOS Arrays", Design Automation Conference (1975), pp. 384-393.

PROVING PRECEDENCE PROPERTIES:
THE TEMPORAL WAY

ZOHAR MANNA
Computer Science Department
Stanford University
Stanford, CA
and
Applied Mathematics Department
The Weizmann Institute of Science
Rehovot, Israel

AMIR PNUELI
Applied Mathematics Department
The Weizmann Institute of science
Rehovot, Israel

Abstract:

The paper explores the three important classes of temporal properties of concurrent programs: invariance, liveness and precedence. It presents the first methodological approach to the precedence properties, while providing a review of the invariance and liveness properties. The approach is based on the ***unless*** operator $\mathcal{U}$, which is a weak version of the ***until*** operator U. For each class of properties, we present a single complete proof principle.

This research was supported in part by the National Science Foundation under grants MCS79-09495 and MCS80-06930, by DARPA under Contract N00039-82-C-0250, by the United States Air Force Office of Scientific Research under Grant AFOSR-81-0014, and by the Basic Research Foundation of the Israeli Academy of Sciences.

1. INTRODUCTION

In studying temporal properties of programs, i.e., properties that go beyond partial correctness, an obvious hierarchy of such properties can be developed. One way of classifying the different sets in this hierarchy is by the syntax of the temporal formulas expressing them.

The first set in this hierarchy is the class of ***invariance*** properties (***safety*** in the terminology of [L1]). These are the properties that can be expressed in terms of a formula of the form:

$$\Box\psi \quad \text{or} \quad \varphi \supset \Box\psi.$$

A formula of the first form, stated for a program P, says that every computation of P continuously satisfies ψ. In the case of the second form, the formula says that whenever φ is true, ψ is immediately realized and will hold continuously throughout the rest of the computation. Properties falling into this class include partial correctness, clean behavior (error freedom), mutual exclusion, and deadlock absence.

The second set in the hierarchy of properties is the class of ***liveness*** properties (***eventualities*** in the terminology of [MP1]). These are properties that are expressible by temporal formulas of the form:

$$\Diamond\psi \quad \text{or} \quad \varphi \supset \Diamond\psi.$$

In both forms these formulas guarantee the occurrence of some event ψ, in the first case unconditionally and in the second case conditionally on an earlier occurrence of the event φ. Among the properties falling into this class are: total correctness, termination, accessibility, lack of individual starvation, and responsiveness.

While most of the researchers in the field tend to agree that these two classes are the first two rungs in a natural hierarchy, there is less of a consensus about what should be the next step in the hierarchy. In previous work we have proposed that the next class to be studied is that of *precedence* properties. In a broad sense, precedence properties are all the properties that are expressible using the *until* operator $\mathcal{U}$. To remind the reader, the expression $p\mathcal{U}q$, read "p until q", means that eventually q must happen and between now and then p must continuously hold.

A more mathematical formulation of this definition is given by:

Let $\sigma = s_0, s_1, s_2, \ldots$ be a sequence of states, then $p\mathcal{U}q$ is true for σ if there exists a $j \geq 0$ such that:

$$q \text{ is true for the sequence } s_j,\ s_{j+1},\ s_{j+2},\ \ldots$$

(if q is a state property then q holds at s_j), and for every i, $0 \leq i < j$:

$$p \text{ is true for the sequence } s_i,\ s_{i+1},\ s_{i+2},\ \ldots$$

(if p is a state property then p holds at s_i). Here, a state property is a property that depends only on the state and not on the full sequence. Note that in the special case that $j = 0$, then q is true on σ and no requirements for p are implied.

A derived operator is the *precede* operator $\mathcal{P}$ that can be defined by:

$$p\mathcal{P}q \ \equiv\ \sim((\sim p)\mathcal{U}q).$$

The meaning of this operator is that "p precede q", i.e., if q ever happens it cannot happen unless p occurs first (strictly before q). In contrast to $p\mathcal{U}q$ which requires that q eventually happens, $p\mathcal{P}q$ is automatically satisfied if q never happens.

We often use nested *until* expressions of the form

$$p_1\mathcal{U}(p_2\mathcal{U}(p_3\mathcal{U}\ldots(p_k\mathcal{U}q)\ldots)),$$

where $p_1, \ldots, p_k, q$ are state properties, i.e., formulas dependent only on the state and containing no temporal operators. By careful examination of the semantic definition of the until operator we arrive at the interpretation that, stated at t_0, this expression means that there exist instants $t_1, \ldots, t_k$,

$$t_0 \leq t_1 \leq t_2 \leq \ldots \leq t_k,$$

such that:

p_1 holds in every t, $t_0 \leq t < t_1$

p_2 holds in every t, $t_1 \leq t < t_2$

$\vdots$

p_k holds in every t, $t_{k-1} \leq t < t_k$, and

q holds in t_k.

Thus, this expression predicts a period of continuous p_1 followed by a period of continuous p_2, and so on, until a period of continuous p_k, followed by an occurrence of q. Note that any of these periods may be empty by having $t_i = t_{i+1}$ for an empty $(i+1)$st period.

Since we are interested only in nested *until* expressions where the nesting is in the second argument, we can omit the parentheses and represent the expression above by:

$$p_1\mathcal{U}p_2\mathcal{U}p_3\ldots p_k\mathcal{U}q.$$

The class of precedence properties that we consider are therefore formulas of one of the forms:

$p \supset (q\mathcal{P}r)$ — a *precede* formula

$p \supset (p_1 \mathcal{U} p_2 \mathcal{U} \ldots p_k \mathcal{U} q)$ — an *until* formula.

Several interesting properties fall into the broad class of precedence properties.

Example:

Let us consider a program G (granter) serving as an allocator of a single resource between several processes (requesters) $R_1, \ldots, R_k$ competing for the resource. Let each R_i communicate with G by means of two boolean variables: r_i and g_i. The variable r_i is set to *true* by the requester R_i to signal a request for the resource. Once R_i has the resource it signals its release by setting r_i to *false*. The allocator G signals R_i that the resource is granted to him by setting g_i to *true*. Having obtained a release signal from R_i, which is indicated by $r_i = \mathit{false}$, some time later, it will reappropriate the resource by setting g_i to *false*.

Several obvious and important properties of this system belong to the invariance and liveness classes. For instance, the property

$$\Box\left(\left(\Sigma_{i=1}^{k} g_i\right) \leq 1\right),$$

ensuring that the resource is granted to at most one requester at a time, is an invariant property. In summing boolean variables we treat *true* as 1 and *false* as 0. Similarly, the important property

$$r_i \supset \Diamond g_i,$$

which ensures ***responsiveness***, is a liveness property. It guarantees that every request r_i will eventually be granted by setting g_i to *true*.

Let us, however, consider some precedence properties which are relevant to the specification of such a system.

(a) ***Absence of Unsolicited Response.***

An important but often overlooked desired feature is that the resource will not be granted to a party who has not requested it. (A similar property in the context of a communication network is that every message received must have been sent by somebody.) This is expressible by the temporal formula

$$\sim g_i \supset (r_i \mathcal{P} g_i).$$

The formula states that if presently g_i is false, i.e., R_i does not presently have the resource, then before the resource will be granted to R_i the next time, R_i must signal a request by setting r_i to *true*.

(b) ***Strict (FIFO) Responsiveness.***

Sometimes the weak commitment of eventually responding to a request is not sufficient. At the other extreme we may insist that responses are ordered in a sequence parallelling the order of arrival of the corresponding requests. Thus if requester R_i succeeded in placing his request before requester R_j the grant to R_i should precede the grant to R_j. A straightforward translation of this sentence yields the following intuitive but slightly imprecise expression:

$$(r_i \mathcal{P} r_j) \supset (g_i \mathcal{P} g_j).$$

A more precise expression which also better conforms to the general form of the class of properties we discuss in this paper is:

$$(r_i \wedge \sim r_j \wedge \sim g_j) \supset (\sim g_j \mathcal{U} g_i).$$

It states that if we ever find ourselves in a situation where r_i is presently on, and r_j and g_j are both off, then we are guaranteed to eventually get a g_i, and until that moment, no grant will be made to R_j. Note that $r_i \wedge \sim r_j$ implies that R_i's request preceded R_j's request, which has not materialized yet. We implicitly rely here on the assumption that once a request has been made it is not withdrawn until the request has been honored.

This assumption can also be made explicit as part of the specification, using another precedence expression:

$$r_i \supset g_i \mathcal{P}(\sim r_i).$$

Note that while all the earlier properties are requirements from the granter, and should be viewed as the "post-condition" part of the specification, this requirement is the responsibility of the requesters. It can be viewed as part of the "pre-condition" of the specification. Without this assumption, we could not hope to implement the granter in any reasonable way, since it would have to respond to very short and intermittent requests.

(c) *Bounded Overtaking.*

The requirement of *FIFO* responsiveness may sometimes be too restrictive and difficult to implement. Any program for the allocator that scans the requests in a certain polling order, $r_1, \ldots, r_k$ and then back to r_1 may respond to requests in, say, the order of their ***detection*** by the program. This order may be different from the arrival order. A more realistic requirement would allow deviations from the *FIFO* discipline, provided they are bounded. For example 1-bounded overtaking would say that for every i and j such that r_i preceded r_j, we may allow g_j to precede g_i at most ***once***. *FIFO* responsiveness may then be regarded as 0-bounded overtaking. In order to express k-bounded overtaking we have to use nested until expressions.

The 1-overtaking property can be expressed by a nested ***until*** expression:

$$(r_i \wedge \sim r_j) \supset (\sim g_j)\mathcal{U} g_j \mathcal{U} (\sim g_j)\mathcal{U} g_i.$$

This expression predicts a period in which R_j does not have the resource, followed by a continuous period in which R_j has got the resource, followed by a period in which R_j does not have the resource, followed by a grant of the resource to R_i. Since any of these periods may be empty, the formula actually states that in the ***worst case***, R_j may gain the resource at most ***once*** before R_i. ┘

Proofs of invariance properties for concurrent programs, have been extensively discussed in the literature (e.g., [OG], [K],[L1], [MP2]). Fewer suggestions have been made for approaches to proving liveness properties (e.g., [OL], [MP2], [MP3]).

In this work we address the problem of verifying properties of the precedence class. Our main conclusion is that the verification of precedence properties does not call for radically new ideas and can actually be viewed as a generalization of the approaches suggested for invariance and liveness properties. In fact, ***precede*** formulas are in many respects generalization of invariance properties, whereas ***until*** formulas can be established by a generalization of the proof principles for liveness properties.

To provide a proper framework, we first introduce an abstract operational model of concurrent programs. We then outline a proof system based on temporal logic; the system has been shown in [MP5] to be relatively complete for proving all properties of concurrent programs. We then discuss some derived proof principles that are tailored directly for the verification of precedence properties. The utility of these principles is demonstrated by proving several examples. A fuller account of this approach that also presents a decision procedure for checking precedence properties over finite state programs appear in [MP6].

2. A COMPUTATIONAL MODEL

We start by defining an abstract computational model; the temporal logic properties will be stated and proven for computations over this model.

The abstract model consists of the following elements:

$\mathcal{S}$ — A set of *computation states*. This is a possibly infinite set. Every element $s \in \mathcal{S}$ represents the full configuration of the computing system; for concrete programs each state includes the values of all the program variables as well as the program pointers for all the processes.

θ — The *initiality predicate*. We will only consider computations originating in a state s_0 such that $\theta(s_0)$ holds.

T — A finite set of *transitions*. With each transition $\tau \in T$ we associate a partial function $f_\tau : \mathcal{S} \rightarrow 2^{\mathcal{S}}$, where $f_\tau(s)$ yields all the possible outcomes of the transition τ on the state $s \in \mathcal{S}$. A transition $\tau \in T$ is said to be *enabled* on a state s if $f_\tau(s) \neq \phi$; otherwise it is called *disabled* on s. A state s such that no transition $\tau \in T$ is enabled on it is called *terminal.*

$\mathcal{J}$ — The *justice family*. This is a (possibly empty) family of sets of transitions $\mathcal{J} = \{T_1^J, \ldots, T_k^J\}$. Each set in $\mathcal{J}$, $T_i^J \subset T$, is called a *justice set* and a justice requirement defined below is to be applid to the set T_i^J.

$\mathcal{F}$ — The *fairness family*. This is a (possibly empty) family of sets of transitions $\mathcal{F} = \{T_1^F, \ldots, T_\ell^F\}$. Each set in $\mathcal{F}$, $T_j^F \subset T$, is called a *fairness set* and a fairness requirement is to be applied to T_j^F.

An *initialized computation* of such a system is a sequence of states with labelled transitions:

$$\sigma: \quad s_0 \xrightarrow{\tau_1} s_1 \xrightarrow{\tau_2} s_2 \xrightarrow{\tau_3} \ldots \quad \text{where } \tau_i \in T,$$

which satisfies the following requirements:

- *Maximality.* The sequence σ is maximal, i.e., either it is infinite or the last state s_k is terminal.
- *Initiality.* The first state s_0 satisfies the initiality predicate, i.e., $\theta(s_0) = \textit{true}$.
- *State-to-State transition.* For each step $s_i \xrightarrow{\tau_{i+1}} s_{i+1}$ in σ we have that $s_{i+1} \in f_{\tau_{i+1}}(s_i)$.
- *Justice.* For each $T^J \in \mathcal{J}$ we impose a *justice requirement*:
  - σ is finite, or
  - σ is infinite and contains an infinite number of states on which no transition in T^J is enabled, or
  - an infinite number of σ-steps are labelled by transitions in T^J.

  This corresponds to the notion that if for all states from a certain point on, some transition in T^J (not necessarily always the same) is always enabled, then some transition of T^J will be taken infinitely many times.
- *Fairness.* For each $T^F \in \mathcal{F}$ we impose a *fairness requirement*:
  - σ is finite, or
  - σ is infinite and from a certain point on no transition of T^F is enabled, or
  - some transition of T^F is taken infinitely many times.

  This corresponds to the notion that if some transitions from T^F are enabled infinitely many times then some transitions from T^F are activated infinitely many times.

An *admissible computation* is any suffix of an initialized computation.

When considering a concrete computational system, we have to identify the five elements described above with more concrete objects. Since our example is based on a shared-variables computational model, we proceed with such identification for the *shared-variables system*. Such a system has the form:

$$\overline{y} := g(\overline{x});\ [P_1 \parallel \cdots \parallel P_m],$$

where $\bar{y} = (y_1, \ldots, y_n)$ are the program (shared) variables, $\bar{x} = (x_1, \ldots, x_\ell)$ are the input variables, and $P_1, \ldots, P_m$ are the concurrent processes of the program. Each P_i is represented by a transition graph with nodes (locations) $L_i = (\ell_0^i, \ldots, \ell_t^i)$ and directed edges $E_i = \{e_1^i, \ldots, e_r^i\}$. The locations ℓ_0^i are the *entry* locations of P_i, respectively. Each edge $e \in E_i$ is labelled by an instruction:

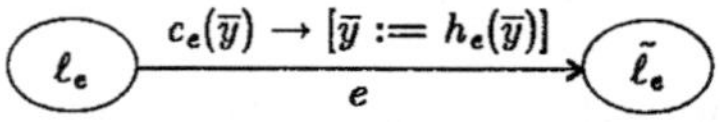

whose meaning is that when $c_e(\bar{y})$ is true, execution may proceed from ℓ_e to $\tilde{\ell}_e$ while assigning the values $h_e(\bar{y})$ to the variables $\bar{y}$. Special cases are the semaphore instructions *request*(y) and *release*(y), equivalent to $(y > 0) \rightarrow [y := y - 1]$ and $true \rightarrow [y := y + 1]$, respectively. We refer the reader to [MP1] for a more detailed discussion of these models.

A program state for this system has the form:

$$\langle \ell^1, \ldots, \ell^m; \; \eta_1, \ldots, \eta_n \rangle,$$

where each $\ell^i \in L_i$ denotes the current location of the execution in the process P_i, and each $\eta_j \in D$ is the current value of the program variable y_j. (The variables $\bar{y}$ are assumed to range over some domain D.) Thus we identify the set of all states $\mathcal{S}$ as the set of all $(m+n)$-tuples $(L_1 \times \cdots \times L_m \times D^n)$.

The initiality predicate is given by:

$$\theta(\ell^1, \ldots, \ell^m; \; \bar{y}) : \quad [\bigwedge_{i=1}^{m} (\ell^i = \ell_0^i)] \; \wedge \; (\bar{y} = g(\bar{x}))$$

ensuring that all the processes are at their initial locations and the values of the program variables are properly initialized.

The set of transitions $\mathcal{T}$ is identified with the set of all edges $\bigcup_{i=1}^{m} E_i$. For $\tau = e \in E_i$ we define

$$(\tilde{\ell}^1, \ldots, \tilde{\ell}^m; \; \tilde{\eta}) \; \in \; f_\tau(\ell^1, \ldots, \ell^m; \; \bar{\eta})$$

if and only if

$$\ell^i = \ell_e, \quad \tilde{\ell}^i = \tilde{\ell}_e, \quad \tilde{\ell}^j = \ell^j \text{ for every } j \neq i\,, \quad c_e(\bar{\eta}) = true \quad \text{and} \quad \tilde{\eta} = h_e(\bar{\eta}).$$

The justice family is given by:

$$\mathcal{J} \;=\; \{E_1, \ldots, E_m\};$$

that is, we require that justice be applied to each *process* individually. This implies that in any infinite computation, each process that has not terminated yet will eventually be scheduled.

The fairness family is given by:

$$\mathcal{F} \;=\; \{\{e\} \mid e \text{ is labelled by a } request(y) \text{ instruction}\}.$$

Thus, each semaphore transition is to be individually treated fairly. This implies that a *request*(y) instruction which is waiting while y turns positive infinitely many times must eventually be performed.

In considering computations of a program as models for temporal formulas that express properties of the program, we define the model $\tilde{\sigma}$ corresponding to a sequence σ,

$$\sigma : \quad s_0 \xrightarrow{\tau_1} s_1 \xrightarrow{\tau_2} s_2 \xrightarrow{\tau_3} \ldots,$$

as follows: If σ is infinite then the corresponding model is

$$\tilde{\sigma} : \quad s_0, \; s_1, \; s_2, \; \ldots .$$

In the case that σ is finite and its last state is the terminal state s_k, we take $\tilde{\sigma}$ to be

$$\tilde{\sigma}: \quad s_0, s_1, \ldots, s_k, s_k, \ldots ,$$

that is, the last state repeats forever.

3. THE PROOF SYSTEM

The proof system consists of three parts.

- Part A, called the *general part*, formalizes the pure temporal logic properties of sequences in general. It is completely independent of the particular program analyzed.
- Part B, called the *domain-dependent* part, formalizes the properties of the domain over which the program operates, such as integers, reals, strings, lists, trees, etc.
- Part C is the *program-dependent* part. It provides a formalization of the properties that result from restricting our attention to the computational sequences of the particular program being analyzed.

We refer the reader to [MP4], [MP5] for a discussion of parts A and B. Here we only repeat part C which we further develop in order to prove precedence properties.

The program-dependent part consists of four axiom schemes corresponding to the four requirements imposed on admissible computations. In the following, a *state formula* is a formula containing no temporal operators and hence interpretable on a single state.

Let φ and ψ be two state formulas. We say that a transition τ *leads from* φ *to* ψ if for every two states s and s' the following is true:

$$\varphi(s) \wedge \big(s' \in f_\tau(s)\big) \ \Rightarrow\ \psi(s').$$

Note that this formula is classical, i.e., contains no temporal operators and should be expressible and provable in the first-order theory over the domain.

For example, in the case of the shared-variables computation model a transition τ would correspond to an edge e in some process P_i:

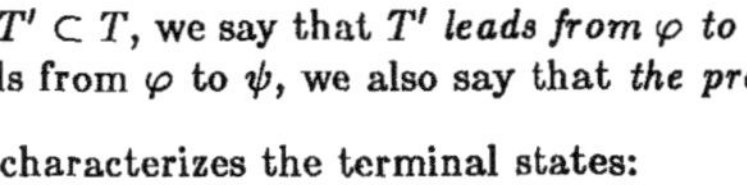

so that the condition above is expressible as

$$\varphi(\ell^1, \ldots, \ell^i, \ldots, \ell^m;\ \overline{y}) \wedge c(\overline{y}) \quad \Rightarrow \quad \psi(\ell^1, \ldots, \tilde{\ell}^i, \ldots, \ell^m;\ h(\overline{y})).$$

Given a subset of transitions $T' \subset T$, we say that T' *leads from* φ *to* ψ if every transition $\tau \in T'$ leads from φ to ψ. If the full set T leads from φ to ψ, we also say that *the program* P *leads from* φ *to* ψ.

The state formula *Terminal*, characterizes the terminal states:

$$Terminal(s) \quad = \quad \bigwedge_{\tau \in T} (f_\tau(s) = \phi).$$

Also, for a subset T' of transitions, the state formula *Enabled* characterizes the enabled transitions in T':

$$Enabled(T')(s) \quad = \quad \bigvee_{\tau \in T'} [f_\tau(s) \neq \phi].$$

Both formulas are expressible by a quantifier-free first-order formula.

Following are the inference rules of the program part:

(INIT) For an arbitrary temporal formula w

$$\frac{\vdash\ \Theta \supset \Box w}{\vdash\ \Box w}$$

This rule states that if w is an invariant for all initialized computations it is also an invariant for all admissible computations. This is because every admissible computation is a suffix of an initialized computation, and a property of the form $\Box w$ is hereditary from a sequence to all of its suffixes.

(TRNS) Let φ and ψ be two state formulas

$$\frac{\begin{array}{l}\vdash\ \text{Every } \tau \in T \text{ leads from } \varphi \text{ to } \psi \\ \vdash\ (\varphi \wedge \mathit{Terminal}) \supset \psi\end{array}}{\vdash\ \varphi \supset \bigcirc \psi}$$

The first premise ensures that as long as at least one transition is enabled, then if the current state satisfies φ, the next state must satisfy ψ. The second premise handles the case that all transitions are disabled, i.e., that of a terminal state. In a computation this means that no further action is possible and the next state is identical to the present. Hence this premise also ensures that in such a case the next state will satisfy ψ.

(JUST) Let φ and ψ be two state formulas, and $T^J \in \mathcal{J}$ a justice set

$$\frac{\begin{array}{l}\vdash\ \text{Every } \tau \in T \text{ leads from } \varphi \text{ to } \varphi \vee \psi \\ \vdash\ \text{Every } \tau \in T^J \text{ leads from } \varphi \text{ to } \psi\end{array}}{\vdash\ [\varphi \wedge \Box \mathit{Enabled}(T^J)] \supset \varphi \mathcal{U} \psi}$$

To justify this rule, consider a computation σ such that $\varphi \wedge \Box\mathit{Enabled}(T^J)$ holds for σ but $\varphi \mathcal{U} \psi$ does not hold. By the first premise, once φ holds it can only stop holding when ψ happens. Hence $\varphi \mathcal{U} \psi$ may fail to hold only if ψ never happens and φ is true forever. Since we assumed that T^J is continuously enabled on σ, some transition in T^J must eventually be activated, and this in a state satisfying φ. Hence, by the second premise, once this transition is activated, it achieves ψ, contrary to our assumption.

A similar rule applies to fairness:

(FAIR) Let φ and ψ be two state formulas, and $T^F \in \mathcal{F}$ a fairness set

$$\frac{\begin{array}{l}\vdash\ \text{Every } \tau \in T \text{ leads from } \varphi \text{ to } \varphi \vee \psi \\ \vdash\ \text{Every } \tau \in T^F \text{ leads from } \varphi \text{ to } \psi\end{array}}{\vdash\ [\varphi \wedge \Box \Diamond \mathit{Enabled}(T^F)] \supset \varphi \mathcal{U} \psi}$$

The justification is similar to that of the JUST rule.

In the following discussion we will consider computations only under the assumption of justice. This amounts to considering an empty fairness family $\mathcal{F} = \phi$. In the shared-variables computation system this means that we consider programs without semaphores. The reintroduction of fairness to the following analysis can be done in a straightforward manner.

In [MP5] the set of the rules above has been shown to be relatively complete. By this we mean that an arbitrary property which is valid for a given program, can be proved using these rules, provided the pure logic and domain dependent parts are strong enough to prove all valid properties. This result implies that the program dependent part is adequate for establishing all the properties that are true for admissible computations. However, while giving full generality, these rules do not provide specific guidance for proving properties of the three important classes that we have discussed: invariance, liveness and precedence.

We will proceed to develop derived rules, one for each class. These rules, while being derivable in the general system, have the advantage of being complete for their classes. By this we mean, that every valid property in the class can be proved using a *single* application of the proposed rule as the only temporal step. All the premises to the rule are first-order over the domain. Thus, for anyone who is interested only in proving properties of these classes, the respective rules are the only temporal proof rules he may ever need, dispensing for example with the general temporal logic part.

We will illustrate these rules on a single example — an algorithm for mutual exclusion (Fig. 0) — taken from [Pe]. The program consists of two concurrent processes, P_1 and P_2 that compete on the access to their critical regions, presented by ℓ_3 and m_3 respectively. Entry into the critical regions is expected to be exclusive, i.e., at no time can P_1 be at ℓ_3 while at the same time P_2 is at m_3. The processes communicate by means of the shared-variables y_1, y_2, t. Process P_i sets y_i $(i = 1, 2)$ to T whenever he is interested in entering his critical region. He then proceeds to set t to i. Following, he reaches a waiting state (ℓ_2 or m_2, respectively). There he waits until either $y_{\bar{i}} = F$ (here $\bar{i}$ is the competing process, i.e., $\bar{1} = 2$ and $\bar{2} = 1$) or $t = \bar{i}$. In the first case he infers that the competitor is not currently interested. In the second case he infers that $P_{\bar{i}}$ is interested but has arrived to his waiting state *after* P_i did, since $P_{\bar{i}}$ was the *last* to set t to $\bar{i}$. In any of these cases P_i enters his critical region. Once he finishes his business there he exits while setting y_i to F, indicating loss of interest in further entries for the present.

This description is of course intuitive and informal. The following discussions will provide more formal proofs of the correctness of the algorithm.

4. INVARIANCE PROPERTIES

A single rule which is complete for this class is:

(INV) — Invariance Rule

Let φ and ψ be state properties

A. $\vdash \; \theta \supset \varphi$

B. $\vdash$ Every $\tau \in T$ leads from φ to φ

C. $\vdash \; \varphi \supset \psi$

$\vdash \; \Box\psi$

A slightly more elaborate rule can similarly be used to establish properties of the form $\varphi \supset \Box\psi$.

Since the rule is derivable from the INIT and TRNS rules above, it is certainly sound.

To argue that it is complete for properties of the form $\Box\psi$, let ψ be a state property such that $\Box\psi$ is true for all computations. Define the predicate:

$$Acc(s) \;=\; \{\text{There exists an initialized computation segment } s_0 \xrightarrow{\tau_1} s_1 \xrightarrow{\tau_2} \ldots \xrightarrow{\tau_k} s_k = s\}.$$

Thus, $Acc(s)$ is true for a state s iff there exists an initialized computation having s as one of its states. We have defined $Acc(s)$ in words rather than by a formula; however, if the underlying domain is rich enough to contain, say, the integers, then this predicate is expressible by a first-order formula over the domain.

We now apply the INV rule with $\varphi = Acc$. Certainly $\theta \supset Acc$, since every state s_0 satisfying θ participates in a computation: $s_0 \to s_1 \to \; \ldots$. It is also easy to see that if s is accessible and $s' \in f_\tau(s)$ then s' is also accessible. This establishes premise B. Premise C says that every accessible state satisfies

ψ, but this follows from our assumption that $\square\psi$ is true on all admissible computations. Consequently the INV rule is always applicable.

Let us consider some invariance properties for the mutual exclusiion program (Fig. 0) presented above.

$I_0:\quad \vdash\ \square((t=1)\vee(t=2))$

Note that for this program

$$\theta:\quad at\,\ell_0\ \wedge\ at\,m_0\ \wedge\ [(y_1,y_2,t)=(F,F,1)].$$

Take $\varphi\ =\ \psi\ =\ (t=1)\vee(t=2)$. It is easy to verify that $\theta\supset\varphi$ since θ implies $t=1$. Similarly by inspecting every transition we see that all of them maintain φ.

$I_1:\quad \vdash\ \square(y_1\equiv\ell_{1..3})$

The proposition $\ell_{1..3}$ is defined as $at\,\ell_1\vee at\,\ell_2\vee at\,\ell_3$, i.e., it holds whenever P_1 is somewhere in $\{\ell_1,\ell_2,\ell_3\}$. Potentially falsifying transitions are:

$\ell_0\rightarrow\ell_1$: setting both y_1 and $\ell_{1..3}$ to T.

$\ell_3\rightarrow\ell_0$: setting both y_1 and $\ell_{1..3}$ to F.

All other transitions do not modify either y_1 or $\ell_{1..3}$.

$I_2:\quad \vdash\ \square(y_2\ \equiv\ m_{1..3})$.

This property is symmetric to I_1.

$I_3:\quad \vdash\ \square\{[\ell_2\ \wedge\ \sim m_2]\ \supset\ (t=1)\}$.

Note that initially ℓ_2 (i.e., $at\,\ell_2$) is false so that the implication is true. Potentially falsifying transitions are:

$\ell_1\rightarrow\ell_2$: sets t to 1.
$m_1\rightarrow m_2$: makes $\sim m_2$ false.
$m_2\rightarrow m_3$ while ℓ_2: by I_1, $y_1=T$ so this transition is possible only when $t=1$.

All other transitions trivially maintain the invariant.

$I_4:\quad \vdash\ \square\{[m_2\ \wedge\ \sim\ell_2]\ \supset\ (t=2)\}$.

Can be shown in a similar way.

We may now obtain the invariant ensuring mutual exclusion:

$I_5:\quad \vdash\ \square(\sim\ell_3\ \vee\ \sim m_3)$.

It is certainly true initially. The potentially falsifying transitions of this invariant are:

$\ell_2\rightarrow\ell_3$ while m_3: but then $y_2=T$ (by I_2) and $t=1$ (by I_3), so that this transition is impossible.

$m_2\rightarrow m_3$ while ℓ_3: impossible, because $y_1=T$ (by I_1) and $t=2$ (by I_4).

Thus mutual exclusion has been formally proved.

5. LIVENESS PROPERTIES

We start by developing a proof rule which is more convenient to apply than the JUST rule.

(J-EVNT) — The Just Eventuality Rule

Let φ and ψ be two state formulas and T^J a justice set

A. $\vdash$ Every $\tau\in T$ leads from φ to $\varphi\vee\psi$

B. $\vdash$ Every $\tau\in T^J$ leads from φ to ψ

C. $\vdash\ \varphi\supset(\psi\ \vee\ Enabled(T^J))$

$\vdash\ \varphi\supset\varphi\,\mathcal{U}\,\psi$

A similar rule exists for fairness. The rule can easily be derived from the JUST rule since by premise C every computation having in it a φ which is not followed by a ψ, will have T^J continuously enabled. This by the JUST rule implies $\varphi \mathcal{U} \psi$.

Let us apply the EVNT rule to our sample mutual exclusion program (Fig. 0). Take for example,

$$\varphi = \varphi_1 : \quad at\,\ell_2 \wedge at\,m_2 \wedge (t=2) \wedge (y_1 = T) \wedge (y_2 = T)$$

$$\psi = \varphi_0 : \quad at\,\ell_3$$

Clearly the only transitions enabled on a state satisfying φ_1 are $\ell_2 \to \ell_3$ and $m_2 \to m_2$. Consequently every transition leads from φ_1 to $\varphi_1 \vee \psi$. Taking T^J to be P_1, i.e., all transitions within P_1, we have premises A and B obviously satisfied. Also φ_1 implies that $\ell_2 \to \ell_3$ and hence P_1 is enabled. Thus we obtain $\vdash \varphi_1 \supset (\varphi_1 \mathcal{U} \varphi_0)$. From this we can certainly obtain

$$\vdash \varphi_1 \supset \Diamond \varphi_0$$

since $p \mathcal{U} q$ implies $\Diamond q$.

Next let us take

$$\varphi = \varphi_2 : \quad at\,\ell_2 \wedge at\,m_1 \wedge (y_1 = T) \wedge (y_2 = T)$$

$$\psi = \varphi_1 \vee \varphi_0 .$$

We now take T^J to be P_2. Certainly, the only transitions possibly enabled under φ_2 are $\ell_2 \to \ell_2$, $\ell_2 \to \ell_3$ and $m_1 \to m_2$. The first transition preserves φ_2. The second transition leads from φ_2 to φ_0. The third transition which is guaranteed to be enabled under φ_2, leads from φ_2 to φ_1. Thus every transition leads from φ_2 to $\varphi_1 \vee \varphi_0$. We conclude $\vdash \varphi_2 \supset \Diamond(\varphi_1 \vee \varphi_0)$. From this we may conclude by temporal reasoning and the previously established $\vdash \varphi_1 \supset \Diamond \varphi_0$ that

$$\vdash \varphi_2 \supset \Diamond \varphi_0 .$$

We may proceed and define additional φ_j, $j = 3, \ldots, 6$, such that for each j, $\vdash \varphi_j \supset \Diamond(\bigvee_{k<j} \varphi_k)$ which eventually leads to $\vdash \varphi_j \supset \Diamond \varphi_0$. This proof strategy of constructing a finite chain of assertions, each eventually leading to an assertion of lower index can be summarized by:

(CHAIN) — The Chain Reasoning Proof Principle

Let $\varphi_0, \varphi_1, \ldots, \varphi_r$ be a sequence of state formulas.

A. $\vdash$ Every $\tau \in T$ leads from φ_i to $\bigvee_{j \le i} \varphi_j$,

B. For every $i > 0$ there exists a justice set $T^J = T_i^J$ such that
$\vdash$ Every $\tau \in T_i^J$ leads from φ_i to $\bigvee_{j<i} \varphi_j$

C. For every $i > 0$ and T_i^J as above:
$\vdash \varphi_i \supset [(\bigvee_{j<i} \varphi_j) \vee \mathit{Enabled}(T_i^J)]$

$$\vdash (\bigvee_{i=0}^{r} \varphi_i) \supset \Diamond \varphi_0$$

The scheme of a proof according to the CHAIN principle is best presented in a form of a diagram. In this diagram we have a node for each φ_i. For each transition τ leading from a state satisfying φ_i to a state satisfying φ_j with $j \neq i$ (and hence by A, $j < i$) we draw an edge from φ_i to φ_j. This edge is labelled by the appropriate justice set to which the transition belongs. Edges belonging to the justice set which is known by premise C to be enabled in φ_i are drawn as double edges. For example, Fig. 1 contains a proof diagram for proving $\vdash at\,\ell_1 \supset \Diamond\, at\,\ell_3$ for the mutual exclusion program. By the CHAIN rule we actually proved $\vdash \left(\bigvee_{i=0}^{6}\varphi_i\right) \supset \Diamond\, at\,\ell_3$, but since φ_6 is $at\,\ell_1$ this establishes the desired result. The diagram representation of the CHAIN rule resembles closely the proof lattice advocated in [OL] for proving liveness properties.

In the application of the CHAIN rule we may freely use any previously derived invariances of the program. Thus, if $\vdash \Box I$ is any previously derived invariance, we may use $\varphi_i \wedge I$ instead of φ_i to establish any of the premises. This amounts to considering the sequence $\varphi_0 \wedge I, \ \ldots, \varphi_r \wedge I$ instead of the original sequence of assertions. Thus in the diagram (Fig. 1) we did not have an assertion corresponding to (ℓ_3, m_3) since by the previously established invariances such a situation is impossible, in particular no transition could lead from $I \wedge \varphi_4$ to (ℓ_3, m_3). Similarly no transition from (ℓ_2, m_1) to ℓ_3 has been drawn in view of I_3.

The chain reasoning principle assumed a finite number of links in the chain. It is quite adequate for finite state programs, i.e., programs where the variables range over finite domains. However, once we consider programs over infinite domains, such as the integers, it is no longer sufficient to consider only finitely many assertions. In fact, sets of assertions of quite high cardinality are needed. The obvious generalization to infinite sets of assertions is to consider a single state assertion $\varphi(\alpha, s)$, parametrized by a parameter α taken from a well-founded ordered set $(\mathcal{A}, \prec)$. Obviously, an important feature of our chain of assertions is that program transitions led from φ_i to φ_j with $j < i$. This property can also be stated for an arbitrary well-founded ordering. Thus a natural generalization of the chain reasoning rule is the following:

(WELL) — The Well Founded Liveness Principle

Let $(\mathcal{A}, \prec)$ be a well-founded ordered set.

Let $\varphi(\alpha) = \varphi(\alpha, s)$ be a parametrized state formula, and ψ a state formula.

Let $h : \mathcal{A} \rightarrow \mathcal{J}$ be a helpfulness function identifying for each $\alpha \in \mathcal{A}$ the helpful justice set $h(\alpha) \in \mathcal{J}$.

A. $\vdash$ Every transition $\tau \in T$ leads from
$$\varphi(\alpha) \quad \text{to} \quad \psi \vee \exists\beta((\beta \preceq \alpha) \wedge \varphi(\beta))$$

B. $\vdash$ Every transition $\tau \in h(\alpha)$ leads from
$$\varphi(\alpha) \quad \text{to} \quad \psi \vee \exists\beta((\beta \prec \alpha) \wedge \varphi(\beta))$$

C. $\vdash \varphi(\alpha) \supset [\psi \vee \exists\beta((\beta \prec \alpha) \wedge \varphi(\beta)) \vee Enabled(h(\alpha))]$

$$\vdash (\exists\alpha.\varphi(\alpha)) \supset \Diamond\psi$$

In order to obtain a complete rule for liveness properties we have to treat the parametrized assertion $\varphi(\alpha, s)$ as an auxiliary assertion:

(LIVE) — A Complete Principle for Liveness

Let p, q be state formulas and $\varphi(\alpha)$, ψ a parametrized assertion pair as in WELL.

Assume premises A, B, C as in WELL, and

D. $\vdash \Box p$, i.e., p is an invariant

E. $\vdash (q \wedge p) \supset (\exists\alpha.\varphi(\alpha))$

$$\vdash q \supset \Diamond\psi$$

We refer the reader to [LPS] for a completeness proof of the LIVE principle. Completeness here means that given two state properties q and ψ such that $q \supset \Diamond\psi$ is a valid statement over all the computations of the program P, it is always possible to find state predicates p, $\varphi(\alpha, s)$ with $\alpha \in \mathcal{A}$ and $(\mathcal{A}, \prec)$, h as in WELL that satisfy premises A to E. Note that premise D requires preliminary derivation of the invariance of p which can be done using the INV rule.

6. PRECEDENCE PROPERTIES

As a key operator in expressing and establishing precedence properties we take the weak until operator, $\mathfrak{U}$, to which we will refer here as the *unless operator.*

The *unless* operator may be defined in terms of the standard *until* operator as:

$$p \,\mathfrak{U}\, q \;\equiv\; \Box p \vee (p \,\mathcal{U}\, q).$$

Thus, in contrast to $p\mathcal{U}q$ it does not require that q eventually happen. But in the case that q never happens p is required to hold forever.

Even though it is introduced here as a derived operator, it can be adopted as the basic operator for establishing precedence properties. This is because both the *until* and *precede* operators can be expressed in terms of the *unless* operator:

$$p \,\mathcal{U}\, q \;\equiv\; (p \,\mathfrak{U} q) \wedge \Diamond q$$

$$p \,\mathcal{P}\, q \;\equiv\; (\sim q) \,\mathfrak{U} (p \wedge \sim q).$$

We can also express the nested *until* operator by considering the nested *unless* operator. Let ψ_r, ψ_{r-1}, $\ldots$, ψ_1, ψ_0 be a sequence of formulas then

$$\psi_r \,\mathfrak{U} \psi_{r-1} \,\mathfrak{U} \ldots \psi_1 \,\mathfrak{U} \psi_0 \;\equiv\; \psi_r \,\mathfrak{U} (\psi_{r-1} \,\mathfrak{U} (\ldots (\psi_1 \,\mathfrak{U} \psi_0))\ldots)$$

holds on a sequence $\sigma = s_0, s_1, \ldots$ if there exists a sequence of indices $0 = i_r \leq i_{r-1} \leq \ldots \leq i_1 \leq i_0 \leq \omega$ such that for every $\ell > 0$ and j, $i_\ell \leq j < i_{\ell-1}$, ψ_ℓ holds on

$$\sigma^{(j)} \;=\; s_j, s_{j+1}, \ldots$$

and if $i_0 < \omega$ then ψ_0 holds on $\sigma^{(i_0)}$. Note that some of the i_ℓ may be equal to one another, and also to ω in which case some of the ψ_ℓ hold in empty periods.

An alternative description is that $\psi_r \,\mathfrak{U} \ldots \psi_1 \,\mathfrak{U} \psi_0$ holds on σ iff either σ satisfies $\psi_r \mathcal{U} \ldots \psi_1 \mathcal{U} \psi_0$ or for some j, $0 < j \leq r$, σ satisfies $\psi_r \mathcal{U} \ldots \psi_{j+1} \mathcal{U} \Box \psi_j$. In the case $j = r$, σ satisfies $\Box \psi_r$.

Then we can express the nested *until* by an extension of the previous formula for a simple *until*:

$$\psi_r \mathcal{U} \psi_{r-1} \mathcal{U} \ldots \psi_1 \mathcal{U} \psi_0 \;\equiv\; (\psi_r \,\mathfrak{U} \psi_{r-1} \,\mathfrak{U} \ldots \psi_1 \,\mathfrak{U} \psi_0) \wedge \Diamond \psi_0.$$

Let us justify this equivalence. The direction in which the nested *until* implies the nested *unless* and the eventual ocurrence of ψ_0 is obvious. Let us therefore consider the other direction.

Assume that $\psi_r \,\mathfrak{U} \ldots \psi_1 \,\mathfrak{U} \psi_0$ and $\Diamond \psi_0$ both hold on a sequence σ. By the interpretation of nested *unless* there exists a partition:

$$0 = i_r \leq i_{r-1} \leq \ldots \leq i_1 \leq i_0 \leq \omega$$

such that ψ_ℓ holds between i_ℓ and $i_{\ell-1}$ for $\ell > 0$ and ψ_0 holds at i_0 if it is finite. Since ψ_0 must occur somewhere in σ let j be the minimal index such that ψ_0 holds on $\sigma^{(j)}$. If $j = i_0 < \omega$, then the same partition justifies $\psi_r \mathcal{U} \ldots \psi_1 \mathcal{U} \psi_0$ on σ. Otherwise there exists some ℓ such that $i_\ell \leq j < i_{\ell-1}$. In this case the partition up to i_ℓ and then j justifies $\psi_r \mathcal{U} \ldots \psi_\ell \mathcal{U} \psi_0$ from which

$$\psi_r \mathcal{U} \ldots \psi_\ell \mathcal{U} \psi_{\ell-1} \ldots \psi_1 \mathcal{U} \psi_0$$

follows by letting $\psi_{\ell-1}, \ldots, \psi_1$ hold over empty periods.

Thus, expressively at least, the *unless* operator seems to be an appropriately basic operator. But we claim that the choice of the *unless* operator is appropriate on proof theoretic grounds as well. By inspecting the expression of *until* formulas in terms of *unless* formulas we find a resemblance to the relation between the concepts of total and partial correctness. Total correctness, which is a liveness property, can be expressed as the conjunction of partial correctness, which is an invariance property, and termination, which is another liveness property but simpler than the original. In quite the same way we can express the *until* property as a conjunction of an *unless* property, which we regard as extended invariance property and the simpler liveness property $\Diamond \psi_0$.

In practice, if we want a single proof principle that will cover properties of the following three subclasses

(a) $\varphi \supset (p \,\mathcal{U}\, q)$

(b) $\varphi \supset (p \,\mathcal{P}\, q)$

(c) $\varphi \supset (p \,\mathfrak{U}\, q)$

then the *unless* operator is a good choice.

In order to establish (a) we establish separately

$$\vdash \ (\varphi \supset p \,\mathfrak{U}\, q) \qquad \text{and} \qquad \vdash \ \varphi \supset \Diamond q,$$

which are implied by (a). The first will be established by using the *unless* proof principle. The second is a liveness property and can be established by the WELL rule or its extensions.

Similarly in order to establish (b) it is sufficient to establish $\varphi \supset (\tilde{p} \,\mathfrak{U}\, \tilde{q})$ where $\tilde{p}$ is $\sim q$ and $\tilde{q}$ is $p \wedge \sim q$.

We could not have used the *until* operator in a similar role, i.e., reducing proofs of properties of the subclasses (b) and (c) to these of (a). This is for example because if $\varphi \supset (p \,\mathfrak{U}\, q)$ is a valid statement, then certainly so is $\varphi \supset (\Box p \vee (p \mathcal{U} q))$, but it does not imply that either $\varphi \supset \Box p$ or $\varphi \supset (p \mathcal{U} q)$ are valid statements. Proving *precede* statements would cause similar problems.

The fact that the weak form of the *until* operator is more basic than its strong form seems to have been intuitively sensed in [L2] where a *while* operator is introduced which is equivalent to $p \,\mathfrak{U} \sim q$.

Consequently, we will proceed by developing proof principles for the *unless* operator $\mathfrak{U}$. We begin by formulating a core rule:

> (CORE-U) — Core Rule for Unless Properties
>
> Let $\varphi_r, \varphi_{r-1}, \ldots, \varphi_0$ be state formulas
>
> A. For every $i > 0$,
>
> $\vdash$ Every $\tau \in T$ leads from φ_i to $\bigvee_{j \leq i} \varphi_j$
>
> ---
>
> $$\vdash \ \left(\bigvee_{i=0}^{r} \varphi_i\right) \supset (\varphi_r \,\mathfrak{U}\, \varphi_{r-1} \,\mathfrak{U}\, \ldots \varphi_1 \,\mathfrak{U}\, \varphi_0)$$

Let σ be a computation whose first state s_0 satisfies φ_j for some $0 \leq j \leq r$. Assume first that $j > 0$. Define $i_r = i_{r-1} = \ldots = i_j = 0$. By premise A, s_1 must satisfy some φ_ℓ for $\ell \leq j$. If $\ell = j$ we proceed until we find an s_k that satisfies φ_ℓ for $\ell < j$. If we never find such a state we may take $i_{j-1} = \ldots = i_0 = \omega$. Otherwise we take $i_{j-1} = \ldots = i_\ell = k$ and proceed similarly beyond s_k unless $\ell = 0$. This construction shows that if s_0 satisfies φ_j for some j then σ satisfies $\varphi_r \,\mathfrak{U} \ldots \mathfrak{U}\, \varphi_0$. The case $j = 0$ is even simpler.

We can make a complete rule out of the CORE-U rule by strengthening the preconditions and weakening the post conditions.

(UNLS) — Complete Rule for Unless Properties

Let $\varphi_r, \ldots, \varphi_0, \psi_r, \ldots, \psi_0, p, q$ be state formulas such that:

A. For every $i > 0$,

$\vdash$ Every $\tau \in T$ leads from $\varphi_i \wedge p$ to $\bigvee_{j \leq i} \varphi_j$

B. $\vdash \Box p$

C. $\vdash (q \wedge p) \supset (\bigvee_{i=0}^{r} \varphi_i)$

D. For every i, $0 \leq i \leq r$

$\vdash (\varphi_i \wedge p) \supset \psi_i$

$\vdash q \supset (\psi_r \,\mathcal{U}\, \psi_{r-1} \,\mathcal{U} \ldots \psi_1 \,\mathcal{U}\, \psi_0)$

Let us consider the application of this rule to the analysis of the mutual exclusion algorithm. We take (the φ_i's refer to the assertions in Fig. 1):

$q: \quad at\,\ell_2$

$\tilde{\varphi}_0 = \psi_0: \quad at\,\ell_3$

$\tilde{\varphi}_1 = \varphi_{1..3}: \quad \ell_2 \wedge [m_{0,1} \vee (m_2 \wedge (t = 2))]$

$\tilde{\varphi}_2 = \varphi_4: \quad \ell_2 \wedge m_3$

$\tilde{\varphi}_3 = \varphi_5: \quad \ell_2 \wedge m_2 \wedge (t = 1)$

$\psi_1 = \psi_3 = \sim m_3, \qquad \psi_2 = m_3$

p — the conjunction of all the invariants $I_0 \wedge \ldots \wedge I_5$

The diagram certainly establishes that $\tilde{\varphi}_i$, $i > 0$, leads to $\bigvee_{j \leq i} \tilde{\varphi}_j$.

It is also easy to show that $(q \wedge p) \supset (\bigvee_{i=1}^{3} \tilde{\varphi}_i)$ and that $\tilde{\varphi}_i \supset \psi_i$ for $i = 0, \ldots, 3$. Thus we may conclude:

$$\vdash \ell_2 \supset (\sim m_3 \,\mathcal{U}\, m_3 \,\mathcal{U} \sim m_3 \,\mathcal{U}\, \ell_3).$$

This establishes the property of 1-bounded overtaking from ℓ_2. This means that once P_1 is at ℓ_2, P_2 may be at m_3 at most once before P_1 gets to his critical section at ℓ_3.

An alternative derivation of the same result could have been achieved by taking the φ's in the rule to be identical to the φ's in the diagram. This leads to:

$$\vdash \ell_2 \supset (\varphi_5 \,\mathcal{U}\, \varphi_4 \,\mathcal{U}\, \varphi_3 \,\mathcal{U}\, \varphi_2 \,\mathcal{U}\, \varphi_1 \,\mathcal{U}\, \varphi_0).$$

We may now use the collapsing theorem for the *unless* operator:

$$(p \,\mathcal{U}\, q \,\mathcal{U}\, r) \supset ((p \vee q) \,\mathcal{U}\, r)$$

to obtain:

$$\vdash \ \ell_2 \supset (\varphi_5 \,\mathcal{U}\, \varphi_4 \,\mathcal{U}\, (\varphi_1 \vee \varphi_2 \vee \varphi_3) \,\mathcal{U}\, \varphi_0),$$

which is equivalent to the above after we replace each of the φ_i's by the weaker ψ_i.

Having obtained 1-bounded overtaking from the point that P_1 is at ℓ_2 we may inquire whether the same holds from the point that P_1 is at ℓ_1. As the analysis shows in Fig. 2 the best we can hope for is 2-bounded overtaking. The diagram in Fig. 2 establishes

$$\vdash \ \ell_1 \supset (\varphi_8 \,\mathcal{U}\, \varphi_{5..7} \,\mathcal{U}\, \varphi_4 \,\mathcal{U}\, \varphi_{1..3} \,\mathcal{U}\, \varphi_0)$$

from which 2-bounded overtaking is easily established.

7. COMPLETENESS OF THE UNLS RULE

Next we will show that the UNLS rule presented above is complete for establishing nested *unless* properties.

Proof:

Let q, $\psi_r, \ldots, \psi_0$ be state properties such that the statement $q \supset (\psi_r \,\mathcal{U}\, \psi_{r-1} \ldots \psi_1 \,\mathcal{U}\, \psi_0)$ is valid on all admissible computations. We will show that there exist state properties p, $\varphi_r, \ldots, \varphi_0$, which are first-order expressible over the integers, such that all the premises of the UNLS rule are satisfied.

As p we choose

$$p(s) \ \equiv \ Acc(s) \ \equiv \ \{\text{There exists an initialized computation containing } s\}.$$

Clearly p is an invariant of all admissible computations so that premise B is satisfied.

Let $\tilde{\sigma}$ be a finite segment of a computation, i.e., a finite sequence

$$\tilde{\sigma} \ = \ s_0 \xrightarrow{\tau_1} s_1 \xrightarrow{\tau_2} \ldots \xrightarrow{\tau_k} s_k$$

such that $s_{i+1} \in f_\tau(s_i)$ for each $i = 0, \ldots, k-1$.

We say that $\tilde{\sigma}$ satisfies a temporal formula w if $\tilde{\sigma}$'s infinite extension $s_0, s_1, \ldots, s_k, s_k, s_k, \ldots$ satisfies w.

Let σ be a computation satisfying $\psi_r \,\mathcal{U} \ldots \psi_1 \,\mathcal{U}\, \psi_0$. It can be verified that any finite prefix of σ is a computation segment that also satisfies $\psi_r \,\mathcal{U} \ldots \psi_1 \,\mathcal{U}\, \psi_0$.

Let us define now φ_i for $i = 0, 1, \ldots, r$ by $\varphi_i(s) = \textit{true}$ iff

- (a) Every computation segment originating at s satisfies $\psi_i \,\mathcal{U}\, \psi_{i-1} \ldots \psi_1 \,\mathcal{U}\, \psi_0$
- (b) The index i is the smallest index for which (a) holds.

Let us show that the sequence of φ_i's defined in this way satisfies premises A, C and D of the UNLS rule.

Consider first premise A. Let s be a state satisfying φ_i, for $i > 0$. Let s' be a state such that $s' \in f_\tau(s)$. Consider any computation segment originating in s':

$$\tilde{\sigma}' : \ \ s' \xrightarrow{\tau_1} s_1 \xrightarrow{\tau_2} \ldots \xrightarrow{\tau_k} s_k.$$

We can obtain from it a computation segment:

$$\tilde{\sigma}: \quad s \xrightarrow{\tau} s' \xrightarrow{\tau_1} s_1 \xrightarrow{\tau_2} \ldots \xrightarrow{\tau_k} s_k.$$

By our assumption about s, $\tilde{\sigma}$ must satisfy $\psi_i \mathcal{U} \ldots \mathcal{U} \psi_0$. It can be shown that due to $i > 0$, and the minimality of i this implies that $\tilde{\sigma}'$ must also satisfy $\psi_i \mathcal{U} \ldots \mathcal{U} \psi_0$. Thus we have identified at least one index, i, such that clause (a) is satisfied for i and s'. Let $j \geq 0$ now be the minimal index satisfying (a) for s'. Then (b) is also satisfied and we have that s' satisfies φ_j for $j \leq i$. This establishes premise A.

Next, consider premise C. Let s be a state satisfying q and p. It is therefore an accessible state satisfying q. By the assumption that $q \supset (\psi_r \mathcal{U} \ldots \mathcal{U} \psi_0)$ is a valid statement for all admissible computations, every computation originating in s saisfies $\psi_r \mathcal{U} \ldots \mathcal{U} \psi_0$. Consequently every computation segment originating in s satisfies $\psi_r \mathcal{U} \ldots \mathcal{U} \psi_0$. Thus, clause (a) of the definition of φ_i is satisfied for $i = r$. Let j be the minimal index satisfying clause (a). Then $\varphi_j(s)$ holds and $j \leq r$.

To show premise D, let s be a state saisfying φ_i. Consider first $i = 0$. The zero version of $\psi_i \mathcal{U} \ldots \mathcal{U} \psi_0$ is ψ_0 by itself. Since every finite computation segment originating in s must saisfy ψ_0 which is a state property, it follows that s satisfies ψ_0. Consider next, $i > 0$. Since i was the minimal index satisfying clause (a), there must exist a computation segment σ originating in s which satisfies $\psi_i \mathcal{U} \ldots \mathcal{U} \psi_0$ but not $\psi_{i-1} \mathcal{U} \ldots \mathcal{U} \psi_0$. Consequently the initial section of $\tilde{\sigma}$ satisfying ψ_i must be non-empty and therefore s must satisfy ψ_i. Thus, we have $\varphi_i \supset \psi_i$.

We claimed that the φ_i's defined above are first-order expressible over the integers. This is due to the fact that clause (a) refers only to *finite* computation segments. This is a direct consequence of the fact that we deal with the *unless* operator. No similar first-order definition is possible for the *until* operator.

8. DIRECT PROOFS OF UNTIL PROPERTIES

In spite of our recommendation of splitting a proof of *until* property into a proof of a similar *unless* property, followed by a liveness proof of $\Diamond \psi$, there are many cases in which an *until* property can be directly obtained by a small modification of the liveness proof. As we have seen both the CHAIN rule and the UNLS rule call for a sequence of assertions, such that the computation always lead from φ_i to φ_j with $j \leq i$. The CHAIN rule stipulates in addition a strict decrease under certain conditions. It is often the case that the same chain of assertions used in the CHAIN rule can be used to establish a nested *until*. In fact, in much the same way that we have justified the CHAIN rule we can with the same premises obtain a stronger result:

Taking $0 < p_1 < p_2 < \ldots < p_s = r$ be a partition of the index range $[0...r]$ into s contiguous segments, we may formulate the following chain principle for *until* properties:

(U-CHAIN) — The Chain Rule for Until Properties

Let $\varphi_0, \varphi_1, \ldots, \varphi_r$ be a sequence of state formulas, and $0 < p_1 < p_2 < \ldots < p_s = r$ a partition of $[1...r]$.

A. $\vdash$ Every $\tau \in T$ leads from φ_i to $(\bigvee_{j \leq i} \varphi_j)$ for $i = 1, \ldots, r$.

B. for every $i > 0$ there exists a justice set $T^J = T_i^J$ such that:

$\vdash$ Every $\tau \in T_i^J$ leads from φ_i to $(\bigvee_{j<i} \varphi_j)$

C. for $i > 0$ and T_i^J as above:

$\vdash \varphi_i \supset [(\bigvee_{j<i} \varphi_j) \vee \mathit{Enabled}(T_i^J)]$

$$\vdash (\bigvee_{i=0}^{r} \varphi_i) \supset \left[(\bigvee_{j=p_{s-1}+1}^{p_s} \varphi_j)\,\mathcal{U}\,(\bigvee_{j=P_{s-2}+1}^{p_{s-1}} \varphi_j)\,\mathcal{U} \ldots (\bigvee_{j=1}^{p_1} \varphi_j)\,\mathcal{U}\,\varphi_0\right]$$

The conclusion states that starting at a state that satisfies one of the φ_i's, $i = 0, \ldots, r$, we are guaranteed to have a period in which $(\bigvee_{j=p_{s-1}+1}^{p_s} \varphi_j)$ continuously hold, followed by a period in which $(\bigvee_{j=p_{s-2}+1}^{p_{s-1}} \varphi_j)$ continously holds, etc., until finally φ_0 is realized. Any of these periods may be empty.

To justify the soundness of this conclusion we first prove it for the most refined partition possible, namely:

$$(*) \qquad (\bigvee_{i=0}^{r} \varphi_i) \supset (\varphi_r \mathcal{U} \varphi_{r-1} \mathcal{U} \varphi_{r-2} \mathcal{U} \ldots \varphi_1 \mathcal{U} \varphi_0).$$

This is proved in a way similar to the justification of the corresponding liveness principle. We show by induction on n, $n = 0, 1, \ldots, r$, that

$$\vdash (\bigvee_{i=0}^{n} \varphi_i) \supset (\varphi_n \mathcal{U} \varphi_{n-1} \mathcal{U} \ldots \varphi_1 \mathcal{U} \varphi_0).$$

For $n = 0$ we have $\vdash \varphi_0 \supset \varphi_0$ from which follows trivially

$$\vdash \varphi_0 \supset \varphi_0 \mathcal{U} \varphi_0.$$

Assume that the statement $(*)$ above has been proved for a certain n and consider its proof for $n+1$.

Consider the EVNT rule with $\varphi = \varphi_{n+1}$, $\psi = (\bigvee_{i=1}^{n} \varphi_i)$. As shown in the proof of the liveness case all the premises of the EVNT rule are satisfied. Consequently we may conclude:

$$\vdash \varphi_{n+1} \supset \varphi_{n+1} \mathcal{U} (\bigvee_{i=1}^{n} \varphi_i).$$

By the induction hypothesis and the monotonicity of the $\mathcal{U}$ operator this yields

$$\vdash \varphi_{n+1} \supset (\varphi_{n+1} \mathcal{U} \varphi_n \mathcal{U} \ldots \varphi_1 \mathcal{U} \varphi_0).$$

Due to $\vdash v \supset (u \mathcal{U} v)$, the induction hypothesis can also be written as

$$\vdash \left(\bigvee_{i=0}^{n} \varphi_i\right) \supset (\varphi_{n+1} \mathcal{U} \varphi_n \mathcal{U} \ldots \varphi_1 \mathcal{U} \varphi_0).$$

Taking the disjunction of the last two statements gives

$$\vdash \left(\bigvee_{i=0}^{n+1} \varphi_i\right) \supset (\varphi_{n+1} \mathcal{U} \varphi_n \mathcal{U} \ldots \varphi_1 \mathcal{U} \varphi_0),$$

which is the required statement $(*)$ for $n+1$.

Consider now a coarser partition:

$$0 < p_1 < p_2 < \ldots < p_s = r.$$

By consecutively merging any two contiguous assertions that fall into the same cell, using the collapsing rule:

$$\vdash (\varphi_{i+1} \mathcal{U} (\varphi_i \mathcal{U} \varphi)) \supset ((\varphi_{i+1} \vee \varphi_i) \mathcal{U} \varphi),$$

we obtain the coarser conclusion:

$$\vdash \left(\bigvee_{i=0}^{r} \varphi_i\right) \supset \left(\left(\bigvee_{j=p_{s-1}+1}^{p_s} \varphi_j\right) \mathcal{U} \left(\bigvee_{j=p_{s-2}+1}^{p_{s-1}} \varphi_j\right) \mathcal{U} \ldots \left(\bigvee_{j=1}^{p_1} \varphi_j\right) \mathcal{U}\, \varphi_0\right).$$

In our mutual exclusion program, by reference to Fig. 1 it is easy to use the U-CHAIN rule and obtain:

$$\ell_2 \supset (\varphi_5 \mathcal{U} \varphi_4 \mathcal{U} \varphi_{1..3} \mathcal{U} \varphi_0),$$

from which the 1-bounded overtaking from ℓ_2 is obtained by the monotonicity of the *until* operator (i.e., replacing formulas by weaker formulas).

A natural extension of the U-CHAIN rule to programs that require infinite chains of assertions uses again well-founded ordered sets.

Let $(\mathcal{A}, \prec)$ be a well-founded ordered set. We require however that the ordering is total (or linear). That is, for every two distinct elements, $\alpha_1, \alpha_2 \in \mathcal{A}$ either $\alpha_1 \prec \alpha_2$ or $\alpha_2 \prec \alpha_1$.

(U-WELL) — Well-Founded Until Rule

Let $(\mathcal{A}, \prec)$ be a well-founded totally ordered set.

Let $\varphi(\alpha) = \varphi(\alpha, s)$ be a parametrized state formula.

Let $h : \mathcal{A} \to \mathcal{J}$ be a helpfulness function identifying for each $\alpha \in \mathcal{A}$ the helpful justice set $h(\alpha) \in \mathcal{J}$.

Let $\alpha_1 \prec \alpha_2 \prec \ldots \prec \alpha_s$ be a *finite* sequence of elements of $\mathcal{A}$.

A. $\vdash$ Every transition $\tau \in T$ leads from
$\varphi(\alpha)$ to $\psi \vee \exists \beta((\beta \preceq \alpha) \wedge \varphi(\beta))$

B. $\vdash$ Every transition $\tau \in h(\alpha)$ leads from
$\varphi(\alpha)$ to $\psi \vee \exists \beta((\beta \prec \alpha) \wedge \varphi(\beta))$

C. $\vdash \varphi(\alpha) \supset [\psi \vee \exists \beta((\beta \prec \alpha) \wedge \varphi(\beta)) \vee \mathit{Enabled}(h(\alpha))]$

$$\begin{aligned}\vdash \exists \alpha((\alpha \preceq \alpha_s) \wedge \varphi(\alpha)) \supset \\ [\exists \beta((\alpha_{s-1} \prec \beta \preceq \alpha_s) \wedge \varphi(\beta)) \mathcal{U} \\ \exists \beta((\alpha_{s-2} \prec \beta \preceq \alpha_{s-1}) \wedge \varphi(\beta)) \mathcal{U} \ldots \\ \exists \beta((\beta \preceq \alpha_1) \wedge \varphi(\beta)) \mathcal{U}\, \psi]\end{aligned}$$

By a combination of the completeness of the WELL rule for liveness properties and the UNLS rule for *unless* properties we can extend the above rule to a complete rule for *until* properties.

Acknowledgement:

We would like to thank Yoni Malachi, Ben Moszkowski, and Frank Yellin for careful and critical reading of the manuscript.

9. REFERENCES

[K] Keller, R.M., "Formal verification of parallel programs," CACM, Vol. 19, No. 7 (July 1976), pp. 371–384.

[L1] Lamport, L., "Proving the Correctness of Multiprocess Programs," IEEE Trans. Soft. Eng. SE-3, 2 (Mar. 1977), pp. 125-143.

[L2] Lamport, L., " 'Sometime' is Sometimes 'Not Never': On the Temporal Logic of Programs," 7th Annual ACM Symposium on Principles of Programming Languages (1980), pp. 174-185.

[LPS] Lehmann, D., A. Pnueli, and J. Stavi, "Impartiality, justice and fairness: the ethics of concurrent termination," in *Automata Languages and Programming*, Lecture Notes in Computer Science 115, Springer Verlag (1981), pp. 264–277.

[MP1] Manna, Z. and A. Pnueli, "Verification of Concurrent Prorams: The Temporal Framework," in *The Correctness Problem in Computer Science* (R.S. Boyer and J S. Moore, eds.), International Lecture Series in Computer Science, Academic Press, London (1982), pp. 215-273.

[MP2] Manna, Z. and A. Pnueli, "Verification of Concurrent Programs: Temporal Proof Principles," Proc. of the Workshop on Logic of Programs (D. Kozen, ed.), Yorktown-Heights, N.Y. (1981). Springer-Verlag Lecture Notes in Computer Science 131, pp. 200-252.

[MP3] Manna, Z. and A. Pnueli, "Verification of Concurrent Programs: Proving Eventualities by Well-Founded Ranking," TOPLAS (1983, to appear).

[MP4] Manna, Z. and A. Pnueli, "Verification of Concurrent Programs: a Temporal Proof System," Proc. 4th School on Advanced Programming, Amsterdam, Holland (June 1982).

[MP5] Manna, Z. and A. Pnueli, "How to Cook a Temporal Proof System for Your Pet Language," in the Proc. of the Symposium on Principles of Programming Languages, Austin, Texas (Jan. 1983).

[MP6] Manna, Z. and A. Pnueli, "Proving Precedence Properties: The Temporal Way," Technical Report, Computer Science Dept., Stanford University, Stanford, CA(1983, to appear).

[OL] Owicki, S. and L. Lamport, "Proving Liveness Properties of Concurrent Programs," ACM Transactions on Programming Languages and Systems, Vol. 4, No. 3 (July 1982), pp. 455-495.

[OG] Owicki, S. and D. Gries, "An Axiomatic Proof technique for Parallel Programs," Acta Informatica, Vol. 6, No. 4 (1976), pp. 319–340.

[Pe] Peterson, G.L., "Myths about the Mutual Exclusion Problem," Information Processing Letters, Vol. 12, No. 3 (June 1981), pp. 115-116.

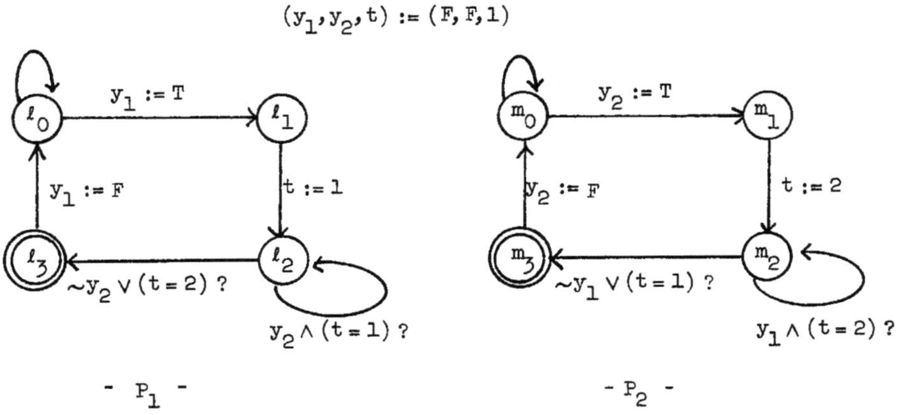

Figure 0

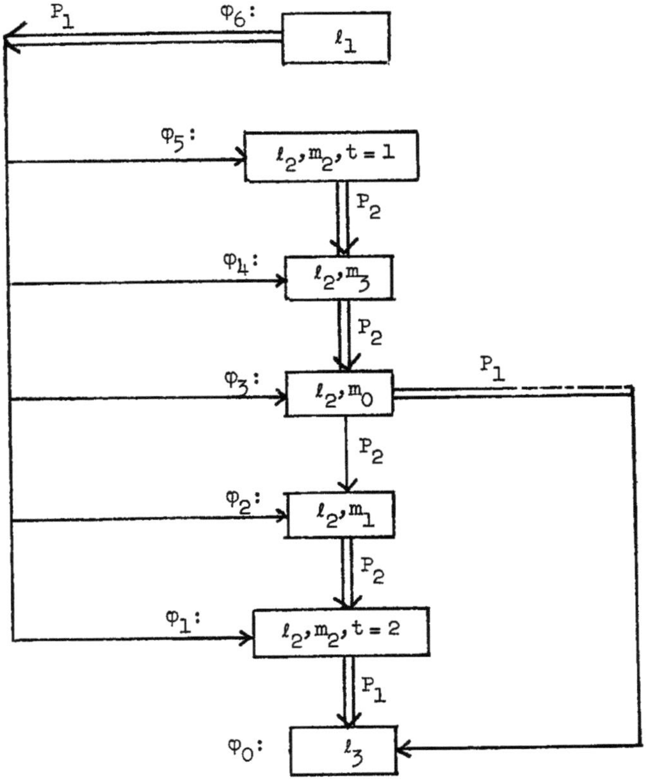

Fig. 1. Proof Diagram for $\vdash \ell_1 \supset \Diamond \ell_3$

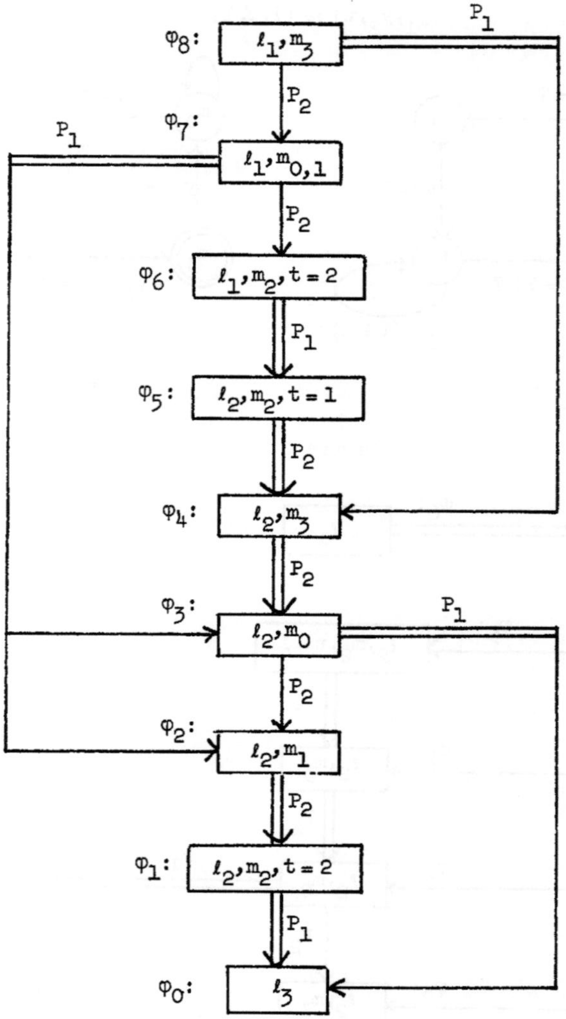

Fig. 2. Proof Diagram for 2-bounded overtaking from ℓ_1

An Algebraic Semantics for Busy (Data-Driven) and Lazy (Demand-Driven) Evaluation and its Application to a Functional Language [1)]

Bernhard Möller

Institut für Informatik
Technische Universität München
Arcisstr. 21, D-8000 München 2, Fed. Rep. Germany

1. Introduction

In recent years ideas on "non-conventional" machines and languages have become more and more important. One aim is to move towards a more flexible use of parallelism. Another idea is the use of "infinite objects". Suitable operational semantics for these concepts are provided by the techniques of data-driven (or busy) and demand-driven (or lazy) evaluation (see e.g. [18] for these notions). The present paper shows how equationally defined continuous algebras can be employed for deriving these two kinds of operational semantics from the least-fixpoint-semantics of recursive definitions.

The general method used is similar to the well-known techniques for evaluating recursively defined functions, viz. repeated unfolding and subsequent simplification. Here, the simplification rules are obtained from equations specifying a continuous algebra whose carrier sets serve as semantic domains. This has the advantage that the simplification rules are correct by construction. Moreover, a syntactic criterion (safety) guarantees that the resulting term rewriting system is confluent and noetherian so that finding normal forms is uncritical. In this way the algebraic approach permits a coherent presentation of mathematical semantics (satisfaction of equations in a continuous algebra) and operational semantics (deductions using equations as term rewriting rules).

The algebraic approach allows a uniform treatment of data and control structures. This is shown by a safe equational specification of a functional programming language a la Backus [3] over (finite and infinite) sequences of natural numbers. The techniques developed in the paper provide a mathematical as well as lazy and busy operational semantics for it.

Detailed proofs of the theorems and lemmas are contained in [16]. I would like to thank F.L.Bauer, M.Broy, W.Dosch, and the referees for a number of valuable suggestions.

1) This work was partially sponsored by the Sonderforschungsbereich 49, Programmiertechnik, Munich, Fed. Rep. Germany

2. Equationally Defined Continuous Algebras

A signature $\Sigma = (S,F)$ consists of a set S of sort symbols and a set F of operation symbols. Each $f \in F$ has a functionality $s_1 x \ldots x s_n \text{-->} s$ with $s_1,\ldots,s_n$, $s \in S$. If n=0 then f is called a constant symbol.

Given a signature Σ, an ordered Σ-algebra consists of a family $(s^A)_{s \in S}$ of nonempty (partially) ordered carrier sets s^A with least elements $\bot_s^A$ and a family $(f^A)_{f \in F}$ of monotonic operations f^A from $s_1^A x \ldots x s_n^A$ to s^A. A is continuous if its carriers s^A are complete, i.e. contain the supremum sup M for each directed subset $M \subseteq s^A$, and its operations are continuous, i.e. satisfy $f^A(\sup M_1,\ldots,\sup M_n) = \sup f^A(M_1,\ldots,M_n)$ for all directed $M_i \subseteq s_i^A$.

Every ordered Σ-algebra A may be embedded into a continuous Σ-algebra A^∞, the ideal-completion of A (see e.g. [20, 17]). The carrier s^{A^∞} consists of all ideals, i.e. all downward closed directed subsets of s^A, ordered by inclusion. For ideals $I_1,\ldots,I_n$, $f^{A^\infty}(I_1,\ldots,I_n)$ is defined as the smallest ideal containing $f^A(I_1,\ldots,I_n)$. A is embedded into A^∞ by assigning to each element the smallest ideal containing it.

A^∞ has the property of being inductive (cf. e.g. [2,9]): every element of a carrier is finitely approximable, i.e. it is the supremum of a directed set of finite elements. Here, an element x of an ordered set N is called finite if for every directed subset $D \subseteq N$, $x \leq \sup D$ implies $x \leq d$ for some $d \in D$. The non-finite elements in an inductive algebra are called infinite elements or limit points.

A family $(\leq_s)_{s \in S}$ of quasiorderings on the carriers s^A of a Σ-algebra A is called Σ-compatible if the operations of A are monotonic wrt. the $\leq_s$.

Let $\Sigma=(S,F)$ be a signature such that for all $s \in S$ F contains a constant symbol $\bot_s$. For a family $X=(X_s)_{s \in S}$ of variables, $W\Sigma(X)$ denotes the usual algebra of Σ-terms with free variables taken from X. The equality of terms is denoted by $\equiv$. $W\Sigma(X)$ is ordered by Nivat's syntactic ordering [17], i.e. by the smallest Σ-compatible family $\sqsubseteq = (\sqsubseteq_s)_{s \in S}$ of partial orderings on $W\Sigma(X)$ satisfying $\bot_s \sqsubseteq_s t$ for all terms $t \in {}_sW\Sigma(X)$.

The ideal-completion $W\Sigma(X)^\infty$ of $W\Sigma(X)$ can be interpreted as the algebra of finite and infinite Σ-terms with free variables (cf. the free complete magma in [17] or $CT_{\Sigma(X)}$ in [1]).

A valuation of X in an ordered Σ-algebra A is a family $v = (v_s)_{s \in S}$ of mappings $v_s\colon X_s \text{-->} s^A$ assigning values to the variables. Let V_A denote the set of valuations of X in A. We order V_A by $v \leq w$ iff $v_s(x) \leq w_s(x)$ for all $x \in X_s$ and $s \in S$. If A is continuous then V_A is complete under this ordering. The interpretation $t[v]$ of a Σ-term t under a valuation $v \in V_A$ is defined by structural induction: $x[v] := v_s(x)$ for a variable $x \in X_s$, and $f(t_1,\ldots,t_n)[v] := f^A(t_1[v],\ldots,t_n[v])$ for $f: s_1 x \ldots x s_n \text{-->} s$ in F.

An equation over a signature Σ is a pair (t_1, t_2) of Σ-terms of the same sort; we also write $t_1 = t_2$. A Σ-algebra A satisfies an equation $t_1 = t_2$ if for all valuations $v \in V_A$ $t_1[v] = t_2[v]$.

For a set E of equations over Σ let $\lesssim_E$ be the smallest Σ-compatible family of quasiorderings on $W\Sigma(X)$ such that $\sqsubseteq \subseteq \lesssim_E$ and for all equations $t_1=t_2$ in E and all valuations $v \in V_{W\Sigma(X)}$ $t_1[v] \lesssim_E t_2[v]$.

Theorem 1 (cf.e.g. [6,9]):

(1) The quotient algebra $W\Sigma(X)/\lesssim_E$ of $W\Sigma(X)$ by the congruence induced by $\lesssim_E$ satisfies E.

(2) If an ordered Σ-algebra A satisfies E, so does A^∞.

This guarantees the existence of a continuous algebra satisfying a given set of equations.

3. The Semantics of Terms over Recursively Defined Objects

A system of recursion equations is a valuation e of X in $W\Sigma(X)$. Over a Σ-algebra A, e defines a valuation transformer $e_A : V_A \text{-->} V_A$ by $e_A(v)_s(x) := e_s(x)[v]$ for $x \in X_s$.

Example: Let $\Sigma_0 = (S_0, F_0)$ where $S_0 = \{\underline{nat}, \underline{sequ}\}$ and F_0 consists of

$\bot$: --> nat,	$\bot$: --> sequ,
0 : --> nat,	() : --> sequ,
succ : nat-->nat,	add : nat x sequ --> sequ.

Let $X_{\underline{sequ}}=\{x\}$ and e be the system x --> add(0, x) over Σ_0. It will be interpreted as the recursion equation sequ x = add(0, x). For an arbitrary valuation v in a Σ_0-algebra A we have $e_A(v)$: x --> $add^A(0^A, v(x))$.
Over $W\Sigma_0(X)$ we may take e itself for v and obtain $e_{W\Sigma_0(X)}(e)$: x --> add(0, add(0, x)), i.e. the result of "unfolding" x once in e.

Lemma 1: If A is continuous then e_A is continuous.

Therefore, if A is continuous, by the fixpoint theorem (cf. e.g. [15]) e_A has a least fixpoint $|e_A|$. We call $|e_A|$ the solution of e in A (cf. [1]).

Example: In $W\Sigma_0(X)^\infty$ the system e from the previous example has as its solution the valuation which assigns to x the ideal generated by

$$\{\bot, add(0, \bot), add(0, add(0, \bot)), \ldots\}$$

which may be interpreted as the infinite term add(0, add(0, add(0,...))).

For a term t from $W\Sigma(X)$ and a system e of recursion equations we call the pair $r = (e; t)$ a representation and $r^A := t[|e_A|]$ the object represented by r in A.

This defines the mathematical semantics of terms over recursively defined objects completely. An operational semantics for such terms can be developed from the approximation sequence given by the fixpoint theorem. It uses repeated unfolding of the recursive definitions and was first described in [14] (see also the Herbrand-Kleene-Machine in [5]).

Let e be a system of recursion equations over $W\Sigma(X)$, A a continuous Σ-algebra, and O^A the valuation which assigns the least element $\bot_s^A$ to every $x \in X_s$. This valuation is used to interpret terms with (not yet unfolded) variables: forming $t[O^A]$ for some term $t \in W\Sigma(X)$ means interpreting t such that the variables are considered as carrying no information.

For a term $t \in W\Sigma(X)$ and a system e of recursion equations we define $t_0^\# := t$, $t_{n+1}^\# := t_n^\#[e]$. Thus the $t_i^\#$ evolve from t by repeatedly unfolding the variables according to their definitions in e.

Lemma 2: $t[|e_A|] = \sup \{t_n^\#[O^A] : n \in \mathbb{N}\}$, i.e. the object represented by (e; t) is the supremum of the interpretations of the $t_n^\#$.

Thus, a first operational semantics for a representation $r_n = (e; t_n^\#)$ is given by Kleene's approximation process:

(1) (Interpretation) Form $u_n := t_n^\#[O^A]$.

(2) (Unfolding) Replace in $t_n^\#$ simultaneously all variables by their definitions according to e, i.e. form $t_{n+1}^\# := t_n^\#[e]$, and apply the process to $r_{n+1} := (e; t_{n+1}^\#[e])$.

Then $\sup \{u_m : m \geq n\} = r_n^A$, the object represented by r_n in A.

If the carrier of the sort of $t_n^\#$ in A is a flat domain then by the continuity of the operations involved there is an index $k \geq n$ such that $t_k^\#[O^A] = t_n^\#[|e_A|]$ and the process can stop as soon as a maximal element is reached.

4. Operative Algebras

In general, the interpretation step (1) in Kleene's approximation process is not "algorithmic". However, Under certain restrictions the equations E defining the ordered algebra $W\Sigma(X)/\lesssim_E$ can be used as term rewriting rules. This will allow to make step (1) effective.

The basic idea is to partition the set of operations into "constructors" which suffice for generating all elements of the algebra, and "extensions" which are defined essentially by primitive recursion over the constructors. This is related to the criterion for sufficient completeness given in [11]. We require that every extension has certain "critical arguments" which control the primitive recursion. They will allow a precise treatment of lazy evaluation. Let us now formalize these notions; for the rest of this section we identify terms which differ only by a consistent variable-renaming.

Let $\Sigma = (S,F)$ be a signature and $C, Z \subseteq F$ form a partition of F. The operation symbols in C are called constructors, those in Z extensions. We write C also for the subsignature (S,C) of Σ. We want to impose conditions on a set E of Σ-equations under which every variable-free Σ-term can be rewritten into a pure (also variable-free) C-term using E.

A ZC-combination is a term $t \equiv z(t_1,\dots,t_n)$ with an extension $z \in Z$ and constructor terms $t_i \in WC(X)$ such that every variable occurs at most once in t.

Now let E consist only of equations $t_1 = t_2$ in which t_1 is a ZC-combination. Let E be unambiguous, i.e. assume that no two left-hand-sides in E are identical. For every $z \in Z$ let the number of equations whose left-hand-side starts with z be finite. Then $|z|_j$ denotes the maximal height of terms occurring as j-th arguments of z in left-hand-sides in E (the height of variables is 0). If $|z|_j > 0$, the j-th argument of z is called critical. E is called C-complete for the j-th argument of z if in all j-th arguments of z in left-hand-sides of E, variables occur only at nesting depth $|z|_j +1$ and every C-term of height $\leq |z|_j$ occurs as j-th argument of z in some left-hand-side of E (cf. also the notion "complete for C" in [13]).

Let $Q \subseteq Z$ be a subfamily of extensions. An equation $z(t_1,\dots,t_n) = t \in E$ is called reducing wrt. Q if only extensions from $Q \cup \{z\}$ occur in t, all variables of t also occur in the left-hand-side, and, if z actually occurs in t, every critical argument of z in t is a proper subterm of some critical t_i. E is called safe wrt. Q if all its equations are reducing wrt. Q, if for all $z \in Z\setminus Q$ E is C-complete for all arguments of z, and if it is monotonic, i.e. if for equations $t_1 = t_2$, $u_1 = u_2$ in E, $t_1 \sqsubseteq u_1$ implies $t_2 \sqsubseteq u_2$. E is called safe if it is safe wrt. $\emptyset$.

For a safe set E of equations, C-completeness means that the left-hand-sides in E provide a complete case-analysis; together with the unambiguity it also implies that at most one equation can be "applied" at any "place" in a given term.

A <u>context</u> K is a term in which exactly one variable x occurs exactly once. For a term t of the sort of x we denote by K[t] the term resulting from K by replacing x by t. For Σ-terms t_1, t_2 we say that $t_1 \rightarrow t_2$ if there is a context K, an equation $u_1 = u_2$ in E and a valuation v of X in $W\Sigma(X)$ such that $t_i = K[u_i[v]]$ $(i=1,2)$. $\rightarrow^*$ is the reflexive-transitive closure of $\rightarrow$.

<u>Theorem 2</u>:
For safe E, $\rightarrow^*$ is confluent and noetherian. Therefore every term $t \in W\Sigma(X)$ has a unique normal form NF[t] wrt. $\rightarrow^*$, and there are no nonterminating computations under $\rightarrow^*$.

<u>Theorem 3</u>:
For safe E the carrier sets of $W\Sigma/\leq_E$ are isomorphic to those of WC. This means that WC (WC^{∞}) can be extended to an ordered (continuous) Σ-algebra satisfying E by interpreting the extensions suitably.

For the proofs see [16].

Thus, interpreting a Σ-term in the algebra WC means reducing it to its normal form. By theorem 2 this process is effective. Therefore, for safe E, we call $W\Sigma/\leq_E$ an operative algebra. More generally, $W\Sigma/\leq_E$ is <u>operative</u>, if there is a sequence $\emptyset = Z_0 \subseteq Z_1 \subseteq \ldots$ with $\bigcup_{i \in \mathbb{N}} Z_i = Z$ and a sequence $(E_i)_{i \in \mathbb{N}}$ with $\bigcup_{i \in \mathbb{N}} E_i = E$, such that for $i > 0$ E_i is safe wrt. Z_{i-1} with Z_i as extensions and C as constructors.

<u>Example</u>: We enrich Σ_0 to Σ_1 by the extensions
pred : <u>nat</u> --> <u>nat</u>, head : <u>sequ</u> --> <u>nat</u>, tail : <u>sequ</u> --> <u>sequ</u>.
Then the equations

pred($\perp$) = $\perp$,	head($\perp$) = $\perp$,	tail($\perp$) = $\perp$,
pred(0) = $\perp$,	head(()) = $\perp$,	tail(()) = $\perp$,
pred(succ(x)) = x,	head(add(x, s)) = x,	tail(add(x, s)) = s

are safe if we take $C := \Sigma_0$ and $Z := \Sigma_1 \backslash \Sigma_0$.
Note that by these equations add is required to be nonstrict in both arguments.

From now on we restrict ourselves to operative algebras. Over such algebras, Kleene's approximation process is fully "algorithmic"; note, however, that in the case of a carrier with limit points nontermination may be <u>necessary</u> for the correctness of the operational semantics. In this case one may view the process as producing more and more output (the sequence of the u_n, for which $u_0 \sqsubseteq u_1 \sqsubseteq u_2 \sqsubseteq \ldots$ holds) which approximates the exact value "to any degree of precision desired".

5. Busy and Lazy Evaluation

In the form of Kleene's process considered so far, in every interpretation step the normal form is computed anew. This section aims at avoiding these repeated computations. We exploit the fact that - by construction - interpretation and term rewriting are compatible, and simplify the terms $t_n^{\#}$ before the interpretation step proper. This saves rewriting work in later interpretation steps. The process terminates if eventually all variables are eliminated by some simplification step so that further unfolding becomes unnecessary.

The two evaluation techniques we are now going to derive from Kleene's process differ only in the way they select the variables to be unfolded and the subterms to be simplified. Thus they are different operational semantics, leading however, by construction, to the same mathematical semantics.

First we consider a method which strives for "maximal increase in information". It therefore reduces the term under consideration as far as possible and afterwards unfolds all variables. It can therefore be called busy evaluation [7], or, since it starts reducing terms as soon as sufficient information about the arguments of the extensions in the term is available, also data-driven evaluation (see e.g. [18]).

In terms of parallel execution, this method can be viewed as starting an evaluation process for each argument t_i of the outermost operation f of a term $f(t_1,\ldots,t_n)$. These subprocesses (which recursively apply the same method) communicate approximations of the arguments to f as soon as possible; if f can determine the final value already from the "current" approximations, it stops all the (possibly infinite) processes which compute the arguments t_i. This is effected by the simplification steps.

Essential for the correctness of this method is the use of nonstrict operations. However, these are already crucial for the existence of infinite objects in our algebras: If for all operations strictness were required by the axioms E, the carriers of $(W\Sigma/\leq_E)^{\infty}$ would be flat domains and could not contain limit points.

For a given representation $r_n = (e; t_n)$ the busy evaluation works as follows:

(0) (Simplification) Determine the normal form $t_n' := NF[t_n]$.

(1) (Interpretation) Interpret the resulting term, i.e. form $u_n := NF[t_n'[\Omega^{W\Sigma(X)}]]$.

(2) (Unfolding) Unfold the recursive definitions in t_n', i.e. form $t_{n+1} := t_n'[e]$, and apply the process to the new representation $r_{n+1} := (e; t_{n+1})$.

We give two criteria for terminating the process:

(0a) If t'_n does not contain variables, $u_n = r_n^{W\Sigma\infty}$ and the process may stop.

(1a) If u_n is maximal in the respective carrier set (i.e. if it does not contain $\perp$) then $u_n = r_n^{W\Sigma\infty}$ and the process may stop.

The correctness of this operational semantics is stated in

Theorem 4:

(1) For the u_m evolving during busy evaluation of r_n and the object $r_n^{W\Sigma\infty}$ represented by r_n in $W\Sigma^\infty$ one has $r_n^{W\Sigma\infty} = \sup \{u_m : m \geq n\}$.

(2) If the carrier set of the sort of r_n is flat and neither of the termination criteria is ever satisfied then $r_n^{W\Sigma\infty} = \perp$.

Second, we consider a method which strives to avoid term manipulations which are irrelevant for the further progress of computation. Because the applicability of the equations of a safe set E is determined by the critical arguments of the extensions, this method avoids reducing terms which "at the moment" are not critical (they may, however, become critical by subsequent rewriting steps), and unfolds only those variables which "at the moment" prevent further evaluation of the critical arguments. Thus this method simplifies only as far as necessary and unfolds as little as possible; it can therefore be called lazy evaluation [12,10,4] or demand-driven evaluation [18].

For the precise formulation of this method we need two technical notions. The normal form KNF[t] wrt. the critical arguments of a term t is the term that results from t by reducing only those subterms which are (critical arguments of ...) critical arguments of extensions in t until no further progress is possible. KNF[t] is formally defined by

(1) KNF[x] := x for $x \in X$

(2) For a term $t \equiv f(t_1,\dots,t_n)$, KNF[t] := f(KNF[$t_1$],...,KNF[$t_n$]) if f is a constructor. If f is an extension, we set $\bar{t} := f(\bar{t}_1,\dots,\bar{t}_n)$ where $\bar{t}_j$:= KNF[t_j] if t_j is critical for f and $\bar{t}_j := t_j$ otherwise. If there is an equation $u_1 = u_2$ in E such that $u_1[v] = \bar{t}$ for some valuation v (by the safety of E there is at most one such equation) then KNF[t] := KNF[u_2[v]], otherwise KNF[t] := $\bar{t}$.

In general, KNF[t] $\neq$ NF[t], however one always has $t \to^* \text{KNF}[t] \to^* \text{NF}[t]$.

If t has been reduced to KNF[t], further progress in the reduction of critical arguments (and hence in the elimination of extensions) is "blocked" by those variables that appear in critical positions and are not yet unfolded. Thus, for $t \in W\Sigma(X)$ we define the set K(t) of critical variables by

(1) $K(x) := \emptyset$ for a variable $x \in X$.

(2) $K(f(t_1,\dots,t_n)) := \bigcup_{j \in M_f} K(t_j)$ where M_f is the set of all j such that an extension occurs in t_j if f is a constructor, and the set of critical argument indices if f is an extension.

Finally, for the method of demand-driven evaluation it is important not to neglect the noncritical variables completely: the operations of a continuous algebra in general are not sequential in the sense of [19], so that the evaluations of their arguments have to be advanced "sufficiently uniformly", "in a fair manner in parallel".

For a representation $r_n = (e;\ t_n)$ the process of lazy evaluation works as follows:

(A) (Reduction of extensions) Determine an arbitrary natural number $k_n > 0$, set $v_{n0} := t_n$, $l := k_n$, and $\overline{r}_{n0} := (e;\ v_{n0})$.

(A0) If l=0 apply step (B). Otherwise

(A1) (Simplification) For the given representation $\overline{r}_{nm} = (e;\ v_{nm})$ determine the normal form $v'_{nm} := KNF[v_{nm}]$ wrt. the critical variables.

(A2) (Interpretation) Form $u_{nm} := NF[v'_{nm}[0^{W\Sigma(X)}]]$.

(A3) (Unfolding) Determine the set $K(v'_{nm})$ of critical variables and unfold them in v'_{nm}, i.e. form $v_{nm+1} := v'_{nm}[e_{nm}]$ where $e_{nm}(x) := e(x)$ if $x \in K(v'_{nm})$ and $e_{nm}(x) := x$ otherwise. Afterwards apply step (A0) to the new representation $\overline{r}_{nm+1} := (e;\ v_{nm+1})$ and to l-1.

(B) (General unfolding) Form $t_{n+1} := v_{nk_n}[e]$ and apply step (A) to $r_{n+1} := (e;\ t_{n+1})$.

The termination criteria are analogous to those for data-driven evaluation:

(A1a) If v'_{nm} does not contain variables then $v'^{W\Sigma^\infty}_{nm} = r^{W\Sigma^\infty}_n$ and the process may stop.

(A2a) If u_{nm} is maximal in the respective carrier set then $u_{nm} = r^{W\Sigma^\infty}_n$ and the process may stop.

Theorem 5:

(1) For the u_{nm} evolving during lazy evaluation of r_n and the object $r^{W\Sigma^\infty}_n$ represented by r_n in $W\Sigma^\infty$ one has $r^{W\Sigma^\infty}_n = \sup\{u_{mp} : m \geq n,\ p = 1,\dots,k_m\}$.

(2) If the carrier set of the sort of t_n is flat and none of the termination criteria is ever satisfied then $r^{W\Sigma^\infty}_n = \bot$.

Example: We enrich Σ_1 to Σ_2 by a sort bool and the operations

$\bot$, true, false : --> bool,
not : bool --> bool,
iszero : nat --> bool,
if . then . else . fi : bool x nat x nat --> nat,

incr : sequ --> sequ,

sel : nat x sequ --> nat .

If we take true, false, 0, succ, (), add and the ⊥'s as constructors, the following equations are operative:

not(⊥) = ⊥, if ⊥ then m else n fi = ⊥,

not(true) = false, if true then m else n fi = m,

not(false) = true, if false then m else n fi = n,

iszero(⊥) = ⊥, incr(⊥) = ⊥,

iszero(0) = true, incr(()) = (),

iszero(succ(n)) = false, incr(add(n, x)) = add(succ(n), incr(x)),

sel(n, ⊥) = ⊥,

sel(n, ()) = ⊥,

sel(n, add(m, x)) = if iszero(n) then m else sel(pred(n), x) fi.

The solution of the system

e : sequ nats = add(0, incr(nats))

is the infinite sequence add(0, add(1, add(2,...))).

Still the busy as well as the lazy evaluation of a representation (e; sel($succ^k(0)$, nats)) terminates with the value $succ^k(0)$.

To summarize: The busy evaluation simplifies a given term wherever possible; it computes the normal forms of all subterms "in advance" for the case that they might be needed in some later computation step. It seems therefore more suitable in a parallel environment where the overall computation time does not so much depend on the actual number of reduction steps. The lazy evaluation, on the contrary, defers all computations until they become unavoidable. Therefore it seems more appropriate for a sequential environment where the overall time is "proportional" to the actual number of reduction steps.

6. An Equational Specification of a Functional Language

This section contains our main example for the techniques described. We shall give an equational specification of functionals of arbitrary order over sequences of natural numbers. For this purpose we first extend the set of sorts S_2 of signature Σ_2 by infinitely many new sorts for functionals to a set of sorts S_3 as follows:

(1) $S_2 \subseteq S_3$

(2) If $s_1,\dots,s_n$, $s \in S_3$ ($n > 0$) then funct($s_1,\dots,s_n$)$s \in S_3$.

(3) S_3 is the smallest set satisfying (1) and (2).

The carrier of sort $\underline{funct}(s_1,\dots,s_n)s$ in the Σ_3-algebra to be constructed will contain denotations of function(al)s with argument sorts $s_1,\dots,s_n$ and result sort s. Some sorts of S_3 are

funct(nat)nat, funct(nat,funct(bool,sequ)sequ)nat,
funct(funct(nat)sequ, funct(sequ,sequ)bool) funct(nat)nat .

The operation symbols F_3 for the signature Σ_3 are the following:

$\bot^{s}_{s_1\dots s_n}$: --> $\underline{funct}(s_1,\dots,s_n)s$ for all $s_1,\dots,s_n,s \in S_3$

$\underline{if}.\underline{then}.\underline{else}.\underline{fi}_s$: $\underline{bool}$ x s x s --> s for all $s \in S_3$
if.then.else.fi denotes the usual conditional.

$apply^{s}_{s_1\dots s_n}$: $\underline{funct}(s_1,\dots,s_n)s \times s_1 \times\dots\times s_n$ --> s for all $s_1,\dots,s_n$, $s \in S_3$
apply denotes the operation of applying a function denotation to its arguments.

f' : --> $\underline{funct}(s_1,\dots,s_n)s$ for all operation symbols f : $s_1 \times \dots \times s_n$ --> s (n>0)
f' is a syntactic construct for lifting a function f to a functional constant of the next-higher order.

$p^{j}_{s_1\dots s_n}$: --> $\underline{funct}(s_1,\dots,s_n)s_j$ for all $s_1,\dots,s_n \in S_3$ and $1 \le j \le n$
p^j is a syntactic construct for denoting the j-th projection (or selection).

$const^{s}_{s_1\dots s_n}$: s --> $\underline{funct}(s_1,\dots,s_n)s$ for all $s_1,\dots,s_n$, $s \in S_3$
const is a syntactic construct for denoting constant functions.

$comp^{s_1\dots s_n s}_{u_1\dots u_m}$: $\underline{funct}(s_1,\dots,s_n)s \times \underline{funct}(u_1,\dots,u_m)s_1 \times \dots \times$
$\underline{funct}(u_1,\dots,u_m)s_n$ --> $\underline{funct}(u_1,\dots,u_m)s$ for all $u_1,\dots,u_m$, $s_1,\dots,s_n$, $s \in S_3$
comp is a syntactic construct for denoting function composition.

$cond^{s}_{s_1\dots s_n}$: $\underline{funct}(s_1,\dots,s_n)\underline{bool} \times \underline{funct}(s_1,\dots,s_n)s \times \underline{funct}(s_1,\dots,s_n)s$
--> $\underline{funct}(s_1,\dots,s_n)s$ for all $s_1,\dots,s_n$, $s \in S_3$
cond is a syntactic construct for denoting the conditional.

We take as constructors all operations in $F_3 \backslash F_2$ besides if.then.else.fi and apply; they correspond to the syntactic constructs found in most functional (applicative) programming languages. From now on we drop the indices of the operation symbols.

The semantics of the operations is specified by the following operative equations:

$\underline{\text{if}}\ \bot\ \underline{\text{then}}\ x\ \underline{\text{else}}\ y\ \underline{\text{fi}} = \bot,$
$\underline{\text{if}}\ \text{true}\ \underline{\text{then}}\ x\ \underline{\text{else}}\ y\ \underline{\text{fi}} = x,$
$\underline{\text{if}}\ \text{false}\ \underline{\text{then}}\ x\ \underline{\text{else}}\ y\ \underline{\text{fi}} = y,$

$\text{apply}(\bot, x_1,\dots,x_n) = \bot,$
$\text{apply}(f', x_1,\dots,x_n) = f(x_1,\dots,x_n),$
$\text{apply}(p^j, x_1,\dots,x_n) = x_j,$
$\text{apply}(\text{const}(z), x_1,\dots,x_n) = z,$
$\text{apply}(\text{comp}(g, h_1,\dots,h_n), x_1,\dots,x_m) = \text{apply}(g, \text{apply}(h_1, x_1,\dots,x_m), \dots, \text{apply}(h_n, x_1,\dots,x_m)),$
$\text{apply}(\text{cond}(p, g, h), x_1,\dots,x_n) =$
$\quad \underline{\text{if}}\ \text{apply}(p, x_1,\dots,x_n)\ \underline{\text{then}}\ \text{apply}(g, x_1,\dots,x_n)\ \underline{\text{else}}\ \text{apply}(h, x_1,\dots,x_n)\ \underline{\text{fi}}.$

Note that only the first arguments of if.then.else.fi and apply are critical; in the case of apply this is the function argument.

Let us now illustrate the semantics with an example: The while-combinator of [3] can be denoted by the recursive definition

funct(funct(s)bool, funct(s)s) funct(s)s while =
comp(cond', p^1, comp(comp', while, p^2), const(id))

where the identity function id can again be realized by a projection (we have not done this in order to avoid distinguishing projections with different indices).

Let F abbreviate the term apply(while, comp(not', iszero'), pred'), or, in Backus' notation, (while not o iszero pred). A busy or lazy evaluation of the term apply(F, succ(0)) (or F:succ(0)) first unfolds while once (since no simplifications are possible) giving

```
apply(apply(comp(cond', p1,
                         comp(comp', while, p2),
                         const(id)),
            comp(not', iszero'), pred'),
      succ(0)).
```

This has the KNF

apply(F, apply(apply(p^2, comp(not', iszero'), pred'), succ(0)))

and the NF

apply(F, 0).

This means that the lazy evaluation has deferred the application of pred to the original argument succ(0) to a later stage, whereas the busy evaluation already has performed it.

Now again while is unfolded, and this time both the KNF and the NF are 0 so that busy as well as lazy evaluation stop here.

Since the busy evaluation of a term containing identifiers of recursively defined functionals unfolds all these identifiers, it corresponds to the full computation rule of [19]. Moreover, it evaluates functions and their arguments "in parallel" as in [7]. In lazy evaluation, only those variables which are critical for apply are unfolded. Because we represent a nested function application

f(f(x, y), f(u, v))

as

apply(f, apply(f, x, y), apply(f, u, v))

and only the first argument of apply is critical, lazy evaluation of functionals here corresponds to a restricted and more economical form of the parallel outermost rule (not all outermost occurrences of recursively defined functions are expanded but only those occurring within some critical argument of an extension).

8. Conclusion

The method of algebraic specification, when extended to inductive continuous algebras, is a convenient tool for defining and describing domains with nonstrict operations and with limit points. This replies to a number of remarks in [8] on the "restrictiveness" of algebraic specifications. Moreover, our approach has the advantage that the characteristic properties define the semantic domains, whereas in [8] they have to be proved.

Our main aim was to show how correct operational semantics can be derived from a mathematical semantics in terms of operative continuous algebras. Such algebras are defined by equations of a certain restricted form which provide a reduction calculus for the evaluation of terms over the algebras. By organizing the application of the rules suitably various operational realizations (here lazy and busy evaluation) of the mathematical semantics can be obtained.

Further research should concern techniques for implementing continuous algebras specified by more general kinds of axioms (e.g. conditional equations, see [16]) in terms of operative ones. In this way a first specification could be free of operational details which should only be introduced in a later stage of the development process.

References

[1] J.A.Goguen, J.W.Thatcher, E.G.Wagner, J.B.Wright: Initial algebra semantics and continuous algebras. JACM 24, 68-95 (1977)

[2] J.B.Wright, E.G.Wagner, J.W.Thatcher: A uniform approach to inductive posets and inductive closure. MFCS 1977. LNCS 53. Berlin: Springer 1977, 192-212

[3] J.Backus: Can programming be liberated from the von Neumann style? A functional

style and its algebra of programs. CACM 21, 613-641 (1978)

[4] F.L.Bauer: Detailization and lazy evaluation, infinite objects and pointer representation. In: F.L.Bauer, M.Broy (eds.): Program construction. LNCS 69. Berlin: Springer 1979, 406-420

[5] F.L.Bauer, H.Wössner: Algorithmic language and program development. Berlin: Springer 1982

[6] S.L.Bloom: Varieties of ordered algebras. JCSS 13, 200-212 (1976)

[7] M.Broy: Transformation parallel ablaufender Programme. Fakultät für Mathematik der TU München, Dissertation, 1980. Institut für Informatik der TU München, TUM-I8001, 1980

[8] R.Cartwright, J.Donahue: The semantics of lazy (and industrious) evaluation. Conf. Record of the 1982 ACM Symposium on LISP and Functional Programming, 253-264

[9] B.Courcelle, M.Nivat: Algebraic families of interpretations. 17th FOCS 1976, 137-146

[10] D.P.Friedman, D.S.Wise: CONS should not evaluate its arguments. In: S.Michaelson, R.Milner (eds.): Automata, languages and programming. Edinburgh: Edinburgh University Press 1976, 257-285

[11] J.V.Guttag: The specification and application to programming of abstract data types. Ph.D. Thesis, University of Toronto, Dept. of Computer Science, Rep. CSRG-59, 1975

[12] P.Henderson, J.H.Morris: A lazy evaluator. 3rd POPL 1976, 95-103

[13] G.Huet, J.-M.Hullot: Proofs by induction in equational theories with constructors. 21st FOCS 1980, 96-107

[14] S.C.Kleene: Introduction to metamathematics. New York: Van Nostrand 1952

[15] Z.Manna: Mathematical theory of computation. New York: McGraw-Hill 1974

[16] B.Möller: Unendliche Objekte und Geflechte. Fakultät für Mathematik und Informatik der TU München, Dissertation, 1982. Institut für Informatik der TU München, TUM-I8213, 1982

[17] M.Nivat: On the interpretation of recursive polyadic program schemes. Istituto Nazionale di Alta Matematica, Symposia Mathematica XV. London: Academic Press 1975, 255-281

[18] P.C.Treleaven, D.R.Brownbridge, R.P.Hopkins: Data-driven and demand-driven computer architecture. Computing Surveys 14, 93-143 (1982)

[19] J.Vuillemin: Correct and optimal implementations of recursion in a simple programming language. JCSS 9, 332-354 (1974)

[20] J.Vuillemin: Syntaxe, semantique et axiomatique d'une langage de programmation simple. Basel: Birkhäuser 1975

Searchability in Merging and Implicit Data Structures †

J. Ian Munro
Data Structuring Group
Department of Computer Science
University of Waterloo
Waterloo, Ontario, Canada
N2L 3G1

Patricio V. Poblete *
Computer Science Division
University of Chile
Santiago, Chile

ABSTRACT

We introduce the notion of searchability as a property of an in place merging algorithm. It is shown that a pair of sorted arrays can be merged in place in linear time so that a logarithmic time search may be performed at any point during the process. This method is applied to devise an implicit data structure which can support searches in $O(\log^2 n)$ time and insertions in $O(\log n)$ time.

1. Introduction

In studying the process of merging sorted blocks of data, three properties have been considered (i) minimizing the number of comparisons [7], (ii) performing the merge in place [12] (also in [10], ex. 5.2.4–10) and (iii) maintaining stability [6],[14]. We introduce the notion of *searchability* as a property of a merging algorithm. A merging algorithm is said to support $f(n)$ searchability if at any stage in the process a search for an arbitrary element can be performed in $f(n)$ comparisons. The standard merging algorithm is $O(\log n)$ searchable. Like stability, this property is of greater interest in considering in place merging schemes such as that of Kronrod [12]. His technique involves totally "randomizing" a block of n elements and so is only $\Theta(\sqrt{n})$ searchable. Searchability of merge algorithms can be viewed as a paradigm for the more general issue of performing basic operations while reorganizing a database.

Our interest in this problem was sparked by the development of an implicit (i.e., pointer free) structure for performing searches and insertions. In developing the technique outlined in section 3 for the implicit structure, our major hurdle was that of performing an in place $O(\log n)$ searchable merge. It is surprising that this problem does not appear to have come up else-

† This work was supported by NSERC grant A8237.
* This work was done while on leave at the University of Waterloo.

where in the literature. We were relatively content with an $O(n \log n)$ technique before developing the $O(n)$ method outlined in section 2. This method is applied in section 3 to solve the original problem of forming an implicit structure to support searches in time $O(\log^2 n)$ worst case and $O(\log n)$ on the average and $O(\log n)$ (worst case) for an insertion. We also present a scheme to perform deletions on this structure and conjecture that it runs in $O(\log^2 n)$ time on the average.

2. A Merging Algorithm

Theorem 1: Two sorted arrays of n elements can be merged in place by usings $O(n)$ time and $O(1)$ pointers in such a manner that a search can be conducted at any time using $O(\log n)$ comparisons.

Proof: In order to prove the theorem an $O(n \log n)$ algorithm is presented first. It is used in the linear algorithm which follows. The notions of Wong [15] were useful in the development of these methods. Assume A[1::n] and B[1::n] are to be merged and that B immediately follows A. For notational convenience assume n is a power of 2.

```
Procedure Slowmerge
begin
    For i = 1 log n - 1 do
    begin
        A and B at this point have been partitioned so that each consists of n/2^(i-1) blocks of 2^(i-1)
        elements of consecutive range in A U B.
        In a single scan (n/2^(i-2) comparisons and n moves) swap blocks of size 2^(i-1) so that A and
        B can each be viewed as n/2^i blocks of 2^i elements of consecutive rank.
        This is done by repeatedly finding the three blocks of smallest elements. At least two
        of them will be contiguous. Move the two blocks of smaller elements into that seg-
        ment of 2^i locations and the third to the remaining block.
    end
    Exchange A and B if necessary
end
```

It should be clear that this algorithm requires about $4n$ comparisons but an unfortunate $O(n \log n)$ moves. Throughout Slowmerge both A and B remain in sorted order with one exception. In the process of swapping two blocks one may have a point of non-monotonicity. This leads to a $3 \log n$ search algorithm.

Now consider a linear technique.

Procedure Searchable merge

begin

1) Find the $2 \log n$ smallest elements of the whole set, and move them to the first $2 \log n$ locations of A. This can be done in time $O(n)$ by merging the elements that must be moved out of A with the elements that remain in B, using the block of elements that will be taken from B as a scratch area.

2) Scan the $n-2 \log n$ remaining elements of A and the n elements of B from left to right, forming blocks of size $\log n$ contiguous elements. This can be done in a single pass using the first $2 \log n$ locations of A as a scratch area.

3) Sort the first $2 \log n$ locations of A.

4) Conceptually divide A and B in blocks of size $\log n$. Each block consists of a first element, header (j), the next $\log n - 2$ elements middle (j) and the last, trailer (j). Apply Slowmerge to the $2n/\log n$ elements {header (i)}. At this point, these "headers" are in their final positions.

5) For $i = 1$ $2n/\log n$ do
   While middle (i) is not in its final position do
   begin
      By binary search on the headers, find the final position of middle (i) and swap middle (i) with that block.
   end

6) Apply Slowmerge to {trailer(i)}

end

Each of the 6 labelled steps requires at most linear time and so the entire algorithm is linear. Note that when Slowmerge is called, it is applied to lists of $n/\log n$ elements. In step 5) no element is moved more than twice and the $O(\log n)$ binary search is applied to each middle at most once. The $O(\log n)$ searchability follows by arguments similar to those applied to Slowmerge, note that during step 5) searches are performed by two binary searches, on the headers and on the trailers.

A quick scan through the algorithm shows that about $4n$ comparisons are made ($2n$ in each of steps 2) and 5) and $O(n)$ elsewhere). At the cost of complication, the $2n$ in step 5) can be reduced to $O(n/\log n)$ without increasing the number of moves above $O(n)$. Hence Theorem 1 can be strengthened to say the number of comparisons is within a lower order term of optimal.

This merging algorithm suggests an approach to merge sort by which the sort can reasonably be suspended at any time for a search to be performed. (The cost of searching will depend on the state of the sort.) We perform a merge sort by pairing single elements; then all pairs, etc.. Observe that this scheme has two advantages. First, only a constant number of pointers are required to keep track of the state of the sort. The second advantage is that all sorted subfiles are of roughly the same size. The cost of performing a search after P "sorting" comparisons have been performed will be $O(n/2^{P/n} + \log n)$. This is within a constant factor of the lower bound of Borodin et al. [3]. (They also give a matching upper bound but are not concerned with space considerations nor "on-line" queries.) This yields the following result.

Theorem 2: A file can be sorted in place using a constant number of points and a number of comparisons within a lower order term of optimal, such that the sort may be interrupted at any point and a search performed on the file. This search requires a number of comparisons within a constant factor of any scheme which has used the same number of comparisons in preprocessing the file.

3. An Application to Implicit Data Structures

An implicit data structure [13] is an array of n data elements organized in some fashion to support appropriate operations without the use of pointers. Clearly a sorted list is a very effective implicit structure for searching. A sorted list is, of course, disastrous for insertions and deletions. If the operations insert, delete and find are to be supported, then a structure suggested by Frederickson [5] is the present champion, permitting searches in $O(\log n)$ time and insertions and deletions in $O(\log^{3/2} n\ 2^{\sqrt{2\log n}})$ steps in the worst case, provided all the keys are different. Bentley et al. [1] have considered a restricted version of this problem in which no deletions are permitted. They are able to achieve searches in $O(\log^2 n)$ comparisons in the worst case and $O(\log n)$ on the average while spending $\Theta(n \log n)$ time for a sequence of n insertions. Their scheme may require $\Theta(n)$ for a single insertion but does achieve $O(\log n)$ average behaviour. We build on their scheme, and our merging algorithm to achieve $O(\log n)$ behaviour in the worst case for insertions.

The basic idea of the Bentley et al. scheme is to retain up to $\log_2 n$ sorted subarrays or blocks, one of length 2^i if the ith digit in the binary representation of n is a 1. A search is performed by applying binary search to the blocks in decreasing order by size. Insertion is similar to binary addition: a new element is a new block of length 1. Each time two blocks of length 2^i appear, they are merged into a single block of length 2^{i+1}. It follows that, although increasing the structure from $n = 2^k - 1$ to 2^k elements will spawn k merges and $\Theta(n)$ work, the average number of comparisons per insertion is $O(\log n)$. In order to avoid additional storage in the merge phase they employ Kronrod's algorithm [12].

To convert the $O(\log n)$ average insertion cost to a worst case bound, we must (i) amortize the merging cost and (ii) maintain $\Theta(\log n)$ searchability while doing so. One way to achieve the former subgoal is to apply what Bentley and Saxe [2] have dubbed the "online binary transform". The cost of merging is spread over several insertions in a manner that can be viewed as counting in a *redundant* binary system, using the digits 0, 1 *and* 2. The presence of a 2 in a given position indicates that the two corresponding blocks are being merged. If we delay, as much as possible the expansion $2 \rightarrow 10$, then there will always be at least one block of each possible size, and it is not hard to see that the merging of two blocks of size n can be spread over n steps. Under such a time sharing arrangement $\log n$ merges could not only be "active" but actually "worked on" in a single $O(\log n)$ "time slice". In practice one would clearly use $O(\log n)$ words of $\Theta(\log n)$ bits each to monitor the progress of the merges. One could, of course, carry out a purely implicit implementation. A cache of $O(\log n)$ elements can be used to encode each pointer. The cost of encoding and decoding this information is kept under control by adopting the policy of always working on the smallest uncompleted merge. This implies that if a "large" number of merges are worked on, then "most" of them are small and so less time is required to decode their status. Hence decoding is not a dominant issue.

The maintenance of searchability during the process follows by using the merging algorithm presented in the preceding section. Hence:

Theorem 3: There is an implicit data structure under which insertions can be performed in $O(\log n)$ steps and searches require $O(\log n)$ time on the average and $O(\log^2 n)$ in the worst case.

4. Conclusions and Further Work

We have introduced the notion of $O(\log n)$ searchability as a desirable property of an (in place) merging scheme. In addition to showing that this new property can be achieved in linear time we have shown the usefulness of the concept by demonstrating an implicit data structure requiring only $\Theta(\log^2 n)$ comparisons for a search and $O(\log n)$ for an insertion. This is the first such scheme guaranteeing both operations in "polylog" time.

An interesting area of further work is to try to accommodate deletions. We do not have a deletion scheme which performs well in the worst case. However, the following scheme appears to do well, $O(\log^2 n)$), on the average. A slightly modified version of the Bentley et al. scheme [1], using a redundant binary decomposition guarantees that there is always at least one block of each possible size. Then to delete element x

```
Find and "remove" x, this leaves a hole in a block of 2^r locations
For i = r step -1 until do
begin
    Using a binary search, find the element in a block of size 2^(i-1) which fits as
    closely as possible to the hole
    Move this element into the hole
end
This may leave no list of length 1; if so, initiate a sequence of "unmerges" analo-
gous to the merges required for insertion.
```

For purposes of discussing the run time, let us assume that n is of the form $2^k - 1$ and that each update consists of the deletion of a randomly chosen element and the insertion of a random value. Clearly the interesting metric is the number of "internal moves" required to shift the empty spot to the appropriate position for the element promoted from the smaller list. Unfortunately the analysis of this quantity, even in considering the first update, is tricky. A quick computation shows that the expected number of internal moves, after a random deletion, to make room for the new element from the list below is .8. If this implied all elements in the list below were equally likely to be promoted we would expect about $.8\ ((\log n) - 2)$ internal moves to be made in the first update. (Deletion of an element in the top level causes $\lceil \log n \rceil - 1$ promotions; and on the average 1 less promotion will be made.) This simple analysis is, however, inaccurate; and, our experiments support the hypothesis that $\frac{1}{2}((\log n) - 2)$ internal moves are expected for the first update. (Forming 128 structures of sizes $2^8 - 1$ and $2^{11} - 1$ we found averages of 3.01 and ± .02 and 4.48 ± .03 respectively.)

A number of experiments were performed, updating structures of various sizes. The basic conclusion is that the structure degenerates somewhat. The experiments involved creating a structure by forming sorted lists of random numbers. The process continues by repeatedly making a number of random updates and determining the average cost (over all elements currently in the structure) of performing an update by replacing that element. Note that although each value we determine is a mean it is not the average of independent values; hence, we do not expect (or find) that means of these means are normally distributed.

For structures of size $255 = 2^8 - 1$ the mean update cost quickly rose from 3.0 to 4.0 ± .2 (variance 3). With $2095 = 2^{11} - 1$ elements, the degeneration moved the update cost from an average of 4.5 to 8.1 ± .3 (variance 8). Both of these experiments were repeated several times picking up 128 observations of the structure spaced n updates apart. One run of the same experiment was performed with $n = 2^{14} - 1 = 16767$ and the mean update cost degenerated from roughly 7 to 15 ± 1 (variance 27). The structure appeared to degenerate to a condition under which the average search cost was a random variable from a distribution which look vaguely Poisson. Convergence to this state seemed to require only n updates in all cases. We observe, however, that the degeneracy was greater, in both absolute and relative terms, in the larger structure than the smaller ones. From our limited evidence, however, we are inclined to feel that this degeneration is not only $O(\log^2 n)$ but indeed $< \frac{1}{2} \log^2 n$ for all n, and so dominated by the comparisons required.

An analogy with updates made at random in binary search trees is natural. The analysis of the behaviour of such trees is a well known open problem [8], [9], [10]. Recently, Jeffrey Eppinger [4] has performed some very extensive simulations, using a month or so of CPU time. His experiments, like ours, involve deleting a random element and inserting a new one. When an element is to be deleted and it happens to be an internal node, it is natural to simply replace its value by that of its rightmost left descendant or its leftmost right descendant. If this choice is made randomly with equal probability (or even by alternating) it is said to be symmetric. If the same relative descendant is always chosen, the update method is aymmetric. Effinger discovered that, for symmetric updates, the average search time decreases from $2 \ln n (\approx 1.4 \log n)$ to roughly $1.2 \log n$ after about $n^2/4$ updates, where it stabilizes. Asymmetric updates also improve behaviour for about $n^2/4$ updates before the structure starts to degenerate until after n^2 updates the average search path seems to be $\Theta(\log^2 n)$.

Our observations are not as dramatic. The initial structure is better than one would naively estimate. It does degenerate, but apparently converges after $O(n)$ updates to something which, even if $\omega(\log n)$ is $O(\log^2 n)$, and hence is not the dominant term in the total cost.

There is, however, another interesting twist to our experiments. In some early work it was arbitrarily decided to delete only elements in the largest list (update cost is still the mean over all elements in the entire structure). The degeneration was substantially greater and continued for more updates than outlined above. Indeed it was this behaviour which truly sparked our interest in the experimental work. For 2^8-1 elements 5 ± 1 internal moves were required for an update, rather than 4. With $2^{11}-1$ elements, 23 ± 2 (variance 150) rather than 8.1 and with $2^{14}-1$, 85 ± 3 (variance 2200) rather than 15. (Note the huge variances of these mean values.) A general explanation of this phenomenon may be that random deletions in level i tend to pull up elements in level $i-1$ which differ greatly from the others in that level. The effect is to produce clusters of values at level $i-1$. The random deletion of elements at level $i-1$ seems to substantially reduce the impact of this process. We feel these preliminary experiments suggest a number of lines for mathematical and emperical work.

5. Acknowledgement

We thank Gaston Gonnet, Pedro Celis and the other members of the Data Structuring Group for a number of productive discussions on the mathematical and experimental aspects of this work, and Vitus Chan for some preliminary experimentation.

6. References

[1] Bentley, J.L., D. Detig, L. Guibas and J.B. Saxe: An Optimal Data Structure for Minimal-Storage Dynamic Member Searching, Carnegie-Mellon University, 1978.

[2] Bentley, J.L. and J.B. Saxe: Decomposable Searching Problems I. Static-to-Dynamic Transformation, Journal of Algorithms, 1, 4 (Dec. 1980), 301-358.

[3] Borodin, A.B., L.J. Guibas, N.A. Lynch and A.C. Yao: Efficient Searching Using Partial Ordering, IPL (12,2) April 1981, 71-75.

[4] Eppinger, J.L., An Empirical Study of Insertion and Deletion in Binary Trees (Sept. 1982) unpublished manuscript.

[5] Frederickson, G.N.: Implicit Data Structures with Fast Update, 21st Annual Symposium on Foundations of Computer Science, 1980, 255-259.

[6] Horvath, E.C.: Stable Sorting in Asymptotically Optimal Time and Extra Space, Journal of the ACM, 25, 2 (April 1978), 177-199.

[7] Hwang, F.K. and S. Lin: A Simple Algorithm for Merging Two Disjoint Linearly Ordered Sets, SIAM Journal on Computing, 1, 1 (March 1972), 31-39.

[8] Jonassen, A.T. and D.E. Knuth: A Trivial Algorithm Whose Analysis Isn't, Journal of Computer and System Sciences, 16, 3 (June 1978), 301-322.

[9] Knott, G.D.: Deletion in Binary Storage Trees, Dept. of Computer Science, Stanford University, Rep. STAN-CS-75-491, May 1975.

[10] Knuth, D.E.: The Art of Computer Programming, Vol. 3: Sorting and Searching, Addison-Wesley, Reading, MA., 1973.

[11] Knuth, D.E.: Deletions that Preserve Randomness, IEEE Transactions on Software Engineering, SE-3, 5 (Sept. 1977), 351-359.

[12] Kronrod, M.A.: An Optimal Ordering Algorithm Without a Field of Operation, Dok. Akad. Nauk SSSR, 186 (1969), 1256-1258.

[13] Munro, J.I. and H. Suwanda: Implicit Data Structure for Fast Search and Update, Journal of Computer and System Sciences, 21 2 (Oct. 1980), 236-250.

[14] Trabb Pardo, L.: Stable Sorting and Merging with Optimal Space and Time Bounds, SIAM Journal on Computing, 6, 2 (June 1977), 351-372.

[15] Wong, J.K.: Some Simple In-place merging Algorithms, BIT 21 (1981), 157-166.

STRONG ABSTRACT INTERPRETATION USING POWER DOMAINS (Extended Abstract)

A. Mycroft,(*) F. Nielson
Dept. of Computer Science
University of Edinburgh, Scotland.

Abstract Using a suitable notion of powerdomain we extend Abstract Interpretation to deal with partial functions so that non-termination is regarded as a specific value. We use this to validate a data flow analysis aimed at justifying when call-by-name can be implemented as call-by-value.

1. Introduction

In program optimisation, program transformation and program verification it is necessary to determine properties of the computations performed by a program. Often it suffices to know only properties of the values possible at points in the program. Abstract Interpretation is a general framework for performing such analyses which was mainly developed by Cousot and Cousot [2,3,4]. It is related to the lattice theoretic approach to data flow analysis of Kildall [10], Kam and Ullman [11] and further developed by Rosen and others [19]. Abstract Interpretation has a semantic basis not explicit in the lattice theoretic approach and enables one to concentrate on the data flow analysis problems independently of the actual algorithms used to compute their (approximate) solutions.

An introduction to Abstract Interpretation can be found in [2] from which we take the following motivating example: "An intuitive example (which we borrow from Sintzoff) is the rule of signs. The text -1515×17 may be understood to denote computations on the abstract universe $\{(+),(-),(\pm)\}$ where the semantics of arithmetic operators is defined by the rule of signs. The abstract execution $-1515 \times 17 \Rightarrow -(+) \times (+) \Rightarrow (-) \times (+) \Rightarrow (-)$, proves that -1515×17 is a negative number. Abstract Interpretation is concerned by a particular underlying structure of the universe of computation (the sign, in our example). It gives a summary of some facets of the actual executions of a program. In general this summary is simple to obtain but inaccurate (e.g. $-1515 + 17 \Rightarrow -(+) + (+) \Rightarrow (-) + (+) \Rightarrow (\pm)$)."

Traditionally, Abstract Interpretation has been considered in an operational setting for a flowchart-like language, but Donzeau-Gouge [5] and Nielson [15] carry the framework across to a denotational setting for while-programs. But in that work, and [2] as well, one can only infer information such as: "if control reaches this point then the set of values are such and such". One cannot determine whether for some input value some piece of program might not have terminated. This is perhaps not too important for the traditional applications of Abstract Interpretation to data flow analysis of a flowchart, but when Abstract Interpretation is extended to include applicative programs this becomes important. For then it is the parameter mechanism (e.g. call-by-value or call-by-name) that determines whether non-termination of eval-

(*):Current Address: Dept. of Comp. Sci., Chalmers Tekniska Högskolan, Göteborg, Sweden.

uation of an argument should lead to non-termination of the entire construct. So for program transformations (including procedure expansion) that may effectively change the parameter mechanism we believe it to be essential to have a data flow analysis that treats non-termination as a value in itself.

In this paper we provide such an extension of Abstract Interpretation. After the preliminaries (section 2) we define in section 3 a simple applicative programming language and its semantics. In section 5 we investigate the collecting semantics (static semantics [2], deductive semantics [4]). This is the "lifting" of the standard semantics of section 2 to operate on sets of values rather than the values themselves, and for this we use the theory of powerdomains developed in section 4. In section 6 we extend Abstract Interpretation to deal directly with non-termination and the collecting semantics is the most precise analysis of all. An important ingredient is to assume that abstraction spaces are equipped with two partial orders ($\sqsubseteq$,$\subseteq$) that were previously always identical. We shall explain that $\sqsubseteq$ can be viewed as improvement in evaluation in the sense of Scott, whereas $\subseteq$ represents approximation in the process of computing the sets of values arising. We apply this framework in section 7 to show that the traditional framework (e.g. [2]) is a special case of ours and we use it to validate the data flow analysis used by Mycroft [13] to justify transforming call-by-name into call-by-value.

Other work aimed at analysing applicative programs include Sharir [20] for call-by-value only, and Jones [8] who analyses the states processed by an interpreter for the language. An attempt at validating [13] by means of Abstract Interpretation was made in [14] but failed because it used the powerdomain of [17]. To some extent the notion of termination for flowcharts with procedures (but not call-by-name) is already implicit in Abstract Interpretation when based on Dijkstra's weakest precondition predicate transformer (as in [4]) or a forward predicate transformer from sets of values to sets of pairs of values (as in [3]). In contrast our denotational development is explicit in extending the notion of abstraction to express whether non-termination is possible. The idea of using two partial orders has already been used to give semantics of non-deterministic languages (e.g. [6]) but the idea of abstraction between objects with two partial orders is believed to be new.

2. Preliminaries

We now state general information on partial orders and fixed-points. Consult [1] for details not given here. A cpo (complete partial order) is a partially ordered set $D = (D,\sqsubseteq)$ with a least element, denoted by $\perp$, and where every directed subset Y of D has a least upper bound, denoted by $\bigsqcup Y$. For any set S one can obtain a cpo $S_\perp$ with elements $S \cup \{\perp\}$ ordered by $x \sqsubseteq y$ iff $x = \perp$ or $x = y$. If $D_1,\ldots,D_m$ are cpo's we write their cartesian product as $D_1\times..\times D_m$ and D^m if all D_i equal D. When ordered pointwise $D_1\times..\times D_m$ is a cpo with least upper bounds given pointwise. If D and E are cpo's we denote by D -> E the set of monotonic functions from D to E. It is ordered pointwise and gives a cpo with least upper bounds being pointwise.

A predicate Q on D is viewed as a subset of D. It is admissible if $\perp \in Q$ and we have $Y \subseteq Q$ implies $\bigsqcup Y \in Q$ for each directed subset Y of Q. If Q is a property on D -> E then we write $D \to_Q E$ for the set of monotonic functions from D to E that satisfy Q. If Q is admissible then $D \to_Q E$ is a cpo with least element and least upper bounds of directed sets as in D -> E. Example admissible properties are strictness (f is strict iff $f(\perp) = \perp$) and continuity (f is continuous iff $f(\bigsqcup Y) = \bigsqcup_{y \in Y} f(y)$ for any directed subset Y).

If f is a monotonic function from a cpo D to itself it has a least fixed-point LFP(f). For one can define by transfinite induction $f^{(\lambda)} = f(\bigsqcup_{\kappa<\lambda} f^{(\kappa)})$ for each ordinal λ. This is well-defined because D is a cpo and for a natural number n we may verify $f^{(n)} = f^{n+1}(\perp)$ where $f^0 = \lambda d.d$ and $f^{n+1} = f^n \circ f$. By transfinite induction one can prove $f^{(\lambda)} \sqsubseteq d$ whenever $f(d) \sqsubseteq d$ and that $f^{(\kappa)} \sqsubseteq f^{(\lambda)}$ whenever $\kappa < \lambda$. There is an ordinal λ such that $f^{(\lambda)} = f(f^{(\overline{\lambda})})$ and thus LFP(f) exists and is $f^{(\lambda)}$. Corresponding to this existence of least fixed-points there is the following induction principle: if D is a cpo, f is a monotonic function from D to D, Q is an admissible predicate on D and $\forall d.Q(d) \Rightarrow Q(f(d))$ then Q(LFP(f)). By the above remarks it merely suffices to show $Q(f^{(\lambda)})$ for arbitrary ordinals λ.

By an augmented cpo $D = ((D,\sqsubseteq),\subseteq)$ we mean a cpo $(D,\sqsubseteq)$ together with an additional partial order $\subseteq$. We call the augmentation admissible if $\subseteq$ is admissible when viewed as a predicate on D^2. Hence choosing $\subseteq$ as $\sqsubseteq$ turns a cpo into an admissibly augmented cpo. If D and E are augmented cpo's a function f from D to E is called $\subseteq$-monotonic iff $d_1 \subseteq d_2$ implies $f(d_1) \subseteq f(d_2)$ and we also use $\subseteq$ to name this monotonicity property on D -> E. When the augmentation of E is admissible then $\subseteq$ is admissible on D -> E, which means that $D \to_{\subseteq} E$ is a cpo with least element and least upper bounds of directed sets as in D -> E.

3. The Language and its Semantics

The applicative programming language we consider is a kind of recursion equation schema. Its expressions E and programs U are given by the following abstract syntax:

$$\begin{aligned} E ::= \; & X_i && (1 \le i \le k) \\ & |\, F_i(E_1,\ldots,E_k) && (1 \le i \le n) \\ & |\, A_i(E_1,\ldots,E_k) \end{aligned}$$

$$U ::= \text{let } F_1(X_1,\ldots,X_k)=E_1 \;\&\ldots\&\; F_n(X_1,\ldots,X_k)=E_n \text{ in } E_0$$

Here n and k are fixed natural numbers. The variables are $X_1,\ldots,X_k$, and $F_1,\ldots,F_n$ are the functions defined by mutual recursion, and $A_1,\ldots$ are predefined functions. The free variables in a program U (they occur in E_0) are taken to be input variables and we intend the parameter mechanism to be call-by-name. To keep the notation simple in this extended abstract we have assumed all functions take the same number of arguments and that all arguments are of the same type. In examples we ignore some of these restrictions.

We need several semantics for this language. All will be specified by the same set of semantic equations, but the basic operations will vary from semantics to semantics. To this end we introduce the notion of an interpretation which is a 6-tuple $(L_k, Q, L_1, \square, \pi_i, a_i)$ such that L_k, L_1 and $L = L_k \to_Q L_1$ are cpo's, $\pi_i \in L$, $a_i \in L$ and $\square : L \times L^n \to L$. Each interpretation gives a semantics to the language by

$$\mathcal{E}[\![E]\!] : L^n \to L; \quad \mathcal{U}[\![U]\!] : L$$

where, writing $\rho = \langle \rho_1, \ldots, \rho_n \rangle$, we have

$$\begin{aligned}
\mathcal{E}[\![X_i]\!]\rho &= \pi_i \\
\mathcal{E}[\![F_i(E_1,\ldots,E_k)]\!]\rho &= \rho_i \ \square \ \langle \mathcal{E}[\![E_1]\!]\rho, \ldots, \mathcal{E}[\![E_k]\!]\rho \rangle \\
\mathcal{E}[\![A_i(E_1,\ldots,E_k)]\!]\rho &= a_i \ \square \ \langle \mathcal{E}[\![E_1]\!]\rho, \ldots, \mathcal{E}[\![E_k]\!]\rho \rangle \\
\mathcal{U}[\![\text{let} \ldots \text{in } E_0]\!] &= \mathcal{E}[\![E_0]\!] (\mathrm{LFP}\ \lambda\rho . \langle \mathcal{E}[\![E_1]\!]\rho, \ldots, \mathcal{E}[\![E_n]\!]\rho \rangle)
\end{aligned}$$

This can easily be used to obtain the standard semantics [12] of the language: Let S be any set and a_i any continuous functions $a_i : S_\perp{}^k \to S_\perp$. By taking $L_1 = S_\perp$, $L_k = S_\perp{}^k$, Q continuity, $\pi_i \langle s_1, \ldots, s_k \rangle = s_i$ and

$$f_0 \ \square \ \langle f_1 \ldots f_k \rangle = \lambda(s_1 \ldots s_k).f_0(f_1(s_1 \ldots s_k), \ldots, f_k(s_1 \ldots s_k))$$

the above gives the standard semantics as substitution in the above parameterized semantics will verify. We will use the subscript S to indicate the standard semantics $(\mathcal{E}_S, \mathcal{U}_S)$. The details of S and a_i are of no further concern in this paper.

4. Powerdomains

In this section we develop the theory of powerdomains that we shall need and then compare the powerdomain with those of [17,18]. We first define the Egli-Milner order $\sqsubseteq_{EM}$ between subsets of a cpo D by $X \sqsubseteq_{EM} Y$ iff $\forall x \in X \exists y \in Y$: $x \sqsubseteq y$ and $\forall y \in Y \exists x \in X$: $x \sqsubseteq y$ as in [17]. This is a natural way of defining $\sqsubseteq$ pointwise on sets and gives a preorder. A subset X of D is convex if $d_1 \sqsubseteq d_2 \sqsubseteq d_3$ with $d_1, d_3 \in X$ implies $d_2 \in X$. If we restrict sets to being convex the Egli-Milner order becomes a partial order. Below we shall need the "left closure" of X defined by $LC(X) = \{d \in D \mid \exists x \in X: d \sqsubseteq x\}$ and the "right closure" defined by $RC(X) = \{d \in D \mid \exists x \in X: x \sqsubseteq d\}$. Then a subset X is convex iff $X = LC(X) \cap RC(X)$ and $X \sqsubseteq_{EM} Y$ iff $LC(X) \subseteq LC(Y)$ and $RC(X) \supseteq RC(Y)$.

We only need powerdomains of certain cpo's. An fdcpo is a cpo D with the finite domination property that $\{d' \in D \mid d' \sqsubseteq d\}$ is finite for each $d \in D$. Clearly $S_\perp$ is an fdcpo for an arbitrary set S and the cartesian product of fdcpo's is an fdcpo. We then define $\mathcal{P}(D) = (\{X \subseteq D \mid X \neq \emptyset \text{ and } X \text{ convex}\}, \sqsubseteq_{EM})$.

Lemma 1 If D is an fdcpo then $\mathcal{P}(D)$ is a cpo with least upper bound of any directed set $\mathcal{Y}$ given by $\bigsqcup \mathcal{Y} = (\bigcup_{Y \in \mathcal{Y}} LC(Y)) \cap \bigcap_{Y \in \mathcal{Y}} RC(Y)$. ∎

The condition that D is an fdcpo is sufficient but not necessary to ensure $\mathcal{P}(D)$ is a cpo. Next define a continuous semi-lattice to be a pair $(M,\cup)$ where M is a cpo and $\cup: M^2 \to M$ is continuous, associative, commutative and absorptive $(x\cup x=x)$. Defining $x \subseteq y$ by $x\cup y=y$ makes $(M,\subseteq)$ into an admissibly augmented cpo. For subsets X,Y of D we define $X \uplus Y = LC(X \cup Y) \cap RC(X \cup Y)$.

Lemma 2 If D is an fdcpo then $(\mathcal{P}(D),\uplus)$ is a continuous semi-lattice. ∎
The partial order obtained from $\uplus$ is ordinary set inclusion.

For fdcpo's D and E we may define $\biguplus\mathcal{Y} = (\bigcup_{Y\in\mathcal{Y}} LC(Y)) \cap \bigcup_{Y\in\mathcal{Y}} RC(Y)$ and if $\mathcal{Y}$ is a non-empty subset of $\mathcal{P}(D)$ then $\biguplus\mathcal{Y}$ is an element of $\mathcal{P}(D)$. A function $g: \mathcal{P}(D) \to \mathcal{P}(E)$ is completely linear iff $g(\biguplus\mathcal{Y}) = \biguplus_{Y\in\mathcal{Y}} g(Y)$ for all non-empty subsets $\mathcal{Y}$ of $\mathcal{P}(D)$. Let $\mathcal{L}$ name this property of complete linearity. Also define the singleton function $\{\cdot\}: D \to \mathcal{P}(D)$ by $\{\cdot\}(d) = \{d\}$.

Lemma 3 If D,E are fdcpo's and $f: D \to \mathcal{P}(E)$ then there is a unique completely linear $f^\dagger: \mathcal{P}(D) \to \mathcal{P}(E)$ such that $f^\dagger \circ \{\cdot\} = f$. It is given by $f^\dagger(Y) = \biguplus_{y\in Y} f(y)$. Furthermore, $\lambda f.f^\dagger$ is an isomorphism of partial orders from $D \to \mathcal{P}(E)$ to $\mathcal{P}(D) \to_{\mathcal{L}} \mathcal{P}(E)$ whose inverse is $\lambda g.g\circ\{\cdot\}$. ∎
We can use lemma 3 to "lift" a function $f: D \to E$ to $\hat{f}: \mathcal{P}(D) \to_{\mathcal{L}} \mathcal{P}(E)$ by defining $\hat{f} = (\{\cdot\}\circ f)^\dagger = \lambda Y.\biguplus_{y\in Y}\{f(y)\}$. For $g: \mathcal{P}(D) \to \mathcal{P}(E)$ we define $\bar{g}: \mathcal{P}(D) \to_{\mathcal{L}} \mathcal{P}(E)$ by $\bar{g} = (g\circ\{\cdot\})^\dagger = \lambda Y.\biguplus_{y\in Y} g\{y\}$. Lemma 3 then shows that $\mathcal{P}(D) \to_{\mathcal{L}} \mathcal{P}(E)$ is a cpo with least upper bound of a directed set G given by $\overline{\lambda Y.\bigsqcup_{g\in G} g(Y)}$ which need not be the pointwise least upper bound, because complete linearity is not in general an admissible property. For example if $f_i: \mathcal{P}(N_\perp) \to \mathcal{P}(N_\perp)$ are defined by $f_i(Y) = \{\perp \mid \exists n \in Y: n \geq i\} \cup \{0 \mid \exists n \in Y: n<i\}$ then all f_i are completely linear but $\lambda Y.\bigsqcup_{i\in N}(f_i(Y))$ is not.

We now compare our powerdomain to other definitions. Let N be the set of integers. Our $\mathcal{P}(N_\perp)$ clearly differs from the powerdomain of [17] in that we allow infinite subsets of $N_\perp$ to be elements of $\mathcal{P}(N_\perp)$ even when they do not contain $\perp$. Our powerdomain extends the Egli-Milner powerdomain of [1] where powerdomains are only defined for flat countable cpo's. In [18] a powerdomain is defined to be a pair consisting of the inclusion (our $\{\cdot\}$) and the partial order (our $\mathcal{P}(N_\perp^2)$). Our $(\{\cdot\}, \mathcal{P}(N_\perp^2))$ is not isomorphic (in the sense of [18]) to either of the two powerdomains defined there. The crucial observation is that $(\lambda\langle n_1,n_2\rangle.\{n_1\})^\dagger$ is not continuous in our case (consider the chain $Y_j = \{\langle 0,0\rangle,\ldots,\langle 0,j\rangle,\langle\perp,j+1\rangle,\ldots\}$) but that this is always the case in [18]. As a consequence we avoid assuming functions to be continuous. A disadvantage of our definition is that it is not clear how to extend it to domains of infinite height.

5. The Collecting Semantics

The standard semantics of section 3 has functionality $\mathcal{U}_S[[U]] : S_\perp^k \to S_\perp$ and thus operates on values. When performing abstract interpretation we have a semantic function $\mathcal{U}_L[[U]] : L_k \to L_1$ that operates on representations of sets of values. As in the traditional framework [2] one can consider a semantics that is as precise as possible, by which we mean that it equals the "lifting" $\widehat{\mathcal{U}_S[[U]]}$ of the standard semantics as defined in section 4. We call this semantics the collecting semantics (static semantics [2], deductive semantics [4]) and denote it $\mathcal{U}_C[[U]]$. Intuitively, the collecting semantics is the extension to sets of values and functions over them from the standard semantics of values and functions over them. It will be specified by the collecting interpretation $<\mathcal{P}(S_\perp^k), Q, \mathcal{P}(S_\perp), \Box, \hat{\pi}_i, \hat{a}_i>$ where $S_\perp, \pi_i, a_i$ are as section 3 and the choice of Q and $\Box$ is made below.

One possibility for $\Box$ is $\Box_i$ defined by $g_0 \Box_i <g_1,\ldots,g_k> = \lambda Y.g_0(g_1(Y)\times\ldots\times g_k(Y))$ which is our formulation of the "independent attribute method" of [9] and occurs in [7] as well. This is not an appropriate choice for the collecting semantics as $\mathcal{U}_C[[\text{let}\ldots\text{in } X_1 * X_1]]$ when applied to $\{1,2\}$ would produce $\{2,3,4\}$ contrary to the $\{2,4\}$ produced by $\widehat{\mathcal{U}_S[[\ldots]]}$. Another possibility then is $\Box_r$ defined by $g_0 \Box_r <g_1,\ldots,g_k> = \overline{g_0 \Box_i <g_1,\ldots,g_k>}$ (see section 4) which corresponds to the "relational method" of [9]. Then the above phenomenon does not arise whereas it would for all the alternatives to $\Box_i$ considered in [7]. So define the collecting interpretation C to have $\Box_r$ for $\Box$ and $\subseteq$-monotonicity for Q. Also let C' have $\Box_r$ for $\Box$ and complete linearity for Q. Since $\hat{}$ produces completely linear functions one might regard C' as the natural choice for the collecting interpretation but we prefer C because in general we can enforce $\subseteq$-monotonicity but not complete linearity in the development of Abstract Interpretation in section 6. Clearly C and C' are interpretations in the sense of section 3 as is C'' with $\Box_i$ for $\Box$ and $\subseteq$-monotonicity (but not complete linearity) for Q.

The overall correctness condition of the collecting semantics is

Proposition 1 ("lifting"). $\mathcal{U}_C[[U]] = \widehat{\mathcal{U}_S[[U]]}$ for all programs U. ∎

This result holds for C' as well but we have already seen it fails for C''. For the proof observe that $\mathcal{U}_{C'}[[U]]$ evidently is completely linear and the use of $\Box_r$ in C turns out to make $\mathcal{U}_C[[U]]$ completely linear as well. It therefore suffices to show the pointwise correctness condition that $\mathcal{U}_C[[U]] \circ \{\bullet\} = \{\bullet\} \circ \mathcal{U}_S[[U]]$ which also holds for C' and C''. If we let $Q(\rho_S,\rho_C)$ stand for $\forall i.(\rho_C)_i \circ \{\bullet\} = \{\bullet\} \circ (\rho_S)_i$ the proof amounts to showing $Q(\rho_S,\rho_C) \Rightarrow \mathcal{E}_C[[E]]\,\rho_C \circ \{\bullet\} = \{\bullet\} \circ \mathcal{E}_S[[E]]\,\rho_S$ by structural induction on E. To infer the result for programs we use the induction principle stated in section 2 on the function $\lambda<\rho_S,\rho_C>.<F_S(\rho_S),F_C(\rho_C)>$ where $F(\rho) = <\ldots,\mathcal{E}[[E_i]]\,\rho,\ldots>$. One can show that $LFP(F_C) = F_C(\bigsqcup_{n=0}^{\infty} F_C^n(\perp))$ which differs from $\bigsqcup_{n=0}^{\infty} F_C^n(\perp)$ in general (F_C need not be continuous).

6. Abstract Interpretation

The collecting semantics is not decidable in general and as explained in the introduction the purpose of abstract interpretation is to obtain approximate results by easy (and hence decidable) calculations. The idea is then to replace $\mathcal{P}(S_\perp^k)$ and $\mathcal{P}(S_\perp)$ of the collecting interpretations by suitable structures L_k and L_1. We then need concretization functions [2,3] $\gamma_k : L_k \to \mathcal{P}(S^k)$ and $\gamma_1 : L_1 \to \mathcal{P}(S_\perp)$ to express the intended meaning of L_k and L_1. If L_1 is the universe of signs used in the introduction we would have $\gamma_1((+)) = \{0,1,2,\ldots\}$. If the collecting semantics specifies a set $Y \in \mathcal{P}(S_\perp)$ of values to be possible and a more "abstract" (or approximate) semantics specifies z then we want z to be a safe description of Y, that is $Y \subseteq \gamma_1(z)$. It will not do to use $Y \sqsubseteq_{EM} \gamma_1(z)$: If Y does not contain $\perp$ we would in effect require $Y = \gamma_1(z)$ which is too demanding and if Y did contain $\perp$ we would be allowed to forget it and this is not a safe basis for program transformations that may change the parameter mechanism. Also $Y \subseteq \gamma_1(z)$ is the notion of safe approximation well-known in data flow analysis. So if $\mathcal{U}_C[\![U]\!] : \mathcal{P}(S_\perp^k) \to \mathcal{P}(S_\perp)$ is to be approximated by $\mathcal{U}_L[\![U]\!] : L_k \to L_1$, we will require that the following diagram "commutes":

$$\begin{array}{ccc}
\mathcal{P}(S_\perp^k) & \xrightarrow{\ \mathcal{U}_C[\![U]\!]\ } & \mathcal{P}(S_\perp) \\
\uparrow \gamma_k & & \cap\!\!\!\!\mid\ \ \uparrow \gamma_1 \\
L_k & \xrightarrow{\ \mathcal{U}_L[\![U]\!]\ } & L_1
\end{array}$$

That is we want $\forall z \in L_k : \mathcal{U}_C[\![U]\!](\gamma_k(z)) \subseteq \gamma_1(\mathcal{U}_L[\![U]\!](z))$ and we abbreviate this to $\mathcal{U}_L[\![U]\!] \geq_{\gamma_k \gamma_1} \mathcal{U}_C[\![U]\!]$ and sometimes $\mathcal{U}_L[\![U]\!] \geq \mathcal{U}_C[\![U]\!]$.

We next must determine what structure we expect L_k and L_1 to possess and what properties functions in $L_k \to L_1$ should fulfil. As before we shall need L_k and L_1 to be equipped with a partial order $\sqsubseteq$ resembling $\sqsubseteq_{EM}$, that is $\sqsubseteq$ will correspond to improvement in evaluation in the sense of Scott. This order will be used when computing least fixed points and we shall assume functions are monotonic with respect to this partial order. It is also natural to assume L_k and L_1 are equipped with an additional partial order $\subseteq$ resembling subset-inclusion, that is $\subseteq$ will correspond to making more approximate computations of the sets of values that may arise. This will enable us to compare "approximate" interpretations with one another. Functions will be assumed to be monotonic with respect to this partial order ($\subseteq$-monotonic). This is natural because computations on an approximated set of values should give an approximation to the computations on the set itself. From the collecting semantics one might expect that functions should be completely linear, but even the weaker property of binary linearity ($f(X \cup Y) = f(X) \cup f(Y)$) does not hold in general even in the traditional framework of Cousot and Cousot. This discussion motivates the following definition of interpretations that are "like the collecting interpretation".

Definition An approximate interpretation is an interpretation $(L_k, \subseteq, L_1, \square, l_i, f_i)$ where L_k and L_1 are augmented cpo's with the augmentation of L_1 admissible. Writing $L = L_k \to_{\subseteq} L_1$ we have $l_i \in L$ and $f_i \in L$ and we require that $\square : L \times L^n \to L$ is not only monotonic but also $\subseteq$-monotonic (where we extend $\subseteq$ pointwise on cartesian products and function spaces for this to make sense). ■

The collecting interpretation C is an approximate interpretation as is C" but not C':

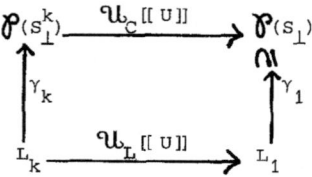

any approximate interpretation has least upper bounds to be pointwise but this is not the case for C'.

We now study connections between interpretations such that one semantics is an approximation of the other. A function γ from augmented cpo M to augmented cpo L is pseudo-strict iff $\gamma(\bot) \supseteq \bot$ and pseudo-continuous iff $\bigsqcup_{Y\in\mathcal{Y}}\gamma(Y) \subseteq \gamma(\bigsqcup\mathcal{Y})$ for directed subsets $\mathcal{Y}$ of M. Strictness implies pseudo-strictness and continuity implies pseudo-continuity, which is essentially the dual notion of the quasi-continuity considered in [18].

Definition Let $L = (L_k, \subseteq, L_1, \square_L, l_i, f_i)$ be an approximate interpretation and $M = (M_k, Q, M_1, \square_M, m_i, g_i)$ be an interpretation with Q admissible (as would hold if M is an approximate interpretation). A pair $\langle\gamma_k: M_k \to L_k, \gamma_1: M_1 \to L_1\rangle$ is called a correct concretization from M to L provided:

- γ_1 is pseudo-strict and pseudo-continuous
- $m_i \geq_{\gamma_k\gamma_1} l_i$ and $g_i \geq f_i$
- $g_i \geq f_i$ implies $g_0 \square_M \langle g_1,\ldots,g_k\rangle \geq f_0 \square_L \langle f_1,\ldots,f_k\rangle$ ∎

The prime example of L is of course the collecting interpretation C.

Proposition 2 ("correctness") If $\langle\gamma_k, \gamma_1\rangle$ is a correct concretization from M to L, where M and L are as above, then $\mathcal{U}_M[\![U]\!] \geq_{\gamma_k\gamma_1} \mathcal{U}_L[\![U]\!]$ for all programs U. ∎

If we write $\rho_M \geq \rho_L$ for $\forall i.(\rho_m)_i \geq (\rho_L)_i$ the proof amounts to showing $\rho_M \geq \rho_L \Rightarrow \mathcal{E}_M[\![E]\!]\rho_M \geq \mathcal{E}_L[\![E]\!]\rho_L$ by structural induction on E and then infer the result for programs by using the induction principle of section 2. A simple application of proposition 2 with γ_k and γ_1 being the identities shows that $\mathcal{U}_{C''}[\![U]\!]Y \supseteq \mathcal{U}_C[\![U]\!]Y$ as the example in section 5 has already suggested. By proposition 1 this means $\mathcal{U}_{C''}[\![U]\!]\,Y \supseteq \{\mathcal{U}_S[\![U]\!]\,y \mid y \in Y\}$.

So far we can use proposition 2 to prove an approximate semantics correct with respect to the collecting semantics and thus the standard semantics. It is also possible to "induce" an approximate semantics from the collecting semantics. To specify this we need the following generalisation of [4]:

Definition If L and M are augmented cpo's we call $\langle\alpha: L \to M, \gamma: M \to L\rangle$ a pair of adjoined functions iff α (the abstraction function) and γ are monotonic and $\subseteq$-monotonic and additionally $\alpha \circ \gamma \subseteq id$ and $\gamma \circ \alpha \supseteq id$ (for id the identity function). ∎

The key ingredient in this definition is $\forall z \in L.\gamma(\alpha(z)) \supseteq z$ which is the notion of safe approximation already discussed.

Proposition 3 ("induced interpretations"). Let $L = (L_k, \subseteq, L_1, \square_L, l_i, f_i)$ be an approximate interpretation, M_k and M_1 augmented cpo's with M_1 admissible, and $\langle\alpha_k: L_k \to M_k, \gamma_k\rangle$, $\langle\alpha_1, \gamma_1\rangle$ pairs of adjoined functions. The induced interpretation is the approximate interpretation $M = \langle M_k, \subseteq, M_1, \square_M, \alpha_1 \circ l_i \circ \gamma_k, \alpha_1 \circ f_i \circ \gamma_k\rangle$ with

$g_0 \square_M \langle g_1,\ldots,g_k \rangle = \alpha_1 \circ [(\gamma_1 \circ g_0 \circ \alpha_k) \square_L \langle \ldots,\gamma_1 \circ g_i \circ \alpha_k,\ldots \rangle] \circ \gamma_k$. If γ_1 is pseudo-strict and pseudo-continuous then $\langle \gamma_k,\gamma_1 \rangle$ is a correct concretization from M to L. ■
In the applications in section 7 we shall use this proposition as a handy means of specifying an approximate interpretation. It is also helpful to be able to perform the abstractions in several stages and then compose them. That this is possible follows from:

Proposition 4 ("transitivity of abstraction") Let approximate interpretations L,M and N be related in the obvious manner by pairs of adjoined functions $\langle \alpha_k: L_k \to M_k,\gamma_k \rangle, \langle \alpha_1,\gamma_1 \rangle$ from L to M and $\langle \alpha_k',\gamma_k' \rangle, \langle \alpha_1',\gamma_1' \rangle$ from M to N. Then $\langle \alpha_k' \circ \alpha_k,\gamma_k \circ \gamma_k' \rangle$ and $\langle \alpha_1' \circ \alpha_1,\gamma_1 \circ \gamma_1' \rangle$ are pairs of adjoined functions from L to N. If additionally $\langle \gamma_k,\gamma_1 \rangle$ and $\langle \gamma_k',\gamma_1' \rangle$ are correct concretizations then so is $\langle \gamma_k \circ \gamma_k', \gamma_1 \circ \gamma_1' \rangle$. ■
Further, this gives a hierarchy of approximate interpretations along the lines of [2,4].

We have not compared the solutions obtained by Abstract Interpretation in this framework to more traditional data flow analyses like [20]. We believe this could be done by adapting [15] to this framework.

7. Applications

We give three applications. The first is to show an "external" and an "internal" reason for why our framework generalises the traditional theory [2,3,4,5,15]. The third is to sketch how the data flow analysis of [13] can be justified in our framework. We believe it can at most very indirectly be justified by means of the traditional framework. Yet another application is given in [16] where it is shown that the ideas developed above can also be used as a new framework for defining the semantics of non-deterministic programs.

For the "external" explanation we note that [2,3,4] do not distinguish between $\sqsubseteq$ and $\subseteq$ and thus have $\subseteq$ to be $\sqsubseteq$. Also [2,3,4] essentially have k = 1 in that the only parameter is the entire state; for this remark to be fully correct we would need to treat conditional as a special construct. Composition $\square$ is always taken to be ordinary functional composition. Then our definition of adjoined functions coincides with [4] and pseudo-strictness and pseudo-continuity are vacuously fulfilled. Further, an approximate interpretation $(L_k,\sqsubseteq,L_1,\square,l_i,f_i)$ is specified by the tuple (L_1,f_i) much as in [4] and we only need one pair of adjoined functions.

An "internal" construction can be given by specifying the equivalent of the collecting interpretation of [2,5,15] as induced from our collecting interpretation (proposition 3). Instead of $\mathcal{P}(S_\perp)$ use $((2^S,\sqsubseteq),\sqsubseteq)$ with $\gamma_1: 2^S \to \mathcal{P}(S_\perp)$ given by $\gamma_1(Y) = Y \cup \{\perp\}$. This formalises the intuition that [2,5,15] ignore the issue of non-termination. We define $\alpha_1(Y) = Y \cap S$ and similarly for γ_k,α_k. Ordering 2^S and $2^{(S^k)}$ by subset ($\sqsubseteq$) satisfies all requirements of proposition 3. As an example

$(\alpha_1 \circ \hat{a}_i \circ \gamma_k)(Y) = \{a_i(y) | y \in Y\}$ provided $a_i: S_\perp^k \to S_\perp$ satisfies $a_i(y) = \perp$ $\Leftrightarrow \exists j: \pi_j(y) = \perp$ (where π_j is as in section 3).

A second application is mainly used as a stepping-stone to the third, and consists of the justification of a data flow analysis ("independent attribute method" in [9]) which analyses parts of programs without considering their mutual connection. Beginning with the collecting semantics C we use proposition 3 to obtain an approximate interpretation induced from C by means of $\gamma_k(Y_1,\ldots,Y_k) = Y_1\times\ldots\times Y_k$, $\alpha_k(Y) = \langle\{y_1 | y \in Y\},\ldots,\{y_k | y \in Y\}\rangle$ and $\gamma_1 = \alpha_1 = \lambda Y.Y$. This gives an approximate interpretation $I = (\mathcal{P}(S_\perp)^k, \subseteq, \mathcal{P}(S_\perp), \square_I, \pi_i^I, a_i^I)$ where $\pi_i^I(Y_1,\ldots,Y_k) = Y_i$ and $a_i^I(Y_1,\ldots,Y_k) = \{a_i(y_1,\ldots y_k) | y_i \in Y_i\}$. We can also use proposition 2 to replace $\square_I$ with the simpler $\square_I'$ defined by $f_0 \square_I' \langle f_1,\ldots,f_k\rangle = \lambda(Y_1,\ldots,Y_k).\ f_0(\ldots,f_i(Y_1,\ldots,Y_k),\ldots)$. We call I the independent attribute interpretation.

For the third application we show how the data flow analyses of Mycroft [13] can be justified in this framework. The results of the data flow analyses can be used to detect situations where call-by-name can safely be replaced by call-by-value and we refer to [13] for an explanation of this. It may be helpful to illustrate the results of the data flow analyses by means of the following program (U):

$$\begin{aligned}&\text{let } F(X_1,X_2,X_3,X_4,X_5) = \text{if } X_1 = 1\\ &\qquad\qquad\qquad\qquad\qquad\ \text{then } X_2 \times X_3\\ &\qquad\qquad\qquad\qquad\qquad\ \text{else } F(X_1-1,X_3,X_2,X_5,X_4)\\ &\text{in } F(X_1,X_2,X_3,X_4,X_5)\end{aligned}$$

Here $X_2 \times X_3$ should really be written $A_i(X_2,X_3,X_3,X_3,X_3)$ with a_i (the meaning of A_i in the standard semantics) fulfilling $a_i(x_1,x_2,x_3,x_4,x_5) = x_1 \times x_2$ and similarly for the other constructs. We assume only one type, the integers, and code true and false by odd and even numbers respectively (†). The standard semantics is given by the standard interpretation $(N_\perp^k$, continuity, $N_\perp, \square, \pi_i, a_i)$ and the definitions of the a_i are the obvious ones.

Let D by the cpo $\{0,1\}$ ordered by $0 \sqsubseteq 1$. By setting $\subseteq$ equal to $\sqsubseteq$ this gives an admissibly augmented cpo. The intention is to let 0 represent non-termination and 1 possible termination. We then specify $L = (D^k, \subseteq, D, \square_L, \pi_i^L, a_i^L)$ as induced from I by $\gamma_k\langle d_1,\ldots,d_k\rangle = \langle\gamma_1(d_1),\ldots,\gamma_1(d_k)\rangle$ and $\alpha_k\langle Y_1,\ldots,Y_k\rangle = \langle\alpha_1(Y_1),\ldots,\alpha_1(Y_k)\rangle$. We choose $\gamma_1(1) = N_\perp$, $\gamma_1(0) = \{\perp\}$ and $\alpha_1(Y) = 1$ except for $\alpha_1(\{\perp\}) = 0$. So 0 in the abstract interpretation means that non-termination is guaranteed in the standard interpretation and because $a_i^L \geq a_i^I$ this means that if $a_i^L(0,1,\ldots) = 0$ then $a_i(\perp,n_2,\ldots,n_k) = \perp$ for all choices of $n_i \in N$. So $A_i(E_1,\ldots,E_k)$ cannot terminate unless E_1 does. We may calculate $\pi_i^L(d_1,\ldots,d_k) = d_i$ and $(g_0\square_L\langle g_1,\ldots,g_k\rangle)\langle d_1,\ldots,d_k\rangle$ $g_0\langle\ldots,g_i\langle d_1,\ldots,d_k\rangle,\ldots\rangle$ and $(\cdot+\cdot)^L\langle d_1,d_2\rangle = d_1 \sqcap d_2$. Then/

(†) This coding trick is not inherently necessary. In the full version we extend the framework to allow several types (and thus avoid the trick) and characterise $\mathcal{P}(N_\perp^k)$ as the k-fold tensor-product $\mathcal{P}(N_\perp) \otimes \ldots \otimes \mathcal{P}(N_\perp)$.

Then $\mathcal{U}_L[[U]] = \lambda<d_1,d_2,d_3,d_4,d_5>.d_1 \sqcap d_2 \sqcap d_3$ so let... in $F(E_1,E_2,E_3,E_4,E_5)$ cannot terminate unless all of E_1,E_2,E_3 do.

Next we specify M. Here we turn D into an admissibly augmented cpo by setting $\sqsubseteq$ equal to $\sqsupseteq$ which could not be done in the traditional framework. The intention now is to let 1 represent termination and 0 possible non-termination. Again we induce $M = (D^k,\sqsubseteq,D,\sqcup_M,\pi_i^M,a_i^M)$ from C by letting γ_k' and α_k' on tuples be γ_1' and α_1' pointwise and $\gamma_1'(0) = N_\perp$, $\gamma_1'(1) = N$ and $\alpha_1'(Y-\{\perp\}) = 1$, $\alpha_1'(Y \cup \{\perp\}) = 0$. So 1 in the abstract interpretation means that termination is guaranteed in the standard interpretation and because $a_i^m \geq a_i^I$ this means that if $a_i^M(0,1,...) = 1$ then $a_i(\perp,n_2,...,n_k) \neq \perp$ for all choices of $n_i \neq \perp$. So $A_i(E_1,...E_k)$ will terminate if $E_2,...,E_k$ all do. Formulae for π_i^M and $\sqcup_M$ are as for π_i^L and $\sqcup_L$, and $(\cdot + \cdot)^M<d_1,d_2> = d_1 \sqcap d_2$ so $E_1 + E_2$ terminates if both E_1 and E_2 do. As expected $\mathcal{U}_M[[U]] = \lambda<d_1,...,d_5>.0$.

To gain perspective on the method note that if $X_1 = 1$ was replaced by $X_1 = 0$ (to give U') one would have $\alpha_1' \circ \mathcal{U}_I[[U']] \circ \gamma_k' = \lambda<d_1,...,d_5>.d_1 \sqcap d_2 \sqcap d_3$ but $\mathcal{U}_M[[U']]$ equals $\mathcal{U}_M[[U]]$. So the analysis does not detect that termination of the modified program is guaranteed. This is not only due to the choice of M but more fundamentally it is because Abstract Interpretation has here been formulated in a first-order manner where we only express the set of possible results of a function and not how results are related to their inputs (e.g. X_1 has been decreased). This is satisfactory for data flow analysis and by a suitable choice of M it should be possible to detect termination for programs with a fixed upper bound upon the depth of recursion. To use Abstract Interpretation to prove termination of "all" programs it would need to be formulated in a second-order manner and [3] is a first step in that direction.

Acknowledgements

This work was supported by the British Science and Engineering Research Council and the Danish Natural Science Research Council.

References

[1] K. Apt, G. Plotkin: A Cook's Tour of Countable Nondeterminism, Proceedings ICALP 1981, Lecture Notes in Computer Science 115, pp. 479-494, (Springer-Verlag, Berlin, 1981).

[2] P. Cousot, R. Cousot: Abstract Interpretation: A Unified Lattice Model for Static Analysis of Programs by Construction or Approximation of Fixpoints, Conf. Record of the 4th ACM Symposium on Principles of Programming Languages, 1977.

[3] P. Cousot, R. Cousot: Static Determination of Dynamic Properties of Recursive Procedures, in: E.J. Neuhold, Ed., Formal Descriptions of Programming Concepts, pp. 237-277, (North-Holland, Amsterdam, 1978).

[4] P. Cousot, R. Cousot: Systematic Design of Program Analysis Frameworks, Conf. Record of the 6th ACM Symposium on Principles of Programming Languages, 1979.

[5] V. Donzeau-Gouge: Utilisation de la Sémantique Dénotationelle Pour l'Étude d'Interprétations Non-Standard, Rapport de Recherche, No. 273, INRIA, Rocquencourt, Le Chesnay, France, 1978.

[6] M. Hennessy, G. Plotkin: Full Abstraction for a Simple Parallel Programming Language, Proceedings MFCS 1979, Lecture Notes in Computer Science 74, pp. 108-120, (Springer-Verlag, 1979).

[7] M. Hennessy: Powerdomains and Nondeterministic Recursive Definitions, 5th Int. Symp. on Programming, Lecture Notes in Computer Science 137, (Springer-Verlag, 1982).

[8] N. Jones: Flow Analysis of Lambda Expressions, Proceedings ICALP 1981, Lecture Notes in Computer Science 115, pp. 114-128, (Springer-Verlag, Berlin, 1981).

[9] N. Jones, S. Muchnick: Complexity of Flow Analysis, Inductive Assertion Synthesis and a Language Due to Dijkstra, in S. Muchnick and N. Jones, Eds., Program Flow Analysis: Theory and Applications, pp. 380-393, (Prentice-Hall, New Jersey, 1981).

[10] G. Kildall: A Unified Approach to Global Program Optimization, Conf. Record of ACM Symposium on Principles of Programming Languages, 1973.

[11] J. Kam, J. Ullman: Monotonic Data Flow Analysis Frameworks, Acta Informatica 7, 1977.

[12] R. Milne, C. Strachey: A Theory of Programming Language Semantics, Chapman and Hall, London, 1976.

[13] A. Mycroft: The Theory and Practice of Transforming Call-by-need into Call-by-value. Proc. 4th Int. Symp. on Programming, Lecture Notes in Computer Science 83, (Springer-Verlag, 1980).

[14] A. Mycroft: Abstract Interpretation and Optimising Transformations for Applicative Programs, Ph.D. thesis, University of Edinburgh, 1981.

[15] F. Nielson: A Denotational Framework for Data Flow Analysis, Acta Informatica 18, 265-287 (1982).

[16] F. Nielson: Towards Viewing Nondeterminism as Abstract Interpretation, University of Edinburgh, 1983.

[17] G. Plotkin: A Powerdomain Construction, Siam J. Comput. 5,3 (1976), pp.452-487.

[18] G. Plotkin: A Powerdomain for Countable Nondeterminism, Proceedings ICALP 1982, Lecture Notes in Computer Science 140, pp. 418-428, (Springer-Verlag, Berlin, 1982).

[19] B. Rosen: Monoids for Rapid Data Flow Analysis, Siam J. Comput. 9, 1 (1980).

[20] M. Sharir: Data Flow Analysis of Applicative Programs, Proceedings ICALP 1981, Lecture Notes in Computer Science 115, pp. 98-113, (Springer-Verlag, Berlin, 1981).

TESTING EQUIVALENCES FOR PROCESSES

R. de Nicola and M.C.B. Hennessy
Dept. of Computer Science
University of Edinburgh
Edinburgh EH9 3JZ, Scotland

Abstract

Given a set of processes and a set of tests on these processes we show how to define in a natural way three different equivalences on processes. These equivalences are applied to a particular language CCS. We give associated complete proof systems and fully abstract models. These models have a simple representation in terms of trees.

Introduction

In this paper we present a new semantic theory for processes. By this we mean a structured collection of objects which can be used to adequately model the behaviour of processes as represented by programs in a language with concurrent features. If the language were purely sequential, such as PASCAL, then the relevant semantic theory would be some suitable collection of functions. It is well-known that if the language has concurrent features the behaviour of its programs cannot be adequately represented in this way. However if we are to build a semantic theory then a counterpart to functions is needed; if we model programs written in such languages what are the objects in the models?

Various suggestions have been made, [8],[10],[12],[14]. For example in [12], communication trees are put forward but unfortunately they need to be factored by certain equivalences. Moreover the behaviour which they describe seems too detailed in certain respects, [1],[11]. The models presented here, called representation trees, are similar to those discussed in [9],[11],[14]. However we show that they can be motivated in a very simple and appealing manner.

The behaviour of programs or processes, can be investigated by a series of tests. For example with sequential programs we can consider a test as a pair consisting of a predicate on the input domain and a predicate on the output domain. In general we can say that two processes are equivalent if they pass exactly the same set of tests. In §1 we formalise this natural notion of equivalence. Processes are inherently non-deterministic and so different applications of a particular test to a particular process may yield different results. Because of this phenomenon we obtain three different behavioural preorders on processes based on their ability to pass tests and their inability not to fail tests. In the remainder of the paper we apply these notions to a particular language, CCS [12]. In §3 we give sound and complete proof systems for the substitutive relation generated by each of the three behavioural preorders. These systems consist essentially of a set of axioms together with a form of induction. Fully abstract models arise naturally from the proof systems and in §4 we show that these models have a very intuitive representation in terms of certain kinds of trees, called representation trees. Informally such a tree describes the possible sequence of actions a process can perform together with a set of subsets of actions representing the possible future of the process.

We omit all proofs from this presentation. They may be found in the complete version of the paper, [2].

§1. General Setting

We assume a predefined set of states, States, and we let s range over States. A computation is any non-empty sequence of states. Let Comp denote the set of computations, ranged over by c. Note that a computation may be finite or infinite. Let $\mathcal{O}$, $\mathcal{P}$ (ranged over by o, p respectively) be sets of predefined observers and processes. Observers may be thought of as agents which perform tests. The effect of observers performing tests on processes may be formalised by saying that for every o and p there is a non-empty set of computations Comp(o,p). If $c \in$ Comp(o,p) then the result of o testing p may be the computation c. To indicate that a process passes a test we choose some subset of States, denoted Success, to be successful states. Then a computation is successful if it contains a successful state. On the other hand a computation will be called unsuccessful if it contains no successful state. To develop a useful theory we need one further ingredient. The semantic theory of sequential computations, developed in [15],[17], was greatly facilitated by hypothesising the existence of "partial objects". For example the symbol Ω is often used to denote a partial program whose behaviour is totally undefined. It will also be convenient for us to consider such partial objects. To this end we assume the existence of a unary post-fixed predicate on states, $\uparrow$. Informally $s\uparrow$ means that s is a partial-state, whose properties are under-defined. We can now define divergence, a unary post-fixed predicate on computations, which we denote by $\Uparrow$:

$c\Uparrow$ if i) c is unsuccessful

or ii) c contains a state s, such that $s\uparrow$ and is not preceded by a successful state.

By convention a state precedes itself.

We may now tabulate the effect of an observer o testing a process p by noting the types of computations in Comp(o,p). For every $o \in \mathcal{O}$, $p \in \mathcal{P}$ let $R(o,p) \subseteq \{\top,\bot\}$, the result set, be defined by:

i) $\top \in R(o,p)$ if $\exists c \in$ Comp(o,p) such that c is successful.

ii) $\bot \in R(o,p)$ if $\exists c \in$ Comp(o,p) such that $c\Uparrow$.

Note that we do not differentiate between an experiment which deadlocks, i.e. the computation is finite without reaching a successful state and an experiment which diverges, i.e. the computation goes on forever without ever reaching a successful state: they both contribute $\bot$ to the result set. From the observers point of view both computations are equally useless; they yield no information on the nature of the process. Using this tabulation we can distinguish between processes which cannot fail a test (the result set is {T}) and processes which may pass a test (the result set is {⊥,T}). This will be elaborated upon shortly.

A natural equivalence between processes immediately suggests itself:

$p \sim^{\mathcal{O}} q$ if for every $o \in \mathcal{O}$, $R(o,p) = R(o,q)$.

However it will be more fruitful to consider instead preorders, i.e. relations which are transitive and reflexive. In general preorders (or partial orders) are easier to deal with mathematically and we can easily recover the equivalence $\sim^{\mathcal{O}}$ by studying a preorder which generates it. This gives us a certain amount of freedom since in general there may be more than one preorder which generates any given equivalence. Finally preorders are more primitive than equivalences and therefore we may use them to concentrate on more primitive notions which combine to form the equivalence $\sim^{\mathcal{O}}$.

The set {T,⊥} may be viewed as the simple two point lattice $\mathbb{O}$, given in Fig. 1.a. So every result set can be viewed as a subset of this lattice. The theory of Powerdomains [13],[16], provides us with general methods of ordering subsets of (complete) partial orders. In [5] it was argued that three different powerdomain constructions arise naturally and that they correspond to three natural views of nondeterministic computations. Here we use these three constructions to give three different orderings on result sets. Since the partial order $\mathbb{O}$ is so trivial we can avoid descriptions of the powerdomain constructions completely and give the resulting orderings on the subsets of $\mathbb{O}$. These are given in Fig. 1 b,c,d. The first ordering, Fig. 1.b, corresponds to the Egli-Milner Powerdomain of $\mathbb{O}$, and we will denote it by $\underset{\sim}{\sqsubset}_1$.

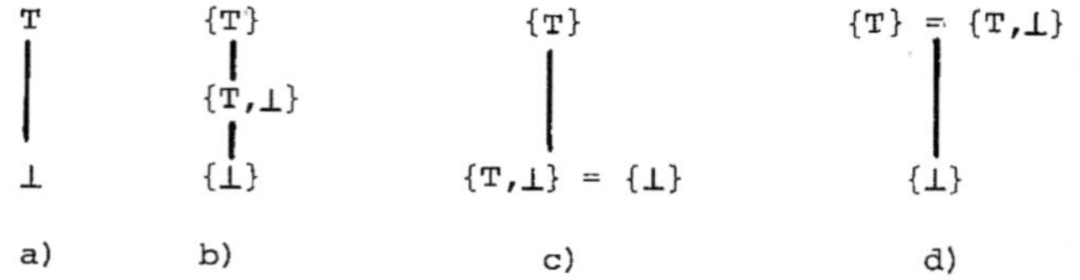

Figure 1

The second ordering, Fig. 1.c, corresponds to the Smyth Powerdomain of $\mathbb{O}$. The sets {T,⊥} and {⊥} are identified and they are less than {T}. This corresponds to the view that possible divergence is catastrophic. We denote this order by $\underset{\sim}{\sqsubset}_2$. The third ordering, Fig. 1.d, corresponds to the dual of the Smyth construction and was called the Hoare Powerdomain in [5]. The sets {T}, {T,⊥} are identified and both are greater than {⊥}. This ordering corresponds to the view that divergence is unimportant and is therefore ignored. We denote it by $\underset{\sim}{\sqsubset}_3$.

These three different orderings on result sets generate three different orderings on processes.

Definition 1.1 For given sets of observers and processes, $\mathcal{O}$, $\mathcal{P}$ respectively, let

$\underset{\sim i}{\sqsubset}^{\mathcal{O}} \subseteq \mathcal{P} \times \mathcal{P}$, i = 1,2,3, be defined by:

p $\underset{\sim i}{\sqsubset}^{\mathcal{O}}$ q if $\forall$o $\varepsilon \mathcal{O}$ R(o,p) $\underset{\sim i}{\sqsubset}$ R(o,q). □

We denote the related equivalences by $\overset{\sim}{-}{}^{\mathcal{O}}_i$, i.e. $\overset{\sim}{-}{}^{\mathcal{O}}_i = \underset{\sim i}{\sqsubset}^{\mathcal{O}} \cap {}^{\mathcal{O}}_{i}\underset{\sim}{\sqsupset}$. The following results are trivial to establish.

Proposition 1.2 a) p $\sim^{\mathcal{O}}$ q if and only if p $\overset{\sim}{-}_1$ q

b) p $\underset{\sim 1}{\sqsubset}^{\mathcal{O}}$ q if and only if p $\underset{\sim 2}{\sqsubset}^{\mathcal{O}}$ q and p $\underset{\sim 3}{\sqsubset}^{\mathcal{O}}$ q. □

Thus we have reformulated the natural equivalence $\sim^{\mathcal{O}}$ as the equivalence generated by a preorder $\underset{\sim 1}{\sqsubset}^{\mathcal{O}}$. This preorder is further broken down into two more primitive preorders $\underset{\sim 2}{\sqsubset}^{\mathcal{O}}$, $\underset{\sim 3}{\sqsubset}^{\mathcal{O}}$. The relevance of these primitive preorders can be motivated in the following manner.

If T ε R(o,p) we say that p may satisfy o. If {T} = R(o,p) we say that p must satisfy o.

Thus (if we ignore the role of the under-defined predicate $\uparrow$) p may satisfy o if there is a resulting successful computation whereas p must satisfy o if every resulting computation is successful. Then it is trivial to establish that:

p $\underset{\sim 3}{\sqsubset}^{\mathcal{O}}$ q if $\forall$ o $\varepsilon \mathcal{O}$ p may satisfy o implies
q may satisfy o

p $\underset{\sim 2}{\sqsubset}^{\mathcal{O}}$ q if $\forall$ o $\varepsilon \mathcal{O}$ p must satisfy o implies
q must satisfy o □

In the remainder of the paper we apply this general theory to the language CCS [12]. To do so we need to specify -

$\mathcal{P}$ - a set of processes (closed CCS terms)

$\mathcal{O}$ - a set of observers

States - a set of states, together with a subset of successful states and the under-defined-predicate $\uparrow$ on states

Comp - a method of assigning to every observer and process a non-empty set of computations (sequences of states).

The three resulting preorders have many interesting mathematical properties. We will give three complete proof systems for these orders and three fully-abstract denotational models.

§2. CCS

§2.1 In this section we review the definition of CCS and its operational semantics. For simplicity we consider the "pure" calculus without taking into account value passing. Let Δ denote a set of unary operators, ranged over by α,β. Let $\bar{\Delta} = \{\bar{\alpha} | \alpha \in \Delta\}$. The operator $\bar{\alpha}$ is said to be the complement of α and $\bar{\bar{\alpha}}$ will denote α. Let $\Lambda = \Delta \cup \bar{\Delta} \cup \{\tau\}$, where τ is a distinguished unary operator not occurring in $\Delta \cup \bar{\Delta}$. Λ is often referred to as the set of basic actions, and we use μ to range over it. We use λ to range over $\Delta \cup \bar{\Delta}$. Let PER denote the set of partial functions over Λ, such that if S ε PER then $S(\tau) = \tau$, $S(\lambda) = \gamma$ implies $S(\bar{\lambda}) = \bar{\gamma}$ and $S(\lambda) = S(\lambda')$

implies $\lambda = \lambda'$. Let X be a set of variables, ranged over by x and Σ denote $\cup\{\Sigma_k | k \geq o\}$ where Σ_k is a set of operators of arity k. If we have

$\Sigma_0 = \{NIL, \Omega\}$
$\Sigma_1 = \{M | M \in \Lambda\} \cup \{[S] | S \in PER\}$
$\Sigma_2 = \{+, |\}$
$\Sigma_n = \emptyset,\ n \geq 3$

the set of CCS terms is defined by the following BNF-like form

$t ::= x | op(t_1, \ldots, t_k),\ op \in \Sigma_k | rec\ x.t$

The operation rec x._ binds occurrences of x in the subterm x of rec x.t. This leads to the usual notions of free and bound variables in a term. Let FV(t) be the set of free variables in t. If FV(t) = $\emptyset$ we say that t is closed. Let $CREC_\Sigma$ denote the set of closed terms and we use p,q, as meta-variables to range over this set. A term is finite if it is closed and contains no occurrence of rec x._ . Let $FREC_\Sigma$ denote the set of finite terms, and we use d,e as meta-variables. Let t[u/x] denote the term which results from substituting u for every free occurrence of x in t. More generally let SUB be the set of substitutions, i.e. mappings from variables to terms. We use ρ as a meta-variable over SUB. Let $t\rho$ denote the result of substituting $\rho(x)$ for every free occurrence of x in t, for every x in X. A substitution is closed if for every x in X, $\rho(x)$ is closed.

The operational semantics is given in terms of labelled rewrite rules over closed terms.

Definition 2.1.1 Let $\xrightarrow{\mu}$ be the least relation over closed terms which satisfies

i) $\mu p \xrightarrow{\mu} p$
ii) $p_1 \xrightarrow{\mu} q$ implies $p_1 + p_2 \xrightarrow{\mu} q,\ p_2 + p_1 \xrightarrow{\mu} q,\ p_1|p_2 \xrightarrow{\mu} q|p_2,\ p_2|p_1 \xrightarrow{\mu} p_2|q$
iii) $p \xrightarrow{\mu} q$, $S(\mu)$ defined, implies $p[S] \xrightarrow{S(\mu)} q[S]$
iv) $p_1 \xrightarrow{\lambda} q_1,\ p_2 \xrightarrow{\bar{\lambda}} q_2$ implies $p_1|p_2 \xrightarrow{\tau} q_1|q_2$
v) $t[rec\ x.t/x] \xrightarrow{\mu} q$ implies $rec\ x.t \xrightarrow{\mu} q$. □

We also need the following unary predicate on closed terms.

Definition 2.1.2 Let be the least predicate on closed terms which satisfies

i) $NIL\downarrow$, $ap\downarrow$
ii) $p\downarrow, q\downarrow$ implies $(p+q)\downarrow, (p|q)\downarrow, p[S]\downarrow$
iii) $t[rec\ x.t/x]\downarrow$ implies $rec\ x.t\downarrow$ □

Let $p\uparrow$ if not $p\downarrow$. So for example $\Omega\uparrow$ and $rec\ x.(ap+x)\uparrow$. Informally $p\uparrow$ means that there is an unguarded recursion or an unguarded occurrence of Ω.

§2.2 In this section we show how to view CCS as a particular example of the general setting explained in §1. The set of processes is simply the closed CCS-terms i.e. $CREC_\Sigma$, and the set of observers $\mathcal{O}$ is $CREC_{\Sigma\cup\{\omega\}}$ where ω is a distinguished action symbol, not in Λ, used to report success.

Example The term $o \equiv \bar{\alpha}\ \bar{\beta}\ \omega\ NIL$ is an observer for testing whether a process can perform an α-action followed by a β-action. The process p = $\alpha(\beta NIL + \gamma NIL)$ passes this test because $o|p \xrightarrow{\tau} \bar{\beta}\omega NIL\ |(\beta NIL + \gamma NIL) \xrightarrow{\tau} \omega\ NIL \xrightarrow{\omega}$ □

Moreover States = $CREC_{\Sigma\cup\{\omega\}}$, Success = $\{p \mid \exists p'.p \overset{\omega}{\to} p'\}$ and $\uparrow$ is the one implied by def. 2.1.2. A computation is any sequence of terms $\{p_n \mid n \geq 0\}$, (finite or infinite), such that

i) if p_n is the final element in the sequence then $p_n \overset{\tau}{\not\to} p'$ for no p'

ii) otherwise $p_n \overset{\tau}{\to} p_{n+1}$.

Finally for $o \in \mathcal{O}$, $p \in \mathcal{P}$, let Comp(o,p) be the set of computations whose initial element is the term $(o|p)$.

These definitions immediately give three different preorders on $\mathcal{P}$, the set of closed CCS-terms. To emphasise their import we translate the predicates may satisfy and must satisfy into this setting:

a) p may satisfy o if $(o|p) \overset{\tau}{\to}{}^* q$ for some q such that $q \overset{\omega}{\to}$

b) p must satisfy o if whenever $o|p = o_0|p_0 \overset{\tau}{\to} o_1|p_1 \overset{\tau}{\to} \ldots$ is a computation from $o|p$ then i) $\exists n \geq 0$ such that $o_n \overset{\omega}{\to}$ and ii) $o_k|p_k\uparrow$ implies $o_{k'} \overset{\omega}{\to}$ for some $k' \leq k$.

We have used $q \overset{\mu}{\to}$ as a shorthand for $\exists q'.q \overset{\mu}{\to} q'$. In the remainder of the paper we will use $\underset{\sim}{\sqsubset}_i$ in place of $\underset{\sim}{\sqsubset}_i^{\mathcal{O}}$. These preorders, defined on closed terms, may be extended in the usual way to arbitrary terms by:

$t \underset{\sim}{\sqsubset}_i u$ if, for every closed substitution ρ, $t\rho \underset{\sim}{\sqsubset}_i u\rho$.

In general the relations $\underset{\sim}{\sqsubset}_1, \underset{\sim}{\sqsubset}_2$, are not preserved by the operator +. For example $\alpha NIL \underset{\sim}{\sqsubset}_2 \tau\alpha NIL$ but $\lambda NIL+\alpha NIL \not\underset{\sim}{\sqsubset}_2 \lambda NIL+\tau\alpha NIL$: if o denotes $\bar{\lambda}\omega NIL$ then $\lambda NIL+\alpha NIL$ must satisfy o whereas $(\lambda NIL+\tau\alpha NIL)|o \overset{\tau}{\to} \alpha NIL|o$.

By and large the preorders $\underset{\sim}{\sqsubset}_i$ are well-behaved. It is very simple to prove that they are preserved by the remaining operators in CCS. As in [12] we can define $\underset{\sim}{\sqsubset}_i^c$ to be the relations obtained by closing under contexts:

$t \underset{\sim}{\sqsubset}_i^c u$ if for every context C[ ], $C[t] \underset{\sim}{\sqsubset}_i C[u]$

and $\underset{\sim}{\sqsubset}_i^+$ by:

$t \underset{\sim}{\sqsubset}_i^+ u$ if for every term r, $r+t \underset{\sim}{\sqsubset}_i r+u$.

We can now characterise $\underset{\sim}{\sqsubset}_i^c$:

Thm. 2.2.1 $t \underset{\sim}{\sqsubset}_i^c u$ if and only if $t \underset{\sim}{\sqsubset}_i^+ u$, i=1,2,3 □

§2.3 In this section we give some examples and counter-examples. These will mainly concern only the equivalence $\overset{\sim}{-}_1$, which in the sequel we will abbreviate by $\overset{\sim}{-}$. Moreover in the example the occurrences of NIL will be omitted; αNIL will be rendered as α.

Example 1 For any X,Y

$\lambda X + \lambda Y \overset{\sim c}{-} \lambda X + \lambda Y + \lambda(X+Y)$.

Using the representation of terms by trees of [12] these may be described as

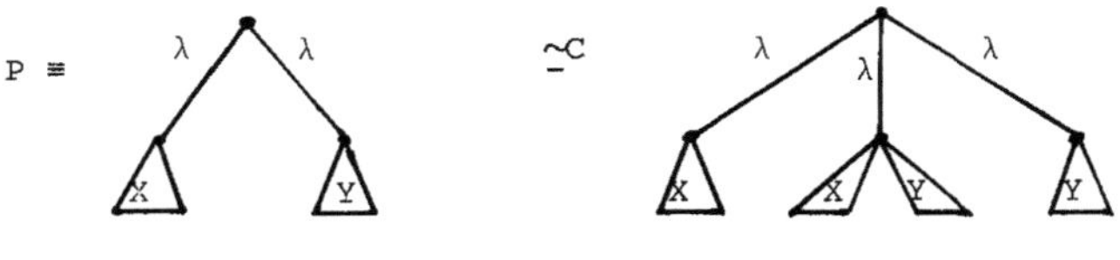

The reader may like to convince himself that for any observer o, p <u>may satisfy</u> o if and only if q <u>may satisfy</u> o and p <u>must satisfy</u> o if and only if q <u>must satisfy</u> o.

<u>Example 2</u> For any X,Y,Z

$$\lambda X + \lambda(X+Y+Z) \simeq^{c} \lambda X + \lambda(X+Y) + \lambda(X+Y+Z). \qquad \square$$

However we can distinguish very similar pairs of trees.

<u>Example 3</u> a) $p \equiv \lambda\alpha + \lambda(\alpha+\beta+\gamma) \not\simeq^{c} \lambda\alpha + \lambda(\alpha+\beta+\gamma) + \lambda\beta \equiv q$. This follows since p <u>must satisfy</u> $\bar\lambda\bar\alpha\omega$ whereas $q \mid \bar\lambda\bar\alpha\omega \xrightarrow{\tau} \beta \mid \bar\alpha\omega$.

b) $p \equiv \lambda\alpha + \lambda(\beta+\gamma) \not\simeq^{c} \lambda\alpha + \lambda\beta + \lambda(\beta+\gamma) \equiv q$, since p <u>must satisfy</u> $\bar\lambda(\bar\alpha\omega + \bar\gamma\omega)$ whereas $q \mid \bar\lambda(\bar\alpha\omega+\bar\gamma\omega) \xrightarrow{\tau} \beta \mid (\bar\alpha\omega + \bar\gamma\omega)$. $\square$

<u>Example 4</u> $\alpha(\beta x + \beta y) \simeq^{c} \alpha\beta x + \alpha\beta y,$

$\simeq^{c} \alpha\beta(\tau x + \tau y).$

In terms of trees

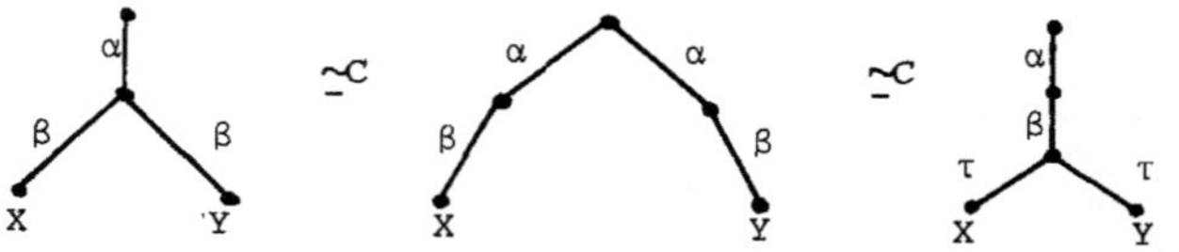

The two examples show that $\simeq^{c}$ tends to abstract from "when choices are made". $\square$

<u>Example 5</u>

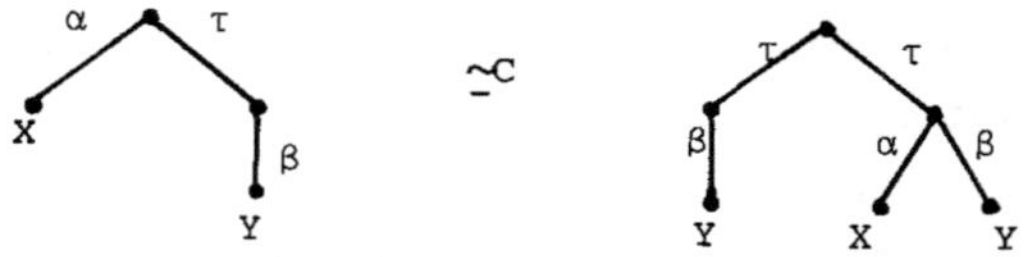

$$\alpha X + \tau\beta Y \quad \simeq^{c} \quad \tau(\alpha X + \beta Y) + \tau\beta Y.$$

This will in fact be one of our more useful axioms. With it we may transform terms so that they represent processes in which all choices are either purely external or purely internal. $\square$

<u>Example 7</u> a) $\tau x + \tau y \underset{\sim}{\sqsubset}^{c}_{2} \tau x$

The presence of τ on the left hand side is important. For example $\alpha+\beta \not\underset{\sim}{\sqsubset}_{2} \tau\alpha$. This follows since $\alpha+\beta$ <u>must satisfy</u> $\bar\beta\omega$ while $\tau\alpha \mid \bar\beta\omega \xrightarrow{\tau} \alpha \mid \bar\beta\omega$.

b) $\lambda x + \lambda x \simeq^{c}_{3} \lambda(x+y)$

Thus the relation $\simeq^{c}_{3}$ ignores all the tree structure of terms. Moreover $\tau X \simeq^{c}_{3} X$, so that $\simeq^{c}_{3}$ is a very weak relation. $\square$

§3. <u>Proof Systems</u>

In this section we examine the complete proof systems for the three relations $\underset{\sim i}{\sqsubset}^{c}$ defined in the previous section for CCS. The basic axioms and the proof systems are given in Table 1. Most of the axioms are given in terms of "=", and they are designed to be used in conjunction with the rule R1. The axioms A1-A4, S1-S3, C1, Ω1, Ω2 are essentially taken from [7], [6]. The summation notation used in C1 is justified by the axioms A1-A4. As in [12] $\sum_{i\in\emptyset} t_i$ denotes NIL. The notation $t\{+\Omega\}$ is

$$X + X = X \qquad \text{A1}$$

$$X + Y = Y + X \qquad \text{A2}$$

$$X + (Y + Z) = (X + Y) + Z \qquad \text{A3}$$

$$X + NIL = X \qquad \text{A4}$$

$$\mu X + \mu Y = \mu(\tau X + \tau Y) \qquad \text{N1}$$

$$X + \tau Y \sqsubseteq \tau(X + Y) \qquad \text{N2}$$

$$\mu X + \tau(\mu Y + Z) = \tau(\mu X + \mu Y + Z) \qquad \text{N3}$$

$$\tau X \sqsubseteq X \qquad \text{N4}$$

$$NIL[S] = NIL \qquad \text{S1}$$

$$(X + Y)[S] = X[S] + Y[S] \qquad \text{S2}$$

$$\mu X[S] = S(\mu)\ X[S] \text{ if } S(\mu) \text{ defined, NIL otherwise} \qquad \text{S3}$$

Let t denote $\sum_{i \in I} \mu_i t_i \{+\Omega\}$, u denote $\sum_{j \in J} \gamma_j u_j \{+\Omega\}$.

$$t|u = \sum_{i \in I} (t_i|u) + \sum_{\mu_i = \bar{\gamma}_j} \tau(t_i|u_j) + \sum_{j \in J} \gamma_j (t|u_j) + \{\Omega \mid \Omega \text{ is a summand of } t \text{ or } u\} \qquad \text{C1}$$

$$\Omega[S] = \Omega \qquad \Omega 1$$

$$\Omega \sqsubseteq X \qquad \Omega 2$$

$$t[\mathrm{rec}\ x.t/x] \sqsubseteq \mathrm{rec}\ x.t \qquad \text{REC1}$$

$$\tau X + \tau Y \sqsubseteq X \qquad \text{E1}$$

$$X \sqsubseteq \tau X + \tau Y \qquad \text{F1}$$

R1 (Equality) $\dfrac{t = u}{t \sqsubseteq u,\ u \sqsubseteq t}$ $\qquad \dfrac{t \sqsubseteq u,\ u \sqsubseteq t}{t = u}$

R2 (Partial Order) $\dfrac{t \sqsubseteq u,\ u \sqsubseteq r}{t \sqsubseteq r}$ $\qquad \dfrac{}{t \sqsubseteq t}$

R3 (Substitutivity)

i) $\dfrac{t \sqsubseteq u}{t\rho \sqsubseteq u\rho}$ ii) $\dfrac{t \sqsubseteq u}{\mathrm{rec}\ x.t \sqsubseteq \mathrm{rec}\ x.u}$ iii) $\dfrac{t_i \sqsubseteq u_i,\ 1 \le i \le k}{op(t_1,\ldots,t_k) \sqsubseteq op(u_1,\ldots,u_k)}$

for every $op \in \Sigma_k$

R4 (General Induction) $\dfrac{d \sqsubseteq u,\ \forall d \in Fin(t)}{t \sqsubseteq u}$

TABLE 1

meant to denote that the term Ω is optional as a summand. The axioms of particular interest are N1-N4, which replace the τ-laws of [12]. Indeed these new axioms imply these τ-laws.

Let A_1 denote the set of axioms A1-A4, N1-N4, S1-S3, C1, Ω1-Ω2, REC1. Let A_2 be the set A_1 together with E1 and A_3 be the set A_1 together with F1. These sets of axioms give rise to the three different proof systems. Each of these will have the rules R1-R4 in common. R4 is introduced to deal with the recursion operator rec x._. The set Fin(t) represents the set of finite approximants of t, [3], [4]. For example Fin(rec x.ax) = $\{\Omega, a\Omega, aa\Omega, \ldots\}$.
We now state the main results of the paper.

Thm. 3.1 For i=1,2,3, $A_i \vdash t \sqsubseteq u$ implies $t \sqsubset^c_{\sim i} u$. □

Thm. 3.2 For i=1,2,3, and closed terms p,q, $p \sqsubset^c_{\sim i} q$ implies $A_i \vdash p \sqsubseteq q$. □

The Rule R4 is infinitary since it has an infinite number of premises. However since CCS contains all the power of Turing machines recursively enumerable complete axiomatisations of any of the relations $\sqsubset^c_{\sim i}$, i=1,2,3 do not exist. Recursively enumerable proof systems can be obtained from our systems by replacing R4 with some finitary form of induction. Indeed Fixpoint Induction or Scott Induction, [17], can be derived from R4.

§ 4. Fully Abstract Denotational Models

We have presented pure CCS as the set of recursive terms over a set of operators. This enables us to give a denotational semantics in a straightforward way, [3], [17]. If D is a Σ-cpo then we can define a mapping

$$\mathcal{V}_D : REC_\Sigma \to ENV_D \to D$$

where ENV_D is the set of mappings from X to D.
Let I_i be the initial Σ-cpos which satisfy the axioms A_i, i=1,2,3.
As a simple corollary to Thm. 3.1, Thm. 3.2, we have

Thm. 4.1 $t \sqsubset^c_{\sim i} u$ if and only if $\mathcal{V}_{I_i}[[t]] < \mathcal{V}_{I_i}[[u]]$. □
This theorem states that the models I_i are fully-abstract with respect to $\sqsubset^c_{\sim i}$. These models are of particular interest as they have a simple characterisation in terms of trees, which we now explain.

If L is a set of labels let PCT_L denote the set of (finite or infinitely branching) trees whose branches are labelled by labels from L in such a way that for every $\lambda \in L$ every node has at most one outgoing branch labelled by λ. Every node in such a tree, tr, can be uniquely identified by a string from L^*. We denote the node in tr identified by s as tr(s). We let N(tr) denote the set of strings which identify every node in tr. N(tr) is prefixed closed, i.e. $s \in N(tr)$ and $s = s_1 s_2$ implies $s_1 \in N(tr)$. There is in fact an isomorphism between PCT_L and the set of prefixed closed strings from L. We prefer however the more graphical notation of trees. We also let S(tr(s)) denote the set of labels on the branches from the node tr(s) and $tr(s)_\lambda$ denote the successor tree of tr(s) along the unique branch λ from tr(s), if it exists. Our model will consist of trees from PCT_L whose nodes are labelled by sets of subsets of $\Delta \cup \bar{\Delta}$. Such a set $\mathcal{A}$ is <u>saturated</u> if it satisfies:

i) $X,Y \in \mathcal{A}$ implies $X \cup Y \in \mathcal{A}$

ii) $X,Y \in \mathcal{A}$, $X \subseteq Z \subseteq Y$ implies $Z \in \mathcal{A}$.

<u>Definition 4.1</u> Let RT denote the set of trees in $PCT_{\Delta \cup \bar{\Delta}}$ such that

a) every node is either open (represented by o) or closed (represented by ●)

b) every closed node tr(s) is labelled by a saturated set of subsets of S(tr(s)), denoted by $\mathcal{A}$(tr(s)) and the following conditions hold

i) if a node has an infinite number of successors it is open

ii) if a node is open every successor is open

iii) if $\mathcal{A}$(tr(s)) is empty then tr(s) is the root

iv) if $\mathcal{A}$(tr(s)) is not empty then $\lambda \in S(tr(s))$ implies $\exists A \in \mathcal{A}(tr(s))$ such that $\lambda \in A$. □

The sets $\mathcal{A}$(tr(s)) are called acceptance sets. By definition they are finite collections of finite subsets of actions. Note that we distinguish between the empty acceptance set $\emptyset$ and the acceptance set containing the empty subset, $\{\emptyset\}$. Thus the two trees

● $\emptyset$ ● $\{\emptyset\}$

are different. In fact one will represent NIL, the other τNIL. Examples of trees are given in Table 2. We let RT_2 denote the set of trees in RT whose only open nodes are leaves and we let RT_3 denote those who have only open nodes. It will be convenient to replace RT by RT_1.

<u>Definition 5.2</u>

a) For $tr,tr' \in RT_1$ let $tr <_3 tr'$ if $N(tr) \subseteq N(tr')$

b) For $tr,tr' \in RT_1$ let $tr <_2 tr'$ if for every $s \in N(tr')$ either there exists a prefix s' of s such that tr(s') is open or $s \in N(tr)$ and if tr(s) is closed then

i. tr'(s) is closed

ii. $\mathcal{A}(tr'(s)) \subseteq \mathcal{A}(tr(s))$

iii. $\mathcal{A}(tr'(s)) = \emptyset$ implies $\mathcal{A}(tr(s)) = \emptyset$ and $S(tr'(s)) = S(tr(s))$

or

$S(tr'(s)) \in \mathcal{A}(tr(s))$

c) For $tr,tr' \in RT_1$ let $tr <_1 tr'$ if $tr <_2 tr'$ and $tr <_3 tr'$. □

Referring to Table 2 we have that $p_1 <_1 q_1$, $p_2 <_2 q_2$, $p_3 <_1 q_3$. Note that, if $\mathcal{A}(tr(s)) \neq \emptyset$, $\mathcal{A}(tr(s)) \supseteq \mathcal{A}(tr'(s))$ implies $S(tr(s)) \supseteq S(tr'(s))$. This follows from condition iv) in the definition of RT. Therefore if $tr <_2 tr'$ we have that $S(tr'(s)) \subseteq S(tr(s))$ whenever tr(s) is closed. If $tr <_1 tr'$ then $S(tr(s)) \subseteq S(tr'(s))$ for every $s \in N(tr)$ and $S(tr(s)) = S(tr'(s))$ if tr(s) is closed.

<u>Thm. 4.2</u> $\langle RT_i, <_i \rangle$ is a Σ-cpo isomorphic to I_i, i=1,2,3 □

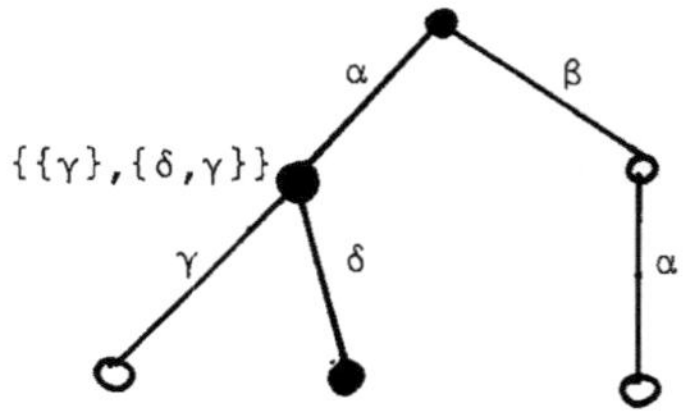

$p_1 \equiv \alpha(\tau\gamma\Omega + \tau(\gamma\Omega + \delta)) + \beta(\alpha\Omega + \Omega)$

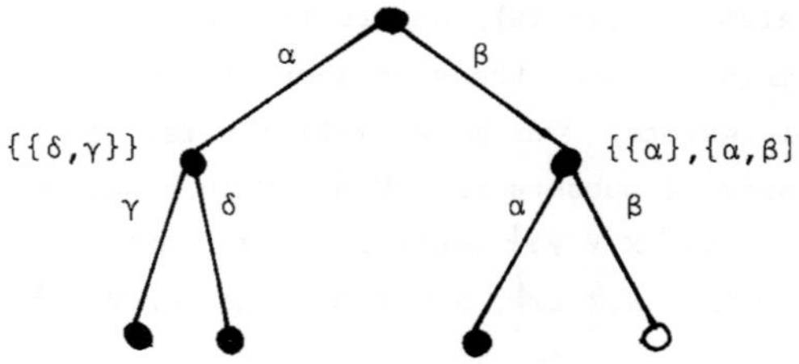

$q_1 \equiv \alpha(\tau(\gamma + \delta)) + \beta(\tau\alpha + \tau(\alpha + \beta\Omega))$

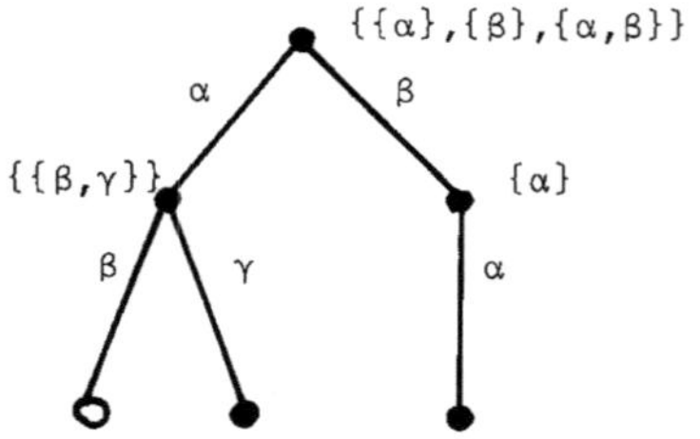

$p_2 \equiv \tau\alpha\tau(\beta\Omega + \gamma) + \tau\beta\tau\alpha$
$+ \tau(\alpha\tau(\beta\Omega + \gamma) + \beta\tau\alpha)$

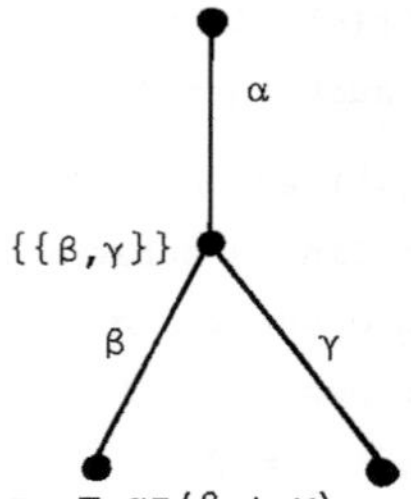

$q_2 \equiv \alpha\tau(\beta + \gamma)$

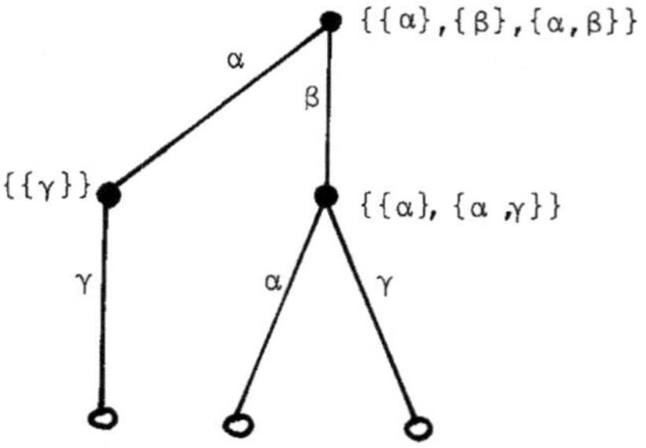

$p_3 \equiv \tau\alpha r_1 + \tau\beta r_2 + \tau(\alpha r_1 + \beta r_2)$
where $r_1 \equiv \tau\gamma\Omega$ and $r_2 \equiv \tau\alpha\Omega + \tau(\alpha\Omega + \gamma\Omega)$

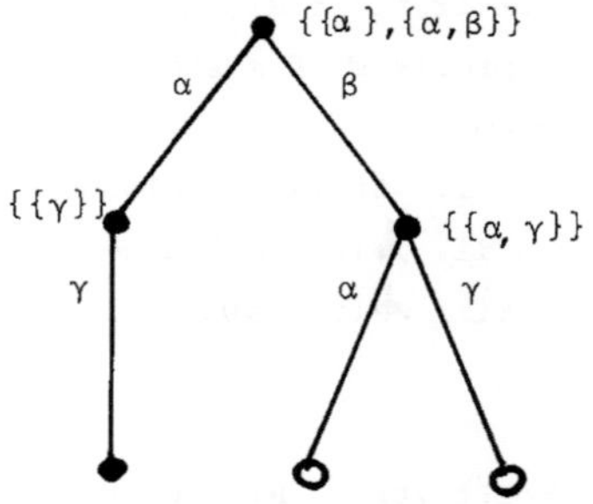

$q_3 \equiv \tau\alpha\tau\gamma + \tau(\alpha\tau\gamma + \beta(\tau(\alpha\Omega + \gamma\Omega))$

TABLE 2

Conclusion

We first of all recapitulate on the results of the paper. We started with a rather general notion of equivalence between processes based on a simple tabulation of the possible effects of interactions between observers and processes. This equivalence was in turn decomposed into three different preorders in a natural way. In the remainder of the paper we investigated these preorders in the language CCS. For each of these we gave a complete proof system based on a set of axioms and a rule of induction. These proof systems lead in a natural way to fully abstract denotational models. These are constructed as term models but in the last section of the paper we showed that they have very intuitive representations as particular kinds of trees.

We end with a brief comparison with related work. The original observation equivalence for CCS, [12], [7] is much smaller than $\simeq_1$. For guarded terms, terms in which every bound variable is within a subterm of the form λt, we can show that $\simeq_3$ coincides with $\approx_1$ and $\simeq_1$ lies between $\approx_1$ and $\approx_2$. (The equivalences $\simeq_n$ are defined on page 99 of [12].) So the observation equivalence of CCS distinguishes many more terms than we do. Some of these distinctions are concerned only with the internal structure of processes and an interesting critique of this equivalence is given in [1]. There the author gives an alternate equivalence. However it applies only to finite terms and there is no obvious extension to recursive terms. Even for finite terms his language is less expressive than ours. Nevertheless the exact relationship between $\simeq_i$ and his equivalence is not known.

A mathematical model of processes, called the refusal set model was introduced in [9] and developed further in [14] as refusal-acceptance-machines. Basically the refusal set model defines a process as a set of pairs $<s,X>$ where s is a string of actions and X is a non-empty set of sets of actions, the refusal sets. Such a pair means that the process may perform the sequence of actions s and then may refuse any set of actions in X. This is quite similar to our RT_2 with our acceptance sets being the complement of the refusal sets. There are seemingly minor but important differences. For example it is crucial for us to have the empty set as an acceptance set in order to handle τ and it is not clear what the corresponding refusal set is. An ordering is defined on this model which is somewhat similar to $<_2$ defined on RT_2 (at least the version of the ordering in [14]). There is however a crucial difference between $<_2$ and their order. There are two reasons why $p <_2 q$. The first is that intuitively p is more nondeterministic than q, the second that some undefined component of p (specified by Ω or an open leaf) has been improved upon in q. The second component seems to be absent from their ordering. Nevertheless this ordering turns out to be a complete partial order and various operators are shown to be continuous. (A notable omission from the relevant theorem, theorem 4.6.1 of [14], is their version of "hiding" direct image.) These operators form the basis of a language for processes and the model is then a denotational model in the sense of [17]. As of yet there does not appear to be a related proof theory or a relationship with an operational semantics.

A direct comparison with our work is somewhat hampered by the very different set of operators used. Nevertheless we hope that at the semantic level we can, with a few minor adjustments on both sides, get a strong relationship between RT_2 and a version of the refusal set model.

Acknowledgements

The authors would like to thank R. Milner and G. Plotkin for many useful discussions. The first author would like to acknowledge the financial assistance of the Italian Research Council (C.N.R.) and the second author wishes to express his gratitude to the University of Genoa for their hospitality. Credit for the excellent typing is due to E. Kerse.

References

LNCS n denotes Lecture Notes in Computer Science Volume n, Springer-Verlag

[1] Darondeau,Ph. An enlarged definition and complete axiomatization of observational congruence of finite processes, LNCS 137, pp. 47-62, 1982.

[2] De Nicola,R. and Hennessy,M. Testing equivalences for processes, Technical Report CSR-123-82, University of Edinburgh.

[3] Goguen,J.A., Thatcher,J.W., Wright,J.B. Initial algebra semantics and continuous algebras, JACM Vol. 24, No. 1, pp. 68-95, 1977.

[4] Guessarian,I. Algebraic semantics, LNCS 99, 1981.

[5] Hennessy,M. Powerdomains and nondeterministic recursive definitions, LNCS 137, pp. 178-193, 1982.

[6] Hennessy,M., Plotkin,G. A term model for CCS, LNCS 88, pp. 261-274, 1980.

[7] Hennessy,M., Milner,R. On observing nondeterminism and concurrency, LNCS 85, pp. 299-309, 1980.

[8] Hoare,C.A.R. A model for communicating sequential processes, Technical Monograph Prg-22, Computing Laboratory, University of Oxford, 1981.

[9] Hoare,C.A.R., Brookes,S.D. and Roscoe,A.D. A theory of communicating sequential sequential processes, Technical Monograph Prg-16, Computing Laboratory, University of Oxford, 1981.

[10] Kennaway,J.K. and Hoare,C.A.R. A theory of nondeterminism, LNCS 85, pp. 338-350, 1980.

[11] Kennaway,J.K. Formal semantics of nondeterminism and parallelism, Ph.D. thesis, University of Oxford, 1981.

[12] Milner, R. A calculus of communicating systems, LNCS 92, 1980.

[13] Plotkin,G. A powerdomain construction, SIAM J. on Computing, No. 5, pp. 452-486, 1976.

[14] Rounds,W.C., and Brookes,S.D. Possible futures, acceptances, refusals and communicating processes, Proc. of 22nd FOCS Annual Symposium, Nashville Tennessee, October 1981.

[15] Scott, D.S. Data types as lattices, SIAM J. on Computing, Vol. 5, No. 3, 1976.

[16] Smyth,M.B. Power domains, JCSS, Vol. 2, pp. 23-36, 1978.

[17] Stoy,J. Denotational semantics: the Scott-Strachey approach to programming language theory, MIT Press, 1977.

SPECIFICATION-ORIENTED SEMANTICS FOR COMMUNICATING PROCESSES

E.-R. Olderog and C.A.R. Hoare

Programming Research Group, Oxford University
Institut für Informatik, Universität Kiel*)

1. Introduction

For concurrent programs - even when restricted to a particular style like Communicating Processes - a variety of semantical models have been proposed (e.g. [2,11,12]). Each of these different models can be viewed as describing certain aspects of a complex behaviour of programs. It seems therefore desirable to bring some "order" into these semantical models so that one will finally be able to recommend each model for the purposes and applications for which it is best suited.

This leads us to pursue the following aims:

(1) The semantics of concurrent programs should lead to a *simple correctness criterion*, and simple proofs of correctness.

(2) Systematic methods should be developed for *generating sound semantical models* for different purposes and applications.

(3) Existing semantical models should be *related to each other* in a clear system of classification.

In this paper we concentrate on an application to Communicating Processes and present concrete steps towards aims (1)-(3). In different settings such steps can also be found in recent work by [2,4,13,14]. Let us now outline the approach of our paper.

Ad (1): Informally, a program P is called correct w.r.t. a given specification S, abbreviated by P sat S, if every observation we can make about the behaviour of P is allowed by S. To realize this idea we start in Sections 2-4 from a set M of observations and define the space of specifications S as a certain family of subsets of M. A *specification-oriented semantics* assigns denotationally to every program P a specification $[\![P]\!]$ such that P sat S holds if $[\![P]\!] \subset S$ is true. This approach deals very simple with nondeterminism, which is expressed just as the set union of sets of observations. Technically, a *specification space* is a complete partial order and the semantics $[\![\cdot]\!]$ maps every syntactic constructor of the programming language onto a continuous operator on specifications. This enables us to treat recursion in the usual way.

Ad (2): The simplest way of defining an operator on specifications is by pointwise application of a relationship g between observations, i.e. to consider

$$O_g(S) = \{y \mid \exists x\colon x \in S \,\&\, x\,g\,y\} .$$

But this operator is not necessarily continuous. By viewing specification spaces as *information systems* in the sense of [17] we arrive at a definition C_g from g which is guaranteed to be continuous. Unfortunately, the result of this construction is too abstract for our purposes. Our main result is that under certain assumptions about g the operator C_g can be represented simply as

$$C_g = O_g \quad \text{or} \quad C_g = O_g \cup O_g^{\infty}$$

where O_g^{∞} is defined explicitly in terms of g, and models the possibility of divergence. The details are given in Sections 5-6.

Ad (3): In Sections 7-10 we apply the methods developed so far to generate and relate three semantical models for Communicating Processes. These models differ in the structure of their observations which influences both the number of representable

---

*) Authors' present address: Oxford University Computing Laboratory, Programming Research Group, 8-11 Keble Road, Oxford OX1 3QD, United Kingdom

operators and the notion of correctness.

The simplest model is the *Counter Model C* which can deal only with acyclic or tree-like networks of processes [10]. Arbitrary networks require the *Trace Model T* which still cannot model global nondeterminism [8]. In *C* and *T* only *safety properties* (partial correctness) can be described by P sat S. Dealing with the full language of Communicating Processes and with *liveness properties* (total correctness) calls for the more sophisticated *Readiness Model R* [7,10].

Special attention is given to the hiding operators which localise communications on internal network channels. These are complicated because the possibility of *infinitely many* hidden communications has to be considered. We show that in all three models the hiding operators can be represented as $C_g = O_g \cup O_g^\infty$. The remaining operators are simply of the form $C_g = O_g$.

Proofs of our results will appear in the full version of this paper.

2. Algebraic Preliminaries

This section describes the general format of our programming language and denotational semantics.

A *signature* Σ consists of a set $(\xi\in)$ V_Σ of variables and a set $(f \in)$ F_Σ of *operator symbols* each one with a certain arity $n \geq 0$. Every signature Σ determines a simple *programming language* $(P,Q \in)$ $L(\Sigma)$, namely the set of all *recursive terms* over Σ as defined by the following BNF-syntax:

$$P :: \xi \mid f(P_1,\ldots,P_n) \text{ where f has arity n } \mid \mu\xi.P \,.$$

The construct $\mu\xi.\_$ [1] defines a binding occurrence of ξ and induces the usual notions of free and bound variables. A *program* is a recursive term without free variables.

Let D be a partial order w.r.t. $\sqsubseteq$. A subset $X \subset D$ is *directed* if every finite subset of X has an upper bound in X. D is a *cpo* (*complete partial order*) if it has a least element $\perp$ and every directed subset $X \subset D$ has a lub (least upper bound) $\bigsqcup X$ in D. If D is a cpo, then so is $D^n = D \times \ldots \times D$ (n times), with componentwise ordering.

An operator $\phi: D \to E$ from one cpo D into another cpo E is ($\sqsubseteq$-) *continuous* if it preserves lubs of directed subsets, i.e. if $\phi(\bigsqcup X) = \bigsqcup\phi(X)$ holds for every directed $X \subset D$. And ϕ is called *strict* if it preserves the least element. We remark that an operator $\phi: D^n \to D$ is continuous iff it is continuous in all its arguments. Every continuous operator $\phi : D \to D$ has a least fixed point $\underline{\text{fix}}\ \phi$ in D, namely

$$\underline{\text{fix}}\ \phi = \bigsqcup\{\phi^n(\perp) \mid n \geq 0\} \quad \text{where } \phi^0(d) = d \text{ and } \phi^{n+1}(d) = \phi(\phi^n(d)).$$

A *model A* for $L(\Sigma)$ consists of a cpo D_A and a family $([\![f]\!]_A \mid f \in F_\Sigma)$ of continuous operators $[\![f]\!]_A : D_A \times \ldots \times D_A \to D_A$. A induces a straightforward *denotational semantics* of $L(\Sigma)$, also denoted by $[\![\cdot]\!]_A$. Let $(\rho\in)$ Env be the set of *environments*, i.e. mappings $\rho : V_\Sigma \to D_A$. Then

$$[\![\cdot]\!]_A : L(\Sigma) \to Env \to D_A$$

is given by

(i) $[\![\xi]\!]_A(\rho) = \rho(\xi)$

(ii) $[\![f(P_1,\ldots,P_n)]\!]_A(\rho) = [\![f]\!]_A([\![P_1]\!]_A(\rho),\ldots,[\![P_n]\!]_A(\rho))$

(iii) $[\![\mu\xi.P]\!]_A(\rho) = \underline{\text{fix}}\ (\lambda d.\ [\![P]\!]_A(\rho[d/\xi]))$

where $\rho[d/\xi]$ denotes the redefinition of ρ at argument ξ by d. For programs P we write $[\![P]\!]_A$ instead of $[\![P]\!]_A(\rho)$.

For signatures Σ^1 and Σ^2 we write $\Sigma^1 \subset \Sigma^2$ if $F_{\Sigma^1} \subset F_{\Sigma^2}$ holds. Let A be a model for $L(\Sigma^2)$ and $\Sigma^1 \subset \Sigma^2$. Then the Σ^1-*reduct* $A \upharpoonright \Sigma^1$ is that model for $L(\Sigma^1)$ which consists of the cpo D_A of A and the restricted family $([\![f]\!]_A \mid f \in F_{\Sigma^1})$ of operators.

Let A,B be models for $L(\Sigma)$. A *homomorphism* from A to B is an operator $\phi: D_A \to D_B$ such that

$$\phi([\![f]\!]_A(d_1,\ldots,d_n)) = [\![f]\!]_B(\phi(d_1),\ldots,\phi(d_n))$$

holds for all $f \in F_\Sigma$.

3. Observations and Specifications

This section formalises the concepts of observation and specification. We are interested in observations we can make about the behaviour of a program P during its operation. This intuition leads us to postulate a certain relation $\longrightarrow\!\!\!\triangleright$ between observations which is intended to reflect that P usually produces the observations in a *step-by-step* manner. Thus $x \longrightarrow\!\!\!\triangleright y$ means that observation y may be made immediately *after* x, without any intervening observation. This relation will be crucial later in Section 6. First we need an auxiliary notion. A relation $g \subset M \times N$ between sets M and N is *domain finite* if for every $y \in N$ the set $\{x \mid x\,g\,y\}$ is finite.

Definition 1. An *observation space* is a structure $(M, \longrightarrow\!\!\!\triangleright)$ where M is a set of so-called *observations* and $\longrightarrow\!\!\!\triangleright$ is a relation $\longrightarrow\!\!\!\triangleright \subset M \times M$ such that $\longrightarrow\!\!\!\triangleright^+$ (the transitive closure of $\longrightarrow\!\!\!\triangleright$) is non-reflexive and domain finite.

Thus $(M, \longrightarrow\!\!\!\triangleright^+)$ is a simple well-founded order where every $x \in M$ has at most finitely many immediate predecessors $y \longrightarrow\!\!\!\triangleright x$. Note that $\longrightarrow\!\!\!\triangleright$ may be empty. Some notation:

$$Min = \{x \in M \mid \neg\exists y \in M: y \longrightarrow\!\!\!\triangleright x\} \ , \quad pred(x) = \{y \in M \mid y \longrightarrow\!\!\!\triangleright x\} \ .$$

By a *grounded chain* of length $n \geq 0$ for x we mean a chain $x_0 \longrightarrow\!\!\!\triangleright \ldots \longrightarrow\!\!\!\triangleright x_n = x$ with $x_0 \in Min$. Associated with every observation x there are two *levels*:

$$\text{min-level}(x) = \min\{n \in N_0 \mid \exists \text{ grounded chain of length } n \text{ for } x\}$$

and analogously max-level(x).

Specifications are certain sets of observations which reflect the sructure $\longrightarrow\!\!\!\triangleright$ on observations according to

Definition 2. Let $(M, \longrightarrow\!\!\!\triangleright)$ be an observation space. A subset $X \subset M$ is *generable* w.r.t. $\longrightarrow\!\!\!\triangleright$ if $\forall x \in X \setminus Min\ \exists y \in X: y \longrightarrow\!\!\!\triangleright x$.

We say that an observation x *satisfies* a specification S or that S *allows* x if $x \in S$ holds. Specifications are ordered in a *Smyth-like* manner [18]:

$$S_1 \sqsubseteq S_2 \quad \text{iff} \quad S_1 \supset S_2 \ .$$

$S_1 \sqsubseteq S_2$ means that S_2 is *stronger* or *more deterministic* than S_1 resp. S_1 is *weaker* than S_2. M is the weakest specification allowing every observation.

Definition 3. A *specification space* over an observation space $(M, \longrightarrow\!\!\!\triangleright)$ is a subset $\mathcal{M} \subset \mathcal{P}(M)$ of so-called *specifications* such that the following holds:

(S1) $M \in \mathcal{M}$.

(S2) $\emptyset \notin \mathcal{M}$.

(S3) Every $S \in \mathcal{M}$ is generable w.r.t. $\longrightarrow\!\!\!\triangleright$.

(S4) $(\mathcal{M}, \supset)$ is a cpo.

$\mathcal{M}$ is called a *simple* specification space if Min is finite and $\mathcal{M}$ consists of *all* non-empty, generable subsets of M.

For observation spaces $(M, \longrightarrow\!\!\!\triangleright_M)$ and $(N, \longrightarrow\!\!\!\triangleright_N)$ the *product* is given by $(M \times N, \longrightarrow\!\!\!\triangleright_{M \times N})$ where $\longrightarrow\!\!\!\triangleright_{M \times N}$ is the following binary relation on $M \times N$:

$$(x_1,y_1) \longrightarrow\!\!\!\triangleright_{M \times N} (x_2,y_2) \text{ if either } x_1 \longrightarrow\!\!\!\triangleright_M x_2 \text{ and } y_1 = y_2$$
$$\text{or} \quad x_1 = x_2 \text{ and } y_1 \longrightarrow\!\!\!\triangleright_N y_2 \ .$$

Definition 4. For specification spaces $\mathcal{M}$ over $(M, \longrightarrow\!\!\triangleright_M)$ and $\mathcal{N}$ over $(N, \longrightarrow\!\!\triangleright_N)$ the *product specification space* is $\mathcal{M}\times\mathcal{N}$ over $(M\times N, \longrightarrow\!\!\triangleright_{M\times N})$.

4. Specification-oriented Semantics

We now bring together the concepts described in the previous two sections.

Definition 5. A *specification-oriented semantics* of the programming language $L(\Sigma)$ is a semantics $[\![\cdot]\!]_A$ induced by a model A for $L(\Sigma)$ which consists of a specification space $\mathcal{M}_A$ and a family $([\![f]\!]_A \mid f\in F_\Sigma)$ of $\supset$-continuous operators on specifications.

Correctness of programs $P \in L(\Sigma)$ w.r.t. a specification $S\in\mathcal{M}_A$ is expressed by *correctness "formulas"* P sat S interpreted as follows:

$$\models_A P \text{ sat } S \quad \text{iff} \quad [\![P]\!]_A \subset S \ .$$

Informally P sat S holds if every observation we can make about P is allowed by S. In Sections 8-10 we shall see that both safety and liveness properties of Communicating Processes can be expressed within this framework.

5. Continuous Operators

So far we have developed a rather general framework of talking about observations and specifications. But despite of this generality we can already derive some results on the construction and representation of continuous operators on specifications which will prove useful in applications to Communicating Processes.

Let in this and the subsequent section $\mathcal{M}$ and $\mathcal{N}$ always denote *simple* specification spaces over $(M, \longrightarrow\!\!\triangleright_M)$ resp. $(N, \longrightarrow\!\!\triangleright_N)$. We wish to construct $\supset$-continuous operators $C_g: \mathcal{M}\to\mathcal{N}$ working on specifications by starting from certain relations $g\subset M\times N$ which describe the desired effect of C_g "pointwise" for single observations. Following Scott (e.g. [17]) there is a standard construction of such operators C_g provided we know what the *finite elements* of the domains $\mathcal{M}$ and $\mathcal{N}$ are. To help to identify these elements Scott has set up the concept of an *information system* [17].

First we explain how to view every *simple* specification space $\mathcal{M}$ as an *example of an information system* I such that the elements of I are just the specifications in $\mathcal{M}$. Well almost, because we have to face the problem that Scott's approach automatically leads to $\subset$-continuity whereas we are interested in $\supset$-continuity according to the Smyth-like order. But this difficulty is easy to overcome by constructing I so that its elements are exactly the *complements* of specifications in $\mathcal{M}$. So I is actually dealing with *counterobservations* to specifications.

An *information system* is a structure $I=(D, \text{Con}, \vdash)$ where D is a set of *data objects*, Con is a set of finite subsets of D called *consistent* sets of data objects, and $\vdash$ is a binary relation between Con and D called the *entailment relation*. According to [17] the components D, Con, and $\vdash$ of I have to satisfy certain axioms.

For a given simple specification space $\mathcal{M}$ over $(M, \longrightarrow\!\!\triangleright)$ we define $I_\mathcal{M} = (D_\mathcal{M}, \text{Con}_\mathcal{M}, \vdash_\mathcal{M})$ as follows:

(i) $D_\mathcal{M} = M$: set of counterobservations.

(ii) $\text{Con}_\mathcal{M}$ consists of all *finite* subsets $X\subset M$ such that $\exists S\in\mathcal{M} : X\subset M\setminus S$. Intuitively, X is a consistent set of counterobservations w.r.t. S.

(iii) $\vdash_\mathcal{M}\subset \text{Con}_\mathcal{M}\times D_\mathcal{M}$ is defined as follows:
$X \vdash_\mathcal{M} y$ holds if every grounded chain for y will eventually hit some counterobservation in X (see Figure 1). Informally $X\vdash_\mathcal{M} y$ means that y can be *excluded* as a possible observation provided that every

member of X has been excluded.

Figure 1. $X \vdash_M y$

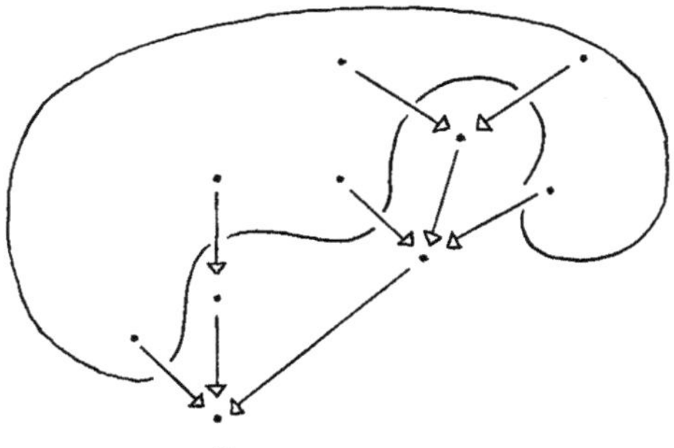

Every information system I determines a set $\langle I \rangle$ of *elements* [17]. For I_M the set $\langle I_M \rangle$ consists of all proper subsets $X \subset M$ with

$$\forall x \in M \setminus Min: \ pred(x) \subset X \rightarrow x \in X .$$

The set $\langle I_M \rangle_{fin}$ of *finite elements* of I_M consists by definition of all closures

$$\bar{X} = \{x \in M \mid X \vdash_M x\}$$

of finite sets $X \in Con_M$. To get the corresponding sets of observations we take complements. Indeed

$$\mathcal{M} = \{M \setminus X \mid X \in \langle I_M \rangle\}$$

holds. Thus I_M exactly determines the simple specification space $\mathcal{M}$.

Definition 6. (i) The complements of finite elements $\bar{X}$ of I_M are called *finitary specifications*. Let $(F,G \in)\ \mathcal{M}_{fin} \subset \mathcal{M}$ be the set of these.
(ii) A relation $g \subset M \times N$ is called *well-formed* if $g(F) \in \mathcal{N}_{fin}$ holds for every $F \in \mathcal{M}_{fin}$.

We can now describe the construction of the operator C_g mentioned above.

Theorem 1. Let $g \subset M \times N$ be well-formed and $C_g\colon \mathcal{M} \rightarrow \mathcal{N}$ defined by

$$C_g(S) = \bigcap \{G \in \mathcal{N}_{fin} \mid \exists F \in \mathcal{M}_{fin}: \ S \subset F \ \& \ g(F) \subset G\} .$$

Then C_g is properly defined, i.e. $C_g(S) \in \mathcal{N}$ holds for every $S \in \mathcal{M}$, and C_g is $\supset$-continuous.

6. Explicit Representations

Theorem 1 is a general continuity result, but it is *too abstract* for our purposes. When applying the operator C_g to a specification S we are not interested in how exactly S is approximated by finitary specifications F and we don't want to follow the tedious construction of $C_g(S)$ described in Theorem 1. This would correspond to the *completion technique* used in [2]. We would rather like to apply the relation g directly to S. In the rest of this section we investigate this idea and derive *explicit representations* of $C_g(S)$ in terms of g. The advantage of Theorem 1 is that it relieves us of the obligation of proving continuity of these representations directly.

First we compare C_g with the standard operator O_g: $M \to P(N)$ induced by g, namely

$$O_g(S) = \{y \in N \mid \exists x \in S: x\,g\,y\} = g(S).$$

Clearly, if g is well-formed, then $O_g(S) \subset C_g(S)$ holds for every $S \in M$.

Theorem 2. If g is well-formed and domain finite, then $C_g(S) = O_g(S)$ holds for every $S \in M$.

As we shall see in Sections 8-10, most operators for Communicating Processes are induced by domain finite relations g. But the crucial hiding operators are not. We therefore present an abstract analysis of such hiding operators based on the relation $\longrightarrow\!\!\triangleright$ between observations.

First we introduce a new operator O_g^∞: $M \to P(N)$ by defining

$$O_g^\infty(S) = \{y' \mid \exists y \longrightarrow\!\!\triangleright^* y' \ \overset{\infty}{\exists} x \in S: x\,g\,y \ \&\ y' \in g(M)\}$$

where $\overset{\infty}{\exists}$ means "there exist infinitely many".

Definition 7. A relation $g \subset M \times N$ is called *level finite* if for every $y \in N$ and $l \in N_0$ there exist only finitely many $x \in g^{-1}(y)$ with min-level$(x) = l$ or max-level$(x) = l$.

Definition 8. A relation $g \subset M \times N$ is called *downward consistent* if whenever

$$\begin{array}{ccc} x_0 & & \\ \downarrow{*} & & \\ x & g & y \end{array} \quad \text{holds there exists some } y_0 \text{ with} \quad \begin{array}{ccc} x_0 & g & y_0 \\ \downarrow{*} & & \downarrow{*} \\ x & g & y \end{array}$$

Definition 9. A relation $g \subset M \times N$ is called *upward consistent* if whenever

$$\begin{array}{ccc} x_0 & g & y_0 \\ & & \downarrow{*} \\ & & y \end{array} \quad \text{with } y \in g(M) \text{ holds then there exists some } x \text{ with} \quad \begin{array}{ccc} x_0 & g & y_0 \\ \downarrow{*} & & \downarrow{*} \\ x & g & y \end{array}$$

And g is called *consistent* if g is both upward and downward consistent.

We can now state our main result.

Theorem 3. Let $g \subset M \times N$ be well-formed, level finite, and consistent. Then

$$C_g(S) = O_g(S) \cup O_g^\infty(S)$$

holds for every $S \in M$.

If the relations $\longrightarrow\!\!\triangleright$ are empty, Theorem 3 reduces to Theorem 2. - So far we considered only simple specification spaces. When dealing with *non-simple* ones, Theorems 1-3 yield of course $\supset$-continuous operators C_g: $M \to P(N)$. But it remains to be shown that indeed $C_g(S) \in N \subset P(N)$ holds for every $S \in M$. An example of a non-simple specification space will be studied in Section 10. Dealing with operators C_g of *several arguments* is easy: we just take the product of the argument specification spaces.

7. Communicating Processes

A process can engage in certain observable communications. We are interested in networks of such processes which work in parallel and communicate with each other in a synchronised way. *Communicating Processes* is a language $L(\Sigma)$ which describes how such networks can be constructed.

Formally, we start from a finite set $(a,b\in)$ Comm of *communications*. (Usually Comm is structured as Comm = Cha $\times M$ where Cha is a set of channel names and M is a set of messages. But for simplicity we shall not exploit this structure here.) The signature Σ for Communicating Processes is given by a set V_Σ of variables ξ and the following set

$$F_\Sigma = \{\underline{stop}, \underline{chaos}\} \cup \{a \rightarrow \ \mid a \in \mathrm{Comm}\} \cup \{\underline{or}, \Box\} \cup \{\|_A \mid A \subset \mathrm{Comm}\} \cup \{\setminus b \mid b \in \mathrm{Comm}\}$$

of operator symbols. To fix the arities and some notational conventions we exhibit $L(\Sigma)$:

$$P ::= \xi \mid \underline{stop} \mid \underline{chaos} \mid a \rightarrow P \mid P \ \underline{or}\ Q \mid P \Box Q \mid P \|_A Q \mid P \setminus b \mid \mu\xi.P \quad .$$

Some intuition: stop denotes a process which engages in no communication at all. chaos is wholly arbitrary and can exhibit every possible behaviour. $a \rightarrow P$ first engages in communication a and then behaves like P. P or Q models *local nondeterminism* [6]: it behaves like P or like Q, but the choice between them is nondeterministic and not controlable from outside. In contrast $P \Box Q$ models *global nondeterminism* [6]: the environment can control whether $P \Box Q$ behaves like P or like Q by choosing in the first step either to communicate with P or with Q. $P \|_A Q$ behaves as if P and Q are working in parallel where all communications in the set A have to be synchronised. $P \setminus b$ behaves like P, but with all communications b *hidden* or *unobservable* from outside. Hiding brings the concept of *abstraction* into Communicating Processes.

Besides the "full" language $L(\Sigma)$ we consider two sublanguages $L(\Sigma^1)$ and $L(\Sigma^2)$ of $L(\Sigma)$ with $\Sigma^1 \subset \Sigma^2 \subset \Sigma$.

- Σ^2 is obtained from Σ by removing $\Box$ from F_Σ.
- Σ^1 is obtained from Σ^2 by restricting parallel composition $\|_A \in F_{\Sigma^1}$ to the case $|A| \leq 1$.

8. The Counter Model C

We start with the simplest language $L(\Sigma^1)$. We postulate that the only thing we can observe about a process P is how many times each communication $a \in$ Comm has occurred up to a given moment [10]. Formally, we define the set of *observations* by

$$(h\in) \quad \mathrm{Obs}_C = \mathrm{Comm} \rightarrow N_0$$

i.e. for each communication a there is a separate *counter*. Obs_C is an observation space with the following relation $\longrightarrow$:

$$h \longrightarrow h' \quad \text{iff} \quad \exists a \in \mathrm{Comm}: h' = h[h(a)+1 \,/\, a] .$$

Then $h \longrightarrow^* h'$ (reflexive, transitive closure) means $h(a) \leq h'(a)$ for every $a \in$ Comm ($h \leq h'$ for short). Let ZERO denote the constant mapping h with $h(a) = 0$ for $a \in$ Comm. Let the set Spec_C of *specifications* consist of all generable w.r.t. $\longrightarrow$ subsets $S \subset \mathrm{Obs}_C$ with ZERO $\in S$. Then Spec_C is a simple specification space over $(\mathrm{Obs}_C, \longrightarrow)$.

The *Counter Model* C consists of the specification space Spec_C and the family $(\,[\![f]\!]_C \mid f \in F_{\Sigma^1}\,)$ of operators (for simplicity we drop subscripts C).

(i) $[\![\underline{\text{stop}}]\!] = \{ZERO\}$

(ii) $[\![\underline{\text{chaos}}]\!] = Obs_C$

(iii) $[\![a \to P]\!] = \mathcal{C}_g([\![P]\!])$ where we use the notation of Theorem 1 with $g \subset Obs_C \times Obs_C$ as follows:

$$h\ g\ h' \quad \text{iff} \quad h' = ZERO \quad \text{or} \quad h' = h[\,h(a)+1\,/\,a\,].$$

Since g is well-formed and domain finite, Theorem 2 implies $\mathcal{C}_g = \mathcal{O}_g$ yielding as explicit definition

$[\![a \to P]\!] = \{ZERO\} \cup \{h[\,h(a)+1\,/\,a\,] \mid h \in [\![P]\!]\}$

which is continuous and properly defined by Theorem 1.

(iv) $[\![P \parallel_A Q]\!] = \mathcal{C}_g([\![P]\!], [\![Q]\!])$ where g relates the product $Obs_C \times Obs_C$ with Obs_C by

$$(h_1,h_2)\ g\ h \quad \text{iff} \quad \forall a \in A: h_1(a) = h_2(a) \;\&\; h(a) = \begin{cases} h_1(a) & , a \in A \\ h_1(a)+h_2(a) & , a \notin A \end{cases}$$

This formalises the intuition that P and Q work independently except for the communications mentioned in A. Clearly g is domain finite, but well-formedness holds only thanks to the restriction $|A| \leq 1$ in Σ^1. Theorem 2 yields now $\mathcal{C}_g = \mathcal{O}_g$. Thus the explicit definition for $[\![\parallel_A]\!]$ is

$[\![P \parallel_A Q]\!] = \{h \mid \exists h_1 \in [\![P]\!]\ \exists h_2 \in [\![Q]\!] : (h_1,h_2)\ g\ h\}$

For $|A| \leq 1$ the relation g does not necessarily preserve generability of specifications. This is due to the fact that we cannot observe the *relative timing* between different communications in the Counter Model C. A similar problem, known as *merge anomaly*, can arise in loosely coupled nondeterministic dataflow networks [3,4].

(v) $[\![P\ \underline{\text{or}}\ Q]\!] = [\![P]\!] \cup [\![Q]\!]$

(vi) $[\![P \setminus b]\!] = \mathcal{C}_g([\![P]\!])$ where $g \subset Obs_C \times Obs_C$ is given by

(+) $\quad h\ g\ h' \quad \text{iff}\ h'(b) = 0 \;\&\; \forall a \neq b: h(a) = h'(a)$.

Intuitively, g hides all communications b in h. Note that g is not domain finite any more. And indeed, $\mathcal{O}_g$ is not continuous. But at least g is *level finite*. Also it is well-formed and consistent. Thus Theorem 3 yields $\mathcal{C}_g = \mathcal{O}_g \cup \mathcal{O}_g^{\infty}$ which leads to

(++) $[\![P \setminus b]\!] = \{h \mid h(b) = 0 \;\&\; \exists n \geq 0: h[n/b] \in [\![P]\!]\}$
$\qquad \cup \{h' \mid \exists h \leq h': h'(b) = 0 \;\&\; \overset{\infty}{\exists} n \geq 0: h[n/b] \in [\![P]\!]\}$.

Here it is advantageous to have Theorem 3 available because it is not easy to prove continuity of (++) directly. Moreover, Sections 5 and 6 tell us that (++) is the *natural* continuous operator induced by the intuitive hiding relation (+).

If we picture processes $P_1,\dots,P_n$ working in parallel as networks with $P_1,\dots,P_n$ as nodes and synchronised communications between P_i and P_j as edges, the restriction $|A| \leq 1$ in Σ^1 means that we can only deal with *acyclic* or *tree-like* networks. Typical applications for such networks are buffers and protocols [5].

9. The Trace Model $\mathcal{T}$

To deal with $L(\Sigma^2)$ allowing *cyclic* networks of processes, we must be able to observe also the *relative order* of communications. This leads to the new *observation* set

$$(s,t\in)\quad Obs_{\mathcal{T}} = Comm^*$$

of *words* or *traces* over Comm [8] with ε denoting the empty trace. The relation

$$s \longrightarrow t \quad \text{iff} \quad \exists a\in Comm: s\cdot a = t$$

turns $Obs_{\mathcal{T}}$ into an observation space. Then $s \longrightarrow^* t$ holds iff s is a *prefix* of t ($s\leqslant t$ for short). A subset $S\subset Comm^*$ is called *prefix-closed* if $t\in S$ and $s\leqslant t$ always imply $s\in S$. Let the set $Spec_{\mathcal{T}}$ of *specifications* consist of all prefix-closed subsets $S\subset Obs_{\mathcal{T}}$ with $\varepsilon\in S$. Then $Spec_{\mathcal{T}}$ is a simple specification space over $(Obs_{\mathcal{T}}, \longrightarrow)$.

The *Trace Model* $\mathcal{T}$ consists of $Spec_{\mathcal{T}}$ and the family $(\llbracket f\rrbracket_{\mathcal{T}} \mid f\in F_{\Sigma 2})$ of operators where we state only the explicit definitions of $\llbracket \,\|_A\, \rrbracket$ and $\llbracket \backslash b\rrbracket$:

$$\llbracket P \,\|_A\, Q\rrbracket = \left\{ r \;\middle|\; \begin{array}{l}\exists s\in\llbracket P\rrbracket\ \exists t\in\llbracket Q\rrbracket: r \text{ is an interleaving of s and t synchronising}\\ \text{communications in A}\end{array}\right\}$$

$$\llbracket P\backslash b\rrbracket = \{s\backslash b \mid s\in\llbracket P\rrbracket\}$$
$$\cup\{(s\backslash b)\cdot t \mid \forall n\geqslant 0: s\cdot b^n\in\llbracket P\rrbracket \,\&\, t\in(A\backslash\{b\})^*\}$$

where $s\backslash b$ results from s by removing all occurrences of b in s. As with the Counter Model these explicit definitions can be derived systematically from appropriate relations g on traces.

To relate the models $\mathcal{T}$ and $\mathcal{C}$ we introduce a relation $g\subset Obs_{\mathcal{T}}\times Obs_{\mathcal{C}}$ with

$$s\ g\ h \quad \text{iff} \quad \forall a\in A: h(a) = a\# s$$

where $a\# s$ denotes the number of occurrences of a in s. Since g is well-formed and domain finite, we obtain:

<u>Proposition 1.</u> The operator $\mathcal{O}_g$ is a continuous and strict homomorphism from the reduct $\mathcal{T}\upharpoonright\Sigma^1$ to $\mathcal{C}$. Thus for every program $P\in L(\Sigma^1)$ we have $\mathcal{O}_g(\llbracket P\rrbracket_{\mathcal{T}}) = \llbracket P\rrbracket_{\mathcal{C}}$.

What is the notion of correctness induced by $\mathcal{T}$ (and $\mathcal{C}$)? For a program $P\in L(\Sigma^2)$ and a specification $S\subset Spec_{\mathcal{T}}$

$$(*)\qquad \models_{\mathcal{T}} P\ \underline{sat}\ S \quad \text{iff} \quad \llbracket P\rrbracket_{\mathcal{T}}\subset S\ .$$

Note that there is a particular program P which satisfies *every* specification $S\subset Spec_{\mathcal{T}}$, namely P = <u>stop</u>. This shows that (*) expresses only *safety properties* [15] of P in the sense that P does nothing that is forbidden by S (cf. the concept of "counterobservation" in Section 5). The situation has its analogue in the theory of *partial correctness* for sequential programs where the diverging program <u>div</u> satisfies every partial correctness formula {P} <u>div</u> {Q} . In the next section we study a refinement of the Trace Model which can deal also with *total* correctness or better *liveness properties* [15].

10. The Readiness Model $\mathcal{R}$

We now consider the full language $L(\Sigma)$ of Communicating Processes. We postulate that not only the "past" of a process can be observed via traces, but also a part of the "future" via so-called ready sets indicating which communications can happen next [7,9]. Thus the set of *observations* is now given by

$((s,X),(t,Y) \in)\quad Obs_R = Comm^* \times P(Comm)$.

The second component X of an observation (s,X) is a *ready set*. On Obs_R we define a relation $\longrightarrow\!\!\!\triangleright$ as follows:

$$(s,X) \longrightarrow\!\!\!\triangleright (t,Y) \text{ iff } \exists a \in Comm: s \circ a = t .$$

Then $(Obs_R, \longrightarrow\!\!\!\triangleright)$ is an observation space where all observations (ε,X) are minimal. Let the set $Spec_R$ of *specifications* consist of all non-empty subsets $S \subset Obs_R$ which are generable w.r.t. $\longrightarrow\!\!\!\triangleright$ and *extensible* in the following sense:

$$(s,X) \in S \ \& \ a \in X \ \rightarrow \ \exists Y: (s \circ a, Y) \in S .$$

Extensibility formalises the intuition that all communications in a ready set X *can* happen next. $Spec_R$ is a non-simple specification space over $(Obs_R, \longrightarrow\!\!\!\triangleright)$. The existence of observations $(s,\emptyset)$ enable us to specify and prove of particular programs that they will not occur. This is why the correctness criterion P <u>sat</u> S deals now with both safety and liveness properties. For example, the specification

$$S = \{(a^n, \{a\}) \mid n \geq 0\}$$

forces a program P with P <u>sat</u> S to be live and to "send" and infinite stream of communications a.

The *Readiness Model R* consists of $Spec_R$ and the family $([\![f]\!]_R \mid f \in F_\Sigma)$ where we only state the explicit definitions of $[\![\Box]\!]$ and $[\![\setminus b]\!]$:

$$\begin{aligned}[\![P \Box Q]\!] = &\{(\varepsilon, X \cup Y) \mid (\varepsilon,X) \in [\![P]\!] \ \& \ (\varepsilon,Y) \in [\![Q]\!] \} \\ \cup &\{ (s,X) \mid s \neq \varepsilon \ \& \ (s,X) \in [\![P]\!] \cup [\![Q]\!] \}\end{aligned}$$

Ready sets enable us to model *global nondeterminism*: in $P \Box Q$ the environment can control whether this process behaves like P or like Q by choosing either a communication in the ready set X of P or in Y of Q.

$$\begin{aligned}[\![P \setminus b]\!] = &\{(s \setminus b, Y) \mid (s,X) \in [\![P]\!] \ \& \ Y = X \setminus \{b\} \} \\ \cup &\left\{((s \setminus b) \circ t, Y) \ \middle| \ \begin{array}{l} \forall n \geq 0 \ \exists X: (s \circ b^n, X) \in [\![P]\!] \\ \& \ t \in (Comm \setminus \{b\})^* \ \& \ Y \subset Comm \setminus \{b\} \end{array}\right\}\end{aligned}$$

Again we use Theorems 1-3 for deriving these explicit operator definitions from the corresponding relations on observations. Additionally, we must prove that each constructor preserves the extensibility property of its operands (cf. Section 6). This reflects the fact that extensibility is independent of the concept of continuity.

To relate the models R and T, let $g \subset Obs_R \times Obs_T$ be the projection

$$(s,X) \ g \ t \quad \text{iff} \quad s = t .$$

<u>Proposition 2.</u> The operator O_g is a continuous and strict homomorphism from $R \upharpoonright \Sigma^2$ to T. Thus for every program $P \in L(\Sigma^2)$ we have $O_g([\![P]\!]_R) = [\![P]\!]_T$.

11. Conclusion

We are aiming at a classification of semantical models for Communicating Processes that will enable us to recommend certain models which are just detailed enough for particular applications. But before such an aim can be fully realised, more sophisticated models of processes should be studied.

For example, we have not considered the notion of state so far. This would allow to add assignment and explicit value passing between processes, thus combining sequential programs with Communicating Processes.

It is also important to ensure that the operators satisfy the usual algebraic laws, for example parallel composition should be associative. And the relationship between specification-oriented denotational semantics used here and the operational semantics used in [12,13,16] should be studied. This requires an explicit concept of divergence. In particular, it is interesting to investigate how the criterion P sat S can be derived systematically from the operational semantics. A significant step in this direction has already been made in [14].

Finally, an explicit syntax for specifications and proof systems for the relation P sat S should be developed. First proposals for such proof systems can be found in [5,9].

Acknowledgement. The first author was supported by the German Research Council (DFG) under grant No. La 426/3-1, and by the University of Kiel in granting him leave of absence.

References

[1] J.W. de Bakker, Mathematical Theory of Program Correctness (Prentice Hall, London, 1980).

[2] J.W. de Bakker, J.I. Zucker, Denotational semantics of concurrency, in: Proc. 14th ACM Symp. on Theory of Computing (1982) 153-158.

[3] J.D. Brock, W.B. Ackermann, Scenarios: a model for nondeterminate computations, in: J. Diaz, I. Ramos, Eds., Formalisation of Programming Concepts, LNCS 107 (Springer, Berlin-Heidelberg-New York, 1981) 252-267.

[4] M. Broy, Fixed point theory for communication and concurrency, in: D. Bjørner, Ed., Formal Description of Programming Concepts II, Preliminary Proc. IFIP TC-2 Working Conference (North Holland, Amsterdam, 1982) 104-126.

[5] Z. Chaochen, C.A.R. Hoare, Partial correctness of communicating processes, in: Proc. 2nd International Conference on Distributed Computing Systems, Paris (1981).

[6] N. Francez, C.A.R. Hoare, D.J. Lehmann, W.P. de Roever, Semantics of nondeterminism, concurrency and communication, JCSS 19 (1979) 290-308.

[7] E.C.R. Hehner, C.A.R. Hoare, A more complete model of communicating processes (to appear in Theoret. Comp. Sci.) 1982.

[8] C.A.R. Hoare, A model for communicating sequential processes, in: R.M. McKeag, A.M. McNaghton, Eds., On the Construction of Programs (Cambridge University Press, 1980) 229-243.

[9] C.A.R. Hoare, A calculus of total correctness for communicating processes, Sci. Comp. Programming 1 (1981) 49-72.

[10] C.A.R. Hoare, Specifications, programs and implementations, Tech. Monograph PRG-29, Oxford Univ., Progr. Research Group, Oxford 1982.

[11] C.A.R. Hoare, S.D. Brookes, A.W. Roscoe, A theory of communicating sequential processes, Tech. Monograph PRG-16, Oxford Univ., Progr. Research Group, Oxford 1981.

[12] R. Milner, A calculus of communicating systems, LNCS 92 (Springer, Berlin-Heidelberg-New York, 1980).

[13] R. Milner, Four combinators for concurrency, in: Proc. ACM SIGACT-SIGOPS Symp. on Principles of Distributed Computations, Ottawa, 1982.

[14] R. de Nicola, M.C.B. Hennessy, Testing equivalences for processes, Internal Report CSR-123-82, Univ. of Edinburgh, Computer Science Dept., 1982.

[15] S. Owicki, L. Lamport, Proving liveness properties of concurrent programs, ACM TOPLAS 4 (1982) 455-495.

[16] G.D. Plotkin, An operational semantics for CSP, in: D. Bjørner, Ed., Formal Description of Programming Concepts II, Preliminary Proc. IFIP TC-2 Working Conference (North Holland, Amsterdam, 1982) 185-208.

[17] D.S. Scott, Domains for denotational semantics, in: M. Nielsen, E.M. Schmidt, Eds., Proc. 9th ICALP, LNCS 140 (Springer, Berin-Heidelberg-New York, 1982) 577-613.

[18] M.B. Smyth, Power domains, JCSS 16 (1978) 23-26.

COMPLEXITY CLASSES OF ALTERNATING MACHINES WITH ORACLES

Pekka Orponen
Department of Computer Science
University of Helsinki

ABSTRACT

Relativized complexity theory based on alternating Turing machines is considered. Alternating complexity classes are shown to provide natural counterexamples to the long-standing conjecture that known proofs of complexity class inclusion results relativize. In particular, there exist oracle sets separating classes APSPACE and E (of languages recognizable in alternating polynomial space and deterministic exponential time, respectively), although the classes are known to be equal in the unrelativized case. Classes APSPACE and E may even be shown to differ for almost all oracles, thus providing a counterexample also to the so called random oracle hypothesis. A complexity hierarchy built by quantifying over oracle sets for alternating machines is also defined, with its first Σ-level coinciding with class NE (nondeterministic exponential time). This representation of NE is noted not to relativize. Problems about the structure of this second-order hierarchy are shown to be related to open problems concerning the polynomial-time hierarchy.

1. INTRODUCTION

While the fundamental problems concerning complexity classes have remained unsolved, relativizations of these classes have been used to study what is likely to be provable with current methods. By evidence from recursion theory, it has long been argued that proofs by ordinary simulation-based techniques (e.g. by diagonalization) are insensitive to whether an oracle set is present or not [2,15]. In view of the results by Baker, Gill and Solovay [2], truth of this *relativization hypothesis* would imply that new techniques would be needed to solve the P = NP question and its like.

Recently, Bennett and Gill [3] have suggested using relativization results also as a basis for inferences about the unrelativized case. Admittedly, the theorems in e.g. [2], relying heavily on carefully designed oracles, are not useful for this purpose. However, computation with a completely *random* oracle might resemble computation without one at all because, intuitively taken, a random oracle should be of no help to an algorithm except by a rare accident. Bennett and Gill formulate this idea as the *random oracle hypothesis*, stating that "acceptable" relations between complexity classes that hold with probability 1 for a random oracle are also true in the unrelativized case. (A formal definition of "acceptable" is used in [3] to rule out certain pathologies.)

Contrary to the relativization hypothesis, Ladner and Lynch [9] have shown that certain results related to log space bounded complexity classes appear not to relativize. Their point is that these results, unrelativized, are proved by *indirect* simulations. By this they mean constructions where a machine investigates the computation of another machine in a more complicated manner than simply by following through it step by step.

Unfortunately, the results in [9] seem to depend on minor details of the model used for relativized log space computation [10,13]. A particularly problematic feature of the machine model in [9] is that it doesn't count the space used to make oracle questions. Since then, Angluin [1] has proved nonrelativizability results without this defect for auxiliary pushdown automata. (Yet these too have a free space component, the pushdown store.) Further nonrelativizability results, concerning in a sense incompletely relativized classes, are presented in [5] and [8].

The random oracle hypothesis has been criticized by Kurtz [8]. His criticism is based on artificially constructed counterexamples, and is therefore rather more effective against the precise formulation of the hypothesis in [3] than the intuition behind it.

Alternating Turing machines [6] will be seen to provide simple and natural examples of nonrelativizability phenomena. Some of the theorems in [6] relating time, space and alternation are proved by indirect simulations that cannot be relativized. These phenomena are invariant over most reasonable changes in the machine model. Depending on whether space on oracle tape is counted or not, different constructions fail to relativize. It can even be shown that these nonrelativizations occur with probability 1, contrary to what the random oracle hypothesis would imply.

With the help of alternating oracle machines, a complexity-theoretic analogue to the analytical hierarchy [11] can be defined. The interesting fact about this hierarchy is that its first existential, or Σ-level contains exactly the sets recognizable in nondeterministic exponential time (as already discovered by Simon [14], in a slightly different context). This representation for the NE-sets cannot be relativized. The oracle-quantification hierarchy is also directly related to the polynomial-time hierarchy [16].

2. PRELIMINARIES

In what follows, the reader is assumed to be familiar with the concept of alternating

Turing machines [6]. Ordinary alternating machines are extended to alternating *oracle Turing machines* (OTM's) by distinguishing one of the work tapes as an oracle tape and adding six distinguished states: the *universal* and *existential query*, *yes* and *no* states. When attached to oracle set A, the machine moves from a query state to the yes or no state of the same type (universal/existential), according to whether the string currently on the oracle tape belongs to A or not.

The set of strings, or language recognized by machine M with oracle A is denoted by $L(M^A)$. Language $L(M^{\emptyset})$ is denoted simply by L(M). If $\underline{M}$ is a class of alternating OTM's and C is the unrelativized, or *absolute* language class recognized by them,

$$C = \{L(M) \mid M \in \underline{M}\},$$

class C *relativized to oracle set* A is defined as

$$C^A = \{L(M^A) \mid M \in \underline{M}\}.$$

An alternating OTM *runs in time* (*space*) f(n), if for any oracle set, for all n and for all inputs of length n, each computation of the machine halts within f(n) moves (uses at most f(n) work tape squares).

Polynomial complexity classes P, NP, Σ_k^p, Π_k^p, PH (the polynomial-time hierarchy), PSPACE and APSPACE are defined as usual. For exponential classes the following notation is used:

$$(N)E = \{L(M) \mid M \text{ is a (non)deterministic Turing machine running in time } 2^{p(n)}, \text{ for some polynomial } p(n)\},$$

$$ESPACE = \{L(M) \mid M \text{ is a deterministic Turing machine running in space } 2^{p(n)}, \text{ for some polynomial } p(n)\},$$

and for every $k \geq 0$,

$$\Sigma_k E\ (\Pi_k E) = \{L(M) \mid M \text{ is a } \Sigma_k\ (\Pi_k) \text{ machine [6] running in time } 2^{p(n)}, \text{ for some polynomial } p(n)\}.$$

The input alphabet of each machine is assumed to contain symbols 0 and 1. Numbers are represented in binary notation, without leading zeros. No distinction will be made between a number and its representation. Some simple standard pairing function $\langle x,y \rangle$ is used to code pairs of strings to strings.

3. NONRELATIVIZABILITY RESULTS

Recall that AP = PSPACE and APSPACE = E [6]. The first theorem below proves, by a minor variation to a diagonalization in [2] (Theorem 3), that the equality APSPACE = E doesn't relativize. More precisely, the proof exhibits an oracle set A such that

$APSPACE^A \subsetneq E^A$. The simple intuitive explanation for this result is that a machine running in polynomial space cannot in general ask oracle questions of exponential length.

3.1 Theorem. There exists a recursive set A such that $APSPACE^A \neq E^A$.

Proof. Let X be a set of strings. Consider the set

$$LOG(X) = \{0^n \mid 0^{2^n} \in X,\ n \geq 0\}.$$

Obviously $LOG(X) \in E^X$ for any X. However, an oracle A can be constructed that has $LOG(A) \notin APSPACE^A$.

Let $M_0, M_1, \ldots$ be an effective enumeration of polynomial space alternating OTM's, such that M_i runs in space $p_i(n)$, a polynomial, and

$$APSPACE^X = \{L(M_i^X) \mid i \geq 0\},$$

for any X (see, e.g. [2]). Note that if machine M_i on input of length n queries its oracle of string y, then $|y| \leq p_i(n)$.

Set A is constructed in stages. Let A_i, $i \geq 0$, denote the set of strings placed in A prior to stage i; define

$$A = \cup\{A_i \mid i \geq 0\}.$$

At stage i set A_i is extended to A_{i+1} in a way that guarantees

$$LOG(A) \neq L(M_i^A).$$

For each i, n_i is an upper bound on the length of strings in A_i. In the beginning set $A_0 = \emptyset$, $n_0 = 0$.

Stage i. Choose $n \geq n_i$ so large that $2^n > p_i(n)$. Simulate the computation of machine M_i on input 0^n and oracle set A_i. If M_i rejects, set $A_{i+1} = A_i \cup \{0^{2^n}\}$, otherwise set $A_{i+1} = A_i$. Set $n_{i+1} = 2^n$. This guarantees that no string queried in the computation is added to A at a later stage. Go to stage i + 1.

For any i, the sets LOG(A) and $L(M_i^A)$ differ at least at string 0^n for the n considered at stage i. Hence $LOG(A) \notin APSPACE^A$. Furthermore, the construction of A is effective, so A is recursive. □

An examination of the proof of the absolute inclusion $E \subseteq APSPACE$ ([6], Theorem 3.4) shows that it is by an indirect simulation in the sense of Ladner and Lynch. Intuitively, the computation sequence of the exponential time machine to be simulated is distributed in small pieces in the computation tree of the alternating machine, which checks the pieces for consistency. Each node in the tree knows only one symbol of a configuration of the simulated machine. Consequently, no single node has enough information to simulate an oracle question.

Theorem 3.1 is obviously insensitive to most reasonable modifications to the definition of OTM's, such as increasing the number of oracle tapes, erasing the oracle tape in connection with queries, and not requiring termination on all computation paths. (Invariance over these variations is listed by Lynch in [10] as desirable for nonrelativizability results; the results in [9] fail this reqirement.) The theorem is *not* insensitive to not counting space on the oracle tape. However, then the following nonrelativization occurs.

3.2 Theorem. If oracle tape space is not counted, there exists a recursive set B such that $AP^B \neq PSPACE^B$.

Remark. The use of a free tape must of course be limited in some way, so assume that the oracle tape is write-only, and is erased at every query move.

Proof. Consider the sets LOG(X) of the previous theorem. There exists a polynomial (even linear) space deterministic OTM that on input 0^n counts up to 2^n, simultaneously constructing 0^{2^n} on the oracle tape. Hence $LOG(X) \in PSPACE^X$ for any X. To construct B such that $LOG(B) \notin AP^B$, diagonalize over an enumeration of alternating polynomial time machines as before. □

In [12] it is suggested that a free oracle tape really causes problems only when machines are allowed to write on it nondeterministically. However, restricting alternating machines to use their oracle tapes deterministically only serves to strengthen the previous proof.

4. NONRELATIVIZABILITY WITH PROBABILITY 1

Let Ω denote the class of all oracle sets. Bennett and Gill [3] define a probability measure μ on Ω by having each string belong to a random oracle with probability 1/2, independent of other strings. (This measure is equivalent to the Lebesgue measure on the unit interval via the identification of languages with their characteristic functions, i.e. with infinite binary strings.) By a slight modification to a construction in [3] (Theorem 2) it can be shown that the inequality $APSPACE^A \neq E^A$ holds for almost all oracle sets A, with respect to measure μ.

Bennett and Gill prove (a version of) the following important lemma:

4.1 Lemma. Let L(X) be an oracle-dependent language (cf. LOG(X) in Theorem 3.1) and C a language class recognized by alternating OTM's $\{M_1, M_2, \ldots\}$, both satisfying certain computability conditions ([3], p. 98). If for some $r < 1$,

$$\mu\{A \mid L(A) = L(M_i^A)\} < r, \quad i = 1,2,\ldots,$$

then

$$\mu\{A \mid L(A) \in C^A\} = 0.$$

Proof. See [3], pp. 98-99. □

4.2 Theorem. $\mu\{A \mid \text{APSPACE}^A \neq E^A\} = 1$.

Proof. As in Theorem 3.1, define

$$\text{LOG}(X) = \{0^n \mid 0^{2^n} \in X, n \geq 0\}.$$

Since $\text{LOG}(X) \in E^X$ for any X, the result follows when it is shown that

$$\mu\{A \mid \text{LOG}(A) \in \text{APSPACE}^A\} = 0.$$

By the Lemma above, it is enough to prove that for each alternating OTM M running in polynomial space,

$$\mu\{A \mid L(M^A) = \text{LOG}(A)\} \leq 1/2.$$

Let M be an alternating OTM running in polynomial space. For shortness, denote

$$E = \{A \mid L(M^A) = \text{LOG}(A)\}.$$

Since M may ask the oracle questions of only polynomial length, for some large enough n its accepting or rejecting string 0^n is independent of whether string 0^{2^n} is a member of the oracle set or not. Define

$$C = \{A \mid 0^n \in L(M^A) \text{ iff } 0^n \in \text{LOG}(A)\}.$$

Clearly $E \subseteq C$, so $\mu(E) \leq \mu(C)$.

Consider the measure-preserving transformation f of oracles that changes each oracle at string 0^{2^n}:

$$f(A) = \begin{cases} A \cup \{0^{2^n}\}, & \text{if } 0^{2^n} \notin A \\ A - \{0^{2^n}\}, & \text{if } 0^{2^n} \in A. \end{cases}$$

Changing oracle A at 0^{2^n} changes the truth of $0^n \in \text{LOG}(A)$, but not of $0^n \in L(M^A)$, so

$$C \cap fC = \emptyset.$$

It follows that

$$\mu(C) + \mu(fC) = \mu(C \cup fC) = 1,$$

and since $\mu(fC) = \mu(C)$, that $\mu(C) \leq 1/2$. (It was tacitly assumed that C is a measurable set. Indeed, C is open in the topology of Ω corresponding to the usual topology of the unit interval.) □

5. ORACLE QUANTIFICATION

In this chapter a complexity analogue to the analytical hierarchy of recursion theory [11] will be considered. The basic theorem relating this hierarchy to exponential complexity classes (Theorem 5.2) was proved by Simon in [14] (and re-discovered by the author). A simpler proof using alternating OTM's will be given here. As will be shown, this basic result cannot be relativized.

Let $<A_1,\ldots,A_k>$ be an efficient disjoint union of sets $A_1,\ldots,A_k$, e.g.

$$<A_1,\ldots,A_k> = \{<i,x> \mid x \in A_i,\ i = 1,\ldots,k\}.$$

Recall that set A belongs to class Σ_k^1, $k \geq 0$, of the analytical hierarchy if there is a "relativized" arithmetical set B, such that for all x,

$$x \in A \quad \text{iff} \quad \exists A_1 \forall A_2 \ldots QA_k (x \in B^{<A_1,\ldots,A_k>}),$$

where Q is $\exists$, if k is odd and $\forall$, if k is even. Class Π_k^1 is defined similarly, except that the quantifier sequence begins with $\forall$. As a special case, note that classes Σ_0^1 and Π_0^1 contain exactly the sets in the arithmetical hierarchy.

Analogously, define set A to belong to class Σ_k^e of the *exponential-time hierarchy* if there is a polynomial time constant-alternation OTM M such that for all x,

$$x \in A \quad \text{iff} \quad \exists A_1 \forall A_2 \ldots QA_k (\text{M accepts x with oracle } <A_1,\ldots,A_k>).$$

Class Π_k^e is defined by interchanging existential and universal quantifiers. In this case, classes Σ_0^e and Π_0^e contain the sets in the polynomial-time hierarchy. (Polynomial time constant-alternation machines recognize exactly the sets in PH [6].) Denote the totality of this hierarchy by

$$EH = \cup\{\Sigma_k^e \cup \Pi_k^e \mid k \geq 0\}.$$

Here is a list of some basic properties of the hierarchy.

5.1 Proposition. For all $k \geq 0$,

(i) $\Sigma_k^e = \text{co-}\Pi_k^e$;

(ii) $\Sigma_k^e \cup \Pi_k^e \subseteq \Sigma_{k+1}^e \cap \Pi_{k+1}^e$;

(iii) if $k \geq 1$ and $\Sigma_k^e = \Pi_k^e$, then $EH = \Sigma_k^e$.

Proof. By simple codings and induction. □

The exponential-time hierarchy is interesting mostly because set quantifiers mediate a connection between polynomial and exponential time bounded complexity classes, as the following theorem shows.

5.2 Theorem. $\Sigma_1^e = NE$.

Proof. To show the inclusion of Σ_1^e in NE, consider an alternating OTM M with running time bounded by a polynomial p(n). On input x of length n, M queries its oracle of strings of length at most p(n). Hence, if M has a work tape alphabet of size t, there are at most $(p(n) + 1)\cdot t^{p(n)}$ possible queries. The existence of an oracle set A leading M to accept x may be verified by a nondeterministic algorithm that first makes a guess of the strings up to length p(n) in A, and then evaluates the computation tree M associates with x and A, replacing queries to A by investigations of the guess (see [6], Theorem 3.2). A simple analysis shows that such an algorithm may be constructed to work in time $2^{q(n)}$, for some polynomial q(n).

In the other direction, let M be a nondeterministic Turing machine with time bound $2^{q(n)}$, for some polynomial q(n). W.l.o.g. assume that M has only one tape, initially containing the input string, and that it actually runs in time at least n and at most $2^{q(n)}-3$. Let # be a symbol not in the tape alphabet of M.

Consider the possible computation sequences of M on input x of length n. For shortness, denote $2^{q(n)}$ by e. A configuration of M may in this context be represented as a string

$$\alpha = uqv\#\ldots\#, \quad |\alpha| = e - 1,$$

meaning that M is in state q, has string uv on its tape, and is scanning the first symbol of string v. Symbol # is used only to pad configurations to the same length. A computation may be represented as a sequence of configuration strings $\alpha_0,\alpha_1,\ldots,\alpha_e$, with $\alpha_0 = q_0x\#\ldots\#$, $\alpha_e = uqv\#\ldots\#$ for some final state q, and for each $i \leq e - 1$, either $\alpha_i \vdash \alpha_{i+1}$ or $\alpha_i = \alpha_{i+1} = \alpha_e$. (Here $\vdash$ denotes the single-move relation of M.) M accepts x if and only if there is some sequence of length e ending in an accepting configuration.

A computation sequence may be coded characterwise in an oracle set:

$$C = \{\langle i,j,\alpha_{ij}\rangle \mid i,j \leq 2^{q(n)}\},$$

where α_{ij} denotes the symbol configuration α_i has in position j. Since the alphabet of M is finite, α_{ij} may be recovered from C by a bounded number of oracle queries, given i and j.

A polynomial time Π_1 (or co-nondeterministic) OTM may be constructed to check whether an oracle set codes an accepting computation of M on a given input. This is possible because number representations are short ($i,j \leq 2^{q(n)} - 1$ iff $|i|,|j| \leq q(n)$), and because symbol $\alpha_{i+1,j}$ only depends on symbols $\alpha_{i,j-1}$, α_{ij}, $\alpha_{i,j+1}$ and $\alpha_{i,j+2}$ (assuming these are defined). On input x of length n and oracle set C the machine, call it COMP, operates according to the following instructions:

1. Check that for all j with $|j| \leq q(n)$, α_{0j} (according to C) equals the corresponding symbol in the initial configuration on input x.
2. Check that for all i,j with $|i|, |j| \leq q(n)$, $\alpha_{i,j-1}$, α_{ij}, $\alpha_{i,j+1}$ and $\alpha_{i,j+2}$ correctly determine $\alpha_{i+1,j}$.
3. Check that for all j with $|j| \leq q(n)$, if $\alpha_{2^{q(n)},j}$ is a state symbol, it denotes an accepting state.

Clearly,

$x \in L(M)$ iff $\exists C$(COMP accepts x with oracle C). □

The previous proof may be generalized to show:

5.3 Theorem.

(i) For all $k \geq 1$, $\Sigma_k^e = \Sigma_k E$ and $\Pi_k^e = \Pi_k E$.

(ii) $EH \subseteq ESPACE$.

Proof. (i) is proved by a straightforward generalization of the constructions above; (ii) follows, since classes $\Sigma_k E$ and $\Sigma_k E$ are included in class ESPACE for all $k \geq 0$ [6]. □

The exponential-time hierarchy could be relativized by defining set A to belong to class $\Sigma_k^{e,B}$ if there is a polynomial time constant-alternation OTM M such that for all x,

$x \in A$ iff $\exists A_1 \forall A_2 \ldots QA_k$(M accepts x with oracle $\langle B, A_1, \ldots, A_k \rangle$).

Class EH^B would be the union of classes $\Sigma_k^{e,B}$, $k \geq 0$. However, with these definitions the following could be proved:

5.4 Theorem. There exists a recursive set B such that $E^B \not\subseteq EH^B$.

Remark. This implies that $\Sigma_1^{e,B} \neq NE^B$.

Proof (sketch). As noted above, a polynomial time constant-alternation OTM can make use of only a bounded initial segment of its oracle. Construct an indexing of class EH by enumerating polynomial time constant-alternation machines together with finite quantifier sequences. Diagonalize over this indexing as in Theorem 3.1, only modifying the diagonalization step so that the oracle quantifiers are taken into account. This means simulating each machine on several combinations of oracle segments, and deciding acceptance according to the associated quantifier sequence. The set B resulting from the diagonalization will have $LOG(B) \in E^B - EH^B$. □

The next simple theorem connects the exponential-time hierarchy directly to the polynomial-time hierarchy.

5.5 Theorem. For all $k \geq 1$, $\Sigma_k^p = \Pi_k^p$ implies $\Sigma_k^e = \Pi_k^e$.

Proof. The proof generalizes a padding argument from [4] (Theorem 4.1). Assume $\Sigma_k^p = \Pi_k^p$, $k \geq 1$, and let $A \in \Sigma_k^e$. Since $\Sigma_k^e = \Sigma_k E$, set A is recognized by some Σ_k-machine M in time $2^{q(n)}$, for some polynomial q(n). Pad strings in A to give set

$$A' = \{ \langle x,0^k \rangle \mid |\langle x,0^k \rangle| = 2^{q(|x|)} \}.$$

From M one easily obtains a polynomial time Σ_k-recognizer for A'. Since $\Sigma_k^p = \Pi_k^p$, there exists also a polynomial time Π_k-recognizer M' for A'. This may again be modified to give an exponential time Π_k-recognizer for A. Hence $A \in \Pi_k E = \Pi_k^e$. □

Recall that in the polynomial-time hierarchy one usually defines

$$\Sigma_{k+1}^p = NP^{\Sigma_k^p}, \quad k \geq 0.$$

The following corollary shows that proving the analogous result for the exponential-time hierarchy would require a major breakthrough.

5.6 Corollary. If $\Sigma_2^e = NE^{\Sigma_1^e}$, then $NP \neq$ co-NP.

Proof. The standard diagonalization showing $P \subsetneq E$ (e.g.[7], pp. 299-300) relativizes. Choose oracle A to be an NE-complete set. Then

$$\Sigma_1^e = NE \subseteq P^A \subsetneq E^A \subseteq NE^A \subseteq NE^{\Sigma_1^e}.$$

Hence, if $NE^{\Sigma_1^e} = \Sigma_2^e$, then $\Sigma_1^e \neq \Sigma_2^e$, implying that $\Sigma_1^e \neq \Pi_1^e$ and $\Sigma_1^p \neq \Pi_1^p$. □

6. CONCLUDING REMARKS

Certain representations of exponential time recognizable sets by polynomial time or space bounded alternating machines have been shown not to relativize in the obvious model for alternating machines with oracles. The absolute representations are based on machines that use their capability for parallel computation to investigate exponentially long computation sequences in pieces of polynomial size. These machines, however, cannot in general simulate exponentially long oracle questions.

The simplicity of these results leads one to suspect that they are due to some defect in the manner of relativizing alternating computation. Some alternative models were considered, but were seen to be as vulnerable to nonrelativizability as the basic one. To gain a clear understanding of the role of relativization in complexity theory, this seeming incongruence of alternation and relativization should be clarified.

Unless a different way of relativizing alternation can be found, the fact that equality APSPACE = E fails to relativize with probability 1 suggests very strongly that the random oracle hypothesis is in error. However, it may be that the intuition behind the hypothesis has merely been misrepresented by Bennett and Gill in [3]. Assuming this intuition is made precise by the idea that a random oracle should rarely be of help in computing, then it is obvious that oracle-dependent test languages (such as LOG(X) above and RANGE(X) and CORANGE(X) in [3]) shouldn't be used in working out its consequences. From the point of view of an oracle-dependent language the oracle is far from random. To use the idea to study whether, say, P = NP, one should most likely compute the probability that a random oracle helps some polynomial time deterministic machine to recognize an NP-complete language.

ACKNOWLEDGEMENTS

The author would like to thank Esko Ukkonen for several helpful conversations. This research has been supported by the Academy of Finland.

REFERENCES

[1] Angluin,D., On relativizing auxiliary pushdown machines. *Math. Systems Theory 13* (1980), 283-299.

[2] Baker,T., J.Gill and R. Solovay, Relativizations of the P =? NP question. *SIAM J. Comput. 4* (1975), 431-442.

[3] Bennett,C.H. and J.Gill, Relative to a random oracle A, $P^A \neq NP^A \neq co\text{-}NP^A$ with probability 1. *SIAM J. Comput. 10* (1981), 96-113.

[4] Book,R.V., Comparing complexity classes. *J. Comput. System Sci. 9* (1974), 213-229..

[5] Book,R.V., Bounded query machines: on NP and PSPACE. *Theor. Comput. Sci. 15* (1981), 27-29.

[6] Chandra,A.K., D.C.Kozen and L.J.Stockmeyer, Alternation. *J. Assoc. Comput. Mach. 28* (1981), 114-133.

[7] Hopcroft,J.E. and J.D.Ullman, *Introduction to Automata Theory, Languages, and Computation*. Addison-Wesley, Reading, Mass. (1979).

[8] Kurtz,S.A., On the random oracle hypothesis. *Proc. 14th Ann. ACM Symp. on Theory of Computing* (1982), 224-230.

[9] Ladner,R.E. and N.A.Lynch, Relativization of questions about log space computability. *Math. Systems Theory 10* (1976), 19-32.

[10] Lynch,N.A., Log space machines with multiple oracle tapes. *Theor. Comput. Sci. 6* (1978), 25-39.

[11] Rogers,H.,Jr., *Theory of Recursive Functions and Effective Computability*. McGraw-Hill, New York (1967).

[12] Ruzzo,W.L., J.Simon and M.Tompa, Space-bounded hierarchies and probabilistic computations. *Proc. 14th Ann. ACM Symp. on Theory of Computing* (1982), 215-223.

[13] Simon,I., *On Some Subrecursive Reducibilities*. Ph.D. dissertation. Report STAN-CS-77-608, Dept. of Computer Science, Stanford University, Stanford, Ca. (1977).

[14] Simon,J., *On Some Central Problems in Computational Complexity*. Ph.D. dissertation. Report TR 75-224, Dept. of Computer Science, Cornell University, Ithaca, N.Y. (1975)

[15] Sipser,M., On relativizations and existence of complete sets. *Proc. 9th Int. Colloq. on Automata, Languages, and Programming*, Aarhus, Denmark (1982), 523-531.

[16] Stockmeyer,L.J., The polynomial-time hierarchy. *Theor. Comput. Sci. 3* (1976), 23-33.

A propos d'une conjecture de F. Dejean
sur les répétitions dans les mots

Jean-Jacques Pansiot
Université Louis Pasteur
Centre de Calcul de l'Esplanade
7, rue René Descartes
67084 STRASBOURG Cédex
FRANCE

Abstract. We show that with a four letter alphabet the largest unavoidable repetitions in arbitrarily long words are of the form uvu where the length of uvu is $7/5^{th}$ of the length of uv. This proves part of a conjecture of F. Dejean.

Résumé. Nous montrons que pour un alphabet à 4 lettres, les plus grands répétitions inévitables dans des mots arbitrairement longs sont de la forme uvu où la longueur de uvu est 7/5 de la longueur de uv. Ceci prouve une partie d'une conjecture de F. Dejean.

1. Introduction.

Les répétitions dans les suites de symboles ont été beaucoup étudiées depuis le travail d'Axel Thue au début du siècle [11, 12] qui démontra qu'on peut construire un mot infini sur deux lettres ne contenant pas de facteur de la forme uuu (cube), ainsi qu'un mot infini sur trois lettres ne contenant pas de facteur de la forme uu (carré). Dès lors se pose la question de savoir pour un nombre de lettres donné quelles sont les répétitions inévitables dans un mot infini. Pour des alphabets à deux et à trois lettres, la réponse est connue [5, 11, 12]. Dans cet article nous résolvons le cas d'un alphabet à quatre lettres, en donnant une réponse affirmative à une conjecture de Dejean [5].

Donnons d'abord quelques définitions et notations. Un mot (fini) est un élément du monoïde libre A^* engendré par l'ensemble de lettres ou alphabet A. La longueur d'un mot u est notée $|u|$ et le mot vide ε.

Définition. Une t-répétition, pour t rationnel, est un mot de la forme u^t, où u^t est le plus court préfixe de $u^{\lceil t \rceil}$ de longueur au moins $|u|.t$, pour un certain mot u non vide.

Par exemple pour $u = abcd$, $u^{5/2} = abcdabcdab$, et $u^{4/3} = u^{3/2} = abcdab$. Une 2-répétition est un carré, une 3-répétition un cube. Les mots ne contenant pas de carré (square-free) ont été l'objet de nombreux travaux [1, 10, 11, 12], avec un regain d'intérêt récent [2, 3, 4, 8].

<u>Définition.</u> Un mot u contient au plus des t-répétitions si pour toute occurrence d'une t'-répétition dans u on a $t' \leq t$. Notons $RMAX_k(t)$ l'ensemble des mots sur un alphabet à k lettres et contenant au plus des t-répétitions.

Si $t' \leq t$, alors $RMAX_k(t') \subseteq RMAX_k(t)$. De plus pour tout $k \geq 2$, $RMAX_k(1)$ est fini, et $RMAX_k(2)$ est infini d'après les résultats de Thue [11, 12]. On a aussi $RMAX_k(t) \subseteq RMAX_{k+1}(t)$ en considérant qu'un alphabet à k lettres est un sous-ensemble d'un alphabet à k+1 lettres.

<u>Définition.</u> Le seuil de répétition, noté s(k) , est le plus petit nombre t tel que $RMAX_k(t)$ soit infini.

Si $RMAX_k(t)$ est infini, il contient des mots arbitrairement longs. En définissant un mot infini (à droite) comme une application des entiers dans l'alphabet A , on peut étendre aux mots infinis les notions de facteur, préfixe (finis). On dira qu'un mot infini est sans t-répétition si c'est le cas de chacun de ses facteurs finis. Avec ces conventions, $RMAX_k(t)$ est infini si et seulement s'il contient un mot infini. Une façon simple de construire un mot infini est d'itérer un morphisme. Soit m un morphisme ε-free de A^* dans A^* , et a_0 une lettre telle que $m(a_0)$ soit de la forme a_0u pour un mot non vide u. Alors la suite a_0, $m(a_0)$, $m^2(a_0)$, ..., $m^i(a_0)$, ... est telle que chaque mot est un préfixe des suivants et elle définit donc bien un mot infini, noté $m^{\omega}(a_0)$.

Dans ses travaux [11, 12] Thue a montré que si on itère le morphisme f défini sur $\{a, b\}^*$ par $f(a) = ab$, $f(b) = ba$, on obtient un mot infini $f^{\omega}(a) = abbabaabbaababbabaaba...$ ayant la propriété de ne pas contenir de facteur de la forme xuxux , $x \in \{a, b\}$, $u \in \{a, b\}^*$, c'est-à-dire pas de t-répétition, $t > 2$, donc $RMAX_2(2)$ est infini. Comme tout mot de $\{a, b\}^*$ de longueur au moins 4 contient un carré, $RMAX_2(t)$ est fini pour $t < 2$. En conséquence $s(2) = 2$.

Le cas d'un alphabet à trois lettres a été résolu par F. Dejean [5]. Elle donne un morphisme uniforme, c'est-à-dire tel que toutes les lettres ont des images de même longueur, qui a la propriété d'envoyer $RMAX_3(7/4)$ dans lui-même. Donc si on itère ce morphisme on obtient un mot infini dans $RMAX_3(7/4)$. Comme tout mot de $\{a, b, c\}^*$ de longueur au moins 39 contient une 7/4-répétition, on a $s(3) = 7/4$.

Pour des alphabets à plus de trois lettres, Dejean montre que $s(4) \geq 7/5$ et $s(k) \geq k/k-1$ pour $k \geq 5$, et conjecture que ces minorations sont en fait des valeurs exactes. Dans ce qui suit nous allons montrer qu'on a effectivement $s(4) = 7/5$. Le moyen utilisé pour construire un mot infini dans $RMAX_4(7/5)$ est plus compliqué que l'itération de morphisme employée par Thue et Dejean. Ce n'est pas surprenant au vu de résultats de Brandenburg [4] : Soit A un alphabet à k lettres. Si $s(k) < 3/2$ il n'existe pas de morphisme envoyant $RMAX_k(s(k))$ dans lui-même, ni de morphisme uniforme h tel que $h^i(x)$ appartienne à $RMAX_k(s(k))$ pour un certain x et pour tout i.

Pour construire notre mot infini N dans $RMAX_4(7/5)$, nous construisons d'abord un mot infini M sur deux lettres 0 et 1 en itérant un morphisme, puis nous lui appliquons une machine séquentielle pour obtenir N. Au Paragraphe 2 nous justifions le passage par un alphabet à deux lettres et donnons quelques propriétés de la machine séquentielle. Au Paragraphe 3 nous étudions les facteurs du mot M, en particulier les répétitions. Finalement au Paragraphe 4 nous montrons que les répétitions de N proviennent de répétitions de M d'une certaine forme, ce qui permet de majorer les répétitions par 7/5. Nous en déduisons aussi un phénomène curieux, à savoir qu'à une permutation près de l'alphabet il y a une seule 7/5-répétition inévitable, le mot abcdbacbdcabcd, toutes les autres répétitions de N étant au plus égales à 4/3. Ceci permet aussi de montrer que N ne peut pas être engendré par morphisme itéré.

2. Passage à un alphabet à deux lettres et machine séquentielle.

Soit A un alphabet à k lettres, $k \geq 2$, et $m = a_1 \dots a_n$, $a_i \in A$, $n \geq k$, un mot ne contenant pas de t-répétition, $t \geq (k-1)/(k-2)$. On constate que $k-1$ lettres consécutives de m doivent être distinctes. En particulier a_k est différent de $a_2, \dots, a_{k-1}$ et il n'y a que deux valeurs possibles pour a_k, soit a_1 soit b, l'unique lettre distincte de $a_1, \dots, a_{k-1}$. De même $a_1 \dots a_i$, $i \geq k-1$ étant fixé, il n'y a que deux possibilités pour a_{i+1}. Un tel mot m peut donc être codé par le couple $(a_1 \dots a_{k-1}, x_k \dots x_n)$ où $a_1 \dots a_{k-1}$ est le préfixe de longueur $k-1$ de m et x_i vaut 0 ou 1 selon que $a_i = a_{i-k+1}$ ou que $a_i = b$, l'unique lettre distincte de $a_{i+1-k}, \dots, a_{i-1}$. Bien entendu ce codage est injectif mais pas surjectif. Le passage du couple au mot correspondant peut s'effectuer au moyen de la machine séquentielle complète (voir [9, Chapter XI] pour une définition) S_k définie par :

- un alphabet d'entrée $X = \{0, 1\}$ et un alphabet de sortie A à k lettres.

- un ensemble d'état E identifié à l'ensemble des mots multilinéaires de A^{k-1}. Les états sont donc en bijection avec les permutations de A.

- les fonctions de sortie σ et de changement d'état δ sont données par

$$\sigma(a_1 \ldots a_{k-1}, 0) = a_1 \quad , \quad \sigma(a_1 \ldots a_{k-1}, 1) = b$$
$$\delta(a_1 \ldots a_{k-1}, 0) = a_2 a_3 \ldots a_{k-1} a_1, \quad \delta(a_1 \ldots a_{k-1}, 1) = a_2 \ldots a_{k-1} b$$

où b est l'unique lettre de A distincte de $a_1, \ldots, a_{k-1}$.

On remarque que $\delta(e, u)$ n'est rien d'autre que le facteur droit de $e\,\sigma(e, u)$ de longueur $k-1$, la sortie de la machine encode donc la suite des états. D'autre part la sortie de la machine est indépendante de l'état de départ à une permutation près de l'alphabet de sortie A.

L'intérêt de la machine séquentielle S_k est justifié par le lemme suivant.

Lemme 2.1. Pour tout mot $m \in A^*$, $m \in RMAX_k(t)$, $t < (k-1)/(k-2)$, il existe un état e et un mot $u \in X^*$ tels que $\sigma(e, u) = m$.

Corollaire. Pour $k = 4$, tout mot de $RMAX_4(7/5)$ est de la forme $\sigma(e, u)$, donc si $s(4) = 7/5$ il existe un mot infini M sur X tel que $\sigma(e, M) \in RMAX_4$ $(7/5)$. Dans le prochain paragraphe nous étudions un tel mot M construit par morphisme itéré.

3. Propriétés du mot infini M.

Soit $X = \{0, 1\}$. On considère le morphisme φ de X^* défini par $\varphi(1) = 10$, $\varphi(0) = 101101$, et on note M le mot infini $\varphi^{\omega}(1)$ obtenu par itération de φ. On a $M = 10101101101011011010101101101010101101 \ldots$. L'ensemble $\{\varphi(0), \varphi(1)\}$ est un code suffixe, donc tout mot fini u s'écrit d'au plus une façon $u = \varphi(v)$. De plus on a

Propriété 3.1. Tout facteur u de M, $|u| \geq 7$, se factorise sous la forme $u = u_1 u_2 u_3$ avec $u_2 \neq \varepsilon$, de telle sorte que si $M = \alpha u \beta$, alors $M = v_1 v_2 v_3$ avec $\varphi(v_1) = \alpha u_1$, $\varphi(v_2) = u_2$, $\varphi(v_3) = u_3 \beta$. Cette factorisation est dite standard si u_1 et u_3 sont choisis minimaux.

Remarque. Dans toutes les factorisations finies de mots infinis que l'on considèrera, on admettra implicitement que le facteur de droite (suffixe) est infini, et tous les autres facteurs sont finis.

Dans la suite, les facteurs de M qui peuvent être suivis (ou précédés) dans M à la fois par 0 et par 1 jouent un grand rôle, nous allons donc les caractériser.

Propriété 3.2. Soit u , $|u| \geq 7$, un mot tel que 0u et 1u (resp. u0 et u1) soient facteurs de M . Alors u commence (resp. finit) par 1010110 (resp. 0110101).

Soit $\mu : X^* \to X^*$ l'application définie par $\mu(u) = \varphi(u)101$. Notons que $\mu(u) = \varphi(u)\mu(\epsilon)$ et $\mu^i(u) = \varphi^i(u)\mu^i(\epsilon) = \varphi^i(u)\varphi^{i-1}(101)\ldots\varphi(101)101$.

Propriété 3.3. Les mots 0u, 1u, u0, u1 sont facteurs de M si et seulement si u est de la forme $\mu^i(v)$, $i \geq 0$, où v est l'un des mots 1, 101, 101101 . De plus si 0u0, 0u1, 1u0, 1u1 sont facteurs de M alors u est de la forme $\mu^i(101)$, $i \geq 0$.

Preuve. Si 0u, 1u, u0, u1 sont facteurs de M , $|u| \geq 7$, u commence par 1010110 et finit par 0110101 (Propriété 3.2), et la factorisation standard de u est de la forme $(\epsilon)(1010110\ldots01101)(101)$ donc $u = \mu(u')$. De plus si $M = \alpha u \beta$, il existe α' et β' tels que $\varphi(\alpha') = \alpha$, $\varphi(\beta') = 101\beta$, $M = \alpha' u' \beta'$. Alors α se termine par 1 si et seulement si α' se termine par 0 et β commence par 1 si et seulement si β' commence par 0 , donc 0u' , 1u', u'1 sont facteurs de M . En répétant ce raisonnement tant que $|u'| \geq 7$, on obtient bien $u = \mu^i(v)$, $|v| \leq 6$. Les seuls mots v possibles sont 1, 101, 10101, 101101, de plus $10101 = \mu(1)$. Finalement parmi les trois mots 1, 101, 101101, seul 101 peut apparaître dans M avec les quatre contextes possibles, ce qui achève la démonstration. ∎

Nous allons maintenant caractériser les répétitions de M . Une occurrence d'un carré uu de M est cadrée à gauche si on a $M = \alpha u u \beta$ avec la dernière lettre de α différente de la dernière lettre de u . Un carré est cadré à gauche si une de ses occurrences l'est, de plus tout carré est conjugué d'un carré cadré à gauche (deux mots α et β sont conjugués s'il existe un mot γ tel que $\alpha\gamma = \gamma\beta$).

Propriété 3.4. a) Tout carré cadré à gauche uu , $|u| \geq 7$ est l'image par φ d'un carré cadré à gauche plus court.

b) Le mot uu (resp. uuu) est un carré (resp. cube) cadré à

gauche de M si et seulement s'il est de la forme $\varphi^i(vv)$ (resp. $\varphi^i(vvv)$), $i \geq 0$, où v est l'un des mots 1, 101, 10110 (resp. 10, 101).

En fait le mot M contient des t-répétitions pour $t > 3$. Si on appelle inextensible une répétition cadrée à la fois à gauche et à droite on a

<u>Propriété 3.5.</u> Les t-répétitions inextensibles de M, $t \geq 3$ sont de la forme $\mu^i(1010101)$ et $\mu^i(101101101)$, $i \geq 0$.

Soit u_n le nombre de facteurs distincts de M de longueur n. D'après un résultat de Ehrenfeucht, Lee et Rozenberg [7], on sait que u_n est au plus proportionnel à n log n et même à n si le mot infini peut être engendré par un morphisme uniforme. Nous allons voir (Propriété 3.6) que u_n est linéaire, bien que M ne soit pas engendrable par morphisme uniforme (Propriété 3.8). On observe qu'il y a soit un soit deux facteurs qui peuvent être suivis à la fois par 0 et par 1 dans M. Plus précisément :

<u>Propriété 3.6.</u> La suite u_n vérifie la récurrence

$$u_{n+1} = \begin{cases} u_n+2 & \text{si } \exists\, i \geq 0 \quad |\mu^i(101)|+1 \leq n \leq |\mu^i(101101)| . \\ u_n+1 & \text{sinon.} \end{cases}$$

En particulier pour $n \geq 2$, $n < u_n < 2n$.
Les premières valeurs de u_n pour n = 1, 2, ... sont 2, 3, 4, 5, 7, 9, 11, 12, 13, 14 ... .

Nous allons montrer que M ne peut être engendré par un morphisme uniforme. Ceci n'est qu'une conséquence d'un résultat plus fort.

<u>Définition.</u> Deux morphismes f et g de X^* sont conjugués s'il existe un mot u de X^* tel que pour toute lettre x, $f(x)u = u\,g(x)$.

<u>Propriété 3.7.</u> Un morphisme engendre un mot infini ayant les mêmes facteurs que M si et seulement si c'est un conjugué d'une puissance de φ.

<u>Preuve.</u> Soit $M' = \psi^\omega(x_0)$ un mot infini ayant les mêmes facteurs que M. Comme $(10)^3$ et $(101)^3$ sont des cubes de M, donc de M', $(\psi(10))^3$ et $(\psi(101))^3$ sont des cubes de M', donc de M. Par la propriété 3.4, $\psi(10)$ et $\psi(101)$ sont des conjugués de mots de la forme $\varphi^i(v)$, $i \geq 0$, v = 10 ou 101. On a les relations $|\psi(10)| < |\psi(101)| < 2|\psi(10)|$ et $|\varphi^i(u)| > 2|\varphi^{i-1}(u)|$. Si $\psi(10)$ était un

conjugué de $\varphi^i(101)$, alors $\psi(101)$ serait un conjugué de $\varphi^{i+1}(10) = \varphi^i(10101101)$, d'où $|\psi(1)| > |\psi(10)|$ ce qui est impossible. Donc $\psi(10)$ est un conjugué de $\varphi^i(10)$, et $\psi(101)$ un conjugué de $\varphi^i(101)$, ce qui entraîne $|\psi(x)| = |\varphi^i(x)|$, $x = 0, 1$. La plus grande répétition contenant $(\varphi^i(10))^3$ est $\mu^i(1010101)$ (Propriété 3.5), donc

$$\mu^i(1010101) = \alpha\, \psi(1010101)\beta \;,\; |\alpha| \le \mu^i(\varepsilon) \;. \tag{1}$$

D'autre part on montre aisément par récurrence que $\mu^i(\varepsilon)$ est le plus long préfixe commun de $\varphi^i(0)$ et $\varphi^i(1x)$ pour une lettre quelconque x. Si dans (1) on considère les préfixes de longueur $\varphi^i(10)\mu^i(\varepsilon)$ on obtient $\varphi^i(10)\mu^i(\varepsilon) = \alpha\, \psi(10)\gamma$, donc $\psi(0)$ est un facteur de $\varphi^i(0)\mu^i(\varepsilon)$, soit $u\, \psi(0)\gamma = \varphi^i(0)\mu^i(\varepsilon)$. Si on pose $\mu^i(\varepsilon) = v\,\gamma$, on a $u\, \psi(0) = \varphi^i(0)\, v$. De plus v est un préfixe de $\mu^i(\varepsilon)$, donc de $\varphi^i(0)$ et $u = v$. Il reste $\varphi^i(1)\, u\, \psi(0) = \alpha\psi(10)$, donc $\varphi^i(1)\, u = \alpha\, \psi(1)$, et α est un préfixe de $\varphi^i(10)$ donc de $\mu^i(\varepsilon)$ et $\alpha = u$. On a bien $\varphi^i(1)u = u\, \psi(1)$ et $\varphi^i(0)\, u = u\, \psi(0)$ donc φ^i et ψ sont conjugués.

Réciproquement si ψ est un conjugué de φ^i , si $M' = \psi^\omega(x_0)$, M' a pour facteur 11, donc $\psi^j(11)$ donc $\varphi^{ij}(1)$, et tout facteur de M est facteur d'un $\varphi^{ij}(1)$ donc de M'. Symétriquement tout facteur de M' est facteur d'un $\psi^j(1)$, donc de $\varphi^i(11)$ donc de M et les deux mots infinis M et M' ont les mêmes facteurs ∎

Le mot M n'étant pas périodique, deux morphismes distincts conjugués d'une puissance de φ engendrent des mots infinis distincts d'où :

<u>Corollaire 3.8.</u> Tout morphisme engendrant M est une puissance de φ , en particulier il ne peut être uniforme.

<u>Corollaire 3.9.</u> Il existe une infinité de mots infinis distincts engendrés par morphisme itéré et ayant les mêmes facteurs que M.

4. Propriétés des répétitions de N.

Nous allons d'abord donner quelques propriétés de la machine séquentielle appliquée à M. Notons $\equiv$ la congruence de X^* définie par $u \equiv v$ si et seulement si u et v provoquent le même changement d'état. En particulier $u \equiv \varepsilon$ ssi $\delta(e, u) = e$.

<u>Propriété 4.1.</u> On a les relations $\varphi(u) \equiv 110\, u\, 0011$, $u \equiv 0011\varphi(u)110$, $\varphi^3(u) \equiv u$. En particulier $u \equiv v$ si et seulement si $\varphi(u) \equiv \varphi(v)$ et $u \equiv \varepsilon$ si et seulement si $\varphi(u) \equiv \varepsilon$.

Preuve. On vérifie que $000 \equiv 1111 \equiv (110)^3 \equiv (0011)^3 \equiv \varepsilon$, donc toutes ces relations se déduisent de la première. Celle-ci se démontre par récurrence sur la longueur de u . Elle est vraie pour $u = \varepsilon$, et si $u = vx$, $x \in X$, on vérifie que $0011\ \varphi(x) \equiv x\ 0011$ ∎

Comme $u1 \equiv \varepsilon$ entraîne $u \equiv 111$ entraîne $1u \equiv \varepsilon$ et $u0 \equiv \varepsilon$ entraîne $u \equiv 00$ entraîne $0u \equiv \varepsilon$ on a

Propriété 4.2. Un mot est congru à ε si et seulement si ses conjugués le sont.

On définit le mot infini N sur 4 lettres par $N = \sigma(p_0, M)$. L'état initial p_0 n'a pas d'importance, à une permutation près de l'alphabet A. Par exemple en prenant $p_0 = cbd$ on obtient

$N = abcadbacdabcdacbdcadbacdabca...$

Nous allons voir qu'à toute répétition assez longue de N correspond une répétition de M d'une forme particulière, appelée N-répétition (de M). L'idée principale est la suivante : la suite N donne non seulement la sortie de la machine, mais aussi la suite des états, donc si un mot de longueur supérieure à 3 , par exemple $abcU$, $a, b, c \in A$, $U \in A^*$ a deux occurrences dans N alors ces deux occurrences de U ont été produites à partir du même état abc, donc à partir de deux occurrences du même facteur u de M . Si $abcUWabcU$, pour $W \in A^*$ est un facteur de N , le facteur correspondant de M est $a'b'c'uwa''b''c''u$, et le mot $uwa''b''c''$ fait passer la machine de l'état abc à lui-même, d'où

Définition. Une N-répétition de M est un facteur de M de la forme uvu, $uv \equiv \varepsilon$, $|v| \geq 3$.

Propriété 4.3. Si un mot de la forme $abcUWabcU$ est facteur de N , $a, b, c \in A$, $U, W \in A^*$, alors M contient une N-répétition uvu, avec $\sigma(abc, u) = U$, $\sigma(abc, uv) = UWabc$.

Définition. L'exposant d'une N-répétition uvu, noté $E(uvu)$ est le rapport $(|uvu|+3)/|uv|$.

L'image par σ d'une N-répétition d'exposant t est donc une t-répétition de N . Considérons une occurrence de la N-répétition uvu, $M = \alpha uvu\beta$. Sans perte de généralité on peut supposer que cette répétition est cadrée à gauche, c'est-à-dire que la dernière lettre de v est différente de la dernière lettre de α . Si ce n'est pas le cas, on a $\alpha = \alpha'x$, $xu = u'y$, $yv = v'x$, $\beta' = y\beta$ et $M = \alpha'u'v'u'\beta'$. De plus

$|v'| = |v| \geq 3$, et $u'v'$ est un conjugué de uv, donc $u'v' \equiv \epsilon$ (Propriété 4.2), et $u'v'u'$ est une N-répétition. En répétant ce décalage on obtient bien une N-répétition cadrée à gauche, de même exposant que la première, et conjuguée de celle-ci. On a

Propriété 4.4. La suite N ne contient pas de t-répétition, $t \geq 2$. Elle est donc sans carré (square-free).

En effet on vérifie aisément que N ne contient pas de facteur de la forme u^t , $t \geq 2$, $|u| = 1, 2$, donc si N contenait une t-répétition, $t \geq 2$, celle-ci commencerait par abcUabcU..., et la N-répétition correspondante uvu vérifierait $|v| = 3$. Or il n'existe pas de N-répétition uvu , $|v| = 3$. Des Propriétés 4.3 et 4.4 on déduit

Propriété 4.5. Le mot N contient une t-répétition u^t , $|u| \geq 3$ si et seulement si M contient une N-répétition d'exposant t .

Il nous faut maintenant démontrer que M ne contient pas de N-répétition d'exposant supérieur à 7/5. En fait nous montrerons même qu'il y a essentiellement une seule N-répétition d'exposant 7/5 , toutes les autres étant d'exposant au plus 4/3. La preuve se décompose en plusieurs étapes. On montre d'abord que les N-répétitions assez longues sont images par μ de répétitions plus courtes. On montre ensuite que l'application de μ fait décroitre l'exposant. Il suffit ensuite d'examiner les N-répétitions les plus courtes.

Comme ce sont les N-répétitions de plus grand exposant possible qui nous intéressent, on pose

Définition. Une N-répétition uvu est dite inextensible si on a $M = \alpha uvu\beta$, où la première lettre de v diffère de la première lettre de β , et la dernière lettre de v diffère de la dernière lettre de α .

Une N-répétition inextensible a donc une occurrence cadrée à la fois à gauche et à droite.

Propriété 4.6. a) Toute N-répétition peut être étendue en une N-répétition inextensible d'exposant au moins égal,

b) Si uvu est inextensible, avec $|u| \geq 7$, alors il existe une N-répétition u'v'u', avec $\mu(u'v'u') = uvu$, $\varphi(u'v') = uv$, $\mu(u') = u$, $|u'| < |u|$,

c) Toute N-répétition inextensible uvu est de la forme $uvu = \mu^i(u'v'u')$, $uv = \varphi^i(u'v')$, $u = \mu^i(u')$, $i \geq 0$, $u' \in \{\varepsilon, 1, 101, 101101\}$, où $u'v'u'$ est une N-répétition inextensible.

<u>Propriété 4.7.</u> a) Pour toute N-répétition uvu, $E(\mu^2(uvu))$ est strictement inférieur au maximum de $E(uvu)$ et de $E(\mu(uvu))$,

b) Les N-répétitions uvu, $u \in \{\varepsilon, 1, 101, 101101\}$, vérifient $E(\mu(uvu)) < E(uvu)$,

c) Le maximum de $E(\mu^i(uvu))$, $i \geq 0$, $u \in \{\varepsilon, 1, 101, 101101\}$ est atteint pour $i = 0$.

Par examen des différents cas on obtient :

<u>Propriété 4.8.</u> La suite M ne contient pas de N-répétition uvu avec $E(uvu) > 7/5$. De plus la seule N-répétition uvu d'exposant supérieur à 4/3 est obtenue pour $u = 1$, $v = 011010110$.

Les propriétés 4.5 et 4.8 donnent notre résultat principal :

<u>Théorème 4.9.</u> Le mot infini sur 4 lettres N contient au plus des 7/5 répétitions. Le seuil de répétition s(4) est donc égal à 7/5.

D'après la Propriété 4.8, la seule 7/5 répétition, et même la seule répétition supérieure à 4/3 de N est, à une permutation près de l'alphabet, abcdbacbdcabcd. On peut montrer par énumération que tout mot assez long de RMAX (7/5) contient cette répétition d'où

<u>Propriété 4.10.</u> Le mot abcdbacbdcabcd, à une permutation près de l'alphabet, est inévitable dans tout mot suffisemment long de RMAX (7/5), et c'est la seule répétition supérieure à 4/3 ayant cette propriété.

Nous allons utiliser ces propriétés pour montrer que le mot infini N ne peut pas être engendré par morphisme itéré. Nous avons d'abord besoin du résultat suivant sur les facteurs de N.

Soit v_n le nombre de facteurs distincts de N de longueur n. On a

<u>Propriété 4.11.</u> Si un mot u est facteur de N, alors tous les mots obtenus de u en permutant l'alphabet sont aussi facteurs de N, donc $v_n = 4!u_n$, en par-

ticulier $24n < v_n < 48n$, $n \geq 2$.

Ceci vient du fait que lorsqu'on applique σ à M , on rencontre chaque facteur u de M dans chacun des 24 états de la machine, c'est-à-dire que pour tout état p il existe un préfixe $\alpha(u, p)$ de M tel que $\alpha(u, p)u$ est un préfixe de M et $\delta(p_0, \alpha(u, p)) = p$.

Propriété 4.12. Le mot infini N ne peut être engendré par morphisme itéré.

Preuve. Par la propriété précédente w = abcdbacbdcabcd et tous les mots obtenus de w en permutant l'alphabet sont facteurs de N . Supposons que N soit obtenu en itérant un morphisme ψ . Alors $\psi(w)$ est aussi un facteur de N , et $\psi(w)$ est au plus une 4/3 répétition, donc

$$|\psi(abcdbacbdcabcd)| / |\psi(abcdbacbdc)| \leq 4/3 ,$$

ce qui entraîne $|\psi(ad)| = 0$. Comme cette propriété doit rester vraie par permutation de l'alphabet, on obtient que ψ est le morphisme trivial ce qui est impossible ■

5. Conclusion.

Nous avons construit un mot infini sur quatre lettres ayant au plus des 7/5 répétitions, prouvant ainsi un cas de la conjecture de F. Dejean. Le cas des alphabets à plus de quatre lettres reste ouvert. Les techniques utilisées ici peuvent sans doute s'appliquer pour d'autres valeurs de k , le raisonnement du Paragraphe 2 s'appliquant dès que $s(k) < (k-1)/(k-2)$. Il est à noter que la notion de seuil de répétition est très locale puisque par exemple le mot N ne contient pas de 7/5-répétition de longueur supérieure à 14. Des résultats analogues ont été obtenus pour les carrés dans les mots sur un alphabet à deux lettres [6] . Il pourrait donc être intéressant d'étudier les répétitions u^t en fonction non seulement de t et du nombre de lettre, mais aussi de la longueur de u .

Références.

1. S. Aršon, Démonstration de l'existence de suites asymétriques infinies Mat. Sb. 44 (1937), 769-777.

2. J. Berstel, Sur les mots sans carré définis par un morphisme, Proceedings 6th International Colloquium in Automata, Language and Programming, Lecture Notes in Computer Science 71 (1979), 16-29.

3. J. Berstel, Mots sans carrés et morphismes itérés, Discrete Math. 29 (1979), 235-244.

4. F.-J. Brandenburg, Uniformly Growing k-th power-free homomorphisms, Theoretical Computer Science 23 (1983), 69-82.

5. F. Dejean, Sur un Théorème de Thue, J. of Comb. Theory (A) 13 (1972), 90-99.

6. F. M. Dekking, On repetitions of blocs in binary sequences, J. of Comb. Theory (A) 20 (1976), 292-299.

7. A. Ehrenfeucht, K. P. Lee, G. Rozenberg, Subword complexities of various classes of deterministic developmental languages without interaction, Theoretical Computer Science 1 (1975), 59-75.

8. A. Ehrenfeucht and G. Rozenberg, On the subword complexity of square-free DOL languages, Proceedings 5th GI Conference in Theoretical Computer Science, Lecture Notes in Computer Science 104 (1981), 1-4.

9. S. Eilenberg, Automata, languages and machines, volume A (Academic Press, New York, 1974).

10. M. Morse and G. A. Hedlund, Unending chess, symbolic dynamics, and a problem in semigroups, Duke Math. J. 11 (1944), 1-7.

11. A. Thue, Über unendliche Zeichenreihen, Norske Vid. Selsk. Skr. I, Mat.-Nat. Kl. christiana 7 (1906), 1-22.

12. A. Thue, Über die gegenseitige Lage gleicher Teile gewisser Zeichenreihen, Norske Vid. Selsk. Skr. I, Mat.-Nat. Kl. christiana 1 (1912), 1-67.

PARALLEL DICTIONARIES ON 2-3 TREES

W. Paul*
IBM Research Laboratory
San Jose, California 95193

U. Vishkin**
Courant Institute of Mathematical Sciences
New York University, 251 Mercer Street
New York, New York 10012

and

H. Wagener
Technische Universitaet Berlin
Institut fuer Software and Theoretische Informatik
Strasse des 17. Juni 135, D-1000 Berlin 10, West Germany

ABSTRACT

Our model of computation is a parallel computer with k synchronized processors $P_1,\ldots,P_k$ sharing a common random access storage, where simultaneous access to the same storage location by two or more processors is not allowed. Suppose a 2-3 tree T with n leaves is implemented in the storage, suppose $a_1,\ldots,a_k$ are data that may or may not be stored in the leaves, and for all i, $1 \le i \le k$, processor P_i knows a_i. We show how to search for $a_1,\ldots,a_k$ in the tree T, how to insert these data into the tree and how to delete them from the tree in $O(\log n + \log k)$ steps.

1. Introduction

Technology will make it possible to build computers with a large number of cooperating processors in the near future. However, building such computers will only be worthwhile if the increased computing power can be used to reduce considerably the execution time of sufficiently many basic computational problems. In particular, one would like to have datastructures, where k processors can solve many problems about k times faster than a single processor. 2-3 trees are one such datastructure as will be demonstrated here. Protocols that avoid read or write conflicts, if several processors are working simultaneously on the same balanced

*Part of this research was done while the first author was visiting the InInstitut de Programmation of the Université Paris VI.

**Visiting from the Computer Science Department, Technion, Haifa, Israel.

tree, have been studied previously [BS], [S], but apparently no attempt was made to design fast algorithms and to analyze their running time.

In the sequel, we say very little about how to avoid read or write conflicts. In the situations where they are possible, there are easy ways to avoid them. We will, however, have to say some words about storage allocation.

2. 2-3 Trees

A 2-3 tree T is a tree in which all leaves have the same depth and each interior mode v has two or three sons: the left son $\ell(v)$, the right son $r(v)$, and in case there are three sons, the middle son $m(v)$. Data from a totally ordered domain are stored in the leaves with smaller data to the left of larger ones. For each node v, the value $L(v)$ (resp. $R(v)$) of the largest element stored in the subtree of T with root $\ell(v)$ (resp. $r(v)$) is stored in v. Recall that in the sequential use of 2-3 trees $R(v)$ is not stored. If v has three sons, then the value $M(v)$ of the largest element stored in the subtree of T with root $m(v)$ is also stored in v. The depth of a node v in T is its distance from the root, the height of v is its distance from the leaves. We assume the reader to be familiar with the usual search, insertion and deletion routines as described say in [AHU]. There, a datastructure that supports these routines, is called a dictionary.

Suppose a 2-3 tree T with n leaves is implemented in the storage, suppose $a_1,\dots,a_k$ are data that may or may not be stored in the leaves, suppose $a_1 < \dots < a_k$ and for all i processor P_i knows a_i. We show how to perform any of three dictionary operations with respect to these elements by these k processors in $O(\log n + \log k)$ steps.

If the elements $a_1,\dots,a_k$ arrive unsorted they can be sorted in $O(\log k)$ time (see [AKS]). Their solution can readily be modified into our model of computation using k processors (see [V2] for similar arguments).

3. Search

If simultaneous access by several processors to the same storage location for read purposes is allowed (as in the PRAM model of parallel computation of [FW]) then search is very simple. Processor P_i $(1 \leq i \leq k)$ performs the standard sequential search of a_i in $O(\log n)$ time ([AHU]).

Since no writes into the shared memory are required, this is done in parallel by all k processors in time O(log n). Since such simultaneous reads are not allowed in this presentation, we need another solution.

A chain is a subsequence $a_f, a_{f+1}, \ldots, a_\ell$ of the input sequence $a_1, \ldots, a_k$. Such a chain corresponds in a natural way to a chain of processors $P_f, P_{f+1}, \ldots, P_\ell$. The search algorithm starts with the chain $a_1, \ldots, a_k$ at the root of the 2-3 tree T. This chain is subsequently split into many subchains which are wandering down the tree. Among the processors of a chain $a_f, \ldots, a_\ell$ only the first one, i.e., P_f, is active. P_f knows ℓ and of course f. If at some time the chain is split into $a_f, \ldots, a_{m-1}$ and $a_m, \ldots, a_\ell$, then processor P_f will invoke processor P_m and transmit the value ℓ to P_m.

The search algorithm proceeds in stages. During each stage s, the active processor of each chain C will access the data in some node v of the 2-3 tree T. We say that C is in node v at stage s. The chain $a_1, \ldots, a_k$ is in the root at stage 1. During each stage, each active processor processes its chain once. We describe how this is done.

Suppose a chain $C = a_f, \ldots, a_\ell$ is in node v at stage s, the node v has two or three sons and the labels L(v) and possibly M(v) are stored in v. We say that C hits a label X, if $a_f \leq X < a_\ell$. The label R(v) does not play any role in the present discussion.

Chains C that hit no label are sent to the appropriate son of v; more precisely: C is at stage s+1 in node

$\ell(v)$ if $a_\ell \leq L(v)$

m(v) if $L(v) < a_f$ and $a_\ell \leq M(v)$ and v has 3 sons

r(v) if $M(v) < a_f$ and v has 3 sons
or $L(v) < a_f$ and v has 2 sons.

For chains $C = a_f, \ldots, a_\ell$ let $C_1 = a_f, \ldots, a_{m-1}$ and $C_2 = a_m, \ldots, a_\ell$ with $m = \lceil (f+\ell)/2 \rceil$. If C hits a label, then it is split into C_1 and C_2. If C_i, i = 1,2, hits no label, then it is sent to the appropriate son, else it remains in v, i.e., C_i is in node v at stage s+1. Clearly, a chain can be processed in O(1) steps.

<u>Claim</u>. (a) (resp. (b)). Say that elements $a_f, a_{f+1}, \ldots, a_\ell$ only have passed through edge e of T through stage s, for any $s \geq 1$. If a chain C

such that $a_j \in C$ and $j > \ell$ (resp. $j < f$) passed through e at stage s+1 then $a_{\ell+1} \in C$ (resp. $a_{f-1} \in C$).

Corollary. No more than two chains may pass each edge e of T at any single stage.

Proof of Claim. By induction on the depth of e in T. The claim obviously holds for each edge e that emanates from the root of T. This completes the base of the induction. Assume that both parts (a) and (b) of the claim hold for all edges of depth k. Let $e_1 = (v,w)$ be an edge of depth k+1 and $e_2 = (u,v)$ its father edge in T. We will show that part (a) of the claim holds for e. The proof of part (b) is similar.

Elements $a_f, a_{f+1}, \ldots, a_\ell$ (resp. a_j) passed e_2 through stage s-1 (resp. s). By the inductive hypothesis $a_{\ell+1}$ passed e_2 no later than stage s.

Case 1. w is a left son of v.

If $a_{\ell+1}$ passed e_2 at stage s then, by the inductive hypothesis, $a_{\ell+1}$ passed e_2 at the same chain as a_j. If $a_{\ell+1}$ passed e_2 before stage s then $a_{\ell+1}$ and a_j were, again, in the same chain at e_2 since otherwise $a_{\ell+1}$ would not have been delayed at v. Since left chops of hit chains are sent to left sons and $a_{\ell+1}$ did not pass e_1 before stage s+1, $a_{\ell+1}$ and a_j pass e_1 in the same chain at stage s+1.

Case 2. w is a right son of v.

The chain in which a_ℓ passed e_2 did not contain $a_{\ell+1}$ because if it did then $a_{\ell+1}$ would have passed e_1 not later than a_ℓ. So, since a_j (and $a_{\ell+1}$) could not have delayed at v it passed e_2 at stage s and by the inductive hypothesis its chain included $a_{\ell+1}$. This chain passed e_1 at stage s+1.

Case 3. w is a middle son of v.

If the chain in which a_ℓ passed e_2 contained $a_{\ell+1}$ then it must have contained a_j and large enough elements to hit label M(v); now, if it did not hit L(v) then the left-choping arguments (see Case 1) imply that $a_{\ell+1}$ and a_j passed e_1 in the same chain. If it hit L(v) then this chain (or later subchains of it) are cut into pieces that separate a_ℓ and a_j; $a_{\ell+1}$ must be in the right one with a_j (otherwise it is sent on e_1 no later than a_ℓ) and, again, the left-choping arguments apply. If the chain in which a_ℓ passed e_2 did not contain $a_{\ell+1}$ then the analysis of Case 1 applies. This completes the proof of the claim.

The corollary implies that for each s and v at most 4 chains are in v at stage s. Thus, each stage lasts O(1) steps. Once a chain $a_f, \ldots, a_\ell$ has arrived in a leaf b, the processors $P_{f+1},\dots,P_\ell$ have to be informed of the value of b. This is done recursively in $\lceil \log k \rceil$ stages. In stage j, $0 \le j \le \lceil \log k \rceil - 1$, processor P_i that knows where a_i falls informs P_{i+2^j}, if this later processor does not know yet where a_{i+2^j} falls. See [V1] for more details. Whenever a chain hits a label it is halved. Thus, any element may be contained in chains that hit labels no more than $\lceil \log k \rceil$ times; therefore it arrives to a leaf in at most $\lceil \log n \rceil + \lceil \log k \rceil$ stages, and the search takes $O(\log n + \log k)$ time.

4. Insertions

The tree T has n leaves $b_1 < b_2 < \dots < b_n$. The elements $a_1,\dots,a_k$ are to be inserted into T.

We first run the search algorithm. This results in splitting the input into chains (a_i and a_j, $1 \le i < j \le k$, belong to the same chain if there is no leaf b_q, $1 \le q \le n$, such that $a_i \le b_q < a_j$). There are n+1 possible chains $C_o, C_1, \dots, C_n$. Let $|C_q|$ denote the number of input elements in chain C_q. (For most q, $0 \le q \le n$, $|C_q| = 0$ since it makes sense to insert elements to a tree rather than building it from scratch only if $k \ll n$.) We say that by the insertion algorithm elements of chain C_q (resp. C_o) <u>arrive</u> to leaf b_q (resp. b_1) and <u>fall</u> to its right (resp. left) hand side, for $1 \le q \le n$.

First, we describe a simple algorithm for the special case $|C_o| = 0$ and $|C_q| \le 1$ for all $1 \le q \le n$. This algorithm works in stages. In stage 1, for all i processor P_i makes a_i a son of a father of b_i and then stands by on a_i. Now the algorithm works such that for all s after stage s the following holds:

All leaves in the tree have the same depth, all interior nodes of height $\ne$ s have two or three sons. Between each pair of "old" nodes (resp. to the right of the rightmost old node) of height s-1, there is at most one "new" node of height s-1. Each such new node has a processor standing by. So an (old) node v of height s has at most three new sons. It also has no more than three old sons. In an obvious way the processor standing by at a leftmost new son of a node of size s "takes over," while the other two processors become inactive. In case the total number of old and new sons of v is $\le$ 3 the new son becomes an "ordinary" son of v and the processor becomes inactive. In case this total number of sons is > 3, a new internal node v′ of height s which becomes the right brother of v is created and the new and old sons of height s-1 are partitioned properly among v and v'. The processor then stands by on v'. Updating the L, M and R fields of v and v' in both cases is easy. So stage s takes O(1) steps. We showed that in each stage, several new nodes of the tree may be created simultaneously. We will say later how to do this without occupying too much storage space.

Let us go back to the general problem of insertion. If $|C_o| > 0$, start by inserting a_1 by the sequential algorithm. The new C_o (with respect to the new tree and $a_2, a_3, \ldots, a_k$) satisfies $|C_o| = 0$.

The problem of inserting a long chain $C_j = a_f, \ldots, a_\ell$ at leaf b_j, for $1 \leq j \leq n$, is reduced to the problem of inserting shorter chains. This is done by first inserting the middle element a_m $(m = \lceil (f+\ell)/2 \rceil)$ at leaf b_j and then inserting recursively $a_f, \ldots, a_{m-1}$ at b_j and $a_{m+1}, \ldots, a_\ell$ at a_m. This is done for all chains in parallel and the middle elements are inserted by the simple algorithm described above. After the chains have been split $\lceil \log k \rceil$ times, they are reduced to length one. Thus, running first the algorithm for C_o and then the simple algorithm $\lceil \log k \rceil$ times would do the job in $O(\log n \log k)$ steps. For $i \leq \lceil \log k \rceil$, let T_i be the tree obtained by running the algorithm for C_o and then the simple algorithm i times. Now for all i running the simple algorithm the i'th time results in a wave of processors running up T_{i-1} at a speed of one level per stage, and below this wave, the tree already looks like T_i. Thus, pipelining can be applied; this is since before starting the (i+1)-st run of the simple algorithm and with it the (i+1)-st wave of processors, one has not to wait until the i'th wave has reached the root, but only long enough to ensure that the two waves will not overlap. Three stages will certainly suffice.

5. Deletions

Two deletion algorithms are presented. The first algorithm is fairly simple. The second algorithm, however, is more involved but has the advantage of presenting some new ideas. We hope that these ideas will be found useful for routines on 2-3 trees which are more complicated than the dictionary routines which are discussed here.

5.1. The First Deletion Algorithm

For deleting the elements $a_1 < a_2 < \ldots < a_k$ from the 2-3 tree T, we first run the search algorithm. Similar to the description of the insertion algorithm we have elements of chain C_q (resp. C_o) which arrive to leaf b_q (resp. b_1) and fall to its right (resp. left) hand side, for $1 \leq q \leq n$. C_o cannot contain an element which is in a leaf and therefore can be ignored. For each (non-empty) chain C_q $(1 \leq q \leq n)$ the processor of its left-most element checks if its element is the same as the one stored in leaf b_q. If it is so, the processor marks leaf b_q for deletion and stands by on this leaf. All other processors become inactive.

First, we describe a simple algorithm for the special case where each node of height 1 has at least one non-marked son. This algorithm works in stages.

In stage 1 all the marked leaves are deleted. Following stage 1 a node of height 1 may either remain a node of height 1 or become a node of height 0 (a leaf). Say that a node v of height 1 had one or two son-leaves which were deleted. If it remained of height 1 (it is possible if it had three sons and only one was deleted) then the processor of this deleted leaf becomes inactive. Otherwise the processor of a deleted son-leaf stands by on v and v is marked. The processor of a (possibly existing) second deleted son-leaf becomes inactive.

The algorithm works such that, for all s $(s \geq 1)$, the following holds after stage s:

1. Each marked node is a root of a 2-3 tree of height s-1 and is a son of a node of height s+1 in T. It has a processor standing by on it.
2. Each internal node has two or three sons.
3. Each node of height s in T which is not marked is a root of a 2-3 tree of height s.

It is easy to verify that each node v of height s+1 in T which has a marked son must have between two and seven sons and grandchildren of height s-1. All, but one, of the processors which stand by on a marked son of v become inactive. This processor does the following in stage s+1:

- if v has ≥ 4 sons and grandchildren of height s-1 then they are partitioned in the usual way into sons of v so as to make v of height s+1 as before. The processor becomes inactive.

- else the nodes of height s-1 become sons of v_1 in the usual way, v is marked and the processor is standing by on v.

Care has to be taken in order to avoid, read or write conflicts and to choose at each stage the processors which become inactive. This as well as updating the L, M and R fields is easy. The algorithm runs in O(log n) time.

Let us go back to the general case. We run the following algorithm A. It works in stages. Denote our 2-3 tree T by T_o. Let T_t be the 2-3 tree which is the output of stage t for $t \geq 1$.

Stage t ($t \geq 1$)

T_{t-1} is the input 2-3 tree for stage t. For each node of height 1 in T_{t-1} such that all its son-leaves have to be deleted marks all leaves, but one, for deletion. For each node such that not all its son-leaves have to be deleted mark the ones that have to be deleted. Processors of these marked leaves stand by on them. Processor of leaves that have to be deleted but have not yet been marked do not take part in the rest of this stage. The stage proceeds, now, in the same way as the algorithm for the special case given above.

In each stage we delete at least half of the leaves that have to be deleted but have not been deleted by previous stages. Therefore, algorithm A runs in $\leq \lceil \log k \rceil$ stages. Similar to Section 4 (insertions) we pipeline the stages of algorithm A thereby obtaining an overall time complexity of O(log n + log k).

5.2. The Second Deletion Algorithm

In order to clarify the presentation, let us start with a solution for the corresponding sequential deletion problem, i.e., we give an algorithm which employs a single processor for the deletion of a simple element a from a 2-3 tree.

1. Using the standard search algorithm, find the path $\pi(a) = (p_1,\dots,p_t)$ from the root of T to a. Delete the whole path $\pi(a)$ and all edges adjacent to it from T.

One is left with a forest of subtrees of T some of which were to the left of the path $\pi(a)$ and the others were to the right of $\pi(a)$. Let us call these subtrees of T the left (resp. right) side trees of path $\pi(a)$. If a was not stored in the tree, then a was eventually compared to a leaf b of T with the result $a < b$ or $a > b$. In the first [second] case treat b and possibly its right [left] brothers as right [left] side trees of $\pi(a)$. Our problem is to join this forest of subtrees into a new 2-3 tree. This is done in two steps.

2. Join the left (resp. right) subtrees of $\pi(a)$ into a 2-3 tree L (resp. R).

We describe this step for the left subtrees only. Right subtrees are handled similarly. This is done in stages which are described recursively. Before starting stage s we have a 2-3 tree S that contains the leaves of all left subtrees of height $< s-1$. The height of S is $h < s$. There are either none or one or two left subtrees of height s. In the second (resp. third) case we denote them L (resp. L_1 and L_2). In the first case S is the "output" of stage s. In the third case L_1 and L_2 are joined into a 2-3 tree of height s+1 in the obvious way. Let us denote this new tree by L, too. No confusion will arise. In both the second and third cases we reach, down the rightmost path in L, a node of height h+1. The root of S becomes its son and the insertion is propagated in the standard way up in L. (The possibility where S is of height s and we are in the second case is simple and has to be added to the description.) This completes the description of one step. Note that the height of the new S is $< s+1$.

Throughout step 2 we did not visit any level more O(1) time; in stage s we never go below the height h of S before the stage started. Each time we visit a level O(1) operations are performed. Therefore, Step 2 takes O(log n) time.

3. Join L and R into a 2-3 tree.

A fairly awkward way of performing Step 3 is given. However, this technique is useful in the parallel algorithm since it enables pipelining. Start at the rightmost leaf of L and the leftmost leaf of R. Climb, level by level, simultaneously in L and R, till the first root of either L or R is encountered. Then join L and R to one tree and propagate the update, in the standard way, to form a 2-3 tree. The algorithm requires O(log n) time. See [AHU] for all "standard ways" mentioned above.

We now parallelize and pipeline this algorithm in order to delete simultaneously elements $a_1,\ldots,a_k$ from a 2-3 tree T:

1. Run the search algorithm for $a_1,\ldots,a_k$ and mark the paths $\pi(a_1),\ldots,\pi(a_k)$. As we do not require the elements a_i to be stored in the tree T, these paths are not necessarily distinct.

For all i, we define the <u>left</u> [<u>right</u>] <u>forest</u> LF(i) [RF(i)] of path $\pi(a_i)$ as the set of left [right] side trees of $\pi(a_i)$ whose root is not marked and that are not left [right] side trees of $\pi(a_{i-1})$ [$\pi(a_{i+1})$]. The example of Fig. 1 shows the only case where RF(i) and LF(i+1) may have a tree in common. "Correct" our definition for this case, so that this tree belongs to LF(i+1) only.

2. Rerun the search algorithm, but for all chains $a_f,\dots,a_\ell$ that are created have the processors p_f and p_ℓ both active. Processor P_f [P_ℓ] keeps track which trees are in LF(f) [RF(ℓ)]. Also delete in this run the paths $\pi(a_1),\dots,\pi(a_k)$ and the adjacent edges. For all chains $a_f\dots a_\ell$ that have reached a leaf only processors P_f and P_ℓ remain active. P_f remembers the index ℓ of the next active processor. The following two commands are executed by active processors P_i only, similar to Step 2 of the sequential algorithm.

3. For all P_f processors: join the left forest of path $\pi(a_f)$ into a 2-3 tree L_{f-1}.

4. For all P_ℓ processors: join the right forest of path $\pi(a_\ell)$ into a 2-3 tree R_ℓ. (All R_i and L_i that were not affected by the last two commands are empty.)

5. (a) Processor P_1: Insert L_o into $T_o^{(o)}$.
   Processor P_k: Insert R_k into $T_k^{(o)}$.

   (b) For all P_i processors $(1 < i < k)$: Join L_i and R_i into a 2-3 tree $T_i^{(o)}$. (The "insertion" into the T_i trees should be understood as renaming rather than copying.)

6. We are left with the problem of joining the trees $T_o^{(o)},T_1^{(o)},\dots,T_k^{(o)}$. This is done in phases $j = 0,1,\dots$.

For any tree let $\lambda(T)$ (resp. $\rho(T)$) denote the leftmost (resp. rightmost) leaf of T. For all odd i, processor P_i determines: $\lambda(T_{i-1}^{(o)})$, $\rho(T_{i-1}^{(o)})$, $\lambda(T_i^{(o)})$ and $\rho(T_i^{(o)})$.

The following is true for $j = 0$ and will remain true: At the beginning of phase j we are left with $\lceil (k+1)/2^j \rceil$ trees $T^{(j)},T^{(j)},\dots$ where for each $v \in \{0,\dots,\lceil (k+1)/2^j\rceil -1\}$ the tree $T_v^{(j)}$ is a 2-3 tree obtained by joining $T_{v2^j},\dots,T_{(v+1)2^j-1}$. For each v we have not yet used processor P_{v2^j} and processor P_{v2^j} knows $\rho(T_{v-1}^{(j)})$, $\lambda(T_{v-1}^{(j)})$, $\rho(T_v^{(j)})$ and $\lambda(T_v^{(j)})$.

The following is done in phase j: For each odd v processor P_{v2^j} runs up the right branch of $T_{v-1}^{(j)}$ and the left branch of $T_v^{(j)}$ and joins the two trees into $T_{(v-1)/2}^{(j+1)}$, as in Step 3 of the sequential algorithm. This processor performs also,

$$\lambda(T_{(v-1)/2}^{(j+1)}) \leftarrow \begin{cases} \lambda(T_{v-1}^{(j)}) & \text{if } T_{v-1}^{(j)} \neq \phi \\ \lambda(T_v^{(j)}) & \text{otherwise.} \end{cases}$$

and

$$\rho(T_{(v-1)/2}^{(j+1)}) \leftarrow \begin{cases} \rho(T_v^{(j)}) & \text{if } T_v^{(j)} \neq \phi \\ \rho(T_{v-1}^{(j)}) & \text{otherwise.} \end{cases}$$

Finally, observe that the phases can be pipelined, i.e., for all j, phase j+1 can be started a constant number of steps after phase j. The deletion algorithm takes O(log n + log k) time.

Note that throughot this section we omitted the updates of the fields L(v), M(v) and R(v). It is always easy to complete these details.

6. Storage Allocation

Nodes of a 2-3 tree with n leaves are stored in the first, say N, locations of some vector A. During the insertion algorithm, each processor P_i may create $n_i \leq \log n$ new nodes. Therefore, for each processor P_i log n consecutive locations of some other vector B are reserved, where the new nodes are created. For each i let $N_i = \Sigma_{j<i}\, n_j$. After the insertion algorithm, the numbers N_i are computed in parallel (in O (log k) time) and for all i processor P_i copies the nodes that it created into rows $N+N_i+1,\ldots,N+N_i+n_i$ of A.

During command 2 of the second deletion algorithm, each processor P_i may cancel $m_i \leq \log n$ nodes, i.e., locations in A. Each processor P_i stores the numbers of these rows in its private section in the vector B. After command 2 of the deletion algorithm $M = \Sigma_{i=1}^{k} m_i$ is computed. Now the rows with numbers > N-M that were not cancelled have to be copied into the rows with numbers < N-M, that have been cancelled: locations N-M+1,...,N of A are partitined into blocks $B_1,\dots,B_k$, each consisting of at most log n consecutive locations of A. Each processor P_i determines the number d_i of locations in B_i that were not cancelled. The numbers $D_i = \Sigma_{j<i} d_j$ are computed. Similar considerations apply for the first deletion algorithm.

Next, each processor P_i determines the set ρ_i of indices < N-M that were cancelled by processor P_i and its cardinality r_i. The numbers $R_i = \Sigma_{j<i} r_j$ are computed. Each processor P_i writes the indices in ρ_i in places $R_i+1,\dots,R_i+r_i$ of some vector C. Once all processors are done with this, P_i copies the locations of block B_i that were not cancelled in those locations of A whose indices are in places $D_i+1,\dots,D_i+d_i$ of vector C.

Later in the deletion algorithms, every processor may create O(log n) new nodes Storage allocation is handled as in the case of insertions.

Acknowledgments

The authors thank Professor J. Berstel for inspiring discussions.

REFERENCES

[AHU] A. Aho, J. Hopcroft and J.D. Ullman, The design and analysis of computer algorithms, Addison-Wesley, Reading, Massachusetts, 1974.

[AKS] M. Ajtai, J. Komlos and E. Szemerdi, "An O(n log n) sorting network", Proc. Fifteenth ACM Symp. on Theory of Computing, 1983, to appear.

[BS] R. Bayer and M. Schkolnick, "Concurrency of operations on B-Trees", Acta Informatica 9, 1-21 (1977).

[FW] S. Fortune and J. Wyllie, "Parallelism in random access machines", Proc. Tenth ACM Symp. on Theory of Computing, 114-118 (1978).

[S] Ellis C. Schlatter, "Concurrent search and insertion in 2-3 trees", Acta Informatica 14, 63-86 (1980).

[V1] U. Vishkin, "Implementation of simultaneous memory access in models that forbid it", TR 210, Dept. of Computer Science, Technion, Haifa, Israel (1981), and J. of Algorithms 4, 45-50, (1983).

[V2] U. Vishkin, "Parallel-Design space Distributed-Implementation space (PDDI) general purpose computer", RC 9541, IBM T.J. Watson Research Center, Yorktown Heights, N.Y. 10598, 1982.

[W] H. Wagener, "Parallele Bearbeitung von 2-3-Bäumen", Diplomarbeit, Fakltät für Mathematik, Universität Bielefeld, 1982.

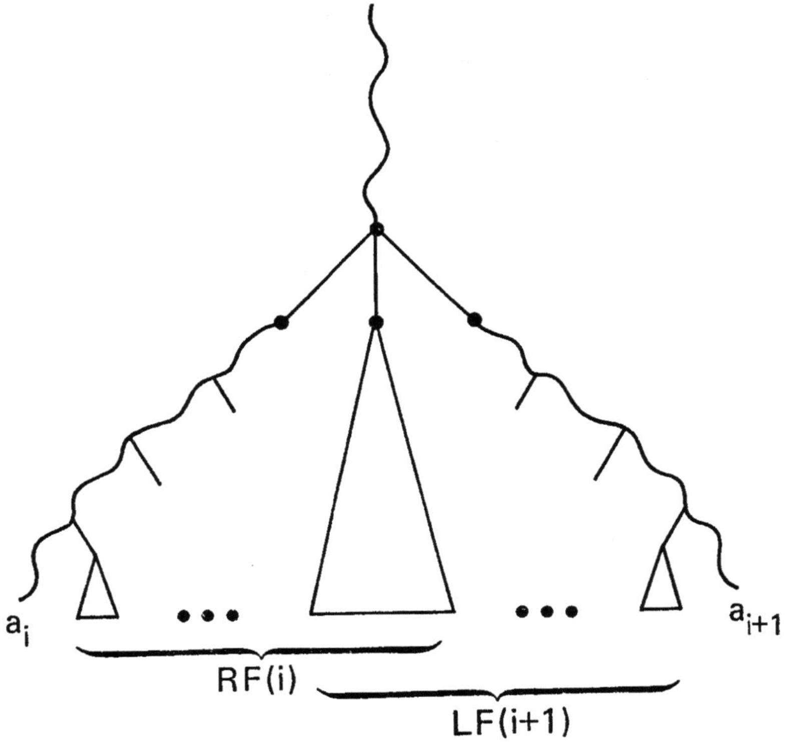

FIGURE 1

VARIETES DE SEMIGROUPES
ET MOTS INFINIS

Dominique PERRIN
LITP
Université de Rouen,
Laboratoire d'Informatique
B.P. 67, 76130 Mont-Saint-Aignan

I. INTRODUCTION

Il existe essentiellement deux façons de définir le comportement d'un automate fini sur un mot infini. La première correspond à ce que l'on appelle un automate de Büchi. Elle consiste à vérifier que l'automate, qui peut être non déterministe, passe une infinité de fois par un état terminal. La seconde est ce que l'on appelle un automate de Müller : l'automate est supposé déterministe et l'on vérifie que l'ensemble des états atteints infiniment souvent appartient à une famille donnée de parties de l'ensemble des états. Le théorème fondamental, dû à Büchi et McNaughton, dit que ces deux procédés sont équivalents : ils définissent la même famille de langages de mots infinis.

Dans cet article nous établissons une généralisation du Théorème de Büchi/McNaughton. Pour cela, nous considérons une variété $\underline{V}$ de semigroupes et la variété correspondante $\mathcal{V}$ de langages (cf. plus bas pour une définition de ces termes). Nous montrons que si la variété de langages $\mathcal{V}$ est fermée par concaténation, les familles de langages de mots infinis définies par des automates de Büchi ou de Müller, dont le semigroupe de transitions appartient à cette variété $\underline{V}$, sont les mêmes. Le cas où la variété $\underline{V}$ est celle de tous les semigroupes finis donne le théorème de Büchi/McNaughton. Le cas où la variété $\mathcal{V}$ est celle des langages sans étoile ('star free') redonne un résultat obtenu par W.Thomas [7]. Des exemples donnés plus bas montrent que le résultat est faux si la variété n'est pas fermée par concaténation.

II. RESULTAT PRINCIPAL

Soit A un alphabet. On note A^* le monoïde libre sur A et $A^+=A^*-1$ le semigroupe libre sur A. On note A^ω l'ensemble des mots infinis

$$\alpha = a_0 a_1 a_2 \ldots$$

avec $a_i \in A$.

Pour une partie X de A^+, on note $\vec{X}$ l'ensemble des mots infinis $\alpha \in A^\omega$ qui ont un nombre infini de facteurs gauches dans X. On dit que $\vec{X}$ est la limite de X.

Pour une partie X de A^+, on note X^ω l'ensemble des mots infinis $\alpha \in A^\omega$ de la forme

$$\alpha = x_0\, x_1\, x_2 \ldots$$

avec $x_i \in X$.

Rappelons qu'une variété de semigroupes finis est une famille $\underline{V}$ de semigroupes finis satisfaisant les trois propriétés suivantes :

(i) si $f: S \to T$ est un morphisme de semigroupes et si $S \in \underline{V}$ alors $f(S) \in \underline{V}$.

(ii) si S est un sous-semigroupe de T et si $T \in \underline{V}$ alors $S \in \underline{V}$.

(iii) si S, $T \in \underline{V}$ alors le produit direct SxT est dans $\underline{V}$.

Si $\underline{V}$ est une variété de semigroupes, il lui correspond une famille noté $\mathcal{V}$ de parties de A^+. C'est la famille des $X \subset A^+$ tels qu'il existe un morphisme $f: A^+ \to S$ de A^+ sur un semigroupe $S \in \underline{V}$ tel que $f^{-1}f(X)=X$. On dit que $\mathcal{V}$ est la + variété associée à la variété de semigroupes $\underline{V}$.

On dit que $\mathcal{V}$ est fermée par produit si pour tous X, $Y \in \mathcal{V}$ on a $XY \in \mathcal{V}$. On obtient un exemple typique de variété fermée par produit de la façon suivante soit $\underline{U}$ une variété de groupes finis et soit $\underline{V}$ la famille de tous les semigroupes finis S tels que pour tout groupe G contenu dans S on ait $G \in \underline{U}$. Alors $\underline{V}$ est une variété des semigroupes et la + variété correspondante $\mathcal{V}$ est fermée par produit. Signalons aussi qu'une caractérisation des variétés de semigroupes dont la + variété associée est fermée par produit a été donnée par Straubing [6].

On note $\mathcal{V}^\omega$ la famille des parties de A^ω obtenues par un nombre fini d'unions portant sur des parties de la forme

$$XY^\omega$$

pour des parties X,Y de A^+ telles que XY^*, $Y^+ \in \mathcal{V}$.

Observons que si $\mathcal{V}$ est fermée par produit X,$Y^+ \in \mathcal{V}$ implique $XY^* \in \mathcal{V}$.

On note $\vec{\mathcal{V}}$ la famille des parties de A^ω obtenues par un nombre fini d'unions et de complémentations portant sur des parties $\vec{X}$ pour $X \in \mathcal{V}$.

Théorème : Si $\mathcal{V}$ est fermée par produit, on a l'égalité

$$\vec{\mathcal{V}} = \mathcal{V}^\omega.$$

Dans le cas où la variété $\underline{V}$ est celle de tous les semigroupes finis, le théorème précédent donne le théorème de Mc Naughton (cf. |1| p. 382).

La variété des semigroupes ne contenant que des groupes triviaux est connue sous le nom de variété des semigroupes <u>apériodiques</u>, notée $\underline{A}$; la + variété correspondante est notée $\mathcal{A}$. La variété $\vec{\mathcal{A}}$ correspondante a été considérée par R. Ladner |3| et par W. Thomas |7|, |8|. Ce dernier a montré que $\vec{\mathcal{A}}=\mathcal{A}^{\omega}$, ce qui est donc un cas particulier du théorème précédent pour $\underline{V}$ = A. Le théorème n'est pas vrai en général sans l'hypothèse que $\mathcal{V}$ est fermée par produit, comme le montrent les exemples suivants.

Exemple 1. Soit A alphabet fini et soit $\underline{V}$ la variété des semigroupes S vérifiant

$$eS=e$$

pour tout idempotent $e \in S$. La + variété correspondante $\mathcal{V}$ est formée des $XA^* \cup Y$ avec X, Y des parties finies de A^+ (cf. |2| p. 214).
On a visiblement

$$\vec{\mathcal{V}} = \{XA^{\omega} \mid X \text{ partie finie de } A^+ \}$$

et donc $\vec{\mathcal{V}} \subset \mathcal{V}^{\omega}$. Posons $A=\{a,b\}$. On a $(ba^*)^{\omega} \in \mathcal{V}^{\omega}$ puisque $(ba^*)^+=bA^*$. Par contre on n'a pas $(ba^*)^{\omega} \in \vec{\mathcal{V}}$ comme on le vérifie facilement. Cet exemple montre qu'en général, on n'a pas $\mathcal{V}^{\omega} \subset \vec{\mathcal{V}}$.

Exemple 2. Soit $\underline{V}$ la variété des groupes finis. Posons $A=\{a,b\}$ et soit X_0(resp. X_1) l'ensemble des mots de A^+ ayant un nombre pair (resp. impair) d'occurrences de b. On a $X_0, X_1 \in \mathcal{V}$. D'autre part $\vec{X}_0$(resp. $\vec{X}_1$) est constitué des mots infinis ayant un nombre pair (resp. impair) ou infini d'occurrences de b. Ainsi $\vec{X}_0 \cap \vec{X}_1$ est l'ensemble $(a^*b)^{\omega}$ des mots ayant un nombre infini d'occurrences de b. On a donc $(a^*b)^{\omega} \in \vec{\mathcal{V}}$. Par contre on n'a pas $(a^*b)^{\omega} \in \mathcal{V}^{\omega}$. En effet si $(a^*b)^{\omega} = \bigcup_{i=1} X_i Y_i^{\omega}$ avec $X_i Y_i^*$, $Y_i^* \in \mathcal{V}$, l'un au moins des couples (X_i, Y_i), soit (X_1, Y_1), doit être formé de deux parties non vides. Comme $Y_1^+ \in \mathcal{V}$, il existe un morphisme f de A^+ sur un groupe fini G tel que $f^{-1} f\, Y^+ = Y^+$. L'ensemble $f(Y^+)$ est un sous semigroupe d'un groupe fini et donc un sous groupe. Il existe donc un entier $k \geq 1$ tel que $a^k \in Y^+_1$. On a ainsi $xa^{\omega} \in X_1 Y_1^{\omega}$ pour tout $x \in X_1$, une contradiction.

III. PREUVE DU THEOREME

La preuve du théorème repose sur une série d'énoncés.Commençons par la partie la plus facile. Elle repose sur une caractérisation de $\vec{\mathcal{V}}$ en termes d'automates de Müller.

Proposition 1. Si $\vec{V}$ est fermée par produit, on a

$$\vec{V} \subset V^{\omega}$$

Démonstration : Considérons la famille $\mathcal{F}$ de parties de A^{ω} ainsi définies : on a $Z \in \mathcal{F}$ ssi il existe un morphisme $f : A^{+} \to S$ sur un semigoupe $S \in \underline{V}$ et une famille $\underline{T}$ de parties de S tels que $\alpha \in Z$ ssi l'ensemble des $s \in S$ tels que

$$s = f(\alpha_0 \alpha_1 \ldots \alpha_n)$$

pour une infinité d'entiers n est dans $\underline{T}$. On note $Z = ||(f,S,\underline{T})||$.

Pour tout $X \in V$, on a $\vec{X} \in \mathcal{F}$. En effet, soit $f : A^{+} \to S$ un morphisme de A^{+} sur $S \in \underline{V}$ tel que $f^{-1}fX = X$.

On a $\alpha \in \vec{X}$ ssi l'ensemble des $s \in S$ tels que $s = f(\alpha_0 \alpha_1 \ldots \alpha_n)$ pour une infinité d'entiers n rencontre $f(X)$. Il suffit donc de poser $\underline{T} = \{T \subset S \mid T \cap f(X) \neq \emptyset\}$.

Ensuite $\mathcal{F}$ est fermé par union et complémentation :
pour l'union de Z et Z' définis par $(f,S,\underline{T})$ et $(f',S',\underline{T'})$, il suffit de considérer le morphisme $f \times f'$ de A^{+} sur le produit direct $S \times S'$ (qui est encore dans $\underline{V}$) et de considérer la famille des parties de $S \times S'$ égale à $\underline{T} \times \mathcal{P}(S') \cup \mathcal{P}(S) \times \underline{T'}$). Le complément de $Z = ||(f,S,\underline{T})||$ est $||(f,S,\mathcal{P}(S) - \underline{T})||$. Ceci montre que $\vec{V} \subset \mathcal{F}$. Enfin, on a $\mathcal{F} \subset V^{\omega}$:

Soit en effet $S \in \underline{V}$, $f : A^{+} \to S$ un morphisme et $\underline{T} \subset \mathcal{P}(S)$. On a

$$||(f,S,\underline{T})|| = \bigcup_{T \in \underline{T}} ||(f,S,\{T\})||.$$

Posons $T = \{t_0, t_1, \ldots, t_n\}$ et

$$X = f^{-1}(t_0), Y_i = f^{-1}\{s \in S \mid t_i s = t_{i+1}, 0 \leq i \leq n,\}$$

où on a posé $t_{n+1} = t_0$. On a

$$||(f,S,\{T\})|| = XY^{\omega}$$

avec $Y = Y_0 Y_1 Y_2 \ldots Y_n - f^{-1}\{s \in S \mid t_0 s \notin T\} A^{*}$. On a $X, Y_i \in V$ par définition.
Comme V est fermée par produit, on a $Y \in V$. Comme de plus $Y^{+} = Y$, on a $XY^{\omega} \in V^{\omega}$.
Ceci montre que $||(f,S,\underline{T})||$ appartient à V^{ω} et achève de prouver que $\vec{V} \subset V^{\omega}$.

■

Remarquons que l'on a toujours $\vec{X} \in V^{\omega}$ pour $X \in V$, même si V n'est pas fermée par produit. Par contre l'inclusion $\vec{V} \subset V^{\omega}$ est fausse en général sans cette hypothèse (cf. Exemple 2).

Pour montrer l'inclusion inverse, on utilise le résultat suivant qui est une conséquence du théorème de Ramsey. On peut aussi l'établir directement de façon simple (cf. |5| par exemple). Notons que dans cet énoncé l'alphabet A peut être infini.

Proposition 2. Soit $f : A^+ \to S$ un morphisme de A^+ sur un semigroupe fini. Pour tout mot infini $\alpha \in A^\omega$, il existe un $s \in S$ et un idempotent $e \in S$ tels que

$$\alpha \in f^{-1}(s)\,[f^{-1}(e)]^\omega .$$

Disons qu'un élément Z de A^ω est $\mathcal{V}$-simple s'il existe un morphisme f de A^+ sur un semigroupe $S \in \underline{V}$, un $s \in S$ et un idempotent $e \in S$ tels que

$$Z = f^{-1}(s)\,[f^{-1}(e)]^\omega .$$

Proposition 3. Si $\mathcal{V}$ est fermée par produit, tout élément de $\mathcal{V}^\omega$ est une union finie de parties $\mathcal{V}$-simples.

Démonstration : Considérons un élément de $\mathcal{V}^\omega$ de la forme XY^ω avec $XY^*, Y^+ \in \mathcal{V}$. Il existe un morphisme $f : A^+ \to S$ avec $S \in \underline{V}$ tel que l'on ait simultanément $f^{-1}f(XY^*) = XY^*$ et $f^{-1}f(X^+) = X^+$.

Soit P l'ensemble des couples (s,e) formés d'un $s \in S$ d'un idempotent $e \in S$ tels que $s \in f(XY^*)$, $e \in f(Y^+)$.

On a $XY^\omega = \cup\{f^{-1}(s)[f^{-1}e)]^\omega \mid (s,e) \in P\}$. En effet, l'inclusion $\supset$ est évidente et l'inclusion inverse résulte de l'application de la Proposition 2 à un alphabet B en correspondance biunivoque avec $X \cup Y$. Ceci montre que XY^ω est une union finie de parties $\mathcal{V}$-simples. ■

Proposition 4. Si $\mathcal{V}$ est fermée par produit, on a

$$\mathcal{V}^\omega \subset \vec{\mathcal{V}}$$

Démonstration : D'après la Proposition 3, il suffit de prouver que toute partie $\mathcal{V}$-simple est dans $\vec{\mathcal{V}}$. Soit donc $f : A^+ \to S$ un morphisme de A^+ sur un semigroupe $S \in \underline{V}$, soit $s \in S$ et e un idempotent de S. Posons $X = f^{-1}(s)$ et soit Y l'ensemble générateur minimal du semigroupe $f^{-1}(e)$. On a $X, Y^+ \in \mathcal{V}$ et comme $Y = f^{-1}(e) - [f^{-1}(e)]^2$ on a $Y \in \mathcal{V}$. Posons encore

$$F = \{g \in S \mid g = g^2,\ e \notin SgS\}$$

et pour $g \in F$

$$K_g = f^{-1}(g) - A^+ f^{-1}(g) A^+ - A^+ f^{-1}(g) - f^{-1}(g) A^+ .$$

Posons enfin

$$R = \cup\{A^* K_g \mid g \in F\}\ ,\quad D = Y - YA^+ .$$

D'après le résultat de Schützenberger |5| on a

$$XY^{\omega} = \vec{Y}^{+}D-\vec{R}$$

(ce résultat est aussi redémontré en |4|). Comme Y^{+}, $D \in V$ on a $Y^{+}D \in V$. Comme chacun des K_g est dans V, on a aussi $R \in V$. Ceci montre que $XY^{\omega} \in \vec{V}$. ■

Remarque. Il est possible de donner une troisième définition de la famille $\vec{V} = V^{\omega}$. C'est la plus petite famille de parties A^{ω} contenant la partie vide et fermée par les opérations booleennes et le produit à gauche par les éléments de V. Dans le cas où V est fermée par produit on obtient une définition équivalente à celle de $\vec{V} = V^{\omega}$. En effet, V^{ω} est fermée par produit à gauche par les éléments de V. D'autre part pour tout $X \in V$ le complémentaire de $\vec{X}$ peut être mis sous la forme d'une union finie de parties de la forme

$$Y(A^{\omega} - ZA^{\omega})$$

avec $Y, Z \in V$. Ceci donne l'équivalence des définitions. Dans le cas de la + variété A, ce résultat a été obtenu par W. Thomas [8].

IV. REFERENCES

1 Eilenberg, S., Automata, Languages and Machines, Vol. A, Academic Press, 1974

2 Eilenberg, S., id., Vol. B, 1976.

3 Ladner, R., Applications of model-theoretic games to discrete linear orders and finite automata, Inform. Contr. (1977), 33, 281-303.

4 Nivat, M., Perrin, D., Ensembles reconnaissables de mots bi infinis, 18th ACM Conf. on Theory of Computing, San Francisco, 1982, 47-59.

5 Schützenberger, M.P. A propos des relations rationnelles fonctionnelles, in Automata, Langages and Programming (M.NIVAT ed.) 103-114, North Holland, 1973.

6 Straubing, H., Aperiodic homomorphisms and the concatenation product of recognizable sets, J. Pure and Applied Algebra, 15, 1979, 319-327.

7 Thomas, W., Star-free regular sets of ω-sequences, Inform. Contr. 42 (1979) 148-156.

8 Thomas, W., A combinatorial approach to the theory of ω-automata, Inform. Contr. 48 (1981) 261-283.

ARBRES ET HIERARCHIES DE CONCATENATION

Jean-Eric PIN

Laboratoire d'Informatique Théorique et de Programmation
Université Paris VI et CNRS - Tour 55-65, 4 Place Jussieu

75230 PARIS Cedex 05 FRANCE

INTRODUCTION

Le produit de concaténation est, avec l'étoile, l'opération la plus importante pour l'étude des langages rationnels. Schützenberger a d'abord caractérisé la classe des langages apériodiques (star-free en anglais), obtenus à partir des lettres à l'aide des opérations booléennes et du produit. Par la suite, plusieurs sous-classes des langages apériodiques ont été étudiées, notamment par Brzozowski, Simon, Fich, Schützenberger, Eilenberg, Mc Naughton, Zalcstein, etc. Une étude plus systématique a été entreprise par Brzozowski, qui a défini une hiérarchie remarquable baptisée "dot-depth hierarchy". Ultérieurement Brzozowski, Simon puis Straubing ont défini d'autres hiérarchies, toutes basées sur le produit de concaténation.

Le but de cet article est de présenter une nouvelle hiérarchie qui englobe toutes les hiérarchies précédentes. **Les caractéristiques de cette hiérarchie sont les suivantes :**

(a) chaque niveau de la hiérarchie est une variété de langages

(b) la hiérarchie est indexée non par les nombres entiers comme dans les hiérarchies précédentes, mais par des arbres ou par des familles d'arbres.

On sait depuis Eilenberg que les variétés de langages sont en bijection avec les variétés de semigroupes. Aussi construisons-nous, parallèlement à notre hiérarchie de langages, une hiérarchie de variétés de semigroupes, elle aussi indexée par des arbres. Ceci permet en particulier de donner une description purement algébrique des semigroupes syntactiques des langages de hauteur n dans les hiérarchies de Brzozowski, Simon ou Straubing. On retrouve également d'autres variétés classiques telles que la variété des monoides R-triviaux. Enfin nous montrons que l'opération qui à un arbre t associe l'arbre  est liée d'une part à une opération simple sur les langages et d'autre part au produit semidirect des semigroupes.

Ces résultats ne conduisent malheureusement pas à un algorithme permettant de calculer la hauteur d'un langage dans la hiérarchie de Straubing ou dans celle de Brzozowski. Toutefois nous montrons que la hiérarchie construite à partir de la variété triviale est décidable. Il en découle en particulier que la "γ_1-hiérarchie" considérée par Simon est décidable.

Pour terminer, nous montrons que si un arbre t est un sous-arbre de t' (en un sens qui sera précisé plus loin), alors la variété associée à t est une sous-variété de la variété associée à t'. Ce résultat, relativement formel, a des conséquences plus inattendues en termes de langages ou de semigroupes.

1.- Rappels et notations

Les références de base sont Eilenberg [4] et Lallement [7] dont j'adopterai la plupart des notations. Si S est un semigroupe, on note E(S) l'ensemble des idempotents de S.

Une variété de semigroupes (monoïdes) est une classe de semigroupes (monoïdes) finis $\underline{V}$ telle que

(1) Si $S \in \underline{V}$ et si T est un sous-semigroupe de S, alors $T \in \underline{V}$

(2) Si $S \in \underline{V}$ et si T est un quotient de S, alors $T \in \underline{V}$

(3) Si $(S_i)_{i\in I}$ est une famille d'éléments de $\underline{V}$, le produit direct $\prod_{i\in I} S_i$ est dans $\underline{V}$.

Eilenberg a montré l'existence d'une bijection entre les variétés de semigroupes (monoïdes) et certaines classes de langages, les +variétés (*-variétés) de langages. De façon formelle une +-variété de langages $\mathcal{V}$ associe à chaque alphabet fini A un ensemble $A^+\mathcal{V}$ de langages reconnaissables de A^+ tels que

(1) Pour tout alphabet A, $A^+\mathcal{V}$ est fermée pour les opérations booléennes finies

(2) Pour tout alphabet A, si $a \in A$ et $L \in A^+\mathcal{V}$, alors $a^{-1}L, La^{-1} \in A^+\mathcal{V}$

(3) Pour tout morphisme de semigroupes $\varphi : A^+ \to B^+$, $L \in A^+\mathcal{V}$ entraîne $L\varphi^{-1} \in A^+\mathcal{V}$

La définition des *-variétés s'obtient en remplaçant + par * et semigroupe par monoïde.

Les hiérarchies de concaténation fournissent des exemples particulièrement intéressants de variétés de langages. La hiérarchie de Brzozowski [1] $\mathcal{B}_n$ est définie comme suit : pour tout alphabet A, $A^+\mathcal{B}_o$ est l'ensemble des langages finis ou cofinis de A^+ et $A^+\mathcal{B}_{n+1}$ est l'algèbre de Boole engendrée par les langages de la forme $L_o\ldots L_k$ avec $k \geq o$ et $L_o,\ldots,L_k \in A^+\mathcal{B}_n$.

On peut définir une sous-hiérarchie à l'intérieur de $\mathcal{B}_{n+1}$ en considérant pour chaque entier $r \geq o$ l'algèbre de Boole $A^+\mathcal{B}_{n+1,r}$ engendrée par les langages de la forme $L_o \ldots L_k$ avec $L_o, \ldots, L_k \in A^+\mathcal{B}_n$ et $o \leq k \leq r$. On définit ainsi une suite de variétés $\mathcal{B}_{n,r}$. On notera que $\mathcal{B}_{n+1,0} = \mathcal{B}_n$ pour tout $n \geq o$. On montre également que $\mathcal{B}_{1,2k} = \mathcal{B}_{1,2k+1}$ pour tout $k > o$.

La hiérarchie de Straubing [15] $\mathcal{V}_n$ est la suite des $*$-variétés ainsi définie : pour tout alphabet A, $A^*\mathcal{V}_o$ est constitué de ϕ et de A^* et $A^*\mathcal{V}_{n+1}$ est l'algèbre de Boole engendrée par les langages de la forme $L_o a_1 L_1 \ldots a_k L_k$ avec $k > o$, $L_o, \ldots, L_k \in A^*\mathcal{V}_n$ et $a_1, \ldots, a_k \in A$.

On démontre que les $\mathcal{V}_n$ (resp $\mathcal{B}_n, \mathcal{B}_{n,k}$) sont effectivement des $*$-variétés ($+$-variétés). Les variétés de monoïdes (resp. semigroupes) correspondantes sont notées $\underline{V}_n$ (resp $\underline{B}_n, \underline{B}_{n,k}$). Le problème majeur concernant ces variétés demeure leur caractérisation algébrique. Rappelons les résultats connus à ce jour.

Théorème 1.1 (Simon [13]) On a $\underline{V}_1 = \underline{J}$, la variété des monoïdes $\mathcal{J}$-triviaux. En particulier un monoïde M est dans $\underline{J}$ ssi pour tout $x,y \in M$ $(xy)^n = (yx)^n$ et $x^n = x^{n+1}$ avec $n = \text{Card } M$.

Si $\underline{V}$ est une variété de monoïdes, on note $\underline{LV}$ la variété de semigroupes "locale" associée à $\underline{V}$:

$$\underline{LV} = \{S \mid eSe \in \underline{V} \text{ pour tout } e \in E(S)\}$$

On note $\underline{J}_1$ la variété des monoïdes idempotents et commutatifs (appelés aussi demi-treillis).

Théorème 1.2 [3] On a $\underline{B}_{1,2} = \underline{LJ}_1$.

Les langages de $\mathcal{B}_{1,2}$ sont appelés localement testables. Pour chaque alphabet A, $A^+\mathcal{B}_{1,2}$ est l'algèbre de Boole engendrée par les langages de la forme uA^*, A^*v et A^*wA^* où u,v et w sont des mots de A^+.

Simon avait conjecturé l'égalité $\underline{B}_1 = \underline{LJ}$. En fait, on a bien $\underline{B}_1 \subset \underline{LJ}$ mais Knast a montré que l'inclusion était stricte :

Théorème 1.3 [5,6] Un semigroupe S est dans $\underline{B}_1$ ssi il satisfait la condition suivante :

(K) il existe $m > o$ tel que pour tout $e_1, e_2 \in E(S)$, pour tout $x,y,u,v \in S$
$$(e_1xe_2y)^m e_1x\, e_2ve_1(ue_2ve_1)^m = (e_1xe_2y)^m e_1(ue_2ve_1)^m$$

Si M est un monoïde, on note $\mathcal{P}(M)$ le monoïde des parties de M, muni du produit usuel des parties.

Théorème 1.4 [10] On a $\underline{V}_2 = \underline{PJ}$, la variété engendrée par les monoïdes $\mathcal{P}(M)$ où $M \in \underline{J}$.

Malheureusement ni cette description de $\underline{V}_2$ ni les autres caractérisations connues [10] ne permettent de résoudre le problème suivant : peut-on décider si un monoïde fini M est dans $\underline{V}_2$?

On ne connaît à ce jour aucun résultat sur les variétés $\underline{B}_n$ pour $n \geq 2$ $\underline{V}_n$ pour $n \geq 3$, hormis les résultats généraux suivants :

Théorème 1.5 [2], [14] La hiérarchie $\underline{B}_n$ est infinie.

Théorème 1.6 [15] On a $\underline{B}_n = \underline{V}_n * \underline{LI}$ pour tout $n > o$. En particulier la hiérarchie $\underline{V}_n$ est infinie.

Dans ce dernier énoncé, la notation $\underline{V}_n * \underline{LI}$ désigne la variété engendrée par les produits semidirects $M * S$ d'un monoïde $M \in \underline{V}_n$ et d'un semigroupe $S \in \underline{LI}$. $\underline{LI}$ est la variété des semigroupes localement triviaux, i.e. $S \in \underline{LI}$ ssi $eSe = e$ pour tout $e \in E(S)$.

2; Le produit de Schützenberger

Si S est un semigroupe, on note $\mathcal{P}(S)$ le semianneau des parties de S, muni de l'union comme addition et du produit des parties comme multiplication. On note S^1 le monoïde ainsi défini

$S^1 = S$ si S est un monoïde

$S^1 = S \cup \{1\}$ si S n'est pas un monoïde (1 est évidemment alors l'élément neutre de S^1).

Soient $S_1,\dots,S_n$ des semigroupes. Le produit de Schützenberger de $S_1,\dots,S_n$, noté $\Diamond_n(S_1,\dots,S_n)$ est le semigroupe des matrices $n \times n$ à coefficients dans $\mathcal{P}(S_1^1 \times \dots \times S_n^1)$ de la forme $p = (p_{ij})_{1 \leq i,j \leq n}$ et vérifiant les trois conditions suivantes :

(1) $p_{ij} = \emptyset$ si $i > j$

(2) $p_{ii} = \{(1,\dots,1, s_i, 1,\dots,1)\}$ pour un certain $s_i \in S_i$

(3) $p_{ij} \subset \{(s_1,\dots,s_n) \in S_1^1 \times \dots \times S_1^n \mid s_1 = \dots = s_{i-1} = 1 = s_{j+1} = \dots = s_n\}$

Il est à noter que le produit de Schützenberger n'est pas "associatif" c'est-à-dire qu'en général les semigroupes $\Diamond_2(\Diamond_2(S_1,S_2),S_3)$, $\Diamond_3(S_1,S_2,S_3)$ et $\Diamond_2(S_1,\Diamond_2(S_2,S_3))$ sont distincts.

Straubing a établi le résultat suivant :

Théorème 2.1 [14] Si les langages $L_i (0 \leq i \leq n)$ de A^* (resp. de A^+) sont reconnus par des monoïdes (resp. par des semigroupes) S_i, alors le langage

$L_0a_1L_1a_2\dots a_nL_n$, où les a_i sont des lettres, est reconnu par $\diamond_{n+1}(S_0,\dots,S_n)$.

Nous proposons ici une réciproque de ce résultat. Le cas $n = 1$ a été traité par Reutenauer [11] et la preuve s'inspire en partie de ses arguments.

Théorème 2.2 Si un langage L de A^*(resp. A^+) est reconnu par $\diamond_{n+1}(S_0,\dots,S_n)$, alors L est dans l'algèbre de Boole engendrée par les langages de la forme $L_{i_0}a_1L_{i_1}a_2\dots a_rL_{i_r}$ $(0 \le i_0 < i_1\dots<i_r \le n)$ où les a_k sont des lettres et où $L_{i_0},L_{i_1},\dots,L_{i_r}$ sont des langages reconnus respectivement par $S_{i_0},\dots,S_{i_r}$.

3.- Hiérarchies de concaténation

Dans cette section, je construis des hiérarchies de variétés qui contiennent en particulier les hiérarchies proposées par Brzozowski [1] Simon [12] et Straubing [15].

On note T l'ensemble des arbres (ou mots bien parenthésés) sur l'alphabet $\{a,\bar{a}\}$. De façon formelle, T est l'ensemble des mots de $\{a,\bar{a}\}^*$ congrus à 1 dans la congruence engendrée par la relation $a\bar{a} = 1$. De façon intuitive les mots de T sont obtenus par le procédé suivant : on dessine un arbre (au sens naïf du terme) et on le parcourt en partant de la racine (suivant le sent trigonométrique) en codant a pour une descente et $\bar{a}$ pour une montée. Par exemple

est codé par $aa\bar{a}aa\bar{a}a\bar{a}a\bar{a}\bar{a}\bar{a}a\bar{a}$.

Le nombre de feuilles d'un mot u de $\{a,\bar{a}\}^*$, noté $d(u)$, est par définition le nombre d'occurrences du facteur $a\bar{a}$ dans u. Dans le cas des arbres, cette définition est bien conforme à l'intuition.

Je rappelle ci-dessous quelques propriétés classiques des arbres que j'utiliserai par la suite :

(1) tout arbre u se factorise de façon unique en $u = au_1\bar{a}au_2\bar{a}\dots au_n\bar{a}$ où $n \ge 0$ et où les u_i sont des arbres. On a alors $d(u) = \sum_{1\le i\le n} d(u_i)$.

L'interprétation intuitive de cette propriété est illustrée par le schéma suivant :

(2) Soit u un arbre et soit $u = u_1 a u_2 \bar{a} u_3$ une factorisation de u. On dit que les occurrences de a et $\bar{a}$ définies par cette factorisation sont <u>liées</u> si u_2 est un arbre. On démontre que toute occurrence de a dans u est liée à une <u>unique</u> occurrence de $\bar{a}$. L'interprétation intuitive de cette propriété est très simple : les occurrences de a et $\bar{a}$ sont liées ssi elles codent respectivement la descente et la montée sur une même arête de l'arbre.

<u>Exemple</u>

est codé par $a\bar{a}aa\bar{a}a\bar{a}\bar{a}$ où les occurrences liées sont indiquées par des crochets.

Nous pouvons maintenant définir nos hiérarchies de langages indexées par des arbres. Comme toujours, on part d'une algèbre de Boole de langages de A^+ (resp. A^*) donnée arbitrairement et on l'associe à l'arbre trivial réduit à un point (et donc codé par le mot vide 1). Cette algèbre de Boole est notée $\mathcal{F}_1$. La récurrence se fait ainsi :

si $t =$

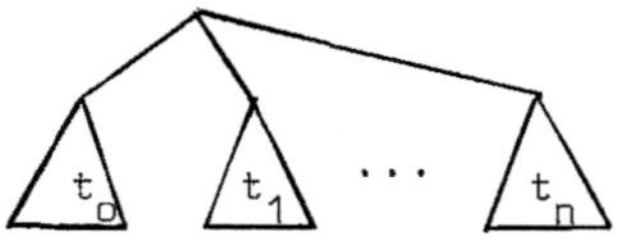

alors $\mathcal{F}_t$ est l'algèbre de Boole engendrée par les langages de la forme

$L_{i_0} a_1 L_{i_1} a_2 \dots a_k L_{i_k}$ où $0 \le i_0 < i_1 \dots < i_k \le n$ et pour $0 \le j \le k$, $a_j \in A$ et $L_{i_j} \in \mathcal{F}_{t_j}$.

On peut utiliser le produit de Schützenberger pour construire de manière analogue des hiérarchies de variétés de semigroupes (ou de monoides) que l'on notera $(\Diamond_t(\underline{V}))_{t \in T}$. Comme précédemment on fixe arbitrairement la variété $\underline{V}$ associée à l'arbre trivial. Autrement dit, on pose par définition $\Diamond_1(\underline{V}) = \underline{V}$. Maintenant

si $t =$

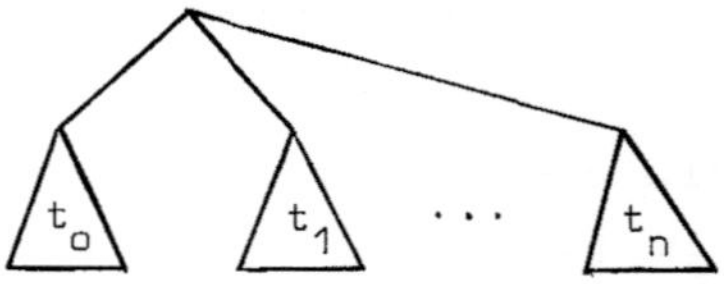

$\Diamond_t(\underline{V})$ est la variété engendrée par tous les produits de Schützenberger de la forme $\Diamond_{n+1}(S_0, \dots, S_n)$ où pour $0 \le i \le n$, $S_i \in \Diamond_{t_i}(\underline{V})$.

Le lien entre les deux constructions précédentes est assuré par l'important résultat suivant, qui est une conséquence du théorème 2.2.

<u>Théorème 3.1</u> Soit $\mathcal{V}$ une +-variété et soit $\underline{V}$ la variété de semigroupes correspondante. Pour chaque alphabet A, soit $(A^+\mathcal{V}_t)_{t \in T}$ la hiérarchie de langages construite à partir de $A^+\mathcal{V}$ comme point de départ. Alors pour tout arbre $t \in T, \mathcal{V}_t$

est une +-variété et la variété de semigroupes correspondante est $\Diamond_t(\underline{V})$.

Notons que le théorème précédent demeure valable si on remplace partout "+" par "*" et semigroupe par monoïde. Si $L \subset T$ est un ensemble d'arbres, on note $\Diamond_L(\underline{V})$ la plus petite variété contenant $\Diamond_t(\underline{V})$ pour tout $t \in L$.

Nous allons maintenant retrouver les hiérarchies classiques comme cas particuliers. Notre premier exemple est la "γ_1-hiérarchie" considérée par Simon [12]. Pour tout alphabet A, on note $A^*\mathcal{J}_n$ l'algèbre de Boole engendrée par les langages de la forme $A^*a_1A^*a_2\ldots A^*a_kA^*$ avec $o \leq k \leq n$ et $a_i \in A$ pour $1 \leq i \leq k$. On démontre que $\mathcal{J}_n$ est une $*$-variété et on note $\underline{J}_n$ la variété de langages correspondante. La variété $\mathcal{J}$ définie dans la section 2 est bien sûr la réunion des variétés $\mathcal{J}_n$.

Proposition 3.2

(1) Si $u = a\bar{a}a\bar{a}$ (arbre ), $\Diamond_u(\underline{I}) = \underline{J}_1$, la variété des monoides idempotents et commutatifs

(2) Si $u = (a\bar{a})^{n+1}$ (arbre  à (n+1) feuilles, $\Diamond_u(\underline{I}) = \underline{J}_n$

(3) Si $L = (a\bar{a})^*$, $\Diamond_L(\underline{I}) = \underline{J}$, la variété des monoides $\mathcal{J}$-triviaux.

Preuve C'est une conséquence immédiate du théorème 3.1 □

La hiérarchie de Straubing $\underline{V}_n$ peut se décrire de façon analogue. Soit L_n la suite de langages définie par $L_o = \{1\}$ et $L_{n+1} = (aL_n\bar{a})^*$. Pour guider l'intuition on peut représenter ces langages par des arbres "infinis en largeur"

L_o

L_1

L_2

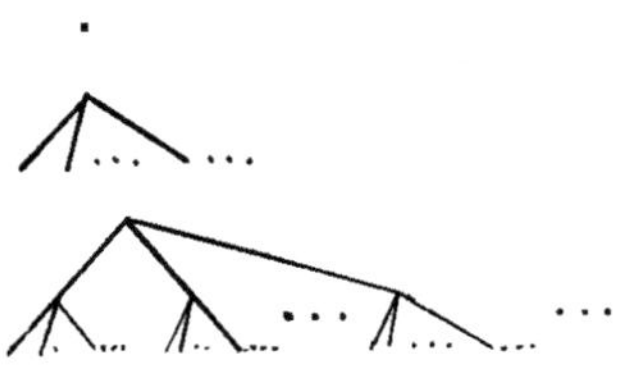

Proposition 3.3 Pour tout $n \geq o$, $\Diamond_{L_n}(\underline{I}) = \underline{V}_n$. En particulier

$$\Diamond_{L_o}(\underline{I}) = \underline{I}\ ,\ \Diamond_{L_1}(\underline{I}) = \underline{J}\ ,\ \Diamond_{L_2}(\underline{I}) = \underline{PJ}$$

Preuve Là encore la proposition résulte immédiatement du théorème 3.1 □

La hiérarchie de Brzozowski s'obtient en considérant des variétés de la forme $\Diamond_L(\underline{Nil})$ où $\underline{Nil}$ désigne la variété des semigroupes nilpotents. De façon plus précise

<u>Proposition 3.4</u> Pour tout $n, k \geq o$, on a

(a) $\underline{B}_n = \Diamond_{L_n}(\underline{Nil})$

(b) $\underline{B}_{n+1,k} = \Diamond_{(aL_n\bar{a})^{k+1}}(\underline{Nil})$

D. Thérien (communication personnelle) a proposé de modifier la hiérarchie de Brzozowski en partant de la variété $\underline{LI}$ au lieu de $\underline{Nil}$. On définit alors des +-variétés $\mathcal{B}'_{n,k}$ de la façon suivante :

pour tout alphabet A

(1) $A^+\mathcal{B}'_o$ est constitué des langages de la forme $XA^*Y \cup Z$ où X, Y et Z sont des langages finis de A^+.

(2) $A^+\mathcal{B}'_{n+1,r}$ est l'algèbre de Boole engendrée par les langages de la forme $L_o a_1 L_1 \ldots a_k L_k$ avec $o \leq k \leq r$, $a_1, \ldots, a_k \in A$ et $L_o, \ldots, L_k \in A^+\mathcal{B}'_n$.

(3) $A^+\mathcal{B}'_{n+1} = \bigcup_{r \geq o} A^+\mathcal{B}'_{n+1,r}$

On sait que $\mathcal{B}'_o$ est la variété de langages correspondant à $\underline{LI}$. Par conséquent il résulte aisément du théorème 3.1 :

<u>Proposition 3.5</u> : pour tout $n, k \geq o$, $\mathcal{B}'_n$ et $\mathcal{B}'_{n+1,k}$ sont des variétés de langages. Les variétés de semigroupes correspondantes sont respectivement $\underline{B}'_n = \Diamond_{L_n}(\underline{LI})$ et $B'_{n+1,k} = \Diamond_{(aL_n\bar{a})^{k+1}}(\underline{LI})$

Le lien entre les variétés $\underline{B}_{n,k}$ et $\underline{B}'_{n,k}$ est précisé par l'énoncé suivant, dû à D. Thérien :

<u>Proposition 3.6</u> (1) Pour tout $k > o$ $\underline{B}_{1,2k} = \underline{B}_{1,2k+1} = \underline{B}'_{1,k}$

(2) Pour tout $n > o$ et $k \geq o$ $\underline{B}_{n+1,k} = \underline{B}'_{n+1,k}$

et $\underline{B}_n = \underline{B}'_n$

Comme on le voit les hiérarchies $\underline{B}_{n,k}$ et $\underline{B}'_{n,k}$ ne diffèrent que pour $n = 1$. Cependant la hiérarchie $\underline{B}'_n$ me paraît plus intéressante. Par exemple, comme me l'a fait remarquer D. Thérien, le théorème 1.5 peut s'écrire $\underline{B}'_n = \underline{V}_n * \underline{LI}$ pour tout $n \geq o$, alors que le cas $n = o$ était curieusement éliminé dans la version donnée plus haut.

Le théorème qui suit donne une caractérisation algébrique intéressante des opérations $t \to \overset{\diagdown}{\triangle_t}$ et $t \to \overset{\diagup}{\triangle_t}$.

<u>Théorème 3.7</u> Pour tout arbre t, on a :

(a) $\Diamond_{at\bar{a}a\bar{a}}(\underline{I}) = \underline{J}_1 * \Diamond_t(\underline{I})$

(b) $\Diamond_{a\bar{a}at\bar{a}}(\underline{I}) = \Diamond_t(\underline{I}) * \underline{J}_1$

Notons au passage l'interprétation de l'opération $\underline{V} \to \underline{J}_1 * \underline{V}$ en termes de langages.

<u>Proposition 3.8</u> : soit $\underline{V}$ une variété de monoïdes et soit $\mathcal{V}$ la variété de langages correspondante. Soit $A^*\bar{\mathcal{V}}$ l'algèbre de Boole engendrée par les langages de la forme L ou LaA^* avec $a \in A$ et $L \in A^*\mathcal{V}$. Alors $\bar{\mathcal{V}}$ est une variété de langages et la variété de monoïdes correspondante est $\underline{J}_1 * \underline{V}$.

<u>Corollaire 3.9</u> 1) Si $u = a^n(\bar{a}a\bar{a})^n$ (arbre  à $(n+1)$ feuilles)

$\Diamond_u(\underline{I}) = \underline{J}_1{}^n = \underline{J}_1 * \underline{J}_1 \ldots * \underline{J}_1$ (n fois)

2) Si $L = \{a^n(\bar{a}a\bar{a})^n \mid n \geq 0\}$, $\Diamond_L(\underline{I}) = \underline{R}$, la variété des monoïdes $\mathcal{R}$-triviaux.

<u>Preuve</u> : (1) Par récurrence à l'aide des théorèmes 3.1 et 3.7

(2) Un résultat de théorie des semigroupes affirme qu'un monoïde est $\mathcal{R}$-trivial ssi il divise un produit en couronne de la forme $U_1 \circ U_1 \ldots \circ U_1$. En termes de variétés cet énoncé se traduit par l'égalité :

$$\underline{R} = \bigcup_{n \geq 0} \underline{J}_1{}^n \quad \text{ce qui établit (2).} \qquad \square$$

<u>Corollaire 3.10</u> Soit $\underline{V}$ une variété de monoïdes et $\mathcal{V}$ la variété de langages correspondante. Soit, pour tout alphabet A, $A^*\bar{\mathcal{V}}$ la plus petite algèbre de Boole contenant $A^*\mathcal{V}$ et fermée pour opérations $L \to LaA^*$ (resp $L \to A^*aL$) où $a \in A$. Alors $\bar{\mathcal{V}}$ est une variété de langages et la variété de monoïdes correspondante est $\underline{R} * \underline{V}$ ($\underline{V} *_r \underline{R}$).

<u>Preuve</u> : l'énoncé résulte de la proposition 3.8 et de l'égalité $\underline{R} = \bigcup_{n \geq 0} \underline{J}_1^n$. $\square$

Il est intéressant de comparer entre elles les variétés $\Diamond_t(\underline{V})$. La proposition qui suit montre que les variétés associées aux arbres t et  sont les mêmes.

<u>Proposition 3.11</u> Soit t un arbre. Alors pour toute variété $\underline{V}$, on a :

$$\Diamond_t(\underline{V}) = \Diamond_{at\bar{a}}(\underline{V}) = \Diamond_{a\bar{a}}(\Diamond_t(\underline{V})).$$

Plus généralement, si un arbre t contient un noeud d'arité 1, l'arbre t' obtenu en supprimant ce noeud vérifie $\Diamond_t(\underline{V}) = \Diamond_{t'}(\underline{V})$. Plus formellement :

<u>Proposition 3.12</u> Soit $t = t_1aat_2\bar{a}\bar{a}t_3$ un arbre. Si t_2 est un arbre, on a pour toute variété $\underline{V}$, $\Diamond_t(\underline{V}) = \Diamond_{t_1at_2\bar{a}t_3}(\underline{V})$

Soient t et u deux arbres. On dit que t est un sous-arbre de u si t s'obtient à partir de u en supprimant un certain nombre de branches. Par exemple si dans l'arbre u =  on supprime la branche marquée d'une croix, on obtient le sous-arbre t =  . De façon plus formelle, t est un sous-arbre de u si t s'obtient en supprimant un certain nombre d'occurrences liées de a et $\bar{a}$ dans u. Ainsi dans notre exemple $t = a\bar{a}a\bar{a}a\bar{a}$ est sous-arbre de $u = aa\bar{a}a\bar{a}\bar{a}a\bar{a}$ car $u = a(a\bar{a}a\bar{a})\bar{a}(a\bar{a})$. On peut alors énoncer :

Théorème 3.13 Si t est un sous-arbre de u, on a pour toute variété $\underline{V}$, $\Diamond_t(\underline{V}) \subset \Diamond_u(\underline{V})$

Voici une conséquence inattendue de ce résultat. Notons K_n le monoïde multiplicatif des matrices booléennes de taille n x n de la forme $\begin{pmatrix} 1 & & \varepsilon \\ & \ddots & \\ 0 & & 1 \end{pmatrix}$

Corollaire 3.14 Pour tout $n > 0$, K_n divise un produit en couronne de $(n-1)$ monoïdes idempotents et commutatifs (ou demi-treillis).

Preuve Straubing a montré que $K_n \in \underline{J}_{n-1}$. Or d'après la proposition 3.2, on a $\underline{J}_{n-1} = \Diamond_{(a\bar{a})^n}(\underline{I})$. Maintenant $(a\bar{a})$ est un sous-arbre de $a^n(\bar{a}a\bar{a})^n$ et donc d'après 3.13 et 3.9, $\underline{J}_{n-1} = \Diamond_{(a\bar{a})^n}(\underline{I}) \subset \Diamond_{a^n(\bar{a}a\bar{a})^n}(\underline{I}) = \underline{J}_1^{n-1}$. Par conséquent $K_n \subset \underline{J}_1^{n-1}$, ce qui établit le résultat.

La réciproque du théorème 3.13 est fausse en général. Par exemple si $\underline{V} = \underline{A}$, la variété des semigroupes apériodiques, on a $\Diamond_t(\underline{V}) = \underline{V}$ pour tout arbre t. Même dans le cas $\underline{V} = \underline{I}$, les énoncés 3.11 et 3.12 montrent qu'il faut se restreindre à l'ensemble T' des arbres dont chaque noeud est d'arité différente de 1. On peut alors avancer la conjecture suivante :

Conjecture soient $t, u \in T'$. Alors $\Diamond_t(\underline{I})$ est contenu dans $\Diamond_u(\underline{I})$ si et seulement si t est un sous-arbre de u.

4.- Problèmes de décidabilité

On dit qu'une variété de semigroupes (ou de monoïdes) $\underline{V}$ est décidable s'il existe un algorithme qui permet de tester si un semigroupe fini donné est ou n'est pas dans $\underline{V}$.

Pour les variétés $\underline{V}_n$ et $\underline{B}_n$ des hiérarchies de Straubing et de Brzozowski, le problème de la décidabilité est toujours ouvert puisque seul le cas $n = 1$ a pu être résolu positivement (cf. les théorèmes de Simon et de Knast rappelés dans la section 1). Le résultat qui suit constitue peut-etre une première étape ver la solution générale du problème.

Théorème 4.1 Pour tout arbre u la variété $\diamond_u(\underline{I})$ est décidable.

Le théorème repose sur une propriété de $\diamond_u(\underline{I})$ intéressante pour elle-même.

Proposition 4.2 Soit u un arbre et soit V_u la variété de langages associée à $\diamond_u(\underline{I})$. Pour tout alphabet A, A^*V_u est un ensemble fini effectivement descriptible.

Preuve Le résultat est évident si $u = 1$. Si $u = au_1\bar{a}au_2\bar{a}\ldots au_n\bar{a}$ avec $u_1,\ldots,u_n \in P$, on a $\diamond_u(\underline{V}) = \diamond_{(a\bar{a})^n}(\diamond_{u_1}(\underline{V}),\ldots,\diamond_{u_n}(\underline{V}))$. Par récurrence les ensembles $A^*V_{u_1},\ldots,A^*V_{u_n}$ sont des ensembles finis effectivement descriptibles. Le théorème 3.1 donne alors un algorithme pour construire A^*V_u, qui est un ensemble fini puisque c'est l'algèbre de Boole engendrée par un nombre fini de langages. □

Preuve du théorème 4.1 Soit M un monoïde fini et A un alphabet en bijection avec M. Il existe alors un morphisme subjectif naturel $\pi : A^* \rightarrow M$. D'après [4, p. 188], on a pour tout $m \in M$ la double inégalité

$$M(m\pi^{-1}) < M < \prod_{m \in M} M(m\pi^{-1})$$

On en déduit que M est dans la variété $\diamond_u(\underline{I})$ si et seulement si, pour tout $m \in M$, le langage $m\pi^{-1}$ est dans A^*V_u. La proposition 4.2 fournit donc un algorithme pour tester si $M \in \diamond_u(\underline{I})$. □

On en déduit en particulier à l'aide du corollaire 3.9, un résultat de pure théorie des semigroupes.

Corollaire 4.3 Pour tout entier n, la variété $\underline{J}_1^n = \underline{J}_1 * \ldots * \underline{J}_1$ (n fois) est décidable.

On en déduit également que la "γ_1-hiérarchie" de Simon est décidable :

Corollaire 4.4 Pour tout entier n, la variété $\underline{J}_n$ est décidable.

Preuve En effet d'après la proposition 3.2, $\underline{J}_n = \diamond_{(a\bar{a})^{n+1}}(\underline{I})$.

BIBLIOGRAPHIE

[1] J.A. Brzozowski, Hierarchies of aperiodic languages, RAIRO, Informatique Théorique, vol. 10, 1976, 33-49.

[2] J.A. Brzozowski et R. Knast, The dot-depth hierarchy of star-free languages is infinite, J. Computer and System Sciences, vol. 16, 1978, 37-55.

[3] J.A. Brzozowski et I. Simon, Characterizations of locally testable events Discrete Mathematics, vol. 4, 1973, 243-271.

[4] S. Eilenberg, Automata, languages and machines, vol. B, Academic Press, New York (1976)

[5] R. Knast, Some theorems on graph congruences. A paraître dans la RAIRO, Informatique Théorique.

[6] R. Knast, A semigroup characterization of dop-depth one languages. A paraître dans la RAIRO, Informatique Théorique.

[7] G. Lallement, Semigroups and Combinatorial applications, Wiley, New-York, 1979.

[8] J.E. Pin, Variétés de langages et variétés de semigroupes. Thèse, Paris, 1981.

[9] J.E. Pin et J. Sakarovitch, Une application de la représentation matricielle des transductions. A paraître.

[10] J.E. Pin et H. Straubing, Monoids of upper-triangular matrices, à paraître.

[11] C. Reutenauer, Sur les variétés de langages et de monoîdes, Lect. Notes in Computer Science n° 67, Springer Verlag, Berlin (1979) 260-265.

[12] I. Simon, Hierarchies of events with dop-depth one, These, Université de Waterloo (1972).

[13] I. Simon, Piecewise testable events, Lect. Notes in Computer Science n° 33, Springer Verlag, Berlin (1975), 214-222.

[14] H. Straubing, A generalization of the Schützenberger product of finite monoids, Theor. Comp. Sc. 13 (1981), 137-150.

[15] H. Straubing, A study of the dot-depth hierarchy (à paraître).

A MULTIPROCESS NETWORK LOGIC WITH TEMPORAL AND SPATIAL MODALITIES*

John Reif and Aravinda Prasad Sistla
Aiken Computation Laboratory
Harvard University
Cambridge, MA 02138

SUMMARY

We introduce a modal logic which can be used to formally reason about synchronous fixed connection multiprocess networks such as of VLSI. Our logic has both *temporal* and *spatial* modal operators. The various temporal modal operators allow us to relate properties of the current state of a given process with properties of succeeding states of the given process. Also, the spatial modal operators allow us to relate properties of the current state of a given process with properties of the current state of neighboring processes. Many interesting properties for multiprocessor networks can be elegantly expressed in our logic. We give examples of the diverse applications of our logic to packet routing, firing squad problems, and systolic algorithms.

We also present some results in the decidability and complexity issues in this logic.

1. INTRODUCTION

One of the fundamental models of parallel computation is a collection of synchronous processors with fixed inter-connections. For example, the iterative linearly connected, mesh connected, and multidimensional arrays of [Ko69] and [Co69], the shuffle exchange networks of [St71] and ultracomputer of [Sc80], and the cube connected cycle networks of [PV79].

Parallel algorithms for such networks are difficult to formally describe and prove correct. For example, the systolic algorithms of [KL78] are not formally proved correct in that paper; instead informal "picture proofs" are presented.

An informal description of a program or algorithm for a fixed connection network would likely make reference to the spatial relationships between neighboring processes and properties holding for all processes, as well as the transformations over time. Indeed, natural English allows expression of spatial modal operators such as "everywhere", "somewhere", "across such and such connection", as well as temporal modal operators such as "until", "eventually", "hereafter", and "next-time". However, natural English cannot suffice for formal semantics. This paper proposes a formal logic allowing use of these modal operators in the context of a fixed connection network. Section 2 defines our logic's syntax and semantics.

*This work was supported by the National Science Foundation Grants NSF MCS79-21024 and NSF MCS79-08365 and the Office of Naval Research Contract N00014-80-0674.

Previous program logics contained only temporal modal operations [Pn77], [MP81] or modal operations for the effect of program statements [FL79]. Temporal logic has been used to reason about parallel programs; however it is impractical to use this logic to reason about large number of processes operating synchronously and communicating through fixed connections. Our use of spatial as well as temporal modal operators is a new idea. (Note: our spatial modal operators differ in an essential way from the modal operators of dynamic logic; see Section 2.3). This combination of temporal and spatial modal operators allows us to formally reason about computations on networks with complex connections.

The contribution of this paper is more than simply the definition of our logic; we also describe applications and investigate certain complexity problems.

Section 2 defines the logic. Section 3 describes some interesting applications of our logic to routing on the shuffle exchange network, to the firing squad problem on a linear array, and to systolic computations on arrays. We felt these examples to multiprocess networks illustrate the general applicability.

Section 4 investigates the problem of testing validity of formulae of our logic. We show the set of valid formulas are Π^1_1-complete. However, in practice we are generally only interested in deciding validity of a propositional formula with respect to a given finite network. We show this problem is PSPACE-complete. Also, we show in the full paper that it is decidable to test validity of proportional formulae with restricted modalities (for example formulae with all temporal operators, but only the "somewhere" spatial operator, and also formulae with all spatial operators, but only the "eventually" temporal operator).

We conclude in Section 5 with a summary of our results.

2. DEFINITIONS

2.1 Networks

Let L be a countable set of symbols, which we call *links*. A *network* $G = (P,E)$ contains a countable set of *processes* P and a partial mapping $E: L \times P \to P$. For each process $p \in P$ and label $\ell \in L$, $E(\ell,p)$ is (if defined) the *process connected to* p *by link* ℓ. For example, a square grid network might have links *up*, *down*, *left*, and *right*. The links are different from atomic programs of PDL due to the restrictions given in the next page.

2.2 Syntax of the Logic

We distinguish as *temporal* modal operators the symbols *eventually*, *hereafter*, *until*, and *nexttime*. The *spatial* modal operators are *somewhere*, *everywhere*, and any symbol in the set of links L, which we assume contains none of the previously mentioned modal operators.

Let $\mathcal{F}_0$ be an infinite set of *atomic formulae*. The set of formulae $\mathcal{F}$ is the minimal set of strings containing $\mathcal{F}_0$ and such that if $f_1, f_2 \in \mathcal{F}$ then the following are in $\mathcal{F}$: $f_1 \wedge f_2$, $\neg f_1$, *eventually* f_1, *hereafter* f_1, f_1 *until* f_2, *nexttime* f_1, *somewhere* f_1, *everywhere* f_1, and also $\ell f_1 \in \mathcal{F}$ for each link $\ell \in L$.

2.3 Semantics of Our Logic

A *model* $\mathcal{M}$ is a 5-tuple (S,Ψ,Δ,G,π) where:

(i) S is the set of *states*,

(ii) $\Psi: S \to 2^{\mathcal{F}_0}$,

(iii) $\Delta: (L \cup \{\textit{nexttime}\}) \times S \to S$, is a partial function

(iv) $G = (P,E)$ is a network, and

(v) $\pi: S \to P$.

Thus for each state $s \in S$, $\Psi(s)$ is the set of atomic formulas which hold at s, and $\pi(s)$ is the process associated with state s. Also, $\Delta(\textit{nexttime}, s)$ is the state occurring in the time instance just after state s, and $\Delta(\ell,s)$ is the current state of the process connected to process $\pi(s)$ by link ℓ.

We extend Δ as a partial mapping to the domain $(L \cup\{\textit{nexttime}\})^* \times S$ so that for all $s \in S$ $\Delta(\varepsilon,s) = s$, and $\Delta(\ell_1 \circ \ell_2,s)$ is defined iff $\Delta(\ell_1,s)$ and $\Delta(\ell_2,\Delta(\ell_1,s))$ are defined and in this case $\Delta(\ell_1 \circ \ell_2,s) = \Delta(\ell_2,\Delta(\ell_1,s))$. Similarly we also extend E as a partial mapping to the domain $L^* \times P$.

A model $\mathcal{M}$ is *proper* iff

R1: For each link $\ell \in L$ and each state $s \in S$, $\Delta(\ell \circ \textit{nexttime},s) = \Delta(\textit{nexttime} \circ \ell,s)$ (thus *nexttime* commutes with respect to each link; this presumes the processes are synchronous.

R2: For each state $s \in S$, $\Delta(\textit{nexttime},s)$ is defined and $\pi(s) = \pi(\Delta(\textit{nexttime},s))$ (thus the name of each process is invariant over time).

R3: For each state $s \in S$ and link $\ell \in L$, $E(\ell,\pi(s))$ is defined iff $\Delta(\ell,s)$ is defined and in this case, $E(\ell,\pi(s)) = \pi(\Delta(\ell,s))$.

R4: For any $\alpha, \alpha' \in L^*$ and states $s, s' \in S$ if $E(\alpha,\pi(s))$, $E(\alpha',\pi(s'))$ are defined and $E(\alpha,\pi(s)) = E(\alpha',\pi(s'))$ then $\Delta(\alpha,s) = \Delta(\alpha',s')$. (Thus the relationship between the states of two processes is independent of the particular paths of links over which they are connected.)

R5: If $\pi(s_1) = \pi(s_2)$ then for some $i \geq 0$ $\Delta(\textit{nexttime}^i,s_1) = s_2$ or $\Delta(\textit{nexttime}^i,s_2) = s_1$.

Hereafter, we consider only proper models.

Let us fix the model $\mathcal{M}$. We define truth of a formulae at a given state $s \in S$ by structural induction.

For each atomic formula $F \in \mathcal{F}_0$, $s \models F$ iff $F \in \Psi(s)$. For any formulas f_1, $f_2 \in \mathcal{F}$,

$s \models f_1 \wedge f_2$ iff $s \models f_1$ and $s \models f_2$

$s \models \neg f_1$ iff $s \not\models f_1$

$s \models$ *nexttime* f_1 iff $\Delta(\textit{nexttime},s) \models f_1$

$s \models$ *eventually* f_1 iff $\exists k \geq 0,\ \Delta(\textit{nexttime}^k,s) \models f_1$

$s \models$ *hereafter* f_1 iff $\forall k \geq 0,\ \Delta(\textit{nexttime}^k,s) \models f_1$

$s \models f_1$ *until* f_2 iff $\exists k \geq 0,\ \Delta(\textit{nexttime}^k,s) \models f_2$ and
$\forall i,\ 0 \leq i < k,\ \Delta(\textit{nexttime}^i,s) \models f_1$

$s \models \ell f_1$ iff $\Delta(\ell,s)$ is defined and $\Delta(\ell,s) \models f_1$

$s \models$ *somewhere* f_1 iff $\exists \alpha \in L^*$, such that $\Delta(\alpha,s)$ is defined and $\Delta(\alpha,s) \models f_1$

$s \models$ *everywhere* f_1 iff $\forall \alpha \in L^*$ $(\Delta(\alpha,s)$ is defined $\Rightarrow \Delta(\alpha,s) \models f_1)$

We let $\models_{\mathcal{M}}$ denote truth with respect to a given model $\mathcal{M}$.

2.4 Decision Problems

Formula $f \in \mathcal{F}$ is *satisfiable (valid)* if $s \models_{\mathcal{M}} f$ for some (all, respectively) model $\mathcal{M}$ and state s. Given a network G, formula $f \in \mathcal{F}$, is *G-satisfiable (G-valid)* if $s \models_{\mathcal{M}} f$ for some (all, respectively) model $\mathcal{M}$ and state s with given network G.

2.5 Extensions to a First Order Logic

The first order version of this logic consists of the additional symbols like local variables, global variables, constant symbols, function and relation symbols, and the universal quantifier $\forall$. A term is defined as in the case of first order predicate calculus. An atomic formula is an atomic proposition or of the form $R\, t_1 t_2 \ldots t_k$ where R is k-any relation symbol (R can be equality in which case $k=2$). The additional requirement for the set of formulae is that if f is a formula and x is a global variable so is $\forall x(f)$. A model $\mathcal{M}$ is a 5-tuple (Σ,S,Δ,G,π) where $\Sigma=(D,\alpha,\beta)$ in which D is a countable domain in which the variables take values, α interprets relation and function symbols, β is a mapping associating with each global variable and constant symbol a value from the domain; S is the set of states where each state is a mapping that associates a truth value with each atomic proposition and a value from D with each local variable; Δ, G, π are the same as in the propositional case. A proper model should satisfy the same conditions as for the propositional case, modified in a natural way. We consider only proper models. Truth of an atomic formula in a state of a model is defined as in the case of first order predicate calculus; and truth of a formula in a state of a model is defined inductively as in the propositional version with the following addition; $\mathcal{M},s \models \forall x f$ iff for each $c \in D\ \mathcal{M}^c,s \models f$ where $\mathcal{M}^c$ is exactly same as $\mathcal{M}$ except that the global variable x is given the value c in $\mathcal{M}^c$. Satisfiability and validity of formulae are defined as usual.

3. APPLICATIONS

This section gives some examples of the use of our logic to various multi-process network applications.

3.1 Routing on a Shuffle-Exchange Network

A Shuffle-Exchange network G is a pair (P,E) where $P=\{0,1\}^n$ and

$E: \{exchange, shuffle\} \times P \to P$

is defined as follows:

$$E(exchange,(a_{n-1},a_{n-2},\ldots,a_0)) = (a_{n-1},a_{n-2},\ldots,\bar{a}_0)$$

$$E(shuffle,\ (a_{n-1},a_{n-2},\ldots,a_0)) = (a_0,a_{n-1},\ldots,a_1)$$

for all $a_{n-1},a_{n-2},\ldots,a_0 \in \{0,1\}$.

Intuitively, the exchange edge connects processes p_1 and p_2 if all the bits of p_1 and p_2 are the same excepting the least significant bits which are distinct. The shuffle edge connects two processes p_1 and p_2, if p_2 is obtained by one cyclic shift of bits in p_1.

The routing problem in this network is to route a packet present at some process to a given destination traversing only along the shuffle and exchange edges.

We capture the name of a process by the atomic propositions $A_{n-1},A_{n-2},\ldots,A_0$. The formula f_0 asserts that the name of a process is invariant over time;

$$f_0 = \bigwedge_{0\leqslant i<n} (\textit{hereafter}\ A_i \vee \textit{hereafter}\ \neg A_i)$$

f_1, f_2 assert that exchange and shuffle edges are properly connected.

$$f_1 = \bigwedge_{1\leqslant i<n} (A_i \leftrightarrow \textit{exchange}\ A_i) \wedge A_0 \leftrightarrow \textit{exchange}\ \neg A_0$$

$$f_2 = \bigwedge_{0\leqslant i<n} (A_i \leftrightarrow \textit{shuffle}\ A_{(i-1)\bmod n})$$

The presence of the packet at any process will be indicated by the atomic proposition X, and the destination by $D_{n-1},D_{n-2},\ldots,D_0$. We assume that the name of the destination travels with the message. Let g_0 assert that X is true in at most one place. It is not difficult to see that this can easily be expressed.

$$g_1 = X \supset \left[\bigwedge_{0\leqslant i<n} \begin{array}{l} (D_i \supset \textit{hereafter everywhere}\ (X \supset D_i)) \wedge \\ (\neg D_i \supset \textit{hereafter everywhere}\ (X \supset \neg D_i)) \end{array} \right]$$

asserts that the name of the destination process travels with the packet.

$$g_2 = X \supset \textit{nexttime}\ (X \vee (\textit{shuffle}\ X) \vee \textit{exchange}\ X)$$

asserts that the packet travels along shuffle or exchange edges only.

The main correctness property is g_3 which asserts that the packet reaches its destination eventually.

$$g_3 = \mathit{eventually\ somewhere} \left(X \wedge \bigwedge_{0 \leq i \leq n-1} (A_i \leftrightarrow D_i) \right) .$$

Let r be a formula which describes the actual routing algorithm. Then $(\mathit{hereafter\ everywhere}\ (r \wedge f_0 \wedge f_1 \wedge f_2 \wedge g_0 \wedge g_1 \wedge g_2)) \supset g_3$ is a valid formula iff the algorithm correctly routes packets.

Next we describe a specific routing algorithm for the shuffle exchange network and derive the corresponding formula r for its semantics. The packet will be routed in n stages, where for $i = 0,\ldots,n-1$, if at the start of the i-th stage the packet is located at a process whose lowest order address bit is not the value of D_i, then the packet traverses an *exchange* link. In either case, the packet next traverses a *shuffle* link and reaches the $i+1$ stage.

To define a formula r for this routing algorithm, it is useful to introduce proportional variables $S_0,\ldots,S_{n-1}$ and require that only unique S_i be true at any processes, and that the S be invariant or traversing an *exchange* link but that $S_{(i+1) \bmod n}$ be true on traversing a *shuffle* link. Thus we let

$$r_0 = \bigvee_{0 \leq i < n} \left(S_i \wedge \left(\bigwedge_{\substack{0 \leq j < n \\ i \neq j}} \neg S_j \right) \wedge (\mathit{nexttime\ exchange}\ S_i) \wedge (\mathit{nexttime\ shuffle}\ S_{(i+1) \bmod n}) \right) .$$

The formula for semantics of this routing algorithm is therefore:

$$r_1 = r_0 \wedge \left(X \supset \bigvee_{0 \leq i < n} (S_i \wedge ((A_0 \leftrightarrow D_i) \supset \mathit{nexttime\ exchange}(X)) \wedge ((A_0 \leftrightarrow \neg D_i) \supset \mathit{nexttime\ shuffle}(X)) \right) .$$

3.2 The Firing Squad Problem for a Linear Array

We briefly describe the problem and show how its correctness can be specified by our logic. A solution to the firing squad problem consists of a linear array of deterministic finite state processes as shown in Figure 1. The next move of each process is a function of its present state and the states of its neighbors. All the privates are identical processes. The problem is to obtain the program for the lieutenant, the sergeant and the privates so that whenever the lieutenant is in a designated initial state, then eventually all the processes simultaneously enter a special state called the firing state, and none of them enters this state before this time. The solution should work for linear arrays of *all sizes*.

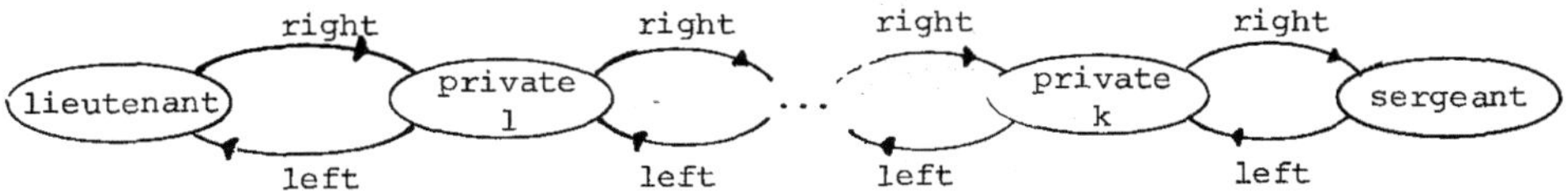

Figure 1

We assume that all processes have the state set $Q = \{0,1,2,...,m\}$, and the state 0 is the initial state of each process. State 1 is the specific state into which the lieutenant enters to start the operation, state m is the firing state. All the privates are identical. We use atomic propositions $P_0, P_1, ..., P_m$ to indicate the state of a process (P_i is true at a place iff the corresponding process is in a state i at that instance). Now we assert the operation of the system as follows.

(i) 'I' asserts that each process is in at most one state at any instant of time.

$$I = \mathit{everywhere\ hereafter} \left[\bigwedge_{\substack{0 \leq i,j \leq k \\ i \neq j}} (P_i \supset \neg P_j) \right]$$

(ii) f_0 asserts that the moves of lieutenant is according to its next move partial function $\delta_0 : Q^2 \to Q$.

$$f_0 = \mathit{everywhere} \left[\neg \mathit{left}(\text{true}) \supset \Big((P_0 \vee P_1) \wedge \mathit{hereafter} \bigwedge_{i,j} ((P_i \wedge \mathit{right}\ P_j) \supset \mathit{nexttime}\ P_{\delta_0(i,j)}) \Big) \right]$$

Note that $\neg \mathit{left}(\text{true})$ is true only on the lieutenant, the left most processor.

(iii) Similarly, let f_1, f_2 be the formulae that define the moves of all privates and the sergeant, respectively. The positions of privates is identified by the truth of the formula

$(\mathit{left}(\text{true}) \wedge \mathit{right}(\text{true}))$.

Note that the position of the sergeant is identified by the formula

$\neg \mathit{right}(\text{True})$.

(iv) Let g_0 be the formula that asserts that if any process (other than the lieutenant) and all its neighbors are in state 0 then it remains in state 0 in the next step. It is easily seen that this can also be asserted.

Now we assert that if all the above conditions are met and at any time the lieutenant enters the state 1 then all processes will eventually enter the firing state simultaneously at some future instance, and none of them will be in the firing state before that instance. This is captured by the formula g.

$$g = (I \wedge f_0 \wedge f_1 \wedge g_0) \supset \textit{hereafter}[\textit{somewhere}(\neg \textit{left}(\text{true}) \wedge P_1) \supset ((\neg \textit{somewhere}\ P_m)\ \textit{until}\ (\textit{everywhere}\ P_m))]$$

g is valid on all models with linear arrays as networks iff the given solution to the firing squad problem is correct. A similar construction can be given for the firing squad problem over any given network.

3.3 Systolic Arithmetic Computations

The systolic algorithms of [KL78] are not formally proved correct in their paper; instead they present informal "picture proofs". Our logic is thus particularly useful here when extended to first order formulae (as described in Section 2.5).

We consider an interesting example of a network for matrix-vector multiplication due to [KL78]. The matrix is an infinite band matrix of bandwidth (n+1). The network architecture is shown in Figure 2.

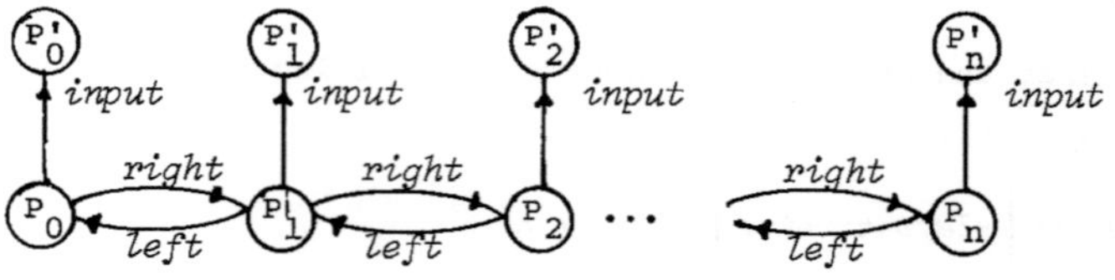

Figure 2

The main processors are $P_0, P_1, \ldots, P_n$. The processors $P'_0, P'_1, \ldots, P'_n$ are the input processors, each of them contains a variable Z. The values of Z in P'_i change with time and they represent the values of the i-th diagonal of the matrix. Each processor P_i has two variables X, Y. The values of the variable X in P_0 over time represent the input vector. The values of X move right with each time instance.

Thus

$$g_1 = \textit{left}(\text{true}) \supset \forall\alpha(\textit{left}(X=\alpha) \leftrightarrow \textit{nexttime}(X=\alpha))$$

asserts that the value of X at the nexttime instance in a process $P_i (i > 0)$, is the present value of X in the process left to P_i.

At each step $P_i (i < n)$ computes its value of Y to be the sum of the previous value of Y in process P_{i+1}, plus the product of X in P_i times Z in P'_i. This is captured by

$$g_2 = \textit{right}(\text{true}) \supset \forall\alpha\forall\beta(\textit{right}(Y=\alpha) \wedge \textit{nexttime}\ \textit{input}(Z=\beta) \supset \textit{nexttime}(Y = \alpha + X\cdot\beta))\ .$$

At each step P_n computes its value of Y to be the product of the value of X in P_n and the value of Z in P_n'. This can also be easily asserted by formula

$$g_3 = \mathit{right}(\text{false}) \wedge \mathit{input}(\text{true}) \supset \forall\alpha\forall\beta(X=\alpha \wedge \mathit{input}(Z=\beta)) \supset \mathit{nexttime}(Y=\alpha\cdot\beta)) \ .$$

(note that $\mathit{right}(\text{false}) \wedge \mathit{input}(\text{true})$ holds only for process P_n)

The correctness property at P_n can thus be expressed in our logic as

$$\mathit{hereafter}\ \mathit{everywhere}(g_1 \wedge g_2 \wedge g_3) \supset \mathit{hereafter}\ \ h$$

where

$$h = \mathit{left}(\mathit{false}) \wedge \mathit{input}(\text{true}) \supset$$

$$\forall\alpha_0\ldots\alpha_n\forall\beta_0\ldots\beta_n\left(\bigwedge_{i=0}^{n} \mathit{nexttime}^i(X=\alpha_i) \wedge \mathit{nexttime}^{n+i}(Z=\beta_i)) \supset \mathit{nexttime}^{2n}\ \ Y=\sum_{i=0}^{n}\alpha_i\cdot\beta_i\right)$$

4. DECIDABILITY AND COMPLEXITY ISSUES

In this section we consider issues of decidability and complexity of different versions of our logic. Recall that a formula is said to be satisfiable iff there exists a model and a state at which the formula is true. A formula is said to be valid if it is true in all states of all models. We say that a formula is satisfiable (valid) on finite networks if the formula is true in a (all) model with finite networks.

THEOREM 1. *The set of satisfiable formulae of multiprocessor network logic is* Σ_1^1*-complete and the set of valid formulae is* Π_1^1*-complete.*

Proof Sketch. First we show that the set of satisfiable formulae is a Σ_1^1-complete set. From this result it can easily be shown that the set of valid formulae is Π_1^1-complete.

We consider a deterministic Turing machine M on infinite strings. M has one read only infinite input tape, and an infinite work tape. An infinite string is input to M on its input tape. M never halts. M is said to accept an input if during its computation it goes into any of a set of final states infinitely often. The set of encodings of all Turing machines that accept at least one input, is shown to be Σ_1^1-complete in [SCFG82]. We reduce this set to the set of satisfiable formulae. An ID of M is the part of input is seen thus far, the contents of the work tape, the position of the head on the work tape. We define a sequence of IDs of M during its computation on an input and express this sequence using a formula in the logic. We also assert that in this sequence final IDs (IDs having a final state) appear infinitely often. Thus given an encoding of a Turing machine we obtain a formula that is satisfiable iff the Turing machine accepts at least one input. The details will be given in the full paper. □

Let $\mathcal{M} = (S,\Psi,\Delta,G,\pi)$ be a model where $G = (P,E)$ is a finite network. Let $\phi: P \to S$. ϕ is said to be consistent with $\mathcal{M}$, if $\pi(\phi(p)) = p$ for all $p \in P$, and for all p_i, p_j if $p_j = E(\ell,p_i)$ for some $\ell \in L$, then $\phi(p_j) = \Delta(\ell,\phi(p_i))$. Let $\Phi = \{\phi | \phi$ is consistent with $\mathcal{M}\}$, and let *next*: $\Phi \to \Phi$ be such that for all $\phi \in \Phi$ and for all p $next(\phi)(p) = \Delta(nexttime,\phi(p))$. $\mathcal{M}$ is said to be *ultimately periodic* with starting index ℓ and period m, if for all $\phi \in \Phi$ $next^i(\phi) = next^{i+m}(\phi)$ for all $i \geq \ell$. For any formula f, let $SF(f)$ be the set of subformulae of f, and for any $\phi \in \Phi$, let $[\phi]: P \to 2^{SF(f)}$ such that $[\phi](p) = \{g | g \in SF(f)$ and $\phi(p) \models g\}$. We require a technical lemma characterizing satisfiability.

LEMMA 1. f *is satisfiable in a model over a finite network iff* f *is satisfiable over an ultimately periodic model over a finite network.* □

THEOREM 2. *The set of formulae that are satisfiable in a model over a finite network is* Σ_1^0*-complete, and the set of valid formulae in models over finite networks is* Π_1^0*-complete.*

Proof. As in the previous theorem, we can reduce the halting problem of Turing machines over finite strings to the set of satisfiable formulae in a model over a finite network. We give a Turing machine M which accepts the above set. M guesses a finite network and an ultimately periodic model over this network. It next verifies that f is satisfiable in this model. M halts only on the input formulae that are satisfiable in a model over a finite network. □

THEOREM 3. *The following problem is* PSPACE*-complete. Given a finite network* G*, and a formula* f*, is* f *satisfiable in a model over the network* G?

Proof. The PSPACE-hardness of the problem follows from the PSPACE-hardness of satisfiability for linear time temporal logic [SC82]. We give a polynomial space bounded Turing machine M that checks if f is satisfiable in a model over the network G. M guesses $[\phi]$, and verifies for consistency and that $f \in [\phi](p)$ for some $p \in P$. At each subsequent instance M guesses $[next(\phi)]$ and checks that it is consistent with $[\phi]$. It continues this each time keeping $[\phi]$ and $[next](\phi)$. At a certain instance it guesses the beginning of the period and saves the corresponding $[\phi]$. It continues the previous process, each time guessing either $[next(\phi)]$ or guessing that it is the end of the periodic part. In the latter case it takes $[next(\phi)]$ to be the saved value at the beginning of the period. Each time M guesses $[next(\phi)]$ it verifies that $[\phi]$ is consistent with $[next(\phi)]$. M also verifies that certain formulae are fulfilled in the periodic part. M clearly uses space polynomial in the size of G and the size of f. Further, we can show: □

THEOREM 4. *The set of valid formulae of first order multiprocessor network logic over models on finite networks is* Π_1^1*-complete.* □

5. CONCLUSIONS

We have proposed a logic to reason about computations of multiprocessor networks. We feel that our logic will be useful to specify the semantics and prove correctness of multiprocess networks. No such formal system for multiprocessor networks had been proposed previously. We have examined the application of our logic to some diverse multiprocess network problems, and presented some results in decidability and complexity of our logic.

All the applications we presented are synchronous systems. However, our logic can also be used for asynchronous distributed systems. We intend to consider these problems in a later paper.

BIBLIOGRAPHY

[BMP81] M. Ben-ari, Z. Manna, A. Pnueli, "The temporal logic of branching time," 8th ACM Symposium on Principles of Programming Languages, Williamsburg, VA, 1981.

[CE81] E.M. Clarke, A. Emerson, "Design and synthesis of programming skeletons using branching time temporal logic," IBM Conference of Logics of Programs, May 1981.

[Co69] S.N. Cole, "Real time computations by n-dimensional iterative arrays of finite state machines, IEEE Trans. on Computers, 18 (1969), pp. 349-365.

[FL79] M. Fischer, R. Ladner, "Propositional dynamic logic of regular programs," JCSS, 18(2), 1979.

[GPSS] D. Gabbay, A. Pnueli, S. Shealah, J. Stavi, "Temporal analysis of fairness," 7th ACM Symposium on Principles of Programming Languages, Las Vegas, NV.

[HR81] J.Y. Halpern, J.H. Reif, "The propositional dynamic logic of deterministic, well-structured programs," 22nd Symposium on Foundations of Computer Science, Nashville, TN, 1981.

[MP81] Z. Manna, A. Pnueli, "Verification of concurrent programs," *The Correctness Problem in Computer Science*, Academic Press, London, 1981.

[Ko69] S.R. Kosaraju, "Computations on iterative automata," Ph.D. Thesis, University of Pennsylvania, PA, 1969.

[Pn77] A. Pnueli, "The temporal logic of programs," Proceedings of 18th Symposium on Foundations of Computer Science, Providence, RI, Nov. 1977.

[PV79] F.P. Preparata, J. Vuillemin, "The cube connected cycles: A versatile network for parallel computation," FOCS 1979, pp. 140-147.

[Sc80] J.T. Schwartz, "Ultracomputers," ACM Trans. on Programming Languages and Systems, Vol. 12, No. 4, Oct. 1980, pp. 484-521.

[SCFG82] A.P. Sistla, E.M. Clarke, N. Francez, Y. Gurevich, "Are message buffers characterizable in linear temporal logic?", Proceedings of the Symposium on Principles of Distributed Computing, Ottawa, Canada, August 1982.

[SC82] A.P. Sistla, E.M. Clarke, "The complexity of propositional linear temporal logics," ACM Symposium on Theory of Computing 1982, pp. 159-167.

[St71] H.S. Stone, "Parallel processing with the perfect shuffle," IEEE Trans. on Computers, Vol. C-20, No. 2, Feb. 1971, pp. 153-161.

[KL78] H.T. Kung, C.E. Leiserson, Symposium on Sparse Matrix Computations and Their Applications, Knoxville, Tennessee, Nov. 1978.

ENUMERATION OF SUCCESS PATTERNS

IN LOGIC PROGRAMS

Taisuke Sato
(Electrotechnical Laboratory, Ibaraki, Japan)

Hisao Tamaki
(Ibaraki University, Ibaraki, Japan)

1. Introduction

Since the proposal of logic programming by Horn clauses[Ko 74] Prolog [Wa 79] has been gaining popularity because of the unified treatment of declarative semantics and procedural semantics. It has been successfully applied to natural language processing[Co 78], data base query[Ga 78] and so on. Pattern directed invocation and built-in backtracking mechanism of Prolog proved to be very suitable for symbolic manupulation.

A Prolog program is a finite set of Horn cluases. There are two types of Horn clauses. One type, termed definite clause, has the form A0 <- A1,...,Am (m >= 0). A0 is called a head and the literal sequence A1,...,Am is called a body. Each Ai is called a subgoal. If m = 0 it is called a unit clause which asserts that A0 is true. In case of m > 0 it works as a procedure to compute the relation A0 by the subgoals A1,...,Am. A Prolog program consists of definite clauses. It can be seen as an axiom. For example S = { add(0,x,x)<-, add(s(x), y, s(z)) <- add(x,y,z) } is an addition program (axiom) where "s" is a successor function. It defines an addition-relation in the domain of terms (Herbrand universe). The other type, called a goal clause, has the form <-A1(x),...,Am(x)(m >= 1) which is supplied by a user as a top goal. This requires Prolog interpreter to find the value of x which satisfies A1,...,Am simultaneously. For example, <-add(s(0), s(s(0)), x) is a goal to compute 1+2. Prolog interpreter would compute the value of x by invoking clauses in S and return s(s(s(0))). Procedure invocation and parameter passing are done by the pattern match (unification) of a subgoal with a head. The computation by an interpreter can be seen as a (refutation) proof for the given goal and program.

Since a Prolog progrm is basically nondeterministic and an interpreter (compiler) lacks ablity to detect the determinacy in a program, it always prepares for backtrackings even if a careful inspection shows the determinacy of the program. Preparations for backtracking are time and memory consuming tasks so that they are the main causes of slow computations. Therefore the detection of the determinacy in a program and the elimination of preparations for backtracking can save time and memory at a time.

In this paper we show a method to analyze Prolog programs. It gives us run-time instantiation patterns of clauses in a program. Especially it reveals:

(1) all of the possible calling patterns for a clause and,
(2) the necessary conditions for a clause to have a successful computation.

The first information enables us to detect the possible values of variables of a clause at calling time, which would be of much use to a compiler or a program transformation system for Prolog[Ta 82].

More important is the second information since it enables us to avoid backtrackings. This is because if an invoked clause does not meet the condition, backtracks will inevitably occur in the subsequent computation. Therefore, eliminating such invocation has the effect of avoinding backtrackings. This leads to the detection of determinacy of Prolog programs as is exemplified by the parsing program in the section 5.

Our analysis technique consists in the combination of term abstraction and item set construction for a Prolog program and a goal. By the term abstraction we mean the identification of two terms from some abstract point of view which can reduce an infinite set of items to a finite set. Our item set construction resembles the one in LL(k) or LR(k) parsing theory except that we always store abstracted items.

The resulting item set for a program and a goal covers all of the clause instantiation patterns that may appear during the computation for the goal.

We first introduce the term depth abstraction and the item set construction for a Prolog program S and a top goal <- δ. Next we reveal the relation between the item set for S and <- δ and the states of Prolog interpreter and/or the proof trees for <- δ by S. Finally as an example, we take a nondeterministic parsing program and transform it to a deterministic one according to the information obtained from the item set for the program. Readers are assumed to be familiar with clausal logic[Ch 73]. In what follows α , β ,... stand for a sequence of literals and θ , λ ... for substitutions.

2. Term-depth abstraction

Term-depth abstraction converts a term t to the term s whose instantiation is t. It is applied to literals and clauses too.

[Def. 1 Level and subterm]

a) For given a term t, t has level 0.
   t is called a level 0 subterm of t.
b) If the subterm f(t1,...,tn) of t has level k(>= 0)
   then each ti has level k+1 and called a level k+1 subterm of t.

[Def. 2 Depth k abstraction]

For a given term t and an integer k, replace every level k subterm of t by a newly created variable. The reulting term, denoted by [t]k, is called the depth k abstraction of the term t or simply k-term of t. Obviously the original t is an instantiation of [t]k for every integer k. For an expression E (term, literal, clause, item (see def. 3)), replace every term t in the argument position of E by [t]k. Then the resulting expression, denoted by [E]k, is called the depth k abstraction of E.

Example. Let a term t = f(g(x,a),y,b) and u1,v1,v2,v3,w1,w2 be new variables other than x,y. 0-term of t is u1. 1-term of t is f(v1,v2,v3). 2-term of t is f(g(w1,w2),y,b). k-term of t (k >= 3) is f(g(x,a),y,b) which is the same as t.

3. Item set

We define an item set for a program and a goal. Hereafter $(E)\theta$ means the application of a substitution θ to an expression E.

[Def. 3 Item]

A Horn clause including a dot in the body is called an item. An item of the form $A \leftarrow .\alpha$ is called an initial item. An item of the form $A \leftarrow \alpha .$ is called a closed item. We say an item is a k-item if every subterm occurring in the item has level at most k.

[Def. 4 Variant]

If an expressin E (term, literal, clause, item) is identical to an expression F or different from F only in the variable names, E is called a variant of F. If E and F are variants, we write E = F (modulo renaming). This applies to sets of expressions too.

To construct the item set for a program S and a goal $\leftarrow \delta$, first we set up the initial item set for S and $\leftarrow \delta$.

[Def. 5 Initial item set]

For a program S, an integer k and a goal $\leftarrow \delta$, An item set $Init(S, \delta) = \{ \leftarrow . \delta \} \cup \{ A \leftarrow . \mid A \leftarrow \text{ is a unit clause in } S \}$ is called the initial item set for S and $\leftarrow \delta$.

Second we add items to $Init(S, \delta)$ by taking the downward closure and the upward closure of the preceeding item set alternately.

[Def. 6 Downward k-Closure]

For a finite item set I, a program S and an integer k, we define the downard k-closure, denoted by D-closure(I, S, k), as the minimum item set J such that :

(1) J includes I (modulo renaming).

(2) Suppose there is an item $A \leftarrow \alpha .X\beta$ in J and a definite clause $B \leftarrow \gamma$ in S whose head B is unifiable with X. Let the mgu(most general unfier) of B and X be θ . Then C, a variant of $[(B \leftarrow . \gamma)\theta]k$, is included in J. C is called a k-item generated from $B \leftarrow \gamma$ or from S.

[Def. 7 Upward k-closure]

For a finite item set I and integer k, we define the upward k-closure, denoted by U-closure(I, k), as the minimum item set J such that :

(1) J includes I (modulo renaming).

(2) Suppose there are an item A <- α .Xβ and a closed item B <- γ . in J whose head B is unifiable with X. Let the mgu of B and X be θ. Then C, a variant of [(A <- α X.β) θ]k, is also included in J. C is called a k-item generated from the item A <- α.Xβ. Besides if A <-α.Xβ is an item generated from a clause D in a program S, we say C is a k-item generated from D or from S.

[Def. 8 Son(parent) item and descendant(ancestor) item]

The closed item B <- γ. in the above definition or its variant is called a son item of C = [(A <- α X.β) θ]k. Conversely C or its variant is called a parent item of B <-γ.. If a closed item has already been defined as a son item of A <- α.Xβ then it is a son item of C too. Based on the son-item-relation we define the descendant-item-of relation as the transitive closure of son-item-of relation. Similarly we define ancestor-item-of relation.

The exsistence of D-closure(I, S, k) and U-closure(I, k) is easily verified. Since k-items are finite for a given integer k, D-closure(I, S, k) is finite (modulo renaming). Similarly U-closure(I, k) is finite too.

Starting with the initial item set I0 = Init(S, δ) for a program S, a goal <- δ and an integer k, we construct a series I0,I1,I2,... of item sets by taking altenately the downward closure and the upward closure of the preceding item set. At some m-th stage of the construction the downward closure and the upward closlure of Im is the same as Im-1(modulo renaming) because the possible k-items generated from S U { <- δ } are finite(modulo renaming). We define :

[Def. 9 Closure]

For a program S, a goal <- δ and an integer k, define a series of item sets I0,I1,I2,... and the item set for S and <-δ, denoted by I(S, δ , k), as follows:

I0 = Init(S, δ).

Ii+1 = U-closure(D-closure(Ii,S,k),k) for i >= 0.

I(S, δ , k) = I0 U I1 U I2 U ...

[Proposition 1]

Let S be a program, <- δ be a goal, k be an integer. And let I = I(S,δ,k) be the k-item set for S and <-δ, then:

(1) I is finite.

(2) I = D-closure(I,S,k) (modulo renaming).

(3) I = U-closure(I,k) (modulo renaming).

Proof) (1) is obvious. Since both D-closure and U-closure are monotonous and continuous as a function of an item set, next relation (modulo renaming) derives (2) and (3) easily.

I =< D-closure(I,S,k) =< U-closure(D-closure(I,S,k), k) = I

4. Relation between I(S, δ , k) and the computation of <- δ

In this section we investigate the relation I(S,δ,k) and the computation process of <-δ by Prolog interpreter. We introduce a model of Prolog interpreter. The intermediate state of the interpreter can be represented by the pair, < α (goals), θ (substitutions) >. The actual value of the goals is (α)θ. For example, if the state is < A(x,y)B(y,z), {x\a, z\f(y)} >, the actual goals are A(a,y)B(y,f(y)). In the following |A|(A may be empty) means that A is an ancestor goal for the current goals. It is usually called an A-literal in the context of resolution [Ch 73].

Suppose an initial goal is <- δ and a program is S = {C1,...,Cn}. The initial state is < δ | |, ε > where ε is a null substitution. The state transition is defined by two ways:

(1) expansion (procedure call)

Let the current state be <Aα ,θ>. The interpreter always attacks the left-most goal. To solve or compute the current goal (A)θ the interpreter selects a clause B0 <- β in S, whose head B0 is unifiable with (A)θ (renaming is assumed implicitly). Let the mgu be λ. Then next state is <β|B0|α, θ *λ>.

(2) truncation (procudure return)

Let the current state be $<|A|\alpha, \theta>$. Since $|A|$ in the left most position means that A has already been solved, the interpreter truncates $|A|$. Then next state is $<\alpha, \theta>$.

The interpreter model described above does not take consideration of unsuccessful computations, i.e. backtracks. But it suffices for showing the relation between a Prolog program and the item set.

When the state becomes $<|\ |, \theta>$ the computation halts successfully. The answer substitution is θ and the goal proved is $(\delta)\theta$. The relation between I(S, δ,k) and the computation process for <- δ by an interpreter is shown by the proposition 2.

[Proposition 2]

Let S be a program, <- δ be a goal, k be an integer respectively. Construct the k-item set I(S, δ,k) for S and <- δ. Suppose the state of the interpreter is $<\beta 2|B0|\alpha, \theta>$ and also suppose B0 <- β1 β2 is <- δ or included in S, then:

(1) There is an item B0′ <- β1′.β2′ in I(S, δ, k) generated from B0 <- β1 β2 and,
(2) There is a substitution λ for the variables in B0′ <- β1′.β2′ such that $(B0)\theta = (B0')\lambda$ and $(\beta 2)\theta = (\beta 2')\lambda$.

The proof is based on the induction on the number of the steps up to the current state. It is lengthy so that we omit it.

[Corollary 1]

For a program S, a goal <- δ and an integer k, construct the item set I(S,δ,k) for S and <- δ. If a clause A <- α is called in the the computation for solving <- δ, then there exists an initial item A′ <- .α′ from A <- α in I(S,δ,k) and the unified head of the clause A <- α is an instantiation of A′.

The corollary 1 is useful in two ways. First if none of the initial items from A <- α exsist in I(S,δ,k), A <- α is never called in the computation for solving <- δ. Thus it enables us to detect redundant clauses to eliminate from the program S. Second it teaches us possible calling patterns of a clause in a computation for <- δ. In other words it informs us of the possible values of variables in the head of a clause after unification. This would be of great use to a Prolog complier or a Prolog program transformation system [Ta 82]. We can not go into details of such applications baecause of space limitation.

Then we turn our attention to the instantiation patterns of a clause in the successful computation, i.e. global success patterns of the clause. We already know by the proposition 2 that if a clause A <- α is called in the computation for a top goal <- δ and the subgoal α is successfully solved, then there is a closed item A′ <- α′. in I(S,δ,k) of which instantiation (A′ <- α′)λ is (A <- α)θ where θ is the substitution obtained up to the time when the subgoal α is solved. Therefore the set of closed items from A <- α teaches us the instantiation patterns of A <- α at the time when its subgoal has been successfully solved, i.e. the local success patterns of A <- α . It is possible, however, that this local success becomes in vain because of subsequent backtrackings. Consequently the closed items from A <- α in I(S,δ,k) does not necessarily mean global success patterns of A <- α . The construction of the item set I(S,δ,k) does not suffice.

To get the global success patterns of a clause contributory to solving <- δ by way of the item set I(S,δ,k), we enumerate the closed items generated from the clauses participating in the successful computations of <- δ. This is done in such a way that starting with the closed item <- δ′. generated from the goal δ, we trace downward the descendant closed items of <- δ′.. At the same time we propagate instantiations from parent items to their closed sons. The global success pattern of a clause must be an instantiation of one of the enumerated and instantiation-propagated items that are called success items in the following. We define the success item set I-suc(S,δ,k) based on I(S,δ,k) as follows:

[Def. 10 Success item set]

For a program S, a goal <- δ and an integer k, construct the item set I(S,δ,k) for S and <- δ.

(1) Let I-suc = { <- δ′. | a closed item from the goal clause <- δ }

(2) If A0 <- A1,...,Am. is in I-suc then choose its son item B <- β. from I(S,δ,k). Let λ be a subtitution such that Ai = (B)λ for some i.

(3) Add [(B <- β .) λ]k to I-suc.

(4) Repeat the step (2) and (3) until no new closed items are added to I-suc (modulo renaming).

(5) The resulting I-suc set is the success item set I-suc(S, ,k) for S and <- δ.

[Proposition 3]

For a program S, a goal <- δ and an integer k, construct the success item set I-suc(S, δ ,k) for S and <- δ. If a clause A <- α is used in the successful computation for <- δ with an answer substitution θ , then there are a closed item A′ <- α ′. generated from A <- α in I-suc(S, δ ,k) and a substitution λ such that (A <- α) θ = (A′ <- α ′) λ holds. (Proof omitted)

[Corollary 2]

For a program S, a goal <- δ and an integer k, construct I-suc(S, δ ,k) for S and <- δ. Suppose that a clause A <- α is invoked in the computation for <- δ. It will be instantiated further in the subsequent computation. But in order for it to have a global success, the instantiated clause must be unifiable with some closed item generated from A <- α in I-suc(S, δ ,k) at any time during the computation.

Corollary 2 shows the necessary condition for a clause to have a global success. Recall that the corollary 1 teaches us the possible calling patterns of each clause. Thus combining the corollary 1 and 2 we can foresee the possiblities of backtracks if there is a clause whose calling pattern does not satisfy the necessary condition by the corollary 2 for its global success. Our aim is to show how to eliminate such foreseeable backtracks from a program.

5. Success values for variables and the necessary condition for a global success

In this section we show the application of the corollary 2 to Prolog programs. We take a parsing program for a small regular language. It is a nondeterministic top-down parser witout left recursive rules. We show, based on the information obtained from the success item set for the program, that the original program can be transformed to a LL(1) parser.

```
% GRAMMAR-1 for the regular expressions over { a, b, emp }
% <exp>      ::= <term> <exp1>
% <exp1>     ::= + <term> <exp1> | e
% <term>     ::= <factor> <term1>
% <term1>    ::= <factor> <term1> | e
% <factor>   ::= ( <exp> ) <factor1> | a <factor1> |
%                b <factor1> | emp <factor1>
% <factor1> ::= * <factor1> | e
```

In this grammar "e" denotes an empty symbol. Below is a DEC-10 Prolog([Wa 79]) program S1 for GRAMMAR-1.

```
%---------------- Prolog program  S1 --------------------
 %1%    exp(X1,Z1) :-term(X1,Y1),exp1(Y1,Z1).
 %2%    exp1(['+'|X2],Z2):- term(X2,Y2),exp1(Y2,Z2).
 %3%    exp1(X3,X3).
 %4%    term(X4,Z4):- factor(X4,Y4),term1(Y4,Z4).
 %5%    term1(X5,Z5):-factor(X5,Y5),term1(Y5,Z5).
 %6%    term1(X6,X6).
 %7%    factor(['('|X7],Z7):-exp(X7,[')'|Y7]),factor1(Y7,Z7).
 %8%    factor([a|X8],Y8):- factor1(X8,Y8).
 %9%    factor([b|X9],Y9):- factor1(X9,Y9).
%10%    factor([emp|X10],Y10):- factor1(X10,Y10).
%11%    factor1(['*'|X11],Y11):- factor1(X11,Y11).
%12%    factor1(X12,X12).
```

Each predicate name(exp, exp1, term, etc..) corresponds to a non-terminal symbol in GRAMMAR-1. A string with an upper case letter at its head (X1,Y1,Z1, etc..) is a variable. Other strings are constants. "[a|b]" and "[a,b,c...]" denote cons(a,b) and list(a,b,c...) in LISP respectively. ":-" is an implication symmbol.

Every predicate p(X,Y) in S1 has two arguments both of which are lists of words (terminals). p([w1,...,wi,wi+1,...,wn],[wi+1,...,wn]) has declarative meaning as: The category < p > has derived [w1,...,wi] in the entire sentence [w1,...,wn] and the rest of sentence to parse is [wi+1,..., wn].

The program S1 may cause a number of backtracks partly because of ungrammatical input sentences, partly because of nondeterministic computations in S1. For example because ['*',a] is not a grammatical sentence in GRAMMAR-1, :-exp(['*',a],[]) invokes clasuse-1,4 then clause-7,8,9,10 and backtrack occurs. On the other hand though [a,'+',a] is a grammatical sentence, a goal :- exp([a,'+',a],[]) causes a backtrack too. In the parsing of [a,'+',a], there appears a subgoal < term1(['+',a],[]) > which calls the cluase-5. Then occurs a backtrack.

We show how to reduce or eliminate the backtracks in the parsing process of an input sentence either be it grammatical or not using the information obtained from the (success) item set for S1. Let us call the value of a variable in a clause success value if it enables the clause to have a global success. The corollary 2 suggests that we can detect the success values of variables in the heads of clause-1,...,clause-12 by the unification of clauses with success items in the success item set for S1. For example if the success values of the variable X1 in clause-1 is {a, b, emp, '(' }, X1 must be able to take one of {a, b, emp, '(' } as its value at any time during the parsing process for clause-1 to have a global success.

Since all of the possible parsing computations by S1 is included in solving a general goal :- exp(X0,[]) where X0 is a variable, we construct the success item set for S1 and :-exp(X0,[]). We choose 2 for the level of term-depth abstraction because we are interested in the first element of a list in the argument position. The item set I(S1,exp(X0,[]), 2) for S1 and :-exp(X0,[]) includes 201 items.

Next we construct the success item set I-suc(S1,exp(X0,[]),2) for S1 and :-exp(X0,[]) from I(S1,exp(X0,[]),2). It includes 133 items. Then we extract the success values for head variables from I-suc(S1,exp(X0,[]),2). (These item set constructions were done by a LISP program).

In order to extract the success values for X1 of clause-1, for example, exp(X1,Z1), the head of clause-1, is unified with the head patterns of the success items generated from clause-1. Since the head patterns of success items from clause-1 are { exp([a],[]), exp([a|X],[]), exp([a|X],[')'|*]), ..., exp(['(',X|Y],[')',X|Y]), exp(['(',X|Y],[')',X|Y]), exp(['(',X|Y],[]) (15 different patterns) }, the success values for X1 are { a, b, emp, '('}. The corollary 2 teaches us that if the value of X1 is not one of { a,b,emp,'(' }, the computation containning the cluase-1 never succeeds globally. As readers notice, the set { a, b, emp, '(' } is the First(1) symbol set for the category <exp>. In this fashion we can extract the success values for X3, X4, X5, X6, X12. (See fig. 1).

Variable	Success values
X1	a, b, emp, '('
X3	')', []
X4	a, b, emp, '('
X5	a, b, emp, '('
X6	'+', ')', []
X12	a, b, emp, '(', ')', '+', []

Fig. 1 Success values for head variables in S1

What do these success values imply after all ? Let us return to the previous example. Suppose that we are going to parse a (-n illegal) sentence ['*', a]. The first call is :-exp(['*', a],[]) with X1 = '*'. But since '*' is not a success value for X1(see fig. 1) we can immediately return with failure without further computations that would be discarded by backtrackings. Suppose that we are going to parse a (legal) sentence [a, '+', a]. The call term1(['+',a],[]) occurs. There are two possible callees (nondeterminacy !), the clause-5 and the clause-6. The success values in the fig. 1 suggest that we should choose not clause-5 but clause-6 because '+' is a success value for X6, not for X5.

As this example shows, we can avoid backtrackings and/or eliminate nondeterminacies in a program by checking success values for the variables in the program since taking a success value is a necessary condition for a clause to have a global success.

In case of the example program, we can convert it to the deterministic one, LL(1) parser, for the GRAMMAR-1 using the success values in the fig. 1. This is not accidental. When a grammar is LL(k) and a parsing program like S1 for the grammar is given, we are always able to detect the LL(k)-ness of the program by extracting success values from the success item set and convert it to the deterministic program. Even if a grammar is not LL(k), it is evident that we can optimize a parsing program by examing the success values.

We applied similar optimization technique via success values to a bottom-up parser program for the GRAMMAR-1 too. The resultant program is a LR(1) like deterministic parser as was expected. But in general we can not expect the conversion to an exact LR(k) parser because in order to realize LR(k) parser, Prolog interpreter would need to invoke several clauses at a time which corresponds to a GO-TO action.

6. Conclusion

We have proposed the concept of item set for a Prolog program. It is inspired by the item set construction in parsing theories. Difficulties due to the exsistence of variables are overcome by the term-depth abstraction technique which reduces an in finite set of items to the finite one.

Since our technique relies on the item set construction combined with term-depth abstraction, another kind of term abstraction, instead of term-depth abstraciton, would bring forth the new kind of item set construction. For example, looking at a term from data type point of view would produce an item set which contains information about data types of arguments in a clause. Such is an area of future research.

ACKNOWLEDGEMENT: The authers are grateful to Dr. Tanaka, Chief of Machine Inference Section of Electrotechnical Laboratory and other members of the section for helpful discussion.

REFERENCES:

[Aho 77] Aho,A.V. and Ullman,J.D.:"Principles of Compiler Design", Addison-Wesley, 1977.

[Chang 73] Chang,C.C. and Lee,R.C.T.:"Symbolic Logic and Mechanical Theorem Proving", Academic Press, New York, 1973.

[Colmerauer 78] Colmerauer, A.: "Metamorphosis grammars", Lec. note in Comp. Sci. No. 63, Springer Verlag, 1978.

[Gallaire 78] Gallaire,H. and Minker, J.(eds) :"Logic and Data Bases", Plenum Press, New York, 1978.

[Kowalski 74] Kowalski,R.A.:"Predicate logic as programming language", Proc. IFIP-74 Congress, 1974.

[Tamaki 82] Tamaki,H. and Sato,T.:"A Transformation System for Logic Programs which preserves equivalence", in preparation.

[Warren 79] Warren,D., Pereira,L.M. and Pereira,F. :"User's Guide to DEC system-10 Prolog", occasional paper 15, Dep. of AI, Edinburgh Univ., 1979.

IMMUNITY

(Extended Abstract)

Uwe Schöning
Institut für Informatik
Universität Stuttgart
7000 Stuttgart 1
West Germany

Ronald V. Book
Department of Mathematics
University of California
at Santa Barbara
Santa Barbara, Ca. 93106, U.S.A.

1. Introduction

There are a number of results about the separation of relativized complexity classes specified by deterministic or nondeterministic machines [1,4,11,12]. In the case of time-bounded machines, some individuals have taken the view that such results say little about the difference between determinism and nondeterminism in ordinary computation but rather illustrate the power of nondeterministic oracle machines to generate a large set of strings to be queried. Recently, Xu, Doner, and Book [19] provided strong evidence for this thesis by establishing a general separating theorem in the context of "degrees of nondeterminism" (that is, refined nondeterminism in the sense of Kintala [11,12]). The result of Xu, Doner, and Book is proved for classes specified by oracle machines where both the number of nondeterministic steps and also the number of oracle queries allowed in computations are bounded by functions of the length of the input. (See [4,6,7,18] for other results about classes specified by machines with these parameters bounded.)

In the present paper we consider "strong separation" theorems: to witness $\mathcal{C}_1 \neq \mathcal{C}_2$, exhibit $L \in \mathcal{C}_2$ such that L is infinite but no infinite subset of L is in $\mathcal{C}_1$. The first context in which this is done is that of polynomial time-bounded oracle machines: for any A, a set L is $P(A)$-immune if L is infinite but has no infinite subset in $P(A)$. Our first result shows the existence of a recursive set A such that $NP(A)$ has a $P(A)$-immune set. (This was first established by Homer and Maass [9].) Our proof does not depend on polynomial time-bounds as such, but rather on polynomial bounds on the number of nondeterministic steps and the number of oracle queries in computations.

†This research was supported in part by the Deutsche Forschungsgemeinschaft and by the National Science Foundation under Grant MCS80-11979.

This result is then extended to two general settings that allow us to establish "immunity" theorems. Several applications of each of these theorems are given.

The notion of immunity with respect to complexity classes was first discussed by Flajolet and Steyaert [8]. Ko and Moore [13] studied this notion in the context of the "P =? NP" problem, and Bennett and Gill [3] considered immunity in terms of random oracles. Balcázar [2] has developed results parallel to those in the present paper in the context of "simplicity." Schöning [17] has compared the notions of "bi-immune" sets, "complexity cores," and "splitting," and obtained surprising results.

This investigation was motivated by interest in the "P =? NP" problem; however, our results do not appear to speak to this problem. While Book, Long, and Selman [5] have studied restricted relativizations of P( ) and NP( ) such that a separation would imply $P \neq NP$, the witnesses for separations developed here do not meet the specifications of Book, Long, and Selman. The results reported here contribute to the growing literature on complexity-bounded reducibilities, nondeterminism in relativized computation, and refining nondeterminism.

2. The Basic Proof

The Immunity Theorems are essentially invariant under a variety of changes in the model of computation with the exception that inputs are assumed to be strings and the oracle queries are of the form "is the string on the query tape in the oracle set?" However, the examples given are in terms of classes specified by various types of restricted oracle Turing machines.

An _oracle machine_ is a multitape Turing machine M with a distinguished work tape, the _query_ tape, and three distinguished states, QUERY, YES, and NO. At some step of a computation on an input string w, M may transfer into the state QUERY. In state QUERY, M transfers into the stage YES if the string currently appearing on the query tape is in an _oracle set_ A; otherwise, M transfers into the state NO; in either case the query tape is instantly erased. The set of strings _accepted by_ M _relative to the oracle set_ A is $L(M,A) = \{w \mid$ there is an accepting computation of M on input w when the oracle set is $A\}$.

Oracle machines may be deterministic or nondeterministic. An oracle machine may operate within some time bound T, where T is a function of the length of the input string, and the notion of operation within a time bound for an oracle machine is just the same as that notion for an ordinary Turing machine. An oracle machine may operate within some space bound S, where S is a function of the length of the input string, and here we require that the query tape as well as the ordinary work tapes be bounded in length by S.

We assume that every machine has nondeterministic fanout at most two.

We assume that the reader is familiar with the elements of machine-based complexity theory at the level of a textbook such as [8] and with relativized complexity classes such as $P(A)$, $NP(A)$, $PSPACE(A)$, etc.

For a string w, $|w|$ denotes the length of w.

The formal definition of "immunity" is made in a general context.

Definition 1. Let $\underset{\sim}{C}$ be a (possibly, relativized) complexity class. A set L is $\underset{\sim}{C}$-immune if L is infinite and no infinite subset of L is in $\underset{\sim}{C}$.

Now we have the first result.

Proposition. There exists a recursive set A such that $NP(A)$ has a set that is $P(A)$-immune.

Proof. We construct a recursive set A such that $L(A) = \{0^m \mid$ there exists a word of length m in $B\}$ does not have an infinite subset in $P(A)$. Clearly, $L(A)$ is in $NP(A)$.

Let $P_0, P_1, \ldots$ be an effective enumeration of the deterministic oracle machines that run in polynomial time. For each i, let q_i be a polynomial that bounds P_i's running time. The set A will be constructed in stages so that for each m at most one string of length m will be put into A.

Stage 0

$A_0 := \emptyset$.

$\mu(0) := 0$.

$R_0 := \{0\}$.

Stage n ($n \geq 1$)

Let $\mu(n)$ be the least integer k such that the following conditions hold:

(i) $2^k > \Sigma_{i \leq n} q_i(k)$;

(ii) $k > \max\{q_i(\mu(n-1)) \mid i < n\}$.

Search for the smallest $j \in R_{n-1}$ such that $0^{\mu(n)} \in L(P_j, A_{n-1})$.

Case 1. No such j is found.

Search for a string w, $|w| = \mu(n)$, such that no machine P_i, $i \leq n$, on input $0^{\mu(n)}$ queries its oracle for "$w \in A_{n-1}$?" Such a string exists since on input $0^{\mu(n)}$, P_i can query its oracle at most $q_i(\mu(n))$ times, the number of strings in $\{0,1\}^*$ of length $\mu(n)$ is $2^{\mu(n)}$, and $\mu(n)$ was chosen so that condition (i) is satisfied.

Let w be the least such string in some effective enumeration of strings and let $A_n := A_{n-1} \cup \{w\}$. Let $R_n := R_{n-1} \cup \{n\}$.

Case 2. Some such j is found.

Let $R_n := (R_{n-1} - \{j\}) \cup \{n\}$ and let $A_n := A_{n-1}$.

End of construction

Define A as $A := \bigcup_{n\geq 0} A_n$.

Clearly, $L(A)$ is infinite if and only if A is infinite. Suppose that A is finite. Then there exists n_0 such that at each stage $n \geq n_0$, Case 2 occurs so that an index is cancelled from R_n. Thus, at each stage $n \geq n_0$, the size of R_n remains constant, the size of R_{n_0}. But the set $\{i \mid L(P_i,A) = \emptyset\}$ is infinite so that no index in this set is cancelled from R_n in an occurrence of Case 2. Hence, A must be infinite.

Suppose there exists an infinite subset C of $L(A)$ such that for some j, $C = L(P_j,A)$. Since C is infinite, $C \subseteq L(A)$, and $L(A) \subseteq \{0^{\mu(n)} \mid n \geq 0\}$, there are infinitely many n such that $0^{\mu(n)} \in C = L(P_j,A)$. The index j was put into T at stage j. Since there are only finitely many indices less than j, there must be a stage $k \geq j$ such that Case 2 with index j occurs so that $0^{\mu(k)} \in L(P_j,A_{k-1})$. But then A_k is chosen so that $0^{\mu(k)} \notin L(A_k)$ and, hence, $0^{\mu(k)} \notin L(A)$ since no string of length $\mu(k)$ is put into A at a stage greater than k because condition (ii) is satisfied when choosing $\mu(n)$. Thus, $0^{\mu(k)} \notin C$ since $C \subseteq L(A)$, contradicting $0^{\mu(k)} \in L(P_j,A_{k-1}) \subseteq L(P_j,A) = C$.

Hence, $L(A)$ is $P(A)$-immune. □

The existence of a recursive set A such that $NP(A)$ has a $P(A)$-immune set was shown by Homer and Maass [9] and, independently, by Schöning [16]. The proof of the Proposition is from [16] and serves as the outline of the proofs of our more general results.

3. The First Immunity Theorem

The First Immunity Theorem is a straightforward generalization of the Proposition to settings other than deterministic and nondeterministic polynomial time. It illustrates how nondeterminism is used to generate more strings than a deterministic machine can query when the number of queries that the deterministic machine can make is restricted.

Definition 2. Let M be an oracle machine. For each set B and each input string x of M, let $Q(M,B,x)$ be the set of strings y such that in some computation of M relative to D on input x, the oracle is queried about y. Let $\#Q(M,D,x)$ be the cardinality of $Q(M,D,x)$.

Consider the proof of the Proposition. Since each P_i is deterministic and runs in time q_i, for every set B and input string x, $\#Q(P_i,B,x) \leq q_i(|x|)$. Thus, condition (i) implies that $2^{|x|} > \Sigma_{i \leq n} \#Q(P_i,B,x)$ for all sets B and x, and there are $2^{|x|}$ strings in $\{0,1\}^*$ of length $|x|$. Hypotheses forcing this to happen allow one to consider more general classes of oracle machines. This leads to the First Immunity Theorem.

First Immunity Theorem

Let $\underset{\sim}{M} = \{M_i \mid i \geq 0\}$ be a class of nondeterministic oracle machines, and let $\underset{\sim}{F}$ be a class of nondecreasing functions (on the natural numbers) that are running times. Suppose that the following conditions hold:

(i) for each i there exists $f \in \underset{\sim}{F}$ such that for every set B and every string x, $\#Q(M_i,B,x) \leq f(|x|)$;

(ii) for each $f \in \underset{\sim}{F}$ and integer $c \geq 0$, there exists $g \in \underset{\sim}{F}$ such that for all but finitely many n, $cf(n) \leq g(n)$;

(iii) for every f and g in $\underset{\sim}{F}$, $\log f = o(g)$;

(iv) for every set B there is a finite set S such that for infinitely many i, $S = L(M_i,B)$.

Then there exists a set A and a set L in $\mathrm{NTIME}(\underset{\sim}{F},A)$ such that L is $\{L(M_i,A) \mid i \geq 0\}$-immune.

Consider the following applications of the First Immunity Theorem.

1. Let $\underset{\sim}{M}$ be the class of deterministic oracle machines that run in exponential (i.e., 2^{cn}) time. Let $\underset{\sim}{F}$ be the set of functions $\{2^{in} \mid i \geq 1\}$. For each set B, denote $\{L(M_i,B) \mid i \geq 0\}$ by $\mathrm{DEXT}(B)$ and $\mathrm{NTIME}(\underset{\sim}{F},B)$ by $\mathrm{NEXT}(B)$. Then there exists a set A and a set L in $\mathrm{NEXT}(A)$ that is $\mathrm{DEXT}(A)$-immune.

2. For each integer $i > 0$, define $\exp(2,1,in) = 2^{in}$. For each integer $i > 0$ and $j > 0$, define $\exp(2,j+1,in) = 2^{\exp(2,j,in)}$. Fix an integer $h > 1$ and let $\underset{\sim}{F} = \{\exp(2,h,in) \mid i > 0\}$. Let $\underset{\sim}{M}$ be the class of deterministic oracle machines that have time bounds in $\underset{\sim}{F}$, so that for every set B, $\{L(M_i,B) \mid i > 0\} = \mathrm{DTIME}(\underset{\sim}{F},B)$. Then there exists a set A and a set L in $\mathrm{NTIME}(\underset{\sim}{F},A)$ such that L is $\mathrm{DTIME}(F,A)$-immune.

3. Let $\underset{\sim}{M}$ be the class of deterministic oracle machines that use polynomial work space and are restricted so that only a polynomial

number of oracle queries are allowed in any computation. For each set B, denote $\{L(M_i, B) \mid i \geq 0\}$ by PQUERY(B); see [4,6,7,19] for properties of classes of this form. Let $\underset{\sim}{F}$ be the set of polynomials, so that for any set B the class NTIME(F,B) is NP(B). Then there exists a set A and a set L in NP(A) such that L is PQUERY(A)-immune.

For other examples of settings where the First Immunity Theorem is applicable, see [6,19].

4. The Second Immunity Theorem

Now we establish the definitions that enable us to formulate the Second Immunity Theorem.

Definition 3. A machine M operates in nondeterminism $g(n)$ if for every input string x to M, any computation of M on x has at most $g(|x|)$ nondeterministic steps.

Definition 4. Let $\underset{\sim}{M}$ be a set of nondeterministic oracle machines. Let $\underset{\sim}{T}$ be a set of nondecreasing functions with the property that for each $M \in \underset{\sim}{M}$, there is a function $t \in \underset{\sim}{T}$ such that for every n, in any computation on an input of length n, M can query its oracle at most $t(n)$ times, and, conversely, for every $t \in \underset{\sim}{T}$, there is an $M \in \underset{\sim}{M}$ satisfying this condition. Let $\underset{\sim}{G}$ be a set of nondecreasing functions with the property that for each $M \in \underset{\sim}{M}$, there is a function $g \in \underset{\sim}{G}$ such that M operates in nondeterminism g, and, conversely, for every $g \in \underset{\sim}{G}$, there is an $M \in \underset{\sim}{M}$ satisfying this condition. Assume that every deterministic Turing machine that operates simultaneously in real time and log space is in $\underset{\sim}{M}$ so that the class of languages recognized by such machines is in $\{L(M,\emptyset) \mid M \in \underset{\sim}{M}\} \subseteq \{L(M,A) \mid M \in \underset{\sim}{M}\}$, A arbitrary. Any such triple $\langle \underset{\sim}{M}, \underset{\sim}{T}, \underset{\sim}{G} \rangle$ will be called a proper oracle machine class.

Definition 5. Let $\langle \underset{\sim}{M}, \underset{\sim}{T}, \underset{\sim}{G} \rangle$ be a proper oracle machine class. For any set A and any $g \in \underset{\sim}{G}$, define $D(\underset{\sim}{M},A)_g = \{L(M,A) \mid M \in \underset{\sim}{M}$ operates in nondeterminism $g\}$. For any set A, define $D(\underset{\sim}{M},A)_0 = \{L(M,A) \mid M \in \underset{\sim}{M}$ operates deterministically$\}$ and define $D(\underset{\sim}{M},A)_\infty = \{L(M,A) \mid M \in \underset{\sim}{M}\}$.

Since we have assumed that every deterministic Turing machine that runs simultaneously in real time and log space is in $\underset{\sim}{M}$ when $\langle \underset{\sim}{M}, \underset{\sim}{T}, \underset{\sim}{G} \rangle$ is a proper oracle machine class, every language recognized by such a machine is in $D(\underset{\sim}{M},\emptyset)_0 \subseteq D(\underset{\sim}{M},\emptyset)_g \subseteq D(\underset{\sim}{M},\emptyset)_\infty$ for every $g \in \underset{\sim}{G}$. Further, if $M_1, M_2, \ldots$ is an enumeration of M, then for every language L recognized by a real time, log space machine, there are infinitely many i such that $L = L(M_i,\emptyset)$.

Now we can state our result.

<u>Second Immunity Theorem</u>. Let $\langle \underset{\sim}{M}, \underset{\sim}{G}, \underset{\sim}{T} \rangle$ be a proper oracle machine class. Suppose that $\underset{\sim}{G} = \{g[n] \mid n > 0\}$ and $\underset{\sim}{T} = \{t_n \mid n > 0\}$ have the following properties:

(i) $\log n \leq g[1](n)$ for all but finitely many n;

(ii) $i < j$ implies $g[i] = o(g[j])$;

(iii) for every $t \in \underset{\sim}{T}$, $\log t = o(g[1])$;

(iv) for every integer $i > 0$ and every set X, the set $\{0^p \mid$ there exists $w \in X$ such that $|w| = g[i](p)\}$ is in $D(M,X)_{g[i]}$.

Then there exists a set A with the property that for every i, j with $0 \leq i < j \leq \infty$, there is a set $L \in D(M,A)_{g[j]}$ that is $D(M,A)_{g[i]}$-immune.

Consider the following applications of the Second Immunity Theorem.

1. Let $\underset{\sim}{M}_1$ be the collection of clocked nondeterministic oracle machines that run in polynomial time. Let $\underset{\sim}{M}_2$ be the collection of oracle machines that are obtained from $\underset{\sim}{M}_1$ be adding clocks that bound the amount of nondeterminism allowed, say $g[i](n) = n^i$ for all $n \geq 0$, $i \geq 0$. Thus, $D(\underset{\sim}{M}_1,\emptyset)_0 = D(\underset{\sim}{M}_2,\emptyset)_0 = P$ and $D(\underset{\sim}{M}_1,\emptyset)_\infty = D(\underset{\sim}{M}_2,\emptyset)_\infty = NP$, and for each i, $D(\underset{\sim}{M}_1,\emptyset)_{g[i]}$ is the class of languages accepted by polynomial time machines that are allowed to make at most $g[i](n) = n^i$ nondeterministic steps in any computation on an input of length n. The theorem states that there exists a set A such that for every i, j with $0 \leq i < j \leq \infty$, there is a set L in $D(\underset{\sim}{M},A)_{g[j]}$ that is $D(\underset{\sim}{M},A)_{g[i]}$-immune. In the notation of [8,9], L is in $P(A)_{n^j}$ and L is $P(A)_{n^i}$-immune. When $i = 0$ and $j = \infty$, L is in $NP(A)$ and is $P(A)$-immune. If the machines in $\underset{\sim}{M}_2$ are enumerated so that M_i runs in time t_i, a polynomial, then the function t_i also serves as a bound on the number of oracle queries that M_i can make. Thus, the existence of clocks for the t_i and the $g[j]$ allows one to claim that the set A is recursive.

2. As in 1, consider oracle machines that run in polynomial time but now restrict the nondeterminism by means of the functions $g[i](n) = (\log n)^{i+1}$. It is known that there is a set A such that for all i, $P(A)_{\log^i n} \subsetneq P(A)_{\log^{i+1} n}$ [11,12]. The theorem states that there is a set A such that for every i, j with $1 \leq i < j \leq \infty$, there is a set L in $P(A)_{\log^j n}$ that is $P(A)_{\log^i n}$-immune. As in 1, A can be chosen so as to be recursive.

3. Let $\underset{\sim}{M}_1$ be the collection of clocked nondeterministic oracle machines that operate in polynomial space. Let both $\underset{\sim}{T}$ and $\underset{\sim}{G}$ be the collection of polynomials $\{n^k \mid k \geq 0$ and integer$\}$. Let $\underset{\sim}{M}_2$ be

the collection of clocked oracle machines obtained from M_1 by adding clocks from $\underset{\sim}{G}$ that bound the amount of nondeterminism and clocks from $\underset{\sim}{T}$ that bound the number of oracle queries allowed in any computation. Thus, $D(\underset{\sim}{M}_1,\emptyset)_0 = D(\underset{\sim}{M}_1,\emptyset)_\infty = D(\underset{\sim}{M}_2,\emptyset)_0 = D(\underset{\sim}{M}_2,\emptyset)_\infty$ = PSPACE and for every set A, $D(\underset{\sim}{M}_2,A)_0$ = PQUERY(A) and $D(\underset{\sim}{M}_2,A)_\infty$ = NPQUERY(A) (see [4]). Extending the notation of [11,12] to classes PQUERY(?), if $g[i] = n^i$, then for every set A, $D(\underset{\sim}{M}_2,A)_{g[i]} = \mathrm{PQUERY}(A)_{n^i}$ is the class of languages accepted relative to A by polynomial space-bounded oracle machines that make at most a polynomial number of oracle queries in any computation and that operate in nondeterminism $g[i] = n^i$. It is known that there is a set A such that PQUERY(A) $\neq$ NPQUERY(A) [4] and that there is a set B such that for all i, j with $0 \leq i < j \leq \infty$, $\mathrm{PQUERY}(B)_{n^i} \subsetneq \mathrm{PQUERY}(B)_{n^j}$ [19]. The theorem states that there exists a set A such that for every i, j with $0 \leq i < j \leq \infty$, there is a set L in $D(\underset{\sim}{M}_2,A)_{g[j]}$ that is $D(\underset{\sim}{M}_2,A)_{g[i]}$-immune, that is, L is in $\mathrm{PQUERY}(A)_{n^j}$ and L is $\mathrm{PQUERY}(A)_{n^i}$-immune. As in 1, the set A can be chosen to be recursive.

For other examples of settings where the theorem is applicable, see [6,19].

In the statement of the Second Immunity Theorem, nothing is said about the set A being recursive; indeed, generally A is not recursive. However, if $\underset{\sim}{M}$ is a class of machines that halt on every input and if the functions in $\underset{\sim}{G}$ and $\underset{\sim}{T}$ meet certain "honesty" conditions such that the sets in $D(\underset{\sim}{M},?)_g$ can be specified by clocked machines for every oracle set, then one can choose A to be a recursive set.

References

1. Baker, T., Gill, J. and Solovay, R., Relativizations of the P =? NP question. SIAM J. Computing, 4(1975), 431-442.

2. Balcázar, J., Simplicity for relativized complexity classes, submitted for publication.

3. Bennett, C. and Gill, J., Relative to a random oracle A, $P^A \neq NP^A \neq$ co-NP^A with probability 1. SIAM J. Computing, 10(1981), 96-113.

4. Book, R., Bounded query machines: on NP and PSPACE. Theoret. Comput. Sci., 15(1981), 27-39.

5. Book, R., Long, T. and Selman, A., Controlled relativizations of P and NP. Theoret. Comput. Sci., Lecture Notes in Computer Science, 145(1983), 85-90.

6. Book, R., Wilson, C. and Xu Mei-rui, Relativizing time, space, and time space. SIAM J. Computing, 11(1982), 571-581.

7. Book, R. and Wrathall, C., Bounded query machines: on NP( ) and NPQUERY. Theoret. Comput. Sci., 15(1981), 41-50.

8. Flajolet, P. and Steyaert, J., On sets having only hard subsets. 2nd International Colloquium on Automata, Languages, and Programming, Lecture Notes in Computer Science, 14(1974), 446-457. Also, Une généralization de la notion d'ensemble immune, R.A.I.R.O. Informatique Théorique, 8(1974), 37-48.

9. Homer, S. and Maass, W., Oracle dependent properties of the lattice of NP sets. Theoret. Comput. Sci., to appear.

10. Hopcroft, J. and Ullman, J., Introduction to Automata Theory, Languages, and Computation. Addison-Wesley, 1979.

11. Kintala, C.M.R., Computations with a Restricted Number of Nondeterministic Steps. Ph.D. dissertation, Pennsylvania State University, 1977.

12. Kintala, C.M.R. and Fischer, P., Refining nondeterminism in relativized polynomial time-bounded computations. SIAM J. Computing, 9(1980), 46-53.

13. Ko, K and Moore, D., Completeness, approximation, and density. SIAM J. Computing, 10(1981), 787-796.

14. Long, T., Relativizing nondeterministic time. Unpublished manuscript, 1981.

15. Schöning, U., A low and a high hierarchy within NP. J. Comput. Syst. Sci., (1983), to appear.

16. Schöning, U., Relativization and infinite subsets of NP sets. Unpublished manuscript, 1982.

17. Schöning, U., Bi-immune sets for complexity classes, in preparation.

18. Selman, A., Xu Mei-rui and Book, R., Positive relativizations of complexity classes. SIAM J. Computing, 12(1983), to appear.

19. Xu Mei-rui, Doner, J. and Book, R., Refining nondeterminism in relativized complexity classes. J. Assoc. Comput. Mach., 30(1983), to appear.

POWER DOMAINS AND PREDICATE TRANSFORMERS: A TOPOLOGICAL VIEW

M.B. Smyth
Department of Computer Science
University of Edinburgh
Edinburgh, EH9 3JZ, Scotland

Abstract

The broad theme of the paper is that topological concepts are basic to computer science. Such concepts as "specifications", "predicate transformer", and "nondeterminism" can be greatly illuminated by being formulated in topological terms. The specific tasks we undertake are: to provide a more adequate framework for power-domain constructions; and to show that the connection between (Dijkstra's) weakest preconditions and the Smyth powerdomain, established by Plotkin for the case of flat domains, actually holds in full generality.

The broad theme of this paper is that topological concepts are basic to computer science. The recognition of this relationship brings both conceptual and technical benefits. Such concepts as "specification", "predicate transformer", and "nondeterminism" can be greatly illuminated by being formulated in topological terms. The topological formulation enables a more adequate technical treatment to be given, by drawing on a well-established body of mathematical knowledge.

One main area of application is that of powerdomain theory. We show that the ideas of [15], [20] are in perfect harmony with topological treatments of multifunctions and spaces of subsets (or "hyperspaces") going back at least to Vietoris [22]. One obstacle to perceiving this has been that the mathematicians have, for the most part, been interested only in Hausdorff spaces. We propose (Definition 5) a finitary notion of "power space" which includes the existing (finitary) powerdomain and hyperspace constructs as special cases, and which is at the same time more direct and accessible (given a minimal acquaintance with topology) than the versions of [15], [20]. But, for reasons of space, we do not develop the power space theory here and, in particular, we consider the possibility of extending it to cover infinitary powerdomains (as in [1], [17]) only in passing. Instead, we consider Dijkstra's predicate transformers. Here, the topological interpretation is even more direct and compelling than in the case of the power domains. It immediately shows us how to generalize the weakest precondition semantics, and its connection with the upper (or Smyth) powerdomain (cf. Plotkin [16]), to arbitrary domains. (The treatment in [6] and [16] is, of course, restricted to flat, or discrete, domains.) The removal of the restriction to flat domains should permit the development of more adequate programming logics.

The key to the work of generalization presented here, as to much recent mathematical work that seeks to escape the limitations of the traditional insistence on Hausdorff separation, is the use of sober spaces, frames, and related concepts ("pointless topology"). These, along with more standard topological material, are briefly introduced in Section 1.

1. Topology

A) Preliminaries. In this sub-section we recall some rudimentary topological notions which will be used repeatedly in the sequel.

A topology on a set S is a collection of subsets of S that is closed under finite intersection and arbitrary union. A set S together with a topology $\mathcal{T}$ on S is a topological space $(S,\mathcal{T})$; the elements of $\mathcal{T}$ are the open sets of the space. We also use the notation $\Omega(X)$ for the (complete) lattice of open sets of the space X.

A base of the topology $\mathcal{T}$ on S is a subset $\mathcal{B} \subseteq \mathcal{T}$ such that every open set is the union of elements of $\mathcal{B}$. A subbase of $\mathcal{T}$ is a subset $\mathcal{A} \subseteq \mathcal{T}$ such that every open set is the union of finite intersections of elements of $\mathcal{A}$. $\mathcal{T}$ is then the least topology such that $\mathcal{A} \subseteq \mathcal{P}$; any collection $\mathcal{A} \subseteq \mathcal{P}$ S may be taken as the subbase of a (unique) topology.

The topologies on a set S, ordered by inclusion, form a complete lattice: the lub $\bigvee T$, for T a set of topologies, is the topology with subbase $\bigcup T$. The least topology on S is the trivial topology $\{\emptyset,S\}$, while the greatest is $\mathcal{P}S$ (the discrete topology).

Notation. For a poset $(P,\leq)$, $x \in P$, $X \subseteq P$, we write

$\uparrow x$ for $\{y|x\leq y\}$

$\uparrow X$ for $\bigcup\{\uparrow x|x \in X\}$.

X is $\uparrow$-closed if $X = \uparrow X$. Similarly for $\downarrow x$, $\downarrow X$, $\downarrow$-closed.

Examples. (1) Euclidean space R^n, with base the open rational intervals. We are more interested in non-Hausdorff (indeed, non T_1) spaces, such as:

(2) Alexandroff topology of a poset, consisting of the $\uparrow$-closed sets; and especially

(3) Scott topology of a poset (usually a cpo) $(P,\leq)$. A set $O \subseteq P$ is open iff O is $\uparrow$-closed and, for any directed set $Y \subseteq P$, if $\bigvee Y \in O$ then some element of Y is in O. We are mainly interested in the case that P is an ω-algebraic cpo (there are countably many finite elements, and each element is the sup of a chain of finite elements). Here the Scott topology is very simply described: it has as base the sets $\uparrow a$, a finite.

For any topology $\mathcal{T}$ on S, we have the specialization preorder $\leq_{\mathcal{T}}$ on S, defined by:

$$x \leq_{\mathcal{T}} y \equiv_{df} \forall O \in \mathcal{T}. x \in O \rightarrow y \in O.$$

If $\mathcal{T},\mathcal{T}'$ are topologies on S, then $\leq_{\mathcal{T}\vee\mathcal{T}'} = \leq_{\mathcal{T}} \cap \leq_{\mathcal{T}'}$.

A subset Q of a space X is compact provided that any family of open sets whose union contains X (so that the family covers X) has a finite subfamily which covers X. (In Bourbaki, Q is allowed to be only quasi-compact under these circumstances, unless X is Hausdorff; but this convention seems unnecessary.)

If X,Y are (topological) spaces, a map f: X -> Y is *continuous* if the inverse $f^{-1}(O)$ of each set O open in Y is open in X (equivalently, if the inverse of each closed set is closed).

Fact. If D,D' are cpo's, then f: D -> D' is continuous w.r.t. the Scott topologies of D,D' iff f preserves lubs of directed sets.

Miscellaneous notation. We use B_D for the basis (set of finite elements) of an algebraic cpo D; $\mathcal{P}_{fin}(S)$ for the collection of finite subsets of S; *Top* for the category of topological spaces with continuous functions as morphisms.

B) *Computational significance of topological ideas.* We think of a topological space as a "data type", with the open sets as the (*computable*) *properties* defined on the type. Taking a *predicate* on a space X to be a continuous map from X into the Boolean cpo B = ff ⟍ ⟋ tt, we have (trivially) that a subset S of X is open iff S is $p^{-1}(tt)$
⊥
for some predicate p. (To make more of a theorem out of this: there is an order-isomorphism between Ω(X) and [X -> $\mathbb{O}$], where $\mathbb{O}$ is the two-point cpo.)

Another reasonable notion of computable property would be that in which P is considered computable iff the set of (codes, or indices) of (computable) elements satisfying P can be effectively enumerated (so that P is a completely r.e. class, cf. Rogers [19]). The theorem of Rice *et al* (Rogers p.76) shows, in effect, that in the case of the domain $\mathcal{P}\omega$, the two notions of computable property are equivalent. A generalization of the Rice theorem (Plotkin [18], Sec. 7, p.9) shows that the equivalence holds in any "effectively given" algebraic cpo.

Intuitively, the idea of a computable property is simply this: we have a uniform procedure that, given (a code for) an element x, tells us within a finite time that P(x) holds, whenever that is true. Of course, this is just the idea of semi-decidability.

An idea that will surface from time to time, although we are not going to develop it in detail here, is that a *specification* of an object (say, a program) is a (finite or countable) list of properties that the object is to satisfy. In view of our identification of properties with open sets, this means that what is specified is always a countable intersection of open sets, in other words a $\mathcal{G}_\delta$-set (see Kuratowski [13]).

The notion of a compact set is a little harder to motivate: but it will have the significance for us of a "finitarily specifiable" set or, alternatively, of a set of results attainable by a boundedly non-deterministic process (we will elaborate on these points in Sec. 2).

Computability/continuity. We are not going to stress "effectiveness" in this paper. But one requirement (for a computationally reasonable space) which we make use of is that there should be a countable base of open sets. Computability concepts will, in general, be relative not just to the topologies of the spaces involved, but to the particular open bases chosen. It is not strictly correct that arbitrary open sets represent computable properties; the computable properties will, rather, be the basic open sets and "effective" unions of them.

We can now give a simple reason why computable functions should be expected to be continuous. Let $f: X \to Y$ be computable, where X,Y are "effective" spaces (so that, among other things, particular bases are assumed for X,Y). Let B be a basic, hence computable, property (open set) in Y. Thus B is $p^{-1}(tt)$ for some computable $p: Y \to \mathbb{O}$. Then $f^{-1}(B)$ is $(p \cdot f)^{-1}(tt)$, hence (assuming that computable functions compose) a computable property, therefore an open set, in X. So f^{-1} takes basic open sets, hence arbitrary open sets, of Y to open sets of X.

C) Points vs. properties. Pointless topology.

(i) T_0-spaces. If we really think of the (basic) open sets of a space as the fundamental properties of interest in that space, then, presumably points having the same neighbourhoods should not be distinguished. We thus require spaces to have the "T_0 separation property":

Definition 1. A space X is T_0 provided

$$\forall x,y \in X \; ((\forall O \in \Omega(X).\; x \in O \equiv y \in O) \to x = y).$$

Equivalently, X is T_0 provided that its specialization preorder is a partial order. Note that for any space X we have the T_0-ification of X, got by identifying points having the same neighbourhood systems. Alternatively - the procedure we shall adopt in Section 2 - one forms the T_0-ification by selecting a distinguished element from each equivalence class in the specialization preorder.

(ii) Sober spaces. A more radical position would be that, since we can be concerned only with the (ascertainable/computable) properties of points, points should be treated as logical constructions out of properties. Points, in this approach, will be mere "bundles of properties". But which bundles are appropriate?

If X is a space with topology $\mathcal{J}$, and $x \in X$, let us write $\mathcal{J}(x)$ for $\{O \in \mathcal{J} \mid x \in O\}$ (more generally, if $\mathcal{B}$ is any base for the topology, we may write $\mathcal{B}(x)$ for the set of basic open neighbourhoods of x). Any subset $\mathcal{F}$ of $\mathcal{J}$ such that $\mathcal{F} = \mathcal{J}(x)$ for some x satisfies the three conditions:

(1) if $U \in \mathcal{F}$, $V \in \mathcal{J}$ and $U \subseteq V$, then $V \in \mathcal{F}$;

(2) if $U,V \in \mathcal{F}$ then $U \cap V \in \mathcal{F}$;

(3) for any family $(U_i)_{i \in I}$ of open sets, if $\bigcup_i U_i \in \mathcal{F}$ then $U_i \in \mathcal{F}$ for some i.

A subset $\mathcal{F}$ of $\mathcal{J}$ satisfying (1) and (2) is a filter in $\mathcal{J}$. A filter satisfying (3) is said to be completely prime; the intuitive meaning of (3) is that a point which possesses the disjunction of the properties U_i, possesses at least one of these properties. Clearly, the notion of a completely prime filter can be formulated for $\mathcal{J}$ an arbitrary complete lattice.

Now, as one may readily check, the statement that a space X is T_0 is equivalent to :

for any completely prime filter in $\Omega(X)$, there is at most one point x such that $\mathcal{F} = \Omega(X)(x)$. Informally: a space is T_0 iff there is at most one point with a given bundle of properties. A sober space is one in which there is a perfect correspondence between points and bundles of properties. That is:

Definition 2. The space X is sober provided, for every completely prime filter $\mathcal{F}$ in $\Omega(X)$, there is exactly one point x such that $\mathcal{F} = \Omega(X)(x)$.

Loosely, we may say that a space is sober iff it is completely determined by its lattice of properties. For sober spaces X,Y, if $\Omega(X)$, $\Omega(Y)$ are isomorphic lattices, then X,Y are homeomorphic spaces.

For any space X we have its soberification (least sober extension), Sobr(X), which we may take as the set of all completely prime filters in $\Omega(X)$ (instead of just those which happen to correspond to points in X), with base for the topology the sets $\Phi_0 = \{\mathcal{F} | 0 \in \mathcal{F}\}$, where 0 ranges over $\Omega(X)$.

We note in passing that, for a more "effective" treatment of the definitions and constructions considered here, one can work with an arbitrarily chosen countable base $\mathcal{B}$ in place of $\mathcal{Y}(=\Omega(X))$.

Examples (1) Every Hausdorff space is sober.

(2) Every algebraic cpo (indeed, continuous poset) is sober. In detail, for D algebraic: if $\mathcal{F}$ is a completely prime filter in $\Omega(D)$, then $0 \in \mathcal{F}$ iff $\uparrow a \in \mathcal{F}$ for some $a \in 0$, by the third condition. In consequence, the completely prime filters may be identified with the filters of basic opens $\uparrow a$. These filters in turn are in (order-preserving) bijection with the ideals in B_D, and hence with the points of D. One observes here that completion by ideals may be considered as a special case of soberification. That is: for any poset B, the Scott topology on the completion of B coincides with the soberification of the Alexandroff topology on B.

It is interesting that not every cpo is sober in its Scott topology (Johnstone [10]). On the other hand, every sober space is directedly complete in its specialization order.

Several alternative characterizations of the sober spaces are discussed in works such as [3], [7]. The most adequate is in terms of an adjunction between **Top** and a suitable category of lattices - namely, **Frm**, the category of frames (= complete Heyting algebras) and maps which preserve finite meets and arbitrary joins. The left half of the adjunction is in effect Ω, the right half is a functor Pt which acts on objects by sending a frame to its space of completely prime filters. A space is sober iff it is Pt(L) for some frame L; there is a corresponding notion of spatial frames, namely those which are values of Ω. The adjunction cuts down to an equivalence (or rather, a duality, since the morphisms in **Top** and **Frm** are in "opposite" directions) between the sober spaces and the spatial frames. Recent work has shown that there may be significant advantages, not least with respect to constructivity, in avoiding commitment to "points" by working with Frm rather than Top (a striking example is Johnstone [11]). This viewpoint informs much of what we are doing in this paper; it is not made more explicit, so as to spare the introduction of too much unfamiliar machinery.

Example. What frames are of the form $\Omega(D)$ for D an algebraic cpo? The open sets of D are in bijection with the $\uparrow$-closed subsets of B_D. Now B_D can be any poset, for suitable choice of D (namely the completion of B_D). Thus, adapting the Representation Theorem 4.1.12 of [23] (for elementary event structures) we find that the frames in question are the prime algebraic complete lattices.

2. Power domains and Vietoris topology

In the study of the semantics of nondeterminism one strangely neglected avenue of approach is that of seeing what mathematicians have had to say about continuity notions for many-valued functions, and about spaces of subsets. On investigation, one finds much of relevance there; the power domains, in particular, are closely related to ideas expounded as long ago as 1921 (Vietoris [22], cf. Kuratowski [13]).

For inverses of many-valued (or multi-) functions, we adopt the notation of Berge [2]: if $\Gamma: X \to Y$ is a multifunction, then $\Gamma^+(S)$ is $\{x \mid \Gamma x \subseteq S\}$ for $S \subseteq Y$, while $\Gamma^-(S)$ is the relational inverse $\{x \mid \Gamma x \cap S \neq \emptyset\}$.

Definition 3. A multifunction $\Gamma: X \to Y$ is upper semicontinuous (usc) if $\Gamma^+(O)$ is open in X whenever O is open in Y; and lower semicontinuous (lsc) if $\Gamma^-(O)$ is open in X whenever O is open in Y (equivalently, if $\Gamma^+(Q)$ is closed whenever Q is closed). Finally, Γ is continuous if it is both usc and lsc.

Example. The fair merge function FM: $\Sigma^\infty \times \Sigma^\infty \to \Sigma^\infty$ is lsc but not usc. Say Σ is $\{0,1\}$. Taking S as $\uparrow\{01,10\}$, we find that $\langle 0,1\rangle \in FM^+(S)$, but $\langle 00,1\rangle \notin FM^+(S)$; thus $FM^+(S)$ is not open, so FM is not usc. On the other hand, if S is an arbitrary open set $\uparrow B$, where B is a set of finite sequences, then $FM^-(S) = \{\langle x,x'\rangle \mid \exists$ finite initial segments a,a' of x,x' $\wedge\ \exists b \in B$ such that some merge of a,a' extends b$\}$, and this is clearly open.

Given a notion of continuity for multifunctions $\Gamma: X \to Y$, it is natural to ask whether there is a reasonable topology on Y such that Γ is continuous as a multifunction iff it is continuous in the ordinary sense as a function from X to $\mathcal{P}Y$. In the case of the three continuities of Definition, there are indeed easily defined topologies on $\mathcal{P}Y$ which agree in this sense.

We will arrive at these topologies by considering some notions of "properties of subsets" which readily suggest themselves. Given a notion of "property", i.e. a topology, over X we have, then, two obvious derived notions of property over subsets S of X: every element of S has a given property P; or, some element of S has P. Combinations of these are also possible.

Formally:

Definition 4. Given a space X and a subset $\mathcal{S}$ of $\mathcal{P}X$, the upper topology on $\mathcal{S}$ has as a base the collection of sets of the form U_0 (0 open in X), where $U_0 = \{S | S \subseteq 0\}$; the lower topology has as subbase the L_0, where $L_0 = \{S | S \cap 0 \neq \emptyset\}$; while the Vietoris (or convex) topology takes as subbase both the L_0 and the U_0.
(The name convex is non-standard; finite is more usual.)

Remark. The Vietoris topology is the (least) common refinement, that is, the lub (in the lattice of topologies), of the upper and lower topologies. The glb of the upper and lower topologies is trivial, in general.

Our definition of the three topologies is more general than those usually given (e.g. [13]) in that we have parameterized on $\mathcal{S}$ (usually a particular collection $\subseteq$ X is fixed); and we give no priority to T_1-spaces.

Why do we not simply take $\mathcal{S}$ to be $\mathcal{P}X$? One reason for restricting the class of sets is to ensure that the resulting space is T_0; we ensure this by picking distinguished elements from the equivalence classes. It is easy to see, for example, that two sets are equivalent with respect to the upper topology iff they have the same $\uparrow$-closure (in the specialization order); it is therefore reasonable to restrict to $\uparrow$-closed sets when considering the upper topology. Similar remarks apply to the other two topologies (details in Theorem 2).

A further restriction (in the case of the upper and convex topologies) arises from the desire to capture the idea of bounded non-determinism. A boundedly non-deterministic process can, we suppose, be represented as a finitely branching tree T such that the possible results of the computation form the "frontier" of T (limits along paths of T). A little more precisely, we suppose that with each point of T is associated a set R(p) of "potential" results, and that the sets occurring along any path from a decreasing sequence having a unique limit point. (The generating trees of [20] are a special case of this. The "set of potential results" associated with a point of one of those trees, labelled with finite element a, is of course $\uparrow$a.)
We claim that the frontier F of such a tree T is compact. Indeed, suppose $F \subseteq \bigcup_{\iota \in I} 0_\iota$. The set $\{p \in T | \exists \iota . R(p) \subseteq 0_\iota\}$ must be finite; for if not, König's lemma implies that there is an infinite path $p_0, p_1, \ldots$, such that for all j, ι, $R(p) \not\subseteq 0$, which implies that $\lim_j p_j \notin 0$ (for all ι). It follows that there is a (finite) cross-section of T for which each associated set is contained in a single 0_ι; thus a finite collection of the 0_ι suffices to cover this cross-section and hence F. (The justification of the restriction to compact sets is taken up again at the end of this section.)

If Γ: X -> Y is a multifunction, we denote by $\hat{\Gamma}$: X -> $\mathcal{P}$Y the corresponding function.
Theorem 1. Let Y be a space, $\mathcal{S}$ a (non-empty) subset of $\mathcal{P}$Y. Then, for any space X, a multifunction Γ: X -> Y with (multi)values in $\mathcal{S}$ is usc iff $\hat{\Gamma}$: X -> $\mathcal{S}$ is continuous w.r.t. the upper topology on $\mathcal{S}$; similarly for lower semi-continuity w.r.t. the lower topology, and for continuity w.r.t. the convex topology. Moreover, the three

topologies on $\mathcal{S}$ are uniquely determined by the requirement that they agree with the continuity notions for multifunctions, in this sense.

Proof The (sub-)bases of the three topologies on $\mathcal{S}$ are so chosen as to make the first statement of the Theorem trivial (notice that a function is continuous if the inverse image of each subbasic open set is open). For uniqueness, notice that distinct topologies $\mathcal{J}$, $\mathcal{J}'$ on a set Z cannot yield the same set of continuous functions with Z as codomain: the identity functions between $(Z,\mathcal{J})$ and $(Z,\mathcal{J}')$ cannot both be continuous. □

We now introduce our definition of the three "power spaces" of a (sober) space.

Notation. Let X be a space. For $S \subseteq X$, $\bar{S}$ denotes the closure of S, while conv(S) is $\bar{S} \cap \uparrow S$. Also, CL(X), UC(X) and COMP(X) are the sets of closed, $\uparrow$-closed and compact sets of X respectively; CONV(X) is the set of fixed points of conv. We use $\leq_L$ for the specialization order derived from the lower topology; similarly for $\leq_C$, $\equiv_L$, etc.

Definition 5. The lower power space of X, $PS_L(X)$, is CL(X) taken with the lower topology; the upper power space, $PS_U(X)$, is COMP(X) $\cap$ UC(X) with the upper topology; and the convex power space, $PS_C(X)$ is COMP(X) $\cap$ CONV(X) with the convex topology.

Theorem 2. $PS_L(X)$, $PS_U(X)$ and $PS_C(X)$ are the T_0-ifications of X, COMP(X) and COMP(X) taken with the lower, upper and convex topologies, respectively.

Proof PS_L: Clearly, it suffices to show that $S \equiv_L S'$ (in the lower topology) iff $\bar{S} \equiv_L \overline{S'}$. But, by definition, a point x is in $\bar{S}$ iff every open set containing x meets S. It follows at once that $\bar{S}$ is the largest set equivalent to S and that $S \equiv_L S'$ iff $\bar{S} \equiv_L \overline{S'}$.

PS_U: Evidently, an open set O contains a set S iff $\uparrow S \subseteq O$. Hence $S \equiv_U \uparrow S$, and if S is compact then so is $\uparrow S$. Moreover, $\uparrow S$ is the largest set equivalent to S: since if $x \notin \uparrow S$ then for each $y \in S$ there is an open neighbourhood O_y of y such that $x \notin O_y$, so that, putting $U = \bigcup_{y \in \uparrow S} O_y$, we have $S \subseteq U$ while $x \notin U$. The conclusion follows as before.

PS_C: Since $S \subseteq \text{conv}(S) \subseteq \bar{S}$, $S \equiv_L \text{conv}(S)$; similarly, $S \equiv_U \text{conv}(S)$. Hence, $S \equiv_C \text{conv}(S)$ An easy calculation shows that conv(conv(S)) = conv(S). Further, if $Y \equiv_C S$ then $Y \subseteq \bar{S}$ (since $Y \equiv_L S$) and $Y \subseteq \uparrow S$ (since $Y \equiv_U S$); hence $Y \subseteq \text{conv}(S)$. Finally, if S is compact, then conv(S), as the intersection of a closed set with a compact set, is also compact. We have thus shown that the elements of $PS_C(X)$ are the canonical (largest) elements of the $\equiv_C$-equivalence classes in (COMP(X),C). □

The "hyperspace" most usually studied is CL(X) with the Vietoris topology. We have restricted to compact sets as we are interested in modelling bounded non-determinism (but see remarks at end of this section). The standard treatment is, in effect, restricted to T_1-spaces (see [14]). Now, if X is T_1, all sets are $\uparrow$-closed, CONV(X) = CL(X) and, modulo the restriction to compactness, our theory is equivalent to the usual one. But it seems clear that to have a good theory applicable to non-T_1-spaces one needs to work with convex and not just closed sets (this is one of the main contributions of Plotkin [15]).

It has been proposed by de Bakker and Zucker [4] to use, as a power space construct, the Hausdorff metric on the closed subsets of a metric space X. Now it is not difficult to show that, for the compact (and therefore closed) subsets of X, the Hausdorff metric topology coincides with the Vietoris topology. It is true that they do not coincide in the non-compact case, and that de Bakker and Zucker allow arbitrary closed sets. However, there is a question as to which is the best topology to use in the non-compact situation; Michael [14] argues that the Hausdorff metric topology is mathematically less satisfactory than the Vietoris topology.

We will next show that, in case D is an algebraic cpo, the power spaces reduce to the usual power domains over D. Following [20], we shall define the power domains of D as completions of M(D) under suitable orderings, where M(D) is the set of non-empty finite subsets of B_D. For completeness we treat, along with the upper, or Smyth, powerdomain [20], its dual, sometimes known as the Hoare power domain.

<u>Definition 6</u>. Let D be an ω-algebraic cpo. Define the pre-orders $\sqsubseteq_L, \sqsubseteq_U, \sqsubseteq_C$ on M(D) by:

$A \sqsubseteq_L B$ iff $\forall a \in A.\exists b \in B.a \sqsubseteq b$

$A \sqsubseteq_U B$ iff $\forall b \in B.\exists a \in A.a \sqsubseteq b$

$A \sqsubseteq_C B$ iff $A \sqsubseteq_L B \wedge A \sqsubseteq_U B$.

Then the <u>lower</u> (or Hoare), <u>upper</u> (or Smyth), and <u>convex</u> (or Plotkin) power domains of D, denoted $PD_L(D)$, $PD_U(D)$, $PD_C(D)$, are the completions by ideals of M(D), under the respective orderings $\sqsubseteq_L, \sqsubseteq_U, \sqsubseteq_C$.

Actually we find it convenient, most of the time, to work with (equivalence classes of) ω-chains rather than directed ideals. If $(E,\sqsubseteq)$ is a preorder then $(\omega CH(E), \sqsubseteq_L)$, where ωCH(E) is the set of ω-chains of E, is a preorder equivalent to the completion $\bar{E}$ of E. To show that $\bar{E}$ is isomorphic to a cpo D it suffices to show that there is a (pre-) order-preserving and -reflecting surjection of $(\omega CH(E), \sqsubseteq_L)$ onto D. We write [X] for the ideal generated by an ω-chain X. We usually omit the subscript L for the preorder on chains.

<u>Lemma 1</u>. Let D be ω-algebraic, $S \subseteq D$ compact and non-empty. Then the set $U_S = \{A \in M(D) \mid A \sqsubseteq_U S\}$ is $\sqsubseteq_U$-directed; and $C_S = \{A \in M(D) \mid A \sqsubseteq_C S\}$ is $\sqsubseteq_C$-directed. Moreover $\bigcap\{\uparrow A \mid A \in U_S\} = \bigcap\{\uparrow A \mid A \in C_S\} = \uparrow S$.

<u>Proof</u> If 0 is an open superset of S, we can find an element K_0 of M(D) such that $K_0 \subseteq 0$ and $K_0 \sqsubseteq_C S$. For, since S is compact, $\exists A \in M(D).\ A \subseteq 0 \wedge S \subseteq \uparrow A$; then choose K_0 to be a minimal such A. The last assertion of the lemma follows at once, since $\uparrow S = \bigcap_{S \subseteq 0} 0$. It also follows that U_S is $\sqsubseteq_U$-directed, since if $A,B \sqsubseteq_U S$ we have $A,B \sqsubseteq_U K_{\uparrow A \cap \uparrow B} \sqsubseteq_U S$.

Finally, suppose $A,B \sqsubseteq_C S$. Write K for $K_{\uparrow A \cap \uparrow B}$. For each $a \in A$ such that $\exists c \in K.a \sqsubseteq c$, augment K by adding to it an element A' chosen as follows. Find $x \in S$ such that $a \sqsubseteq x$. Find $b \in B$ such that $b \sqsubseteq x$. Then choose a' such that $a,b \sqsubseteq a' \sqsubseteq x$. Also, for each $b \in B$ such that $\exists c \in K.b \sqsubseteq c$, augment K by a similarly chosen b'.

Let K' be the result of all these augmentations of K. Then $A,B \sqsubseteq_C K' \sqsubseteq_C S$. □

In defining the power domains, the empty set is usually excluded from consideration. For the comparison of power spaces with power domains we therefore define $PS_L^+(X)$ to be the subspace of the non-empty elements of $PS_L(X)$, and similarly for $PS_U^+(X)$, $PS_C^+(X)$.

Theorem 3. Let D be an ω-algebraic cpo, taken with its Scott topology. Then $PS_L^+(D)$, $PS_U^+(D)$ and $PS_C^+(D)$ are isomorphic, in their specialization orders, with $PD_L(D)$, $PD_U(D)$ and $PD_C(D)$ respectively.

Proof (i) $PD_L(D)$: if I is a (directed) ideal in $(M(D), \sqsubseteq_L)$, let $L(I) = \{a \mid \{a\} \in I\}$. Then L(I) is a ↓-closed subset of B_D, and indeed L is an isomorphism of $PS_L^+(D)$ onto $(\mathcal{L}, \subseteq)$, where $\mathcal{L}$ is the set of non-empty ↓-closed subsets of B_D (with L^{-1} as $\mathcal{P}_{fin}$). If $Z \in \mathcal{L}$ then $\bar{Z} = \{x \mid {\downarrow}x \cap B_D \subseteq Z\}$, and closure is an isomorphism of $(\mathcal{L}, \subseteq)$ onto $(CL(D), \subseteq)$, with inverse $S \mapsto {\downarrow}S \cap B_D$. Thus $(\bar{\ }) \circ L$ is the required isomorphism of $PD_L(D)$ onto $PS_L^+(D)$ (i.e. $(CL(D), \subseteq)$).

(ii) $PD_U(D)$: For an ω-chain $H = H_0 \sqsubseteq_U H_1 \sqsubseteq_U \ldots$ in $(M(D), \sqsubseteq_U)$, define $\Phi_U(H) = \bigcap_i {\uparrow}H_i$. Then Φ_U is order-preserving: indeed, if $H \sqsubseteq K$ then for each i there exists j with ${\uparrow}H_i \supseteq {\uparrow}K_j$, so that $\bigcap_i {\uparrow}H_i \supseteq \bigcap_j {\uparrow}K_j$. On the other hand, suppose $\bigcap_i {\uparrow}H_i \supseteq \bigcap_j {\uparrow}K_j$. We consider the generating tree (cf. [20]) whose finite paths are all the sequences $\langle b_0, \ldots, b_n \rangle$, where $b_i \in K_i$ and $b_i \sqsubseteq b_{i+1}$. The cross-sections of this tree are (multisets whose corresponding sets are) the K_j. For each i there must be a cross-section K_j such that $H_i \sqsubseteq_U K_j$; for if not, we could by König's Lemma find an infinite path $b_0 \sqsubseteq b_1 \sqsubseteq \ldots$ with each $b_j \notin {\uparrow}H_i$, hence $\bigsqcup_j b_j \notin {\uparrow}H_i$, hence $\bigcap_j K_j \not\subseteq {\uparrow}X_i$. This shows that Φ_U is order-reflecting. Further, every compact ↑-closed set Q is $\Phi_U(H)$ for some H: by Lemma 1, we have only to choose an H cofinal with U_Q. Thus Φ_U determines an isomorphism of $PD_U(D)$ onto $PS_U^+(D)$.

(iii) $PD_C(D)$: For an ω-chain $H = H_0 \sqsubseteq_C H_1 \sqsubseteq_C \ldots$, define

$$\Phi(H) = \Phi_U(H) \cap \Phi_L([H]),$$

where $\Phi_L = (\bar{\ }) \circ L$ is the isomorphism considered in (i). First, ${\uparrow}\Phi(H) = \Phi_U(H)$. For, obviously ${\uparrow}\Phi(H) \subseteq \Phi_U(H)$. On the other hand, suppose $x \in \Phi_U(H)$. This means (using König's Lemma) that there is a chain $a_0 \sqsubseteq a_1 \sqsubseteq \ldots$ with $a_i \in H_i$ and $\bigsqcup_i a_i \sqsubseteq x$. But then $\bigsqcup_i a_i \in \Phi_U(H) \cap \Phi_L([H])$, and so $x \in {\uparrow}\Phi(H)$. Similarly, $\overline{\Phi(H)} = \Phi_L([H])$: the left-to-right inclusion is again trivial, while if $a \in \Phi_L([H])$ we have $a \sqsubseteq a_i$ (for some $a_i \in H_i$) and $a_i \sqsubseteq a_{i+1} \sqsubseteq \ldots$ (for suitable $a_{i+k} \in H_{i+k}$), so that $a \sqsubseteq \bigsqcup_i a_i \in \Phi(H)$. Thus $\Phi(H) \leq_C \Phi(K)$ iff $\Phi_U(H) \leq_U \Phi_U(K)$ and $\Phi_L([H]) \leq_L \Phi_L([K])$. At the same time, it is clear that $H \sqsubseteq_C K$ iff $H \sqsubseteq_U K$ & $H \sqsubseteq_L K$ (notice that if $H_i \sqsubseteq_U K_j$ and $H_i \sqsubseteq_L H_K$ then $H_i \sqsubseteq_C K_{max(j,k)}$) and that $H \sqsubseteq_L K$ iff $[H] \subseteq [K]$. Hence, by (i) and (ii), $H \sqsubseteq_C K$ iff $\Phi(H) \leq_C \Phi(K)$.

For surjectivity, suppose $Q \in PS_C^+(D)$. Let H be an ω-chain cofinal with C_Q (see Lemma 1); then $\Phi_U(H) = {\uparrow}Q$. Further, it is clear that $\Phi_L([H]) \subseteq \bar{Q}$. To show that $\Phi_L([H]) \supseteq \bar{Q}$, suppose $a \in \bar{Q}$ (a finite). Then $\{a\} \cup H_0 \sqsubseteq_C Q$. Hence, for some j,

$\{a\} \cup \Sigma_0 \sqsubseteq_C \Sigma_j$. Thus $a \in \Phi_L([H])$; we have shown that $\Phi(H) = Q$. □

Plotkin has observed that the powerdomains over an algebraic cpo have a convenient universal characterisation, namely as free continuous semilattices (see [8]). One naturally tries to extend this to power spaces, in terms of free topological semilattices. Unfortunately this does not work, except for the relatively uninteresting lower power space (for details, see [21]). It seems that the justification of the power spaces, in the general case, has to be rather indirect. A little has been said above to justify the choice of compact sets; we can now add something to that in terms of "specifications". A specification, we have suggested, can be taken to be a countable collection of open sets. Since the set of properties to be satisfied is obviously closed under conjunction (intersection) and logical implication (inclusion), we may as well say that a specification is a countably-generated filter of open sets. We shall say that a specification, $\mathcal{F}$, is finitary if the following condition holds: whenever the union O of an increasing sequence $O_0 \subseteq O_1 \subseteq \dots$ is in $\mathcal{F}$, some O_i is already in $\mathcal{F}$. To say that the filter $\mathcal{F} \subseteq \Omega(X)$ is finitary is thus equivalent to saying that it is itself an open set in the complete lattice $\Omega(X)$, taken with the Scott topology; or, following the ideas of Section 1, that it is computable, in the sense, e.g. that one can effectively enumerate all (the indices of) the properties which belong to it. The special interest of open filters, in the present context, is due to the following remarkable

FACT Let X be a sober space. A set $Q \subseteq X$ is compact iff the set $\mathcal{F}^*(Q) = \{O \in \Omega(X) \mid Q \subseteq O\}$ is an open filter. Moreover, if $\mathcal{F}$ is any open filter in $\Omega(X)$, then $\bigcap\mathcal{F}$ is compact (and, of course, $\uparrow$-closed), and if O is any open superset of $\bigcap\mathcal{F}$ then $O \in \mathcal{F}$. Hence the maps $\mathcal{F}^*$, $\bigcap$ define an order-isomorphism between $(\mathcal{P}S_U(X), \supseteq)$ and $(O\,\mathrm{Filt}(\Omega(X)), \subseteq)$, where O Filter L, for L a complete lattice with Scott topology, is the collection of open filters in L.

(See Hofmann & Mislove [9], and references given there.)

Open filters provide the link by which we connect the upper power space with weakest precondition semantics, in the next section.

An equally satisfactory description does not seem to be available for the convex power space, in the general case; these matters are explored in [21].

We conclude this section with some brief remarks on the infinitary powerdomains introduced recently by Apt and Plotkin [1], Plotkin [17] for handling unbounded (countable) nondeterminism. Consider first the case of a flat, countable domain $S_\perp$, as in [1]. Then the upper topology on $\mathcal{P}(S_\perp) - \{\emptyset\}$ gives exactly the infinitary upper (or Smyth) powerdomain of $S_\perp$. This upper topology is not sober, nor is the upper domain a cpo. At the same time, the Vietoris topology gives exactly the convex (Plotkin) powerdomain ($\mathcal{P}(S_\perp) - \{\emptyset\}$, Egli-Milner ordering); in this case the topology is sober, and the powerdomain is a cpo. The lower topology and powerdomain are not very interesting: they are the same as in the finite case.

As for general domains, one suggestion is to treat the infinitary power spaces/ domains analogously to the finitary ones, replacing finite sets by countable sets. That is, one observes that the (finitary) convex power space of an algebraic cpo, D, is the soberification of the Vietoris topology on $\mathcal{P}_{fin}(D)$, and similarly for the upper and lower power spaces. For the infinitary construct, then, one could try the soberification of the space of countable subsets. But whether this leads anywhere is not known at present.

3. Predicate Transformers

Recall that we have defined the "upper" inverse f^+ of a (multi-)map f: X -> Y as $f^+: \mathcal{P}Y \to \mathcal{P}X: S \to \{x \mid f(x) \subseteq S\}$. When f is usc, f^+ cuts down to a function from $\Omega(Y)$ to $\Omega(X)$, which we might denote by $\Omega^+(f)$; the point being that, just as Ω is a functor from Top into Frm, Ω^+ (with $\Omega^+ = \Omega$ on objects) is a functor from the category of spaces and usc maps into a modified category of frames. But we will not dwell on the categorical aspect here.

Since we identify predicates, or properties, with open sets, maps from $\Omega(Y)$ to $\Omega(X)$ are (the appropriate generalization of) predicate transformers in our framework. The upper inverse can be said to correspond to the weakest precondition: $wp(f,S) = f^+(S)$.

In justification of these remarks, consider the predicate transformers as introduced by Dijkstra [6] and their correspondence, investigated by Plotkin [16], with non-deterministic state transformations. Here we are concerned with discrete state sets X,Y. A predicate transformer from Y to X, satisfying Dijkstra's healthiness conditions, is a strict, multiplicative, continuous function from $\mathcal{P}(Y)$ to $\mathcal{P}(X)$. Plotkin observes that there is an order isomorphism between the (cpo of) healthy predicate transformers from Y to X and the domain of non-deterministic state transformations taken as $[X \to PD_U(Y_\perp)]$. Now, the topology of $Y_\perp$ is $\mathcal{P}(Y) \cup \{Y_\perp\}$, while that of X is $\mathcal{P}(X)$. In order to regard a predicate transformer P: $\mathcal{P}(Y) \to \mathcal{P}(X)$ as a map from $\Omega(Y_\perp)$ to $\Omega(X)$, then, we have only to give it a value for the argument $Y_\perp$; naturally, we assume $P(Y_\perp) = X$. Thus, we consider the domain of (healthy) predicate transformers to be the (pointwise ordered) poset of maps $\Omega(Y_\perp) \to \Omega(X)$ which are strict and continuous and preserve finite intersections (including the null intersection). Our claim is that, with this view of predicate transformers, the correspondence with non-deterministic maps can be extended far beyond the case of discrete spaces considered by Dijkstra and Plotkin; indeed it extends to arbitrary sober spaces.

For Y a sober space, the points of $PS_U(Y)$, as well as of Y itself, can be identified with suitable filters in $\Omega(Y)$, by the above FACT. We will be able to treat deterministic and non-deterministic ST's (state transformations) in a uniform way by regarding them as maps from X into the space $Filt(\Omega(Y))$ of filters in $\Omega(Y)$ (with basic open sets the $\Phi_O = \{\mathcal{F} \mid O \in \mathcal{F}\}$, for $O \in \Omega(Y)$).

Theorem 4. Let X,Y be sober spaces. For a continuous map f: X -> Filt(Ω(Y)), let π(f): Ω(Y) -> Ω(X) be defined by $\pi(f)(O) = \{x \mid O \in f(x)\}$ (π(f)(O) is open in X by continuity of f, since $\pi(f)(O) = \{x \mid f(x) \in \Phi_O\}$). Then π defines an order-isomorphism between [X -> Filt(Ω(Y))] and the poset of PT's (predicate transformers) p ∈ [Ω(Y) -> Ω(X)] which satisfy

(1) p is monotonic and strict, and preserves finite meets. Moreover, π cuts down to an order-isomorphism between [X -> PS_U(Y)] and the poset of PT's satisfying (1) and

(2) p is continuous (i.e. preserves directed sups; equivalently, under our assumption that spaces are second countable, p preserves sups of ω-chains).

It cuts down further to an order-isomorphism between [X -> Y] and the poset of PT's satisfying (1) and

(2') p is completely additive (i.e. preserves arbitrary sups).

Remark. The final part of the theorem (concerning [X -> Y]) is essentially the (well-known) duality result mentioned at the end of Section 1.

Proof of Theorem 4. It is straightforward to check that, for any f: X -> Filt(Ω(Y)), the PT π(f) satisfies (i) (for preservation of meet, for example, one uses the fact that, for any filter $\mathcal{F}$, $O \cap O' \in \mathcal{F} \equiv O \in \mathcal{F} \wedge O' \in \mathcal{F}$). For any p: Ω(Y) -> Ω(X) satisfying (1), define T(p): X -> Filt(Ω(Y)) by:

$T(p)(x) = \{O \mid x \in p(O)\}$;

again, one readily checks that condition (1) implies that T(p)(x) is a filter. To prove the theorem, it suffices to show that (A) T is a right inverse of π (i.e. that $T \circ \pi(f)(x) = f(x)$), and that this remains true on cutting down in the ways indicated; and (B) T is strictly monotonic (i.e. $T(p) \leq T(q)$ iff $p \leq q$).

A) For the right inverse property, we have

$T \circ \pi(f)(x) = \{O \mid x \in \pi(f)(O)\} = \{O \mid O \in f(x)\} = f(x)$.

It remains to show that π and T cut down appropriately. Suppose that f: X -> O Filt(Ω(Y)) (recall that this codomain is identified with PS_U(Y)), and let $O_1 \subseteq O_2 \subseteq \ldots$ be an increasing sequence in Ω(Y). Suppose also that $x \in \pi(f)(\bigcup_i O_i)$. This means that $\bigcup_i O_i \in f(x)$. Since f(x) is (Scott-)open, $O_i \in f(x)$ for some i; thus $x \in \pi(f)(O_i)$ for some i. This shows that π(f) is continuous. One shows similarly that if p satisfies (1) and (2), then T(p) maps X into O Filt(Ω(Y)).

Suppose now that f: X -> Y (here we are of course identifying Y with the space of completely prime filters in Ω(Y)). Let $(O_\iota)_{\iota \in I}$ be a family of open sets in Y. Suppose that $x \in \pi(f)(\bigcup_\iota O_\iota)$, in other words $\bigcup_\iota O_\iota \in f(x)$. Since f(x) is completely prime, some $O_\iota \in f(x)$. Thus $x \in \pi(f)(O_\iota)$ for some ι.. This shows that π(f) is additive. Again, it is easy to see that if p satisfies conditions (1) and (2'), then π(p) maps X into Y.

B) Suppose $p \leq q$, that is $p(O) \subseteq q(O)$ for all $O \in \Omega(Y)$. Then, for each x ∈ X, $T(p)(x) = \{O \mid x \in p(O)\} \subseteq \{O \mid x \in q(O)\} = T(q)(x)$; that is, $T(p) \leq T(q)$. On the other hand, suppose $\neg(p \leq q)$. Then for some x ∈ X, O ∈ Y we have $x \in p(O)$ while $x \notin q(O)$. But then $T(p)(x) \not\subseteq T(q)(x)$; that is, $\neg(T(p) \leq T(q))$. Thus strict monotonicity obtains; the theorem is proved.

The significance of this theorem (more precisely, of part (2) of the theorem) is that it gives us an equivalence, in a very general setting, between a denotational semantics using the upper power domain/space and axiomatic semantics in the manner of Dijkstra.

The viewpoint of the upper powerdomain/predicate transformer approach is, of course, that a process passes a test (satisfies a property) iff all its possible computations do so - that is, it must pass the test. Also to be considered is the view which corresponds to the lower topology (the process may pass the test), and the conjunction of the two (convex topology). Given a notion of successful computation, the resulting specialization orders will give three preorders and equivalence notions for processes. It is interesting to note that (independently of the above) de Nicola and Hennessy [5] have recently developed exactly this approach to the equivalence of processes.

Acknowledgements

Discussions with Gordon Plotkin have been very helpful. The comprehensive treatise [7] has proved to be a continuing, almost inexhaustible, source of inspiration. Financial support has been provided by the (U.K.) SERC.

References

1. Apt, K., Plotkin, G., A Cook's tour of countable non-determinism. Proc. ICALP 1981, Springer-Verlag LNCS 115, pp. 479-494 (1981).
2. Berge, C., Espaces Topologiques: Fonctions Multivoques. Dunod, Paris (1959).
3. Continuous Lattices, Proceedings Bremen 1979, ed. Banaschewski and Hoffman, Springer LN Math. 871 (1981).
4. de Bakker, J., Zucker, J., Denotational semantics of concurrency, Proc. 14th ACM STOC, pp. 153-158 (1982).
5. de Nicola, R., Hennessy, M., Testing equivalences for processes, CSR-123-82, Dept. of Computer Science, Edinburgh (1982).
6. Dijkstra, E., A Discipline of Programming, Prentice-Hall (1976).
7. Gierz, G., Hofmann, K., Keimel, K., Lawson, J., Mislove, M., Scott, D., A Compendium of Continuous Lattices. Springer (1980).
8. Hennessy, M., Plotkin, G., Full abstraction for a simple parallel programming language. Proc. MFCS, Springer LNCS 74, pp. 108-120 (1979).
9. Hofmann, K., Mislove, M., Local compactness and continuous lattices: in [3] (pp, 209-248).
10. Johnstone, P., Scott is not always sober: in [3] (pp. 283-284).
11. Johnstone, P., Tychonoff's theorem without the axiom of choice, Fund. Math. 113, pp. 21-35 (1981).
12. Johnstone, P., Stone Spaces, Cambridge U.P. (198?).
13. Kuratowski, K., Topology. Revised edition, Academic Press and PWN (1966).
14. Michael, E., Topologies on spaces of subsets, Trans. AMS 71,pp.152-182 (1951).
15. Plotkin, G., A powerdomain construction, SIAM J. Comput. 5,pp. 452-487 (1976).
16. Plotkin, G., Dijkstra's predicate transformers and Smyth's powerdomains, Abstract Software Specifications (ed. D. Bjørner) LNCS 86 (1980).
17. Plotkin, G., A powerdomain for countable non-determinism, Proc. ICALP 1982.
18. Plotkin, G., Domains: notes for lecture course, Edinburgh (1981).
19. Rogers, H., Theory of Recursive Functions.
20. Smyth, M., Power domains, JCSS 16 (1978).
21. Smyth, M., Powerdomain and hyperspace. To appear.
22. Vietoris, L., Monatsh. f. Math. u. Phys. 31, pp. 173-204 (1921).
23. Winskel, G., Events in Computation, Thesis, Edinburgh (1980).

Recognition and Isomorphism of Two Dimensional Partial Orders

Jeremy Spinrad
Department of Computer and Information Sciences
Georgia Institute of Technology, Atlanta, Ga.

Jacobo Valdes
Department of Electrical Engineering and Computer Science
Princeton University, Princeton, NJ

Abstract:

This paper presents an algorithm for recognizing two dimensional partial orders. The algorithm accepts as input an arbitrary partial order G and responds "yes" if the dimension of G is less than or equal to two and responds "no" otherwise. As part of the recognition process, the algorithm decomposes the partial order in a canonical way which can be used to determine whether two partial orders of dimension two are isomorphic. Both the recognition and the isomorphism algorithms can be implemented to run in time $O(n^2)$ when the input is a partial order on n elements. The best previously known algorithms for these two tasks had a worst case behavior of $O(n^3)$.

1. Introduction

Dushnik and Miller [DM] defined the *dimension* of a partial order as the minimum number of total orders whose intersection defines the partial order. They showed that any partial order has a unique dimension, and gave several necessary and sufficient conditions for a partial order to have dimension less than or equal to two.

This paper is concerned with the *recognition* of two dimensional partial orders: the problem of determining whether the dimension of a given partial order is less than or equal to two. Determining whether a partial order has dimension one is a trivial problem since it must be a total order. Determining the dimension of a partial order is NP-complete for dimension greater than two [YA].

The recognition problem is interesting because of the following fact: there are important problems for which no polynomial algorithm that works for arbitrary inputs is known yet have polynomial time algorithms when the input is restricted to the class of two dimensional partial orders . Some examples are the chromatic number and vertex cover problems [EL], problems involving vertex deletion and scheduling [SP] -- all of which are NP-complete in the general case -- and directed graph isomorphism [COL]. A fast recognition algorithm allows testing a partial order given as input to decide whether an exact solution or a heuristic method should be used on it for a particular problem.

The class of two dimensional partial orders is also interesting because it properly includes the class of *vertex series-parallel* partial orders, and the class of *interval orders*. Vertex series-parallel partial orders have proved to be quite useful in scheduling [LAW]; they arise quite naturally as representations of scheduling constraints and admit very efficient algorithms for important problems which are intractable in the general case. We hope that similar algorithms can be discovered for two dimensional partial orders as well. The recognition algorithm that we are about to describe produces a representation of the structure of its input which may in fact help the design of such algorithms.

Our algorithm determines whether a partial order on a set of size n is two dimensional in $O(n^2)$ steps, whereas the best previously known algorithm required $O(n^3)$. It can also be used to test two dimensional partial orders for isomorphism in $O(n^2)$, another problem for which the best previously known algorithm required $O(n^3)$ steps.

The remainder of this paper contains a small number of definitions, an outline of the algorithm and the details of some parts of it. A complete description of the algorithm can be found in [SP].

2. Basic definitions

In this paper we will think of a partial order R on a set V as represented by a *directed acyclic graph (dag)* with vertex set V and edges between any pair of vertices u,v such that uRv. Note that a dag that represents a partial order must be transitive.

Let G be a partial order and u, v two of its vertices. If there is an edge from u to v in G, we will say u *dominates* v and that v *is dominated* by u. Two vertices u, v are said to be *related* (opposite *unrelated*) if u dominates v or v dominates u.

A dag $G=(V,E)$ is a *two dimensional partial order* if there exists a pair of total orders L_1, L_2 on V such that for any two vertices u and v of G, u precedes v in both total orders if and only if (u,v) is a (directed) edge in G. The two total orders are each called *listings*, and together, they form a *representation* of G. A listing L of the vertices of a dag G is *nonseparating* if the following two conditions hold:

-1- For any two vertices u and v of G, if u dominates v, u precedes v in L.

-2- For any three vertices u, v, w, such that u dominates v, and w is unrelated to both u and v, w does not occur between u and v in L.

A partial order G is two dimensional if and only there is a nonseparating listing of its vertices [DM]. This fact will be used in our recognition algorithm.

3. An outline of the algorithm

Our recognition algorithm resembles in certain respects the algorithm of Lueker and Booth [LB] for recognizing interval graphs. Their algorithm uses a data structure called PQ-trees, while ours represents the structure of its input as a peculiar tree that we call the *modular representation* or *modular decomposition.*

In the modular representation tree of a dag G, internal nodes are labeled either *series*, *parallel*, or *neighborhood* and leaves represent the vertices of G. If the graph is a two dimensional partial order, children of a series node (which corresponds to a chain) must appear in a unique order in any nonseparating listing for G, children of a parallel node may appear in any order, and children of a neighborhood node may appear in one of exactly two different orders which are particular to the neighborhood node.

The recognition algorithm consists of several parts. Given a graph G, we first construct the modular representation of G (this can be done for any dag). From the modular representation we then compute a nonseparating listing for G, and from it we compute a pair of listings. Finally we verify that the pair of listings we have constructed represents the graph correctly: G is two dimensional if and only if it is represented by our candidate representation.

The modular representation of G is constructed by a recursive method that repeatedly selects a vertex u and splits the vertex set of the subgraph being considered based on the relationship of these vertices to u.

The nonseparating listing of G is constructed by a traversal of its modular decomposition in which we compute a partial listing for each node of the tree from the partial listings of its children. The difficult part of the construction is the one that deals with the neighborhood modules and it involves a partition refinement scheme: we consider the vertices in the module one at a time in an arbitrary sequence; for each new vertex we refine a partition representing the possible set of nonseparating listings for the module on the basis of the relationship of the new vertex to all other vertices previously considered; when all vertices have been considered, the partition represents a single possible choice.

From the nonseparating listing, it is relatively straightforward to compute a pair of listings that represent G if and only if G is two dimensional.

4. The modular decomposition of a dag

We will now describe the modular decomposition of a dag. We begin by defining some terms, then prove a few facts about the modular decomposition and finally outline an algorithm that uses these facts to compute the modular decomposition of an arbitrary dag with n vertices in $O(n^2)$ steps.

4.1. Definitions

Let $G=(V,E)$ be a dag. A *module* is a set M of vertices of V with the property that for any two vertices $u \in M$, $w \in M$ and $v \in V-M$, v is related to u if and only if v is related to w. A module M is said to be a *maximal submodule* of another module N if $M \subset N$ and no proper submodule of N contains M.

Let M be a module and let M_c be the undirected graph that has M as its vertex set and edge set defined as follows: (u,v) is an edge of M_c if and only if u is related to v. Similarly, let M_{cc} be the undirected graph having M as vertex set ant the following edge set: (u,v) is an edge of M_{cc} if and only if u is not related to v. We say that a module M is *connected* if the graph M_c defined above is connected. We say that M is *complement-connected* if M_{cc} is connected.

Suppose a module M is not connected. We can partition M into M_1 and M_2 such that no vertex in M_1 is related to a vertex in M_2. We call such unconnected submodules *parallel modules* because of their similarity to subgraphs of a vertex series-parallel graph which are connected in parallel.

If a module M is not complement-connected, it can be partitioned into M_1 and M_2 such that every vertex in M_1 is related to every vertex in M_2. Modules which are not complement-connected are called *series modules*, again because of their similarity with series-connected subgraphs of a vertex series parallel graph.

Modules which are both connected and complement-connected are called *neighborhood modules*.

By definition, a module cannot be both a neighborhood module and a series or parallel module. A module M cannot be both a series module and a parallel module: if M_c is not connected, every vertex in one component of M_c will be connected to every vertex not in that component in M_{cc} and the module would then be complement-connected.

4.2. Some facts about modules

We will now define precisely the modular decomposition of a graph by proving some simple facts about modules.

Lemma 1:

Let M_1 and M_2 be modules of G with $M_1 \cap M_2 \neq \emptyset$. One of the following three conditions must be true: (i) one module contains the other or (ii) both modules are parallel modules or (iii) both modules are series modules.

Proof:

Suppose lemma 1 is false. Then $M_1-(M_1 \cap M_2) \neq \emptyset$, and $M_2-(M_1 \cap M_2) \neq \emptyset$ or (i) would be true. We show that in that case either (ii) or (iii) must be true by assuming that M_1 is connected and that M_2 is complement-connected and deriving a contradiction.

Since M_1 is connected, there must be some vertex x in $M_1-(M_1 \cap M_2)$ which is related to a vertex in $M_1 \cap M_2$. Such a vertex must be related to every vertex in M_2 because M_2 is a module,

Since M_2 is complement-connected, there must be some vertex y in $M_2-(M_1 \cap M_2)$ which is unrelated to a vertex in $M_1 \cap M_2$. Again, every vertex in M_1 must be unrelated to y because M_1 is a module.

We have derived a contradiction: vertex x must be related to y because y belongs to M_2 but y must be unrelated to x since x belongs to M_1. We conclude that either (ii) or (iii) must be true.

Lemma 2:

Let M_1 and M_2 be modules of G with $M_1 \cap M_2 \neq \emptyset$ and such that neither one contains the other. $M_1 \cup M_2$ is a module of the same type as M_1 and M_2.

Proof:

By lemma 1, we know that M_1 and M_2 are both series modules or both parallel modules.

Because M_1 and M_2 are modules every vertex x in $V-(M_1 \cup M_2)$ is related to every vertex in M_1 and M_2 if and only if x is related to some vertex in $M_1 \cap M_2$. Therefore, $M_1 \cup M_2$ is a module.

Every vertex x in M_1 - $(M_1 \cap M_2)$ is related to every vertex in $M_1 \cap M_2$ if and only if x is related to every vertex in M_2. If some vertex in M_1 is related to every vertex in M_2 while some other vertex is not, M_1 would not be a module. Therefore, either every vertex in $M_1-(M_1 \cap M_2)$ is unrelated to every vertex in $(M_1 \cap M_2)$, or every vertex in $M_1-(M_1 \cap M_2)$ is related to every vertex in $(M_1 \cap M_2)$.

If every vertex in $M_1-(M_1 \cap M_2)$ is unrelated to every vertex in $M_1 \cap M_2$, M_1 and M_2 must be parallel modules. Also $M_1 \cup M_2$ must be a parallel module, since every vertex in M_1 is unrelated to every vertex in M_2.

If every vertex in $M_1-(M_1 \cap M_2)$ is related to every vertex in $M_1 \cap M_2$, M_1 and M_2 are series modules, and every vertex in M_1 is related to every vertex in M_2. Therefore, $M_1 \cup M_2$ is a series module.

Corollary 1:

Every vertex contained in a neighborhood module N is in a unique maximal submodule of N.

Proof:

Suppose vertex x in N is contained in the distinct maximal submodules M_1, M_2 of N. By lemma 1, M_1 and M_2 are both series modules, or both parallel modules. By lemma 2, $M_1 \cup M_2$ is a proper submodule of N, so M_1 and M_2 are not both maximal.

4.3. Computing the modular decomposition of a dag

We will now outline a recursive algorithm that takes a graph G as input and produces a *unique* tree structure that we call the *modular decomposition* or *representation* of G. The uniqueness of the structure we compute is guaranteed in part by corollary 1. Fig. 1 is intended to give the reader an idea what this structure looks like.

The algorithm begins by considering the module M consisting of the entire graph. If M is a single vertex, we halt and produce as output the tree containing the single vertex as its root and only node. Otherwise M is either a series, parallel, or neighborhood module. We then create a node in the structure labeled with S, P, or N, depending on the type of the module.

Let k be a node representing a parallel (series) module M, and let $M_1, M_2, \dots, M_p$ be the connected components of the undirected graph M_c (M_{cc}) defined in section 4.1. We construct the modular decomposition for M by finding the modular representation of each M_j as an independent graph, and making the roots of these trees the children of node k.

Let k be a node representing a neighborhood module M, and let $M_1, M_2, \dots, M_p$ be the maximal submodules of M. We construct the modular decomposition of M by finding the modular decomposition of each M_j, and making these the children of node k.

The result of this process is a tree with the vertices of G as leaves. We note that this is a simple extension of the tree representation of vertex series-parallel graphs in [VTL]. In fact, vertex series-parallel graphs are exactly those dags which have no neighborhood nodes in their modular representation.

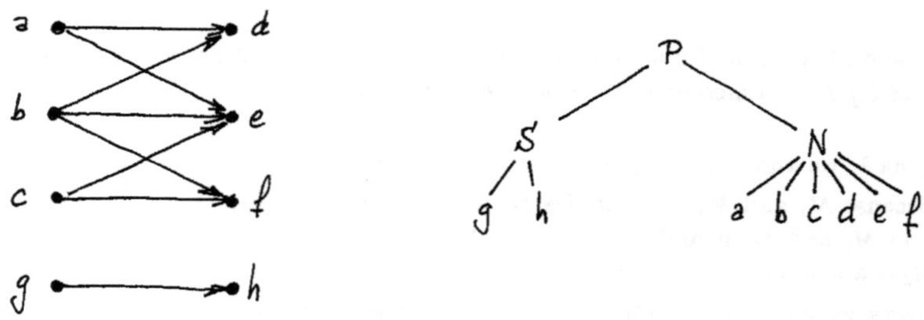

Fig. 1:
A dag and its modular representation

Although the algorithm just outlined is relatively simple, it must be implemented carefully so that it runs in $O(n^2)$ steps on a dag with n vertices. Given below is a brief outline of a possible implementation described in full detail in [SP].

To find the decomposition of a module M we begin by choosing any vertex u of M. If every vertex is related to u, we have found a series module, and partition the graph into three components: (i) vertices which dominate u, (ii) u itself, and (iii) vertices dominated by u. We find the modular representation of each partition, and make the resulting trees the children of the node representing M, which is marked with an S to denote that the module is a series module. If any of the roots of the subtrees is labeled S also, we make the children of that component children of the root of the tree representing M so as to avoid having any node labeled S with the same label as its parent.

For the rest of the section we will address the case where, after selecting u, some vertex v exists which is unrelated to u.

We first find $M_{u,v}$, the smallest module which contains both u and v. This module must contain all vertices which are related to u and unrelated to v, so we compute this set first and call it M_u. We then grow M_u in stages: during a stage, we select a vertex $w \in M_u$ and add to M_u all vertices which are either related to v and unrelated to w or unrelated to v and related w. We continue to add vertices to M_u in this manner until we cannot add any more. Note that $M_u \subset M_{u,v}$ and that v may or may not end up in M_u.

If $v \notin M_u$, we grow M_v in the same way we constructed M_u. If $v \notin M_u$, and $u \notin M_v$, then we will have $M_{u,v} = M_u \bigcup M_v$ and the modular representation of $M_{u,v}$ will have a root labeled P and the representations of M_u and M_v as children of that root. We then proceed to find the modular decomposition for $(M - M_{u,v})$ by treating $M_{u,v}$ as a single vertex which is related to all others in the same way as u (we say that u is the *representative* of $M_{u,v}$). When we are finished with $M - M_{u,v}$, we find the modular representation of M_u and M_v and make the roots of the subtrees thus obtained children of the node representing $M_{u,v}$. If during this process we find that the root of the tree representing $M_{u,v}$ is the child of a node n labeled P, we make the trees representing M_u and M_v children of n and do not create any node for $M_{u,v}$. This is done so that there is no node labeled P that has the same label as its parent.

We now consider the case when $v \in M_u$, in which case we will have $M_{u,v} = M_u$. (If $v \notin M_u$ and $u \in M_v$, we use the procedure that we are about to describe interchanging the roles of u and v). The representation of $M_{u,v}$ is a tree whose root is labeled N. Once again we treat $M_{u,v}$ as a single vertex while finding the modular representation of the rest of the graph, and come back to decompose $M_{u,v}$. To decompose $M_{u,v}$ we partition it initially into two sets: M_v containing all vertices that were added to $M_{u,v}$ at the same time as v, and $M_{u,v} - M_v$. We refine this initial partition so as to insure that when we are done any two vertices in a partition relate in the same manner to all vertices of all other partitions. This refinement can be performed so that the relationship between any two vertices x and y which are in the same submodule is never examined, except if they happen to be in the same submodule as u. (This is important if the whole decomposition process has to run in $O(n^2)$). Every partition generated in this manner will be a submodule in the final decomposition. For each of them, except that which includes u, we find now their modular representation by treating each as a separate dag (applying this method recursively) and make the roots of the trees thus obtained children of the node labeled N which represents $M_{u,v}$.

We complete this outline by describing how to find the modular decomposition of the module M_u, the submodule produced by the growing process described earlier. The method is identical to that which we used to find the modular representation of M_u and M_v when $M_{u,v}$ was a parallel module. Let x be a vertex brought into $M_{u,v}$ during the last stage of its growth and which is also in M_u. We find $M_{u,x}$ just as we did for $M_{u,v}$ except that now we consider only vertices of $M_{u,v}$. Enough information can be saved from the construction of M_u so that we never have to look at relationships between two vertices more than once until they are put in separate partitions. We then refine M_x and M_u as before. This process is iterated again and again (now we would take a vertex y brought into $M_{u,x}$ during the last stage of its growth that is also in M_u, and find the module $M_{u,y}$) until M_u consists of a single vertex. All submodules created during the iteration are treated as separate graphs, and reduced to their modular representations. These are then placed as children of the node representing $M_{u,v}$.

If the procedure just outlined is implemented carefully, the relationship between any pair of vertices x and y will be examined at most three times: once when they are brought into a common module, and twice when the vertices are put into separate modules (once when the module containing x is refined with respect to relatedness with y, and once when the module containing y is refined with respect to relatedness with x). This is enough to guarantee a running time of $O(n^2)$ for this method of computing the modular decomposition of an arbitrary dag.

5. Constructing a nonseparating listing from the modular decomposition

We now discuss the following problem: given the modular decomposition of a dag G, find a nonseparating listing of the vertices of G. We outline an algorithm that will construct such a listing provided that it exists, i.e., that G is two dimensional.

The method we use is the following. The modular decomposition tree for the dag is traversed from the leaves to the root so when a node is being processed all its children have been processed already. At each node x we compute a nonseparating listing for the module represented by x from the nonseparating listings of the children of x. The nonseparating listing for the complete dag is the listing computed for the root of the modular decomposition tree.

5.1. Computing a nonseparating list: the simple cases

Generating a nonseparating listing for a module consisting of a single vertex is trivial since the listing consists only of the node itself. Let M be a series or parallel module in the modular decomposition of G. Given a nonseparating listing for all children of M in the modular decomposition of G it is easy to construct a nonseparating listing for M. If M is a parallel module its listing is computed by concatenating the listings for all of its children in any order whatsoever.

The case of series modules is equally simple. Choose any two children M_1 and M_2 of a series module M. Since M is a series module, either every vertex in M_1 dominates every vertex in M_2, or every vertex in M_2 dominates every vertex in M_1. This defines a total order among the children of a series module and gives us an easy way to create the nonseparating listing for it. The listing is obtained by concatenating the listings of its children so that the listing for M_i precedes the listing for M_j if and only if every vertex of M_i dominates every vertex of M_j.

5.2. The complex case: neighborhood modules

Computing a nonseparating list for a neighborhood module from the listings of its children is considerably more complicated. Our algorithm uses a partition refinement schema based on the fact that the listings for the neighborhood module will be obtained by concatenating the lists for its children. Because no shuffling of the listings for the children may occur, our task is reduced to finding a total order for the children of the module M under consideration that preserves nonseparability.

Because M is a neighborhood module, the children of M in the modular representation must be maximal submodules of M. Let these maximal submodules be $M_1, M_2 \ldots M_k$. We create a set D containing one vertex, chosen arbitrarily, from each maximal submodule of M. The vertex v_i chosen from M_i will be called the *representative descendant* of M_i; from now on, all processing is done using these representatives to stand for the complete submodules. This is done to save computation and can be done because any vertex in a submodule must relate to any other vertex in a different submodule exactly the way the representative vertices for the two modules do.

To compute the listing for M, we first arrange the elements of D in a nonseparating list called the *target listing*. We then replace each v_i in the target listing by the nonseparating listing for M_i and the result is a nonseparating list for M. A more detailed description of this process is given below; it is, however, too complicated a process to permit a thorough description in a few pages, so the interested reader should look the details up in [SP].

At any point during the running of the algorithm, we keep a concise representation of all the possible target listings consistent with the information considered up to that time. As more and more information is considered the number of possible target listings will decrease until only one possibility remains.

The choices of nonseparating listings still possible at a given time will be represented in our algorithm by a *partition list*: a linear order of disjoint subsets of D. The partition list $|P_1, P_2, .. , P_m|$, will represent all listings in which all vertices in P_i precede every vertex in P_{i+1}.

The elements of the partition list at a given time during execution is determined by the following equivalence relationship on D. For any two vertices $x \in D$ and $y \in D$, and every vertex $v \in D$ already processed by the algorithm, x and y are in the same partition if and only if both x and y are unrelated to v or both dominate v or both are dominated by v.

The algorithm consists of two parts. First, we create an initial partition list. We then refine the partitions in the partition list (i.e., narrow the number of possible nonseparating listings) by selecting a vertex of D not yet processed and guaranteeing that the equivalence relation still holds. Vertices of D that have been used to refile the partition list will be called *used* (opposite *unused*); the refinement process terminates when every member of D is used.

5.2.1. Creating an initial partition list

The process we use to compute an initial partition list is the following. We select a vertex v of D, split D into two partitions and then refine them so they represent all possible nonseparating listings consistent with how all other vertices of D relate to v.

Choose any vertex v as the first vertex in a partition P, and let x be any vertex of D which is unrelated to v; such a vertex must exist since we are dealing with a neighborhood module. Initially, add to P all vertices that relate differently to v and x, that is, those that are either related to v and unrelated to x or related to x and unrelated to v. We will now add vertices to P in stages until no more vertices can be added.

Each stage in the process of growing P is performed as follows. We select from P a vertex w, compute the set $S_{v,w}$ of vertices that relate differently to v and w and add all vertices of $S_{v,w}$ to P. Eventually, no new vertices can be added to P and the process terminates. The choice of w at each step is arbitrary as long as (i) no vertex is chosen twice and (ii) when a vertex y is chosen no vertex added to P_1 at an earlier stage than y remains to be chosen.

We now split off a portion of P to create the original partition list as follows. Let z be the last vertex chosen at the beginning of a stage which is unrelated to v and consider the set $S_{v,z}$ of vertices added to P during that stage. The initial partition list consists of $|P_1,P_2|$ where $P_1=P-S_{v,z}$ and $P_2=S_{v,z}$.

Because M is connected, every vertex in v will be in one of the two partitions in the list, and because M is complement-connected, v must be unrelated to every vertex in P_2.

An example of this process is shown in fig.2, where the stages of the computation of P for the neighborhood module of the graph of fig. 1 is shown.

$P_1 = \{ a \}$ $\quad S_{a,f} = \{ d, e \}$
$P_1 = \{ a, d, e \}$ $\quad S_{a,d} = \{ b \}$
$P_1 = \{ a, d, e, b \}$ $\quad S_{a,e} = \{ c \}$
$P_1 = \{ a, d, e, b, c \}$ $\quad S_{a,b} = \{ f \}$

******* *Initial Partition list:* $| \{ a, d, e, b, c \}, \{ f \} |$

Fig.2
An example of the process of computing the initial partition for the neighborhood module of the graph of fig. 1. The module is $\{ a, b, c, d, e, f \}$, the initial vertex chosen is a.

Let u be any vertex in P_2. If G is a two dimensional partial order, there must be some non-separating listing L for G such that v precedes u in L, since u and v are unrelated (all vertices of P_2 are unrelated to v). This is the basic fact needed to prove the following lemma about the listing that we are trying to compute (see [SP] for a complete proof).

Lemma 3:
There exists a nonseparating listing L in which for every pair of vertices $x \in P_1$ and $y \in P_2$, y precedes x in L only if y dominates x.

The partition refinement step that we will describe shortly assumes that every vertex in P_i precedes every vertex in P_{i+1} in the target listing. In order to guarantee this, we have to do some further work to the partition just computed. Namely, we have to form new partitions to insure that vertices of P_2 that dominate vertices of P_1 are in partitions that appear in the appropriate order.

To do this, we perform an *adjustment* process on the pair P_1, P_2, (this process is described in more detail in the next subsection). This process produces a new partition list such that for any two vertices y which was originally in P_2 and x originally in P_1, y ends up in a partition that precedes the partition of x if and only if y dominates x.

The partition resulting from this process can be used as the starting point for the refinement process that we will now describe.

5.2.2. Refining the partition list

The refinement process can be described as follows. Repeatedly select a partition P which includes at least one unused vertex. For each such partition, repeatedly choose any unused vertex u from P and refine (i.e., split) all partitions except P on the basis of the relationship between their elements and u. When all vertices are used, the process terminates.

Let us describe the inner loop of the refinement process more precisely. Let $L=|P_1, \cdots P_k|$ be the current partition list, let u be an unused vertex which is in some partition P_j and let Z be the set of vertices related to u. Split each partition P_i in the current partition list (different from P_j) into $P_{i,u}=P_i \cap Z$ and $P_{i,n}=P_i-P_{i,u}$.

Suppose partition P_j preceded partition P_i in the partition list. Because of the way we maintain our partition lists this guarantees that u will appear before every vertex of $P_{i,n}$ in the target listing. We also know -- because the final list has to be nonseparating -- that for any $x \in P_{i,u}$ and $y \in P_{i,n}$, y precedes x in the target listing if and only if y dominates x. We thus have to make sure that this information is reflected in the partition list after the subdivision of P_i so it represents exactly all target listings still possible. In order to do this we may have to ***adjust*** the pair of partitions $P_{i,u}$, $P_{i,n}$ as we adjusted the two partitions computed in the previous section in order to produce the initial partition list.

The adjustment process is not symmetric as we will see shortly. Hence, if P_i preceded P_j in the partition list, we adjust $P_{i,n}$, $P_{i,u}$ and if P_j preceded P_i we adjust the pair $P_{i,u}$, $P_{i,n}$.

We conclude the description of this process by explaining the process of ***adjusting*** the pair P_1, P_2. First P_1 and P_2 are divided into a collection of partitions each, $P_{1,1}, P_{1,2}, \cdots P_{1,k}$ and $P_{2,1}, P_{2,2}, \cdots P_{2,k}$ by the following criterion. The partition $P_{1,1}$ consists of vertices which are not dominated by any vertex in P_2 and $P_{2,i}$ consists of vertices in P_2 which dominate every vertex in $P_1-P_{1,i}-P_{1,i-1}-\cdots-P_{1,1}$. Finally $P_{1,i}$ for $i>1$ consists of vertices in P_1 which are not dominated by any vertex in $P_2-P_{2,i-1}-P_{2,i-2}-\cdots-P_{2,1}$. Clearly $P_{1,1}$ and $P_{2,k}$ may be empty. We then interleave these partitions to create a new partition list $L_{new}=|P_{1,1},P_{2,1},P_{1,2},P_{2,2},\cdots,P_{1,j},P_{2,j}|$.

If the partitions just split contained used vertices some extra work must be done during this adjustment process, because of the following reason. During the partition refinement, partitions that are composed exclusively of used vertices are never examined to see if they comply with the equivalence relationship that defines the partitions in the partition list. Therefore, when a partition composed exclusively of used vertices is split, further refining of the pieces may be needed. In that case, we simply refine L_{new} recursively and substitute the result for the partition being split in the partition list.

We note that when the refinement is done, no partition in the partition list may contain more than one vertex. If some partition list consisted of more than one vertex, the union of the submodules represented by the vertices would be a submodule of the neighborhood module being processed. This is not possible, however, because the vertices represent maximal submodules. Therefore,there is only one nonseparating listing for the children of a neighborhood module once an initial partition has been fixed. This property allows us to use the modular representation to test pairs of two dimensional partial orders for isomorphism. The full details of this procedure can be found in [SP].

In summary, a refinement step consists of iteratively splitting the partitions in the current partition list, and ***adjusting*** the pairs of partitions thus created. The adjustment operation may, in turn, require that a sublist of the partition list be refined, therefore introducing a recursive call to the refinement process on a portion of the partition list. At the end, a partition list in which each partition contains a single vertex is produced; either this is a nonseparating listing of the neighborhood module or no such list exists.

An example of the way the initial partition list of fig. 2 is refined to produce a nonseparating list for the neighborhood module of the graph of fig. 1 is shown in fig. 3.

Split { *a, d, e, b, c* } with respect to *f* yielding { *a, d, e* } and { *b, c*}
Adjust { *a, d, e* } and { *b, c* } yielding { *a* } { *b* } { *d* } { *c* } { *e* }
Final partition list: | { *a* } { *b* } { *d* } { *c* } { *e* } { *f* } |
Nonseparating listing: *a, b, d, c, e, f*

Fig. 3
The refinement of the initial partition shown in fig. 2

5.3. Time complexity

Let us now analyze briefly the running time of the algorithm just described for computing a nonseparating list from the modular decomposition.

All the process does effectively is to compute, for every node in the modular decomposition, a total order on its children. That computation is trivial for parallel nodes: any total order works. The computation is only slightly more complex for series nodes: the total order is defined by the adjacency matrix of the input graph and all we have to do is read it. Thus, except for neighborhood nodes, the process would run in time proportional to the number of nodes in the modular decomposition tree.

Unfortunately, the process of computing the appropriate total order for neighborhood nodes requires time proportional to the square of the number of children of the node. We show that it is no worse than that by counting the number of times that we need to find out whether two vertices x and y are related or unrelated, as this is the most frequent elementary action performed.

We may examine the relationship between vertices x and y once in the initial partition step, once during an *adjustment* step when the two are assigned to separate partitions, once when we refine the partition containing x with respect to y, and once when we refine the partition containing y with respect to x. We therefore examine the relationship between pairs of vertices a constant number of times, so the time complexity of constructing the nonseparating listing for a neighborhood module with k children is $O(k^2)$.

The time needed to compute the listing for the complete graph is thus dominated by the time needed to compute the listings of the neighborhood nodes, and may be as high as $O(n^2)$ for a graph having n vertices.

6. Constructing the total orders from the nonseparating listing

Let L be the nonseparating list for a dag G produced by the process just described. We will use L as one of the two total orders with which we will represent G. The second listing is created by assigning a number n_i to each vertex v_i in L. The value of n_i is the total number of vertices x in G such that either v_i dominates x, or x precedes v_i in L and x is unrelated to v_i. We construct L' -- the second total order to represent G -- by sorting the vertices by their values n_i.

It is now a trivial matter to check whether this pair of listings L and L' represent G: for each pair of vertices u, v, we check that that u dominates v if and only if u precedes v in both L and L'. If the listings do not represent G properly, G is not a two dimensional partial order; if they do we have a representation of G.

Figure 4 shows a nonseparating listing of the vertices of the graph shown in fig. 1 -- trivially derived from the sublisting shown in fig. 3 -- and the two total orders obtained from it.

Nonseparating Listing : g, h, a, b, d, c, e, f

Two dimensional representation: g, h, a, b, d, c, e, f
c, b, f, a, e, d, g, h

Fig. 4
A nonseparating listing of the vertices of the graph of fig. 1 and the representation of the graph obtained from this listing.

7. Conclusions

We have presented the outline of an $O(n^2)$ algorithm for recognizing two dimensional partial orders. This algorithm can also be used to determine whether a pair of two dimensional partial orders are isomorphic. Since two dimensional partial orders are transitive graphs (i.e., dense), the time complexity will be often linear in the size of the input. Nevertheless, it would be interesting to find an $O(n+e)$ algorithm to solve these problems.

The ideas used in this algorithm should allow the solution of two related problems: recognition of permutation graphs (undirected graphs which can be oriented to be two dimensional partial orders) and transitively orientable graphs (undirected graphs which can be oriented so that they become transitive dags). One of us has already made some progress in this direction [SP2].

We believe that the modular representation my become a useful way to describe various classes of graphs for certain purposes. For examples of the uses of modules and modular representations in scheduling algorithms see [LAW].

Another interesting question is whether we can update the two dimensional representation of a graph in $O(n)$ time when presented with an additional vertex and all edges incident to it. If this is feasible it might allow us to represent two dimensional graphs by two total orders in many problems, saving space and time to process certain types of queries about the graph represented.

8. Acknowledgements

The work of Jacobo Valdes was supported in part by the National Science Foundation under grant MCS-8203693.

9. References

[COL] C.J. Colbourn, "On Testing Isomorphism of Permutation Graphs", *Networks*, vol. 11, pp. 13-21 (1981).

[DM] B. Dushnik, E.W. Miller, "Partially Ordered Sets", *American Journal of Mathematics*, vol. 63, pp. 600-610 (1941).

[EL] S. Even, A. Lempel, A. Pnueli, "Transitive Orientation of Graphs and Identification of Permutation Graphs", *Canadian Journal of Mathematics*, vol. 23, pp. 160-175 (1971).

[LAW] E. L. Lawler, "Sequencing Jobs to Minimize Total Weighted Completion Time Subject to Precedence Constraints", *Annals of Discrete Mathematics*, vol. 2, pp. 75-90 (1978).

[LB] G. Luecker, K. Booth, "A Linear Time Algorithm for Deciding Interval Graph Isomorphism", *J. ACM*, vol. 26, pp. 183-195 (1979).

[SP] J. Spinrad, *Two Dimensional Partial Orders*, Ph.D. Thesis, Department of Electrical Engineering and Computer Sciences, Princeton University, (1982).

[SP2] J. Spinrad, "Transitive Orientation in $O(n^2)$ time", to appear in the *Proceedings of the 15th Annual ACM symposium on Theory of Computing*, Boston, Mass. (1983).

[VTL] J. Valdes, R. E. Tarjan, E. Lawler, "The Recognition of Series-Parallel Digraphs", *Proceedings of the 11th Annual ACM Symposium on Theory of Computing*, Atlanta, Georgia, pp. 1-12, (1979).

[YA] M. Yannakakis, "The Complexity of the Partial Order Dimension Problem", to appear.

ON THE SIMULATION OF MANY STORAGE HEADS BY A SINGLE ONE*

(Extended Abstract)

Paul M.B. Vitányi†

Mathematisch Centrum, Amsterdam

ABSTRACT

Each multitape Turing machine, of which the storage heads scan $O(\log n)$ *distinct squares in each interval of* n *steps, for all* $n \geq 1$*, can be real-time simulated by an oblivious one-head tape unit. There exist multitape Turing machines, e.g. the normal pushdown store, for which the fastest on-line simulation by an oblivious one-head tape unit requires* $\Omega(n\sqrt{n})$ *time.*

1. Introduction

It is generally the case, that additional access pointers in storage enhance computing power. In real-time, $(k+1)$-tape Turing machines are more powerful than k-tape Turing machines. Analogous results hold with all heads placed on the same tape [V1,PSS], head-to-head jumps added [PSS], and for multihead finite automata with and without head-to-head jumps [J,SV]. Recently it was shown that k-tape Turing machines require nonlinear time to on-line simulate $k+1$-tape Turing machines [P]. With respect to upper bounds there are essentially two facts known. Each multitape machine can be on-line simulated by a one-head tape unit in square time [HU], and also by a two-tape Turing machine in time‡ $O(n \log n)$ [HS]. Both of these simulations can be made oblivious [PF], retaining the same simulation time. In [PF] it was furthermore shown that each oblivious multitape Turing machine on-line simulating a single

* This work is registered at the Mathematical Centre.

† Author's Address: Mathematisch Centrum, Kruislaan 413, 1098 SJ Amsterdam, The Netherlands

‡ We use the customary notation, viz.:
$f(n) \in O(g(n))$ if there is a positive constant c such that $f(n) \leq c\, g(n)$ for all n.
$f(n) \in \Omega(g(n))$ if there is a positive constant c such that $f(n) \geq c\, g(n)$ for all n.
$f(n) \in \Theta(g(n))$ if $f(n) \in O(g(n)) \cap \Omega(g(n))$.
$f(n) \in o(g(n))$ if $f(n) \in O(g(n)) - \Omega(g(n))$.

pushdown store requires $\Omega(n \log n)$ time. Thus, for on-line simulation of multitape Turing machines by one-head tape units the fastest simulation time is somewhere in between a nonlinear lower bound and a square upper bound, while for on-line simulation by oblivious one-head tape units the lower bound is $n \log n$ and the upper bound n^2. We improve this situation in two ways. First, we show that for a restricted class of multitape Turing machines, viz. machines of which the storage heads scan $O(\log n)$ distinct squares in each interval of n steps, for all $n \leq 1$, each member can be real-time simulated by an oblivious one-head tape unit belonging to that class. Second, it is demonstrated that each oblivious one-head tape unit, on-line simulating a single pushdown store, requires $\Omega(n\sqrt{n})$ time.

Turing machines, simulation and oblivousness. We regard machines as *transducers*, that is, as abstract storage devices connected with input- and output terminals. Thus we consider the machine as hidden in a black box, and the presented simulation results concern the input/output behaviour of black boxes and are independent of input/output conventions or whether we want to recognize or to compute. By a k-tape Turing machine we mean an abstract storage device, consisting of a finite control connected with k single-head linear storage tapes, and an input- and an output terminal. A one-tape Turing machine is the same as a one-head tape unit. The transducers effect a transduction from input strings to output strings by producing the i-th output just before reading the $(i+1)$-th input command. A machine A *on-line simulates* a machine B in time $T(n)$ if, for all $n>0$, the input/output behaviour of B, during the first n steps, is exactly mimicked by A within the first $T(n)$ steps. That is, for each input sequence $i_1, i_2, \ldots, i_k, \cdots$, read from the input terminal, the output sequences written to the output terminal are the same for A and B, and if $t_1 \leq t_2 \leq \cdots \leq t_k \leq \cdots$ are the steps at which B reads or writes a symbol, from or to the terminals, then there are corresponding steps $t_1' \leq t_2' \leq \cdots \leq t_k' \leq \cdots$ at which A reads or writes the same symbols and $t_i' \leq T(t_i)$, for all $i \geq 1$. In the sequel we write *simulation* for *on-line simulation*. Simulation in time $T(n)=n$ is called *real-time* simulation; simulation in time $T(n) \in O(n)$ is called *linear time* simulation. A Turing machine is *oblivious* if the movements of the storage tape heads are fixed functions of time, independent of the particular inputs to the machines, see e.g. [PF]. There are many reasons why one may want to restrict attention to oblivous computations. For instance, oblivious Turing machine computations translate efficiently to combinational logic networks, while ordinary Turing machine computations do not. We mention two less often cited motives, of a more heuristic nature, for focussing attention on oblivious computations, of which the second one is pure conjecture. Suppose we can simulate some abstract storage device S in time $T(n)$ by an oblivious one-head tape unit M. Then we can also simulate k copies of S, say $S_1, S_2, \ldots, S_k$, interacting through a common finite control, by dividing M's tape into k tracks, modifying M's finite control, and letting the head on each track do the same job as it formerly did on the total tape. Thus, the resulting oblivious one-head tape unit M', with modified finite control and expanded tape alphabet, uses the same time and space as did M.

Lemma 1. *If we can simulate a pushdown store by an oblivous one-head tape unit in time $T(n)$ then we can simulate each multitape Turing machine by an oblivious one-head tape unit in time $T(n)$, using just the same space.*

Proof. Replace each tape of the multitape Turing machine by two pushdown stores and apply the preceding argument to multipushdown store machines. □ □

Conjecture. If we can simulate each multitape Turing machine by a one-head tape unit in time $T(n)$ then we can also simulate each multitape Turing machine by an oblivious one-head tape unit in time $T(n)$.

2. Uniform space and fast simulation of many heads by a single oblivious one

For on-line computations (viz. the transducer type of computations) it is, perhaps, unreasonable that the workspace accessed in any length input interval may be arbitrary large, for unbounded storage complexity, if the machine has been computing long enough previously. For example, if a real-time Turing machine M has storage complexity $\Theta(\log n)$ then in the 1-step interval, from the 2^n-th step through the 2^n+1-th step, the machine M can access $\Theta(n)$ storage squares. Thus, we propose a space complexity measure, independent from the origin of the time scale, and only depending on the size of the intervals of steps.

Definition. Let M be a multitape Turing machine, and let for any unbounded input sequence ω the interval of steps by M, executed in processing ω, from the $(m+1)$-th through $(m+i)$-th *step*, be denoted by $I_{m,i}^{\omega}$, $m \geq 0$ and $i \geq 1$. The *uniform space complexity* $U(n)$ of M is defined as

$$U(n) = \sup\{U_m^{\omega} \mid U_m^{\omega} \textit{ is the number of distinct squares, on all of } M\textit{'s storage tapes, visited by } M\textit{'s heads during } I_{m,n}^{\omega}, \textit{for } m \geq 0 \textit{ and } \omega \textit{ an unbounded input sequence}\}.$$

Thus, finite automata correspond to Turing machines with uniform space complexity $O(1)$. If the (ordinary) space complexity of some Turing machine is $S(n)$ and the time complexity $T(n)$, then its uniform space complexity $U(n) \in \Omega(S(T^{-1}(n))) \cap O(n)$. Recall that finite automata have the exceptional property that a storage facility consisting of a collection of k finite automata, interacting through a common finite control, can be replaced by a single finite automaton, without slowing down the computation, see e.g. [HU]. Below we show that additional tapes, or nonobliviousness, likewise do not increase the power of an (oblivious) one-head tape unit in uniform logarithmic space.

Lemma 2. *Each multitape Turing machine of uniform space complexity $O(\log n)$ can be real-time simulated by an oblivious one-head tape unit of also uniform space complexity $O(\log n)$.*

Proof Sketch. The proof uses a complicated tape manipulation technique developed in [V2], to real-time simulate multicounter machines by oblivious one-head tape units. Without going into details, an oblivious one-head tape unit M can be constructed such that, for each $i \geq 1$, the pair of squares, or rather square contents or *cells*, originally in positions i, $i+1$ is scanned at least once in each time interval of c^i

steps for some small constant c, say c is about 3. Moreover, the head recognizes such pairs when they are scanned (knows they are cells i, $i+1$ for some $i \geq 1$) and has always cells 1, 2 under scan. The tape unit M works by, in each step, interchangeing cells residing on the currently simultaneously scanned tapesquares. (M's fat head scans a few adjacent cells simultaneously.) In this process, the identity of the underlying squares is not important, the identity (index i above) of the cells, however, is fixed wherever they end up. The oblivious one-head tape unit M has uniform space complexity $\Theta(\log n)$. By Lemma 1 we only have to show that any pushdown store P of uniform space complexity $O(\log n)$ can be real time simulated by the described oblivious one-head tape unit. So, let P be a pushdown store which does not change its stack height by more than $O(\log i)$ elements in each interval of steps $I^{\omega}_{m,i}$, for all $m \geq 0$, $i \geq 2$ and any ω. In the simulating M each cell (square contents) can contain an ordered segment of P's stack consisting of 0, d, or $2d$ elements, and the first cell can contain an initial segment of P's stack of in between 0 and $2d$ elements. Each cell $i \geq 1$ strives for an occupancy of stack elements as follows. If it contains $2d$ elements when cells i, $i+1$ are scanned then the last d elements are shifted to cell $i+1$. If it contains 0 elements when cells i, $i+1$ are scanned, and cell $i+1$ contains d or $2d$ elements, then the first d elements are shifted from cell $i+1$ to cell i. Cell 1, being distinguished, shifts d elements out, if it contains $2d$ elements, and shifts d elements in, if it contains $d-1$ (or less) elements, to and from cell 2. According to the current input, elements are added/deleted from the segment in cell 1 in each step. Thus, a segment of d stack elements can be shifted from the 1-th cell to the i-th cell, or vice versa, in $\sum_{j=1}^{i-1} c^j < c^i$ $(c \geq 2)$ steps, and thus in c^i steps id elements can be pushed or popped. Starting with an empty stack, it can be proved that at all times $t \geq 0$, for any input,

(i) no cell contains more than $2d$ stack elements;

(ii) if any cell contains stack elements then cell 1 contains stack elements,

provided the stack height does not change more than id elements in I^{ω}_{m,c^i}, for all m, i, ω. Choosing d appropriately, which is possible since the stack height varies $O(\log i)$ elements in each interval $I^{\omega}_{m,i}$, for all m, i, ω, (i) and (ii) show that the arrangement can real-time implement a uniform $O(\log n)$ space pushdown store. □ □

The next question is which computations, or problems, are in uniform logarithmic space. [V2] shows that each multicounter computation is of this space complexity. Uniform log space is, however, more extensive. Recall that multicounter machines consist of a set of counters numbered say, 1,2, . . . , k, which can execute one-step arithmetic/boolean instructions as "add [subtract] 1 from counter i" and "test counter i for 0", $1 \leq i \leq k$. Several other one-step instructions can be synthesized, by using concealed auxiliary counters, such as tests for equality amongst counters (by maintaining all the differences on extra counters). Instructions for which it is known [FMR] that they cannot be so synthesized as one-step instructions are "set counter i to 0" or "set counter i to the value of counter j". Call multicounter machines with those one-step instructions added *augmented counter machines* [*ACMs*]. It can be proved [V3] that:

Lemma 3. *Each augmented counter machine can be real-time simulated by a uniform log space oblivious one-head tape unit.*

None the less, uniform log space computations are *not very* powerful if we impose time restrictions.

Lemma 4. *There are (ordinary) log space/real-time Turing machines such that the fastest uniform log space Turing machines simulating them use exponential time.*

Proof Sketch. Take as an example the on-line recognition of

$$L = \{\star w_1 \star w_2 \star \cdots \star w_{2^i} \star \cdots \mid w_j \text{ is a palindrome in } \{0,1\}^*, j \geq 1, \ \&$$

$$\& \ \# w_{2^i} = \# w_{2^i+1} = \cdots = \# w_{2^{i+1}-1} = 2(i+1), \ i \geq 0\ \}.$$

Recognition in real-time/ $\log n$ *space:* on one track of its single storage tape the recognizer maintains a binary count of the number of $\star$'s. During the update of the $\star$ count, it writes the first half of the current word $w_{current}$ on another track and, while proceeding back to the origin, compares it with the second half. *Recognition in uniform* $\log n$ *space:* to on-line check whether w_{2^i} is a palindrome, the machine must access $\Omega(i)$ tape squares. By definition it takes $\Omega(2^i)$ steps to do so. □ □

Obviously, any real-time multitape Turing machine computation can be simulated on a uniform $\log n$ space Turing machine in exponential time. Thus, by Lemma's 1-4:

Theorem 1. *(i). In real-time, multicounter machines are less powerful than uniform* $\log n$ *space Turing machines.*
(ii). In real-time, uniform $\log n$ *space multitape Turing machines are equally powerful as uniform* $\log n$ *space oblivious one-head tape units.*
(iii). There are $\log n$ *space/real-time one-tape Turing machines which cannot be simulated by uniform* $\log n$ *space multitape Turing machines in less than exponential time.*

The question to consider next is: 'what is the most extensive uniform space complexity class for which nonobliviousness and extra storage heads do not increase the computation power of the device under the real-time restriction?'. We can give an upper bound on the uniform space complexity allowing linear time simulation, of multitape Turing machines, by oblivious one-head tape units.

Theorem 2. *Each real-time multitape Turing machine, which can be linear time simulated by an oblivious one-head tape unit, has uniform space complexity* $o(n / \log n)$.

Proof Sketch. Similar to the overlap argument in [PF] that an oblivious Turing machine, simulating a single pushdown store, needs $\Omega(n \log n)$ time. The argument leads in fact to the more general trade-off:

$$\sum_{i=1}^{\log n} 2^{-i} U(2^i) \in O(T(n)/n),$$

with $U(n)$ the uniform space complexity of the simulated real-time machine and $T(n)$ the simulation time of the oblivious simulator. □

3. Improved lower bound on the time to simulate multitape Turing machines by oblivious one-head tape units

In view of Lemma 1, any lower bound on the simulation time of multitape Turing machines by oblivious one-head tape units also holds for the simulation of a single pushdown store by the same (and obviously, vice versa). The following Theorem improves the known lower bounds. The proof makes extensive use of *crossing sequence* arguments, as is to be expected. It depends on a fairly precise selection and interdependence of the involved constants of proportionality. The proofsketch below gives the intuition behind the proof.

Theorem 3. *Any oblivious one-head tape unit simulating a (typical) pushdown store requires* $\Omega(n\sqrt{n}\,)$ *time.*

Proof Sketch. Let M be the fastest oblivious one-head tape unit for simulating a typical pushdown store in, say, time $T(n)$. It is known that $T(n) \in \Omega(n \log n) \cap O(n^2)$. Let $I_{m,i}$ denote the interval of steps by machine M to process the (m+1)-th through $(m+i)$-th *input command.* (Do not confuse these intervals with the I-intervals of the previous section. The subscripts refer to the sequence of input commands, instead of the sequence of steps, and since M is oblivious a superscript referring to particular input sequences is unnecessary, and therefore suppressed. For simplicity we assume that in an oblivious machine the steps at which it reads or writes a symbol are the same for all input streams. However, it is not necessary to assume this subtility in order to derive the desired results.) Assume that M's tape is one-way infinite, and let $[0,o(n)]$ be some initial $o(n)$ length tape segment, let $[\Theta(n),\infty]$ be a final tapesegment, consisting of all of the tape but an initial $\Theta(n)$-length tape segment, and let $(o(n),\Theta(n))$ be the elusive segment in between. See the picture below.

The idea is to show that there is an integer m, $m \in \Theta(n)$, such that the storage head stays on the right tapesegment $[\Theta(n),\infty]$ during the interval of steps $I_{m,\sqrt{m}}$. Consequently, all information originally recorded on the initial tapesegment $[0,o(n)]$, must have been transported over the intervening tapesegment $(o(n),\Theta(n))$, in order to be accessed during the interval of steps $I_{m,\sqrt{m}}$. This then entails long crossing sequences associated with *each* square of $(o(n),\Theta(n))$, the sum of which yields the claimed lower bound on $T(n)$. Below we define three functions, viz. S, P and Q, from the cartesian product of the positive rationals and the natural numbers into the powerset of the natural numbers. Let

$$S(c,n) \overset{def}{=} \{j \mid 1 \leq j \leq n \textit{ and the tapesegment visited in } I_{j,1} \textit{ is contained in } [0,cn]\}.$$

With $[0,cn]$ we mean the initial tapesegment consisting of the first $\lceil cn \rceil$ squares. Similar statements are tacitly assumed in all cases hereafter where comparable issues crop up.

Claim 1. If $T(n) \in o(n^2)$ then $\#S(c,n) \in O(cn)$.

Proof Sketch. Assume $T(n) \in o(n^2)$ and $\#S(c,n) \in \Theta(n)$, that is, there is a constant $\delta > 0$ such that, for each $c > 0$, we have $\#S(c,n) \geqslant \delta n$ for all n. By a crossing sequence argument we can show that then $T(n) \in \Omega(n^2)$: contradiction. □ □

Let

$$P(c,n) \stackrel{def}{=} \{j \mid 1 \leqslant j \leqslant n \textit{ and the tapesegment visited in } I_{j,\sqrt{j}} \textit{ has at least length } cj\ \}.$$

Claim 2. If $T(n) \in o(n\sqrt{n})$ then $\#P(c,n) \in O(cn)$.

Proof Sketch. Assume $T(n) \in o(n\sqrt{n})$ and $\#P(c,n) \in \Theta(n)$, that is, there is a constant $\delta > 0$ such that, for each $c > 0$, we have $\#P(c,n) \geqslant \delta n$ for all n. Then there are $\Theta(n)$ values of j, $1 \leqslant j \leqslant n$, for which $T(j+\sqrt{j}) - T(j) \in \Omega(j)$, so it follows that $T(n) \geqslant \sum_{j=1}^{\Theta(n)} \Omega(\sqrt{j}) \in \Omega(n\sqrt{n})$: contradiction. □ □

Assume $T(n) \in o(n\sqrt{n})$. Then from Claims 1 and 2 it follows that, for

$$Q(c,n) \stackrel{def}{=} \{j \mid 1 \leqslant j \leqslant n \textit{ and the tapesegment visited in } I_{j,\sqrt{j}} \textit{ is contained in } [cn,\infty]\ \},$$

we have

$$Q(c,n) \supseteq \{1,2,\ldots,n\} - S(2c,n) - P(c,n).$$

Therefore, $\#Q(c,n) \geqslant n - \epsilon n$, for arbitrary small $\epsilon > 0$, depending on the choice of c. Hence, for $m(c,n) \stackrel{def}{=} \max(Q(c,n))$ we can, for each $\epsilon > 0$, choose a $\delta > 0$ such that $m(\delta,n) \geqslant n - \epsilon n$. Since $T(n) \in o(n\sqrt{n})$, we have $T(\sqrt{n}) \in o(n^{3/4})$. Considering the input ensemble

$$\{push\ 0, push\ 1\}^{\sqrt{n}} \{skip\}^{m(\delta,n)-\sqrt{n}} \{pop\}^{\sqrt{n}} ,$$

we must pop an arbitrary sequence of 0's and 1's of length $\sqrt{n}$, originally recorded on the initial $o(n)$ length tapesegment $[0, o(n)]$, completely, while never leaving the tapesegment $[\Theta(n),\infty]$, see picture. Again using a crossing sequence argument, we obtain the contradictory $T(n) \in \Omega(n\sqrt{n})$, and hence the Theorem. □

REFERENCES

[A] Aanderaa, S.O., [1974], On k-tape versus $(k+1)$-tape real-time computation, SIAM-AMS Proceedings, Vol. 7 (*Complexity of Computation*), 75-96.

[FMR] Fischer, P.C., A.R. Meyer & A.L. Rosenberg, [1968], Counter machines and counter languages, *Math. Systems Theory*, **2**, 265-283.

[HS] Hennie, F.C. & R.E. Stearns, [1966], Two-tape simulation of multitape Turing machines, *J. ACM*, **13** , 533-546.

[HU] Hopcroft, J.E. & J.D. Ullman, [1969], *Formal languages and their relations to automata*, Addison-Wesley.

[J] Janiga, L., [1979], Real-time computations of two-way multihead finite automata, Fundamentals of Computation Theory (FCT '79), L. Budach ed., Akademie Verlag, Berlin, DDR, 1979, 214-218.

[P] Paul, W., [1982], On-line simulation of $k+1$ tapes by k tapes requires nonlinear time, 23rd IEEE Symp. on Foundations of Computer Science, 53-56.

[PSS] Paul, W., J. Seiferas & J. Simon, [1980], An information-theoretic approach to time bounds for on-line computation, 12th ACM Symp. on Theory of Computing, 357-367.

[PF] Pippenger, N. & M.J. Fischer, [1979], Relations among complexity measures, *J. ACM*, **26** , 361-384.

[SV] Savitch, W.J. & P.M.B. Vitányi, [1982], On the power of real-time two-way multihead finite automata with jumps. Tech. Rept. CS-056, Dept. EECS, Univ. of California, San Diego.

[V1] Vitányi, P.M.B., [1980], On the power of real-time Turing machines under varying specifications, 7th Coll. on Automata, Languages and Programming (ICALP '80), *Lecture Notes in Computer Science*, **85** , Springer Verlag, Berlin, 658-671.

[V2] Vitányi, P.M.B., [1982], Real-time simulation of multicounters by oblivious one-tape Turing machines, 14th ACM Symp. on Theory of Computing, 27-36.

[V3] Vitányi, P.M.B., [1983], An optimal simulation of counter machines: the ACM case. Tech. Rept. IW 225, Mathematisch Centrum, Amsterdam, March 1983.

SYNCHRONISATION TREES

by

Glynn Winskel

Department of Computer Science

Carnegie-Mellon University

Pittsburgh, Pennsylvania 15213

0. Introduction.

We present a collection of categories of labelled trees useful in giving denotational semantics to parallel programming languages such as Milner's "Calculus of communicating Systems" , CCS [M1], his synchronous CCS, called SCCS [M2], and languages derived from Hoare's CSP as presented in [HBR] and [B]. Enough results are given to provide denotational semantics to any of the languages in [M1, M2, HBR] though at the rather basic level of labelled trees—called synchronisation trees in [M1].

Synchronisation trees are a basic interleaving model of parallel computation in which processes communicate by mutual synchronisation. A synchronisation tree is a tree in which the nodes represent states and the arcs represent event occurrences, labelled to show how they synchronise with events in the environment. Tree semantics arise naturally once concurrency is simulated by nondeterministic interleaving and for this reason synchronisation-tree semantics underlie much of the work on the semantics of synchronising processes. For example in [M1] it is made clear how every equivalence on CCS programs presented there factors through a synchronisation-tree semantics while [B] shows a similar result for the failure-set semantics in [HBR].

In order to cover a wide range of synchronisation disciplines between synchronising processes we express synchronisation disciplines between processes as synchronisation algebras. They are algebras on sets of labels which specify how pairs of labelled events combine to form a synchronisation event and what labels such combinations carry. They also specify what labelled events can occur asynchronously. The parallel composition is derived from a product in a category of trees; essentially one restricts the product of trees to those synchronised events allowed by the synchronisation algebra. By varying the synchronisation algebra we obtain many forms of parallel composition in the literature. Other useful operations are defined on synchronisation trees. They are all continuous with respect to a natural complete partial order of trees and so can be used to give denotations to processes defined recursively in terms of them by using least-fixed points—the standard tool of Scott-Strachey semantics.

Many of the results below follow from the report [W2], which dealt with the broader framework of event structures [NPW,W,W1]. However more direct proofs will also be given in the full version of this paper to appear in the journal "Theoretical Computer Science". There a wider range of issues will be addressed.

1. A category of trees.

Assume in any finite history a process can perform a sequence of events. Because a process need not be deterministic, such a sequence need not be extended in a unique way, but rather form a tree of sequences.

1.1 Definition. A *tree* is subset $T \subseteq A^*$ of finite sequences of some set A which satisfies

(i) $<>\in T$ and,

(ii) $< a_0, a_1, \ldots a_n, \ldots > \in T \Rightarrow < a_0, a_1, \ldots a_n > \in T$.

1.2 Notation. Let T be a tree with $T \subseteq A^*$. We say T *is over* A iff every element of A is in some sequence of T. We shall often call elements of A *events.*

The following convention is very useful to avoid treating the null sequence $<>$ as a special case. Often we shall write a typical sequence as $< a_0, a_1, \ldots, a_{n-1} >$ where n is an integer representing the length of the sequence. We shall allow the length n to be 0 when by convention we agree that the above sequence represents $<>$.

Let t be a sequence $< a_0, a_1, \ldots, a_{n-1} >$ and b some element. Write

$$bt = < b, a_0, a_1, \ldots, a_{n-1} > \quad \text{and} \quad tb = < a_0, a_1, \ldots, a_{n-1}, b > .$$

Let T be a tree. Let b be an element. By bT we mean the tree

$$bT = \{ <> \} \cup \{ bt \mid t \in T \}.$$

Let T be a tree. For $t, t' \in T$ write

$$t \longrightarrow_T t' \Leftrightarrow \exists a. t' = ta.$$

Clearly the elements T correspond to the nodes of a tree T while arcs correspond to pairs (t, t') where $t \longrightarrow_T t'$. The nodes are thought of as states of a process and the arcs as occurrences of events. A *morphism* from a tree S to a tree T shows the way in which the occurrence of an event of the process S implies the synchronised occurrence of an event in the process T. Formally it is a map on nodes which preserves the root-node and either preserves or collapses arcs. A special kind of morphism are the *synchronous morphisms* which always preserve arcs.

1.3 Definition. A *morphism* of trees from S to T is a map $f : S \to T$ such that

(i) $f(<>) = <>$ and,
(ii) $s \longrightarrow_S s' \Rightarrow f(s) = f(s')$ or $f(s) \longrightarrow_T f(s')$.

A *synchronous morphism* of trees from S to T is a map $f : S \to T$ such that

(i) $f(<>) = <>$ and,
(ii) $s \longrightarrow_S s' \Rightarrow f(s) \longrightarrow_T f(s')$.

Let $f : S \to T$ be a morphism of trees. Assume $s \longrightarrow_S s'$ in S, representing the occurrence of an event a of S so that $s' = sa$. If $f(s) \longrightarrow_T f(s')$ there is an event b such that $f(s') = f(s)b$. Intuitively the occurrence of the event a implies the occurrence of the event b, synchronised with that of a. If instead $f(s) = f(s')$ then the occurrence of a is not synchronised with an event occurrence in T. The latter possibility is disallowed for synchronous morphisms. We shall see that morphisms and synchronous morphisms give rise to a product and synchronous product of trees. Events of the products will essentially be pairs of events of the two trees, representing events of synchronisation between two processes. Their occurrence will project via tree morphisms to occurrences of component events in the constituent processes.

1.4 Proposition. *Trees with tree morphisms form a category with composition and identities those usual for functions. Similarly trees with synchronous morphisms form a subcategory.*

1.5 Definition. Let **Tr** be the category of trees with tree morphisms. Let $\mathbf{Tr}_{syn}$ be the subcategory of trees with synchronous morphisms.

Remark. The above categories are equivalent but not equal to the categories of the same name in [W1,W2].

2. Categorical constructions on trees..

Some major categorical constructions on **Tr** and $\mathbf{Tr}_{syn}$ are presented. The basic category theory used can be found in [AM] or [Mac].

2.1 Definition. (Coproducts in Tr and $\mathbf{Tr}_{syn}$) Let $\{ T_i \mid i \in I \}$ be an indexed set of trees. Define their coproduct by

$$\sum_{i \in I} T_i = \bigcup_{i \in I} \{ < (i, a_0), \ldots, (i, a_{n-1}) > \mid < a_0, \ldots, a_{n-1} > \in T_i \}.$$

Define the obvious injections $in_i : T_i \to \sum_{i \in I} T_i$ by $in_i(< a_0, \ldots, a_{n-1} >) = < (i, a_0), \ldots, (i, a_{n-1}) >$ for $i \in I$. We write $T_0 + T_1$ for the coproduct of the $\{0, 1\}$-indexed trees T_0, T_1.

The coproduct construction just "glues" trees together at their roots.

2.2 Theorem. *The construction $\sum_{i \in I} T_i$, in_i for $i \in I$, above forms a coproduct of $\{ T_i \mid i \in I \}$ in the categories* **Tr** *and* $\mathbf{Tr}_{syn}$.

It is easier to define the product of trees in the category $\mathbf{Tr}_{syn}$ than the product in **Tr** . We call the product in $\mathbf{Tr}_{syn}$ the *synchronous* product. The synchronous product of two trees basically "zips" their sequences together.

2.3 Definition. (Synchronous product in the category $\mathbf{Tr}_{syn}$) Let S and T be trees. Define their synchronous product by

$$S \bigotimes T = \{ < (a_0, b_0), (a_1, b_1), \ldots, (a_{n-1}, b_{n-1}) > \mid < a_0, a_1, \ldots, a_{n-1} > \in S \ \& < b_0, b_1, \ldots, b_{n-1} > \in T \}.$$

Define projections $\pi_0 : S \otimes T \to S$ and $\pi_1 : S \otimes T \to T$ by

$$\pi_0 :< (a_0, b_0), \ldots, (a_{n-1}, b_{n-1}) > \mapsto < a_0, \ldots, a_{n-1} >,$$
$$\pi_1 :< (a_0, b_0), \ldots, (a_{n-1}, b_{n-1}) > \mapsto < b_0, \ldots, b_{n-1} > .$$

2.4 Theorem. *The construction $S \otimes T, \pi_0, \pi_1$ above is a product of S and T in the category* $\mathbf{Tr}_{syn}$.

2.5 Example.

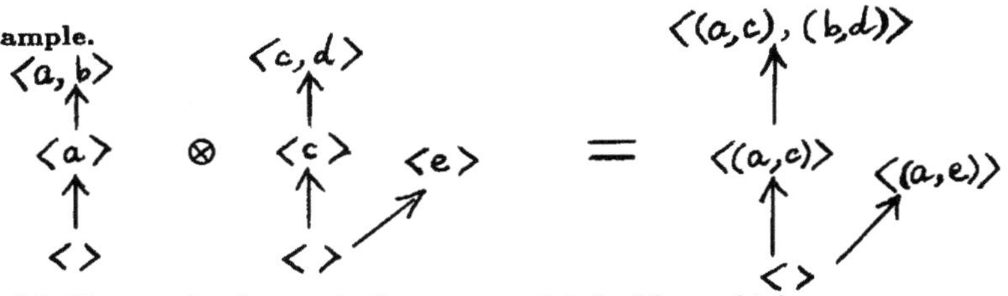

Or, labelling arcs by the events they are associated with we obtain:

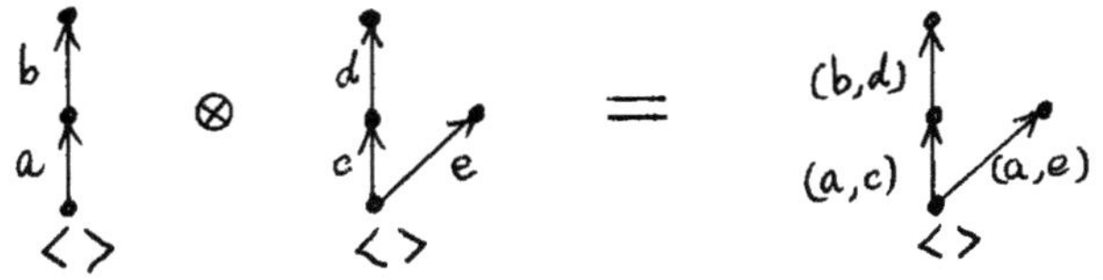

For example $\pi_0(< (a, c), (b, d) >) = < a, b >$ and $\pi_1(< (a, c), (b, d) >) = < c, d >$. Notice how projections "unzip" sequences of pairs in the synchronous product.

Clearly we have the following synchronous product

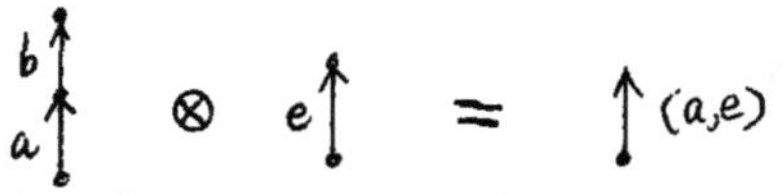

so projections need not be onto—consider the projection $\pi_0 :< (a,e) >\mapsto< a >$.

To give an explicit construction of a product in the category **Tr** we use partial functions. Represent undefined by the symbol $*$ and regard a partial function from A to B as a total function from A to $B \cup \{*\}$. Write a partial function, represented by $\theta : A \to B \cup \{*\}$, as $\theta : A \to_* B$—we shall always assume $* \notin B$ for such functions. Compose partial functions as follows: Let $\theta : A \to_* B$ and $\phi : B \to_* C$. Define their composition $\phi\theta : A \to_* C$ to be

$$\phi\theta(a) = \begin{cases} \phi(\theta(a)) & \text{if } \theta(a) \neq *, \\ * & \text{otherwise.} \end{cases}$$

Denote by $\mathbf{Set}_*$ the category of sets (not containing $*$) with partial functions as morphisms. Now $\mathbf{Set}_*$ itself has a useful product. The product in $\mathbf{Set}_*$ of two sets A and B is given by

$$A \times_* B = \{(a,*) \mid a \in A\} \cup \{(a,b) \mid a \in A \;\&\; b \in B\} \cup \{(*,b) \mid b \in B\}$$

with projections $\rho_0 : A \times_* B \to A$ and $\rho : A \times_* B \to B$ given by $\rho_i(x_0, x_1) = x_i$ for $i = 0, 1$.

Now we define the product in **Tr** .

2.6 Definition. (Product in the category Tr) Let S and T be trees. Assume S is over A and T is over B. Define $S \times T$ to consist of sequences over $A \times_* B$ which project via $\rho_0 : A \times_* B \to_* A$ and $\rho_1 : A \times_* B \to_* B$ to sequences in S and T as follows:

$$< c_0, \ldots, c_n > \in S \times T \Leftrightarrow c_0, \ldots, c_n \in A \times_* B \;\&\; \pi_0(< c_0, \ldots, c_n >) \in S$$
$$\& \; \pi_1(< c_0, \ldots, c_n >) \in T,$$

where, for $i = 0, 1$, we take

$$\pi_i(<>) = <>$$
$$\text{and} \quad \pi_i(< c_0, c_1, \ldots, c_{n-1} >) = \begin{cases} \rho_i(c_0)\pi_i(< c_1 \ldots, c_{n-1} >) & \text{if } \rho_i(c_0) \neq * \\ \pi_i(< c_1, \ldots, c_{n-1} >) & \text{otherwise.} \end{cases}$$

2.7 Theorem. *The construction $S \times T, \pi_0, \pi_1$ above is a product in the category* **Tr** .

2.8 Example. We show the product of two simple trees. For neatness we label arcs by their associated events.

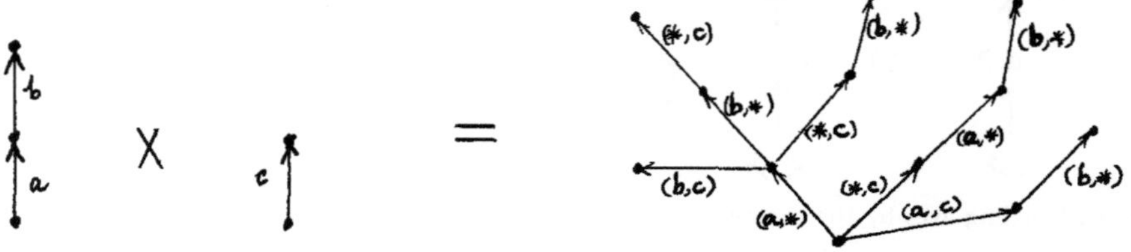

The projections π_0, π_1 act for example so that $\pi_0 :< (*,c), (a,*), (b,*) >\mapsto< a, b >$ and $\pi_1 :< (*,c), (a,*), (b,*) >\mapsto< c >$. Notice how the projections "unzip" sequences of pairs of events with $*$. By introducing $*$ we allow the possibility of asynchrony; events in the product of two trees are not made to occur in step.

In the categories **Tr** and $\mathbf{Tr}_{syn}$ there are pleasing relations between product and coproduct. This result indicates the relation between the parallel compositions of synchronisation trees (in *e.g.*[M1, B]) and the product of trees.

2.9 Proposition. *Let S and T be trees. Then*

$$S = \bigcup_{a\in A} aS_a \cong \sum_{a\in A} aS_a \quad \text{and} \quad T = \bigcup_{b\in B} bT_b \cong \sum_{b\in B} bT_b$$

for some trees A and B and trees S_a and T_b indexed by $a \in A$ and $b \in B$ respectively. We have the following characterisation of the product of S and T:

$$S \times T = \bigcup_{a\in A} (a,*)S_a \times T \cup \bigcup_{a\in A, b\in B} (a,b)S_a \times T_b \cup \bigcup_{b\in B} (*,b)S \times T_b$$
$$\cong \sum_{a\in A} (a,*)S_a \times T + \sum_{a\in A, b\in B} (a,b)S_a \times T_b + \sum_{b\in B} (*,b)S \times T_b;$$

and the following characterisation of their synchronous product:

$$S \bigotimes T = \bigcup_{a\in A, b\in B} (a,b)S_a \bigotimes T_b \cong \sum_{a\in A, b\in B} (a,b)S_a \bigotimes T_b.$$

Parallel compositions will be defined as some kind of restriction of the product. In fact the parallel composition of synchronisation trees appropriate to Milner's synchronous calculi will be a restriction of of the synchronous product $\bigotimes$. We define the operation of restriction in the next section.

3. Complete partial orders of trees.

We consider two natural complete partial orderings on trees. One is based on the idea of restricting a tree to a subset of events—an operation natural in itself—and the other is just inclusion of trees. Our operations on trees will be continuous with respect to both orderings so we shall be able to define trees recursively following now standard lines—see *e.g.*[S]—by taking least fixed-points in either of the two cpo's.

3.1 Definition. (Restriction) Let T be a tree over a set A. Let B. Define the *restriction* of T to B, written $T\lceil B$, by

$$t \in T\lceil B \Leftrightarrow t \in T \;\&\; (\forall b_0, \ldots, b_n . t = <b_0, \ldots, b_{n-1}> \Rightarrow \forall i < n . b_i \in B).$$

In other words the restriction of a tree to a subset of events is just the subtree consisting of sequences in T for which all elements are in B. Restriction induces a partial order on trees; one tree is below another if it is a restriction of the other. This ordering makes a complete partial order (c.p.o.) of trees, apart from the fact that trees form a class and not a set. Of course there is another natural c.p.o. of trees induced by simple inclusion. All the above operations on trees are continuous with respect to the two c.p.o. structures.

3.2 Definition. Let S and T be trees over A and B respectively. Define

$$S \leq T \Leftrightarrow A \subseteq B \;\&\; S = T\lceil A.$$

3.3 Proposition. *(i) The null tree $\{<>\}$ is the $\leq$-least tree i.e.for all trees T, $\{<>\} \leq T$. Let $T_0 \leq T_1 \cdots T_n \leq \cdots$ be an ω-chain of trees. Then it has a least upper bound $\bigcup_{n\in\omega} T_n$.*

(ii) The null tree $\{<>\}$ is the $\subseteq$-least tree i.e.for all trees T, $\{<>\} \subseteq T$. Let $T_0 \subseteq T_1 \cdots T_n \subseteq \cdots$ be an ω-chain of trees. Then it has a least upper bound $\bigcup_{n\in\omega} T_n$.

3.4 Definition. Say a unary operation operation *op* on trees is $\leq$-(respectively $\subseteq$-) *continuous* iff it preserves least upper bounds of ω-chains of trees *i.e.*if $T_0 \leq T_1 \cdots T_n \leq \cdots$ (respectively $T_0 \subseteq T_1 \cdots T_n \subseteq \cdots$) is an ω-chain of trees then $op(\bigcup_{n\in\omega} T_n) = \bigcup_{n\in\omega} op(T_n)$. If *op* is an n-ary operation on trees, say it is $\leq$-(respectively $\subseteq$-) *continuous* iff it is continuous in each argument separately.

3.5 Proposition. *Each operation* $T \mapsto bT, T \mapsto T\lceil B, +, \otimes, \times$ *for an arbitrary element* b *and set* B *is* $\leq$*-continuous and* $\subseteq$*-continuous.*

Consequently each of the above operations can be used in the recursive definition of trees.

4. Synchronisation algebras.

We shall label events of processes to specify how they interact with the environment. We shall obtain trees in which the arcs are labelled just like the synchronisation trees of CCS in [M1]. However our approach is more abstract. We shall label trees by elements of a *synchronisation algebra* which shows how labelled events synchronise with labelled events in the environment. Associated with any particular sychronisation algebra is a particular parallel composition of synchronisation trees. So, by specialising to particular synchronisation algebras we obtain Milner's parallel composition of synchronisation trees [M1], the parallel composition that underlies his synchronous calculi [M2], and the parallel compositions defined in [B] which underlie the parallel compositions on failure sets given in [HBR].

The intuitions behind synchronisation algebras are given in [W1,W2]. To recap, a synchronisation algebra is a binary, commutative, associative operation $\bullet$ on a set of labels which always includes two distinguished elements $*$ and 0. The binary operation $\bullet$ says how labelled events combine to form synchronisation events and what labels such combinations carry. No real events are ever labelled by $*$ or 0. However their introduction allows us to specify the way labelled events synchronise without recourse to partial operations on labels. These two forms of undefined should not be confused with another "undefined" $\perp$ used in the theory of domains.

The constant 0 is used to specify when sychronisations are disallowed. If two events labelled λ and λ' are not supposed to synchronise then their composition $\lambda \bullet \lambda'$ is 0. For this reason 0 does indeed behave like a zero with respect to the "multiplication" $\bullet$.

We have already seen the constant $*$ in the definition of product. Recall the partial functions ρ_0, ρ_1 which projected from the events in the product to events in one of the components. An event $(e_0, *)$ in the product $S \times T$ of trees S and T projected down to the event e_0 in S and the undefined "event" $* = \rho_1((e_0, *))$ in T. This meant the event e_0 of S occurred asynchronously, unsynchronised with any event of T. In a synchronisation algebra, the constant $*$ is used to specify when a labelled event can or cannot occur asynchronously. An event labelled λ can occur asynchronously iff $\lambda \bullet *$ is not 0. We insist that the only divisor of $*$ is $*$ itself, essentially because we do not want a synchronisation event to disappear.

4.1 Definition. A *synchronisation algebra* (S.A.) is an algebra $(L, \bullet, *, 0)$ where L is a set of *labels* so $L \setminus \{*, 0\} \neq 0$ and $\bullet$ is a binary commutative associative operation on L which satisfies

(i) $\forall \lambda \in L. \lambda \bullet 0 = 0$ and

(ii) $* \bullet * = *$ and $\forall \lambda, \lambda' \in L. \lambda \bullet \lambda' = * \Rightarrow \lambda = *$.

(It follows that $*$ and 0 are distinct.)

Synchronisation algebras have an obvious divisor relation which intuitively says when one labelled event can be a component of a synchronisation event.

3.4 Definition. Say a unary operation operation *op* on trees is $\leq$-(respectively $\subseteq$-) *continuous* iff it preserves least upper bounds of ω-chains of trees *i.e.*if $T_0 \leq T_1 \cdots T_n \leq \cdots$ (respectively $T_0 \subseteq T_1 \cdots T_n \subseteq \cdots$) is an ω-chain of trees then $op(\bigcup_{n\in\omega} T_n) = \bigcup_{n\in\omega} op(T_n)$. If *op* is an n-ary operation on trees, say it is $\leq$-(respectively $\subseteq$-) *continuous* iff it is continuous in each argument separately.

3.5 Proposition. *Each operation $T \mapsto bT, T \mapsto T[B, +, \otimes, \times$ for an arbitrary element b and set B is $\leq$-continuous and $\subseteq$-continuous.*

Consequently each of the above operations can be used in the recursive definition of trees.

4. Synchronisation algebras.

We shall label events of processes to specify how they interact with the environment. We shall obtain trees in which the arcs are labelled just like the synchronisation trees of CCS in [M1]. However our approach is more abstract. We shall label trees by elements of a *synchronisation algebra* which shows how labelled events synchronise with labelled events in the environment. Associated with any particular sychronisation algebra is a particular parallel composition of synchronisation trees. So, by specialising to particular synchronisation algebras we obtain Milner's parallel composition of synchronisation trees [M1], the parallel composition that underlies his synchronous calculi [M2], and the parallel compositions defined in [B] which underlie the parallel compositions on failure sets given in [HBR].

The intuitions behind synchronisation algebras are given in [W1,W2]. To recap, a synchronisation algebra is a binary, commutative, associative operation $\bullet$ on a set of labels which always includes two distinguished elements $*$ and 0. The binary operation $\bullet$ says how labelled events combine to form synchronisation events and what labels such combinations carry. No real events are ever labelled by $*$ or 0. However their introduction allows us to specify the way labelled events synchronise without recourse to partial operations on labels. These two forms of undefined should not be confused with another "undefined" $\perp$ used in the theory of domains.

The constant 0 is used to specify when sychronisations are disallowed. If two events labelled λ and λ' are not supposed to synchronise then their composition $\lambda \bullet \lambda'$ is 0. For this reason 0 does indeed behave like a zero with respect to the "multiplication" $\bullet$.

We have already seen the constant $*$ in the definition of product. Recall the partial functions ρ_0, ρ_1 which projected from the events in the product to events in one of the components. An event $(e_0, *)$ in the product $S \times T$ of trees S and T projected down to the event e_0 in S and the undefined "event" $* = \rho_1((e_0, *))$ in T. This meant the event e_0 of S occurred asynchronously, unsynchronised with any event of T. In a synchronisation algebra, the constant $*$ is used to specify when a labelled event can or cannot occur asynchronously. An event labelled λ can occur asynchronously iff $\lambda \bullet *$ is not 0. We insist that the only divisor of $*$ is $*$ itself, essentially because we do not want a synchronisation event to disappear.

4.1 Definition. A *synchronisation algebra* (S.A.) is an algebra $(L, \bullet, *, 0)$ where L is a set of *labels* so $L \setminus \{*, 0\} \neq 0$ and $\bullet$ is a binary commutative associative operation on L which satisfies

(i) $\forall \lambda \in L.\, \lambda \bullet 0 = 0$ and

(ii) $* \bullet * = *$ and $\forall \lambda, \lambda' \in L.\, \lambda \bullet \lambda' = * \Rightarrow \lambda = *$.

(It follows that $*$ and 0 are distinct.)

Synchronisation algebras have an obvious divisor relation which intuitively says when one labelled event can be a component of a synchronisation event.

4.2 Definition. Let $(L, \bullet, *, 0)$ be an S.A.. For $\lambda, \lambda' \in L$ define

$$\lambda \; \textit{div} \; \lambda' \Leftrightarrow \lambda = \lambda' \text{ or } \exists \mu \in L. \lambda \bullet \mu = \lambda'.$$

When λ *div* λ' we say "λ divides λ'".

We might wish to specify that no event can occur asynchronously. An event will be labelled by a non-$*$, non-0 label so this can be specified by ensuring the composition of such labels with $*$ always gives 0. Milner's synchronous calculi [M2] fit into this scheme, as we shall see later in proposition 6.14.

4.3 Definition. Let $(L, \bullet, *, 0)$ be an S.A.. We say L is *synchronous* when it satisfies the law

$$\forall \lambda \in L \setminus \{*\}. \lambda \bullet * = 0.$$

As examples and for future reference we now present some synchronisation algebras. We present the algebras in the form of multiplication tables. In fact the synchronisation algebras correspond to the parallel composition of CCS and the two forms of parallel composition in [HBR, B]. A justification of these facts appears later. For the moment though, the reader can probably see what each synchronisation algebra is saying so we shall try to give the intuition. The tie-up with Milner's monoids and groups of actions for his synchronous calculi will be made later.

4.4 Example. (The synchronisation algebra for CCS [M1]) In CCS events are labelled by $\alpha, \beta, \cdots$ or by their complementary labels $\overline{\alpha}, \overline{\beta}, \cdots$ or by the label τ. The idea is that only two events bearing complementary labels may synchronise to form a synchronisation event labelled by τ. Events labelled by τ cannot synchronise further. All labelled events may occur asynchronously. Hence the synchronisation algebra for CCS takes the following form. We call the algebra L_1.

$\bullet$	$*$	α	$\overline{\alpha}$	β	$\overline{\beta}$	$\cdots$	τ	0
α	α	0	τ	0	0	$\cdots$	0	0
$\overline{\alpha}$	$\overline{\alpha}$	τ	0	0	0	$\cdots$	0	0
β	β	0	0	τ	0	$\cdots$	0	0
.	.	.	.	.	.	$\cdots$	.	.

4.5 Example. (The synchronisation algebra for $\|$ in [HBR, B]) In [HBR] and [B] events are labelled by $\alpha, \beta, \cdots$ or τ. For the parallel composition $\|$ in [HBR, B] events must "synchronise on" $\alpha, \beta, \cdots$. In other words non-τ-labelled events cannot occur asynchronously. Rather, an α-labelled event in one component of a parallel composition must synchronise with an α-labelled event from the other component in order to occur; the two events must synchronise to form a synchronisation event again labelled by α. The S.A. for this parallel composition takes the following form. We call the algebra L_2.

$\bullet$	$*$	α	β	$\cdots$	τ	0
$*$	$*$	0	0	$\cdots$	τ	0
α	0	α	0	$\cdots$	0	0
β	0	0	β	$\cdots$	0	0
.	.	.	.	$\cdots$	.	.

4.6 Example. (The synchronisation algebra for $|||$ in [HBR, B]) The parallel composition $|||$ in [HBR] and [B] is called the "interleaving" operation in [HBR, B]. The reason is that no synchronisations are allowed, but every event can occur asynchronously, so in the framework of [HBR, B] where processes are coerced so they perform only one event at a time the parallel composition $|||$ interleaves the sequences of events of the two component processes. Events are labelled exactly as they are for L_2 but the

4.2 Definition. Let $(L, \bullet, *, 0)$ be an S.A.. For $\lambda, \lambda' \in L$ define

$$\lambda \; div \; \lambda' \Leftrightarrow \lambda = \lambda' \text{ or } \exists \mu \in L. \lambda \bullet \mu = \lambda'.$$

When $\lambda \; div \; \lambda'$ we say "λ divides λ'".

We might wish to specify that no event can occur asynchronously. An event will be labelled by a non–$*$, non–0 label so this can be specified by ensuring the composition of such labels with $*$ always gives 0. Milner's synchronous calculi [M2] fit into this scheme, as we shall see later in proposition 6.14.

4.3 Definition. Let $(L, \bullet, *, 0)$ be an S.A.. We say L is *synchronous* when it satisfies the law

$$\forall \lambda \in L \setminus \{*\}. \lambda \bullet * = 0.$$

As examples and for future reference we now present some synchronisation algebras. We present the algebras in the form of multiplication tables. In fact the synchronisation algebras correspond to the parallel composition of CCS and the two forms of parallel composition in [HBR, B]. A justification of these facts appears later. For the moment though, the reader can probably see what each synchronisation algebra is saying so we shall try to give the intuition. The tie–up with Milner's monoids and groups of actions for his synchronous calculi will be made later.

4.4 Example. (The synchronisation algebra for CCS [M1]) In CCS events are labelled by $\alpha, \beta, \cdots$ or by their complementary labels $\overline{\alpha}, \overline{\beta}, \cdots$ or by the label τ. The idea is that only two events bearing complementary labels may synchronise to form a synchronisation event labelled by τ. Events labelled by τ cannot synchronise further. All labelled events may occur asynchronously. Hence the synchronisation algebra for CCS takes the following form. We call the algebra L_1.

$\bullet$	$*$	α	$\overline{\alpha}$	β	$\overline{\beta}$	$\cdots$	τ	0
α	α	0	τ	0	0	$\cdots$	0	0
$\overline{\alpha}$	$\overline{\alpha}$	τ	0	0	0	$\cdots$	0	0
β	β	0	0	τ	0	$\cdots$	0	0
.	.	.	.	.	.	$\cdots$	.	.

4.5 Example. (The synchronisation algebra for || in [HBR, B]) In [HBR] and [B] events are labelled by $\alpha, \beta, \cdots$ or τ. For the parallel composition || in [HBR, B] events must "synchronise on" $\alpha, \beta, \cdots$. In other words non–τ–labelled events cannot occur asynchronously. Rather, an α–labelled event in one component of a parallel composition must synchronise with an α–labelled event from the other component in order to occur; the two events must synchronise to form a synchronisation event again labelled by α. The S.A. for this parallel composition takes the following form. We call the algebra L_2.

$\bullet$	$*$	α	β	$\cdots$	τ	0
$*$	$*$	0	0	$\cdots$	τ	0
α	0	α	0	$\cdots$	0	0
β	0	0	β	$\cdots$	0	0
.	.	.	.	$\cdots$	.	.

4.6 Example. (The synchronisation algebra for ||| in [HBR, B]) The parallel composition ||| in [HBR] and [B] is called the "interleaving" operation in [HBR, B]. The reason is that no synchronisations are allowed, but every event can occur asynchronously, so in the framework of [HBR, B] where processes are coerced so they perform only one event at a time the parallel composition ||| interleaves the sequences of events of the two component processes. Events are labelled exactly as they are for L_2 but the synchronisation algebra takes a different form, shown below. We call this algebra L_3.

$\bullet$	$*$	α	β	$\cdots$	τ	0
$*$	$*$	α	β	$\cdots$	τ	0
α	α	0	0	$\cdots$	0	0
β	β	0	0	$\cdots$	0	0
.	.	.	.	$\cdots$	.	.

5. Synchronisation trees.

A synchronisation tree is a tree with arcs labelled by elements of synchronisation algebra. It is convenient to label arcs via the underlying events from which the tree is built.

5.1 Definition. Let L be a synchronisation algebra. An *L–synchronisation tree* is a pair (T, l) where T is a tree over A and $l : A \to L \setminus \{*, 0\}$.

5.2 Notation. Let (T, l) be an L–synchronisation tree. Write $t \xrightarrow{\lambda} t'$ when $t \to t'$ and $l(a) = \lambda$ for the unique a such that $t' = ta$.

Frequently we shall omit the prefix "L–" when discussing synchronisation trees. When it is important the appropriate synchronisation algebra should be clear from the context.

We produce a category of synchronisation trees by restricting the tree–morphisms in accord with the synchronisation algebra. We insist the label of the image of an arc should divide the label of the arc because the image of an event is imagined to be a component of the event. Of course an arc may be collapsed in the image corresponding to the intuition that the event is not synchronised with any event of the image. But then we insist $*$ divides the original label.

5.3 Definition. Let L be a synchronisation algebra. Define an *L–morphism* of L–synchronisation trees from (S, l_S) to (T, l_T) to be a map $f : S \to T$ such that

$$f(<>) = <> \quad \text{and}$$

$$s \xrightarrow{\lambda} s' \Rightarrow (f(s) = f(s') \ \& \ * \ div \ \lambda) \text{ or } (f(s) \xrightarrow{\lambda'} f(s') \ \& \ \lambda' \ div \ \lambda).$$

5.4 Proposition. *Let L be a synchronisation algebra. Then L–synchronisation trees with L–morphisms form a category under the usual function composition and with the usual identity functions.*

Let (S, l_S) and (T, l_T) be two L-synchronisation trees. Then (S, l_S) and (T, l_T) are isomorphic in this category iff there is a bijection $f : S \to T$ such that

$$s \longrightarrow s' \Leftrightarrow f(s) \longrightarrow f(s')$$

and such that labels of corresponding arcs divide each other.

In particular, if div is an antisymmetric relation on L (i.e.λ div λ' div $\lambda \Rightarrow \lambda = \lambda'$) then (S, l_S) and (T, l_T) are isomorphic iff there is a bijection $f : S \to T$ such that

$$s \xrightarrow{\lambda} s' \Leftrightarrow f(s) \xrightarrow{\lambda} f(s').$$

5.5 Definition. Write $\mathbf{Tr}_L$ for the category of L–synchronisation trees with L–morphisms.

Remark. Note this category is equivalent but not equal to the category $\mathbf{Tr}_L$ in [W1, W2].

5.6 Proposition. *Let L be a synchronisation algebra. If $f : (S, l_S) \to (T, l_T)$ is an L–morphism of synchronisation trees then $f : S \to T$ is a morphism of trees. Assume that L is synchronous, so $\lambda \bullet * = 0$ for all $\lambda \in L \setminus \{ * \}$. Then for any L–morphism $f : (S, l_S) \to (T, l_T)$ the map $f : S \to T$ is a synchronous morphism of trees.*

Thus we see how assumptions made on the synchronisation algebra influence the morphisms we allow. In fact, particular synchronisation algebras give us categories isomorphic to **Tr** and $\mathbf{Tr}_{syn}$.

5.7 Proposition. *Let A and S be the synchronisation algebras given by:*

A

$\bullet_A$	$*$	T	0
$*$	$*$	T	0
T	T	T	0
0	0	0	0

S

$\bullet_S$	$*$	T	0
$*$	$*$	0	0
T	0	T	0
0	0	0	0

Then $\mathbf{Tr}_A \cong \mathbf{Tr}$ and $\mathbf{Tr}_S \cong \mathbf{Tr}_{syn}$.

6. Operations on synchronisation trees.

Throughout this section let $(L, \bullet, *, 0)$ be a synchronisation algebra. Define the following operations on synchronisation trees.

6.1 Definition. (Lifting) Let $\lambda \in L \setminus \{ *, 0 \}$ and (T, l) be a synchronisation tree. Define $\lambda(T, l)$ to be the synchronisation tree (T', l') where

$$t \in T' \Leftrightarrow t = <> \text{or } t = < (0,0), (1, a_0), \cdots, (1, a_{n-1}) >$$

for some $< a_0, \ldots, a_{n-1} > \in T$, and the new labelling function acts so

$$l'((0,0)) = \lambda \text{ and } l'((1,a)) = l(a).$$

The process represented by λT must first do a λ–labelled event before becoming the process represented by a copy of T.

6.2 Definition. (Indexed Sum) Let (T_i, l_i) be a set of synchronisation trees indexed by $i \in I$. Define their *sum* by

$$\sum_{i \in I} (T_i, l_i) = (\sum_{i \in I} T_i, l)$$

where $l(c) = l_i(a)$ if $c = (i, a)$ for $i \in I$. We write $(T_0, l_0) + (T_1, l_1)$ for the sum of two synchronisation trees indexed by $\{ 0, 1 \}$.

The sum just sticks synchronisation trees together at their roots.

6.3 Definition. (Restriction) Let $\Lambda \subseteq L \setminus \{ *, 0 \}$ which satisfies the property: $\lambda \in \Lambda$ & λ *div* λ' & λ' *div* $\lambda \Rightarrow \lambda' \in \Lambda$. Let (T, l) be a synchronisation tree over A. Define

$$(T, l) \lceil \Lambda = (T \lceil B, l')$$

where

$$B = \{ b \in A \mid l(b) \in \Lambda \} \quad \text{and} \quad l'(b) = l(b) \quad \text{for } b \in B.$$

The operation $(T, l) \lceil \Lambda$ restricts events to those which are labelled by elements of Λ. There are several alternative definitions of restriction in the literature [M1, M2, HBR, B]. Ours is chosen to be general and such that it still preserves isomorphism; it is like that in [M2].

6.4 Definition. (Relabelling) Let Ξ be an endomorphism of the synchronisation algebra L by which we mean that $\Xi : L \to L$ and Ξ preserves $\bullet$, $*$, 0 and

$$\forall \lambda \in L.(\Xi(\lambda) = 0 \Rightarrow \lambda = 0) \;\&\; (\Xi(\lambda) = * \Rightarrow \lambda = *).$$

Let (T, l) be a synchronisation tree. Define $(T, l)[\Xi] = (T, \Xi l)$.

We have chosen this definition of relabelling because it extends to a functor on $\mathbf{Tr}_L$. (Of course there are other possible definitions which are also continuous with respect to $\leq_L$ given below. One example is the make–α–labels–into–τ–labels definition of hiding given in [HBR, B].)

6.5 Definition. (Parallel Composition) Let (S, l_S) and (T, l_T) be synchronisation trees. Assume S is over A and T is over B. Then $S \times T$ is over $A \times_* B$, the product in **Set**$_*$with projections $\rho_0 : A \times_* B \to A$ and $\rho_1 : A \times_* B \to B$. Define the parallel composition of (S, l_S) and (T, l_T) by

$$(S, l_S) \textcircled{L} (T, l_T) = (S \times T\lceil C, l)$$

where

$$C = \{\, c \in A \times_* B \mid l_S \rho_0(c) \bullet l_T \rho_1(c) \neq 0 \,\} \quad \text{and,}$$
$$l(c) = l_S \rho_0(c) \bullet l_T \rho_1(c).$$

Remark. Note we assume that the projection function compositions occur in **Set**$_*$; so if, for example, $\rho_0(c) = *$ then $l_S \rho_0(c) = *$.

Apart from restriction all the above operations extend to functors on $\mathbf{Tr}_L$ in an obvious way. Not surprisingly, sum corresponds to coproduct in the category of synchronisation trees.

6.6 Proposition. *Let L be a synchronisation algebra. Let (T_i, l_i) be an I–indexed set of synchronisation trees. Let $in_i : T_i \to \sum_{i \in I} T_i$ be the injections of trees into the coproduct of trees given in 2.1. Then $\sum_{i \in I}(T_i, l_i)$, in_i for $i \in I$, is a coproduct in $\mathbf{Tr}_L$ of the family (T_i, l_i).*

Generally the parallel composition of synchronisation trees is defined recursively—see *e.g.*[M1, B]. Instead we can give a recursive characterisation of our definition of parallel composition, which fortunately agrees with those in the literature when we specialise to particular synchronisation algebras. Because here we serialise all events, parallel composition, like product, can be expressed as an indexed sum.

6.7 Proposition. *Let L be a synchronisation algebra. Let S an T be L–synchronisation trees. Then*

$$S \cong \sum_{i \in I} \lambda_i S_i \quad \text{and} \quad T \cong \sum_{j \in J} \mu_j T_j$$

for some indexed sets of labels and synchronisation trees. Moreover, the parallel composition of S and T can be characterised as follows:

$$S \textcircled{L} T \cong \sum_{\lambda_i \bullet * \neq 0} (\lambda_i \bullet *)(S_i \textcircled{L} T) + \sum_{\lambda_i \bullet \mu_j \neq 0} (\lambda_i \bullet \mu_j)(S_i \textcircled{L} T_j) + \sum_{* \bullet \mu_j \neq 0} (* \bullet \mu_j)(S \textcircled{L} T_j).$$

The above result means we can show how by specialising to particular synchronisation algebras we obtain various parallel compositions of synchronisation trees present in the literature. Before this we pause to show how parallel composition relates to product in the categories of synchronisation trees. Although there are obvious projection functions parallel composition does not always coincide with product. It does however when the operation $\bullet$ in the algebra behaves like the least common multiple (L.C.M.) operation.

6.8 Proposition. *Let L be a synchronisation algebra. Parallel composition extends to a functor* Ⓛ *from* $\mathbf{Tr}_L \times \mathbf{Tr}_L$ *to* $\mathbf{Tr}_L$ *in the following way. Let $f : (S, l_S) \to (S', l_{T'})$ and $g : (T, l_T) \to (T', l_{T'})$ be two morphisms in* $\mathbf{Tr}_L$. *Define f Ⓛ $g = f \times g$, the image of f and g under the product functor $\times$ on* $\mathbf{Tr}$. *Then f Ⓛ g is a morphism in* $\mathbf{Tr}_L$. *In fact this definition extends* Ⓛ *to a functor.*

Let (S, l_S) and (T, l_T) be two L–synchronisation trees over A and B respectively. Let $\pi_0' : S$ Ⓛ $T \to S$ and $\pi_1' : S$ Ⓛ $T \to T$ be the obvious restrictions of the projections $\pi_0 : S \times T \to S$ and $\pi_1 : S \times T \to T$. Then S Ⓛ T, π_0', π_1' is a product in the category $\mathbf{Tr}_L$ *iff*

$$\forall \gamma \in L \forall \alpha \in l_S A \forall \beta \in l_T B. \alpha \ div\ \gamma \ \&\ \beta \ div\ \gamma \Rightarrow (\alpha \bullet \beta) \ div\ \gamma.$$

It follows that parallel composition is always a categorical product in $\mathbf{Tr}_L$ *iff the synchronisation algebra satisfies*

$$\forall \alpha, \beta, \gamma \in L. \alpha \ div\ \gamma \ \&\ \beta \ div\ \gamma \Rightarrow (\alpha \bullet \beta) \ div\ \gamma.$$

(This law expresses that $\bullet$ behaves like an L.C.M..)

Let us run through, in a series of propositions, some parallel compositions in the literature. We refer to the synchronisation algebras L_1, L_2, L_3 of the earlier examples—4.4, 4.5, 4.6.

6.9 Proposition. (Parallel composition in CCS) *Let L_1 be the synchronisation algebra for CCS presented above. Write the parallel composition* Ⓛ *as $|$, as in [M1]. Then two L_1–synchronisation trees*

$$S \cong \sum_{i \in I} \lambda_i S_i \quad \text{and} \quad T \cong \sum_{j \in J} \mu_j T_j$$

have a parallel composition given by

$$S \mid T \cong \sum_i \lambda_i (S_i \mid T) + \sum_{\lambda_i = \overline{\mu}_j \text{ or } \mu_j = \overline{\lambda}_i} \tau (S_i \mid T_j) + \sum_j \mu_j (S \mid T_j).$$

Because, for L_1, $\alpha \ div\ \tau$ yet $0 = \alpha \bullet \alpha$ and $0 \not{div}\ \tau$ the parallel composition $|$ for CCS does not coincide with product in the category of synchronisation trees.

Now we examine the parallel compositions $||$ and $|||$ given in [B] to support the failure set semantics in [HBR]. Here $||$ does coincide with product in the appropriate category of synchronisation trees only for trees which have no τ–labelled events.

6.10 Proposition. (Parallel composition $||$ in [B]) *Let L_2 be the synchronisation algebra presented above. Write the parallel composition* Ⓛ *as $||$, as in [B]. Then two L_2–synchronisation trees*

$$S \cong \sum_i \lambda_i S_i + \sum_k \tau S_k \quad \text{and} \quad T \cong \sum_j \lambda_j T_j + \sum_l \tau T_l,$$

where λ_i, λ_j are non–τ labels, have a parallel composition given by

$$S \mid\mid T \cong \sum_{i,j : \lambda_i = \lambda_j} \lambda_i (S_i \mid\mid T_j) + \sum_k \tau (S_k \mid\mid T) + \sum_l \tau (S \mid\mid T_l).$$

The synchronisation algebra does not satisfy the L.C.M. law above because $\tau \ div\ \tau$ and yet $\tau \bullet \tau = 0 \not{div}\ \tau$. However for trees without τ–labels $||$ coincides with product in the category of L_2–synchronisation trees.

6.11 Proposition. (The parallel composition $|||$ in [B]) *Let L_3 be the synchronisation algebra presented above. Write the parallel composition* Ⓛ *as $|||$, as in [B]. Then two L_3–synchronisation trees*

$$S \cong \sum_{i \in I} \lambda_i S_i \quad \text{and} \quad T \cong \sum_{j \in J} \mu_j T_j$$

have a parallel composition given by

$$S \parallel\mid T \cong \sum_i \lambda_i (S_i \parallel\mid T) + \sum_j \mu_j (S \parallel\mid T_j).$$

For L_3 we have α div α and yet $\alpha \bullet \alpha = 0$ so ($\alpha \bullet \alpha$ $\not{div}$ α). Therefore $\parallel\mid$ does not coincide with product in the category of L_3-synchronisation trees.

As a final example we exhibit how Milner's synchronous calculi fit into the picture. In [M2] algebras of actions are presented. They are closely related to synchronisation algebras though because the algebras do not contain $*$ they cannot express asynchrony in the way synchronisation algebras can. The most general algebras of actions described in [M2] are Abelian monoids of the form $(M, \bullet, 1)$. The identity element serves to label delay events. We show how Milner's monoids of actions determine synchronisation algebras which satisfy the synchronous law of definition 4.3.

6.12 Definition. Let $(M, \bullet_M, 1)$ be an Abelian monoid (assumed to not contain $*$ or 0). Define $L[M]$ to be the algebra $(M \cup \{*, 0\}, \bullet, *, 0)$ where $\bullet$ extends the monoid operation $\bullet_M$ so $* \bullet * = *$, $* \bullet \mu = \mu \bullet * = 0$ for $\mu \in M \cup \{0\}$, $0 \bullet \mu = \mu \bullet 0 = 0$ for $\mu \in M \cup \{*, 0\}$ and $\mu \bullet \mu' = \mu \bullet_M \mu'$ for $\mu, \mu' \in M$.

6.13 Lemma. *The algebra $L[M]$ defined above is a synchronisation algebra which satisfies the synchronous law*

$$\forall \lambda \neq *. \lambda \bullet * = 0.$$

Further, the algebra $L[M]$ satisfies the L.C.M. law

$$\alpha \ div\ \gamma \ \&\ \beta \ div\ \gamma \Rightarrow \alpha \bullet \beta \ div\ \gamma$$

iff M satisfies the L.C.M. law—the divides relation for M is defined exactly as that for L.

6.14 Proposition. *Let L be a synchronisation algebra which satisfies the synchronous law. Then the parallel composition of L-synchronisation trees*

$$S \cong \sum_i \lambda_i S_i \quad \text{and} \quad T \cong \sum_j \mu_j T_j$$

has the form

$$S \, Ⓛ \, T \cong \sum_{\lambda_i \bullet \mu_j \neq 0} (\lambda_i \bullet \mu_j)(S_i \, Ⓛ \, T_j).$$

So then parallel composition Ⓛ is obtained by restricting $\otimes$ the synchronous product.

Let $(M, \bullet_M, 1)$ be an Abelian monoid. Write $\times_M$ for the parallel composition with respect to the synchronisation algebra $L[M]$. Then for two M-labelled synchronisation trees

$$S \cong \sum_i \lambda_i S_i \quad \text{and} \quad T \cong \sum_j \mu_j T_j$$

we have

$$S \times_M T \cong \sum_{i,j} (\lambda_i \bullet_M \mu_j)(S_i \times_M T_j).$$

The operation $\times_M$ coincides with product in the category of synchronisation trees iff the operation $\bullet_M$ in $(M, \bullet_M, 1)$ behaves like an L.C.M.. If $(M, \bullet_M, 1)$ is an Abelian group $\times_M$ coincides with product.

7. Denotational semantics.

We present a denotational semantics to a simple parallel programming language which involves the constructs we have defined earlier. The class of languages is parameterised by the synchronisation algebra L.

7.1 Definition. Let L be a synchronisation algebra. The language **Proc**$_L$is defined to be given by the following grammar:

$$t ::= NIL \mid x \mid \lambda t \mid t + t \mid t\lceil\Lambda \mid t[\Xi] \mid t \textcircled{L} t \mid x \textbf{ isrec } t$$

where x is in some set of variables X over processes, $\lambda \in L \setminus \{*, 0\}$, $\Lambda \subseteq L \setminus \{*, 0\}$ is closed under $div \cap div^{-1}$, and Ξ is an endomorphism of L.

In order to give a meaning to the recursively defined processes of the form x **isrec** t we use the fact that the operations are continuous with respect to a c.p.o. of synchronisation trees. Fortunately the two c.p.o.'s of trees $\leq$ and $\subseteq$ extend to synchronisation trees in such a way that the operations of the previous section are continuous.

7.2 Definition. Let L be a synchronisation algebra. Define the orderings $\leq_L$ and $\subseteq_L$ on synchronisation trees by:

$$(S, l_S) \leq_L (T, l_T) \Leftrightarrow S \leq T \;\&\; l_S = l_T\lceil A,$$
$$(S, l_S) \subseteq_L (T, l_T) \Leftrightarrow S \subseteq T \;\&\; l_S = l_T\lceil A.$$

7.3 Proposition. *The null synchronisation tree* $(\{<>\}, \emptyset)$ *is the least L–synchronisation tree with respect to both orderings* $\leq_L$ *and* $\subseteq_L$. *Both orderings* $\leq_L$ *and* $\subseteq_L$ *possess least upper bounds of* ω*–chains.*
All the operations lifting $T \mapsto \lambda T$, *sum* $+$, *restriction* $T \mapsto T\lceil\Lambda$, *relabelling* $T \mapsto T[\Xi]$ *and parallel composition* $\textcircled{L}$, *of section 6, are continuous with respect to* $\leq_L$ *and* $\subseteq_L$.

Thus we can give a denotational semantics to **Proc**$_L$by representing recursively defined processes as the least fixed points of continuous functionals.

7.4 Definition. (Denotational semantics for Proc$_L$) Let L be a synchronisation algebra. Define an *environment* for process variables to be a function $\rho : X \rightarrow \mathbf{Tr}_L$. For a term T and an environment ρ, define the denotation of t with respect to ρ written $[\![t]\!]\rho$ by the following structural induction. Note syntactic operators appear on the left and their semantic counterparts on the right.

$$\begin{array}{llll} [\![NIL]\!]\rho & = (\{<>\}, \emptyset) & [\![t\lceil\Lambda]\!]\rho & = [\![t]\!]\rho\lceil\Lambda \\ [\![x]\!]\rho & = \rho(x) & [\![t[\Xi]]\!]\rho & = [\![t]\!]\rho[\Xi] \\ [\![\lambda t]\!]\rho & = \lambda([\![t]\!]\rho) & [\![t_1 \textcircled{L} t_2]\!]\rho & = [\![t_1]\!]\rho \textcircled{L} [\![t_2]\!]\rho \\ [\![t_1 + t_2]\!]\rho & = [\![t_1]\!]\rho + [\![t_2]\!]\rho & [\![x \textbf{ isrec } t]\!]\rho & = fix\, \Gamma \end{array}$$

where $\Gamma : \mathbf{Tr}_L \rightarrow \mathbf{Tr}_L$ is given by $\Gamma(T) = [\![t]\!]\rho[x/T]$ and fix is the least–fixed point operator so that $fix\, \Gamma = (\bigcup_n T_n, \bigcup_n l_n)$ where $(T_0, l_0) = (\{<>\}, \emptyset)$ and $(T_{n+1}, l_{n+1}) = \Gamma(T_n, l_n)$ inductively.

Remark. A structural induction shows that Γ above is indeed continuous with respect to either order $\leq_L$ or $\subseteq_L$ so the denotation of a recursively defined process is really the least fixed point of the associated functional Γ.

Choosing L to be the appropriate synchronisation algebra we immediately obtain denotational semantics for CCS and SCCS.

Of course we cannot expect all languages to fit into the simple scheme **Proc**$_L$; for instance the CSP–language of [HBR, B] does not quite because it has two parallel compositions corresponding to two synchronisation algebras on the same set of labels. However the semantics for this language and that for CCS with value–passing follow similar lines to that for **Proc**$_L$. Some languages like those in [H, Mi] have a parallel composition which depends on *sorts* being associated with processes. They need a slightly more intricate definition of parallel composition which uses combinations of our parallel composition, with respect to some synchronisation algebra, together with restriction and relabelling.

Naturally one wishes to use semantics to prove properties of programs. This can often be reduced to the problem of whether or not two programs have equivalent behaviour with respect to some natural notion of equivalence. Thus much work is involved with inventing natural equivalences and proof rules for them—see *e.g.*[M1], [B], [HM], [HN], [HP]. Consider the programming language $\mathbf{Proc}_L$ for some synchronisation algebra L. There is an obvious equivalence on closed terms of the language: Say two closed terms are equivalent iff they have isomorphic denotations. (The idea extends to open terms; say two terms are equivalent if the closed terms obtained by an arbitrary assignment of closed terms to free variables are always equivalent.)

7.5 Definition. Let L be a synchronisation algebra. Let t and t' be closed terms of $\mathbf{Proc}_L$. Write

$$t \sim t' \Leftrightarrow [\![t]\!]\rho \cong [\![t']\!]\rho$$

for some arbitrary enviroment ρ.

We immediately know some properties of the equivalence: firstly it really is an equivalence—is reflexive, symmetric and transitive—because these properties hold for isomorphism, and then the commutativity and associativity of sum $+$ with respect to $\sim$ follows directly from the properties of coproduct. Less immediate are the commutativity and associativity of parallel composition $\textcircled{L}$, but these facts follow easily from the corresponding properties of product $\times$ of trees and $\bullet$ in the synchronisation algebra L. Because all our operations preserve isomorphism—all but restriction are functors anyhow and functors must preserve isomorphism—we know that the equivalence $\sim$ is also a congruence with respect to the operations of $\mathbf{Proc}_L$.

Particular laws follow from particular properties of the synchronisation algebra L. One useful property, when it is valid, is that of the distributivity of parallel composition over sum. This property holds for the equivalence $\sim$ precisely when the synchronisation algebra satisfies the synchronous law.

7.6 Proposition. *Let L be a synchronisation algebra. The following conditions are equivalent:*

(i) $t \textcircled{L} (u + v) \sim (t \textcircled{L} u) + (t \textcircled{L} v)$ *for all closed terms t, u, v of $\mathbf{Proc}_L$, that is parallel composition distributes over sum,*

(ii) $NIL \textcircled{L} t \sim NIL$ *for all closed terms t of $\mathbf{Proc}_L$, that is NIL is a $\textcircled{L}$-zero,*

(iii) $\lambda \bullet * = 0$ *for λ an element of $L \setminus \{*\}$, that is L satisfies the synchronous law.*

Of course a semantics for a language of synchronising processes may well ensure that parallel composition distributes over sum without the synchronisation algebra being synchronous. The above result only implies that any abstract semantics which factors through our synchronisation tree semantics will satisfy the distributivity. For example the synchronous calculi SCCS do because the equivalences in [M2] could be based on synchronisation trees and the synchronisation algebras associated with monoids of actions are synchronous by lemma 6.13.

In the full version we present a sound and complete proof system for the non-recursive processes of $\mathbf{Proc}_L$and show the relation with the operational semantics based on labelled transition systems, an approach followed in [M1] for example. Interestingly a similar story can be told in categories of event structures [W1,2] and Petri nets [W3] which do not simulate concurrency by interleaving; the categorical set-up makes a smooth relationship between the different approaches.

Acknowledgements.

Thanks are due to Mogens Nielsen of the Computer Science Department, Aarhus University, Denmark for encouragement and many helpful discussions. This work was supported in part by a postdoctoral fellowship from the Royal Society of Great Britain, to work at Aarhus, and in part by Carnegie-Mellon University.

References.

[AM] Arbib, M.A.,and Manes,E.G., Arrows, Structures and Functors, The categorical imperative. Academic Press (1975).

[B] Brookes, S.D., On the relationship of CCS and CSP, ICALP 1983.

[H] Hoare, C.A.R., A Model for Communicating Sequential Processes. Report of the Programming Research Group, Oxford University (1978).

[HBR] Hoare, C.A.R., Brookes, S.D., and Roscoe, A.W., A Theory of Communicating Processes, Technical Report PRG-16, Programming Research Group, University of Oxford (1981); to appear also in JACM.

[HM] Hennessy, M.C.B. and Milner, R., On observing nondeterminism and concurrency, Springer LNCS Vol. 85. (1979).

[HN] Hennessy, M.C.B., and de Nicola, R., Testing Equivalences for Processes, Internal Report, University of Edinburgh, (July 1982).

[HP] Hennessy, M.C.B. and Plotkin, G., A term model for CCS, Proceedings of the 9th Conference on Mathematical Foundations of Computer Science, Springer-Verlag LNCS Vol. 88. (1980)

[Mac] Maclane, S., Categories for the Working Mathematician. Graduate Texts in Mathematics,Springer-Verlag (1972).

[Mi] Milne, G., Synchronised Behaviour Algebras; a model for interacting systems. Report of Comp. Sc. Dept., University of Southern California (1979).

[M1] Milner, R., A Calculus of Communicating Systems. Springer-Verlag Lecture Notes in Comp. Sc. vol. 92 (1980).

[M2] Milner, R., Calculi for Synchrony and Asynchrony, Dept. of Comp. Sci. report, University of Edinburgh (1982).

[NPW] Nielsen, M., Plotkin, G., Winskel, G., Petri nets, Event structures and Domains, part 1 . Theoretical Computer Science, vol. 13 (1981) pp.85–108.

[S] Scott, D., Domains for Denotational Semantics, Springer-Verlag Lecture Notes in Comp. Sc. 140 (1982).

[W] Winskel, G., Events in Computation. Ph.D. thesis, University of Edinburgh (1980).

[W1] Winskel, G., Event structure semantics of CCS and related languages, Springer-Verlag Lecture Notes in Comp. Sc. 140 (1982).

[W2] Winskel, G., Event structure semantics of CCS and related languages, Report of the Computer Sc. Dept., University of Aarhus, Denmark (1982).

[W3] Winskel, G., A new definition of morphism on Petri nets. Submitted to FCT 1983.

Cutting and Partitioning a Graph after a Fixed Pattern
(Extended Abstract)

Mihalis Yannakakis
Bell Labs
Paris C. Kanellakis
Brown Univ.
Stavros S. Cosmadakis
MIT
Christos H. Papadimitriou
MIT and Nat. Tech. Univ. of Athens

1. Introduction

The problems we study in this paper are those of finding optimal ***cuts and partitions*** of a given (directed or undirected) graph, so that the graph resulting from this cutting and partitioning has a property specified by a fixed ***pattern*** graph. These problems arise when heuristic "divide-and-conquer" methods are used to solve hard graph-theoretic questions. The general flavor of our results is characterizing the classes of patterns for which such problems are in P, and for which they become NP-complete.

We first consider the problem of finding ***a minimum weight set of edges of a graph, whose deletion breaks all paths between certain specified pairs of nodes.*** This is one example of a generalization of the familiar max flow/min cut problem in a direction different from multicommodity flow problems. It also gives rise to a whole family of problems, one for each fixed pattern of paths that we wish to eliminate. We classify the complexity of problems in this family according to the structure of the fixed pattern of paths. Our analysis leads to sufficient conditions for NP-completeness [Y],[PY]. Our main result in this area is that, for the directed graph family of problems, only for patterns of paths, which are very similar to full bipartite directed graphs, do we have efficient algorithms. For all other patterns the problems are NP-complete. A similar family of problems and classification scheme are the "fixed node-fixed graph H" SUBGRAPH HOMEOMORPHISM questions in [FHW],[GJ].

The second family of problems we examine are also based on constraints specified by a fixed pattern. We are now searching for ***a partition of the nodes of a graph in a fixed number of bounded sets, so that only certain sets in this partition contain adjacent nodes in the graph.*** We specify, which sets of the partition are allowed to contain adjacent nodes, by a pattern graph (i.e., the nodes of this graph are the member sets of the partition and the edges connect sets of the partition that may contain adjacent nodes). We show that in the undirected, directed and directed acyclic cases, unless the pattern is essentially a collection of cliques the partitioning problems are NP-complete.

In general, the task of partitioning the node set V of a graph G into disjoint sets $\{V_1, V_2, \ldots, V_m\}$, so that the subgraphs of G induced by the V_i's have desirable properties (e.g., are isomorphic to a fixed pattern H, are of bounded size and connected, or are directed acyclic graphs) is an NP-complete problem [GJ], [J]. However, the partitioning problems examined here are much closer to the spirit of "divide-and-conquer" methods [L]. What is important for "divide-and-conquer" is, not so much the structure of the subgraphs of $G=(V,E)$ induced by the sets V_i of the partition, but the properties of the edges or arcs with endpoints in different sets of the partition and the fact that the sets of the partition are suitably bounded. General versions of such problems in [GJ] are GRAPH PARTITIONING, ACYCLIC PARTITION, and MIN-CUT-INTO-BOUNDED-SETS.

We can always partition the nodes of a dag (i.e., directed acyclic graph) into two equal pieces, so that the only arcs between them are directed from the first to the second piece. In the last section we examine minimization and maximization versions of this problem. If we do not require that the sets of the partition are bounded, then these problems can be solved in polynomial time, otherwise they are NP-complete. They can also be interpreted as more constrained versions of the (directed) MINIMUM-CUT-LINEAR-ARRANGEMENT problem [GJ]. We also investigate the notion of *directed separators* for dags.

Finally let us note that all the above NP-complete problems have efficient solutions, when the graphs to be disconnected or partitioned are restricted to trees.

The classification of graph cutting problems is contained in Section 2, and that of graph partitioning problems in Section 3. The minimization and maximization of directed bounded cuts is the subject of Section 4. The graph theoretic terminology used is from [PS] and [AHU]. Full proofs will appear in the final paper.

2. The Complexity of Disconnecting a Graph

The computation of minimum cuts separating a source s from a sink t in a directed or an undirected graph is one of the central themes of algorithmic graph theory. An important open problem in this area (i.e. not known to be in P or to be NP-complete) is the *triangle problem:*
Given an undirected graph and three of its nodes u, v, w, what is the smallest set of edges whose removal breaks every path connecting any two of these nodes?
In this section we present two sets of problems naturaly related to this open question, and we completely classify the complexity of the problems in the directed case.

UCUT

Instance: An undirected graph $H=(N,F)$ ("the pattern"); an undirected graph $G=(V,E)$; positive edge weights $w:E \to Z^+$; a one-to-one mapping $f:N \to V$; and a positive integer K.
Question: Is there a subset E' of E such that: $\sum_{e \in E'} w(e) \leq K$, and, if $\{u,v\} \in F$, then there is no undirected path from $f(u)$ to $f(v)$ in $(V,E-E')$? ▪

Let UCUT(H) be the previously described problem, with the pattern fixed to a graph H. If H consists only of an edge $\{u,v\}$ we have the max flow problem for undirected graphs [PS]. If H is a clique on three points (with no self loops) and all edge weights are 1 we have the ***triangle problem***.

DCUT

Instance: A directed graph $H=(N,F)$ ("the pattern"); a directed graph $G=(V,A)$; positive arc weights $w:A \to Z^+$; a one-to-one mapping $f:N \to V$; and a positive integer K.
Question: Is there a subset A' of A such that: $\sum_{a \in A'} w(a) \leq K$, and, if $(u,v) \in F$, then there is no directed path from $f(u)$ to $f(v)$ in $(V,A-A')$? ▪

Once again DCUT(H) is DCUT with the pattern fixed to a graph H, and if H consists only of an arc (u,v) we have the max flow problem for directed graphs [PS].

Intuitively, the pattern H and the mapping f specify which paths to break (between which nodes) in G; e.g. $H =$ 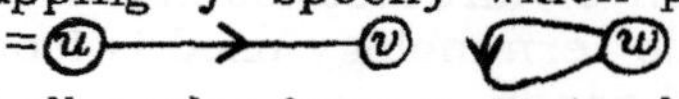 means "break all directed paths from s_1 to t_1 and all cycles from s_2 to itself, where $s_1=f(u)$, $t_1=f(v)$ and $s_2=f(w)$". This has to be done by removing a set of arcs or edges with minimum total weight. The pattern H may have self loops. A number of simple observations lead to the following lemmas.

Lemma 1: If H contains at most m edges, then UCUT(H) is polynomially reducible to UCUT(H_m), where H_m consists of m edges sharing no common endpoint and has no self loops. Moreover, UCUT(H_2) can be solved in $O(n^3)$ time by max flow techniques. ▪

In the case of UCUT(H_2) (see Figure 1) the edges removed should also break;
(1) all paths from u to v or from v to u',
(2) all paths from u to v or from u to v',
(3) all paths from u' to v' or from v' to u,
(4) all paths from u' to v' or from u' to v.
It follows from a simple case analysis that UCUT(H_2) reduces to solving UCUT(H_a) and UCUT(H_b) and taking the minimum (see Figure 1). Both these problems correspond to UCUT(H), with H a complete bipartite undirected graph. This is a case solvable by a max flow algorithm.

Lemma 1 illustrates that, for the UCUT(H) family of problems, the patterns H, for which there are efficient solutions, are not essentially constrained to the complete bipartite graphs. As we shall see the situation is different for DCUT(H).

Lemma 2: If the input graphs G are constrained to be trees, then all UCUT(H) and DCUT(H) problems are in P. ▪

This is a consequence of the fact that H is fixed and G contains at most one of the "bad" paths we wish to break. Therefore, for an H with k edges or arcs we need only examine edge or arc subsets of G of at most size k. In most of the problems we examine, in this and other sections, fixing H and constraining G to trees leads to similar results. We now proceed to the family of problems DCUT(H).

Lemma 3: Let H' be the directed graph we obtain from H by replacing each node v with non-zero indegree and non-zero outdegree by two nodes v_{in}, v_{out} such that: all arcs incoming to (outgoing from) v, become arcs incoming to v_{in} (outgoing from v_{out}).Then DCUT(H) and DCUT(H') are polynomial time equivalent. ▪

The transformation of Lemma 3 is illustrated in Figure 2.

For every fixed $H=(N,F)$ the nodes of $H'=(N',F')$ so obtained can be partitioned into a set S_1 of sources (with indegree 0) and a set S_2 of sinks (with outdegree 0), and the arc set F' of H' is a subset of $S_1 \times S_2$. We call H ***full*** if for H' we have $F'=S_1 \times S_2$. The condition H ***is full*** can also be stated as follows:
if $H=(N,F)$ then there are $N_1,N_2 \subseteq N$ such that $N=N_1 \cup N_2$ and $F=N_1 \times N_2$.

(a) If H is full, then DCUT(H') and consequently DCUT(H) can be solved by max flow techniques.

(b) If H is not full, then H' either contains Figure 3a or Figure 3b as a node induced subgraph. In both cases we can show that DCUT(H') is NP-complete. Thus:

Theorem 1: DCUT(H) is in P if H is full, otherwise it is NP-complete, even when all arc weights are 1.

Sketch of Proof: We show that $DCUT(H)$ is NP-complete if H is either Figure 3a or 3b, by a reduction from EXACT COVER BY 3-SETS [GJ]:
"Given a collection C of 3 element subsets of a set X with $|X|=3n$, does C contain an ***exact cover*** for X, i.e. a subcollection $K \subseteq C$ such that every element of X occurs in exactly one member of K?"

Given an instance of EXACT COVER BY 3-SETS, we construct an input to $DCUT(H)$, with H either one of Figures 3a or 3b as follows:

Our input graph contains four nodes a_1,a_2,b_1,b_2 that correspond to the nodes with the same names in the patterns. It also contains paths that correspond to the elements of X and the members of the collection C.

For each $s_i \in C$, $(1 \le i \le m)$, we put in a path from a_1 to a_2 as shown in Figure 4a, with weight $k > 2m$. To break this path, either (u_i, v_i) or (v_i, a_2) should be removed, corresponding to $s_i \in K$, $s_i \notin K$.

Now for each $x \in X$, we put in a path from b_1 to b_2, which will be broken iff some 3-set containing x is included in the cover. This path is illustrated in Figure 4b, where we assume that x appears in s_1, s_2, s_3.

Now C contains an exact cover K for X, $(|K| = n)$ iff we can break all paths from a_1 to a_2 and from b_1 to b_2, by removing a set of arcs of total weight $2n + (m - n) = m + n$. Observe that this also breaks all paths from b_1 to a_2, thus handling both Figure 3a and 3b.

Finally, all arc weights can be made equal to 1, by substituting weighted arcs of weight k with k parallel paths of lenght 2. ▪

3. The Complexity of Partitioning a Graph

In this section we will provide necessary and sufficient conditions for NP-completeness of graph partitioning problems. We wish to partition the node set of a graph into sets of bounded size, so that the edges or arcs between these sets conform to some fixed pattern. The families of related questions UPAR(H), DPAR(H) and APAR(H) are defined below:

UPAR

Instance: An undirected graph $H = (N, F)$ ("the pattern"), where $N = \{1, 2, \ldots, m\}$; and an undirected graph $G = (V, E)$, where $|V| = n$.
Question: Is there a partition of the node set V into m disjoint sets $\{V_1, V_2, \ldots, V_m\}$ of equal size (i.e. $|V_i| = n/m$), such that, the undirected graph $H' = (N, F')$ is a subgraph of H, where $\{i, j\} \in F'$ iff $i \ne j$ and $\{u, v\} \in E$ for some $u \in V_i$ and some $v \in V_j$?

In these partitioning problems we wish to divide the input graph into pieces with the same number of nodes, so that only certain of these pieces have adjacent nodes in the input graph. For directed graphs the related problem is as follows:

DPAR

Instance: A directed graph $H = (N, F)$ ("the pattern"), where $N = \{1, 2, \ldots, m\}$; and a directed graph $G = (V, A)$, where $|V| = n$.
Question: Is there a partition of the node set V into m disjoint sets $\{V_1, V_2, \ldots, V_m\}$ of equal size (i.e. $|V_i| = n/m$), such that the directed graph $H' = (N, F')$ is a subgraph of H, where $(i, j) \in F'$ iff $i \ne j$ and $(u, v) \in A$ for some $u \in V_i$ and some $v \in V_j$?

Now let UPAR(H) and DPAR(H) be UPAR and DPAR, respectively, with the pattern fixed to graph H. In the particular case, where both H and G are restricted to dags (i.e. directed acyclic graphs) we call DPAR and DPAR(H), APAR and APAR(H).

Intuitively the pattern H specifies, which parts of the partition of G are allowed to be adjacent in G, without forcing them to be adjacent. In these problems, it makes no sense for the patterns to have self loops. No quantity is minimized or maximized, but the sets of the partition are bounded. We could have easily formulated the problems in terms of individual bounds of the form $B_i \geq |V_i|$, where the B_i's are part of the instance, and obtained very similar results. Let us first consider the undirected case.

If H is a collection of cliques then UPAR(H) is in P. Without loss of generality we might assume that m, the number of nodes in H, divides n, the number of nodes in V. In this case let every connected component of G be considered as a number coded in unary (the number of nodes in this component), and each clique of H on k nodes can be considered as a bin of capacity $k(n/m)$. The desired partition of G exists iff the numbers fit exactly in the bins. Since the numbers are coded in unary and there is a fixed number of bins (H is fixed), we can solve the bin packing problem in polynomial time. In fact we can show that these are the only cases, for which UPAR(H) is in P.

Theorem 2: UPAR(H) is in P if H is a collection of cliques, otherwise it is NP-complete. Moreover, if the graphs G are restricted to trees, UPAR(H) is in P for all H.

Sketch of Proof: We first prove that UPAR(H^*) is NP-complete for $H^*=$①—②—③, provided we also require that $|V_1| \leq B_1$, $|V_2| \leq B_2$ and $|V_3| \leq B_3$, (where B_1, B_2, B_3 are part of the input). For this we use a reduction from: "Does a regular undirected graph F of high valence contain a clique of size k?" We transform an arbitrary F of n nodes and m edges into a graph $G(F)$ of $n + m$ nodes and $2m + m(m-1)/2 + n(n-1)/2$ edges. There are two kinds of nodes in $G(F)$, n nodes representing the nodes of F and forming a size n clique, and m nodes representing the edges of F and forming a size m clique. Moreover, the node of $G(F)$ representing edge $\{i,j\}$ of F is connected in $G(F)$ with the nodes representing i and j. There is a clique of size k in F iff it is possible to divide the nodes of $G(F)$ in three parts such that $|V_1| \leq k(k-1)/2$, $|V_2| \leq m-k(k-1)/2+k$ and $|V_3| \leq n-k$ and this partition respects the pattern H^* constraint.

An elaborate padding argument generalizes the reduction to all H's that contain O—O—O, as a node induced subgraph and guarantees the equal size of all member sets of the partition.

If the graph G is restricted to be a tree we can use a dynamic programming algorithm, which, based on the assumption that H is fixed and that the bounds on the $|V_i|$'s are in fact numbers coded in unary, will run in polynomial time (the exponent will depend on H) ▪

For DPAR(H) we can perform a similar analysis, for patterns that are sets of directed cliques and graphs G that are restricted to trees.

A particularly interesting case is that of APAR(H), where both pattern and G are dags (i.e. directed acyclic graphs). A part of the next section will be devoted to the pattern  . Let H be a collection of transitively closed dags, each one being a total order. In this case we call H ***total*** and it is easy to see that APAR(H) is in P. We can show that these are the only "nice" patterns. The argument as in Theorem 2 involves reductions from CLIQUE, for the three cases of node induced subgraphs,    and a suitable padding argument.

Theorem 3: APAR(H) is in P if H is total, otherwise it is NP-complete. ▪

Note that DPAR(H) is NP-complete, when H is the pattern  , which is total but not a directed clique. This is because the strongly connected components [AHU] of the directed graph G, must be contained in one set of the partition. Therefore DPAR(H) corresponds to partitioning a dag, whose nodes have weights in unary, in two equal weight parts, so that no node in the second part has an arc to a node in the first part. This is a strongly NP-complete scheduling problem [GJ].

4. Separators for Directed Acyclic Graphs

Although graph partitioning is a hard problem in general, particular classes of graphs (i.e. planar graphs) can be partitioned in a regular fashion based on *separator* theorems [LT1, LT2]. As a result, "divide-and-conquer" can be successfully applied to a variety of graph-theoretic problems.

We will examine "small" separators for directed acyclic graphs. In this case the partition of the dag is also required to satisfy a direction constraint. Let $G=(V,A)$ be a dag. We will call a partition of the node set V into sets V_1 and V_2 a ***directed cut*** (V_1,V_2) of G, if all arcs in A with one endpoint in V_1 and the other in V_2 are directed from V_1 to V_2.

A ***directed separator*** corresponds to a directed cut of specified size, that partitions the dag into approximately equal pieces. Formally, for graphs with valence bounded by a constant d, we have:

Definition: Let Ψ be a family of dags closed under the subgraph relation, and let $\alpha<1$ and β be positive constants. If every dag on n nodes in Ψ can be partitioned into two disconnected components, each having no more than αn nodes, by removing no more than $\beta f(n)$ arcs and if, in addition, this partition is a directed cut, then Ψ has an $f(n)$- ***directed separator*** theorem.

Although there is no $\sqrt{n}$-directed separator theorem for planar dags, (planarity and arbitrary directions do not combine gracefully as illustrated by the dag of Figure 5a), some classes of dags do have "small" separator theorems. We can show that:

(a) A directed tree of size n and maximum valence d, can be partitioned into two parts V_1 and V_2, with no more than $2n/3$ nodes each, by removing no more than d arcs. These arcs are incident on one node and directed from part V_1 to part V_2. Using a similar embedding argument with that of [BL], we can also bisect the tree into parts V_1 and V_2 of almost equal sizes, by removing at most $O(\log n)$ arcs directed from V_1 to V_2.

(b) The class of planar bipartite dags G=(V,U,A), with all arcs directed from V to U has a $\sqrt{n}$-directed separator theorem. This is no longer true if arcs are also directed from U to V, even for transitively reduced dags (see Figure 5a).

(c) A ***directed grid graph*** is any subgraph of the infinite directed two-dimensional grid illustrated in Figure 5b. Using a geometric argument and inclusion-exclusion type counting we can show that a $\sqrt{n}$-directed separator theorem holds for the class of directed grid graphs.

Searching for "small" directed separators is related to a weighted minimization version of the APAR(H) problem, with $H= \circ\!\!\rightarrow\!\!\circ$. In fact, we will examine a number of similar partitioning problems, some of which differ from their undirected counterparts.

DMINCUT

Instance: A dag $G=(V,A)$; positive arc weights $w: A \to Z^+$; two nodes s,t in V; and a positive integer K.
Question: Is there a directed cut (V_1, V_2) of G, such that, if A' is the set of arcs of G with one endpoint in V_1 and the other in V_2 then $\sum_{a \in A'} w(a) \le K$, moreover s is in V_1 and t in V_2?

DMAXCUT

Instance: A dag $G=(V,A)$; positive arc weights $w: A \to Z^+$; and a positive integer K.
Question: Is there a directed cut (V_1, V_2) of G, such that, if A' is the set of arcs of G with one endpoint in V_1 and the other in V_2 then $\sum_{a \in A'} w(a) \ge K$?

Since every strongly connected component of a directed graph can only belong to one node set of a directed cut (V_1, V_2), there is no loss of generality in assuming the input to DMAXCUT or DMINCUT to be acyclic.

If in addition we are given a positive integer B as part of the above instances and we require that $|V_1| \le B$ and $|V_2| \le B$ in the directed cut (V_1, V_2) of G, we have the problems BOUNDED-DMAXCUT and BOUNDED-DMINCUT. The undirected counterpart for these is MINIMUM-CUT-INTO-BOUNDED-SETS from [GJ], which is NP-complete in general and open for planar graphs. Using reductions from CLIQUE we can show that:

Theorem 4: BOUNDED-DMAXCUT and BOUNDED-DMINCUT are NP-complete, even if all weights are 1, and $B = |V/2|$. ▪

However, we also have that:

Theorem 5: DMAXCUT and DMINCUT are in P. BOUNDED-DMAXCUT for transitively closed dags and all weights equal is also in P, (for general weights it is NP-complete).

Sketch of Proof: For the input dag $G=(V,A)$, with $|V|=n$ we consider the 0−1 variables x_i, $1 \le i \le n$, where $x_i=0$ means node i belongs to V_1 and $x_i=1$ means node i belongs to V_2. Also let c_i for $1 \le i \le n$ be the difference between the sums of weights of arcs outgoing from node i and the sum of weights of arcs incoming to node i. DMAXCUT and DMINCUT correspond to maximizing and minimizing the linear function $\sum_{i=1}^{n} c_i x_i$ under the constraints:

$$x_i \ge x_j \text{ if } (i,j) \in A$$

$$1 \ge x_i \ge 0 \text{ for } 1 \le i \le n$$

$$x_s = 1,\ x_t = 0 \text{ and } x_i \ in\ Z$$

These constraints are unimodular, so both integer programs are in P, [PS].

DMINCUT can also be reduced to a max flow problem from s to t [H] (use the same network with source s and sink t, with arc weights as capacities, and add the inverses of all arcs in A with capacities ∞).

DMAXCUT can be shown in P using the "line-digraph" of the given dag and finding a maximum weight independent set in a comparability graph [G]. There are also similarities between DMAXCUT and Dilworth's theorem for partial orders [D]. The undirected version (i.e. MAXCUT) is NP-complete [GJ], in general, and in P for planar graphs.

Finally for BOUNDED-MAXCUT we must add the constraints
$\sum_{i=1}^{n} x_i \le B$ and $\sum_{i=1}^{n} (1-x_i) \le B$,
which destroy the unimodular character of the integer program. However, for all arc weights equal and G transitively closed a greedy algorithm can be used to solve this integer program [H]. For transitively closed dags and arbitrary arc weights there is a reduction from the CLIQUE problem. ▪

5. Discussion and Open Problems

We have investigated minimum cuts and partitions, that satisfy constraints described by a fixed pattern, both in directed and undirected graphs. Our analysis is in the form of necessary and sufficient conditions for NP-completeness, based on the structure of a fixed pattern graph H, resulting in a sharpening of previously known bounds. We have also examined the special partition problems of directed cuts and directed separators in dags.

Some of these questions, of considerable graph-theoretic interest, are still unresolved. Among these we would like to point out the triangle problem or UCUT(H_3), and UPAR(H) when the input is a planar graph.

Acknowledgements

We would like to thank Larry Stockmeyer, Ashok Chandra and Alan Hoffman for many helpful discussions. The directed separator for grid graphs was obtained jointly with Ashok Chandra and parts of Theorem 5 were pointed out by Alan Hoffman. The research of the second author was supported by NSF grant MCS-8210830.

References

[AHU] Aho, A.V., J.E. Hopcroft, J.D. Ullman, "The Design and Analysis of Computer Algorithms", Addison-Wesley, 1974.

[BL] Bhatt, S.N., C.E. Leiserson, "How to Assemble Tree Machines" Proc. 14th SIGACT, pp.77-84, 1980.

[D] Dilworth, R.P., "A Decomposition Theorem for Partially Ordered Sets", Ann. of Math. (1), vol. 51, pp. 161-166, 1950.

[FHW] Fortune S., J.E. Hopcroft, J. Wyllie, "The Directed Subgraph Homeomorphism Problem", Theor. Comput. Sci. (10), pp. 111-121, 1980.

[G] Golumbic, M. C., "The Complexity of Comparability Graph Recognition and Coloring", Computing (18), pp. 199-208, 1977.

[GJ] Garey, M.R., Johnson, D.S., "Computers and Intractability: A Guide to the Theory of NP-Completeness" Freeman, 1979.

[H] Hoffman A., private communication, 1982.

[J] Johnson, D. S., "The NP-Completeness Column: An Ongoing Guide", J. of Algorithms (3), pp. 182-195, 1982.

[L] Leighton, F.T., "A Layout Strategy for VLSI which is Provably Good", Proc. 14th SIGACT, pp. 85-98, 1980.

[LT1] Lipton, R.J., Tarjan, R.E., "A Separator Theorem for Planar Graphs", SIAM J. Applied Math., vol. 36, no. 2, pp. 177-189, 1979.

[LT2] Lipton, R.J., Tarjan, R.E., "Applications of a Planar Separator Theorem", SIAM J. Comput., vol. 9, no. 3, pp. 615-626, 1980.

[PS] Papadimitriou, C.H., K. Steiglitz, "Combinatorial Optimization: Algorithms and Complexity" Prentice Hall, 1982.

[PY] Papadimitriou, C.H., M. Yannakakis, "The Complexity of Restricted Spanning Tree Problems" JACM, vol 29, no. 2, pp. 285-310, 1982.

[Y] Yannakakis M., "Node- and Edge-deletion NP-complete Problems" Proc. 10th SIGACT, pp. 253-264, 1978.

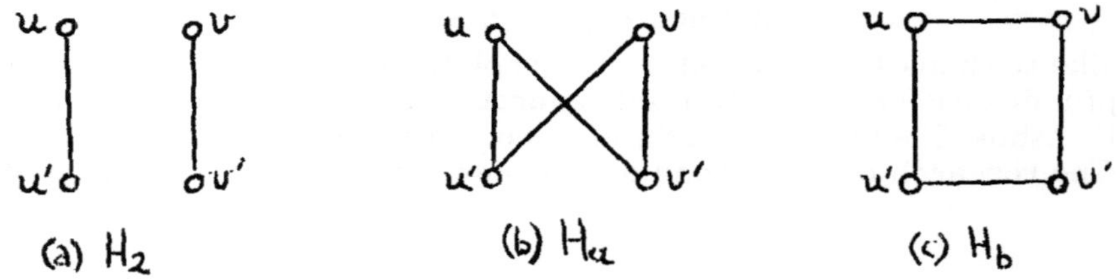

Figure 1

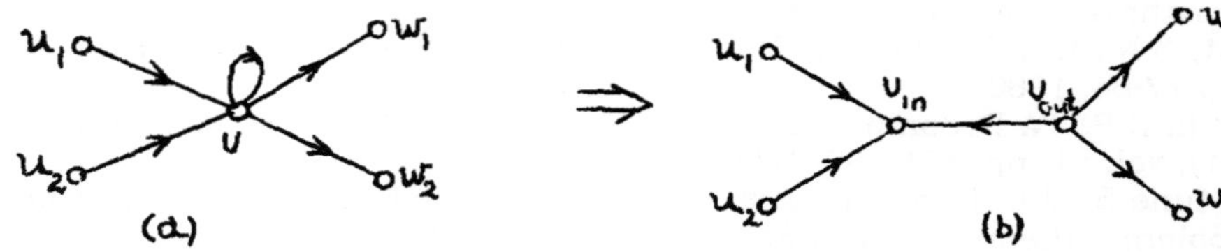

Figure 2

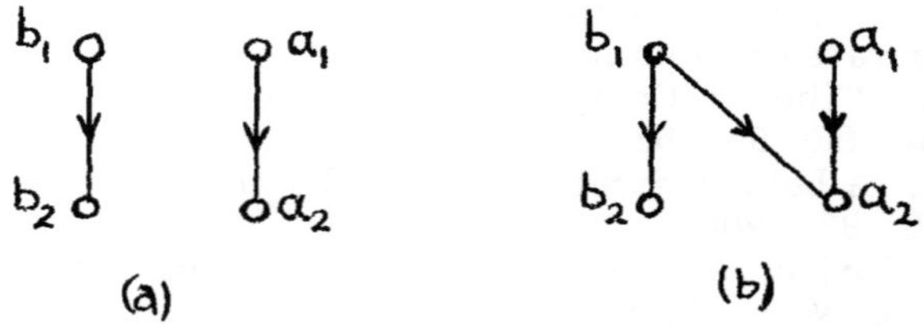

Figure 3

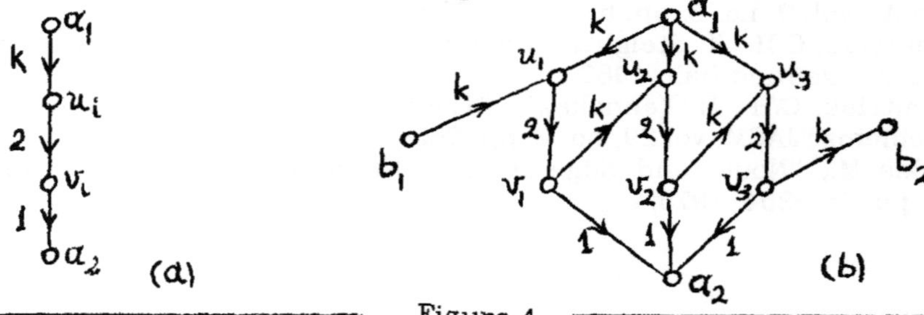

Figure 4

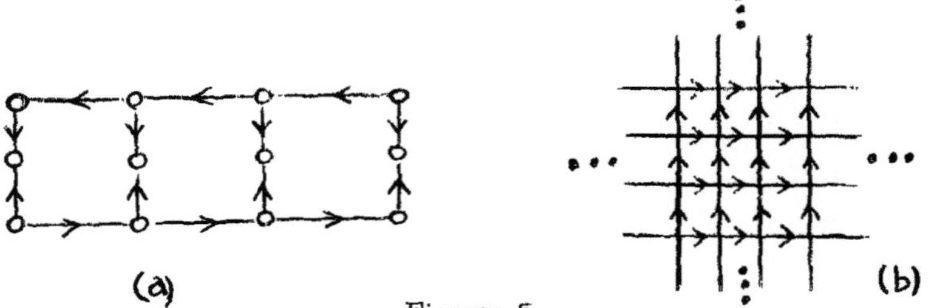

Figure 5

CONTEXT - FREE CONTROLLED ETOL SYSTEMS

Klaus - Jörn Lange
Fachbereich Informatik, Universität Hamburg
Schlüterstraße 70, 2000 Hamburg 13, West Germany

ABSTRACT

The following results concerning context-free controlled ETOL systems are shown:

- (CF)ETOL = (D_2)ETOL = (DCF)ETOL
- (RMOL)EDTOL $\subset$ LOG(CF)
- EOL $\not\subset$ (CF)EDTOL
- OI $\cap$ IO $\not\subset$ (CF)ETOL.

INTRODUCTION

Regulated rewriting is an important tool in formal language theory. One way to regulate derivations of a rewriting system is to restrict the set of permitted sequences of applied rules by control languages (see [S 1]). This method works also in the (parallel) case of iterated substitutions and homomorphisms, i.e. of L systems, very well (see [A 2]). Thus for an ETOL system G = (V,Ψ,S,U) (where V is a finite alphabet, Ψ a finite set of finite substitutions, $S \in V^*$ the axiom and $U \subset V$ the set of terminals,) and a control set $\Gamma \subset \Psi^*$ we define $L(G,\Gamma) := \{w \in U^* : S \xrightarrow{\theta} w \text{ for } \theta \in \Gamma\}$. If Γ is an element of a fixed class $\mathfrak{A}$, called the control family, the elements of which are called control sets, we call the pair (G,Γ) an $(\mathfrak{A})$ETOL system and $L(G,\Gamma)$ an $(\mathfrak{A})$ETOL language. The class of all $(\mathfrak{A})$ETOL languages is denoted by $(\mathfrak{A})$ETOL. In a corresponding way we get $(\mathfrak{A})$EDTOL systems and languages and the class $(\mathfrak{A})$EDTOL as well. A very fundamental result in this area was the 'no-control' result of Ginsburg and Rozenberg [G R]: (REG)ETOL = ETOL and (REG)EDTOL = EDTOL. Therefor, to get a proper extension of ETOL it is necessary to choose a control family $\mathfrak{A}$ fulfilling REG $\subsetneq \mathfrak{A}$. On the other hand, it seems reasonable to demand that $\mathfrak{A}$ is 'feasible', hence ETOL $\not\subset \mathfrak{A}$, because ETOL contains NP-complete sets. If we further forbid hyperexponential growth in $(\mathfrak{A})$ETOL by requiring that the elements of $\mathfrak{A}$ have semilinear Parikh images, then any additional language generating power is not caused by mere growth reasons, but rather by structural properties, demonstrated by non-indexed languages like $\{(\$a^\mu)^\mu : \mu \in \mathbb{N}\}$, which is an element of $(\{\alpha^\mu\beta^\mu : \mu \in \mathbb{N}\})$EDTOL. If we look in the Chomsky hierarchy for an $\mathfrak{A}$ with theese properties, our only choice is $\mathfrak{A}$ = CF. By some results of Asveld and Engelfriet in [A 1] and [A E] we know that (CF)ETOL is a full AFL and (CF)EDTOL is a full a-GSM-closed QAFL, which is not contained in INDEX = OI (the families of indexed and outside-in macro languages). Asveld conjectured in [A 2] that vice-versa neither OI nor IO (the family of inside-out macro languages) are contained in (CF)ETOL and proposed the Language of Cuts L_{Cut} (see [E Sch vL]) as a candidate for $OI \cap IO \setminus (CF)EDTOL$. In the following we show that L_{Cut} is not contained in (CF)ETOL by application of the seldom used theory of f-random words (see [Eh R 2]) on languages of the type $ANTICOP(L) := \{\$v_1\$v_2 \cdots \$v_k : k \in \mathbb{N},\ v_i \in L \text{ and } v_i \neq v_j \text{ for all } i \neq j\}$, where L is an arbitrary language and \$ a new symbol not occurring in any word of L. ANTICOP languages are closely related to problems like the well-declaration problem of variables in Algol-like languages, i.e. the problem whether each variable occurring in a programm is declared at most once.

New bounds on the derivation length in (CF)EDTOL systems (based on ideas in [P]) allow us to show $EOL \not\subset (CF)EDTOL$ in extension of $ETOL \not\subset (CF)EDTOL$ by [E R S1].

Concerning the complexity of the membership problem we show $(RMOL)EDTOL \subset LOG(CF)$, where RMOL (see [Cu O]) is the smallest AFL containing EOL. As a direct corollary we get $(CF)EDTOL \subset P \cap DSPACE((\log n)^2)$, which seems to be hardly improvable because (CF)EDTOL contains both CF and EDTOL.

This work is based on the authors Ph. D. thesis [L], which contains in detail most of the results below and was partially carried out under the auspices of a Canada Council Grant.

1. PRELEMINARIES

We assume the reader to be familiar with the notation and basic results of formal language theory and complexity theory as outlined in [H U] as well as the theory of L systems as contained in [R S]. In addition we remind the reader of the following notations:

- For a finite M we denote its cardinality by CARD(M).
- If $v \in V^*$ is a word, /v/ denotes the length of v, $\pi(v)$ its Parikh vector, and ALPH(v) the set of all letters occurring in v. The empty word is denoted by Λ.
- $\Pi(f)$ stands for the growth matrix of a homomorphism f.
- A deterministic general sequential machine with accepting states (a-GSM) is a construct $T = (Q, \Phi, \Psi, f, g, q_0, Q_F)$, where Q is a finite set (of states), Φ and Ψ are finite sets, called the input and output alphabets $f: Q \times \Phi \longrightarrow Q$ and $g: Q \times \Phi \longrightarrow \Psi^*$ are mappings, $q_0 \in Q$ is called the initial state, and $Q_F \subset Q$ is called the set of accepting states (see [A 1]). For $\Gamma \subset \Phi^*$ we set $T(\Gamma) := \{g^*(\theta) : \theta \in \Gamma \text{ and } f^*(\theta) \in Q_F\}$.
- If Ψ is a set of substitutions over V^*, then with each $\alpha_1\alpha_2 \cdots \alpha_n \in \Psi^*$, $\alpha_i \in \Psi$, we associate the substitution generated by the composition of

the α_i. If $\Gamma \subset \Psi^*$ and $L \subset V^*$, then $\Gamma(L) := \{w \in V^* : w \in \theta(v), v \in L, \theta \in \Gamma\}$.

1.1 Definition: A (CF)ETOL system is a pair (G,Γ), where $G = (V,\Psi,S,U)$ is an ETOL system and $\Gamma \subset \Psi^*$ is a context-free language, called the control set. If the underlying system G is deterministic or propagating, we call (G,Γ) a (CF)EDTOL or (CF)EPTOL system. The set $L(G,\Gamma) := \Gamma(S) \cap U^*$ is called the language generated by (G,Γ). The class of all languages generated by (deterministic) (CF)ETOL systems is denoted by (CF)ETOL ((CF)EDTOL). If we assume the control sets to be regular or to coincide with a particular language Γ we use the notations (REG)ETOL and (Γ)ETOL. By some results of Asveld [A 1] we know:

1.2 Theorem: a) (CF)ETOL is a full AFL containing ETOL and (CF)EDTOL.
b) (CF)EDTOL is a full a-GSM-closed QAFL containing CF and EDTOL.
c) $\{L \setminus \{\Lambda\} : L \in$ (CF)ETOL$\}$ = (CF)EPTOL and $\{L \setminus \{\Lambda\} : L \in$ (CF)EDTOL$\}$ = (CF)EPDTOL.

Each regular language is an a-GSM image of $\{\alpha,\beta\}^*$ where α and β are two arbitrary but distinct symbols. The 'two-table' result ETOL = $(\{\alpha,\beta\}^*)$ETOL of Rozenberg in [R] and the 'no-control' result (REG)ETOL = ETOL of Ginzburg and Rozenberg [G R] lead to the equation $(\{\alpha,\beta\}^*)$ETOL = (REG)ETOL. This combination of results holds in general:

1.3 Theorem: For each ETOL system $G = (V,\Psi,S,U)$ and each a-GSM $T = (Q,\Phi,\Psi,f,g,q_0,Q_F)$ there exists an ETOL system $G' = (V',\Phi,S',U)$ such that for every $\Gamma \subset \Phi^*$ we have $L(G,T(\Gamma)) = L(G',\Gamma)$.

Proof: Set $V' := V \times Q \cup V \cup \{F\}$, where F is a new ('garbage') symbol. For each $q \in Q$ define the homomorphism $h_q : V^* \longrightarrow V'^*$ by $h_q(a) := \langle a,q \rangle$ for all $a \in V$. Then set $S' := h_{q_0}(S)$. Furtheron, associate with each $\phi \in \Phi$ the table of productions: $\{a \longrightarrow F : a \in V \cup \{F\}\} \cup \{\langle a,q \rangle \longrightarrow h_{q'}(w) : w \in g(q,\phi)(a)$ and $q' = f(q,\phi)\} \cup \{\langle a,q \rangle \longrightarrow w : w \in g(q,\phi)(a)$ and $f(q,\phi) \in Q_F\}$. Obviously, we then have $L(G,T(\Gamma)) = L(G',\Gamma)$.

Let D_2 denote the (semi-)Dyck language of degree two. Then we get by the Chomsky-Schützenberger theorem:

1.4 Corollary: (CF)ETOL = (D_2)ETOL = (DCF)ETOL
where DCF denotes the set of deterministic context-free languages.

Simularly we get for LIN, the set of linear context-free languages and $S_2 := \{wcw^R : w \in \{a,b\}^*\}$:

1.5 Corollary: (LIN)ETOL = (S_2)ETOL.

The statements of corollaries 1.4 and 1.5 hold for EDTOL systems, too, although the proofs are a little bit more complicated.

2. THE COMPLEXITY OF THE WORD PROBLEM

It is quite easy to see that (CF)ETOL, just like ETOL, is contained in NP and contains languages with an NP-complete word problem. The deterministic case is more interesting.

We will use nondeterministic augmented pushdown automata as introduced in [C] and [Su 2]. The following theorem is based on theorem 3.3 in [A 3], where space restricted automata without pushdown store were considered. Let $NAPDA(\log n)_{PT}$ denote the class of languages accepted by nondeterministic pushdown automata augmented with logarithmically bounded working tapes, which are working in polynomial time. If we restrict this machine modell further to have one-way input we get the family $1\text{-}NAPDA(\log n)_{PT}$. In [Su 2] $NAPDA(\log n)_{PT}$ = LOG(CF) was shown.

2.1 Theorem: Let $\mathfrak{A}$ be a full AFL, which is closed under reversal and contained in $1\text{-}NAPDA(\log n)_{PT}$. Then $(\mathfrak{A})EDTOL \subset LOG(CF)$.

Sketch of proof: By lemma 2.3 of [A 3] we know, that each L in $(\mathfrak{A})$EDTOL can be generated in a way, that for every word w in L there is a controlled derivation of w, the length of which is bounded in a linear way by the length of w. Now consider the method of Jones and Skyum for nondeterministic recognition of EDTOL languages in logarithmic. Asveld modified their construction for the controlled case [A 3]. In his algorithm a control string θ is nondeterministically guessed in reversed order. This we take as one-way input for an $1\text{-}NAPDA(\log /\theta/)_{PT}$, which recognizes the reversal of the control set. If the guessed control string θ becomes longer than $c \cdot /w/$ for some fixed $c > 0$, which we can test in $\log(/w/)$-space, we reject the input. We accept w, if w is generated by the underlying EDTOL system, if the guessed control string is not to long, and if it is contained in the control set. Obviously, the whole construction works in logarithmic space and polynomial time.

The condition of $\mathfrak{A}$ being a full AFL could be weakened. Essentially, we only need the closure of $\mathfrak{A}$ under reversal and finite, but erasing substitution.

Of course every context-free language is in $1\text{-}NAPDA(\log n)_{PT}$ and hence (CF)EDTOL $\subset$ LOG(CF), which was also indicated recently in (E). But even RMOL (see [Cu O]), which is the AFL generated by EOL, is contained in $1\text{-}NAPDA(\log n)_{PT}$, which can be shown with the results in [S 2] and [Su 1].

2.2 Corollary: (CF)EDTOL $\subset$ (RMOL)EDTOL $\subset$ LOG(CF) $\subset$ P $\cap$ $DSPACE((\log n)^2)$.

It should be quite difficult to get better complexity bounds, since (CF)EDTOL contains CF and EDTOL and for CF the best known space bound is $DSPACE((\log n)^2)$, while for EDTOL the best known time bound is P. In the context of cor. 1.4 and cor. 2.2 it is remarkable that we have (D_1)EDTOL $\subset$ NSPACE(log n) by theorem 3.3 in [A 3].

3. THE DERIVATION STRUCTURE OF (CF)EDTOL SYSTEMS

In this section we briefly present two approaches to analyse the structure of (CF)EDTOL languages. The first method is based on the intercalation lemma of Perrault [P]. (Because we consider deterministic systems, in the following the substitutions of the underlying ETOL systems are regarded as homomorphisms.

3.1 Definition: Let $G = (V,\Psi,S,U)$ be an EDTOL system, $\Gamma \subset \Psi^*$ a context-free set, and θ an element of Γ. We say that θ contains a control loop, if there is a decomposition $\theta = \alpha\beta\gamma'\gamma\gamma''\delta\varepsilon$ such that

i) $\beta\delta \neq \Lambda$,
ii) $\alpha\beta^n\gamma'\gamma\gamma''\delta^n\varepsilon \in \Gamma$ for all $n \in \mathbb{N}_0$,
iii) $\Pi(\gamma') \leq \Pi(\beta\gamma')$ and $\Pi(\gamma'') \leq \Pi(\gamma''\delta)$, and
iv) For all $a \in V$ we have $ALPH(\gamma'(a)) = ALPH(\gamma'(\beta(a)))$ and $ALPH(\gamma''(a)) = ALPH(\delta(\gamma''(a)))$.

3.2 Lemma: For each (CF)EPDTOL system (G,Γ) there exists an integer k such that each $\theta \in \Gamma$ of length $/\theta/ \geq k$ contains a control loop $\theta = \alpha\beta\gamma'\gamma\gamma''\delta\varepsilon$ with $/\beta\gamma'\gamma\gamma''\delta/ \leq k$.

The proof of lemma 3.2 is similar to that one of Perrault's intercalation lemma. But because of the context-free control we have to consider matrices of the type $\begin{pmatrix} M & O \\ O & N \end{pmatrix}$ where $N = \Pi(\delta)$ and M is the transpose of $\Pi(\beta)$ for some control word $\alpha\beta\gamma\delta\varepsilon$ in Γ.(see [L]).

3.3 Definition: Let $L \subset U^*$ be an infinite language.

i) The length density of L at length n is defined by $LD(L,n) := CARD(\{/v/ : v \in L,\ /v/ \leq n\})$.
ii) L is quick(ly growing), iff $\lim_{n\to\infty} LD(L,n)/n = 0$.
iii) L is exponential(ly growing), iff $\limsup_{n\to\infty} \log(n)/LD(L,n) > 0$.
iv) L is exhaustive (w.r.t. U), $U^n \cap L = \emptyset$ or $U^n \subset L$ for all $n \in \mathbb{N}$.

3.4 Theorem: For each (CF)EDTOL language L there exist a PDTOL system $G = (V,\Psi,S)$, i.e. an EPDTOL system (V,Ψ,S,U) with $V = U$, a context-free control set $\Gamma \subset \Psi^+$, and an integer k' such that

i) $L\setminus\{\Lambda\} = L(G,\Gamma)$ and
ii) $/\theta/ \leq k'\cdot LD(L,/\theta(S)/)$ for all $\theta \in \Gamma$.

Sketch of proof: By a combination of some results in [G R] and [A 3] it is possible to generate $L\setminus\{\Lambda\}$ by a (CF)PDTOL system (G,Γ) such that in every derivation controlled by Γ every derivation step except the last one is strictly length increasing. Now let k be the constant derived in lemma 3.2

If $\theta \in \Gamma$ is of length $/\theta/ \geq k$, then θ is decomposable to $\theta = \alpha\beta\gamma'\gamma\gamma''\delta\varepsilon$ such that $\eta := \alpha\gamma'\gamma\gamma''\varepsilon$ is of length $/\theta/ - k \leq /\eta/ < /\theta/$. Hence we have $/\eta(S)/ < /\theta(S)/$ in the case $\varepsilon \neq \Lambda$, i.e. if the reduction from θ to η does not affect the last derivation step of θ. But a careful analysis shows that this could happen only once. Thus we know that after $LD(L,/\theta(S)/) + 1$ reduction steps we get an element $\eta' \in \Gamma$ which does not contain any control loop. Then we know $/\eta'/ < k$ and $/\theta/ < k\cdot(LD(L,/\theta(S)/) + 1)$. Setting $k' := 2\cdot k$ we have the result.

It should be noted, that theorem 3.4, of course, pertains also to the subcase of EDTOL languages.

3.5 Corollary: No quick (CF)EDTOL language is exhaustive w.r.t. any alphabet which has at least two elements.

Proof: Let $L \subset U^*$ be a quick (CF)EDTOL language with $CARD(U) \geq 2$. Furtheron, let $G = (V,\Psi,S)$, $\Gamma \subset \Psi^+$, and k' be constructed according to theorem 3.4. Then we know, that for each $n \in \mathbb{N}$ and each $\theta \in \Gamma$ with $n = /\theta(S)/$ we have $/\theta/ \leq k'\cdot LD(L,n)$. Hence $CARD(L \cap U^n) \leq (CARD(\Psi))^{k'LD(L,n)+1}$. But the last expression is of order $o(2^n) = o(CARD(U^n))$. In total we have $\lim_{n\to\infty} CARD(L \cap U^n)/CARD(U^n) = 0$, which implies the result.

3.6 Corollary: EOL is not contained in (CF)EDTOL.

Proof: If the homomorphism $g:\{a,b\}^* \longrightarrow \{a\}^*$ is defined by $g(a) := g(b) := a$ then languages like $g^{-1}(\{a^{2^n} : n \in \mathbb{N}\})$ or $g^{-1}(\{a^{n^2} : n \in \mathbb{N}\})$ are in EOL, but according to cor. 3.5 not in (CF)EDTOL.

Corollary 3.6 also shows that (CF)EDTOL is not closed under inverse Λ-free homomorphism. For arbitrary homomorphism this was already shown in [E R S]

In the second part of this section we present the application of the method of f-random words [Eh R 2] to (CF)EDTOL systems. Because of the size of this complex we only sketch the main ideas.

3.7 Definition: A mapping $f:\mathbb{N} \longrightarrow \mathbb{N}$ is called slow, if $\lim_{n\to\infty} f(n)/n^c = 0$ for all $c > 0$. A word w is called f-random, if $w = xuyvz$ and $/u/ \geq f(/w/)$ imply $u \neq v$.

It should be noted that for non-unary alphabets almost all words are f-random, if $f(n) \geq 4\cdot\log(n)$ [Eh R 2, Theorem 3].

Corresponding to the notion of a neat subderivation in [Eh R 2] we call a derivation controlled by a table sequence θ CF-structured, if θ is decomposable in $\theta = \alpha\beta_1\cdots\beta_n\gamma\delta_n\cdots\delta_1\varepsilon$ such that each pair (β_i,δ_i) is pumpable w.r.t. the context-free control language and either $(\alpha,\beta_1,\beta_2,\cdots,\beta_n,\gamma\delta_n\cdots\delta_1\varepsilon)$ or $(\alpha\beta_1\cdots\beta_n\gamma,\delta_n,\cdots,\delta_2,\delta_1,\varepsilon)$ is a neat subderivation of θ. Now it is possible to show that each derivation of an f-random word controlled by a control word θ contains a CF-structured subderivation of length $\log(\log(/\theta/))$, if f is a slow function. This is done by applying the main theorem of |Eh R 2| which gives us a neat subderivation of the derivation controlled by θ and by that a decomposition of θ. This decomposition is embedded into the context-free derivation of θ in the way of Ogden's Iteration Theorem and further refined until we get a CF-structured subderivation. With this result we get for arbitrary slow function f, that each infinite (CF)ETOL language contains infinitely many words, which are not f-random and that each exponential (CF)EDTOL language contains only finitely many f-random words.

Another consequence is a kind of pumping theorem for (CF)EDTOL languages corresponding to the main result of |Eh R 1|.

3.8 Theorem: For each (CF)EDTOL system (G,Γ), $G = (V,\Psi,S,U)$, and each slow function f there exists an integer p such that every derivation controlled by some control word $\theta \in \Gamma$ of any f-random word $\theta(S)$ of length $/\theta(S)/ \geq p$ contains a subderivation, i.e. a decomposition $\theta = \alpha\beta\gamma\delta\varepsilon$, with the following properties:

i) $\alpha\beta^n\gamma\delta^n\varepsilon \in \Gamma$ for each $n \in \mathbb{N}_0$,

ii) $\mathrm{ALPH}(\alpha(S)) = \mathrm{ALPH}(\alpha\beta(S))$,

iii) $\mathrm{ALPH}(\alpha\beta\gamma(S)) = \mathrm{ALPH}(\alpha\beta\gamma\delta(S))$, and

iv) a) there are words $x_0,x_1,\cdots,x_n,y_1,\cdots,y_n$ such that $y_1y_2\cdots y_n \neq \Lambda$ and $\alpha\beta^{m+1}(S) = x_0y_1^mx_1y_2^m\cdots y_n^mx_n$ for all $m \in \mathbb{N}_0$

or

b) for each $t \in \mathbb{N}$ there are words $x_0,x_1,\cdots,x_n,y_1,\cdots,y_n$ such that $y_1y_2\cdots y_n \neq \Lambda$ and $\alpha\beta^t\gamma\delta^{m+1}(S) = x_0y_1^mx_1y_2^m\cdots y_n^mx_n$ for all $m \in \mathbb{N}_0$.

The proof follows directly the way shown in |Eh R 1|, but using CF-structured subderivations instead of neat ones.

4. ANTICOP - LANGUAGES

4.1 Definition: For $L \subset U^*$ and $\$ \notin U$ we set $\mathrm{ANTICOP}(L) := \{\$v_1\$v_2\cdots\$v_n : n \in \mathbb{N},\ v_i \in L, \text{ and } v_i \neq v_j \text{ if } i \neq j \text{ for } 1 \leq i,j \leq n\}$.

While $\mathrm{COPY}(L) := \{(\$v)^n : n \in \mathbb{N},\ v \in L\}$ is a (CF)EDTOL language for every L in (CF)EDTOL, we will show that ANTICOP(L) is in (CF)EDTOL for finite L only. This implies that $\mathrm{ANTICOP}(a^*)$ or in general $\mathrm{ANTICOP}(U^*)$, which is the formal representation of problems like well-declaration of program variables or well-definition of mappings, is not in (CF)EDTOL. Before we can derive this result, we need the following notation.

4.2 Definition: If a control word θ contains two control loops, that is two decompositions $\theta = \alpha_i\beta_i\gamma_i'\gamma_i\gamma_i''\delta_i\varepsilon_i$ for $i = 1,2$, we say that theese are independent if for some $i \in \{1,2\}$ either $\alpha_i\beta_i\gamma_i'$ is a prefix of α_{3-i} and $\gamma_i''\delta_i\varepsilon_i$ is a suffix of ε_{3-i} or $\alpha_i\beta_i\gamma_i'\gamma_i\gamma_i''\delta_i$ is a prefix of α_{3-i}.

In extension of lemma 3.2 it is possible to show the following lemma, which we state without proof.

4.3 Lemma: For each (CF)EDTOL language L there exist a PDTOL system $G = (V,\Psi,S)$, a context-free set $\Gamma \subset \Psi^+$, and an integer k" such that $L(G,\Gamma) = L\setminus\{\Lambda\}$ and for all $\theta \in \Gamma$ with $/\theta/ \geq n\cdot k''$ θ contains n independent control loops, where n is an arbitrary integer.

4.4 Theorem: If ANTICOP(L) is a (CF)EDTOL language, then L is finite.

Sketch of proof: If L is infinite, we can define $d(j) := \min\{/v/ : v \in \text{ANTICOP}(L) \cap (\$L)^j\}$ and $W(j) := \{v : v \in \text{ANTICOP}(L) \cap (\$L)^j,\ /v/ = d(j)\}$ for each $j \in \mathbb{N}$. Obviously $\text{CARD}(W(j)) \geq j!$ for all j. Furtheron, we know that each $v \in \text{ANTICOP}(L)$ with $/v/ < d(j)$ contains at most $j-1$ \$-symbols. Now assume that ANTICOP(L) is a (CF)EDTOL language. Then let $G = (V,\Psi,S)$, Γ, and k" be defined according to lemma 4.3. As in the proof of theo. 3.4 it is possible to construct G and Γ in a way that in each derivation controlled by Γ the length of the sentential form is strictly increased in each derivation step except the last one. If $\theta \in \Gamma$ derives for some $j \in \mathbb{N}$ an element of W(j), which we denote by $\theta(S)$, then each control loop $\theta = \alpha\beta\gamma'\gamma\gamma''\delta\varepsilon$ affects the number of \$-symbols, because for $\eta := \alpha\gamma'\gamma\gamma''\varepsilon$ we know that $/\eta(S)/ < /\theta(S)/$ and hence $\eta(S)$ contains less \$-symbols than $\theta(S)$. This implies that θ contains at most j independent control loops and hence $/\theta/ < j\cdot k''$. For all $j \in \mathbb{N}$ we have $\text{CARD}(L(G,\Gamma) \cap W(j)) \leq (\text{CARD}(\Psi))^{j\cdot k''+1}$. But the last expression is of order $o(j!)$, i.e. $\lim_{n\to\infty} c^j/j! = 0$ for each fixed c. This contradicts the fact $\text{CARD}(W(j)) \geq j!$ and $W(j) \subset \text{ANTICOP}(L) = L(G,\Gamma)$.

The last part of this section uses theorem 3.8 in connection with ANTICOP languages.

4.5 Theorem: Let $g: \mathbb{N} \longrightarrow \mathbb{N}$ be a monotonous mapping fulfilling $\lim_{n\to\infty} n^k/g(n) = 0$ for all $k \in \mathbb{N}$. If $L \subset \text{ANTICOP}(U^*)$ and $L \cap (\$U^n)^{g(n)}$ is infinite, then L is not a (CF)EDTOL language.

Sketch of proof: Assume (G,Γ) is a (CF)EDTOL system, such that $L = L(G,\Gamma) \subset \text{ANTICOP}(U^*)$ and $L \cap (\$U^n)^{g(n)}$ is not empty for infinitely many $n \in \mathbb{N}$. If we define $f(n) := \max\{2\cdot j : j\cdot g(j-1) \leq n\}$, then f is a slow function and for each $j \in \mathbb{N}$ and each $w \in L \cap (\$U^j)^{g(j)}$ w is an f-random word. By our assumption L contains f-random words of arbitrary large length. Hence we can apply theorem 2.8. A careful analysis shows that it is possible to get a 'pumpable' derivation $\theta = \alpha\beta\gamma\delta\varepsilon \in \Gamma$ such that the (iterated) word $y_1y_2\cdots y_n$ in condition iv) of theorem 3.8 contains at least one \$-symbol. But then the control word $\alpha\beta^4\gamma\delta^4\varepsilon$ derives a word, which cannot be a member of ANTICOP(U^*) contradicting the assumption.

If $\prec$ is a total order on U^*, $\$ \notin U$, and $L \subset U^*$, we set ANTICOP(L,$\prec$):= $\{\$v_1\$v_2\cdots\$v_n \in$ ANTICOP(L) $: v_i \prec v_j$ for $i < j\}$. A direct consequence of theorem 4.5 is:

<u>4.6 Corollary</u>: If CARD(U) > 2, then ANTICOP(U^*,$\prec$) is not in <u>(CF)EDTOL</u>.

The last result could be interpreted, that also the problem of well-declaration for ordered (variable) names is not expressable by a (CF)EDTOL syntax. The next result proves a conjecture of Asveld,stated in |A 2|.

<u>4.7 Corollary</u>: The language of cuts (which is the set of all yields of complete binary trees, where each leaf is labelled with the binary coded path, which leads from the root to this leaf; see |E Sch vL|) is not a (CF)EDTOL language.

Proof: Setting U:= {0,1} and g(j):= 2^j the conditions of theorem 4.5 are fulfilled.

Since the language of cuts has the property P_3 of |E Sk| (see |E Sch vL|), it is not contained in <u>(CF)ETOL</u> either. Hence we have:

<u>4.8 Corollary</u>: Neither <u>OI</u> nor <u>IO</u> are contained in <u>(CF)ETOL</u>.

Of course, corollary 4.8 holds for all families of languages, which contain the language of cuts, e.g. <u>DS</u>, the class of deterministic one-way stack languages |E Sch vL|.

The results of the previous sections are summarized in the diagramm aside, which compares <u>(CF)ETOL</u> and <u>(CF)EDTOL</u> with other well-known families of formal language theory.

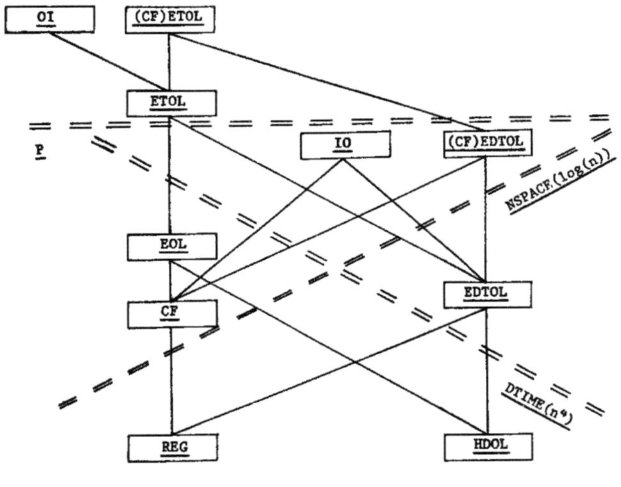

ACKNOWLEDGEMENT

I would like to thank W. Brauer, G. Rozenberg, and D. Wood for discussing this work and refereeing my Ph.D. thesis.

REFERENCES

[A 1] P.R.J. Asveld, Controlled iteration grammars and full hyper-AFL's, Inform. and Control 34 (1977), 248-269. in [A 2].

[A 2] P.R.J. Asveld, Iterated Context-Independent Rewriting, Ph.D. thesis, Technische Hogeschool Twente, 1978.

[A 3] P.R.J. Asveld, Space-bounded complexity classes and iterated deterministic substitution, Inform. and Control 44 (1980), 282-299.

[A E] P.R.J. Asveld and J. Engelfriet, Iterated deterministic substitution, Acta Informatica 8 (1977), 285-302. in [A 2].

[C] S.A. Cook, Characterizations of pushdown machines in terms of time-bounded computers, J. Assoc. Comput. Mach. 18 (1971), 4-18.

[Cu O] K. Culik II and J. Opatrny, Macro OL-systems, Internat. J. of Comput. Math. 4 (1975), 327-342.

[Eh R 1] A. Ehrenfeucht and G. Rozenberg, A pumping theorem for deterministic ETOL languages, Rev. Fr. Automat. Inform. Rech. Opér., Sér. Rouge 9 (1975), 13-23.

[Eh R 2] A. Ehrenfeucht and G. Rozenberg, On the structure of derivations in deterministic ETOL systems, J. Comput. System Sci. 17 (1978), 331-347.

[E] J. Engelfriet, The complexity of languages generated by attribute grammars, Technical Report, Memorandumnr. INF-82-13, Twente University of Technology, 1982.

[E R Sl] J. Engelfriet, G. Rozenberg, and G. Slutzki, Tree transducers, L-systems and two-way machines, J. Comput. System Sci. 20 (1980), 150-202.

[E Sch vL] J. Engelfriet, E.M. Schmidt, and J. van Leeuwen, Stack machines and classes of nonnested macro languages, J. Assoc. Comput. Mach. 27 (1980), 96-117.

[E Sk] J. Engelfriet and S. Skyum, Copying theorems, Inform. Process. Lett. 4 (1976), 157-161.

[G R] S. Ginsburg and G. Rozenberg, TOL schemes and control sets, Inform. and Control 27 (1974), 109-125.

[H U] J.E. Hopcroft and J.D. Ullman, Introduction to Automata Theory, Languages, and Computation, Addison Wesley, Reading, 1979.

[L] K.-J. Lange, Kontextfrei Kontrollierte ETOL-Systeme, Dissertation, Universität Hamburg, 1983.

[P] C.R. Perrault, Intercalation lemmas for tree transducer languages, J. Comput. Syste, Sci 13 (1976), 246-277.

[R] G. Rozenberg, Extension of tabled OL systems and languages, Internat. J. Comput. Inform. Sci. 2 (1973), 311-334.

[R S] G. Rozenberg and A. Salomaa, The Mathematical Theory of L Systems, Academic Press, New York, 1980.

[S 1] A. Salomaa, Formal Languages, Academic Press, New York, 1973.

[S 2] A. Salomaa, Iteration grammars and Lindenmayer AFL's, Lecture Notes in Computer Science 15 (1974), 250-253.

[Su 1] I.H. Sudborough, The complexity of the membership problem for some extensions of context-free languages, Internat. J. Comput. Math. 6 (1977), 191-215.

[Su 2] I.H. Sudborough, On the tape complexity of deterministic context-free languages, J. Assoc. Comput. Mach. 25 (1978), 405-414.

REFEREES FOR ICALP-83

V. AMBRIOLA
A. ARNOLD
A. ASHCROFT
E. ASTESIANO
P. ASVELD
G. ATTARDI
J.M. AUBERT

F. BAIARDI
J.L. BALCAZAR
J. BEAUQUIER
F. BELLEGARDE
M. BELLIA
J. BERSTEL
M. BLATTNER
S.L. BLOOM
R. BOOK
F.J. BRANDERBURG
J. BRZOZOWSKI

R. CASAS
G. COMYN
B. COURCELLE
G. COUSINEAU

A. D'ATRI
P.P. DEGANO
M. DEKKING
P.A. DEVIJVER
M. DEZANI-CIANCAGLINI
J. DONAHUE

J. ENGELFRIED
P. ENJALBERT

E. FEHR
G. FILÈ
I.S. FILOTTI
J.P. FINANCE
N. FRANCES
P. FRANCHI-ZANNETTACCI
J. FRANÇON

S. GAL
W.I. GASARCH
G. GERMANO
C. GHEZZI
J.A. GOGUEN
O. GOLDREICH
A. GONZALEZ DEL RIO

J. HALPERN
T. HARJU
M. HARRISON
M. HOFNI

A. ITAI

D. JANSSENS
M. JANTZEN
J.P. JOUANNAUD

A. KANDA
J. KARHUMÄKI
S. KATZ
J.A. KENTONEN
H.A. KLAEREN
H.C.M. KLEIJN
L. KOTT
H.J. KREOWSKI

J.C. LAFON
D. LAZARD
D. LEHMANN
O. LEHVMANN
P. LESCANNE
G. LEVI
H. LEWIS
M. LINNA
A. LLAMOSÍ

A. MAGGIOLO
B. MAHR
B. MANDRILI
J.A. MAKOWSKY
P. MARCHAND
A. MARCHETTI-SPACCAMELA
J. MARIN
A. MARTELLI
G.F. MASCARI
G. MAURI
D. McQUEEN
E. MEINECHE SCHMIDT
MEMMI
G. MICHELIS
P. MIGLIOLI
M. MIGNOTTE
C. MONTANGERO
S. MORAN
F.L. MORRIS
M. MUÑOZ

A. NIJHOLT
M. NIELSEN
NORBERT

F. OREJAS
R. ORSINI

J. PAREDAENS
K. PARSHAYE-GHOMI
A. PAZ
F.C. PEREIRA
J.E. PIN
D.A. PLAISTED

A. PNUELI
V. PRATT
G.A. PRINI
M. PROTASI
C. PUECH

M. RABIN
Y. RAZ
M. REGNIER
J. REIF
J.C. REYNOLDS
J.L. REMY
J.A. ROBINSON
M. RODEH
Z. ROSBERG
K. RUOHONEN

T. SALES
A. SALOMAA
P.L. SCHWARTZ
R. SEDGEWICK
E.SHAMIR
Y. SHILOACH
R. SHOSTAK
R. SPRUGNOLI
M. STEINBY
J.M. STEYAERT
M.E. STICKEL
L. STOCKMEYER
H. STRAUBING

P.S. THIAGARAJAN
C. TORRAS
P. TORRIJIANI
F. TURINI

M. VANNESCHI
M. VARDI
R. VALK
M. VENTURINI
M. VERGES
VERRAEDT
G. VIDAL

P. WOLPER
J. WILLIAMS

Y. YACOBI
M. YOELI

S. ZAKZ

Vol 107: International Colloquium on Formalization of Programming Concepts Proceedings. Edited by J. Diaz and I Ramos VII, 478 pages. 1981

Vol 108 Graph Theory and Algorithms Edited by N. Saito and T Nishizeki. VI, 216 pages. 1981.

Vol. 109. Digital Image Processing Systems. Edited by L Bolc and Zenon Kulpa. V, 353 pages 1981.

Vol 110· W. Dehning, H. Essig, S Maass, The Adaptation of Virtual Man-Computer Interfaces to User Requirements in Dialogs X, 142 pages 1981

Vol 111: CONPAR 81. Edited by W. Handler. XI, 508 pages. 1981

Vol. 112. CAAP '81. Proceedings. Edited by G Astesiano and C. Bohm VI, 364 pages 1981

Vol. 113· E-E Doberkat, Stochastic Automata Stability, Nondeterminism, and Prediction. IX, 135 pages. 1981

Vol 114: B Liskov, CLU, Reference Manual. VIII, 190 pages 1981.

Vol. 115· Automata, Languages and Programming Edited by S Even and O Kariv. VIII, 552 pages. 1981

Vol 116: M A Casanova, The Concurrency Control Problem for Database Systems. VII, 175 pages. 1981.

Vol. 117. Fundamentals of Computation Theory Proceedings, 1981 Edited by F. Gécseg. XI, 471 pages. 1981

Vol 118 Mathematical Foundations of Computer Science 1981 Proceedings, 1981 Edited by J Gruska and M. Chytil. XI, 589 pages 1981.

Vol 119 G. Hirst, Anaphora in Natural Language Understanding. A Survey. XIII, 128 pages 1981.

Vol 120: L. B. Rall, Automatic Differentiation Techniques and Applications. VIII, 165 pages. 1981.

Vol. 121 Z. Zlatev, J. Wasniewski, and K. Schaumburg, Y12M Solution of Large and Sparse Systems of Linear Algebraic Equations IX, 128 pages 1981.

Vol 122: Algorithms in Modern Mathematics and Computer Science Proceedings, 1979 Edited by A. P. Ershov and D E Knuth. XI, 487 pages 1981

Vol 123· Trends in Information Processing Systems Proceedings, 1981. Edited by A. J. W Duijvestijn and P C Lockemann XI, 349 pages. 1981.

Vol 124: W. Polak, Compiler Specification and Verification XIII, 269 pages. 1981.

Vol. 125. Logic of Programs Proceedings, 1979 Edited by E Engeler V, 245 pages. 1981.

Vol. 126· Microcomputer System Design. Proceedings, 1981 Edited by M J. Flynn, N R Harris, and D P McCarthy VII, 397 pages 1982

Voll. 127. Y.Wallach, Alternating Sequential/Parallel Processing X, 329 pages 1982.

Vol 128: P. Branquart, G. Louis, P Wodon, An Analytical Description of CHILL, the CCITT High Level Language VI, 277 pages 1982

Vol. 129: B T Hailpern, Verifying Concurrent Processes Using Temporal Logic VIII, 208 pages 1982

Vol. 130 R. Goldblatt, Axiomatising the Logic of Computer Programming XI, 304 pages. 1982

Vol. 131: Logics of Programs Proceedings, 1981 Edited by D Kozen. VI, 429 pages. 1982

Vol 132. Data Base Design Techniques I Requirements and Logical Structures Proceedings, 1978 Edited by S B Yao, S B Navathe, J.L Weldon, and T L Kunii V, 227 pages 1982

Vol. 133 Data Base Design Techniques II Proceedings, 1979 Edited by S.B Yao and T L. Kunii. V, 229–399 pages. 1982.

Vol 134. Program Specification. Proceedings, 1981 Edited by J. Staunstrup. IV, 426 pages 1982

Vol. 135: R.L. Constable, S.D. Johnson, and C.D Eichenlaub, An Introduction to the PL/CV2 Programming Logic. X, 292 pages 1982

Vol. 136. Ch M. Hoffmann, Group-Theoretic Algorithms and Graph Isomorphism VIII, 311 pages. 1982

Vol. 137: International Symposium on Programming Proceedings, 1982. Edited by M Dezani-Ciancaglini and M. Montanari VI, 406 pages. 1982

Vol. 138 6th Conference on Automated Deduction Proceedings, 1982. Edited by D.W. Loveland. VII, 389 pages 1982

Vol 139 J Uhl, S. Drossopoulou, G Persch, G. Goos, M. Dausmann, G. Winterstein, W Kirchgassner, An Attribute Grammar for the Semantic Analysis of Ada. IX, 511 pages. 1982

Vol 140 Automata, Languages and programming Edited by M Nielsen and E.M. Schmidt VII, 614 pages 1982

Vol 141 U Kastens, B. Hutt, E. Zimmermann, GAG. A Practical Compiler Generator. IV, 156 pages. 1982.

Vol. 142: Problems and Methodologies in Mathematical Software Production Proceedings, 1980 Edited by P C Messina and A Murli VII, 271 pages 1982

Vol. 143 Operating Systems Engineering. Proceedings, 1980 Edited by M. Maekawa and L.A Belady. VII, 465 pages 1982

Vol. 144 Computer Algebra. Proceedings, 1982 Edited by J Calmet XIV, 301 pages 1982

Vol 145 Theoretical Computer Science Proceedings, 1983 Edited by A.B. Cremers and H.P Kriegel X, 367 pages 1982

Vol 146 Research and Development in Information Retrieval Proceedings, 1982 Edited by G. Salton and H.-J Schneider IX, 311 pages 1983

Vol. 147 RIMS Symposia on Software Science and Engineering. Proceedings, 1982. Edited by E Goto, I. Nakata, K Furukawa, R. Nakajima, and A. Yonezawa. V 232 pages 1983.

Vol 148 Logics of Programs and Their Applications Proceedings, 1980 Edited by A Salwicki. VI, 324 pages. 1983

Vol. 149· Cryptography Proceedings, 1982. Edited by T Beth VIII, 402 pages. 1983

Vol. 150 Enduser Systems and Their Human Factors Proceedings, 1983 Edited by A Blaser and M Zoeppritz III, 138 pages 1983

Vol 151 R. Piloty, M. Barbacci, D. Borrione, D Dietmeyer, F Hill, and P Skelly, CONLAN Report XII, 174 pages. 1983.

Vol. 152 Specification and Design of Software Systems Proceedings, 1982 Edited by E. Knuth and E. J. Neuhold V, 152 pages. 1983

Vol. 153. Graph-Grammars and Their Application to Computer Science. Proceedings, 1982 Edited by H Ehrig, M. Nagl, and G Rozenberg. VII, 452 pages 1983

Vol. 154· Automata, Languages and Programming Proceedings, 1983 Edited by J. Diaz. VIII, 734 pages. 1983.

MIX
Papier aus verantwortungsvollen Quellen
Paper from responsible sources
FSC® C105338

If you have any concerns about our products,
you can contact us on
ProductSafety@springernature.com

In case Publisher is established outside the EU,
the EU authorized representative is:
Springer Nature Customer Service Center GmbH
Europaplatz 3, 69115 Heidelberg, Germany

Printed by Libri Plureos GmbH
in Hamburg, Germany